1,000
GLUTEN-FREE
Recipes

CAROL FENSTER

WILEY

John Wiley & Sons, Inc.

Fenster, Carol Lee.

1,000 gluten-free recipes / Carol Fenster.

p. cm.

Includes bibliographical references and index.

ISBN 978-0-470-06780-2 (cloth)

1. Gluten-free diet—Recipes. I. Title. II. Title: One thousand gluten-free recipes.

RM237.86.F462 2008

641.5'638—dc22

2007046850

Printed in the United States of America

10 9 8 7

Publisher: Natalie Chapman

Senior Editor: Linda Ingroia

Senior Editorial Assistant: Charleen Barila

Senior Production Editor: Amy Zarkos

Cover Design: Jeffrey Faust

Interior Design: Holly Wittenberg

Production by Wiley Indianapolis Composition Services

Manufacturing Manager: Kevin Watt

Cover Illustration: Linda Ayriss

Key to Cover Illustration

1. Gingerbread People, Chocolate Chip Cookies, Holiday Cutout Cookies
2. French Yeast Bread
3. bagels
4. Breakthrough Ready-to-Bake Yeast Bread
5. grapes
6. Gluten-Free Granola with Nuts and Dried Fruit
7. Focaccia with Herbs
8. Asparagus with Hollandaise
9. onion
10. tomato
11. Spaghetti and Meatballs with Marinara
12. Lemon Meringue Tart
13. Grilled Salmon with Minted Pineapple Salsa
14. lemon
15. pear
16. apple
17. Crown Roast of Lamb
18. gluten-free beer
19. Pepperoni Cheese Pizza
20. Chocolate Vegan Cupcakes with Chocolate Mocha Frosting; Yellow Cupcakes with Fluffy Pink Frosting; Orange-Coconut Cupcakes with Fluffy Orange-Coconut Frosting; White Cupcakes with Cream Cheese Frosting (sprinkled with confetti)
21. Devil's Food Layer Cake with Fudge Frosting

Dedication

To my family: Larry, Brett, Helke, Keene, Romi, and baby Cole—who arrived just in time to get his name in this book.

ACKNOWLEDGMENTS

Writing this cookbook has been a fascinating experience, and I appreciate the inspiration from my family, friends, professional colleagues, attendees at cooking classes and speaking engagements, visitors to my trade-show booths and book signings, and chefs in restaurants here and abroad.

I am very grateful to my wonderful testers who made these recipes in their own kitchens to make sure they were perfect for you: Nate Amundsen, Janet L. Armil; Tristan Armil; Lori Baird, Mary Lou Baltz, Suzanne Bowland, founder/producer, GF Culinary Productions, Inc.; Bev Chevalier; Jean Duane, Alternative Cook; Nancy Patin Falini, RD, and Francesco, Analisa, Teresa, and Patrick Falini; Helen Foreman, CSA Resource Person #2011, San Diego Chapter #57; Donna Furr; Andrea Levario and Pablo; Beckee Moreland; Jennifer Parker; Karin Parker; Genevieve Potts; Judy Sarver; Virginia Schmuck; Ellen Switkes, San Francisco Bay Area Celiac Support Group; Karel Anne Tieszen, Kitchen Friends Cooking School; Patty Tobias, patron services, Arapahoe Library District; Anne Burton Washburn, GF wife, mom, and lover of good food; Cecile Weed, CSA Chapter 14; and Steve Zeiden. You were all so generous and helpful.

Several chefs provided recipes for this book. They include Jane Bauer, member, Slow Food Utah; Aaron Flores, executive chef, Doubletree Hotels; Susan Cox-Gilbertson, cooking school assistant, Bob's Red Mill; Lorna Sass, author of *Whole Grains: Every Day, Every Way*; Joel Schaefer, CCC, CHT; Mary Schaefer, CEPC, director of education, Notter School of Pastry Arts; Matt Selby, executive chef/partner, Vesta Dipping Grill and Steuben's; Lori Sobelson, program director, Bob's Red Mill; Eric Stein, MS, RD, chef-instructor, Johnson & Wales University; Elise Wiggins, executive chef, Panzano Restaurant; and Renee Zonka, RD, CEC, MBA, CHE, associate dean of culinary, Kendall College.

Many companies provided samples of ingredients that weren't in stores yet so I could use them to develop these recipes. Many thanks to Bob's Red Mill, Corn Products International, Cream Hill Estates, Enjoy Life Natural Brands, Farm Pure (Only Oats), Food for Life, Gluten-Free Oats, Gifts of Nature, Heartland's Finest, La Tortilla Factory, Mary's Gone Crackers, and Pamela's Products.

I owe a special thanks to my wonderfully inspirational and supportive agent, Lisa Ekus-Saffer, who believes in the importance of cookbooks for people on special diets. Lisa and her staff are absolutely terrific.

I am deeply grateful to my marvelous editor at Wiley, Linda Ingroia, who suggested this book in this first place, and her wonderful assistant, Charleen Barila. Together, they guided this book through the process with their great wisdom and insights. I also appreciate the help of Adam Kowit and the rest of the Wiley team: Amy Zarkos, production editor; Jeffrey Faust, cover art director; Holly Wittenberg, interior designer; Linda Ayriss, cover designer; and Helen Chin, copyeditor.

As always, thanks to my wonderful husband, Larry, for his loving support in my quest for delicious gluten-free food.

CONTENTS

GLUTEN-FREE: A NEW DIET FOR THE 21ST CENTURY

Twenty years ago, I walked out of my doctor's office with a single phrase ringing in my ears: "Don't eat wheat." It seemed simple enough at the time. My first inkling of trouble came that night as I searched the cupboards for something to eat. I hadn't realized how wheat-laden our American diet was until then. So began my quest for a new way to live without wheat and it couldn't have been a more unlikely turn of events, given my history.

You see, I'm the daughter of a Nebraska farmer—a farmer who raised wheat. Wheat was a good thing at our house. It put food on the table and paid my college tuition. After college, I married into a wheat-farming family. In fact, that's all they raise on their farm in western Nebraska. Furthermore, my father-in-law is an internationally known Professor Emeritus of Agronomy at the University of Nebraska. What is his main area of expertise? You guessed it: wheat!

When I first discovered my sensitivity to the gluten protein in wheat, I thought I was the only person in the world who had to avoid this seemingly healthy food. At least, I certainly didn't know anyone else with this life-altering situation, and back in 1988, there wasn't much information on the topic. Access to internet research and support groups as we know it today, didn't exist. I was in a state of denial for some time, bewildered by this unexpected turn of events that disrupted

my otherwise wonderful life. There were virtually no gluten-free foods in grocery stores, so I revamped my entire repertoire of dishes and continued my solitary gluten-free lifestyle for another five years without meeting anyone else who ate like I did.

When I was told to avoid wheat in 1988, celiac disease was virtually unknown to the general public. The medical community didn't pay much attention, either, calling it a "rare" condition. And, there was no support for people like me who weren't celiac patients, but still sickened by gluten. I was told that it was all "in my head," and that I was simply using a "fake" food reaction to gain attention. Over time, however, I met more and more people who also avoided wheat, and I realized that my newly revised recipes and hard-won wisdom could help others. So, I resigned from my corporate marketing position and founded Savory Palate, Inc., a publishing and consulting firm with a single mission: I help people eat.

GLUTEN-FREE IS FOR REAL

Today, the need for a gluten-free diet is accepted as a viable medical condition. It turns out that I am actually one of several million people with a gluten-free lifestyle. Compared to 1988, when I couldn't find anything to eat in the grocery store, we now have a wonderful array of ready-made foods, mixes, and ingredients from retail stores and online vendors, and many restaurants now serve gluten-free dishes. Leading universities and clinics have established celiac research centers. In addition, we have national gluten-free associations, gluten-free magazines, and the American Celiac Disease Alliance—comprised of associations, companies, and individuals who present a unified voice to the government, the food industry, and the public on various issues, including food labeling. As a result, we have the Food Allergen Labeling and Consumer Protection Act (FALCPA), which has required manufacturers to identify the eight major food allergens, including wheat, on any food manufactured since January 1, 2006. And, by late 2008, manufacturers will have official gluten-free standards to guide them. But just what is this mysterious thing called gluten? Keep reading.

WHAT IS GLUTEN?

Most people can easily go through life never knowing—or caring—about gluten. For those who can't eat it, however, it's foremost in our minds. But just what is it? Gluten is that mysterious protein that food experts talk about in terms of baking. For example, gluten provides wonderful elasticity in bread dough, but it can toughen pie crusts and biscuits if you handle the dough too much.

From a scientific standpoint, gluten is actually a storage protein of wheat. For people with celiac disease it is the gliadin fraction of gluten in particular that is problematic. For those who are sensitive to wheat but don't have celiac disease, there may be other proteins in gluten that affect us but we don't know which proteins are actually the culprits.

Other grains have proteins that chemically resemble gluten. Barley contains secalins, and rye contains hordeins. Other members of this botanical tribe include spelt, kamut, and triticale, and that's why you see all of these grains—wheat, barley, rye, spelt, kamut, and triticale—on the "do not eat" list for gluten-free people.

SOURCES OF GLUTEN

OBVIOUS SOURCES OF GLUTEN

- Bagels
- Breads
- Cakes
- Cereals
- Cookies
- Crackers
- Muffins
- Pancakes
- Pastas
- Tortillas
- Waffles
- Anything made with wheat and related grains of barley, rye, spelt, and kamut

SURPRISING SOURCES OF GLUTEN

- Bouillons
- Broths
- Deli meats
- Imitation seafoods
- Licorice candy
- Malt vinegar
- Salad dressings
- Seasonings
- Soup and soup mixes
- Tea

Oats may appear on this list because of the possibility that they are contaminated by wheat, not because they inherently contain gluten. There are now pure, uncontaminated gluten-free oats on the market that, according to Dr. Peter Green, a leading gastroenterologist at Columbia University, can be tolerated by over 98 percent of those with celiac disease. So, I offer recipes in this book that use those special oats. For more about the various positions on oats, go to www.gluten.net or www.glutenfreediet.ca, or to learn more about gluten-free oats, go to the manufacturers' websites: www.bobsredmill.com, www.creamhillestates.com, www.glutenfreeoats.com, www.giftsofnature.net., and www.onlyoats.com.

WHY CAN'T SOME PEOPLE EAT GLUTEN?

There are several reasons why some people can't eat gluten.

Celiac Disease

When everything goes well with our digestive system we are blissfully unaware of it. We eat food, digest it, and the nutrients silently nourish our bodies. But when celiac disease disrupts that process, the damage may start in the digestive system but can affect the entire body.

Celiac disease is an inherited autoimmune disorder that affects the digestive process of the small intestine. When a person who has celiac disease consumes gluten, the individual's immune system regards this otherwise normal food as an invader and attacks the small intestine. In an effort to protect the body from this invasion, the villi—hairlike cilia that line the small intestine and absorb nutrients from food—become inflamed and eventually flatten, thus inhibiting the absorption of important nutrients into the body. Classic symptoms include gas, bloating, diarrhea, and fatigue. However, only one-third to one-half of people with celiac disease exhibit these symptoms—making celiac disease less likely to be the suspect in the first place. But these symptom-free people are still damaging their intestines when they eat gluten.

The University of Chicago Celiac Disease Center suggests that undiagnosed and untreated celiac disease can lead to the development of other autoimmune disorders, as well as osteoporosis, infertility, neurological conditions, and in rare cases, cancer. Another form of the disease is dermatitis herpetiformis (DH), with symptoms of skin rashes and blisterlike spots.

Once deemed "extremely rare," celiac disease is far more common than originally thought. Dr. Alessio Fasano, Medical Director of the Center for Celiac Research, says that approximately one in 133 Americans—ten times more than originally expected—have celiac disease and he calls it "the most prevalent genetically transmitted condition in the world." This means that nearly 3 million Americans are living with this disease, and it takes an average of eleven years to get a correct diagnosis, according to Dr. Peter Green and Rory Jones in *Celiac Disease: A Hidden Epidemic*.

Unlike many other diseases, there is no pill, no vaccine, and no surgical procedure to cure celiac disease. It is an autoimmune condition for which there is no cure. A strict, lifelong adherence to a gluten-free diet is the only treatment. Eating food with gluten will cause damage to the intestines.

Celiac disease must be managed with the help of a gastroenterologist, who performs a series of tests—including a small-bowel endoscopy while the patient is sedated—before a final diagnosis can be made. For more information on celiac disease, go to www.americanceliac.org, www.celiaccentral.org, www.celiaccenter.org, www.celiacdisease.net, www.gluten.net, www.celiac.org, www.csaceliacs.org, www.celiac.com, and www.glutenfreediet.ca.

Allergies and Intolerances

According to the Food Allergy & Anaphylaxis Network (FAAN at www.foodallergy.org), about 12 million Americans suffer from true food allergies. Eight percent of children under the age of three have food allergies, compared to three percent for adults. Wheat is one of the top eight food allergens affecting these allergic individuals.

True food allergies involve the immune system's IgE antibodies, and reactions—such as skin rashes or respiratory stress—are usually sudden and more pronounced than reactions in food intolerances. Few people have this type of severe allergy, but for those who do, it's *very* serious, and many carry an EpiPen® (an injectable shot of epinephrine) to buy more time until they can get to an emergency room.

In contrast to the few people with wheat allergies, some experts estimate that 10 to 15 percent of Americans have intolerances to gluten (*Dangerous Grains,* James Braly, MD, and Ron Hoggan, MA). Unlike true food allergies, the reactions involved in food intolerances involve IgG antibodies and may be delayed, are usually more subtle, and can take many different forms. Some people—like me—experience nasal congestion and stuffiness, a feeling of fatigue, and what we ruefully call "brain fog." Others have headaches (sometimes migraines), stomachaches, rashes, achy joints, and a host of other maladies that are easily associated with other ailments. That's why it's often difficult to pinpoint food intolerances.

While food intolerances won't kill you, they can certainly compromise the quality of your life. Furthermore, the treatment for the symptoms can be as devastating as the symptoms themselves. In my case, endless rounds of antibiotics had a profound and lasting effect on my digestive system.

Diagnosis of a food allergy or intolerance should be made by a board-certified allergist or a health professional that specializes in this area. There are a variety of tests and procedures used to confirm a diagnosis. Testing for food allergies and intolerances remains a somewhat controversial area, and not all experts agree on a single approach.

Autism—A Special Case

According to www.autismspeaks.org, approximately one in 150 children are estimated to have autism, a neurobiological disorder that perplexes families and the medical community alike. As part of the overall treatment (but not as a substitute for other treatment or as a cure for autism), several experts advocate a gluten-free, casein-free (GFCF) diet (casein is a milk protein). According to these experts, some autistic children don't process these proteins properly, and removing them from the children's diet helps their behavior. The use of a gluten-free diet for autistic children is controversial and I am not an expert in autism, but many families use my gluten-free recipes to prepare food for their autistic children. For more information on autism and the gluten-free, casein-free diet, go to www.gfcfdiet.com, www.autismndi.com, and www.autismspeaks.org.

Other conditions may warrant a gluten-free diet. For example, people with food-triggered asthma are sometimes placed on gluten-free diets. You should rely on the advice of your physician as to whether a gluten-free diet is appropriate for you. If it is, this book will help you. All of the recipes avoid wheat and any wheat-related grains such as barley, rye, spelt, or kamut by using gluten-free flours and by specifying gluten-free substitutes for other ingredients.

READ FOOD LABELS EVERY TIME YOU SHOP

The key to successful living without gluten is to read labels on everything. Gluten is in many products, but it doesn't always appear as "gluten." It is often listed as all-purpose flour, unbleached flour, bread flour, cake flour, whole-wheat flour, graham flour, farina, semolina, bulgur, or durum—all of which indicate the presence of wheat and, therefore, gluten. The Food Allergen Labeling and Consumer Protection Act (FALCPA) requires that wheat-containing foods must list the word "wheat" on the ingredient label.

Gluten is present in other well-known grains such as barley, rye, and spelt. But it's also in lesser-known grains like triticale, kamut, einkorn, and farro. They are still part of the wheat family and contain gluten. By law, the label doesn't have to say "wheat" if the food contains these wheat-related grains, but when those ingredients are used they are usually named in the ingredient list, so you'll know that particular food contains gluten.

You should carefully read the labels of *everything* you buy, each time you buy it—even if you've bought the item many times before, are familiar with the manufacturer, and have confidence in that company. Manufacturers might change their ingredients or their procedures, and foods that you thought were safe in the past might suddenly contain gluten.

While gluten might not be one of the main ingredients in the food you buy, that food may be prepared in the same receptacle or manufacturing equipment as gluten-containing foods. If the facility isn't dedicated to gluten-free foods, find out how the company cleans its equipment between runs. Is there any possibility of contamination with gluten? Some manufacturers state on the package that their product is processed on equipment that also processes food containing other allergens, including wheat. It is up to you to decide whether to eat that food or not, but this also raises the issue of what "gluten-free" truly means.

This issue becomes much clearer when the Food and Drug Administration (FDA) implements its definition of "gluten-free," which will affect food product labeling. Although the final ruling is scheduled for release after *1,000 Gluten-Free Recipes* is published, you can check on the ruling yourself at www.gluten.net, www.americanceliac.org, or www.glutenfreediet.ca.

You may see gluten-free certification logos on some foods. The Gluten-Free Certification Organization (www.gfco.org), a branch of the Gluten Intolerance Group certifies companies as gluten-free and authorizes them to display a certification logo on the food item, as does the Celiac Sprue Association (www.csaceliacs.org). These certifying organizations help consumers identify safe foods, though they act independently of the FDA. Food manufacturers must list wheat if it is an ingredient, but displaying a gluten-free claim is voluntary. Companies that don't use these logos don't necessarily manufacture unsafe foods, but these logos are yet another tool for you to use when you shop.

For updates, subscribe to newsletters from gluten-free associations such as Savory Palate, the Celiac Disease Foundation, Celiac Sprue Association, and Gluten Intolerance Group, and read gluten-free magazines like *Gluten-Free Living*, *Living Without*, and *Scott-Free*.

COOKING WITH GLUTEN-FREE INGREDIENTS

Gluten-Free Flours

Sorghum: The Mainstay of My Flour Blend

Sorghum (also called "milo") grows in places around the world and in the central United States, including our family farm in Nebraska during the 1960s—long before I became gluten-free. I began experimenting with sorghum in 1996 when it was called *jowar,* its name in India. I wanted an alternative to rice flour to make better baked goods with flour that wasn't gritty and contained more protein. I really began to use sorghum extensively after 2000, when the grade we call sweet white sorghum or food sorghum was developed and began to be readily available from Bob's Red Mill. This meant I could use it in my cookbooks knowing that consumers could find it. So, I developed this sorghum blend that has become the basis for my personal baking and my cookbooks.

How to Modify Carol's Sorghum Blend

You can modify the sorghum blend right at the point of baking, which makes this versatile blend all the more adaptable. For example, I often do one or more of the following "customized" tweaks to achieve my particular baking goals:

Carol's Sorghum Blend

1½ cups sorghum flour	35%
1½ cups potato starch/cornstarch	35%
1 cup tapioca flour	30%

Whisk the ingredients together until well blended. Store, tightly covered, in a dark, dry place. You may refrigerate or freeze the blend, but bring to room temperature before using. Makes 4 cups. You may double or triple the recipe.

- **For extra pliability in a pie crust, add sweet rice flour.** Making pie crust is probably one of the most intimidating tasks for gluten-free bakers. I add sweet rice flour to the sorghum blend as I combine all of the pie crust ingredients in a mixing bowl or food processor. It makes the pie crust very easy to roll, without the usual breaking and tearing usually associated with gluten-free pie crusts. In fact, the pie crust is so supple that I can drape it across the palm of my hand and it will not tear or break.

- **For breads and biscuits with a light crumb and high rise, add more potato starch or cornstarch.** There is already some potato starch (or cornstarch) in the sorghum blend, but adding even more makes the dough or batter extremely light, thus increasing the possibility for baked goods that are less dense. If I want airier, lighter baked bread, for example, I might add more potato starch or cornstarch in relation to the protein flours because the starchy flours don't weigh down the dough. If I want a soft cookie, I might add more potato starch or cornstarch in relation to the protein-based flours, much like the softer cookies enjoyed for the Jewish holiday Passover.

- **For a well-browned or crisp texture in cookies and bars, add a fair amount of tapioca flour** because tapioca flour lends chewiness and also helps the browning process.

- **For heartier, more nutritious muffins and breads, add fiber-rich grains and nuts** (ground or chopped nuts, flax meal, cooked quinoa, uncooked cream of buckwheat cereal, or whole grain teff). I love breads and muffins, but I know that they will be healthier if I add some fiber to them. This fiber, in turn, adds important nutrients and a more interesting texture.

- **For greater density or "chew" in cookies, add protein flours** (potato flour, almond meal, pure Montina supplement, or flax meal.) Gluten-free flour blends are especially high in carbohydrates because starches are added to them for maximum performance. I like to add a little more protein to breads and muffins to give them more substance.

6. **For higher rise, moist texture, more natural-looking crumb, and longer shelf-life, add Expandex** (modified tapioca starch). I often replace ¼ cup of the flour blend with Expandex in muffins, cornbread, yeast bread, and hamburger bun recipes for better texture. I use 2 tablespoons Expandex in cream puffs for a crispier crust. My general rule of thumb is to replace about 12 percent of the total flour blend with Expandex but others may use it in larger quantities. For more information from the manufacturer, see www.expandex-glutenfree.com.

Expandex

Modified starches were typically unavailable to the home cook, but that changed in 2005 with the introduction of Expandex modified tapioca starch by Corn Products International (www.expandexglutenfree.com). It offers many benefits to the gluten-free home cook, it is certified gluten-free by the Gluten-Free Certification Organization, and I use it in many recipes in this cookbook.

Some particularly important benefits of Expandex for gluten-free baking include:

- Enhances the appearance, texture, and flavor of baked products;
- Creates a moist and expanded bread crumb, with a texture similar to regular bread;
- Improves crispy texture in thin baked foods such as cookies or crackers;

- Reduces the amount of xanthan or guar gums needed in baking;
- Extends shelf life as compared to existing gluten-free foods.

This means Expandex can make gluten-free baked goods look and taste more like food that contains gluten. I have experimented quite a bit with Expandex since it became available, and it is now an important part of my gluten-free pantry.

Here is a brief summary of how I use it in my home cooking and in certain recipes in this cookbook:

ROLE OF EXPANDEX MODIFIED FOOD TAPIOCA STARCH IN BAKING

	AMOUNT	WHAT EXPANDEX DOES
French Bread	Replace 2 tablespoons of the flour in a recipe with 3 cups flour	Produces a crispier crust and more rounded loaf with a higher rise
Muffins	Replace ¼ cup of the flour in a recipe with 2 cups flour	Rises higher, produces more normal looking and less dense texture, and improves shelf life. Crust is crispier
Corn Bread	Replace ¼ cup of the flour in a recipe with 2 cups of flour	Rises higher, produces more normal looking and less dense texture, and improves shelf life
Biscotti	Replace ¼ cup of the flour in a recipe with 2¼ cups of flour	Produces crispier, crunchier texture especially in recipes where the dough is patted or rolled thinly
Cream Puffs	Replace 2 tablespoons of the flour in a recipe with ¾ cup flour	Produces a crispier texture and higher rise
Graham Crackers	Replace 2 tablespoons of the flour in a recipe with 1½ cups of flour	Produces crispier, crunchier texture
Shortbread	Replace ¼ cup of the flour in a recipe with 2¼ cups of flour	Produces crispier texture, especially in recipes where the dough is patted or rolled thinly

Measuring Flours

In baking, precise ingredient measurements are important, because even a small error in measuring can mean the difference between success and failure. This means no "eyeballing" or loosely guessing amounts. You should use standard measuring cups or measuring spoons and follow these steps when measuring flour: I do it this way every time.

1. Fluff or aerate the flour with a whisk, especially if it has been sitting in the container for a long time. Spoon the flour lightly into the measuring cup.

2. Never pack the flour down into the measuring cup or measure flour in a cup designed to measure liquids (they usually have pour spouts). It can add up to 20 percent more flour and can ruin a recipe.

3. Level off the top of the flour with the straight edge of a knife.

Whenever you purchase a new cookbook, read the front pages to find out how the author measures ingredients. Some cooks use the "dip and sweep" method, which means dipping the measuring cup itself into the flour and then leveling or sweeping it off with a straight edge. I never use that method because it packs the flour too densely.

Storing Flours

Use storage containers that fit with your storage needs. Any of the following options will work:

- Heavy-duty freezer (food-quality) bags
- Plastic (food-quality) storage containers, made of polystyrene or polycarbonate
- Original containers the flours are sold in

Be sure to refrigerate or freeze flours if you live in a warm climates; otherwise store them in a dark, dry area. Certain flours should be refrigerated at all times (e.g., brown rice flour, amaranth, millet, or any flours with high amounts of oil because they have a tendency to turn rancid). Don't allow storage containers to sit in direct sunlight or near any heat source that causes condensation to form inside. This will cause the flour to clump and deteriorate quicker. Be sure to clean out storage containers periodically to assure that old flours are used up or thrown away before you add new flour to the container.

Ingredients that Affect Baking

Baking involves a complex interplay of various ingredients. Here is a brief explanation of the role of these ingredients in gluten-free baking.

Acids: Generally speaking, acids act as a catalyst or food for the yeast, encouraging the bread to rise higher and faster. Vinegar is an acid, as is lemon juice, and both can be used interchangeably in bread. Unbuffered Vitamin C, also known as ascorbic acid, is also acidic and can be used in place of vinegar or lemon juice. Usually about ¼ teaspoon of ascorbic acid per recipe will do the trick.

If you've ever sprinkled lemon juice or citric acid on fruit to keep it from discoloring, then you know that acids also discourage browning. So there has to be a balance between being a catalyst for yeast and inhibiting the necessary browning process that makes baked goods look attractive. All of the bread recipes in this book state the exact amount of vinegar or lemon juice, so be sure to follow the recipe exactly.

Nonfat Dry Milk Powder: Most people confuse this ingredient with Carnation instant milk granules. In fact, the two are vastly different. According to food science expert Harold McGee, nonfat dry milk powder—a very fine, dense powder—is made by pasteurizing milk and removing 90 percent of its water. The remaining 10 percent is misted into a dry chamber where it dries into particles or milk solids. It can be reconstituted into milk for drinking, but we usually use it in yeast breads to add protein, calcium, and sugar, which feed the yeast, smooth the crust, and tenderize the crumb in bread. It is especially useful in breads made from rice flour. Milk powder can be used either in larger quantities as a flour or in smaller quantities as a helper.

Carnation instant milk, on the other hand, is coarser and less dense than nonfat dry milk powder, so it doesn't measure the same. That is, one-quarter cup of nonfat dry milk powder is far denser and, therefore, contains far more protein, sugar, and calcium than one-quarter cup of Carnation granules. The effect on your baking will be noticeable because the Carnation requires far less water than the nonfat dry milk powder.

Fiber: Adding fiber to baked items is an important way to improve the nutrient value as well as the fiber level of baked goods. Fiber can take many forms, but in baking we usually think of flax meal, rice bran, cereal, or chopped nuts. There is a great deal of interest in adding fiber to our diets to comply with recommendations from many nutrition experts for anywhere from 25 to 35 grams a day, depending on your calorie intake. For some newly diagnosed celiac patients, too much fiber during the early stages of healing might be upsetting to their digestive systems, but for the rest of us it is an important component of a healthy diet.

Adding fiber is especially important in recipes that are based primarily on low-fiber, low nutrient flours such as rice flour, potato starch, and tapioca flour blends—which characterize many gluten-free recipes. If fiber isn't added, these baked goods are basically pure carbohydrate and provide little nutritive value.

In general, adding fiber to baked goods such as breads weighs them down and makes them heavier and less likely to rise as high. In larger quantities, fiber can make baked goods quite dense. And, certain forms of fiber such as flax meal and nuts add fat, so you may need to cut down on the amount of butter or oil in the recipe. Also, some forms of fiber, such as cereal (for example, buckwheat cereal) will soak up liquid at a rate different from the other ingredients. For all of my recipes, I specify how much fiber to add so you should follow the recipe closely to make sure it works.

Unflavored Gelatin Powder: This is the familiar ingredient we all know as Knox or Grayslake gelatin, the stuff that makes Jell-O (but without the color or flavoring). I began using gelatin back when rice flour was about the only flour we had for gluten-free baking. Gelatin added important protein (virtually lacking in white rice flour) and it helped bind the ingredients together, plus it added moisture, which in turn helped prevent baked goods from drying out so fast. With today's improved, more nutritious flours—such as the sorghum flour I routinely use—I rarely use gelatin powder. But it is still useful when baking without eggs because it provides important protein and binding, traits that eggs bring to baking.

Lecithin: Lecithin is a natural emollient and emulsifier found in egg yolks and soybeans. As an emulsifier, it binds water and oil together and promotes a finer texture. I especially like to use soy lecithin in egg-free baked goods because it promotes a better texture and greater stability. Lecithin is typically sold in the supplement section of health food stores and can be stored on your pantry shelf.

Salt: According to food science expert Shirley Corriher in *Cookwise,* salt plays three important functions: it enhances flavor, controls bacteria, and strengthens gluten. Since we're not concerned with gluten, the latter benefit is irrelevant to us. However, salt also slows down yeast action, so it is important to strike a balance between bread flavor and its ability to rise effectively. If you've ever tasted bread without salt—like the salt-free, flat-tasting breads of Tuscany—then you'll realize its importance. I prefer flavorful bread, so I use the maximum amount of salt in my bread recipes. Tip: If you want to cut down on the salt to get a better rise, you can try adding ¼ teaspoon of salt to the egg wash so that the crust has a slightly salty taste, but the rising action won't be affected.

The recipes in this book also use salt in sweet breads, as well as desserts such as cakes and cookies because they benefit from its flavor-enhancing properties. I use table salt in all recipes, unless the recipe specifically calls for kosher salt.

Water: Some bakers will only bake bread with filtered water because they believe that highly chlorinated water inhibits yeast action. Other bakers prefer not to use softened water because of its higher sodium content (the softening process involves sodium and high amounts of sodium can inhibit yeast). You should use the water that best suits your situation.

Xanthan gum: Xanthan gum is a polysaccharide, made from a pure culture fermentation of any carbohydrate (most likely corn) with the plant bacteria *xanthomonas campestris*. The mixture is then purified, yielding a polysaccharide gum. In plain English, xanthan gum is the glue that holds our baked goods together by performing a function similar to gluten.

Picture millions of tiny cells or balloons in your batter or dough. As the leavening (baking powder, baking soda, or yeast) starts expanding, the cells created by xanthan gum act like little containers to hold the carbon dioxide released by the leavening agent. As these little containers get bigger to hold the increasing carbon dioxide, your baked goods rise instead of falling flat as a pancake.

Xanthan gum also acts an emulsifier by helping the water and oil stay together once they're blended. That's why we say it "stabilizes" the baked item.

Guar Gum: Guar gum can be used instead of xanthan gum. Guar gum, also a polysaccharide, is a legume called *Cyanmopsis tetragonoloba*. It is extracted from the guar bean found in India and Pakistan, although some is also grown in the United States. If your recipe calls for 1 teaspoon xanthan gum, use 1½ teaspoons guar gum. Some particularly sensitive people think that guar gum irritates their intestines since large amounts of guar gum are used to make laxatives. Make sure you know if it is guar gum that causes your symptoms so you don't unnecessarily exclude this important ingredient because baked goods will fall apart without a gum. Of course, if guar gum bothers you in any way, don't use it. However, the small amounts used in our baking shouldn't have that much of an effect. For example, a loaf of bread with 2 teaspoons of guar gum that is cut into 12 slices has about one-sixth of a teaspoon per slice—not very much at all.

You have probably seen other types of binding in commercially-prepared foods such as carrageenan and locust bean gum but these ingredients are not readily available to consumers, so you won't find them in my recipes.

One of the curious findings in gluten-free baking is that a combination of xanthan and guar gum makes a nicer baked good—better texture, prettier crust, and slightly higher rise—than using one or the other alone. My discovery was one of those marvelous, but serendipitous events that I accidentally stumbled onto—but now use regularly. So, when you see my recipes with both forms of gum listed as ingredients, please be assured that it isn't a mistake. But you can use one or the other gum, as you please.

Natural and Dutch-Processed Cocoa Powder: Many cooks wonder how natural cocoa powder differs from Dutch-processed cocoa powder and how this affects cakes. Cocoa powder is made from the cocoa solids left over when cocoa beans are pressed to form chocolate liquor. About three-fourths of the cocoa butter is removed, leaving behind the remaining one-fourth cocoa butter which is processed to form cocoa powder. If the cocoa powder is left natural, then it is called natural cocoa powder and has a full, intense chocolate flavor. It is quite acidic, making it necessary to pair it with baking soda for balance.

If the cocoa powder is treated with alkali to neutralize this acid, then it is called Dutch-processed (or sometimes European). The alkali treatment reduces the bitterness of the cocoa powder, but—because it is now alkaline—it must be balanced with baking powder as the leavening agent in baking. The two cocoa powders are not interchangeable in gluten-free baking, so it is always important to use the type of cocoa powder and leavening agent specified in your recipe. There are other factors that can affect your choice of leavening agents such as buttermilk, molasses, and brown sugar, but basically it is important to

How Much Xanthan Gum or Guar Gum?

When using either xanthan gum or guar gum, mix with dry ingredients first (e.g., salt, spices), then add liquids.

WHERE?	HOW MUCH?
Salad Dressings	Xanthan: ⅛ to ¼ teaspoon per cup of liquid Guar: ¼ to ⅜ teaspoon per cup of liquid
Cookies	Xanthan: ¼ teaspoon per cup of flour Guar: ⅜ teaspoon per cup of flour
Pancakes and Waffles	Xanthan: ¼ teaspoon per cup of flour Guar: ⅜ teaspoon per cup of flour
Cakes	Xanthan: ½ teaspoon per cup of flour Guar: ¾ teaspoon per cup of flour
Muffins, Quick Breads	Xanthan: ¾ teaspoon per cup of flour Guar: 1 teaspoon per cup of flour
Bread	Xanthan: 1 to 1½ teaspoons per cup of flour Guar: 1½ to 2¼ teaspoons per cup of flour
Pizza	Xanthan: 2 teaspoons per cup of flour Guar: 3 teaspoons per cup of flour
Thickener for Sauces	Xanthan: 1 teaspoon in place of each tablespoon of original thickener (e.g., wheat flour or cornstarch) Guar: 1½ teaspoons in place of each tablespoon of original thickener

use the type of cocoa powder as well as the type of leavening agent specified in the recipe.

Converting Your Own Recipes to Gluten-Free

One of the most frequent questions at my cooking classes is, "How can I make my own recipes gluten-free?" When I eventually conceded that I couldn't eat my favorite homemade baked goods anymore, I asked myself the same question. This brings us to the topic of converting your everyday favorites—or perhaps family heirloom recipes—to be gluten-free.

I usually recommend that, as a new gluten-free cook, you make recipes from gluten free cookbooks before modifying your own. That way, you can see what the dough or batter should look like and get a feel for how gluten-free cooking differs from the way you used to cook. But I can readily identify with your need to resume eating your old favorites. The following box shows an example of one cake conversion (text continues on page xix).

When I first started baking gluten-free food—when

CONVERTING A CAKE RECIPE

This cake is a family heirloom; my mother made it frequently during my childhood. It is a small cake, sometimes called a "snacking cake," and it is perfectly suited for converting. Why?

1. Cakes with baking soda are more often successful than those with baking powder. It's not known exactly why, but baked goods leavened with baking soda seem to perform better than those leavened with baking powder. Baking soda, which is alkaline, requires acidic ingredients (such as the cocoa in this recipe) to achieve the proper pH balance. Since gluten-free flour blends are generally low-protein (once they're blended with the high-carbohydrate flours of potato starch and tapioca) and are more acidic, they work well in cakes that are leavened with baking soda because the alkalinity of the baking soda helps balance the acidity of the flours and other ingredients.

2. This cake uses natural cocoa rather than Dutch cocoa, which often requires baking powder.

3. The cake is small (under 2 cups of flour), so it bakes more successfully than a larger cake because you can use smaller baking pans that allow the heat to penetrate to the center of the batter more readily.

You will see the original cake ingredients in the first column. The second column shows how I modified them to use Carol's Sorghum Blend (page x), followed by the recipe directions.

MOTHER'S CHOCOLATE CAKE	GLUTEN-FREE CHOCOLATE CAKE
1½ cups all-purpose flour	1¼ cups Carol's Sorghum Blend
½ cup natural cocoa	½ cup natural cocoa
1 teaspoon salt	1 teaspoon xanthan gum
1 teaspoon baking soda	1 teaspoon baking soda
1 cup sugar	¾ teaspoon salt
½ cup shortening	1 cup packed light brown sugar
½ cup milk	½ cup unsalted butter or buttery spread, such as Earth Balance
1 large egg	½ cup milk
¾ cup hot brewed coffee	1 large egg
1 teaspoon vanilla	2 teaspoons pure vanilla extract
	¾ cup hot brewed coffee

1. Place a rack in the middle of the oven. Preheat the oven to 350°F. Generously grease a 9-inch round nonstick (gray, not black) or 11 × 7-inch rectangular pan.

2. Sift the flour blend, cocoa, xanthan gum, soda, and salt together in a small bowl; set aside.

3. In a medium mixing bowl, beat the sugar and butter with an electric mixer until well blended. Beat in milk, egg, and vanilla. Add sifted flour blend alternately with hot coffee, beginning and ending with flour. Transfer to prepared pan.

4. Bake 30 to 35 minutes or until a toothpick inserted into center of cake comes out clean. Cool the cake in the pan on a wire rack.

How Much Thickener?

Many people wonder how to thicken foods—such as gravy—without wheat. Here is a summary to help you choose the right thickener for your needs.

In place of **1 tablespoon of wheat flour,** use the following:

INGREDIENT/ AMOUNT?	TRAITS	SUGGESTED USES
Agar (Kanten) 1½ teaspoons	A jellylike thickening agent made from seaweed. Follow package directions. Colorless, flavorless. Sets at room temperature. Gels acidic liquids. Thin sauces need less.	Puddings, pie fillings, gelatin desserts, ice cream, glazes. Holds moisture and improves texture in pastry products.
Arrowroot 1½ teaspoons	Powdered tropical root. Mix with cold water before using. Thickens at lower temperature than wheat flour or cornstarch; better for eggs or sauces that can't be boiled. Add during last 5 minutes of cooking. Serve right away. Clear, shiny. Semisoft when cool.	Foods requiring clear, shiny sauce; good for egg or starch dishes where high heat is undesirable. Gives appearance of oil even when none used. Don't overcook or sauce will thin somewhat.
Cornstarch 1½ teaspoons	Mix with cold lquid before use. Stir just to boilling. Transparent, shiny sauce. Slight starchy flavor. Thicker and rigid when cool.	Puddings, pie fillings, fruit sauces, soups. Gives appearance of oil even when none used.
Gelatin Powder (unflavored) 1½ teaspoons	Animal-based powder. Dissolve in cold water. Then heat until clear before using.	Cheesecakes, gelatin salads, puddings, aspics. Won't gel acidic fruit like pineapple.
Kudzu (kuzu) Powder 1½ teaspoons	Derived from a plant root, Dissolve in cold water before using. Odorless, tasteless. Makes transparent, silky-smooth sauces with soft consistency.	Puddings, pie fillings, and gelled preparations. May need to experiment to find exact amount to use.
Potato Starch 1½ teaspoons	Mix with cold liquid before using.	Soups, stews, gravies
Rice Flour (brown or white) 1 tablespoon	Mix with cold water before using. Grainy texture. Consistency the same hot or cold.	Soups, stews, gravies
Sweet Rice Flour 1 tablespoon	Made from sticky white rice. Excellent thickening agent.	Sauces such as vegetable sauces
Tapioca Flour 1½ tablespoons	Tapioca is ground from the manioc or cassava plant. Mix with cold water before using. Add during last 5 minutes of cooking to avoid stringy consistency. Makes transparent, shiny sauce. Thick, soft gel when cool.	Soups, stews, gravies, potato dishes
Quick-Cooking Tapioca (precooked) 2 teaspoons	This is the granular form of tapioca flour. Mix with fruit. Let stand 15 minutes before baking.	Fruit pies, cobblers, and tapioca pudding

rice flour was the norm—my approach was to reduce the total flour amount by 10 to 15 percent to compensate for the dense nature of rice flour. I added xanthan gum (using the guides earlier) and three-fourths of the liquid. I then checked the consistency of the batter or dough and then added the remaining liquid, if needed, in small amounts. I always kept notes on what I did so I could replicate these same results the next time. You can do the same thing with your personal recipes.

Gluten-free and dairy-free

Lactose intolerance is one of the leading food sensitivities in America and goes hand in hand with celiac disease, at least in the initial stages of recovery. A 2005 online survey by the Gluten Intolerance Group found that nearly half of the gluten-free respondents had additional food sensitivities.

There are several replacements for dairy in cooking. You can use rice, soy, nut, or potato milk in place of cow's milk. Or try the new hemp milk. Each substitute has a unique taste, and most people go through a palate adjustment phase until the new flavors become tolerable or enjoyable.

Of course, butter makes food taste great, but if you avoid animal products or can't have dairy, you may use nondairy margarine or buttery spread. I'm particularly fond of the Earth Balance buttery spreads, buttery sticks, and shortening. They are nonhydrogenated—which means they do not contain transfat—and work just as well in most recipes. You can also use Spectrum Vegetable buttery spread in baking, but it does not melt.

Additionally, there are now soy-based cream cheeses called cream cheese alternatives by Soyco and Tofutti. Soyco makes a soy-based and rice-based Parmesan cheese, although the rice version still contains the milk protein casein. Soyco also makes sour cream alternatives that have emulsifiers and gums for extra body, but these additions may affect your baked items.

Instead of whipped cream, you can use Soyatoo or the nondairy whipped toppings that are sold in tubs. Many of these contain hydrogenated oils, which I avoid, but use them if you wish. Or, make your own soy-based whipped topping with my nondairy Whipped Topping (page 624) in this cookbook. Some recipes simply work best with dairy, but when an alternative is acceptable, I mention it by brand to help you locate that particular product. I used the Clan Thompson service called Celiac SmartList (www.clanthompson.com). But even though I suggest a brand, you must always read the label of that particular product because the manufacturer may change the ingredients or their manufacturing practices.

If you have sensitivities to any other foods you will have to read labels even more carefully, since some dishes in this book use prepared foods that have a wider variety of ingredients than you would ordinarily find in homemade versions. I've tried to make these recipes as versatile as possible so you can choose the right alternative for you.

MENUS

There are hundreds, even thousands, of ways you could combine the recipes in this book to make great meals. Here are a few ideas for everyday menus and for special occasions.

Weeknight Dinner
Warmed Olives in Herbs
Linguini with Red Clam Sauce
Italian-Style Spinach
Canadian Cookies

Comfort Food Supper
Meat Loaf
Garlic Mashed Potatoes
Broiled Tomatoes
Corn Spoon Bread
Chocolate Pudding

Kids-Will-Love-It Dinner
Cream of Tomato Soup
Macaroni and Cheese

After-Soccer-Practice Dinner
Oven-Baked Tortilla Chips with Guacamole
Chicken Enchiladas
Fresh baby carrots

Vegetarian Dinner
Vegetable Tempura with Dipping Sauce
Curried Chickpeas on Basmati Rice
Herb-Garlic Muffins
Pavlova

Sunday Morning Brunch
Leek-Pasta Strata
Fresh Fruit Salad with Coconut-Apricot Sauce
Blueberry-Lemon Coffee Cake

Sunday Dinner
Baked Ham with Clementine Marmalade Glaze
Mashed Garlic Potatoes and Celery Root
Waldorf Salad
Creamed Corn
Dinner Yeast Rolls
Cherry Pie

Breakfast Buffet for Weekend Guests
Breakfast Cheese and Egg Strata
Spiced Applesauce Waffles
Lemon Poppy Seed Scones with Lemon Glaze
Granola Orange-Strawberry Parfait

Summertime Luncheon
Gazpacho
Spinach Salad with Orange-Basil Dressing
Grilled Vegetables on Brown Rice
Basic Popovers
Strawberries and Cream Layer Cake

Tailgate Party or Picnic
Barbecued Brined Chicken
Home-Style Potato Salad
Tomato-Cucumber Salad with Feta Cheese
Quinoa Tabbouleh
Breakthrough Ready-to-Bake Bread
Chocolate Brownies

Dinner Party
Sage-Dusted Pork Chops with Autumn Spiced Apples
Crisp Potato Wedges

Baby Carrots with Dill-Maple Syrup
Mixed Greens Salad with Champagne Vinaigrette
French Bread
Sacher Torte

July 4th Bash
Barbecued Baby-Back Ribs
Home-Style Potato Salad
Baked Beans
Cabbage Coleslaw
Cornbread
Oatmeal Raisin Cookies
Vanilla Ice Cream

Thanksgiving or Christmas Meal
Brined Turkey
Corn Bread Stuffing with Sausage and Fruit
Sweet Potato Casserole with Pineapple-Pecan Topping
Green Bean Casserole with Onion Topping
Dinner Yeast Rolls or Sweet Potato Biscuits
Praline Pumpkin Pie

Super Bowl Party
Corn Chips with Guacamole
Fresh Vegetables with Creamy White Bean Dip
Buffalo Wings with Blue Cheese Dipping Sauce
Cincinnati Turkey Chili
Corn Bread Muffins with Chives
Chocolate Peanut Butter Cookies

Valentine's Day Romantic Dinner
Mediterranean Red Snapper en Papillote
Mixed Green Salad with Sherry Walnut Vinaigrette
Asparagus with Hollandaise Sauce
Dilled Rice Pilaf
Breadsticks
Chocolate-Espresso Souffles

Children's Party
Corn Dogs
Cheese Quesadillas
Fresh Vegetables with Ranch Dressing
Ice Cream Cones with Strawberry Ice Cream

Bridal Shower Luncheon
Asparagus Soup
Poached Salmon with Cucumber-Dill Sauce
Spinach, Strawberry, and Walnut Salad with
Lemon-Pomegranate Vinaigrette
Savory Biscotti Sticks
Old-Fashioned Strawberry Shortcake

PANCAKES, WAFFLES, AND OTHER BREAKFAST FOODS

Pancakes, Waffles, and French Toast

Basic Pancakes

Buttermilk Pancakes

Buckwheat Pancakes

Sweet Potato Pancakes with Maple Butter

Blueberry Millet Pancakes

Mesquite Pancakes

Cottage Cheese Pancakes

Sour Cream–Raisin Pancakes

Coconut Pancakes

Peanut Butter and Jelly (PB&J) Pancakes

Pumpkin Pancakes with Pomegranate Syrup

Spiced Applesauce Waffles

Baked Cinnamon Raisin French Toast

Savory French Toast

Cereal and Granola

Naked Gluten Free Granola

Gluten-Free Granola with Nuts and Dried Fruit

Thin, Crispy Granola Bars

Chewy Granola Bars

Cranberry-Ginger Cereal Bars

Granola Orange-Strawberry Parfait

Muesli

Eggs, Quiches, and Casseroles

Eggs Baked in French Bread

Eggs in a Nest

Cheese Blintzes

Egg Crepes with Brie and Almonds

Breakfast Egg and Cheese Strata

Leek-Pasta Frittata

Wild Morel Frittata

Bacon, Leek, Tomato, and Goat Cheese Quiche

Sweet Potato Hash

Turkey Hash

Egg Tortilla Casserole with Chipotle Mole Sauce

Breakfast Pizza

Breakfast—the foundation of a healthy diet—is also the most wheat-laden meal. Bagels, muffins, toast, pancakes, waffles, and cereal—they all contain wheat, leading some newly diagnosed people to skip breakfast entirely for fear of getting sick. But the many recipes offered in this chapter leave no reason to skip this critical meal.

Many of us eat breakfast at our desk or on-the-run, but there is something very comforting about eating a breakfast that you prepare in your own home. If you're short on time during the week, set aside time on weekends to try some of these terrific recipes.

Yes, you can use store-bought mixes for pancakes and waffles; in fact, you can buy basic gluten-free waffles and muffins, as well as bread for your morning toast. Instead, mix up a batch of my versatile Carol's Sorghum Blend (page x) ahead of time so you're ready to make the flavorful pancakes and waffles in this chapter anytime. Or use it to make muffins and quick breads in the Quick Breads and Muffins chapter. Or English muffins and Bagels in the Yeast Breads chapter. These recipes provide a wider variety of flavors and much more diversity than any store-bought versions.

Wholesome, nutritious cereals—hot or cold, and made from amaranth, sorghum, quinoa, corn, rice, beans, buckwheat, and teff—are widely available in natural food stores and grocery stores. Oats—an inherently gluten-free grain that can be contaminated during growing or processing—are now available in a pure, uncontaminated, gluten-free form. Make your own granola, granola bars, or muesli, using gluten-free oats, for a hearty start to your day. Be sure to get your physician's approval before you indulge; some gluten-intolerant people still may react to these oats for a number of other reasons, even though they are uncontaminated. For more information on the issue of gluten-free oats, go to www.gluten.net or see *Gluten-Free Diet* (Expanded Edition, 2006) by Shelley Case, RD.

Finally, I offer innovative ways to prepare eggs—beyond sunny-side-up, over-easy, or scrambled—such as frittatas, hash, quiche, and even pizza, for special days.

PANCAKES, WAFFLES, AND FRENCH TOAST

Basic Pancakes

MAKES 8 PANCAKES (4 INCHES EACH)

Make this easy batter for those mornings when the comfort of homemade pancakes seems absolutely necessary. You can use any milk but, of course, the flavor will change a little bit. For pancakes later in the week, double all of the ingredients (except the baking powder and baking soda) and refrigerate the remaining batter for up to 3 days. A teaspoon of fresh lemon juice will revive the reserved batter and make the pancakes nice and light.

1 cup Carol's Sorghum Blend (page x)

2 tablespoons sugar

2 teaspoons baking powder

½ teaspoon baking soda

⅛ teaspoon salt, or to taste

¼ teaspoon xanthan gum

⅓ to ½ cup 1% milk (cow's, rice, soy, potato, or nut)

2 tablespoons unsalted butter or buttery spread, such as Earth Balance, melted, or canola oil

1 large egg, at room temperature

1 teaspoon pure vanilla extract

Additional butter, buttery spread, or canola oil for frying

1 In a mixing bowl or large measuring cup, sift together the sorghum blend, sugar, baking powder, baking soda, salt, and xanthan gum.

2 Gradually whisk in the milk, butter, egg, and vanilla until very smooth. Let the batter stand 5 minutes and then adjust the consistency, if needed (see Tips for Perfect Pancakes, right).

3 In a large, nonstick (gray, not black) skillet, heat the butter over medium-high heat until hot but not smoking. Pour ¼ cup batter onto the skillet and cook until bubbles appear on top of the pancake, about 2 to 3 minutes. Turn and cook until browned on other side. Serve immediately.

TIPS FOR PERFECT PANCAKES

- Let the pancake batter stand 5 minutes before frying the pancakes to give the liquid and dry ingredients time to meld and reach the proper consistency.

- For the recipes in this book, start with the smaller amount of milk. If the batter looks too thick, add another 2 to 3 tablespoons milk to reach the desired consistency. The batter should be thick enough to spread only slightly when it hits the hot griddle, yet not so thick that it doesn't spread at all. If it spreads very rapidly, add more sorghum blend, 1 tablespoon at a time.

- Browning time will vary with the ingredients in your pancake batter, but generally the pancakes are ready to be turned when bubbles start to appear on the surface of the batter. You can also determine if the underside is browned enough by gently lifting the pancake with a spatula and taking a peek. Frying a "test" pancake is always a good idea to see if the skillet heat and the pancake batter are correctly calibrated.

Buttermilk Pancakes

MAKES 4 PANCAKES (4 INCHES EACH)

Homey and comforting, these pancakes are sure to please your family and guests. Buttermilk makes pancakes lighter, but you can achieve a similar effect using the homemade Buttermilk option (page 677). To make small silver-dollar pancakes, use 2 tablespoons of batter per pancake; for 4-inch pancakes, use ¼ cup of batter; for large 5-inch pancakes, use ⅓ cup of batter.

1 cup Carol's Sorghum Blend (page x)

2 tablespoons sugar

1 teaspoon baking powder

½ teaspoon baking soda

¼ teaspoon salt

¼ teaspoon xanthan gum

½ cup buttermilk, or homemade Buttermilk (page 677), well-shaken, or more as needed

2 tablespoons unsalted butter or buttery spread, such as Earth Garden, melted, or canola oil

1 large egg

1 teaspoon pure vanilla extract

Additional butter, buttery spread, or canola oil for frying

1 In a mixing bowl or large measuring cup sift together the sorghum blend, sugar, baking powder, baking soda, salt, and xanthan gum.

2 Gradually whisk in the buttermilk, butter, egg, and vanilla until very smooth. Let the batter stand 5 minutes and then adjust the consistency, if needed (see Tips for Perfect Pancakes, page 3).

3 In a large nonstick (gray, not black) skillet, heat the butter over medium-high heat until hot but not smoking. Pour ¼ cup batter onto the skillet and cook until bubbles appear on top of the pancake, about 2 to 3 minutes. Turn and cook until browned on other side. Serve immediately.

Buckwheat Pancakes

MAKES 8 PANCAKES (4 INCHES EACH)

Buckwheat is related to rhubarb and is not actually a grain; it is a seed in the fruit family. Rather than buy buckwheat flour, I always have Bob's Red Mill Creamy Buckwheat Cereal on hand for my breakfast. I quickly grind what I need for these pancakes with my little coffee grinder. Start with ½ cup of milk, adding more if necessary until the batter reaches the right consistency.

½ cup buckwheat flour

½ cup potato starch

2 teaspoons baking powder

1 teaspoon sugar

½ teaspoon baking soda

¼ teaspoon xanthan gum

¼ teaspoon salt

½ to ⅔ cup 1% milk (cow's, rice, soy, potato, or nut)

2 tablespoons unsalted butter or buttery spread, such as Earth Balance, melted, or canola oil

1 tablespoon fresh lemon juice

1 large egg

1 teaspoon pure vanilla extract

Additional butter, buttery spread, or canola oil for frying

1 In a mixing bowl or large measuring cup, sift the flour, potato starch, baking powder, sugar, baking soda, xanthan gum, and salt.

2 Whisk in milk, butter, lemon juice, egg, and vanilla until very smooth. Let the batter stand 5 minutes and then adjust the consistency, if needed (see Tips for Perfect Pancakes, page 3).

3 In a large nonstick (gray, not black) skillet, heat the butter over medium-high heat until hot but not smoking. Pour ¼ cup batter onto the skillet and cook until bubbles appear on top of the pancake, about 2 to 3 minutes. Turn and cook until browned on other side. Serve immediately.

Sweet Potato Pancakes with Maple Butter

MAKES 8 PANCAKES (4 INCHES EACH)

Joel Schaefer is a chef at a major resort, where his responsibilities include meeting the requests of guests with food allergies and intolerances. He provides guests with innovative choices, such as these pancakes with sweet potatoes—one of the least allergenic foods on earth.

MAPLE BUTTER

1 pound unsalted butter or buttery spread, such as Earth Balance, at room temperature
½ cup (4 ounces) pure maple syrup
Salt to taste

PANCAKES

1 cup Carol's Sorghum Blend (page x)
2 teaspoons sugar
2 teaspoons baking powder
½ teaspoon baking soda
1 large egg
½ cup 1% milk (cow's, rice, soy, potato, or nut)
1 tablespoon canola oil
¼ teaspoon salt
½ cup sweet potato, roasted, peeled, and pureed
Additional canola oil for frying

1 Make the Maple Butter: Place the butter in a mixing bowl and beat with a stiff whisk or spatula. Add the maple syrup and mix until combined. If you are using an electric mixer, use the paddle attachment to combine the ingredients. Transfer the Maple Butter to a container and store in the refrigerator until needed. Bring to room temperature before serving.

2 Make the pancakes: In a small mixing bowl, sift together the sorghum blend, sugar, baking powder, and baking soda. Whisk until well blended.

3 In another mixing bowl, whisk together the egg, milk, oil, and salt. Add the sweet potato puree and blend with a handheld mixer or a wire whisk just until smooth.

4 Add the sweet potato mixture to the dry ingredients and stir until combined.

5 Heat a 10-inch skillet or electric griddle on medium heat. Lightly oil the pan or griddle with canola oil, wiping off any excess oil with a paper towel.

6 Pour ¼ cup batter in the skillet and cook until bubbles appear on top of the pancake, about 1 to 2 minutes. Turn and cook until browned on the other side, about another 1 to 2 minutes. Serve immediately with Maple Butter.

Blueberry Millet Pancakes (V)

MAKES 8 PANCAKES (4 INCHES EACH)

I developed this recipe to showcase the mild flavor of millet, an incredibly healthy grain that adds wonderful nutrients to gluten-free meals. Rather than buy millet flour (which has a fairly short shelf life), buy whole-grain millet and grind it as you need it in a small coffee grinder. Keep the millet grains in your freezer or refrigerator to keep them fresh. If you buy frozen blueberries, just toss them into the batter in their frozen state to keep the batter from turning blue.

¼ cup millet flour
¼ cup tapioca flour
½ cup potato starch
2 tablespoons sugar
1½ teaspoons baking powder
1 teaspoon baking soda
¼ teaspoon salt
¼ teaspoon xanthan gum
⅓ cup 1% milk (cow's, rice, soy, potato, or nut)
2 tablespoons unsalted butter or buttery spread, such as Earth Balance, melted, or canola oil
2 teaspoons grated lemon zest
1 large egg
1 teaspoon pure vanilla extract
1 cup fresh or frozen blueberries, preferably small
Additional butter, buttery spread, or canola oil for frying

1 In a mixing bowl or large measuring cup, sift the flours, potato starch, sugar, baking powder, baking soda, salt, and xanthan gum.

2 Whisk in the milk, butter, lemon zest, egg, and vanilla until very smooth. Gently stir in the blueberries. Let the batter stand 5 minutes and then adjust the consistency, if needed (see Tips for Perfect Pancakes, page 3).

3 In a large nonstick (gray, not black) skillet, heat the butter over medium-high heat until hot but not smoking. Pour ¼ cup batter onto the skillet and cook until bubbles appear on top of the pancake, about 2 to 3 minutes. Turn and cook until browned on other side. Serve immediately.

Mesquite Pancakes

MAKES 8 PANCAKES (4 INCHES EACH)

If you've only thought of mesquite as the wood that lends a wonderful flavor to grilled meats, this will be a pleasant surprise. Mesquite flour, ground from the pods of mesquite shrubs that grow in arid regions, has a wonderful cinnamonlike taste that can be used in a variety of foods. It has a high protein and fiber content. I devised this simple recipe so you can substitute other high-protein and high-fiber flours such as amaranth, teff, Montina, or millet.Use the same quantity as the mesquite flour, though you may need to add a few additional tablespoons of milk to reach the proper consistency. You can also increase the mesquite flour to ¼ cup if you like, and add more milk as needed.

1¾ cups Carol's Sorghum Blend (page x)
2 tablespoons mesquite flour*
2 tablespoons sugar
1½ teaspoons baking powder
½ teaspoon baking soda
⅛ teaspoon salt, or to taste
¼ teaspoon xanthan gum
⅓ to ½ cup 1% milk (cow's, rice, soy, potato, or nut)
2 tablespoons unsalted butter or buttery spread, such as Earth Balance, melted, or canola oil
1 large egg
1 teaspoon pure vanilla extract
Additional butter, buttery spread, or canola oil for frying

1 In a mixing bowl or large measuring cup sift together the sorghum blend, mesquite flour, sugar, baking powder, baking soda, salt, and xanthan gum.

2 Gradually whisk in the milk, butter, egg, and vanilla until very smooth. Let the batter stand 5 minutes and then adjust the consistency, if needed (see Tips for Perfect Pancakes, page 3).

3 In a large nonstick (gray, not black) skillet, heat the butter over medium-high heat until hot but not smoking. Pour ¼ cup batter onto the skillet and cook until bubbles appear on top of the pancake, about 2 to 3 minutes. Turn and cook until browned on other side. Serve immediately.

Available at www.therubyrange.com or www.casadefruta.com.

Cottage Cheese Pancakes **V**

MAKES 8 PANCAKES (4 INCHES EACH)

Adding cottage cheese to pancakes gives them a nice, substantial texture while boosting their calcium content. As with all pancakes, I recommend making a "test" pancake first, to see if the skillet is the right temperature.

1 cup Carol's Sorghum Blend (page x)

2 tablespoons sugar

1 teaspoon baking powder

1 teaspoon Expandex modified tapioca starch,
    or 1 teaspoon Carol's Sorghum Blend

½ teaspoon baking soda

¼ teaspoon xanthan gum

¾ cup buttermilk or homemade Buttermilk (page
    677), well-shaken

2 tablespoons unsalted butter or buttery spread,
    such as Earth Balance, melted

1 large egg

½ teaspoon pure vanilla extract

½ cup small curd cottage cheese

Additional butter, buttery spread, or canola oil for
    frying

1 In a medium mixing bowl, sift the sorghum blend, sugar, baking powder, modified tapioca starch, baking soda, and xanthan gum.

2 Whisk in the buttermilk, butter, egg, and vanilla until very smooth. Gently stir in the cottage cheese. Let the batter stand 5 minutes and then adjust the consistency, if needed (see Tips for Perfect Pancakes, page 3). If it is too thick, add more water, a tablespoon at a time.

3 In a large nonstick (gray, not black) skillet, heat the butter over medium-high heat until hot but not smoking. Pour ¼ cup batter onto the skillet and cook until bubbles appear on top of the pancake, about 2 to 3 minutes. Turn and cook until browned on other side. Serve immediately.

Sour Cream–Raisin Pancakes **V**

MAKES 8 PANCAKES (4 INCHES EACH)

Sour Cream–Raisin Pie (page 597) was my inspiration for these pancakes. The sour cream makes these pancakes deliciously rich, and they are all the more irresistible with chewy raisins tucked inside.

1 cup Carol's Sorghum Blend (page x)

2 tablespoons sugar

1 teaspoon baking powder

½ teaspoon baking soda

¼ teaspoon salt

¼ teaspoon xanthan gum

½ cup sour cream or sour cream alternative, such as
    Tofutti

¼ to ⅓ cup 1% milk (cow's, rice, soy, potato, or nut)

1 large egg

1 teaspoon pure vanilla extract

1 teaspoon grated lemon zest

¼ cup dark raisins or dried currants

Butter, buttery spread, such as Earth Balance, or
    canola oil for frying

1 In a mixing bowl or large measuring cup, sift together the sorghum blend, sugar, baking powder, baking soda, salt, and xanthan gum.

2 Gradually whisk in the sour cream, milk, egg, vanilla, and lemon zest until very smooth. Let the batter stand 5 minutes and then adjust the consistency, if needed (see Tips for Perfect Pancakes, page 3). Stir in the raisins.

3 In a large nonstick (gray, not black) skillet, heat the butter over medium-high heat until hot but not smoking. Pour ¼ cup batter onto the skillet and cook until bubbles appear on top of the pancake, about 2 to 3 minutes. Turn and cook until browned on other side. Serve immediately.

Coconut Pancakes

MAKES 8 PANCAKES (4 INCHES EACH)

Coconut flour is made by drying and defatting coconut meat and then finely grinding it into flour. It lends a delicious coconut flavor and is a great ingredient for gluten-free baking because of its high fiber, high protein, and low carbohydrate content. I especially like using it with coconut flakes, which further intensify the lovely coconut flavor in these yummy pancakes.

¾ cup Carol's Sorghum Blend (page x)
¼ cup coconut flour
2 tablespoons sugar
2 teaspoons baking powder
½ teaspoon baking soda
⅛ teaspoon salt, or to taste
¼ teaspoon xanthan gum
¾ to 1 cup 1% milk (cow's, rice, soy, potato, or nut)
2 tablespoons unsalted butter or buttery spread, such as Earth Balance, melted, or canola oil
1 large egg, at room temperature
1 teaspoon pure vanilla extract
1 teaspoon coconut-flavored extract (optional)
¼ cup sweetened shredded coconut
Additional butter, buttery spread, or canola oil for frying

1 In a mixing bowl or large measuring cup, sift the sorghum blend, coconut flour, sugar, baking powder, baking soda, salt, and xanthan gum.

2 Gradually whisk in the milk, butter, egg, vanilla, and coconut extract, if using, until very smooth. Stir in the coconut. Let the batter stand 5 minutes and then add more milk, if necessary, just until the batter is thin enough to pour (see Tips for Perfect Pancakes, page 3).

3 In a large nonstick (gray, not black) skillet, heat the butter over medium-high heat until hot but not smoking. Pour ¼ cup batter onto the skillet and cook until bubbles appear on top of the pancake, about 2 to 3 minutes. Turn and cook until browned on other side. Serve immediately.

Peanut Butter and Jelly (PB&J) Pancakes

MAKES 8 PANCAKES (4 INCHES EACH)

You can have the delicious flavors of the traditional peanut butter and jelly sandwich in this breakfast version of every kid's favorite.

1 cup Carol's Sorghum Blend (page x)
2 tablespoons sugar
1½ teaspoons baking powder
1 teaspoon baking soda
¼ teaspoon salt
¼ teaspoon xanthan gum
⅓ cup 1% milk (cow's, rice, soy, potato, or nut)
⅓ cup crunchy peanut butter, at room temperature
2 tablespoons unsalted butter or buttery spread, such as Earth Balance, melted, or canola oil
1 large egg
1 teaspoon pure vanilla extract
Additional butter, buttery spread, or canola oil for frying
½ cup grape jelly

1 In a medium mixing bowl, sift the sorghum blend, sugar, baking powder, baking soda, salt, and xanthan gum.

2 Whisk in the milk, peanut butter, butter, egg, and vanilla until very smooth. Let the batter stand 5 minutes and then adjust the consistency, if needed (see Tips for Perfect Pancakes, page 3).

3 In a large nonstick (gray, not black) skillet, heat the butter over medium-high heat until hot but not smoking. Pour ¼ cup batter onto the skillet and cook until bubbles appear on top of the pancake, about 2 to 3 minutes. Turn and cook until browned on other side. Serve immediately with 1 tablespoon jelly per pancake.

Pumpkin Pancakes with Pomegranate Syrup

MAKES 8 PANCAKES (4 INCHES EACH)

Subtly flavored with autumn accents, these pancakes are a perfect way to use up that little bit of pumpkin left over from your holiday baking. They are also a great way to add important nutrients to your diet and the pomegranate syrup provides important antioxidants—not to mention that it's delicious!

⅓ cup 100% pumpkin puree (not pumpkin pie filling)

1 large egg, at room temperature

½ cup 1% milk (cow's, rice, soy, potato, or nut)

2 tablespoons unsalted butter or buttery spread, such as Earth Balance, melted, or canola oil

1 teaspoon pure vanilla extract

½ cup Carol's Sorghum Blend (page x)

½ cup potato starch

2 tablespoons sugar

2 teaspoons baking powder

½ teaspoon baking soda

½ teaspoon ground cinnamon

½ teaspoon ground ginger

¼ teaspoon salt

⅛ teaspoon freshly grated nutmeg

⅛ teaspoon ground cloves

1 tablespoon fresh lemon juice (optional)

Additional butter, buttery spread, or canola oil for frying

Store-bought pomegranate syrup or homemade Pomegranate Syrup (page 649) or maple syrup

1 In a medium bowl, whisk the pumpkin puree, egg, milk, butter, and vanilla until smooth. In a separate bowl, whisk the sorghum blend, potato starch, sugar, baking powder, baking soda, cinnamon, ginger, salt, nutmeg, and cloves until blended. Or, put all the ingredients in a blender and process until very smooth. Let the batter stand 5 minutes and then adjust the consistency, if needed (see Tips for Perfect Pancakes, page 3). For lighter pancakes, squeeze a tablespoon of fresh lemon juice into the batter just before frying.

2 In a large nonstick (gray, not black) skillet, heat the butter over medium-high heat until hot but not smoking. Pour ¼ cup batter onto the skillet and cook until bubbles appear on top of the pancake, about 2 to 3 minutes. Turn and cook until browned on other side. Serve immediately with pomengranate syrup.

Spiced Applesauce Waffles V

MAKES 8 WAFFLES (4 INCHES EACH)

This is a wonderful breakfast to serve your family or guests on a leisurely autumn weekend when you want something special. You can double this recipe if you need to serve more than four, but there's no need to increase the baking powder or baking soda.

2 large eggs, at room temperature, separated

¼ cup unsalted butter or buttery spread, such as Earth Balance, melted, or canola oil

1 container (4 ounces) unsweetened applesauce

1 teaspoon cider vinegar

1 teaspoon pure vanilla extract

1 cup Carol's Sorghum Blend (page x)

1 tablespoon sugar

2 teaspoons baking powder

1½ teaspoons pumpkin pie spice or apple pie spice (or use 1 teaspoon ground cinnamon, plus ¼ teaspoon ground nutmeg or allspice)

½ teaspoon baking soda

¼ teaspoon salt

¼ teaspoon xanthan gum

Topping of your choice, such as warmed applesauce, syrup, or honey

1 If you want to keep the cooked waffles warm while preparing the others, line a 15 × 10-inch baking sheet with foil and place in a preheated 200°F oven.

2 In a large bowl, whisk together the egg yolks, butter, applesauce, vinegar, and vanilla until smooth.

3 In a small bowl, sift together the sorghum blend, sugar, baking powder, pumpkin pie spice, baking soda, salt, and xanthan gum and then whisk into the liquid ingredients until the batter is smooth.

4 In a small bowl, beat the egg whites with an electric mixer on medium speed until soft peaks form, about 30 to 45 seconds. Increase the speed to high and beat until stiff peaks form, about 2 minutes. Fold half of the whites into the batter and then carefully fold in the remaining whites.

5 Coat a waffle iron with cooking spray and heat, following manufacturer's directions. Pour about ⅓ cup for each 4-inch waffle onto the surface, spreading the batter evenly to the edges. Cook 3 to 4 minutes or until the waffles are golden brown. Transfer cooked waffles to the baking sheet in the oven while cooking the remaining waffles, if necessary. Top with warmed applesauce, syrup, or honey.

Baked Cinnamon Raisin French Toast Ⓥ

MAKES 6 SERVINGS

French toast is always a treat, but my simple version is an exceptionally easy way to have a hot breakfast for your family on a weekday or to serve weekend house guests. Prepare it the night before so all you have to do the next morning is bake it.

6 slices (½-inch thick) homemade gluten-free Cinnamon Raisin Yeast Bread (page 84)
6 large eggs
2 cups 1% milk (cow's, rice, soy, potato, or nut)
2 tablespoons sugar
2 teaspoons pure vanilla extract
½ teaspoon ground cinnamon
¼ teaspoon freshly grated nutmeg
½ teaspoon salt

1 Arrange bread slices in 2 rows in a generously buttered 13 × 9-inch nonstick (gray, not black) baking dish.

2 In a large bowl, combine the eggs, milk, sugar, vanilla, cinnamon, nutmeg, and salt and whisk until blended. Pour the mixture over the bread slices, making sure all are covered evenly. Cover with foil and refrigerate overnight.

3 Place a rack in the middle of the oven. Preheat the oven to 350°F. Bake 35 to 40 minutes or until puffed and lightly browned. Serve immediately with your favorite syrup, honey, or jam.

French Toast with Candied Almond Topping: Just before baking, blend together ¼ cup (½ stick) unsalted butter, ¼ cup packed light brown sugar, ½ cup sliced almonds, 1 tablespoon light corn syrup, ½ teaspoon ground cinnamon, ½ teaspoon freshly grated nutmeg, and ¼ teaspoon salt in a medium bowl. Spread evenly over slices of the French toast. Bake and serve as directed in Step 3.

Savory French Toast

MAKES 4 SERVINGS

French toast doesn't have to be sweet as this savory version illustrates. You can still top it with a little marmalade or apple butter for a sweet contrast to the melted cheese.

2 large eggs, beaten

½ cup milk (cow's, rice, soy, potato, or nut)

1 cup shredded Monterey Jack cheese or cheese alternative, such as Vegan Gourmet

1 tablespoon chopped fresh chives

4 teaspoons unsalted butter or buttery spread, such as Earth Balance

1 homemade gluten-free French Baguette (page 100), cut into ½-inch slices

¼ cup grated Parmesan cheese or soy alternative, such as Soyco

½ cup orange marmalade, apple butter, or fruit preserves of choice for topping

1 In a shallow bowl, whisk together the eggs, milk, cheese, and chives. In a large nonstick (gray, not black) skillet, melt the butter over medium heat. Dip slices of bread into the egg mixture and place them in the hot skillet.

2 Cook 3 to 5 minutes per side, or until the toast is golden and crispy. Dust the tops with Parmesan cheese. Serve hot with a small dollop of marmalade, apple butter, or fruit preserves.

CEREAL AND GRANOLA

Naked Gluten-Free Granola

MAKES 4 CUPS

This is a simple, lightly sweetened yet tasty version of granola. Without the nuts and fruit, it becomes even more versatile in your repertoire of quick dishes for your family. For a sweeter granola, increase the honey to ½ cup.

DRY INGREDIENTS

3 cups rolled soy flakes (available at health food stores) or gluten-free rolled oats*†

1 cups raw natural coconut or sweetened coconut flakes

1 teaspoon ground cinnamon

¼ teaspoon salt

LIQUID INGREDIENTS

⅓ cup honey

¼ cup very hot water

¼ cup canola oil

1 teaspoon pure vanilla extract

1 Place a rack in the middle of the oven. Preheat the oven to 300°F. Line a 15 × 10-inch baking sheet (not nonstick) with parchment paper or lightly coat it with cooking spray.

2 In a very large bowl, place the dry ingredients and toss to thoroughly combine.

3 In a small bowl, combine the liquid ingredients and stir until the honey is dissolved. Pour over the dry ingredients and toss with a spatula until thoroughly combined. (The mixture will be fairly wet.) Place the granola on the prepared sheet and spread to a thin layer.

4 Bake 15 minutes and stir. Bake another 15 minutes and stir again. Continue baking in 10-minute increments until granola is browned to desired degree. Cool the granola on the pan 20 minutes on a wire rack. Refrigerate up to 2 weeks.

*Available from www.bobsredmill.com, www. creamhillestates.com, www.giftsofnature.net, www. glutenfreeoats.com, or www.onlyoats.com.

†Check with your physician before using gluten-free oats.

Gluten-Free Granola with Nuts and Dried Fruit

MAKES 5 CUPS

You can enjoy this wonderful cereal for breakfast, as a topping for fruit crisps, as a granola bar, or just by the handful as a snack.

DRY INGREDIENTS
2 cups rolled soy flakes* or gluten-free rolled oats**†
1 cup unsweetened coconut flakes
¼ cup sunflower seeds
¼ cup almond slices
¼ cup pumpkin seeds
¼ cup walnuts or pecans
1 teaspoon ground cinnamon
¼ teaspoon salt

LIQUID INGREDIENTS
½ cup honey
¼ cup very hot water
¼ cup canola oil
1 teaspoon pure vanilla extract

DRIED FRUITS AND NUTS
½ cup whole almonds
¼ cup dried bananas
¼ cup dark raisins
¼ cup finely chopped dried apricots

1 Place a rack in the middle of the oven. Preheat the oven to 300°F. Line a 15 × 10-inch baking sheet (not nonstick) with parchment paper or lightly coat it with cooking spray.

2 In a very large bowl, place the dry ingredients and toss to thoroughly combine.

3 In a small bowl, combine the liquid ingredients and stir until the honey is dissolved. Pour over dry ingredients and toss with a spatula to thoroughly combine. The mixture will be fairly wet. Place the granola on the prepared sheet and spread to a thin layer.

4 Bake 15 minutes and then stir. Bake another 15 minutes and stir again. Continue baking in 10-minute increments until the granola is browned to the desired degree. Cool the granola on the pan 20 minutes on a wire rack. Stir in dried fruits and nuts. Refrigerate up to 2 weeks.

*Available at natural food stores.

**Available from www.bobsredmill.com, www. creamhillestates.com, www.giftsofnature.net, www. glutenfreeoats.com, or www.onlyoats.com.

†Check with your physician before using gluten-free oats.

Thin, Crispy Granola Bars

MAKES 24 BARS

Granola bars can take a variety of different textures. Use your homemade granola to make this thin, crispy version, or try rolled soy flakes in place of the oats in the Naked Gluten-Free Granola (page 11). You can bake the bars in a 13 × 9 × 2-inch cake pan, but I recommend a 13 × 9-inch rimmed baking sheet (not nonstick) to make it easier to remove the bars. They are perfect for lunch boxes or hiking snacks, sealed tightly in individual food storage bags.

¾ cup almonds, pecans, or walnuts
2 cups homemade Naked Gluten-Free Granola
   (page 11)*†
¼ cup honey
¼ cup packed light brown sugar
1 tablespoon boiling water
1 tablespoon canola oil
1 teaspoon pure vanilla extract
¾ teaspoon ground cinnamon

1 Place a rack in the middle of the oven. Preheat the oven to 325°F. Line a 13 × 9-inch rimmed baking sheet (not nonstick) with foil or parchment paper. Coat with cooking spray.

2 In a food processor, pulse the nuts until very finely chopped. Add the remaining ingredients and process until thoroughly combined.

3 With a wet spatula, spread the mixture in the pan. Lay a piece of plastic wrap over the mixture and flatten to a ¼-inch thickness with your palms.

4 Bake 45 to 50 minutes, or until golden brown. Cool the pan 10 minutes on a wire rack. Cut into bars with a very sharp knife. Remove from pan and cool the bars completely on a wire rack.

*Made with gluten-free oats from www.bobsredmill.com, www.creamhillestates.com, www.giftsofnature.net, www. glutenfreeoats.com, and www.onlyoats.com.

†Check with your physician before using gluten-free oats.

Chewy Granola Bars

MAKES 24 BARS

These bars can be served warm with a dollop of whipped cream. Or, they make a great breakfast as you're rushing out the door to school or work.

¼ cup unsalted butter or buttery spread, such as Earth Balance, at room temperature
¼ cup honey
¼ cup packed light brown sugar
1 teaspoon pure vanilla extract
2 cups homemade Naked Gluten-Free Granola (page 11)*†
1 cup nutty flax cereal, such as Perky's
½ teaspoon ground cinnamon
½ teaspoon xanthan gum
¼ teaspoon salt
¼ cup gluten-free dairy-free chocolate chips, such as Tropical Source

1 In a medium saucepan, combine butter, honey, and brown sugar. Bring to boil and cook, stirring, until sugar is melted. Remove from heat and stir in vanilla.

2 Stir in granola, flax cereal, cinnamon, xanthan gum, and salt with wooden spoon until blended. Then stir in chocolate chips. Spread in a 13 × 9-inch *ungreased* glass pan. Refrigerate 2 hours or until firm.

*Made with gluten-free oats from www.bobsredmill.com, www.creamhillestates.com, www.giftsofnature.net, www. glutenfreeoats.com, and www.onlyoats.com.

†Check with your physician before using gluten-free oats.

Cranberry-Ginger Cereal Bars

MAKES 24 BARS

You will enjoy the wonderful flavors in this no-bake snack bar. It makes a quick breakfast meal on the run or a nutritious after-school snack.

2 cups gluten-free puffed rice cereal, such as Erewhon
2 cups homemade Naked Gluten-Free Granola*† (page 11) or Enjoy Life or Bakery on Main
1 cup almond slices
1 cup dried cranberries
½ cup sweetened coconut flakes
½ cup ground flax meal
¼ cup finely chopped crystallized ginger
2 teaspoons pure vanilla extract
1 teaspoon xanthan gum
½ teaspoon salt
⅔ cup honey
1 tablespoon unsalted butter or buttery spread, such as Earth Balance, or canola oil

1 Place a rack in the middle of the oven. Preheat the oven to 325°F. Generously grease an 11 × 7-inch nonstick (gray, not black) pan.

2 In a large bowl, mix all the ingredients, except the honey and butter, until thoroughly blended.

3 Heat the honey and butter in the microwave on low for 1 minute or until the butter is melted; stir to combine. Pour over the dry ingredients and toss until thoroughly combined. Transfer the mixture to the prepared pan, spreading it evenly with a spatula, then press the mixture down firmly with a spatula or oiled hands.

4 Bake 10 to 15 minutes or just until the edges of the bars turn golden. Cool the bars in the pan on a wire rack at least 1 hour before cutting.

*Made with gluten-free oats from www.bobsredmill.com, www.creamhillestates.com, www.giftsofnature.net, www.glutenfreeoats.com, and www.onlyoats.com.

†Check with your physician before using gluten-free oats.

COOKED WHOLE GRAINS FOR BREAKFAST

Hot cereal makes a great breakfast year-round, not just in the cold winter months. There are several gluten-free whole grains besides wheat that cook up into marvelous hot cereals.

For breakfast, I like to stir a teaspoon of vanilla into the cooked cereal for a flavor boost. You can also use salt to taste if you wish. My favorite toppings include cinnamon, honey, maple syrup, pancake syrup, brown sugar, fresh fruit, jam, jelly, or applesauce.

Look for Bob's Red Mill Mighty Tasty Gluten-Free Cereal, which is made from brown rice, corn, buckwheat, and sorghum; or Bob's Red Mill Creamy Buckwheat hot cereal in your local natural food store.

Cooking times for whole grains can vary slightly depending on the age of the grains and their moisture content. The height and depth of your pot will also affect cooking time. Use the table below as a guide; if the grains are not done when the allotted time is up, add a little more water and continue cooking.

GRAIN (1 CUP)	WATER	COOKING TIME	YIELD
Amaranth	2 cups	15 to 20 minutes	3½ cups
Brown rice	2½ cups	30 to 45 minutes	3½ to 4 cups
Buckwheat (kasha)	1 cup	15 to 20 minutes	4 cups
Millet	2½ to 4 cups	35 to 40 minutes	4 cups
Quinoa	2 cups	15 to 20 minutes	3 cups
Sorghum (soak overnight)	2 cups	45 to 60 minutes	3 cups
Wild Rice	4 cups	40 minutes	3½ to 4 cups

Granola Orange-Strawberry Parfait

MAKES 4 SERVINGS

I am especially fond of using Bakery on Main granola for this recipe because it is delicious and comes in a wide variety of flavors. This recipe makes four individual parfaits for families, but I sometimes double or even triple the recipe and serve it in a glass trifle bowl for large brunches. It makes a dramatic presentation and guests love it. To keep the granola crunchy, assemble the parfait just before serving rather than preparing it ahead of time. You can use any number of different yogurt and fruit combinations, such as blueberry yogurt with fresh blueberries or raspberry yogurt with fresh raspberries.

2 containers (8 ounces each) lemon or orange-flavored yogurt (cow's, soy)

½ cup orange marmalade or homemade Clementine Marmalade (page 678)

2 cups gluten-free granola, such as Bakery on Main

2 cans (8 ounces each) mandarin oranges, drained

2 cups sliced fresh hulled strawberries

Fresh mint leaves for garnish

In a small bowl, whisk together the yogurt and marmalade. For each parfait, layer ½ cup yogurt-marmalade mixture, ½ cup granola, ½ can mandarin oranges, and ½ cup hulled strawberries. For larger parfait glasses or the trifle bowl, repeat the layers as needed. Reserve some of the fruit to use as a garnish on top. Serve immediately, garnished with fresh mint leaves.

Muesli

MAKES 4 SERVINGS

This hearty breakfast dish can be kept in the refrigerator and served throughout the week. It is commonly served in European countries and is a "stick-to-your-ribs" kind of meal.

2 cups gluten-free rolled oats*†

½ cup raw coconut flakes

¼ cup chopped dried apricots

¼ cup raw pumpkin seeds

¼ cup sunflower seeds

¼ cup dried cranberries

2 apples (Gala, Fuji, or your choice), cored, and diced

1 container (8 ounces) plain low-fat yogurt (cow's, soy)

1 cup 1% milk (cow's, rice, soy, potato, or nut)

1 tablespoon honey, or to taste

1 teaspoon pure vanilla extract

In a large bowl, toss all the ingredients until combined. Cover and refrigerate overnight or until the liquids are absorbed, at least 4 hours. Serve cold or gently reheated in the microwave oven on medium for 3 to 5 minutes or until warm.

Available from www.bobsredmill.com, www.creamhillestates.com, www.giftsofnature.net, www.glutenfreeoats.com, or www.onlyoats.com.

†Check with your physician before using gluten-free oats.

EGGS, QUICHES, AND CASSEROLES

Eggs Baked in French Bread

MAKES 4 SERVINGS

When everyone tires of the usual scrambled eggs and toast, this is an innovative way to serve these two breakfast staples.

1 loaf homemade gluten-free French Yeast Bread (page 100), sliced in half horizontally
Cooking spray (preferably olive oil)
2 large eggs
¼ cup chopped fresh thyme
¼ cup grated Parmesan cheese or soy alternative, such as Soyco
¼ teaspoon salt
⅛ teaspoon white pepper
Fresh parsley for garnish

1 Place a rack in the middle of the oven. Preheat the oven to 350°F. With your fingers, hollow out the loaf of bread, leaving the crust intact. Reserve the hollowed-out bread. Generously spray the loaf halves with cooking spray.

2 Place the loaf halves cut side down on a baking sheet (not nonstick) and bake 10 minutes or until the inside of the loaf begins to brown. Remove from oven and let cool slightly.

3 While the bread bakes, in a mixing bowl, combine the eggs, thyme, Parmesan cheese, salt, and pepper. Whisk together until smooth. Stir in reserved bread pieces. Arrange the mixture in each half of the cooled loaf.

4 Bake 30 to 35 minutes or until eggs are set. If the bread browns too much, cover with foil. Remove from oven, cut each half into 4 pieces, and serve immediately with a garnish of fresh parsley.

Eggs in a Nest

MAKES 4 SERVINGS

This is a particularly good way to use up gluten-free bread that has hardened, but is not quite stale. Gently heat it in a microwave oven on low for 1 to 2 minutes or until it is soft and pliable and then proceed with this recipe.

4 slices gluten-free bread of choice (see Yeast Breads chapter)
2 tablespoons chopped green onion
2 tablespoons chopped fresh thyme, divided
4 large eggs
¼ teaspoon salt
¼ teaspoon freshly ground black pepper
¼ cup shredded Gruyère or Swiss cheese, or cheese alternative, such as Vegan Gourmet
Dash paprika

1 Put a rack in the lowest position of the oven. Preheat the oven to 325°F. Generously grease four 6-ounce ramekins. Place the ramekins on a baking sheet (not nonstick).

2 Trim the crusts from the bread. With a rolling pin, flatten each slice of bread to ⅛-inch thickness, and push and press into a ramekin.

3 Divide the green onion and half of the thyme evenly among the ramekins, reserving some thyme for garnish. Break an egg into each ramekin and season it with salt and pepper. Top with cheese and sprinkle with paprika.

4 Bake 20 to 25 minutes or to desired doneness for eggs. Remove from the oven, garnish with a sprinkle of remaining fresh thyme, and serve immediately.

Cheese Blintzes

MAKES 8 BLINTZES

Cheese blintzes, with their sweet topping, are an excellent choice for brunch or dessert. Serve them anytime you wish. They are especially pretty topped with cherry pie filling, but other fruit toppings such as blueberry will also work well.

CREPES

¾ cup 1% milk (cow's, rice, soy, potato, or nut)

⅔ cup Carol's Sorghum Blend (page x)

2 large eggs

6 teaspoons unsalted butter, buttery spread, such as Earth Balance, melted, or canola oil

¼ teaspoon xanthan gum

⅛ teaspoon salt

Additional butter, buttery spread, or canola oil for frying

FILLING AND TOPPING

1 cup ricotta cheese or firm silken tofu, such as Mori-Nu

1 small package (3 ounces) cream cheese or cream cheese alternative, such as Tofutti, softened

3 tablespoons powdered sugar + ½ cup powdered sugar, for dusting

Grated zest of 1 lemon

1 large egg, at room temperature

1 can (20 ounces) cherry pie filling

1 Make the crepes: In a blender, combine all the ingredients, except the additional butter and process until the mixture is smooth. Refrigerate 1 hour. Just before frying the crepes, blend again to reincorporate ingredients.

2 Heat an 8-inch skillet or seasoned crepe pan over medium-high heat until a drop of water dances on the surface. Brush the surface with butter and replenish after each crepe is cooked.

3 For each crepe, pour a scant ¼ cup batter into the pan and immediately tilt and swirl the pan to coat the bottom evenly with crepe batter. Cook until the underside of the crepe is crispy brown, then flip the crepe with a thin spatula and cook the other side for about 20 to 30 seconds, or until the crepe batter sets. (The first crepe will often not cook as well as the pan reaches the right temperature.) Stack the cooked crepes between sheets of foil, plastic wrap, or parchment paper to prevent drying out. Repeat with the remaining batter.

4 Place a rack in the middle of the oven. Preheat the oven to 400°F. Coat a 13 × 9-inch glass baking dish with cooking spray.

5 Make the filling: In a medium bowl, beat the ricotta cheese and cream cheese together on medium speed until smooth. Gradually, beat in the 3 tablespoons powdered sugar, lemon zest, and egg until smooth. Spoon ¼ cup of the cheese mixture in a line along the lower third of each crepe. Fold the bottom edge away from you to just cover the cheese filling; then fold the 2 sides in to the center. Roll the crepe away from you a couple of times to make a package, ending with the seam side down. Place the blintzes in the baking dish.

6 Bake 10 to 15 minutes, or until the egg is cooked and the cheese sets. Using a spatula, transfer the blintzes to serving plates. Dust with powdered sugar, spoon cherry pie filling on top, and serve warm.

Egg Crepes with Brie and Almonds ⓥ

MAKES 4 SERVINGS

You're probably familiar with crepes made with flour, but these lacy beauties are made from very thin layers of fried egg.

2 teaspoons olive oil

6 large eggs

2 tablespoons 1% milk (cow, rice, soy, potato, or nut)

¼ teaspoon salt

¼ teaspoon freshly ground pepper

1 small round (8 ounces) Brie, cut into ½-inch cubes, or cheese alternative, such as Vegan Gourmet, divided

¼ cup sliced almonds, divided

1 bunch fresh chives, snipped

1 In a large heavy nonstick (gray, not black) skillet, heat the oil over medium heat.

2 In a medium bowl, whisk the eggs with the milk, salt, and pepper until smooth. Pour ½ cup egg mixture into the skillet and tilt and rotate to make eggs coat the bottom of the pan evenly. Cover and cook until the eggs are barely set, about 2 minutes. Lay ¼ of the Brie cubes in a row down the middle of the crepe and sprinkle with 1 tablespoon of the almonds. Loosen eggs from the pan with a silicon spatula and fold sides over the Brie.

3 Transfer Brie-filled crepe to a serving plate and repeat the process to make another 3 crepes. Serve immediately or place Brie-filled crepes on a baking sheet and keep warm in a 180°F oven until all the crepes are cooked. The Brie will soften slightly. Garnish with snipped fresh chives and serve.

Breakfast Egg and Cheese Strata

MAKES 8 SERVINGS

This dish is perfect for a weekend family visit or for entertaining because you can assemble it the day before and refrigerate it overnight. It bakes while you're preparing the rest of the meal. For added flavor, replace ¼ of the milk with your favorite dry white wine.

10 slices store-bought gluten-free bread, such as Whole Foods or Enjoy Life, or homemade White Sandwich Yeast Bread (page 85) or homemade Cornbread (page 68), cut in 1-inch cubes

2 cups Canadian-style bacon, finely diced

2 cups coarsely grated Gruyère (about 6 ounces), or cheese alternative, such as Vegan Gourmet

1 cup finely grated Parmesan cheese or soy alternative, such as Soyco, divided

½ cup store-bought basil pesto or homemade Basil Pesto (page 672)

2 tablespoons extra-virgin olive oil

2 tablespoons fresh grated onion or 1 tablespoon dried minced onion

4 large eggs

3 cups 1% milk (cow's, rice, soy, potato, or nut)

1 tablespoon Dijon mustard

1 teaspoon salt

½ teaspoon freshly ground black pepper

¼ teaspoon freshly grated nutmeg

2 tablespoons chopped fresh parsley

1 Generously grease a 13 × 9-inch baking dish; set aside.

2 In a very large bowl, place the bread cubes, bacon, Gruyère, and ¾ cup of the Parmesan cheeses; toss until thoroughly combined. Combine the pesto, oil, and onion, and toss with the bread until thoroughly blended. Spread the mixture evenly in the bottom of the baking dish.

3 In the same large bowl, whisk together the eggs, milk, mustard, salt, pepper, and nutmeg and pour evenly over the bread cubes. Cover with plastic wrap and refrigerate overnight.

4 Place a rack in the middle of the oven. Preheat the oven to 350°F. Remove the plastic wrap and sprinkle with the remaining ¼ cup Parmesan. Bake 45 minutes to 1 hour, or until the top of the casserole is brown. Let stand 5 minutes before serving sprinkled with chopped parsley.

Leek-Pasta Frittata

MAKES 4 SERVINGS

Most people throw away leftover pasta, but there are many flavorful ways to use it up. Any brand will work in this flavorful frittata, but I like the linguine from Heartland's Finest because it holds its shape quite well and has a high protein content.

1 tablespoon canola oil, divided
2 cups thinly sliced leeks (about 2 medium), white section only, halved lengthwise, and washed thoroughly
1 slice prosciutto or pancetta, finely chopped
4 large eggs
¼ cup 1% milk (cow's, rice, soy, potato, or nut)
¼ cup grated Parmesan cheese or soy alternative, such as Soyco
½ teaspoon salt
¼ teaspoon freshly ground black pepper
2 teaspoons fresh oregano or 1 teaspoon dried
2 teaspoons fresh basil or 1 teaspoon dried
1½ cups (about 4 ounces) cooked gluten-free linguini, such as Heartland's Finest
½ cup shredded mozzarella cheese or cheese alternative, such as Vegan Gourmet
2 tablespoons fresh parsley or 1 tablespoon dried

1 In a 10-inch nonstick (gray, not black) skillet, heat 2 teaspoons of oil over low-medium heat. Add the leeks and prosciutto and cook until the leeks are softened, about 4 minutes. Remove the skillet from the heat.

2 In a medium bowl, whisk together the eggs, milk, Parmesan cheese, salt, pepper, oregano, and basil. Stir in the cooked linguine.

3 Return the skillet to medium heat. Add the remaining teaspoon canola oil. Pour the egg mixture

into pan, cover, and cook 10 minutes or until the top is set. Uncover, sprinkle with mozzarella cheese, and cover again. Cook another 1 to 2 minutes or until the cheese is melted and eggs are cooked through. Garnish with parsley and serve immediately.

Wild Morel Frittata

MAKES 4 SERVINGS

Morels are mushrooms that resemble little corn cobs. In fact, that is what we called them when we gathered them in the timberland near my childhood home. Today, dried morels can be found near the produce section of your grocery store when fresh ones aren't available. Substitute 1 cup of any fresh mushroom or dried mushroom variety, and this dish will still taste just as great.

1 tablespoon canola oil
2 teaspoons unsalted butter or buttery spread, such as Earth Balance
½ pound reconstituted dried morels (follow package directions)
¼ cup sliced green onions
1 slice pancetta or bacon, finely chopped
4 large eggs
¼ cup 1% milk (cow's, rice, soy, potato, or nut)
¼ cup grated Parmesan cheese or soy alternative, such as Soyco
½ teaspoon salt
¼ teaspoon freshly ground black pepper
2 teaspoons snipped fresh chives or 1 teaspoon dried
2 teaspoons chopped fresh parsley or 1 teaspoon dried
2 teaspoons chopped fresh chervil or 1 teaspoon dried
1½ cups cooked gluten-free linguine (about 4 ounces), such as Heartland's Finest or Tinkyada
Juice of 1 lemon
2 tablespoons chopped fresh parsley or 1 tablespoon dried

1 In a 10-inch nonstick (gray, not black) skillet, heat the oil and butter over medium-low heat. Add the morels, onions, and pancetta and cook until onions have softened, about 5 minutes. Remove the skillet from heat.

2 In a medium bowl, whisk together the eggs, milk, cheese, salt, pepper, chives, parsley, and chervil. Stir in the cooked linguini.

3 Return the skillet to medium heat. Pour the egg mixture into the skillet. Cover and cook 10 minutes or until the top is set. Uncover and sprinkle with lemon juice. Cover again and cook another 1 to 2 minutes or until the eggs are cooked through. Garnish with parsley. Serve immediately.

Bacon, Leek, Tomato, and Goat Cheese Quiche

MAKES 4 SERVINGS

Quiche is a wonderful flavorful option for brunch, lunch, or a light dinner. Pair it with a tossed green salad and some crusty French bread and you have a delightful meal. Keep a few pie crusts rolled out and stored flat in your freezer, and this quiche will come together quickly.

Basic Pastry Crust for a 9-inch pie, single crust (page 587), unbaked

2 leeks, white section only, halved lengthwise, thinly sliced and washed thoroughly

4 slices cooked bacon, cut in 1-inch pieces

4 large eggs

¾ cup whole milk (cow's, rice, soy, potato, or nut)

1 teaspoon Dijon mustard

1½ teaspoons chopped fresh thyme or ½ teaspoon dried

1 small package (4 ounces) goat cheese, crumbled, or cheese alternative, such as Vegan Gourmet

1 tablespoon sweet rice flour or potato starch

¼ teaspoon salt

⅛ teaspoon white pepper

½ cup finely diced sun-dried tomatoes

1 Place a rack in the bottom position and another rack in the middle position of the oven. Preheat the oven to 400°F. Fit the pie crust into 9-inch pie plate and flute edges; set aside.

2 In a heavy skillet over medium heat, cook the leeks and bacon together, stirring constantly, until the bacon is crisp and leeks are tender. Transfer the leeks and bacon to drain on paper towels.

3 In a separate bowl, whisk together the eggs, milk, mustard, thyme, goat cheese, sweet rice flour, salt, and pepper. Stir in the leeks, bacon, and tomatoes. Pour the mixture into the crust.

4 Bake 15 minutes on the bottom rack of the oven. Move the quiche to the middle rack. Lay a sheet of foil over it and continue baking 30 minutes or until the quiche is set and a knife inserted in center comes out clean. Serve immediately.

Sweet Potato Hash

MAKES 4 SERVINGS

You've no doubt heard of corned beef hash, but this version uses chopped Canadian-style bacon and sweet potatoes instead. And if your potatoes are already mashed, that's fine, too. Unlike many hash dishes where the eggs are cooked separately and then served on top of the hash, this version goes into the oven with the raw eggs resting on top and they cook together. If you prefer, you can always cook the eggs separately from the hash and arrange them on the cooked hash at serving time.

2 tablespoons olive oil, divided

1 tablespoon unsalted butter or buttery spread, such as Earth Balance

1 small red bell pepper, cored and diced

1 small yellow onion, peeled and diced

1 garlic clove, minced

1 large sweet potato, peeled and cut in ¼-inch dice

2 cups diced Canadian-style bacon

½ teaspoon salt

½ teaspoon freshly ground black pepper

4 large eggs

2 green onions, thinly sliced

Dash paprika

1 tablespoon chopped fresh parsley or 1 teaspoon dried

1 In a heavy cast-iron skillet, heat 1 tablespoon of the oil and the butter over medium heat. Add the bell pepper and onion and cook, stirring occasionally, about 4 to 5 minutes, or until lightly browned. Add the garlic and stir 30 seconds.

2 In a large bowl, stir together the potatoes, bacon, salt, and pepper until well blended and transfer it to the skillet. With a spatula, press the mixture firmly to compress it. Cook until the bottom sets, about 3 to 4 minutes. To turn the hash, set a plate the size of the skillet on top of the pan. Invert the pan carefully so the hash falls intact onto the plate. Heat the remaining tablespoon of oil in the skillet. Slide the hash cooked-side up back into the skillet. (If the hash breaks apart during this process, simply reshape it with a spatula.) Cook 3 to 5 minutes more, or until the bottom of the hash starts to brown. (Browning time may vary due to the amount of moisture in the potatoes.)

3 Make 4 (3-inch) holes in the hash and break an egg into each hole. Sprinkle the hash with the green onions. Reduce the heat to low, cover, and cook 4 to 5 minutes or until the eggs are cooked to the desired degree of doneness. You can also bake the hash in a preheated 350°F oven until the eggs are set. Dust with paprika, sprinkle with fresh parsley, and serve immediately.

Turkey Hash
MAKES 4 SERVINGS

This is an excellent way to use up leftover turkey from your holiday meals, and it is a hearty breakfast. Once you make a hash, you'll see that there are no hard and fast rules—you can vary the ingredients based on what you have available at the time.

2 tablespoons olive oil, divided

1 tablespoon unsalted butter or buttery spread, such as Earth Balance

2 cups diced cooked russet potatoes

1 cup chopped or shredded cooked turkey or chicken

¼ cup gluten-free, low-sodium chicken broth, such as Swanson's Natural Goodness, or homemade Chicken Broth (page 676)

1 tablespoon gluten-free Worcestershire sauce, such as French's

1 tablespoon Dijon mustard

2 tablespoons finely diced fresh onion or 2 teaspoons dried minced onion

½ teaspoon celery salt

½ teaspoon freshly ground black pepper

4 large eggs

Additional salt and pepper

Paprika, for garnish

2 tablespoons chopped fresh parsley or 1 tablespoon dried for garnish

1 In a heavy cast-iron skillet, heat 1 tablespoon of the oil and the butter over medium heat. Place the potatoes and turkey in the skillet and cook until heated through.

2 While the mixture heats, in a medium bowl, whisk together the broth, Worcestershire sauce, mustard, onion, celery salt, and pepper. Pour over the potatoes and turkey.

3 With a spatula, press the mixture firmly down to compress it; and cook until deeply browned and crispy on the bottom. Flip the hash, add the remaining tablespoon of oil to the skillet, and cook the other side until deeply browned and crisp.

(The cooking time will depend on the temperature and size of the potatoes and turkey.)

4 Transfer the hash to a plate, season with additional salt and pepper, and cover with foil to keep warm.

5 Add eggs to the same skillet and fry each to the desired degree of doneness. Add salt and pepper to taste. Place an egg on top of each serving. Dust with paprika and parsley and serve immediately.

Egg Tortilla Casserole with Chipotle Mole Sauce Ⓥ

MAKES 4 SERVINGS

This makes the perfect brunch dish, and the mole sauce is sure to capture the interest of your guests. Mole sauce can take many forms, but in the United States, this term typically refers to a dried chile sauce that contains unsweetened chocolate—an unusual ingredient that gives it a unique flavor. Coffee further complements these flavors. This recipe works great with corn tortillas, but I also make it for large brunch groups by frying the eggs in a 10-inch skillet, using the larger gluten-free flour tortillas by Food for Life or La Tortilla Factory, and assembling the casserole in a skillet large enough to accommodate this size. If you don't want to use the homemade sauce, just use a 16-ounce jar of gluten-free prepared salsa.

MOLE SAUCE

1 can (14 to 15 ounces) fire-roasted tomatoes, drained

½ cup strong brewed coffee

2 tablespoons chopped onion

1 large garlic clove, chopped

1 teaspoon homemade Chipotle Adobo Sauce (page 673)

1 teaspoon unsweetened cocoa powder

½ teaspoon sugar

CASSEROLE

6 large eggs

2 tablespoons 1% milk (cow's, rice, soy, potato, or nut)

¼ teaspoon salt

⅛ teaspoon freshly ground black pepper

¼ cup canola oil for frying eggs

5 white corn tortillas (6-inch size), such as Tamxico's

1 cup grated mild Cheddar cheese or cheese alternative, such as Vegan Gourmet

GARNISHES

2 tablespoons chopped fresh cilantro

2 tablespoons chopped black olives

2 tablespoons chopped green onion

1 Make the sauce: Place all the ingredients in a blender and puree until very smooth. Transfer the sauce to a small, heavy pan and simmer over low heat 15 minutes.

2 While the sauce simmers, make the casserole. In a mixing bowl, whisk together the eggs, milk, salt, and pepper until smooth. Heat a tablespoon of the oil in a 6-inch nonstick (gray, not black) skillet over medium heat. Pour ¼ of the egg mixture into the skillet and cook until lightly browned. Repeat with the remaining egg mixture, using ¼ of the egg mixture for each of the 3 remaining layers and using more oil as needed.

3 Place a corn tortilla on an 8-inch round microwave-safe rimmed serving platter or shallow bowl. As each egg layer cooks, cover it with a tortilla, ending with the fifth tortilla. Pour the sauce over the tortillas. Heat the casserole in a microwave oven on medium for 2 to 3 minutes or until heated through. Garnish with cilantro, black olives, and green onion. Serve immediately.

Breakfast Pizza

MAKES 6 SERVINGS (12-INCH PIZZA)

My pizza crust has won national acclaim as a lunch or dinner item, but few people consider pizza for breakfast. In fact, it's a great choice because it can be eaten on the run, if necessary, and it won't crumble or fall apart. And, you still get all the sausage-and-egg flavors of a typical breakfast.

1 (12-inch) homemade gluten-free Pizza Crust (page 117)

¼ pound gluten-free pork sausage, such as Jennie-O or Hormel

2 tablespoons each diced red bell and green bell pepper

¾ cup shredded Cheddar cheese or cheese alternative, such as Vegan Gourmet

3 large eggs, beaten

1 tablespoon finely diced fresh onion or 1 teaspoon dried minced onion

½ teaspoon salt

¼ teaspoon freshly ground black pepper

2 tablespoons grated Parmesan cheese or soy alternative, such as Soyco

1 Place a rack in the bottom position and another rack in the middle position of the oven. Preheat the oven to 425°F. Prepare the gluten-free Pizza Crust (page 117), making the edges high to contain the toppings. Bake 10 minutes on the bottom rack.

2 While the crust bakes, in a heavy skillet, cook the sausage and bell pepper over medium-high heat until the sausage is no longer pink. Sprinkle it evenly on the pizza crust. Sprinkle the cheese evenly on top.

3 In a medium bowl, whisk the eggs together with the onion, salt, pepper, and Parmesan cheese. Pour over the pizza crust and bake on the middle rack for another 20 to 25 minutes or until the eggs are set. Cut into wedges and serve immediately.

QUICK BREADS AND MUFFINS

Muffins

Basic Muffins

Hearty Muffins with Dried Fruit

Egg-Free Multi-Grain Muffins

Blueberry-Lemon Muffins with Lemon-Sugar Crust

Raspberry Muffins with Streusel Topping

Apple Cinnamon Muffins

Mesquite Flour Apple Muffins

Lemon Poppy Seed Muffins with Lemon Crust

Almond Muffins with Fig Filling

Oatmeal Muffins with Dried Plums and Walnuts

Orange-Cranberry Muffins with Orange Glaze

Rhubarb Muffins with Streusel Topping

Chestnut Flour Chocolate Chip Muffins

Chocolate Latte Muffins

Cappuccino-Chocolate Muffins with White Chocolate Drizzle

Millet Flour Sour Cream–Raisin Muffins

Chestnut Flour Banana-Pecan Muffins

Mesquite Flour Banana-Nut Muffins

Chickpea Flour Muffins with Clementine Marmalade

Cinnamon Pecan-Streusel Muffins

French Vanilla Muffins with Vanilla Sugar Crust

Buckwheat Flour Pumpkin Muffins with Molasses-Cinnamon Glaze

Amaranth Spice Muffins

Rice Bran Spice Muffins

Teff Flour Gingerbread Muffins

Salba Coconut Muffins

White Bean Flour Muffins with Molasses-Cinnamon Glaze

Corn Muffins with Chives

Herb-Garlic Muffins

Biscuits and Scones

Buttermilk Biscuits

Chive Biscuits with Parmesan Topping

Onion-Bacon Biscuits

Sweet Potato Biscuits

Cheddar-Pepperoni Scones

Chai Almond Scones

Chocolate Chip Scones with Fresh Raspberries

Cranberry-Clementine Scones with Clementine Glaze

Lemon Poppy Seed Scones with Lemon Glaze

Popovers

Basic Popovers

Bacon and Cheddar Cheese Popovers

Herb Popovers

Parmesan Cheese Popovers

Yorkshire Pudding

Gougères

Quick Breads

Irish Soda Bread

Navy Bean Flour Beer Cheese
Quick Bread

Boston Brown Bread

Old-Fashioned Molasses Quick
Bread

Chestnut Flour Banana-Almond
Mini Quick Breads

Montina Flour Banana
Mini Quick Bread

No-Egg Banana Bread

Cranberry-Orange Mini Quick
Breads with Orange-Sugar Crust

Amaranth Flour–Ginger Quick
Bread with Ginger-Sugar Crust

Piña Colada Quick Bread

Quinoa Flour Zucchini
Mini Quick Breads

Spoon Breads

Corn Spoon Bread

Green Chile–Cheddar
Spoon Bread

Sour Cream–White Cheddar
Spoon Bread

Cornbreads

Cornbread

Cornbread with Pancetta

Green Chile Cornbread with
Cheddar Cheese Topping

Hush Puppies

Arepas

Hoe Cakes

Flatbreads

Corn Tortillas

Flour Tortillas

Farinata with Sage and Onion

Savory Biscotti Sticks

Oatcakes

Parmesan Shortbread

Savory White Cheddar
Shortbread Squares

Fry Bread

Chapatis

Potato Lefse

Ethiopian Flatbread

Matzoh

Q = Quick   V = Vegetarian

Quick breads are a satisfying way to make bread because they're, well . . . quick!! They rely on baking powder, baking soda, cream of tartar, eggs, or steam rather than yeast. You don't have to wait for the yeast to proof, you don't have to let the bread rise before baking, you don't have to knead the dough, and baking time—at least for most versions—is comparatively short.

Try making your own quick breads with the easy, straightforward recipes in this chapter. Create hearty muffins for breakfast or home-style corn bread for dinner. Enjoy the fabulous flatbreads that you can't buy in a store or order in a restaurant, such as oatcakes, potato lefse, arepas, chapatis, farinata, injera, and matzoh. Fluffy biscuits, rich scones, crispy popovers, hoe cakes, gougères, and hush puppies are easier to make than you think. You can even make your own corn or flour tortillas.

These recipes use a wide variety of nutritious flours such as amaranth, buckwheat, chickpea, Montina (Indian ricegrass), millet, quinoa, and teff in muffins, quick breads, and flatbreads that add variety and flavor to your diet.

Some techniques may surprise you. For example, I don't use the "muffin method" of making a well in the dry ingredients, then briefly and lightly stirring in the liquid ingredients to form a batter. Instead, I recommend mixing the batter with an electric mixer, which gives you a taller (and better-looking) gluten-free muffin.

Another novel technique is using a food processor to mix batter for flatbreads. It is far quicker and does a better job of blending gluten-free ingredients than a handheld electric mixer. I often use modified tapioca starch (Expandex) which improves the texture and shelf-life of gluten-free breads. Read more about it in "Cooking with Gluten-Free Ingredients" (page x).

If you avoid dairy, I offer substitutions for cow's milk and butter. I use 1% milk in most of these recipes because it is lower in fat and calories, but you can use the milk of your choice. When working with buttermilk, be sure to shake store-bought varieties thoroughly before measuring; the solids tend to settle on the bottom of the carton, making the first few cups much thinner than the final cup. If your buttermilk is extremely thick, thin it with a little water. While everything tastes wonderful with real butter, you can substitute nondairy buttery spreads such as Earth Balance; Spectrum Naturals also works well in baking, though it doesn't melt. You will also find some egg-free recipes in this section.

MUFFINS

Basic Muffins

MAKES 12 MUFFINS

This is a basic muffin recipe that you can modify to suit your taste. It's pretty simple, and sometimes that's exactly what you need. Feel free to add your own personal touch: replace the lemon zest with orange zest; add a teaspoon of your favorite extract; or add ½ cup of any of the following after you have mixed the batter: chopped nuts, finely chopped dried fruit, or chocolate chips.

LIQUID INGREDIENTS

2 large eggs, at room temperature
¾ cup 1% milk (cow's, rice, soy, potato, or nut)
½ cup canola oil
1 tablespoon grated lemon zest
1 teaspoon pure vanilla extract

DRY INGREDIENTS

2 cups Carol's Sorghum Blend (page x)
¼ cup Expandex modified tapioca starch, or ¼ cup
     Carol's Sorghum Blend (page x)
¾ cup sugar
1 tablespoon baking powder
1½ teaspoons xanthan gum
1 teaspoon salt

1 Place a rack in the middle of the oven. Preheat the oven to 375°F. Generously grease the cups of a standard 12-cup nonstick (gray, not black) muffin pan or line them with paper liners and coat with cooking spray.

2 In a medium mixing bowl, beat the eggs with an electric mixer on low speed until light yellow and frothy, about 30 seconds. Add the milk, oil, lemon zest, and vanilla and beat just until blended.

3 In a small bowl, whisk together the dry ingredients. With the mixer on low speed, gradually beat the dry ingredients into the liquid ingredients until the batter is smooth and slightly thickened. Divide the batter evenly in the muffin pan.

4 Bake 25 to 30 minutes or until the muffin tops are firm and the edges start to pull away from the pan. Cool the muffins in the pan 10 minutes. Transfer the muffins to a wire rack to cool another 5 minutes. Serve warm.

Hearty Muffins with Dried Fruit Ⓥ

MAKES 12 MUFFINS

Eat these hearty muffins for breakfast and you'll have a very nutritious start to your day. Montina is the commercial name given to Indian ricegrass, which grows in several states in the Northwest. It is particularly high in fiber and protein and has a hearty, nutty flavor similar to whole wheat.

1 cup gluten-free rolled oats^† or rolled soy flakes**
½ cup boiling water

DRY INGREDIENTS

1 cup Carol's Sorghum Blend (page x)
2 tablespoons Montina Pure Supplement
2 tablespoons rice bran or ground flax meal
¾ cup packed light brown sugar
1½ teaspoons baking soda
1 teaspoon ground cinnamon
¾ teaspoon salt
1½ teaspoon xanthan gum
¼ cup pitted, finely chopped dates
¼ cup raisins (dark or golden)
¼ cup dried cranberries
¼ cup chopped walnuts

LIQUID INGREDIENTS

1 cup buttermilk, well shaken, or homemade
     Buttermilk (page 677)
¼ cup canola oil
2 teaspoons pure vanilla extract

1 Place a rack in the middle of the oven. Preheat oven to 375°F. Generously grease the cups of a standard 12-cup nonstick (gray, not black) muffin pan.

2 In a small bowl, combine the rolled oats and boiling water and let stand 10 minutes.

3 Meanwhile, in a medium bowl whisk together the dry ingredients except the dried fruit and walnuts. Add the oat mixture, and liquid ingredients, and beat with an electric mixer on low speed until well blended. Gently stir in dates, raisins, cranberries, and nuts. Divide the batter evenly in the muffin pan.

4 Bake 20 to 25 minutes or until the muffin tops are firm and the edges start to pull away from the pan. Cool the muffins in the pan 10 minutes. Transfer the muffins to a wire rack to cool another 5 minutes. Serve warm.

* Available at www.bobsredmill.com, www. creamhillestates.com, www.giftsofnature.net, www. glutenfreeoats.com, or www.onlyoats.com.

**Available at natural food stores.

†Check with your physician before using gluten-free oats.

Egg-Free Multi-Grain Muffins Ⓥ

MAKES 6 LARGE MUFFINS

These muffins have an ultra-high nutrient and fiber content without eggs, sugar, or dairy. I often make these when I'm on the run; they are large muffins (a good size for me on the road), and they travel well. If you prefer the rolled oats and oat flour, make sure you use the pure, gluten-free version.

½ cup fresh orange juice

¼ cup canola oil

1 container (4 ounces) prune baby food

¼ cup agave nectar or honey

Grated zest of 1 orange

½ cup Carol's Sorghum Blend (page x) or oat flour ground from rolled oats* with your spice grinder

¼ cup gluten-free rolled oats*† or sweetened shredded coconut

¼ cup rice bran or Montina Pure Supplement

¼ cup ground flax meal

1 tablespoon sesame seed

1 tablespoon baking powder

1 teaspoon xanthan gum

½ teaspoon salt

¾ cup finely chopped dried plums

½ cup finely chopped pecans

1 Place a rack in the middle of the oven. Preheat the oven to 375°F. Generously grease the cups of a 6-cup nonstick (gray, not black) large muffin pan or line them with paper liners and coat with cooking spray. Or use 6 free-standing paper muffin molds placed on a baking sheet.

2 In a medium mixing bowl, whisk together the orange juice, oil, baby food, agave nectar, and orange zest until smooth. Add the sorghum blend, oats, bran, flax, sesame seed, baking powder, xanthan gum, and salt and whisk until the batter is smooth. Stir in the dried plums and pecans. Divide the batter evenly in the muffin pan.

3 Bake 20 to 25 minutes or until the muffin tops are browned and firm and the edges start to pull away from the pan. Cool the muffins in the pan 10 minutes. Transfer the muffins to a wire rack to cool another 5 minutes. Serve warm.

* Available at www.bobsredmill.com, www. creamhillestates.com, www.giftsofnature.net, www. glutenfreeoats.com, or www.onlyoats.com.

†Check with your physician before using gluten-free oats.

Blueberry-Lemon Muffins with Lemon-Sugar Crust Ⓥ

MAKES 12 MUFFINS

Blueberries and lemons team up to make a delightful breakfast treat or snack. The Lemon-Sugar Crust adds wonderful crispiness.

LIQUID INGREDIENTS

2 large eggs, at room temperature

¾ cup 1% milk (cow's, rice, soy, potato, or nut)

½ cup canola oil

1 tablespoon grated lemon zest

1 teaspoon pure vanilla extract

DRY INGREDIENTS

2 cups Carol's Sorghum Blend (page x)

¼ cup Expandex modified tapioca starch, or ¼ cup Carol's Sorghum Blend (page x)

¾ cup sugar

1 tablespoon baking powder

1½ teaspoons xanthan gum

1 teaspoon salt

1 cup fresh blueberries, washed and patted dry

TOPPING

Cooking spray

½ cup sugar

1 teaspoon grated lemon zest

1 Place a rack in the middle of the oven. Preheat the oven to 375°F. Generously grease the cups of a standard 12-cup nonstick (gray, not black) muffin pan or line with paper liners and coat them with cooking spray

2 In a medium mixing bowl, beat the eggs with an electric mixer on low speed until light yellow and frothy, about 30 seconds. Add the milk, oil, lemon zest, and vanilla and beat just until blended.

3 In a small bowl, whisk together the dry ingredients except the blueberries. With the mixer on low speed, gradually beat the dry ingredients into the liquid ingredients until the batter is smooth and slightly thickened. Gently stir in the blueberries. Divide the batter evenly in the muffin pan.

4 Bake 25 to 30 minutes or until the muffin tops are firm and the edges start to pull away from the pan. Cool the muffins in the pan 10 minutes. Transfer the muffins to a wire rack. Spray the tops with cooking spray.

5 Make the topping: In a small bowl, combine the sugar and lemon zest. Dip each muffin top into the sugar mixture and let stand on a wire rack for 5 minutes. Serve warm.

Raspberry Muffins with Streusel Topping Ⓥ

MAKES 12 MUFFINS

This muffin is best made with fresh raspberries, which will hold their shape better during baking than frozen ones. The streusel topping is a nice crunchy contrast to the soft raspberries.

LIQUID INGREDIENTS

2 large eggs, at room temperature

⅓ cup 1% milk (cow's, rice, soy, potato, or nut)

⅓ cup canola oil

2 teaspoons grated lemon zest

1 teaspoon pure vanilla extract

DRY INGREDIENTS

1½ cups Carol's Sorghum Blend (page x)

¼ cup Expandex modified tapioca starch, or ¼ cup Carol's Sorghum Blend (page x)

¾ cup packed light brown sugar

1 tablespoon baking powder

1½ teaspoons xanthan gum

1 teaspoon ground cinnamon

1 teaspoon salt

1 cup (6 ounce container) fresh raspberries, gently washed and patted dry

¾ cup Streusel Topping (page 566)

1 Place a rack in the middle of the oven. Preheat the oven to 375°F. Generously grease the cups of a standard 12-cup nonstick (gray, not black) muffin pan or line them with paper liners and coat with cooking spray.

2 In a medium bowl, beat the eggs with an electric mixer on low speed until light yellow and frothy, about 30 seconds. Add the milk, oil, lemon zest, and vanilla and beat on low speed until the batter is smooth and slightly thickened.

3 In a small bowl, whisk together the dry ingredients except the raspberries. With the mixer on low speed, gradually beat the dry ingredients into the liquid ingredients until the batter is smooth and slightly thickened. Gently stir in the fresh raspberries. Divide the batter evenly in the muffin pan. Sprinkle 1 tablespoon of Streusel Topping on each muffin, gently pressing the topping lightly into the batter.

4 Bake 20 to 25 minutes or until the muffin tops are firm and the edges start to pull away from the pan. Cool the muffins in the pan 10 minutes. Transfer the muffins to a wire rack to cool another 5 minutes. Serve warm.

Apple-Cinnamon Muffins Ⓥ

MAKES 6 LARGE MUFFINS

These muffins will fill your kitchen with the unmistakable aroma of apples and cinnamon. They are dense and moist, and they travel and store well, so make a batch and freeze them for a future trip.

LIQUID INGREDIENTS

1 large egg, at room temperature
⅓ cup canola oil
1 teaspoon pure vanilla extract
2 cups peeled and coarsely grated Granny Smith apples (about 2 medium apples)

DRY INGREDIENTS

1 cup Carol's Sorghum Blend (page x)
½ cup packed light brown sugar
2 teaspoons xanthan gum
1 teaspoon ground cinnamon
¾ teaspoon salt
¼ teaspoon ground nutmeg
½ cup dark raisins
½ cup chopped walnuts

1 Place a rack in the middle of the oven. Preheat the oven to 325°F. Generously grease the cups of a 6-cup large nonstick (gray, not black) muffin pan or line them with paper liners and coat with cooking spray.

2 In a medium mixing bowl, whisk the egg, oil, and vanilla together just until blended. Stir in the apples.

3 In a small bowl, whisk together the dry ingredients except the raisins and walnuts. With a spatula, gradually stir in the dry ingredients just until they are incorporated. Stir in the raisins and walnuts. Divide the batter evenly in the muffin pan.

4 Bake 25 to 30 minutes or until the muffin tops are firm and the edges start to pull away from the pan. Cool the muffins in the pan 10 minutes. Transfer the muffins to a wire rack to cool another 5 minutes. Serve warm.

Mesquite Flour Apple Muffins Ⓥ

MAKES 12 MUFFINS

These muffins are especially wonderful in the fall when McIntosh or Jonathan apples—with their characteristic sweet-tart flavor—are at their best. Mesquite flour, one of the newest flours available for gluten-free baking, lends complex flavors to any dish, including a sweet hint of cinnamon. It is derived from mesquite pods, which are found on mesquite trees in the Southwest, and has only recently become widely available to consumers. Serve these muffins with apple butter or pumpkin butter for a great flavor combination.

LIQUID INGREDIENTS

1 large egg, at room temperature

1 cup applesauce

⅓ cup unsalted butter or buttery spread, such as Earth Balance, melted, or canola oil

1 teaspoon pure vanilla extract

DRY INGREDIENTS

1 cup Carol's Sorghum Blend (page x)

½ cup mesquite flour*

¼ cup Expandex modified tapioca starch, or ¼ cup Carol's Sorghum Blend (page x)

½ cup packed light brown sugar

2 teaspoons baking powder

1½ teaspoons xanthan gum

1 teaspoon ground cinnamon

1 teaspoon salt

1 medium apple (Jonathan or McIntosh), peeled, cored, and very finely chopped

½ cup chopped walnuts

TOPPING

2 tablespoons sugar

½ teaspoon ground cinnamon

Cooking spray

1 Place a rack in the middle of the oven. Preheat the oven to 375°F. Generously grease the cups of a standard 12-cup nonstick (gray, not black) muffin pan or line them with paper liners and coat with cooking spray.

2 In a medium mixing bowl, beat the egg with an electric mixer on low speed until light yellow and frothy, about 30 seconds. Add the applesauce, melted butter, and vanilla and beat on low speed until well blended.

3 In a small bowl, whisk together the dry ingredients except the apples and walnuts. With the mixer on low speed, gradually beat the dry ingredients into the liquid ingredients until the batter is smooth and slightly thickened. Stir in the apple and walnuts. Divide the batter evenly in the muffin pan.

4 Bake 20 to 25 minutes or until the muffin tops are firm and the edges start to pull away from the pan. Baking time may take longer depending on the water content of the apples. If so, bake longer—in

5-minute increments—until done. Cool the muffins in the pan 10 minutes. Transfer the muffins to a wire rack.

5 While the muffins are still warm, make the topping: Mix the sugar and cinnamon in a small bowl. Coat each muffin top with cooking spray and sprinkle with ½ teaspoon sugar-cinnamon mixture. Serve immediately.

*Available at www.therubyrange.com and www. casadefruta.com.

Lemon Poppy Seed Muffins with Lemon Crust Ⓥ

MAKES 12 MUFFINS

If you like lemons, you will love this morning treat. For added flavor, serve these muffins with store-bought lemon curd.

LIQUID INGREDIENTS

2 large eggs, at room temperature

¾ cup 1% milk (cow's, rice, soy, potato, or nut)

½ cup canola oil

1 teaspoon grated lemon zest

1 teaspoon pure vanilla extract

DRY INGREDIENTS

2 cups Carol's Sorghum Blend (page x)

¼ cup Expandex modified tapioca starch, or ¼ cup Carol's Sorghum Blend (page x)

¾ cup sugar

1 tablespoon poppy seeds

1 tablespoon baking powder

1½ teaspoons xanthan gum

1 teaspoon salt

TOPPING

3 tablespoons sugar

1 teaspoon grated lemon zest

1 Place a rack in the middle of the oven. Preheat the oven to 375°F. Generously grease the cups of a standard 12-cup nonstick (gray, not black) muffin pan or line them with paper liners and coat with cooking spray.

2 In a medium mixing bowl, beat the eggs with an electric mixer on low speed until light yellow and frothy, about 30 seconds. Add the milk, oil, lemon zest, and vanilla extract and beat on low speed until well blended.

3 In a small bowl, whisk together the dry ingredients. With the mixer on low speed, gradually beat the dry ingredients into the liquid ingredients until the batter is smooth and slightly thickened. Divide the batter evenly in the muffin pan.

4 Make the topping: In a small bowl, combine the sugar and lemon zest and sprinkle ¼ teaspoon on each muffin.

5 Bake 20 to 25 minutes or until the muffin tops are firm and the edges start to pull away from the pan. Cool the muffins in the pan 10 minutes. Transfer the muffins to a wire rack to cool another 5 minutes. Serve warm.

Almond Muffins with Fig Filling Ⓥ

MAKES 12 MUFFINS

The flavors of almond and fig marry nicely in this unique and tasty muffin. Almond meal is available at health food stores, or you can make your own by processing 1 cup whole almonds in a food processor, along with 2 tablespoons of the sugar from this recipe, until it reaches a meal-like consistency.

LIQUID INGREDIENTS
2 large eggs, at room temperature
1 cup milk 1% (cow's, rice, soy, potato, or nut)
⅓ cup canola oil
2 teaspoons almond extract
1 teaspoon pure vanilla extract

DRY INGREDIENTS
¾ cup almond meal
¾ cup potato starch
¾ cup sugar
½ cup tapioca flour
¼ cup Expandex modified tapioca starch, or ¼ cup Carol's Sorghum Blend (page x)
1 tablespoon baking powder
1 teaspoon xanthan gum
1 teaspoon salt

2 tablespoons fig marmalade

1 Place a rack in the middle of the oven. Preheat the oven to 375°F. Generously grease the cups of a standard 12-cup nonstick (gray, not black) muffin pan or line them with paper liners and coat with cooking spray.

2 In a medium mixing bowl, beat the eggs with an electric mixer on low speed until they are light yellow and frothy, about 30 seconds. Add the milk, oil, and almond and vanilla extracts and beat just until blended.

3 In a small bowl, whisk together the dry ingredients. With the mixer on low speed, gradually beat the dry ingredients into the liquid ingredients until the batter is smooth and slightly thickened.

4 Fill each muffin cup with 3 tablespoons of batter. Place a scant ½ teaspoon of fig marmalade in the center of each muffin, pressing it firmly into the batter. Top each muffin cup with another 3 tablespoons of batter.

5 Bake 20 to 25 minutes or until the muffin tops are firm and the edges start to pull away from the pan. Cool the muffins in the pan 10 minutes. Transfer the muffins to a wire rack to cool another 5 minutes. Serve warm.

Oatmeal Muffins with Dried Plums and Walnuts Ⓥ

MAKES 12 MUFFINS

This is my adaptation of a scrumptious muffin I ate at a health food store in northern California some years ago and remembered long after. It is packed with fiber and important nutrients. If your diet won't allow gluten-free oats, rolled soy flakes will work just fine in this muffin.

1 cup gluten-free rolled oats*† or rolled soy flakes**

¾ cup buttermilk, well shaken, or homemade Buttermilk (page 667)

2 large eggs, at room temperature

½ cup canola oil

2 tablespoons molasses (not blackstrap)

Juice and grated zest from 1 orange

1 teaspoon pure vanilla extract

1 cup Carol's Sorghum Blend (page x)

¼ cup Expandex modified tapioca starch, or ¼ cup Carol's Sorghum Blend (page x)

½ cup packed light brown sugar

1½ teaspoons xanthan gum

2 teaspoons baking powder

½ teaspoon baking soda

½ teaspoon salt

½ cup finely chopped dried plums

½ cup chopped walnuts

1 About 30 minutes before making the muffins, combine the oats and buttermilk in a medium mixing bowl. Cover and let stand so oats (or soy flakes) soften in the buttermilk.

2 Place a rack in the middle of the oven. Preheat the oven to 375°F. Generously grease the cups of a standard 12-cup nonstick (gray, not black) muffin pan or line them with paper liners and coat with cooking spray.

3 Add the remaining ingredients, except the dried plums and walnuts, to the buttermilk-oat mixture and beat with an electric mixer on low speed just until blended. Increase the speed to medium and beat until the batter thickens slightly, about 30 seconds. Stir in the dried plums and walnuts. Divide the batter evenly in the muffin pan.

4 Bake 20 to 25 minutes or until the muffin tops are firm and the edges start to pull away from the pan. Cool the muffins in the pan 10 minutes. Transfer the muffins to a wire rack to cool another 5 minutes. Serve warm.

*Available at www.bobsredmill.com, www. creamhillestates.com, www.giftsofnature.net, www. glutenfreeoats.com, or www.onlyoats.com.

**Available at natural food stores.

†Check with your physician before using gluten-free oats.

Orange-Cranberry Muffins with Orange Glaze Ⓥ

MAKES 12 MUFFINS

The combination of cranberry and orange is especially inviting in this wonderful muffin; they are even more delightful when the sweet-tart flavors are enhanced with a dab of orange marmalade.

LIQUID INGREDIENTS

2 large eggs, at room temperature

¾ cup 1% milk (cow's, rice, soy, potato, or nut)

½ cup canola oil

1 tablespoon grated orange zest

1 teaspoon pure vanilla extract

DRY INGREDIENTS

2 cups Carol's Sorghum Blend (page x)

¾ cup sugar

¼ cup Expandex modified tapioca starch, or ¼ cup Carol's Sorghum Blend (page x)

1 tablespoon baking powder

1½ teaspoons xanthan gum

1 teaspoon salt

1 cup dried sweetened cranberries

ORANGE GLAZE

1 cup powdered sugar

1 teaspoon grated orange zest

2 teaspoons water, or enough to form a thick glaze

1 Place a rack in the middle of the oven. Preheat the oven to 375°F. Generously grease the cups of a standard 12-cup nonstick (gray, not black) muffin pan or line them with paper liners and coat with cooking spray.

2 In a medium bowl, beat the eggs with an electric mixer on low speed until light yellow and frothy, about 30 seconds. Add the milk, oil, vanilla, orange zest, and vanilla and beat on low speed until well blended.

3 In a small bowl, whisk together the dry ingredients except the cranberries. With the mixer on low speed, gradually beat the dry ingredients into the liquid ingredients until the batter is smooth and slightly thickened. Stir in the cranberries. Divide the batter evenly in the muffin pan.

4 Bake approximately 20 to 25 minutes or until muffin tops are firm and the edges start to pull away from the pan. Cool the muffins in the pan 10 minutes. Transfer the muffins to a wire rack to cool another 5 minutes.

5 Make the glaze: In a small bowl, combine the powdered sugar, orange zest, and water to form a thick glaze. Dip each muffin top into the glaze and then cool another 10 minutes on the wire rack. Serve immediately.

Rhubarb Muffins with Streusel Topping Ⓥ

MAKES 12 MUFFINS

This recipe works best with fresh rhubarb, so make it in the spring when rhubarb is in season. I have a rhubarb plant in my garden that has provided me with rhubarb every spring for fifteen years. You can find fresh rhubarb in the produce section of supermarkets and at farmer's markets.

LIQUID INGREDIENTS

2 large eggs, at room temperature
½ cup canola oil
¼ cup 1% milk (cow's, rice, soy, potato, or nut)
1 teaspoon pure vanilla extract

DRY INGREDIENTS

1½ cups Carol's Sorghum Blend (page x)
¾ cup packed light brown sugar
¼ cup Expandex modified tapioca starch, or ¼ cup Carol's Sorghum Blend (page x)
1 tablespoon baking powder
1½ teaspoons xanthan gum
1 teaspoon ground cinnamon
1 teaspoon salt
1½ cups finely diced fresh rhubarb
¼ cup chopped pecans

¾ cup Streusel Topping (page 566)

1 Place a rack in the middle of the oven. Preheat oven to 375°F. Generously grease the cups of a standard 12-cup nonstick (gray, not black) muffin pan or line them with paper liners and coat with cooking spray.

2 In a medium bowl, beat the eggs with an electric mixer on low speed until light yellow and frothy, about 30 seconds. Add the oil, milk, and vanilla and beat on low speed until the batter is smooth and slightly thickened.

3 In a small bowl, whisk together the dry ingredients, except the rhubarb and pecans. With the mixer on low speed, gradually beat the dry ingredients into the liquid ingredients until the batter is smooth and slightly thickened. Gently stir in the rhubarb and pecans. Divide the batter evenly in the muffin pan. Sprinkle 1 tablespoon Streusel Topping on each muffin, pressing topping lightly into batter with fingers.

4 Bake 20 to 25 minutes or until the muffin tops are firm and the edges start to pull away from the pan. Cool the muffins in the pan 10 minutes. Transfer the muffins to a wire rack to cool another 5 minutes. Serve warm.

Chestnut Flour Chocolate Chip Muffins Ⓥ

MAKES 12 MUFFINS

Chestnut flour is ground from dried chestnuts and commonly used in many Italian dishes. Although chestnuts are often associated with autumn, the flour's mildly nutty flavor and silky texture—and its year-round availability—make it a great choice for gluten-free baking any time.

LIQUID INGREDIENTS

2 large eggs, at room temperature

¾ cup 1% milk (cow's, rice, soy, potato, or nut)

¼ cup canola oil

1 teaspoon pure vanilla extract

DRY INGREDIENTS

¾ cup packed light brown sugar

⅔ cup chestnut flour*

⅔ cup potato starch

⅓ cup tapioca flour

¼ cup Expandex modified tapioca starch, or ¼ cup Carol's Sorghum Blend (page x)

1 tablespoon baking powder

1 teaspoon xanthan gum

1 teaspoon salt

½ cup gluten-free dairy-free chocolate chips, such as Tropical Source

1 Place a rack in the middle of the oven. Preheat the oven to 375°F. Generously grease the cups of a standard 12-cup nonstick (gray, not black) muffin pan or line them with paper liners and coat with cooking spray.

2 In a medium mixing bowl, beat the eggs with an electric mixer on low speed until light yellow and frothy, about 30 seconds. Add the milk, oil, and vanilla and beat on low speed just until blended.

3 In a small bowl, whisk together the dry ingredients except for the chocolate chips. With the mixer on low speed, gradually beat the dry ingredients into the liquid ingredients until the batter is smooth and slightly thickened. Stir in the chocolate chips. Divide the batter evenly in the muffin pan.

4 Bake 20 to 25 minutes or until the muffins are firm and the edges start to pull away from the pan. Cool the muffins in the pan 10 minutes. Transfer the muffins to a wire rack to cool another 5 minutes. Serve warm.

*Available at natural food stores and from www. dowdandrogers.com

Chocolate Latte Muffins Ⓥ

MAKES 12 MUFFINS

My husband makes so many café or coffee lattes each day that he's known as "Latte Larry." Here I replicate that latte flavor in a chocolate muffin; I think this recipe comes pretty close.

LIQUID INGREDIENTS

2 large eggs, at room temperature

¾ cup 1% milk (cow's, rice, soy, potato, or nut)

½ cup canola oil

2 teaspoons pure vanilla extract

DRY INGREDIENTS

1¼ cups Carol's Sorghum Blend (page x)

¾ cup unsweetened cocoa powder (not Dutch-process or alkali)

¼ cup Expandex modified tapioca starch, or Carol's Sorghum Blend (page x)

¾ cup packed light brown sugar

1½ teaspoons xanthan gum

½ teaspoon baking soda

2 teaspoons instant coffee granules or espresso powder, such as Medaglia d'Oro

1 teaspoon salt

1¼ cups gluten-free dairy-free chocolate chips, such as Tropical Source, divided

1 tablespoon 1% milk (cow's, rice, soy, potato, or nut) plus enough to make a thin frosting

1 Place a rack in the middle of the oven. Preheat the oven to 375°F. Generously grease the cups of a standard 12-cup nonstick (gray, not black) muffin pan or line them with paper liners and coat with cooking spray.

2 In a medium mixing bowl, beat the eggs with an electric mixer on low speed until light yellow and frothy, about 30 seconds. Add the milk, oil, and vanilla extract and beat on low speed until well blended.

3 In a small bowl, whisk together the dry ingredients except chocolate chips. With the mixer on low speed, gradually beat the dry ingredients into the liquid ingredients until the batter is smooth and slightly thickened. Stir in ¾ cup of the chocolate chips. Divide the batter evenly in the muffin pan.

4 Bake 20 to 25 minutes or until the muffin tops are firm and the edges start to pull away from the pan. Cool the muffins in the pan 10 minutes. Transfer the muffins to a wire rack to cool another 5 minutes.

5 Make the drizzle: In a small bowl, heat the remaining ½ cup chocolate chips and 1 tablespoon milk on low in the microwave just until the chips are melted. Stir with a spatula until smooth, adding more milk a teaspoon at a time, if necessary, to make a thin drizzle. Use the spatula to drizzle the chocolate mixture back and forth across the muffins. Serve immediately.

Cappuccino-Chocolate Muffins with White Chocolate Drizzle Ⓥ

MAKES 12 MUFFINS

Coffee and chocolate are probably my two favorite flavors so I couldn't resist making a muffin with them. Without the drizzle this makes a nice breakfast or midday treat; add the drizzle, and suddenly

you have a scrumptious dessert. Serve this boldly flavored muffin with an equally strong coffee, such as a French roast. These are best served slightly warm so that the chocolate chips are still soft.

LIQUID INGREDIENTS

2 large eggs, at room temperature

¾ cup 1% milk (cow's, rice, soy, potato, or nut)

½ cup canola oil

2 teaspoons pure vanilla extract

DRY INGREDIENTS

1¼ cups Carol's Sorghum Blend (page x)

¾ cup unsweetened cocoa powder (not Dutch-process or alkali)

¼ cup Expandex modified tapioca starch, or ¼ cup Carol's Sorghum Blend (page x)

¾ cup packed light brown sugar

1½ teaspoons xanthan gum

½ teaspoon baking soda

2 teaspoons instant espresso powder, such as Medaglia D'Oro

1 teaspoon salt

½ teaspoon ground cinnamon

¾ cup gluten-free dairy-free chocolate chips, such as Tropical Source

¼ cup slivered almonds

TOPPING

½ cup white chocolate chips, or white chocolate baking bar, such as Ghirardelli

1 tablespoon 1% milk (cow's, rice, soy, potato, or nut) plus enough to make a thin frosting

1 Place a rack in the middle of the oven. Preheat the oven to 375°F. Generously grease the cups of a standard 12-cup nonstick (gray, not black) muffin pan or line them with paper liners and coat with cooking spray

2 In a medium mixing bowl, beat the eggs with an electric mixer on low speed until light yellow and frothy, about 30 seconds. Add the milk, oil, and vanilla and beat just until blended.

3 In a small bowl, whisk together the dry ingredients except the chocolate chips and almonds. With the mixer on low speed, gradually beat the dry ingredients into the liquid ingredients until the batter is smooth and slightly thickened. Stir in the chocolate chips and almonds. Divide the batter evenly in the muffin pan.

4 Bake 20 to 25 minutes or until the muffin tops are firm and the edges start to pull away from the pan. Cool the muffins in the pan 10 minutes. Transfer the muffins to a wire rack to cool another 5 minutes.

5 Make the drizzle: In a small bowl, heat the chocolate and milk on low in the microwave until the chips are melted. Stir with a spatula until smooth, adding more milk a teaspoon at a time, if necessary. Use the spatula to drizzle the white chocolate mixture back and forth across the muffins. Serve immediately.

Millet Flour Sour Cream– Raisin Muffins Ⓥ

MAKES 12 MUFFINS

This muffin contains all the delicious flavors of traditional sour cream–raisin pie. Millet is a lightly flavored, but highly nutritious, flour ground from whole grain millet. I keep whole grain millet in my freezer and when I want flour for this recipe I grind the proper amount in my small coffee or spice grinder.

LIQUID INGREDIENTS
2 large eggs, at room temperature
½ cup sour cream or sour cream alternative, such as Tofutti
¼ cup 1% milk (cow's, rice, soy, potato, or nut)
1 teaspoon pure vanilla extract
1 teaspoon grated lemon zest

DRY INGREDIENTS
⅔ cup millet flour
⅔ cup potato starch
⅓ cup tapioca flour
¾ cup sugar
1 tablespoon baking powder
1 teaspoon xanthan gum
1 teaspoon salt
½ teaspoon ground cinnamon
¼ teaspoon ground cloves
¾ cup dark raisins

TOPPING
Cooking spray
1 teaspoon ground cinnamon
2 teaspoons sugar

1 Place a rack in the middle of the oven. Preheat the oven to 375°F. Generously grease the cups of a standard 12-cup nonstick (gray, not black) muffin pan or line them with paper liners and coat with cooking spray.

2 In a medium mixing bowl, beat the eggs with an electric mixer on low speed until light yellow and frothy, about 30 seconds. Add the sour cream, milk, vanilla, and lemon zest and beat on low speed until well blended.

3 In a small bowl, whisk together the dry ingredients, except the raisins, until thoroughly blended. With the mixer on low speed, gradually beat the dry ingredients into the liquid ingredients until the batter is smooth and slightly thickened. Stir in raisins. Divide the batter evenly in the muffin pan. Lightly coat muffins with cooking spray.

4 Make the sprinkle: Combine sugar and cinnamon and sprinkle about ¼ teaspoon on each muffin.

5 Bake 20 to 25 minutes or until the muffin tops are firm and the edges start to pull away from the pan. Cool the muffins in the pan 10 minutes. Transfer the muffins to a wire rack to cool another 5 minutes. Serve warm.

Chestnut Flour Banana Pecan Muffins Ⓥ

MAKES 12 MUFFINS

Eating freshly roasted chestnuts from a street vendor or roasted in your own oven is certainly one way of enjoying them. But chestnuts can also be ground into a nutty, silky-textured flour that pairs well with the flavorful ripe bananas and pecans in this muffin.

LIQUID INGREDIENTS

2 large eggs, at room temperature

1 large very ripe banana, mashed

1 cup 1% milk (cow's, rice, soy, potato, or nut)

¼ cup canola oil

1 teaspoon pure vanilla extract

DRY INGREDIENTS

⅔ cup chestnut flour*

⅔ cup potato starch

⅓ cup tapioca flour

¼ cup Expandex modified tapioca starch, or ¼ cup Carol's Sorghum Blend (page x)

¾ cup packed light brown sugar

1 tablespoon baking powder

1 teaspoon xanthan gum

1 teaspoon salt

1 teaspoon ground cinnamon

⅓ cup chopped pecans

1 Place a rack in the middle of the oven. Preheat the oven to 375°F. Generously grease the cups of a standard 12-cup nonstick (gray, not black) muffin pan or line it with paper liners and coat them with cooking spray

2 In a medium mixing bowl, beat the eggs with an electric mixer on medium speed until light yellow and frothy, about 30 seconds. Add the banana, milk, oil, and vanilla extract and beat on low speed until well blended.

3 In a small bowl, whisk together the dry ingredients, except the pecans. With the mixer on low speed, gradually beat the dry ingredients into the liquid ingredients until the batter is smooth and slightly thickened. Stir in the pecans. Divide the batter evenly in the muffin pan.

4 Bake 20 to 25 minutes or until the muffins are firm and the edges start to pull away from the pan. Cool the muffins in the pan 10 minutes. Transfer the muffins to a wire rack to cool another 5 minutes. Serve warm.

*Available at natural food stores and from www. dowdandrogers.com.

Mesquite Flour Banana-Nut Muffins Ⓥ

MAKES 12 MUFFINS

The cinnamon-like flavor of mesquite flour, ground from the pods that grow on mesquite trees in the Southwest, complements the banana in this delicious muffin.

LIQUID INGREDIENTS

2 large eggs, at room temperature

1 large very ripe banana, mashed

½ cup 1% milk (cow's, rice, soy, potato, or nut)

¼ cup canola oil

1 teaspoon pure vanilla extract

DRY INGREDIENTS

2 cups Carol's Sorghum Blend (page x)

¼ cup mesquite flour*

¾ cup packed dark brown sugar

2 teaspoons baking powder

1½ teaspoons xanthan gum

¾ teaspoon salt

½ cup chopped walnuts

2 tablespoons sugar, for sprinkling (optional)

1 Place a rack in the middle of the oven. Preheat oven to 375°F. Generously grease the cups of a standard 12-cup nonstick (gray, not black) muffin pan or line it with paper lines and coat with cooking spray; set aside.

2 In a medium mixing bowl, beat the eggs with an electric mixer on low speed until light yellow and frothy, about 30 seconds. Add the banana, milk, oil, and vanilla and beat on low speed until well blended.

3 In a small bowl, whisk together the dry ingredients except the walnuts. With the mixer on low speed, gradually beat the dry ingredients into the liquid ingredients until the batter is smooth and slightly thickened. Gently stir in walnuts. Divide the batter evenly in the muffin pan. Sprinkle muffins tops with sugar.

4 Bake 20 to 25 minutes or until the muffin tops are firm and the edges start to pull away from the pan. Cool the muffins in the pan 10 minutes. Transfer the muffins to a wire rack to cool another 5 minutes. Serve warm.

*Available at health food stores, www.therubyrange.com, and www.casadefruta.com.

Chickpea Flour Muffins with Clementine Marmalade Ⓥ

MAKES 12 MUFFINS

Chickpeas or garbanzo beans make great muffins, as shown here, where this nutritious flour is enhanced with homemade Clementine Marmalade (page 678). If you can't find clementines (also known as seedless tangerines) in your area, or you don't want to make clementine marmalade yourself, substitute a good quality store-bought orange marmalade.

LIQUID INGREDIENTS
2 large eggs, at room temperature
1 cup 1% milk (cow's, rice, soy, potato, or nut)
⅓ cup canola oil
1 teaspoon pure vanilla extract

DRY INGREDIENTS
¾ cup chickpea flour*
¾ cup potato starch
¾ cup sugar
½ cup tapioca flour
¼ cup Expandex modified tapioca starch, or Carol's Sorghum Blend (page x)
1 tablespoon baking powder
1 teaspoon xanthan gum
1 teaspoon salt

½ cup Clementine Marmalade (page 678) or store-bought orange marmalade

1 Place a rack in the middle of the oven. Preheat the oven to 375°F. Generously grease the cups of a standard 12-cup nonstick (gray, not black) muffin pan or line them with paper liners and coat with cooking spray.

2 In a medium mixing bowl, beat the eggs with an electric mixer on low speed until light yellow and frothy, about 30 seconds. Add the milk, oil, and vanilla and beat on low speed until well blended.

3 In a small bowl, whisk together the dry ingredients. With the mixer on low speed, gradually beat the dry ingredients into the liquid ingredients until the batter is smooth and slightly thickened. Beat in the Clementine Marmalade. Divide the batter evenly in the muffin pan.

4 Bake 20 to 25 minutes or until the muffins are firm and the edges start to pull away from the pan. Cool the muffins in the pan 10 minutes. Transfer the muffins to a wire rack to cool another 5 minutes. Serve warm.

*Also called garbanzo flour, it is available at natural food stores or www.bobsredmill.com.

Cinnamon Pecan-Streusel Muffins ⓥ

MAKES 12 MUFFINS

The heavenly aroma of cinnamon wafting through your kitchen will entice everyone to the kitchen to see what smells so wonderful. The streusel provides just the right crunch.

TOPPING

½ cup packed light brown sugar

½ cup finely chopped pecans

¼ cup Carol's Sorghum Blend (page x)

1 teaspoon ground cinnamon

1 teaspoon grated lemon zest

2 tablespoons unsalted butter or buttery spread, such as Earth Balance, melted

LIQUID INGREDIENTS

2 large eggs, at room temperature

⅔ cup 1% milk (cow's, rice, soy, potato, or nut)

½ cup canola oil

1 teaspoon pure vanilla extract

DRY INGREDIENTS

2 cups Carol's Sorghum Blend (page x)

¾ cup sugar

¼ cup Expandex modified tapioca starch, or Carol's Sorghum Blend (page x)

1 tablespoon baking powder

1½ teaspoons xanthan gum

1 teaspoon ground cinnamon

1 teaspoon salt

1 Make the topping: In a small bowl, mix the streusel ingredients together with a pastry blender until thoroughly blended; set aside.

2 Place a rack in the middle of the oven. Preheat the oven to 375°F. Generously grease the cups of a standard 12-cup nonstick (gray, not black) muffin pan or line them with paper liners and coat with cooking spray.

3 In a medium mixing bowl, beat the eggs with an electric mixer on low speed until light yellow and frothy, about 30 seconds. Add the milk, oil, and vanilla extract and beat on low speed until well blended.

4 In a small bowl, whisk together the dry ingredients. With the mixer on low speed, gradually beat the dry ingredients into the liquid ingredients until the batter is smooth and slightly thickened. Place a heaping tablespoon of batter in the bottom of each of the 12 muffin cups. Sprinkle a tablespoon of the topping on top of the batter in each muffin cup. Divide the remaining batter among the 12 muffin cups.

5 Sprinkle the top of each muffin with 2 teaspoons of the topping, lightly pressing the streusel down into the muffin batter with your fingers.

6 Bake approximately 20 to 25 minutes or until the muffin tops are firm and the edges start to pull away from the pan. Cool the muffins in the pan 10 minutes. Transfer the muffins to a wire rack to cool another 5 minutes. Serve warm.

French Vanilla Muffins with Vanilla Sugar Crust Ⓥ

MAKES 12 MUFFINS

If you're a big fan of vanilla—like I am—you'll love this muffin. You can find whole vanilla beans in the spice section of your grocery store. The white vanilla powder used here is the type served with coffee in coffee shops, but you can also buy it in the spice section of your grocery store or order it from www.giftsofnature.net or www.authenticfoods.com. Try stirring ½ cup of your favorite chocolate chips (milk, dark, or white) into the batter after it's mixed for added variety.

LIQUID INGREDIENTS

¾ cup 1% milk (cow's, rice, soy, potato, or nut)

1 whole vanilla bean

2 large eggs, at room temperature

½ cup canola oil

2 teaspoons pure vanilla extract

DRY INGREDIENTS

2 cups Carol's Sorghum Blend (page x)

¾ cup sugar

¼ cup Expandex modified tapioca starch, or Carol's Sorghum Blend (page x)

1 tablespoon baking powder

1½ teaspoons xanthan gum

1 teaspoon white vanilla powder (optional)

1 teaspoon salt

CRUST

2 tablespoons sugar

1 teaspoon white vanilla powder

¼ cup sliced almonds

1 Place a rack in the middle of the oven. Preheat oven to 375°F. Generously grease the cups of a standard 12-cup nonstick (gray, not black) muffin pan or line them with paper liners and coat with cooking spray.

2 Place milk in a small saucepan. Split the vanilla bean in half, lengthwise, to expose the seeds inside the pod. Scrape the seeds from the pod with a knife and add to the milk. Heat the milk over medium heat just until bubbles form around the edges of the pan. Remove the milk from the heat and cool 10 minutes. Remove the vanilla bean and pat dry.

3 In a large mixing bowl, beat the eggs, oil, and vanilla extract with an electric mixer on low speed just until blended. Beat in the milk until blended.

4 In a small bowl, whisk together the dry ingredients. With the mixer on low speed, gradually beat the dry ingredients into the liquid ingredients until the batter is smooth and slightly thickened. Divide the batter evenly in the muffin pan.

5 Make the crust: Spray the muffin tops with cooking spray. In a small bowl, combine the sugar and white vanilla powder. Sprinkle a heaping ½ teaspoon on each muffin. Sprinkle a few almond slices on each muffin.

6 Bake approximately 20 to 25 minutes or until the muffin tops are firm and the edges start to pull away from the pan. Cool the muffins in the pan 10 minutes. Transfer the muffins to a wire rack to cool another 5 minutes. Serve warm.

Note: Store used vanilla bean pods in a container of granulated sugar or powdered sugar to make vanilla sugar.

Buckwheat Flour Pumpkin Muffins with Molasses-Cinnamon Glaze

MAKES 6 LARGE MUFFINS

Cream of buckwheat hot cereal is a wonderful staple to have in your kitchen pantry because it not only makes very quick hot cereal on a cold morning, but it also gives these flavorful muffins wonderful fiber and nutrients.

LIQUID INGREDIENTS

2 large eggs, at room temperature

1 cup pumpkin puree (not pumpkin pie filling)

½ cup canola oil

¼ cup molasses (not blackstrap)

1 teaspoon pure vanilla extract

DRY INGREDIENTS

1½ cups Carol's Sorghum Blend (page x)

¾ cup sugar

½ cup cream of buckwheat cereal, such as Birkett Mills

¼ cup Expandex modified tapioca starch, or ¼ cup Carol's Sorghum Blend (page x)

2 teaspoons pumpkin pie spice

1½ teaspoons xanthan gum

1 teaspoon salt

¾ teaspoon baking soda

½ teaspoon ground allspice

¼ cup chopped raw pumpkin seeds

¼ cup finely chopped crystallized ginger

GLAZE

1½ cups powdered sugar

1 tablespoon molasses (not blackstrap)

1½ teaspoons water

1 Place a rack in the middle of the oven. Preheat the oven to 375°F. Generously grease the cups of a large 6-cup nonstick (gray, not black) large muffin pan or line them with paper liners and coat with cooking spray.

2 In a medium mixing bowl, beat the eggs with an electric mixer on low speed until light yellow and frothy, about 30 seconds. Add the pumpkin, oil, molasses, and vanilla and beat on low speed just until blended.

3 In a small bowl, whisk together the dry ingredients except the pumpkin seeds and ginger. With the mixer on low speed, gradually beat the dry ingredients into the liquid ingredients until the batter is smooth and slightly thickened. Stir in the pumpkin seeds and ginger. Divide the batter evenly in the muffin pan.

4 Bake 35 to 40 minutes or until the muffin tops are firm and the edges start to pull away from the pan. Cool the muffins in the pan 10 minutes. Transfer the muffins to a wire rack.

5 Make the glaze: In a small bowl, blend the powdered sugar, water, and molasses until smooth. With a small spatula or knife, spread the glaze over each muffin. Serve warm.

Amaranth Spice Muffins

MAKES 12 MUFFINS

Amaranth, an ancient grain once used by the Aztecs, is enjoying new popularity since it is safe for gluten-free diets. It is very nutritious and can be purchased as a whole grain (simply grind it in a little spice or coffee grinder for use in muffins or other baked goods) or as flour at most natural food stores.

LIQUID INGREDIENTS

2 large eggs, at room temperature

¾ cup 1% milk (cow's, rice, soy, potato, or nut)

½ cup canola oil

1 tablespoon molasses (not blackstrap)

1 teaspoon pure vanilla extract

DRY INGREDIENTS

2 cups Carol's Sorghum Blend (page x)

1 cup packed light brown sugar

¼ cup amaranth flour

1 tablespoon baking powder

1½ teaspoons xanthan gum

1 teaspoon pumpkin pie spice (or ¼ teaspoon each ground cinnamon, cloves, nutmeg, and allspice)

1 teaspoon salt

½ cup dark raisins

1 Place a rack in the middle of the oven. Preheat the oven to 375°F. Generously grease the cups of a standard 12-cup nonstick (gray, not black) muffin pan or line them with paper liners and coat with cooking spray.

2 In a medium mixing bowl, beat the eggs with an electric mixer on low speed until light yellow and frothy, about 30 seconds. Add the milk, oil, molasses, and vanilla and beat on low speed just until blended.

3 In a small bowl, whisk together the dry ingredients except the raisins. With the mixer on low speed, gradually beat the dry ingredients into the liquid ingredients until the batter is smooth and slightly thickened. Stir in the raisins. Divide the batter evenly in the muffin pan.

4 Bake 20 to 25 minutes or until the muffin tops are firm and the edges start to pull away from the pan. Cool the muffins in the pan 10 minutes. Transfer the muffins to a wire rack to cool another 5 minutes. Serve warm.

Rice Bran Spice Muffins

MAKES 12 MUFFINS

Rice bran is the outside layer of the rice kernel that is removed to make brown rice. It contains the bran and part of the rice germ and adds fiber and protein to baked goods—along with a nutty, earthy flavor. Serve these muffins with pumpkin or apple butter for a sumptuous morning treat.

LIQUID INGREDIENTS

2 large eggs, at room temperature

½ cup 1% milk (cow's, rice, soy, potato, or nut)

½ cup canola oil

2 tablespoons molasses (not blackstrap)

1 teaspoon pure vanilla extract

DRY INGREDIENTS

1¾ cups Carol's Sorghum Blend (page x)

½ cup rice bran, such as Ener-G

¼ cup Expandex modified tapioca starch, or ¼ cup Carol's Sorghum Blend (page x)

¾ cup packed light brown sugar

1 tablespoon baking powder

1½ teaspoons ground cinnamon

1½ teaspoons xanthan gum

1 teaspoon salt

½ teaspoon ground nutmeg

¼ teaspoon ground cloves

¼ teaspoon ground allspice

½ cup dark raisins

½ cup chopped pecans

3 tablespoons granulated sugar

1 Place a rack in the middle of the oven. Preheat oven to 375°F. Generously grease the cups of a standard 12-cup nonstick (gray, not black) muffin pan or line them with paper liners and coat with cooking spray.

2 In a medium bowl, beat the eggs with an electric mixer on low speed until light yellow and frothy, about 30 seconds. Add the milk, oil, molasses, and vanilla and beat on low speed until the batter is smooth and slightly thickened.

3 In a small bowl, whisk together the dry ingredients except the raisins, pecans, and granulated sugar. With the mixer on low speed, gradually beat the dry ingredients into the liquid ingredients until the batter is smooth and slightly thickened. Stir in the raisins and pecans. Divide batter evenly in muffin pan. Sprinkle the 3 tablespoons of sugar (¼ teaspoon per muffin) on the muffins.

4 Bake 20 to 25 minutes or until the muffin tops are firm and the edges start to pull away from the pan. Cool the muffins in the pan 10 minutes. Transfer the muffins to a wire rack to cool another 5 minutes. Serve warm.

Teff Flour Gingerbread Muffins Ⓥ

MAKES 12 MUFFINS

Teff flour comes in brown and ivory colors, but it doesn't matter which you use in this muffin; both are equally nutritious and taste the same. The spices in this gingerbread-style muffin complement teff's earthy flavor.

LIQUID INGREDIENTS

2 large eggs, at room temperature
⅔ cup 1% milk (cow's, rice, soy, potato, or nut)
¼ cup canola oil
2 tablespoons molasses (not blackstrap)
1 teaspoon pure vanilla extract

DRY INGREDIENTS

1 cup packed light brown sugar
⅔ cup teff flour*
⅔ cup potato starch
⅓ cup tapioca flour
¼ cup Expandex modified tapioca starch, or ¼ cup Carol's Sorghum Blend (page x)
1 tablespoon baking powder
1 teaspoon xanthan gum
1 teaspoon salt
1 teaspoon ground ginger
1 teaspoon ground cinnamon
½ teaspoon grated nutmeg
½ teaspoon ground allspice
⅛ teaspoon ground cloves
1 cup dark or golden raisins

1 Place a rack in the middle of the oven. Preheat oven to 375°F. Generously grease the cups of a standard 12-cup nonstick (gray, not black) muffin pan or line them with paper liners and coat with cooking spray.

2 In a medium bowl, beat the eggs with an electric mixer on low speed until light yellow and frothy, about 30 seconds. Add the milk, oil, molasses, and vanilla and beat on low speed until the batter is smooth and slightly thickened.

3 In a small bowl, whisk together the dry ingredients except the raisins. With the mixer on low speed, gradually beat the dry ingredients into the liquid ingredients until the batter is smooth and slightly thickened. Stir in the raisins. Divide the batter evenly in the muffin pan.

4 Bake 20 to 25 minutes or until the muffin tops are firm and the edges start to pull away from the pan. Cool the muffins in the pan 10 minutes. Transfer the muffins to a wire rack to cool another 5 minutes. Serve warm.

Available at natural food stores and at www.teffco.com

Salba Coconut Muffins

MAKES 12 MUFFINS

Salba is a whole grain that has been used for more than five hundred years in South America. Because of its high iron, fiber, calcium, magnesium, and Omega-3 fatty acid content, it is extremely nutritious, but has little taste of its own so it virtually disappears into the muffin.

LIQUID INGREDIENTS

2 large eggs, at room temperature

1 cup 1% milk (cow's, rice, soy, potato, or nut)

½ cup canola oil

1 teaspoon pure vanilla extract

1 teaspoon coconut-flavored extract

DRY INGREDIENTS

1¾ cups Carol's Sorghum Blend (page x)

¾ cup sugar

¼ cup Expandex modified tapioca starch, or ¼ cup Carol's Sorghum Blend (page x)

2 tablespoons salba*

2 teaspoons baking powder

1½ teaspoons xanthan gum

1 teaspoon salt

½ cup shredded sweetened coconut

1 Place a rack in the middle of the oven. Preheat the oven to 375°F. Generously grease the cups of a standard 12-cup nonstick (gray, not black) muffin pan or line them with paper liners and coat with cooking spray.

2 In a medium mixing bowl, beat the eggs with an electric mixer on low speed until light yellow and frothy, about 30 seconds. Add the milk, oil, vanilla, and coconut extract and beat just until blended.

3 In a small bowl, whisk together the dry ingredients except coconut. With the mixer on low speed, gradually beat the dry ingredients into the liquid ingredients until the batter is smooth and slightly thickened. Stir in the coconut. Divide the batter evenly in the muffin pan.

4 Bake 25 to 30 minutes or until the muffin tops are firm and the edges start to pull away from the pan. Cool the muffins in the pan 10 minutes. Transfer the muffins to a wire rack to cool another 5 minutes. Serve warm.

*Available at natural food stores

White Bean Flour Spice Muffins with Molasses-Cinnamon Glaze

MAKES 12 MUFFINS

White bean flour provides a wonderful wholesomeness while the molasses glaze intensifies the spices in these muffins.

LIQUID INGREDIENTS

2 large eggs, at room temperature

1 cup 1% milk (cow's, rice, soy, potato, or nut)

⅓ cup canola oil

1 tablespoon molasses (not blackstrap)

1 teaspoon pure vanilla extract

DRY INGREDIENTS

2 cups Carol's Sorghum Blend (page x)

⅔ cup sugar

⅓ cup white bean flour*

1 tablespoon baking powder

1½ teaspoons xanthan gum

1 teaspoon salt

½ teaspoon ground nutmeg

¼ teaspoon ground cloves

¼ teaspoon ground allspice

½ cup dark raisins

GLAZE

1 cup powdered sugar

¼ teaspoon ground cinnamon

1 tablespoon molasses (not blackstrap)

2 tablespoons water

1 Place a rack in the middle of the oven. Preheat the oven to 375°F. Generously grease the cups of a 12-cup nonstick (gray, not black) muffin pan or line them with paper liners and coat with cooking spray.

2 In a medium bowl, beat the eggs with an electric mixer on low speed until light yellow and frothy, about 30 seconds. Add the milk, oil, molasses, and vanilla and beat on low speed until smooth and slightly thickened.

3 In a small bowl, whisk together the dry ingredients except raisins. With the mixer on low speed, gradually beat the dry ingredients into the liquid ingredients until the batter is smooth and slightly thickened. Stir in the raisins. Divide the batter evenly in the pan.

4 Bake 20 to 25 minutes or until the muffin tops are firm and the edges start to pull away from the pan. Cool the muffins in the pan 10 minutes. Transfer the muffins to a wire rack to cool another 5 minutes.

5 Make the glaze: In a small bowl, stir together the powdered sugar, cinnamon, molasses, and water with a spatula. Using the spatula, drizzle the glaze over the muffins. Serve immediately.

*Available at www.bobsredmill.com.

Corn Muffins with Chives
MAKES 12 MUFFINS

These muffins taste like cornbread (with the addition of chives), but are easier to make in muffin pans. They are best served straight from the oven, ideally with butter and honey. While yellow cornmeal results in beautiful-looking muffins, white cornmeal will taste just as great here.

LIQUID INGREDIENTS

2 large eggs, at room temperature
¾ cup 1% milk (cow's, rice, soy, potato, or nut)
½ cup light olive oil

DRY INGREDIENTS

1 cup gluten-free yellow cornmeal, such as Albers, Lamb's, Kinnikinnick, or Shiloh Farms
1 cup Carol's Sorghum Blend (page x)
⅓ cup sugar
¼ cup Expandex modified tapioca starch, or ¼ cup Carol's Sorghum Blend (page x)
1 tablespoon baking powder
1½ teaspoons xanthan gum
1 teaspoon salt
½ cup snipped fresh chives or finely sliced green onions

1 Place a rack in the middle of the oven. Preheat the oven to 375°F. Generously grease the cups of a standard 12-cup nonstick (gray, not black) muffin pan or line them with paper liners and coat with cooking spray.

2 In a medium bowl, beat the eggs with an electric mixer on low speed until light yellow and frothy, about 30 seconds. Add the milk and oil and beat on low speed until the batter is smooth and slightly thickened.

3 In a small bowl, whisk together the dry ingredients except chives. With the mixer on low speed, gradually beat the dry ingredients into the liquid ingredients until the batter is smooth and the consistency of thick cake batter. Stir in the chives. Divide the batter evenly in the muffin pan.

4 Bake 25 to 30 minutes or until the muffin tops are firm and the edges start to pull away from the pan. Cool the muffins in the pan 10 minutes. Transfer the muffins to a wire rack to cool another 5 minutes. Serve warm.

Herb-Garlic Muffins

MAKES 12 MUFFINS

These muffins go well with a hearty stew for dinner and they're best served straight from the oven.

LIQUID INGREDIENTS

2 large eggs, at room temperature

1 cup 1% milk (cow's, rice, soy, potato, or nut)

¼ cup unsalted butter or buttery spread, such as Earth Balance, melted

1 garlic clove, minced

DRY INGREDIENTS

2 cups Carol's Sorghum Blend (page x)

⅓ cup Expandex modified tapioca starch, or ¼ cup Carol's Sorghum Blend (page x)

2 tablespoons sugar

1 tablespoon baking powder

1½ teaspoons xanthan gum

1 teaspoon salt

HERBS

⅓ cup chopped fresh parsley

⅓ cup green onions or fresh chives

2 tablespoons chopped fresh thyme

1 tablespoon grated lemon zest

1 Place a rack in the middle of the oven. Preheat oven to 375°F. Generously grease the cups of a standard 12-cup nonstick (gray, not black) muffin pan or line them with paper liners and coat with cooking spray.

2 In a medium bowl, beat the eggs with an electric mixer on low speed until light yellow and frothy, about 30 seconds. Add the milk, butter, and garlic and beat on low speed until the batter is smooth and slightly thickened.

3 In a small bowl, whisk together the dry ingredients. With the mixer on low speed, gradually beat the dry ingredients into the liquid ingredients until the batter is smooth and is the consistency of thick cake batter. Gently stir in herbs. Divide the batter evenly in the muffin pans.

4 Bake 20 to 25 minutes or until muffin tops are firm and the edges start to pull away from the pan. Cool the muffins in the pan 10 minutes. Transfer the muffins to a wire rack to cool another 5 minutes. Serve warm.

BISCUITS AND SCONES

Buttermilk Biscuits

MAKES 10 BISCUITS

Don't be puzzled by the soft biscuit dough—this texture is necessary for the biscuits to rise properly. When dusted with white rice flour, the ultra-soft dough becomes more manageable. Serve these biscuits with Honey Butter (page 678) or your favorite jam.

White rice flour for dusting and rolling
¾ cup Carol's Sorghum Blend (page x)
¾ cup potato starch
4 teaspoons sugar
1 tablespoon baking powder
1 teaspoon xanthan gum
1 teaspoon guar gum
½ teaspoon baking soda
½ teaspoon salt
¼ cup shortening, such as Crisco, Earth Balance, or Spectrum Vegetable
1 cup buttermilk or homemade Buttermilk (page 677), well-shaken and at room temperature
2 tablespoons milk (cow's, rice, soy, potato, or nut) or heavy cream for brushing

1 Place a rack in the middle of the oven. Preheat the oven to 375°F. Generously grease a 13 × 9-inch nonstick (gray, not black) baking sheet or line with parchment paper. Dust the surface lightly with white rice flour.

2 In a food processor, pulse the sorghum blend, potato starch, sugar, baking powder, xanthan gum, guar gum, baking soda, and salt until thoroughly mixed. Add the shortening and buttermilk and process just until the dough forms a ball, scraping down the sides with a spatula, if necessary. The dough will be very, very soft.

3 Place the dough on the baking sheet. Lightly dust the dough with white rice flour to facilitate easier handling. Gently pat the dough to a 1-inch-thick circle. Cut into 10 biscuits, 2 inches in diameter, with floured metal biscuit cutter. For better rising, push the biscuit cutter straight down on the dough rather than twisting it while cutting. Pat the remaining dough to 1 inch thick and cut again, lightly dusting with white rice flour to prevent sticking, if necessary. Arrange the biscuits evenly on the baking sheet and gently brush the biscuit tops with milk.

4 Bake 12 to 15 minutes or until the biscuits are nicely browned and crisp. Serve immediately.

Chive Biscuits with Parmesan Topping

MAKES 10 BISCUITS

Serve these savory biscuits with a luncheon soup, a simple salad, or with dinner. They bake very quickly so be sure the rest of your meal is ready so you can begin eating right after you take them out of the oven.

White rice flour for dusting and rolling
¾ cup Carol's Sorghum Blend (page x)
¾ cup potato starch
4 teaspoons sugar
1 tablespoon baking powder
1 teaspoon xanthan gum
1 teaspoon guar gum
½ teaspoon baking soda
½ teaspoon salt
¼ cup shortening, such as Crisco, Earth Balance, or Spectrum Vegetable
1 cup buttermilk, well-shaken, or homemade Buttermilk (page 677), at room temperature
2 teaspoons minced chives
2 tablespoons milk (cow's, rice, soy, potato, or nut) or heavy cream for brushing
2 tablespoons grated Parmesan cheese or soy alternative, such as Soyco, for sprinkling on biscuit tops

1 Place a rack in the middle of the oven. Preheat the oven to 375°F. Generously grease a 13 × 9-inch nonstick (gray, not black) baking sheet or line with parchment paper. Dust the surface lightly with white rice flour.

2 In a food processor, pulse the sorghum blend, potato starch, sugar, baking powder, xanthan gum, guar gum, baking soda, and salt until thoroughly mixed. Add the shortening and buttermilk and process just until the dough forms a ball, scraping down the sides with a spatula, if necessary. Pulse in the chives. The dough will be very, very soft.

3 Place the dough on the baking sheet. Lightly dust the dough with white rice flour to facilitate easier handling. Gently pat the dough to a 1-inch thick circle. Cut into 10 biscuits, 2 inches in diameter, with floured metal biscuit cutter. For better rising, push the biscuit cutter straight down on the dough rather than twisting it while cutting. Shape the remaining dough to 1 inch thick and cut again, lightly dusting with white rice flour to prevent sticking, if necessary. Arrange the biscuits evenly on the baking sheet and gently brush the biscuit tops with milk. Dust with Parmesan cheese.

4 Bake 12 to 15 minutes or until the biscuits are nicely browned and crisp. Remove from the oven and serve immediately.

Onion-Bacon Biscuits

MAKES 10 BISCUITS

Hearty, warm biscuits piping hot from the oven always lend a comforting touch to any meal. The addition of onion and bacon make these luscious, and they work really well with soup or chowder.

White rice flour for dusting and rolling
¾ cup Carol's Sorghum Blend (page x)
¾ cup potato starch
4 teaspoons sugar
1 tablespoon baking powder
1 teaspoon xanthan gum
1 teaspoon guar gum
½ teaspoon baking soda
½ teaspoon salt
¼ cup shortening, such as Crisco, Earth Balance, or Spectrum Vegetable
1 cup buttermilk or homemade Buttermilk (page 677), well-shaken, at room temperature
4 slices cooked bacon, drained and crumbled
1½ tablespoons finely diced fresh onion or 2 teaspoons dried minced onion
2 tablespoons milk (cow's, rice, soy, potato, or nut) or heavy cream for brushing

1 Place a rack in the middle of the oven. Preheat oven to 375°F. Generously grease a 13 × 9-inch nonstick (gray, not black) baking sheet or line with parchment paper. Dust surface lightly with white rice flour.

2 In a food processor, pulse the sorghum blend, potato starch, sugar, baking powder, xanthan gum, guar gum, baking soda, and salt to mix thoroughly. Add shortening and buttermilk. Blend just until the dough forms a ball, scraping down the sides with spatula, if necessary. Add the chopped bacon and onion and pulse just a few times to incorporate the bacon, but not pulverize it. The dough will be very, very soft.

3 Place the dough on the baking sheet. Lightly dust the dough with white rice flour to facilitate easier handling. Gently pat the dough to a 1-inch-thick circle. Cut into 10 biscuits, 2 inches in diameter, with a floured metal biscuit cutter. For better rising, push the biscuit cutter straight down on the dough rather than twisting it while cutting. Shape and press the remaining dough to a 1-inch thickness and cut again, lightly dusting with white rice flour to prevent sticking, if necessary. Arrange the biscuits about 1½ inches apart on the baking sheet and gently brush the biscuit tops with milk.

4 Bake 15 to 18 minutes or until the biscuits are nicely browned and crisp to your liking. Depending on your oven, the biscuits may start browning at 12 minutes and will brown much more rapidly from that point on, so watch them carefully to prevent burning. Serve immediately.

Sweet Potato Biscuits

MAKES 10 BISCUITS

These slightly sweet, mild-tasting biscuits are a great way to use leftover mashed sweet potatoes. The result is heavier, but wonderfully tasty nonetheless. Some consider these biscuits a Southern tradition; in other families, regardless of region, they accompany the turkey and stuffing at Thanksgiving dinner.

White rice flour for dusting and rolling
¾ cup Carol's Sorghum Blend (page x)
¾ cup potato starch
2 tablespoon sugar
1 tablespoon baking powder
1 teaspoon xanthan gum
1 teaspoon guar gum
½ teaspoon baking soda
½ teaspoon salt
¼ cup shortening, such as Crisco, Earth Balance, or Spectrum Vegetable
1 cup buttermilk or homemade Buttermilk (page 677), well-shaken, at room temperature
½ cup mashed sweet potatoes
2 tablespoons milk (cow's, rice, soy, potato, or nut) or heavy cream for brushing

1 Place a rack in the middle of the oven. Preheat the oven to 375°F. Generously grease a 13 × 9-inch nonstick (gray, not black) baking sheet or line with parchment paper. Dust the surface lightly with white rice flour.

2 In a food processor, pulse the sorghum blend, potato starch, sugar, baking powder, xanthan gum, guar gum, baking soda, and salt to mix thoroughly. Add the shortening, buttermilk, and sweet potatoes and process just until the dough forms a ball, scraping down the sides with a spatula, if necessary. The dough will be very soft.

3 Place the dough on the baking sheet. Lightly dust the dough with white rice flour to facilitate easier handling. Gently pat the dough to a 1-inch-thick circle. Cut into 10 biscuits, 2 inches in diameter, with floured metal biscuit cutter. For better rising, push the biscuit cutter straight down on the dough rather than twisting it while cutting. Shape the remaining dough to 1 inch thick and cut again, lightly dusting with white rice flour to prevent sticking, if necessary. Arrange the biscuits evenly on the baking sheet and gently brush the biscuit tops with milk.

4 Bake 15 to 18 minutes or until the biscuits are nicely browned and crisp. Serve immediately.

Cheddar-Pepperoni Scones

MAKES 8 SCONES

This unique approach to scone making calls for baking the dough on a baking sheet then cutting it into wedges. Shaping the scones in a uniformly thick circle—rather than making the edges thinner—lets them bake more evenly. Scones are best eaten hot, right out of the oven. These taste great plain, but are even more delicious topped with a little butter.

⅓ cup unsalted butter or buttery spread, such as Earth Balance, at room temperature

1 large egg, at room temperature

2 tablespoons sugar

1½ cups Carol's Sorghum Blend (page x)

¾ cup milk (cow's, rice, soy, potato, or nut)

½ cup tapioca flour

1 tablespoon baking powder

1 tablespoon finely diced fresh onion or 1 teaspoon dried minced onion

1 teaspoon xanthan gum

1 teaspoon guar gum

1 teaspoon ground mustard

¾ teaspoon salt

⅛ teaspoon crushed red pepper

¾ cup (3 ounces) grated sharp Cheddar cheese or cheese alternative, such as Vegan Gourmet

½ cup finely chopped gluten-free pepperoni, such as Hormel

2 tablespoons heavy cream or whole milk (cow's, rice, soy, potato, or nut)

1 tablespoon grated Parmesan cheese or soy alternative, such as Soyco

1 Place a rack in the middle of the oven. Preheat the oven to 375°F. Generously grease a 13 × 9-inch nonstick (gray, not black) baking sheet or line it with parchment paper.

2 In a food processor, blend the butter, egg, and sugar until well blended. Add the sorghum blend, milk, tapioca, baking powder, onion, xanthan gum, guar gum, mustard, salt, and red pepper, and process just until blended. Evenly distribute the cheese and pepperoni around the perimeter of the bowl and pulse just until they are evenly blended into the dough. The dough will be very soft.

3 Transfer the dough to the baking sheet, shaping it with a wet spatula into a smooth, 8-inch circle, ¾-inch thick. Use the wet spatula to shape straight sides (rather than rounded) for more

even browning. Brush the dough with cream and sprinkle with Parmesan cheese.

4 Bake 20 minutes or until the dough is lightly browned. Remove the baking sheet from the oven and, using a sharp knife, cut the circle of dough into 8 wedges. Pull the wedges away from the center so they are at least 1 inch from each other and return to the oven. Bake 5 to 7 minutes longer, or until all sides of each scone are browned. (This makes all edges of the scones crisp, rather than the just the tops.) Cool the scones 5 minutes on the pan on a wire rack. Serve warm.

Chai Almond Scones
MAKES 8 SCONES

Scones are a delightful way to serve guests a home baked treat, without much fuss. In this version, Altiplano Gold's Chai Almond Instant Hot Breakfast Cereal provides a hint of chai flavor and part of the sugar for scones. The heavenly chai aroma wafting through the kitchen invites everyone to gather around the breakfast table. For variety, consider using the other delicious flavors of their quinoa-based hot cereal in the same amounts, as well.

¼ cup (½ stick) unsalted butter or buttery spread, such as Earth Balance, at room temperature

½ cup 1% milk (cow's, rice, soy, potato, or nut)

1 large egg, at room temperature

1 teaspoon pure vanilla extract

¾ cup Carol's Sorghum Blend (page x)

½ tapioca flour

1 packet (48 grams) Altiplano Chai Almond Instant Hot Cereal

¼ cup sugar, divided

2 teaspoons xanthan gum

1½ teaspoons cream of tartar

¾ teaspoon baking soda

½ cup currants or dried cranberries

1 Place a rack in the middle of the oven. Preheat the oven to 375°F. Generously grease a 13 × 9-inch nonstick (gray, not black) baking sheet or line it with parchment paper.

2 In a food processor, blend the butter, milk, egg, and vanilla until smooth. Add sorghum blend, tapioca flour, cereal, 3 tablespoons of the sugar, xanthan gum, cream of tartar, and baking soda, and process until smooth, scraping down sides of bowl with a spatula if necessary. Add the currants and pulse a few times to incorporate. The dough will be very soft.

3 Place the dough on the baking sheet, patting it with a wet spatula into a smooth, uniform 8-inch circle, ¾-inch thick. Use the wet spatula to shape straight sides (rather than rounded) for more even browning. Sprinkle with remaining sugar.

4 Bake 20 minutes or until the dough is lightly browned. Remove the baking sheet from the oven and, using a sharp knife, cut the circle of dough into 8 wedges. Pull the wedges away from the center so they are at least 1 inch from each other and return to the oven. Bake 5 to 7 minutes longer, or until all sides of each scone are browned. (This makes all edges of the scones crisp, rather than just the tops.) Cool the scones 5 minutes on the pan on a wire rack. Serve immediately.

Chocolate Chip Scones with Fresh Raspberries Ⓥ

MAKES 8 SCONES

Scone pans, available in kitchen stores, already have scone shapes built into them, for easy use. Simply fill the (generously greased) indentations and bake as directed by the manufacturer. If you don't have a scone pan, the directions in this recipe will help you shape any of the scone recipes in this book, using a regular baking sheet.

5 tablespoons unsalted butter or buttery spread, such as Earth Balance, at room temperature

1 large egg, at room temperature

½ cup sugar

¾ cup 1% milk (cow's, rice, soy, potato, or nut)

2 teaspoons pure vanilla extract

1½ cups Carol's Sorghum Blend (page x)

½ cup tapioca flour

1 tablespoon baking powder

1 teaspoon xanthan gum

1 teaspoon guar gum

¾ teaspoon salt

½ cup gluten-free dairy free chocolate chips, such as Tropical Source

1 cup (6-ounce package) fresh raspberries, gently washed and patted dry

2 tablespoons heavy cream or whole milk (cow's, rice, soy, potato, or nut)

2 tablespoons sugar for sprinkling on top of scones

1 Place a rack in the middle of the oven. Preheat the oven to 375°F. Generously grease a 13 × 9-inch nonstick (gray, not black) baking sheet or line it with parchment paper. Or, generously grease a scone pan (see headnote).

2 In a food processor, process the butter, egg, and sugar until blended. Add the milk, vanilla, sorghum blend, tapioca, baking powder, xanthan gum, guar gum, and salt, and process just until blended. The dough will be very soft. Transfer the dough to a large bowl and gently stir in the chocolate chips and fresh raspberries.

3 Place the dough on the baking sheet, shaping it with a wet spatula into a smooth, 8-inch circle, ¾-inch thick. Use the wet spatula to shape straight sides (rather than rounded) for more even browning. Brush the dough with cream and sprinkle with sugar.

4 Bake 20 minutes or until the dough is lightly browned. Remove the baking sheet from the oven and, using a sharp knife, cut the circle of dough into 8 wedges. Pull the wedges away from the center so they are at least 1 inch from each other and return to the oven for the final 5 to 7 minutes of baking, or until all sides of each scone are browned. (This makes all edges of the scones crisp, rather than the just the tops.) Cool the scones 5 minutes on the pan on a wire rack. Serve warm.

Cranberry-Clementine Scones with Clementine Glaze Ⓥ

MAKES 8 SCONES

Serve these scones with Clementine Marmalade (page 678) or store-bought orange marmalade. Sparkling sugar is especially beautiful on these scones, but regular sugar makes a fine substitute. If fresh clementines (or tangerines) aren't available, use oranges instead for the juice and zest.

⅓ cup unsalted butter or buttery spread, such as Earth Balance, at room temperature

1 tablespoon grated clementine or tangerine zest

1 large egg, at room temperature

⅓ cup sugar

½ cup 1% milk (cow's, rice, soy, potato, or nut)

1½ cups Carol's Sorghum Blend (page x)

½ cup tapioca flour

1 tablespoon baking powder

1½ teaspoons xanthan gum

1 teaspoon guar gum

1 teaspoon salt

¾ cup dried sweetened cranberries

2 tablespoons heavy cream or milk (cow's, rice, soy, potato, or nut) for brushing

1 tablespoon sparkling sugar (or regular sugar) for sprinkling

GLAZE

1 cup powdered sugar

2 tablespoons fresh clementine juice, or enough to make a thin glaze

1 Place a rack in the middle of the oven. Preheat the oven to 375°F. Generously grease a 13 x9-inch nonstick (gray, not black) baking sheet or line it with parchment paper.

2 In a food processor, process the butter, clementine zest, egg, and sugar until blended. Add the milk, sorghum blend, tapioca, baking powder, xanthan gum, guar gum, and salt, and process just until blended. Add cranberries and pulse just until the cranberries are incorporated into the dough. The dough will be very soft.

3 Place the dough on the baking sheet, patting it with a wet spatula into a smooth, uniform 8-inch circle, ¾-inch thick. Use the wet spatula to shape straight sides (rather than rounded) for more even browning. Brush the dough with cream and sprinkle with sugar.

4 Bake 20 minutes or until the dough is lightly browned. Remove the baking sheet from the oven and, using a sharp knife, cut the circle of dough into 8 wedges. Pull the wedges away from the center so they are at least 1 inch from each other and return to the oven. Bake 5 to 7 minutes longer, or until all sides of each scone are browned. (This makes all edges of the scones crisp, rather than just the tops.) Cool the scones 5 minutes on the pan on a wire rack.

5 Make the glaze: Stir together powdered sugar and clementine juice until smooth. Using a pastry brush, brush the glaze onto the warm scones. Serve immediately.

Lemon Poppy Seed Scones with Lemon Glaze Ⓥ

MAKES 8 SCONES

The lemon glaze on these scones is like the frosting on the classic cake. The scones taste fantastic without it, but the glaze provides that perfect finishing touch.

SCONES

⅓ cup unsalted butter or buttery spread, such as Earth Balance, at room temperature

1 tablespoon grated lemon zest

½ cup sugar

1 large egg, at room temperature

½ cup 1% milk (cow's, rice, soy, potato, or nut)

1 teaspoon pure vanilla extract

1½ cups Carol's Sorghum Blend (page x)

½ cup tapioca flour

1 tablespoon baking powder

1 teaspoon xanthan gum

1 teaspoon guar gum

1 teaspoon salt

4 teaspoons poppy seed

2 tablespoons heavy cream or milk (cow's, rice, soy, potato, or nut) for brushing

1 tablespoon sugar for sprinkling

GLAZE

1 cup powdered sugar

2 tablespoons fresh lemon juice

1 Place a rack in the middle of the oven. Preheat the oven to 375°F. Generously grease a 13 × 9-inch nonstick (gray, not black) baking sheet or line it with parchment paper.

2 In a food processor, process the butter, lemon zest, sugar, and egg until blended. Add the milk, vanilla, sorghum blend, tapioca, baking powder, xanthan gum, guar gum, and salt. Process just until blended. Sprinkle poppy seeds around perimeter of bowl and pulse until blended into dough. The dough will be very soft.

3 Place the dough on the baking sheet, patting it with a wet spatula into a smooth, uniform 8-inch circle, ¾-inch thick. Use the wet spatula to shape straight sides (rather than rounded) for more even browning. Brush the dough with cream and sprinkle with sugar.

4 Bake 20 minutes or until the dough is lightly browned. Remove the baking sheet from the oven and, using a sharp knife, cut the circle of dough into 8 wedges. Pull the wedges away from the center so they are at least 1 inch from each other and return to the oven for the final 5 to 7 minutes of baking, or until all sides of each scone are browned. (This makes all edges of the scones crisp, rather than the just the tops.) Cool the scones 5 minutes on the pan on a wire rack.

5 Make the glaze: Stir together the powdered sugar and lemon juice until smooth. Using a pastry brush, brush the glaze onto the warm scones. Serve immediately.

POPOVERS

Basic Popovers

MAKES 6 POPOVERS

Popovers may not come to mind when thinking of bread, but they are much like a dinner roll: they can be filled to make a sandwich, and they satisfy a craving for something crispy. You can purchase popover pans in kitchen stores and discount stores for around twenty dollars, which is a good investment for bread that is so easy. Muffin pans or custard cups are also an option, but their wide shape and short height won't allow the popovers to rise as high. To guarantee success, keep all your ingredients at room temperature, and heat the popover pan before filling it with batter.

3 large eggs, at room temperature

1 cup 1% milk (cow's, rice, soy, potato, or nut), at room temperature

⅓ cup potato starch

⅓ cup Expandex modified tapioca starch, or ⅓ cup Carol's Sorghum Blend (page x)

¼ cup Carol's Sorghum Blend (page x)

1 tablespoon unsalted butter or buttery spread, such as Earth Balance, melted

½ teaspoon salt

¼ teaspoon xanthan gum

1 Place a rack in the lower-middle position of the oven. Preheat the oven to 450°F. Lightly oil each cup of a standard 6-cup popover pan with shortening.

2 In a blender, thoroughly blend all the ingredients. The batter will be almost as thin as crepe batter but not as thick as pancake batter.

3 Place the pan in the hot oven 5 minutes to heat it. Wearing oven mitts, carefully remove the hot pan from the oven, divide the batter among the cups, and return the pan to the oven.

4 Bake 20 minutes at 450°F and then reduce the heat to 350°F. Continue baking another 10 to 15 minutes or until the sides of the popovers become rigid. (Do not open the oven door during this time.) Quickly—and carefully—remove the pan from the oven. Pierce each popover along the rigid side with a toothpick to release the steam; return the pan to the oven to bake another 5 minutes. Remove from oven and cool the pan on a wire rack 5 minutes. Remove the popovers from the pan and serve immediately.

Bacon and Cheddar Cheese Popovers

MAKES 6 POPOVERS

These savory popovers won't rise quite as high as the Basic Popovers (left) because the bacon and cheese weigh them down a little. But they are simply delicious and make a nice addition to any meal. Serve them within 10 minutes of removing them from the oven, but if necessary you can reheat them at 200°F for 5 minutes.

3 large eggs, at room temperature

1 cup 1% milk (cow's, rice, soy, potato, or nut), at room temperature

⅔ cup potato starch

¼ cup Carol's Sorghum Blend (page x)

1 tablespoon unsalted butter or buttery spread, such as Earth Balance, melted

¼ teaspoon salt

¼ teaspoon xanthan gum

¾ cup grated extra-sharp Cheddar cheese or cheese alternative, such as Vegan Gourmet

4 slices cooked lean bacon, finely crumbled

2 tablespoons finely snipped fresh chives

1 Place a rack in the lower-middle position of the oven. Preheat the oven to 450°F. Lightly oil each cup of a standard 6-cup popover pan.

2 In a blender, thoroughly blend all of the ingredients, except the cheese, bacon, and chives. Add the cheese, bacon, and chives and pulse just a few times to incorporate them, but not chop them.

3 Place the pan in the hot oven 5 minutes to heat it. Wearing hot mitts, carefully remove the hot pan from the oven and fill each cup halfway with batter. Divide remaining batter evenly among the cups. Place the pan on the lower-middle rack of the oven.

4 Bake 20 minutes at 450°F, then reduce the heat to 350°F. Continue baking another 10 minutes or until the sides of the popover are rigid. Do not open the oven door during this time. Quickly—and carefully—remove the pan from the oven. Pierce each popover along the rigid side with a toothpick to release the steam; return the pan to the oven to bake another 5 minutes. Cool in the pan 5 minutes on a wire rack. Remove the popovers from the pan and serve immediately.

Herb Popovers

MAKES 6 POPOVERS

You can vary the herbs in this popover depending on what ingredients you have on hand. In summer, I just step outside my back door to harvest many different varieties of fresh herbs. If fresh herbs aren't available, you can use 1 teaspoon dried herbs in place of each tablespoon of fresh herbs. Simply crush the herbs a bit before using to release their flavor and aroma.

3 large eggs, at room temperature
1 cup 1% milk (cow's, rice, soy, potato, or nut), at room temperature
⅔ cup potato starch
¼ cup Carol's Sorghum Blend (page x)
1 tablespoon unsalted butter or buttery spread, such as Earth Balance, melted
½ teaspoon salt
¼ teaspoon xanthan gum
1 tablespoon finely snipped fresh chives
1 tablespoon finely snipped fresh rosemary
2 teaspoons finely chopped fresh sage

1 Place a rack in the lower-middle position of the oven. Preheat the oven to 450°F. Lightly oil each cup of a standard 6-cup popover pan.

2 In a blender, thoroughly blend all of the ingredients, except the chives, rosemary, and sage. Add the herbs and pulse just a few times to incorporate them, but not chop them.

3 Place the pan in the hot oven 5 minutes. Using pot holders or mitts, carefully remove the hot pan from the oven and fill each cup halfway with batter. Divide remaining batter evenly among the cups. Place the pan on the lower-middle rack of the oven.

4 Bake 20 minutes at 450°F, then reduce the heat to 350°F and continue baking 10 minutes or until the sides of the popover are rigid. Do not open the oven door during this time. Quickly—and carefully—remove the pan from the oven. Pierce each popover along the rigid side with a toothpick to release the steam; return the pan to the oven to bake another 5 minutes. Cool in the pan 5 minutes on a wire rack. Remove the popovers from the pan and serve immediately.

Parmesan Cheese Popovers

MAKES 6 POPOVERS

The salt amount called for in this recipe is smaller than the other popover varieties because the Parmesan cheese adds a nice salty flavor on its own. I often serve these at my dinner parties because they look so impressive as they come out of the oven.

3 large eggs, at room temperature
1 cup 1% milk (cow's, rice, soy, potato, or nut)
⅔ cup potato starch
½ cup grated Parmesan cheese, or soy alternative, such as Soyco
¼ cup Carol's Sorghum Blend (page x)
1 tablespoon unsalted butter or buttery spread, such as Earth Balance, melted
¼ teaspoon salt
¼ teaspoon xanthan gum

1 Place a rack in the lower-middle position of the oven. Preheat the oven to 450°F. Lightly oil each cup of a standard 6-cup popover pan.

2 In a blender, thoroughly blend all of the ingredients. The batter will be almost as thin as crepe batter but not as thick as pancake batter.

3 Place the pan in the hot oven 5 minutes. Wearing hot mitts, carefully remove the hot pan from the oven and fill each cup halfway with batter. Divide remaining batter evenly among the cups. Place the pan on the lower-middle rack of the oven.

4 Bake 20 minutes at 450°F, then reduce the heat to 350°F and continue baking 10 minutes or until the sides of the popover are rigid. Do not open the oven door during this time. Quickly—and carefully—remove the pan from the oven. Pierce each popover along the rigid side with a toothpick to release the steam; return the pan to the oven to bake another 5 minutes. Cool in the pan 5 minutes on a wire rack. Remove the popovers from the pan and serve immediately.

Yorkshire Pudding

MAKES 6 POPOVERS

Despite their interesting name, these English breads are simply a form of popover. Make them when a roast beef or other roast is on the menu; the roast produces luscious pan drippings. Pan drippings are quite flavorful because they include the browned bits of meat clinging to the pan as well as the seasonings. Not only do they flavor Yorkshire pudding, but if strained they can also serve as the foundation for a sauce.

6 teaspoons hot meat drippings, from the bottom of a roasting pan

3 large eggs at room temperature

1 cup 1% milk (cow's, rice, soy, potato, or nut)

⅓ cup potato starch

⅓ cup Expandex modified tapioca starch, or ⅓ cup Carol's Sorghum Blend (page x)

¼ cup Carol's Sorghum Blend (page x)

1 tablespoon unsalted butter or buttery spread, such as Earth Balance, melted

½ teaspoon salt

¼ teaspoon xanthan gum

1 Place a rack in the lower-middle position of the oven. Preheat the oven to 450°F. Lightly oil each cup of a standard 6-cup popover pan. Pour 1 teaspoon of hot meat drippings into each cup of the pan.

2 In a blender, thoroughly blend all of the ingredients. The batter will be almost as thin as crepe batter but not as thick as pancake batter.

3 Place the pan in the hot oven 5 minutes. Wearing hot mitts, carefully remove the hot pan from the oven and fill each cup halfway with batter. Divide remaining batter evenly among the cups. Place the pan on the lower-middle rack of the oven.

4 Bake 20 minutes at 450°F, then reduce the heat to 350°F and continue baking 10 minutes or until the sides of the popover are rigid. Do not open the oven door during this time. Quickly—and carefully—remove the pan from the oven. Pierce each popover along the rigid side with a toothpick to release the steam; return the pan to the oven to bake another 5 minutes. Cool in the pan 5 minutes on a wire rack. Remove the popovers from the pan and serve immediately.

Gougères Ⓥ

MAKES 12 ROLLS

Pronounced "gu-SHARE," these little French puffs are best served right out of the oven when they're crispy on the outside yet warm and chewy on the inside. I serve them at dinner parties, but they're also perfect for cocktail parties in the miniature size. To make sure the gougères are equal in size, use a 2-tablespoon measure such as a coffee measure or a #24 spring-action metal ice-cream scoop for larger ones, or a 1-tablespoon measuring spoon for the smaller ones.

½ cup white rice flour

¼ cup potato starch

2 tablespoons Expandex modified tapioca starch

2 large eggs + 1 egg white, at room temperature

⅔ cup water

¼ cup unsalted butter or buttery spread, such as Earth Balance

1 teaspoon sugar

½ teaspoon salt

1 cup (4 ounces) grated Gruyère cheese, or cheese alternative, such as Vegan Gourmet

2 tablespoons grated Parmesan cheese, or soy alternative, such as Soyco

¼ teaspoon freshly ground black pepper (optional)

1 Place a rack in the middle of the oven. Preheat the oven to 400°F. Line a 15 × 10-inch baking sheet (not nonstick) with parchment paper.

2 In a small bowl, whisk together the rice flour, potato starch, and modified tapioca starch and have them ready by the stove. Have the eggs ready in another small bowl beside the stove as well.

3 In a medium heavy saucepan, bring the water, butter, sugar, and salt to a boil over medium-high heat. When the mixture starts to boil, add the flour mixture all at once and stir it with a wooden spoon until the dough pulls away from the sides of the pan and leaves a film on the bottom of the pan.

4 Remove the pan from the heat and let the dough cool at least 5 minutes, but no longer than 8 minutes. Using a hand mixer, add the eggs one at a time, beating until smooth after each addition. The dough will separate each time an egg is added, yet will form a paste again after beating with the mixer. Beat in the cheeses and pepper (if using) until smooth.

5 For larger gougères, drop 12 mounds, 2 tablespoons each, on the baking sheet, spacing them evenly. For mini-gougères, use 1 tablespoon for each. With wet fingers, shape the mounds into uniformly shaped balls, smooth any points that protrude, and then nudge the mounds into circles for even baking.

6 Bake larger gougères 35 to 40 minutes; 25 to 30 minutes for mini-gougères or until they turn a deep golden brown. For crisper gougères, remove the pan from the oven and cut a ½-inch slit in the side of each one. Bake another 5 minutes. Cool the pan 5 minutes on a wire rack. Serve immediately.

QUICK BREADS

Irish Soda Bread

MAKES 10 SERVINGS

Irish soda bread originated in the mid-1800s in Ireland when baking soda was first introduced. Back then, it was simply made from flour, buttermilk, baking soda, and salt. This gluten-free version is more complex but it is ideal for those who avoid yeast breads. Great for sandwiches, it can also be toasted for breakfast. For a unique twist, use a cast-iron skillet, which will give it a nice, crispy crust.

2 cups Carol's Sorghum Blend (page x)

3 tablespoons sugar

1 teaspoon baking soda

1 teaspoon baking powder

1½ teaspoons xanthan gum

1 teaspoon salt

1 large egg, at room temperature

1 cup buttermilk thinned with ¼ cup water, well-shaken, or homemade Buttermilk (page 677), at room temperature

¼ cup (½ stick) unsalted butter or buttery spread, such as Earth Balance, at room temperature

½ cup dried currants

1 tablespoon caraway seeds, toasted for fuller flavor

1 Place a rack in the middle of the oven. Preheat the oven to 375°F. Generously grease an 8 × 4-inch nonstick (gray, not black) loaf pan or a 10-inch cast-iron skillet.

2 In a large mixing bowl, whisk together the sorghum blend, sugar, baking soda, baking powder, xanthan gum, and salt. Add the egg, milk, butter, currants, and caraway seeds. With an electric mixer on low speed, mix all the ingredients just until thoroughly blended. Spread the batter evenly in the pan and smooth the top with a wet spatula. With a very sharp knife, cut a ⅛-inch deep "X" on the top to allow the bread to expand as it rises.

3 Bake 55 to 60 minutes or until the top is deeply browned and the loaf sounds hollow when tapped. The internal temperature should reach 205°F when an instant-read thermometer is inserted into center of loaf. Cool the bread in the pan 10 minutes on a wire rack. Remove the bread from the pan and cool completely on the wire rack. Slice with an electric or serrated knife.

Navy Bean Flour Beer Cheese Quick Bread

MAKES 12 SERVINGS

Bean flours have been around for some time, but navy bean flour—ground from navy beans, naturally—is relatively new and very appropriate for this beer-based bread. It supplies important protein and fiber to a gluten-free diet and its hearty flavor complements the beer. Now, with gluten-free beer available, there's no reason not to enjoy beer in food as well as with it.

1 cup Carol's Sorghum Blend (page x)

1 cup navy bean flour*

1 cup potato starch

2 tablespoons sugar

1 tablespoon baking powder

2 teaspoons xanthan gum

1 tablespoon finely diced fresh onion or 1 teaspoon dried minced onion

1 teaspoon Dijon mustard

1 teaspoon salt

1 bottle (12 ounces) or 1½ cups gluten-free beer, such as Bard's Tale or Redbridge, at room temperature

2 large eggs, at room temperature

½ cup grated Cheddar cheese, or cheese alternative, such as Vegan Gourmet, divided

¼ cup unsalted butter or buttery spread, such as Earth Balance, melted, or canola oil

Cooking spray

1 Generously grease a 9 × 5-inch nonstick (gray, not black) loaf pan.

2 In a large mixing bowl, whisk together the sorghum blend, navy bean flour, potato starch, sugar, baking powder, xanthan gum, onion, mustard, and salt. Open the beer over a deep bowl so you capture any overflow if it foams up. Add the beer, eggs, all but 2 tablespoons of the cheese, and the butter to the flour mixture and beat with an electric mixer on low speed just until the batter is blended and slightly thickened.

3 Pour the batter into the pan and smooth the top with a wet spatula. Lightly coat the top of the loaf with cooking spray and sprinkle the reserved 2 tablespoons of cheese on top. Lay a piece of wax paper over the pan and put in a warm place (75°F to 80°F) 15 to 20 minutes.

4 While the bread rests, place a rack in the middle of the oven. Preheat the oven to 375°F. Bake 60 minutes, or until the crust is very firm and a toothpick inserted into the center of the loaf comes out clean. Cover with foil after 15 minutes of baking to prevent overbrowning. Cool the bread in the pan 10 minutes on the wire rack. Remove the bread from the pan and cool completely on the wire rack. Slice with an electric or serrated knife.

Available at www.heartlandsfinest.com.

Boston Brown Bread

MAKES 12 SERVINGS

I bake this beloved bread in mini-loaf pans, rather than the coffee cans of the classic version. It's a little less sweet than some versions, but it is delicious served with cream cheese. Great as a simple tea bread, it also makes for an easy, portable breakfast. These mini-loaves travel very well; I often tuck them into the minibar in my hotel room.

LIQUID INGREDIENTS
1 large egg, at room temperature
1 cup buttermilk, well-shaken, or homemade Buttermilk (page 677)
¼ cup molasses (not blackstrap)
¼ cup canola oil
1 teaspoon pure vanilla extract

DRY INGREDIENTS
1½ cups Carol's Sorghum Blend (page x)
⅓ cup Expandex modified tapioca starch, or ⅓ cup Carol's Sorghum Blend (page x)
¼ cup gluten-free cornmeal, such as Albers, Lamb's, Kinnikinnick, or Shiloh Farms
¼ cup packed light brown sugar
1 teaspoon baking soda
1 teaspoon xanthan gum
½ teaspoon salt
½ teaspoon ground cinnamon
¼ teaspoon ground allspice
¼ teaspoon ground ginger
⅛ teaspoon ground cloves
½ cup dark raisins

1 Place a rack in the middle of the oven. Preheat the oven to 350°F. Generously grease 3 mini 5 × 3-inch nonstick (gray, not black) loaf pans.

2 In a medium bowl, beat the egg with an electric mixer on medium speed until light yellow and frothy, about 30 seconds. Add the buttermilk, molasses, oil, and vanilla, and beat on low speed until well blended.

3 In a small bowl, whisk together the dry ingredients except the raisins. With the mixer on low speed, gradually beat the dry ingredients into the liquid ingredients until the batter is smooth and slightly thickened. Stir in the raisins. Spread the batter evenly in the pans.

4 Bake 30 to 35 minutes or until the tops are browned and a toothpick inserted into the center of a loaf comes out clean. Cool the breads in the pans 10 minutes on a wire rack. Remove the breads from the pans and cool completely on the wire rack. Slice with an electric or serrated knife.

Old-Fashioned Molasses Quick Bread ⓥ

MAKES 12 SERVINGS

Serve this slightly sweet bread with savory soups or entrées, or spread it with apple butter or pumpkin butter for a quick breakfast.

½ cup 1% milk (cow's, rice, soy, potato, or nut)

1 tablespoon cider vinegar or fresh lemon juice

2 cups Carol's Sorghum Blend (page x)

½ cup gluten-free yellow cornmeal, such as Albers, Lamb's, Kinnikinnick, or Shiloh Farms

½ cup potato starch

1½ teaspoons xanthan gum

1 teaspoon salt

1 teaspoon baking soda

2 large eggs, at room temperature

½ cup molasses (not blackstrap)

¼ cup canola oil

1 teaspoon sesame seeds, for sprinkling on top (optional)

1 Place a rack in the middle of the oven. Preheat the oven to 325°F. Generously grease a 9 × 5-inch nonstick (gray, not black) pan; set aside. In a small measuring cup, whisk together the milk and vinegar and let stand 5 minutes.

2 In a large mixing bowl, whisk together the sorghum blend, cornmeal, potato starch, xanthan gum, salt, and baking soda. Using an electric mixer on low speed, beat in the milk, eggs, molasses, and oil until the batter is smooth. Transfer the batter to the prepared pan and smooth top with a wet spatula. Sprinkle with the sesame seeds.

3 Bake 45 to 60 minutes, or until a toothpick inserted into the center of the loaf comes out clean. Cool the bread in the pan 10 minutes on a wire rack. Remove the bread from the pan and cool completely on the wire rack. Slice with an electric or serrated knife. Serve warm.

Chestnut Flour Banana-Almond Mini Quick Breads ⓥ

MAKES 12 SERVINGS

Baking this quick bread in three mini-loaf pans (rather than one 8 × 4-inch pan) allows you to serve one loaf and freeze the other two for another day. The small slices are easy to handle, especially for kids.

LIQUID INGREDIENTS

2 large eggs, at room temperature

1 large very ripe banana, mashed

½ cup 1% milk (cow's, rice, soy, potato, or nut)

½ cup canola oil

1 teaspoon pure vanilla extract

DRY INGREDIENTS

⅔ cup chestnut flour*

⅔ cup potato starch

⅓ cup tapioca flour

¼ cup Expandex modified tapioca starch, or Carol's Sorghum Blend (page x)

¾ cup packed light brown sugar

1 tablespoon baking powder

1 teaspoon xanthan gum

1 teaspoon salt

1 teaspoon ground cinnamon

½ cup sliced almonds, divided

1 Place a rack in the middle of the oven. Preheat the oven to 375°F. Generously grease 3 mini 5 × 3-inch nonstick (gray, not black) loaf pans.

2 In a medium bowl, beat the eggs with an electric mixer on medium speed until light yellow and frothy, about 30 seconds. Add the banana, milk, oil, and vanilla and beat on low speed until well blended.

3 In a small bowl, whisk together the dry ingredients except the almonds. With the mixer on low speed, gradually beat the dry ingredients into the liquid ingredients until the batter is smooth and slightly thickened. Stir in all but 3 teaspoons of almonds. Divide the batter evenly in pans. Sprinkle 1 teaspoon of almonds on each loaf, lightly pressing them into the batter with your fingers.

4 Bake 35 to 45 minutes or until a toothpick inserted into the center of the loaves comes out clean. Cool the bread in the pans 10 minutes on a wire rack. Remove the bread from the pans and cool completely on the wire rack. Slice with an electric or serrated knife.

*Available at www.dowdandrogers.com.

Montina Flour Banana Mini Quick Breads Ⓥ

MAKES 12 SERVINGS

Montina has one of the highest protein and fiber contents of all the gluten-free flours, making this traditional banana bread very nutritious. Don't confuse the Montina Pure Supplement (pure Indian ricegrass) with Montina Flour Blend (a mixture of Indian ricegrass, rice flour, and tapioca flour). Substitute the same amount of Carol's Sorghum Blend (page x) instead of the Montina, if you prefer—the results will still be delicious.

LIQUID INGREDIENTS

2 large eggs, at room temperature
1 large very ripe banana, mashed
½ cup canola oil
¼ cup 1% milk (cow's, rice, soy, potato, or nut)
1 tablespoon molasses (not blackstrap)
1 teaspoon pure vanilla extract

DRY INGREDIENTS

1½ cups Carol's Sorghum Blend (page x)
¾ cup packed light brown sugar
¼ cup Montina Pure Supplement* or Carol's Sorghum Blend (page x)
¼ cup Expandex modified tapioca starch, or Carol's Sorghum Blend (page x)
1 tablespoon baking powder
1½ teaspoons xanthan gum
1 teaspoon ground cinnamon
1 teaspoon salt
½ cup dark raisins
¼ cup chopped pecans

TOPPING

3 tablespoons sugar

1 Place a rack in the middle of the oven. Preheat the oven to 375°F. Generously grease 3 mini 5 × 3-inch nonstick (gray, not black) loaf pans.

2 In a medium bowl, beat the eggs with an electric mixer on medium speed until light yellow and frothy, about 30 seconds. Add the banana, oil, milk, molasses, and vanilla and beat on low speed until well blended.

3 In a small bowl, whisk together the dry ingredients except the raisins and pecans. With the mixer on low speed, gradually beat the dry ingredients into the liquid ingredients until the batter is smooth and slightly thickened. Stir in the raisins and nuts. Divide the batter evenly in pans. Sprinkle 1 tablespoon of sugar evenly on each loaf.

4 Bake 40 to 45 minutes or until a toothpick inserted into the center of the loaves comes out clean. Cool the bread in the pans 10 minutes on a wire rack. Remove the bread from the pans and cool completely on the wire rack. Slice with an electric or serrated knife.

*Available at natural food stores and www.amazinggrains.com.

No-Egg Banana Bread

MAKES 12 SERVINGS

If your diet requires you to avoid gluten, dairy, and eggs, you can still enjoy banana bread with this recipe: just use a nondairy buttery spread or ⅓ cup of canola oil in place of the butter. Because it lacks eggs, this bread will be heavier and take longer to bake than regular banana bread, but it will still look and taste delicious.

LIQUID INGREDIENTS

½ cup soft silken tofu, such as Mori-Nu, drained

½ cup unsalted butter or buttery spread, such as Earth Balance, at room temperature

¾ cup packed light brown sugar

1½ cups mashed very ripe bananas

1 teaspoon pure vanilla extract

DRY INGREDIENTS

1½ cups Carol's Sorghum Blend (page x)

1 teaspoon xanthan gum

½ teaspoon salt

2 teaspoons baking powder

1 teaspoon ground cinnamon

½ cup chopped pecans

½ cup dark raisins

1 Place a rack in the middle of the oven. Preheat the oven to 350°F. Generously grease 3 mini 5 × 3-inch nonstick (gray, not black) loaf pans.

2 In a medium bowl, beat the tofu with an electric mixer on medium until it is smooth. Add the butter, sugar, banana, and vanilla and beat until the banana is no longer chunky.

3 In a separate bowl, whisk together the sorghum blend, xanthan gum, salt, baking powder, and cinnamon. With the mixer on low speed, gradually beat the dry ingredients into the liquid ingredients until they are well blended. Stir in the pecans and raisins. The batter will be somewhat grainy.

4 Bake 45 to 50 minutes, or until a toothpick inserted into the center of the loaf comes out clean. Cool the bread in the pan 10 minutes on a wire rack. Remove the bread from the pans and cool completely on the wire rack. Slice with an electric or serrated knife.

Cranberry-Orange Mini Quick Breads with Orange-Sugar Crust

MAKES 12 SERVINGS

These tasty little loaves make great gifts for the holidays. Simply let them cool completely, wrap them tightly in holiday-themed plastic wrap, and tie with a festive ribbon.

LIQUID INGREDIENTS

2 large eggs, at room temperature

¾ cup 1% milk (cow's, rice, soy, potato, or nut)

½ cup canola oil

1 tablespoon grated orange zest

1 teaspoon pure vanilla extract

DRY INGREDIENTS

2 cups Carol's Sorghum Blend (page x)

¼ cup Expandex modified tapioca starch, or ¼ cup Carol's Sorghum Blend (page x)

¾ cup sugar

1 tablespoon baking powder

1½ teaspoons xanthan gum

1 teaspoon salt

1 cup dried sweetened cranberries

CRUST

3 tablespoons sugar

1 teaspoon grated orange zest

1 Place a rack in the middle of the oven. Preheat the oven to 375°F. Generously grease 3 mini 5 × 3-inch nonstick (gray, not black) loaf pans.

2 In a medium bowl, beat the eggs with an electric mixer on medium speed until light yellow and frothy, about 30 seconds. Add the milk, oil, orange zest, and vanilla and beat on low speed until well blended.

3 In a small bowl, whisk together the dry ingredients except the cranberries. With the mixer on low speed, gradually beat the dry ingredients into the liquid ingredients until the batter is smooth and slightly thickened. Beat in the cranberries. Divide the batter equally in the pans.

4 Make the crust: In a small bowl, combine the sugar and orange zest and sprinkle 1 tablespoon on each loaf.

5 Bake approximately 35 to 45 minutes or until the loaves are golden brown and a toothpick inserted into the center of the loaves comes out clean. Cool the bread in the pans 10 minutes on a wire rack. Remove the bread from the pans and cool completely on the wire rack. Slice with an electric or serrated knife.

Amaranth Flour–Ginger Quick Bread with Ginger-Sugar Crust ⓥ

MAKES 12 SERVINGS

The high nutritional content of amaranth makes this bread special, but paired with aromatic spices it becomes irresistible. I like it with cream cheese, but it is delicious just plain or with a simple brush of butter.

LIQUID INGREDIENTS
2 large eggs, at room temperature
⅔ cup 1% milk (cow's, rice, soy, potato, or nut)
¼ cup canola oil
2 tablespoons molasses (not blackstrap)
1 teaspoon pure vanilla extract

DRY INGREDIENTS
1 cup packed dark brown sugar
⅔ cup amaranth flour
⅔ cup potato starch
½ cup tapioca flour
1 tablespoon baking powder
1½ teaspoons xanthan gum
1 teaspoon salt
1 teaspoon ground ginger
1 teaspoon ground cinnamon
½ teaspoon grated nutmeg
½ teaspoon ground allspice
⅛ teaspoon ground cloves
½ finely chopped crystallized ginger
¼ cup finely chopped walnuts

CRUST
2 tablespoons sugar
½ teaspoon ground ginger

1 Place a rack in the middle of the oven. Preheat the oven to 375°F. Generously grease an 8 × 4-inch nonstick (gray, not black) loaf pan.

2 In a medium bowl, beat the eggs with an electric mixer on medium speed until light yellow and frothy, about 30 seconds. Add the milk, oil, molasses, and vanilla and beat on low speed until well blended.

3 In a small bowl, whisk together the dry ingredients except the crystallized ginger and walnuts. With the mixer on low speed, gradually beat the dry ingredients into the liquid ingredients until the batter is smooth and slightly thickened. Gently stir in the crystallized ginger and walnuts. Spread the batter evenly in the pan.

4 Make the crust: In a small bowl, whisk together the sugar and ground ginger and sprinkle evenly on the batter.

5 Bake 40 to 45 minutes or until a toothpick inserted into the center of the loaf comes out clean. Cool the bread in the pan 10 minutes on a wire rack. Remove the bread from the pan and cool completely on the wire rack. Slice with an electric or serrated knife.

Piña Colada Quick Bread

MAKES 12 SERVINGS

If you love the combination of coconut and pineapple—as in the famous Piña Colada drink—you'll want to serve this delightful bread often. The sweet flavor makes this a wonderful tea bread or tasty afternoon snack.

LIQUID INGREDIENTS

1 large egg, at room temperature

½ cup 1% milk (cow's, rice, soy, potato, or nut)

¼ cup canola oil

1 teaspoon pure vanilla extract

1 teaspoon coconut extract

DRY INGREDIENTS

1½ cups Carol's Sorghum Blend (page x)

1 tablespoon baking powder

1½ teaspoons xanthan gum

¾ teaspoon salt

½ cup sugar

½ cup sweetened coconut flakes

½ cup finely chopped dried pineapple

1 Place a rack in the middle of the oven. Preheat the oven to 350°F. Generously grease an 8 × 4-inch nonstick (gray, not black) loaf pan.

2 In a medium bowl, beat the eggs with an electric mixer on medium speed until light yellow and frothy, about 30 seconds. Add the milk, oil, vanilla, and coconut extract and beat on low speed until well blended.

3 In a small bowl, whisk together the dry ingredients except the coconut and pineapple. With the mixer on low speed, gradually beat the dry ingredients into the liquid ingredients until the batter is smooth and slightly thickened. Stir in the

coconut and pineapple. Spread the batter evenly in the pan.

4 Bake 35 to 40 minutes or until the top is browned and a toothpick inserted into the center of the loaf comes out clean. Cool the bread in the pan 10 minutes on a wire rack. Remove the bread from the pan and cool completely on the wire rack. Slice with an electric or serrated knife.

Quinoa Flour Zucchini Mini Quick Breads

MAKES 12 SERVINGS

Quinoa is one of the most nutritious "super foods." If you can't find quinoa flour, buy quinoa grains or quinoa flakes and grind them into flour with your coffee grinder.

LIQUID INGREDIENTS

2 large eggs, at room temperature

½ cup canola oil

1 teaspoon pure vanilla extract

DRY INGREDIENTS

1 cup Carol's Sorghum Blend (page x)

¾ cup quinoa flour* or quinoa flakes*

¾ cup packed light brown sugar

¼ cup Expandex modified tapioca starch, or Carol's Sorghum Blend (page x)

1 tablespoon baking powder

1½ teaspoons ground cinnamon

1 teaspoon xanthan gum

1 teaspoon salt

2 cups finely grated zucchini (3 small or 2 medium zucchini)

¾ cup dark raisins

½ cup chopped pecans

TOPPING

Cooking spray

3 teaspoons sugar

1 Place a rack in the middle of the oven. Preheat the oven to 375°F. Generously grease 3 mini 5 × 3-inch nonstick (gray, not black) loaf pans.

2 In a medium bowl, beat the eggs with an electric mixer on medium speed until light yellow and frothy, about 30 seconds. Add the oil and vanilla and beat on low speed until well blended.

3 In a small bowl, whisk together the dry ingredients except the zucchini, raisins, and pecans. With the mixer on low speed, gradually beat the dry ingredients into the liquid ingredients until the batter is smooth and slightly thickened. Stir in the zucchini, raisins, and nuts. Spread the batter evenly in the pans. Lightly coat the loaf tops with cooking spray. Sprinkle 1 teaspoon sugar on each loaf.

4 Bake 40 to 45 minutes or until the tops are browned and a toothpick inserted into the center of a loaf comes out clean. Cool the bread in the pans 10 minutes on a wire rack. Remove the bread from the pans and cool completely on the wire rack. Slice with an electric or serrated knife.

*Quinoa grains or quinoa flour are available at natural food stores and www.bobsredmill.com. Quinoa flakes are available at natural food stores and www.ancientharvest.com.

SPOON BREADS

Corn Spoon Bread

MAKES 6 SERVINGS

Spoon bread is described as bread so soft that you can eat it with a spoon. Since it is often made with cornmeal, it tastes like extra soft cornbread. This version is very simple with no additional seasonings, so that the flavor of the corn shines through. Feel free to add your favorite herbs or seasoning blends if you want an even more flavorful dish.

2 cups gluten-free, low-sodium chicken broth, such as Swanson's Natural Goodness, or homemade Chicken Broth (page 676)

¾ cup gluten-free yellow cornmeal, such as Albers, Lamb's, Kinnikinnick, or Shiloh Farms

1 tablespoon sugar

1 teaspoon baking powder

1 teaspoon salt

¼ teaspoon white pepper

4 large eggs, separated and at room temperature

1 cup fresh corn kernels or frozen, thawed

1 Place a rack in the middle of the oven. Preheat the oven to 350°F. Generously grease a 2-quart glass or ceramic baking dish.

2 In a medium saucepan, heat the broth over medium heat. Gradually whisk in the cornmeal and stir until very thick, about 2 minutes. Remove from the heat and whisk in the sugar, baking powder, salt, and pepper. Combine the egg yolks and corn and blend well. Stir into the cornmeal mixture.

3 In a medium bowl, beat the egg whites to stiff peaks. Gently fold the beaten egg whites into the cornmeal mixture. Spread the batter in the dish.

4 Bake 40 minutes, or until spoon bread is just firm in center. Serve immediately.

Green Chile–Cheddar Spoon Bread Ⓥ

MAKES 6 SERVINGS

Spoon bread makes a great homey side dish for a hearty winter's meal. Serve it right out of the oven because like soufflés made with lots of beaten egg whites, it falls right away. The green chiles give this spoon bread a little kick.

1 cup gluten-free yellow cornmeal, such as Albers, Lamb's, Kinnikinnick, or Shiloh Farms

1½ teaspoons baking powder

1 teaspoon salt

1 teaspoon onion powder

1 teaspoon fresh oregano or ½ teaspoon dried

¼ teaspoon garlic powder

2 cups 1% milk (cow's, rice, soy, potato, or nut)

3 large eggs, at room temperature

2 tablespoons unsalted butter, or buttery spread, such as Earth Balance, at room temperature

1 cup (8 ounces) plain yogurt or soy yogurt

2 cups coarsely grated Cheddar cheese or cheese alternative, such as Vegan Gourmet (about 8 ounces), divided

1 can (4 ounces) diced green chiles

½ teaspoon paprika

1 Place a rack in the middle of the oven. Preheat oven to 375°F. Generously grease 1-quart (4-cup) baking dish or 10-inch cast-iron skillet.

2 In large bowl, whisk together cornmeal, baking powder, salt, onion powder, oregano, and garlic powder.

3 In a medium saucepan, heat milk over medium heat until bubbles form around edges. Whisk in cornmeal mixture and continue to whisk until blended. Remove from heat and cool 5 minutes.

4 In another bowl, whisk together the eggs, butter, yogurt, and 1¾ cups of the cheese. Whisk egg mixture into hot cornmeal mixture until thoroughly blended. Stir in the green chiles. Spread the batter in the pan and sprinkle the remaining cheese on top; dust with paprika.

5 Bake 40 minutes, or until the top is firm and browned and a knife inserted in the center comes out clean. Serve immediately.

Sour Cream–White Cheddar Spoon Bread Ⓥ

MAKES 6 SERVINGS

I like to bake this in a 9-inch square, porcelain-coated cast-iron baking dish because the thick metal base makes the crust brown and crispy. You can achieve a similar effect in a cast-iron skillet. Unlike the soufflé version of spoon bread, which falls immediately, this version holds its shape after baking because of its crispier crust.

1 cup gluten-free white cornmeal, such as Albers, Lamb's, Kinnikinnick, or Shiloh Farms

1½ teaspoons baking powder

1 teaspoon salt

1 teaspoon onion powder

¼ teaspoon garlic powder

2 cups 1% milk (cow's, rice, soy, potato, or nut)

3 large eggs, at room temperature

2 tablespoons unsalted butter or buttery spread, such as Earth Balance, at room temperature

1 container (8 ounces) sour cream or sour cream alternative, such as Tofutti

2 cups (8 ounces) coarsely grated white Cheddar cheese, or cheese alternative, such as Vegan Gourmet

½ teaspoon paprika

1 Place a rack in the middle of the oven. Preheat the oven to 375°F. Generously grease a 1-quart (4-cup) baking dish or 10-inch cast-iron skillet.

2 In a large bowl, whisk together the cornmeal, baking powder, salt, onion powder, and garlic powder.

3 In a medium saucepan, heat the milk over medium heat until bubbles form around edges. Whisk in the cornmeal mixture and continue to whisk until blended. Remove from the heat and cool 5 minutes.

4 In another bowl, whisk together the eggs, butter, sour cream, and cheese. Whisk egg mixture into hot cornmeal mixture until thoroughly blended. Spread in the pan and sprinkle with paprika.

5 Bake 40 minutes or until the spoon bread is firm and browned and a knife inserted in center comes out clean. Serve immediately.

CORNBREADS

Cornbread

MAKES 12 SERVINGS

Cornbread is easy to make, as this simple recipe shows. Southerners like their cornbread more savory, while Midwesterners like me prefer it sweeter. I compromised with this moderately sweet version, but you can always add more sugar if you wish. For a better crumb and longer shelf life, replace 2 tablespoons of Carol's Sorghum Blend with Expandex modified tapioca starch.

LIQUID INGREDIENTS

2 large eggs, at room temperature

¾ cup 1% milk, at room temperature

¼ cup canola oil

1 tablespoon apple cider or fresh lemon juice

DRY INGREDIENTS

1 cup gluten-free yellow cornmeal, such as Albers, Lamb's, Kinnikinnick, or Shiloh Farms

¾ cup Carol's Sorghum Blend (page x)

¼ to ⅓ cup sugar

2 teaspoons baking powder

1½ teaspoons xanthan gum

1 teaspoon salt

1 Place a rack in the middle of the oven. Preheat the oven to 350°F. Generously grease an 8-inch square nonstick (gray, not black) pan.

2 In a medium bowl, beat the eggs with an electric mixer on low speed until light yellow and frothy, about 30 seconds. Add the milk, oil, and cider and beat on low speed until well blended.

3 In a small bowl, whisk together the dry ingredients together. With the mixer on low speed, gradually beat the dry ingredients into the liquid ingredients until thoroughly blended. The batter will be the consistency of thick cake batter. Spread the batter evenly in the pan.

4 Bake 25 to 30 minutes or until the cornbread is firm and the edges are lightly browned. Cool the bread in the pan 10 minutes on a wire rack. Serve warm.

Cornbread in a Cast-Iron Skillet: Bake the batter in a preheated 350°F oven 25 to 30 minutes in a 10-inch cast-iron skillet, which makes a crisp crust. Preheating the skillet intensifies the crispiness of the crust, but if the pan starts to smoke, remove it from the oven until you're ready to fill it with batter.

Cornbread with Pancetta

MAKES 12 SERVINGS

Pancetta, an unsmoked Italian bacon, contributes a salty crunchiness that sets this cornbread apart from its traditional counterparts. The light olive oil (rather than canola oil) adds to the Italian flavor.

LIQUID INGREDIENTS

2 large eggs, at room temperature

1 cup 1% milk (cow's, rice, soy, potato, or nut)

⅓ cup light olive oil

1 tablespoon vinegar or fresh lemon juice

DRY INGREDIENTS

1¼ cups gluten-free yellow cornmeal, such as Albers, Lamb's, Kinnikinnick, or Shiloh Farms

1 cup Carol's Sorghum Blend (page x)

⅓ cup sugar

2 teaspoons baking powder

1½ teaspoons xanthan gum

1 teaspoon salt

½ cup chopped pancetta, fried until crisp and drained

1 Place a rack in the middle of the oven. Preheat the oven to 350°F. Generously grease an 8-inch round or square nonstick (gray, not black) pan.

2 In a medium bowl, beat the eggs and milk until light yellow and frothy, about 30 seconds. Add the oil and vinegar and beat on low speed until well blended.

3 In a small bowl, whisk together the dry ingredients except the pancetta. With the mixer on low speed, gradually beat the dry ingredients into the liquid ingredients until thoroughly blended. Stir in the chopped pancetta. The batter will be the consistency of thick cake batter. Spread the batter evenly in the pan.

4 Bake 25 to 30 minutes or until top is firm and the edges are lightly browned. Cool the bread in the pan 10 minutes on a wire rack. Serve warm.

Green Chile Cornbread with Cheddar Cheese Topping ⓥ

MAKES 12 SERVINGS

As a resident of the Southwest, I've been known to put green chiles in almost everything. For years, when I was in Santa Fe I would buy freshly roasted green chiles and freeze them right away for use throughout the year. Not everyone has access to fresh green chiles, so I use canned green chiles here, which are readily available in grocery stores.

LIQUID INGREDIENTS

2 large eggs, at room temperature

1 cup 1% milk (cow's, rice, soy, potato, or nut)

⅓ cup canola oil

DRY INGREDIENTS

1¼ cups gluten-free yellow cornmeal, such as Albers, Lamb's, Kinnikinnick, or Shiloh Farms

1 cup Carol's Sorghum Blend (page x)

⅓ cup sugar

2 teaspoons baking powder

1½ teaspoons xanthan gum

1 teaspoon salt

1 can (4 ounces) mild diced green chiles, drained

½ cup grated Cheddar cheese or cheese alternative, such as Vegan Gourmet

1 Place a rack in the middle of the oven. Preheat the oven to 350°F. Grease an 8-inch round or square nonstick (gray, not black) pan.

2 In a medium bowl, beat the eggs, milk, and oil with an electric mixer on low speed until light and fluffy, about 30 seconds.

3 In a small bowl, whisk together the dry ingredients except for chiles and cheese. With the mixer on low speed, gradually beat the dry ingredients into the liquid ingredients until thoroughly blended. Stir in the green chiles. The batter will be the consistency of thick cake batter. Spread the batter evenly in the pan.

4 Bake 20 minutes. Sprinkle the cheese on top of the cornbread and return to the oven to bake another 5 to 10 minutes or until the top is firm and the edges are lightly browned. Cool the bread in the pan 10 minutes on a wire rack. Serve warm.

Hush Puppies

MAKES 10 HUSH PUPPIES

Hush puppies are deep-fried cornmeal delights—part cornbread and part fritter. They are surprisingly simple to prepare and are best eaten right after they're made.

1½ cups gluten-free yellow cornmeal, such as Albers, Lamb's, Kinnikinnick, or Shiloh Farms
½ cup Carol's Sorghum Blend (page x)
2 teaspoons baking powder
1 tablespoon sugar
½ teaspoon salt
1 small onion, chopped fine
1 large egg, beaten
⅓ to ½ cup 1% milk (cow's, rice, soy, potato, or nut)
Peanut oil for frying

1 In a small bowl, whisk together the cornmeal, sorghum blend, baking powder, sugar, and salt until thoroughly blended.

2 Whisk in the onion and egg and enough of the milk to form a stiff batter.

3 In a deep pot, heat 3 inches of peanut oil to 365°F, or use an electric deep-fryer (following manufacturer's directions). For regular hush puppies, drop tablespoonfuls of the batter into the hot oil and fry until they're golden brown, about 3

to 4 minutes. For larger hush puppies, use heaping tablespoons of batter. You can vary the size of the hush puppies as you wish. Remove the hush puppies with a slotted spoon and drain on paper towels. Serve immediately.

Arepas

MAKES 8 AREPAS

Pronounced "ah-RAY-pah" in Spanish, these are dense little cakes of corn masa or cornmeal that are fried and slit in half to form a pocket for a cheese or meat filling. They are commonly served in the Southwest. You can eat the filled arepa at room temperature or heat it on a baking sheet in the oven until it is warm.

2 cups water
¾ teaspoon salt
3 tablespoons olive oil
1 cup instant masa harina
½ teaspoon baking powder
½ teaspoon onion powder
¼ teaspoon garlic powder
½ teaspoon xanthan gum
Filling of your choice (optional)

1 In a small saucepan, combine the water, salt, and oil and bring to a boil. Remove the pan from the heat and stir in the masa harina, baking powder, onion power, garlic powder, and xanthan gum with a wooden spoon until well blended. Cover and let stand 10 minutes.

2 Divide the dough into 8 equal portions. With wet hands, shape each portion into a smooth ball, then press each ball into a 3-inch patty, ½ inch thick. Coat the top of each patty with cooking spray.

3 Heat a 10-inch cast-iron skillet over medium heat. Place 4 arepas in the skillet, cooking spray side down, and flatten each slightly with a spatula. Cook until golden brown, about 5 minutes. Coat tops with cooking spray, then turn and cook until golden brown on the other side. Remove from heat and eat immediately or slit in half and add a filling to make a sandwich, if you like.

Hoe Cakes

MAKES 8 HOE CAKES

Hoe cakes are cornmeal flatbreads, fried in oil until browned and crispy. Some say they were originally cooked on a hoe over an open fire (hence the name). There are many variations, ranging from simple recipes using only white cornmeal, salt, water, and oil, to more modern versions like this one that use a little baking powder to lighten the texture. These cakes are quite versatile and can be eaten for breakfast with butter and syrup or as an accompaniment to lunch or dinner. If you can't find gluten-free white cornmeal, just use yellow cornmeal.

1 cup gluten-free white cornmeal, such as Albers
½ teaspoon salt
¼ teaspoon baking powder
1¼ cups boiling water
Bacon fat, butter or buttery spread, such as Earth Balance, or canola oil for frying

1 In a medium bowl, whisk together the cornmeal, salt, and baking powder. Pour in the boiling water in a slow stream, whisking constantly, until the mixture is smooth. Let stand a few minutes for the cornmeal to absorb the water.

2 In a large heavy skillet, heat 2 tablespoons of the bacon fat over medium-high heat. For each hoe cake, drop a tablespoon of the batter on the skillet and pat it into a flat circle, about 2 inches in diameter. (You may also make larger cakes using 2 tablespoons batter, flattened to a 4-inch circle.) Cook the hoe cakes about 2 to 3 minutes on each side or until golden brown, turning them with a wide spatula. Add more fat to the pan as needed for frying the remaining 7 cakes. Serve immediately.

FLATBREADS

Corn Tortillas

MAKES 12 (6-INCH) TORTILLAS

Most of us are so accustomed to eating commercially made corn tortillas that we are unaware of how delicious homemade ones can be. Believe me—there is no comparison. These tortillas are especially easy with a tortilla press, which can be purchased at kitchen stores, but you can also roll them with a regular rolling pin between sheets of wax paper. Some stores carry only plain corn flour while others may have traditional masa harina (corn flour treated with lime), but either works with this recipe.

2 cups corn flour or masa harina (not cornmeal)
1 to 1¼ cups warm (110°F) water

1 In a food processor, blend the corn flour and warm water until a soft ball forms. Remove the dough from the food processor. You should be able to knead the dough in your hands without it sticking to your hands or falling apart. If it isn't right, put the dough back in the food processor. If it is too sticky, blend in more flour, a tablespoon at a time; if it falls apart, add more warm water, a tablespoon at a time. Test the dough by kneading a tablespoon of it in your hands. Divide the dough into 12 equal pieces and shape into balls. Cover tightly to prevent drying out.

2 Cut 24 pieces of wax paper, each about 7 inches square. Put 1 square of wax paper on the bottom half of a tortilla press. Place a ball of dough slightly off-center—closer to the edge that is opposite the handle. Place another piece of wax paper on top of the dough.

3 Lower the top of the tortilla press and press down firmly on the lever. This makes a tortilla about 6 to 6½ inches in diameter. Remove the tortilla, keeping it between the two squares of wax paper, and place on a plate. Repeat with the remaining dough. If you prefer to roll the tortillas with a rolling pin, place the ball of dough between two pieces of wax paper, roll to a 6-inch diameter, and stack on a plate.

4 To fry, heat a griddle or cast-iron skillet over high heat until hot. Hold the tortilla in your left hand and peel off the top layer of wax paper with your right hand (starting with side nearest your left wrist) and pull the wax paper up toward the ceiling. Carefully invert the tortilla onto the griddle. Wait 3 seconds; peel off remaining wax paper. (Do not leave the wax paper on the tortilla for longer than 3 seconds because it will permanently cook into the tortilla.)

5 Cook the tortilla about 2 minutes on each side until it looks dry and has golden flecks on it. Transfer the cooked tortilla to a plate to cool between clean sheets of wax paper. Cook the remaining tortillas. These are best eaten right after they're cooked, but if you have leftovers, let them cool, and refrigerate them between layers of parchment paper in a resealable plastic bag. Reheat tortillas in the microwave on low 1 to 2 minutes.

Flour Tortillas

MAKES 12 (8-INCH) TORTILLAS

The success of these tortillas depends partly on the ingredients and partly on how the tortillas are handled once they're cooked. I recommend making 7- or 8-inch tortillas because they fit into a 10-inch cast-iron skillet and are easier to handle. The yield of this recipe is small, so if you want to make more than 12 tortillas I recommend you whip up a new batch; doubling measurements will upset the delicate balance between wet and dry ingredients.

½ cup Carol's Sorghum Blend (page x)
½ cup tapioca flour
¼ cup sweet rice flour
1 teaspoon sugar
1 teaspoon xanthan gum
½ teaspoon salt
2 tablespoons shortening, such as Crisco, Earth Balance, or Spectrum Vegetable
½ cup 1% milk (cow's, rice, soy, potato, or nut) or water
White rice flour for dusting
1 teaspoon canola oil

1 Wet a tea towel (not terry cloth and not paper towels) and fold it in half on the counter top. Place all the ingredients, except milk, white rice flour, and oil, in a food processor and process until blended. Pour the milk or water over the dry ingredients and process until the mixture forms a ball. The dough will be soft and sticky.

2 Immediately remove the dough from the food processor and knead it into a smooth ball with your hands. Shape the dough into 12 large, egg-size balls, using a spring-action metal ice cream scoop for uniformly-sized balls. Cover the balls tightly to avoid drying out until ready to roll.

3 Place a wet paper towel on a flat surface and top with a 12-inch piece of heavy-duty plastic wrap. Lightly dust the plastic wrap with rice flour, then place a ball of dough in the center. Lightly dust the ball with rice flour, then top with a sheet of wax paper. With a rolling pin, roll the dough as thin as possible to a 7- or 8-inch circle, rolling from the center to the outside of the circle in clockwise fashion to assure a circular, uniformly thick tortilla.

4 Preheat a cast-iron skillet over medium-high heat. Use a pastry brush to spread 1 teaspoon canola oil on the skillet. Remove wax paper from the top of the tortilla, then rest the tortilla on one hand to remove the plastic wrap. Carefully lay the tortilla on the hot skillet and cook until the underside is light brown and spotted, about 1 to 2 minutes. Flip the tortilla with tongs and cook the other side until it is light brown and spotted.

Don't overcook; the goal is to lightly brown tortillas rather than make them crisp.

5 Immediately place the cooked tortilla between the layers of the damp tea towel. Repeat the process with the remaining 11 tortillas, stacking the tortillas in the tea towel up to 30 minutes. The tortillas will soften as they lie in the damp tea towel. You can then fill them and roll into desired shapes. Alternatively, you can place the tortillas in a large, heavy-duty food storage bag and refrigerate. To warm, wrap the tortillas in a damp tea towel and microwave on low 1 to 2 minutes, until the tortillas are soft and supple.

Farinata with Sage and Onion

MAKES 4 SMALL SERVINGS

Farinata is a thin, crisp, pizzalike Italian pancake made from chickpea flour. The name varies depending on where it is made—it's called socca in parts of France. When I first tried this bread, it was so good I ate the whole batch myself. So be prepared to make extra batches for you or your family! Farinata can be made in a regular cast-iron skillet, but it won't be quite as crisp, and the skillet's high sides make the bread a little difficult to remove.

1 cup garbanzo and fava bean flour*
1 tablespoon finely diced fresh onion or 1 teaspoon dried minced onion
1 teaspoon salt
1 teaspoon freshly ground black pepper
1 tablespoon chopped fresh sage or fresh rosemary
1 cup lukewarm (100°F) water
5 tablespoons olive oil, divided

1 In a small bowl, whisk together the flour, onion, salt, pepper, and sage. Slowly whisk in the water until no lumps remain; stir in the 3 tablespoons of the olive oil. Cover and let stand at room temperature 1 hour.

2 Place a rack in the middle of the oven. Preheat the oven to 450°F. While the oven preheats, place a 10-inch cast-iron round griddle, with a ⅜-inch rim that holds about 1 cup batter into the oven. When the batter is ready, remove the griddle with an oven mitt on the handle to protect your hands. Pour the remaining 2 tablespoons of oil into the griddle, tilting it to evenly coat the bottom. Pour the batter into griddle, swirling to cover the pan evenly.

3 Bake 12 to 15 minutes or until the farinata is firm to the touch. Heat the broiler and place the griddle a few inches from broiler. Broil just long enough to brown the top. Cut into wedges and serve immediately.

*Available from www.authenticfoods.com or www. bobsredmill.com.

Savory Biscotti Sticks

MAKES 24 BISCOTTI

Part cracker, part bread—these savory biscotti sticks are a variation of traditional sweet biscotti. I serve these onion-flavored sticks with soups or salads, and I often take them along when I'm traveling so I will always have something crisp to eat with meals. The modified tapioca starch makes the biscotti nice and crispy.

2 cups Carol's Sorghum Blend (page x)
¼ cup Expandex modified tapioca starch
2 tablespoons sugar
1 tablespoon dried minced onion
1½ teaspoons xanthan gum
1 teaspoon baking powder
½ teaspoon salt
¼ cup unsalted butter or buttery spread, such as Earth Balance, at room temperature
¼ cup corn syrup
2 large eggs, at room temperature
3 tablespoons grated Parmesan cheese or soy alternative, such as Soyco (plus more for sprinkling, if desired)
2 tablespoons fresh snipped chives
2 tablespoons sunflower seeds
½ teaspoon butter-flavored salt, for sprinkling

1 Place a rack in the middle of the oven. Preheat the oven to 350°F. Line a 13 × 9-inch nonstick (gray, not black) baking sheet with parchment paper.

2 In a food processor, place the sorghum blend, tapioca starch, sugar, onion, xanthan gum, baking powder, and salt. Pulse a few times until ingredients are thoroughly blended.

3 Add the butter, corn syrup, eggs, and Parmesan cheese to the food processor and pulse on and off about 20 times to moisten the dough. Add chives and sunflower seeds and pulse just until they are incorporated.

4 With wet hands, form the dough into a ball, divide in half, and shape each half into a log 12 inches long, 2 inches wide, and ½ inch thick.

5 Bake 20 minutes, or until the dough browns at the edges. Remove the pan from the oven and cool 10 minutes. Reduce the heat to 300°F, but leave the oven on.

6 With a sharp serrated knife or an electric knife, cut each log on the diagonal into about ¾-inch-thick slices. Arrange the slices, cut side down, ½ inch apart on the baking sheet. Sprinkle with salt and return the sheet to the oven.

7 Bake another 15 to 20 minutes or until the biscotti are browned. Transfer the biscotti to a wire rack for cooling. Sprinkle with additional Parmesan cheese, if desired.

Oatcakes **Ⓥ**

MAKES 18 OATCAKES

Oatcakes originated when British military officers attempted to replicate the flatbreads they ate while stationed in India. Unable to find the same ingredients at home, they used oats instead, and this early attempt led to today's oatcakes. Some oatcake recipes start with quick-cooking oats, but pulverizing rolled oats in your food processor will also give you the right texture.

1 cup gluten-free rolled oats, such as Bob's Red Mill, Cream Hill Estates, Gluten-Free Oats, Gifts of Nature, or Only Oats†
1 cup Carol's Sorghum Blend (page x)
2 tablespoon Expandex modified tapioca starch
2 teaspoons sugar
1 teaspoon xanthan gum
½ teaspoon salt
¼ teaspoon baking soda
¼ cup unsalted butter or buttery spread, such as Earth Balance, melted
½ cup hot water

1 Place a rack in the middle of the oven. Preheat the oven to 325°F. Line a 15 × 10-inch nonstick (gray, not black) baking sheet with parchment paper.

2 In a food processor, process the oats, sorghum blend, modified tapioca starch, sugar, xanthan gum, salt, and baking soda until the ingredients are well blended and the oats are slightly pulverized. While the food processor is running, add the butter and hot water through the feed tube and process until the mixture is well blended and forms a ball on one side of the bowl.

3 Place a wet paper towel on a work surface and top with a 12-inch square piece of plastic wrap. Divide the dough into two portions and massage each into a ball with your hands. Place one ball on the plastic wrap, then place a sheet of plastic wrap on top of the dough. Roll it to a ¼-inch thickness with a rolling pin. Cut the dough into 9 oatcakes, using a sharp knife to cut 2½-inch squares or a 2½-inch biscuit cutter to cut circles. Place the oatcakes ¼ inch apart at one end of the baking sheet. Repeat with the remaining dough and place those 9 oatcakes at the other end of the baking sheet.

4 Bake 20 to 25 minutes or until the oatcakes are slightly browned and crisp. Transfer the parchment with the oatcakes still on it to a wire rack to cool completely.

†Check with your physician before using gluten-free oats.

Parmesan Shortbread

MAKES 8 SERVINGS

Shortbread is simply bread with no leavening that tastes somewhat like a thick cracker. This easy form of bread can be a nice crispy contrast to the smooth, creamy texture of soup. For best results, use the very finely ground Parmesan cheese that you buy in containers rather than grating the cheese yourself. The modified tapioca starch makes the shortbread nice and crisp.

½ cup (1 stick) unsalted butter or buttery spread, such as Earth Balance, at room temperature

2 tablespoons sugar

2 cups Carol's Sorghum Blend (page x)

¼ cup Expandex modified tapioca starch

½ teaspoon xanthan gum

½ teaspoon salt

½ cup 1% milk (cow's, rice, soy, potato, or nut)

⅓ cup store-bought grated Parmesan cheese, or soy alternative, such as Soyco

¼ teaspoon butter-flavored salt, for sprinkling

1 Place a rack in the middle of the oven. Preheat the oven to 350°F. Line a 13 × 9-inch nonstick (gray, not black) pan with parchment paper.

2 In a food processor, process the butter and sugar until well blended. Add the sorghum blend, modified tapioca starch, and xanthan gum. Pulse a few times to blend. Add the milk and cheese and process until the mixture forms a ball, stopping to scrape down sides of bowl if necessary. The dough will be somewhat stiff.

3 Place the dough in the center of parchment paper and roll or pat into an 8-inch circle, ½-inch thick. Flute the outer edges of the circle decoratively with your fingers and prick the center of the circle a few times with a fork. Cut the dough into 8 wedges and sprinkle with salt.

4 Bake 30 to 35 minutes or until the edges are golden brown. Cool the shortbread on the pan 10 minutes on a wire rack. Serve warm or at room temperature.

Savory White Cheddar Shortbread Squares

MAKES 8 SQUARES

The white Cheddar lends a wonderful light cheese flavor to this bread, which can be served with dinner or topped with your favorite filling and served as an appetizer.

½ cup (1 stick) unsalted butter or buttery spread, such as Earth Balance, at room temperature

2 tablespoons powdered sugar

2 cups Carol's Sorghum Blend (page x)

¼ cup Expandex modified tapioca starch

½ teaspoon xanthan gum

½ teaspoon salt

¼ cup 1% milk (cow's, rice, soy, potato, or nut)

½ cup grated white Cheddar cheese or cheese alternative, such as Vegan Gourmet

½ teaspoon butter-flavored salt, for sprinkling

1 Place a rack in the middle of the oven. Preheat the oven to 350°F. Line a 13 × 9-inch baking sheet (not nonstick) with parchment paper.

2 In a food processor, process the butter and sugar until well blended. Add the sorghum blend, modified tapioca starch, xanthan gum, and pulse a few times to blend. Add the milk and cheese and process until the mixture forms a ball, stopping to scrape down sides of bowl if necessary. The dough will be somewhat stiff. Remove the dough from the food processor and knead it into a smooth ball with your hands.

3 Place the dough in the center of the parchment paper and roll or pat dough into an 8-inch square, ½-inch thick. (Or, line an 8-inch pan with plastic wrap and press the dough evenly into it to get a perfectly square shape. Flip the dough onto the baking sheet and remove the plastic wrap.) Flute the outer edges of the circle with your fingers and prick the center of the circle a few times with a fork. With a sharp knife, cut the dough into 8 squares and sprinkle with salt.

4 Bake 30 to 35 minutes or until edges are golden brown. Cool the shortbread on the pan 10 minutes on a wire rack. Serve warm or at room temperature.

Fry Bread

MAKES 4 SERVINGS

Fry bread is a Native American flatbread fried in hot oil. My first taste of this simple yet satisfying bread was nearly thirty-five years ago on the Fort Berthold Indian reservation in North Dakota when I was on the staff of the Cooperative Extension Service. My hosts served it with berry jam—probably elderberry or lingonberry jam. As I recall, I ate my fair share—and then some—and loved every bite, much to the joy of my hosts. I've adapted this recipe to be gluten-free, but the end result is very similar to that first taste long ago.

1 cup Carol's Sorghum Blend (page x)
1 cup potato starch
1 tablespoon baking powder
1 teaspoon salt
½ teaspoon sugar
1 teaspoon xanthan gum
1 cup warm (110°F) 1% milk (cow's, rice, soy, potato, or nut)
1 teaspoon canola oil

1 In a mixing bowl, whisk together the sorghum blend, potato starch, baking powder, salt, sugar, and xanthan gum. Stir in the warm milk and oil to form a dough. Shape the dough into a ball with your hands and knead a few minutes until the dough is very smooth. Cover tightly with plastic wrap and let sit 15 minutes.

2 In a heavy-duty saucepan, heat the oil to 375°F at a depth of 4 inches on the stove or in an electric fryer (following manufacturer's directions). Break off a piece of the dough and roll into a ball about the size of a golf ball. Flatten to 3 inches in diameter and carefully ease the dough into the hot oil.

Fry on one side until browned, then turn with a slotted spatula and brown the other side. Transfer to paper towels and drain. Serve immediately with powdered sugar, jam or jelly, honey, or butter.

Chapatis

MAKES 12 CHAPATIS

Chapati is unleavened Indian flatbread that is usually grilled, then brushed with melted butter. It can be served with Indian dishes or with any main dish as an alternative to more traditional breads. To make this gluten-free version in your own kitchen an unusual, but a readily available array of tools is required—a spray bottle, rolling pin, plastic wrap, and pastry brush. Spraying the breads with water produces steam, which causes their characteristic puffing. Chapatis are best eaten right away, so prepare them just before dining. You can find ghee, or clarified butter, in the dairy section of some grocery stores or natural food stores. Substitute olive oil if ghee is unavailable.

½ cup Carol's Sorghum Blend (page x)
½ cup tapioca flour
¼ cup sweet rice flour
1 teaspoon sugar
1 teaspoon xanthan gum
1 teaspoon salt
½ cup + 1 tablespoon warm (110°F) water
White rice flour for dusting
Canola oil for frying
Spray bottle of tap water
¼ cup ghee or unsalted butter or buttery spread, such as Earth Balance, melted

1 In a food processor, process the sorghum blend, tapioca, sweet rice flour, sugar, xanthan gum, and salt until blended. Pour the water over the dry ingredients and process until the mixture forms a soft ball. The dough will be soft and sticky.

2 Immediately remove the dough from the food processor and shape it into a ball, kneading for a few seconds with your hands into a smooth ball. Shape the dough into 12 large-egg-size balls, using a spring-action metal ice cream scoop. Place the balls in a plastic resealable bag to prevent them from drying out until ready to roll.

3 Place a wet paper towel on a flat surface and top with a 12-inch piece of heavy-duty plastic wrap. Lightly dust the plastic wrap with white rice flour, then place a ball of dough in the center. Lightly dust the ball with rice flour, then top with a second sheet of plastic wrap. With a rolling pin, roll the dough as thin as possible to a 7-inch circle, rolling from the center to the outside in clockwise fashion to assure a circular, uniformly thick chapati.

4 Preheat a cast-iron skillet over medium-high heat. Use a paper towel to spread 1 teaspoon canola oil on the skillet. Remove the top plastic wrap from the chapati, then flip chapati onto one palm to remove the other piece of plastic wrap. Carefully lay chapati on hot skillet and cook until brown spots start to form on the bottom side, about 1 to 2 minutes. Spray the chapati with water and press the outside edges down with a spatula, causing it to puff in the middle. Flip the chapati with tongs and cook the other side until lightly browned, repeating the process of spraying and pressing with the spatula on the chapati's edges. Continue to flip, spray, and press chapati until both sides are browned.

5 Remove the chapati from the skillet and brush the entire chapati with melted ghee, which will soften it and make it ready to eat. Repeat with the remaining 11 balls of dough. These are best eaten immediately after cooking, while they are still warm and pliable.

Potato Lefse

MAKES 24 LEFSE

Lefse is a traditional soft Norwegian flatbread. I was first introduced to lefse several years ago when I lived in Minnesota and North Dakota. I never dreamed I would one day make it gluten-free, but here it is, in a surprisingly easy version. You can eat lefse in any number of ways: with butter and cinnamon-sugar, or smeared with peanut butter and jelly, or (blasphemy!) even wrapped around savory items such as hotdogs or luncheon meat, which your kids will love! The only limitation is your creativity. If you freeze them, reheat them in the microwave oven gently on low 1 to 2 minutes to restore their pliability.

2 large russet potatoes, peeled and quartered
1½ teaspoons salt + ½ teaspoon for boiling potatoes
¼ cup unsalted butter or buttery spread, such as Earth Balance, at room temperature
2 tablespoons 1% milk (cow's, rice, soy, potato, or nut) or half-and-half or evaporated milk
1½ teaspoons sugar
1 cup potato starch
¼ cup sweet rice flour
½ teaspoon xanthan gum
Additional white rice flour or sweet rice flour for dusting

1 In a large pot, boil the potatoes in salted water until tender. Drain thoroughly, then press the hot potatoes through a potato ricer into a large bowl. You should have approximately 4 cups of potatoes. With an electric mixer on low speed, beat in the butter, salt, and sugar until smooth. Sift the potato starch and sweet rice flour into the potato mixture and beat on low speed, until smooth.

2 Place a wet paper towel on the countertop and top with a 12-inch piece of heavy-duty plastic wrap. Shape the dough into walnut-size balls, using a metal spring-action ice cream scoop (3-tablespoon size). Place 4 balls about 3 inches apart on plastic wrap and top with another sheet of plastic wrap.

3 With a rolling pin, roll out balls to about ⅛ inch thick, taking care to make them as uniformly thick as possible. (They may be irregularly-shaped, but they should be the same thickness.) Wet a tea towel (not terry) with hot water and fold it in half, lengthwise, on the countertop.

4 Bake lefse on a hot (400°F) griddle or cast-iron skillet until bubbles start to form and the underside is browned. Flip and cook until the other side is lightly browned. If you have a pizza roller, you can roll the dough again while it is on the griddle. Transfer the lefse to one side of the damp tea towel and fold the other half of the towel over them to keep them soft and supple. If they stick together, separate them with parchment paper. Repeat with remaining dough. Serve immediately.

Ethiopian Flatbread

MAKES 10 FLATBREADS

Known as injera *in Ethiopia, this is a spongy, pancakelike bread made from teff flour. Rather than sourdough starter, which gives injera its characteristic tang and leavening, my easy version uses yogurt for the tang. Baking soda and club soda provide the leavening. Brown teff flour makes the flatbreads dark, while ivory teff flour makes them lighter in color. In Ethiopia,* injera *is typically torn into pieces and used to scoop up food, but you may eat it plain like bread with any meal, or spread it with butter or whatever you like. You can also wrap it around your favorite sandwich filling. Any way you eat it, it's best hot from the skillet.*

2 cups teff flour (ivory or brown), such as Bob's Red Mill or The Teff Company
1 cup Carol's Sorghum Blend (page x)
2 teaspoons baking soda
1 teaspoon salt
½ teaspoon xanthan gum
½ cup plain yogurt (cow's, rice, soy)
3 cups club soda
2 tablespoons unsalted butter or buttery spread, such as Earth Balance, for frying

1 In a blender, whirl the teff, sorghum blend, baking soda, salt, and xanthan gum a couple of times to combine. Add the yogurt and club soda and blend until the mixture is smooth.

2 Wet a tea towel (not terry cloth) with hot water, wring it out, and lay it on the countertop, folded in half. You will place each flatbread between the layers of towel to keep it soft and pliable until serving time.

3 Heat a large nonstick (gray, not black) skillet over medium heat. Lightly coat the skillet evenly with some of the butter. Pour ¼ cup of the batter into the skillet, starting in the center of the skillet and spiraling out as you pour. Cook 15 to 20 seconds or until bubbles appear all over the surface. Flip it over with a wide spatula, and cook, covered, for another 20 to 30 seconds. Place each flatbread between the layers of damp towel. Cook the remaining battes, placing each cooked bread between the layers of damp towel. Serve immediately.

Note: If you prefer to make injera with the traditional sourdough starter, use ½ recipe Sourdough Starter (page 101) and omit the baking soda.

Matzoh

MAKES 12 FLATBREADS

Matzoh (or matzah) is the very thin, unsalted, unleavened flatbread, typically eaten during the Jewish holidays. While commercial varieties are prepared under strict rules, my version is meant for the casual home cook and doesn't conform to any of these rules. Use them as you would crackers. You can also process the breads in your food processor to make matzoh meal.

3 cups Carol's Sorghum Blend (page x)
¼ teaspoon xanthan gum
1 cup warm (110°F) water, or more as needed

1 Place a rack in the middle of the oven. Preheat the oven to 450°F. Have two 15 × 10-inch baking sheets (not nonstick) ready.

2 In a food processor, process the sorghum blend and xanthan gum until blended. With the food processor running, add the water slowly through the food tube and continue to process until the mixture forms a ball. Add more water, a tablespoon at a time, if the mixture does not immediately form a ball. Divide the dough into 12 egg-size balls and keep balls covered until you roll them.

3 Place a 12-inch sheet of parchment paper on a flat surface, anchored by a wet paper towel. Place a ball of dough on the parchment paper and lay a 12-inch piece of heavy-duty (premium) plastic wrap on top.

4 With a rolling pin, roll the dough as thin as possible into an oval. Remove the plastic wrap and place the piece of parchment paper (with the dough on it) on the baking sheet. Repeat with the remaining dough, overlapping the parchment paper pieces to fit 3 matzohs on each baking sheet. Pierce each oval all over with a fork or pastry docker.

5 Bake until crisp and lightly browned around the edges, about 7 to 10 minutes. Cool on a wire rack before eating. Repeat with remaining 6 balls of dough.

YEAST BREADS

Loaf Yeast Breads

Cinnamon Raisin Yeast Bread

Portuguese Sweet Bread

White Sandwich Yeast Bread

Millet Yeast Bread

Italian Parmesan Herb Yeast Bread

Multi-Seed Yeast Bread

Dill-Onion Yeast Bread

Flax Yeast Bread

High-Fiber Bran Yeast Bread

Fennel Yeast Bread

Rosemary-Olive Yeast Bread

Cheddar Cheese–Olive Yeast Bread

Toasted Walnut Cheese Yeast Bread

Green Chile Cheese Bread

Honey Oatmeal Yeast Bread

Light Rye Beer Yeast Bread

Montina–Multi-Seed Yeast Bread

Russian Black Yeast Bread

Quinoa Pumpernickel Yeast Bread

Swedish Rye (Limpa) Yeast Bread

Breakthrough Ready-to-Bake Yeast Bread

French Bread–Style Yeast Breads

French Yeast Bread

Brioche French Yeast Bread

Sourdough Starter

Sourdough French Yeast Bread

Amaranth-Onion French Yeast Bread

Montina–Sunflower Seed French Yeast Bread

Pumpernickel French Yeast Bread

Focaccia, Bagels, Pita, and Other Yeast Breads

Focaccia with Herbs

Sun-Dried Tomato and Kalamata Olive Focaccia

Focaccia with Caramelized Onions, Goat Cheese, and Rosemary

Italian Chestnut Bread

Burger or Hot Dog Buns

Dinner Yeast Rolls

Bagels

Bread Bowls

English Muffins

Crumpets

Naan Bread

Pita Bread

Kolaches

Soft Pretzels

Breadsticks

Melba Toast

Croutons

Plain Bread Crumbs

Pizza

Homemade Pizza Crust

Pepperoni Cheese Pizza

Margarita Pizza

Mediterranean Pizza

White Pizza

Grape–Feta Cheese Pizza

Caramelized Onion, Tomato, and Rosemary Pizza

Barbecued Chicken Pizza

Corned Beef and Cabbage Pizza

Ham, Pineapple, and Green Pepper Pizza

Rosemary Potato Pizza with Basil Pesto

Pizza on Rice Crust

Calzones

Runzas

Holiday and Special Occasion Breads

Brioche

Challah

Greek Holiday Bread

Panettone

Stollen

Ask gluten-free folks which food they miss the most and they'll likely say "bread," particularly yeast breads. Most probably took bread for granted, popping it into the toaster for breakfast, making a sandwich for lunch, or cutting a big slice of French bread to round out dinner. However, if you are gluten-free, you must be very selective about your bread choices.

While you can buy gluten-free bread mixes or store-bought yeast breads in natural food stores or gluten-free bakeries, there's something special about taking a loaf of bread out of the oven that has been crafted with your own hands. Years ago, I baked cracked wheat bread by hand every weekend (long before bread machines became popular). My reward was a hearty loaf with a crunchy exterior. As soon as the loaf came out of the oven, I sliced off a huge chunk of the "heel," slathered it with butter, and devoured it. With a steaming mug of freshly brewed coffee, it was divine.

You can create your own fabulous yeast breads, ranging from basic White Sandwich Bread to crusty French Bread to breakfast favorites like chewy Bagels and English Muffins. Or, try breads that are unique and extraordinarily delightful such as Breadsticks, Naan, and Pita Bread, and holiday favorites such as Challah, Brioche, and Panettone.

You can't forget pizza, America's favorite food. With my easy, fail-proof crust you really can make fabulous pizza at home that's better than anything found in a box.

Here are a few tips to ensure successful bread baking—whether you use a bread machine or a conventional oven.

Preparing the Batter

1. Assemble the correct ingredients; no substitutions (nonfat dry milk powder, not Carnation; potato starch, not potato flour). Have all ingredients at room temperature. Check yeast expiration date; keep yeast refrigerated to make it last longer.

2. Measure flours by referring to Measuring Flours (page xii). Be sure you use the proper blend of flours to maximize each flour's unique culinary performance traits

3. Use the proper type and size of pan. Nonstick pans (gray, not black) conduct heat and brown the bread better than glass, ceramic, or shiny aluminum. Generously grease the pan (and dust with rice flour, if desired, for a slightly higher rise). Use an 8 × 4-inch loaf pan for 1-pound loaves or a 9 × 5-inch loaf pan for 1½-pound loaves. Small pans work better than large ones because they allow the oven's heat to reach the center of the loaf easily.

4. Dough should fall gracefully off beaters in "globs," rather than cling firmly or drip like water. It should look like "fluffy frosting" or stiff cake batter. If you have to pry the dough from the beater, it's too stiff and needs more liquid. If it runs off the beater in a thin stream, it's too wet and needs more flour.

5. Smooth dough in pan with a wet spatula for smoother crust and even rising. The dough will not smooth out as it bakes.

6. Dough should rise no higher than top of pan. "Oven-spring" or rising during baking will cause dough to get even higher.

Baking

7. Don't underbake—this is one of the chief causes of fallen bread. Allow the bread to form a firm crust, then lay a sheet of foil on it to prevent over-browning.

8. Small, narrow breads such as French bread, breadsticks, and bagels can start to bake in a *cold* oven. The recipe will tell you how. This method will not work with full-size loaves—or if your oven preheats with the broiler only. It works better in full-size ovens rather than small ovens.

9. A properly baked loaf registers an internal temperature of 205°F on an instant-read

thermometer inserted into the center of the loaf.

10. After baking, let bread cool in the pan for no longer than 10 minutes on a wire rack, or the bread will get soggy. Then remove bread from the pan and cool completely on the wire rack.

Slicing, Storing, and Reheating

11. Slice thoroughly cooled bread with a serrated or an electric knife. Store the sliced bread in a resealable plastic bag in the refrigerator or the freezer with pieces of parchment paper or wax paper between slices to make it easy to retrieve as many slices as you want without disturbing the others.

12. Most bread can benefit from a gentle reheat in the microwave—especially when it's frozen or a few days old. Use 30-second increments at 30 to 40 percent power until the bread reaches the desired state.

13. To refresh bread that has been frozen or refrigerated, lay a slice on a paper towel and place it in the microwave oven on low 15 to 20 seconds. It should be just warm to the touch, not hot or steaming. If too hot, it will harden very quickly. If it's not warm to the touch, heat it for 10 seconds more and check again. From then on, warm it in 5-second increments because it will warm up progressively quicker each time. For best results, eat it immediately. The thicker the bread, the longer it will take to soften it. Never warm bread or muffins in the microwave oven on high because they will toughen immediately.

Bread Machines

With the constant changes in appliances, it is hard to recommend a specific brand of bread machine. However, there are some general features you should consider, regardless of the brand you choose:

Bucket or Pan Size: I personally think smaller, 1-pound loaves turn out better than larger 2-pound loaves because the heat penetrates more quickly to the center of the loaf, making it more stable.

Cycles: Ideally, a bread machine has an option for one rise, usually called a short or rapid cycle. Most bread machines have two cycles. Do not use the overnight cycle if your recipe contains eggs.

Paddles: Generally, larger paddles are better. Be sure to use the right size recipe for your machine. Some cooks unknowingly use a 1½- to 2-pound recipe in a 1-pound bread machine. The dough overflows, causing a mess.

Shape: Some machines produce loaves that are cylindrical (round); others are square. Still others are loaf shaped. I've found all three acceptable.

TROUBLESHOOTING THE PROBLEM LOAF

Sometimes, things don't go as planned when we're baking bread. Here are some common problems and their recommended solutions.

PROBLEM	SOLUTION FOR THE NEXT TIME YOU BAKE
Cratered top	Too much liquid. Add more sorghum blend, 1 tablespoon at a time.
Mushroom top	Too much yeast. Reduce by ½ teaspoon.
Gnarly, rough top	Not enough liquid. Add liquid, 1 tablespoon at a time. Another tablespoon of sugar may help or using more cornstarch in the sorghum blend.
Unbaked inside	Adjust bread machine cycle to bake longer, or finish baking in a conventional oven, or bake loaves in several smaller pans.

LOAF YEAST BREADS

Cinnamon Raisin Yeast Bread Ⓥ

MAKES 12 SERVINGS (1½-POUND LOAF)

This bread makes fabulous toast or delicious bread pudding. I used currants here as they're smaller and don't weigh down the dough as much as raisins.

1 tablespoon active dry yeast

1 cup warm (110°F) 1% milk (cow's, rice, soy, potato, or nut)

¼ cup packed dark brown sugar

White rice flour for dusting

2 large eggs, at room temperature

1¾ cups potato starch

1 cup Carol's Sorghum Blend (page x)

2 teaspoons xanthan gum

1 teaspoon salt

¾ teaspoon ground cinnamon

⅓ cup canola oil

2 teaspoons cider vinegar

⅔ cup currants or dark raisins tossed with 1 teaspoon of potato starch

Hand Method

1 In a small bowl, combine yeast, warm milk, and 1 teaspoon of the brown sugar. Set aside to foam 5 minutes. Generously grease a 9 × 5-inch nonstick (gray, not black) loaf pan. Dust the bottom and sides of the pan lightly with white rice flour.

2 In the bowl of a heavy-duty stand mixer, beat eggs until light and frothy, about 30 seconds. Add potato starch, sorghum blend, xanthan gum, salt, cinnamon, yeast-milk mixture, oil, vinegar, and remaining brown sugar and beat on low speed until blended, scraping down sides of bowl if necessary. Increase speed to medium and beat 30 seconds, or until dough thickens slightly. Stir in currants. Dough will be somewhat softer than most yeast breads.

3 Transfer dough to prepared pan, smoothing top with a wet spatula. Cover dough lightly with foil and let rise in a warm place (75°F to 80°F) until dough is level with top of pan. (Rising time will vary from 45 minutes to 1 hour or more, depending on altitude, humidity, and temperature of ingredients.)

4 Place a rack in the middle of the oven. Preheat the oven to 375°F. With a sharp knife, make three diagonal slashes (⅛-inch deep) in loaf so steam can escape during baking.

5 Bake 1 hour to 1 hour 5 minutes or until temperature reaches 205°F on an instant-read thermometer inserted into center of loaf. Do not underbake. Cover with foil tent after 20 minutes of baking to reduce overbrowning. Remove from oven and cool bread in pan 10 minutes on a wire rack. Remove bread from pan and cool completely on the wire rack. Slice with an electric knife or a serrated knife.

Bread Machine

Follow bread machine instructions, making sure machine is appropriate size for recipe. With my machine, I whisk together the dry ingredients (including yeast) and add to the pan. Then, I whisk the liquid ingredients together (water at room temperature) and pour carefully over the dry ingredients. Set controls and bake (I use the Normal setting). Add the currants or raisins as directed by your machine directions.

Portuguese Sweet Bread

MAKES 10 SERVINGS (1 POUND LOAF)

Portuguese sweet bread is traditionally made with milk, yeast, and honey to give it a sweet flavor. It is sometimes called Hawaiian Sweet Bread, but is common in New England because of its large Portuguese population. Some people eat it with dinner, but others regard it as more of a dessert.

¼ cup sugar, divided

1 packet (2¼ teaspoons) active dry yeast

1 cup warm (110°F) 1% milk (cow's, rice, soy, potato, or nut)

White rice flour for dusting

1 cup Carol's Sorghum Blend (page x)

1 cup potato starch

¼ cup Expandex modified tapioca starch, or ¼ cup Carol's Sorghum Blend (page x)

2 teaspoons xanthan gum

1 teaspoon salt

Grated zest of 1 lemon

Grated zest of 1 orange

2 large eggs, at room temperature

2 tablespoons unsalted butter or buttery spread, such as Earth Balance, at room temperature, or canola oil

2 teaspoons cider vinegar

1 teaspoon pure vanilla extract

1 teaspoon orange extract

1 teaspoon lemon extract

1 In a small bowl, combine 2 teaspoons of the sugar, yeast, and milk. Set aside to foam 5 minutes.

2 Generously grease an 8 × 4-inch nonstick (gray, not black) pan. Dust the bottom and sides of the pan lightly with white rice flour.

3 In the bowl of a heavy-duty mixer, beat sorghum blend, potato starch, modified tapioca starch, xanthan gum, salt, lemon zest, and orange zest on low speed until blended. Add eggs, butter, vinegar, vanilla, orange and lemon extracts, yeast mixture, and remaining sugar. Beat on low until blended. Increase speed to medium and beat until mixture thickens slightly, about 30 seconds.

4 Transfer dough to prepared pan and smooth top with a wet spatula. Coat with cooking spray, if desired. Let rise in a warm place (75°F to 80°F) until dough is level with top of pan.

5 Place a rack in the middle of the oven. Preheat the oven to 375°F. With a sharp knife, make three slashes (⅛-inch deep) in loaf so steam can escape during baking.

6 Bake 55 minutes to 1 hour 5 minutes or until top of loaf is lightly browned. Cover with foil if loaf browns too quickly. Remove from oven and cool bread in pan 10 minutes on a wire rack. Remove bread from pan and cool completely on the wire rack. Slice with an electric knife or a serrated knife.

White Sandwich Yeast Bread Ⓥ

MAKES 12 SERVINGS (1½-POUND LOAF)

This is the perfect sandwich bread for families who prefer "white" bread. Keep on hand to make bread crumbs or croutons that are lighter in color.

1 packet (2¼ teaspoons) active dry yeast

2 tablespoons sugar

1 cup warm (110°F) water

White rice flour for dusting

3 large egg whites (or ½ cup), at room temperature

2 cups potato starch

1 cup Carol's Sorghum Blend (page x)

2 teaspoons xanthan gum

1 teaspoon guar gum

1 teaspoon salt

¼ cup unsalted butter or buttery spread, such as Earth Balance, at room temperature, or canola oil

2 teaspoons cider vinegar

1 teaspoon sesame seeds

1 In a small bowl, dissolve yeast and sugar in warm water. Set aside to foam 5 minutes.

2 Generously grease 9 × 5-inch nonstick (gray, not black) loaf pan. Dust the bottom and sides of the pan lightly with white rice flour.

3 In the large bowl of a heavy-duty mixer, beat egg whites until thick and foamy. Add sorghum blend, potato starch, xanthan gum, guar gum, salt, butter, vinegar, and yeast mixture. Beat on low speed to gently blend ingredients, then increase speed to medium and beat 30 seconds more or until mixture is thoroughly combined and slightly thickened.

4 Transfer dough to pan and smooth top with a wet spatula. Coat top with cooking spray and sprinkle with sesame seeds, pressing them gently into dough with fingers. Cover lightly with foil, and let rise in a warm place (75°F to 80°F) until dough is level with top of pan.

5 Place a rack in the middle of the oven. Preheat the oven to 375°F. With a sharp knife, make three diagonal slashes (⅛-inch deep) in loaf so steam can escape during baking. Bake 1 hour to 1 hour 5 minutes or until temperature reaches 205°F on an instant-read thermometer inserted into center of loaf. Remove from oven and cool in the pan 10 minutes on a wire rack. Remove bread from pan and cool completely on the wire rack. Slice with electric knife or serrated knife.

Millet Yeast Bread Ⓥ

MAKES 12 SERVINGS (1½-POUND LOAF)

Millet is one of the more nutritious grains for those following a gluten-free diet, and it's one of the least allergenic grains available. Since it is an alkaline grain, it's more easily digested. Always store it in the refrigerator or freezer to preserve freshness and maintain its mild, slightly nutty flavor. If you don't have millet flour, you can grind whole millet grain into flour with a clean coffee or spice grinder.

1 packet (2¼ teaspoons) active dry yeast
2 tablespoons sugar, divided
1 cup warm (110°F) milk (cow's, rice, soy, potato, or nut)
White rice flour for dusting
1 cup millet flour
1 cup Carol's Sorghum Blend (page x)
1 cup potato starch
1½ teaspoons xanthan gum
1 teaspoon guar gum
1 teaspoon salt
¼ cup unsalted butter or buttery spread, such as Earth Balance, at room temperature, or canola oil
2 large eggs, at room temperature
1 teaspoon cider vinegar
½ teaspoon poppy seeds
½ teaspoon sesame seeds

1 In a small bowl, dissolve yeast and 1 teaspoon of the sugar in warm milk. Set aside to foam 5 minutes.

2 Generously grease 9 × 5-inch nonstick (gray, not black) loaf pan. Dust the bottom and sides of the pan lightly with white rice flour.

3 In the bowl of a heavy-duty stand mixer, combine the remaining sugar, millet flour, sorghum blend, potato starch, xanthan gum, guar gum, salt, butter, eggs, vinegar, and yeast-milk mixture. Beat on low speed to blend. Beat on high speed 30 seconds, stirring down sides with spatula. Dough will be soft.

4 Transfer to prepared pan. Smooth top with a wet spatula. Coat top lightly with cooking spray. Sprinkle top with poppy seeds and sesame seeds. Let rise in a warm place (75°F to 80°F) until dough is level with top of pan.

5 Place a rack in the middle of the oven. Preheat the oven to 375°F. With a sharp knife, make three diagonal slashes (⅛-inch deep) in each loaf so steam can escape during baking.

6 Bake 1 hour or until temperature reaches 205°F on an instant-read thermometer inserted into center of loaf.

7 Cool bread in the pan 10 minutes on a wire rack. Remove bread from pans; cool completely on the wire rack before slicing with an electric knife or a serrated knife.

Italian Parmesan Herb Yeast Bread Ⓥ

MAKES 10 SERVINGS (1 POUND LOAF)

Serve this flavorful herb bread with minestrone, lentil, or French Onion Soup (page 161). It's great for sandwiches, especially for Panini (pages 183 to 184).

1 packet (2¼ teaspoons) active dry yeast

1 cup warm (110°F) 1% milk (cow's, rice, soy, potato, or nut)

White rice flour for dusting

2 cups Carol's Sorghum Blend (page x)

1 cup potato starch

1½ teaspoons xanthan gum

1 teaspoon guar gum

1½ teaspoons salt

2 teaspoons fresh dill weed or 1 teaspoon dried

2 teaspoons fresh thyme or 1 teaspoon dried

1 teaspoon chopped fresh rosemary or ½ teaspoon dried, crushed

¼ cup unsalted butter or buttery spread, such as Earth Balance, at room temperature, or canola oil

¼ cup honey

2 large eggs, at room temperature

2 teaspoons cider vinegar

1 teaspoon grated Parmesan cheese or soy alternative, such as Soyco, for sprinkling on top of dough after baking

1 In a small bowl, dissolve yeast in warm milk. Set aside to foam 5 minutes.

2 Generously grease a 9 × 5-inch nonstick (gray, not black) loaf pan. Dust the bottom and sides of the pan lightly with white rice flour.

3 In the bowl of a heavy-duty stand mixer, combine the sorghum blend, potato starch, xanthan gum, guar gum, salt, dill, thyme, rosemary, butter, honey, eggs, vinegar, and yeast-milk mixture. Beat on low speed to blend. Beat on high speed 30 seconds, stirring down sides with spatula. Dough will be soft.

4 Transfer to prepared pan. Smooth top with a wet spatula. Let rise in a warm place (75°F to 80°F) until dough is level with top of pan.

5 Place a rack in the middle of the oven. Preheat the oven to 375°F. With a sharp knife, make three diagonal slashes (⅛-inch deep) in loaf so steam can escape during baking.

6 Bake 1 hour or until temperature reaches 205°F on an instant-read thermometer inserted into center of loaf.

7 Remove from oven and spray crust lightly with cooking spray. Dust with Parmesan cheese. Cool bread in the pan 10 minutes on a wire rack. Remove bread from pan and cool completely on the wire rack. Slice with an electric knife or a serrated knife.

Multi-Seed Yeast Bread

MAKES 12 SERVINGS (1½-POUND LOAF)

Every now and then, I crave hearty robust bread with plenty of texture and fiber—something I can really sink my teeth into. This one fits the bill with four different seeds. It's especially good when you're serving a light meal and want a nutritional boost.

1 tablespoon active dry yeast

2 tablespoons sugar, divided

1 cup warm (110°F) 1% milk (cow's, rice, soy, potato, or nut)

White rice flour for dusting

2 large eggs, at room temperature (reserve 1 tablespoon for egg wash)

1 cup Carol's Sorghum Blend (page x)

2 cups potato starch

1 teaspoon xanthan gum

1 teaspoon guar gum

½ teaspoon onion powder

¾ teaspoon salt

¼ cup unsalted butter or buttery spread, such as Earth Balance, at room temperature, or canola oil

2 teaspoons cider vinegar

2 tablespoons raw, unsalted sunflower seeds

1 tablespoon + ½ teaspoon sesame seeds

1 tablespoon flax meal

1 tablespoon cream of buckwheat cereal, such as Bob's Red Mill

1 tablespoon finely chopped pumpkin seeds

1 In a small bowl, dissolve yeast and 1 teaspoon of the sugar in warm milk. Set aside to foam 5 minutes.

2 Generously grease a 9 × 5-inch nonstick (gray, not black) loaf pan. Dust the bottom and sides of the pan lightly with white rice flour.

3 In the large bowl of a heavy-duty mixer, beat eggs until thick and foamy. Add remaining sugar, and sorghum blend, potato starch, xanthan gum, guar gum, onion powder, salt, butter, vinegar, and yeast mixture. Beat on low speed to gently blend ingredients, then increase speed to medium and beat 30 seconds or until mixture is thoroughly combined and slightly thickened. Add the sunflower seeds, 1 tablespoon of the sesame seeds, flax seeds, cereal, and pumpkin seeds and beat just until blended in.

4 Transfer dough to pan and smooth top with a wet spatula. Whisk reserved 1 tablespoon of egg with 1 tablespoon of water and brush crust. Sprinkle with sesame seeds, pressing them gently into dough with fingers. Cover lightly with foil, and let rise in a warm place (75°F to 80°F) until dough is level with top of pan.

5 Place a rack in the middle of the oven. Preheat the oven to 375°F. With a sharp knife, make three diagonal slashes (⅛-inch deep) in loaf so steam can escape during baking. Bake 1 hour to 1 hour 5 minutes or until temperature reaches 205°F on an instant-read thermometer inserted into center of loaf. Remove from oven and cool bread in the pan 10 minutes on a wire rack. Remove bread from pan and cool completely on the wire rack. Slice with an electric knife or a serrated knife.

Dill-Onion Yeast Bread

MAKES 10 SERVINGS (1 POUND LOAF)

My mother made this bread all through my childhood and she learned to make it from her mother. They usually baked it in a round baking dish, but I prefer to use mini-loaf pans for prettier, more versatile slices. This bread is a flavorful accompaniment to a luncheon salad.

1 packet (2¼ teaspoons) active dry yeast
2 tablespoons sugar, divided
1 cup warm (110°F) water
White rice flour for dusting
2 large eggs, at room temperature
½ cup low-fat cottage cheese, at room temperature
¼ cup canola oil
2 teaspoons cider vinegar
2 cups Carol's Sorghum Blend (page x)
1 tablespoon instant Clear-Gel by King Arthur Flour, optional
2 teaspoons dried minced onions
2 teaspoons dill seed
1 teaspoon xanthan gum
1 teaspoon guar gum
¾ teaspoon salt

1 In a small bowl, combine yeast, 1 teaspoon of the sugar, and warm water. Set aside to foam 5 minutes.

2 Generously grease 2 mini 5 × 3-inch nonstick (gray, not black) loaf pans. Dust the bottom and sides of the pans lightly with white rice flour.

3 In the large bowl of a heavy-duty stand mixer, beat eggs until light and frothy, about 30 seconds. In a large mixing bowl, combine cottage cheese, remaining sugar, oil, and vinegar. Beat until well blended, about 30 seconds. Add yeast mixture and remaining ingredients. Beat on low speed until blended, scraping down sides of bowl if necessary. Increase speed to medium and beat 30 seconds, or until dough thickens slightly. Transfer dough to prepared pans and smooth tops with a wet spatula.

4 Cover dough lightly with foil and let rise in a warm place (75°F to 80°F) until dough is 1 inch above top of pan.

5 Place a rack in the middle of the oven. Preheat the oven to 375°F. With a sharp knife, make three diagonal slashes (⅛-inch deep) in each loaf so steam can escape during baking.

6 Bake 40 to 45 minutes or until temperature reaches 205°F on an instant-read thermometer inserted into center of loaf. Do not underbake. Cover with foil tent after 20 minutes of baking to reduce overbrowning. Remove from oven and cool bread in the pans 10 minutes on a wire rack. Remove bread from pans and cool completely on the wire rack. Slice with an electric knife or a serrated knife.

Bread Machine

Follow machine instructions, making sure machine is appropriate size for recipe. I combine dry ingredients, using 1½ teaspoons active dry yeast. Pour into bread machine. In a small bowl, combine liquid ingredients (water at room temperature) and pour over dry ingredients in bread machine. Set controls (I use Normal setting) and bake.

Flax Yeast Bread

MAKES 12 SERVINGS (1½-POUND LOAF)

Flax seeds have a distinctive, nutty flavor that is highlighted in this moist, dense bread. Flax meal is simply ground flax seeds, which you can make with your spice grinder. The oil in flax helps make this bread moist.

1 tablespoon active dry yeast

2 tablespoons sugar, divided

1 cup warm (110°F) 1% milk (cow's, rice, soy, potato, or nut)

White rice flour for dusting

2 large eggs, at room temperature

1 cup Carol's Sorghum Blend (page x)

2 cups potato starch

1 teaspoon xanthan gum

1 teaspoon guar gum

¾ teaspoon salt

¼ cup unsalted butter or buttery spread, such as Earth Balance, at room temperature, or canola oil

2 teaspoons cider vinegar

2 tablespoons ground flax meal

2 tablespoons flax seeds

1 large egg, beaten to foam for egg wash

½ teaspoon sesame seeds

1 In a small bowl, dissolve the yeast and 1 teaspoon of the sugar in warm milk. Set aside to foam 5 minutes.

2 Generously grease 9 × 5-inch nonstick (gray, not black) loaf pan. Dust the bottom and sides of the pan lightly with white rice flour.

3 In the large bowl of a heavy-duty mixer, beat eggs until thick and foamy. Add the remaining sugar, and the sorghum blend, potato starch, xanthan gum, guar gum, salt, butter, vinegar, and yeast-milk mixture. Beat on low speed to gently blend, then increase speed to medium and beat 30 seconds or until mixture is thoroughly combined and slightly thickened. Add flax meal and flax seeds and beat just until blended.

4 Transfer the dough to the pan and smooth the top with a wet spatula. Brush crust with beaten egg and sprinkle with sesame seeds, pressing them gently into dough with fingers. Cover lightly with foil, and let rise in a warm place (75°F to 80°F) until the dough is level with the top of the pan.

5 Place a rack in the middle of the oven. Preheat the oven to 375°F. With a sharp knife, make three diagonal slashes (⅛-inch deep) in loaf so steam can escape during baking.

6 Bake 1 hour to 1 hour 5 minutes or until temperature reaches 205°F on an instant-read thermometer inserted into center of loaf. Remove from oven and cool bread in the pan 10 minutes on a wire rack. Remove bread from pan and cool on the wire rack. Slice with an electric knife or a serrated knife.

High-Fiber Bran Yeast Bread

MAKES 12 SERVINGS (1½-POUND LOAF)

High fiber breads require more yeast and a somewhat longer rising time, but your reward is hearty, nutritious bread that makes pleasantly chewy toast for breakfast. Brushing the crust with egg white makes it crispier and slightly shiny.

1 tablespoon active dry yeast

2 tablespoons sugar, divided

1¾ cups warm (110°F) 1% milk (cow's, rice, soy, potato, or nut)

White rice flour for dusting

2 large eggs, at room temperature

1½ cups potato starch

½ cup Carol's Sorghum Blend (page x)

¼ cup rice bran, such as Ener-G

2 tablespoons Montina pure supplement

2 tablespoons almond meal or hemp seed, such as Manitoba Harvest

1 tablespoon apple pectin (available at natural food stores)

1 teaspoon xanthan gum

1 teaspoon guar gum

1 teaspoon salt

¼ cup canola oil

2 teaspoons cider vinegar

2 tablespoons sesame seeds, divided

1 egg white, beaten until foamy, for egg wash (optional)

1 In a small bowl, dissolve yeast and 1 teaspoon of the sugar in warm milk. Set aside to foam 5 minutes.

2 Generously grease a 9 × 5-inch nonstick (gray, not black) loaf pan. Dust the bottom and sides of the pan lightly with white rice flour.

3 In the large bowl of a heavy-duty mixer, beat eggs until light and frothy, about 30 seconds. Add potato starch, sorghum blend, rice bran, Montina, almond meal, apple pectin, xanthan gum, guar gum, salt, oil, vinegar, remaining sugar and yeast-milk mixture. Beat on low speed to blend, then increase speed to medium and beat 30 seconds or until mixture is thoroughly combined and slightly thickened. Stir in all but ½ teaspoon of the sesame seeds.

4 Transfer dough to pan and smooth top with a wet spatula. Brush top of crust with egg-white wash, if using. Sprinkle remaining ½ teaspoon of sesame seeds on top, gently pressing into dough

with fingers. Cover loosely with foil and let rise in a warm place (75°F to 80°F) until dough is 1 inch above top of pan.

5 Place a rack in the middle of the oven. Preheat the oven to 375°F. With a sharp knife, make three diagonal slashes (⅛-inch deep) in loaf so steam can escape during baking.

6 Bake 1 hour to 1 hour 5 minutes or until temperature reaches 205°F on an instant-read thermometer inserted into center of loaf. Remove from oven and cool in the pan 10 minutes on a wire rack. Remove bread from pan and cool completely on the wire rack. Slice with an electric knife or a serrated knife.

Fennel Yeast Bread

MAKES 12 SERVINGS (1½-POUND LOAF)

Fennel, the seed of the fennel plant, provides a pleasant licorice-like taste to this bread. I ate this unique and delicious bread many years ago at a relative's home and continued making it for several years until I became gluten-free. This gluten-free adaptation tastes just like the original.

1 packet (2¼ teaspoons) active dry yeast

1 cup warm (110°F) 1% milk (cow's, rice, soy, potato, or nut)

2 tablespoons packed dark brown sugar, divided

White rice flour for dusting

2 large eggs, at room temperature

2 cups Carol's Sorghum Blend (page x)

1 cup potato starch

1 teaspoon xanthan gum

1 teaspoon guar gum

1 teaspoon salt

¼ cup canola oil

1 tablespoon molasses (not blackstrap)

2 teaspoons cider vinegar

1 tablespoon fennel seed

1 large egg, beaten to foam for egg wash

1 In a small bowl, dissolve yeast and 1 teaspoon of the sugar in warm milk. Set aside to foam 5 minutes.

2 Generously grease 9 × 5-inch nonstick (gray, not black) loaf pan. Dust the bottom and sides of the pan lightly with white rice flour.

3 In the large bowl of a heavy-duty mixer, beat eggs until thick and foamy. Add sorghum blend, potato starch, xanthan gum, guar gum, salt, oil, molasses, vinegar, fennel, remaining sugar, and yeast-milk mixture. Beat on low to blend, then increase speed to medium and beat 30 seconds or until mixture is thoroughly combined and thickens slightly. Stir in fennel.

4 Transfer dough to pan and smooth top with a wet spatula. Brush crust with beaten egg. Cover loosely with foil, and let rise in a warm place (75°F to 80°F) until dough is level with top of pan.

5 Place a rack in the middle of the oven. Preheat the oven to 375°F. With a sharp knife, make three diagonal slashes (⅛-inch deep) in loaf so steam can escape during baking. Bake 1 hour to 1 hour 5 minutes or until temperature reaches 205°F on an instant-read thermometer inserted into center of loaf. Remove from oven and cool bread in the pan 10 minutes on a wire rack. Remove bread from pan and cool completely on the wire rack. Slice with an electric knife or a serrated knife.

Rosemary-Olive Yeast Bread Ⓥ

MAKES 10 SERVINGS (1 POUND LOAF)

I'm always curious about the rosemary-olive bread served in bread baskets in Italian restaurants. Everyone, including my husband, always raves about it. Here is a delectable gluten-free version.

1 packet (2¼ teaspoons) active dry yeast
1 cup warm (110°F) 1% milk (cow's, rice, soy, potato, or nut)
White rice flour for dusting
2 cups potato starch
1 cup Carol's Sorghum Blend (page x)
1½ teaspoons xanthan gum
1 teaspoon guar gum
1 teaspoon salt
½ to 1 teaspoon finely snipped fresh rosemary
½ teaspoon onion powder
¼ cup unsalted butter or buttery spread, such as Earth Balance, at room temperature, or canola oil
¼ cup honey, at room temperature
2 large eggs, at room temperature
2 teaspoons cider vinegar
⅓ cup thinly sliced black olives
Cooking spray
1 tablespoon grated Parmesan cheese or soy alternative, such as Soyco, for sprinkling on top of loaf

1 In a small bowl, dissolve yeast in warm milk. Set aside to foam 5 minutes.

2 Generously grease 9 × 5-inch nonstick (gray, not black) loaf pan. Dust the bottom and sides of the pan lightly with white rice flour.

3 In the bowl of a heavy-duty stand mixer, combine the potato starch, sorghum blend, xanthan gum, guar gum, salt, rosemary, onion powder, butter, honey, eggs, vinegar, and yeast-milk mixture. Beat on low speed to blend. Beat on medium speed 30 seconds, stirring down sides with spatula. Stir in olives. Dough will be soft.

4 Transfer to prepared pan. Smooth top with a wet spatula. Let rise in a warm place (75°F to 80°F) until dough is level with top of pan.

5 Place a rack in the middle of the oven. Preheat the oven to 375°F. With a sharp knife, make three diagonal slashes (⅛-inch deep) in loaf so steam can escape during baking.

6 Bake 1 hour or until temperature reaches 205°F on an instant-read thermometer inserted into center of loaf.

7 Remove from oven and spray crust lightly with cooking spray. Sprinkle with Parmesan cheese. Cool bread in the pan 10 minutes on a wire rack. Remove bread from pan and cool completely on the wire rack. Slice with an electric knife or a serrated knife.

Cheddar Cheese–Olive Yeast Bread Ⓥ

MAKES 12 SERVINGS (1½-POUND LOAF)

This bread is a wonderful choice when your entrée is fairly plain and you want something a little more flavorful for balance. The Cheddar cheese and slightly salty olives add lots of flavor.

1 tablespoon active dry yeast

2 tablespoons sugar, divided

1 cup warm (110°F) 2% milk (cow's, rice, soy, potato, or nut)

White rice flour for dusting

2 large eggs, at room temperature

¼ cup light olive oil

2 teaspoons cider vinegar

2 cups potato starch

1 cup Carol's Sorghum Blend (page x)

1 teaspoon xanthan gum

1 teaspoon guar gum

1 teaspoon salt

½ cup shredded sharp Cheddar cheese or cheese alternative, such as Vegan Gourmet

¼ cup chopped pitted black olives

1 large egg, beaten to foam for egg wash

1 In a small bowl, dissolve yeast and 1 teaspoon of the sugar in warm milk. Set aside to foam 5 minutes.

2 Generously grease 9 × 5-inch nonstick (gray, not black) loaf pan. Dust the bottom and sides of the pan lightly with white rice flour.

3 In the large bowl of a heavy-duty mixer, beat eggs until thick and foamy. Blend in oil and vinegar. Add remaining sugar, potato starch, sorghum blend, xanthan gum, guar gum, salt, and yeast-milk mixture. Beat on low to blend, then increase speed to medium and beat 30 seconds or until mixture is thoroughly combined. Stir in cheese and olives.

4 Transfer dough to pan. Smooth top with a wet spatula. Brush top of crust with egg wash. Cover pan loosely with foil and let rise in a warm place (75°F to 80°F) until dough is level with top of pan.

5 Place a rack in the middle of the oven. Preheat the oven to 375°F. With a sharp knife, make three diagonal slashes (⅛-inch deep) in loaf so steam can escape during baking. Bake 1 hour to 1 hour 5 minutes or until temperature reaches 205°F on an instant-read thermometer inserted into center of loaf. Remove from oven and cool bread in the pan 10 minutes on a wire rack. Remove bread from pan and cool completely on the wire rack. Slice with an electric knife or a serrated knife.

Toasted Walnut Cheese Yeast Bread Ⓥ

MAKES 12 SERVINGS (1½-POUND LOAF)

This bread works especially well baked in mini 5 × 3-inch loaves, yielding delicate little slices that taste great with a salad or a hearty winter soup. I happen to love rosemary, but you can reduce the amount, if you like. During summer when I have fresh rosemary in outdoor pots, I use a tablespoon of very finely chopped rosemary instead of the dried.

1 packet (2¼ teaspoons) active dry yeast

2 tablespoons sugar, divided

1 cup warm (110°F) water

White rice flour for dusting

2 large eggs, at room temperature

2 cups Carol's Sorghum Blend (page x)

1 cup potato starch

1 teaspoon xanthan gum

1 teaspoon guar gum

1 teaspoon salt

¼ cup light olive oil

2 teaspoons cider vinegar

4 teaspoons fresh chopped rosemary or 2 teaspoons
dried rosemary, crushed (or to taste)

1 cup finely chopped toasted walnuts

¼ cup grated Pecorino Romano cheese, or Parmesan
cheese, or soy alternative, such as Soyco

1 In a small bowl, dissolve yeast and 1 teaspoon of the sugar in warm water. Set aside to foam 5 minutes.

2 Generously grease 9 × 5-inch nonstick (gray, not black) loaf pan. Dust the bottom and sides of the pan lightly with white rice flour.

3 In the large bowl of a heavy-duty mixer, beat eggs until light and frothy, about 30 seconds. Add sorghum blend, potato starch, xanthan gum, guar gum, salt, oil, vinegar, rosemary, remaining sugar, and yeast-water mixture. Beat on low to blend, then increase speed to medium and beat 30 seconds or until mixture is thoroughly combined and thickens slightly. Gently stir in walnuts and cheese.

4 Transfer dough to pan, cover loosely with foil, and let rise in a warm place (75°F to 80°F) until dough is level with top of pan.

5 Place a rack in the middle of the oven. Preheat the oven to 375°F. With a sharp knife, make three diagonal slashes (⅛-inch deep) in loaf so steam can escape during baking. Bake 1 hour to 1 hour 5 minutes or until temperature reaches 205°F on an

instant-read thermometer inserted into center of loaf. Remove from oven and cool bread in the pan 10 minutes on a wire rack. Remove bread from pan and cool completely on the wire rack. Slice with an electric knife or a serrated knife.

Green Chile Cheese Bread

MAKES 12 SERVINGS (1½-POUND LOAF)

Many Southwestern restaurants serve variations of this bread. It's yet another indication that we will put green chiles in just about anything!

1 packet (2¼ teaspoons) active dry yeast

2 tablespoons sugar

1 cup warm (110°F) water

White rice flour for dusting

2 large eggs, at room temperature

2 cups Carol's Sorghum Blend (page x)

1 cup potato starch

1 teaspoon xanthan gum

1 teaspoon guar gum

1 teaspoon salt

¼ cup light olive oil

1 teaspoon cider vinegar

1 can (4 ounces) diced green chiles

1 cup shredded sharp Cheddar cheese or cheese
alternative, such as Vegan Gourmet

1 In a small bowl, dissolve yeast and 1 teaspoon of the sugar in warm water. Set aside to foam, 5 minutes.

2 Generously grease a 9 × 5-inch nonstick (gray, not black) loaf pan. Dust the bottom and sides of the pan lightly with white rice flour.

3 In the large bowl of a heavy-duty mixer, beat eggs until light and frothy, about 30 seconds. Add sorghum blend, potato starch, xanthan gum, guar gum, salt, olive oil, vinegar, remaining sugar, and yeast-water mixture. Beat on low to blend, then increase speed and beat on medium for 30 seconds or until mixture is thoroughly combined. Gently stir in green chiles and cheese.

4 Transfer dough to pan and let rise in a warm place (75°F to 80°F) until dough is level with top of pan.

5 Place a rack in the middle of the oven. Preheat the oven to 375°F. Make three diagonal slashes (⅛-inch deep) in loaf so steam can escape during baking. Bake 1 hour or until temperature reaches 205°F on an instant-read thermometer inserted into center of loaf. Remove from oven and cool bread in the pan 10 minutes on a wire rack. Remove bread from pan and cool completely on the wire rack. Slice with an electric knife or a serrated knife.

Honey Oatmeal Yeast Bread

MAKES 12 SERVINGS (1½-POUND LOAF)

My first taste of this bread was years ago—our hostess made fabulous sandwiches from it—as we cruised on a yacht in search of lighthouses along the beautiful Maine coast. Now that gluten-free rolled oats are available (and as long as your physician approves) you can enjoy it, too.

½ cup gluten-free rolled oats*†, divided
1 cup boiling water
1 cup warm (110°F) water
1 packet (2¼ teaspoons) active dry yeast
1 teaspoon sugar
White rice flour for dusting
2 large eggs, at room temperature
2 cups Carol's Sorghum Blend (page x)
1 cup potato starch
1 teaspoon xanthan gum
1 teaspoon guar gum
1 teaspoon salt
¼ cup honey
¼ cup canola oil
2 teaspoons cider vinegar

1 In a small bowl, stir all but 1 teaspoon of the oats into the boiling water and let sit while assembling remaining ingredients.

2 In another small bowl, dissolve yeast and sugar in warm water. Set aside to foam 5 minutes.

3 Generously grease a 9 × 5-inch nonstick (gray, not black) loaf pan. Dust the bottom and sides of the pan lightly with white rice flour. Set aside.

4 In the large bowl of a heavy-duty mixer, beat eggs until light and frothy. Add sorghum blend, potato starch, xanthan gum, guar gum, salt, honey, oil, vinegar, and yeast-water mixture, plus rolled oats-water mixture. Beat on low to gently blend ingredients, then increase speed to medium and beat 30 seconds or until mixture is thoroughly combined and thickens slightly.

5 Transfer dough to pan and smooth top with a wet spatula. Coat top with cooking spray and sprinkle remaining teaspoon of rolled oats on top, gently pressing oats into dough with your fingers. Cover loosely with foil, and let rise in a warm place (75°F to 80°F) until dough is level with top of pan.

6 Place a rack in the middle of the oven. Preheat the oven to 375°F. With a sharp knife, make three diagonal slashes (⅛-inch deep) in loaf so steam can escape during baking. Bake 1 hour 10 minutes to 1 hour 15 minutes or until temperature reaches 205°F on an instant-read thermometer inserted into center of loaf. Cover bread with foil after 25 minutes of baking to avoid overbrowning. Remove from oven and cool bread in the pan 10 minutes on a wire rack. Remove bread from pan and cool on the wire rack. Slice with an electric knife or a serrated knife.

Available in natural food stores and at www.bobsredmill. com, www.creamhillestates.com, www.giftsofnature.net, www.glutenfreeoats.com, and www.onlyoats.com.

†*Check with your physician before using gluten-free oats.*

Light Rye Beer Yeast Bread Ⓥ

MAKES 12 SERVINGS (1½ POUND LOAF)

Perfect for deli sandwiches, this light rye bread can be made with club soda rather than beer, if you wish, but the flavor will not be as fully developed.

1 tablespoon active dry yeast
¼ cup warm (110°F) 1% milk (cow's, rice, soy, potato, or nut)
White rice flour for dusting
¾ cup (half of 12-ounce bottle) gluten-free beer, such as Bard's Tale or Redbridge
2 large eggs, at room temperature (1 tablespoon reserved for egg wash)
2 tablespoons canola oil
2 tablespoons molasses (not blackstrap)
1½ tablespoons packed light brown sugar
1 teaspoon grated orange zest
2 cups Carol's Sorghum Blend (page x)
1 cup potato starch
2 tablespoons caraway seeds
1 teaspoon instant espresso powder or instant coffee powder
1 teaspoon salt
1 teaspoon xanthan gum
½ teaspoon onion powder

1 In the mixing bowl of a heavy-duty stand mixer, dissolve the yeast in the milk. Set aside to foam 5 minutes.

2 Generously grease a 9 × 5-inch nonstick (gray, not black) pan. Dust the bottom and sides of the pan lightly with white rice flour.

3 In the mixing bowl, add the beer, eggs, oil, molasses, brown sugar, and orange zest and beat on low speed until blended. In a separate bowl, whisk together the sorghum blend, potato starch, caraway seeds, espresso powder, salt, xanthan gum, and onion powder. With the mixer on low speed, gradually beat the dry ingredients into the wet ingredients until the dough is smooth.

4 Transfer dough to prepared pan and smooth top with a wet spatula. Let the dough rise in a warm place (75°F to 80°F) until dough is level with the top of the pan.

5 Place a rack in the middle of the oven. Preheat the oven to 375°F. Whisk reserved 1 tablespoon of egg with 1 tablespoon water until very smooth and brush it on top of the dough. With a sharp knife, make three diagonal slashes (⅛-inch deep) in loaf so steam can escape during baking. Bake 1 hour or until temperature reaches 205°F on an instant thermometer inserted into the center of the loaf. Cover with foil if bread browns too much.

6 Remove from oven and cool bread in the pan 10 minutes on a wire rack. Remove bread from pan and cool completely on the wire rack. Slice with an electric knife or a serrated knife.

Montina–Multi-Seed Yeast Bread Ⓥ

MAKES 12 SERVINGS (1½ POUND LOAF)

Montina is the commercial name for Indian rice-grass grown in the Northwest. It is a fairly new grain for the gluten-free diet and nutritious, packing a huge punch of protein and fiber. Since it is quite heavy, it works best when blended in small amounts with other flours; the dough also takes longer to rise due to this heaviness. Be sure to use the pure supplement in this recipe, not the blend of rice flour and Montina.

1 packet (2¼ teaspoons) active dry yeast

1 cup warm (110°F) 1% milk (cow's, rice, soy, potato, or nut)

White rice flour for dusting

2 large eggs, at room temperature

¼ cup honey

2 cups potato starch

1 cup Carol's Sorghum Blend (page x)

⅓ cup Montina pure supplement

2 teaspoons xanthan gum

¾ teaspoon salt

¼ cup canola oil

2 teaspoons cider vinegar

¼ cup raw, unsalted sunflower seeds

3 tablespoons sesame seeds, divided

1 egg white, beaten to a foam, for egg wash (optional)

1 In a small bowl, dissolve yeast in warm milk. Set aside to foam 5 minutes.

2 Generously grease a 9 × 5-inch nonstick (gray, not black) loaf pan. Dust the bottom and sides of the pan lightly with white rice flour.

3 In the large bowl of a heavy-duty mixer, beat eggs and honey until thick and foamy. Add potato starch, sorghum blend, Montina, xanthan gum, salt, oil, vinegar, and yeast-milk mixture. Beat on low to blend. Add sunflower seed and all but 1 teaspoon of the sesame seeds. Beat on low 30 for seconds.

4 Transfer dough to pan and smooth top with a wet spatula. Brush each loaf with egg wash for glossier crust. Sprinkle remaining teaspoon of sesame seeds on top of loaf and gently press into dough with fingers. Cover loosely with foil and let rise in a warm place (75°F to 80°F) until dough is 1 inch above top of pan.

5 Place a rack in the middle of the oven. Preheat the oven to 375°F. With a sharp knife, make three diagonal slashes (⅛ inch deep) in loaf so steam can escape during baking.

6 Bake 1 hour to 1 hour 5 minutes or until temperature reaches 205°F on an instant-read thermometer inserted into center of loaf. Remove pan from oven and cool bread in pan 10 minutes on a wire rack. Remove bread from pan and cool completely on the wire rack. Slice with an electric knife or a serrated knife.

Russian Black Yeast Bread

MAKES 12 SERVINGS (1½-POUND LOAF)

This hearty bread derives its dark color from the coffee powder and cocoa, but it is also flavored with caraway, fennel, and onion. It is especially good for deli sandwiches and Reuben Sandwiches (page 185).

1 packet (2¼ teaspoons) active dry yeast

2 tablespoons packed dark brown sugar, divided

1¼ cups warm (110°F) 1% milk (cow's, rice, soy, potato, or nut)

White rice flour for dusting

2 cups Carol's Sorghum Blend (page x)

1 cup cornstarch

1 tablespoon caraway seeds

½ teaspoon fennel seeds

1 teaspoon gluten-free instant espresso powder or instant coffee powder

1 teaspoon onion powder

1½ teaspoons xanthan gum

1 teaspoon guar gum

1 teaspoon salt

¼ cup unsweetened cocoa powder (not Dutch-process or alkali)

2 large eggs, at room temperature

¼ cup canola oil

1 teaspoon cider vinegar

¼ cup molasses (not blackstrap)

1 In a small bowl, dissolve yeast and 1 teaspoon brown sugar in the warm milk. Set aside to foam 5 minutes.

2 Generously grease 3 mini 5 × 3-inch nonstick (gray, not black) loaf pans or a 9 × 5-inch nonstick (gray, not black) loaf pan. Dust the bottom and sides of the pan(s) lightly with white rice flour.

3 In the large bowl of a heavy-duty mixer, combine yeast mixture with remaining ingredients, including remaining brown sugar. With mixer on low speed, blend. Then increase speed to high and beat 30 seconds or until the mixture thickens slightly.

4 Place dough in greased pan(s). Smooth top(s) with a wet spatula. Cover loosely with foil and let rise in a warm place (about 75°F to 80°F) until dough is level with top of pan.

5 Place a rack in the middle of the oven. Preheat the oven to 375°F. With a sharp knife, make three diagonal slashes (⅛-inch deep) in loaf so steam can escape during baking. Bake small loaves 45 to 50 minutes and large loaf 55 minutes to 1 hour or until internal temperature of bread registers 205°F on an instant-read thermometer inserted into center of loaf. Baking times can vary significantly; some loaves take less time, others more. Cover with foil if bread browns too much.

6 Remove from oven and cool bread in the pan 10 minutes on a wire rack. Remove bread from pan and cool completely on the wire rack. Slice with an electric knife or a serrated knife.

Bread Machine

Follow bread machine instructions. With my machine, I whisk together dry ingredients and add to bread machine. Then I combine liquid ingredients (water at room temperature). Pour carefully over dry ingredients in bread machine. Set controls (I use Normal setting) and bake.

Quinoa Pumpernickel Yeast Bread Ⓥ

MAKES 12 SERVINGS (1½-POUND LOAF)

Use this bread for hearty sandwiches. Quinoa is one of the most nutritious grains on earth, with its rich amounts of protein, iron, potassium, and other vitamins and minerals, making it a good source of dietary fiber. Its distinctive flavor gives a boost to the pumpernickel.

1 packet (2¼ teaspoons) active dry yeast

2 tablespoons sugar, divided

1 cup warm (110°F) 1% milk (cow's, rice, soy, potato, or nut)

White rice flour for dusting

2 large eggs, at room temperature

2 cups potato starch

¾ cup Carol's Sorghum Blend (page x)

¼ cup quinoa flakes, such as Ancient Harvest

2 tablespoons unsweetened cocoa powder (not Dutch-process or alkali)

1 teaspoon xanthan gum

1 teaspoon guar gum

1 teaspoon onion powder

1 teaspoon caraway seeds

1 teaspoon instant espresso powder or instant coffee powder

¾ teaspoon salt

¼ cup canola oil

1 tablespoon molasses (not blackstrap)

2 teaspoons cider vinegar

1 teaspoon grated orange zest (optional)

¼ cup sunflower seeds

2 tablespoons sesame seeds, divided

1 egg white, beaten, for egg wash (optional)

1 In a small bowl, dissolve yeast and 1 teaspoon of the sugar in warm milk. Set aside to foam 5 minutes.

2 Generously grease a 9 × 5-inch nonstick (gray, not black) loaf pan. Dust the bottom and sides of the pan(s) lightly with white rice flour.

3 In the large bowl of a heavy-duty mixer, beat eggs until light and frothy. Add potato starch, sorghum blend, quinoa flakes, cocoa powder, xanthan gum, guar gum, onion powder, caraway seeds, espresso powder, salt, oil, molasses, remaining sugar, vinegar, orange zest, if using, and yeast-milk mixture. Beat on low to blend, then increase speed to medium and beat 30 seconds or until mixture is thoroughly combined and thickens slightly. Stir in sunflower seeds and all but ½ teaspoon of the sesame seeds.

4 Transfer dough to pan and smooth top with a wet spatula. Brush with egg-white wash, if using. Sprinkle remaining ½ teaspoon of sesame seeds on top. Cover loosely with foil and let rise in a warm place (75°F to 80°F) until dough is 1 inch above top of pan.

5 Place a rack in the middle of the oven. Preheat the oven to 375°F. With a sharp knife, make three diagonal slashes (⅛-inch deep) in loaf so steam can escape during baking.

6 Bake 1 hour to 1 hour 5 minutes or until temperature reaches 205°F on an instant-read thermometer inserted into center of loaf. Cover with foil after 25 minutes of baking to prevent over-browning. Remove from oven and cool bread in the pan 10 minutes on a wire rack. Remove bread from pan and cool completely on a wire rack. Slice with an electric knife or a serrated knife.

Swedish Rye (Limpa) Yeast Bread Ⓥ

MAKES 12 SERVINGS (1½-POUND LOAF)

Known in Swedish as limpa, *this is a particularly moist form of rye bread, flavored with fennel or anise, cumin, and orange peel. It makes terrific deli sandwiches or Reuben sandwiches.*

1 packet (2¼ teaspoons) active dry yeast
1 tablespoon packed light brown sugar
1 cup warm (110°F) 1% milk (cow's, rice, soy, potato, or nut)
White rice flour for dusting
2 cups Carol's Sorghum Blend (page x)
1 cup potato starch
1½ teaspoons xanthan gum
1 teaspoon guar gum
1½ teaspoons salt
1 tablespoon caraway seeds
1 tablespoon anise seeds
1 teaspoon onion powder
1 teaspoon instant espresso powder or instant coffee powder
¼ cup molasses (not blackstrap)
¼ cup unsalted butter or buttery spread, such as Earth Balance, at room temperature, or canola oil
2 large eggs, at room temperature
2 teaspoons grated orange zest
1 teaspoon cider vinegar
1 teaspoon poppy seeds for sprinkling on top of dough before baking

1 In a small bowl, dissolve yeast and brown sugar in warm milk. Set aside to foam 5 minutes.

2 Generously grease a 9 × 5-inch nonstick (gray, not black) loaf pan. Dust the bottom and sides of the pan(s) lightly with white rice flour.

3 In the bowl of heavy-duty stand mixer, combine sorghum blend, potato starch, xanthan gum, guar gum, salt, caraway and anise seeds, onion powder, espresso, molasses, butter, eggs, orange zest, vinegar, and yeast-milk mixture. Beat on low speed to blend. Beat on high speed 30 seconds, stirring down sides with spatula. Dough will be soft.

4 Transfer dough to prepared pan. Smooth top with a wet spatula. Let rise in a warm place (75°F to 80°F) until dough is level with top of pan.

5 Place a rack in the middle of the oven. Preheat the oven to 375°F. With a sharp knife, make three diagonal slashes (⅛-inch deep) in each loaf so steam can escape during baking. Sprinkle with poppy seeds, pressing them gently into dough with fingers.

6 Bake 1 hour or until internal temperature reaches 205°F on an instant-read thermometer inserted into center of the loaf.

7 Remove from oven and cool bread in the pan 10 minutes on a wire rack. Remove bread from pans and cool completely on a wire rack before slicing with an electric knife or a serrated knife.

Breakthrough Ready-to-Bake Yeast Bread Ⓥ

MAKES FOUR 5 X 3-INCH MINI-LOAVES
(5 ONE-INCH SLICES EACH),
THREE 10-INCH FRENCH BAGUETTES
(7 ONE-INCH SLICES EACH), OR
TWO 10-INCH FRENCH BREAD LOAVES
(10 ONE-INCH SLICES EACH)

Even though we don't knead gluten-free breads, the "no-knead" bread craze credited to professional baker Jim Lahey and the extended fermentation period of this now famous process led me to my own innovation that produces gluten-free bread with a marvelous crumb. You mix the bread dough and refrigerate it, tightly covered, for up to 5 days. This is so helpful because you don't have to mix the dough each time you want to bake bread and you can bake as much (or as little) as needed within that 5 day refrigeration period. It reduces the number of steps required to have homemade bread with no loss in quality. When you're ready to bake, remove dough for as many loaves as you wish (return unused dough to the refrigerator). Shape the dough in a nonstick (gray, not black) pan, let it rise, then bake in a preheated oven.

1 tablespoon active dry yeast
1 cup milk, room temperature (cow's, rice, soy, potato, or nut)
2 tablespoons sugar
1 teaspoon flaxmeal stirred into ½ cup boiling water, then cooled to room temperature
2 cups potato starch
1 cup Carol's Sorghum Blend (page x)
1¼ teaspoons salt (1½ teaspoons if using canola oil)
1 teaspoon xanthan gum
1 teaspoon guar gum
¼ cup unsalted butter or buttery spread, such as Earth Balance, melted, or canola oil
1 tablespoon cider vinegar
1 teaspoon sesame seeds, for sprinkling

1 Dissolve yeast in milk. Set aside 5 minutes.

2 In bowl of heavy-duty stand mixer, beat all ingredients (except sesame seeds) on low speed just to blend ingredients. Increase speed to medium and beat 30 seconds, stirring down sides with spatula. Dough will be soft. Refrigerate, tightly covered, for up 5 days.

3 When ready to bake, generously grease up to four mini 5 × 3-inch pans or line a French bread pan or French baguette pan with parchment paper.

4 Using a #12 metal spring-action ice cream scoop or a well-greased one-third cup measuring cup, place dough in pan(s) and shape with wet spatula as follows:

2 level scoops bread dough per 5 × 3-inch loaf, top of loaf smoothed flat.

2 heaping scoops bread dough per French baguette loaf, shaped to 10-inch log(s).

4 level scoops bread dough per French bread loaf, shaped to 10-inch log(s).

Sprinkle with sesame seeds. Place dough in warm place (75° to 80°F) to rise until level with top of pan. With a sharp knife, make 3 diagonal slashes (⅛-inch deep) in loaf so steam can escape during baking.

5 Position a rack in the middle of the oven. Set the oven to 400°F. Bake 5 x 3-inch loaf 20 to 25 minutes, French baguette 25 to 30 minutes, or French bread 30 to 35 minutes, or until nicely browned. Cover loaves with aluminum foil after 15 minutes of baking to prevent overbrowning.

6 Remove bread from pans; cool 15 minutes on wire rack before slicing with an electric knife or a serrated knife. Serve slightly warm or at room temperature.

FRENCH BREAD–STYLE YEAST BREADS

French Yeast Bread

MAKES 20 SERVINGS

A crispy crust makes this loaf bread a delight to eat. It makes fantastic bruschette and crostini. Bake it in the 2-loaf French bread pan for regular French bread, or in the 3-loaf French baguette pan for baguettes (see below). Notice that the bread starts baking in a cold oven, an unusual but very effective method for this type of bread because it produces a crisper crust and airier texture.

2 tablespoons active dry yeast

2 tablespoons sugar, divided

1 cup + 2 tablespoons warm (110°F) water

3 large egg whites (or ½ cup), at room temperature

2 cups potato starch

1 cup Carol's Sorghum Blend (page x)

1 teaspoon xanthan gum

1 teaspoon guar gum

1 teaspoon salt

¼ cup unsalted butter or buttery spread, such as Earth Balance, at room temperature, or canola oil

2 teaspoons cider vinegar

1 tablespoon egg white whisked with 1 tablespoon water for egg wash

1 teaspoon sesame seeds

1 In a small bowl, dissolve yeast and 1 teaspoon sugar in warm water. Set aside to foam 5 minutes.

2 Grease French bread pan (one with two indentations) or line with parchment paper.

3 In the bowl of a heavy-duty stand mixer, combine egg whites, potato starch, sorghum blend, xanthan gum, guar gum, salt, butter, and vinegar plus the remaining sugar and yeast-water mixture. Beat on low speed to blend. Beat on medium speed 30 seconds, stirring down sides with spatula. Dough will be soft.

4 Divide dough in half on prepared pan. (A #12 metal spring-action ice cream scoop helps make loaves of the same size.) Shape each half into 10-inch log with a wet spatula, taking care to make each loaf the same length and equal thickness, with blunt rather than tapered ends. Brush with egg wash for glossier crust. With a sharp knife, make three diagonal slashes (⅛-inch deep) in each loaf so steam can escape during baking. Sprinkle with sesame seeds.

5 Place immediately on middle rack in a *cold* oven. Set the oven to 425°F and bake approximately 30 to 35 minutes, or until nicely browned. Cover loaves with foil after 15 minutes of baking to prevent overbrowning.

6 Remove bread from pans and cool completely on a wire rack before slicing with electric knife or serrated knife. Makes 2 loaves.

French Baguettes: Make the dough as directed above, shaping dough into 3 loaves. Use a French baguette pan with 3 rather than 2 indentations. Bake 25 to 30 minutes. Makes 3 loaves.

Brioche French Yeast Bread

MAKES 20 SERVINGS

Brioche is a bread from France typically made of flour, eggs, and yeast. By baking it in a French bread pan and starting it in a cold oven, we get bread that bakes quickly, yet has that wonderful brioche texture.

2 tablespoons active dry yeast

1 cup warm (110°F) 1% milk (cow's, rice, soy, potato, or nut)

2 cups Carol's Sorghum Blend (page x)

1 cup potato starch

2 tablespoons sugar

2 teaspoons xanthan gum

1 teaspoon guar gum

3 large eggs, at room temperature

1 teaspoon salt

¼ cup (½ stick) unsalted butter or buttery spread,
   such as Earth Balance, at room temperature
2 teaspoons fresh lemon juice or cider vinegar
1 large egg, beaten, for egg wash (optional)

1 In a small bowl, combine yeast and warm milk. Set aside to foam 5 minutes.

2 Generously grease a French bread pan (with two indentations) or line with parchment paper. Sift together sorghum blend, potato starch, sugar, xanthan gum, and guar gum. Set aside.

3 In the bowl of a heavy-duty stand mixer, beat eggs on high speed for 1 minute. Add salt, butter, lemon juice, and yeast-milk mixture. Beat on low speed to blend. Beat on high speed 30 seconds or until dough thickens slightly, stirring down sides with spatula. Dough will be soft and should fall in "graceful globs" from beaters.

4 Place half of dough in each indentation. Smooth each half into 10-inch log with a wet spatula, taking care to make each loaf an even width and height. Brush with egg wash, if using, for glossier crust. Make three diagonal slashes (⅛-inch deep) in each loaf so steam can escape during baking.

5 Place immediately on middle rack in a *cold* oven. Set the oven to 425°F and bake approximately 30 to 35 minutes, or until nicely browned and temperature of bread reads 205°F on an instant-read thermometer inserted into center of loaf.

6 Remove bread from pans and cool completely on a wire rack. Slice with an electric knife or serrated knife.

Sourdough Starter

MAKES 3 CUPS

I have always wanted to make a sourdough starter, so I turned to my antique 1940s cookbook, which instructed me to use potato water rather than plain tap water. I use white rice flour in place of the traditional wheat flour because its neutral

flavor and white color won't interfere with the flavor or color of my baked goods. Although my nostalgic cookbook doesn't mention it, today we know that it is better to use filtered or bottled spring water because the chlorine in regular tap water interferes with yeast fermentation and leaves a chlorinated aftertaste.

1½ cups warm (110°F) potato water (leftover water
   from boiling potatoes)
1 packet (2¼ teaspoons) active dry yeast
1 teaspoon sugar
1½ cups white rice flour

1 In a 2-quart glass bowl or crock, whisk potato water, yeast, and sugar and stir until combined. Whisk in flour until mixture is smooth and about the consistency of pancake batter. Cover loosely with plastic wrap and let sit for 1 to 3 days on your countertop to ferment. It will bubble up at first and you'll need to stir it down then.

2 Once the starter is fermented, store it tightly covered in a glass jar or bowl in the refrigerator. Bring it to room temperature right before you are ready to bake and stir it before using. To replenish the starter after you make 1 loaf of bread, whisk in 1 cup lukewarm filtered or bottled water and 1 cup white rice flour until smooth. If you make 2 loaves of bread, replenish the starter with 2 cups water and 2 cups flour. Store tightly covered in refrigerator.

Sourdough French Yeast Bread (V)

MAKES 20 SERVINGS

This is undoubtedly one of my favorite bread recipes of all time. It bakes up so beautifully using the cold oven start method described in this recipe, and I just love the sourdough tang. I especially like to time things so that the bread comes out of the oven right after my dinner guests arrive so that they smell the delicious aroma and see those lovely loaves.

2 tablespoons sugar

1 tablespoon active dry yeast

1 cup warm (110°F) water

3 large egg whites (or ½ cup), at room temperature
    (reserve 2 teaspoons for egg wash)

2 cups potato starch

1 cup Carol's Sorghum Blend (page x)

1 teaspoon xanthan gum

1 teaspoon guar gum

1¼ teaspoons salt

¼ cup unsalted butter or buttery spread,
    such as Earth Balance, at room temperature,
    or canola oil

½ cup Sourdough Starter (page 101)

2 teaspoons cider vinegar

1 teaspoon sesame seeds

1 In a small bowl, dissolve sugar and yeast in warm water. Set aside to foam 5 minutes.

2 Grease a French bread pan that has indentations for two loaves or line with parchment paper (especially important if the pans are perforated).

3 In the large bowl of a heavy-duty mixer, beat egg whites on medium speed until thick and foamy. Add potato starch, sorghum blend, xanthan gum, guar gum, salt, butter, sourdough starter, vinegar, and yeast-water mixture. Beat on low speed until ingredients are blended, then increase the speed to medium and beat 30 seconds or until the mixture is slightly thickened.

4 Divide dough between two indentations in prepared pan. (I use 4 scoops of a 2-inch metal spring-action ice cream scoop for each loaf to assure that both loaves are the same size and bake evenly.) Smooth each half into an 11-inch loaf with a wet spatula. Whisk the remaining 2 teaspoons of the egg white with 1 tablespoon water to make egg wash. Brush each loaf with egg wash for glossier crust. With a sharp knife, make three diagonal slashes (⅛-inch deep) in each loaf so steam can escape during baking. Sprinkle sesame seeds on top of loaves.

5 Place immediately on middle rack in a *cold* oven. Set the oven to 425°F and bake approximately 35 to 40 minutes, or until nicely browned and temperature of bread reads 205°F on an instant-read thermometer inserted into center of loaf.

6 Remove bread from pans and cool completely on wire rack. Slice with an electric knife or a serrated knife.

Amaranth-Onion French Yeast Bread

MAKES 20 SERVINGS

Amaranth has a tendency to brown more quickly than other flours, so be sure to cover your bread with aluminum foil during the last 15 minutes of baking.

¼ cup packed light brown sugar

2 tablespoons active dry yeast

1 cup warm (110°F) 1% milk (cow's, rice, soy, potato,
    or nut)

1½ cups Carol's Sorghum Blend (page x)

1 cup cornstarch

½ cup amaranth flour, such as Bob's Red Mill or
    NuWorld Amaranth

2 tablespoons dried minced onion

1 teaspoon onion powder

1 teaspoon xanthan gum

1 teaspoon guar gum

1½ teaspoons salt

¼ cup canola oil

2 large eggs, at room temperature

1 teaspoon cider vinegar

1 large egg, beaten, for egg wash (optional)

1 In a small bowl, dissolve brown sugar and yeast in warm milk. Set aside to foam 5 minutes.

2 Generously grease French bread pans or line with parchment paper.

3 In the bowl of a heavy-duty stand mixer, combine sorghum blend, cornstarch, amaranth flour, onion, onion powder, xanthan gum, guar gum, salt, oil, eggs, vinegar, and yeast-milk mixture. Beat on low speed to blend. Beat on medium speed for 30 seconds, stirring down sides with spatula. Dough will be soft.

4 Divide dough between two indentations in prepared pan. Smooth each half into 10-inch log with a wet spatula. Brush with egg wash, if using, for glossier crust. With a sharp knife, make three diagonal slashes (⅛-inch deep) in each loaf so steam can escape during baking.

5 Place immediately on middle rack in a *cold* oven. Set the oven to 425°F and bake approximately 30 to 35 minutes, or until nicely browned and temperature of bread reads 205°F on an instant-read thermometer inserted into center of loaf.

6 Remove bread from pans and cool completely on wire rack before slicing with an electric knife or a serrated knife.

Montina–Sunflower Seed French Yeast Bread Ⓥ

MAKES 20 SERVINGS

Montina, or Indian ricegrass, brings lots of fiber and protein to this hearty bread, and the sunflower seeds lend a mouth-pleasing crunch.

2 tablespoons active dry yeast
¼ cup packed light brown sugar
1 cup warm (110°F) 1% milk (cow's, rice, soy, potato, or nut)
1¼ cups Carol's Sorghum Blend (page x)
1 cup cornstarch
½ cup Montina pure supplement
¼ cup sunflower seeds
1 teaspoon xanthan gum
1 teaspoon guar gum
1½ teaspoons salt
½ cup canola oil
2 large eggs, at room temperature
1 teaspoon cider vinegar
1 egg white, beaten to a foam, for egg wash (optional)

1 In a small bowl, dissolve yeast and 1 teaspoon of the brown sugar in warm milk. Set aside to foam 5 minutes.

2 Grease French bread pans or line with parchment paper (especially important if you use perforated pans).

3 In the bowl of a heavy-duty stand mixer, combine sorghum blend, cornstarch, Montina, sunflower seeds, xanthan gum, guar gum, salt, oil, eggs, vinegar, remaining sugar, and yeast-milk mixture. Beat on low speed to blend. Beat on medium speed for 30 seconds, stirring down sides with spatula. Dough will be soft.

4 Divide dough between indentations in prepared pan. Smooth each half into 10-inch log with a wet spatula. Brush with egg wash, if using, for glossier crust. With a sharp knife, make three diagonal slashes (⅛-inch deep) in loaf so steam can escape during baking.

5 Place immediately on middle rack in a *cold* oven. Set the oven to 425°F and bake approximately 30 to 35 minutes, or until nicely browned or temperature reaches 205°F on an instant-read thermometer inserted into center of loaf.

6 Remove bread from pans and cool completely on a wire rack before slicing with an electric knife or a serrated knife.

Pumpernickel French Yeast Bread Ⓥ

MAKES 20 SERVINGS

This French bread style of long, thin loaves makes little slices, but they're convenient and easy to use, especially for sandwiches or appetizers.

2 tablespoons active dry yeast

3 tablespoons packed light brown sugar

1 cup warm (110°F) 1% milk (cow's, rice, soy, potato, or nut)

2 cups Carol's Sorghum Blend (page x)

1 cup corn starch

2 tablespoons unsweetened cocoa powder, such as Hershey's Special Dark

2 tablespoons caraway seed

1 teaspoon onion powder

1 teaspoon xanthan gum

1 teaspoon guar gum

1½ teaspoons salt

¼ cup canola oil

1 tablespoon molasses (not blackstrap)

2 large eggs, at room temperature

1 teaspoon grated orange zest

1 teaspoon cider vinegar

1 egg white, beaten, for egg wash (optional)

1 In a small bowl, dissolve yeast and 1 teaspoon of brown sugar in warm milk. Set aside to foam 5 minutes.

2 Generously grease French bread pans or line with parchment paper.

3 In the bowl of a heavy-duty stand mixer, combine sorghum blend, cornstarch, cocoa, caraway seed, onion powder, xanthan gum, guar gum, salt, oil, molasses, eggs, orange rind, and vinegar with remaining sugar and yeast-milk mixture. Beat on low speed to blend. Beat on medium speed for 30 seconds, stirring down sides with spatula. Dough will be soft.

4 Divide dough in half on prepared pan. Smooth each half into 10-inch log with a wet spatula. Brush with egg wash for glossier crust. Make three diagonal slashes (⅛-inch deep) in each loaf so steam can escape during baking.

5 Place immediately on middle rack in a *cold* oven. Set the oven to 425°F and bake approximately 30 to 35 minutes, or until nicely browned or temperature reaches 205°F on an instant-read thermometer inserted into center of loaf.

6 Remove bread from pans and cool completely on wire rack before slicing with an electric knife or a serrated knife.

FOCACCIA, BAGELS, PITA, AND OTHER YEAST BREADS

Focaccia with Herbs

MAKES 10 SERVINGS

Focaccia is a cross between flatbread and pizza; in fact, it is sometimes used as the base for pizza. I use focaccia as an accompaniment for dinner and as a sandwich bread (sliced horizontally), and I use the leftovers for Croutons (page 116) or Bread Crumbs (page 117).

BREAD

1½ teaspoons active dry yeast

2 teaspoons sugar

½ cup warm (110°F) water

White rice flour for dusting

1½ cups Carol's Sorghum Blend (page x)

1½ teaspoons xanthan gum

2 teaspoons chopped fresh rosemary or 1 teaspoon dried, crushed with your hands

½ teaspoon onion powder

½ teaspoon salt

2 large eggs, at room temperature

2 tablespoons extra-virgin olive oil

1 teaspoon cider vinegar

TOPPING

Olive oil cooking spray

2 teaspoons chopped fresh rosemary or 1 teaspoon dried, crushed with your hands

½ teaspoon Italian seasoning

1 teaspoon kosher or coarse sea salt (or to taste)

1 Make the bread: In a small bowl, dissolve yeast and sugar in warm water. Set aside to foam 5 minutes.

2 Generously grease an 11 × 7-inch nonstick (gray, not black) pan. Dust the bottom and sides of the pan lightly with white rice flour.

3 In a mixing bowl, combine sorghum blend, xanthan gum, rosemary, onion powder, salt, eggs, oil, vinegar, and yeast-water mixture. Beat dough with mixer on low speed until thoroughly blended. Increase mixer speed to medium and continue beating for 30 seconds or until dough starts to thicken slightly. Dough will be somewhat soft and sticky.

4 Transfer dough to pan. Spread dough to edges of pan with a wet spatula, making sure dough is uniformly thick.

5 Let dough rise in a warm place (75°F to 80°F) until dough is level with top of pan. Spray dough lightly with cooking spray. Sprinkle dough with rosemary, Italian seasoning, and salt.

6 Place a rack in the lower-middle position of the oven. Preheat the oven to 400°F.

7 Bake 25 to 30 minutes or until top is dark golden brown and firm. Remove from oven and cool focaccia in the pan 10 minutes on a wire rack. Remove focaccia from pan and cool 10 minutes more on the wire rack. Slice with an electric knife or a serrated knife.

Rosemary Focaccia in a Skillet: In Step 4, spread the dough in a 10-inch cast-iron skillet that is generously greased with shortening and dusted with white rice flour. Continue with the rest of the recipe.

Sun-Dried Tomato and Kalamata Olive Focaccia

MAKES 10 SERVINGS

Sun-dried tomatoes and kalamata olives give this focaccia a Mediterranean flavor.

BREAD

1½ teaspoons active dry yeast

2 teaspoons sugar

¾ cup warm (110°F) 1% milk (cow's, rice, soy, potato, or nut)

White rice flour for dusting

1½ cups Carol's Sorghum Blend (page x)

¼ cup Expandex modified tapioca starch

1½ teaspoons xanthan gum

2 teaspoons chopped fresh basil or 1 teaspoon dried

½ teaspoon onion powder

½ teaspoon salt

2 large eggs, at room temperature

1 tablespoon extra-virgin olive oil

1 teaspoon cider vinegar

¼ cup chopped kalamata olives

¼ cup sun-dried tomatoes, chopped

TOPPING

1 teaspoon Italian seasoning

½ teaspoon kosher salt

¼ teaspoon cracked black pepper

1 tablespoon extra-virgin olive oil, divided

1 Make the bread: In a small bowl, dissolve yeast and sugar in warm milk. Set aside to foam 5 minutes.

2 Generously grease an 11 × 7-inch nonstick (gray, not black) pan. Dust the bottom and sides of the pan lightly with white rice flour.

3 In a mixing bowl, combine sorghum blend, modified tapioca starch, xanthan gum, basil, onion powder, salt, eggs, oil, vinegar, olives, tomatoes, and yeast-milk mixture. Beat dough on low speed until thoroughly blended, about 30 seconds. Increase mixer speed to medium and continue beating for 30 seconds or until dough starts to thicken slightly. Dough will be somewhat soft and sticky. Transfer dough to pan. Spread dough to edges of pan with a wet spatula, making sure dough is uniformly thick.

4 Let dough rise in a warm place (75°F to 80°F) until dough is nearly level with top of pan.

5 Place a rack in the lower-middle position of the oven. Preheat the oven to 400°F. Sprinkle dough with Italian seasoning, salt, and pepper. Drizzle evenly with olive oil.

6 Bake 25 to 30 minutes or until top is dark golden brown and firm. Remove from oven and cool focaccia in the pan 10 minutes on a wire rack. Remove focaccia from pan and cool 10 minutes more on the wire rack. Slice with an electric knife or a serrated knife.

Focaccia with Caramelized Onions, Goat Cheese, and Rosemary Ⓥ

MAKES 10 SERVINGS

Onions become quite sweet after extended cooking at moderate temperatures and complement the goat cheese and bread flavor. The toppings make this focaccia more like pizza.

BREAD

1½ teaspoons active dry yeast

2 teaspoons sugar

¾ cup warm (110°F) water

White rice flour for dusting

1½ cups Carol's Sorghum Blend (page x)

¼ cup Expandex modified tapioca starch

1½ teaspoons xanthan gum

2 teaspoons chopped fresh rosemary or 1 teaspoon dried, crushed with your hands

½ teaspoon onion powder

¾ teaspoon salt

2 large eggs, at room temperature

2 tablespoons extra-virgin olive oil

1 teaspoon cider vinegar

TOPPING

3 tablespoons extra-virgin olive oil, divided

½ teaspoon kosher salt, divided

¼ teaspoon freshly ground black pepper

2 medium yellow onions, halved and sliced very thin

2 tablespoons chopped fresh rosemary or 1 tablespoon dried, crushed with your hands

½ cup crumbled goat cheese

1 Make the bread: In a small bowl, dissolve yeast and sugar in warm water. Set aside to foam 5 minutes.

2 Generously grease an 11 × 7-inch nonstick (gray, not black) pan. Dust the bottom and sides of the pan lightly with white rice flour.

3 In a mixing bowl, combine sorghum blend, modified tapioca starch, xanthan gum, rosemary, onion powder, salt, eggs, oil, and vinegar. Add yeast-water mixture and beat on low speed until thoroughly blended, about 30 seconds. Increase mixer speed to medium and continue beating for 30 seconds or until dough starts to thicken slightly. Dough will be somewhat soft and sticky.

4 Transfer dough to pan and smooth top with a wet spatula. Let dough rise in a warm place (75°F to 80°F) until dough is level with top of pan.

5 While dough is rising, make the topping: In a heavy skillet, heat 1½ tablespoons of the oil, ¼ teaspoon of the salt, and ¼ teaspoon pepper. Add onions and cook over medium heat until golden brown, about 20 to 25 minutes.

6 Place a rack in the lower-middle position of the oven. Preheat the oven to 400°F. Sprinkle dough with caramelized onions, rosemary, goat cheese and remaining ¼ teaspoon of the salt. Drizzle evenly with remaining 1½ tablespoons of the olive oil.

7 Bake 25 to 30 minutes or until top is dark golden brown and firm. Cool the focaccia in the pan 10 minutes on a wire rack. Remove focaccia from pan and cool 10 minutes more on the wire rack. Slice with an electric knife or a serrated knife.

Italian Chestnut Bread

MAKES 8 SERVINGS

Chestnut flour is usually used in rich Italian desserts. However, chestnuts were actually a staple in Italy—especially during World War II when food supplies ran short. They were used for a wide variety of everyday dishes, including this rustic bread called castagnaccia. *Cut it in wedges and serve it warm, topped with some sweetened cream cheese.*

1 teaspoon active dry yeast

1 tablespoon sugar

1½ cups warm (110°F) water

2 cups chestnut flour*

1 tablespoon Expandex modified tapioca starch

½ teaspoon xanthan gum

½ teaspoon salt

1 tablespoon extra-virgin olive oil

¼ cup chopped pine nuts

1 teaspoon chopped fresh rosemary or ½ teaspoon dried, crushed

1 In a small bowl, dissolve yeast and sugar in warm water. Set aside to foam 5 minutes.

2 Generously grease a 10-inch nonstick (gray, not black) round cake pan. Line with parchment paper or wax paper.

3 In a medium mixing bowl, place chestnut flour, modified tapioca starch, xanthan gum, and salt. Add yeast-water mixture and beat with an electric mixer on medium speed until well blended, about 30 seconds. Add the oil, pine nuts, and rosemary and beat until smooth, about another 30 seconds. Pour into prepared pan. Cover loosely with foil and let rise in a warm place (75°F to 80°F) until dough is level with top of pan.

4 Place a rack in the middle of the oven. Preheat the oven to 375°F. Bake 30 minutes or until top is crusty. Cool the bread in the pan 10 minutes on a wire rack. Remove bread from pan and cool 10 minutes more on the wire rack. Cut into 8 wedges and serve warm.

Available at some natural food stores and www.dowdandrogers.com.

Burger or Hot Dog Buns

MAKES 16 BUNS

Use these buns for any type of burger or hot dog, simply changing the shape of the foil rings to the burger or hot dog shape. For a nice crispy texture, lightly toast the cut side on the grill or in a toaster oven.

4 teaspoons active dry yeast

2 tablespoons sugar, divided

¾ cup warm (110°F) water

1½ cups potato starch

½ cup Carol's Sorghum Blend (page x)

⅓ cup nonfat dry milk powder (not Carnation)

2 tablespoons Expandex modified tapioca starch

1 teaspoon salt

1 teaspoon xanthan gum

1 teaspoon guar gum

1 large egg, at room temperature

2 teaspoons cider vinegar

1 tablespoon canola oil

¼ cup + 2 tablespoons unsalted butter or buttery spread, such as Earth Balance, melted, for brushing on tops

1 tablespoon poppy seeds or sesame seeds, for sprinkling on buns (optional), or more to taste

1 Generously grease 16 aluminum foil rings shaped as hamburger buns or hot dog buns (see English Muffins, page 111, for information on aluminum foil rings). Place on a 15 × 10-inch baking sheet or jelly roll pan lined with parchment paper. Set aside. For best results, do not use a nonstick baking sheet; this will brown the buns too much on the underside. Bring a tea kettle of water to a boil and have a 13 × 9-inch baking pan ready.

2 In a small bowl, dissolve yeast and 1½ teaspoons of the sugar in the warm water. Set aside to foam 5 minutes.

3 In the mixing bowl of a heavy-duty mixer, combine the yeast-water mixture, potato starch, sorghum blend, dry milk powder, modified tapioca starch, salt, xanthan gum, guar gum, egg, vinegar, oil, and remaining sugar. Beat with regular beaters on medium speed just until blended and smooth, about 30 seconds. The dough will seem fairly soft.

4 Place scant ¼ cup dough into each ring. Smooth dough with a wet spatula, making sure dough reaches all sides of ring. Gently brush tops with ¼ cup of the melted butter and sprinkle with poppy seeds, if desired, pressing them gently into dough with fingers. Cover lightly with foil, and place on middle rack in the oven. Place a 13 × 9-inch pan on the bottom rack of the oven and fill it with boiling water. Close the door and let the dough rise until it is not quite level with top of rings.

5 Set the oven to 350°F. Bake 30 to 35 minutes or until tops are lightly browned, brushing with the remaining 2 tablespoons of melted butter midway through baking and again right after removing pan from oven. Cool buns on pan 10 minutes on a wire rack. Remove buns from rings and cool 10 minutes more on the wire rack. Once they are fully cooled, store in resealable plastic bag to maintain softness.

Dinner Yeast Rolls

MAKES 15 ROLLS

Brushing the dinner rolls lightly with melted butter before, during, and after baking helps keep them soft and pliable yet doesn't compromise their nice crispy exterior.

1 packet (2¼ teaspoons) active dry yeast

2 tablespoons sugar, divided

1 cup warm (110°F) 1% milk (cow's, rice, soy, potato, or nut)

White rice flour for dusting

3 large (½ cup) egg whites, at room temperature

1½ cups potato starch

1 cup Carol's Sorghum Blend (page x)

¼ cup Expandex modified tapioca starch

2 tablespoons nonfat dry milk powder (not Carnation), or Better Than Milk soy powder

2 teaspoons xanthan gum

1 teaspoon guar gum

1 teaspoon salt

¼ cup unsalted butter or buttery spread, such as Earth Balance, at room temperature, or canola oil

1 teaspoons cider vinegar

½ teaspoon poppy seeds or sesame seeds

White rice flour for dusting

¼ cup unsalted butter or buttery spread, such as Earth Balance, melted, or canola oil for brushing on tops of rolls

1 In a small bowl, dissolve yeast and 1 teaspoon of the sugar in warm milk. Set aside to foam 5 minutes.

2 Generously grease an 11 × 7-inch nonstick (gray, not black) pan. Dust the bottom and sides of the pan lightly with white rice flour.

3 In the large bowl of a heavy-duty mixer, beat egg whites on medium speed until thick and foamy. Increase speed to high and beat to soft peak stage (tips of peaks curl over rather than stand straight up). Add remaining sugar, potato starch, sorghum blend, modified tapioca starch, dry milk powder, xanthan gum, guar gum, salt, butter, vinegar, and yeast-milk mixture. Beat on low speed to blend, then increase speed to medium and beat 30 seconds or until mixture is thoroughly combined and slightly thickened.

4 Use 1½-inch metal spring-action ice cream scoop to measure 15 equal pieces of dough. Dust pieces of dough with rice flour. With very lightly oiled hands, gently shape each into round ball. Place balls in prepared pan in 3 rows of 5 each for a total of 15 rolls. Gently brush tops with melted butter and sprinkle with poppy seeds, pressing them gently into dough with fingers. Cover lightly with foil and let rise in a warm place (75°F to 80°F) until dough is level with top of pan.

5 Place a rack in the middle of the oven. Preheat the oven to 375°F. Bake 30 to 35 minutes or until tops are lightly browned, brushing with butter midway through baking and again right after removing pan from oven. Cool rolls in pan 10 minutes on a wire rack. Remove rolls from pan and cool 10 minutes more on the wire rack. Serve warm.

Bagels

MAKES 8 BAGELS

Making your own bagels is not difficult, but it does require several steps and techniques to assure the best results. Your reward is a warm, delicious bagel that can be eaten right out of the oven; sliced, toasted, and slathered with cream cheese for breakfast; or sliced and piled with your favorite deli fillings for a sandwich.

4 teaspoons active dry yeast

3 tablespoons sugar, divided

¾ cup warm (110°F) water

1½ cups potato starch

½ cup Carol's Sorghum Blend (page x)

⅔ cup nonfat dry milk powder (not Carnation), or Better Than Milk soy powder

3 tablespoons Expandex modified tapioca starch

1 teaspoon salt

1 teaspoon xanthan gum

1 teaspoon guar gum

1 large egg + 1 egg white, at room temperature

2 teaspoons cider vinegar

2 tablespoons canola oil, divided

White rice flour for dusting

Spray bottle of water

1 tablespoon sesame seeds or poppy seeds, for sprinkling on bagels (optional)

1 In a small bowl, dissolve yeast and 1½ teaspoons of the sugar in the warm water. Set aside to foam five minutes. Grease a 15 × 10-inch nonstick (gray, not black) baking sheet or line it with parchment paper. Bring a tea kettle of water to a boil and have it ready.

2 In the mixing bowl of a heavy-duty mixer, combine the yeast-water mixture, potato starch, sorghum blend, dry milk powder, modified tapioca starch, salt, xanthan gum, guar gum, 1 egg, vinegar, 1 tablespoon of the canola oil, and 2 tablespoons of the sugar. Beat with regular beaters on medium speed until well blended, about 1 minute. The dough will look stiff, yet seem too soft to handle.

3 Dust your hands with rice flour and divide the dough into 8 equal portions. Generously dust each portion with rice flour to prevent sticking, then shape each portion into a ball with your hands. Gently flatten each ball to a 3-inch circle, dust again with rice flour, and punch a 1-inch hole in the center with your thumbs. Gently pull the

dough away from the hole with your fingers while forming it into a bagel shape that is as uniformly thick and rounded as possible. The hole will grow smaller as the bagel rises. Place the bagels about 1½ inches apart on the baking sheet. Spray with warm water.

4 Place racks in the bottom and middle positions of the oven. Place an ovenproof dish on the bottom rack and fill it with the boiling water. Place the bagels on the middle rack; then turn the temperature to 300°F. Watch until the temperature hits 200°F, then turn off the oven, but keep the door closed. You are creating a small, humid hothouse that encourages the bagels to rise while keeping them moist until they have risen enough. Let the bagels rise for 30 to 45 minutes or until they are doubled in size. Rising time may vary considerably due to a variety of factors, so be patient and allow the bagels to rise fully.

5 While the bagels are rising, bring 3 inches of water, the remaining 1 1/2 teaspoons sugar, and the remaining oil to a boil in a large pan or a Dutch oven or other deep, wide (at least 10 inches across) heavy pot with a tight-fitting lid on the stovetop. Remove the bagels from the oven and preheat the oven to 350°F.

6 Boil the bagels 30 seconds in the water. Lift the bagels out of the boiling water with a slotted spatula and return them to the baking sheet. Whisk the remaining egg white with 1 tablespoon water and brush on top of each bagel for better browning. Sprinkle with sesame seeds, if using.

7 Return the baking sheet to the oven and spray the bagels with warm water. Refill the ovenproof dish of hot water if necessary.

8 Bake 25 to 35 minutes, or until the bagels are browned. Cool on a wire rack. Serve immediately. Rewarm refrigerated bagels gently on Low power in a microwave oven.

Bread Bowls

MAKES 4 BOWLS

First you eat the soup and then you eat the bowl. Yes, you can actually do that when the bowl is made of gluten-free bread. You can make the bread bowls ahead of time and freeze them for later use. This recipe works best with a thick soup or stew, such as Hearty Beef Stew (page 174) rather than a thin soup, which may be absorbed quickly and weaken the walls of the bread bowl.

2 tablespoons sugar

2 tablespoons active dry yeast

1¼ cups warm (110°F) 1% milk (cow's, rice, soy, potato, or nut)

2 cups Carol's Sorghum Blend (page x)

1 cup potato starch

2 teaspoons xanthan gum

1 teaspoon guar gum

¼ cup nonfat dry milk powder (not Carnation), or Better Than Milk soy powder

1 teaspoon salt

1 tablespoon unsalted butter or buttery spread, such as Earth Balance, at room temperature, or canola oil

3 large egg whites (½ cup), at room temperature (with 1 tablespoon egg white reserved for egg wash)

2 teaspoons cider vinegar

Olive oil cooking spray

Thick stew or soup of your choice

1 In a small bowl, dissolve the sugar and yeast in the warm milk. Set aside to foam 5 minutes. Line a 15 × 10-inch baking (not nonstick) with parchment paper.

2 In the large bowl of a heavy-duty mixer, combine sorghum blend, potato starch, xanthan gum, guar gum, dry milk powder, salt, butter, egg whites, vinegar, and the yeast-milk mixture. Beat the ingredients on low speed until well blended, about 30 seconds, stirring down sides with spatula. Increase speed to medium and beat 30 seconds, or until dough thickens slightly. The dough will be somewhat soft.

3 Divide the dough into 4 pieces. With oiled or wet hands or a wet spatula, gently shape each of the 4 pieces into round balls and place them, evenly spaced apart, on the baking sheet. Whisk the reserved egg white with 1 tablespoon water until very smooth and brush each ball. Make a crisscross slash or "x" (⅛-inch deep) on the top of each ball to let the steam escape as the bread rises.

4 Immediately place the dough balls on the middle rack of a *cold* oven. Set the oven to 425°F and bake approximately 30 to 35 minutes, or until the bowls are nicely browned. Cover the balls with foil during baking if they appear to be browning too quickly. Remove the bread from the pans and cool them completely on a wire rack.

5 Prepare the bread bowls for the soup. Preheat the oven to 400°F. Cut a ¼- to ⅓-inch slice from the top of each bowl. With your fingers, tear the bread from the inner part of the ball, leaving a bowl with ½-inch-thick sides. If the sides of the bowl are any thinner, it may collapse with the weight and moisture of the soup or stew. (Save the bread torn from the bowl to make bread crumbs in your food processor.)

6 Coat the inside and outside of the bowls with olive oil cooking spray. Place bread bowls on a large (nonstick) baking sheet and toast in preheated oven 10 minutes. Fill immediately with soup or stew of choice. Serve immediately.

English Muffins

MAKES 8 MUFFINS

The crispy texture of these muffins is sure to delight your senses, especially if you haven't had an English muffin in a long time. The structure of an English muffin relies on a crisp bottom and sides for stability. The only way to achieve this is to encourage the browning process on the sides of the muffin. Baking the muffins in a nonstick (gray, not black) pan is the best way to get this crisp edge, so use mini-springform pans, sometimes called mini-cheesecake pans.

You could also use aluminum foil rings. Cut 12 inches from a 12-inch-wide roll of aluminum foil and fold in half, lengthwise, repeating to make a 1-inch high strip. Secure ends together with masking tape. Spray insides of rings with cooking spray.

English muffins are best toasted, cut side up, in a toaster oven so that just the top (cut side) of the muffin is browned, rather than both sides, as in a conventional toaster.

1¾ cups warm (110°F) 1% milk (cow's, rice, soy, potato, or nut)

1 tablespoon sugar

1 packet (2¼ teaspoons) instant dry yeast

1 tablespoon unsalted butter or buttery spread, such as Earth Balance, melted, or canola oil

2 large egg whites (about ¼ cup), at room temperature

2 cups Carol's Sorghum Blend (page x)

¾ cup potato starch

¼ cup Expandex modified tapioca starch

2 tablespoons potato flour

2 teaspoons xanthan gum

1¼ teaspoons salt

1 In the large bowl of a heavy-duty mixer, combine the warm milk, sugar, and yeast. Set aside to foam 5 minutes. Generously grease eight 4-inch rings from mini-springform pans or make your own rings (see left) and place on a 13 × 9-inch (not nonstick) baking sheet that is lined with parchment paper.

2 Add butter, egg whites, sorghum blend, potato starch, modified tapioca starch, potato flour, xanthan gum, and salt to the mixing bowl. Beat on low speed until well blended, about 30 seconds, then mix on medium speed for 30 seconds. The dough will be soft and sticky. Using a wet #12 metal ice cream scoop or a wet ⅓ cup metal measuring cup, drop a ball of dough into each ring. Pat the dough to the edges of the ring with a wet spatula or wet fingers. Cover the rings loosely with foil and place the baking sheet in a warm place (75°F to 80°F) to rise, 20 to 25 minutes or until the dough is not quite level with the top of the pan.

3 Place a rack in the middle of the oven. Preheat the oven to 375°F. Spray the tops of the muffins with cooking spray. Bake the muffins 20 to 25 minutes or until the tops are light brown and the muffins start to pull away from the rings. Remove the baking sheet from the oven and cool the muffins in the rings 10 minutes on a wire rack. Remove the muffins from the rings and cool 10 minutes more on the wire rack.

4 To serve, slice the muffins in half crosswise and toast, cut side up, in a toaster oven. Serve immediately.

Crumpets V

MAKES 6 CRUMPETS

Crumpets are spongy, mild-flavored yeast cakes. They are similar to English muffins but are not as sweet and are baked on a griddle rather than in the oven. They are usually eaten with butter and served with tea, but you can eat them any way you like.

1½ teaspoons active dry yeast

2 teaspoons honey

¾ cup warm (110°F) 1% milk (cow's, rice, soy, potato, or nut)

2 tablespoons unsalted butter or buttery spread, such as Earth Balance, at room temperature

1 large egg white, at room temperature

2 teaspoons cider vinegar

1½ cups Carol's Sorghum Blend (page x)

¼ cup potato starch

¼ cup Expandex modified tapioca starch

1 teaspoon xanthan gum

¾ teaspoon salt

¼ teaspoon baking soda

1 In a small bowl, dissolve the yeast and honey in the warm milk. Set aside to foam 5 minutes. Generously grease a griddle and place 6 muffins rings on it (or see English Muffins, page 111, for information on aluminum foil rings). Coat the rings with cooking spray.

2 In the medium bowl of a heavy-duty mixer, place the butter, egg white, vinegar, sorghum blend, potato starch, modified tapioca starch, xanthan gum, salt, and baking soda. Add the yeast-milk mixture and beat on low speed until thoroughly blended, about 30 seconds. Increase the speed to medium-high and beat 30 seconds or until mixture thickens slightly.

3 Heat the griddle over medium heat until it is hot and a drop of water dances on the surface. Transfer ¼ cup of dough to each ring, smoothing the dough with a wet spatula to the edge of the ring.

4 Reduce the heat to medium-low and cook the crumpets about 10 minutes or until the tops are full of holes and the batter is set. Remove the crumpets from the rings and cool on a wire rack. Toast the crumpets in a toaster until browned to your liking and serve immediately.

Naan Bread

MAKES 6 SERVINGS

Like chapati, which are unleavened, naan is the term used to refer to a flatbread typically served with Indian dishes. They require your complete attention, so plan to stay nearby as they bake. Your reward is a delectably tender flatbread to serve with your favorite Indian food—or any meal. It works best with butter, milk, and yogurt because of the calcium they contain, which softens the crumb.

1 packet (2¼ teaspoons) instant dry yeast

1 teaspoon sugar

½ cup warm (110°F) 2% milk (cow's, rice, soy, potato, or nut)

½ cup white rice flour

½ cup potato starch

½ teaspoon salt

½ teaspoon onion powder (optional)

½ teaspoon xanthan gum

½ teaspoon guar gum

¼ cup plain yogurt or soy yogurt

¼ cup unsalted butter or buttery spread, such as Earth Balance, at room temperature

White rice flour in shaker for sprinkling

Cooking spray

2 teaspoons poppy, sesame, or nigella seeds (optional)

Spray bottle filled with tap water

1 In a small bowl, dissolve yeast and sugar in the warm milk. Set aside to foam 5 minutes. Generously grease a 15 × 10-inch (not nonstick) heavy-duty baking sheet. Place racks in lowest and highest positions of the oven.

2 In a food processor, combine whiterice flour, potato starch, salt, onion powder (if using) xanthan gum, guar gum, yogurt, and butter. Add yeast-milk mixture and process until dough thickens slightly. Dough will be very soft. Using a #14 spring-action ice cream scoop, place 6 equal-sized and evenly spaced balls of dough (about ¼ cup each) on the baking sheet.

3 Generously sprinkle each ball with white rice flour and using your fingers, press each ball as thinly as possible in a circular or oval shape. Spray each naan with cooking spray, then sprinkle with seeds, if using. Spray each naan with water. Place immediately on the lowest rack in a *cold* oven. Set the oven to 400°F. Bake 5 to 7 minutes, continuing to spray naan every 2 minutes and taking care to avoid spraying the oven light or thermometer.

4 Move baking sheet to top rack of oven and turn oven to broil setting. Broil approximately 5 minutes or until golden brown spots appear on top of each naan. Remove from the oven and cool 1 minute on a wire rack. Serve immediately. Store 1 day in heavy-duty, resealable plastic bag. Reheat by placing naan on baking sheet in a 350°F oven for 2 to 3 minutes.

Pita Bread

MAKES 4 BREADS

Pita breads—round flatbreads that are often cut in half into pockets and stuffed with sandwich fillings—are staples in the Middle East. This plain white pita bread is perfect for light, mild-flavored fillings and is best eaten on the day it's made.

½ cup white rice flour

⅓ cup potato starch

1 tablespoon Expandex modified tapioca starch

1 packet (2¼ teaspoons) instant dry yeast

2 teaspoons sugar

½ teaspoon salt

½ teaspoon xanthan gum

½ teaspoon guar gum

½ cup *very* warm (120°F) 1% milk (cow's, rice, soy, potato, or nut)

¼ cup unsalted butter or buttery spread, such as Earth Balance, at room temperature

1 large egg white

1 Generously grease a 15 × 10-inch (not nonstick) baking sheet or line it with parchment paper.

2 In a food processor, combine the white rice flour, potato starch, modified tapioca starch, yeast, sugar, salt, xanthan gum, guar gum, very warm milk, butter, and egg white. Process until the dough thickens slightly but it will be somewhat soft.

3 Using a #12 metal spring-action ice cream scoop, place 4 equal-size and evenly spaced balls of dough (about ⅓ cup each) on the baking sheet.

4 Lay a sheet of heavy-duty plastic wrap over the balls and, using a rolling pin, roll the balls to 5-inch circles about ¼ inch thick. Cover the sheet loosely with foil and let rise in a warm place (75°F to 80°F) for 20 minutes. Press pita edges lightly with fingers.

5 Place a rack in the bottom position and another in the middle of the oven. Preheat the oven to 425°F. Place the baking sheet on the lowest rack and bake 10 minutes, then shift the sheet to the middle rack of the oven. Bake 10 to 12 minutes more, or until the pita breads are golden brown and slightly puffed.

6 Remove the baking sheet from the oven and place it on a wire rack to cool for 2 minutes. Dampen a tea towel (not terry) and wrap the pita breads in the towel, then seal in a heavy-duty food-storage bag to soften the pita breads slightly. Once they are softened to your liking, cut the pita breads in half and carefully slit each half, starting from the cut edge, to create a pocket for the filling. For a large pita, slit the top edge and stuff the whole pita. Serve immediately. Store 1 day in a heavy-duty, food-storage bag. Reheat the pitas in a microwave oven on low for about 30 seconds.

Kolaches

MAKES 24 ROLLS

Aunt Agnes, who grew up in a Czech community, was one of my favorite aunts, especially on those days when she baked kolaches—Czechoslovakian yeast buns with fruit fillings. She nestled cherry pie filling, apricot preserves, or prune puree in the soft, sweet dough (sometimes she got wild and crazy and used sweetened cream cheese) and then drizzled the kolaches with a powdered-sugar frosting. I have re-created her kolaches as a tribute to those delicious treats. Thanks, Aunt Agnes.

1 cup 1% milk (cow's, rice, soy, potato, or nut)

⅓ cup sugar

1 tablespoon pure vanilla extract

¼ cup (½ stick) + 2 tablespoons unsalted butter or buttery spread such as Earth Balance, at room temperature

1 package (2¼ teaspoons) active dry yeast

1 large egg + 1 egg yolk, at room temperature

2 cups Carol's Sorghum Blend (page x)

1 cup potato starch

2 tablespoons Expandex modified tapioca starch

2 teaspoons xanthan gum

1½ teaspoons salt

½ cup apricot preserves (or prune puree, poppy seed pie filling, cherry pie filling)

1 In a small pan, heat the milk on medium heat until bubbles start to form around the edge of the pan. Stir in the sugar, vanilla, and butter and let stand until lukewarm (about 110°F). Stir in the yeast. Set aside to foam 5 minutes.

2 Line two 15 × 10-inch baking sheets (not non-stick) with parchment paper.

3 In a large mixing bowl, beat egg and egg yolk with an electric mixer on medium speed 2 minutes. Reduce speed to low and add yeast-milk mixture, sorghum blend, potato starch, xanthan gum, and salt gradually until mixture is smooth.

4 Place a rack in the lower-middle position and another in the upper-middle position of the oven. Preheat the oven to 375°F. With wet or oiled hands, shape 24 pieces of dough, each 1½ inches round (or use a wet metal, spring-action ice cream scoop to assure same-size balls). Continue to wet your hands as you shape the pieces of dough into smooth balls and place them on the baking sheets, 12 to a sheet.

5 With wet fingers, pat the dough to form a 2½-inch circle. With the back of a teaspoon, firmly press an indentation in the middle of the dough. Put 1 teaspoon of filling in each indentation.

6 Bake 30 to 35 minutes or until the kolaches are lightly browned, rotating the baking sheets between racks halfway through baking. Remove the baking sheets from the oven and brush the kolaches with melted butter. Cool them in the pan 15 minutes on a wire rack. Drizzle with powdered sugar frosting. Serve slightly warm.

Soft Pretzels

MAKES 12 PRETZELS

Soft pretzels are delicious on their own or with lots of mustard or cheese spread. As you become more experienced with piping the dough onto the baking sheet, you might try creating pretzels with interesting shapes such as circles, strips with knots in the center, or the traditional heart-shaped pretzel.

1 tablespoon active dry yeast

1 tablespoon sugar

⅔ cup warm (110°F) milk (cow's, rice, soy, potato, or nut)

½ cup sorghum flour

½ cup potato starch

1 tablespoon Expandex modified tapioca starch, or nonfat dry milk powder (not Carnation), or Better Than Milk soy powder

2 teaspoons xanthan gum

1 teaspoon onion powder

½ teaspoon salt

1 tablespoon olive oil

2 teaspoons cider vinegar

1 large egg white, beaten to a foam

1 tablespoon coarse kosher salt, or to taste

1 tablespoon poppy seeds, optional

1 In a small bowl, dissolve the yeast and sugar in warm milk. Set aside to foam 5 minutes. Line a 15 × 10-inch baking sheet (not nonstick) with parchment paper; set aside.

2 In the bowl of a heavy-duty mixer, beat the sorghum flour, potato starch, modified tapioca starch, xanthan gum, onion powder, salt, olive oil, vinegar, and the yeast-milk mixture on low speed until well blended, about 30 seconds. Increase the speed to high and beat 30 seconds more, or until the dough thickens slightly.

3 Place the dough in a large, heavy-duty food-storage bag. Cut ⅓ inch from a bottom corner of the bag, making a ⅔-inch circle. Squeeze the dough through the opening onto the baking sheet in the shape of 24 pretzels, each about 3 inches long. It works best to hold the bag upright as you squeeze the dough onto the baking sheet. Brush the pretzels lightly with beaten egg white, then sprinkle them with coarse salt to taste. Let the pretzels rise 20 to 25 minutes in a warm place (80°F to 90°F).

4 Place the baking sheet on the middle rack of a *cold* oven and set the oven to 400°F. Bake the pretzels until they are dry and golden brown, approximately 15 minutes. Remove from the oven and spray lightly with cooking spray. Sprinkle with poppy seeds. Cool the pretzels 15 minutes on the sheet 15 minutes on a wire rack. Remove pretzels from sheet and cool completely on the wire rack.

Breadsticks

MAKES 10 BREADSTICKS

Breadsticks are especially fun with an Italian meal, and gluten-free guests are particularly charmed that you would serve something that they so rarely get to eat.

1 tablespoon active dry yeast

¾ cup warm (110°F) 1% milk (cow's, rice, soy, potato, or nut)

½ cup Carol's Sorghum Blend (page x)

½ cup potato starch

1 tablespoon sugar

2 teaspoons xanthan gum

½ to ¾ teaspoon salt

2 tablespoons grated Parmesan cheese, or Romano cheese, or soy alternative, such as Soyco

1 teaspoon onion powder

1 tablespoon olive oil

2 teaspoons cider vinegar

1 egg white, beaten to foam for the egg wash

1 teaspoon sesame seeds (optional)

1 In a small bowl, dissolve the yeast in warm milk. Set aside to foam 5 minutes. Place a rack in the middle of the oven.

2 Generously grease a 15 × 10-inch baking sheet (not nonstick) or line with parchment paper.

3 In a medium-size mixer bowl, use an electric mixer to blend the yeast-milk mixture, sorghum blend, potato starch, sugar, xanthan gum, salt, Parmesan cheese, onion powder, oil, and vinegar on low speed just until blended. Or, process the ingredients in a food processor until thoroughly combined. The dough will be soft and sticky.

4 Place the dough in a large, heavy-duty food-storage bag. Cut a ½-inch opening diagonally on a bottom corner. Squeeze the dough out of the plastic bag onto the sheet in 10 strips, each 1 inch wide by 6 inches long. For best results, hold the bag of dough upright as you squeeze, rather than at an angle. Also, hold the bag with the corners perpendicular to the baking sheet, rather than horizontal, for a more authentic-looking breadstick. Brush the breadsticks with egg white or coat with cooking spray for a crispier, shinier breadstick. Sprinkle with sesame seeds.

5 Put the baking sheet on the middle rack of a *cold* oven and turn the oven on to 400°F. Bake 15 to 20 minutes, or until the breadsticks are golden brown. Rotate the baking sheet a quarter turn halfway through baking to assure even browning. Cool the breadsticks 15 minutes on the baking sheet. Remove breadsticks from sheet and cool 5 minutes on the wire rack. Serve warm.

Melba Toast

MAKES 8 SLICES

Melba toast, named after Dame Nellie Melba, the stage name of an Australian opera singer, is thinly sliced, double-toasted bread. Quite dry and crisp, it is often served with soup or salads. A lovely Canadian lady named Ute shared her way of making gluten-free melba toast with me and I have modified her technique here. I offer two methods for making melba toast, one in an oven and the other in a toaster.

4 slices gluten-free bread

1 Place a rack in the middle of the oven. Preheat the oven or toaster oven to 350°F. Place the bread on a baking sheet and toast one side until browned. Turn the bread to toast the other half. Toasting times will vary depending on the bread; watch carefully so they don't burn.

2 Cut toasted bread in half horizontally so that you have two full-sized pieces that are very thin (one side toasted).

3 Trim the crusts from the bread with a sharp knife.

4 Place bread, toasted side down, in the oven.

5 Bake 15 to 20 minutes or until the toast is browned and the edges start to curl. Remove toasts from baking sheet and cool completely on a wire rack.

Another method for making melba toast: Lightly toast a slice of bread in a toaster. Once the outsides of the bread are slightly firm, remove it from the toaster and slice it in half horizontally with a bread knife to make two slices. Toast these two thin slices again to make the melba toast.

Croutons

MAKES 4 CUPS

Croutons add wonderful crunch to mixed green salads and soups, so always keep a stash in your freezer.

4 slices gluten-free bread of your choice
Olive oil cooking spray
Garlic powder (optional)
Italian herb seasoning (optional)

1 Place a rack in the middle of the oven. Preheat the oven to 375°F. Line a 13 × 9-inch rimmed baking sheet (not nonstick) with foil.

2 Trim the crusts from the bread and cut the slices into ½-inch cubes. Spray the cubes with cooking spray. Dust with garlic powder or Italian seasoning to taste, if using. Place the cubes in a single layer on the prepared sheet.

3 Toast 5 to 10 minutes, until the croutons are lightly browned. Store tightly covered in the refrigerator for up to 2 weeks and in the freezer for up to 3 months.

Plain Bread Crumbs

MAKES 2 CUPS

Bread crumbs can be made from either yeast bread or quick bread. They help make fried foods crispy and hold flavor, and make a crunchy topping for vegetable dishes. They also bind such foods as meat loaf or meatballs. I prefer to store bread crumbs in a big, heavy-duty food-storage bag in the freezer without seasoning, then add salt or herbs that complement the recipe I'm using them in. If you prefer dry bread crumbs, toast them in a 300°F oven to the desired degree of dryness. For a recipe calling for very fine bread crumbs, put the toasted crumbs back in a food processor and pulse to the desired consistency.

4 cups gluten-free bread of choice, torn into small pieces

Place the bread in a food processor and pulse until the crumbs reach desired consistency. Store tightly covered in the refrigerator for up to 2 weeks and in the freezer up to 3 months.

Italian Bread Crumbs: Add 1 teaspoon onion powder and 4 teaspoons Italian herb seasoning to the recipe above; toss well.

PIZZA

Homemade Pizza Crust

MAKES 6 SERVINGS (12-INCH PIZZA)

Although store-bought gluten-free pizza crusts such as those from Whole Foods are a great time-saver, nothing beats a homemade pizza. Because gluten-free doughs are very, very sticky, you have to pre-bake them for 10 minutes to dry out the dough a bit before topping or freezing them.

If you and your family love pizzas, make extra crusts, bake 10 minutes, then let cool. Freeze the cooled crusts, tightly wrapped in wax paper and foil, for later use.

If you want to use this basic crust recipe for your own pizza inventions, after you pre-bake the crust, brush it with sauce (if using) and arrange the toppings. Bake the pizza at 425°F on the middle rack of the oven 15 to 20 minutes more or until top is nicely browned. Remove pizza from oven and let stand 5 minutes. Brush rim of crust with olive oil before cutting and serving.

1 tablespoon active dry yeast

2½ teaspoons sugar

⅔ cup warm (110°F) 1% milk (cow's, rice, soy, potato, or nut)

⅔ cup potato starch

½ cup Carol's Sorghum Blend (page x)

2 teaspoons xanthan gum

1 teaspoon Italian seasoning

1 teaspoon onion powder

¾ teaspoon salt

1 tablespoon olive oil

2 teaspoons cider vinegar

Shortening for greasing pizza pan, such as Spectrum Vegetable

White rice flour for dusting

1 In a small bowl, dissolve yeast and sugar in warm milk. Set aside to foam 5 minutes. In a food processor, blend yeast mixture, potato starch, sorghum blend, xanthan gum, Italian seasoning, onion powder, salt, oil, and vinegar, until ball forms. Dough will be very soft.

2 Generously grease a 12-inch nonstick (gray, not black) pizza pan with shortening. Do not use cooking spray—it makes it harder to shape the dough. Place dough on prepared pan. Liberally dust dough with white rice flour; then press dough into pan with your hands, continuing to dust dough with flour to prevent sticking as needed. The smoother the dough, the smoother the baked crust will be. Make edges thicker to contain toppings.

3 Place a rack in the bottom position of the oven for the pre-baking and another in the middle position for the secondary baking. Preheat the oven to 425°F.

4 Bake pizza crust 10 minutes on the bottom rack, until crust begins to brown on the bottom. Remove from the oven. The crust is now ready to be used as per your recipe, or one of the following recipes.

Pepperoni Cheese Pizza

MAKES 6 SERVINGS (12-INCH PIZZA)

This is the classic pizza choice at my house for young and old alike. My little grandson likes to sneak a few pieces of pepperoni while I'm making the pizza.

1 (12-inch) homemade Pizza Crust (page 117)

SAUCE

1 can (8 ounces) tomato sauce
2 teaspoons fresh basil or 1 teaspoon dried
2 teaspoons fresh parsley or 1 teaspoon dried
¼ teaspoon fennel seeds
¼ teaspoon garlic powder
¼ teaspoon salt
⅛ teaspoon sugar

TOPPINGS

About 24 pepperoni slices, such as Hormel (or to taste)
1 cup grated mozzarella cheese or cheese alternative, such as Vegan Gourmet
1 tablespoon olive oil

1 Make the crust on a 12-inch nonstick (gray, not black) pizza pan as directed on page 117. Place a rack in the middle position of the oven. Preheat the oven to 425°F.

2 Make the sauce: Combine sauce ingredients in a small saucepan. Simmer 15 minutes and set aside. Makes about 1 cup, enough for one 12-inch pizza.

3 Brush crust with sauce and arrange single layer of pepperoni slices on top. Sprinkle cheese over top. Bake pizza 15 to 20 minutes or until top is nicely browned.

4 Remove pizza from oven and let stand 5 minutes. Brush rim of crust with the olive oil before cutting into 6 slices. Serve immediately.

Margarita Pizza

MAKES 6 SERVINGS (12-INCH PIZZA)

This pizza features fresh tomatoes rather than cooked tomato sauce, and fresh basil. The vibrant colors of green, white, and red (the colors of Italy's flag) make this a very pretty pizza.

1 (12-inch) homemade Pizza Crust (page 117)
2 to 3 medium ripe tomatoes, sliced very thinly
8 fresh basil leaves (or to taste)
1 cup grated mozzarella cheese or cheese alternative, such as Vegan Gourmet
1 tablespoon olive oil

1 Make the crust on a 12-inch nonstick (gray, not black) pizza pan as directed on page 117. Place a rack in the middle position of the oven. Preheat the oven to 425°F.

2 Layer the crust with sliced tomatoes. Sprinkle basil, then cheese evenly over top. Spray crust with olive oil cooking spray at this point, if desired. (Or spray after baking for shinier, softer crust.)

3 Bake pizza 15 to 20 minutes or until top is nicely browned. Remove pizza from oven and let stand 5 minutes. Brush rim of crust with the olive oil before cutting into 6 slices. Serve immediately.

Mediterranean Pizza

MAKES 6 SERVINGS (12-INCH PIZZA)

This pizza was inspired by the wonderful Mediterranean flavors of olives, basil, artichokes, and bell peppers. If you can't find smoked mozzarella, use regular mozzarella cheese.

CRUST
1 (12-inch) homemade Pizza Crust (page 117)

TOPPINGS
1 tablespoon olive oil
1 cup thinly sliced red, yellow, or green bell peppers
Basil Pizza Sauce (page 118)
1 jar (11 ounces) marinated artichokes, drained
½ cup chopped dried tomatoes
1 can (11 ounces) sliced black olives
8 slices smoked mozzarella cheese or cheese alternative, such as Vegan Gourmet

1 Make the crust on a 12-inch nonstick (gray, not black) pizza pan as directed on page 117. Place a rack in the middle position of the oven. Preheat the oven to 425°F.

2 While the crust is baking, make the toppings: In a medium heavy skillet, heat the oil over medium heat. Cook the bell peppers until they become soft, stirring constantly, about 5 to 7 minutes. Set aside.

3 Brush crust with sauce and arrange peppers, artichokes, tomatoes, and olives on crust. Lay smoked mozzarella slices on top. Bake pizza 15 to 20 minutes or until top is nicely browned.

4 Remove pizza from the oven and let stand 5 minutes. Brush rim of crust with the olive oil before cutting into 6 slices. Serve immediately.

White Pizza

MAKES 6 SERVINGS (12-INCH PIZZA)

Who says pizza has to have tomatoes in it? I often get requests for a tomato-free pizza recipe, so here is one you'll love—and you'll never miss the tomatoes!

CRUST
1 (12-inch) homemade Pizza Crust (page 117)

TOPPINGS
3 tablespoons olive oil
1 large garlic clove, minced
1 cup thinly sliced fresh cremini or button mushrooms, or 1 can (8 ounces) sliced mushrooms, drained thoroughly
2 teaspoons finely chopped fresh parsley
1 teaspoon finely chopped fresh rosemary
½ cup chopped cooked pancetta (Italian bacon) or regular bacon
1½ cups grated Manchego or Provolone cheese or cheese alternative, such as Vegan Gourmet

1 Make the crust on a 12-inch nonstick (gray, not black) pizza pan as directed on page 117, using the fresh or dried oregano in place of the Italian seasoning. Place a rack in the middle position of the oven. Preheat the oven to 425°F.

2 Heat the olive oil and garlic in a skillet over medium heat. Add the mushrooms and fry 2 to 3 minutes. Remove the skillet from the heat.

3 With a pastry brush, brush the garlic-infused oil (from the mushrooms) over the pizza crust, including the edges. Spread the mushrooms and the remaining oil on the pizza. Sprinkle with the herbs and pancetta, then the cheese.

4 Bake the pizza 15 to 20 minutes or until cheeses are browned and bubbling. Remove from oven and let sit 5 minutes before cutting into 6 slices. Serve immediately.

Grape–Feta Cheese Pizza

MAKES 6 SERVINGS (12-INCH PIZZA)

Grape focaccia is traditionally made during the grape harvest in Tuscany, so why not a pizza with these flavors? The sweetness of the grapes contrasts nicely with the sharpness of the cheeses. Serve this pizza to your friends and family who like innovative dishes.

1 (12-inch) homemade Pizza Crust (page 117)

1½ cups red seedless grapes, halved lengthwise

2 tablespoons apple jelly, melted

1 cup coarsely grated Manchego or Provolone cheese or cheese alternative, such as Vegan Gourmet

1 package (4 ounces) goat cheese, crumbled, or cheese alternative, such as Vegan Gourmet

¼ cup crumbed feta cheese

1 Make the crust on a 12-inch nonstick (gray, not black) pizza pan as directed on page 117. Place a rack in the middle position of the oven. Preheat the oven to 425°F.

2 In a small bowl, combine grapes and melted apple jelly and arrange evenly on baked crust. Sprinkle with cheeses.

3 Bake pizza 20 minutes or until cheeses are browned and bubbling. Remove from the oven and let stand 5 minutes before cutting into 6 slices. Serve immediately.

Caramelized Onion, Tomato, and Rosemary Pizza V

MAKES 6 SERVINGS (12-INCH PIZZA)

This may seem like an enormous amount of onions, but they reduce in size significantly as you sauté and brown them. Their sweet flavor complements the other toppings.

CRUST

1 (12-inch) homemade Pizza Crust (page 117)

1 tablespoon chopped fresh rosemary or 1 heaping teaspoon dried, crushed

SAUCE

1 can (8 ounces) tomato sauce

1 tablespoon chopped fresh rosemary or 1 heaping teaspoon dried, crushed

2 teaspoons chopped fresh parsley or 1 teaspoon dried

¼ teaspoon garlic powder

¼ teaspoon salt

¼ teaspoon sugar

TOPPINGS

1 teaspoon light olive oil

3 medium onions, halved and thinly sliced

1 cup chopped dried tomatoes

1 cup sliced red bell pepper

½ cup sliced black olives

2 cups shredded smoked mozzarella cheese or cheese alternative, such as Vegan Gourmet

Shortening for greasing pizza pan, such as Spectrum Vegetable

White rice flour for dusting

Olive oil cooking spray (optional)

1 tablespoon olive oil

1 Make the crust on a 12-inch nonstick (gray, not black) pizza pan as directed on page 117, using the rosemary in place of the Italian seasoning. Place a rack in the middle position of the oven. Preheat the oven to 425°F.

2 Make the sauce: In a small saucepan, combine all sauce ingredients. Simmer 15 minutes. Makes about 1 cup, enough for one 12-inch pizza.

3 Make the toppings: Heat oil over medium heat in medium skillet. Cook onions, stirring occasionally, until golden brown, about 15 to 20 minutes. Have tomatoes, bell pepper, olives, and cheese ready.

4 Brush crust with sauce and scatter onions, tomatoes, bell pepper, and olives on top. Add cheese. Spray crust with olive oil cooking spray at this point, if desired. (Or spray after baking for shinier, softer crust.)

5 Bake pizza 15 to 20 minutes more or until top is nicely browned. Remove pizza from oven and let stand 5 minutes. Brush rim of crust with the olive oil before cutting into 6 slices. Serve immediately.

Barbecued Chicken Pizza

MAKES 6 SERVINGS (12-INCH PIZZA)

This pizza is a great way to use up leftover barbecue sauce and cooked chicken, and you will love this combination of old favorites presented in a new way. Add other toppings such as red, yellow, and green bell peppers for additional color, texture, and taste.

CRUST

1 (12-inch) homemade Pizza Crust (page 117)
2 teaspoons chopped fresh oregano or 1 heaping teaspoon dried, crushed

TOPPINGS

¾ cup homemade Barbecue Sauce (page 285) or your favorite sauce, divided
¼ pound (about 1 cup) shredded cooked chicken
½ teaspoon salt
¼ teaspoon freshly ground black pepper
1 cup chopped red onion, sautéed until tender
1 cup grated smoked mozzarella cheese or cheese alternative, such as Vegan Gourmet
2 tablespoons grated Parmesan cheese or soy alternative, such as Soyco
1 tablespoon olive oil
2 tablespoons chopped fresh cilantro, for garnish

1 Make the crust on a 12-inch nonstick (gray, not black) pizza pan as directed on page 117, using the fresh or dried oregano in place of the Italian seasoning. Place a rack in the middle position of the oven. Preheat the oven to 425°F.

2 Brush crust with ½ cup barbecue sauce. Mix remaining ¼ cup of sauce with shredded chicken,

salt, and pepper and arrange in even layer on top. Arrange onions evenly over chicken. Sprinkle cheeses on top.

3 Bake pizza on the middle rack of the oven 15 to 20 minutes or until top is nicely browned. Remove pizza from oven and let stand 5 minutes.

4 Brush rim of crust with the olive oil, garnish with the cilantro, then cut into 6 slices. Serve immediately.

Corned Beef and Cabbage Pizza

MAKES 6 SERVINGS (12-INCH PIZZA)

If you enjoy Reuben sandwiches, then you'll love the wonderful flavors of this unusual pizza recipe. Rather than a traditional pizza sauce, it uses Russian or Thousand Island salad dressing. Use canned sauerkraut or make your own.

1 (12-inch) homemade Pizza Crust (page 117)
2 teaspoons chopped fresh oregano or 1 heaping teaspoon dried, crushed
1 teaspoon caraway seeds
Shortening for greasing pizza pan, such as Spectrum Vegetable
White rice flour for dusting

TOPPINGS

1 can (16 ounces) sauerkraut, very well-drained
1 teaspoon sugar
½ teaspoon caraway seeds
¾ cup gluten-free Russian salad dressing, such as Walden Farms, or homemade Russian Dressing (page 161) or Thousand Island salad dressing, such as Litehouse or Publix
1 cup (about 2 ounces) thinly sliced lean deli corned beef, chopped into small bits
2 cups shredded mozzarella cheese or cheese alternative, such as Vegan Gourmet
2 tablespoons grated Parmesan cheese or soy alternative, such as Soyco
1 tablespoon olive oil

1 Make the crust on a 12-inch nonstick (gray, not black) pizza pan as directed on page 117, using oregano in place of the Italian seasoning and adding the caraway seeds. Place a rack in the middle position of the oven. Preheat the oven to 425°F.

2 Make the topping: Toss sauerkraut with sugar and caraway seeds. Set aside.

3 Spoon Russian salad dressing evenly over crust. Spread sauerkraut mixture evenly on top of sauce. Top with corned beef; sprinkle cheeses on top. Spray crust with olive oil cooking spray at this point, if desired. (Or spray after baking for shinier, softer crust.)

4 Bake pizza 15 to 20 minutes or until top is nicely browned. Remove pizza from oven and let stand 5 minutes. Brush rim of crust with olive oil before cutting into 6 slices. Serve immediately.

Ham, Pineapple, and Green Pepper Pizza

MAKES 6 SERVINGS (12-INCH PIZZA)

Sometimes called Hawaiian Pizza, this combination of pineapple and ham may seem unusual, but the sweet pineapple complements the salty ham. You'll find it on the menu in many pizza restaurants, especially in the western United States. It is my daughter-in-law's favorite, so I serve it often at my house.

CRUST

1 (12-inch) homemade Pizza Crust (page 117)
2 teaspoons chopped fresh basil or 1 teaspoon dried

TOPPINGS

Basil Pizza Sauce (page 118)
1 can (8 ounces) pineapple tidbits, drained
1 small green bell pepper, thinly sliced
6 green onions, thinly sliced
1 cup diced ham or Canadian-style bacon
1 cup grated mozzarella cheese or cheese alternative, such as Vegan Gourmet
1 tablespoon grated Parmesan cheese or soy alternative, such as Soyco
1 tablespoon olive oil

1 Make the crust on a 12-inch nonstick (gray, not black) pizza pan as directed on page 117, using the basil in place of the Italian seasoning. Place a rack in the middle position of the oven. Preheat the oven to 425°F.

2 Brush crust with Basil Pizza Sauce and arrange pineapple, pepper, onion, and ham on top. Sprinkle cheeses on top. Spray crust with olive oil cooking spray, if desired.

3 Bake pizza 15 to 20 minutes or until top is nicely browned. Remove pizza from oven and let stand 5 minutes. Brush rim of crust with the olive oil before cutting into 6 slices. Serve immediately.

Rosemary Potato Pizza with Basil Pesto Ⓥ

MAKES 6 SERVINGS (12-INCH PIZZA)

For those who are allergic to or don't like tomatoes, this pizza is for you. A mandoline will help slice the potatoes extra-thin, but use it very carefully since it is quite sharp. The pizza dough will be quite soft, so dust it with plenty of rice flour so your hands won't stick to it.

CRUST

1 (12-inch) homemade Pizza Crust (page 117)
2 teaspoons chopped fresh rosemary or 1 teaspoon dried, crushed

TOPPINGS

3 tablespoons extra-virgin olive oil
1 large russet potato, sliced into very thin rounds
¼ cup store-bought basil pesto
2 teaspoons chopped fresh rosemary
2 large garlic cloves, minced
¼ teaspoon crushed red pepper flakes
1 cup (4 ounces) shredded smoked or regular mozzarella cheese or cheese alternative, such as Vegan Gourmet
1 tablespoon olive oil

1 Make the crust on a 12-inch nonstick (gray, not black) pizza pan as directed on page 117 using rosemary for the Italian seasoning. Place a rack in the middle position of the oven. Preheat the oven to 425°F.

2 Make the topping: Heat olive oil in heavy skillet over medium heat. Add potato slices in single layer. Cook until just tender, about 5 minutes.

3 Brush crust with pesto. Scatter potato slices on top of dough. Sprinkle with rosemary, garlic, and crushed red pepper. Sprinkle cheese on top.

4 Bake pizza 15 to 20 minutes or until top is nicely browned. Remove pizza from oven and let stand 5 minutes.

5 Brush rim of crust with olive oil before cutting into 6 slices. Serve immediately.

Pizza on Rice Crust

MAKES 6 SERVINGS (12-INCH PIZZA)

If a yeasted pizza crust isn't appropriate for your diet, you can still enjoy a fabulous pizza with this innovative rice crust that uses cooked white rice as the base.

Shortening for greasing pizza pan, such as Spectrum Vegetable

2 cups cooked long-grain white rice, cooled

1 tablespoon Expandex modified tapioca starch

1 teaspoon xanthan gum

1 teaspoon Italian seasoning

1 teaspoon onion powder

½ teaspoon salt

¼ teaspoon garlic powder

1 large egg, at room temperature

1 cup pizza sauce of your choice

Toppings of your choice

1 Place an oven rack on bottom shelf of oven and another rack in middle of oven. Preheat the oven to 425°F. Generously grease a 12-inch nonstick (gray, not black) pizza pan with shortening.

2 In a bowl, combine cooked rice with remaining ingredients except the sauce and toppings. Using a spatula dipped in water, press mixture firmly and evenly in a thin layer on prepared pan. Make edges slighter thicker to contain toppings.

3 Bake pizza crust 10 minutes on bottom rack of oven. Remove from oven.

4 Add your favorite pizza sauce (or see Basil Pizza Sauce on page 118) and your choice of toppings to crust.

5 Bake pizza on middle rack of oven and bake 20 to 25 minutes more or until cheese is nicely browned. Remove from oven and let sit 5 minutes before cutting into 6 slices. Serve immediately.

Calzones

MAKES 8 CALZONES

Calzones are yeast breads formed around the same types of ingredients we put on top of pizza. They are baked in an oven and then drizzled with marinara sauce. Some are quite large so they can be filling; this version is a bit smaller but no less delicious. These may seem complicated at first, but with a little practice they can be assembled quickly.

CRUST

1 packet (2¼ teaspoons) active dry yeast

2 tablespoons sugar, divided

½ cup warm (110°F) 1% milk (cow's, rice, soy, potato, or nut)

1 cup Carol's Sorghum Blend (page x)

¾ cup tapioca flour

½ cup sweet rice flour

1 teaspoon xanthan gum

1 teaspoon guar gum

1 teaspoon Italian seasoning

½ teaspoon onion powder

½ teaspoon salt

¼ teaspoon baking soda

½ cup shortening, such as Spectrum Vegetable

White rice flour for dusting

1 egg yolk + 1 tablespoon water for egg wash (optional)

FILLING

1 teaspoon olive oil

1 pound gluten-free sweet Italian sausage, such as Giant or Johnsonville, raw with casings removed

1 garlic clove, minced

½ cup grated Parmesan cheese or soy alternative, such as Soyco

¼ teaspoon freshly grated nutmeg

2 cups ricotta cheese

1½ cups homemade Marinara Sauce (page 672), or store-bought marinara sauce, such as Classico, divided

1 Make the crust: In a small bowl, dissolve yeast and 1 teaspoon of the sugar in warm milk. Set aside to foam 5 minutes.

2 In a food processor, combine remaining sugar, sorghum blend, tapioca flour, sweet rice flour, xanthan gum, guar gum, Italian seasoning, onion powder, salt, baking soda, and shortening and process until mixture is thoroughly blended. Add yeast mixture and blend until dough forms a ball. If it doesn't form a ball, use a spatula to break up the dough into pieces and process again, scraping down sides if necessary. Remove dough from food processor and knead with hands a few times until thoroughly blended and smooth. Place dough in resealable plastic bag and refrigerate while making filling. You can refrigerate the dough overnight if necessary.

3 Make the filling: In a heavy-duty skillet, heat oil over medium heat. Cook sausage until thoroughly browned, about 7 to 10 minutes, breaking up the pieces with a spatula until it is finely crumbled. Stir in minced garlic just before removing from heat. Drain sausage on paper towels.

4 Place a rack in the middle of the oven. Preheat the oven to 375°F. Remove dough from refrigerator and knead with hands until warm and pliable. Divide dough into 8 equal portions. Wrap 7 pieces in plastic wrap to keep them from drying out.

Place 8th piece of dough on sheet of parchment paper or aluminum foil that is anchored on wet paper towel to prevent slipping. Dust dough with white rice flour and place sheet of plastic wrap on top. Use rolling pin to roll dough to a 7-inch circle. Be sure to move rolling pin from center of dough to outer edge, moving around circle in clockwise fashion to assure uniform thickness.

5 Stir Parmesan cheese and nutmeg into ricotta. Place ¼ cup ricotta mixture on dough, slightly to right of center. Top with ⅛ of browned sausage and 1 tablespoon marinara sauce. Fold crust in half and roll edges together to seal calzone. Crimp the sealed edge with a fork, if you wish. Transfer calzone (and parchment or foil underneath it) to a 13 × 9-inch baking sheet. Repeat with remaining 7 pieces of dough and filling, placing each on a separate piece of parchment paper or foil. Brush each calzone with egg-water mixture.

6 Bake 35 to 40 minutes or until calzones are browned and golden. Remove from oven and cool 5 minutes on baking sheet before serving. To serve, top each calzone with 2 tablespoons warmed marinara sauce.

Runzas

MAKES 8 RUNZAS

These beef and cabbage-filled breads, also spelled runsas, were brought to the United States by German-American immigrants. I remember them from my childhood because a restaurant chain near my home in eastern Nebraska served them, and my family would often make the 20-mile round-trip just to buy them. Before I became gluten-free, I used frozen bread dough to make homemade versions but today I use this lighter version, with equally good results. Some people like to add a slice of American cheese to the filling, as well.

CRUST

1 packet (2¼ teaspoons) active dry yeast

2 tablespoons sugar, divided

½ cup warm (110°F) 1% milk (cow's, rice, soy, potato, or nut)

1 cup Carol's Sorghum Blend (page x)

¾ cup tapioca flour

½ cup sweet rice flour

1 tablespoon Expandex modified tapioca starch

1 teaspoon xanthan gum

1 teaspoon guar gum

½ teaspoon lemon pepper

½ teaspoon onion powder

½ teaspoon salt

¼ teaspoon baking soda

½ cup shortening, such as Spectrum Vegetable

White rice flour for dusting

1 egg yolk + 1 tablespoon water for egg wash

1 tablespoon melted butter, for brushing after baking

FILLING

1 tablespoon olive oil

1 pound lean ground beef

½ teaspoon salt, or to taste

½ teaspoon lemon pepper, or to taste

1 garlic clove, minced

3 cups shredded green cabbage (about ½ head)

1 small onion, finely diced

1 Make the crust: In a small bowl, dissolve yeast and 1 teaspoon of the sugar in warm milk. Set aside to foam 5 minutes. Generously grease a 15 × 10-inch baking sheet (not nonstick) or line it with parchment paper.

2 In a food processor, combine the remaining sugar, sorghum blend, flours, modified tapioca starch, xanthan gum, guar gum, lemon pepper, onion powder, salt, baking soda, and shortening and process until the mixture is thoroughly blended. Add yeast mixture and blend until dough forms a ball. If it doesn't form a ball, use a spatula to break up the dough and process again, scraping down the side of the bowl, if necessary. Remove the dough from the food processor and knead it with your hands a few times until it is very smooth. Place the dough in a plastic food-storage bag and refrigerate while making the filling. You can refrigerate overnight if necessary.

3 Make the filling: In a heavy-duty skillet, heat oil over medium-high heat. Cook the ground beef, salt, and lemon pepper until the beef is thoroughly browned, about 7 to 10 minutes, stirring in the minced garlic just before removing the beef from the heat. Drain the beef on paper towels.

4 In the same skillet, add the cabbage and onions and cook over medium heat until the onion and cabbage start to wilt, about 3 to 5 minutes. In a large bowl, combine the browned beef, onions, and cabbage and toss well; set aside.

5 Place a rack in the middle of the oven. Preheat the oven to 375°F. Remove the dough from refrigerator and knead with your hands until it is warm and pliable. Divide the dough into 8 equal pieces. Place 7 pieces in sealed food-storage bag to keep them from drying out. Tear 8 pieces of parchment or foil, each a 10-inch square. Place 8th piece of dough on sheet of parchment paper or aluminum foil that is anchored on wet paper towel to prevent slipping. Dust the dough with white rice flour and place a sheet of plastic wrap on top. Use a rolling pin to roll the dough to a 7-inch circle. Be sure to move the rolling pin from the center of dough to the outer edge, moving around the circle in clockwise fashion to assure uniform thickness.

6 Place about ¾ cup of filling on the circle of dough, slightly to the right of center. Fold the crust in half and roll the edges together to seal the runza. Transfer the runza (and parchment or foil underneath it) to the baking sheet. Repeat with the remaining 7 pieces of dough, each on a separate piece of parchment paper or foil. Brush each runza with egg wash.

7 Bake 35 to 40 minutes or until runzas are browned and golden. Remove the sheet from the oven and cool 5 minutes on a wire rack. Brush runzas with melted butter and serve immediately.

HOLIDAY AND SPECIAL OCCASION BREADS

Brioche

MAKES 20 SERVINGS (1-INCH SLICES)

Brioche is typically made with lots of eggs and therefore is a golden and has a moist texture. It is somewhat similar to Challah (below) but is not quite as sweet.

1 packet (2¼ teaspoons) active dry yeast

¼ cup sugar, divided

¾ cup warm (110°F) 1% milk (cow's, rice, soy, potato, or nut)

White rice flour for dusting

2 cups Carol's Sorghum Blend (page x)

1 cup potato starch

2 teaspoons xanthan gum

1 teaspoon guar gum

1 teaspoon salt

3 large eggs, at room temperature

¼ cup (½ stick) unsalted butter or buttery spread, such as Earth Balance, at room temperature

1 teaspoon cider vinegar

1 egg, beaten, for egg wash

1 In a small bowl, dissolve yeast and 1 teaspoon of the sugar in warm milk. Set aside to foam 5 minutes.

2 Generously grease a 9 × 5-inch nonstick (gray, not black) loaf pan. Dust the bottom and sides of the pan(s) lightly with white rice flour.

3 Sift together sorghum blend, potato starch, xanthan gum, guar gum, salt, and remaining sugar. Set aside.

4 In the medium bowl of a heavy-duty stand mixer, beat eggs on high speed 2 minutes. Reduce speed to low and add dry ingredients, butter, vinegar, and yeast-milk mixture and beat until blended, then increase speed and beat on medium for 30 seconds or until mixture is thoroughly combined. Transfer dough to prepared pan and smooth top with wet spatula. Cover and let rise in a warm place (75°F to 80°F) until dough is level with top of pan. Gently brush top with beaten egg.

5 Place a rack in the middle of the oven. Preheat the oven to 375°F. Bake 55 minutes to 1 hour or until temperature reaches 205°F on an instant-read thermometer inserted into center of loaf. Remove from oven and cool in pan 15 minutes on a wire rack. Remove loaf from pan and cool completely on the wire rack. Slice with an electric knife or a serrated knife.

Challah

MAKES 12 SERVINGS

Pronounced "HA-lah," this is an egg bread, similar to Brioche, but a bit sweeter. Challah is typically braided, but this dough is far too soft, so bake it in a 9 × 5-inch pan instead.

1 packet (2¼ teaspoons) active dry yeast

½ cup warm (110°F) water

White rice flour for dusting

2 large eggs + 2 egg yolks, divided, at room temperature

½ cup canola oil

⅓ to ½ cup sugar

2 cups Carol's Sorghum Blend (page x)

1 cup potato starch

2 tablespoons Expandex modified tapioca starch

1½ teaspoons salt

1 teaspoon xanthan gum

1 teaspoon guar gum

1 teaspoon cider vinegar

1 In a small bowl, dissolve yeast in warm water. Set aside to foam 5 minutes.

2 Generously grease a 9 × 5-inch nonstick (gray, not black) loaf pan. Dust the bottom and sides of the pan lightly with white rice flour.

3 In the large bowl of a heavy-duty mixer, beat eggs and egg yolk on high speed until thick and foamy, about 2 minutes. Blend in oil and sugar. Add sorghum blend, potato starch, modified tapioca starch, salt, xanthan gum, guar gum, vinegar, and yeast-water mixture. Beat on low to blend, then increase speed and beat on medium for 30 seconds or until mixture is thoroughly combined.

4 Transfer dough to pan and smooth top with wet spatula. Let rise in a warm place (75°F to 80°F) until dough is level with top of pan, or about 1 to 1½ hours. Whisk the remaining egg yolk with 1 tablespoon of water and gently brush top of loaf.

5 Place a rack in the middle of the oven. Preheat the oven to 375°F. Bake 50 minutes to 1 hour or until temperature reaches 205°F on an instant-read thermometer inserted into center of loaf. Remove from oven and cool bread in pan 10 minutes on a wire rack. Remove bread from pan and cool completely on the wire rack. Slice with an electric knife or a serrated knife.

Greek Holiday Bread

MAKES 10 SERVINGS

Tradition dictates that the Greeks bury a wrapped coin in the dough of this bread called vasilopita, *and the lucky person who finds it (or breaks a tooth on it) will have good luck the coming year. You can skip the hidden coin tradition and just enjoy this delightful bread.*

1 packet (2¼ teaspoons) active dry yeast

1 cup warm (110°F) 1% milk (cow's, rice, soy, potato, or nut)

2 tablespoons sugar, divided

White rice flour for dusting

2 large eggs, at room temperature

2 tablespoons unsalted butter or buttery spread, such as Earth Balance, at room temperature

1 cup Carol's Sorghum Blend (page x)

1 cup potato starch

¼ cup Expandex modified tapioca starch

2 teaspoons xanthan gum

¾ teaspoon salt

Grated zest of 1 lemon

Grated zest of 1 orange

2 teaspoons vinegar

1 teaspoon pure vanilla extract

1 egg yolk + 1 teaspoon water for egg wash

6 whole blanched almonds (or slivers)

½ teaspoon sesame seeds, for sprinkling on top

1 In a small bowl, dissolve yeast and 1 teaspoon of the sugar in warm milk. Set aside to foam 5 minutes.

2 Generously grease an 8 × 4-inch nonstick (gray, not black) loaf pan. Dust the bottom and sides of the pan lightly with white rice flour.

3 In the large bowl of a heavy-duty mixer, beat eggs on medium speed until thick and foamy, about 2 minutes. Add remaining sugar and butter and blend well on low speed. Add sorghum blend, potato starch, modified tapioca starch, xanthan gum, salt, lemon zest, orange zest, vinegar, vanilla, and yeast-water mixture. Beat on low to blend, then increase speed to medium and beat 30 seconds or until mixture slightly thickens.

4 Transfer dough to pan and smooth top with wet spatula. Brush dough with egg wash and arrange almonds decoratively on top, gently pressing into dough. Sprinkle with sesame seeds. Let rise in a warm place (75°F to 80°F) until dough is 1 inch above top of pan.

5 Place a rack in the middle of the oven. Preheat the oven to 375°F. Bake 1 hour or until temperature reaches 205°F on an instant-read thermometer inserted into center of loaf. Remove from oven and cool bread in pan 10 minutes on a wire rack. Remove bread from pan and cool completely on the wire rack. Slice with an electric knife or a serrated knife.

Panettone

MAKES 10 SERVINGS (2 PANETTONE LOAVES OR AN 8X4-INCH LOAF)

Panettone is an Italian sweet bread flavored with vanilla or anise and filled with dried fruits and citrus zest. The bread is traditionally baked in a paper panettone mold, which can be purchased at kitchen stores. Make several and give them as gifts to your friends, whether they follow a gluten-free diet or not. If you prefer less fruit, reduce each dried fruit from ¼ cup to 2 tablespoons. If you don't have a panettone mold, you can bake the bread in a Bundt cake pan or even a large clean, dry coffee can.

1 packet (2¼ teaspoons) active dry yeast
¼ cup sugar, divided
1 cup warm (110°F) 1% milk (cow's, rice, soy, potato, or nut)
White rice flour for dusting
1 cups Carol's Sorghum Blend (page x)
1 cup potato starch
¼ cup Expandex modified tapioca starch
2 teaspoons xanthan gum
1 teaspoon salt
Grated zest of 1 lemon
Grated zest of 1 orange

2 large eggs, at room temperature
2 tablespoons unsalted butter or buttery spread, such as Earth Balance, or canola oil
2 teaspoons vinegar
1 teaspoon pure vanilla extract
1 teaspoon crushed anise seed or anise-flavored extract
¼ cup golden raisins
¼ cup dried currants
¼ cup dried cranberries
¼ cup pine nuts
½ cup powdered sugar mixed with 1 tablespoon 1% milk (cow's, rice, soy, potato, or nut)

1 In a small bowl, combine yeast and 2 teaspoons of the sugar in warm milk. Set aside to foam 5 minutes.

2 Generously grease 2 panettone molds or an 8 × 4-inch nonstick (gray, not black) loaf pan. Dust the bottom and sides of the pans lightly with white rice flour.

3 In the bowl of a heavy-duty mixer, beat sorghum blend, potato starch, modified tapioca starch, xanthan gum, salt, lemon zest, orange zest, and remaining sugar on low speed just until blended. Add eggs, butter, vinegar, vanilla, anise, and yeast-milk mixture. Beat on low just until blended, about 30 seconds. Do not overbeat. Stir in dried fruit and nuts.

4 Transfer dough to prepared pan(s) and smooth top with a wet spatula. Coat with cooking spray, if desired. Place pan(s) in a warm place (75°F to 80°F) and allow to rise until dough is level with top of pan. Place a rack in the middle of the oven. Preheat the oven to 375°F. With a sharp knife, cut an "x", ⅛-inch deep, in top of each loaf.

5 Bake 25 to 30 minutes or until top of loaves are lightly browned. Remove pans from oven and cool 10 minutes on wire rack. Remove bread from pan and cool completely. Mix together powdered sugar and milk to form glaze. Drizzle glaze over loaves. Slice with an electric or a serrated knife.

Stollen

MAKES 10 SERVINGS

While traveling in Austria just before Thanksgiving, I saw these holiday breads everywhere—gaily packaged and ready for gift giving. Determined to have my own, I developed this recipe. Since gluten-free dough is too soft to shape like traditional stollen, bake it in mini-loaves or a 9 × 5-inch nonstick (gray, not black) loaf pan instead.

1 packet (2¼ teaspoons) active dry yeast

¾ cup warm (110°F) 1% milk (cow's, rice, soy, potato, or nut)

White rice flour for dusting

¼ cup unsalted butter or buttery spread, such as Earth Balance, melted and cooled + 1 tablespoon for brushing tops

2 large eggs, at room temperature

2 teaspoons pure vanilla extract

½ teaspoon almond-flavored extract

1 tablespoon grated lemon zest

1⅓ cups Carol's Sorghum Blend (page x)

2 tablespoons Expandex modified tapioca starch, or Carol's Sorghum Blend (page x)

½ cup sugar

1 teaspoon xanthan gum

¾ teaspoon salt

¼ teaspoon grated nutmeg

¼ cup sliced almonds or chopped pecans

¼ cup golden raisins

¼ cup dried currants

¼ cup candied citrus peel or orange peel

1 tablespoon canola oil

1 tablespoon sugar

1 In a small bowl, dissolve the yeast in the warm milk. Set aside to foam 5 minutes.

2 Generously grease 3 mini-5 × 3-inch or a 9 × 5-inch nonstick (gray, not black) pan(s). Dust the bottom and sides of the pan(s) lightly with white rice flour.

3 Place a rack in the middle of the oven. Preheat the oven to 350°F.

4 In a large mixing bowl, beat the butter, eggs, vanilla and almond extracts, and lemon zest with an electric mixer on low speed. Beat in yeast-milk mixture until blended. Add sorghum blend, modified tapioca starch, sugar, xanthan gum, salt, and nutmeg and beat on low just until dough thickens slightly. Gently stir in nuts, raisins, currants, and candied orange peel. Transfer dough to prepared pan(s) and smooth top with wet spatula. Brush with canola oil. Sprinkle with sugar.

5 Bake 25 to 30 minutes or until crust is lightly browned. Remove from oven and cool in pan(s) 10 minutes on a wire rack. Slice with an electric or a serrated knife.

APPETIZERS AND SNACKS

Dips and Dippers

Hummus

Creamy White Bean Dip

Pinto Bean Dip

Guacamole

Roasted Artichoke Dip

Crab Cocktail Spread

Crackers

Oven-Baked Tortilla Chips

Nibbles

Savory Spiced Nuts

Sweet and Spicy Cashews

Toasted Pumpkin Seeds

Crispy, Old-Fashioned
Savory Snack Mix

Warmed Olives in Herbs

Fried Onion Flower

Finger Foods

Antipasto Plate

Stuffed Dates

Tapenade-Stuffed Cherry
Tomatoes

Dolmades (Stuffed Grape Leaves)

Lettuce Wraps

Pizza Sticks with Marinara Sauce

Mini Polenta Rounds with Pesto

Empanadas

Roasted Wild Mushroom Tart

Cheese

Brie with Honey and
Chopped Nuts

Feta Cheese Crisps

Olive Puffs

Smoked Salmon Cheesecake
Squares

Simple Cheese Quesadillas

Mini-Refried Bean Quesadillas

Smoked Salmon Quesadillas

Veggie Mini-Quiches

Prosciutto and Chive
Mini-Quiches

"Little bites" aptly describes the offerings in this chapter. These are recipes for appetizers or snacks, foods that can be eaten in very small quantities to tide you over between meals or in combination as a meal.

Many restaurants serve small plates—sometimes called *tapas*—which means "cover" or "lid" in Spanish, and originates from the custom of placing a small hunk of bread over a glass of wine to keep the flies out. Of course, people ate the bread and the idea of little snacks with drinks became a tradition. This style of dining is seen in the Italian antipasti and Greek *meze* traditions, as well as in wine bars everywhere where delicious small-plate offerings cover the globe.

I chose the recipes for this chapter to follow this tradition. Some recipes are based on foods served in restaurants (e.g., lettuce wraps, quesadillas, quiches, or empanadas), and some are items typically thought of as snacks (e.g., crackers, dips, chips, nuts) that are served between meals or as an appetizers before meals. But don't stop there.

You can create appetizers from the main dishes, side dishes, and even the breakfast dishes in this book—just serve them in tiny portions, and if serving several together, try to offer a range of flavors and textures. For example, some restaurants offer egg frittatas as tapas, while others serve vegetable or potato dishes. A main dish such as Shrimp Tempura or Beef Kabobs will work as appetizers. Little panini sandwiches could also be appetizers. Let your imagination be your guide and delight your family and guests with your creativity.

DIPS AND DIPPERS

Hummus Q V

**MAKES 6 SERVINGS
(ABOUT ½ CUP EACH)**

Hummus is a Middle-Eastern dish of pureed chickpeas and tahini, which is sesame seed paste. You can find hummus in many stores, but store-bought versions may be overly seasoned or may not taste fresh. When you make your own, you control the amount of seasonings, and the lemon juice and garlic add a freshness that you can't buy in a jar or a can. Use hummus as a dip with chips or vegetables or as a spread for sandwiches.

1 can (16 ounces) chickpeas, undrained
¼ cup roasted tahini (sesame seed paste)
1 garlic clove, minced (or more to taste)
3 tablespoons olive oil
¼ cup fresh lemon juice
1 teaspoon salt
1 teaspoon ground cumin
1 teaspoon ground coriander
½ teaspoon freshly ground black pepper
¼ teaspoon crushed red pepper flakes

In a food processor, place chickpeas and their juice and all remaining ingredients and puree until smooth, scraping down sides of the bowl frequently. If the mixture is too thick, add water, 1 tablespoon at a time, to reach the desired consistency. Serve at room temperature.

Creamy White Bean Dip Ⓠ Ⓥ

MAKES 4 SERVINGS (A GENEROUS
¼ CUP EACH)

Similar to hummus, this classic bean dip is simple to whip up and always appropriate, even for your vegetarian guests.

1 can (14 to 15 ounces) white kidney beans or cannellini beans, drained and rinsed
2 tablespoons fresh lemon juice
2 tablespoons extra-virgin olive oil, or 1 tablespoon olive oil and 1 tablespoon sesame oil
½ teaspoon ground cumin
¼ teaspoon garlic powder
¼ teaspoon salt
¼ teaspoon freshly ground black pepper
2 teaspoons chopped fresh parsley or ½ teaspoon dried, for garnish
1 package gluten-free crackers, such as Mary's Gone Crackers

1 In a food processor, combine beans, lemon juice, oil, cumin, garlic powder, salt, and pepper and process until the beans are smooth. Scrape down the side of the bowl and process again until all the beans are mashed.

2 Remove the dip from the food processor to a decorative bowl and garnish with parsley. Chill, covered, until serving time. Bring to room temperature before serving with gluten-free crackers.

Pinto Bean Dip Ⓠ Ⓥ

MAKES 4 SERVINGS (A GENEROUS
¼ CUP EACH)

You can certainly buy refried bean dips, but this homemade variety has a fresh flavor that you and your guests will appreciate. Serve this dip with homemade or store-bought tortilla chips or use it in recipes that call for bean dip (such as the Mini-Refried Bean Quesadillas on page 145).

1 garlic clove, minced
1 teaspoon salt
1 can (14 to 15 ounces) pinto beans, drained and rinsed
1 teaspoon chili powder
1 teaspoon extra-virgin olive oil
½ teaspoon ground cumin
½ teaspoon ground coriander
1 teaspoon fresh oregano or ½ teaspoon dried
1 tablespoon hot water, or more as needed
¼ cup chopped fresh cilantro, for garnish
¼ cup chopped fresh green onions, for garnish

1 On a cutting board, mash the garlic and salt together with the flat side of a knife to a coarse paste.

2 In a food processor, combine the garlic-salt mixture, beans, chili powder, oil, cumin, coriander, oregano, and water and blend until smooth, adding another tablespoon of hot water if the mixture is too stiff for spreading or dipping. Serve immediately or refrigerate, tightly covered, for 2 days. Bring to room temperature before serving. Sprinkle with cilantro and green onions. Serve immediately.

Guacamole Ⓠ Ⓥ

MAKES 8 SERVINGS (ABOUT ½ CUP EACH)

Guacamole is made from mashed avocados, and there is a standard set of ingredients that are used in its preparation: lime juice, onion, garlic, peppers, salt, and pepper. But the proportions and other modifications give each cook's guacamole its own personality. This is the one my family loves— even my grandson started eating it when he was eighteen months old. You can vary the heat by how much jalapeño you use; be sure to wear protective gloves when cutting the jalapeño to avoid getting burned by the chile oil.

4 Hass avocadoes, halved, peeled and pitted

2 vine-ripened tomatoes, seeded and finely chopped

½ cup red onion, finely diced

1 small jalapeño chile pepper, seeded and finely diced

½ cup chopped fresh cilantro

2 tablespoons fresh lime juice

1 small garlic clove, minced (optional)

¼ teaspoon salt (or to taste)

⅛ teaspoon white pepper (or to taste)

In a large bowl, mash avocadoes coarsely with a fork. Add tomatoes, onion, jalapeño, cilantro, lime juice, garlic, salt, and pepper and mix until thoroughly blended. Serve immediately or cover tightly and refrigerate up to 1 hour. If you store guacamole any longer, it tends to discolor.

Roasted Artichoke Dip

MAKES 8 SERVINGS (ABOUT ¼ CUP EACH)

I always keep frozen artichokes in my freezer because they are so versatile and bring a wonderful Mediterranean flavor to a wide variety of dishes.

½ cup fresh lemon juice, divided

⅔ cup extra-virgin olive oil, divided

2 large garlic cloves, minced

½ teaspoon salt

¼ teaspoon freshly ground black pepper

1 package (14 ounces) frozen artichokes, thawed

2 teaspoons dried thyme leaves

2 teaspoons dried basil leaves

2 tablespoons grated Parmesan cheese, or soy alternative, such as Soyco

Additional salt and pepper to taste

1 Place a rack in the middle of the oven. Preheat the oven to 350°F. In a large, heavy ovenproof skillet, combine 6 tablespoons of the lemon juice, 2 tablespoons of the olive oil, garlic, salt, and pepper.

Add artichokes and toss to coat with lemon juice mixture. Bring mixture to boil, remove from heat, and place skillet, uncovered, in preheated oven.

2 Bake 30 to 45 minutes, or until artichokes are tender and lightly browned. Remove from oven and cool.

3 Place roasted artichokes in a food processor and add the remaining lemon juice, the remaining oil, and the thyme, basil, and Parmesan cheese. Process until thoroughly blended. Taste and add additional salt and pepper, if desired. Serve immediately.

Crab Cocktail Spread

MAKES 4 SERVINGS (ABOUT ½ CUP EACH)

This classic favorite tastes delicious and is so easy to put together at the last minute.

1 package (8 ounces) cream cheese or cream cheese alternative, such as Tofutti, at room temperature

½ cup gluten-free cocktail sauce, such as Hy-Vee or Safeway

1 can (7.5 ounces) lump crabmeat, picked over

1 package gluten-free crackers, such as Mary's Gone Crackers

Place the softened cream cheese on a serving plate and drizzle the cocktail sauce over the cheese. Gently place the crabmeat on top. Serve with gluten-free crackers.

Crackers

MAKES 6 SERVINGS (3 CRACKERS EACH)

Despite all the delicious gluten-free crackers available these days, you might still want to make your own with this recipe. The Expandex (a modified tapioca starch) makes them crispy, which is an important quality in crackers.

1 cup Carol's Sorghum Blend (page x)

2 tablespoons Expandex modified tapioca starch

1 tablespoon sugar

1 teaspoon onion powder

½ teaspoon xanthan gum

½ teaspoon baking powder

½ teaspoon salt

¼ teaspoon garlic powder

2 tablespoons unsalted butter or buttery spread, such as Earth Balance, at room temperature

2 tablespoons corn syrup

1 large egg

2 tablespoons Parmesan cheese, or soy alternative such as Soyco

1 tablespoon sesame seeds, divided

1 Place a rack in the middle of the oven. Preheat the oven to 350°F. Line a 13 × 9-inch baking sheet (not nonstick) with parchment paper.

2 In a food processor, combine the sorghum blend, modified tapioca starch, sugar, onion powder, xanthan gum, baking powder, salt, and garlic powder. Pulse a few times until the ingredients are thoroughly blended.

3 Add the butter, corn syrup, egg, Parmesan cheese, and 1½ teaspoons sesame seeds. Pulse a few times to moisten the dough and then process until the dough forms a soft ball. Remove the dough from the food processor and knead it with your hands until it is soft and smooth. Shape it into a flat disk.

4 On a flat surface such as the countertop, lay a sheet of parchment paper on a wet paper towel. Place the ball of dough on the parchment paper and lay a sheet of heavy-duty plastic wrap on top. With a rolling pin, roll the dough to ⅛-inch thickness. Remove the plastic wrap and cut the dough into 2-inch circles with a biscuit cutter. Place the crackers on the

baking sheet at least 1 inch apart. Re-roll the scraps to ⅛-inch thickness, cut as many shapes as possible, and transfer the crackers to the baking sheet. Sprinkle with the remaining sesame 1½ teaspoons seeds.

5 Bake 10 minutes, or until the crackers look firm and slightly toasted. Remove from oven and cool the crackers on the pan on a wire rack.

Oven-Baked Tortilla Chips

MAKES 8 SERVINGS (6 CHIPS EACH)

You can buy tortilla chips, of course, but when you make them yourself, you control the amount of fat and salt. Oven baking requires far less fat using my cooking spray method, and salting the chips just after they come out of the oven makes the salt cling better. Plus, I think freshly-baked chips are absolutely delicious.

12 gluten-free white corn tortillas, such as Tamxico
Cooking spray
¼ teaspoon salt

1 Place a rack in the middle of the oven. Preheat the oven to 375°F. Line a 13 × 9-inch baking sheet (not nonstick) with foil.

2 Cut tortillas into wedges and place in single layer on prepared sheet. Spray lightly with cooking spray. Turn wedges over and spray other side. Lay an ovenproof wire rack on top to prevent the chips from curling. (If you want them curled, then don't use the wire rack.)

3 Bake the chips until they are crisp. Baking time will depend on the type and thickness of the tortillas you choose. Sprinkle the tortillas with salt as soon as you remove the chips from the oven and serve immediately.

NIBBLES

Savory Spiced Nuts

MAKES 8 SERVINGS (¼ CUP EACH)

Spiced nuts make a very simple appetizer or snack. They can be made ahead of time and gently warmed in a 200°F oven just before your guests arrive, filling the house with a marvelous aroma. You can also add them to bowls of popcorn, or use them in the Crispy, Old-Fashioned Savory Snack Mix (page 136).

1 teaspoon olive oil
1 teaspoon chili powder
¼ teaspoon ground cumin
½ teaspoon garlic powder
½ teaspoon salt
2 cups shelled nuts such as walnut halves, pecan halves, or almonds or a mixture of nuts of similar sizes

1 Place a rack in the middle of the oven. Preheat the oven to 325°F. In a large bowl, toss olive oil with chili powder, cumin, garlic powder, and salt. Add nuts and toss until thoroughly and evenly coated. Arrange in a single layer on a large baking sheet.

2 Bake 45 minutes to 1 hour, shaking pan occasionally to promote even browning. Serve slightly warm.

Sweet and Spicy Cashews

MAKES 8 SERVINGS (¼ CUP EACH)

Sometimes, the perfect accompaniment to a selection of savory appetizers is a slightly sweet dish, such as these yummy cashews roasted in a simple apple pie spice mixture. In the unlikely event that there are any leftovers, use them as garnish for apple pie, fruit crisps, or your favorite ice cream.

1 large egg white
1 teaspoon water
2 cups whole unsalted cashews
½ cup sugar
2 teaspoons apple pie spice (or pumpkin pie spice), or to taste

1 Place a rack in the middle of the oven. Preheat the oven to 250°F. Lightly grease a 15 × 10-inch baking sheet (not nonstick) or line it with parchment paper.

2 Beat the egg white and water with an electric mixer or by hand with a whisk until very frothy. Toss the cashews in the egg mixture and then place them in a sieve to drain slightly.

3 In a medium bowl, whisk together the sugar and spice until well combined. Add the cashews and toss until the nuts are thoroughly coated. Arrange the cashews in the pan in a single layer.

4 Bake until dry, about 45 minutes to 1 hour. Remove from oven and cool completely on a wire rack. Break the nuts apart if they are stuck together. Serve at room temperature.

Toasted Pumpkin Seeds

MAKES 4 SERVINGS (¼ CUP EACH)

Most people have tried unshelled pumpkin seeds or popped a few of the green, hulled seeds on occasion. But hulled and toasted pumpkin seeds are quite another thing; you won't recognize them! Instead, you'll think you're eating an exotic nut. This nosh is especially appropriate for people with nut allergies since toasted pumpkin seeds may taste like nuts, but they aren't nuts at all—pumpkins are actually members of the squash family.

1 cup raw, hulled pumpkin seeds (green in color)
½ teaspoon extra-virgin olive oil
⅛ teaspoon salt
⅛ teaspoon ground cumin (optional)
Pinch cayenne (optional)

1 Place a rack in the middle of the oven. Preheat the oven to 300°F. Line a 13 × 9-inch baking sheet (not nonstick) with foil.

2 In a small bowl, combine the pumpkin seeds and oil. Spread on the prepared baking sheet.

3 Roast the pumpkin seeds 15 to 20 minutes, until lightly browned (time may vary according to size and moisture in seeds, so watch carefully). Remove from the oven and toss with the salt, cumin, and cayenne, if using, until coated thoroughly. Serve warm.

Crispy, Old-Fashioned Savory Snack Mix

MAKES 8 SERVINGS (A GENEROUS
1 CUP EACH)

Everyone remembers the old-fashioned cereal mixes served at parties in the 1970s and 1980s. This version is only lightly salted and seasoned, making it appropriate for folks of all ages. If your tastes run spicier, use "heaping" amounts when measuring the seasonings next time.

4 cups Rice Chex
2 cups O-shaped cereal, such as CerOs by
    Heartland's Finest or Perky's
½ cup cashew halves
½ cup pecan halves
1 tablespoon unsalted butter or buttery spread, such
    as Earth Balance, melted
1 tablespoon gluten-free Worcestershire sauce, such
    as French's
Dash hot pepper sauce
½ teaspoon sugar
½ teaspoon gluten-free seasoning salt, such as Lawry's
¼ teaspoon onion powder
¼ teaspoon garlic powder
Cooking spray
¼ cup grated Parmesan cheese, or soy alternative,
    such as Soyco
1 cup gluten-free pretzels, such as Glutano or
    Ener-G Foods
1 cup gluten-free corn chips, such as Fritos

1 Place a rack in the middle of the oven. Preheat the oven to 250°F. In a large bowl, combine the cereals and nuts. In a small microwavable measuring cup, combine the butter, Worcestershire sauce, hot pepper sauce, sugar, seasoning salt, onion powder, and garlic powder and heat in the microwave on low 1 to 3 minutes until the butter is melted. Stir thoroughly to blend. Add to cereal mixture, stirring until thoroughly coated. Spray with cooking spray, if desired, and toss to coat the ingredients. Spread the mixture on a large 15 × 10-inch nonstick baking sheet.

2 Bake 45 to 50 minutes, stirring occasionally, until the mixture is lightly browned and crisp. Remove from the oven and immediately sprinkle with Parmesan cheese. Stir in pretzels and corn ships. Cool thoroughly. Store in airtight container.

Asian Savory Snack Mix: Add 3 teaspoons Chinese 5-spice powder. Replace Worcestershire sauce with gluten-free teriyaki sauce, such as Premier Japan.

Warmed Olives in Herbs

MAKES 4 SERVINGS (½ CUP EACH)

Several years ago, I was sitting with friends on their patio in the foothills of the Rocky Mountains, munching on herbed olives. Out of the corner of my eye, I noticed a fox keenly watching us, sitting within three feet of my husband. Soon, another fox crept to the edge of the patio, waiting. It turns out they were expecting their daily snack from the host. It was wonderful to note how easily we were communing with our natural environment (and what good taste these foxes had!).

2 cups olives of your choice, drained
1 sprig fresh rosemary
1 sprig fresh thyme
1 (3-inch) strip lemon zest (no white)
1 garlic clove, halved
¼ teaspoon fennel seeds
¼ teaspoon crushed red pepper
2 tablespoons extra-virgin olive oil

1 Place a rack in the middle of the oven. Preheat the oven to 350°F. Combine all the ingredients on a heavy-duty sheet of foil (or use two sheets of foil). Fold up edges of the foil to create a pocket and place on a small baking sheet.

2 Bake 15 to 20 minutes, or until the olives become fragrant. Serve warm.

Fried Onion Flower

MAKES 4 SERVINGS (¼ OF ONION EACH)

This is the classic fried onion that is commonly served in restaurants. The idea here is that each person peels off one "petal" of onion at a time, and eats it like a potato chip, although this showy dish is so tempting that you'll want to eat all the petals yourself. They may look complicated, but they're quite easy to prepare at home. Vidalia or Spanish onions work better in this dish because they're sweeter.

1 large yellow Vidalia or Spanish onion
½ cup white rice flour
2 tablespoons cornstarch
¼ teaspoon garlic powder
½ teaspoon salt
½ teaspoon fresh oregano or ¼ teaspoon dried
⅛ teaspoon cayenne pepper
¼ teaspoon fresh thyme or ⅛ teaspoon dried
⅛ teaspoon ground cumin
⅛ teaspoon freshly ground black pepper
1 large egg
¼ cup water
Canola oil for frying (do not use olive oil; it will burn)

1 Remove the paper skin from the onion and cut a ¼-inch slice from the top of the onion. With a very sharp knife, cut down from the top of the onion through the center of the onion to within ½ inch of the bottom, leaving the root end intact. Turn the onion 90 degrees, and slice through the center of the onion, again to within ½ inch of the bottom. Now you have an onion with 4 sections. Keep rotating the onion 10 degrees at a time cutting through the center of the onion until you have made 16 slices. Spread the "petals" of the onion apart slightly so the coating can reach the innermost parts of the onion blossom.

2 In a bowl, sift together the flour, cornstarch, garlic powder, salt, oregano, cayenne, thyme, cumin, and pepper; set aside. In a measuring cup, whisk together the egg and water until very foamy and all the egg membrane is broken up. Using a pastry brush, coat the onion petals with the egg mixture. Place the flour mixture in a sieve and liberally dust the onion with the flour mixture.

3 In a deep fryer or a deep pot, heat the oil to 350°F. There should be enough oil to cover the onion. Carefully place the onion right side up in the oil and fry 10 minutes, or until it is browned. With a large slotted spatula or spoon, remove it from the oil and drain it on paper towels. Serve immediately.

FINGER FOODS

Antipasto Plate

MAKES 4 SERVINGS

Relying solely on store-bought ingredients, this appetizer can be assembled in seconds on a pretty tray and served to your guests. I rely on the deli at my local natural food store for these items.

1 jar (4.5 ounces) marinated artichokes, drained
¼ pound fresh mozzarella cheese balls (bocconcini)
¼ pound cured Italian meats of your choice, thinly sliced
¼ pound pitted kalamata olives or a blend of pitted olives
¼ pound roasted red peppers
1 package gluten-free crackers, such as Mary's Gone Crackers

Assemble the artichokes, cheese, Italian meats, olives, and red peppers decoratively on a large tray, preferably one with indentations. Or place each item in its own little bowl on a larger tray. Serve with gluten-free crackers.

Stuffed Dates

MAKES 8 SERVINGS (2 DATES EACH)

The hardest part of this simple appetizer is slitting the date and removing the pit. Once that's done, it's a breeze to stuff them. Dates and almonds are extremely healthy, and the little strip of Swiss cheese adds just the right savory contrast.

16 whole dates
1 slice Swiss cheese or cheese alternative, such as Vegan Gourmet, sliced into ⅛-inch strips
16 small whole almonds

Slit each date lengthwise from end to end and remove the pit. Place a strip of cheese and a whole almond inside each date and press shut. Arrange on a serving plate or a small bowl. These can be made ahead and chilled. Bring to room temperature before serving.

Tapenade-Stuffed Cherry Tomatoes Ⓥ

MAKES 4 SERVINGS (4 TOMATOES EACH)

Tapenade is simply pureed olive spread, and a simple way to add loads of flavor to pretty red cherry tomatoes, which in turn add a festive note to an appetizer plate.

16 cherry tomatoes
¼ cup store-bought tapenade or olive spread
2 tablespoons chopped fresh parsley or 1 tablespoon dried, for garnish

1 With a sharp knife, slice ¼ inch off the stem end and ⅛ inch off the bottom of each tomato. Discard the trimmed parts. Using a ¼-teaspoon measuring spoon, remove the juice and seeds from each tomato, leaving the outside shell intact.

2 Spoon about ¼ teaspoon tapenade into each tomato shell and garnish with the parsley. Arrange on a platter and chill 2 hours. Bring to room temperature before serving.

Dolmades (Stuffed Grape Leaves) Ⓥ

MAKES 6 SERVINGS (5 DOLMADES EACH)

You can buy ready-made stuffed grape leaves (dolmades in Greek) in gourmet food shops, but you can also make your own for a fresher, mellower flavor. Your guests will appreciate this wonderful change from the typical bread and cracker appetizers.

¼ cup extra-virgin olive oil

1 large yellow onion, finely chopped

1 cup long-grain white rice

1½ cups gluten-free, low-sodium chicken broth, such as Swanson's Natural Goodness, or homemade Chicken Broth (page 676)

2 tablespoons finely chopped fresh dill weed

2 tablespoons finely chopped flat-leaf parsley

2 tablespoons finely chopped fresh mint leaves

2 teaspoons fresh oregano or 1 teaspoon dried

1 teaspoon grated lemon zest

Kosher salt and freshly ground black pepper

1 jar (8 ounces) grape leaves

Juice of 2 lemons

1 In a medium heavy pan, heat 2 tablespoons of the oil over medium heat. Add the onion and cook, stirring, until soft, about 10 minutes. Add the rice and cook 2 minutes, stirring to coat the rice with oil. Pour in ½ cup of the broth. Reduce the heat to low and simmer, covered, until the liquid is absorbed and the rice is al dente, about 10 minutes. Transfer the rice mixture to a bowl and stir in the dill, parsley, mint, oregano, lemon zest, and salt and pepper to taste; set aside.

2 Fill a Dutch oven or other deep, heavy pot with a tight-fitting lid with water and bring to a boil over high heat. Reduce the heat to medium-low and blanch the grape leaves in the hot water 5 minutes, or until pliable. Drain the leaves on paper towels and trim away the stems and hard veins. Pat the leaves dry with paper towels. Drain the water from the Dutch oven to ready it for cooking the dolmades.

3 Assemble the dolmades by laying a grape leaf on a work surface, shiny-side down. Put 2 tablespoons of the rice filling near the stem end of the leaf. Fold the stem end over the filling, fold both sides toward the middle, and roll up into a cylinder. (Don't roll the leaves too tightly because the rice will expand as it cooks.) Repeat with the remaining grape leaves and filling placing the rolled leaves in the Dutch oven seam-side down in a single layer. Pour the remaining broth, the remaining

olive oil, and the lemon juice over the dolmades. If the liquid doesn't reach at least halfway up the rolls, add additional water.

4 Cover the Dutch oven and simmer 30 to 40 minutes over low heat, or until the dolmades are tender when pierced with a fork. Serve warm, at room temperature, or cool.

Lettuce Wraps

MAKES 8 SERVINGS (2 WRAPS EACH)

These wraps are most often served as appetizers in restaurants, but they are hearty enough to be a meal for 4 people if you increase the serving size to 4 wraps per person.

1 tablespoon peanut oil or canola oil

1 pound ground pork, turkey, or chicken

1 small red bell pepper, diced

2 cups packaged cabbage and carrot slaw (or 1 cup shredded cabbage and 1 cup shredded carrot)

1 cup chopped fresh cilantro, divided

6 green onions, sliced thinly

1 tablespoon minced fresh ginger

1 garlic clove, minced (or more to taste)

1 tablespoon wheat-free tamari soy sauce, such as Crystal, or San-J

1 tablespoon gluten-free Asian fish sauce, such as A Taste of Thai

1 tablespoon gluten-free Thai sweet chile sauce, such as A Taste of Thai

1 teaspoon Asian sesame oil

1 English (or hothouse) cucumber, diced

16 Boston or Bibb lettuce leaves, washed and patted dry

1 In a large, heavy skillet, heat the peanut oil until hot. Add the pork and cook over medium heat until browned and cooked through, about 5 to 7 minutes. Transfer pork to a plate.

2 In the same skillet, add the bell pepper, cabbage, ¾ cup cilantro, green onions, ginger, garlic, soy sauce, fish sauce, chile sauce, sesame oil, and cucumber. Cook over medium heat, stirring constantly, about 10 to 15 minutes, or until cabbage starts to wilt. Add browned pork and heat to serving temperature. Transfer mixture to serving plate and garnish with remaining cilantro.

3 Arrange the lettuce leaves on a serving platter. To eat, spoon the pork mixture on a lettuce leaf and roll up like a taco or burrito. Serve immediately.

Pizza Sticks with Marinara Sauce

MAKES 4 SERVINGS (3 STICKS EACH)

I've often salivated while watching others eat this appetizer in restaurants, but you can enjoy them at home fresh from your oven.

1 tablespoon active dry yeast

½ cup warm (110°F) 1% milk (cow's, rice, soy, potato, or nut)

½ cup Carol's Sorghum Blend (page x)

½ cup potato starch

1 tablespoon sugar

2 teaspoons xanthan gum

1 teaspoon guar gum

½ to ¾ teaspoon salt

2 tablespoons grated Parmesan or Romano cheese, or soy alternative, such as Soyco

1 teaspoon onion powder

1 teaspoon Italian seasoning, plus additional for sprinkling

1 tablespoon olive oil

1 teaspoon cider vinegar

1 cup store-bought gluten-free marinara or pasta sauce, such as Classico, or homemade Marinara Sauce (page 672), warmed

1 In a small bowl, dissolve the yeast in warm milk. Set aside for 5 minutes to foam.

2 In a medium mixer bowl, blend the yeast-milk mixture, flour blend, potato starch, sugar, xanthan gum, guar gum, salt, Parmesan cheese, onion powder, Italian seasoning, oil, and vinegar with an electric mixer on low speed 1 minute, or process the ingredients in a food processor until thoroughly combined. The dough will be soft and sticky.

3 Place the dough in a large, heavy-duty plastic freezer bag. Cut a ½-inch opening diagonally on a bottom corner to make a 1-inch circle. Generously grease a 13 × 9-inch nonstick (gray, not black) baking sheet or line with parchment paper for best results.

4 Squeeze the dough out of the plastic bag onto prepared sheet in 12 strips, each 1 inch wide by 4 inches long. For best results, hold bag of dough upright as you squeeze, rather than at an angle. Also, hold bag with corners perpendicular to baking sheets, rather than horizontal, for more authentic-looking breadsticks. Lightly sprinkle with Italian seasoning.

5 Place a rack in the middle of the oven. Place the baking sheet on rack and turn on the oven to 400°F. Bake 15 to 20 minutes or until golden brown. Rotate sheet halfway through baking to assure even browning. Remove the baking sheet from the oven and cool the sticks on the pan on a wire rack for 10 minutes. Serve with warmed marinara sauce for dipping.

Mini Polenta Rounds with Pesto Ⓠ Ⓥ

MAKES 4 SERVINGS (3 ROUNDS EACH)

You can cook your own polenta (see page 226) and cut it into rounds, then proceed with this recipe, but using the prepared polenta saves considerable time.

1 tube prepared polenta (in your choice of flavor), such as Food Merchant by Quinoa Corporation

¼ cup cornstarch

2 tablespoons olive oil

Salt and pepper, to taste (optional)

¼ cup store-bought basil pesto or homemade Basil Pesto (page 672)

¼ cup toasted pine nuts

Parmesan cheese, or Soy alternative, such as Soyco for garnish

Paprika, for garnish

1 Cut the polenta into ¼-inch-thick rounds. Dust both sides lightly with the cornstarch.

2 In a heavy, nonstick (gray, not black) skillet heat the oil over medium-high heat. Cook a few polenta rounds at a time, turning occasionally, until golden brown on both sides. Drain on paper towels. Repeat with remaining polenta. Sprinkle with salt and pepper, if desired. Cool slightly.

3 Spread each polenta round with pesto, dividing evenly. Sprinkle with pine nuts, pressing them down with your fingers. Dust with Parmesan cheese and paprika. Serve immediately.

Empanadas Ⓥ

MAKES 4 SERVINGS (4 EMPANADAS EACH)

Empanadas are little half-moon-shaped breads commonly served in Mexico and the Southwest, and filled with just about anything you could imagine. I use a bean paste here because it's easy and flavorful, and the smooth bean paste won't break the delicate dough.

CRUST

1 cup Carol's Sorghum Blend (page x)

¾ cup tapioca flour

¼ cup sweet rice flour

1 tablespoon sugar, divided

2 teaspoons guar gum

½ teaspoon salt

¼ teaspoon baking soda

½ cup shortening, such as Crisco, Earth Balance or Spectrum Vegetable

⅓ cup 1% milk (cow's, rice, soy, potato, or nut)

1 teaspoon vinegar

White rice flour for dusting

1 egg yolk + 1 teaspoon water for egg wash (optional)

FILLING

1 can (9 ounces) bean dip

1 Make the crust: In a food processor, combine sorghum blend, flours, sugar, guar gum, salt, baking soda, and shortening and process until blended. Add the milk and vinegar and blend until the dough forms a ball. If it doesn't form a ball, use a spatula to break dough into pieces and process again, scraping down sides if necessary. Remove dough from food processor and knead with hands a few times until smooth. Flatten the dough to 1-inch disk, place in food storage bag, and chill 1 hour to distribute liquid throughout dough.

2 Place a rack in the middle of the oven. Preheat the oven to 375°F. Line a 13 × 9-inch nonstick (gray, not black) baking sheet with parchment paper or aluminum foil.

3 Massage dough in your hands until it is warm and pliable; this makes the crust easier to handle. Divide the dough into quarters; keep remaining 3 quarters in plastic wrap to avoiding drying out.

4 With a rolling pin, roll ¼ of dough to 7-inch square between two pieces of heavy-duty plastic wrap dusted with rice flour. Place a damp paper towel between countertop and plastic wrap to prevent slipping. Roll from center of dough to outer edge, moving around the circle in clockwise fashion to assure uniform thickness.

5 Remove the top plastic wrap and cut 4 circles using a 3-inch cookie cutter. Place a scant teaspoon of bean dip slightly to the right of center on the dough. Use a thin spatula or knife to lift the left side of the dough up and over the right side to form a half-circle. Using a fork coated with cooking spray, press edges with fork tines to seal. Gently transfer the empanada with a spatula to the baking sheet. Repeat with remaining dough and filling. Brush empanadas with egg-water mixture.

6 Bake 15 to 20 minutes or until nicely browned. Serve immediately.

Roasted Wild Mushroom Tart

MAKES 8 SERVINGS [3 TARTS EACH]

Matt Selby is Executive Chef and Partner at Vesta Dipping Grill in Denver, Colorado, and has been named one of the best chefs in the city. Matt is skilled at meeting the special dietary needs of his customers, as illustrated in this creative tart that uses almond flour in the crust.

PÂTE BRISÉE

2 cups almond flour, such as Bob's Red Mill

¼ cup white bean flour, such as Bob's Red Mill

2½ teaspoons sugar

2½ teaspoons salt

1 teaspoon xanthan gum

½ teaspoon baking powder

½ teaspoon freshly ground black pepper

1 tablespoon truffle oil

½ cup (1 stick) cold unsalted butter or buttery spread, such as Earth Balance, cut into small pieces

¼ cup heavy cream or 3 tablespoons soy milk, as needed

1 tablespoon extra-virgin olive oil, for brushing

MUSHROOMS

⅛ pound specialty mushrooms, such as morels or porcini, cut

⅛ pound crimini mushrooms, sliced thin

⅛ pound oyster mushrooms, sliced thin

1 shallot, chopped

5 garlic cloves, minced

1 teaspoon chopped fresh oregano

½ teaspoon chopped fresh thyme

½ tablespoon extra-virgin olive oil

Salt and pepper, to taste

1 tablespoon grated Parmesan cheese or soy alternative, such as Soyco

1 Make the pâte brisée: In the bowl of an electric mixer, combine the flours, sugar, salt, xanthan gum, baking powder, and pepper on low speed until well blended. Pour in the truffle oil and mix thoroughly.

2 With the mixer on medium speed, add butter pieces in very small amounts to the dry ingredients. Continue beating to incorporate and soften the butter.

3 With the mixer on medium speed, slowly add half of the cream and mix, adding remaining cream as necessary, until the dough forms a ball and does not stick to the sides of the mixing bowl. If the dough is too wet, add almond flour 1 tablespoon at a time.

4 Remove the dough from the bowl and knead with your hands into a ball. Wrap tightly and let stand at room temperature for 1 hour.

5 While the dough rests, prepare the mushrooms: Place a rack in the middle of the oven. Preheat the oven to 400°F. In a large mixing bowl, combine the mushrooms with the shallots, garlic, oregano, and thyme. Toss with the oil, then season with salt and pepper.

6 Place mushrooms on a 13 × 9-inch nonstick (gray, not black) baking sheet and roast for 30 to 35 minutes or until they are half their size. Remove from oven and let cool slightly while rolling out the dough.

7 With a rolling pin, roll or press the dough with your fingers onto a 15 × 10-inch sheet of parchment paper until it is ¹⁄₁₆ inch thick. Transfer the dough and parchment paper to a 15 × 10-inch baking sheet (called a half sheet). Pierce the dough with a fork and bake for 15 minutes, turning the sheet a quarter turn every 5 minutes. Remove the sheet from the oven and brush 1 tablespoon of oil over the surface of the dough.

8 Evenly spread the mushrooms over the tart and sprinkle with Parmesan cheese. Bake another 20 to 25 minutes, turning the tray a quarter-turn every 5 minutes. Remove from the oven and cool on a wire rack for 15 minutes or until it reaches room temperature. Cut into small squares and serve as an appetizer or first course.

CHEESE

Brie with Honey and Chopped Nuts V

MAKES 4 SERVINGS

The creamy smoothness of the Brie pairs nicely with the sweet honey, while crunchy nuts provide a bit of contrasting texture. For extra fun, use honey with a unique flavor such as alfalfa, buckwheat, or lavender.

1 small round of Brie (about 6.5 ounces)
2 tablespoons honey
2 tablespoons chopped walnuts, pecans, or almonds
1 package gluten-free crackers, such as Mary's Gone Crackers
2 crisp apples, such as Gala or Braeburn, unpeeled, washed, cored, and cut in ¼-inch slices

1 Place the Brie on a microwave-safe serving plate and heat gently in the microwave on low 1 to 2 minutes or just until it is slightly softened and can be easily cut with a knife. Don't make it too hot or it will melt all over the plate.

2 Pour the honey over the Brie and sprinkle the chopped nuts on the top. To serve, cut one wedge from the Brie so guests can see what it is and how to eat it. Serve with crackers and sliced apples.

Feta Cheese Crisps

MAKES 4 SERVINGS (5 CRISPS EACH)

These irresistible, salty little crisps make interesting appetizers, or you can add them to salads for a crunchy contrast to salad greens.

1 small tub (4 ounces) goat's milk–feta cheese crumbles
2 tablespoons grated pecorino Romano cheese or soy alternative, such as Soyco
¼ teaspoon fresh oregano or ⅛ teaspoon dried
¼ teaspoon fresh thyme or ⅛ teaspoon dried
⅛ teaspoon freshly ground black pepper

1 Place a rack in the middle of the oven. Preheat the oven to 375°F. Have a 13 × 9-inch nonstick (gray, not black) baking sheet ready.

2 In a food processor, blend the feta, pecorino, oregano, and thyme until crumbly. Remove lid of food processor and gently stir in pepper by hand. Drop rounded teaspoons of cheese mixture onto baking sheet, about 2 inches apart.

3 Bake 7 to 8 minutes until crisps are light golden brown.

4 Remove sheet from oven and cool crisps for 1 minute, then loosen with a thin, metal spatula. Transfer to wire rack to cool thoroughly.

Olive Puffs V

MAKES 6 SERVINGS (4 PUFFS EACH)

I've served these little appetizers for many years. No one ever expects—but everyone is totally delighted—to find a whole olive inside! For easier handling, the dough is chilled for 2 hours. If you're short on time, freeze the formed balls for 15 minutes and then bake. You can also freeze the unbaked balls and bake a few as needed, which is a really great way to have hot appetizers ready quickly for unexpected guests.

½ cup Carol's Sorghum Blend (page x)
2 teaspoons chopped fresh parsley or 1 teaspoon dried
½ teaspoon paprika
⅛ teaspoon onion powder
⅛ teaspoon baking soda
⅛ teaspoon cayenne pepper
1 cup shredded sharp Cheddar cheese or cheese alternative such as Vegan Gourmet
¼ cup (½ stick) unsalted butter or buttery spread, such as Earth Balance, at room temperature but not melted
24 stuffed green olives

1 In a food processor, combine sorghum blend, parsley, paprika, onion powder, baking soda, and cayenne pepper. Pulse a few times to blend. Add cheese and butter and pulse until mixture forms ball. Remove dough from food processor.

2 Shape 1 teaspoon of dough around each olive and place on plate. Cover and chill 2 hours or overnight.

3 Place a rack in the middle of the oven. Preheat the oven to 400°F. Place the chilled balls on a 13 × 9-inch baking sheet that is generously greased or lined with parchment paper. Bake 12 to 15 minutes or until lightly browned. Serve immediately.

Smoked Salmon Cheesecake Squares

MAKES 18 SERVINGS (3 SQUARES EACH)

Save this dish for entertaining a crowd as it serves a lot. Cut it into tiny squares for a stunning appetizer or small plate. Or cut in larger slices and serve as a luncheon dish accompanied by a crisp, tossed salad and popovers.

CRUST

1 cup homemade gluten-free Plain Bread Crumbs (page 117) or crushed gluten-free pretzels, such as Ener-G or Glutano

2 tablespoons unsalted butter or buttery spread, such as Earth Balance, melted

¼ cup shredded Swiss or Gruyère cheese, or soy alternative, such as Soyco

½ teaspoon seafood seasoning, such as Bayou Blast or Emeril's, or dried dill weed

FILLING

2 tablespoons unsalted butter or buttery spread, such as Earth Balance

1 medium onion, finely chopped

3 packages (8 ounces each) cream cheese or cream cheese alternative, such as Tofutti, at room temperature

4 large eggs, at room temperature

1½ teaspoons finely chopped fresh dill weed or ½ teaspoon dried

½ cup shredded Swiss or Gruyère cheese or nondairy cheese, such as Vegan Gourmet

1 package (4 ounces) smoked salmon or trout

1 Place a rack in the middle of the oven. Preheat the oven to 325°F. Generously grease a 9-inch round nonstick (gray, not black) springform pan with a removable bottom.

2 Make the crust: In a food processor, process the bread crumbs, butter, cheese, and seasoning until thoroughly combined. Press the mixture onto the bottom of the springform pan.

3 Make the filling: In a skillet, cook the onions in butter over medium heat until soft, about 5 minutes. Wipe out the food processor and process the cream cheese, eggs, and dill until thoroughly blended. Add the cheese, salmon, and onions and pulse a few times to incorporate, but leave some chunks of salmon. Spread into the springform pan.

4 Bake 1 hour 10 minutes to 1 hour 15 minutes or until the top is firm. Turn the oven off, prop the oven door open, and allow the cheesecake to cool in the pan for 1 hour. Remove the cheesecake from the oven and finish cooling in the pan on a wire rack for 30 minutes. Remove the cheesecake from the pan and cut into wedges. Serve warm or at room temperature. Refrigerate leftovers.

HOW TO GRATE CHEESE

Grate hard cheeses quickly in your food processor. Cut the cheese into small pieces and process until the cheese is grated. One-fourth pound (4 ounces) of hard cheese yields about 1 cup of grated cheese.

Simple Cheese Quesadillas Q V

MAKES 4 SERVINGS (1 QUESADILLA EACH)

Queso means cheese in Spanish; quesadillas are toasted Spanish cheese sandwiches made from tortillas instead of bread. Feel free to add your favorite fillings in addition to the cheese: shredded chicken, beef, or pork; caramelized onions; black olives; or avocado.

FILLING

½ pound shredded or cheddar cheese, or cheese alternative, such as Vegan Gourmet

¼ cup chopped fresh cilantro

TORTILLAS

1 tablespoon canola oil

4 gluten-free tortilla wraps, such as Food for Life or La Tortilla Factory

1 Make the filling: Combine the cheese and cilantro in a small bowl. Set aside.

2 Make the tortillas: Brush half of oil over surface of a flat, nonstick (gray, not black) grill pan or skillet large enough to hold the tortillas. Gently lay a tortilla directly on grill pan. Do not turn on the heat yet.

3 Spoon cheese mixture evenly spaced over tortilla. With a spatula, gently spread filling evenly over tortilla and to within ½ inch of edge. Gently lay second tortilla on top and gently press down.

4 Turn heat to medium and cook, covered with a lid large enough to cover tortillas, until tortillas are gently browned, about 2 to 3 minutes. With a very large spatula or two smaller ones, gently turn quesadilla. Cook 2 to 3 minutes more. Gently place cooked tortilla on a flat surface, such as a large cutting board, and cut into quarters with very sharp knife. Remove grill pan from heat to cool slightly.

5 Repeat with remaining tortillas, filling, and using canola oil. Serve immediately.

Mini-Refried Bean Quesadillas Q V

MAKES 16 SERVINGS
(4 MINI-QUESADILLAS EACH)

Quesadillas are usually cheese filled tortillas, but they can feature any filling you like. This easy version simply uses beans and green onions. Be sure to use a sharp metal cutter; plastic cutters aren't sharp enough to cut through tortillas.

4 gluten-free tortilla wraps, such as Food for Life or LaTortilla Factory

½ cup store-bought refried bean dip, such as El Paco, Snyder's of Hanover, or homemade Pinto Bean Dip (page 132)

4 green onions, washed and very thinly sliced

2 tablespoons chopped fresh cilantro

½ teaspoon ground cumin, for dusting (optional)

Gluten-free Mexican salsa, such as Newman's Own or Pace, for dipping

1 With a 2-inch round metal biscuit or cookie cutter, carefully cut 12 circles from each tortilla and arrange them in a single layer on a sheet of wax paper. You will have 48 circles.

2 Spread 24 of the circles evenly with 1 teaspoon of the bean dip, then sprinkle with green onions and cilantro. Place a circle on top, pressing down firmly to meld them together.

3 Lightly coat a nonstick (gray, not black) flat griddle with cooking spray. Place as many quesadillas as possible in the griddle and toast over medium heat until golden brown on the bottom. Flip carefully with a spatula and toast on the other side. Lightly dust with cumin. Remove to a plate, cover with foil, and set aside until all the quesadillas are toasted. Serve immediately, with Mexican salsa for dipping.

Smoked Salmon Quesadillas

MAKES 4 SERVINGS (1 QUESADILLA EACH)

Smoked salmon—accentuated by dill, onion, and capers—makes this a delightful variation on traditional cheese quesadillas.

FILLING

1 cup shredded Monterey Jack cheese or cheese alternative, such as Vegan Gourmet

1 package (8 ounces) cream cheese or cream cheese alternative, such as Tofutti, softened

8 ounces smoked salmon, finely chopped

2 tablespoons finely diced red onions

2 tablespoons capers, drained

1 tablespoon finely chopped fresh dill weed or 1 teaspoon dried

¼ teaspoon garlic powder

TORTILLAS

1 tablespoon canola oil

4 gluten-free tortilla wraps, such as Food for Life or La Tortilla Factory

GARNISH

3 tablespoons sour cream or sour cream alternative, such as Tofutti

1 tablespoon finely chopped fresh dill weed or 1 teaspoon dried

8 cherry tomatoes, halved

1 Make the filling: Combine the filling ingredients in a small bowl. Set aside.

2 Make the tortillas: Brush half of canola oil over surface of a flat, nonstick (gray, not black) grill pan or skillet large enough to hold the tortillas. Gently lay a tortilla directly on grill pan. Do not turn on the heat yet.

3 Drop filling by teaspoons evenly over tortilla. With a spatula, gently spread filling evenly over tortilla and to within ½ inch of edge. Lay second tortilla on top and gently press down.

4 Turn heat to medium and cook, covered with a lid large enough to cover tortillas, until tortillas are gently browned, about 2 to 3 minutes. With a very large spatula or two smaller ones, gently turn quesadilla. Cook another 2 to 3 minutes. Gently place cooked tortilla on a flat surface, such as a large cutting board, and cut into quarters with very sharp knife. Remove grill pan from heat to cool slightly.

5 Repeat with remaining tortillas, filling, canola oil.

6 Prepare the garnish: Place a teaspoon of sour cream on each quarter, dust with dill weed, and garnish with half a cherry tomato. Serve warm.

*As an alternative, use 6 gluten-free corn tortillas to make 3 smaller quesadillas. Divide the filling into thirds and follow directions above.

Veggie Mini-Quiches

MAKES 8 SERVINGS (3 MINI-QUICHES EACH)

Although I use zucchini in these mini-quiches, you could also use chopped roasted red bell peppers or eggplant, or grated carrots, or a combination of your favorite vegetables.

¼ recipe Basic Pastry Crust dough, (page 587) at room temperature

1 tablespoon canola oil

½ cup finely diced zucchini

1 tablespoon finely diced fresh onion or 1 teaspoon dried minced onion

1 tablespoon chopped fresh basil or 1 teaspoon dried

1 small garlic clove, minced

2 large eggs, at room temperature

½ cup heavy cream or ⅓ cup whole milk (cow's, rice, soy, potato, or nut)

¼ teaspoon salt

1 teaspoon chopped fresh parsley or ½ teaspoon dried, for garnish

½ teaspoon paprika, for garnish

1 Place a rack in the bottom position of the oven. Preheat the oven to 400°F.. Generously grease 2 nonstick (gray, not black) mini-muffin pans (12 cups each). With your fingers, press about ½ teaspoon of pie crust dough into each of the 24 muffin cups. Set aside.

2 In a small skillet, heat the oil over medium heat. Add zucchini, onion, and garlic and cook, stirring constantly, until the vegetables become soft and translucent.

3 In a medium bowl, whisk eggs, cream, and salt together until smooth. Stir vegetable mixture into egg mixture until well blended.

4 Divide mixture evenly among muffin cups, about a heaping tablespoon each. Sprinkle with parsley and paprika.

5 Bake 10 to 12 minutes or until eggs are set. Remove from oven and serve immediately.

Prosciutto and Chive Mini-Quiches Ⓠ

MAKES 8 SERVINGS (3 MINI-QUICHES EACH)

These little delights are incredibly quick to assemble (assuming you have your stash of gluten-free pie crust dough in the freezer) and bake in a little more than 10 minutes. They make great finger food for parties. If you don't have prosciutto, you can use finely chopped ham instead.

¼ recipe Basic Pastry Crust dough (page 587), at room temperature
2 large eggs, at room temperature
½ cup heavy cream or ⅓ cup whole milk (cow's, rice, soy, potato, or nut)
2 tablespoons finely snipped fresh chives
1 tablespoon chopped fresh parsley or 1 teaspoon dried
¼ teaspoon salt (optional)
½ cup finely chopped prosciutto
½ teaspoon paprika for garnish

1 Place a rack in the bottom position of the oven. Preheat the oven to 400°F. Generously grease the cups of 2 nonstick (gray, not black) mini-muffin pans (12 mini-muffins each). With your fingers, press about ½ teaspoon of pie crust dough into each of the 24 muffin cups. Set aside.

2 In a medium bowl, whisk eggs, cream, chives, parsley, salt, and prosciutto together until well-blended.

3 Divide egg mixture evenly among muffin cups, about a heaping tablespoon each. Sprinkle with paprika.

4 Bake 10 to 12 minutes or until eggs are set. Remove from oven and serve immediately.

SALADS AND SOUPS

Mixed Green Salads

Caesar Salad

Mâche Greens with Blueberries
and Asian Dressing

Spinach Salad with Orange-Basil
Dressing

Spinach, Strawberry, and Walnut
Salad with Lemon-Pomegranate
Vinaigrette

Vegetable and Fruit Salads

Cabbage Coleslaw

Red Cabbage Coleslaw

Rainbow Coleslaw

Creamy Lemon Coleslaw

Cucumber Salad

Tomato-Cucumber Salad with
Feta Cheese

Caprese Salad

Panzanella

Porcini and Parmesan Salad

Jicama and Asian Pear Slaw

Waldorf Salad

Orange-Olive Salad

Beet-Orange Salad with
Clementine Vinaigrette

Fresh Fruit Salad with Coconut-
Apricot Sauce

Pasta Salads

Corkscrew Picnic Salad

Penne Pasta Primavera

Soba Noodles with Asian
Dressing

Salad Dressings

Italian Mustard Vinaigrette

Champagne Vinaigrette

Sherry-Walnut Vinaigrette

Ranch Dressing

Easy Russian Dressing

Vegetable and Fruit Soups

French Onion Soup

Asparagus Soup

Beer Cheese Soup

Green Vegetable Soup

Potato-Leek Soup

Cream of Tomato Soup

Mediterranean Tomato Soup with Rice

Pumpkin Soup

Cumin-Scented Pumpkin and Bean Soup

Moroccan Pumpkin–White-Bean Bisque

Red Beet Borscht

Roasted Red Pepper Soup with Basil Pesto

Traditional Gazpacho

Gazpacho with Fruit

Apple-Fennel Soup

Chilled Double Melon Soup

Meat and Fish Soups and Stews

Chicken Noodle Soup with Dumplings

Pho (Vietnamese Chicken Noodle Soup)

Tortilla Soup

Simple Ham and Bean Soup

Tuscan Bean Soup

Minestrone Soup

Cannellini Bean Soup with Italian Sausage

Hearty Beef Stew

Middle Eastern Beef Stew

Italian Meatball Soup

Lamb Stew

Smoky Turkey-Bacon Chili

White Chili

Fish Chowder

Salmon Corn Chowder

Bouillabaisse

Cioppino

reparing salads and soups is an excellent way to add variety, nutrition, texture, and color to any meal. The foundation of a salad can be vegetables or fruit and can be mixed with a wide variety of dressings and vinaigrettes that dramatically change its character. Simple salads can be easily transformed into main dishes by topping them with grilled chicken, fish, or beef. They make excellent lunches or light dinners, appropriate for any time of year.

Bright and/or deeply colored vegetables such as beets, cabbage, tomatoes, bell peppers, and broccoli are full of nutrients and can be deliciously incorporated into salads. I often serve salads to complement a main dish. For example, a citrus-based salad such as the Beet-Orange Salad with Clementine Vinaigrette is great with fish or poultry because the lovely ruby-colored beets and bright oranges add important color alongside the fish and poultry. I also serve slightly sweet salads with fish and poultry, reserving savory salads for beef entrees. So I pair my favorite Waldorf Salad with fish and chicken and serve the Caprese Salad or Panzanella (Tuscan Bread Salad) with beef main dishes. There are a variety of dressings and vinaigrettes in this chapter—some are paired with specific salad recipes because the seasonings can sometimes make or break a dish—and some

dressings stand on their own like Italian Mustard Vinaigrette or Ranch Dressing because they can be adapted for many recipes.

Store-bought soups or those served in restaurants can be thickened by reduction (boiling the liquid until thickened slightly) or by adding one of the following: cornstarch, arrowroot, tapioca flour, gums, eggs, or nuts, and, unfortunately, wheat in the form of flour. The recipes here are safe because you choose the ingredients. You can make family favorites such as Simple Ham and Bean Soup, Hearty Beef Stew, and French Onion Soup. Others are re-creations of soups I've eaten on my travels, including a Pumpkin Soup, a fish soup called Bouillabaisse, and a hearty Tuscan Bean Soup. Brighten your menu with Roasted Red Pepper Soup with Basil Pesto or Chilled Double Melon Soup.

The beauty of soups is that they're easy to create and can be modified to suit your taste. For example, many soups that call for chicken broth but have no other meat, poultry, or fish in them, can be made vegetarian by using a flavorful vegetable broth. The seasonings may need to be adjusted to add flavor, but these soups will still be tasty. Let these recipes be a general guide, and then adapt them as you wish.

MIXED GREEN SALADS

Caesar Salad

MAKES 4 SERVINGS

I love the tangy crispness of a Caesar salad with steak dishes, but my version is egg-free because I don't eat raw eggs. I guarantee you won't miss them.

2 garlic cloves, minced
½ teaspoon salt
¼ cup extra-virgin olive oil
1½ cups gluten-free bread cubes, crusts removed, and cut in ½-inch pieces
1 tablespoon fresh lemon juice
1 teaspoon cider vinegar
1 teaspoon dry mustard
1 teaspoon gluten-free Worcestershire sauce, such as French's
1 teaspoon anchovy paste (optional)
1 head Romaine lettuce, washed, patted dry, and torn
⅓ cup grated Parmesan cheese or soy alternative, such as Soyco

1 Place a rack in the middle of the oven. Preheat the oven to 350°F. Line a 13 × 9-inch baking sheet (not nonstick) with foil; set aside.

2 In a small bowl, mash the minced garlic with salt and oil; set aside.

3 Make the croutons: Place the bread cubes in a single layer on the baking sheet. Bake 10 minutes, or until they are just lightly browned. Transfer the bread cubes to a large bowl, toss them with half of the garlic-oil mixture, and return to the baking sheet to bake 3 to 5 minutes more, or until golden brown and crisp. Remove from oven and set aside to cool slightly.

4 In a large salad bowl, whisk together the remaining garlic-oil mixture, lemon juice, vinegar, mustard, Worcestershire sauce, and anchovy paste, if using. Add the Romaine lettuce and toss thoroughly. Sprinkle with Parmesan cheese and croutons, toss again, and serve immediately.

Mâche Greens with Blueberries and Asian Dressing ⓥ

MAKES 4 SERVINGS

In Europe, mâche is quite popular and is known as "lamb's lettuce." In the United States, mâche can usually be found in the produce section of natural food stores. I appreciate its unusual shape and taste, and it always inspires the curiosity of dinner guests. Blueberries add a sweet contrast to the onion and cheese; when they are not in season, you can substitute seedless grapes.

SALAD

8 ounces (about 3½ cups) mâche greens or spring greens
1 cup fresh blueberries
⅓ cup crumbled feta cheese
2 tablespoons thinly sliced red onion
⅓ cup toasted pine nuts

DRESSING

2 tablespoons fresh lime juice
2 teaspoons rice wine vinegar
1 teaspoon ground ginger
1 teaspoon honey
½ teaspoon sesame oil
¼ teaspoon garlic powder
¼ cup extra-virgin olive oil

1 Make the salad: In a large serving bowl, combine the mâche greens, blueberries, feta cheese, onion, and pine nuts.

2 Make the dressing: In a small bowl, whisk together the lime juice, vinegar, ginger, honey, sesame oil, and garlic powder. Gradually whisk in olive oil, stirring constantly until fully combined.

3 Pour dressing over salad and toss to coat thoroughly. Serve immediately.

Spinach Salad with Orange-Basil Dressing

MAKES 4 SERVINGS

Spinach is tremendously healthy, and the garbanzo beans (also known as chickpeas) add healthy fiber to the dish and are a nice contrast to the other ingredients.

SALAD

6 cups baby spinach, washed and spun dry

1 can (14 to 15 ounces) garbanzo beans, rinsed and drained

2 cups unpeeled sliced English (or hothouse) cucumbers

1 cup halved cherry or grape tomatoes

¼ cup raw pumpkin seeds

2 tablespoons chopped fresh basil

DRESSING

¼ cup extra-virgin olive oil

2 tablespoons orange juice concentrate

2 tablespoons rice vinegar

2 tablespoons chopped fresh basil

2 teaspoons Dijon mustard

½ teaspoon salt

¼ teaspoon freshly ground black pepper

1 Make the salad: In a large bowl, combine the spinach, beans, cucumbers, tomatoes, pumpkin seeds, and basil and toss thoroughly.

2 Make the dressing: In a blender, combine the oil, orange juice concentrate, vinegar, basil, mustard, salt, and pepper, and process until smooth. Pour over salad ingredients and toss to coat thoroughly. Serve immediately.

Spinach, Strawberry, and Walnut Salad with Lemon-Pomegranate Vinaigrette

MAKES 4 SERVINGS

Serve this delightful salad when you need a colorful, surprising dish. Strawberries work well to balance the slight tang of the spinach; it's a wonderful combination.

SALAD

6 cups baby spinach, washed and spun dry

1 pint (2 cups) fresh strawberries, washed, hulled, and halved

½ small red onion, thinly sliced

½ cup toasted walnuts

⅓ cup feta cheese, crumbled

⅛ teaspoon salt

⅛ teaspoon freshly ground black pepper

DRESSING

¼ cup red wine vinegar

¼ cup fresh lemon juice

2 tablespoons pomegranate molasses or melted red currant jelly

2 teaspoons Dijon mustard

¼ teaspoon salt

⅛ teaspoon freshly ground black pepper

¾ cup extra-virgin olive oil

1 Make the salad: In a large serving bowl, combine the spinach, strawberries, onion, walnuts, feta cheese, salt, and pepper; set aside.

2 Make the dressing: Whisk together the vinegar, lemon juice, pomegranate molasses, mustard, salt, and pepper. Slowly whisk in oil, continuing to whisk until blended.

3 Pour just enough dressing over the salad to coat the greens lightly; toss thoroughly. Serve immediately. Store leftover vinaigrette in refrigerator.

VEGETABLE AND FRUIT SALADS

Cabbage Coleslaw

MAKES 4 SERVINGS

This coleslaw can be put together in seconds in a food processor. I don't use the special shredder attachment; I just use the knife blade and pulse the machine a few times to do the job. If you're really in a time crunch, you can start with store-bought shredded cabbage, though it won't be as fresh.

1 small head red or green cabbage, cored and quartered
1 medium carrot, peeled and cut in 1-inch chunks
1 small yellow onion, quartered
3 tablespoons cider vinegar
2 tablespoons honey
1 teaspoon Dijon mustard
¼ cup canola oil
½ teaspoon celery seed
½ teaspoon salt
¼ teaspoon freshly ground white pepper
¼ teaspoon paprika, for garnish

1 Working in batches, cut each quarter of cabbage in half so that it fits in a food processor. Pulse a few times to shred to the desired consistency and transfer the shredded cabbage to a serving bowl. Shred the carrot and onion together to desired consistency and place in the serving bowl.

2 Add the vinegar, honey, mustard, oil, celery seed, salt, and pepper to the food processor and blend. Pour over the coleslaw and toss to coat thoroughly. Sprinkle with the paprika. Cover tightly and refrigerate. Serve chilled.

Red Cabbage Coleslaw

MAKES 8 SERVINGS

I prefer to use my food processor to shred the cabbage quickly and easily when I want coleslaw that I can serve in mounds. Otherwise, I simply slice it very thin with a very sharp knife. This coleslaw makes great leftovers.

1 head (3 pounds) of red cabbage, washed, cored and shredded
½ cup chopped onion
½ cup mayonnaise
3 tablespoons cider vinegar
1 tablespoon honey or agave nectar
2 teaspoons Dijon mustard
1 teaspoon celery seed
1 teaspoon celery salt
¼ teaspoon freshly ground black pepper
2 tablespoons chopped fresh parsley or 1 tablespoon dried, for garnish

Combine the cabbage and onion in a medium serving bowl. In a small bowl, whisk together the mayonnaise, vinegar, honey, mustard, celery seed, celery salt, and pepper. Pour over cabbage and stir with spatula to blend thoroughly. Garnish with parsley. Chill for 2 hours or overnight. Serve chilled.

Rainbow Coleslaw

MAKES 6 SERVINGS

This coleslaw gets its name from the multicolored ingredients of red cabbage, carrots, and bell peppers. It adds a nice touch of color to your plate and makes great leftovers for the next day.

VEGETABLES
1 small head red cabbage
½ small carrot, cut in matchsticks
½ cup diced red bell pepper
½ cup diced yellow bell pepper
1 small onion, chopped
2 tablespoons chopped fresh cilantro

DRESSING

1 small garlic clove, minced

¼ cup rice vinegar

2 tablespoons canola oil

1 tablespoon sugar

1 teaspoon Dijon mustard

¼ teaspoon crushed red pepper

¼ teaspoon salt

⅛ teaspoon freshly ground black pepper

1 Prepare the vegetables: Thinly slice the cabbage and place in a large bowl. Add the carrots, bell peppers, onion, and cilantro, and toss thoroughly.

2 Make the dressing: In a blender, combine the garlic, vinegar, oil, sugar, mustard, crushed red pepper, salt, and pepper and blend until smooth. Pour over cabbage mixture and toss well. Chill until serving time.

Creamy Lemon Coleslaw

MAKES 6 SERVINGS

The lemon in this coleslaw is unexpected but gives it a fresh, springtime taste. For an even prettier presentation, slice the peeled carrot into matchsticks.

¼ cup mayonnaise

2 tablespoons sour cream or sour cream alternative, such as Tofutti

2 teaspoons sugar

Grated zest and juice of 1 lemon

½ teaspoon celery seed

½ teaspoon salt

¼ teaspoon freshly ground black pepper

1 very small head green cabbage, thinly sliced and inner ribs discarded

1 carrot, peeled and cut in thin diagonal slices

1 tablespoon chopped fresh parsley, for garnish

1 In a large bowl, whisk together the mayonnaise, sour cream, sugar, lemon zest, lemon juice, celery seeds, salt, and pepper until smooth.

2 Add cabbage and carrots to serving bowl and toss thoroughly to coat with dressing. Garnish with chopped parsley. Chill 2 hours. Let stand at room temperature 20 minutes before serving.

Cucumber Salad

MAKES 4 SERVINGS

Cucumber salad is so simple and refreshing. My mother always soaked cucumbers in salted water to draw out any bitterness, so I do it, too. I especially like to use English, or hothouse, cucumbers, which have fewer seeds than regular cucumbers and don't have to be peeled, making for a more colorful dish. But don't worry if you can't find English cucumbers—using regular, peeled cucumbers will work as well. I serve this salad with Pork Schnitzel (page 362).

2 medium English (or hothouse) cucumbers, unpeeled and thinly sliced

½ teaspoon salt

1 small thinly sliced white or yellow onion

¼ to ½ cup white wine vinegar (the more vinegar, the more acidic the taste)

2 tablespoons water

2 teaspoons sugar

¼ teaspoon freshly ground black pepper

¾ teaspoon finely chopped fresh dill weed or ¼ teaspoon dried (optional)

1 Place the cucumbers in a shallow serving bowl, sprinkle with the salt, and add water to cover. Refrigerate 30 minutes; drain thoroughly.

2 Add the onions, vinegar, water, sugar, pepper, and dill, if using, and toss to coat thoroughly. Chill up to 2 hours, stirring occasionally.

Tomato-Cucumber Salad with Feta Cheese

MAKES 4 SERVINGS

Feta cheese can be made from cow's milk, sheep's milk, or goat's milk, and lends a nice tang to the salad. But you may also use an alternative cheese to suit your taste.

2 cups cherry tomatoes, halved

1 English (or hothouse) cucumber, unpeeled, sliced in ⅛-inch rounds

¼ pound (4 ounces) feta cheese, cut or crumbled in ¼-inch pieces

1 small red onion, sliced lengthwise in ⅛-inch slices

2 tablespoons champagne vinegar

2 tablespoons extra-virgin olive oil

2 tablespoons chopped fresh basil

¼ teaspoon salt

¼ teaspoon freshly ground black pepper

Gently combine all ingredients in serving bowl, taking care not to crumble feta cheese too much. Refrigerate 1 to 2 hours. Bring to room temperature before serving.

Caprese Salad

MAKES 4 SERVINGS

Caprese *means "in the style of Capri," the stunning island just off the west coast of Italy. I love the traditional version of this salad, but I also really like marinated artichoke hearts, so I modified the classic version to include them. This salad is especially wonderful in summer when fresh tomatoes are at their best.*

1 pound fresh mozzarella cheese, cut in ¼-inch-thick slices

4 plum or Roma tomatoes, washed and sliced crosswise

1 jar (4.5 ounces) marinated artichoke hearts, drained

1 small red onion, thinly sliced

½ cup chopped fresh basil

½ teaspoon salt

½ teaspoon freshly ground black pepper

1 tablespoon extra-virgin olive oil, or to taste

1 Arrange the mozzarella slices on a serving platter. Top with the tomato slices, artichoke hearts, and onion slices.

2 Sprinkle with the basil, salt, and pepper. Drizzle with oil. Serve at room temperature.

Panzanella

MAKES 4 SERVINGS

Panzanella is a classic Tuscan summer bread salad. For added beauty, I like to use yellow and red cherry tomatoes, especially when I have them growing in my garden during the summer. And, you don't have to stop with ½ cup basil. Personally, I love basil and use tons of it in dishes like this. This dish is best when you can serve it immediately after browning the bread cubes and—unlike the classic panzanella—eat the salad right away after it's tossed so the gluten-free bread retains its crispness.

6 slices gluten-free bread, preferably homemade White Sandwich Yeast Bread (page 85)

½ cup extra-virgin olive oil, divided

2 tablespoons unsalted butter or buttery spread, such as Earth Balance

2¼ teaspoons salt, divided

1 garlic clove, minced

2 tablespoons balsamic vinegar (white balsamic vinegar also works well)

½ teaspoon freshly ground black pepper

2 cups cherry or grape tomatoes, washed, stemmed and halved (about 2 pounds)

½ cup sliced red onion

½ cup chopped fresh basil (or to taste) plus a few leaves for garnish

1 Place a rack in the middle of the oven. Preheat the oven to 350°F. Line a large 13 × 9-inch baking sheet (not nonstick) with foil. Cut crusts from bread (you can reserve them for use as bread crumbs or for stuffing) and cut remaining bread into ½-inch cubes. Place bread cubes in a large bowl.

2 In a small pan, combine 6 tablespoons of the oil, butter, ¼ teaspoon of the salt, and garlic and cook over low heat until the butter melts, stirring to blend ingredients thoroughly. Pour the oil mixture over the bread cubes and toss to mix well. Spread the bread cubes in a single layer on the prepared baking sheet.

3 Bake 10 to 20 minutes, or until the bread cubes are golden and fragrant, stirring and turning cubes occasionally halfway through for even browning. The amount of time required to brown bread cubes varies depending on the bread you use, so watch carefully to avoid burning. Remove the baking sheet from the oven and let the bread cubes cool slightly on the baking sheet. (The toasted bread cubes should be used within the next 15 minutes for best results.)

4 In the same large bowl, whisk together the remaining 2 tablespoons oil, the remaining 2 teaspoons salt, vinegar, and pepper. Add the bread cubes, tomatoes, onion, and chopped fresh basil and toss until blended. Serve immediately, garnished with basil leaves.

Porcini and Parmesan Salad

MAKES 4 SERVINGS

This delicious salad illustrates the Tuscan flair for dishes with few ingredients, letting each ingredient deliver a lot of flavor. Porcini mushrooms are an autumn delicacy in Tuscany, and I ate my fair share when I visited, but you may substitute regular cremini (button) mushrooms instead.

2 cups thinly sliced mushrooms (porcini, cremini, or your choice)
½ cup chopped flat-leaf Italian parsley
1 tablespoon extra-virgin olive oil (or just enough to lightly coat vegetables)
1 teaspoon balsamic vinegar or sherry vinegar
1 garlic clove, minced
1 cup thinly sliced (not grated) Parmesan cheese or soy alternative, such as Soyco

In a medium serving bowl, toss mushrooms, parsley, oil, vinegar, and garlic together. Add sliced Parmesan cheese and toss lightly. Serve immediately.

Jicama and Asian Pear Slaw

MAKES 4 SERVINGS

This salad was served at a restaurant that I once dined at regularly. I was so enchanted with it that I went home and recreated this version, and I now serve it often, especially with Southwestern meals. Jicama is a crisp, starchy legume that resembles a turnip in appearance, but tastes somewhat like water chestnuts. Asian pears are also crisp, but a little sweeter than jicama. I especially love the contrast between the crunchy jicama and the sweet mandarin oranges. Use fresh, if you like.

1 small jicama head, peeled and diced
1 small Asian pear, diced
1 can (11 ounces) mandarin oranges, drained
1 stalk celery, fibers removed
¼ cup chopped fresh cilantro
2 green onions, thinly sliced diagonally
½ cup diced red bell pepper
2 tablespoons seasoned rice vinegar
1 tablespoon fresh lime juice
1 tablespoon honey or agave nectar

In a medium serving bowl, toss all ingredients together and refrigerate 1 hour to blend the flavors. Serve chilled.

Waldorf Salad

MAKES 4 SERVINGS

I make this salad at least once a week because my husband and I love it so much. It is our standby salad—always delicious and it complements fish, poultry, and beef entrees. Make it first and refrigerate while preparing dinner.

2 crisp red apples (Gala, Jonathan, or Honey Crisp), unpeeled

2 ribs celery, trimmed and cut in 1-inch diagonal slices

½ cup pecan or walnut pieces

¼ cup dried cranberries, dried cherries, dried currants, or dried dates

1 tablespoon fresh lemon juice

1 tablespoon honey or agave nectar

2 tablespoons gluten-free salad dressing, such as Miracle Whip

Dash salt

1 Quarter and core the apples. Cut into ½-inch pieces and combine with celery, pecans, and cranberries in a serving bowl.

2 In a separate bowl, whisk together the lemon juice, honey, and salad dressing until smooth. Pour over the apple mixture and toss to coat thoroughly. Serve immediately or refrigerate until serving time.

Orange-Olive Salad

MAKES 6 SERVINGS

This salad is gorgeous to look at and simple to create. The saltiness of the olives is a nice balance to the sweetness and tartness of the oranges. To keep the vegetables fresh and crisp, add the dressing just before serving it. I serve this often during the winter when oranges are at their best.

3 oranges (preferably chilled), peeled, seeded, and sliced in rounds

1 red onion, peeled and thinly sliced

½ jar (16 ounces) pitted kalamata olives, or to taste

½ teaspoon salt

½ teaspoon freshly ground black pepper

2 tablespoons extra-virgin olive oil

2 tablespoons red wine vinegar

¼ cup chopped fresh cilantro, for garnish

1 Arrange the oranges in a single layer on a serving platter. Top with a layer of red onion and arrange a black olive in the center of each orange round. Sprinkle salt and pepper on top. You can refrigerate the salad, wrapped, until serving time.

2 Whisk the oil and vinegar together in a small jar. Pour over the oranges. Sprinkle with the cilantro. Serve immediately.

Beet-Orange Salad with Clementine Vinaigrette

MAKES 4 SERVINGS

Save this lovely composed beet salad for a dinner with company and let its gorgeous ruby, orange, and green colors adorn the table. Only you have to know that you're serving some of the most nutritious produce on earth.

SALAD

1 head butter lettuce, washed and leaves separated.

1 can (16 ounces) sliced red beets, drained

3 clementines, tangerines, or navel oranges, peeled and sliced crosswise into rounds

1 small shallot, minced

4 tablespoons goat cheese, or cheese of choice

1 tablespoon chopped fresh cilantro

VINAIGRETTE

3 tablespoons fresh clementine, tangerine, or orange juice

1 tablespoon fresh lemon juice

1 teaspoon grated clementine, tangerine, or orange zest

1 teaspoon grated lemon zest

1 teaspoon dry mustard

1 tablespoon extra-virgin olive oil

⅛ teaspoon xanthan gum

1 Make the salad: Arrange lettuce leaves on a large platter or 4 individual salad plates. Arrange the beets, clementines, and shallots in the bowls formed by the lettuce. Drop teaspoons of goat cheese on top and sprinkle with cilantro.

2 Make the vinaigrette: Whisk the ingredients together in a small bowl or put them in a glass jar with a screw-top lid and shake vigorously until the vinaigrette thickens slightly. Drizzle the salad with vinaigrette and serve immediately.

Fresh Fruit Salad with Coconut-Apricot Sauce

MAKES 6 SERVINGS

Combine all the fruit in a large serving bowl and then toss it in the sauce like a classic fruit salad. Or, cut the fruit in larger pieces and arrange it in groups (e.g., all the strawberries in a single mound) on a lovely platter and use the coconut-apricot sauce as a dip. You can vary the fruit with the seasons.

FRUIT

1 orange, peeled and sectioned

1 pint fresh strawberries, washed, hulled, and patted dry

1 can (8 ounces) pineapple chunks, drained

1 apple, cored and quartered; each quarter cut in ½-inch-thick vertical slices

1 banana, peeled and cut in ½-inch slices

2 kiwi, peeled and cut in ¼-inch slices

2 tablespoons fresh lemon juice

1 tablespoon honey or agave nectar

SAUCE

1 container (8 ounces) sour cream or sour cream alternative, such as Tofutti

¼ cup sweetened coconut flakes, shredded

2 tablespoons apricot preserves

2 tablespoons coarsely chopped walnuts

1 teaspoon pure vanilla extract

1 Assemble the fruit: Toss the fruit with the lemon juice and honey. Place in a serving bowl or arrange attractively on a serving platter.

2 Make the sauce: In a medium bowl, combine all the sauce ingredients. Toss the sauce with the fruit in the serving bowl or place in a small bowl to serve as a dip for fruit on the platter.

PASTA SALADS

Corkscrew Picnic Salad

MAKES 4 SERVINGS

This pasta salad is particularly visually dramatic because of its colorful vegetables—bright green broccoli and snow peas, black olives, and red bell peppers. It is a good dish for a picnic because its flavors complement the typical picnic dishes of ribs, hot dogs, and hamburgers.

2 cups uncooked gluten-free rotini or ziti, such as Tinkyada

1 cup snow peas

1 cup small broccoli florets

¼ cup red wine vinegar

2 tablespoons fresh lemon juice

1 tablespoon Dijon mustard

¼ teaspoon salt, or to taste

¼ teaspoon white pepper, or to taste

2 tablespoons chopped fresh basil or 1 tablespoon dried

1 small garlic clove, minced

¼ cup extra-virgin olive oil

1 small red bell pepper, chopped

½ cup small whole black olives

¼ cup pine nuts, toasted

1 Cook the pasta in a pot of boiling salted water until not quite done. Put the snow peas and broccoli in a sieve and place the sieve over the boiling water. Cover the pot with a lid, and steam the vegetables while the pasta cooks another minute. Immerse the vegetables in ice water to stop cooking, drain well; set aside in a bowl. Drain the pasta well and transfer to a large bowl.

2 In a screw-top jar, combine the vinegar, lemon juice, mustard, salt, pepper, basil, and garlic and shake well. Add the oil and shake vigorously to blend the dressing. Add dressing to pasta and toss. Add the broccoli and snow peas, bell pepper, olives, and pine nuts. Toss again. Serve at room temperature, seasoned with salt and pepper to taste.

Penne Pasta Primavera

MAKES 4 SERVINGS

Primavera *means "springtime" in Italian and aptly describes this dish because the vegetables typically used in it are plentiful during the spring. Asparagus is especially pretty to use in the spring when it is in season—however, I use whatever vegetables I have on hand.*

1 cup diagonal 1-inch slices asparagus

1 cup diagonally halved snow peas

4 cups hot cooked gluten-free penne, such as Tinkyada or Orgran

½ cup grated Parmesan cheese or soy alternative, such as Soyco

2 tablespoons dry white wine

2 tablespoons rice wine vinegar

1 tablespoon extra-virgin olive oil

1 garlic clove, minced

1 teaspoon onion powder

½ teaspoon salt, plus more for cooking asparagus and snow peas

¼ teaspoon white pepper

1 cup red grape tomatoes (or cherry tomatoes, halved)

¼ cup chopped fresh parsley

1 Cook the asparagus and snow peas in a pot of boiling salted water 1 to 2 minutes, or just until barely done. Drain and immerse in ice water to stop the cooking and preserve the color. Add the hot penne and toss with the Parmesan cheese.

2 In a screw-top jar, combine the wine, vinegar, oil, garlic, onion powder, salt, and pepper and shake vigorously until well blended. Pour it over the penne and vegetables and toss until thoroughly coated. Add the tomatoes and parsley and toss to coat thoroughly. Let stand at room temperature 30 minutes to let the flavors blend. Transfer to a serving bowl and serve at room temperature.

Soba Noodles with Asian Dressing

MAKES 4 SERVINGS

Soba *is the term used to refer to Japanese noodles that are typically made with buckwheat and wheat. Be sure to choose 100 percent pure buckwheat noodles, such as those made by Eden Foods, which work just as well as wheat noodles but are gluten-free. Be sure to wear protective gloves when chopping the jalapeño to avoid irritation from the oil.*

1 package (8 ounces) uncooked 100% buckwheat noodles, such as Eden, or gluten-free spaghetti

¼ cup wheat-free, low-sodium tamari soy sauce, such as Crystal or San-J

2 tablespoons toasted sesame oil or regular sesame oil

2 tablespoons water

2 tablespoons sugar or honey

2 tablespoons red wine vinegar

¼ teaspoon salt

1 cup chopped fresh cilantro

½ cup chopped green onions

½ jalapeño pepper, chopped

½ cup diced red bell pepper

½ cup pine nuts, toasted

1 Bring a large pot of salted water to a boil and cook the noodles until just tender, about 10 minutes. Drain thoroughly, then immerse the noodles in ice water to stop cooking. Drain again, and place in a large bowl, patting the noodles with a paper towel to capture any remaining droplets.

2 While the noodles are cooking, in a screw-top jar, combine the soy sauce, oil, water, sugar, vinegar, and salt and shake vigorously until well blended. Pour dressing over the noodles and toss until they are thoroughly coated. Add the cilantro, green onions, jalapeño pepper, and bell pepper and mix well. Sprinkle pine nuts over the salad and serve immediately.

SALED DRESSINGS

Italian Mustard Vinaigrette

MAKES ¾ CUP

This is a very basic dressing that can be used to dress virtually any salad. You can vary the vinegar and change the whole character of the dressing, so try it with champagne vinegar, sherry vinegar, or rice wine vinegar.

¼ cup red wine vinegar
2 tablespoons Dijon mustard
1 teaspoon Italian seasoning
¼ teaspoon sugar
½ cup extra-virgin olive oil
¼ teaspoon salt
⅛ teaspoon freshly ground black pepper

In a small bowl or jar, combine vinegar, mustard, Italian seasoning, and sugar. Slowly whisk in the oil, continuing to whisk until mixture emulsifies. Add salt and pepper. Store, tightly covered, in the refrigerator for up to 1 week.

Champagne Vinaigrette

MAKES ½ CUP

Champagne vinegar is one of my all-time favorite ingredients. The slight sweetness complements salads with a hit of fruity flavor that can't be beat.

¼ cup champagne vinegar
1 tablespoon Dijon mustard
1 tablespoon minced shallots
½ teaspoon minced garlic
½ teaspoon salt
¼ teaspoon freshly ground black pepper
¼ cup extra-virgin olive oil

In a small bowl or jar, combine the vinegar, mustard, shallots, garlic, salt and pepper. Whisk to blend thoroughly. Slowly whisk in the oil, continuing to whisk until mixture thickens. Or place all ingredients in a blender and process until thick and creamy. Store, tightly covered, in refrigerator for up to 1 week.

Sherry-Walnut Vinaigrette

MAKES ¼ CUP

Sherry vinegar is a dramatic flavor so use this recipe when you want the flavor of the vinaigrette to stand out.

1 tablespoon sherry vinegar
1 tablespoon Dijon mustard
1 teaspoon grated fresh onion or ¼ teaspoon dried minced onion
2 tablespoons walnut oil
2 teaspoons extra-virgin olive oil
¼ teaspoon salt
⅛ teaspoon xanthan gum
Dash freshly ground black pepper

In a small bowl or jar, combine the vinegar, mustard, and onion and whisk or shake until thoroughly blended. Add remaining ingredients and whisk or shake jar to blend thoroughly. Store tightly covered in refrigerator, for up to 1 week.

Ranch Dressing

MAKES 1 CUP

Keep the dry mix ingredients on hand so you can quickly whip up ranch dressing for salads or to use as a dip. This recipe calls for a lot of dried herbs, but the end result is worth it. Of course, you can always buy bottled gluten-free ranch dressing, but a homemade version will be fresher and contain no preservatives.

DRY MIX INGREDIENTS

½ teaspoon celery salt

¼ teaspoon freshly ground black pepper

¼ teaspoon dried oregano

¼ teaspoon dried chives

¼ teaspoon dried parsley

¼ teaspoon dried marjoram

¼ teaspoon dried savory

¼ teaspoon sugar

¼ teaspoon onion powder

⅛ teaspoon garlic powder

LIQUID INGREDIENTS

½ cup mayonnaise

½ cup 1% milk (cow's, rice, soy, or nut—if using rice milk, add ⅛ teaspoon xanthan gum)

1 tablespoon white wine vinegar

1 In a blender, process the dry mix ingredients and liquid ingredients together until smooth. Let stand 1 hour for flavors to blend before serving.

2 Store, tightly covered, in refrigerator for up to 1 week.

Easy Russian Dressing

MAKES ABOUT 1 CUP

Russian dressing is a heavy flavorful salad dressing and—in my mind—more suitable as a sauce in savory dishes than as a dressing for salad greens. But it is sometimes hard to find, so here is an easy recipe made from ingredients you likely have in your refrigerator or can easily get from your local grocery store.

½ cup ketchup

¼ cup mayonnaise

2 tablespoons sweet pickle relish

2 tablespoons grated onion

1 tablespoon fresh lemon juice

1 tablespoon cider vinegar

1 teaspoon prepared horseradish, or to taste

In a blender, place all the ingredients and pulse until well blended and the pickle relish is almost smooth. For thinner dressing, add water a tablespoon at a time until desired consistency is reached. Store, tightly covered, in the refrigerator for up to 1 week.

VEGETABLE AND FRUIT SOUPS

French Onion Soup

MAKES 4 SERVINGS

Plan ahead to make this delicious soup because the onions need to cook for about an hour to reach the right consistency. The extraordinary flavor is well worth the effort.

¼ cup olive oil

1 tablespoon butter or buttery spread, such as Earth Balance

6 yellow onions, sliced

½ teaspoon salt

½ teaspoon freshly ground black pepper

2 garlic cloves, minced

3 cups gluten-free, low-sodium beef broth, such as Swanson's, or homemade Beef Broth (page 675)

3 cups gluten-free, low-sodium chicken broth, such as Swanson's Natural Goodness, or homemade Chicken Broth (page 676)

¼ cup dry white wine, sherry, or Vermouth

1 tablespoon brandy

1 teaspoon sugar

2 teaspoons fresh thyme or ½ teaspoon dried

1 bay leaf

1 tablespoon cornstarch

4 slices (about ½-inch thick) homemade French Yeast Bread (page 100)

2 cups grated Gruyère cheese, or cheese alternative, such as Vegan Gourmet

2 tablespoons grated Parmesan cheese or soy alternative, such as Soyco, for garnish

1 In a Dutch oven or other deep, heavy pot with a tight-fitting lid, heat the oil and butter over medium heat. Add the onions, salt, and pepper. Cook, stirring occasionally, until the onions soften, about 10 minutes. Reduce the heat to low and cook slowly, stirring occasionally, until onions are caramelized, about 1 hour 15 minutes. (After 30 minutes of cooking, the onions should be light golden brown; by 45 minutes, the onions will be deep brown—the secret for excellent French onion soup.)

2 After the onions have cooked for 1 hour 15 minutes, slowly stir in the garlic, beef broth, chicken broth, wine, brandy, sugar, thyme, and bay leaf. Simmer, partially covered, 15 minutes. Mix cornstarch with 1 tablespoon water, add to soup, and stir until thickened.

3 Place a rack in the middle of the oven. Preheat the oven to 325°F. Place bread slices on a 13 × 9-inch baking sheet (not nonstick). Bake until dry, 5 minutes per side. (You can do this ahead if you wish.)

4 Heat the broiler. Remove the bay leaf and ladle the soup into heatproof soup bowls. Place the bowls in a 13 × 9 × 2-inch ovenproof baking pan. Place a slice of toasted bread on top of each bowl. Divide Gruyère cheese equally among 4 bowls. Broil until golden brown, about 2 to 3 minutes. Serve hot, garnished with Parmesan cheese.

Asparagus Soup

MAKES 4 SERVINGS

Asparagus is very nutritious and this soup is a simple way to eat more of this tasty vegetable—particularly in spring, its peak season.

2 cans (14 to 15 ounces each) gluten-free, low sodium chicken broth, such as Swanson's Natural Goodness, or homemade Chicken Broth (page 676), divided

½ pound fresh asparagus, chopped, or 1 package (10 ounces) frozen asparagus, thawed

1 leek, white part only, cleaned and diced

1 tablespoon unsalted butter or buttery spread, such as Earth Balance

½ teaspoon salt

¼ teaspoon freshly ground black pepper

1 tablespoon sweet rice flour

1 teaspoon freshly chopped fresh dill weed or ½ teaspoon dried

1 In a medium saucepan, bring 1 can of broth, the asparagus, and the leek to a boil over medium heat. Reduce the heat to low and simmer 5 minutes, or until the asparagus and leek are tender.

2 Using a slotted spoon, transfer the asparagus and leek to a food processor, leaving the broth in pan. Add the remaining can of broth, the butter, salt, pepper, and sweet rice flour to the food processor and process 1 minute, or until completely smooth. Transfer the mixture to the saucepan.

3 Cook the soup over medium heat, whisking constantly, until slightly thickened, about 5 to 7 minutes. Stir in the dill and serve immediately.

Beer-Cheese Soup

MAKES 4 SERVINGS

A small restaurant near my college apartment served a fantastic beer-cheese soup. I made it frequently until my gluten intolerance forced me to give up beer in 1988. With today's gluten-free beer (or hard cider*), there's no reason not to enjoy this soup. Mild cheddar melts better than drier sharp Cheddar.

2 tablespoons unsalted butter or buttery spread, such as Earth Balance

½ cup finely diced onion

½ cup finely diced celery

½ cup finely diced carrot

½ teaspoon salt, or to taste

⅛ teaspoon ground nutmeg

Dash ground cloves

Dash white pepper

2 cups gluten-free, low-sodium chicken broth, such as Swanson's Natural Goodness, divided, or homemade Chicken Broth (page 676), divided

2 tablespoons sweet rice flour

2 cups (8 ounces) grated mild Cheddar cheese

1 bottle (12 ounces) gluten-free beer, such as Bard's Tale or Redbridge

2 teaspoons chopped fresh parsley or 1 teaspoon dried, for garnish

Dash paprika, for garnish

1 Heat the butter in a heavy soup pot over medium heat. Add onions, celery, and carrot and stir for 1 minute. Reduce heat to medium-low, cover, and cook until onions are soft and translucent, about 5 minutes. Add salt, nutmeg, cloves, pepper, and 1¾ cups of the broth. Simmer, covered, 30 minutes.

2 In a bowl, whisk sweet rice flour with remaining ¼ cup broth until smooth and then add to the pot, stirring constantly until the soup thickens slightly. Remove soup from the heat and stir in the cheese until it is thoroughly melted.

3 Just before serving, open the beer bottle over a bowl so that the bowl catches any overflow if the beer foams up. Add the beer to the soup and bring the soup to serving temperature over low heat. Garnish with the parsley and paprika and serve hot.

*Gluten-free hard ciders include Woodchuck or White Winter Winery.

Green Vegetable Soup

MAKES 4 SERVINGS

Even though I eat a varied diet, I always look for ways to eat more vegetables. I also hate to waste food, so this delicious, easy soup is how I make the most of leftover green vegetables. My favorite combination is asparagus and leeks; I always keep chopped leeks in my freezer for this dish, but you can use any vegetable you wish. You can halve or quarter this recipe to make a single serving.

2 cups chopped unseasoned cooked green vegetables (such as broccoli, asparagus, or green beans)
1 cup cleaned and chopped leeks
¼ cup chopped fresh parsley or 2 tablespoons dried
3 cups gluten-free, low-sodium chicken broth, such as Swanson's Natural Goodness, divided, or homemade Chicken Broth (page 676), divided
2 tablespoons sweet rice flour
1 teaspoon herbes de Provence
½ teaspoon salt, or to taste
¼ teaspoon freshly ground black pepper
Pinch of freshly grated nutmeg

1 In a blender, place the vegetables, leeks, parsley, 1 cup chicken broth, and sweet rice flour and process until the vegetables are very smooth. Or for a soup with a little texture, process just until the mixture is not quite smooth.

2 Transfer the mixture to a medium, heavy saucepan. Add the herbes de Provence, salt, pepper, and nutmeg, and cook over medium heat, whisking constantly, until thickened. Serve hot.

Potato-Leek Soup

MAKES 4 SERVINGS

Called vichysoisse *(vee-shee-SWAZ), this French-style soup is rich and creamy. Leeks, a member of the onion family, lend wonderful depth and a hint of nutmeg accents their unique flavor.*

2 large leeks, white parts only
3 tablespoons unsalted butter or buttery spread, such as Earth Balance
3 russet potatoes, peeled and cut in ¼-inch dice
3 sprigs of fresh thyme
Pinch of freshly grated nutmeg
2 teaspoons salt
¼ teaspoon freshly ground black pepper
4 cups water
2 cups half-and-half
Additional salt and pepper, to taste
½ cup finely snipped fresh chives, for garnish

1 Cut the roots from the leeks and slice each in half lengthwise. To remove dirt and sand, rinse in water several times until the water is clear. Remove leeks from water, cut in ¼-inch slices; and pat dry with a paper towel; set aside in a small bowl.

2 In a large pot, melt the butter over medium heat. Add the leeks and cook over medium heat, stirring occasionally, until they are limp. Add the potatoes, thyme, nutmeg, salt, and pepper. Add water and bring to a simmer. Cook, covered, until potatoes are tender, about 20 to 25 minutes.

3 Using an immersion blender, puree the soup until it is very smooth. Stir in the half-and-half. Taste to see if additional salt and pepper are needed. Serve hot or cold, garnished with fresh chives.

Note: You can also puree the soup in a blender. To avoid burns from the hot mixture, puree equal parts of hot potatoes and cold half-and-half and hold a kitchen towel over the blender lid while blending.

Cream of Tomato Soup

MAKES 4 SERVINGS

Lori Sobelson handles the Coronary Health Improvement Program (CHIP) classes offered at the Bob's Red Mill Cooking School in Milwaukie, Oregon. Lori's passion for healthy foods is illustrated in this vegan tomato soup, which contains cooked quinoa and gets marvelous flavor from the vegetables, basil, vinegar, and onions.

2 cups water
1 cup whole grain quinoa, such as Bob's Red Mill or Ancient Harvest
¾ teaspoon salt, divided
2 tablespoons olive oil
1 large yellow onion, diced
2 garlic cloves, minced
1 cup peeled and diced carrots
2 stalks celery, diced
4 cups gluten-free, low sodium vegetable broth, such as Imagine, or homemade Vegetable Broth (page 677)
1 can (28 ounces) diced tomatoes, with juice
4 teaspoons chopped fresh basil or 2 teaspoons dried basil
2 teaspoons red wine vinegar
½ teaspoon freshly ground black pepper
2 cups green onions, chopped
½ cup soy milk

1 In a 2-quart saucepan, bring water to a boil. Add quinoa and ¼ teaspoon of the salt. Reduce the heat to low, and simmer, covered, 8 to 10 minutes or until all the liquid is absorbed. This will yield 4 cups cooked quinoa. Set aside.

2 In a Dutch oven or other deep, heavy pot with a tight-fitting lid, heat the oil over medium heat. Add onion and cook, stirring, for about 3 minutes or until softened. Add garlic and cook, stirring constantly, for 1 minute. Stir in carrots and celery. Reduce heat to low, cover, and cook 12 to 15 minutes or until vegetables are softened.

3 Stir in broth, tomatoes, basil, and vinegar and bring to a boil over medium heat. Reduce heat to low and simmer, uncovered, 10 minutes.

4 Stir in remaining ½ teaspoon of salt, pepper, green onions, and milk and simmer, uncovered, for 20 minutes. Add cooked quinoa and cook 10 minutes more or until soup reaches desired thickness. Serve immediately.

RINSING QUINOA

If you do not use Bob's Red Mill or Ancient Harvest quinoa (or quinoa imported by Inca Organics), you must rinse the quinoa grains at least three times in water or it will taste bitter. While these companies have pre-rinsed the grains for you, other companies might not—leaving the grain's natural coating called *saponin*, which is the plant's natural protection from insects and pests. Although it is harmless to humans, its bitter taste can detract from your enjoyment of this unique grain. If you're unsure about the source of your quinoa, it's best to rinse it before cooking. Simply rinse the quinoa in a sieve, rubbing the grains between your fingers. Drain and repeat until the water runs clear.

Mediterranean Tomato Soup with Rice

MAKES 4 SERVINGS

Brimming with the flavors of southern France, this soup uses cooked instant rice that slightly thickens the soup as it cooks. An easy homemade herb blend makes this recipe a snap to prepare. If you don't like chunks of tomato, puree the tomatoes in a blender before you cook them.

2 cans (14 to 15 ounces each) gluten-free, low-sodium chicken broth, such as Swanson's Natural Goodness, or homemade Chicken Broth (page 676)

1 can (14 to 15 ounces) petite diced tomatoes, including juices

¼ cup diced fresh onion or 1 tablespoon dried minced onion

2 teaspoons homemade Mediterranean Herb Blend (page 667)

½ teaspoon sugar

¼ teaspoon salt

¼ cup instant brown rice

Combine all the ingredients in a 2-quart heavy saucepan. Bring to a boil over high heat, reduce the heat to low, and simmer, covered, 20 minutes. Serve hot.

Pumpkin Soup

MAKES 4 SERVINGS

After traveling for twenty-four hours to get to Vienna, Austria, all my husband and I wanted on our first night was a quick dinner before retiring to our hotel. When I spotted pumpkin soup on the menu that night, I knew I had to try it because pumpkins are a local staple. It turned out to be the most fabulous pumpkin soup of the trip—a little heartier than the others because it used beef broth rather than chicken broth. This is my interpretation of that extraordinary soup, which by the way, is customarily served with a drizzle of pumpkin oil, although you could also use mild extra-virgin olive oil.

1 tablespoon olive oil

1 large leek, cleaned, rinsed, and cut into thin slices

2 garlic cloves, minced

½ teaspoon rubbed sage

1½ teaspoons fresh thyme or ½ teaspoon dried

½ teaspoon salt

¼ teaspoon freshly ground black pepper

1 can (14 to 15 ounces) gluten-free, low-sodium beef broth, such as Swanson's, or homemade Beef Broth (page 676)

¾ cup (about ½ of a 14 to 15 ounce can) pure pumpkin (not pumpkin pie filling)

½ cup dry white wine

¼ cup toasted pumpkin seeds*

Pumpkin oil to taste **

1 In a heavy, medium pan, heat the olive oil over medium heat. Cook the leek and garlic, stirring constantly, until leeks are soft, about 3 to 5 minutes.

2 Add the sage, thyme, salt, pepper, broth, pumpkin, and wine. Reduce heat to low and simmer, covered, 30 minutes. Remove pan from heat and cool slightly. In a blender, puree the mixture in batches or use an immersion blender to puree the soup in the pan until it is very smooth. Strain the soup through a sieve to remove any leek pieces.

3 Bring the soup to serving temperature and serve immediately, garnished with pumpkin seeds and a drizzle of pumpkin oil.

*To toast pumpkin seeds, preheat the oven to 300°F. Spread the pumpkin seeds in a foil-lined 13 × 9-inch baking sheet (not nonstick). Roast until lightly browned, about 15 to 20 minutes (time may vary according to size and moisture in seeds,). Lightly salt to taste.

**Available at health food stores.

Cumin-Scented Pumpkin and Bean Soup

MAKES 4 SERVINGS

This soup is delicious and nutritious, thanks to the white beans and pumpkin. The cumin adds important antioxidants and the beans are the sole thickener.

1 can (14 to 15 ounces) pure pumpkin (not pumpkin pie filling)

1 can (14 to 15 ounces) white navy beans, rinsed and drained

1 can (14 to 15 ounces) gluten-free, low-sodium chicken broth, such as Swanson's Natural Goodness, or homemade Chicken Broth (page 676)

1 tablespoon honey

2 tablespoons grated fresh onion or 1 teaspoon dried minced onion

1 teaspoon ground cumin

½ teaspoon salt

¼ teaspoon garlic powder

¼ cup toasted pumpkin seeds (page 165)

½ teaspoon ground sage

1 In a blender, place pumpkin, beans, broth, honey, onion, cumin, salt, and garlic powder and puree until very, very smooth.

2 Transfer the mixture to a heavy saucepan and heat to serving temperature. Serve in soup bowls or mugs, each garnished with a tablespoon of pumpkin seeds and a dash of sage.

Moroccan Pumpkin–White-Bean Bisque

MAKES 4 SERVINGS

This soup is a powerhouse of nutrients and has a delicious, exotic taste. White beans provide ample nutrients and fiber, plus the pumpkin is no "lightweight," either. The beans thicken the bisque without requiring any other thickener. And the spices—such as turmeric—are very healthy.

1 can (14 to 15 ounces) pure pumpkin (not pumpkin pie filling)

1 can (14 to 15 ounces) white navy beans, rinsed and drained

1 can (14 to 15 ounces) gluten-free, low-sodium chicken broth, such as Swanson's Natural Goodness, or homemade Chicken Broth (page 676)

1 tablespoon honey

2 tablespoons diced onion or 1 teaspoon dried minced onions

½ teaspoon salt

¼ teaspoon ground allspice

¼ teaspoon ground cinnamon

¼ teaspoon paprika (smoked paprika is even better)

¼ teaspoon ground turmeric

¼ teaspoon garlic powder

¼ cup toasted pumpkin seeds (page 165), for garnish

1 Place all the ingredients in a blender and puree until very, very smooth.

2 Transfer to a heavy saucepan and heat over medium heat to serving temperature. Serve in soup bowls or mugs, each garnished with a table-spoon of pumpkin seeds.

Red Beet Borscht

MAKES 4 SERVINGS

I had to learn how to make borscht myself when the Russian restaurant near my home closed. Although some versions are served cold, mine is served hot. The apple lends a touch of sweetness that contrasts nicely with the savory-sweet beets. Like the restaurant, my version leaves small chunks of apples and beets in the soup, but you can also puree the soup to a smooth consistency if you wish.

¾ pound beets (about 5 to 6 medium beets)

Kosher salt and freshly ground black pepper

3 sprigs fresh thyme, savory, or rosemary, divided

3 tablespoons extra-virgin olive oil, divided

1 small onion, diced

1 apple (such as Granny Smith), peeled and finely diced

1 garlic clove, minced

4 cups gluten-free, low-sodium beef broth, such as
    Swanson's or homemade Beef Broth (page 675),
    heated

1 tablespoon champagne or sherry vinegar

1 tablespoon honey, or to taste

1 tablespoon finely chopped fresh dill weed, divided

Additional salt and pepper to taste

4 tablespoons sour cream or sour cream alternative,
    such as Tofutti, for garnish

1 Place a rack in the middle of the oven. Preheat the oven to 400°F. Scrub the beets well and place them on a large piece of aluminum foil. Sprinkle them with salt and pepper, add an herb sprig, and drizzle with 1 tablespoon olive oil. Fold the foil tightly around the beets and bake until they are tender, about 1 hour. Set aside to cool. When the beets are just slightly warm, slip off their skins (wearing plastic gloves to protect your hands from the beet color), and chop them into 1-inch chunks.

2 In a large heavy-bottomed pot, heat the remaining 2 tablespoons oil over medium heat. Add the onion and apple and cook until the onions are soft and translucent, about 7 to 10 minutes. Add the remaining herb sprigs, garlic, and broth and simmer, covered, 20 minutes. Remove the herb sprigs. Set aside to cool 10 minutes.

3 Put the beets, cooked onions, and apples, and most of the cooled broth in a blender. Blend until not quite smooth, leaving a few little chunks of beets and apple. Add more broth if necessary if the mixture is too thick. Add the vinegar, honey, and 1 teaspoon dill. Season with salt and pepper to taste and blend again.

4 Return the borsch to the pot and cook over medium heat until it reaches serving temperature. Serve in bowls, garnished with a tablespoon of sour cream and a sprinkle of the remaining dill.

Roasted Red Pepper Soup with Basil Pesto

MAKES 4 SERVINGS

This soup makes a very colorful main dish. Buy roasted red peppers in a jar and save yourself the work of roasting fresh ones from scratch. This soup could also be served in espresso cups as a first course for a dinner party.

4 roasted red bell peppers (about 1 cup from a jar)

2 teaspoons dried minced onion

1 teaspoon ground cumin

¼ teaspoon garlic powder

¼ teaspoon sugar

3 cups gluten-free, low-sodium chicken broth, such
    as Swanson's Natural Goodness, or homemade
    Chicken Broth (page 676)

¾ cup fresh orange juice

1 tablespoon extra-virgin olive oil

½ teaspoon grated orange zest

¼ teaspoon salt, or to taste

¼ teaspoon freshly ground white pepper

2 tablespoons sweet rice flour stirred into ¼ cup
    cold water until smooth

1 tablespoon homemade Basil Pesto (page 672), for
    garnish

1 tablespoon chopped fresh basil or 1 teaspoon
    dried, for garnish

1 In a blender, place bell peppers, onion, cumin, garlic powder, sugar, broth, orange juice, oil, orange zest, salt and pepper and puree until very smooth. Transfer soup to a heavy medium saucepan over medium heat. Bring to a boil, reduce the heat to low, and simmer, covered, 10 minutes.

2 Raise the heat to medium, stir in the sweet rice flour mixture and continue to cook until slightly thickened, stirring constantly.

3 Divide the soup among 4 soup bowls. Stir ¼ of the basil pesto into each serving and garnish with a sprinkle of basil. Serve immediately.

Traditional Gazpacho

MAKES 4 SERVINGS

Gazpacho is classically made with fresh vegetables that require chopping, but this easy version uses canned diced tomatoes and store-bought salsa—plus a few fresh cucumbers and peppers to add crunch—and is quickly "chopped" in a food processor. This recipe yields a relatively small amount of soup per person, since I usually serve gazpacho as an appetizer rather than a main dish. If you want larger servings or wish to serve more people, simply double the recipe.

1 can (14 to 15 ounces) petite diced tomatoes, including juice

1 small yellow bell pepper, cored and cut in ½-inch slices

1 (4-inch) piece English (or hothouse) cucumber, unpeeled and cut in ½-inch slices

¼ cup store-bought gluten-free Mexican salsa, such as Newman's Own or Pace

¼ cup chopped fresh cilantro, divided

2 teaspoons chopped fresh onion or ½ teaspoon dried minced onion

½ teaspoon ground coriander

¼ teaspoon salt

¼ teaspoon freshly ground black pepper

1 tablespoon red wine vinegar

1 fresh avocado, peeled, seeded, and chopped, for garnish

1 In a food processor, combine half of the tomatoes with the bell pepper and cucumber. Pulse until the bell pepper and cucumber are finely chopped.

2 Transfer the mixture to a large bowl and add the remaining tomatoes, salsa, 3 tablespoons chopped cilantro, onion, coriander, salt, pepper, and vinegar. Refrigerate at least 1 hour or overnight. Serve in coffee cups, goblets, or small bowls, garnished with avocado and remaining chopped fresh cilantro.

Gazpacho with Fruit

MAKES 4 SERVINGS

You may be surprised by pineapple in gazpacho, but a very dear friend served a similar soup at an elegant gluten-free dinner a few years ago and everyone loved it. It was wintertime, but this cool green gazpacho, made without tomatoes, can be served year-round.

Start with a small bit of cilantro and then taste to see if it needs more. Use this taste to determine if it also needs honey, as some brands of pineapple may be sweeter than others. You can substitute fresh pineapple chunks from the supermarket produce section for fresher flavor.

2 cans (8 ounces each) pineapple tidbits in juice, not syrup; drained

1 small English (or hothouse) cucumber, cut into 1-inch chunks, divided

2 stalks celery, fibers removed and cut into 1-inch chunks, divided

2 green onions, white parts only

Juice of 1 lime

¼ teaspoon salt, or to taste

1 tablespoon olive oil

Chopped fresh cilantro to taste (start with ¼ of a bunch)

1 tablespoon honey (if needed)

Dash hot pepper sauce, such as Frank's, or to taste

Paprika, for garnish

1 In a blender, place 1 can pineapple, ½ of the cucumbers, celery, and green onions. Process until very smooth. Add the remaining pineapple, cucumbers, celery, and onions plus lime juice, salt, oil, and cilantro. Pulse blender a few times, but leave a few small chunks. Taste to see if more seasoning is needed. Refrigerate the soup at least one hour or overnight, until serving time.

2 Serve chilled in small coffee cups or bowls as an appetizer. As a main dish for lunch, serve in small bowls, garnished with additional sprigs of fresh cilantro and a sprinkle of paprika.

Apple-Fennel Soup

MAKES 4 SERVINGS

Serve this creamy, refreshing bisque in tiny espresso cups or small bowls as the first course for dinner guests or as a light main course for a fall luncheon.

2 tablespoons canola oil

1 small onion, chopped

1 rib celery, chopped

1 head fennel, chopped

1 medium leek, cleaned, rinsed, and chopped

1 large garlic clove, minced

1 cup apple juice

1 cup gluten-free, low-sodium chicken broth, such as Swanson's Natural Goodness, or homemade Chicken Broth (page 676)

3 apples (such as Granny Smith), peeled and chopped

2 teaspoons fresh ginger, minced

½ teaspoon salt, or to taste

¼ teaspoon white pepper

½ cup half-and-half or plain yogurt or non-dairy creamer of choice

1 tablespoon sweet rice flour (if necessary)

2 tablespoons Calvados (apple brandy), optional, or apple cider

2 tablespoons chopped fresh parsley, for garnish

Dash of paprika, for garnish

1 In a medium sauce pan, heat the oil over medium heat. Cook the onion, celery, fennel, and leek until soft, about 10 minutes. Add the garlic and cook 2 to 3 minutes more, stirring constantly.

2 Add the apple juice, broth, apples, ginger, salt, and pepper and cook over low heat, uncovered, 30 minutes. Remove from heat and let cool 15 minutes.

3 Puree ¼ of the soup with an immersion blender until smooth to give a creamier consistency, yet still leave some crunch. Stir in the half-and-half and cook over low heat, stirring constantly, until hot. (As an alternative to the half-and-half, use yogurt and if the soup isn't thick enough, stir sweet rice flour into 2 tablespoons cold water until smooth. Then whisk into soup and cook over low heat until it thickens.) Serve hot, adding Calvados just before serving, if using. Garnish with parsley and a dash of paprika.

Chilled Double Melon Soup

MAKES 4 SERVINGS

The idea of a fruit soup surprises many people. However, the unexpected sweetness often balances a savory main dish; plus fruit soups provide critical nutrients. Serve this easy melon soup in small portions as a first course for dinner or in larger portions for lunch. It is especially pretty when you pour both soups into opposite sides of the same bowl at the same time, making a soup that is half green and half orange. Salt used as a garnish may seem unusual, but try it—you'll see it enhances the melon flavor.

You can use pre-chopped melon from your produce section for this soup, but if you use a fresh melon, look for one that feels heavy for its size, has no cuts or bruises on the rind, has a yellow spot on its belly where it rested on the ground, yields slightly to gentle pressure on its flesh, and gives off a pleasant melon scent.

1 small very ripe cantaloupe, peeled, seeded, and coarsely chopped

¼ cup orange-juice concentrate

3 tablespoons honey, divided

½ very ripe honeydew melon, peeled, seeded, and coarsely chopped

1 tablespoon fresh lime juice

1 teaspoon minced fresh mint, or to taste, plus additional mint sprigs, for garnish

4 teaspoons sour cream, or sour cream substitute, such as Tofutti, for garnish (optional)

¼ teaspoon salt, for garnish (optional)

1 In a food processor or blender, puree the cantaloupe, orange-juice concentrate, and 1½ tablespoons of the honey in batches until very smooth. Transfer to a large measuring cup with pour spout and chill, covered, at least 3 hours or overnight.

2 In the same food processor or blender, puree honeydew, lime juice, mint, and the remaining 1½ tablespoons honey in batches until very smooth. Transfer to a large measuring cup with pour spout and chill, covered, at least 3 hours or overnight.

3 To serve, pour equal amounts of each soup into chilled serving cups or bowls at the same time and at the same speed so that you have a container with two colors of soup. Garnish each serving with sour cream and mint sprigs, if using. Sprinkle with salt, if using.

MEAT AND FISH SOUPS AND STEWS

Chicken Noodle Soup with Dumplings

MAKES 4 SERVINGS

Chicken noodle soup, brimming with dense, hearty dumplings, is my idea of comfort food. This soup tastes the best when made with your own chicken broth, but don't let that stop you; canned broth works just fine. These proportions are just guidelines. You can start with this recipe and adjust it to your taste. In fact, when I make chicken noodle soup at home, I rarely measure any of the ingredients. I work by instinct.

It's better to boil the dumplings in a separate pot of broth or water rather than to boil them with the soup. Leave the lid on while they are boiling and don't peek until the cooking time is up so the dumplings keep their shape.

DUMPLINGS
Water for boiling dumplings
1½ teaspoons salt
1¼ cups Carol's Sorghum Blend (page x)
⅔ cup potato starch
2 teaspoons baking powder
½ teaspoon baking soda
1 large egg
¼ cup unsalted butter or buttery spread, such as Earth Balance, at room temperature
½ cup well-shaken buttermilk or homemade Buttermilk (page 677)
2 tablespoons chopped fresh parsley

SOUP

1 teaspoon canola oil

½ cup thinly sliced celery

½ cup chopped onion

6 cups gluten-free, low sodium chicken broth, such as Swanson's Natural Goodness, or homemade Chicken Broth (page 676)

1 small carrot, thinly sliced

½ teaspoon poultry seasoning

¼ teaspoon salt, or to taste

¼ teaspoon freshly ground white pepper

⅛ teaspoon ground nutmeg

1 bay leaf

1 cup uncooked gluten-free noodles (or pasta shape of choice), such as Heartland's Finest, DeBoles, or Pastariso

1½ cups diced cooked chicken

1 tablespoon fresh lemon juice

¼ cup chopped fresh parsley or 2 tablespoons chopped dried, for garnish

1 Make the dumplings: Fill a large pot with 4 inches of water and 1 teaspoon of salt. Bring to a boil. Meanwhile, in a medium mixing bowl, whisk together sorghum blend, potato starch, baking powder, baking soda, and the remaining salt.

2 In another small bowl, whisk together the egg and butter. Gradually whisk the egg and butter mixture into the dry ingredients, alternating with the buttermilk, and mixing just until moistened. Stir in parsley. The dough will be stiff.

3 Drop the dough by tablespoonfuls into the boiling water. (Or, use a small spring-action, metal scoop to drop balls of dough into the boiling water). Cover, reduce heat to simmer, and cook, without lifting the lid, for 20 minutes.

4 While the dumplings boil, make the soup: Heat oil in a large, heavy saucepan over medium heat. Add the celery and onion and cook 3 to 4 minutes, until soft and slightly browned. Add the broth, carrot, poultry seasoning, salt, pepper, nutmeg, and bay leaf. Bring to a boil, then reduce heat to low and cook, covered, 10 to 15 minutes.

5 Add the noodles and chicken and simmer, uncovered, until chicken is heated through and

noodles are done, about 3 to 5 minutes for Heartland's Finest noodles and up to 8 to 10 minutes for other brands.

6 Stir in the lemon juice at the last minute; remove the bay leaf. Ladle the soup into 4 bowls, remove dumplings from boiling water with a slotted spoon, and divide evenly among the 4 bowls. Serve, garnished with parsley.

Pho (Vietnamese Chicken Noodle Soup)

MAKES 4 SERVINGS

Pho is simply chicken noodle soup with a Vietnamese twist. I like to add the star anise and cinnamon for added flavor as well. I prefer to use my own homemade chicken broth and add salt to taste, but if you use store-bought chicken broth you might not need any additional salt. Use protective gloves when you cut the chiles to avoid the irritating effects of their oils.

6 cups gluten-free, low-sodium chicken broth, such as Swanson's Natural Goodness, or homemade Chicken Broth (page 676)

2-inch piece of fresh ginger, grated

2 whole star anise

2 whole cinnamon sticks

2 teaspoon ground coriander

2 cups chopped cooked chicken

1 teaspoon Asian fish sauce, such as A Taste of Thai

½ pound (8 ounces) rice noodles, such as Thai Kitchen or Tinkyada

GARNISHES

2 cups fresh bean sprouts

1 cup chopped fresh cilantro

½ cup chopped fresh basil

½ fresh mint leaves

2 limes, cut in half

2 to 3 sliced fresh jalapeño or serrano chiles

1 In a Dutch oven or other deep, heavy pot with a tight-fitting lid, combine broth, ginger, star anise, cinnamon, and coriander. Bring to simmer over medium-high heat. Immediately reduce heat and simmer, covered, 30 minutes. (The broth will remain clearer if not allowed to boil.) Add chicken and fish sauce and simmer 15 minutes more. Add rice noodles to chicken broth and simmer until al dente, following manufacturer's directions for cooking time. Remove star anise and cinnamon.

2 To serve, place ½ cup bean sprouts in each of 4 large soup bowls. Ladle equal amounts of hot soup into bowls. Serve immediately with cilantro, basil, mint, lime wedges, and jalapeño peppers on the side in bowls so everybody can garnish their own soup.

Tortilla Soup

MAKES 4 SERVINGS

Part of the fun of eating this flavorful soup is the fresh garnishes you can sprinkle on it. Don't add the fried tortilla strips until the very last minute so that you can preserve their delicate crispiness.

1 tablespoon canola oil

1 small white onion, finely chopped

1 quart gluten-free, low-sodium chicken broth, such as Swanson's Natural Goodness, or homemade Chicken Broth (page 676)

½ teaspoon salt

1 teaspoon chopped fresh oregano or ¼ teaspoon dried

¼ teaspoon white pepper

Juice of 2 limes

½ pound boneless, skinless cooked chicken, cut into ½-inch cubes

TORTILLA STRIPS

Canola oil for frying

3 gluten-free white corn tortillas, such as Tamxico, (6-inch size), cut in half and then into ¼-inch strips

Salt to taste

GARNISHES

1 ripe avocado, peeled, seeded and coarsely chopped

2 plum tomatoes, seeded and chopped

¼ cup chopped fresh cilantro

¼ cup chopped green onions

1 In a large soup pot, heat the oil over medium heat. Add the onion and cook until tender, about 5 minutes. Add the broth, salt, oregano, and white pepper. Cover and simmer on low while preparing remaining ingredients.

2 Make the tortilla strips: In a heavy skillet, heat ½ inch of oil over medium-high heat. Fry tortilla strips until lightly golden and crisp. Watch carefully; tortilla strips can burn quickly. Drain on paper towels and sprinkle with salt.

3 Add the lime juice and chicken to the soup and bring to serving temperature. Serve immediately in 4 bowls, topped with a handful of tortilla strips and garnished with avocado, tomatoes, cilantro, and onions.

Simple Ham and Bean Soup

MAKES 4 SERVINGS

This dish was a mainstay at our house when I was growing up; however, we always started with dry beans and simmered the soup all day on the stove. This easy version starts with canned beans and provides important fiber that helps you reach your daily goal of 25 to 38 grams of fiber. We served it with cornbread, but I know that some people prefer it served over hot boiled potatoes.

1 tablespoon canola oil

1 small onion, finely chopped

2 stalks celery, chopped

1 large carrot, peeled and sliced

2 cans (14 to 15 ounces each) gluten-free, low-sodium chicken broth, such as Swanson's Natural Goodness or homemade Chicken Broth (page 676)

2 cans (14 to 15 ounces each) white navy beans, rinsed and drained

1 pound ham cut into ½-inch cubes

1 tablespoon sugar or honey

2 teaspoons fresh thyme or 1 teaspoon dried

1 teaspoon chopped fresh marjoram or chervil or ½ teaspoon dried marjoram or chervil (optional)

¼ teaspoon freshly ground black pepper

1 In a Dutch oven or other deep, heavy pot with a tight-fitting lid, heat the oil over medium-high heat. Add the onions, celery, and carrot, and cook until the onions are soft and translucent, about 5 to 7 minutes. Add the remaining ingredients and bring to a boil. Reduce the heat, cover, and cook 20 minutes or until all the vegetables are tender.

2 For a creamier soup, use a handheld or immersion blender to puree as much of the soup as you like to bring it to the desired consistency. Taste and add salt, if desired. Serve hot.

Tuscan Bean Soup

MAKES 4 SERVINGS

This simple bean soup can be expanded to include bits of sausage, prosciutto, or pancetta (Italian bacon), and vegetables such as onions, carrots, tomato, kale, Swiss chard, spinach, celery, potatoes, and cabbage. You can also add rosemary, fennel, or additional parsley for flavor.

¼ cup extra-virgin olive oil

1 small onion, chopped

1 carrot, peeled and chopped

2 cans (14 to 15 ounces each) cannellini (white kidney) beans, drained and rinsed

1 medium ripe tomato, chopped

2 tablespoons chopped Italian parsley

1 teaspoon rubbed sage, or to taste

1 tablespoon tomato paste

Salt and pepper to taste

2 cups gluten-free, low-sodium chicken broth, such as Swanson's Natural Goodness, or homemade Chicken Broth (page 676), or as needed

In a heavy saucepan, heat the oil over medium heat. Add the onion and carrot and cook until soft, about 5 to 7 minutes. Add remaining ingredients and simmer, covered, 30 minutes to 1 hour, until vegetables are tender. Add more broth or water if soup becomes dry. Serve hot.

Minestrone Soup

MAKES 6 SERVINGS

Wonderfully hearty and flavorful, this soup is a perfect choice for a cold, gray winter day. A slice of crusty gluten-free bread completes the meal.

1 teaspoon olive oil

½ pound gluten-free ground Italian sausage, such as Applegate Farms

1 small onion, sliced

1 quart gluten-free, low-sodium beef broth, such as Swanson's, or homemade Beef Broth (page 675)

1 can (14 to 15 ounces) diced tomatoes, including juice

2 large carrots, cut in ½-inch diagonal slices

1 small zucchini, cut in ¼-inch slices

1 garlic clove, minced

1 teaspoon Italian seasoning

½ teaspoon salt, or to taste

¼ teaspoon freshly ground black pepper

1 bay leaf

1 tablespoon chopped fresh parsley

1 can (14 to 15 ounces) cannellini (white kidney) beans, rinsed and drained

½ cup uncooked gluten-free elbow macaroni, such as Heartland's Finest

¼ cup grated Parmesan cheese, or soy alternative, such as Soyco

1 In a Dutch oven or other deep, heavy pot with a tight-fitting lid, heat the oil over medium heat. Add the sausage and onions and cook until sausage is browned and the onions are soft, about 5 to 7 minutes.

2 Add the broth, tomatoes, carrots, zucchini, garlic, Italian seasoning, salt, pepper, bay leaf, parsley, and beans. Bring to a boil, reduce heat to low, and simmer, covered, 30 minutes. Following pasta manufacturer's directions, add pasta and simmer just until pasta is done. Remove bay leaf and serve immediately with dusting of Parmesan cheese.

Cannellini Bean Soup with Italian Sausage

MAKES 4 SERVINGS

Hearty and robust, this is a perfect dish for a cold winter's day. Because Italian sausage is quite flavorful and high in fat I only use one link, but you can always increase it to two links if you wish.

1 tablespoon olive oil

¼ pound (1 link) gluten-free Italian sausage, such as Applegate Farms, casing removed

1 large onion, chopped

1 large carrot, chopped

1 large stalk celery, chopped

2 cans (14 to 15 ounces each) cannellini (white kidney) beans, rinsed and drained

2 cans (14 to 15 ounces each) gluten-free, low-sodium chicken broth, such as Swanson's Natural Goodness, or homemade Chicken Broth (page 676)

1 garlic clove, minced

3 teaspoons chopped fresh thyme

2 teaspoons chopped fresh rosemary

1 bay leaf

1 In a heavy, medium pan, heat the oil over medium-high heat. Add the sausage, onion, carrot, and celery, and cook stirring frequently, until sausage is browned and vegetables begin to soften, about 5 to 7 minutes.

2 Add the beans, broth, garlic, thyme, rosemary, and bay leaf. Bring to a boil, cover, and reduce the heat to low, and simmer, covered, 15 to 20 minutes. Remove the bay leaf. Soup may be eaten as is, or to thicken, carefully insert immersion blender into pot and puree some of the soup. Or, transfer ½ cup soup to blender and carefully puree, placing lid loosely on blender (covered with a dish towel) because soup will be hot and may erupt at the top of the blender. Return pureed soup to pot. Bring to serving temperature and serve immediately.

Hearty Beef Stew

MAKES 4 SERVINGS

Here is a perfect dinner for winter nights when you want something hot and comforting, yet don't want to spend hours in the kitchen. The answer is to let this stew cook all day in a slow cooker. All you have to do is make a tossed salad and pair it with cornbread or French bread.

1 tablespoon canola oil

1 pound top sirloin, cut in 1-inch cubes

3 tablespoons cornstarch (for dredging)

2 cups gluten-free, low-sodium beef broth, such as Swanson's, or homemade Beef Broth (page 675)

½ cup red wine (optional)

1 can (6 ounces) tomato juice

½ cup chopped onion

1 small carrot, sliced in 1-inch diagonal pieces

1 bay leaf

1 teaspoon chopped fresh thyme or ½ teaspoon dried

½ teaspoon salt

¼ teaspoon freshly ground black pepper

½ teaspoon smoked Spanish paprika

1 tablespoon chopped fresh parsley, for garnish

1 In a Dutch oven or other deep, heavy pot with a tight-fitting lid, heat the oil over medium heat. Dust the sirloin cubes with cornstarch, and add to the pot.

2 Cook the beef cubes until they are nicely browned, about 7 to 10 minutes. Add the broth, red wine, tomato juice, onion, carrot, bay leaf, thyme, salt, pepper, and paprika.

3 Reduce the heat to low and simmer 2 to 3 hours or until the vegetables are cooked through. Or put all of the ingredients in a slow cooker and cook 6 to 8 hours on Low setting. Remove the bay leaf and serve immediately, garnished with fresh parsley.

Middle Eastern Beef Stew

MAKES 6 SERVINGS

Dramatically flavorful, this dish is for those who like full-bodied dishes with exotic flavors. The spices are accentuated by the surprising and delicious sweetness of raisins—a combination that is typical of Middle Eastern dishes.

2 tablespoons olive oil

1 pound beef tenderloin, cut 1-inch cubes

1 teaspoon salt

¼ teaspoon freshly ground black pepper

1 medium onion, chopped

½ cup very thinly sliced carrots

1 garlic clove, minced

1 tablespoon smoked paprika

2 teaspoons ground cumin

1½ teaspoons ground cinnamon

½ teaspoon ground ginger

½ teaspoon ground coriander

2 cups gluten-free, low-sodium beef broth, such as Swanson's, or homemade Beef Broth (page 675)

1 can (14 to 15 ounces) diced tomatoes, including juice

1 can (14 to 15 ounces) chickpeas, drained

½ cup halved, pitted kalamata olives

½ cup golden raisins

Juice and half of 1 lemon's grated zest

3 cups hot cooked brown rice

½ cup chopped fresh cilantro, for garnish

1 In a large, heavy pot, heat the oil over medium-high heat. Sprinkle the beef with salt and pepper and cook until lightly browned on all sides, about 3 to 5 minutes per side.

2 Add onions and continue to cook, stirring constantly, until onions are soft and beef is darkly browned, about 5 to 7 minutes. Add carrots, garlic, paprika, cumin, cinnamon, ginger, coriander, broth, tomatoes, and chickpeas. Reduce heat to low and simmer, covered, 30 minutes. Add olives and raisins, and simmer 10 minutes more. Just before serving, stir in lemon zest. Serve 1 cup per person over ½ cup cooked brown rice, garnished with cilantro.

Italian Meatball Soup

MAKES 4 SERVINGS

If you keep meatballs in the freezer, you can put this recipe together in a snap. I prefer the Heartland's Finest pasta for this soup because it holds its shape during cooking. If you store the leftovers, it's wise to remove the pasta, if you can, or it will get mushy. Then, when you reheat it, simply toss in an amount of pasta proportionally appropriate to the amount of soup and cook it until it's done.

1 tablespoon olive oil

½ cup chopped onion

¼ cup chopped celery

2 cups water

2 cans (14 to 15 ounces) gluten-free, low-sodium beef broth, such as Swanson's, or homemade Beef Broth (page 675)

1 can (14 to 15 ounces) petite diced tomatoes, including juice

1 garlic clove, minced

2 tablespoons tomato paste

1 teaspoon dried Italian seasoning

½ teaspoon salt

¼ teaspoon crushed red pepper

16 cooked homemade Meatballs (page 207)

1 cup uncooked gluten-free elbow macaroni, such as Heartland's Finest, or pasta of choice

¼ cup Parmesan cheese, for garnish

1 In a Dutch oven or other deep, heavy pot with a tight-fitting lid, heat the oil over medium heat. Add onion and celery and cook, stirring, until soft, about 3 to 4 minutes. Add water, broth, tomatoes, garlic, tomato paste, Italian seasoning, salt, and crushed red pepper; stir to combine. Cover and simmer 15 minutes.

2 Add the meatballs and macaroni to pot and bring soup to a boil. Reduce heat and simmer just until macaroni is done. Serve immediately, garnished with Parmesan cheese.

Lamb Stew

MAKES 4 SERVINGS

Simmer this stew in the oven for a hearty winter supper that will perfume your house as it cooks. French bread and crisp salad are all you need to round out the meal.

1½ pounds boneless lamb stew meat, fat trimmed away cut into 1½-inch pieces
1 teaspoon salt
½ teaspoon freshly ground black pepper
2 tablespoons canola oil
1 small onion, peeled and chopped
1 carrot, peeled and chopped
1 stalk celery, chopped
1 cup finely chopped cabbage
1 leek, cleaned and chopped
1 garlic clove, minced
1 cup gluten-free, low-sodium beef broth, such as Swanson's, or homemade Beef Broth (page 675), or dry white wine
1 can (14 to 15 ounces) diced tomatoes, including juice
¼ teaspoon ground thyme
⅛ teaspoon fennel seed
⅛ teaspoon ground allspice
6 small new potatoes, scrubbed and halved
Sweet rice flour (if necessary)
1 tablespoon chopped fresh parsley, for garnish

1 Preheat the oven to 325°F. Sprinkle the lamb with salt and pepper. In a Dutch oven or other deep, oven-proof heavy pot with a tight-fitting lid, heat the oil over medium-high heat. Add the lamb and cook until it is dark brown on all sides, about 6 to 8 minutes. Transfer the lamb to a plate.

2 Add the onion, carrot, celery, cabbage, and leek and cook until the vegetables are limp, about 3 to 5 minutes. Add the garlic and stir 30 seconds more. Return the lamb to the Dutch oven.

3 Add the broth, tomatoes, thyme, fennel seed, and allspice and stir to mix well. Cover and bake 45 minutes. Add potatoes and return stew to the oven and bake 30 minutes more. If the stew is not thick enough, stir 1 tablespoon sweet rice flour into 2 tablespoons cold water until smooth and stir it into the stew. Cook over medium heat until the mixture thickens, about 2 to 3 minutes. Serve immediately, garnished with parsley.

Smoky Turkey-Bacon Chili

MAKES 6 SERVINGS

Turkey chili takes on a new set of deeper, richer flavors with the addition of smoked paprika and gluten-free beer. If you don't want to use beer, use gluten-free hard cider such as Woodchuck.

1 strip uncooked bacon
1 pound ground turkey (I use half dark meat and half white meat)
1 small onion, finely diced
1 large garlic clove, minced
1 can (14 to 15 ounces) fire-roasted diced tomatoes, including juice
1 bottle (12 ounces) gluten-free beer, such as Bard's Tale or Redbridge, or hard cider
1 can (14 to 15 ounces) pinto beans, rinsed and drained
1 can (14 to 15 ounces) dark red kidney beans, rinsed and drained
1 tablespoon gluten-free Worcestershire sauce, such as French's
4 teaspoons chili powder
1½ teaspoons smoked Spanish paprika
1½ teaspoons ground cumin
1 teaspoon salt
1 teaspoon chopped fresh oregano or ½ teaspoon dried
¼ teaspoon freshly ground black pepper

1 In a Dutch oven or other deep, heavy pot with a tight-fitting lid, cook the bacon over medium heat until it is cooked through, about 3 to 4 minutes. Remove the bacon from the skillet, leave the bacon drippings in the skillet and reserve the bacon.

2 In the same Dutch oven, add the turkey and onions and cook until the turkey is browned, about 8 to 10 minutes. Add the remaining ingredients including the bacon strip, bring to a boil, and then reduce heat to low. Simmer, covered, 30 minutes, adding water if necessary. Serve hot.

White Chili

MAKES 6 SERVINGS

This is called white chili because it uses white beans and is made with turkey rather than beef. It has a much lighter color than traditional chili, but is still tremendously flavorful.

2 teaspoons canola oil

1 pound ground turkey

2 cans (14 to 15 ounces each) Great Northern beans, rinsed and drained

2 cans (14 to 15 ounces each) petite diced tomatoes with green chiles, including juice

1 can (4 ounces) diced green chiles, drained

1 small onion, peeled and sliced

2 teaspoons chopped fresh oregano or 1 teaspoon dried

1 teaspoon ground cumin

½ teaspoon salt

¼ teaspoon cayenne pepper

1 quart gluten-free, low-sodium chicken broth, such as Swanson's Natural Goodness, or homemade Chicken Broth (page 676)

2 garlic cloves, minced

½ cup chopped fresh cilantro, divided

1 cup shredded Monterey Jack cheese, or cheese alternative, such as Vegan Gourmet, for garnish

In a Dutch oven or other deep, heavy pot with a tight-fitting lid, heat the oil over medium heat. Add the turkey and cook until browned, about 7 to 10 minutes. Add the beans, tomatoes, chiles, onion, oregano, cumin, salt, cayenne, broth, garlic and ¼ cup cilantro. Cover and cook on medium heat for 30 to 40 minutes. Ladle into the soup bowls and serve immediately, garnished with a sprinkle of cheese and the remaining ¼ cup chopped cilantro.

Fish Chowder

MAKES 4 SERVINGS

The beauty of this chowder is that you can use any type of fish you like. It's a great soup for Saturday lunch, but my husband and I have often eaten it for dinner as well. It will be far tastier (and much richer) if you use whole milk.

2 slices uncooked bacon

1 small onion, peeled and chopped

1 rib celery, chopped

1 russet potato, peeled and cubed

½ cup gluten-free, low-sodium chicken broth, such as Swanson's Natural Goodness, or homemade Chicken Broth (page 676) or fish stock or broth (if you can find it)

1 teaspoon salt

1 teaspoon chopped fresh thyme or ½ teaspoon dried

½ teaspoon freshly ground black pepper

1 pound cod or sole fillets, skinned and cut into pieces

2 cups whole or 2% milk (cow's, rice, soy, potato, or nut)

2 tablespoons sweet rice flour

Dash hot pepper sauce, such as Frank's, to taste

Paprika, for garnish

1 In a large, heavy saucepan cook the bacon over medium heat until crispy, about 3 to 4 minutes. Drain bacon on paper towel, leaving bacon grease in saucepan.

2 Add onion and celery to the saucepan, reduce the heat to medium-low, and cook, covered, 10 minutes, or until the onions are soft and translucent. Add the potatoes, broth, salt, thyme, and pepper and cook, covered, 15 to 20 minutes, or until the potatoes are done. Add the fish and cook approximately 8 to 10 minutes or until it is just barely opaque when cut in the thickest part.

3 Stir sweet rice flour into ¼ cup of the milk until smooth, then stir this mixture into the remaining milk and add to the saucepan. Cook over medium-low heat until mixture thickens. Stir in hot pepper sauce. Serve hot, garnished with a dusting of paprika.

Salmon Corn Chowder

MAKES 6 SERVINGS

Fresh, cooked salmon makes a prettier soup than canned salmon, which turns the soup darker. But if all you have is canned salmon, by all means use it. Or, use your favorite fish fillets such as red snapper or halibut. At my house, all soups are served with hot pepper sauce at the table. You'll find it adds a nice kick to this otherwise mild chowder.

1 uncooked bacon strip

1 small onion, finely chopped

1 rib celery, finely chopped

1 garlic clove, minced

1 teaspoon celery salt

1 teaspoon chopped fresh thyme or ½ teaspoon dried

¼ teaspoon dry mustard, such as McCormick

½ cup gluten-free, low-sodium chicken broth, such as Swanson's Natural Goodness, or homemade Chicken Broth (page 676)

3½ cups 2% milk (cow's, rice, soy, potato, or nut), divided

2 tablespoons sweet rice flour

½ cup cooked corn kernels

1 pound cooked salmon fillets or steaks, skin and bones removed and chopped into 1-inch pieces

1 teaspoon chopped fresh dill or parsley or 1 teaspoon dried, for garnish

Paprika, for garnish

1 In a large, heavy saucepan, cook the bacon over medium-high heat until crispy, about 3 to 4 minutes. Set aside to cool; chop coarsely. Leave the bacon drippings in the pan.

2 Add onion and celery to pan and cook over medium heat, covered, 3 to 5 minutes, or until tender. Add the garlic, celery salt, thyme, mustard, and chicken broth. Cover and simmer 5 minutes.

Add all but ¼ cup of the milk and bring to a simmer, but do not boil. Whisk sweet rice flour into reserved milk until smooth and slowly stir into chowder. Cook over medium heat until mixture thickens slightly, about 3 to 5 minutes.

3 Add the corn kernels and salmon and stir gently. Cook on medium-low heat, covered, 1 minute, or until chowder reaches serving temperature. Serve immediately, garnished with a sprinkle of dill or parsley and a dash of paprika.

Bouillabaisse

MAKES 4 SERVINGS

This is the classic French seafood stew. Exotic flavors such as orange zest and fennel seed may seem out of place in such a stew but as you'll see, it's absolutely delightful. You can use any combination of seafood you wish, but be sure to use the herbs and spices suggested here for the best flavor.

1 tablespoon olive oil

1 small onion, finely chopped

1 garlic clove, minced

1 small carrot, peeled and thinly sliced

1 can (14 to 15 ounces) petite diced tomatoes, including juice

2 bottles (8 ounces each) clam juice

½ pound shellfish such as lobster, shrimp, or crab

2 teaspoons seafood seasoning of choice, such as Bayou Blast or Emeril's

½ teaspoon grated orange zest

¼ teaspoon fennel seed

1 teaspoon chopped fresh thyme or ¼ teaspoon dried

⅛ teaspoon saffron

1 bay leaf

½ pound each white fish, red snapper, or other white fish, cut in 2-inch pieces

Salt and pepper to taste

1 In a Dutch oven or other deep, heavy pot with a tight-fitting lid, heat the oil over medium heat. Add the onion, garlic, and carrot and cook until the onion is translucent, about 3 to 5 minutes.

2 Add the tomatoes, clam juice, shellfish, seafood seasoning, orange zest, fennel seed, thyme, saffron, and bay leaf and boil until the shellfish is done, about 8 to 10 minutes. Add the white fish and boil 5 minutes more or until the fish is barely opaque when cut in the thickest part. Add salt and pepper. Remove the bay leaf and serve hot.

Cioppino

MAKES 6 SERVINGS

It has become a family tradition for my husband and me to stay home on New Year's Eve and prepare a sumptuous seafood dinner. Later in the week—after we've eaten our fill but still have seafood in the fridge—we make a fisherman's stew like this one. The beauty of this stew is that you can use almost any kind of fish or seafood you want, in any amount you want. You can make it Italian, as this dish is—with wine, basil, oregano, and a lot of shellfish—or French, as in the Bouillabaisse on the preceding page—with orange, fennel, thyme, and saffron flavors plus a fish and shellfish mix. Serve it with your own freshly baked crusty French bread and perhaps a crisp mixed green salad. It's a delightful way to ring in a Happy New Year.

1 tablespoon olive oil

1 large leek, cleaned, rinsed, and thinly sliced or 1 small onion, finely chopped

1 stalk celery, diced

1 garlic clove, minced

1 carrot, peeled and sliced thinly

1 can (14 to 15 ounces) petite diced tomatoes, including juice

1 bottle (8 ounces) clam juice

1 cup dry red or white wine

1 tablespoon chopped fresh parsley

1 bay leaf

½ teaspoon chopped fresh basil or ¼ teaspoon dried

½ teaspoon chopped fresh oregano or ¼ teaspoon dried

1 dozen peeled, cooked shrimp

1 dozen mussels, scrubbed and debearded

1 dozen little-neck clams, cleaned

1 pound white fish such as halibut, cod, or red snapper, cut in 2-inch pieces

Salt and pepper to taste

1 In a Dutch oven or other deep, heavy pot with a tight-fitting lid, heat the oil over medium heat. Add the leek, celery, garlic, and carrot, and cook, stirring occasionally, until the leeks are translucent and start to brown, about 3 to 5 minutes.

2 Add the tomatoes, clam juice, wine, parsley, bay leaf, basil, and oregano. Simmer over medium heat, covered, for 20 minutes. (You can do this ahead of time and refrigerate until serving.)

3 Add the shrimp, mussels, clams, and white fish to the broth and cook about 8 to 10 minutes. Add the white fish and boil 5 minutes more or until the fish is barely opaque when tested with a fork. Taste the stew before adding salt and pepper since the saltiness of the fish may vary. Remove the bay leaf and serve hot.

SANDWICHES, WRAPS, AND TACOS

Sandwiches

Focaccia Sandwiches

Monte Cristo Sandwiches

Ham (or Prosciutto) and Cheese Panini

Arugula-Pear Focaccia Panini

Turkey and Basil Pesto Panini

Muffaletta Sandwiches

Reuben Sandwiches

Sloppy Joes

Crab Louis Sandwiches

Tuna Burgers with Asian Barbecue Sauce

English Muffin Pepperoni Pizzas

Fajitas, Tacos, and Wraps

Chicken Fajitas

Tequila-Marinated Steak Fajitas with Guacamole and Pico de Gallo

Soft Baja Fish Tacos

Veggie Pizza Wraps

Southwest Chicken Wrap

Thai Chicken Salad Wraps

Moo Shu Pork

 **Q** = Quick **V** = Vegetarian

The phrase "let's grab a sandwich" takes on new meaning when you're gluten-free, but it doesn't mean you have to omit sandwiches altogether from your diet. Just use your family's favorite fillings with gluten-free, store-bought sandwich breads or make your own bread with the easy recipes in this book. Feeling creative? Try Panini or Reuben or Monte Cristo sandwiches—these recipes illustrate that grilling or toasting the sandwich uses gluten-free bread to its best advantage. If your bread is frozen or slightly hardened, wrap it in a paper towel and warm it gently on low in a microwave oven to make the texture softer before assembling the sandwich.

Store-bought, gluten-free tortillas by Food for Life and La Tortilla Factory allow you to enjoy a wide variety of sandwiches such as Tequila-Marinated Steak Fajitas, Thai Chicken Salad Wraps, or Veggie Pizza Wraps—or your own favorite fillings for fajitas or wraps—opening up a whole new array of choices. You can even make one of my Asian favorites, Moo Shu Pork, with these wraps (softening them first with the simple directions in this chapter).

When you're craving down-home food, try the Sloppy Joes—one of America's all-time favorites—using store-bought gluten-free buns or your homemade Hamburger Buns (page 107). There are plenty of ideas here to get you started on your own quest for the perfect sandwich, so use these recipes as an inspiration to jazz up your old favorites or to try something totally new.

SANDWICHES

Focaccia Sandwiches
MAKES 8 SANDWICHES

Focaccia is a flat, oven-baked bread that is similar to pizza and makes terrific sandwiches. Slitting the flatbread horizontally before grilling results in browned top and bottom slices that provide greater stability than slices from regular loaves where only the outer crusts are browned. I also use my homemade focaccia to make tea sandwiches by omitting the toasting, cutting them much smaller, and using the traditional afternoon-tea fillings such as cucumbers, ham salad, or chicken salad.

BREAD

1½ teaspoons active dry yeast

½ cup warm (110°F) water

1½ cups Carol's Sorghum Blend (page x)

1½ teaspoons xanthan gum

1 tablespoon finely snipped fresh rosemary or 1 teaspoon dried, crushed

½ teaspoon onion powder

½ teaspoon salt

1½ teaspoons sugar

2 large eggs, at room temperature

2 tablespoons olive oil

1 teaspoon cider vinegar

TOPPING

Olive oil cooking spray

1 tablespoon finely snipped fresh rosemary or 1 teaspoon dried, crushed

¼ teaspoon kosher or coarse sea salt

FILLING

1 cup store-bought basil pesto or homemade Basil Pesto (page 672)

8 ounces thinly sliced turkey

4 ounces thinly sliced provolone cheese or soy cheese alternative, such as Soyco

1 Generously grease an 11 × 7-inch nonstick gray (not black) pan. Make the bread: In a small bowl, dissolve the yeast in warm water and set aside 5 minutes to foam.

2 In a large mixing bowl, combine all the bread ingredients, including the yeast mixture. Beat with an electric mixer on low speed until the ingredients are blended. Increase the speed to medium and continue beating about 30 seconds or until the dough thickens slightly. The dough will be soft and sticky.

3 Spread the dough evenly in the pan and smooth to a uniform thickness with a wet spatula. Cover and let rise in a warm place (75°F to 80°F) 35 to 45 minutes or until the dough reaches top of pan.

4 Place a rack in the middle of the oven. Preheat the oven to 375°F. Make the topping: Spray the dough lightly with olive oil cooking spray and sprinkle with the rosemary and salt.

5 Bake 30 to 35 minutes or until the top is golden brown. Cool the focaccia in the pan 10 minutes on a wire rack and then transfer the focaccia to the wire rack to cool completely.

6 Make the sandwiches: Slice the focaccia in half crosswise to make 2 halves, each 11 × 7 inches. Place focaccia cut side down on a griddle and cook until heated through and golden brown on bottom, about 2 minutes. Spread the pesto over the toasted sides of the focaccia. Layer the bottom halves of the focaccia with the turkey and provolone. Cover with top half of focaccia, pesto side down. You will now have large sandwich, 11 × 7-inches in size. Cut sandwich into 8 squares and serve immediately.

Monte Cristo Sandwiches

MAKES 4 SMALL SANDWICHES

Monte Cristos are simply sandwiches that are dipped in an egg-milk mixture and then fried— much like we make French Toast. They can be totally immersed in hot oil or fried in a thin layer of oil. You can also use larger slices of sandwich bread, but the smaller French bread slices are easier to handle. For larger appetites, increase to two sandwiches per person by doubling the amounts.

8 slices homemade French Yeast Bread (page 100), sliced ¼- to ⅓-inch pieces

½ cup Dijon mustard

8 slices thin baked deli ham

4 slices Swiss cheese or cheese alternative, such as Vegan Gourmet

3 large eggs

½ cup 1% milk (cow's, rice, soy, potato, or nut)

¼ teaspoon salt

¼ teaspoon freshly ground black pepper

2 tablespoons olive oil

2 tablespoons unsalted butter or buttery spread, such as Earth Balance, or canola oil

½ cup jam flavor of choice, such as grape, black-berry, or orange marmalade

1 Lay 4 slices of bread on a flat surface and spread each with 1 tablespoon of the mustard.

2 On top of the mustard, layer a slice of ham, then a slice of cheese, then another slice of ham. Spread the remaining 4 slices of bread with a tablespoon of the remaining mustard and place, mustard-side down, on top.

3 In a shallow bowl or pan, whisk together the eggs, milk, salt, and pepper. Holding the sandwich together with tongs or two spatulas, dip each sandwich into the egg mixture, turning to coat thoroughly.

4 In a large, heavy, nonstick (gray, not black) skillet heat the oil and butter over medium heat.

Cook sandwiches until golden brown, about 4 minutes. Turn the sandwiches and cook another 3 minutes or until the other side is golden brown. Serve immediately with 2 tablespoons of jam per sandwich.

Ham (or Prosciutto) and Cheese Panini

MAKES 4 SANDWICHES

A panino (singular for panini) is an Italian sand-wich made by slicing bread in half horizontally and filling it with meat or cheese, or both. It is cooked in a panini machine—a hinged grill pan with ridges—that presses the sandwich, molding the ingredients together, much like a compressed grilled cheese sandwich. If you don't have a panini machine, cook the sandwiches in a heavy skillet, pressed down with another heavy skillet or a foil-covered brick.

8 slices gluten-free bread, such as Whole Foods Prairie Seed, or homemade White Sandwich Yeast Bread (page 85)

Cooking spray

4 thin slices Black Forest Ham or prosciutto

4 thin slices Swiss or Gruyère cheese or cheese alternative, such as Vegan Gourmet

4 tablespoons apricot preserves

1 Lay the slices of bread on a flat surface and lightly coat with cooking spray (or brush with melted butter for a richer taste). Turn 4 of the slices over and layer each slice with ham and cheese. Spread a tablespoon of preserves on each. Top with the remaining 4 slices of bread, sprayed side up.

2 Heat a panini machine and grill the sand-wiches, following manufacturer's directions. If you use a skillet, lightly coat the skillet with cooking spray and brown the sandwiches, turning once, and using a heavy object to weigh it down. Serve immediately.

Arugula-Pear Focaccia Panini Ⓥ

MAKES 4 SANDWICHES

Known as "rocket" in Europe, arugula is a leafy green from the mustard family. It has a unique, peppery taste that contrasts nicely with the sweet pears. Add a slice of crunchy red onion for a delightful and unique sandwich. You may also use spinach in place of the arugula and your favorite gluten-free bread instead of the focaccia.

4 squares (4 inches each) gluten-free Focaccia with Herbs bread (page 104), cut in half horizontally to form 8 slices

Cooking spray or olive oil

½ cup cream cheese or cream cheese alternative, such as Tofutti, softened, divided

2 tablespoons honey or agave nectar

⅛ teaspoon salt

⅛ teaspoon freshly ground black pepper

4 slices thin Swiss cheese or cheese alternative, such as Vegan Gourmet

2 large ripe pears, cored and cut in ¼-inch slices

1 small red onion, thinly sliced

3 ounces arugula or spinach, washed and spun dry

1 Lay the slices of focaccia on a flat surface, cut side down, and lightly coat with cooking spray (or brush with olive oil). Turn 4 of the slices over. In a small bowl, combine the cream cheese, honey, salt, and pepper and spread each slice with a tablespoon of this mixture. Layer each with a slice of cheese, a few pear slices, a few red onion rings, and a few of the arugula leaves.

2 Turn the remaining 4 slices of bread over and spread each with a tablespoon of the cream cheese mixture. Put the remaining 4 slices of focaccia on top, sprayed side up.

3 Heat a panini machine and grill the sandwiches, following manufacturer's directions. If you use a skillet, lightly coat the skillet with cooking spray and brown the sandwiches, turning once, using a heavy object to weigh it down. Serve immediately.

PANINI: SANDWICHES WITH ITALIAN FLAIR

For best results, use thin fillings such as thinly sliced deli meat rather than thick chunks of meat. Thick, chunky sauces work better than watery ones. Always include an ingredient that is fairly spicy, very flavorful, or a bit sweet to provide pleasing contrast with the crispy bread and savory meat. Panini do not have to contain meat: They can simply be cheese and bread. Panini can be made ahead, wrapped, and transported to work for reheating in a microwave. You'll lose some of the crispy exterior, but they'll still taste great.

Here are a few more ideas for fillings:

- Cheddar cheese (the infamous grilled cheese sandwich)
- Goat cheese and orange marmalade
- Smoked salmon, cream cheese, and dill weed
- Thinly sliced smoked turkey, brie, and chunky cranberry sauce (or dried cranberries)
- Thinly sliced ham, Swiss cheese, and very thin slices of apple
- Thinly sliced roast beef, provolone cheese, and horseradish sauce
- Thinly sliced Granny Smith apples, Cheddar cheese, and grainy mustard
- Nutella (sweet, creamy chocolate-hazelnut spread) with bananas

Turkey and Basil Pesto Panini

MAKES 4 SANDWICHES

The robust flavor of basil pesto complements the subtle smokiness of deli turkey in this panini sandwich. Cream cheese lends a palate-pleasing richness, but you can also use cheeses such as Swiss, white Cheddar, or provolone.

8 slices gluten-free bread, such as Whole Foods Prairie Seed, or homemade White Sandwich Yeast Bread (page 85)

Cooking spray or olive oil

½ cup cream cheese or cream cheese alternative, such as Tofutti, softened, divided

½ cup store-bought basil pesto or homemade Basil Pesto (page 672), divided

8 slices gluten-free smoked deli turkey, such as Boar's Head

4 slices thin mozzarella cheese or cheese alternative, such as Vegan Gourmet

1 small red onion, thinly sliced

1 Lay the slices of bread on a flat surface and lightly coat with cooking spray (or brush with olive oil). Turn 4 of the slices over and spread each with 1 tablespoon cream cheese and 1 tablespoon basil pesto. Layer a slice of turkey, then cheese, then turkey. Add a layer of onion rings to each.

2 Turn the remaining 4 slices of bread over and spread each with 1 tablespoon cream cheese and 1 tablespoon basil pesto. Put the remaining 4 slices of bread on top, sprayed side up.

3 Heat a panini machine and grill the sandwiches, following manufacturer's directions. If you use a skillet, lightly coat the skillet with cooking spray and brown the sandwiches, turning once, using a heavy object to weigh it down. Serve immediately.

Muffaletta Sandwiches

MAKES 4 SANDWICHES

This traditional sandwich is popular in New Orleans. I offer some ideas here, but you can use any combination of meat, cheese, and sauce you want. Use cheese alternatives in place of the mozzarella and provolone, if you like.

1 recipe gluten-free French Yeast Bread dough (page 100)

1 tablespoon egg white mixed with 1 tablespoon water

¼ cup extra-virgin olive oil

¼ cup mayonnaise

¼ cup Dijon mustard

¼ cup store-bought basil pesto, or homemade Basil Pesto (page 072)

4 ounces deli meat (such as smoked turkey, pastrami, or others), thinly sliced

1 large beefsteak tomato, thinly sliced

4 ounces mozzarella, thinly sliced

4 ounces provolone or fontina cheese, thinly sliced

1 jar (14 to 15 ounces) marinated artichokes, drained and chopped

1 Make the French Yeast Bread dough on page 100.

2 Place the dough in a greased 10-inch springform pan and smooth the top with a wet spatula. Brush the loaf with a mixture of 1 tablespoon egg white mixed with 1 tablespoon water. Bake 30 to 35 minutes or until the top of the bread is a deep, golden brown and registers 205°F when an instant-read thermometer is inserted into the center. Cool bread in the pan 5 minutes on a wire rack. Remove bread from pan and cool completely on the wire rack.

3 Make the muffaletta: Place a rack in the middle of the oven. Preheat the oven to 400°F. Slice the loaf in half, horizontally, and set the top half aside. With your fingers, pull out enough of the bread's interior to create a shell that is 1 inch thick. Brush the bottom and sides of the shell with half of the olive oil, mayonnaise, mustard, and pesto.

4 Brush the cut-side of the top half of the loaf with the remaining olive oil, mustard, mayonnaise, and pesto. Then layer the following items in the bottom shell: deli meat, tomato, cheese, and artichokes. Add more olive oil, mustard, mayonnaise, or pesto on top, if desired.

5 Replace the top of the loaf and press down gently. Wrap the loaf loosely in foil and place on a baking sheet (not nonstick). Bake 20 minutes at 400°F. To serve, slice the loaf into quarters with an electric knife. Serve warm.

Reuben Sandwiches

MAKES 4 SANDWICHES

This is my favorite sandwich and it delivers the unmistakable combination of corned beef, sauerkraut, and cheese (or cheese alternative) that complement each other so well. The crunchy toasted bread also provides a wonderful texture contrast.

8 slices homemade Quinoa Pumpernickel Yeast Bread (page 97) or homemade Swedish Rye Yeast Bread (page 98)

2 teaspoons unsalted butter or buttery spread, such as Earth Balance, melted

½ pound corned beef, sliced very thin

8 slices Swiss or provolone cheese

1 cup store-bought Thousand Island dressing, such as Laura Lynn, Litehouse Foods, or homemade Easy Russian Dressing (page 161)

1 teaspoon caraway seed

1 teaspoon brown sugar

1 cup sauerkraut, rinsed and drained

Additional butter, oil, or cooking spray for frying

1 Place all 8 slices of the bread on a flat surface and brush each with the melted butter. Turn 4 of the slices over and layer with corned beef and 2 slices of cheese, placing about 2 tablespoons of dressing between each layer. In a bowl, combine the caraway seed and sugar with the sauerkraut, mix thoroughly, and spread ¼ cup on each of the 4 slices. Top with remaining slice of bread, buttered side up.

2 Heat a cast-iron skillet or grill pan over medium heat. Lightly brush with butter or oil. You may only be able to cook 2 sandwiches at a time if your skillet isn't large enough to hold all 4 sandwiches. Cook the sandwiches over medium heat on both sides until the bread is lightly browned and the cheese begins to melt, about 3 to 4 minutes per side. Serve immediately.

Sloppy Joes

MAKES 4 SANDWICHES

A Sloppy Joe consists of a bun filled with a seasoned ground beef and tomato mixture. If you don't have gluten-free buns on hand, you can use a tortilla wrap by Food for Life or La Tortilla Factory, instead.

1 pound lean ground beef, browned or planned-over browned ground beef
½ cup finely diced onion
1 cup ketchup
2 tablespoons red wine vinegar
1 tablespoon yellow mustard
1 tablespoon gluten-free Worcestershire sauce, such as French's
1 garlic clove, minced
½ teaspoon chili powder
½ teaspoon celery salt
1 teaspoon chopped fresh oregano or ½ teaspoon dried
Pinch ground cloves
4 homemade gluten-free Hamburger Buns (page 107), or 4 gluten-free tortilla wraps, such as Food for Life or La Tortilla Factory

1 In a large, heavy skillet, brown the ground beef over medium heat until the beef is very brown and all the liquid has evaporated, about 5 to 7 minutes.

2 Add the onion, ketchup, vinegar, mustard, Worcestershire sauce, garlic, chili powder, celery salt, oregano, and cloves to the skillet and bring to a boil. Reduce the heat to low and simmer, covered, for 15 minutes.

3 Serve immediately on buns or softened tortilla wraps (see How to Soften Tortillas, page 189).

Crab Louis Sandwiches

MAKES 4 SANDWICHES

This sandwich borrows its flavors—crab, hard-boiled egg, and Louis (pronounced LOO-ey) dressing—from the famous Crab Louis Salad, and it is one of those sandwiches you can modify as you wish. If you like the dressing spicier, add more cocktail sauce.

⅔ cup mayonnaise
⅓ cup cocktail sauce, such as Hy-Vee or Safeway
½ cup sweet relish
½ cup diced celery, diced
3 tablespoons fresh lemon juice
3 tablespoons finely sliced green onions
2 tablespoons green bell pepper, minced
2 tablespoons red bell pepper, minced
1 tablespoon minced fresh parsley
½ teaspoon hot pepper sauce, such as Frank's
1 cup (two 6-ounce cans) crabmeat
1 avocado, pitted and sliced in thin slices
8 slices gluten-free bread, such as Whole Foods Prairie Seed, or homemade gluten-free White Sandwich Yeast Bread (page 85)

1 In a small bowl, whisk together the mayonnaise, cocktail sauce, relish, celery, lemon juice, green onions, bell peppers, parsley, and pepper sauce until smooth. Gently stir in the crabmeat and toss to coat thoroughly.

2 Divide the mixture evenly on 4 slices of the bread. Layer ¼ of the avocado slices on each slice. Top each sandwich with the remaining slice of bread and cut each sandwich in half diagonally. Serve immediately.

Tuna Burgers with Asian Barbecue Sauce

MAKES 4 BURGERS

Mention the word "burgers" and most of us think of beef. However, tuna makes wonderful burgers, too. You may cook the burgers in a skillet or on the grill. Eat them with homemade Hamburger Buns (page 107) or between slices of your favorite gluten-free bread. The barbecue sauce works on regular burgers as well.

SAUCE

⅓ cup gluten-free hoisin sauce, such as Premier Japan

¼ cup canola oil

1 tablespoon sesame oil

1 tablespoon honey

1 tablespoon gluten-free Worcestershire sauce, such as French's

1 teaspoon ground ginger

1 garlic clove, minced

⅛ teaspoon ground cayenne

BURGERS

3 cans (6 ounces each) canned tuna, drained

½ cup gluten-free bread crumbs, such as Ener-G, or homemade Plain Bread Crumbs (page 117)

1 large egg

1 tablespoon wheat-free tamari soy sauce, such as such as Crystal or San-J

1 tablespoon Dijon mustard

1 teaspoon chopped fresh thyme or ½ teaspoon dried

½ teaspoon salt

½ teaspoon freshly ground black pepper

8 pineapple slices

Paprika, for garnish

1 Make the sauce: In a small bowl, whisk together the Asian Barbecue Sauce ingredients. Refrigerate up to 1 day.

2 Make the burgers: In a medium bowl, combine the tuna, bread crumbs, egg, soy sauce, mustard, thyme, salt, and pepper until well blended. Shape into 4 patties.

3 In a large cast-iron skillet or a nonstick (gray, not black) skillet—or on a grill—cook the burgers until done, turning to brown the burgers on both sides, about 4 to 6 minutes per side. Garnish with dash of paprika. Serve with sauce and pineapple slices.

English Muffin Pepperoni Pizzas Ⓠ

MAKES 4 PIZZAS

English muffins form the crust for these cute little pizzas, which kids love. If you use store-bought marinara sauce and have a stash of your homemade English Muffins (page 111) on hand, you can have these little pizzas ready in just a few minutes.

4 homemade gluten-free English Muffins (page 111), split in half

¾ cup gluten-free marinara sauce, such as Classico, or Homemade Marinara Sauce (page 672)

2 cups shredded mozzarella cheese or cheese alternative, such as Vegan Gourmet

24 slices gluten-free pepperoni sausage, such as Hormel

1 Place a rack in the middle of the oven. Preheat the oven to 375°F. Place the English muffin halves, cut side up, on a 13 × 9-inch nonstick (gray, not black) sheet. Spoon 3 tablespoons of the marinara sauce onto each half. Top each with ¼ cup mozzarella cheese and 4 slices of pepperoni.

2 Bake 5 to 10 minutes or until the cheese is melted. Serve hot.

FAJITAS, TACOS, AND WRAPS

Chicken Fajitas

MAKES 8 FAJITAS

Fajitas are Tex-Mex sandwiches made with tortillas and filled with grilled meat. This name refers to the term faja *which refers to the cut of beef typically used and known as belt or girdle— or skirt steak as it's called today. Fajitas are amazingly versatile and can be made with beef, pork, seafood, or chicken, as this recipe shows.*

1 pound chicken breasts, sliced into ½-inch strips

Juice and grated zest of 1 lime

1 tablespoon Southwest or Mexican seasoning, such as McCormick

3 tablespoons olive oil, divided

2 teaspoons salt, divided

½ teaspoon freshly ground black pepper

1 red bell pepper, seeded and cut in ⅛-inch vertical slices

1 green bell pepper, seeded and cut in ⅛-inch vertical slices

1 yellow bell pepper, seeded and cut in ⅛-inch vertical slices

1 medium onion, peeled and cut in ⅛-inch vertical slices

¼ cup pickled jalapeños, optional

½ cup chopped fresh cilantro

1 cup homemade Guacamole (page 132) or store-bought version such Albertson's or Litehouse

1 cup gluten-free Mexican tomato salsa, such as Pace or Tostito

1 cup shredded mozzarella cheese or Pepper Jack cheese or cheese alternative, such as Vegan Gourmet

2 cups finely chopped iceberg lettuce

8 gluten-free tortillas, such as Food for Life or La Tortilla Factory

1 Place chicken strips in a gallon-size heavy-duty food-storage bag. Add the lime juice, lime zest, seasoning, 2 tablespoons of the oil, 1 teaspoon of the salt, and pepper. Seal the bag and shake until chicken is thoroughly coated. Refrigerate all day or overnight.

2 In a large skillet, heat the remaining oil over medium-high heat. Remove the chicken from the marinade (discard marinade) and add to skillet. Cook chicken until golden brown on all sides, about 8 to 10 minutes. Transfer the chicken to a serving platter and cover with foil to keep warm. Add the bell peppers, onion, and the remaining salt and cook over medium-high heat until they are soft and lightly browned, about 8 to 10 minutes. Add the jalapeños and heat to serving temperature. Add the pepper-onion mixture to the serving plate with the chicken or place it on its own serving plate and cover with foil to keep it warm (or put it in the oven on a foil-lined baking sheet at 200°F).

3 Soften the tortillas as directed on page 189 and assemble the fajitas or let everyone assemble their own, using the chicken, onions, peppers, cilantro guacamole, salsa, shredded cheese, and chopped lettuce.

Tequila-Marinated Steak Fajitas with Guacamole and Pico de Gallo

MAKES 12 FAJITAS

Living in the Southwest, I eat a lot of fajitas prepared in a number of different ways. The classic way to eat a fajita is to place the meat and accompaniments in the center of the fajita, fold it in half or shape it into a cylinder, and eat it out of hand. They're delicious, but somewhat messy to eat, so be sure to have plenty of napkins on hand. It's important to cut the steak on the diagonal (across the grain rather than with the grain) or it will be tough.

MARINADE AND STEAK

¼ cup tequila

¼ cup light olive oil or canola oil, divided

¼ cup fresh lime juice

2 tablespoons balsamic vinegar

2 garlic cloves, minced

1½ teaspoons salt, divided

1½ teaspoons Spice Islands Smokey Mesquite Seasoning or homemade Southwestern Seasoning (page 668), divided

½ teaspoon freshly ground black pepper

1 pound flank steak

FILLING (MAKES ABOUT 8 CUPS TOTAL)

2 tablespoons light olive oil or canola oil, divided

2 red bell peppers, sliced into thin strips

2 yellow bell peppers, sliced into thin strips

1 green bell pepper, sliced into thin strips

1 large yellow onion, thinly sliced

½ jalapeño, seeded and finely diced

½ teaspoon Spice Islands Smokey Mesquite Seasoning or homemade Southwestern Seasoning (page 668)

½ teaspoon salt

ACCOMPANIMENTS

12 gluten-free tortillas, such as Food for Life or La Tortilla Factory, steamed until soft (See How to Soften Tortillas, right)

2 cups iceberg lettuce, chopped

½ cup chopped fresh cilantro

1 ½ cups homemade Guacamole (page 132) or store-bought version such as Albertson's or Litehouse

1 cup sour cream or sour cream alternative, such as Tofutti

3 fresh limes, cut into wedges (for squeezing at serving time)

1 cup homemade Pico de Gallo (page 671) or store-bought version

1 Make the marinade and steak: In a glass casserole or gallon-size heavy-duty food-storage bag, combine the tequila, 2 tablespoons of the oil, lime juice, vinegar, garlic, 1 teaspoon of the salt, 1 teaspoon of the seasoning, and pepper. Add the flank steak and refrigerate overnight.

HOW TO SOFTEN TORTILLAS

Place a splatter guard over a large skillet filled with simmering water. Dip a linen canvas tea towel (not terry cloth) in hot water and wring out completely. Spread it out on the countertop or other flat surface, folded in half crosswise. Place paper towel on splatter guard, then tortilla, then another paper towel. Place over simmering water for a few seconds or until the tortilla is pliable. Remove tortilla from paper towels immediately (or it will stick to paper towels) and place between layers of dampened tea towel, placing waxed paper between tortillas if you have to stack them. Serve immediately.

2 Make the filling: In a heavy skillet (a cast-iron skillet works great) or wok, heat 1 tablespoon oil on medium-high heat. Add the bell peppers, onion, and jalapeño, and cook, stirring constantly until the peppers look blistered, about 7 to 10 minutes. Transfer to a plate and cover with foil.

3 Meanwhile, remove the flank steak from marinade and pat dry; discard the marinade. Sprinkle with the remaining ½ teaspoon of seasoning and the remaining ½ teaspoon salt. Grill over medium heat about 5 minutes per side or to desired degree of doneness. Or add the remaining tablespoon of oil to a heavy skillet and cook the flank steak over medium-high heat for 5 minutes per side or to the desired degree of doneness. Remove from heat and let sit, wrapped in foil, for 10 minutes.

4 At serving time, slice steak diagonally in very, very thin strips. Add salt and pepper to taste, if necessary. Serve with warmed tortillas, bell pepper-onion mixture, lettuce, cilantro, guacamole, sour cream, lime wedges, and Pico de Gallo.

Soft Baja Fish Tacos

MAKES 4 SERVINGS

I often eat fish tacos at a restaurant near my home, and I've re-created this dish for you. Not only does it have restaurant flair, but it's also a great way to use up leftover grilled fish. Tacos are naturally messy to eat, and sometimes fall apart, but these won't because they use two tortillas rather than one for greater strength and stability.

1 pound firm white fish, such as orange roughy, red snapper, or tilapia

3 tablespoons extra-virgin olive oil, divided

1 tablespoon homemade Southwestern Seasoning (page 668) or store-bought fajita seasoning

1 small onion, thinly sliced

2 cups very thinly sliced green cabbage (6 ounces if store-bought pre-sliced)

½ cup chopped fresh cilantro

¼ cup plain yogurt or mayonnaise

2 tablespoons fresh lime juice

2 tablespoons rice vinegar

1 tablespoon sugar

1 teaspoon hot sauce, such as Frank's

½ teaspoon salt

¼ teaspoon freshly ground black pepper

16 gluten-free corn tortillas (6-inch), such as Tamxico

1 cup Monterey Jack cheese, or cheese alternative, such as Vegan Gourmet

1 cup homemade Pico de Gallo (page 671)

1 ripe avocado, pitted and cut in 16 slices

1 can (11 ounces) mandarin oranges, drained

2 limes, halved

1 Brush the fish with 1 tablespoon oil (or coat with cooking spray) and sprinkle with seasoning, pressing seasoning into fish with fingers. Let sit 15 minutes while the grill is heating.

2 Cook the onion in 1 tablespoon olive oil until very browned and soft, about 7 to 10 minutes. Transfer to a plate; cover with foil.

3 Cook fish on grill (use a grill basket coated with cooking spray to prevent the fish from falling apart on the grill) until just done, 8 to 10 minutes, depending on the thickness of the fish or until the crumbs are golden and the fish is just barely opaque when cut in the thickest part. Transfer to a plate and cover with foil to keep warm.

4 In a medium bowl, toss the cabbage with the remaining tablespoon of olive oil, and the cilantro, yogurt, lime juice, vinegar, sugar, hot sauce, salt, and pepper.

5 To assemble the tacos, soften the corn tortillas by wrapping a stack of them in wet paper towels or tea towels and steam them in a microwave on low for 5 minutes. Place two tortillas together and fold them slightly in half. Fill each with ⅛ of the cheese, ⅛ of the onion, ⅛ of the fish, ⅛ of the cabbage, and ⅛ of the Pico de Gallo. Top with slices of avocado and mandarin oranges. Serve immediately with a squeeze of fresh lime juice.

Veggie Pizza Wraps

MAKES 4 WRAPS

Feel free to be creative with this wrap, using combinations of your favorite roasted vegetables— perhaps eggplant or zucchini—or use leftover Roasted Vegetables (page 394) in place of the artichokes and red peppers.

4 gluten-free tortilla wraps, such as Food for Life or La Tortilla Factory

1 cup store-bought pizza sauce, such as Contadina, or homemade Basil Pizza Sauce (page 118)

1 cup grated mozzarella cheese or cheese alternative, such as Vegan Gourmet

1 cup chopped marinated artichokes, drained

1 cup baby spinach, rinsed and spun dry

4 roasted red peppers (12-ounce jar), sliced into thin vertical strips

¼ cup grated Parmesan cheese or soy alternative, such as Soyco

1 Soften the tortillas (see How to Soften Tortillas, page 189) and immediately lay the tortilla on wax paper on a flat surface.

2 Spread ¼ cup pizza sauce over each tortilla. Top each tortilla with ¼ cup each mozzarella cheese, artichokes, and spinach. Add roasted red pepper strips to each tortilla. Sprinkle each tortilla with 1 tablespoon Parmesan cheese. Gently roll each tortilla into a loose wrap and wrap it in wax paper, twisting the ends of the wax paper to hold the wrap in place.

3 Place the tortilla wraps in a microwave oven and heat on low 1 to 3 minutes until the cheese is warm or starts to melt. Remove from the microwave and slice the wraps in half diagonally. Serve immediately.

Southwest Chicken Wrap

MAKES 4 WRAPS

This version of the wrap sandwich features southwestern ingredients. Once you've tried it, feel free to vary the ingredients and their amounts as you wish.

¼ cup mayonnaise
½ cup store-bought guacamole or homemade Guacamole (page 132)
¼ teaspoon hot sauce, such as Frank's
4 gluten-free tortilla wraps, such as Food for Life or La Tortilla Factory
1 cup shredded Monterey Jack cheese or cheese alternative, such as Vegan Gourmet
½ cup cooked corn kernels (from about ½ large ear)
½ cup canned black beans or pinto beans, rinsed and drained
½ cup red onion, sliced very thin
8 ounces smoked turkey, sliced thin

1 In a small bowl, combine mayonnaise, guacamole, and hot sauce. Set aside.

2 Steam each tortilla following directions in How to Soften Tortillas on page 189.

3 Spread 2 tablespoons of mayonnaise-guacamole mixture over each tortilla. Sprinkle ¼ cup of cheese on top. In a small bowl, combine corn, beans, and onion and sprinkle ¼ of mixture on each tortilla. Top with 2 ounces of sliced turkey. Gently roll tortilla tightly, then cut in half diagonally. Repeat with remaining tortillas and filling. Serve immediately.

Thai Chicken Salad Wraps

MAKES 4 WRAPS

This is actually a simple chicken salad wrap dressed up with Thai flavors. The almonds give it some crunchiness, and it gets heat from the Thai curry paste and sweetness from the pineapple.

¼ cup mayonnaise
2 tablespoons fresh grated ginger
2 tablespoons honey
2 tablespoons fresh lime juice
2 tablespoons plain yogurt
1 teaspoon Thai red curry paste, such as A Taste of Thai
1½ cups cooked chicken, diced or shredded in a food processor
½ cup pineapple tidbits, drained
¼ cup chopped fresh cilantro
¼ cup slivered almonds
4 gluten-free tortilla wraps, such as Food for Life or La Tortilla Factory
1 cup baby spinach, washed and spun dry

1 In a medium bowl, stir together the mayonnaise, ginger, honey, lime juice, yogurt, curry paste, chicken, pineapple, cilantro, and almonds, until blended.

2 Soften the tortillas (see How to Soften Tortillas, page 189) and immediately lay the tortillas on wax paper on a flat surface.

3 Spread ¼ of the chicken salad over a tortilla. Top with ¼ cup spinach. Gently roll tortilla into a loose roll, then cut in half diagonally. Repeat with the remaining tortillas, filling, and spinach. Serve immediately.

Moo Shu Pork

MAKES 4 SERVINGS

Although you can make little crepe-like pancakes for this dish, I use ready-made tortillas. I prefer La Tortilla Factory tortillas for this dish over other brands because they are softer and more pliable. You can use the same amount of thinly sliced chicken breast or shrimp in place of the pork.

1 tablespoon peanut oil, divided

½ pound pork tenderloin, cut into thin strips about ¼ inch thick (about 2 cups)

2 cans (8 ounces each) sliced mushrooms, drained, or 1 pound sliced fresh mushrooms

2 large garlic cloves, minced

1 cup shredded carrot

3 green onions, sliced

5 cups Napa cabbage, shredded

1 tablespoon cornstarch

1 tablespoon water

2 tablespoons grated fresh ginger

2 tablespoons wheat-free low-sodium tamari soy sauce, such as Crystal or San-J

2 tablespoons hoisin sauce, such as Premier Japan, plus extra for brushing on tortillas

1 tablespoon dry sherry

1 teaspoon sweet red Thai chili sauce, such as A Taste of Thai

4 gluten-free tortilla wraps, such as Food for Life or La Tortilla Factory

1 In a large, heavy skillet, heat 1½ teaspoons of the oil over medium-high heat. Add the pork and cook, stirring constantly, 1 minute. Add the remaining oil and the mushrooms, garlic, carrots, and green onions; cook another minute, stirring constantly.

2 Reduce the heat to low, stir in the cabbage, cover the skillet, and let stand 2 minutes as cabbage wilts.

3 In a small bowl, whisk together the cornstarch and water until smooth. Whisk in the ginger, soy sauce, hoisin sauce, sherry, and chili sauce until smooth and pour over the cabbage mixture. Increase the heat to medium and cook, stirring constantly, until the mixture thickens slightly.

4 To serve, steam the tortillas until pliable (see How to Soften Tortillas, page 189). Brush the tortillas with hoisin sauce, then fill with pork mixture. Serve immediately.

PASTAS

Meatless Pasta Dishes

Linguini with Toasted Almonds

Pesto Penne

Pasta in Fresh Tomato Sauce

Penne in Tomato-Artichoke Sauce

Pasta with Butternut Squash and Sage

Penne alla Vodka

Spaghetti with Marinara Sauce

Asian-Flavored Buckwheat Noodles

Thai Noodle Bowl

Fettuccine Alfredo

Feta-Truffle Tortellini with Orange-Hazelnut Butter

Macaroni and Cheese

Southwestern Macaroni and Cheese

Pasta with Seafood, Poultry, or Meat

Linguini with Red Clam Sauce

Linguini with White Clam Sauce

Fettuccine with Frutti di Mare

Noodles with Salmon in a Lemon-Ginger Broth

Rice Noodles with Shrimp-Coconut Curry

Pad Thai

Chicken Paprikash on Noodles

Pasta with Turkey Bolognese Sauce

Spaghetti and Meatballs

Pasta with Beef Ragù

Lasagna

Greek Pastitsio

Traditional Tuna Casserole

Tuna Casserole with a Twist

Pasta and Noodles from Scratch

Handmade Pasta

Ravioli in Creamy Marinara Sauce

Potato Gnocchi

Spaetzle

Pierogi

Q = Quick   **V** = Vegetarian

Before I adopted a gluten-free lifestyle, I made noodles on my kitchen counter. I made a mound of flour on the countertop, created a well in the center, and stirred in eggs, water, and salt, then rolled it by hand with a rolling pin and cut it into thin noodles with a paring knife. If there was time, I let the noodles dry, but I usually just dropped them immediately into boiling water and *voilà,* I had fabulous noodles that were better than anything I could buy in the store.

Today, I still make fabulous homemade pasta—with a different set of ingredients—using my recipe for Handmade Pasta (page 211). But if this seems too daunting, don't worry. You can now choose among delicious pastas made from beans, buckwheat, corn, rice, and quinoa, and they come in all shapes and sizes, too—elbow macaroni, spaghetti, linguini, fettuccine, and so on. They are readily available in natural food stores, clearly marked as gluten-free, or online at many gluten-free vendors.

Whether you use fresh or store-bought pasta from the ever-growing list of manufacturers such as Ancient Harvest, Bi-Aglut, DeBoles, Dr. Schar, Orgran, Pastariso, and Tinkyada, there are a few guidelines to help you prepare your perfect pasta:

- Use plenty of water—4 cups for each 8 ounces of pasta.

- Salt the water liberally after it starts to boil—most pasta is mild and salt brings out its flavor.

- Put the pasta into boiling water and stir constantly until it comes to a boil again to prevent clumping.

- Cook the pasta following the manufacturer's directions on the package because, unlike regular pasta which is made from wheat, different brands of gluten-free pasta are made with different grains and therefore cook at different rates. For example, bean pasta can be ready in a couple of minutes, while rice pasta can take up to 10 minutes or more.

- Cook the pasta just until it feels slightly soft when you bite into it—sometimes called *al dente* or "to the tooth"—but not soft. Remove it from the heat and drain; it will continue to cook from residual heat even after it is out of the boiling water.

- Unlike regular pasta, you need to use the cooked pasta immediately; it will get mushy and break apart if it sits in the pot or on a buffet table for an extended period of time. Be gentle when you stir in the sauce so you don't tear the pasta.

- Cooked pasta tends to clump together when chilled, but it will separate when rinsed briefly with hot water.

MEATLESS PASTA DISHES

Linguini with Toasted Almonds Ⓠ Ⓥ

MAKES 4 SERVINGS

My favorite packaged linguini is Heartland's Finest, made with bean flour, because it holds its shape after it's cooked and looks just like wheat linguini. You can also try other noodles such as fettuccine in this recipe; I like the rice-bran fettuccine from Thai Kitchen because it has delicious flavor and a hearty texture.

½ pound (8 ounces) gluten-free linguini, such as Heartland's Finest

¼ cup slivered toasted almond slices or pine nuts*

1 tablespoon chopped fresh parsley

¼ cup grated Parmesan cheese or soy alternative, such as Soyco

1 teaspoon lemon pepper, such as Durkee or Spice Islands

2 tablespoons olive oil

1 In a large pot, bring water to a boil and add salt liberally. Add pasta and cook until done, following package directions.

2 Drain the linguini and toss with almonds, parsley, Parmesan cheese, lemon pepper, and olive oil. Serve immediately.

*See Toasting Nuts footnote on page 510.

Pesto Penne Ⓠ Ⓥ

MAKES 4 SERVINGS

This is a wonderful dish for vegetarians, but if you want to boost the protein content, just add half-inch cubes of cooked chicken or cooked shrimp in whatever amounts you like.

1 pound gluten-free penne, such as Heartland's Finest

½ to ¾ cup prepared basil pesto, such as Shaw's or Select, or homemade Basil Pesto (page 672), or to taste

¼ cup grated Parmesan cheese or soy alternative, such as Soyco, for garnish

In a large pot, bring water to boil and add salt liberally. Add the pasta and cook according to package directions. Toss drained pasta with pesto. Garnish with Parmesan cheese, and serve immediately.

Pasta in Fresh Tomato Sauce Ⓥ

MAKES 4 SERVINGS

This recipe is for those of you who find yourself with an abundance of tomatoes at the end of the summer and don't want to heat the kitchen by simmering tomato sauce on a hot stove. It's "fresh" because you don't cook it, but rather just let it sit for a few hours. If you use anything bigger than a plum tomato or if the tomatoes have large white membranes, you may want to seed them first for a better appearance. If you use Heartland's Finest pasta, you can just let the pasta soak in hot water until tender rather than boiling it.

2 pounds ripe plum tomatoes, stemmed, washed, and diced

2 tablespoons red wine vinegar

2 tablespoons extra-virgin olive oil

1 garlic clove, minced

½ teaspoon salt, plus more for pasta water

¼ cup chopped fresh basil or 1 tablespoon dried

1½ teaspoons chopped fresh oregano or ½ teaspoon dried

1 teaspoon chopped fresh marjoram or ¼ teaspoon dried

¼ teaspoon freshly ground black pepper

½ pound gluten-free penne, such as Dr. Schar

1 In a large bowl, combine tomatoes, vinegar, oil, garlic, salt, basil, oregano, marjoram, and pepper. Stir to combine and cover with plastic wrap. Let sit at room temperature up to 2 hours or refrigerate, covered, overnight.

2 In a large pot, bring water to a boil and salt liberally. Cook pasta according to package directions. Drain well and serve with tomato sauce.

Penne in Tomato-Artichoke Sauce Ⓠ Ⓥ

MAKES 4 SERVINGS

This is a great dish for those nights when you have no idea what to prepare for dinner, but need something fast because everyone is starving. You can also toss in any chopped cooked meats on hand, or even pepperoni.

1 can (14 to 15 ounces) petite diced tomatoes, including juice
2 teaspoons chopped fresh basil or 1 teaspoon dried
1 teaspoon chopped fresh oregano or ½ teaspoon dried
1 teaspoon chopped fresh thyme or ½ teaspoon dried
¼ teaspoon sugar
⅛ teaspoon salt, plus more for pasta water
⅛ teaspoon crushed red pepper
Dash freshly ground black pepper
1 jar (4.5 ounces) marinated artichokes, drained and coarsely chopped
½ pound gluten-free penne, such as DeBoles

1 In a medium, heavy saucepan, heat the tomatoes, basil, oregano, thyme, sugar, salt, crushed red pepper, and black pepper over medium-high heat. Bring to a boil, reduce the heat to low, and simmer, covered, about 10 to 15 minutes.

2 While the sauce cooks, bring a large pot of water to boil. Salt the water liberally, add pasta, and cook according to package directions. Serve sauce over drained pasta.

Pasta with Butternut Squash and Sage Ⓥ

MAKES 4 SERVINGS

Pan-frying the butternut squash in balsamic vinegar brings out its sweet, nutty flavor and makes a colorful and distinctive contrast to the pasta. Fresh squash works far better than frozen because it holds its shape better, but if you like your squash a little softer, use the frozen variety. If butternut squash isn't available, you can use sweet potatoes, which are sweeter and even more colorful.

2 tablespoons extra-virgin olive oil, divided
2 cups cubed peeled butternut squash or Red Garnet sweet potato, cut in ½-inch pieces
3 tablespoons balsamic vinegar
1 teaspoon salt, plus more for pasta water
½ teaspoon freshly ground black pepper
2 tablespoons chopped fresh sage or 2 teaspoons rubbed sage
4 ounces gluten-free linguini, such as Tinkyada
¼ cup chopped toasted walnuts, for garnish
¼ cup grated Parmesan cheese or soy alternative, such as Soyco, for garnish

1 Place 1 tablespoon of the oil in a large, heavy skillet. Toss the squash with the vinegar, salt, and black pepper; add to the skillet and cook over low heat, covered, about 15 to 25 minutes until the squash is tender and lightly browned. Stir occasionally to prevent burning. Remove the squash from the heat and stir in the sage; set aside.

2 Bring a large pot of water to boil. Salt the water liberally, add linguini, and cook according to package directions until al dente—tender yet still firm to the bite; drain well. Add to the skillet, along with the remaining tablespoon of oil (or more, if desired), and toss well. Serve hot, garnished with the chopped walnuts and Parmesan cheese.

Penne alla Vodka Ⓠ Ⓥ

MAKES 4 SERVINGS

My favorite penne brands for this dish are Heartland's Finest or Dr. Schar because they hold their shape very well after cooking. Make your meatless pasta dishes heartier simply by adding smoked salmon, as in the variation, or add your favorite beef, chicken or seafood. Add precooked ingredients at the end of the cooking time to heat and blend the pasta and protein together. If you're using an ingredient that cooks quickly, like cut-up meat or chicken pieces, add them to the sauce early enough to allow the meat to heat through.

1 tablespoon unsalted butter or buttery spread, such as Earth Balance, or canola oil

1 tablespoon olive oil

1 large shallot, minced

1 garlic clove, minced

1 can (14 to 15 ounces) petite diced tomatoes, including juice

⅛ teaspoon sugar

¼ cup vodka or dry white wine

¼ cup heavy cream or plain soy milk, such as Silk

½ pound gluten-free penne, such as Heartland's Finest

1 In a medium skillet, heat the butter and olive oil over medium heat. Add shallot and garlic and cook, stirring constantly, about 2 to 3 minutes until the shallot is soft. Add the tomatoes and sugar and simmer 5 minutes or until the tomatoes reduce down and thicken just slightly.

2 Stir in the vodka and cream and simmer the sauce gently over very low heat.

3 Meanwhile, bring a large pot of water to boil and salt liberally. Add the pasta and cook until al dente—tender yet still firm to the bite. (Avoid overcooking because pasta continues to cook after it is removed from heat.) Drain well and serve with the sauce.

Penne alla Vodka with Green Peas: Add 1 cup cooked green peas to cream sauce.

Penne alla Vodka with Smoked Salmon: Add 2 ounces (half of a 4-ounce package) smoked salmon, finely diced, to cream sauce.

Spaghetti with Marinara Sauce Ⓥ

MAKES 12 SERVINGS

This is surely every child's favorite dish; it is certainly my grandson's first choice. Make a whole batch of the marinara sauce and freeze it in meal-size portions for future use so all you have to do is boil pasta and toss it with the thawed marinara for a quick meal.

SAUCE

1 can (24 ounces) tomato juice

2 cans (6 ounces each) tomato paste

¼ cup chopped fresh basil or 2 tablespoons dried

2 tablespoons chopped fresh parsley or 1 tablespoon dried

2 teaspoons sugar

2 teaspoons chopped fresh oregano or 1 teaspoon dried

2 teaspoons finely snipped fresh rosemary or 1 teaspoon dried, crushed

1 teaspoon salt, or to taste

½ teaspoon crushed red pepper

½ teaspoon freshly ground black pepper

1 garlic clove, minced

1 bay leaf

2 tablespoons grated Romano cheese or soy alternative, such as Soyco (optional)

PASTA

1½ pounds gluten-free spaghetti, such as DeBoles

1 Make the sauce: Whisk together all of the marinara sauce ingredients in a Dutch oven or other deep, heavy pot with a tight-fitting lid until thoroughly blended. Bring to boil, reduce heat to low, and simmer, covered, 30 to 45 minutes. Stir frequently and add ¼ cup water if the sauce appears dry. Remove the bay leaf.

2 Make the pasta: In a large pot, bring water to a boil and add salt liberally. Add the spaghetti and cook according to package directions. Serve each portion topped with about ⅓ cup marinara sauce.

Asian-Flavored Buckwheat Noodles

MAKES 4 SERVINGS

Check the box of buckwheat noodles to make sure it's 100 percent pure buckwheat as many brands contain wheat. Serve this with an Asian-inspired main dish. Note that the toasted sesame oil is much stronger in flavor than regular sesame oil so a little goes a long way.

1 package (8 ounces) soba (100% pure buckwheat) noodles, such as Eden
3 green onions, thinly sliced
1 small red bell pepper, cored, seeded, and thinly sliced
3 tablespoons chopped fresh cilantro, divided
¼ cup peanut oil
2 tablespoons wheat-free tamari soy sauce, such as Crystal or San-J
2 tablespoons unseasoned rice vinegar
1 teaspoon grated fresh ginger
1 teaspoon toasted sesame oil
1 small garlic clove, minced
¼ teaspoon crushed red pepper
1 tablespoon chopped unsalted peanuts, for garnish

1 In a large pot, bring water to a boil and salt liberally. Add noodles and cook according to package directions, taking care not to overcook them. Immediately rinse with cold water to stop the cooking. Place the noodles in a serving bowl and toss with green onions, red bell pepper, and 2 tablespoons cilantro.

2 In a small jar, shake together the peanut oil, soy sauce, vinegar, ginger, sesame oil, garlic, and crushed red pepper. Pour it over noodles and toss to coat thoroughly. Garnish with the remaining tablespoon of chopped cilantro and the chopped peanuts, cover, and refrigerate. Bring to room temperature 30 minutes before serving.

Thai Noodle Bowl Ⓠ

MAKES 4 SERVINGS

Light, yet flavorful, this Thai dish is full of wonderful textures from the crisp vegetables, the soft cellophane noodles, and the crunchy nuts. Serve it in wide, shallow bowls to capture the marvelous sauce.

1 tablespoon canola oil
¼ cup green onions
½ red bell pepper, chopped
1 garlic clove, minced
¼ cup rice vinegar
3 tablespoons wheat-free tamari soy sauce, such as Crystal or San-J
⅓ cup packed light brown sugar
4 teaspoons paprika
1 teaspoon Asian fish sauce, such as A Taste of Thai or Thai Kitchen
¾ teaspoon ground cayenne
1 package (12 ounces) cellophane noodles, cooked according to package directions and drained
2 cups mung bean sprouts, rinsed
1 cup chopped fresh cilantro
¼ cup chopped peanuts or cashews, for garnish

1 In a large, heavy skillet, heat the oil over medium heat. Add green onions and cook, stirring frequently, about 2 to 3 minutes until soft. Add red bell pepper and garlic and cook 1 minute more. Set aside.

2 In a small bowl, combine vinegar, soy sauce, brown sugar, paprika, fish sauce, and cayenne. Add mixture to skillet and cook with vegetables until heated through.

3 Place the cooked noodles in 4 individual serving bowls. Divide the vegetable sauce evenly among the bowls, and top with bean sprouts and cilantro. Garnish with chopped peanuts. Serve immediately.

Fettuccine Alfredo

MAKES 4 SERVINGS

Fettuccine Alfredo, typically made with heavy cream and butter, is a delicious dish, but it can be very high in fat and calories. My version uses less-fattening ingredients without compromising the flavor. Of course, you can use any traditional recipe and just substitute the gluten-free pasta for regular pasta. The texture of this dish will vary with the type of pasta you use—heavier and darker in color if you use rice bran pasta by Tinkyada; lighter in color if you use pasta by DeBoles or Heartland's Finest.

1½ cups low-fat cream cheese or cream cheese alternative, such as Tofutti

3 tablespoons 1% milk (cow's, rice, soy, potato, or nut)

¼ cup grated Parmesan cheese or soy alternative, such as Soyco

1 small garlic clove, minced

2 tablespoons unsalted butter or buttery spread, such as Earth Balance

4 cups gluten-free fettuccine, such as DeBoles, cooked according to package directions or Handmade Pasta (page 211)

¼ cup chopped fresh parsley, for garnish (optional)

1 teaspoon lemon pepper, such as Durkee or Spice Islands, for garnish (optional)

1 In a food processor, combine the cream cheese, milk, Parmesan cheese, garlic, and butter. Process until the sauce is very smooth.

2 Transfer the sauce to a medium, heavy saucepan and whisk over medium heat until the sauce reaches serving temperature.

3 Serve immediately over hot fettuccine, garnished with chopped parsley and lemon pepper, if desired.

Feta-Truffle Tortellini with Orange-Hazelnut Butter

MAKES 4 SERVINGS (6 TORTELLINI EACH)

Elise Wiggins is Executive Chef at Panzano Restaurant in Denver, Colorado, and has been named a Colorado Chef of the Year by the American Culinary Federation. The gluten-free diet is close to Elise's heart, so she provides a variety of gluten-free choices at the restaurant. The recipe title may seem intimidating but this dish is actually quite doable if you have the ingredients. You and your guests will be transported by the amazing flavors in this dish.

PASTA

1 cup amaranth flour, such as Bob's Red Mill or NuWorld Amaranth, plus more as needed

¼ cup tapioca flour

1 large egg, at room temperature, whisked until no membrane exists (reserve 1 tablespoon for egg wash)

1 teaspoon hazelnut oil

1 to 2 tablespoons water

FILLING

½ cup Creamy Feta, such as 34 Degrees, oil drained

½ tablespoon chopped fresh tarragon

2 teaspoons Rosario white truffle oil (available at Whole Foods)

BUTTER

¼ cup unsalted European-style butter or buttery spread, such as Earth Balance

¼ cup hazelnuts, toasted

1 tablespoon grated orange zest

1 Make the pasta: In a medium mixing bowl, combine the flours. Create a well in the center and crack the egg into the center. Add the oil and 1 tablespoon of the water and gently whisk them into the flours with a fork. The dough should gradually pull together and not be sticky to the touch. If it is sticky, add more amaranth, 1 tablespoon at a time. If it is too dry, add the remaining tablespoon of water. Shape the dough into a flat disk, cover tightly with plastic wrap, and allow to rest 1 hour at room temperature.

2 Make the filling: In a small bowl, stir together the feta, tarragon, and oil until smooth; set aside.

3 With a rolling pin, roll the dough between sheets of plastic wrap until it is almost paper-thin. Remove the top piece of plastic wrap and cut the pasta into 2-inch squares.

4 Whisk the reserved tablespoon of egg with 1 teaspoon water until thoroughly blended. Brush the pasta squares with the egg wash and place a teaspoon of filling in the middle of each. Fold into tortellini shape by first folding one corner of the square over to the other and pressing all the

edges together. You now have a triangle. Then fold the two outermost points of the triangle together around your finger and press the ends together to form a circle. Fold the top edge down to make the classic tortellini shape. Set aside to dry slightly.

5 Bring a large pan of water to boiling and add salt liberally. Boil the tortellini for about 3 minutes. Remove from the water with a slotted spoon and place on a serving platter.

6 Make the sauce: Heat the butter and hazelnuts in a small pan over medium heat until the butter melts. Add the orange zest and pour over the tortellini. Serve immediately.

Macaroni and Cheese

MAKES 4 SERVINGS

Hot sauce, dry mustard, and nutmeg enhance the flavors of this American classic in a subtle way—they add depth of flavor to the expected delicious creaminess. You won't detect their presence, but you will appreciate the overall effect.

3 cups 1% milk (cow's, rice, soy, potato, or nut)

3 tablespoons sweet rice flour*

2 tablespoons unsalted butter or buttery spread, such as Earth Balance

2 cups (12 ounces) grated sharp cheddar cheese, or cheese alternative, such as Vegan Gourmet

1 cup (6 ounces) grated Monterey Jack or mild white cheese, or cheese alternative, such as Vegan Gourmet

2 tablespoons grated Parmesan cheese or soy alternative, such as Soyco

1 teaspoon hot pepper sauce, such as Frank's

½ teaspoon dry mustard

⅛ teaspoon freshly grated nutmeg

2 cups (about 8 ounces) gluten-free elbow macaroni, such as Tinkyada, cooked al dente in salted water according to package directions

1 cup gluten-free bread crumbs, such as Ener-G, or homemade Plain Bread Crumbs (page 117)

Paprika, for garnish

1 Place a rack in the middle of the oven. Preheat the oven to 350°F. Generously grease a 2-quart ovenproof baking dish.

2 Place all but ¼ cup of the milk in a heavy medium saucepan. In a small bowl, stir the sweet rice flour with the remaining ¼ cup milk until it is smooth; whisk into the milk. Cook over medium heat, whisking constantly, until the mixture thickens. Add the butter and stir until it is melted.

3 Remove the pan from the heat and stir in the cheeses, hot pepper sauce, mustard, and nutmeg until the cheeses are completely melted. While the pasta is still hot, add it to the sauce and toss to coat the pasta thoroughly with the cheese sauce. Transfer the mixture to the baking dish.

4 Bake 15 minutes. Sprinkle with bread crumbs and a dusting of paprika. Bake 15 minutes more or until the cheese is bubbly and the bread crumbs are browned. For speedier results, place a broiler rack about 6 inches away from the heat source. Preheat the broiler and broil the dish until the bread crumbs are browned and crunchy. Let stand 5 minutes. Serve immediately.

If using rice or potato milk, increase the sweet rice flour to ¼ cup.

Southwestern Macaroni and Cheese Ⓥ

MAKES 4 SERVINGS

Living in Denver, I see many dishes inspired by the city's Southwestern culture. Macaroni and Cheese, delicious in its classic preparation, is not immune from these influences. If you prefer yours the familiar way, use the recipe at left. But if you like to experiment with new tastes, give this innovative version a try.

1½ cups gluten-free elbow macaroni, such as Tinkyada

2 cups (8 ounces) grated Cheddar cheese or cheese alternative, such as Vegan Gourmet, divided

1 tablespoon sweet rice flour

⅛ teaspoon ground coriander, freshly grated nutmeg, or ground cloves

½ cup chopped fresh cilantro

1¼ cups 1% milk (cow's, rice, soy, potato, or nut)

½ cup gluten-free bottled salsa, such as Pace or Tostitos

½ cup lightly crushed tortilla chips

Paprika, for garnish

1 Place a rack in the middle of the oven. Preheat the oven to 400°F. Generously grease an 8-inch square baking dish; set aside.

2 In a large pot, cook the macaroni in boiling salted water, following package directions, until al dente—tender yet still firm to the bite. Drain thoroughly.

3 In a large saucepan, stir sweet rice flour and coriander (or nutmeg or cloves) into ¼ cup of the milk until smooth, then stir in the remaining milk. Heat over medium heat until mixture starts to simmer. Remove from heat and add 1½ cups of the cheese, stirring until smooth. Stir in the cilantro.

4 Add the cooked macaroni to the saucepan and stir until thoroughly mixed. Place half of the macaroni in the prepared dish. Top with dollops of half of the salsa. Add the remaining half of the macaroni and top with dollops of the remaining salsa. Sprinkle with tortilla chips and the remaining ½ cup cheese. Sprinkle with paprika.

5 Bake 15 to 20 minutes, or until the cheese is melted and the mixture is heated through. Serve hot.

PASTA WITH SEAFOOD, POULTRY, OR MEAT

Linguini with Red Clam Sauce ⓠ

MAKES 4 SERVINGS

This dish comes together so quickly that you should have everything else ready before you start preparing it. To round out the meal, all you really need are a crisp tossed salad and some crusty bread.

1 tablespoon extra-virgin olive oil
½ cup diced onion
1 garlic clove, minced
¼ teaspoon crushed red pepper
½ cup dry white wine
1 can (14 to 15 ounces) petite diced tomatoes, including juice
½ teaspoon salt
1 can (6.5 ounces) clams, including juice
½ pound (8 ounces) uncooked gluten-free linguini, such as Tinkyada
2 tablespoons chopped fresh flat-leaf parsley leaves
1 tablespoon Parmesan cheese, or soy alternative, such as Soyco, for garnish

1 In a deep pot, heat oil over medium heat. Add onion and cook, stirring constantly, about 2 to 3 minutes until onion is soft. Add garlic and crushed red pepper and cook 1 minute more.

2 Add wine and cook until nearly evaporated, about 3 minutes. Add tomatoes, salt, and clams. Simmer, uncovered, 5 minutes.

3 Add linguini and gradually push down into sauce so linguini can cook in it. Continue to simmer 5 to 6 minutes or until linguini is almost done. Stir in parsley and cook until sauce thickens a bit more. Linguini will thicken sauce slightly as it cooks and will continue to cook after removing from heat. (If sauce isn't thick enough, mix 1 teaspoon cornstarch with 2 teaspoon cold water and gently stir into sauce.)

4 Transfer linguini and sauce to a large serving bowl. Dust with Parmesan cheese and serve immediately.

Linguini with White Clam Sauce ⓠ

MAKES 4 SERVINGS

A favorite dish for so many and even better if you can use fresh clams.

1 tablespoon extra-virgin olive oil
¼ teaspoon crushed red pepper
1 garlic clove, minced
2 tablespoons chopped fresh thyme or 1 teaspoon dried
1 teaspoon anchovy paste
½ cup dry white wine
1 can (6.5 ounces) clams, including juice
¼ teaspoon lemon pepper
¼ teaspoon salt
½ pound (8 ounces) uncooked gluten-free linguini, such as Tinkyada
2 tablespoons chopped fresh parsley
Dash paprika, for garnish

1 In a deep pot, heat oil over medium heat. Add crushed red pepper, garlic, thyme, and anchovy paste and cook 1 minute. Add wine, clams, lemon pepper, and salt. Simmer over low heat, uncovered, 5 minutes.

2 Add linguini and gradually push down into sauce so linguini can cook in it. Continue to simmer for 5 to 6 minutes or until linguini is almost done. Stir in parsley and cook until sauce thickens a bit more. Linguini will thicken sauce slightly as it cooks and will continue to cook after removing from heat. (If sauce isn't thick enough, mix 1 teaspoon cornstarch with 2 teaspoon cold water and stir into sauce.)

3 Transfer to a large serving bowl and garnish with dash of paprika. Serve immediately.

Fettuccine with Frutti di Mare

MAKES 4 SERVINGS

Frutti di mare means "fruit of the sea", which aptly describes seafood. This is one of my husband's favorite dishes and he often orders it in seafood restaurants but particularly loves it made fresh at home. The fish cooks quickly, so have the rest of the meal ready to serve before you start making the dish.

2 tablespoons olive oil

½ cup chopped onion

1 garlic clove, minced

½ cup dry white wine or vermouth

1 can (8 ounces) tomato sauce

2 tablespoons chopped fresh basil or 1 tablespoon dried

¼ teaspoon crushed red pepper

½ pound red snapper fillets, cut into 1½-inch pieces

1 pound large shrimp

1 pound mussels, scrubbed and debearded

½ pound sea scallops, quartered

½ pound (8 ounces) gluten-free fettuccine, such as Tinkyada

¼ cup grated Parmesan cheese or soy alternative, such as Soyco, for garnish

1 In a heavy, deep skillet, heat oil over medium-high heat. Add onion and cook until it starts to soften and becomes translucent, about 5 minutes. Add garlic and wine and cook until wine is reduced by half, about 3 minutes. Add tomato sauce, basil, and crushed red pepper and bring to boil.

2 Add red snapper and cook 2 minutes. Add shrimp, mussels, and scallops and cook just until shrimp curl and mussels open. Remove from heat. Discard any unopened mussels.

3 While seafood cooks, bring a large pot of water to boil over high heat and salt liberally. Add fettuccine and cook, according to package directions, until al dente—tender yet still firm to the bite. Drain pasta well.

4 Transfer pasta to a large serving bowl and toss with seafood and tomato sauce. Garnish with Parmesan cheese and serve hot.

Noodles with Salmon in a Lemon-Ginger Broth

MAKES 4 SERVINGS

Enjoy this dish on a night when you want something light and healthy. You can try a variety of noodles, or you can serve it with cooked brown rice or basmati rice.

4 ounces Pad Thai, or rice fettuccine noodles, such as Tinkyada, cooked

6 cups gluten-free, low-sodium chicken broth, such as Swanson's Natural Goodness, or homemade Chicken Broth (page 676)

2-inch chunk of fresh ginger, grated

2 tablespoons Asian fish sauce, such as A Taste of Thai or Thai Kitchen

Juice and grated zest of 1 lemon

⅛ teaspoon crushed red pepper

1 garlic clove, minced

4 skinless salmon fillets (6 ounces each)

4 green onions, sliced diagonally

2 small carrots, peeled and sliced diagonally

1 package (3.5 ounces) fresh enoki mushrooms

1 bunch of fresh baby spinach leaves or watercress

½ cup thinly sliced red bell pepper

½ cup chopped fresh cilantro, for garnish

1 Cook noodles according to package directions in liberally salted water. Keep warm.

2 In a large pot, bring the broth to a boil over medium-heat. Add the ginger, fish sauce, lemon zest and juice, crushed red pepper, and garlic. Reduce the heat to low and simmer, covered, 10 minutes.

3 Lay the salmon fillets in the broth and add the onions, carrots, mushrooms, spinach, and bell pepper. Increase the heat to high and bring the broth to a boil. Immediately reduce the heat to low and simmer, covered, 8 to 10 minutes or until salmon is just barely opaque when cut in the thickest part.

4 Place equal portions of cooked noodles in 4 heated soup bowls. Place a salmon fillet in each bowl and pour the broth and vegetables into the bowls. Garnish with the fresh cilantro.

Rice Noodles with Shrimp-Coconut Curry Ⓠ

MAKES 4 SERVINGS

Rice noodles, also called rice sticks, are the foundation of this boldly flavored curry dish. You can control the degree of spiciness by how much Thai curry paste you use. If you prefer, replace the shrimp with chopped boneless chicken and cook until done before removing to a plate.

1 tablespoon canola oil

½ pound medium shrimp, peeled and deveined

2 chopped green onions

1 red bell pepper, julienned

1 large garlic clove, minced

1 tablespoon Asian fish sauce, such as A Taste of Thai or Thai Kitchen

1 tablespoon honey

1 to 2 teaspoons Thai green curry paste, such as A Taste of Thai

1 teaspoon grated fresh ginger

1 teaspoon grated lemon zest

1 teaspoon grated lime zest

¼ teaspoon turmeric

1 can (14 to 15 ounces) coconut milk (not cream of coconut)

Salt and white pepper to taste

1 pound rice noodles, such as Thai Kitchen, or rice sticks, cooked according to package directions, drained, and kept hot

2 cups mung bean sprouts, rinsed

½ cup chopped fresh cilantro, for garnish

1 In a large, heavy skillet, heat the oil over medium heat. Add shrimp and cook just until they turn pink. Transfer shrimp to a plate.

2 Add green onions, bell pepper, and garlic to skillet and cook until onions and bell pepper are slightly softened, about 2 to 3 minutes. Stir in fish sauce, honey, Thai curry paste, ginger, lemon zest, lime zest, turmeric, and coconut milk. Reduce heat to low, and simmer, covered, 7 to 10 minutes. Add cooked shrimp and bring to serving temperature. Add salt and pepper to taste.

3 Divide hot cooked noodles among 4 wide, shallow bowls. Divide the shrimp curry among the 4 bowls, top with bean sprouts, and garnish with fresh cilantro. Serve immediately.

Pad Thai

MAKES 4 SERVINGS

Pad Thai originated in Thailand and is a very popular, hearty, flavor-packed dish served in Asian restaurants around the country. It contains a variety of ingredients, but once you get all of them prepped, this dish comes together in minutes. It's important to have the rest of the meal ready to serve before you assemble this dish.

8 ounces (½ package) rice noodles, such as Thai Kitchen

6 tablespoons Asian fish sauce, such as Taste of Thai or Thai Kitchen

⅓ cup fresh lime juice

¼ cup gluten-free Thai sweet red chile sauce, such as Taste of Thai or Thai Kitchen

¼ cup packed light brown sugar

1 tablespoon sesame oil

¼ teaspoon ground cayenne

2 large garlic cloves, minced

⅓ cup peanut oil

2 large eggs, lightly beaten

½ cup chopped green onions

¼ cup chopped fresh cilantro, divided

3 tablespoons chopped fresh basil or 1½ tablespoons dried

2 cups chopped fresh vegetables (such as asparagus, bok choy, carrots, or snow peas)

1½ pounds cooked, peeled and deveined shrimp

½ pound fresh bean sprouts

4 tablespoons chopped roasted peanuts, divided

1 In a large pot, cover the noodles with hot water and soak while preparing the remainder of the meal. Drain thoroughly before adding to the wok in Step 3.

2 Make the sauce: In a small bowl or measuring cup, combine the fish sauce, lime juice, chile sauce, brown sugar, sesame oil, cayenne, and garlic. Whisk until smooth; set aside.

3 In a wok or large, deep skillet, heat the peanut oil over medium-high heat. Add eggs and stir just until set, but not browned. Chop eggs coarsely with spatula before pushing them to the side of the wok and reduce heat to medium. Add green onions, 3 tablespoons of the cilantro, basil, vegetables, shrimp, and drained noodles. Toss to mix thoroughly. Pour sauce evenly over ingredients and toss again.

4 Cover and simmer 2 to 3 minutes or until mixture is heated through. Add bean sprouts and 3 tablespoons of the peanuts and toss gently. Transfer to serving dish and garnish with the remaining 1 tablespoon cilantro and remaining 1 tablespoon peanuts. Serve immediately.

Chicken Paprikash on Noodles

MAKES 4 SERVINGS

Thinly sliced chicken fillets work better than full-size chicken breast halves because they cook more quickly. For a wonderful flavor boost, use smoked paprika in place of sweet Hungarian paprika.

2 small onions, peeled and thinly sliced

1 tablespoon olive oil, unsalted butter, or buttery spread, such as Earth Balance, or canola oil

1½ pounds thin-sliced chicken fillets

1 teaspoon salt

½ teaspoon freshly ground black pepper

1 tablespoon sweet Hungarian paprika

1 teaspoon chopped fresh thyme or ½ teaspoon dried

¼ teaspoon ground cayenne

1 bay leaf

1 large garlic clove, minced

1 can (8 ounces) sliced mushrooms, drained

1 cup canned whole tomatoes, cut with kitchen shears

1 cup gluten-free, low-sodium chicken broth, such as Swanson's Natural Goodness, or homemade Chicken Broth (page 676)

1½ teaspoons cornstarch, dissolved in 1 tablespoon cold water (optional)

½ cup sour cream or sour cream alternative, such as Tofutti

1 pound hot cooked gluten-free noodles or pasta of choice, such as Orgran, Tinkyada, Dr. Schar

2 tablespoons chopped fresh parsley, for garnish

1 In a large, heavy skillet, heat the olive oil over medium heat. Cook onions until lightly browned. Move onion to side of skillet.

2 Sprinkle chicken with salt and pepper. Add chicken to skillet and brown on all sides, about 5 to 8 minutes, scattering onions among chicken pieces and continuing to cook them as well.

3 Add paprika, thyme, cayenne, bay leaf, garlic,

3 Add paprika, thyme, cayenne, bay leaf, garlic, mushrooms, tomatoes, and broth to skillet. Bring to boil, reduce heat and simmer, covered, 45 minutes to 1 hour, or until chicken is done. Remove bay leaf. If sauce needs thickening, stir in cornstarch mixture and cook, stirring constantly, until mixture thickens slightly. Stir in sour cream and bring to serving temperature, but do not boil or the sour cream will curdle.

4 Meanwhile, in a large pot, bring water to a boil and salt liberally. Add pasta and cook according to package directions until al dente. Drain. Serve the chicken and vegetables over the hot noodles, garnished with fresh parsley.

Pasta with Turkey Bolognese Sauce

MAKES 4 SERVINGS

Bolognese sauce is traditionally made with beef and milk, but this innovative version uses turkey (or chicken) and chicken broth instead. If you prefer the traditional approach, use the same amounts of ground beef instead of turkey and milk instead of chicken broth. A Bolognese sauce starts with a "soffrito" or a mixture of celery, carrots, and onions. Pancetta is a non-smoked Italian bacon that is cured with salt and spices. It is available in the deli or meat sections of grocery stores.

1 ounce pancetta, finely diced (1 slice)

1 small onion, finely chopped

1 large carrot, peeled and finely chopped

2 stalks celery, finely chopped

1 pound ground turkey or chicken (I like half dark meat and half white meat)

¾ teaspoon salt

¼ teaspoon freshly ground black pepper

⅛ teaspoon ground allspice

1 cup dry white wine

1 cup gluten-free, low-sodium chicken broth, such as Swanson's Natural Goodness, or homemade Chicken Broth (page 676)

1 can (14 to 15 ounces) whole tomatoes and juices (chop tomatoes with kitchen shears)

2 garlic cloves, minced

2 teaspoons chopped fresh oregano or ¾ teaspoon dried

2 teaspoons chopped fresh thyme or ¾ teaspoon dried

½ teaspoon chopped fresh rosemary or ¼ teaspoon dried

1 pound gluten-free tube pasta, such as Pastariso, cooked according to package directions, hot

¼ cup grated Parmesan cheese or soy alternative, such as Soyco, for garnish

1 In a Dutch oven or other deep, heavy pot with a tight-fitting lid, cook pancetta over medium heat until crisp. Remove pancetta and set aside, leaving remaining fat in the pan. Add the onion, carrot, and celery and cook in the fat over medium heat, stirring occasionally, about 3 to 4 minutes or until onion is translucent and soft.

2 Add turkey, salt, pepper, and allspice and cook until turkey is cooked through and lightly browned.

3 Stir in wine and cook until wine is almost evaporated. Return pancetta to Dutch oven and add broth, tomatoes, garlic, oregano, thyme, and rosemary. Cover, reduce heat to low, and simmer, 2 to 3 hours, until sauce thickens. Serve on hot cooked pasta, garnished with Parmesan cheese.

Spaghetti and Meatballs

MAKES 12 SERVINGS

Whether or not this is a traditional Italian dish, it is certainly one of my family's favorites. I usually make a big batch of the Marinara Sauce (page 672) and freeze it in meal-size portions for future use. I

also make a whole batch of the meatballs and freeze them in a separate container so I can use a few of them at a time in other dishes or single servings. This comes in handy when my grandson is the only one who wants spaghetti for dinner. The Romano cheese is optional, but adds a very special flavor. You can vary the size of the meatballs as you wish.

SAUCE

Homemade Marinara Sauce (see page 672)

MEATBALLS

1 pound raw lean ground beef, or use half ground beef and half ground pork

¼ cup finely chopped onion

½ cup gluten-free bread crumbs, such as Ener-G, or homemade Plain Bread Crumbs (page 117)

1 large egg, beaten

4 tablespoons chopped fresh parsley or 2 tablespoons dried

1 tablespoon chopped fresh basil or 1½ teaspoons dried

1 teaspoon chopped fresh oregano or ½ teaspoon dried

½ teaspoon salt

½ teaspoon freshly ground black pepper

¼ teaspoon crushed red pepper (optional)

¼ teaspoon garlic powder

2 tablespoons grated Romano cheese, or cheese alternative, such as Soyco (optional)

PASTA

1½ pounds gluten-free spaghetti, such as Pastariso

1 Make the sauce: Prepare the marinara sauce; set aside. Place a rack in the middle of the oven. Preheat the oven to 350°F.

2 Make the meatballs: Line a 13 × 9-inch baking sheet (not nonstick) with foil. In a large bowl, combine the beef, onion, bread crumbs, egg, parsley, basil, oregano, salt, pepper, crushed red pepper if using, garlic, and Romano cheese if using. Mix the ingredients well with your hands and shape into 12 meatballs, each about 1½ inches in diameter. Place them on the prepared baking sheet.

3 Bake 20 minutes, or until the meatballs are nicely browned and firm. Remove the meatballs from the oven and cool 15 minutes on the sheet. Add them to the marinara sauce.

4 Make the pasta: Cook the spaghetti in liberally salted water according to package directions and serve each portion topped with about ⅓ cup marinara sauce and a meatball.

Pasta with Beef Ragù

MAKES 6 SERVINGS

The word ragù *means "meat sauce" in Italian. Years ago, I learned about this dish from Chef Francesco Beconcini at his family's Tuscan restaurant, Il Pino, in San Gimignano, Italy. I have modified his fabulous Tuscan ragù, and served it to many dinner guests over the years. It has evolved to its current version, which I know you will love. It freezes beautifully so keep some on hand for quick thawing on a busy night.*

¼ cup extra-virgin olive oil

1 small onion, finely chopped

1 medium carrot, peeled and finely chopped

1 stalk celery, finely chopped

1 pound lean ground beef

2 tablespoons chopped Italian parsley

2 garlic cloves, minced

2 large sprigs fresh rosemary, chopped, or 2 teaspoons dried, crushed

½ cup dry red wine

1 can (28 ounces) whole plum tomatoes, including juice

2 bay leaves

½ teaspoon sugar

Pinch crushed red pepper

Salt and freshly ground pepper to taste

1 pound penne or other pasta shape, such as Dr. Schar

¼ cup grated Parmesan cheese, or Pecorino Romano cheese, or soy alternative, such as Soyco

1 In a large, heavy skillet, heat the oil over medium-high heat. Add the onions, carrot, and celery and cook until the vegetables are tender, but not brown, about 5 minutes. Add the ground beef and cook until it is darkly browned and all juices have evaporated, about 7 to 10 minutes.

2 Add the parsley, garlic, rosemary, wine, tomatoes, bay leaves, sugar, crushed red pepper, salt, and pepper and let simmer, covered, 20 to 30 minutes. Remove the lid and simmer until the juices are reduced to serving consistency. Remove the bay leaves.

3 Meanwhile, in a large pot, bring water to a boil and salt liberally. Add pasta and cook following package directions. Drain.

4 Serve the beef ragù over the hot pasta. Top with grated cheese.

Lasagna

MAKES 6 SERVINGS

Lasagna is undoubtedly one of America's most popular pasta dishes. I assemble mine in advance and bake it the next day. I use uncooked lasagna noodles; the juices in the sauce moisten the pasta, which then cooks as it bakes—eliminating the need to boil the noodles beforehand.

½ pound lean ground beef or gluten-free Italian sausage, such as Applegate Farms

8 ounces (2 cups) shredded mozzarella cheese or cheese alternative, such as Vegan Gourmet, divided

1 pound ricotta cheese

2 large eggs

½ cup grated Parmesan cheese, or soy alternative, such as Soyco

1 jar (26 ounces) or 3 cups store-bought gluten-free marinara or spaghetti sauce, such as Classico, or Homemade Marinara Sauce (page 672)

9 gluten-free lasagna noodles from an 8-ounce box, uncooked, such as DeBoles or Ener-G

1 In a heavy skillet, cook the ground beef over medium heat until browned and all juices have evaporated, about 5 to 7 minutes.

2 In a large bowl, stir together ½ cup of the mozzarella cheese, the ricotta cheese, eggs, and Parmesan cheese.

3 Generously grease an 11 × 7-inch ovenproof baking dish. Spread ½ cup of the marinara sauce on bottom of dish. In order, lay 3 of the uncooked noodles lengthwise on bottom, ⅓ of the browned ground beef, ⅔ cup of the ricotta cheese mixture, ½ cup of the marinara sauce, and ⅓ cup of the mozzarella cheese. Repeat two times, the third time using all of the remaining marinara sauce and ending with all of the remaining mozzarella cheese.

4 Coat foil with cooking spray, then lay the foil on top of the baking dish and press the lasagna mixture down firmly. Wrap the dish tightly with foil and refrigerate 8 hours or overnight. (You may also freeze lasagna at this point. Thaw completely before baking.)

5 Place a rack in the middle of the oven. Preheat the oven to 350°F. Bake, covered, 30 minutes. Remove the foil and bake 15 minutes more, or until the cheeses are lightly browned. Remove the lasagna from the oven and let stand on a wire rack 10 minutes before cutting.

MAKES 4 SERVINGS

Pastitsio is a Greek baked dish with layers of pasta, ground meat, cheese, and eggs—one of Greece's best comfort foods. It is hearty, delicious, and supremely filling.

2 tablespoons olive oil
1 large onion, diced
1 pound lean ground beef
1 garlic clove, minced
1 can (8 ounces) tomato sauce
¼ cup dry red wine
1 teaspoon chopped fresh oregano or ½ teaspoon dried
½ teaspoon salt
½ teaspoon freshly ground black pepper
¼ teaspoon ground allspice
¼ teaspoon freshly grated nutmeg
1 (3-inch strip) of orange rind (no white part)
1 tablespoon unsalted butter or buttery spread, such as Earth Balance
2 cups 2% milk (cow's, rice, soy, potato, or nut)
¼ cup sweet rice flour
1 cup grated Parmesan cheese + 1 tablespoon for topping, or soy alternative, such as Soyco
2 large eggs, beaten
2 cups gluten-free elbow macaroni, such as Tinkyada*
Cream Sauce (see page 674)

1 In a heavy, medium skillet, heat the oil over medium-high heat. Add the onion and cook until slightly softened. Add the ground beef and cook until deeply browned, about 7 to 10 minutes. Add the garlic, tomato sauce, wine, oregano, salt, pepper, allspice, nutmeg, and orange rind. Reduce the heat to low, cover, and simmer 15 minutes. Remove the orange rind.

2 While the meat sauce simmers, melt the butter in a heavy, medium saucepan over medium heat. Add 1½ cups of the milk. Stir sweet rice flour into remaining ½ cup milk until smooth, add it to the pan, and cook, whisking constantly, until slightly thickened and bubbling. Add 1 cup Parmesan cheese and stir until melted. Stir 2 tablespoons of the milk-cheese mixture into the beaten eggs, then add egg mixture to the pan. Cook 3 to 4 minutes more, whisking constantly. The mixture will thicken slightly.

3 Place a rack in the middle of the oven. Preheat the oven to 350°F. Generously grease an 8-inch nonstick (gray, not black) pan. Spread ½ cup of the cream sauce on the bottom of the prepared pan. Spread half of the macaroni evenly on the bottom of the pan. Spread ground beef mixture evenly on top. Place remaining macaroni evenly on top of ground beef. Pour remaining cream sauce over macaroni. Sprinkle with remaining Parmesan cheese.

4 Bake 1 hour or until the top forms a light golden crust. Remove from oven and cool 15 minutes on wire rack before cutting.

If you use another brand of pasta, boil it for 5 minutes, then drain it thoroughly before adding to casserole.

Traditional Tuna Casserole

MAKES 4 SERVINGS

One of the more shocking findings for any new gluten-free cook is discovering that the old staple for tuna casserole—cream of mushroom soup—is off-limits because it gets its thick consistency from wheat flour. My version replaces the mushroom soup with a white sauce and spices that replicate the flavors of the original version. If you've never tried crushed potato chips on this dish, you'll like it. If you use any pasta other than Heartland's Finest, be sure to boil it for 5 minutes before adding it to the casserole.

¼ cup sweet rice flour

1¼ cups 1% milk (cow's, rice, soy, potato, or nut)

1 cup gluten-free elbow macaroni, such as Tinkyada

1 can (6 ounces) tuna in water, drained

1 can (7 ounces) sliced mushrooms, drained

1 cup frozen green peas

1 tablespoon wheat-free tamari soy sauce, such as Crystal or San-J

¼ cup chopped celery or 1 tablespoon dried celery flakes

1 tablespoon chopped fresh onion or ½ teaspoon dried minced onions

1 teaspoon chopped fresh thyme or ½ teaspoon dried

½ teaspoon salt

¼ teaspoon garlic powder (optional)

¼ teaspoon freshly ground black pepper

1 cup crushed gluten-free potato chips, such as Lay's

1 Place a rack in the middle of the oven. Preheat the oven to 350°F. Generously grease a 1-quart ovenproof casserole dish.

2 In a large bowl, whisk the sweet rice flour into ¼ cup of the milk until smooth. Place this mixture and the remaining 1 cup of milk in a heavy, medium saucepan. Cook over medium heat, stirring constantly, about 1 to 2 minute, until the mixture thickens.

3 Add the macaroni, tuna, mushrooms, peas, soy sauce, celery, onion, thyme, salt, garlic powder, if using, and pepper and stir to combine the ingredients thoroughly. Pour the mixture into the prepared dish. Top with potato chips.

4 Bake 25 to 30 minutes or until the casserole is bubbling and the potato chips start to brown. Serve immediately.

Tuna Casserole with a Twist

MAKES 4 SERVINGS

This is probably not the classic casserole you remember from your childhood. It doesn't contain the customary wheat-laden cream of mushroom soup but this contemporary version gets its wonderful flavors from mushrooms, pimento, spices, and herbs. The bean pasta from Heartland's Finest works best because it holds its shape better during baking than other pasta brands.

½ cup chopped onion

½ cup chopped celery or 2 tablespoons dried celery flakes

1 cup gluten-free, low-sodium chicken broth, such as Swanson's Natural Goodness, or homemade Chicken Broth (page 676)

1 cup 1% milk (cow's, rice, soy, potato, or nut), divided

¼ cup sweet rice flour

½ cup mayonnaise

1 tablespoon Dijon mustard

1 tablespoon wheat-free tamari soy sauce, such as Crystal or San-J

1 teaspoon chopped fresh thyme or ½ teaspoon dried

1 teaspoon salt

1 can (7 ounces) sliced mushrooms

1 cup frozen green peas, thawed

1 can (6 ounces) tuna in water, drained

1 cup gluten-free uncooked noodles, such as Tinkyada

1 jar (4 ounces) pimento, drained

1½ cups gluten-free bread crumbs, such as Ener-G, or homemade Plain Bread Crumbs (page 117)

2 tablespoons grated Parmesan cheese or soy alternative, such as Soyco

1 Place a rack in the middle of the oven. Preheat oven to 350°F. Generously grease an 8 × 8-inch glass or ceramic casserole dish.

2 In a large, medium saucepan, heat the oil over medium heat. Add onions and celery and cook until soft, about 5 minutes. Add broth and ½ cup of the milk to pan. In a small bowl, stir sweet rice flour into remaining ½ cup milk until smooth and then whisk into mixture in pan, along with mayonnaise, mustard, soy sauce, thyme, and salt. Continue whisking until mixture thickens slightly.

3 Remove pan from heat. Stir in mushrooms, peas, tuna, uncooked noodles, and pimento. Transfer to prepared dish. (You may refrigerate it at this point to bake the next day or later that same day. If so, cover tightly with aluminum foil.) Sprinkle with bread crumbs. Top with Parmesan cheese. Lightly coat with cooking spray.

4 Bake 30 minutes or until sauce is bubbly and bread crumbs are browned. Remove from oven and let cool 5 minutes before serving. (Baking time will be extended if casserole is refrigerated.)

PASTA AND NOODLES FROM SCRATCH

Handmade Pasta

MAKES 4 SERVINGS

Use this basic recipe to make hand-cut thin noodles and lasagna noodles, as well as various flavors of pasta. Handmade pasta is delicious and cooks quickly because it is fresh, not dried. Once you get the hang of it you'll be able to make it without a recipe. Be sure to dust white rice flour on the dough to prevent sticking when you roll it.

1 teaspoon olive oil
2 large eggs, at room temperature
¼ cup water
1 tablespoon canola oil
½ cup sorghum flour
½ cup tapioca flour
¼ cup potato starch
½ cup cornstarch
4 teaspoons xanthan gum
½ teaspoon salt
White rice flour, for dusting

1 In a food processor, process the eggs, water, and oil until the eggs are light yellow in color. Add flours, potato starch, cornstarch, xanthan gum, and salt. Process until thoroughly blended and the dough forms a ball. Break up the dough into smaller egg-sized pieces and process until a ball forms again.

2 Remove the dough and knead it with your hands until smooth. Divide the dough in two balls

drying out. Place one ball of dough on a 15 × 15-inch sheet of parchment paper that is dusted with white rice flour. Cover with plastic wrap (using overlapping pieces to cover the parchment paper) and with a rolling pin, roll the dough to 1/16-inch thick or as thin as possible.

3 To make thin noodles: Remove the plastic wrap and use a sharp knife to cut the dough into 1/4-inch wide noodles with a sharp knife or a rolling herb mincer (available at kitchen stores). Repeat with the remaining ball of dough. Use immediately or drape strips over a pasta drying rack. To make lasagna noodles: Remove the plastic wrap and use a sharp knife or a pastry crimper (rolling cutter with scalloped edges) to cut dough in 2-inch wide strips. Use immediately or drape strips over a pasta drying rack.

MACHINE-MADE PASTA

The Handmade Pasta dough may also be shaped in an electric pasta machine, but be sure to follow your machine's directions as different machines require different procedures. My machine calls for placing 1 teaspoon of oil (rather than 1 tablespoon as in the handmade version) in the machine. Then thoroughly whisk the dry ingredients together in a medium bowl and add to the machine.

In a small bowl, whisk together the eggs and water until light yellow and foamy and the egg membranes are thoroughly broken up. Follow machine directions from this point to add the liquid ingredients and to make the sizes and shapes offered by your particular model. It is best to reserve the final 2 tablespoons of egg mixture until you are sure it's needed.

Handmade Basil-Garlic Noodles: Add 2 teaspoons chopped fresh basil or 1 teaspoon dried and 1/2 teaspoon garlic powder with the dry ingredients.

Handmade Tomato Noodles: Use 1/4 cup tomato juice in place of 1/4 cup water.

Handmade Chile Noodles: Add 1 teaspoon New Mexico chili powder with the dry ingredients.

Ravioli in Creamy Marinara Sauce Ⓥ

MAKES 4 SERVINGS

Homemade ravioli take a little patience—to roll out the dough, shape it, and fill it—so save this recipe for a day when you have the time. Your reward is delectable, light ravioli that no store-bought version can beat. You can freeze the uncooked ravioli, too.

RAVIOLI

1 recipe Handmade Pasta (page 211)
1½ cups grated Parmesan cheese or soy alternative, such as Soyco
½ cup ricotta cheese or cream cheese alternative, such as Tofutti
1 teaspoon Italian seasoning
1 large egg, separated
1 tablespoon water

SAUCE

2 cups gluten-free marinara sauce, such as Classico, or homemade Marinara Sauce (page 672)
⅔ cup heavy cream

1 Make the ravioli: Make the handmade pasta and keep dough tightly wrapped in plastic wrap until ready to use. In a small bowl, mix together the cheeses, Italian seasoning, and egg yolk until smooth; set aside.

2 Roll the dough with a rolling pin to a 12-inch square on a sheet of parchment paper. Whisk together the egg white and water until the egg membrane is totally broken up and brush it on half of the dough. Place half-teaspoonfuls of the cheese filling 2 inches apart on the egg-painted side of the dough

3 Fold the unpainted half of the dough over the filled portion and seal the edges with your fingers. Press dough together with fingers between mounds to create mounds every 2 inches.

4 Cut the ravioli into 2-inch squares with a pastry cutter, following the lines where you've pressed the dough together. Or, use a pastry crimper that both cuts and crimps (presses together with a curvy line pattern) the dough at the same time. If the edges are not properly sealed, the filling will fall out when the ravioli are boiled.

5 Make the sauce: In a small pan, heat the marinara sauce over medium heat to serving temperature. Cover and keep warm while cooking the ravioli. Just before serving, stir in cream and bring to serving temperature again.

6 In a large pot, bring water to boil. Salt liberally, add ravioli, and cook 5 to 10 minutes or until done. Serve immediately with sauce. (You may also freeze cooked ravioli for later use, if desired.) Makes about 30 ravioli, enough for 6 to 7 ravioli per person.

Potato Gnocchi

MAKES 4 SERVINGS

Gnocchi means "lumps" in Italian and is the word used for light Italian dumplings. But gnocchi are most often served like pasta and tossed with melted butter, Parmesan cheese, or marinara sauce. You might also serve them chilled as part of a pasta salad. Smaller servings of gnocchi make a great side dish, however you choose to serve it. There are many varieties, but this common version uses mashed potatoes as the base.

2 large russet potatoes, scrubbed, peeled, and cut in 1-inch cubes

2 teaspoons salt, divided

2 tablespoons unsalted butter or buttery spread, such as Earth Balance, at room temperature

1 large egg

1 cup Carol's Sorghum Blend (page x), or more if needed

½ teaspoon xanthan gum

1 In a large pot, place the potatoes and add 1 teaspoon of the salt and enough water to cover. Bring to a boil, reduce the heat to medium, and cook, covered, until tender but still firm, about 15 minutes. Drain the potatoes and cool 5 minutes. Mash them with a potato ricer for best results or with a fork or potato masher.

2 Put the potatoes in a large bowl. Beat in the butter and ½ teaspoon of the salt with an electric mixer on low speed until well blended and then beat in the egg until well blended. Cover the bowl tightly and cool 15 minutes or until the potatoes are cool enough to handle. Beat in the sorghum blend and xanthan gum on low speed. The dough will appear crumbly, but will form a soft ball when shaped with your hands.

3 Divide the dough into 6 portions, keeping unused portions covered tightly in plastic wrap to avoid drying out. On a sheet of wax paper, roll each portion into a long rope with your hands, about ½ inch in diameter, and cut into 1-inch pieces. To make the gnocchi, hold a piece in the palm of your hand and gently press the tines of a fork into the ball to create indentations.

4 Bring a large pot of water to a boil. Add the remaining ½ teaspoon salt. Add gnocchi and cook until they float to the top, then cook them 1 to 2 minutes more. Remove them with a slotted spoon and serve immediately.

Spaetzle

MAKES 4 SERVINGS

Spaetzle (SHPETS-luh) are little pieces of pasta made by pressing dough through a colander or a special spaetzle press* into boiling water, then frying the little gems in oil or butter to lightly brown them. They are typically associated with German cooking and make a great accompaniment to entrées such as Sauerbrauten (page 340) or Pork Schnitzel (page 362).

1¼ cups Carol's Sorghum Blend (page x)
⅔ cup potato starch
2 teaspoons baking powder
½ teaspoon baking soda
½ teaspoon salt
1 large egg
3 tablespoons unsalted butter or buttery spread, such as Earth Balance
¾ cup well-shaken buttermilk or homemade Buttermilk (page 677)
2 tablespoons canola oil (or unsalted butter) or more, for frying
Salt and freshly ground pepper to taste
2 tablespoons chopped fresh parsley, for garnish

1 In a food processor, combine sorghum blend, potato starch, baking powder, baking soda, salt, egg, and butter and process until the dough is crumbly. Pour the buttermilk evenly over the mixture and process again until the dough forms a ball or several clumps on one side of the bowl.

2 Bring a large pot of water to a boil. Add salt liberally. Put dough in a colander or spaetzle press and press the dough through the holes into the boiling salted water. Cook the spaetzle until they pop to the surface, then remove them with a slotted spoon and place on a platter. Repeat with remaining dough.

3 In a large, heavy skillet, heat the oil over medium-high heat. Add about half of the spaetzle and cook until lightly browned, about 2 minutes. Lightly season them with salt and pepper, to taste. Repeat with the remaining spaetzle. Serve immediately, garnished with parsley.

*Spaetzle presses are available at www.cookingwithnana. com and other specialty kitchen suppliers

Pierogi

MAKES 16 PIEROGI

Pierogi (peer-OH-ghee) are half-moon-shaped dumplings typically associated with central and eastern European countries. There are many types of fillings but this one uses mashed potatoes. The dumplings are tossed with butter and garnished with sour cream and sometimes they are served with applesauce. If you wish, you may also pan-fry them in butter until they are lightly browned.

2 cups Carol's Sorghum Blend (page x)
½ teaspoon salt
¼ teaspoon baking powder
¼ teaspoon xanthan gum
1 large egg
2 ounces cream cheese or cream cheese alternative, such as Tofutti
¼ to ⅓ cup warm water, or more as needed
White rice flour, for dusting
⅓ cup mashed potatoes, seasoned to taste with salt and white pepper
2 tablespoons unsalted butter or buttery spread, such as Earth Balance, melted
¼ cup sour cream or sour cream alternative, such as Tofutti

1 In a food processor, pulse together the sorghum blend, salt, baking powder, and xanthan gum.

Add the egg and cream cheese and process until crumbly, about 20 seconds. Add ¼ cup of the water through the tube and process until the dough forms a ball. If it does not, add water—a tablespoon at a time—until it does.

2 With a rolling pin, roll half of the dough on a rice-floured surface to about ¹⁄₁₆ inch thick. Cut 3-inch circles with cookie cutter. Place a teaspoon of mashed potato on the center of the bottom half of each circle and fold the circles in half, pressing the edges together (fork tines work well) until they are sealed. Repeat with remaining dough and mashed potatoes.

3 In a large pot, bring water to a boil. Add salt liberally and cook about 5 to 7 pierogi at a time, not overcrowding them, and stirring constantly to avoid sticking. They are done when they float to the top, anywhere from 3 to 7 minutes. Remove the pierogi with a slotted spoon, transfer them to a plate lined with paper towels, and gently pat them dry. Place them on a warmed serving platter. Cover to keep warm while cooking the remaining dumplings. Drizzle with the melted butter and serve hot, garnished with sour cream.

GRAINS AND BEANS

Rice

Basic Rice

Cilantro Rice

Coconut Rice

Herbed Brown Rice

Grilled Vegetables on Brown Rice

Dilled Rice Pilaf

Curried Rice Pilaf

Saffron Rice Pilaf

Basmati Rice Pilaf with Dried
Fruits and Nuts

Wild Rice Pancakes with Pecans

Orange-Scented Wild Rice with
Dried Fruit

Saffron Risotto

Slow-Cooker Brown Rice Risotto

Fried Risotto Cakes

Vegetable, Rice, and Bean Curry

Pork Fried Rice

Basmati Rice Couscous

Lemony Couscous Salad

Fast Tropical Cashew Couscous

Polenta and Other Grains

Polenta

Teff-Corn Polenta

Baked Quinoa, Wild Rice, and
Cherry Pilaf

Quinoa Tabbouleh

Hazelnut Quinoa Salad

Herbed Quinoa Blend with
Chickpeas, Spinach, and Shrimp

Toasted Quinoa with Mandarin
Oranges and Basil

Oat Salad with Roasted
Vegetables

Steel-cut Oats with Spinach and
Dried Cranberries

Kasha with Toasted Almonds

Sorghum with Grapes and Pecans

Amaranth Pilaf

Job's Tears with Bell Peppers

Legumes

Baked Beans

Drunken Southwestern Beans

Refried Drunken Southwestern
Beans

Spicy Black Beans

Brazilian Black Beans on Rice
and Collard Greens

Cannellini Beans with Spinach

Gigante Beans with Tomato
Sauce

Boraccho Pinto Beans

Curried Chickpeas on Basmati
Rice

Warm Lentils with Herbs

Lentils with Kale

Split Pea Dal

Black-Eyed Peas with Collard
Greens

Q = Quick   **V** = Vegetarian

Today, more Americans are eating whole grains because a variety of new delicious, whole grain products are available. This is important because among their many other health benefits, whole grains—with their high fiber content—help you meet the recommended amount of fiber (25 to 38 grams) per day.

However, on average, Americans still eat less than one serving of whole grains each day—and 40% eat no whole grains at all! A minimum of three servings is recommended by the USDA. This gap may be even higher among the gluten-intolerant because dishes made with whole grain wheat (whole wheat, wheat berries, wheat germ, and bulgur) are off-limits. The good news is that there are other, less familiar—but highly nutritious—whole grains to help you meet your daily servings.

In this chapter you will find recipes for tasty whole grain dishes featuring amaranth, buckwheat, corn, brown rice, wild rice, Job's Tears, quinoa, oats, sorghum, and teff. (Also, see the slow-cooked breakfast grains in the Pancakes, Waffles, and Breakfast Dishes chapter.) These grains are readily available in natural food stores or online.

Some of these grains have magnificent nutrient profiles. Quinoa (KEEN-wa) is called the "mother grain" because it contains more high-quality protein than any other grain. Native to the Andes Mountains of South America, it was one of the three staple foods of the Incas, along with corn and potatoes, but the Spanish conquerors destroyed most of the fields in which quinoa was grown. Introduced to America in the 1980s, quinoa has since become increasingly popular.

Amaranth, an 8,000-year-old crop called the "super food" by the ancient Aztecs, is very high in protein, fiber, iron, and other nutrients. Forbidden by Cortez, it slowly fell out of use. But twenty years ago, the "ancient crop with a future" was re-introduced into the American diet by the National Academy of Sciences.

Sorghum, also known as milo, is high in phosphorus, potassium, protein, and fiber. It makes wonderful baked goods and has been a staple in my kitchen for more than a decade.

Teff, high in protein and calcium, is a tiny grain about the size of a poppy seed. Teff is best known as the foundation of the traditional bread of Ethiopia, *injera*—a flat, pancake-like, slightly sour bread. Much of the teff eaten in the United States is grown in Idaho.

The grain receiving the most attention these days is oats. Long off-limits to the gluten-intolerant because it was contaminated with wheat during processing, several manufacturers now offer oats that are certified gluten-free. I use whole oat groats and steel-cut oats in this chapter and rolled oats in recipes for cookie, bar, and fruit desserts throughout this book. Make sure your physician approves of oats for your diet. To learn more about gluten-free oats, go to www.gluten.net and www.glutenfreediet.ca.

Beans and legumes are an important part of a healthy gluten-free diet because they supply important fiber-rich carbohydrates and B-vitamins, yet are low in fat. They are readily available in grocery stores, either dry or canned, and are inexpensive. This book includes recipes using many types of grains, beans, and legumes—some in this chapter and some in the Salad and Soups, and Vegetables chapters. Many can be vegetarian if made with vegetable broth instead of chicken broth. The recipes here are imagined as side dishes; halve the number of servings if you serve any as a main dish.

RICE

Basic Rice

MAKES 4 SERVINGS

This basic recipe for plain white rice is the foundation for a variety of meals. For heartier flavor, use broth instead of water.

2 cups water
1 cup white rice
¼ teaspoon unsalted butter or buttery spread, such as Earth Balance, or canola oil

Bring water to boil in a medium pan. Add rice and butter, cover, and simmer on low heat for approximately 20 minutes or until rice is done. Serve hot.

Cilantro Rice

MAKES 4 SERVINGS

This lightly spiced rice dish is perfect with a Mexican or Southwestern meal. If you prefer a milder flavor, reduce the green chiles by half.

2 cups gluten-free, low-sodium chicken broth, such as Swanson's Natural Goodness, or homemade Chicken Broth (page 676)
1 teaspoon unsalted butter or buttery spread, such as Earth Balance
1 cup white rice, uncooked
¼ cup chopped fresh onion or 1 tablespoon dried minced onion
1 garlic clove, minced
½ teaspoon salt
1 teaspoon chopped fresh oregano or ½ teaspoon dried
1 can (4 ounces) diced green chiles
2 large ripe tomatoes, seeded, and coarsely chopped
¼ cup chopped red bell pepper
½ cup chopped fresh cilantro

In a medium saucepan, bring the broth and butter to a boil. Add the rice, onion, garlic, salt, oregano,

chiles, tomatoes, and bell pepper. Bring to a boil again, reduce the heat to low and cook, covered, until the liquid is absorbed, about 20 minutes. Stir in cilantro. Serve immediately.

Coconut Rice

MAKES 4 SERVINGS

Use this flavorful recipe to cure the "plain old rice" syndrome at your house. It is especially nice when served with an Asian or Southwestern-inspired main dish. I prefer the larger raw coconut flakes, available at natural food stores, but you can also use unsweetened shredded coconut.

1 tablespoon canola oil
1 cup white or brown basmati rice
2 cups gluten-free, low-sodium chicken broth, such as Swanson's Natural Goodness, or homemade Chicken Broth (page 676)
½ teaspoon salt
¼ teaspoon Asian spice blend, such as Durkee's Oriental 5-Spice
1 cup unsweetened coconut flakes
2 tablespoons fresh parsley or 1 tablespoon dried, for garnish

1 In a large, heavy saucepan, heat the oil over medium heat. Add the rice, broth, salt, and seasoning and cook, covered, 15 to 20 minutes or until rice is tender.

2 Remove pan from heat. Stir in coconut and serve hot, garnished with parsley.

Herbed Brown Rice

MAKES 6 SERVINGS

Brown rice is a whole grain and packs lot of nutrients and fiber, so it is my "go-to" side dish when I feel that a meal needs a nutritional and fiber boost. You can use chicken, beef, or vegetable broth in this dish. Dried herbs work best because fresh herbs will overwhelm the color of the dish and turn it very green. Use instant brown rice if you're short on time.

While baking the rice in the oven works very nicely, also consider using an electric rice cooker. It cooks perfect rice every time and frees up your oven—and you, since it requires no tending or stirring.

1 tablespoon olive oil

1 small onion, finely chopped

1 package (12 ounces) brown rice

2 garlic cloves, minced

1½ cups gluten-free, low-sodium chicken broth, such as Swanson's Natural Goodness, or homemade Chicken Broth (page 676)

1 teaspoon dried thyme

1 teaspoon dried chives

1 teaspoon dried parsley

½ teaspoon freshly ground black pepper

½ teaspoon celery salt

1 Place a rack in the middle of the oven. Preheat the oven to 350°F. In a 3-quart ovenproof saucepan, heat the oil over medium heat. Add the onion and cook 5 minutes, stirring frequently. Add the rice and stir 2 minutes to lightly brown it. Add the remaining ingredients.

2 Cover and bake 40 minutes or until the rice is tender. Serve hot.

Grilled Vegetables on Brown Rice Ⓥ

MAKES 6 SERVINGS

Grilling vegetables enhances their flavors more than steaming and the bold marinade used here further enhances that flavor. Your family and guests—whether they are vegetarians or not—will appreciate the bold flavors. If grilling isn't possible, roast the vegetables in the oven.

2 tablespoons extra-virgin olive oil

⅓ cup champagne vinegar or sherry vinegar

1 teaspoon chopped fresh oregano or ½ teaspoon dried

2 large garlic cloves, minced

½ teaspoon ground coriander

½ teaspoon smoked paprika

¼ teaspoon ground cumin

¼ teaspoon salt

¼ teaspoon freshly ground black pepper

2 tablespoons molasses (not blackstrap)

1 large yellow onion, peeled and quartered

4 large carrots, peeled and halved lengthwise

1 large red bell pepper, stemmed and quartered

1 large yellow bell pepper, stemmed and quartered

4 small red new potatoes, washed and halved

2 medium zucchini, stemmed and halved

2 small yellow squash, halved

2 cups hot cooked brown rice

1 In a large bowl, whisk together the oil, vinegar, oregano, garlic, coriander, paprika, cumin, salt, pepper, and molasses. Add the onion, carrots, bell peppers, potatoes, zucchini, and squash and marinate 30 to 45 minutes. Toss occasionally to make sure vegetables are coated with marinade.

2 Drain the vegetables, reserving the marinade, and arrange in a grill basket that has been liberally coated with cooking spray. (Reserve more delicate vegetables such as red and yellow bell pepper until final 10 minutes of grilling so they don't overcook.)

3 Place a grill rack about 5 to 6 inches away from the heat source. Preheat the grill. Cook vegetables on the grill over medium heat with the lid down about 15 to 20 minutes or until done, turning every 5 minutes. The type and thickness of vegetables determines cooking time. Add remaining vegetables during last 10 minutes. Meanwhile, in a small pan, warm marinade over low-medium heat. Remove vegetables from grill basket and toss with marinade. Serve warm over brown rice.

Roasted Vegetables on Brown Rice: Marinate vegetables in marinade for 30 minutes. Drain, reserving marinade. Roast (uncovered) in a single layer on a 15x10-inch pan (not nonstick) in a preheated 400°F oven, turning occasionally, about 15 to 25 minutes or to desired degree of doneness. Meanwhile, in a small pan, warm marinade over low-medium heat. Remove vegetables from oven and toss with marinade. Serve warm over brown rice.

Dilled Rice Pilaf

MAKES 4 SERVINGS

Fresh dill is fabulous in this recipe, but you can also use dried dill. For a really special presentation, grease small custard cups, timbale forms, or a single large Bundt pan. Gently press hot rice mixture into mold(s). Place a serving plate on top of the form(s), invert, and serve.

1 tablespoon extra-virgin olive oil
3 green onions, thinly sliced
⅓ cup chopped fresh dill or 2 teaspoons dried
1 cup long-grain white or brown rice
2 cups gluten-free, low-sodium chicken broth, such as Swanson's Natural Goodness, or homemade Chicken Broth (page 676)
½ teaspoon salt
⅛ teaspoon freshly grated nutmeg
1 tablespoon freshly-squeezed lemon juice
1 teaspoon grated lemon zest
1 teaspoon chopped fresh dill or ½ teaspoon dried, for garnish

1 In a large saucepan, combine the oil, onions, dill, and rice. Cook over medium heat, 1 minute, stirring constantly, to slightly cook the vegetables and rice. Add the broth, salt, and nutmeg.

2 Bring to boil, reduce heat to low and simmer, covered, until broth is absorbed, about 15 to 20 minutes. Stir in lemon juice and zest. Garnish with dill and serve hot.

Curried Rice Pilaf

MAKES 4 SERVINGS

Basmati rice is a fragrant aromatic rice originally grown in India and Pakistan. It is a favorite for pilafs because of its nutty flavor, but I also love the way it holds its shape during cooking, making for a much prettier presentation than plain white rice. I serve Indian-inspired foods as often as I can because the spices used in them, such as curry and turmeric, offer important health benefits and the dishes are so satisfying.

1 small onion, finely chopped
1½ teaspoons curry powder
1 teaspoon chili powder
¼ teaspoon ground turmeric
1 tablespoon peanut oil or canola oil
2 cups gluten-free, low-sodium chicken broth, such as Swanson's Natural Broth, or homemade Chicken Broth (page 676)
1 cup white basmati rice
½ cup golden raisins
½ teaspoon salt
½ cup toasted sliced almonds (see Toasting Nuts footnote, page 510)

1 In a large, heavy saucepan, cook the onion, curry powder, chili powder, and turmeric in oil over medium heat until the onions are tender, about 5 minutes.

2 Add the broth, rice, raisins, and salt, cover, and simmer about 20 minutes or until the broth is absorbed and the rice is tender. Sprinkle with toasted almonds just before serving. Serve hot.

Saffron Rice Pilaf

MAKES 4 SERVINGS

It takes four thousand crocus flowers to produce a single ounce of saffron. Just a tiny amount adds a light flavor and lovely golden hue to this dish, which contrasts nicely with the red cranberries.

Fluffy pilaf grains also make pretty presentations, such as under fish on a serving platter.

1 teaspoon canola oil

1 small onion, finely chopped

1 cup long-grain white rice

2¼ cups gluten-free, low-sodium chicken broth, such as Swanson's Natural Goodness, such as Chicken Broth (page 676)

¼ teaspoon ground saffron

2 teaspoons grated lemon zest

½ cup dried sweetened cranberries

½ teaspoon salt

1 teaspoon fresh thyme or ½ teaspoon dried

⅛ teaspoon ground cardamom

¼ cup pine nuts, toasted (see Toasting Nuts footnote, page 510)

1 tablespoon chopped fresh parsley, for garnish

1 In a medium heavy saucepan, heat the oil over medium heat. Add the onion and cook until soft, about 5 to 7 minutes, stirring frequently.

2 Stir in the rice and cook 3 to 4 minutes more, stirring frequently. This will lightly toast the rice and produces a fuller flavor. Add the chicken broth, saffron, lemon zest, cranberries, salt, thyme, and cardamom. Stir well.

3 Reduce the heat to low, cover, and simmer until all the liquid is absorbed, about 15 to 20 minutes. Remove from heat. Stir in pine nuts. Garnish with parsley and serve hot.

Basmati Rice Pilaf with Dried Fruits and Nuts

MAKES 6 SERVINGS

This is a very flavorful rice pilaf, packed with lots of texture from the dried fruits and nuts. I love the mouthfeel of the light, fluffy basmati rice grains and the dish has a substantial and attractive visual appeal. It makes a wonderful dish for company and goes well with pork or chicken.

1 tablespoon unsalted butter or buttery spread, such as Earth Balance

½ cup chopped onion

1 garlic clove, minced

½ teaspoon salt

¼ teaspoon ground cloves

⅛ teaspoon ground saffron

⅛ teaspoon ground allspice

1 cup white basmati rice

2 cups gluten-free, low-sodium chicken broth, such as Swanson's Natural Goodness, or homemade Chicken Broth (page 676)

½ cup chopped dried apricots

½ cup golden raisins

½ cup dried cherries or cranberries

½ cup toasted sliced almonds

2 tablespoons chopped fresh parsley, for garnish

1 In a large, heavy pan, melt the butter over medium heat. Add the onion and garlic and cook, stirring until the onion is limp, about 2 to 3 minutes. Add the salt, cloves, saffron, allspice, and rice and cook 1 minute, stirring constantly to lightly toast the spices and the rice.

2 Add the broth, apricots, raisins, and cherries and cook, covered, for about 20 minutes or until the rice is tender. Stir in the almonds and garnish with parsley. Serve hot.

Wild Rice Pancakes with Pecans

MAKES 4 SERVINGS (3 PANCAKES EACH)

Pancakes made with wild rice become an unusual and delectable side dish when served with an elegant dinner. Serve them plain or add a topping of sour cream and chives (and possibly caviar for a really special occasion). Or, treat them like potato pancakes (latkes) and top them with cinnamon-scented applesauce or your favorite gravy.

⅔ cup wild rice, rinsed

3 cups gluten-free, low-sodium chicken broth, such as Swanson's Natural Goodness, or homemade Chicken Broth (page 676)

½ cup Carol's Sorghum Blend (page x)

½ teaspoon baking powder

½ teaspoon baking soda

¼ teaspoon freshly ground black pepper

¼ cup snipped fresh chives or 2 tablespoons dried

½ teaspoon chopped fresh thyme or ¼ teaspoon dried

½ teaspoon salt

1 large egg

½ cup buttermilk or homemade Buttermilk (page 677)

¼ cup finely chopped pecans

Olive oil for frying

1 In a medium saucepan, combine the wild rice and broth. Bring to a boil, reduce heat to low, and simmer until the wild rice is tender, about 40 minutes. Drain. Cool to room temperature.

2 In a medium bowl, mix the sorghum blend, baking powder, baking soda, pepper, chives, thyme, and salt.

3 In a small bowl, whisk together the egg and buttermilk. Add to the flour mixture and stir until well blended. Mix in the cooked wild rice and the chopped pecans.

4 Lightly coat a large nonstick skillet with olive oil. Drop batter onto skillet to form 3-inch pancakes and cook over medium heat until golden brown, about 2 minutes per side. Repeat with remaining batter, using more oil if necessary. Serve hot.

Orange-Scented Wild Rice with Dried Fruits

MAKES 4 SERVINGS

Wild rice is actually not rice at all but a grass seed, usually grown in northern parts of the United States. The texture of nutty, crunchy wild rice and the sweet-tart flavor of dried fruit make this an irresistible dish. It especially complements roast pork or roast chicken.

1 cup wild rice, rinsed

3 cups gluten-free, low-sodium chicken broth, such as Swanson's Natural Goodness, or homemade Chicken Broth (page 676)

½ cup finely sliced green onion

½ cup diced dried apricots

¼ cup golden raisins

2 tablespoons chopped fresh parsley

¼ cup pine nuts, toasted (see Toasting Nuts footnote, page 510)

1 teaspoon extra-virgin olive oil

2 tablespoons balsamic vinegar or champagne vinegar

2 tablespoons fresh orange juice

1 tablespoon grated orange zest

1 small garlic clove, minced

¼ teaspoon salt

⅛ teaspoon freshly ground black pepper

1 In a large pot, cook the wild rice in the broth, covered, about 45 minutes or until tender. Drain.

2 In a large heatproof serving dish, combine the cooked rice with the onions, apricots, raisins, parsley, and toasted pine nuts. Toss gently.

3 In a glass jar with a lid, combine the oil, vinegar, orange juice and zest, garlic, salt, and pepper. Shake vigorously to blend well. Pour over the rice mixture and toss gently. Heat in the oven to serving temperature and serve hot. You may also serve chilled as a cold salad.

Saffron Risotto

MAKES 4 SERVINGS

Risotto isn't hard to make; it just requires a little patience. Saffron gives this classic Italian risotto a wonderful yellow hue and adds a distinct flavor as well. For variety, you can replace it with 1 teaspoon of your favorite chopped fresh herb such as thyme.

3 cups gluten-free, low-sodium chicken broth, such as Swanson's Natural Goodness, or homemade Chicken Broth (page 676)

⅓ cup water

⅓ cup dry white wine

2 tablespoons extra-virgin olive oil

1 teaspoon dried minced onion

1 cup Arborio rice

Pinch saffron

⅓ cup shredded Asiago cheese

½ teaspoon salt, or to taste

¼ teaspoon white pepper, or to taste

1 In a medium saucepan, bring the broth, water, and wine to a simmer. Reduce the heat to low, cover, and keep the warm broth mixture on the stove.

2 In a large heavy saucepan, heat the oil over medium-high heat. Add the onion and rice and stir 1 minute. Add 1¾ cups of the warm broth mixture and the saffron to the rice mixture and bring to a boil, stirring constantly. Reduce the heat to low, cover, and simmer the rice about 10 minutes, until the liquid is absorbed. Add the remaining broth mixture; bring the rice to a boil again and stir 1 minute. Reduce the heat to low; cover, and simmer about 10 minutes, until the liquid is absorbed.

3 Remove the pan from the heat and stir in the Asiago cheese. Add the salt and pepper. Cover the pan and let stand 5 minutes. Transfer the risotto to a serving bowl and serve immediately.

Slow-Cooker Brown Rice Risotto

MAKES 4 SERVINGS

Risotto has a reputation for being a labor-intensive dish. But my easy slow-cooker method using brown rice rather than Arborio rice makes it possible for even the busiest cook. Make it the night before and simply reheat it the next day. It produces a fairly robust risotto with lots of chew and texture, rather than the traditional creamy risotto, but it works very nicely. For best results, have all ingredients at room temperature when you start the slow cooker.

1 teaspoon extra-virgin olive oil

½ cup chopped onion or 2 teaspoons dried minced onion

½ cup uncooked brown rice

1 can (14 to 15 ounces) or 1¾ cups gluten-free, low-sodium chicken broth, such as Swanson's Natural Goodness, or homemade Chicken Broth (page 676)

⅛ teaspoon salt

¼ cup grated Parmesan cheese or soy alternative, such as Soyco

1 Lightly coat the liner of a slow cooker with cooking spray. Add all the ingredients except Parmesan cheese and stir to blend thoroughly.

2 Cover and cook 3 hours on high heat, without removing the lid, or until all liquid is absorbed. Stir in Parmesan cheese and serve. Alternatively, you may cook it 6 to 8 hours on low heat. Stir in Parmesan cheese and serve hot.

Fried Risotto Cakes

MAKES 4 SERVINGS (2 CAKES EACH)

Leftover risotto reemerges as a new delicious side dish with a totally different look and taste.

2 cups Saffron Risotto (page 222)

½ cup (2 ounces) shredded Fontina or provolone cheese

⅓ cup shredded Parmesan cheese

¼ cup chopped fresh chives

1 teaspoon salt

1 large egg

1½ cups homemade gluten-free Plain Bread Crumbs (page 117)

2 tablespoons canola oil

2 tablespoons grated Parmesan cheese or soy alternative, such as Soyco, for garnish

1 tablespoon chopped fresh chives, for garnish

1 Prepare the risotto and chill. Then, in a large bowl, combine the risotto with the cheeses, chives, salt, egg, and ½ cup of the bread crumbs. Shape into eight 1-inch balls and flatten balls to

2 inches in diameter. Roll each ball in remaining 1 cup of bread crumbs.

2 In a large, heavy skillet, heat the oil over medium-high heat. Sauté risotto cakes in batches until crisp and brown, about 2 to 3 minutes per side. Garnish with a sprinkling of Parmesan cheese and chives. Serve hot.

Vegetable, Rice, and Bean Curry Ⓥ

MAKES 8 SERVINGS

I developed this simple recipe for people who want a staple vegetable curry to serve as a nutritious side dish—or a main dish, if you prefer.

1 teaspoon canola oil
1 small onion, chopped
½ cup diced red bell pepper
1 small yellow summer zucchini, cut in ⅛-inch slices
1 small green zucchini, cut in ⅛-inch slices
1 tablespoon grated fresh ginger
¼ teaspoon ground coriander
¼ teaspoon fennel seed
¼ teaspoon salt, or to taste
⅛ teaspoon crushed red pepper
⅛ teaspoon ground cinnamon
1 garlic clove, minced
1 can (14 to 15 ounces) three-bean salad, such as Westbrae, rinsed and drained
¾ cup coconut milk
½ cup water
1 teaspoon packed light brown sugar
2 tablespoons dark raisins
¼ cup chopped fresh cilantro, divided
1 teaspoon cornstarch
4 cups hot cooked brown rice

1 In a medium pot, heat oil over medium heat. Add onion, bell pepper, and zucchinis and cook, stirring constantly, 3 to 5 minutes or until vegetables soften. Add ginger, coriander, fennel, salt, crushed red pepper, cinnamon, and garlic and cook, stirring constantly, 2 minutes more.

2 Add beans, coconut milk, water, brown sugar, raisins, and 2 tablespoons of the cilantro. Bring to a boil, reduce heat to low and simmer, covered, 30 minutes. If the curry isn't thick enough, whisk together cornstarch with 1 tablespoon water and stir into the curry over medium heat until thickened slightly, about 1 to 2 minutes.

3 Serve over hot cooked brown rice, garnished with remaining 2 tablespoons of cilantro.

Pork Fried Rice

MAKES 4 SERVINGS

Fried rice is a delicious way to use up leftover rice. Rather than the traditional approach, my variation uses Clementine Marmalade (page 678) and dried cranberries to add a new twist to an old favorite. You'll find that the combination of sweet and savory flavors is tremendously appealing.

1 tablespoon canola oil
2 large eggs
½ pound ground pork
3 tablespoons wheat-free tamari soy sauce, such as such as Crystal or San-J
2 tablespoons sesame oil
1½ tablespoons grated fresh ginger or 2 teaspoons ground ginger
1 tablespoon dry sherry (optional)
1 tablespoon chopped onion or 1 teaspoon dried minced onion
½ teaspoon garlic powder
Pinch of crushed red pepper
1 cup frozen peas
¼ cup gluten-free, low-sodium beef broth, such as Swanson's, or homemade Beef Broth (page 675)
4 cups cooked white rice, chilled

1 In a wok or large skillet, heat the canola oil over medium heat. Add eggs and cook, stirring constantly, until scrambled. Transfer the eggs to a serving platter or bowl.

2 In the same wok or skillet, add the ground pork and cook until browned thoroughly, about 5 minutes. Add the soy sauce, sesame oil, ginger, sherry, onion, garlic powder, crushed red pepper, and peas. Increase the heat to medium-high and cook, stirring constantly, 2 minutes. Add the broth, and rice and toss to combine thoroughly. Reduce the heat, cover, and cook 2 minutes or until the liquid is absorbed and the mixture is heated through. Stir in the scrambled eggs and bring to serving temperature. Serve hot.

Pork Fried Rice with Fruit: Toss ½ cup homemade Clementine Marmalade (page 678) and ¼ cup dried sweetened cranberries with the fried rice just before serving.

Basmati Rice Couscous

MAKES 4 SERVINGS

You may be surprised to see couscous in this book because traditional couscous is actually wheat pasta. However, this basmati rice version is a good substitute for the classic couscous dish and can be served in the same ways as you would serve couscous. The amount of salt you need will vary with the type of chicken broth—the saltier the broth, the less salt is needed. Start with ½ teaspoon and see if you need more by tasting the cooked dish.

1 cup long-grain basmati rice
2 cups gluten-free, low-sodium chicken broth, such as Swanson's Natural Goodness, or homemade Chicken Broth (page 676)
½ to 1½ teaspoons salt, or to taste

1 Place half of the rice in a blender or food processor and pulse until the rice kernels are broken

into smaller pieces—similar to the size of couscous. Repeat with remaining rice.

2 Spread the rice in a thin layer on a 13 × 9-inch (not nonstick) baking sheet. Place a rack in the middle of the oven and toast in a preheated oven at 350°F until lightly browned, about 25 to 30 minutes, stirring occasionally for even browning.

3 In a medium, heavy pan, add the rice, broth, and salt and bring to a boil. Reduce the heat to low, and simmer 30 minutes, covered, or until the water is absorbed. Fluff with a fork and serve immediately.

Lemony Couscous Salad

MAKES 4 SERVINGS

This makes a great salad for picnics as it can be made ahead of time and its fresh, lemony flavor tastes great whether it's cold or at room temperature.

2 cups (1 recipe) Basmati Rice Couscous (page 225)
½ cup diced celery
¼ cup diced red bell pepper
1 tablespoon grated lemon zest
1 tablespoon chopped fresh mint
1 tablespoon chopped fresh cilantro or flat-leaf parsley, packed
¼ cup extra-virgin olive oil
¼ cup fresh lemon juice
½ teaspoon onion powder
½ teaspoon salt
¼ teaspoon freshly ground black pepper
Dash of paprika, for garnish

1 Prepare the couscous. Then, in a medium bowl, combine the cooked couscous, celery, bell pepper, lemon zest, mint, and cilantro.

2 Make the salad dressing: In a small bowl, whisk together the olive oil, lemon juice, onion powder, salt, and pepper. Mix with rice. Refrigerate 3 to 4 hours. Serve chilled, garnished with paprika.

Fast Tropical Cashew Couscous

MAKES 4 SERVINGS

The addition of cashews and tropical dried fruit turns this otherwise simple couscous into a perfect accompaniment for an island-themed main dish. (Dried cranberries add color, taste, and texture, too.) I don't typically use the microwave for cooking, but this dish comes together in a flash with no ill effect to the texture or taste.

2 cups (1 recipe) Basmati Rice Couscous (page 225)
1 package (6 ounces) dried tropical fruit or a blend of your favorite dried fruits such as pineapple, coconut, banana, mango, and papaya
2 tablespoons dried cranberries
¾ cup salted cashews
¼ cup orange marmalade
¼ teaspoon salt

Prepare the couscous. If the couscous has been chilled ahead of time, bring it to serving temperature in a large bowl on Medium in the microwave oven. Stir in the dried fruit, cashews, marmalade, and salt and toss to coat thoroughly. Let stand 30 minutes to soften dried fruits. Serve warm or at room temperature.

POLENTA AND OTHER GRAINS

Polenta

MAKES 4 SERVINGS

Polenta is Italian cornmeal. This is one of my "go-to" recipes when I want a quick side dish for dinner. It cooks in just minutes and makes a nice bed on which to serve the entrée or vegetables. The 4 cups of chicken broth makes a firmer polenta base; for soft polenta, use 6 cups chicken broth. Remember, fine cornmeal will cook very quickly; coarser grinds will take longer.

4 cups gluten-free, low-sodium chicken broth, such as Swanson's Natural Goodness, or homemade Chicken Broth (page 676)
¼ cup unsalted butter or buttery spread, such as Earth Balance
1 teaspoon salt
1 cup gluten-free yellow cornmeal, such as Albers, Lamb's, Kinnikinnick, or Shiloh Farms
½ to 1 cup grated Parmesan cheese or soy alternative, such as Soyco, or to taste
Freshly ground coarse black pepper

1 In a medium, heavy saucepan, bring the broth to boil over high heat. Stir in the butter, salt, and cornmeal, reduce heat to low, and cook, stirring constantly, about 10 minutes. Cover with lid, remove from heat, and let stand about 15 minutes.

2 Stir in the Parmesan cheese and pepper. Serve immediately.

Polenta Squares: Press leftover polenta to a ½-inch thickness in a greased dish. Chill for 2 hours and then fry in olive oil until crispy and brown.

Teff-Corn Polenta

MAKES 4 SERVINGS

Teff, a tiny Ethiopian grain filled with valuable nutrients, has a unique texture similar to corn polenta when cooked. I blend it with traditional polenta in this innovative dish. Use ivory teff for a lighter colored polenta.

4 cups gluten-free, low-sodium chicken broth, such as Swanson's Natural Goodness, or homemade Chicken Broth (page 676)

1 teaspoon salt

¾ cup gluten-free yellow cornmeal, such as Albers, Arrowhead Mills, Kinnikinnick, or Quaker

¼ cup whole grain teff, such as Bob's Red Mill or The Teff Company

1 cup grated Parmesan cheese or soy alternative, such as Soyco

Freshly ground coarse black pepper

1 In a medium, heavy saucepan, bring the broth to a boil over high heat. Stir in the salt, polenta, and teff, reduce heat, and cook, stirring constantly, about 10 minutes. Cover with lid, remove from heat, and let sit about 15 minutes.

2 Stir in the Parmesan cheese and pepper. Serve immediately.

Polenta Teff Squares: Press leftover teff polenta to a ½-inch thickness in a greased dish. Chill for 2 hours and then fry in olive oil until crispy and brown.

Baked Quinoa, Wild Rice, and Cherry Pilaf

MAKES 6 SERVINGS

Quinoa and wild rice bring a wonderfully nutty flavor and very satisfying texture to this dish. It is especially convenient to make when you already have the oven on to roast meat or bake a cake. I love the unique tang of dried cherries here, but dried cranberries will work well, too.

¾ cup wild rice, rinsed

3 cups gluten-free, low-sodium chicken broth, such as Swanson's Natural Goodness, or homemade Chicken Broth (page 676)

½ cup uncooked quinoa, rinsed (see Rinsing Quinoa, page 164)

⅓ cup dried cherries or sweetened cranberries

⅓ cup golden raisins

1 tablespoon olive oil

⅓ cup toasted sliced almonds

1 Place a rack in the middle of the oven. Preheat the oven to 325°F. In a medium, heavy ovenproof saucepan, combine the wild rice and broth and bring to a boil over high heat. Reduce heat, cover, and simmer 15 minutes.

2 Remove saucepan from the heat. Stir in the quinoa, cranberries, raisins, and oil.

3 Bake, covered, 1 hour or until the wild rice and quinoa are tender and the liquid is absorbed. Sprinkle with almonds and serve immediately.

Quinoa Tabbouleh

MAKES 4 SERVINGS

Most of the quinoa available today has been pre-rinsed to remove the bitter saponin coating, particularly if it is imported through Inca Organics, which then sells it to retailers. If you're not sure about the source, it doesn't hurt to rinse it again. See Rinsing Quinoa (page 164) for more information.

QUINOA

1 teaspoon canola oil

1 cup uncooked quinoa, rinsed

½ teaspoon salt

1 can (14 to 15 ounces) or 1¾ cups gluten-free, low-sodium chicken broth, such as Swanson's Natural Goodness or homemade Chicken Broth (page 676)

¾ cup water

TABBOULEH

¼ cup shelled raw pumpkin seeds

1 English (hothouse) cucumber, unpeeled and chopped

3 green onions, thinly sliced

12 cherry tomatoes, quartered, or 24 grape tomatoes, halved

½ cup chopped fresh parsley

½ cup chopped fresh cilantro

¼ cup chopped fresh mint

¼ cup crumbled feta cheese (optional)

DRESSING

3 tablespoons fresh lemon juice

2 tablespoons extra-virgin olive oil

1 tablespoon white wine vinegar or rice vinegar

¼ teaspoon salt

⅛ teaspoon white pepper

1 Make the quinoa: In a medium saucepan, heat the oil over medium heat and toast the quinoa about 4 minutes, shaking the skillet occasionally, until the seeds are light golden brown.

2 Add the broth, water, and salt and reduce the heat to low, and cook 15 to 20 minutes, covered, or until the quinoa is tender. Remove from heat and cool 10 minutes. Drain the quinoa well.

3 Make the tabbouleh: In a large serving bowl, combine the cooked quinoa with the pumpkin seeds, cucumber, green onions, tomatoes, parsley, cilantro, and mint.

4 Make the dressing: In a screw-top jar, combine the lemon juice, oil, vinegar, salt, and pepper and shake vigorously to blend. Pour over quinoa mixture and toss until all the ingredients are thoroughly coated.

Cover the bowl and refrigerate 4 hours. Let stand at room temperature 20 minutes before serving. Toss with the feta cheese, if using, just before serving.

Hazelnut Quinoa Salad

MAKES 8 SERVINGS

Lori Sobelson is Program Director at Bob's Red Mill Natural Foods and is responsible for bringing chefs to the company's cooking school. Lori's passion for nutritious food is exemplified in her colorful, delicious quinoa salad, which can be served as a main dish or a side.

DRESSING

⅓ cup orange juice

¼ cup strawberry fruit spread

3 tablespoons balsamic vinegar (or white vinegar)

2 tablespoons canola oil

1 tablespoon soft silken tofu, such as Mori-Nu

1 medium garlic clove, minced

¾ teaspoon salt

SALAD

2 cups cooked quinoa

¼ cup hazelnuts, toasted and crushed coarsely

¼ cup green onions, chopped finely

½ cup red seedless grapes cut in half

1 Make the dressing: In a food processor or blender, combine the orange juice, fruit spread, vinegar, oil, tofu, garlic, and salt. Blend for about 1 minute or until smooth. Set aside.

2 Make the quinoa salad: In a medium bowl, combine the quinoa, hazelnuts, green onions, and grapes.

3 Pour ½ to ¾ cup of the dressing over the quinoa mixture to coat it thoroughly, or to your taste. Refrigerate any remaining dressing and use within 2 weeks. Serve the salad at room temperature or chill for 2 hours.

To vary the flavors of this dish, you may use ½ to ¾ cup of Homemade Raspberry Vinaigrette (page 670) in place of the dressing.

Herbed Quinoa Blend with Chickpeas, Spinach, and Shrimp

MAKES 6 SERVINGS

I love developing new and different dishes that showcase healthy foods. All too often the gluten-free diet leans toward baked and processed foods, which can be delicious and satisfying, but you also need to keep sufficient levels of fiber and important nutrients in your diet as well. The quinoa, chickpeas, and spinach in this dish fit the bill.

3 tablespoons olive oil

1 small onion, finely chopped

2 cups gluten-free, low-sodium chicken broth, such as Swanson's Natural Goodness, or homemade Chicken Broth (page 676)

3 ripe plum tomatoes, diced

1 package (5.6 ounces) French Herb Quinoa Blend, by Seeds of Change

1 teaspoon ground coriander

1 teaspoon fresh thyme or ½ teaspoon dried

¼ teaspoon smoked paprika (optional)

1 can (14 to 15 ounces) chickpeas, rinsed and drained

2 cups baby spinach, washed and spun dry

½ pound medium cooked shrimp, peeled and deveined

1 In a large, heavy skillet, heat the oil over medium-high heat. Add the onion and cook until it starts to brown on the edges, about 4 minutes.

2 Add the broth, tomatoes, quinoa blend (and its spice packet), coriander, thyme, and paprika, if using. Reduce the heat to low and simmer, covered, 15 to 20 minutes, or until the liquid is absorbed.

3 Stir in the chickpeas, spinach, and shrimp and bring to serving temperature over medium heat. Serve immediately.

Toasted Quinoa with Mandarin Oranges and Basil

MAKES 4 SERVINGS

Mandarin oranges and citrus vinaigrette provide a nice sweet contrast to the savory quinoa in this dish. Toasting the quinoa accentuates its nutty flavor, but you can skip this step if you wish.

1 teaspoon canola oil

1 cup uncooked quinoa, rinsed (see Rinsing Quinoa, page 164)

1 can (14 to 15 ounces) or 1¾ cups gluten-free low-sodium chicken broth, such as Swanson's Natural Goodness, or homemade Chicken Broth (page 676)

¾ cup water

1 can (11 ounces) mandarin oranges, drained

¼ cup sliced toasted almonds

½ small red bell pepper, thinly sliced

2 tablespoons thinly sliced green onions

½ cup finely chopped fresh basil

½ cup fresh orange juice

2 tablespoons fresh lemon juice

2 tablespoons rice vinegar

1 tablespoon honey

1 tablespoon extra-virgin olive oil

1 teaspoon grated orange zest

1 teaspoon grated lemon zest

½ teaspoon salt

¼ teaspoon freshly ground black pepper

Fresh basil leaves, for garnish

1 In a small heavy-duty saucepan, heat oil over medium heat. Add quinoa and toast about 4 minutes, stirring constantly, until seeds are lightly toasted.

2 Add the broth and water, reduce the heat to low, and cook 15 to 20 minutes, covered, or until the quinoa is tender. Remove from heat and cool 10 minutes. Drain the quinoa well.

3 In a large bowl, combine the cooled quinoa, oranges, almonds, bell pepper, green onions, and basil. Toss to coat thoroughly.

4 In a small jar with a screw-top lid, shake together the orange juice, lemon juice, vinegar, honey, oil, orange zest, lemon zest, salt, and pepper until thoroughly combined. Pour over quinoa mixture and toss thoroughly to coat. Serve warm or cold. Garnish with fresh basil leaves.

Oat Salad with Roasted Vegetables

MAKES 6 SERVINGS

Oat groats are whole grain oats without the husks removed. They make a hearty dish with wonderful texture. I enjoy using sherry vinegar in dishes like this one because of its marvelous tart-sweet flavor. Look for it in gourmet stores or in natural food stores.

3½ cups gluten-free low-sodium chicken broth, such as Swanson's Natural Goodness or homemade Chicken Broth (page 676)

½ teaspoon salt

1 cup whole oat groats†, such as Cream Hill Estates

1 medium yellow zucchini, cut into ½-inch diagonal pieces

1 medium green zucchini, cut into ½-inch diagonal pieces

2 red bell peppers, quartered

1 small red onion, peeled and quartered

1 small garlic clove, minced

3 tablespoons extra-virgin olive oil, divided

¼ teaspoon celery salt

¼ teaspoon freshly ground black pepper

3 tablespoons sherry vinegar or red wine vinegar

1 teaspoon chopped fresh oregano

1 tablespoon chopped flat-leaf parsley + additional parsley sprigs, for garnish

Salt and pepper to taste

1 In a medium saucepan over high heat, bring the broth to a boil. Add the salt and oats and bring to a boil again. Reduce the heat to medium-low and cook, covered, 1 hour or until the broth is absorbed and the oats are tender. This can be done a day ahead of time; cover and refrigerate the cooked oats.

2 Preheat the oven to 400°F. In a large bowl, combine zucchini, bell peppers, and onion with 1 tablespoon of the oil, celery salt, and pepper. Toss to coat vegetables thoroughly. Place a rack in the middle of the oven. Place vegetables on a 13 × 9-inch (not nonstick) baking sheet and roast 15 to 25 minutes until vegetables are done, turning occasionally to assure even cooking.

3 Bring cooked oats to serving temperature. Remove vegetables from oven and combine with hot cooked oats in a large serving bowl. Add the remaining oil, vinegar, oregano, and parsley and toss to coat thoroughly. Add salt and pepper to taste. Serve in the same bowl or on a serving platter. Garnish with a sprig of fresh parsley.

†*Check with your physician before using gluten-free oats.*

Steel-cut Oats with Spinach and Dried Cranberries

MAKES 4 SERVINGS

Steel-cut oats are whole oat kernels (called groats) that are cut into smaller pieces on a steel mill. They are very hearty and satisfying and, although you may think of them as breakfast food, they are marvelous in this flavorful salad that can be served as a side dish or as a luncheon salad on its own.

2 cups gluten-free low-sodium chicken broth, such as Swanson's Natural Goodness, or homemade Chicken Broth (page 676)

¼ teaspoon salt

1 cup gluten-free steel-cut oats, such as Bob's Red Mill†

½ cup spinach leaves, washed, dried, and thinly sliced

½ cup dried sweetened cranberries

½ cup chopped green onion

½ cup chopped fresh cilantro

¼ cup fresh lemon juice

2 tablespoons rice vinegar

2 tablespoons extra-virgin olive oil

Salt and freshly ground pepper to taste

¼ cup sliced almonds, toasted, for garnish

1 In a medium, heavy-duty saucepan over high heat, bring the broth to a boil. Add the salt and oats and bring to a boil again. Reduce the heat to medium-low and cook, covered, 15 to 20 minutes, stirring occasionally.

2 Remove from heat. Place the oats in a wire sieve and rinse with cold water until the water is clear. Drain well.

3 In a large bowl, toss the oats with the spinach, cranberries, green onion, and cilantro.

4 In a small jar with a screw-top lid, shake together the lemon juice, vinegar, and oil until blended. Pour over the oat mixture and toss thoroughly to coat. Add salt and pepper to taste. Sprinkle toasted almonds on top. Chill 1 hour to allow flavor to develop, then let stand at room temperature 20 minutes before serving.

†Check with your physician before using gluten-free oats.

Kasha with Toasted Almonds

MAKES 4 SERVINGS.

Kasha, or toasted buckwheat, is often thought of as breakfast food, but it also makes a very wholesome side dish at any meal.

3 cups gluten-free, low-sodium chicken broth, such as Swanson's Natural Goodness, or homemade Chicken Broth (page 676)
1 cup whole kasha
½ teaspoon salt
½ cup chopped green onions, including green tops
½ cup almond slivers, toasted
1 tablespoon sesame oil
1 teaspoon ground ginger
½ teaspoon crushed red pepper
Chopped fresh parsley or dried parsley, for garnish

1 In a heavy, medium pan, bring broth to a boil. Add the kasha and salt to pan, cover, and simmer on low heat about 20 minutes or until the broth is absorbed. Remove from heat.

2 Stir the almonds, sesame oil, ginger, and crushed red pepper into the cooked kasha. Transfer the kasha to a serving bowl and garnish with the parsley.

Kasha with Almonds and Dried Fruit: For color and flavor, stir in ¾ cup each chopped dried pineapple and dried sweetened cranberries (or other chopped dried fruit) in Step 2.

Sorghum with Grapes and Pecans

MAKES 4 SERVINGS

Sorghum is one of my favorite whole grains, but it is sometimes hard to find, so I order it directly from a grower (www.twinvalleymills.com). Be sure to soak the sorghum grains overnight before you simmer them. This dish is wonderful served warm or cold.

1 cup whole grain sorghum, soaked overnight
3 cups gluten-free low-sodium chicken broth, such as Swanson's Natural Goodness, or homemade Chicken Broth (page 676)
1 tablespoon chopped fresh rosemary or ½ teaspoon dried, crushed
½ teaspoon salt
2 tablespoons extra-virgin olive oil
1 small onion, finely chopped
1 small carrot, thinly sliced
1 stalk celery, sliced diagonally
¼ cup dried cranberries
¼ cup sherry vinegar
2 tablespoons honey or agave nectar
½ cup red seedless grapes, halved
¼ cup chopped pecans
Salt and freshly ground pepper to taste
2 teaspoons chopped fresh parsley or 1 teaspoon dried, for garnish

1 In a medium, heavy saucepan, cook the soaked sorghum with the broth, rosemary, and salt over low heat, 1 hour to 1 hour 15 minutes, or until grains are soft. Or, cook overnight in a slow cooker on low heat, using an additional 1 cup broth. Drain any excess liquid.

2 In a large heavy saucepan, heat oil over medium heat. Add the onion, carrot, and celery, and cook, covered, over low-medium heat about 5 minutes, or just until vegetables are somewhat softened but still al dente.

3 Add the cooked sorghum mixture to the saucepan. Add vinegar and honey and stir to coat grains thoroughly. Stir in grapes and pecans. Add salt and pepper to taste. Garnish with dried parsley. Serve immediately.

Amaranth Pilaf

MAKES 4 SERVINGS

This nutritious dish is somewhat like corn grits—it will be crunchy but darker in color. Serve it as a side dish with dinner.

1 tablespoon olive oil
1 medium onion, peeled and finely chopped
1 cup whole grain amaranth, such as NuWorld Amaranth or Bob's Red Mill
1 small garlic clove, minced
3 cups gluten-free, low-sodium chicken broth, such as Swanson's Natural Goodness, or homemade Chicken Broth (page 676)
½ teaspoon salt
2 tablespoons sliced almonds, toasted
2 ripe plum tomatoes, chopped, for garnish
1 tablespoon chopped fresh parsley, for garnish

1 In a heavy, medium saucepan, heat the oil over medium-high heat. Cook the onion until it is translucent and starts to brown, about 3 minutes. Add the amaranth, garlic, broth, and salt and bring to a boil.

2 Cook, covered, until most of the broth is absorbed, about 20 to 25 minutes. Remove from the heat and let stand, covered, 10 minutes.

3 Stir in the almonds and serve immediately, garnished with tomatoes and parsley.

Job's Tears with Bell Peppers

MAKES 4 SERVINGS

Lorna Sass is the award-winning author of Whole Grains: Every Day, Every Way. *This dish, adapted from Lorna's repertoire, features Job's Tears, a mild-flavored, teardrop-shaped grain. Called* hato mugi *by the Japanese and sometimes mistakenly labeled as wild barley or pearled barley in Asian markets, most of the Job's Tears sold in the United States comes from Thailand. With a taste similar to corn, this grain, when cooked, is chewy and creamy and a good source of protein, potassium, and magnesium. Like most whole grains, it takes a while to cook so use a pressure cooker to speed up the process.*

2 tablespoons olive oil
1 large onion, thinly sliced
1 large yellow bell pepper, seeded and cut in ½-inch strips
1 large red bell pepper, seeded and cut in ½-inch strips
¼ teaspoon salt, or to taste
2 large garlic cloves, minced
2 small serrano peppers, seeded and finely diced
4 teaspoons chopped fresh oregano or 2 teaspoons dried
½ teaspoon smoked paprika
2 cups cooked whole grain Job's Tears (see How to Cook Whole Grain Job's Tears)
1 cup gluten-free, low-sodium chicken broth, such as Swanson's Natural Goodness, or homemade Chicken Broth (page 676)
1 ripe plum tomatoes, seeded and diced
¼ cup chopped fresh cilantro, for garnish
2 limes, cut in wedges

1 In a large skillet, heat the oil over medium heat. Cook the onion, bell peppers, and salt about 3 minutes.

2 Add the garlic, serrano peppers, oregano, and smoked paprika and continue cooking 2 to 3

Whole grain Job's Tears are available in Asian markets or at www.goldminenatural food.com or www.simplynatural.biz.

To start: Sort 1 cup of the grains to remove any debris or any grayish-looking ones. Rinse the grains until the water runs clear. Then cook the Job's Tears in one of two ways:

- **Pressure cooker method.** Following the manufacturer's directions for your pressure cooker, cook 1 cup whole grain Job's Tears with 4 cups water, 1 tablespoon canola oil, and ½ teaspoon salt for 35 minutes. Quick-release the pressure when the cooking time is up.

- **Stovetop method.** Soak the grains overnight in enough water to cover. Drain. In a Dutch oven or other deep, heavy pot with a tight-fitting lid, bring 2 cups water to a boil. Add the grains and a pinch of salt. Cover, reduce the heat, and simmer 20 to 40 minutes or until the grains are tender, adding more hot water if necessary. When the grains are tender, turn off the heat and let the grains stand 10 minutes. Drain off any excess water.

minutes more or until the onion is lightly browned and the peppers are softened slightly.

3 Stir in the cooked Job's Tears, broth, and tomatoes and bring to a boil. Lower the heat to low-medium and cook, stirring frequently, until the flavors meld and a little of the liquid evaporates, about 3 to 5 minutes.

4 Ladle into 4 bowls and serve garnished with a tablespoon of cilantro and a squeeze of fresh lime juice.

LEGUMES

....

Baked Beans

MAKES 10 SERVINGS

This is an authentic, cooked-from-scratch version of baked beans—the kind you soak the day before and then cook all the next day so you can eat them that night. The marvelous flavor, enhanced by coffee and bourbon, make them worth every second of preparation.

2 cups dried navy beans, washed and picked over
Water for soaking
2 cans (14 to 15 ounces each) or 3½ cups gluten-free, low-sodium chicken broth, such as Swanson's Natural Goodness, or homemade Chicken Broth (page 676)
½ cup bourbon or dry white wine
¼ cup strongly brewed coffee
1 small onion, finely chopped
½ cup dark molasses (not blackstrap)
½ cup packed light brown sugar
1 teaspoon Dijon mustard
¼ teaspoon ground cloves
¼ teaspoon chili powder
¼ teaspoon black pepper
½ cup ketchup
½ teaspoon salt

1 Place the beans in a large Dutch oven or other deep, heavy pot with a tight-fitting lid and cover with water to 2 inches above beans. Bring to boil, cover, and let stand overnight. Drain.

2 Add the remaining ingredients to the beans in the Dutch oven and stir to combine. Preheat the oven to 325°F. Cover the Dutch oven and bake 4 to 5 hours or until the beans are done. Serve hot.

Drunken Southwestern Beans

MAKES 6 SERVINGS

Beans are a staple in the Southwest and are prepared in many different ways. Here, they're combined with herbs and spices—plus tequila, the quintessential drink of Mexico and the Southwest—to produce a wonderful blend of flavors and aroma. Although the recipe calls for both spirits and coffee, the final dish won't affect alertness—it all cooks down and what remains is great flavor. This easy dish is great with baby back ribs, fajitas, or tacos.

1 slice bacon, uncooked

1 small onion, finely chopped

1 garlic clove, minced

1 bay leaf

2 tablespoons packed light brown sugar

4 teaspoons chopped fresh oregano or 2 teaspoons dried

1 teaspoon instant coffee powder

1 teaspoon ground cumin

½ teaspoon chipotle chile powder

¼ teaspoon smoked salt or table salt

⅛ teaspoon ground cloves

2 cans (14 to 15 ounces) pinto beans, rinsed and drained

1 can (14 to 15 ounces) or 1¾ cups gluten-free, low-sodium chicken broth, such as Swanson's Natural Goodness, or homemade Chicken Broth (page 676)

¼ cup tequila

1 In a Dutch oven or other deep, heavy pot with a tight-fitting lid, fry the bacon until crisp and brown. Remove the bacon from the skillet and crumble when cool, leaving the bacon fat in the pan.

2 Add the chopped onion to the same pan and cook over medium heat in the bacon fat until golden brown, about 3 to 5 minutes. Return the crumbled bacon to the pan and add remaining ingredients. Bring to boil, reduce heat and cook, covered, 30 minutes. Remove bay leaf and serve warm.

Refried Drunken Southwestern Beans

MAKES 4 SERVINGS

Although my family prefers beans in the "whole" state, I sometimes refry them just for tradition's sake. Rather than frying them in lard, I use lighter canola oil.

2 tablespoons canola oil for frying

2 cups Drunken Southwestern Beans (left)

In a large heavy nonstick (gray, not black) skillet, heat 2 tablespoons oil over medium heat. Add the beans and mash them in the skillet, using a potato masher. Cook, uncovered, over medium heat about 10 minutes or until beans are thick, stirring often. Serve hot.

Spicy Black Beans

MAKES 4 SERVINGS

I always have a can of black beans in the pantry, ready to turn into a side dish, a soup, or even a bean dip. This easy version can be whipped up in less than 10 minutes. If you want the beans a little less spicy, cut the chili powder in half. These beans are great with Southwestern dishes such as tacos, fajitas, or Southwestern-style wraps.

1 can (14 to 15 ounces) black beans, drained and rinsed

1 cup gluten-free, low-sodium chicken broth, Swanson's Natural Goodness, or homemade Chicken Broth (page 676)

1 tablespoon extra-virgin olive oil

1 smoked pork chop, bone removed and extra fat trimmed, cut into ½-inch cubes

1 teaspoon dried minced onion

2 garlic cloves, minced

1 bay leaf

¼ teaspoon salt

¼ teaspoon freshly ground black pepper

1 tablespoon chopped fresh cilantro, for garnish

In a heavy medium saucepan combine the beans, broth, oil, pork, onion, garlic, bay leaf, salt and pepper. Bring to a boil over medium-high heat, reduce heat to low and cook, covered, 15 minutes. Remove bay leaf and serve hot, garnished with cilantro.

Brazilian Black Beans on Rice and Collard Greens

MAKES 4 SERVINGS

Known as the national dish of Brazil, feijoada *(fezsh-WAH-da) is black bean stew served over rice and cooked collard greens, and which often features many types of meat. This version is much simpler. You can make it as spicy as you like with the addition of hot sauce.*

1 tablespoon olive oil

1 small onion, diced

1 small green bell pepper, diced

2 stalks celery, diced

2 garlic cloves, minced

1 bay leaf

1 can (6 ounces) tomato paste

1 pound gluten-free chorizo sausage, such as Publix, browned

2 cans (14 to 15 ounces each) black beans, rinsed and drained

1 can (14 to 15 ounces) or 1¾ cups gluten-free, low-sodium chicken broth, such as Swanson's Natural Goodness, or homemade Chicken Broth (page 676)

Salt and freshly ground pepper to taste

Hot pepper sauce to taste, such as Frank's

4 cups hot cooked brown rice or white rice

1 recipe Collard Greens (page 383)

1 orange, peeled and cut in segments, for garnish

1 In a Dutch oven or other deep, heavy pot with a tight-fitting lid, heat the oil over medium heat. Add the onion, bell pepper, celery, and garlic and cook 3 to 5 minutes, stirring constantly.

Add the bay leaf, tomato paste, sausage, beans, and broth.

2 Cook 15 to 20 minutes more until the sausage is cooked. If the beans are too watery, crush some to thicken the juices. Remove the bay leaf. Add salt, pepper, and hot sauce to taste.

3 Place a mound of rice and a mound of collard greens in a wide, shallow bowl. Ladle bean stew on top. Garnish with orange segments. Serve immediately.

Cannellini Beans with Spinach Ⓥ

MAKES 4 SERVINGS

I prefer cannellini beans (which are actually white kidney beans) for this recipe because these lovely white beans hold their shape nicely. Beans are a marvelous source of fiber and protein and with the nutrients in spinach, this is a tasty, healthy dish.

2 tablespoons extra-virgin olive oil

2 tablespoons unsalted butter or buttery spread, such as Earth Balance

1 can (14 to 15 ounces) cannellini beans, drained

2 garlic cloves, minced

¼ teaspoon crushed red pepper or to taste

2 bunches baby spinach (about 2 pounds), washed

¼ cup grated Parmesan cheese or soy alternative, such as Soyco

Salt and freshly ground pepper to taste

1 In a large, deep skillet, heat the oil and butter over medium heat. Add the beans, garlic, and crushed red pepper and simmer for 10 minutes.

2 Reduce the heat to medium-low, add the spinach, cover, and simmer just until the spinach is cooked, about 5 minutes. Stir in the Parmesan cheese. Add salt and pepper to taste and serve hot.

Gigante Beans with Tomato Sauce Ⓥ

MAKES 4 SERVINGS

Gigante (also called gigande*) beans come from Greece and can be found in Mediterranean markets. You can use dried Great Northern beans instead. The results are absolutely delicious, but the process requires a few steps so plan your time accordingly. This dish is even more flavorful when reheated the next day because the herbs and vegetables have spent a longer time infusing the tomato sauce with their marvelous flavors.*

½ cup dried gigante beans or dried Great Northern beans

1 bay leaf

1 teaspoon salt, divided

½ teaspoon freshly ground black pepper, divided

2 tablespoons extra-virgin olive oil

1 small onion, diced

1 large carrot, peeled and diced

1 large stalk celery, diced

2 medium ripe tomatoes, diced

1 large garlic clove, chopped

½ teaspoon crushed red pepper

1½ teaspoons grated lemon zest, (from 1 lemon)

1½ teaspoons chopped fresh thyme or ¾ teaspoon dried

Additional salt and freshly ground pepper to taste (optional)

1 cup chopped parsley, divided

1 Rinse the beans in a sieve and place in a medium bowl to soak overnight. Drain the beans and rinse them well. Place them in a Dutch oven or other deep, heavy pot with a tight-fitting lid and add water to a height of 5 inches above the beans.

2 Add the bay leaf and bring the beans to a boil over high heat, skimming any foam that rises to the surface. Reduce the heat to low and simmer, covered, 1 1½ to 2 hours or until the beans are tender. Add ½ teaspoon of the salt and ¼ teaspoon

of the black pepper and cook 10 minutes more. Drain the beans and discard the bay leaf.

3 In a large skillet, heat the oil over medium heat. Add the onion, carrot, and celery and the remaining ½ teaspoon salt and remaining ¼ teaspoon black pepper. Reduce the heat to low-medium and cook, covered, until the vegetables are tender, or about 10 minutes. Add the tomatoes, garlic, crushed red pepper, and lemon zest and cook 1 minute.

4 Add the beans and thyme to the skillet and cook on low, covered, about 10 minutes. Taste the beans and add more salt or pepper, if necessary. Cool slightly. Toss with parsley just before serving and serve at room temperature.

Borracho Pinto Beans

MAKES 6 SERVINGS

Borracho *means "drunk" in Spanish and here these beans are cooked—to great results—in beer. They are commonly served as a side dish. However, I add diced cooked pork or chicken and sometimes serve it on cooked brown rice as a hearty main dish. It's a great to way to use leftover cooked meat.*

1 tablespoon olive oil

1 medium onion, peeled and thinly sliced

3 large ripe tomatoes, or 8 ripe plum tomatoes, cored and chopped

1 tablespoon chopped fresh oregano or 1½ teaspoons dried

½ teaspoon ground cumin

½ teaspoon salt

¼ teaspoon freshly ground black pepper

2 cups chopped cooked pork or chicken

1 can (14 to 15 ounces) pinto beans, rinsed and drained

½ can to 1 can (4 ounces) diced green chiles, drained, or to taste

2 garlic cloves, minced

1 bottle (12 ounces) gluten-free beer, such as Bard's Tale or Redbridge

1 cup fresh cilantro, finely chopped

2 limes, each sliced into 3 wedges

1 In a stock pot, heat the oil over medium heat. Add the onion and cook, stirring occasionally, until it starts to turn golden brown, about 7 to 10 minutes. Add the tomatoes, oregano, cumin, salt and pepper and cook, stirring constantly, until the tomatoes are broken up and give off their juices, about 2 to 3 minutes.

2 Add the pork, beans, chiles, garlic, beer, and ½ cup cilantro. Bring to a boil over high heat, then reduce the heat to low and simmer, covered, for 20 minutes. Serve hot, garnished with the remaining ½ cup cilantro and a squeeze of fresh lime juice.

Curried Chickpeas on Basmati Rice

MAKES 4 SERVINGS

Traditionally called kabli chana, *this easy Indian dish is perfect for vegetarians, but you can add chopped cooked chicken or cooked shrimp, if you like.*

1 tablespoons canola oil
½ cup diced red bell pepper
1 small onion, diced
1 garlic clove, minced
1-inch piece fresh ginger, peeled and finely chopped
    or ½ teaspoon ground ginger
1 (2-inch) stick cinnamon
½ teaspoon ground cumin
½ teaspoon ground coriander
½ teaspoon ground turmeric
¼ teaspoon ground cayenne
Pinch ground cloves
1 cup coconut milk, well shaken
2 cans (14 to 15 ounces each) chickpeas, rinsed and
    drained
½ cup chopped fresh cilantro, divided
Salt to taste
4 cups hot cooked basmati rice

1 In a large skillet, heat oil over medium heat. Add bell pepper and onion and cook until soft and translucent, about 2 to 3 minutes.

2 Stir in garlic, ginger, cinnamon, cumin, coriander, turmeric, cayenne, and cloves. Cook 1 minute over medium heat, stirring constantly. Add coconut milk and chickpeas and continue to cook, stirring constantly, until all ingredients are well blended and heated through, about 3 to 4 minutes. Remove from heat. Remove cinnamon stick. Stir in ¼ cup of the cilantro and salt to taste.

3 Spread hot basmati rice evenly on a serving platter. Top with curried chickpeas and sprinkle with remaining cilantro. Serve immediately.

Warm Lentils with Herbs V

MAKES 4 SERVINGS

Try this hearty but sophisticated way of serving lentils by simply placing slices of your most elegant roast, rack of lamb, or chops on top of them. Or, just serve them alongside the main dish. Although I use brown lentils here, you may use red or yellow if you wish.

1 cup brown lentils
1 cup gluten-free, low-sodium chicken broth, such
    as Swanson's Natural Goodness, or home-
    made Chicken Broth (page 676), or homemade
    Vegetable Broth (page 677)
¼ cup diced yellow onion
½ teaspoon salt
1 garlic clove, minced
2 ripe plum tomatoes, diced
2 tablespoons chopped fresh basil or thyme or
    1½ teaspoons dried
2 tablespoons chopped fresh flat-leaf parsley or
    1½ teaspoons dried
2 tablespoons extra-virgin olive oil
1 tablespoon sherry or champagne vinegar
Salt and freshly ground pepper to taste

1 In a medium pan, combine the lentils, broth, onion, salt, and garlic. Bring to a boil over medium heat, reduce the heat to low and simmer, covered, 30 minutes or until the lentils are soft.

2 Stir in the tomatoes, basil, parsley, oil, and sherry and heat to serving temperature. Add salt and pepper to taste. Serve hot.

Lentils with Kale

MAKES 4 SERVINGS

Dried lentils—members of the legume family—are inexpensive, nutritious, and they cook much faster than their dried bean cousins. Kale is a form of cabbage, but it grows in large, dark green leaves rather than a head and is typically found in the produce section of natural food stores. You can substitute your favorite herb in place of the thyme.

1 cup lentils (yellow, red, or green)
2 cups water
1 teaspoon salt
1 tablespoon extra-virgin olive oil
2 white onions, halved and sliced into ½-inch rings
2 garlic cloves, minced
1 bunch fresh kale (about ½ pound)
2 teaspoons chopped fresh thyme or 1 teaspoon dried
¼ teaspoon salt, or to taste
¼ teaspoon freshly ground black pepper, or to taste

1 In a medium saucepan, place the lentils, water, and salt. Bring to a boil over high heat, then reduce the heat to low and simmer, covered, 30 to 35 minutes or until the lentils are soft. Drain any excess water from lentils and return them to the saucepan.

2 While the lentils cook, in a deep pot heat the oil over medium heat. Add the onion and cook 10 minutes or until it begins to turn golden, stirring occasionally. Add the garlic and cook 1 minute more. Remove the pot from the heat.

3 Remove the stems from the kale leaves. Discard the stems and chop the leaves coarsely, then swish the leaves in cold water until they are clean. Add the still-wet leaves to the cooked onion-garlic mixture and return the pot to the heat.

4 Cook the kale, covered, over medium-low heat about 5 to 10 minutes or until the leaves are tender. Cooking time will vary with the size and thickness of the leaves.

5 Add the cooked lentils and thyme to the kale and toss well. Taste and add salt and pepper if needed, reduce the heat to low, and simmer, covered, for 5 minutes. Serve hot.

Split Pea Dal

MAKES 4 SERVINGS

In India, dal *refers to any type of legume or legume dish, and it sometimes refers to soup or stew. This version is a lightly spiced stew served over cooked rice. Legumes are particularly high in protein and fiber, making them a nutritious addition to any diet.*

1 tablespoon canola oil
1 teaspoon ground coriander
1 teaspoon ground cumin
1 teaspoon ground turmeric
¼ teaspoon ground ginger
¼ teaspoon salt
⅛ teaspoon ground cayenne
1 garlic clove, minced
1½ cups split peas (green or red)
4 cups water
2 tablespoons fresh lemon juice
4 cups hot cooked brown or white rice

1 In a stock pot, heat the oil over medium high heat and add the coriander, cumin, turmeric, and ginger and stir constantly for 1 minute. Add the salt, cayenne, garlic, split peas, and water.

2 Bring to a boil, reduce the heat to medium-low, and simmer, covered, about 30 minutes or until peas are tender and the mixture thickens slightly. Stir in the lemon juice. Serve immediately over cooked rice.

Black-Eyed Peas with Collard Greens Ⓥ

MAKES 4 SERVINGS

Black-eyed peas, a staple in the South, are actually pale-colored beans with a prominent black spot (hence their name). High in calcium, they are often served with collard greens for a nutritious, flavorful dish. If you prefer the traditional nonvegetarian version with ham, see the variation below.

2 tablespoons olive oil

1 medium onion, chopped

1 garlic clove, minced

½ pound collard greens, rinsed and cleaned

4 cups gluten-free vegetable broth, such as Imagine, or homemade Vegetable Broth (page 677)

1 can (14 to 15 ounces) black-eyed peas, rinsed and drained

Salt and freshly ground pepper, to taste

1 teaspoon cider or sherry vinegar

4 cups hot cooked brown rice

1 In a Dutch oven or other deep, heavy pot with a tight-fitting lid, heat the oil over medium heat. Add onion and garlic and cook, stirring occasionally, until onion is soft and translucent.

2 While onion mixture is cooking, discard stems and center ribs from collards and finely chop the leaves. Add collards and broth to onion mixture and simmer until collards are tender, about 20 minutes.

3 Rinse and drain the black-eyed peas. In a bowl, mash half of peas with a fork. Stir mashed and whole peas into the onion-collard mixture and simmer 5 minutes. Add salt and pepper to taste and stir in vinegar. Serve hot over cooked rice.

Black-Eyed Peas with Ham and Collard Greens: Dice a 4-ounce piece of ham hock and add it to the pot with the collard greens.

FISH AND SEAFOOD

Fillets and Steaks

Broiled Soy-Glazed Salmon

Broiled Salmon with Bell-Pepper Salsa

Honey-Glazed Grilled Salmon with Pineapple Chutney

Grilled Salmon with Minted Pineapple Salsa

Grilled Cedar-Plank Salmon

Grilled Teriyaki Tuna

Grilled Swordfish with Mango Salsa

Grilled Grouper with Ginger-Orange Glaze

Grilled Halibut with Romesco Sauce

Blackened Tilapia with Goat Cheese Mashed Potatoes

Pan-Fried Red Snapper with Lemon-Dill Sauce

Cornmeal-Crusted Red Snapper with Cucumber-Onion Relish

Pan-Seared Grouper in Thai Curry Sauce

Pan-Seared Red Snapper with Ginger-Pear Salsa

Caribbean Red Snapper with Banana-Coconut Salsa

Pan-Seared Red Snapper with Apple-Pear Chutney

Macadamia-Crusted Fish Fillets with Spicy Pineapple Salsa

Tuna Provençal on Rice

Sole Piccata

Baked Red Snapper in Foil

Mediterranean Red Snapper en Papillote

Salmon en Papillote

Baked Salmon with Indian Spices

Prosciutto-Wrapped Fish Fillets with Mediterranean Salsa

Roasted Halibut on Mediterranean Vegetables

Fish and Chips

Braised Halibut in Curry Broth

Braised Salmon on a Bed of Leeks and Tomatoes with Dill

Poached Salmon with Cucumber-Dill Sauce

Salmon Simmered in Beer

Stir-Fries, Casseroles, and Mixed Seafood

Pan-Fried Coconut Shrimp with Apricot-Mustard Dip

Pan-Seared Shrimp with Andouille Sausage

Lemon-Dijon Grilled Prawns

Shrimp and Grits

Shrimp with Tabbouleh

Shrimp Creole

Shrimp deJonghe

Shrimp Etouffée

Shrimp Newburg

Shrimp Scampi

Shrimp Vindaloo

Thai Shrimp Curry

Shrimp and Vegetable Tempura with Dipping Sauce

Shrimp, Sausage, and Red Beans and Rice

Baked Scallops in White Wine

Pan-Seared Scallops with Caper Gremolata

Pan-Seared Scallops with Risotto and Morels

Scallop and Lobster Stir-Fry

Crab and Spinach Enchiladas

Crab Cakes with Rémoulade Sauce

Southwestern Crab Cakes with Spicy Avocado Sauce

Crab Casserole

Deviled Crab

Fried Calamari

Tuna Croquettes

Salmon Patties

Seafood Gumbo

Seafood Rice Casserole

Seafood Jambalaya

My first taste of fish was the catfish my family caught in the Platte River in Eastern Nebraska where I grew up. Fresh-caught and fried in cornmeal, they were fantastic. Today—after sampling some of the world's finest finned and shelled creatures in Europe, Asia, Australia, and, of course, Alaska and the continental United States—I now realize that there are many wonderful species out there, and fish has become my first choice when I dine out.

Fish is very healthy, with a strong "good-fat" (HDL) content, and the generally mild flavor lends itself to many preparations. Plus, it is generally lower in calories than other main-dish choices.

But for people avoiding gluten, fish—just like meat and poultry—can be a risky choice when ordered in restaurants. It might be dredged in wheat flour before it is fried, or the seasoning blend might contain wheat flour. To be safe, I always order my fish grilled, with only salt, pepper, and fresh lemon wedges, unless the restaurant can assure me that the seasoning is gluten-free.

Happily, the fish cooked in your own home is safe because you control what goes into the dish. This chapter includes fish and seafood recipes adapted from my travels around the world, plus some of the regional specialties from the United States. For example, Tuna Provençal on Rice, Shrimp Vindaloo, and Fish and Chips bring you flavors from France, India, and Great Britain. Regional dishes such as Shrimp Etouffée and Creole Crab Cakes hail from the South, while Blackened Tilapia on Goat Cheese Mashed Potatoes is my re-creation of a contemporary dish from a restaurant in Denver, Colorado.

When buying fresh seafood or fish, the fresher the better. Although the flavors differ, many types of fish cook similarly and are interchangeable in most recipes—for example: halibut, red snapper, and grouper; orange roughy and sole; cod and haddock; shrimp and scallops; swordfish and salmon.

FILLETS AND STEAKS

Broiled Soy-Glazed Salmon
MAKES 4 SERVINGS

Salmon is my favorite fish because I like its flavor and texture, and it is so versatile. It is good almost any way you cook it, but this version is extremely easy and flavorful. For a quick meal, serve it with basmati rice and steamed broccoli.

¼ cup wheat-free tamari soy sauce, such as Crystal or San-J
2 tablespoons honey
1 tablespoon unseasoned rice vinegar
1 tablespoon ground ginger
¼ teaspoon ground cayenne
Dash of freshly ground black pepper
4 salmon fillets (about 4 ounces each)

1 In a large shallow bowl, combine soy sauce, honey, vinegar, ginger, cayenne, and pepper. Marinate the salmon, flesh side down, for 2 hours in the refrigerator.

2 Place a broiler rack about 6 inches away from the heat source. Preheat the broiler. Remove salmon from marinade and discard the marinade. Broil the salmon, skin side down, 8 to 10 minutes, depending on the thickness of the fish or until fish is just barely opaque when cut in the thickest part or when it flakes easily with a fork. Serve immediately.

Broiled Salmon with Bell-Pepper Salsa
MAKES 4 SERVINGS

Bell peppers provide lovely color and wonderful flavor to this salsa and the sherry or champagne vinegar further accentuates the salsa flavors. You may also grill the salmon rather than broiling if you wish.

SALMON

4 salmon fillets (about 4 ounces each)

1 teaspoon salt

¼ teaspoon freshly ground black pepper

1 tablespoon Southwest seasoning, such as McCormick (fajita or taco)

Cooking spray

1 fresh lemon, quartered, for garnish

SALSA

½ cup diced red onion

½ cup diced red bell pepper

½ cup diced yellow bell pepper

½ cup diced green bell pepper

½ cup diced plum tomato

¼ cup chopped fresh cilantro

2 tablespoons sherry or champagne vinegar

1 teaspoon extra-virgin olive oil

½ teaspoon Southwest seasoning, such as McCormick (fajita or taco)

1 Prepare the salmon: Sprinkle salmon fillets with salt, pepper, and Southwest seasoning. Let stand 15 minutes.

2 While salmon stands, place a broiler rack about 6 inches away from the heat source. Preheat the broiler. Make the salsa: In a bowl, combine all the salsa ingredients and toss well to mix ingredients thoroughly. Let stand while salmon broils.

3 Coat broiler and salmon fillets with cooking spray. Broil the salmon, skin side down, to the desired degree of doneness, about 8 to 10 minutes, depending on the thickness of the fish or until fish is just barely opaque when cut in the thickest part or when it flakes easily with a fork. Serve immediately with salsa and fresh lemon wedges.

Honey-Glazed Grilled Salmon with Pineapple Chutney

MAKES 4 SERVINGS

This delicious salmon with its honey glaze and pineapple chutney is just the ticket when you want an entree that is filling and a little sweet. Any left-over chutney can be refrigerated for 2 to 3 days to use on other dishes or lightly spread on sandwiches or added to tuna salad to kick up the flavor.

SALMON

4 salmon fillets (about 4 ounces each)

¼ cup wheat-free tamari soy sauce, such as Crystal or San-J

2 tablespoons champagne vinegar

2 tablespoons honey

1 tablespoon Dijon mustard

¼ teaspoon garlic powder

⅛ teaspoon ground cayenne

¼ cup finely snipped fresh chives, for garnish

CHUTNEY

1 can (14 to 15 ounces) pineapple tidbits, drained and ¼ cup juice reserved

¼ cup white wine vinegar

2 tablespoons honey

2 tablespoons chopped fresh cilantro

1 tablespoon grated fresh ginger

1 teaspoon ground cumin or chili powder

1 Prepare the salmon: Place salmon in a heavy-duty food-storage bag and add soy sauce, vinegar, honey, mustard, garlic, and cayenne. Refrigerate 2 hours.

2 While the salmon marinates, make the chutney: In a small saucepan, place all the chutney ingredients and bring to a boil over medium-high heat. Reduce heat to low, cover, and simmer 15 minutes. Remove from heat and let stand at room temperature.

3 Place a barbecue grill about 6 inches away from the heat source. Preheat the grill. Remove the salmon from the marinade, reserving marinade. Grill salmon, skin-side down, to the desired degree of doneness, basting occasionally with marinade, about 8 to 10 minutes, depending on the thickness of the fillet, or until the fish is just barely opaque when cut in the thickest part or flakes easily with fork. Transfer salmon to serving platter and cover with foil to keep warm. Bring remaining marinade and ¼ cup reserved pineapple juice to a boil in a small saucepan, reduce heat to low, and simmer 3 minutes. Pour over salmon, garnish with fresh chives, and serve with pineapple chutney.

Grilled Salmon with Minted Pineapple Salsa

MAKES 4 SERVINGS

I often serve salmon at home with a salsa, such as Minted Pineapple Salsa (page 671). I love the contrast of a sweet fruit against a savory dish like salmon. This dish is a fun and flavorful way to enjoy the nutritious benefits of fish, fruits, and vegetables.

1 recipe Minted Pineapple Salsa (page 671)
4 salmon steaks or fillets (about 6 ounces each)
2 tablespoons olive oil, for brushing on fish
½ teaspoon salt
½ teaspoon freshly ground black pepper
2 tablespoons fresh lemon juice

1 Prepare the salsa; set aside. Brush each piece of salmon with olive oil. Sprinkle with salt and pepper.

2 Place a barbecue grill or broiler rack about 6 inches away from the heat source. Preheat the grill or broiler. Grill the salmon, skin side down, to desired degree of doneness, about 8 to 10 minutes, depending on the thickness of the fish or until the fish is just barely opaque when cut in the thickest part or flakes easily with a fork. Remove the salmon from the heat and sprinkle with fresh lemon juice. Serve salmon immediately topped with salsa.

Grilled Cedar-Plank Salmon

MAKES 6 SERVINGS

Susan Cox-Gilbertson, an accomplished cook who works at Bob's Red Mill Cooking School, grew up on the Southern Oregon coast where her family often enjoyed wild salmon. I like to serve Susan's dish with Crispy Potato Wedges (page 387) or Saffron Rice Pilaf (page 220) for entertaining or even a weeknight dinner.

Cedar planks for grilling are sold at gourmet food shops, houseware stores, and lumberyards. Make sure the lumber hasn't been treated with preservatives or other chemicals. The plank can ignite when exposed to flames, so it is best to keep a spray bottle of water close at hand to keep flames to a minimum. Each plank can only be used once and should be discarded afterward.

1 untreated cedar plank, 24 × 8 × 1 inches
6 salmon fillets (about 4 ounces each), with the skin
½ cup extra virgin olive oil, divided
Salt and freshly ground pepper to taste
12 sprigs of fresh thyme or lemon thyme
12 fresh lemon slices

1 Submerge cedar plank in plain water overnight

2 Place a barbecue grill about 6 inches away from the heat source. Preheat the grill to high heat.

3 Rinse salmon under cold running water and pat dry with paper towel.

4 Remove cedar plank from water and let the water drip off. Lay plank on a baking sheet or cutting board. Rub 2 tablespoons of olive oil on the skin side of each salmon fillet.

5 Place salmon on the plank, skin side down, and brush the flesh with remaining olive oil. Add salt and pepper to taste. Lay a couple sprigs of fresh thyme on each fillet of fish. Top with slices of lemon.

6 Turn grill down to medium high or move charcoals to the side. Place plank directly on the grill and close the lid. The wood will start to smoke in about 10 minutes, producing a smoky flavor. Check periodically to make sure that the plank is smoking but not on fire. If the edges catch fire, mist with a spray bottle of water. Continue to cook 20 to 30 minutes, depending on thickness of the fillets, or until opaque when cut in the thickest part and easily flakes with a fork. The internal temperature should reach 135°F.

7 Transfer the salmon and plank to a platter and serve right off the plank.

Grilled Teriyaki Tuna

MAKES 4 SERVINGS

You may use halibut fillets instead of tuna, if you wish. Assemble the marinade right in the plastic bag, eliminating an extra dish to wash. Save this dish for nights when you know you'll be rushed but still want a great meal.

4 yellowfin tuna fillets (about 4 ounces each)
½ cup gluten-free teriyaki sauce, such as Crystal or Premier Japan
2 tablespoons sesame oil
2 tablespoons packed light brown sugar
1 tablespoon grated lime zest
1 teaspoon ground ginger
⅛ teaspoon crushed red pepper
1 teaspoon toasted sesame seeds, for garnish

1 Place the tuna fillets in a heavy-duty food-storage bag. Add the teriyaki sauce, oil, brown sugar, lime zest, ginger, and crushed red pepper. Seal the bag and shake to coat the tuna. Refrigerate 8 hours or overnight.

2 Place a barbecue grill about 6 inches away from the heat source. Preheat the grill to the desired temperature. Remove the tuna from the bag and reserve the marinade. Cook the tuna until it reaches the desired degree of doneness, about 8 to 10 minutes, depending on the thickness of the fillet or until the fish is just barely opaque when cut in the thickest part.

3 Bring the reserved marinade to a boil in a small saucepan, reduce heat to medium and boil for 3 minutes. Transfer to a pitcher to serve as a sauce. Remove the tuna from the grill and arrange it on a serving platter. Drizzle the heated marinade over the tuna and sprinkle with sesame seed. Serve immediately.

Grilled Swordfish with Mango Salsa

MAKES 4 SERVINGS

Mangos are powerhouses of nutrition and are increasingly available in the grocery store at reasonable prices. Their gorgeous color easily enhances any dish. I enjoy adding something red (like red bell pepper) to the dish for contrast; eye-catching food is always more tempting and seems delicious even before the first bite.

SWORDFISH
1¼ pounds swordfish steaks, divided into 4 pieces
½ teaspoon salt
½ teaspoon freshly ground black pepper
2 tablespoons fresh lemon juice

SALSA
1 ripe mango, peeled, seeded, and finely diced
¼ cup diced red bell pepper
¼ cup diced red onion
Juice and zest of 1 lemon
1 teaspoon olive oil
1 teaspoon rice vinegar
¼ teaspoon salt
¼ teaspoon freshly ground black pepper
¼ cup chopped fresh cilantro

1 Sprinkle the swordfish with the salt and pepper.

2 Place a barbecue grill or broiler rack about 6 inches away from the heat source. Preheat the grill or broiler. Grill the swordfish until it reaches the desired degree of doneness, about 8 to 10 minutes, depending on the thickness of the steak

or until the crumbs are golden and the fish is just barely opaque when cut in the thickest part or flakes easily with a fork. Remove the swordfish from the heat and sprinkle with fresh lemon juice.

3 While the swordfish is on the grill, make the salsa: In a small bowl, combine the mango, bell pepper, red onion, lemon juice, lemon zest, oil, vinegar, salt, pepper, and cilantro. Serve immediately with swordfish.

Grilled Grouper with Ginger-Orange Glaze

MAKES 4 SERVINGS

Grouper is a thick, white fish and one of my favorites, but you may substitute thick red snapper or salmon if you wish. If you don't want to grill this dish, you may broil it in the oven instead; watch the cooking time.

¼ cup wheat-free low-sodium tamari soy sauce, such as Crystal or San-J
¼ cup Dijon mustard
¼ cup orange juice concentrate, thawed
1 tablespoon grated fresh ginger
4 grouper fillets (about 4 ounces each)
1 fresh orange, cut into wedges, for garnish

1 In a heavy-duty food-storage bag, combine soy sauce, mustard, orange juice concentrate, and ginger. Add grouper and refrigerate 30 minutes. Remove grouper from bag and transfer marinade to a small pan.

2 Place a barbecue grill about 6 inches away from the heat source. Preheat the grill to medium-high heat. Grill grouper to desired degree of doneness or until the crumbs are golden and the fish is just barely opaque when cut in the thickest part or flakes easily with a fork about 8 to 10 minutes, depending on thickness of the fish. Remove fish from grill and cover with foil to keep warm.

3 Meanwhile, while fish grills bring marinade to boil over medium heat and boil 3 minutes. Marinade will reduce down slightly. Pour a little of the marinade over cooked fish and serve hot with fresh orange wedges.

Grilled Halibut with Romesco Sauce

MAKES 4 SERVINGS

Romesco sauce, of Spanish origin, is a roasted red pepper-based sauce often made with bread to thicken it. My version omits the bread, but is still rich and thick. Although I use halibut here, any firm fish, such as grouper or swordfish, will work.

4 ripe plum tomatoes
2 garlic cloves, peeled and halved
½ cup olive oil
¼ cup sliced almonds
2 tablespoons red wine vinegar
½ teaspoon salt
¼ teaspoon crushed red pepper
¼ teaspoon sugar
2 roasted red bell peppers from jar
4 halibut steaks (about 4 ounces each)

1 Place a rack in the middle of the oven. Preheat the oven to 450°F. Place tomatoes and garlic on sheet of aluminum foil that's coated with cooking spray. Roast 12 to 15 minutes or until tomatoes blacken. Remove from oven and let cool.

2 Place tomatoes and garlic in a blender. Add oil, almonds, vinegar, salt, crushed red pepper, sugar and roasted red bell peppers. Blend until smooth, adding water a tablespoon at a time if sauce is too thick.

3 Place a barbecue grill about 6 inches away from the heat source. Preheat the grill to medium heat. Coat steaks with cooking spray. Cook steaks to the desired degree of doneness, about 8 to 10 minutes, depending on the thickness of the steak or until fish is just barely opaque when cut in the thickest part or when it flakes easily with a fork.

Serve hot with 2 tablespoons Romesco sauce on each steak.

Blackened Tilapia with Goat Cheese Mashed Potatoes

MAKES 4 SERVINGS

Tilapia is a delicate, white freshwater fish that is available fresh in fish markets or frozen in grocery stores. To "blacken" food means to coat it with dry spices to add flavor and then fry or bake it. For best results, transfer the Blackening Seasoning to a shaker-type bottle (an empty spice bottle with a perforated plastic snap-on lid works quite nicely) so you can quickly and evenly coat the fillets with the seasonings. Make the creamy, rich mashed potatoes first and keep them hot while preparing the quick-cooking tilapia.

MASHED POTATOES

Water to cover potatoes

4 large russet potatoes, peeled and quartered

2 teaspoons salt

1 package (4 ounces) plain goat cheese, at room temperature

Additional salt and freshly ground pepper to taste

TILAPIA

2 tablespoons homemade Blackening Seasoning (page 669), or to taste

¼ cup unsalted butter or buttery spread, such as Earth Balance

4 tilapia fillets (about 6 ounces each)

¼ cup fresh snipped chives

1 whole lemon, quartered, for garnish

1 Make the mashed potatoes: Bring water to a boil in a medium saucepan. Add potatoes and salt and bring to a boil again. Reduce heat to medium, cover, and cook potatoes about 20 minutes on low heat, or until done. Drain potatoes, reserving ¼ cup of the potato liquid. Mash potatoes with a potato masher; adding enough of the reserved potato liquid to reach desired consistency. Add goat cheese and mash into the potatoes until smooth. Add salt and pepper to taste. Cover the pan and let stand while preparing the fish.

2 Make the tilapia: Prepare the blackening seasoning. Then, heat a cast-iron skillet over high heat for about 10 minutes. Melt the butter in the skillet and then pour the butter on a plate. Pat the fillets dry with paper towels. Dip each fillet in the butter, coating both sides. Sprinkle 1 side of each fillet with blackening seasoning. Place the fillet in the hot skillet, seasoned side down, and then sprinkle the top side with blackening seasoning. Cook about 2 minutes or until the underside looks charred. Turn and cook 2 more minutes until the underside looks charred. Reduce heat to low and continue cooking 6 to 8 minutes, depending on the thickness of the fish or until the fish is just barely opaque when cut in the thickest part.

3 Place a mound of mashed potatoes on each of 4 dinner plates. Place the fish on top of the mashed potatoes. Sprinkle with chives. Garnish with lemon wedges. Serve immediately.

Pan-Fried Red Snapper with Lemon-Dill Sauce

MAKES 4 SERVINGS

I like to serve this lemony snapper dish on a bed of steamed greens such as spinach or kale. It also works nicely on a bed of rice pilaf.

4 red snapper fillets (or mahi-mahi, or other firm-flesh fillets—about 6 ounces each)

¾ teaspoon salt

½ teaspoon lemon pepper

1 tablespoon olive oil

2 large eggs, at room temperature

¼ cup fresh lemon juice

¼ cup dry white wine

½ teaspoon grated lemon zest

¼ teaspoon white pepper

2 tablespoons chopped fresh dill + 1 tablespoon for garnish

1 Sprinkle the fillets with ½ teaspoon of the salt and the lemon pepper. In a heavy skillet, heat the oil over medium heat. Cook the fish to the desired degree of doneness, about 8 to 10 minutes, depending on the thickness of the fish or until the crumbs are golden and the fish is just barely opaque when cut in the thickest part or flakes easily with a fork. When the fish is done, cover the skillet with a lid and remove the skillet from the heat while you prepare the sauce.

2 In a small heavy saucepan, beat the eggs with an electric mixer on low speed until frothy, about 30 seconds. Place the pan over medium-low heat and add the lemon juice and wine. Cook the sauce, beating constantly with the electric mixer on low speed, until the sauce thickens slightly, about 3 to 4 minutes. Do not let the sauce boil or the eggs will curdle.

3 Remove the pan from the heat and stir in the lemon zest, white pepper, 2 tablespoons of the dill, and the remaining ¼ teaspoon of the salt. If the sauce is too thick, thin with a little more lemon juice or wine. Serve immediately, drizzled over the fish and garnished with the remaining 1 tablespoon of fresh dill.

Cornmeal-Crusted Red Snapper with Cucumber-Onion Relish

MAKES 4 SERVINGS

The crisp-coated mild fish works nicely with the flavorful juicy relish. Japanese pickled ginger is similar to the pink ginger strips usually served with sushi, and lends a wonderful flavor to this relish. It is normally available at natural food stores, but if you can't find it, just use ½ teaspoon grated fresh ginger.

RELISH

½ cup finely diced English (hothouse) cucumber

¼ cup sweet white onion, finely diced

½ cup finely chopped red bell pepper

2 tablespoons chopped fresh cilantro

1 tablespoon canola oil

1 tablespoon finely chopped Japanese pickled ginger

1 tablespoon rice vinegar

½ teaspoon wasabi powder, such as McCormick

¼ teaspoon cane sugar

¼ teaspoon salt

¼ teaspoon freshly ground black pepper

RED SNAPPER

4 red snapper fillets (or mahi-mahi, or other firm-flesh fillet—about 6 ounces each)

1 teaspoon salt

¼ teaspoon freshly ground black pepper

1 cup gluten-free yellow cornmeal, such as Albers, Arrowhead Mills, Kinnikinnick, or Quaker

2 tablespoons canola oil

1 Make the relish: At least an hour before serving, combine all of the relish ingredients in a small serving bowl, cover, and let sit at room temperature.

2 Prepare the red snapper: Pat fillets dry with paper towel and sprinkle with salt and pepper. Press cornmeal onto both sides of fish.

3 In a heavy-duty skillet, heat the oil and cook fillets until lightly browned and crisp, approximately 8 to 10 minutes, depending on thickness of the fillet or until the crumbs are golden and the fish is just barely opaque when cut in the thickest part. Serve immediately with ⅓ cup relish per serving.

Pan-Fried Grouper in Thai Curry Sauce

MAKES 4 SERVINGS

This is one of the dishes that reminds me that many ethnic foods are totally gluten-free—naturally—and anyone can enjoy them. The heat in this dish comes from the green curry paste. Start with 1 teaspoon and taste the sauce before adding any more.

RICE

2 cups water

1 cup white rice

½ teaspoon salt

¼ teaspoon unsalted butter or buttery spread, such as Earth Balance, or canola oil

SAUCE

¼ cup finely snipped chives

1 tablespoon Asian fish sauce, such as Taste of Thai or Thai Kitchen

1 tablespoon honey

1 to 2 teaspoons Thai green curry paste

1 teaspoon ground ginger

1 teaspoon olive oil

1 teaspoon grated lemon peel

1 teaspoon grated lime peel

¼ teaspoon turmeric

1 garlic clove, minced

1 can (14 to 15 ounces) coconut milk (not cream of coconut)

⅛ teaspoon salt (or more to taste)

1 tablespoon olive oil

1 whole lime or lemon, quartered, for garnish

GROUPER

1 tablespoon olive oil

4 grouper or red snapper fillets (about 4 ounces each)

⅛ teaspoon salt

⅛ teaspoon black pepper

¼ cup chopped cilantro for garnish (optional)

1 Make the rice: In a medium pan, bring water to boil. Add rice, salt, and butter, cover, and simmer on low heat approximately 20 minutes or until rice is done. Remove from heat and keep warm.

2 Make the sauce: In a medium pan, combine all sauce ingredients and simmer, uncovered, over medium heat, stirring often, for about 10 minutes. Mixture will thicken slightly.

3 Meanwhile, prepare the grouper: In a medium, nonstick skillet, heat oil over medium-high heat.

Sprinkle both sides of grouper with salt and pepper. Cook grouper over medium-high heat to desired degree of doneness, about 8 to 10 minutes, depending on the thickness of the fish or until the crumbs are golden and the fish is just barely opaque when cut in the thickest part or flakes easily with a fork

4 For each serving, place ½ cup Thai curry sauce in each of 4 bowls. Add ½ cup cooked white rice and one fillet of grouper. Garnish with chopped cilantro, if using.

Pan-Seared Red Snapper with Ginger-Pear Salsa

MAKES 4 SERVINGS

You can use any fish you like in this recipe, but I find that red snapper works especially well. I think that fruit salsas not only complement the flavors of fish, they also provide important nutrients.

RED SNAPPER

4 red snapper fillets (about 4 ounces each)

1 teaspoon salt

½ teaspoon freshly ground black pepper

1 whole lime or lemon, quartered, for garnish

SALSA

1 large ripe Bosc pear, peeled, halved, cored, and cut in ½-inch dice

1 can (11 ounces) mandarin oranges, drained

2 tablespoons chopped candied ginger

2 tablespoons diced red onion

2 tablespoons chopped fresh cilantro

2 tablespoons fresh lime juice

1 tablespoon olive oil

Dash of hot pepper sauce, such as Frank's, or to taste

1 small garlic clove, minced

¼ teaspoon salt

Dash of freshly ground black pepper

1 Prepare the red snapper: Sprinkle red snapper with salt and pepper and set aside while preparing salsa.

2 Make the salsa: In a medium bowl, combine pear, oranges, candied ginger, red onion, cilantro, lime juice, oil, hot pepper sauce, garlic, salt, and pepper. Toss together gently. Set aside.

3 In a heavy skillet, heat the oil over medium-high heat. Cook red snapper to the desired degree of doneness, about 8 to 10 minutes, depending on the thickness of the fish or until the crumbs are golden and the fish is just barely opaque when cut in the thickest part or flakes easily with a fork. Serve red snapper with salsa and a lemon or lime wedge.

Caribbean Red Snapper with Banana-Coconut Salsa

MAKES 4 SERVINGS

This unusual and tasty salsa is pleasantly mild and will make you feel like you are in the Caribbean. If you want to increase the heat, simply shake a few drops of hot pepper sauce into it. This salsa is best when it is made just before serving, so that the bananas look their freshest.

4 red snapper fillets (about 4 ounces each)
½ teaspoon salt
¼ teaspoon freshly ground black pepper
2 tablespoons canola oil

SALSA
1 medium ripe banana, peeled and cut in ½-inch dice
2 tablespoons fresh lime juice
¼ cup seeded, diced red bell pepper
2 tablespoons chopped fresh cilantro
2 tablespoons almond slices
2 tablespoons natural coconut flakes
    (not sweetened or shredded)
2 chopped green onions, including green tops
1 tablespoon honey
1 tablespoon canola oil
¼ teaspoon salt
¼ teaspoon freshly ground black pepper

1 Prepare the red snapper: Sprinkle fillets with salt and pepper and set aside.

2 Make the salsa: In a small bowl, combine all salsa ingredients and toss gently, making sure to coat bananas thoroughly with lime juice to prevent discoloration. Do not prepare any more than 30 minutes prior to serving.

3 In a heavy skillet, heat the oil over medium-high heat. Cook red snapper fillets to desired degree of doneness, about 8 to 10 minutes, depending on the thickness of the fish or until the crumbs are golden and the fish is just barely opaque when cut in the thickest part or flakes easily with a fork. Serve hot, garnished with salsa.

Pan-Seared Red Snapper with Apple-Pear Chutney

MAKES 4 SERVINGS

This dish is especially welcome in the fall when the aroma of scented apples fills the air. If you prefer your food less spicy, you can omit the chili powder on the snapper and just use salt and pepper. Granny Smith apples are good to cook with because they tend to hold their shape. If you prefer a less firm apple, use Yellow Delicious or Gala apples.

RED SNAPPER
4 red snapper fillets (about 4 ounces each)
1 tablespoon chili powder
¼ teaspoon salt
¼ teaspoon freshly ground black pepper
1 tablespoon olive oil

CHUTNEY
1 tablespoon unsalted butter or buttery spread, such as Earth Balance, or canola oil
1 ripe Bosc pear, peeled, cored, and cut in ½-inch dice
1 small apple (such as Granny Smith), peeled, cored, and cut in ½-inch slices
¼ cup chopped white onion

2 tablespoons cider vinegar

1 tablespoon fresh lemon juice

1 tablespoon honey

1 tablespoon dried cranberries

1 garlic clove, minced

⅛ teaspoon ground cinnamon

⅛ teaspoon freshly grated nutmeg

⅛ teaspoon ground allspice

⅛ teaspoon ground ginger

Dash salt and freshly ground pepper to taste

1 Prepare the red snapper: Pat red snapper fillets dry with paper towel. Mix chili powder, salt, and pepper together and press onto both sides of snapper. Set aside while preparing chutney.

2 Make the chutney: In a heavy skillet, heat butter over medium heat. Add pear and apple and cook until slightly softened, about 5 minutes. Add onion, vinegar, lemon juice, honey, cranberries, garlic, cinnamon, nutmeg, allspice, ginger, salt, and pepper and cook over medium heat until mixture comes to boil. Remove from heat and let stand while preparing red snapper.

3 In a heavy, nonstick (gray, not black) skillet, heat the oil over medium-high heat. Cook red snapper to desired degree of doneness, about 8 to 10 minutes, depending on the thickness of the fish or until the crumbs are golden and the fish is just barely opaque when cut in the thickest part or flakes easily with a fork. Serve red snapper topped with chutney.

Macadamia-Crusted Fish Fillets with Spicy Pineapple Salsa

MAKES 4 SERVINGS

This is a commonly served dish in the Hawaiian Islands. Unfortunately, I had to avoid it on my last trip to Kauai because the chef used bread crumbs along with the macadamia nuts. When I came home I quickly invented my own version. Wear plastic gloves when you work with serrano chiles to avoid burns, and don't touch your eyes— the chile oil will irritate them.

SALSA

1 cup chopped fresh pineapple or 1 can (8 ounces) pineapple tidbits, drained

½ cup finely diced red bell pepper

½ cup chopped fresh cilantro

¼ cup finely diced red onion

1 tablespoon fresh lime juice

1 tablespoon rice vinegar

1 teaspoon olive oil

1 serrano chile pepper, seeded and finely diced

1 teaspoon Asian fish sauce, such as a Taste of Thai or Thai Kitchen

¼ teaspoon salt

FISH FILLETS

4 tablespoons olive oil, divided

1 cup coarsely ground macadamia nuts or almonds

¼ cup cornstarch

1 teaspoon ground ginger

1 teaspoon ground coriander

1 teaspoon paprika + additional for dusting

4 fish fillets (red snapper, mahi-mahi, or firm-flesh fillets—about 6 ounces each)

1 teaspoon salt

½ teaspoon freshly ground black pepper

Additional salt and freshly ground pepper to taste

1 Make the salsa: At least an hour before serving, in a small serving bowl, combine all of the salsa ingredients, cover, and let sit at room temperature so the flavors can develop.

2 Prepare the fish fillets: Place a rack in the middle of the oven. Preheat the oven to 400°F. Lightly grease a rimmed 13 × 9-inch nonstick baking sheet (gray, not black) with 1 tablespoon of the olive oil or line the pan with foil and lightly coat with cooking spray.

3 In a food processor, grind the nuts and cornstarch (the cornstarch prevents the nuts from sticking together). Spread the nuts evenly on a large dinner plate.

4 In a small bowl, combine the remaining 3 tablespoons of the oil, ginger, coriander, and paprika. Brush each fillet with this mixture; sprinkle both sides with salt and pepper. Dredge each fillet in the nuts, pressing the mixture on the fish with your fingers to cover it evenly on both sides. Gently transfer fish to prepared baking dish. Dust with paprika.

5 Bake fillets until they are cooked through, about 8 to 10 minutes, depending on the thickness of the fish or until the crumbs are golden and the fish is just barely opaque when cut in the thickest part. Season with additional salt and pepper, to taste. Serve immediately topped with ⅓ cup salsa.

Tuna Provençal on Rice

MAKES 4 SERVINGS

This tuna dish evokes the flavors of Mediterranean dishes made with tomatoes, capers, olives, and artichokes—a combination most often connected to Provence, France. Provence captured my heart a few years ago because of its inviting warm, dry climate and spectacular food.

1 tablespoon olive oil

4 fresh tuna steaks (about 4 ounces each)

1 can (14 to 15 ounces) or 1½ cups petite diced tomatoes, including juice

½ cup dry white wine

2 teaspoons chopped fresh thyme or 1 teaspoon dried

1 teaspoon chopped fresh oregano or ½ teaspoon dried

3 tablespoons chopped onion or 2 teaspoons dried minced onion

½ teaspoon crushed red pepper

Juice and grated zest of 2 lemons

¼ teaspoon garlic powder

½ teaspoon salt

¼ teaspoon freshly ground black pepper

1 jar (6.5 ounces) marinated artichoke hearts, drained

2 tablespoons capers, drained

¼ cup pitted kalamata olives, sliced

2 cups hot cooked white rice

2 tablespoons chopped fresh parsley or 1 tablespoon dried, for garnish

1 In a large, heavy-duty skillet, heat oil over medium heat. Add tuna steaks and cook until browned on all sides and the fish is just barely opaque when cut in the thickest part. Transfer tuna from skillet to plate and cover to keep warm.

2 In the same skillet, add tomatoes, wine, thyme, oregano, minced onion, crushed red pepper, lemon juice and zest, garlic, salt, and pepper. Bring to boil over medium-high heat, reduce heat to low, and simmer, uncovered, 8 to 10 minutes. Add browned tuna steaks, artichokes, capers, and olives and gently bring to serving temperature, spooning liquid evenly over the fish.

3 Place hot cooked rice in a large, shallow serving bowl or dish. Place tuna steaks on rice and pour tomato sauce on top. Garnish with parsley. Serve immediately.

Sole Piccata Ⓠ

MAKES 4 SERVINGS

Piccata is an Italian dish, and the word itself translates to "piquant," which is fitting due to the tartness of the lemon juice, capers, and wine. You can use any flaky white fish such as cod or haddock if you don't have sole. Sole is quite thin and it will cook very quickly, so have any other dishes ready to serve before you start to prepare this one.

¼ cup white rice flour
¼ teaspoon salt
¼ teaspoon freshly ground black pepper
4 sole fillets (about 6 ounces each), patted dry with paper towels
2 tablespoons unsalted butter or buttery spread, such as Earth Balance, or olive oil, divided
¼ cup dry white wine
¼ cup fresh lemon juice
1 tablespoon capers, rinsed and drained
1 tablespoon chopped fresh parsley
1 lemon, quartered, for garnish

1 In a shallow bowl, combine the rice flour, salt, and pepper and dredge the fish in it. Shake off any excess flour.

2 In a large, nonstick (gray, not black) skillet, heat 1 tablespoon of the butter over medium-high heat. Add the fish and cook 1 to 2 minutes per side or until the fish flakes easily with a fork. Transfer the fish to a warmed serving platter and cover with foil to keep warm.

3 Add the wine and lemon juice to the skillet and bring to a boil; simmer 30 seconds. Add the remaining tablespoon of butter and stir until slightly thickened. Add the capers and parsley and bring sauce to serving temperature. Pour sauce over fish and serve immediately, with fresh lemon wedges for garnish.

Baked Red Snapper in Foil

MAKES 4 SERVINGS

This super-easy dish can be prepared one night then baked the next night for dinner. Once you get the idea, you can vary the herbs and spices as you wish. I often improvise these little packets using whatever happens to be in my refrigerator at the time.

⅓ cup (roughly 5 tablespoons) unsalted butter or buttery spread, such as Earth Balance, or olive oil, at room temperature
2 tablespoons chopped fresh thyme
2 tablespoons chopped fresh chives
1 tablespoon fresh lemon juice
1 tablespoon grated lemon zest
2 dashes of hot pepper sauce, such as Frank's, or ⅛ teaspoon ground cayenne
1 teaspoon celery salt
½ teaspoon lemon pepper
4 sheets of foil (12 inches square each)
4 cups baby spinach, washed and spun dry
1 small red pepper, seeded, cored, and sliced in ⅛-inch strips
4 (1-inch-thick) red snapper fillets (4 ounces each)
8 lemon slices
1 lemon cut into 4 quarters, for garnish

1 Place a rack in the middle of the oven. Preheat the oven to 425°F. In a small bowl, blend the butter with the thyme, chives, lemon juice, lemon zest, hot pepper sauce, celery salt, and lemon pepper.

2 Arrange four squares of foil, each 12 inches square, on the countertop and place 1 cup of spinach and ¼ of the sliced red pepper in the center of each square. Place a red snapper fillet on top. Top each fillet with the butter mixture, dividing evenly. Place 2 lemon slices on each fillet. Wrap the foil around the fillet, pleating the top and twisting the ends securely. Arrange packets on a rimmed 13 × 9-inch baking sheet.

3 Bake 12 to 15 minutes, or until the fish flakes easily with a fork. Transfer packets to serving plates, roll back the foil to form a decorative boat, and serve immediately with fresh lemon wedges.

Mediterranean Red Snapper en Papillote

MAKES 4 SERVINGS

You can be flexible in your choice of fish for this recipe: I've used cod, flounder, and sole instead of red snapper, which all work well with the arti-chokes and seasonings. This makes an especially nice choice for company since you can assemble the packets the night before and bake them just before dinner, leaving you time to concentrate on other dishes in the meal.

¼ cup unsalted butter or buttery spread, such as Earth Balance, or olive oil, at room temperature
¼ cup blend of chopped fresh chervil, chives, pars-ley, or thyme
Grated zest and juice of 1 lemon
½ teaspoon salt
½ teaspoon freshly ground black pepper
4 sheets of parchment paper, each 12 inches square
1½ pounds red snapper, cut into 4 equal-sized fillets
1 jar (6.5 ounces) marinated artichokes, drained
Cooking spray

1 In a small bowl, mash butter, herbs, lemon zest and juice, salt, and pepper together until smooth. Refrigerate until firm, about 1 hour.

2 Arrange 4 pieces of parchment paper on flat surface. Lay a piece of red snapper on each. Top each with ¼ of the butter-herb mixture and ¼ of the drained artichoke hearts. Bring two edges of parchment paper together and crimp or fold together to seal. Twist ends together to seal. Refrigerate at this point or proceed to baking.

3 Place a rack in the middle of the oven. Preheat the oven to 425°F. Place packets on a rimmed 13 × 9-inch baking sheet. Coat packets with cook-ing spray.

4 Bake 15 to 20 minutes if chilled, 12 to 15 minutes if not chilled. Packets will puff up and brown. Remove from oven and place each packet on a serving plate. Slowly cut open the packets with kitchen scissors to allow steam to release gently. Serve immediately.

Salmon en Papillote

MAKES 4 SERVINGS

En papillote loosely means "wrapped in packets." Cooking food wrapped in parchment (or foil) helps seal in and blend the flavor and juices of the foods in the packet. They are also quite healthful because they require very little fat. I love to entertain with these easy-to-make parcels. The dramatic unwrapping of the packets makes the meal special and festive. I often prepare the packets the night before so I can devote more time to the other dishes at the last minute.

4 sheets of parchment paper (each 12 inches square)
4 salmon fillets (about 4 ounces each)
1 small carrot, peeled and julienne
1 small leek, white part only, root-end cut off and sliced and rinsed thoroughly to remove grit
1 teaspoon grated fresh ginger
1 garlic clove, minced
1 teaspoon salt, divided
½ teaspoon freshly ground black pepper
2 teaspoons sesame oil
2 teaspoons extra-virgin olive oil
Cooking spray

1 Arrange 4 pieces of parchment paper on flat surface. Place salmon fillet on each piece. Combine carrot, leek, ginger, garlic, and half of the salt and pepper. Place ¼ of this mixture on each piece of salmon. Top each with ¼ of the remaining salt and pepper. Drizzle with sesame oil and olive oil. Bring two edges of parchment paper together and crimp or fold together to seal tightly. Twist ends together to seal tightly. Refrigerate packets at this point or proceed to baking.

2 Place a rack in the middle of the oven. Preheat the oven to 425°F. Place packets on 13 × 9-inch baking sheet. Coat with cooking spray.

3 Bake 15 to 20 minutes if chilled, 12 to 15 minutes if not chilled. Packets will puff up and brown. Remove from oven and place each packet on a serving plate. Slowly cut open the packets with kitchen scissors to allow steam to release gently. Serve immediately.

Baked Salmon with Indian Spices

MAKES 4 SERVINGS

Save time by mixing up the dry spices and herbs in advance and keep them in a sealed jar or container in the refrigerator until you need them. Or if you can find a pre-mixed Indian spice blend, you may use that instead. The salmon is baked in the oven, but you can also grill it. The cooking time will vary with the thickness of the salmon, so be sure to watch it carefully because the honey in the glaze makes it more likely to burn.

4 salmon fillets (about 4 ounces each)
2 tablespoons olive oil
2 tablespoons honey
1 teaspoon ground coriander
½ teaspoon fennel seeds, ground
½ teaspoon ground cumin
½ teaspoon ground turmeric
½ teaspoon salt
¼ teaspoon ground cayenne
⅛ teaspoon ground allspice
2 tablespoons chopped fresh cilantro, for garnish
Fresh lemon wedges for garnish

1 Place salmon fillets on a flat surface or plate and pat dry. In a small bowl, combine oil, honey, coriander, fennel, cumin, turmeric, salt, cayenne, and allspice and mix into smooth paste. Brush paste on tops of salmon fillets. Let salmon stand for 30 minutes at room temperature.

2 Place a rack in the middle of the oven. Preheat the oven to 375°F. Place salmon on a wire rack that has been coated with cooking spray. Place the rack in a 13 × 9-inch baking pan.

3 Bake 15 to 20 minutes or to desired degree of doneness or until salmon is just barely opaque when cut in the thickest part. Place a broiler rack about 6 inches away from the heat source. Preheat the broiler. Place salmon under broiler and broil until lightly browned. Serve salmon immediately, garnished with fresh cilantro and lemon wedges.

Prosciutto-Wrapped Fish Fillets with Mediterranean Salsa

MAKES 4 SERVINGS

This dish will transport you to the Mediterranean. Large tomatoes have seeds that you may want to remove before chopping, so I use grape or cherry tomatoes instead, to avoid seeding. Though mango isn't Mediterranean, it complements the other salsa ingredients nicely and provides just the right touch of sweetness to balance the acidity in the tomatoes and olives.

FISH FILLETS
4 orange roughy, red snapper, or tilapia fillets (about 4 ounces each, no more than 1 inch thick)
1 teaspoon salt
¼ teaspoon freshly ground black pepper
3 tablespoons extra-virgin olive oil, divided
2 tablespoons fresh lemon juice
¼ cup chopped fresh thyme or 2 teaspoons dried
8 thin prosciutto slices

SALSA
1 whole mango, peeled, seeded, finely chopped
½ cup chopped grape or cherry tomatoes
¼ cup chopped kalamata olives
¼ cup finely chopped red onion
2 tablespoons fresh lemon juice
2 tablespoons chopped fresh thyme
1 tablespoon chopped fresh oregano
1 tablespoon extra-virgin olive oil
¼ teaspoon salt
⅛ teaspoon freshly ground black pepper

1 Make the fish: Earlier in the day or the night before, sprinkle fillets with salt and pepper and drizzle with 2 tablespoons of the oil and lemon juice. Press thyme onto top of each fillet. Wrap each fillet in 2 overlapping slices of prosciutto and place seam side down on a plate. Wrap plate with aluminum foil and refrigerate. Proceed to next step.

2 Place a rack in the middle of the oven. Preheat the oven to 375°F. In a heavy-duty ovenproof skillet, heat the remaining tablespoon of oil over medium heat. Add prosciutto-wrapped fillets, seam side down, and cook until prosciutto is browned, about 1 minute. Gently turn and cook remaining side until browned.

3 Cover skillet with lid and roast in oven to desired degree of doneness about 8 to 10 minutes, depending on the thickness of the fish or until the crumbs are golden and the fish is just barely opaque when cut in the thickest part or flakes easily with a fork.

4 While the fish is roasting, make the salsa: In a small bowl, combine all salsa ingredients and toss gently until well blended. Hold at room temperature.

5 Remove pan from oven, using hot mitts on handle and lid, and let stand 5 minutes. Serve immediately with ¼ of the salsa on each fillet.

Roasted Halibut on Mediterranean Vegetables

MAKES 4 SERVINGS

This dish is so simple yet so delicious, with its rich, Mediterranean flavors. You just put everything in the baking dish and let the oven do the work. It may seem like a lot of spinach, but it will shrink during the roasting process.

1 bag (10 ounces) baby spinach, washed and dried
1 jar (6.5 ounces) marinated artichokes, drained
2 garlic cloves, minced
1 cup yellow or red grape tomatoes, or a mix of both, halved
4 halibut fillets (about 5 ounces each)
2 tablespoons extra-virgin olive oil
2 tablespoons vermouth or dry white wine
½ teaspoon salt
¼ teaspoon freshly ground black pepper or lemon pepper
1 teaspoon homemade Mediterranean Herb Seasoning (page 667) or spice blend of choice

1 Place a rack in the middle of the oven. Preheat the oven to 400°F. In a large bowl, toss the spinach, artichokes, and garlic together and then place on the bottom of a 2-quart ovenproof baking dish. Place the tomatoes around the edges.

2 Arrange the halibut fillets on top of the vegetables; drizzle them with olive oil and vermouth or wine, and sprinkle with the salt, pepper, and seasoning blend. Cover tightly with a lid or foil.

3 Roast 10 minutes; remove the lid and roast 8 to 10 minutes more, depending on the thickness of the fish or until the fish is just barely opaque when cut in the thickest part or flakes easily with a fork. Serve immediately.

Fish and Chips

MAKES 4 SERVINGS

This is my version of the classic English dish. You can slice the potatoes by hand, but a mandoline makes it easier to cut very thin slices.

1 cup cornstarch

¾ teaspoon baking powder

1 teaspoon salt

½ teaspoon freshly ground black pepper

1 large egg, lightly beaten

½ cup (one-third of 12-ounce-can) soda water or gluten-free beer, such as Bard's Tale or Redbridge

½ cup white rice flour, for dredging

Peanut oil, for frying

4 large russet potatoes, peeled and cut into ¹⁄₁₆-inch slices

1½ pounds cod or haddock fillets, patted dry with paper towels and cut in 3-inch pieces

Additional salt to taste

1 Place a rack in the middle of the oven. Preheat the oven to 200°F. Line a 13 × 9-inch baking sheet (not nonstick) with foil; set aside.

2 In a large mixing bowl, make the batter by combining the cornstarch, baking powder, salt, pepper, and egg. Pour in the soda water and whisk to a smooth batter; set aside. Spread the rice flour on a plate; set aside.

3 In a deep saucepan or deep fryer, heat 3 inches of oil to 360°F. Pat the potatoes dry with paper towels. Add the potatoes to the oil and fry in batches 2 to 3 minutes or until nicely browned. Remove the chips with a slotted spoon and drain on paper towels. Transfer chips to the prepared baking sheet and place in the oven to keep warm. Let oil return to 360°F between batches.

4 Dredge the fish pieces in the rice flour and then dip them into the batter. Carefully lay the battered fish in the bubbling oil and fry 4 to 5 minutes, or until crispy and brown and the fish is just opaque when cut in the thickest part or flakes easily with a fork. Remove the fish with a slotted spoon and drain on paper towels. Sprinkle lightly with salt. If you are frying a lot of fish, place fried fish on baking sheet with chips in the oven to keep warm. Serve immediately.

Braised Halibut in Curry Broth

MAKES 4 SERVINGS

Substitute grouper or any other thick, white fish, if you can't find halibut. I like to serve this light, flavorful dish with a scoop of brown basmati rice. Increase the curry powder for a spicier dish. Cook the fish in a skillet that is just big enough so that all pieces are immersed in the broth.

2 teaspoons canola oil

4 shallots, finely chopped (about ¾ cup)

2 teaspoons curry powder, or more to taste

2 cups gluten-free, low-sodium chicken broth, such as Swanson's Natural Goodness, or homemade Chicken Broth (page 676)

½ cup light coconut milk

2 tablespoons grated fresh ginger

1 tablespoon packed light brown sugar

1 large garlic clove, minced

¾ teaspoon salt, divided

4 halibut fillets (about 6 ounces each)

1 cup red bell pepper, cut in matchsticks

1 cup yellow bell pepper, cut in matchsticks

½ cup coarsely chopped fresh cilantro leaves

2 green onions, thinly sliced

2 tablespoons fresh lime juice

Additional salt and freshly ground black pepper to taste

1 In a medium skillet, heat the oil over medium heat. Add the shallots and cook 3 to 5 minutes, stirring occasionally, until they are soft and translucent. Add the curry powder and cook 30 seconds, stirring constantly. Add the broth, coconut milk, ginger, brown sugar, garlic, and ½ teaspoon of the salt; simmer 5 to 10 minutes, or until the liquid has reduced to 2 cups.

2 Sprinkle the halibut fillets with the remaining ¼ teaspoon salt. Arrange the fillets in the skillet. Add the bell pepper around the fillets. Cover and cook 8 to 10 minutes or until the fish is just barely opaque when cut in the thickest part or flakes easily with a fork.

3 With a slotted spatula, transfer each fillet to a warmed soup bowl. Stir the cilantro, green onions, and lime juice into the sauce and season to taste with more salt and pepper, if necessary. Ladle the sauce over the fish and serve immediately.

Braised Salmon on a Bed of Leeks and Tomatoes with Dill

MAKES 4 SERVINGS

Braising is a cooking method not often used with fish, yet it works wonderfully. The beauty of this dish is that it cooks with little tending from you, freeing you to work on other parts of the meal. And, it's fail-proof. After the allotted cooking time, simply remove it from the heat and let it sit, covered, in the braising liquid until you're ready to serve it. Leeks are often forgotten as a vegetable, but they make a very tasty base for the salmon.

1 tablespoon olive oil

2 large leeks, cleaned and chopped

2 garlic cloves, minced

1 cup dry white wine

½ cup chopped tomato (from 1 large tomato)

1 tablespoon chopped fresh dill, divided, or 1 teaspoon dried, divided

¼ teaspoon salt

¼ teaspoon freshly ground black pepper

4 salmon fillets (about 4 ounces each)

1 teaspoon cornstarch whisked into 1 tablespoon cold water until smooth

1 lemon, quartered

1 In a heavy skillet, heat the oil over medium-high heat. Cook leeks until softened, about 5 minutes. Add garlic, wine, tomato, ⅔ of the dill, salt, and pepper and bring to boil.

2 Push leeks and tomatoes to edges of pan. Add salmon, skin side down. Reduce heat to medium-low and simmer, covered, about 8 to 10 minutes depending on the thickness of the fish or until the fish is just barely opaque when cut in the thickest part or flakes easily with a fork. Transfer salmon to plate and cover with foil to keep warm.

3 Simmer leek-tomato sauce uncovered over medium heat to reduce liquids. For thicker sauce, whisk in just enough cornstarch mixture to thicken sauce. Return salmon to skillet to bring it to serving temperature. Serve salmon on bed of leek-tomato mixture, sprinkled with remaining ⅓ of the dill and garnish with lemon wedges.

Poached Salmon with Cucumber-Dill Sauce

MAKES 4 SERVINGS

Poached salmon is great hot or cold. But I especially like to serve it in the summer when I don't want to heat up the kitchen while preparing a meal. If you poach it in the cool of the morning and chill it for a few hours, you can serve it as a luncheon or supper dish. The cooling cucumber-dill sauce is a refreshing complement.

SALMON

1½ cups white wine

1 small onion, peeled and sliced

1 large carrot, peeled and sliced

1 fresh lemon, sliced

2 teaspoons salt

2 bay leaves

1 garlic clove, minced

1 bunch fresh parsley (no need to chop)

1 bunch fresh thyme (no need to chop)

4 skin-on salmon fillets (about 1 pound total)

1 tablespoon chopped fresh parsley, for garnish

SAUCE

½ cup plain low-fat yogurt or soy yogurt

½ cup peeled and chopped cucumber

1 tablespoon grated onion

1 tablespoon drained capers, minced

1 tablespoon fresh lemon juice

1 small garlic clove, minced

1 teaspoon chopped fresh dill

⅛ teaspoon salt or to taste

1 Prepare the salmon: Bring wine, onion, carrot, lemon, salt, bay leaves, garlic, parsley, and thyme to boil in Dutch oven or other deep, heavy pot with a tight-fitting lid wide enough to hold 4 salmon fillets in a single layer. Reduce heat to low and simmer, covered, 15 minutes.

2 Place salmon in Dutch oven, adding water if necessary to make sure salmon is covered by liquid. Cover and cook until salmon is opaque and flakes easily, about 8 to 10 minutes, depending on the thickness of the fish or until the fish is just barely opaque when cut in the thickest part. Using a wide, slotted spatula, carefully transfer salmon from poaching liquid to serving platter. Discard poaching liquid and bay leaves.

3 While the fish poaches, make the sauce: In a small bowl, combine yogurt, cucumber, onion, capers, lemon juice, garlic, dill, and salt. Stir until ingredients are thoroughly combined. Cover and refrigerate until ready to use. Serve salmon warm or cold, with sauce and garnished with fresh parsley.

Salmon Simmered in Beer

MAKES 4 SERVINGS

Now that gluten-free beer is available, you can enjoy main dishes cooked in this flavorful liquid. If you don't want to use the grill, simmer the salmon in a covered skillet.

1 pound salmon fillet or 4 salmon steaks

2 tablespoons packed light brown sugar

2 teaspoons onion powder

1 teaspoon salt

½ teaspoon seafood seasoning, such as McCormick's Old Bay

½ teaspoon freshly ground black pepper

1 bottle (12 ounces) gluten-free beer, such as Bard's Tale or Redbridge

1 fresh lemon, quartered, for garnish

1 Place a barbecue grill about 6 inches away from the heat source. Preheat the grill to medium-high heat. Place salmon in a heavy-duty aluminum-foil baking pan that is large enough to hold all of the salmon in a single layer. In a small bowl, combine sugar, onion powder, salt, seafood seasoning, and pepper until thoroughly blended. Sprinkle around and over salmon. Pour beer into the pan. Cover pan tightly with aluminum foil.

2 Cook salmon on grill until the fish is just barely opaque when cut in the thickest part or flakes easily with a fork, about 8 to 12 minutes, depending on the thickness of the fish. Spoon beer over salmon, then remove salmon from beer and serve immediately with a wedge of lemon.

STIR-FRIES, CASSEROLES, AND MIXED SEAFOOD

Pan-Fried Coconut Shrimp with Apricot-Mustard Dip

MAKES 4 SERVINGS

This dish is delicious and quick to make since the shrimp cooks quickly. The dry grittiness of white rice flour makes it a perfect choice for coating the shrimp, making it nice and crunchy.

DIP

½ cup apricot preserves
2 tablespoons mayonnaise
1 teaspoon Dijon mustard

SHRIMP

1 pound medium shrimp, peeled and deveined, tails on
1 large egg, at room temperature
⅔ cup sparkling water or gluten-free beer, such as Bard's Tale or Redbridge
1½ teaspoons baking powder
1 cup white rice flour, divided
¼ teaspoon Creole seasoning, such as Spice Hunter Cajun Creole (optional)
1 small package (7 ounces or about 2 cups) flaked coconut
¼ cup canola oil or peanut foil, for frying

1 Make the dip: In a small bowl, stir together the apricot preserves, mayonnaise, and mustard; set aside at room temperature.

2 Prepare the shrimp: Pat the shrimp dry with paper towels. In a medium bowl, whisk together the egg, water, baking powder, ½ cup of the white rice flour, and the Creole spice, if using, until smooth. Place the remaining ½ cup white rice flour in a shallow dish. Place the coconut in a separate shallow dish. Roll the shrimp in the white rice flour, shake off any excess, then dip each shrimp

in the batter and turn to coat thoroughly. Roll the shrimp in the coconut until all sides are coated.

3 In a large skillet, heat the oil over medium-high heat. For best results, the oil should be at 360°F, Add the shrimp and cook about 2 minutes per side, or until cooked through and opaque. Serve immediately with the dip.

Pan-Seared Shrimp with Andouille Sausage

MAKES 4 SERVINGS

Flavorful spices and sausage blend with pan-seared shrimp for a dish that can be ready in less than 15 minutes and is perfect served over white rice.

2 tablespoons olive oil
1 pound medium shrimp, peeled, and deveined
1 gluten-free andouille sausage link, such as Johnsonville, cut in ¼-inch slices
1 small onion, peeled and cut in ¼-inch vertical slices
½ red bell pepper, sliced vertically in ¼-inch strips
2 garlic cloves, minced
¾ cup gluten-free, low-sodium chicken broth, such as Swanson's Natural Goodness, or homemade Chicken Broth (page 676)
¼ cup Dijon mustard
1 tablespoon Creole seasoning, such as Spice Hunter Cajun Creole
1 teaspoon gluten-free Worcestershire sauce, such as French's
1 teaspoon chopped fresh thyme or ½ teaspoon dried
Pinch allspice
4 cups hot cooked white rice
1 tablespoon chopped fresh parsley, for garnish

1 In a heavy skillet, heat 1 tablespoon of the oil over medium heat. Cook shrimp until pink and lightly seared, about one minute per side. Transfer shrimp to plate.

2 In the same skillet, add remaining tablespoon of oil and sausage, onion, bell pepper, and garlic.

Cook over medium heat until sausage is lightly browned and onion begins to soften.

3 Add broth, mustard, Creole seasoning, Worcestershire sauce, thyme, and allspice to skillet. Bring mixture to boil and cook 2 minutes. Return shrimp to skillet and heat to serving temperature. Serve over hot cooked rice, garnished with parsley.

Lemon-Dijon Grilled Prawns
MAKES 4 SERVINGS

Prawns are large shrimp. You can prepare the delightfully lemony marinade ahead of time, if you like.

2 tablespoons chopped fresh dill or 1 tablespoon dried
2 tablespoons rice wine vinegar
Juice and grated zest of 1 lemon
1 teaspoon salt
½ teaspoon lemon pepper
1 tablespoon honey
1 tablespoon Dijon mustard
¼ teaspoon hot pepper sauce, such as Frank's
1 garlic clove, minced
¼ cup dry white wine
¼ cup extra-virgin olive oil
2 pounds jumbo shrimp, peeled and deveined, tails on
½ teaspoon freshly ground black pepper, for dusting
1 lemon, quartered, for garnish

1 In a blender, combine dill, vinegar, lemon juice and zest, salt, lemon pepper, honey, mustard, pepper sauce, garlic, and wine. Process until thoroughly blended. Add oil slowly while motor is running and process until mixture thickens slightly. Reserve ¼ cup of the marinade for basting.

2 Place remaining marinade in a glass dish or heavy-duty food-storage bag. Add shrimp, make sure they are thoroughly covered, and marinate 20 to 30 minutes. Remove shrimp from marinade and discard marinade.

3 Heat grill to medium-high heat. Place shrimp on grill and cook until done, about 2 minutes on each side, basting frequently with reserved ¼ cup marinade. Watch shrimp carefully because they will cook quickly and burn easily. Remove from heat, dust with pepper and serve with lemon wedges.

Shrimp and Grits
MAKES 4 SERVINGS

For a more flavorful version of this Southern dish, use half-and-half instead of milk or broth in the grits and stir in some white cheddar cheese or Parmesan cheese. If you don't want to use dairy, use soy or rice milk in place of the half-and-half and use a soy-based Parmesan cheese. The type of grits you buy will affect how long they need to cook. For example, instant grits cook in less than a minute while most regular grits take about 15 minutes. There are also long-cooking grits that take nearly 45 minutes, but I recommend the 15-minute variety.

3 cups 1% milk (cow's, rice, soy, potato, or nut) or gluten-free, low-sodium chicken broth, such as Swanson's Natural Goodness, or homemade Chicken Broth (page 676)
1 bay leaf
¾ cup gluten-free yellow cornmeal or grits, such as Albers, Lamb's Kinnikinnick, or Shiloh Farms
¼ teaspoon salt
¼ teaspoon freshly ground black pepper
2 tablespoons unsalted butter or buttery spread, such as Earth Balance
1 tablespoon extra-virgin olive oil
1 small onion, finely chopped
1 link spicy gluten-free andouille sausage, such as Johnsonville, cut in ¼-inch slices
1 pound medium shrimp, peeled and deveined
1 garlic clove, minced
2 tablespoons chopped fresh parsley, for garnish

1 In a medium saucepan, bring milk to boil over medium-high heat. Stir in bay leaf, cornmeal, salt, and pepper. Reduce heat to low. Cook, stirring occasionally, until silky and smooth, about 10 minutes (cooking time may vary by type and brand of cornmeal).

2 While cornmeal cooks, in a medium, heavy skillet, heat butter and oil over medium heat. Add onion and sausage and cook until onions are tender and sausage is browned on both sides. Add shrimp and garlic and cook 4 to 5 minutes, or until shrimp turn pink. Stir shrimp mixture into grits, and continue cooking for 10 to 15 minutes over medium heat. Remove bay leaf. Serve hot, garnished with parsley.

Shrimp with Tabbouleh

MAKES 4 SERVINGS

Tabbouleh is traditionally made with bulgur, but whole grain brown rice makes a nutty and chewy substitute. If you're fortunate to have pots of fresh herbs outside your kitchen door, as I do, then it will be easy to prepare the herbs for this flavorful dish. If you can't find fresh herbs, use ⅓ the amount in dried herbs.

Juice and grated zest of 2 lemons
1 garlic clove, minced
¼ teaspoon salt
¼ teaspoon freshly ground black pepper
⅓ cup chopped fresh mint
⅓ cup chopped fresh basil
2 tablespoons chopped fresh dill
2 green onions, chopped
2 cups cooked brown rice (you may use instant)
20 cooked large shrimp, peeled and deveined
½ cup pine nuts, toasted
¼ cup feta cheese, crumbled

1 Place lemon juice and zest, garlic, salt, and pepper in shallow glass dish with tight-fitting lid. Stir

to combine. Add mint, basil, dill, and green onions. Toss to combine thoroughly.

2 Add rice and shrimp and marinate overnight or at least 8 hours. Just before serving add pine nuts and feta cheese and mix thoroughly.

Shrimp Creole

MAKES 4 SERVINGS

This dish is my idea of comfort food from the sea and I often serve it to guests. Although it is usually served on a mound of rice, I like to make an attractive presentation: I tightly pack white rice into a greased Bundt pan or angel food pan. Then I unmold it onto a serving platter and put hot cooked green peas in the center opening. The Shrimp Creole can be kept hot in a slow cooker or chafing dish for big dinners.

1 tablespoon olive oil
½ cup onion, chopped
1 cup finely chopped celery
½ cup diced green bell pepper
1 garlic clove, minced
1 can (28 ounces) petite, diced tomatoes, including juices
1 can (8 ounces) tomato sauce
1 teaspoon seafood seasoning, such as McCormick's Old Bay
1 teaspoon sugar
1 teaspoon chopped fresh oregano or ½ teaspoon dried
1 teaspoon chopped fresh basil or ½ teaspoon dried
⅛ teaspoon ground cayenne
1 pound medium shrimp, peeled and deveined
Additional salt and freshly ground pepper to taste
2 teaspoons cornstarch stirred into 1 tablespoon cold water (optional)
4 cups hot cooked white rice
¼ cup chopped fresh parsley

1 In a Dutch oven or other deep, heavy pot with a tight-fitting lid, heat oil. Add onion, celery, bell pepper, and garlic and cook over medium heat until tender, but not brown. Add tomatoes, tomato sauce, Old Bay seasoning, sugar, oregano, basil, and cayenne. Simmer, uncovered, 30 minutes. Sauce will reduce a bit.

2 Add shrimp, cover, and simmer 5 minutes more or until shrimp are cooked. Taste and add salt and pepper, if necessary. If sauce needs thickening, stir cornstarch mixture into sauce. Cook, stirring until mixture thickens slightly. Serve over hot cooked rice, garnished with chopped fresh parsley.

Shrimp deJonghe

MAKES 4 SERVINGS

Shrimp deJonghe is named after the Chicago restaurant in which it was first served. It is basically a shrimp casserole, topped with bread crumbs. As a young bride, I found this recipe in a booklet accompanying a wedding gift. At the time, I thought it was quite sophisticated; I have continued to make it over the years with a few adjustments and some new spices; it is still a favorite.

1 pound cooked large shrimp, shelled and deveined
1 cup gluten-free bread crumbs, such as Ener-G, or homemade Plain Bread Crumbs (page 117), divided
1 large garlic clove, minced
1 tablespoon finely diced fresh onion or 1 teaspoon dried minced onion
1 tablespoon chopped freshly parsley or 1 teaspoon dried
1 teaspoon chopped fresh tarragon or ½ teaspoon ground
½ teaspoon chopped fresh thyme or 1 teaspoon dried
½ teaspoon salt
¼ teaspoon freshly ground black pepper
⅛ teaspoon freshly grated nutmeg
¼ cup grated Parmesan cheese or soy alternative, such as Soyco
¼ cup (½ stick) unsalted butter or buttery spread, such as Earth Balance, melted
⅓ cup dry white wine
Dash of paprika

1 Place a rack in upper-middle position of the oven. Preheat the oven to 350°F. Generously grease a 1½- to 2-quart wide shallow ceramic baking dish. Arrange shrimp in the bottom of the dish.

2 In a bowl, combine the bread crumbs, garlic, onion, parsley, tarragon, thyme, salt, pepper, nutmeg, and Parmesan cheese, and toss to combine thoroughly. Stir in the melted butter and wine. Toss shrimp with all but ¼ cup of the bread crumb mixture. Distribute the remaining ¼ cup bread crumbs evenly over the shrimp. Sprinkle bread crumbs with paprika.

3 Bake 15 to 20 minutes or until the mixture is browned and bubbly. If the topping hasn't browned, place a broiler rack about 6 inches away from the heat source. Preheat the broiler. Place dish under broiler and broil, until the crumbs are golden brown, about 2 minutes. Serve immediately.

Shrimp Etouffée

MAKES 4 SERVINGS

In French, the word etouffée *(ay-too-FAY) means "smothered." This dish is often made with crawfish, but nost of us don't have access to this Southern shellfish so I use shrimp instead. Etouffée is similar to gumbo but it is spicier, thicker, and uses a darker roux. For best results, taste the etouffée before serving to determine whether more spices or salts and pepper are needed.*

2 tablespoons sorghum flour

2 tablespoons cornstarch

¼ cup canola oil

½ cup finely diced onion

1 rib celery, finely diced

¼ cup finely diced green bell pepper

1 garlic clove, minced

1 link (¼ pound) andouille sausage, such as
    Johnsonville, cut in ¼-inch slices

1 bottle (8 ounces) clam broth

1 cup dry white wine or gluten-free, low-sodium
    chicken broth, such as Swanson's Natural
    Goodness, or homemade Chicken Broth
    (page 676)

1 cup petite diced tomatoes, including juice

1 tablespoon gluten-free Worcestershire sauce, such
    as French's

2 teaspoons packed light brown sugar

¼ cup chopped fresh parsley

½ teaspoon Creole seasoning, such as Spice Hunter
    Cajun Creole

½ teaspoon chopped fresh thyme or ¼ teaspoon dried

1 bay leaf

½ pound cooked medium shrimp, peeled and deveined

1 Make the roux: In a 10-inch cast-iron skillet, sift together the sorghum flour and cornstarch. Add into the oil and whisk until smooth before turning on the heat. Cook over medium-low heat 30 to 35 minutes, constantly scraping back and forth with a flat metal spatula, rather than stirring. The roux will darken to light-beige; continue scraping back and forth as the roux gradually becomes dark brown. Add onion, celery, bell pepper, and garlic and cook, scraping back and forth occasionally with the spatula, until onion and bell pepper are softened, about 2 to 3 minutes. Remove skillet from heat.

2 In another small skillet, cook the sausage over medium heat until browned, about 2 to 3 minutes. Add to the cast-iron skillet, along with the broth, wine, tomatoes, Worcestershire sauce, brown sugar, parsley, Creole seasoning, thyme, and bay leaf. Increase heat to medium-high and bring to a boil.

Reduce the heat to low and simmer, covered, 15 to 20 minutes.

3 Add shrimp to the pot and cook until heated through. Taste and adjust seasonings, if necessary. Remove the bay leaf and serve hot.

Shrimp Newburg

MAKES 4 SERVINGS

Newburg typically refers to a sauce flavored with cheese, nutmeg, and sherry. It is wonderful on its own, but for added interest toss in one thinly sliced Andouille sausage for a little extra flavor.

1 tablespoon sweet rice flour

1 tablespoon cornstarch

2 cups whole milk or soy milk, divided

3 tablespoons unsalted butter or buttery spread,
    such as Earth Balance

3 large egg yolks

1 teaspoon seafood seasoning, such as McCormick's
    Old Bay

½ teaspoon salt

¼ teaspoon ground paprika

⅛ teaspoon freshly grated nutmeg

⅛ teaspoon ground cayenne

¼ teaspoon white pepper

1 pound cooked medium shrimp, peeled and deveined

¼ cup dry sherry

2 tablespoons fresh lemon juice

4 slices gluten-free toast (see Bread chapter) or
    homemade Waffles (page 9), toasted

1 tablespoon chopped chives or fresh parsley, for
    garnish

1 In a bowl, whisk sweet rice flour and cornstarch into ½ cup of the milk until it is very smooth. Add it to a medium saucepan, along with the remaining 1½ cups milk, butter, egg yolks, seafood seasoning, salt, paprika, nutmeg, cayenne, and white pepper.

2 Whisk the mixture over medium heat until it is smooth, continuing to cook and whisk until the mixture thickens, about 10 minutes. Remove the pan from the heat and add shrimp, sherry, and lemon juice. Reduce the heat to low, return the pan to the burner and bring the mixture to serving temperature, stirring constantly. Serve hot over toasted bread, or waffles. Garnish with chives or parsley.

Shrimp Scampi Ⓠ

MAKES 4 SERVINGS

Rich and flavorful, this is one of the easiest recipes to prepare; no wonder everyone loves it! Make your own at home and delight your family and guests. (It's also often a safe gluten-free choice in restaurants.)

1 tablespoon unsalted butter or buttery spread, such as Earth Balance
1 tablespoon extra-virgin olive oil
2 pounds large shrimp, peeled and deveined
4 garlic cloves, minced
½ cup dry white wine
½ teaspoon salt
¼ teaspoon crushed red pepper
¼ cup chopped fresh parsley
Grated zest and juice of 1 lemon
Freshly ground black pepper

1 In a large, heavy skillet, heat the butter and oil over medium heat. Add the shrimp and cook 1 minute. Add the garlic and sauté 1 minute more. Add the wine, salt, and red pepper and simmer 30 seconds. Add the parsley and lemon zest and juice and cook 30 seconds more, tossing to coat the shrimp thoroughly with the juices.

2 Serve hot with a dusting of pepper.

Shrimp Vindaloo

MAKES 4 SERVINGS

This is a typical Indian restaurant dish, but was actually brought to India by Portuguese traders. The term vindaloo *is used to describe a hot, vinegary curry. This recipe is an exuberantly flavorful way to satisfy your cravings for Indian food.*

Although pork is traditionally used in this dish, it is especially easy when you have precooked shrimp in the freezer.

1 teaspoon ground ginger
½ teaspoon dry mustard
½ teaspoon ground coriander
½ teaspoon ground cumin
½ teaspoon ground curry powder
½ teaspoon ground turmeric
½ teaspoon salt
¼ to ½ teaspoon ground cayenne
⅛ teaspoon ground cloves
2 tablespoons olive oil
1½ cups finely chopped onion
2 tablespoons minced peeled fresh ginger
2 garlic cloves, minced
1 can (14 to 15 ounces) or 1¾ cups gluten-free, low-sodium chicken broth, such as Swanson's Natural Goodness, or homemade Chicken Broth (page 676)
2 tablespoons red wine vinegar
¼ cup golden raisins, chopped
1 pound cooked medium shrimp, peeled and deveined
1 tablespoon cornstarch stirred into 2 tablespoons cold water until smooth (optional)
2 cups hot cooked brown rice
¼ cup chopped fresh cilantro, for garnish

1 In a small bowl or jar, combine the ground ginger, mustard, coriander, cumin, curry powder, turmeric, salt, cayenne, and cloves. Set aside.

2 In a large nonstick skillet, heat the oil over medium-high heat. Add onion and sauté for 2 minutes. Add fresh ginger and garlic and cook 20 seconds. Add spices; cook 30 seconds, stirring constantly. Stir in broth, vinegar, and raisins. Simmer, uncovered, 10 minutes. Add shrimp and cook until heated through, stirring occasionally. Thicken the vindaloo with cornstarch, if desired, and serve it over the rice, garnished with cilantro. Or, you can serve the vindaloo in a bowl as a broth-based dish, with a ½ cup cooked rice mound of shrimp mixture sitting in the broth.

Thai Shrimp Curry

MAKES 4 SERVINGS

Curry is the term typically used in Indian and other Asian countries to describe a spicy, saucy dish. Start out with the ½ teaspoon red curry paste and see how you like it. If you want it spicier, add a little more. You can always add more spice, but you can't remove the spice once it's in the dish.

2 tablespoons olive oil, divided
1 pound cooked medium shrimp, peeled and deveined
1 small red bell pepper, cored and cut into ¼-inch vertical slices
2 green onions, cut in ¼-inch slices
1 (2-inch) piece of fresh ginger, peeled and finely chopped
½ to 1 teaspoon Thai red curry paste, such as Taste of Thai
1 teaspoon Asian fish sauce, such as Thai Kitchen or Taste of Thai
1 can (14 ounces) unsweetened coconut milk
1 cup frozen green peas
4 cups hot cooked jasmine rice
1 tablespoon chopped fresh cilantro, for garnish
1 lime, quartered, for garnish

1 In a heavy skillet or wok, heat 1 tablespoon of the oil over medium heat. Add shrimp and cook until lightly seared, about one minute per side. Transfer shrimp to plate.

2 In the same skillet, add remaining tablespoon of oil and bell pepper, green onions, ginger, curry paste, and fish sauce. Cook over medium heat until onions start to soften, stirring constantly. Add coconut milk and cook 3 to 5 minutes more.

3 Return shrimp to pan, add peas and bring to serving temperature. Serve over hot rice, garnished with fresh cilantro and a squeeze of fresh lime juice.

Shrimp and Vegetable Tempura with Dipping Sauce

MAKES 4 SERVINGS

Long before I became gluten-free, I sat in a restaurant in Tokyo and blissfully ate piles of light and crispy tempura. This easy recipe allows me to relive that ecstasy—minus the Asian atmosphere and the gluten. You can use calamari or scallops instead of shrimp and any type of vegetables you wish; I have provided a list of suggestions for you below.

BATTER

1½ cups white rice flour, divided
¼ cup cornstarch
1 cup cold sparking mineral water
1 egg yolk, fresh from the refrigerator
Peanut oil, for frying
Salt for sprinkling

SHRIMP AND VEGETABLES

1 pound large shrimp, peeled, deveined, and butterflied, or calamari or scallops
6 thin asparagus stalks, tough ends trimmed off
⅓ pound broccoli, cut into 1-inch florets (1 cup)
2 medium carrots, peeled and sliced diagonally in very thin strips
1 Japanese eggplant, halved and cut in ¼-inch slices
1 sweet potato, peeled and cut in ¼-inch slices
1 cup mushrooms, thinly sliced
1 red bell pepper, seeded and cut in very thin strips
Salt for sprinkling

DIPPING SAUCE

2 tablespoons wheat-free tamari soy sauce, such as Crystal or San-J
1 tablespoon sherry
1 tablespoon rice wine vinegar
1 tablespoon water
1 teaspoon onion powder
1 teaspoon grated fresh ginger
1 teaspoon honey

1 Make the batter: Whisk together 1 cup of the rice flour and the cornstarch in a bowl. Whisk in the sparkling water until the batter is smooth. Add the egg yolk and whisk until the batter is the consistency of heavy cream.

2 Make the shrimp and vegetables: Heat 2 to 3 inches of oil to 375°F in a wok or deep fryer. Pat the fish and vegetables dry with paper towels and dust with the remaining ½ cup rice flour; shake off excess. Dip the shrimp and vegetable pieces into the batter and gently place 4 or 5 pieces of the same type of vegetable or fish at a time in the hot oil. Do not overcrowd the wok or fryer. Fry the shrimp, asparagus, broccoli, carrots, eggplant, potato, mushrooms, and bell pepper until golden brown, turning once, about 3 minutes. Between batches, skim off the small bits of batter that float in the oil. Drain the shrimp and vegetables on paper towels; sprinkle them with salt.

3 Make the dipping sauce: In a small bowl, whisk together the ingredients until smooth. Serve with the tempura.

Shrimp, Sausage, and Red Beans and Rice

MAKES 4 SERVINGS

Brown rice takes nearly an hour to cook, so start it first. Or, use instant brown rice to save some time. All you need with this dish is some French bread and a crisp mixed greens salad.

1 tablespoon olive oil
1 small onion, chopped
1 stalk celery, chopped
1 small green pepper, cored, seeded, and chopped
¼ pound gluten-free andouille sausage (1 link), such as Johnsonville, cut in ¼-inch slices
1 can (14 to 15 ounces) diced tomatoes, with juice
1 can (14 to 15 ounces) red beans, rinsed and drained
2 garlic cloves, mashed
1 teaspoon chopped fresh basil or ½ teaspoon dried
1 teaspoon chopped fresh oregano or ½ teaspoon dried
½ to 1 teaspoon hot pepper sauce, such as Frank's, or to taste
16 cooked medium shrimp, peeled and deveined
⅛ teaspoon ground allspice
4 cups hot cooked white or brown rice
¼ cup chopped cilantro

1 In a heavy, large skillet, heat oil over medium-high heat. Add onion, celery, green pepper, and sausage and cook, stirring frequently, until onion softens. Add tomatoes, beans, garlic, basil, oregano, and hot pepper sauce.

2 Bring to a boil over medium-high heat, reduce heat to low and simmer, covered, about 15 minutes. Add shrimp and allspice and cook 1 to 2 minutes or until shrimp is heated through. Serve over hot rice, garnished with cilantro.

Baked Scallops in White Wine

MAKES 4 SERVINGS

This lightly seasoned dish is perfect for those who like milder flavors or for menus with richer side dishes. The bread crumbs provide a nice crunchy contrast to the smooth scallops.

1½ pounds fresh sea scallops

½ teaspoon salt

½ teaspoon garlic powder

1 teaspoon paprika, divided

¼ teaspoon freshly ground white pepper

1 teaspoon olive oil

1 cup dry white wine

¼ cup finely chopped fresh thyme leaves

1 green onion finely chopped

1 can (8 ounces) sliced mushrooms

2 tablespoons unsalted butter or buttery spread, such as Earth Balance, or canola oil

¾ cup gluten-free bread crumbs, such as Ener-G, or homemade Plain Bread Crumbs (page 117)

2 tablespoons Parmesan cheese or soy alternative, such as Soyco

1 tablespoon chopped fresh parsley, for garnish

1 Generously grease four ovenproof 4-inch ramekins; set aside. Pat scallops dry with paper towels. Sprinkle with salt, garlic powder, ½ teaspoon of the paprika, and white paper.

2 In a heavy skillet, heat the oil over medium-high heat. Add the scallops and sear, about 2 minutes on each side until golden brown. Resist the urge to turn them too soon; they must brown fully to release from the pan. Transfer scallops to the prepared ramekins, dividing evenly.

3 Reduce heat to medium and add wine, thyme, onion, and mushrooms to skillet. Cook approximately 3 to 4 minutes, or until mixture reduces slightly. Divide evenly among four baking dishes. Mix butter, bread crumbs, and Parmesan cheese and sprinkle on top of each dish, dividing evenly. Dust each dish with remaining ½ teaspoon paprika, dividing evenly. Place ramekins on a baking sheet (not nonstick). Place a broiler rack about 6 inches away from the heat source. Preheat the broiler. and place sheet in the oven.

4 Broil 1 minute, or until bread crumbs are browned. Garnish each dish with a sprinkle of fresh parsley and serve immediately.

Pan-Seared Scallops with Caper Gremolata

MAKES 4 SERVINGS

Gremolata is a mixture of lemon, parsley, and garlic and complements these scallops beautifully in what is truly a very simple dish to prepare. Be sure to thoroughly dry the scallops or else their juices will simply steam, rather than brown them. If possible, buy scallops that aren't treated with sodium tripolyphosphate or STP. This treatment inhibits the browning process; part of the visual appeal of this dish is the dramatically browned surface of the scallops. This dish is lovely served on a bed of fluffy white basmati rice with a side of sautéed red, green, and yellow bell peppers.

GREMOLATA

Grated zest of 1 lemon (reserve juice for sauce)

2 tablespoons chopped parsley

1 small garlic clove, minced

1 tablespoon rinsed and drained capers

SCALLOPS

1 cup gluten-free, low-sodium chicken broth, such as Swanson's Natural Goodness, or homemade Chicken Broth (page 676)

2 teaspoons cornstarch

¼ teaspoon salt

¼ teaspoon freshly ground black pepper

1 tablespoon unsalted butter or buttery spread, such as Earth Balance, or canola oil

1½ pounds sea scallops, patted dry

4 cups hot cooked white basmati rice

1 Make the gremolata: In a small bowl, combine lemon zest, parsley, garlic, and capers. Toss together and set aside.

2 Prepare the scallops: Put ¼ cup of chicken broth in 2-cup measure and whisk in cornstarch until smooth. Add remaining broth, salt, and pepper, and whisk again. Set aside.

3 In a heavy skillet, melt the butter over medium-high heat. Add scallops and cook until browned, turning once, about 4 to 5 minutes. Transfer scallops to plate.

4 Add broth mixture and reserved lemon juice to skillet and bring to boil, stirring constantly until thickened. Remove from heat and add scallops. Add half of gremolata and toss gently. Serve with rice, sprinkled with remaining gremolata.

Pan-Seared Scallops with Risotto and Morels

MAKES 4 SERVINGS

I met Chef Aaron Flores, from Oakbrook, Illinois, years ago at a gluten-free conference. He wanted to learn more about gluten-free cooking to better meet the needs of his guests at Disneyland, where he was then a chef. He has since been a guest speaker at several gluten-free group conferences and continues to delight guests with his gluten-free menus. You will need to prepare the risotto ahead of time, omitting the saffron. Morels are a special mushroom with wonderful flavor; you can substitute other exotic mushrooms such as shitake.

RISOTTO AND MORELS

2 cups Saffron Risotto (page 222), saffron omitted

1 tablespoon olive oil

2 garlic cloves, minced

1 shallot minced

½ pound morels

Salt and freshly ground pepper, to taste

½ cup white wine

2 cups gluten-free, low-sodium chicken broth, such as Swanson's Natural Goodness, or homemade Chicken Broth (page 676), hot

¼ cup heavy cream or soy milk

2 tablespoons unsalted butter or buttery spread, such as Earth Balance

Juice of 1½ lemons

SCALLOP SAUCE

2 tablespoons olive oil, divided

¼ cup toasted walnuts

2 teaspoons chopped fresh thyme

Salt and freshly ground pepper, to taste

SCALLOPS

1 pound sea scallops

Salt and freshly ground pepper, to taste

1 tablespoon chopped fresh parsley, for garnish

Grated zest of 1 orange, for garnish

1 Make the risotto and morels: Prepare the risotto, but omit the saffron; set aside. In a medium skillet, heat the olive oil over medium heat. Add the garlic and shallots and sauté until translucent, about 3 to 5 minutes. Add the morels and season with salt and pepper. Add the 2 cups risotto and toss. Add the white wine and chicken broth and simmer, covered, for 10 to 12 minutes. Stir in the cream, butter, and lemon juice. Season again with salt and pepper; set aside, covered to keep warm.

2 Make the sauce: In a small saucepan, heat 1 tablespoon of the oil over medium heat. Add the toasted walnuts, thyme, and a pinch of salt and black pepper. Toss together, remove pan from heat; set aside, covered to keep warm.

3 Prepare the scallops: Pat the scallops dry and season both sides with salt and pepper. Add the remaining tablespoon of olive oil to a medium skillet and cook the scallops for 4 minutes on each side or until golden brown.

4 To serve, divide the risotto among 4 large, shallow soup bowls. Place an equal number of scallops on top of each bowl. Spoon sauce on top and garnish with parsley and orange zest. Serve immediately.

Scallop and Lobster Stir-Fry

MAKES 4 SERVINGS

Stir fries are a creative way to blend delicious flavors, interesting textures, and appealing colors. For added interest, cut the vegetables in differing shapes—the onions, carrots, and snow peas in diagonals and the red bell pepper in long, narrow strips. If scallops and lobster aren't available, use shrimp and chunks of swordfish instead.

1 tablespoon olive oil

1 teaspoon sesame oil

3 green onions, diagonally cut in 1-inch pieces

2 medium carrots, diagonally cut in ½-inch pieces

1 cup fresh snow peas, cut in half diagonally

1 small red bell pepper, cut vertically in ¼ -inch strips

1 small yellow bell pepper, cut vertically in ¼-inch strips

¼ cup wheat-free tamari soy sauce, such as Crystal or San-J

¼ cup fresh lemon juice

¼ cup water

1 tablespoon grated lemon zest

1 tablespoon honey or agave nectar

½ teaspoon crushed red pepper

2 garlic cloves, minced

1 teaspoon grated fresh ginger

1 tablespoon cornstarch

½ pound cooked lobster

½ pound cooked scallops

4 cups hot cooked brown rice

Additional chopped green onion and lemon peel strips for garnish

1 In a heavy skillet, heat the olive oil and sesame oil over medium-high heat. Add the onions and carrots and cook, stirring constantly, until crisp-tender, about 3 to 5 minutes. Add the snow peas and bell peppers and cook, stirring constantly, another minute.

2 In a small bowl, whisk soy sauce, lemon juice, water, lemon zest, honey, crushed red peppers, garlic, ginger, and cornstarch until smooth. Reduce the heat to medium, stir the sauce into the vegetables, and cook, stirring constantly, just until thickened.

3 Add the lobster and scallops to the skillet and simmer gently, without stirring, until heated through. Serve immediately over hot cooked rice. Garnish with additional chopped green onions and lemon strips.

Crab and Spinach Enchiladas

MAKES 4 SERVINGS (8 ENCHILADAS)

This recipe uses half of a 1-pound can of lump crabmeat, leaving you the remaining half can to use in crab cakes or seafood chowder later in the week.

ENCHILADA SAUCE

2 cans (8 ounces) tomato sauce

1 teaspoon red chili powder, such as Dixon, medium

½ teaspoon chipotle chile powder, such as McCormick's, or homemade Chipotle Adobo Sauce (page 673), optional

½ teaspoon sugar

½ teaspoon ground cumin

1 teaspoon chopped fresh oregano or ½ teaspoon ground oregano

1 small garlic clove, minced, or ¼ teaspoon garlic powder

¼ teaspoon salt

ENCHILADAS

2 cups (½ of 1-pound can) lump crabmeat, such as Phillip's, picked over for shells and cartilage

5 ounces (½ of 10 ounce box) frozen chopped spinach, squeezed dry

2 cups (about 8 ounces) shredded Monterey Jack cheese or cheese alternative, such as Vegan Gourmet, divided

1 large egg

1 teaspoon Southwest or fajita seasoning, such as McCormick's

Enchilada Sauce (above) or 1 jar (16 ounces) gluten-free medium-hot tomato salsa, such as Albertson's, Hy-Vee, Newman's Own, or Publix

¼ cup canola or corn oil

8 gluten-free white corn tortillas, such as Tamxico

¼ cup sour cream or sour cream alternative, such as Tofutti, for garnish

1 Make the sauce: Place all the ingredients in a small saucepan and bring to a boil over medium-heat high. Reduce heat to low, cover, and simmer 10 minutes. Keep warm.

2 Make the enchiladas: Place a rack in the middle of the oven. Preheat the oven to 350°F. Generously grease an 11 × 7-inch baking dish; set aside.

3 In a medium bowl, combine the crabmeat, spinach, 1 cup of the cheese, egg, seasoning, and ½ cup of the enchilada sauce. Toss the ingredients until thoroughly blended.

4 In a medium skillet, heat the oil over low heat. Using tongs, dip each tortilla—one at a time—into the hot oil just until they are limp and pliable, about 5 seconds. Or, steam the tortillas—one at a time—on a splatter screen over simmering water (see How to Soften Tortillas, page 189).

5 Spread ¼ cup of the enchilada sauce over the bottom of the baking dish. Fill each tortilla with an equal amount of the crab filling. Roll each tortilla up and arrange it in the dish, seam side down. Pour the remaining 1¼ cups enchilada sauce evenly over the top. Cover the dish with foil.

6 Bake 15 to 20 minutes or until the enchiladas are heated through. Remove the foil and sprinkle with remaining 1 cup of cheese. Return the dish

to the oven and bake 5 to 10 minutes more or until the cheese is melted. Serve hot, garnished with a dollop of sour cream.

Crab Cakes with Rémoulade Sauce

MAKES 4 SERVINGS (2 CRAB CAKES EACH)

A rémoulade is an herb-flavored mayonnaise that complements fish extremely well. Shape the mixture into 6 mini-cakes!

SAUCE

½ cup mayonnaise

2 green onions, finely chopped

2 teaspoons rinsed and chopped capers

1 tablespoon sweet pickle relish

1 tablespoon Dijon mustard

1 tablespoon chopped fresh parsley

1 small garlic clove, minced

¼ teaspoon white pepper

CRAB CAKES

1 cup gluten-free bread crumbs, such as Ener-G, or homemade Plain Bread Crumbs (page 117)

2 tablespoons finely chopped red bell pepper

¼ cup finely chopped onion

2 tablespoons finely chopped celery

2 tablespoons mayonnaise

2 tablespoons chopped fresh parsley or 1 tablespoon dried

1 tablespoon Dijon mustard

1 large egg

1 tablespoon fresh lemon juice

2 teaspoons gluten-free Worcestershire sauce, such as French's

2 teaspoons seafood seasoning, such as McCormick's Old Bay

½ teaspoon salt

¼ teaspoon ground cayenne

1 pound lump crabmeat, such as Phillips, picked over for shells and cartilage

2 tablespoons canola oil for frying

Lemon wedges

1 Make the sauce: In a small bowl, combine mayonnaise, green onions, capers, relish, mustard, parsley, garlic, and white pepper. Refrigerate until serving time.

2 Make the crab cakes: Prepare the bread crumbs; set aside. Then, place a rack in the middle of the oven. Preheat the oven to 300°F. In a heavy skillet over medium heat, sauté red bell pepper, onion; and celery until soft, about 5 minutes.

3 In a large bowl, combine sautéed vegetables with mayonnaise, parsley, mustard, egg, lemon juice, Worcestershire sauce, seafood seasoning, salt, and cayenne. Gently fold in crabmeat and bread crumbs.

4 Shape mixture into 8 large cakes about 1 inch thick. The crab cakes can be refrigerated overnight at this point, if needed.

5 In a large ovenproof skillet, heat the oil over medium-high heat. Add crab cakes and cook over moderate heat until golden and crisp, 2 to 3 minutes per side. Transfer crab cakes to preheated oven to keep warm until serving time. Serve with lemon wedges and the rémoulade sauce or your favorite gluten-free cocktail sauce.

Southwestern Crab Cakes with Spicy Avocado Sauce

MAKES 4 SERVINGS (2 CRAB CAKES EACH)

These crab cakes are moist inside, but holding them in the oven until serving time makes the crust a little crispier. Most crab cake recipes call for chilling them before frying to make the cakes less likely to fall apart, but I sometimes skip that step. Simply using two spatulas for turning the cakes works fine. Be sure to wear rubber gloves when cutting the jalapeño to avoid transferring the chile oil to your skin or face.

CRAB CAKES

1 cup gluten-free bread crumbs, such as Ener-G, or homemade Plain Bread Crumbs (page 117)

2 tablespoons mayonnaise

1 tablespoon dried minced onion or ¼ cup finely chopped onion

2 tablespoons chopped cilantro

1 tablespoon Dijon mustard

2 teaspoons Mexican seasoning, such as McCormick's

1 large egg

1 tablespoon gluten-free Worcestershire sauce, such as French's

1 tablespoon fresh lime juice

½ teaspoon ground coriander

½ teaspoon salt

¼ teaspoon ground cayenne

1 can (4 ounces) mild diced green chiles

1 small jalapeno chile, finely diced (optional)

1 pound lump crabmeat, such as Phillips, picked over for shells and cartilage

2 tablespoons canola oil for frying

Lime wedges

SAUCE

½ cup mayonnaise

1 ripe avocado, mashed

1 tablespoon fresh lime juice

4 drops hot pepper sauce such as Frank's, or to taste

⅛ teaspoon salt

1 Make the crab cakes: Prepare the bread crumbs; set aside. Then, place a rack in the middle of the oven. Preheat the oven to 300°F. In a large bowl, combine mayonnaise, onion, cilantro, mustard, Mexican seasoning, egg, Worcestershire sauce, lime juice, coriander, salt, cayenne, green chiles, and jalapeno (if using). Gently fold in crabmeat and bread crumbs.

2 Shape mixture into 8 large cakes, about 1 inch thick. The crab cakes can be refrigerated overnight at this point, if needed.

3 In a large ovenproof skillet, heat the oil over medium-high heat. Add crab cakes and cook over moderate heat until golden and crisp, 2 to 3 minutes per side. Transfer crab cakes to oven to keep warm until serving time.

4 Make the sauce: In a small bowl, blend together the mayonnaise, avocado, lime juice, hot pepper sauce, and salt until well blended. Remove the crab cakes from the oven and serve hot with the sauce and lime wedges.

Crab Casserole

MAKES 4 SERVINGS

This recipe comes together fairly quickly. Pair it with a salad and some gluten-free bread to make a delicious meal. Although it is good year-round, I especially like to make it in the summer when zucchini and tomatoes are at their best.

2 tablespoons olive oil

1 small red bell pepper, cored, seeded, and chopped

2 stalks celery, chopped

1 small zucchini, thinly sliced

3 medium ripe tomatoes, seeded and chopped

1 cup shredded Swiss, Gruyère, or Manchego cheese, or cheese alternative, such as Vegan Gourmet

1 heaping tablespoon chopped onion or 1 teaspoon dried minced onion

1 teaspoon salt

1 teaspoon freshly ground black pepper

2 teaspoons chopped fresh basil or 1 teaspoon dried

¼ teaspoon garlic powder

1 cup gluten-free bread crumbs, such as Ener-G, or homemade Plain Bread Crumbs (page 117), divided

½ cup grated Parmesan cheese or soy alternative, such as Soyco, divided

½ pound lump crabmeat, such as Phillips, picked over for shells and cartilage

Cooking spray

1 Place a rack in the middle of the oven. Preheat the oven to 375°F. Generously grease a 2-quart casserole.

2 In a heavy skillet over medium-low heat, sauté bell pepper, celery, and zucchini in olive oil until vegetables are soft—about 3 to 5 minutes. Remove from heat.

3 In a large bowl, combine tomatoes, shredded cheese, onion, salt, pepper, basil, garlic, ¾ cup of the bread crumbs, and ¼ cup of the Parmesan cheese. Gently stir together with spatula. Add sautéed vegetables and crabmeat. Mix lightly, but thoroughly. Turn mixture into prepared casserole. Sprinkle top with remaining bread crumbs and remaining ¼ cup Parmesan cheese. Coat with cooking spray.

4 Bake, uncovered, 35 to 40 minutes. Remove from oven and let stand 5 minutes before serving.

Deviled Crab

MAKES 4 SERVINGS

The term deviled *means that the crab is minced and tossed with a spicy dressing or sauce. Serve this dish as a light lunch or supper, with a crisp tossed salad and gluten-free French bread. You can use fresh crab, but I find the Phillips brand in 1-pound cans to be a terrific time-saver.*

½ cup (1 stick) unsalted butter or buttery spread, such as Earth Balance

½ cup finely chopped onion

½ cup finely chopped celery

1 pound lump crabmeat, such as Phillips, picked over for shells and cartilage

2 tablespoons finely chopped fresh parsley

1 teaspoon Dijon mustard

¼ teaspoon salt

⅛ teaspoon freshly grated nutmeg

⅛ teaspoon ground cayenne

2 tablespoons fresh lemon juice

2 tablespoons medium-dry sherry

1 cup gluten-free bread crumbs, such as Ener-G, or homemade Plain Bread Crumbs (page 117)

2 tablespoons grated Parmesan cheese or soy alternative, such as Soyco

Dash of paprika for garnish

1 lemon, quartered, to squeeze on crab after baking

1 Place a rack in the middle of the oven. Preheat the oven to 425°F. In a heavy skillet, melt the butter over medium-low, removing 6 tablespoons once butter is melted to reserve for topping. Cook onion and celery in remaining 2 tablespoons butter over medium-low heat until transparent, about 3 to 5 minutes.

2 In a bowl, combine onion and celery with crabmeat, parsley, mustard, salt, nutmeg, and cayenne. Toss to mix thoroughly. Combine lemon juice and sherry, pour over crab mixture and toss again. Combine 6 tablespoons reserved melted butter with bread crumbs and Parmesan cheese. Gently stir ½ cup bread crumb mixture into crab mixture.

3 Divided crab mixture among four 4-ounce ramekins. Sprinkle remaining ½ cup bread crumb mixture over crab, 2 tablespoons per ramekin. Dust with paprika. Place ramekins on baking sheet.

4 Bake until mixture is bubbling and bread crumbs are golden brown, about 10 minutes. Serve immediately with a squeeze of lemon.

Fried Calamari

MAKES 4 SERVINGS

Fried calamari, or squid, is very popular because of its crunchy coating. You can find fresh calamari at your local seafood market or in the frozen seafood section of your grocery store. Serve fried calamari by itself, with your favorite dip (such as a marinara sauce), or added to mixed greens salads after tossing with the salad dressing. Eat it right after it's fried; once it becomes cool, the coating becomes soggy and the calamari tastes rubbery.

¾ cup cornstarch
½ teaspoon baking powder
½ teaspoon salt
½ teaspoon freshly ground black pepper
1 large egg, lightly beaten
½ cup (one-third of 12-ounce-can) soda water
1 cup white rice flour, for dredging
½ teaspoon seafood seasoning, such as McCormick's Old Bay
1 pound cleaned calamari, patted dry with paper towels with tubes cut into ¼-inch rings
Additional salt to taste

1 Place a rack in the middle of the oven. Preheat the oven to 200°F. Line a rimmed 13 × 9-inch baking sheet (not nonstick) with foil; set aside.

2 In a large mixing bowl, make the batter by combining the cornstarch, baking powder, salt, pepper, and egg. Whisk in the soda water until the mixture is smooth; set aside. Combine the rice flour and seasoning and spread on a plate; set aside.

3 In a deep saucepan or deep fryer, heat 3 inches of the oil to 360°F. Dredge the calamari in the rice flour and then dip each piece into the batter. Carefully lay it in the bubbling oil and fry 4 to 5 minutes, or until the calamari is light brown and crispy. Remove the calamari with a slotted spoon and drain it on paper towels. Sprinkle lightly with salt immediately after removing it from the oil. If you are frying a lot of calamari, place the fried calamari on the baking sheet and keep it warm in the preheated oven. Serve immediately.

Tuna Croquettes

MAKES 4 SERVINGS

Fresh tuna fillets really brighten this dish, but if that's not possible then use four (8-ounce) cans of tuna (drained). Use oil-packed tuna for fuller flavor.

1 pound tuna fillets, skinned and cut into 2-inch pieces
½ cup gluten-free bread crumbs, such as Ener-G, or homemade Plain Bread Crumbs (page 117)
¼ cup mayonnaise
2 finely chopped green onions
1 garlic clove, minced
2 tablespoons chopped fresh herbs, such as dill or flat-leaf parsley
1 tablespoon Dijon mustard
1 tablespoon fresh lemon juice
1 large egg
2 dashes hot pepper sauce, such as Frank's
½ teaspoon salt or celery salt
½ teaspoon freshly ground black pepper
¼ cup white rice flour, for coating
2 tablespoons canola or other vegetable oil

1 Place tuna in a food processor and pulse briefly until chopped medium fine, then transfer it to a bowl. If the fish is chopped too fine, the croquettes will be dry.

2 In a medium bowl, place the tuna and add the bread crumbs, mayonnaise, green onions, garlic, herbs, mustard, lemon juice, egg, hot pepper sauce, salt, and pepper. Mix thoroughly with your hands or a wooden spoon. Shape the mixture into 4 patties, each about ¾ inch thick. Spread the rice flour on a plate and dip the patties in it, one at a time, to coat on both sides, shaking off any excess.

3 Heat the oil in a large heavy skillet over medium heat. Fry the croquettes until cooked through and golden brown on both sides, about 5 minutes per side. Transfer them to paper towels to drain; serve immediately.

Salmon Patties

MAKES 6 PATTIES

These patties, sometimes called croquettes, fry up quickly and are a good choice for nights when you don't have much time to fix dinner. Make the patties the night before and chill them. If you don't have bread crumbs on hand, just tear 2 slices of gluten-free bread into 1-inch pieces and quickly shred them in your food processor. While you're at it, make a little extra and freeze it for another recipe.

1 can (15 ounces) canned salmon or 1 pound cooked salmon, chilled and de-boned
1 rib celery, finely chopped
2 tablespoons chopped fresh parsley or 1 tablespoon dried
½ cup finely chopped onion
¾ cup mayonnaise or salad dressing
1 cup gluten-free bread crumbs, such as Ener-G, or homemade Plain Bread Crumbs (page 117)
1 tablespoon capers (optional)
1 tablespoon gluten-free Worcestershire sauce, such as French's
½ teaspoon celery salt
¼ teaspoon garlic powder
¼ teaspoon ground cayenne
¼ teaspoon freshly ground black pepper
2 tablespoons canola oil

1 In a medium bowl, use a fork to flake the salmon. Add the celery, parsley, onions, mayonnaise, bread crumbs, capers (if using), Worcestershire sauce, celery salt, garlic powder, cayenne, and pepper and combine thoroughly. Shape into 8 patties, about ½ cup each. Place patties on a plate, cover tightly, and chill for at least 1 hour or overnight. Or, place in freezer for 15 minutes. (If you don't have time to chill the patties, proceed to Step 2, but the patties will be easier to handle if they're chilled.)

2 In a large, heavy skillet or flat grill pan, heat the oil over medium-high heat. Gently place chilled patties in skillet and cook until browned, about 5 to 7 minutes. Turn and cook until browned on the other side. Drain on paper towels. Serve immediately.

Seafood Gumbo

MAKES 4 SERVINGS

There are several steps to making a gumbo, so allow plenty of time. First, make the shrimp stock—the best gumbo is made from homemade Shrimp Stock (page 676) using the shells from the shrimp. But you can also use clam broth instead. Gumbo also requires a roux, which is just thickened, browned gravy. Both the shrimp stock and the roux can be made ahead and refrigerated. Serve this southern classic on cooked white rice with a bottle of hot pepper sauce nearby.

1½ pounds large shrimp in shell, peeled and deveined; shells reserved to make Shrimp Stock (page 676)

2 tablespoons canola oil or corn oil

2 tablespoons corn flour (grind gluten-free cornmeal, such as Albers, Lamb's, Kinnikinnick, or Shiloh Farms, with coffee grinder)

2 tablespoons cornstarch

1 large onion, chopped

1 large garlic clove, minced

1 rib celery, chopped

½ cup chopped green bell pepper

¼ pound (1 link) gluten-free andouille sausage, such as Johnsonville, cut in ¼-inch pieces

1 teaspoon salt

½ teaspoon seafood seasoning, such as McCormick's Old Bay

1 teaspoon chopped fresh oregano, or ½ teaspoon dried

1 teaspoon chopped fresh basil or ½ teaspoon dried

¼ teaspoon ground cayenne, or to taste

1½ cups (half of 10 ounce package) frozen baby okra, thawed, and cut into ¼-inch slices

½ cup thinly sliced green onions

Salt to taste (optional)

Hot pepper sauce, such as Frank's to taste (optional)

File powder to taste

THE ROUX RUSE

It is possible to make a gluten-free roux, traditionally made with wheat flour. I use a mixture of half white corn flour (ground from gluten-free white cornmeal in my coffee/spice grinder) and half cornstarch. Cornstarch, a typical thickener in gluten-free entrées, is an excellent thickener for dessert sauces and makes them translucent and shiny, but using it alone lends too much sheen for savory dishes such as gumbo. White corn flour provides body, tones down the sheen from the cornstarch, and lends opaqueness that makes the gumbo more authentic-looking.

1 Prepare shrimp shells and make shrimp stock; refrigerate shelled shrimp up to 1 day.

2 Make the roux: Stir together the oil, corn flour, and cornstarch in a 10-inch cast iron skillet with a flat nylon or wooden spatula. Cook over medium-low heat 20 to 25 minutes, constantly scraping the spatula back and forth, rather than stirring. The roux will darken to a light beige; continue scraping back and forth as the roux gradually darkens to the color of cream-in-your-coffee. Add onion, garlic, celery, and bell pepper and cook, scraping back and forth occasionally with the spatula, until onion is softened, about 4 to 5 minutes. Remove skillet from heat.

3 In a 6- to 8-quart pot, cook the sausage until lightly browned. Add roux and 5 cups shrimp stock and bring to a boil, stirring occasionally. Reduce heat, add salt, seafood seasoning, oregano, basil, and cayenne and simmer, uncovered, 20 minutes. Add okra and simmer until tender, 5 to 8 minutes. Stir in shrimp and simmer until just cooked through, 2 to 3 minutes. Stir in green onions. Add salt, hot pepper sauce and file powder to taste, if desired. Serve immediately.

Seafood Rice Casserole

MAKES 4 SERVINGS

This creamy, home-style casserole can be assembled ahead of time and baked the next day. You may substitute a variety of seafood in place of the types used here.

TOPPING

½ cup gluten-free bread crumbs, such as Ener-G, or homemade Plain Bread Crumbs (page 117)

¼ cup sliced almonds

1 tablespoon grated Parmesan cheese or soy alternative, such as Soyco

¼ teaspoon seafood seasoning, such as McCormick's Old Bay

2 tablespoons unsalted butter or buttery spread, such as Earth Balance, melted, or canola oil

CASSEROLE

2 cups cooked unseasoned wild rice and long grain rice blend, such as Lundberg's, or cooked brown rice

1 cup shredded cooked crabmeat, such as Phillips, picked over for shells and cartilage and drained

1 cup cooked medium shrimp, peeled, deveined, and chopped

1 cup cooked scallops, chopped

1 rib celery, chopped

1 small onion, peeled and finely chopped

1 can (7 ounces) sliced mushrooms, drained

½ jar (2 ounces) diced pimiento, drained

2 tablespoons grated Parmesan cheese or soy alternative, such as Soyco

1 teaspoon seafood seasoning, such as McCormick's Old Bay

1 cup 1% milk (cow's, rice, soy, potato, or nut)

½ cup mayonnaise

2 tablespoons sweet rice flour

1 tablespoon gluten-free Worcestershire sauce, such as French's

½ teaspoon paprika, for dusting

1 Make the topping: In a bowl, combine bread crumbs, almonds, Parmesan cheese, seasoning, and butter and mix thoroughly. Set aside.

2 Make the casserole: Place a rack in the middle of the oven. Preheat the oven to 375°F. In 2-quart, greased casserole dish, mix together the wild rice, crabmeat, shrimp, scallops, celery, onion, mushrooms, pimiento, Parmesan cheese, and seafood seasoning.

3 In a 2-cup measuring cup, whisk together milk, mayonnaise, sweet rice flour, and Worcestershire sauce until smooth. Pour over casserole mixture and mix thoroughly.

4 Bake 20 minutes. Sprinkle topping evenly over casserole and dust with paprika. Bake 10 to 15 minutes more or until sauce is bubbly and topping is browned. Serve hot.

Seafood Jambalaya

MAKES 4 SERVINGS

Jambalaya is a spicy Cajun or Creole dish made with combinations of rice and different forms of seafood. Serve it with a crisp mixed greens salad and some gluten-free French bread. The sausage, tomatoes, broth, and Creole seasoning contain salt, so wait until the end to add any more salt.

1 teaspoon extra-virgin olive oil

¼ pound gluten-free andouille sausage, such as Johnsonville, sliced

1 small onion, peeled and diced

1 rib celery, chopped

½ cup finely chopped green bell pepper

1 can (14 to 15 ounces) petite diced tomatoes, including juice

1 can (14 to 15 ounces) or 1¾ cups gluten-free, low-sodium chicken broth, such as Swanson's Natural Goodness, or homemade Chicken Broth (page 676)

2 garlic cloves, minced

¼ teaspoon Creole seasoning, such as Spice Hunter Cajun Creole, or to taste

1½ cups cooked brown rice

½ pound cooked large shrimp, peeled, and deveined

½ cup frozen green peas, thawed

Additional salt, to taste(optional)

Additional Creole seasoning, to taste (optional)

1 tablespoon chopped fresh parsley or 1 teaspoon dried, for garnish

1 In a heavy skillet, heat the oil over medium heat. Add the sausage, onion, celery, and bell pepper and cook until lightly browned, about 3 to 5 minutes.

2 Add tomatoes, broth, garlic, and Creole seasoning. Bring the mixture to a boil, reduce the heat to low, and simmer, covered, 10 minutes. Add the rice, shrimp, and green peas and cook until the mixture is heated through. Taste and add salt if necessary and more Creole seasoning, if desired. Transfer to a serving dish and sprinkle with the parsley. Serve immediately.

POULTRY

Chicken or Turkey Parts

Grilled Chicken with Cilantro-Pesto Sauce

Grilled Bourbon-Molasses Barbecued Chicken

Grilled Tandoori Chicken

Jamaican Jerk Chicken with Mango Chutney

Barbecued Apricot-Mustard Chicken

Barbecued Brined Chicken

Chicken Satay with Peanut Sauce

Chicken-Fried Chicken with White Gravy

Chicken Marsala with Mushrooms

Chicken Parmesan

Chicken Piccata

Chicken Cordon Bleu

Chicken Scaloppine with Madeira Sauce

Bourbon-Orange Chicken

Pan-Roasted Chicken Breasts with Apricot-Teriyaki Glaze

Pan-Seared Chicken Breasts with Vermouth-Ginger Sauce

Pan-Seared Chicken Breasts in Spicy Orange-Cilantro Sauce

Chicken Breasts with Mango and Pomegranate Salsa

Lemon Chicken

Mediterranean Chicken with Artichoke Salad

Moroccan Chicken with Caramelized Onions & Coconut Rice

Spicy Asian Chicken

Indian-Spiced Chicken Over Basmati Rice

Baked Herbed Chicken

Slow-Baked Herbed Chicken

Buffalo Wings

Roasted Lemon-Rosemary Chicken

Roasted Turkey Legs with Port-Cherry Sauce

Ground, Pulled, or Shredded Poultry

Turkey Meat Loaf

Turkey Meatballs with White Parmesan Gravy

Cincinnati Turkey Chili

Maple-Mustard-Glazed Turkey Bacon

Casseroles and Slow-Cooked Dishes

Chicken and Rice Casserole

Chicken–Chile Relleno Casserole

Turkey Rice Casserole`

Arroz con Pollo

Baked Aloha Pineapple Chicken

Paella

Chicken Divan

Chicken Pot Pie

Chicken Artichoke Mushroom Casserole

Coq au Vin

Chicken Cacciatore

Chicken Fricassee

Chicken Curry

Chicken Mole

Chicken Provençal

Chicken Saltimbocca

Chicken Stroganoff

Chicken Tagine in a Slow Cooker

Chicken Enchiladas

Creole Chicken Gumbo

Turkey Bacon–Onion Pie

Turkey Tetrazzini

Whole Birds

Simple Roasted Chicken

Roast Chicken with Cranberry Chutney

Southwestern Roast Chicken with Avocado Salsa

Chicken Under a Brick

Herbes de Provence Roasted Chicken on Garlic Croutons

Middle-Eastern Spiced Chicken with Homemade Harissa Sauce

Cornish Game Hens with Orange-Apricot Glaze

Cornish Game Hens with Gremolata Pesto

Roasted Cornish Hens with Root Vegetable Puree

Brined Turkey

Stuffings

Bread Pudding Stuffing

Cornbread Stuffing with Sausage and Fruit

Cornbread Stuffing with Dried Fruit and Pomegranate Seeds

Chicken is inspiringly versatile, making it the focus of some of the most popular dishes. There are dozens of recipes here, but if you're creative, you could put your own imaginative spins on these dishes and enjoy chicken every night of the week. You can have it fried, baked, battered, grilled, or boiled.

As with other main dishes served in restaurants, gluten lurks in unsuspecting places such as the sauces, the flour in which chicken is dredged before frying, or the batter it's coated with. This chapter offers you a wide variety of mouth-watering ways to prepare chicken without any of these concerns.

You can serve whole birds as a Simple Roasted Chicken, or dress them up to become tender and flavorful Chicken Under a Brick, or make Cornish Game Hens with Orange-Apricot Glaze. Chicken parts such as breasts, wings, and legs can be become all-American dishes like Baked Herb Chicken or Buffalo Wings.

Try adding aromatic herbs and spices to transform chicken parts into Chicken Cacciatore, Chicken Mole, or Creole Chicken Gumbo—dishes with bold flavors and fascinating ethnic origins.

For the health conscious, many of the entrées use skinless, boneless chicken breasts to reduce calories and fat. However, you can interchange different chicken parts in the recipes, if you wish.

If you eat healthfully and have access to local farms or carefully raised chicken and other poultry—such as free-range, organically raised—investigate your options and choose the foods that make sense based on your taste and budget.

CHICKEN OR TURKEY PARTS

Grilled Chicken with Cilantro-Pesto Sauce

MAKES 4 SERVINGS

This was one of my son's favorite dishes when he was a teenager, but the whole family loved its fresh cilantro taste. The sauce is best served right after you make it, but if you must prepare ahead of time, be sure to cover it with a layer of olive oil to prevent darkening.

CHICKEN
4 boneless skinless chicken breast halves (about 1¼ pounds)
2 tablespoons extra-virgin olive oil
½ teaspoon salt
¼ teaspoon freshly ground black pepper

SAUCE
1 bunch fresh cilantro (1 large bunch)
¼ cup grated Parmesan cheese or soy alternative, such as Soyco
¼ cup pine nuts
1 garlic clove, minced
2 tablespoons fresh lime juice
1 teaspoon chili powder
1 teaspoon ground cumin
½ teaspoon crushed red pepper
½ teaspoon salt
¼ cup olive oil
¼ cup gluten-free, low-sodium chicken broth, such as Swanson's Natural Goodness, or homemade Chicken Broth (page 676)

1 Make the chicken: Brush chicken breasts with olive oil and season with salt and pepper. Place a barbecue grill about 6 inches away from the heat source. Preheat the grill to desired temperature and coat grill with oil to prevent sticking.

2 Grill chicken until lightly browned on both sides and until juices run clear when cut in the thickest part, about 5 minutes per side depending on size.

3 While chicken is on the grill, make the sauce: In a food processor, combine cilantro, Parmesan cheese, pine nuts, garlic, lime juice, chili powder, cumin, crushed red pepper, and salt. Puree, using on/off pulses and scraping down sides until finely chopped. With motor running, add oil and broth through food chute. Process about 3 seconds or until the sauce is well blended.

4 Remove chicken from grill and serve immediately, drizzled with sauce.

Grilled Bourbon-Molasses Barbecued Chicken

MAKES 4 SERVINGS

This sauce is rich and irresistible with sweetness from the sugar and molasses and heat from the chili and black powder. The bourbon (which is gluten-free because the gluten peptides don't survive the distillation process) mellows out the flavor, but if you prefer not to use it, use orange juice instead. This is one you'll make over and over again.

8 chicken drumsticks

1 teaspoons salt

½ teaspoon freshly ground black pepper

2 tablespoons unsalted butter or buttery spread, such as Earth Balance, or canola oil

½ cup diced onion

1 cup ketchup

2 tablespoons molasses (not blackstrap)

2 tablespoons red wine vinegar

2 tablespoons packed light brown sugar

2 tablespoons gluten-free Worcestershire sauce, such as French's

2 teaspoons Dijon mustard

¾ teaspoon freshly ground black pepper, divided

¼ teaspoon chili powder

2 tablespoons bourbon, such as Jim Beam, or orange juice

1 Place a barbecue grill about 6 inches away from the heat source. Preheat the grill to medium-high temperature. Season chicken with salt and pepper.

2 Grill chicken until lightly browned on both sides and until juices run clear when cut in the thickest part, about 5 minutes per side, depending on size.

3 While chicken is grilling, in a heavy saucepan, heat the butter over medium heat. Add onion and cook until soft, about 3 to 5 minutes. Add ketchup, molasses, vinegar, sugar, Worcestershire sauce, mustard, pepper and chili powder and stir together. Remove pan from heat and stir in bourbon. Return pan to heat, reduce heat to low, and simmer 10 minutes. Transfer half of the sauce to a small pitcher or bowl for serving with the chicken. Keep warm.

4 Brush chicken with remaining half of the sauce during last 10 minutes of grilling, watching chicken carefully since it will have a greater tendency to burn with the sauce on it. Remove chicken from grill and serve with sauce.

Grilled Tandoori Chicken

MAKES 4 SERVINGS

Hearty and spicy, this is Indian food at its best. I always choose this dish when my husband and I go out for Indian food. Restaurant versions use red and/or yellow food coloring to achieve the characteristically bright tandoori color—you can do the same at home; it won't affect the taste at all. The smoked paprika adds depth of flavor (and color), but you can use regular paprika if you wish. If you don't want to grill the chicken, roast it on a lightly oiled, foil-lined 13 × 9-inch baking sheet (not nonstick) in a 375°F oven for 40 to 45 minutes, turning once during roasting.

8 skinless, bone-in chicken thighs, trimmed of fat (about 1¼ pounds)

1 cup plain, low-fat yogurt or soy yogurt

¼ cup fresh lemon juice

1 tablespoon canola oil

1 (2-inch) piece fresh ginger, peeled and finely chopped

2 large garlic cloves, minced

1½ teaspoons garam masala, such as Spice Islands

1½ teaspoons ground coriander

1 teaspoon ground cumin

1 teaspoon salt

½ teaspoon ground allspice

½ teaspoon smoked paprika

¼ teaspoon ground cayenne

Pinch of ground cloves

1 small onion, peeled and thinly sliced (vertically) for garnish

2 fresh lemons, for garnish

1 Slash chicken thighs diagonally with a sharp knife to a depth of ⅛ inch to allow marinade to penetrate more deeply. In a heavy-duty, food-storage bag or glass or ceramic dish, whisk together all of the remaining ingredients except onions and lemon. Add chicken and marinate overnight.

2 Place a barbecue grill about 6 inches away from the heat source. Preheat the grill, oiling grates liberally to prevent the chicken from sticking. Remove chicken from marinade and discard marinade. Cook chicken on grill, turning when grill marks appear. Turn chicken and continue cooking, until juices run clear or meat is no longer pink near the bone, about 5 minutes per side, depending on size. Remove from grill and let chicken rest, covered with foil, for 10 minutes.

3 While chicken cooks on grill, spray onions with cooking spray and cook in grill basket until softened and browned. To serve, arrange grilled onion alongside chicken and serve with a squeeze of fresh lemon juice.

Jamaican Jerk Chicken with Mango Chutney

MAKES 4 SERVINGS

Jerk, a style of cooking native to Jamaica, involves marinating the meat in lots of seasonings and grilling it for even more vibrant flavor, which is tempered by the sweet mango chutney. Chicken legs work well in this recipe because they are smaller than other chicken parts, allowing the flavorful marinade to penetrate better.

MARINADE

2 teaspoons onion powder

2 teaspoons crushed red pepper

½ teaspoon salt

½ teaspoon sugar

½ teaspoon ground allspice

½ teaspoon chopped fresh basil or ¼ teaspoon dried

½ teaspoon chopped fresh thyme or ¼ teaspoon dried

¼ teaspoon ground ginger

¼ teaspoon ground cloves

¼ teaspoon garlic powder

¼ teaspoon freshly ground black pepper

2 tablespoons canola oil

1 tablespoon wheat-free tamari soy sauce, such as Crystal or San-J

1 tablespoon cider vinegar

1 tablespoon lime juice

CHUTNEY

1 ripe mango, peeled and diced
½ cup diced red bell pepper
¼ cup diced red onion
¼ cup chopped fresh cilantro
1 tablespoon balsamic vinegar
1 tablespoon fresh lime juice
1 tablespoon extra-virgin olive oil
1 tablespoon honey
¼ teaspoon crushed red pepper
¼ teaspoon salt
¼ teaspoon freshly ground black pepper

CHICKEN

12 chicken legs (about 1¼ pounds)
1 teaspoon salt
½ teaspoon freshly ground black pepper

1 Make the marinade: Combine onion powder through black pepper in a heavy-duty, food-storage resealable bag. Shake to blend spices thoroughly. Add oil, soy sauce, vinegar, and lime juice and shake thoroughly. Add chicken legs, squeezing to make sure all pieces are coated with marinade. Refrigerate overnight or all day.

2 Make the chutney: About 1 hour prior to eating, combine all of the chutney ingredients in a small bowl. Cover and set aside at room temperature.

3 Prepare the chicken: Place a barbecue grill about 6 inches away from the heat source. Preheat the grill to medium temperature. Remove chicken legs from marinade and pat dry. Sprinkle the chicken legs with salt and pepper. Cook on grill until browned, about 5 to 7 minutes per side, basting occasionally with reserved marinade, until juice is no longer pink when centers of thickest pieces are cut. Serve immediately with chutney.

Barbecued Apricot-Mustard Chicken

MAKES 4 SERVINGS

I prefer to partially precook the chicken pieces in the microwave before placing it on the grill. That shortens the grilling time and lessens the chances of burning the chicken skin when trying to make sure it's cooked through.

CHICKEN

8 chicken pieces, preferably legs or thighs
1 teaspoon salt
½ teaspoon freshly ground black pepper

GLAZE

⅓ cup apricot jam or preserves
¼ cup apple cider vinegar
2 tablespoons Dijon mustard
1 tablespoon canola oil
1 garlic clove, minced
½ teaspoon onion powder
½ teaspoon salt
¼ teaspoon chili powder
¼ teaspoon freshly ground black pepper

1 Prepare the chicken: Sprinkle chicken with salt and pepper. Partially cook by microwaving on High power about 10 minutes, Let stand. Place a barbecue grill about 6 inches away from the heat source. Preheat the grill.

2 Make the glaze: In a small bowl, stir jam, vinegar, mustard, oil, garlic, onion powder, salt, chili powder, and pepper until smooth.

3 Transfer chicken to heated grill. Cook over medium-low heat, skin-side down, until skin starts to brown. Turn chicken skin-side up and continue cook, brushing chicken with glaze periodically until it's done. If chicken starts to brown too quickly, turn heat down to low and watch carefully.

Barbecued Brined Chicken

MAKES 4 SERVINGS

Brining infuses the chicken with wonderful flavor, but you can skip this step if time is short and go directly to cooking the chicken.

BRINE

2 tablespoons kosher salt

2 quarts water

2 tablespoons brown sugar

8 bone-in chicken thighs and legs (about 1¼ pounds)

SAUCE

1 cup ketchup

½ cup orange juice

¼ cup cider vinegar

2 tablespoons packed light brown sugar

1 tablespoon molasses (not blackstrap)

1 tablespoon gluten-free Worcestershire sauce, such as French's

1 tablespoon Dijon mustard

1 teaspoon onion powder

1 teaspoon chili powder

2 teaspoons chopped fresh oregano or 1 teaspoon dried

1 teaspoon grated orange zest (optional)

½ teaspoon crushed red pepper

½ teaspoon salt

¼ teaspoon ground cloves

1 garlic clove, minced

1 Make the brine: Dissolve salt in ½ cup of the water by boiling it. Combine with remaining water and other brine ingredients in a large 2-gallon, heavy-duty or freezer food-storage bag. Add chicken and refrigerate at least 2 hours and no more than 4 hours.

2 Make the sauce: In a medium saucepan, combine all ingredients on low heat. Simmer, uncovered, on low heat for 15 minutes. Use immediately or store in refrigerator. Reserve 1¼ cups to serve with chicken during the meal. Use remaining sauce to baste chicken during its final minutes of grilling.

3 Place a barbecue grill about 6 inches away from the heat source. Preheat the grill to medium heat. Remove chicken from brine, rinse, and pat dry. Spray with cooking spray and cook over grill until both sides are nicely browned and show definite grill marks. Cook until chicken is done, about 5 to 7 minutes per side, or until juice is no longer pink when centers of thickest pieces are cut. Brush chicken pieces with sauce during last few minutes of grilling. Serve immediately.

Chicken Satay with Peanut Sauce

MAKES 4 SERVINGS

A satay is a strip of marinated meat threaded on a skewer and grilled. This dish makes a delightful meal served atop a bed of cooked rice. Or, present as an appetizer (8 servings), with the peanut sauce as a dip.

MARINADE AND CHICKEN

1 cup unsweetened coconut milk

1 tablespoon wheat-free tamari soy sauce, such as Crystal or San-J

1 tablespoon sugar

1 teaspoon sesame oil

1 teaspoon grated fresh ginger

1 teaspoon ground coriander

½ teaspoon ground turmeric

¼ teaspoon ground cumin

2 pounds boneless skinless chicken breast halves, cut into ½-inch slices

8 bamboo skewers, soaked in water

SAUCE

½ cup smooth peanut butter

3 tablespoons wheat-free low-sodium tamari soy sauce, such as Crystal or San-J

1 small garlic clove, minced

¼ teaspoon crushed red pepper

1½ tablespoons packed dark brown sugar

Juice of 1 lime

¼ cup hot water (you may not use it all)

1 tablespoon finely chopped peanuts for garnish

1 Prepare the marinade and chicken: Combine marinade ingredients in heavy-duty food storage bag. Add chicken and refrigerate 2 hours. Remove chicken from marinade (discard marinade) and thread 3 to 4 chicken pieces on each bamboo skewer, stretch out meat to fill skewer. Heat barbecue grill to high heat. Grill skewers, about 4 to 5 minutes per side, until chicken is browned and cooked through.

2 Make sauce: In a food processor or blender, combine peanut butter, soy sauce, garlic, red pepper, brown sugar, and lime juice. Puree to combine. With motor of the food processor or blender running, add enough of the hot water to thin sauce. Pour sauce into serving bowl and garnish with chopped peanuts. Serve immediately with chicken.

Chicken-Fried Chicken with White Gravy

MAKES 4 SERVINGS

"Chicken-fried" steak is an American country favorite, but chicken-fried chicken suits those who prefer chicken to steak. There's something about this dish's crispy coating that gluten-free folks absolutely crave, but here it's created with cornstarch rather than wheat flour.

CHICKEN

1 cup cornstarch

2 teaspoons gluten-free seasoned salt, such as Lawry's

¼ teaspoon freshly ground black pepper

½ cup 1% milk (cow's, rice, soy, potato, or nut)

2 large eggs

4 boneless skinless chicken breast halves (about 1¼ pounds)

¼ cup canola oil for frying

GRAVY

2½ cups 1% milk (cow, rice, soy, potato, or nut)

1 tablespoon cider vinegar

4 teaspoons sweet rice flour

½ teaspoon salt

½ teaspoon onion powder

½ teaspoon freshly ground black pepper

1 Prepare the chicken. In a shallow bowl, combine cornstarch, seasoned salt, and pepper. In another shallow bowl, whisk milk and eggs together until egg membrane is broken up and mixture is very smooth.

2 With a meat mallet, pound chicken between two sheets of plastic wrap until it is ¼ to ⅓ inch thick. Dip chicken first in cornstarch mixture, then in egg mixture, then in cornstarch mixture again. Repeat with each chicken breast.

3 In a large, heavy nonstick skillet, heat the oil over medium-high heat. Fry chicken until golden brown, about 4 to 5 minutes per side, turning only once. If you turn them more than once, the coating falls off. Remove chicken to platter, cover with foil to keep warm.

4 Make the gravy: Pour off all but 1 tablespoon of oil, leaving browned bits in skillet. Add 2 cups of the milk and the vinegar to skillet and cook over medium-high. Stir sweet rice flour, salt, onion powder, and pepper into remaining ½ cup of milk until very smooth. Stir mixture into skillet, whisking constantly until mixture thickens, about 7 to 10 minutes. Pour over chicken. Serve immediately.

Chicken Marsala with Mushrooms

MAKES 4 SERVINGS

This is a classic Italian dish made with Marsala wine and mushrooms. A hint of nutmeg lends a mysterious but complementary flavor to the wine. It is a rich and satisfying dish that will please family or dinner guests, and it's simple enough to make often.

1½ pounds thin-sliced boneless skinless chicken breasts

¼ cup cornstarch

1 teaspoon salt

½ teaspoon freshly ground black pepper

2 tablespoons unsalted butter or buttery spread, such as Earth Balance, or olive oil

2 garlic cloves, minced

1 can (8 ounces) sliced mushrooms, drained

Pinch of freshly grated nutmeg

1 cup Marsala wine

1 teaspoon cornstarch stirred into 1 tablespoon water (optional)

2 tablespoons grated Parmesan cheese or soy alternative, such as Soyco

1 With a meat mallet, pound chicken breasts to ½-inch thickness between two sheets of plastic wrap. In a shallow bowl, dredge chicken in cornstarch, then season with salt and pepper.

2 In a large skillet, heat the butter over medium-high heat. Cook chicken about 4 to 5 minutes per side, until deep golden brown and until juice is no longer pink when centers of thickest pieces are cut. Remove from pan and cover with foil to keep warm.

3 In the same skillet, add garlic, mushrooms, nutmeg, and wine. Stir to loosen browned bits from bottom of skillet. Bring mixture to boil, reduce heat to medium-low and cook until mixture is reduced by a third. If you prefer a thicker sauce with more body, stir in the cornstarch-water mixture and cook until mixture thickens.

4 Return chicken to pan and cook 1 to 2 minutes or until it reaches serving temperature. Serve chicken with pan juices poured on top, garnished with Parmesan cheese

Chicken Parmesan

MAKES 4 SERVINGS

I learned to make this dish in graduate school, when getting dinner on the table quickly was essential so I would have more time to study. The easy-to-make Parmesan Herb Blend makes this dish very tasty—with very little effort and is a good item to keep in the refrigerator for chicken or for other meats. Pounding the chicken breasts to an even thickness with a meat mallet makes them cook a lot faster, so don't skip this important step. It can be done the night before, if necessary.

PARMESAN HERB BLEND

3 tablespoons grated Parmesan cheese or soy alternative, such as Soyco

4 tablespoons chopped fresh basil or 2 tablespoons dried

4 teaspoons chopped fresh thyme or 2 teaspoons dried

½ teaspoon garlic powder

¼ teaspoon salt

CHICKEN

½ cup gluten-free bread crumbs, such as Ener-G, or homemade Plain Bread Crumbs (page 117)

2 tablespoons cornstarch

4 boneless skinless chicken breasts (about 4 ounces each)

½ teaspoon salt

½ teaspoon freshly ground black pepper

2 tablespoons canola oil

½ cup gluten-free marinara sauce, such as Classico, or homemade Marinara Sauce (page 672)

½ cup shredded mozzarella cheese or cheese alternative, such as Vegan Gourmet

1 Make the herb blend: In a small bowl, combine all ingredients until thoroughly blended. Set aside.

2 Prepare the chicken: With a meat mallet, lightly pound chicken breasts to about ½-inch thickness between sheets of plastic wrap. Sprinkle with salt and pepper. In a shallow dish or plate, combine bread crumbs, ¼ cup Parmesan herb blend, and cornstarch. Dip both sides of chicken breasts in crumb mixture, pressing it onto chicken with fingers.

3 In a large, heavy skillet, heat the oil over medium-high heat. Cook chicken breasts until lightly browned on both sides, about 7 to 10 minutes. Turn heat to low. While chicken breasts are still in skillet, top each with 2 tablespoons marinara sauce and 2 tablespoons mozzarella cheese. Cover skillet with lid or aluminum foil and cook 2 minutes more or until marinara sauce is heated through and cheese melts. Serve immediately.

Chicken Piccata

MAKES 4 SERVINGS

Chicken Piccata is an Italian dish flavored with lemon and capers. When pounded to ½-inch thickness, the chicken breasts are quite large. If you don't have an extra-large skillet to hold all 4 pieces at one time, brown the chicken in 2 batches or cut the breasts in half before pounding them. The rosemary may not be traditional, but it tastes great in this dish.

4 boneless, skinless chicken breasts halves (about 1¼ pounds)

1 teaspoon salt

½ teaspoon freshly ground black pepper

¼ cup cornstarch

2 tablespoons unsalted butter or buttery spread, such as Earth Balance

1 tablespoon extra-virgin olive oil

½ cup gluten-free, low-sodium chicken broth, such as Swanson's Natural Goodness, or homemade Chicken Broth (page 676)

2 tablespoons fresh lemon juice

¼ cup brined capers, rinsed

1 teaspoon chopped fresh rosemary or ½ teaspoon dried (optional)

⅓ cup chopped fresh parsley, for garnish

1 With a meat mallet, pound each of the 4 chicken pieces to ½-inch thickness between sheets of plastic wrap. Season with salt and pepper. In a shallow bowl, dredge chicken in cornstarch and shake off excess.

2 In a very large skillet, heat the butter and olive oil over medium-high heat. When they start to sizzle, add 2 pieces of chicken and cook 3 minutes. When chicken is browned, flip and cook other side 3 minutes, until juice is no longer pink when centers of thickest pieces are cut. Transfer chicken to plate.

3 Add broth, lemon juice, capers, and rosemary, if using, to skillet and bring to boil, scraping up brown bits from bottom of pan. Return chicken to pan (overlapping to make all 4 pieces fit) and simmer 5 minutes. Transfer chicken to serving platter and pour sauce over chicken. Garnish with parsley. Serve hot.

Chicken Cordon Bleu

MAKES 4 SERVINGS

Despite its sophisticated French name, this dish is quite easy to prepare. It is simply thin slices of chicken, prosciutto, and cheese rolled into a cylinder and then fried in a crispy batter. Be careful not to pound the chicken so thin that it breaks. Prosciutto works much better than the traditional deli ham because it is thinner and more pliable.

4 boneless skinless chicken breast halves, not tenders (about 1¼ pounds)

2 teaspoons salt, divided

1 teaspoon chopped fresh thyme leaves or ½ teaspoon dried

½ cup shredded Gruyère or Swiss cheese, or cheese alternative, such as Vegan Gourmet, divided

4 thin slices prosciutto

2 tablespoons white rice flour

½ teaspoon freshly ground black pepper

1 large egg, beaten

1 teaspoon water

½ cup gluten-free bread crumbs, such as Ener-G, or homemade Plain Bread Crumbs (page 117)

1 tablespoon unsalted butter or buttery spread, such as Earth Balance

1 tablespoon olive oil

1 tablespoon chopped fresh parsley, for garnish

1 Place a rack in the middle of the oven. Preheat the oven to 350°F. Sprinkle chicken with 1 teaspoon of salt and the thyme. With a meat mallet, gently pound the chicken to ¼-inch thickness between sheets of plastic wrap. Sprinkle the breasts evenly with all but 2 tablespoons of the cheese, followed by a slice of prosciutto. Leave a ½-inch margin on all sides of the chicken. Roll the sides of chicken in toward the center before rolling the chicken up tight like a jellyroll. Squeeze log gently to seal and insert toothpick to hold roll together, if necessary.

2 Select 3 wide, shallow bowls. In first bowl, combine the white rice flour and the remaining salt and the black pepper. In the second bowl, beat egg and water until smooth. In the third bowl, place the bread crumbs. Coat the chicken with the white rice flour, then dip it in the egg mixture. Gently roll the chicken in the bread crumbs.

3 In a heavy ovenproof skillet, heat the butter and olive oil over medium heat. Gently place the chicken rolls in the skillet and cook until golden brown on one side. Turn the browned side up and place the skillet in the oven.

4 Bake 20 to 25 minutes, or until the chicken is browned and until juice is no longer pink when centers of thickest pieces are cut. During the last 5 minutes of baking, sprinkle the remaining 2 tablespoons of cheese on the chicken. Serve immediately, garnished with parsley.

Chicken Scaloppine with Madeira Sauce

MAKES 4 SERVINGS

Scaloppine means "cutlet" in Italian. In Italy and in America, thin cuts of chicken can be prepared in a wide variety of ways. This easy version relies on Madeira, a sweet wine, for extraordinary flavor and heavy cream as the finishing touch.

4 boneless, skinless chicken breast halves, (about 1¼ pounds)

1 teaspoon salt

½ teaspoon freshly ground black pepper

¼ cup cornstarch

2 tablespoons unsalted butter or buttery spread, such as Earth Balance

1 tablespoon extra-virgin olive oil

2 shallots, minced

2 garlic cloves, minced

1 can (8 ounces) sliced mushrooms, drained

½ cup gluten-free, low-sodium chicken broth, such as Swanson's Natural Goodness, or homemade Chicken Broth (page 676)

½ cup Madeira

¾ cup heavy cream or ½ cup whole milk (cow, rice, soy, potato, or nut)

1 teaspoon arrowroot stirred into 1 tablespoon water

2 tablespoons chopped fresh parsley, for garnish

1 With a meat mallet, pound each of the 4 chicken pieces to ½-inch thickness between sheets of plastic wrap. Season with salt and pepper. In a shallow bowl, dredge chicken in cornstarch and shake off excess.

2 In a very large skillet, melt butter with olive oil over medium-high heat. When butter and oil start to sizzle, add 2 pieces of chicken and cook 3 minutes. When chicken is browned, flip and cook other side for 3 minutes and until juice is no longer pink when centers of thickest pieces are cut. Transfer chicken to plate. Repeat with remaining 2 pieces of chicken. Transfer to plate and cover.

3 Add shallots and garlic to pan and cook 1 to 2 minutes. Add mushrooms, broth, and Madeira to skillet and bring to a boil, scraping up brown bits from bottom of pan. Reduce heat to low and simmer, uncovered, 5 minutes or until mixture reduces slightly. Stir in cream. For thicker sauce, stir in arrowroot mixture and cook until thickened. Return all of chicken to pan (overlapping to make all 4 pieces fit, if necessary) and simmer until chicken is cooked through. Transfer chicken to serving platter and pour pan juices on top; garnish with parsley.

Bourbon-Orange Chicken

MAKES 4 SERVINGS

You don't have to drink bourbon to appreciate its remarkable flavor. It complements the orange in this dish and lends depth and complexity.

4 boneless skinless chicken breast halves (about 1¼ pounds)

1 teaspoon salt

½ teaspoon freshly ground black pepper

¼ cup cornstarch, divided

2 tablespoons olive oil

½ cup orange juice concentrate, thawed

2 garlic cloves, minced

1 green onion with green top, washed, and finely chopped

1 tablespoons champagne vinegar

½ cup bourbon, such as Jim Beam, or orange juice

2 tablespoons chopped fresh parsley or chives for garnish

1 Cut each chicken breast half into 2 pieces. Sprinkle the chicken with salt and pepper and place in a single layer in a gallon-size food-storage plastic bag. With a meat mallet, pound the chicken to about ½-inch thickness. Remove chicken from bag and discard bag. In a shallow bowl, dredge chicken in 3 tablespoons of the cornstarch.

2 In a large skillet, heat the oil and cook chicken over medium-high heat until lightly browned and crisp, about 4 to 5 minutes per side, or until juice is no longer pink when centers of thickest pieces are cut. Transfer the chicken to a serving platter and cover with foil to keep it warm. Remove skillet from heat.

3 Mix remaining tablespoon of cornstarch into the orange juice concentrate until smooth. Add to the skillet along with remaining ingredients except parsley or chives. Return skillet to burner and stir on low heat for 2 minutes or until sauce thickens. Pour sauce over chicken and serve, garnished with parsley or chives.

Pan-Roasted Chicken Breasts with Apricot-Teriyaki Glaze

MAKES 4 SERVINGS

Sweet apricot jam and savory soy sauce make a delightful glaze on these chicken breasts. Pan-roasting involves browning the chicken breasts in a skillet, then transferring them—skillet and all—to finish cooking in a preheated oven. It's a great timesaver, too, because it frees you up to complete the remainder of the meal.

4 boneless skinless chicken breast halves (about 1¼ pounds)
½ teaspoon salt
¼ teaspoon freshly ground black pepper
2 tablespoons canola oil
⅔ cup apricot jam
½ cup fresh orange juice
2 tablespoons Dijon mustard
2 tablespoons wheat-free tamari soy sauce, such as Crystal or San-J
1 teaspoon grated fresh ginger
¼ cup almond slices
1 tablespoon sesame seed
1 tablespoon chopped fresh parsley, for garnish

1 Place a rack in the middle of the oven. Preheat the oven to 350°F. With a meat mallet, pound the chicken breasts to ½-inch thickness between two sheets of plastic wrap. Sprinkle with salt and pepper.

2 In a large, heavy ovenproof skillet, heat the oil over medium-high. Brown the chicken breasts, about 5 minutes per side depending on size, or until juice is no longer pink when centers of thickest pieces are cut.

3 While chicken is browning, mix together apricot jam, orange juice, mustard, soy sauce, and ginger. Pour over chicken and bake in oven, uncovered, approximately 15 to 20 minutes or until chicken is cooked through. The glaze will thicken slightly as chicken bakes.

4 During the last 5 minutes of baking, spoon glaze over chicken breasts and then sprinkle almonds and sesame seeds over chicken. Remove skillet from oven and transfer chicken to serving platter, spooning glaze around breasts on platter. Garnish with chopped parsley and serve.

Pan-Seared Chicken Breasts with Vermouth-Ginger Sauce

MAKES 4 SERVINGS

Vermouth isn't just for martinis. It is a wine fortified with herbs that brings a nice touch to savory dishes, like this pan-seared chicken. You can substitute a dry white wine if you like.

4 boneless skinless chicken breast halves (about 1¼ pounds)
½ teaspoon salt
¼ teaspoon freshly ground black pepper
2 tablespoons canola oil
½ cup vermouth or white wine
2 tablespoons fresh minced ginger
2 tablespoons minced shallots
1 tablespoon fresh lemon juice
1 tablespoon wheat-free tamari soy sauce, such as Crystal or San-J
1 tablespoon unsalted butter or buttery spread, such as Earth Balance
1 teaspoon cornstarch mixed with 1 tablespoon cornstarch for thickening pan juices (optional)
1 tablespoon fresh minced chives, for garnish

1 With a meat mallet, pound chicken breast halves to ½-inch thickness between two sheets of plastic wrap. Season with salt and pepper. In a heavy skillet, heat the oil over medium-high heat. Add chicken breasts and cook until lightly browned, about 5 minutes per side, or until juice is no longer pink when centers of thickest pieces are cut.

2 Transfer chicken to plate and cover with foil to keep warm.

3 Add vermouth, ginger, shallots, lemon juice, and soy sauce to skillet and bring to a boil, scraping up browned bits on the bottom of the skillet as it cooks, about 5 to 7 minutes. Add butter and cook until butter melts. Return chicken breasts to pan and bring to serving temperature. If pan juices are too thin, stir in cornstarch mixture until it comes to a boil and thickens. Serve chicken with pan juices poured on top, garnished with a sprinkle of fresh chives.

Pan-Seared Chicken Breasts in Spicy Orange-Cilantro Sauce

MAKES 4 SERVINGS

Pounding the breasts with a meat mallet is a good trick for making meat cook faster. It evens out the thick parts of the chicken so it cooks more consistently. You can purchase a meat mallet at your local kitchen store.

4 boneless skinless chicken breast halves (about 1¼ pounds)
½ teaspoon salt
¼ teaspoon freshly ground black pepper
½ cup orange juice
2 tablespoons honey
1 tablespoon Dijon mustard
1 teaspoon sweet paprika
½ teaspoon grated orange zest (optional)
¼ teaspoon ground cayenne
¼ teaspoon garlic powder
1 tablespoon unsalted butter, buttery spread, such as Earth Balance, or canola oil
¼ cup chopped fresh cilantro, divided

1 Pat chicken breasts dry and place between sheets of plastic wrap. With a meat mallet, pound a few times to flatten chicken slightly, but evenly, for faster, more even cooking. Sprinkle with salt and pepper. Let rest while preparing sauce.

2 In a small bowl, whisk together orange juice, honey, mustard, paprika, orange zest, cayenne, and garlic powder. Set aside.

3 In a heavy, large lidded skillet, heat the butter over medium-high heat. Add chicken breasts and cook until lightly browned, about 5 minutes per side depending on size or until juice is no longer pink when centers of thickest pieces are cut. Pour sauce over chicken and sprinkle with 2 tablespoons of the cilantro. Cover with lid or tent of aluminum foil.

4 Reduce heat to low and simmer chicken in sauce for 5 to 7 minutes If chicken is done before you're ready to serve the meal, simply remove skillet from burner and let sit a few minutes up to 10 minutes with the lid to keep it warm. Transfer chicken to serving platter. Pour remaining sauce over chicken and sprinkle with the remaining 2 tablespoons cilantro.

Chicken Breasts with Mango and Pomegranate Salsa

MAKES 4 SERVINGS

Mango, a tropical fruit, and the seeds of the pomegranate, grown mainly in California and Arizona, combine as nutritional powerhouses in the salsa. They are also delicious in this very colorful savory dish of simply seasoned baked chicken.

SALSA
1 mango, peeled, seeded, and chopped
½ cup pomegranate seeds
½ cup green onions, chopped
½ jalapeño chile, seeded and finely chopped
2 tablespoons chopped fresh parsley
1 tablespoon chopped fresh basil
1 tablespoon rice vinegar

CHICKEN BREASTS

4 boneless skinless chicken breast halves (about 1¼ pounds)

1 teaspoon salt

½ teaspoon freshly ground black pepper

2 tablespoons olive oil

1 Make the salsa: In a small bowl, combine all the salsa ingredients and stir together. Let stand at room temperature 30 minutes before serving.

2 Prepare the chicken: Place a rack in the middle of the oven. Preheat the oven to 350°F. With a meat mallet, pound the chicken breasts to ½-inch thickness between two sheets of plastic wrap. Season with salt and pepper.

3 In a large, ovenproof skillet, heat the oil over medium-high heat. Cook chicken until deep golden brown, about 4 to 5 minutes per side. Transfer skillet to oven and roast chicken 20 minutes more or until juice is no longer pink when centers of thickest pieces are cut. Serve with mango-pomegranate salsa.

Lemon Chicken

MAKES 4 SERVINGS

This dish is often found in Chinese restaurants, but it is so easy to make at home. Just brown the chicken breasts and then create a simple pan sauce to pour over them.

4 boneless skinless chicken breast halves (about 1¼ pounds)

½ cup cornstarch + 2 tablespoons, divided

½ teaspoon salt

2 tablespoons canola oil

1 teaspoon ground ginger

1 cup gluten-free, low-sodium chicken broth, such as Swanson's Natural Goodness, or homemade Chicken Broth (page 676)

2 tablespoons honey

2 tablespoons fresh lemon juice

1 tablespoon cider vinegar

1 teaspoon grated lemon zest

2 tablespoons dried chives or ½ cup green onions, finely chopped diagonally, for garnish

4 cups hot cooked basmati rice

1 Pat chicken breasts dry with paper towels. With a meat mallet, pound chicken to flatten just slightly.

2 Place ½ cup cornstarch and salt in a medium-size bowl. Dip each chicken breast in cornstarch to coat thoroughly.

3 In a large, heavy skillet, heat the oil over medium-high heat. Cook chicken breasts 5 minutes on each side, depending on size, or until nicely browned and cooked through and juice is no longer pink when centers of thickest pieces are cut. Remove from skillet and cover with foil to keep warm.

4 Stir remaining 2 tablespoons cornstarch and ginger into ¼ cup of the chicken broth until smooth. Add to skillet, along with remaining chicken broth and honey. Cook over medium heat, stirring frequently, until mixture thickens and comes to boil. Remove from heat. Stir in lemon juice, vinegar, and lemon zest.

5 Cut each chicken breast into 4 slices, slightly at a diagonal. Arrange on serving plate and pour sauce over chicken. Sprinkle with chives and serve immediately over rice.

Mediterranean Chicken with Artichoke Salad

MAKES 4 SERVINGS

Artichokes are a classic ingredient in Mediter-ranean cooking and contribute wonderful flavor to this dish. If you use cow's milk feta cheese, which is saltier than goat's milk feta cheese, taste the salad before you add any more salt.

SALAD

1 jar (6.5 ounces) marinated artichokes, drained and chopped

½ cup finely chopped red bell pepper

2 tablespoons finely chopped red onion

2 tablespoons chopped green onions (tops included)

2 tablespoons sliced black olives (about 6 whole olives)

2 tablespoons toasted pine nuts

1 tablespoon red wine vinegar

1 tablespoon extra-virgin olive oil

½ cup crumbled goat feta cheese, or cheese of choice

Salt and freshly ground pepper to taste

CHICKEN

1½ tablespoons extra-virgin olive oil

4 boneless skinless chicken breast halves (about 1¼ pounds), pounded to ½-inch thickness

½ teaspoon salt

¼ teaspoon freshly ground black pepper

1 teaspoon chopped fresh oregano or ½ teaspoon dried

1 Make the artichoke salad: In a small bowl, toss together artichokes, red bell pepper, onion, olives, nuts, vinegar, and olive oil. Set aside at room temperature to blend flavors. Just before serving, gently stir in feta cheese and salt and pepper to taste.

2 Prepare the chicken: In a large, heavy skillet, heat olive oil over medium-high heat. Sprinkle chicken with salt, pepper, and oregano and cook 5 to 6 minutes on each side or until it is nicely browned and cooked through or until juice is no longer pink when centers of thickest pieces are cut. Serve each chicken breast topped with ½ cup of salad.

Moroccan Chicken with Caramelized Onions and Coconut Rice

MAKES 4 SERVINGS

Moroccan food is typically infused with a myriad of spices so cooking this dish fills your kitchen with enticing aromas as it cooks. The caramelized onions do their share of adding flavor and tanta-lizing aroma, as well.

1 recipe Coconut Rice (page 218)

4 boneless skinless chicken breast halves (about 1¼ pounds)

1½ teaspoons salt, divided

½ teaspoon freshly ground black pepper

1 tablespoon cornstarch

3 tablespoons olive oil, divided

2 large onions, peeled and sliced

1 teaspoon ground ginger

1 teaspoon ground cinnamon

1 teaspoon ground cumin

1 teaspoon ground Hungarian paprika

1 tablespoon packed light brown sugar

1 can (14 to 15 ounces) or 1¾ cups gluten-free, low-sodium chicken broth, such as Swanson's Natural Goodness, or homemade Chicken Broth (page 676)

½ cup petite diced tomatoes, including juice

2 tablespoons fresh lemon juice

2 tablespoons honey

2 large garlic cloves, minced

Additional salt and pepper, to taste

Chopped fresh cilantro, for garnish

1 Prepare the coconut rice; set aside. Sprinkle chicken with 1 teaspoon of the salt and the pepper. Dust with cornstarch. Set aside.

2 In a large, heavy skillet, heat 2 tablespoons of the oil over medium heat. Add onions and remaining ½ teaspoon salt and cook, covered, for 20 minutes. Add brown sugar, ginger, cinnamon, cumin, and paprika and cook 10 minutes more, stirring constantly until browned. Transfer onions from skillet to a platter.

3 In the same skillet, add remaining tablespoon of oil and the chicken to skillet and cook until golden brown, about 5 minutes per side or until juice is no longer pink when centers of thickest pieces are cut. Transfer chicken to plate.

4 Gradually whisk in chicken broth, tomatoes, lemon juice, honey, and garlic. Bring mixture to boil, then reduce heat to medium-low and cook, uncovered, until mixture thickens slightly, about 10 minutes. Return chicken and caramelized onions to skillet. Simmer until heated through, about 3 to 5 minutes. Taste and add additional salt and pepper, if desired. Spread hot cooked rice on serving platter and top with chicken mixture. Pour sauce over platter and sprinkle with cilantro. Serve immediately.

Spicy Asian Chicken

MAKES 4 SERVINGS

The chicken will cut more easily if it is partially frozen. For a milder version, reduce the crushed red pepper to ½ teaspoon. If that isn't spicy enough, add ¼ teaspoon and then taste it. You can always add more until it satisfies your taste buds.

CHICKEN AND MARINADE

1 pound boneless skinless chicken breasts, cut into ¼-inch strips

2 tablespoons sesame oil

2 tablespoons wheat-free tamari soy sauce, such as Crystal or San-J

2 tablespoons rice vinegar

SAUCE

2 tablespoons peanut oil (for sautéing chicken)

2 cups gluten-free, low-sodium chicken broth, such as Swanson's Natural Goodness, or homemade Chicken Broth (page 676)

3 tablespoons balsamic vinegar

2 tablespoons molasses (not blackstrap)

2 teaspoons grated fresh ginger

1 teaspoon gluten-free Asian fish sauce, such as A Taste of Thai

1 teaspoon crushed red pepper

1 garlic clove, minced

2 tablespoons wheat-free tamari soy sauce, such as Crystal or San-J

1½ tablespoons cornstarch

1⅓ pounds broccoli, cut into 1-inch florets (4 cups)

1 small red bell pepper, cut in ¼-inch vertical slices

2 green onions, finely chopped

¼ cup shelled roasted peanuts

4 cups hot cooked white rice

1 In a shallow bowl, combine marinade ingredients and add sliced chicken. Refrigerate 1 hour.

2 In a large, heavy skillet, heat the peanut oil over medium-high heat. Remove chicken from marinade (reserve marinade) and sauté chicken in peanut oil until lightly browned on both sides, stirring frequently. Transfer chicken to a plate.

3 In a large bowl, combine ¼ cup of the chicken broth with cornstarch and stir until smooth. Add remaining chicken broth, reserved marinade, and vinegar, molasses, ginger, fish sauce, crushed red pepper, soy sauce, and garlic and stir until cornstarch is thoroughly blended.

4 Return skillet to medium heat and add chicken broth mixture, whisking constantly until sauce thickens slightly. Add broccoli, red bell pepper, green onions, and peanuts to skillet, cover, and reduce heat to low to gently steam vegetables for 2 to 3 minutes for slightly al dente; steam them a little longer for softer vegetables. Return chicken to skillet and bring to serving temperature. Serve with hot rice.

Indian-Spiced Chicken Over Basmati Rice

MAKES 4 SERVINGS

Indian food is extraordinarily tasty because of a wide variety of aromatic spices, and this dish is no exception. Any leftovers reheat quite nicely the next day.

¼ cup wheat-free tamari soy sauce, such as Crystal or San-J

2 tablespoons fresh lime juice

2 tablespoons dry sherry

2 garlic cloves, minced

2 teaspoons peeled, minced fresh ginger

4 boneless skinless chicken breasts, cut in 1-inch cubes

2 tablespoons ground cumin

1 teaspoon freshly grated nutmeg

1 teaspoon ground allspice

¼ teaspoon curry powder

¼ teaspoon ground white pepper

¼ cup canola oil

1 can (14 to 15 ounces) stewed tomatoes, including juice

2 teaspoons cornstarch dissolved in 1 tablespoon cold water

4 cups hot cooked basmati rice

2 tablespoons chopped fresh cilantro, for garnish

1 In a glass or ceramic dish large enough to hold 4 chicken breasts, combine soy sauce, lime juice, sherry, garlic, and ginger. Add cubed chicken and refrigerate for 4 hours. Remove chicken from marinade and pat dry with paper towels; reserve marinade.

2 In a small bowl combine cumin, nutmeg, allspice, curry powder, and white pepper. Toss chicken with spice mixture.

3 In a large skillet, heat the oil over medium heat. Cook chicken 5 to 10 minutes or until lightly browned on both sides. Add tomatoes and reserved marinade to skillet, gently scraping bottom of skillet around chicken to loosen browned bits. Simmer chicken, covered, for 15 minutes. Remove lid and continue to simmer. Whisk cornstarch mixture into skillet and continue to whisk until mixture thickens. Serve over hot rice, garnished with cilantro.

Baked Herb Chicken

MAKES 4 SERVINGS

For me, the aroma of this dish conveys fond childhood memories of long autumn walks in the woodlands of eastern Nebraska, gathering bittersweet (a vine with bright red berries) along the way. My mother and my aunts would keep the chicken warm in the oven until we returned from our walk, all rosy-cheeked and famished.

½ cup cornstarch

8 small chicken pieces, drumsticks and thighs (or your preference)

2 teaspoons salt or gluten-free seasoned salt, such as Lawry's, or to taste

½ teaspoon freshly ground black pepper

2 tablespoons canola oil

1 Place a rack in the middle of the oven. Preheat the oven to 300°F. Put cornstarch in a wide shallow bowl or on wax paper. Over a clean work surface or bowl, season all sides of chicken pieces with salt and pepper. Dip each piece in cornstarch and shake to remove excess. Transfer each coated piece to a tray.

2 In a Dutch oven or other deep, heavy pot with a tight-fitting lid, heat the oil over medium-high heat. Cook chicken until deeply browned on all sides, about 15 to 20 minutes. Cover Dutch oven with lid or aluminum foil and place in oven.

3 Bake 1 to 2 hours. Remove from oven and serve immediately.

Baked Caraway Chicken: Sprinkle 1 tablespoon caraway seed over chicken before baking.

Slow-Baked Herbed Chicken

MAKES 4 SERVINGS

Rather than deep-frying chicken, this easy method uses very little oil and requires very little attention once it's in the oven. You can vary the herb seasoning as you wish, perhaps using your own favorite herb seasoning blend instead. It may remind you of "shake and bake" seasoning, but this one uses cornstarch instead of wheat flour and is made fresh each time.

8 small chicken pieces, drumsticks or thighs (or your preference)

2 teaspoons salt, divided

1 teaspoon freshly ground black pepper, divided

¾ cup cornstarch

4 teaspoons chopped fresh parsley or 2 teaspoons dried

2 teaspoons dry mustard

1 teaspoon paprika

2 teaspoons chopped fresh thyme or 1 teaspoon dried

½ teaspoon garlic powder

½ teaspoon onion powder

½ teaspoon ground cayenne

1 Place a rack in the middle of the oven. Preheat the oven to 375°F. Line a 13 × 9-inch baking sheet (not nonstick) with foil and coat with cooking spray. Set aside.

2 Season chicken pieces with 1 teaspoon of the salt and ½ teaspoon of the pepper. In a shallow bowl or small paper bag, combine cornstarch, parsley, mustard, paprika, thyme, garlic powder, onion powder, and cayenne. Dip chicken pieces into cornstarch mixture and then lay them on baking sheet. Sprinkle chicken with remaining 1 teaspoon salt and remaining ½ teaspoon black pepper. Coat the chicken pieces with cooking spray.

3 Bake 40 to 45 minutes or until chicken pieces are golden brown and until juice is no longer pink when centers of thickest pieces are cut. Turn chicken after 30 minutes to assure even browning on all sides. Serve immediately.

Buffalo Wings

MAKES 4 SERVINGS

I much prefer oven-roasting over deep-frying—it's healthier, tastes better, and is less dangerous than handling lots of hot oil. I guarantee that you will like these oven-roasted wings as much as the fried version.

SAUCE

1 can (8 ounces) tomato sauce

¼ cup (½ stick) unsalted butter or buttery spread, such as Earth Balance, or canola oil

¼ cup hot pepper sauce, such as Frank's

2 tablespoons cider vinegar

2 tablespoons packed brown sugar

1 tablespoon gluten-free Worcestershire sauce, such as French's

4 teaspoons fresh oregano or 2 teaspoons dried

½ teaspoon onion powder

½ teaspoon garlic powder

½ teaspoon chili powder

¼ teaspoon ground cayenne

¼ teaspoon white pepper

WINGS

4 pounds chicken wing drummettes

1 teaspoon salt

¼ teaspoon white pepper

Blue Cheese Dipping Sauce (page 674)

1 Make the cooking sauce: In a small saucepan, combine all sauce ingredients. Cook over low-medium heat, stirring until butter melts and all ingredients are combined. Cover, reduce heat to low, and simmer 15 minutes. Set aside until ready to use with wings.

2 Prepare the wings: Place a rack in the middle of the oven. Preheat the oven to 400°F. Arrange wings in single layer in foil-lined, rimmed baking sheet (not nonstick). Sprinkle with salt and pepper.

3 Bake wings 30 minutes or until thoroughly browned. During last 10 minutes of baking, baste wings with sauce. Remove wings from oven and arrange on serving plate. Drizzle some of the sauce on wings. Pass remaining sauce in a small pitcher and serve wings with Blue Cheese Dipping Sauce.

Roasted Lemon-Rosemary Chicken

MAKES 4 SERVINGS

Fresh rosemary sprigs add aroma and flavor to this dish. I keep several pots of rosemary growing in various spots in my yard so I always have a good supply. Barring that, you should also be able to find some fresh rosemary at a well-stocked grocery store.

8 chicken drumsticks
¼ cup fresh lemon juice
¼ cup extra-virgin olive oil
1 teaspoon grated lemon zest
4 teaspoons chopped fresh rosemary or 2 teaspoons dried, crushed, divided
2 garlic cloves, minced
2 tablespoons canola oil
2 white russet potatoes, unpeeled, cut in 2-inch pieces
1 small yellow onion, peeled and cut lengthwise in ¼-inch pieces
1 teaspoon salt, or to taste
½ teaspoon lemon pepper, or to taste
Olive oil cooking spray

1 Place drumsticks in a heavy-duty, food-storage bag. Add lemon juice, olive oil, lemon zest, 3 teaspoons of the fresh rosemary or 1½ teaspoons of the dried, and garlic. Seal bag and shake to thoroughly blend ingredients. Refrigerate overnight or all day.

2 Place a rack in the middle of the oven. Preheat the oven to 400°F. Coat bottom of roasting pan with canola oil. Remove chicken from marinade and discard marinade. Place chicken in bottom of roasting pan. Scatter potatoes and onions around chicken. Sprinkle chicken and potatoes with salt, lemon pepper, and remaining rosemary. Coat chicken, potatoes, and onions with cooking spray.

3 Roast 40 to 45 minutes or until chicken is cooked through and juice is no longer pink when centers of thickest pieces are cut. Serve hot.

Roasted Turkey Legs with Port-Cherry Sauce

MAKES 4 SERVINGS

My favorite part of the turkey is the leg; in fact, I could be happy dining on turkey legs forever, forgetting the rest of the bird (except for the thighs, perhaps). The rich, hearty port sauce is the perfect complement to the dark, succulent leg meat.

4 small turkey legs
1 teaspoon salt
1 teaspoon poultry seasoning or dried thyme
½ teaspoon freshly ground black pepper
½ cup ruby port
2 tablespoons balsamic vinegar
2 teaspoons sugar
1 teaspoon unsalted butter or buttery spread, such as Earth Balance, or canola oil
1 teaspoon onion powder
¼ teaspoon chopped fresh thyme
¼ cup sweetened dried cherries (or cranberries)

1 Place a rack in the middle of the oven. Preheat the oven to 400°F. Sprinkle turkey legs with salt, poultry seasoning, and pepper. Place on a rack in roasting pan, cover, and roast until the skin is crispy brown and the internal temperature reaches 160°F on an instant-read temperature inserted into the thickest part of the thigh or is cooked through. Remove from the heat, wrap in foil, and let stand 10 minutes.

2 While turkey legs are roasting, in a small saucepan, combine the port, vinegar, sugar, butter, onion powder, thyme, and cherries over medium-high heat. Bring to boil, reduce heat, and cook about 2 to 3 minutes or until port reduces by one-third. Remove from heat; the mixture will thicken as it cools. You should have about ⅔ cup sauce.

3 Serve each leg garnished with a drizzle of cherry-port sauce. Heat sauce over low heat if it becomes too thick and serve warm.

GROUND, PULLED, OR SHREDDED POULTRY

Turkey Meat Loaf

MAKES 6 SERVINGS

Meat loaf, a delicious comfort food staple, typically uses regular bread crumbs but can easily be made with alternate binders. If this is a family favorite, try different options to see which your family likes best. Traditionally made with ground beef, meat loaf can be far less calorie-laden and just as tasty if you use ground turkey. Or, use a combination of ground turkey, chicken, beef, and pork.

1 can (8 ounces) tomato sauce

2 tablespoons packed light brown sugar, divided

1 tablespoon Dijon mustard

2 tablespoons gluten-free Worcestershire sauce, such as French's

1 pound ground turkey (I use half dark meat and half white meat)

4 tablespoons finely diced fresh onion or 2 tablespoons dried minced onions

2 teaspoons chopped fresh thyme or 1 teaspoon dried

1 teaspoon chopped fresh rosemary or ½ teaspoon dried

1 large egg, beaten

2 tablespoons chopped fresh parsley or 1 tablespoon dried

1 teaspoon celery salt

2 teaspoons chopped fresh oregano or ½ teaspoon dried

½ teaspoon freshly ground black pepper

⅛ teaspoon ground allspice

½ cup gluten-free bread crumbs, such as Ener-G, or homemade Plain Bread Crumbs (page 117), uncooked cream of rice cereal, or instant potato flakes

2 strips uncooked bacon

1 Place a rack in the middle of the oven. Preheat the oven to 325°F. Generously grease an 8 × 4-inch nonstick (gray, not black) loaf pan. Or, line a 13 × 9-inch nonstick (gray, not black) baking sheet with aluminum foil.

2 In a small bowl, combine the tomato sauce, 1 tablespoon of the brown sugar, mustard, and Worcestershire sauce. Stir until thoroughly blended.

3 In a large mixing bowl, place half of the tomato sauce mixture and remaining tablespoon of brown sugar. Add all remaining ingredients, except bacon to the bowl and mix with your hands until thoroughly blended. Transfer the mixture to the pan or baking sheet. Spread the remaining half of the tomato sauce mixture evenly on top. Lay two strips of bacon lengthwise on the meat loaf.

4 Bake 45 minutes to 1 hour or until the internal temperature reaches 160°F on an instant-read temperature or is cooked through. Baking time will depend on how thick the turkey meat loaf is. Let stand 10 minutes before slicing. Serve hot, at room temperature, or cold in a sandwich.

Turkey Meatballs with White Parmesan Gravy

MAKES 4 SERVINGS (16 MEATBALLS)

This recipe can be used for ground pork, beef, or chicken instead of turkey. Make the meatballs any size you like, but giant meatballs are quicker to make and more fun to eat so try making them into 8 large balls next time, rather than 16 smaller ones. Serve them with red sauce on pasta, cut in pieces for meatball sandwiches, or added to soups.

MEATBALLS

½ cup grated Parmesan cheese or soy alternative, such as Soyco

⅓ cup finely diced fresh onion or 1½ tablespoons dried minced onion

1 tablespoon Dijon mustard

2 tablespoons chopped fresh parsley or 1 tablespoon dried

¾ teaspoon salt

½ teaspoon freshly ground black pepper

¼ teaspoon garlic powder

1 large egg, beaten

1½ cups 1% milk (cow, rice, soy, potato, or nut) or gluten-free, low-sodium chicken broth, such as Swanson's Natural Goodness, or homemade Chicken Broth (page 676)

1½ cups gluten-free bread crumbs, such as Ener-G, or homemade Plain Bread Crumbs (page 117)

2 pounds ground turkey (I use half dark and half white meat)

Cooking spray

GRAVY

2 cups 1% milk (cow's, rice, soy, potato, or nut)

4 teaspoons sweet rice flour (2 tablespoons if using rice milk or potato milk)

1 teaspoon onion powder

¾ teaspoon salt

½ teaspoon freshly ground black pepper

⅛ teaspoon freshly grated nutmeg

¼ cup grated Parmesan cheese or soy alternative, such as Soyco

2 tablespoons chopped fresh parsley or 1 tablespoon dried, for garnish

1 Place a rack in the middle of the oven. Preheat the oven to 350°F. Line 13 × 9-inch baking sheet (not nonstick) with foil and spray with cooking spray for easy clean-up.

2 Make the meatballs: In a medium bowl, combine cheese, onion, mustard, parsley, garlic, salt, and pepper. Stir to thoroughly combine. Add egg and milk and stir until mixture is smooth. Add bread crumbs and turkey and mix with hands or spatula until thoroughly combined. Shape into 16 balls, each about 1¼ inches in diameter. Place on prepared sheet. Coat balls with cooking spray.

3 Roast 25 to 30 minutes or until meatballs are brown and firm. Remove from oven.

4 While the meatballs are roasting, make the gravy: In a medium pan, heat 1½ cups of the milk until it bubbles around the edge of the pan. Stir sweet rice flour, onion powder, salt, pepper, and nutmeg into remaining ½ cup of milk until mixture is very smooth. Stir mixture into pan and cook, whisking constantly, until mixture thickens, about 7 to 10 minutes. Remove from heat and stir in Parmesan cheese. Serve meatballs hot with gravy, garnished with parsley.

Cincinnati Turkey Chili

MAKES 4 SERVINGS

This regional chili is usually made with ground beef, but ground turkey or ground pork also work well in my tasty version. Cincinnati-style chili, unlike Southwestern chili, is served on top of something—such as spaghetti—rather than by itself. The garnishes make it even more unique so be sure to have plenty on hand.

1 tablespoon canola oil

1 pound ground turkey (I use half dark and half white meat)

1 cup finely chopped onions

1 tablespoon tomato paste

1 tablespoon chili powder

4 teaspoons chopped fresh oregano or 2 teaspoons dried

1 teaspoon ground cinnamon

½ teaspoon salt

½ teaspoon freshly ground black pepper

¼ teaspoon ground allspice

1 can (14 to 15 ounces) or 1¾ cups gluten-free, low-sodium chicken broth, such as Swanson's Natural Goodness, or homemade Chicken Broth (page 117)

2 cans (8 ounces each) tomato sauce

1 garlic clove, minced

1 tablespoon cider vinegar

1 teaspoon packed light brown sugar

Water (if mixture is too thick)

Additional salt and freshly ground pepper to taste

GARNISHES

Chopped green onions

Grated Cheddar cheese or cheese alternative, such as Vegan Gourmet

Cooked pinto beans

1 In a Dutch oven or other deep, heavy pot with a tight-fitting lid, heat the oil over medium-high heat. Add turkey and onions and cook until onions are soft and turkey is browned, about 10 to 12 minutes. Add tomato paste, chili powder, oregano, cinnamon, salt, pepper, and allspice and cook, stirring constantly, for 1 minute.

2 Add chicken broth, tomato sauce, garlic, vinegar, and brown sugar. Bring to a boil, reduce heat to low, and simmer, uncovered, for 25 to 30 minutes. Chili will thicken slightly, but if it gets too thick stir in more water, ¼ cup at a time, and bring to serving temperature. Add more salt and pepper to taste, if desired. Serve hot, garnished with onions, cheese, and beans.

Maple-Mustard-Glazed Turkey Bacon Ⓠ

MAKES 1 POUND

This maple-mustard glaze can be used on pork bacon, too, but it works especially well with the mild flavor of turkey bacon. Cook up a batch and then use it—not only for breakfast—but also to flavor main dishes as well.

1 pound turkey bacon, sliced

¼ cup Dijon mustard

¼ cup pure maple syrup

1 Place a rack in the middle of the oven. Preheat the oven to 350°F. Lay bacon strips in single layer on a foil-lined rimmed baking sheet.

2 Combine mustard and maple syrup. Brush on bacon.

3 Bake 10 to 15 minutes or until bacon is cooked through. Remove from oven. Serve hot.

CASSEROLES AND SLOW-COOKED DISHES

Chicken and Rice Casserole

MAKES 4 SERVINGS

You can use any combination of vegetables you wish, even a pre-blended bag of vegetables. While most casseroles of this type would use mushroom soup, you'll find that the potato-leek or sweet corn flavors by Imagine work well.

2 cups (16-ounce box) Imagine Potato Leek or Creamy Sweet Corn Soup

¾ cup uncooked long-grain white rice

½ cup fresh or frozen sliced carrots, thawed

½ cup fresh or frozen peas, thawed

½ cup fresh or frozen corn, thawed

½ teaspoon onion powder

4 boneless skinless chicken breasts (about 1¼ pounds)

1 teaspoon salt

½ teaspoon freshly ground black pepper

½ cup grated sharp Cheddar cheese or cheese alternative, such as Vegan Gourmet

2 tablespoons chopped fresh parsley, for garnish

1 Place a rack in the middle of the oven. Preheat the oven to 375°F. Generously grease 11 × 7-inch or 12 × 8-inch ovenproof baking dish.

2 In a bowl, combine soup, rice, carrots, peas, corn, and onion powder. Pour into prepared dish. Sprinkle chicken pieces with salt and pepper and place in pan.

3 Bake 45 minutes to 1 hour or until chicken and vegetables are done. Uncover and sprinkle chicken with cheese. Bake 5 minutes more or until cheese is melted. Remove from oven and cool 5 minutes before serving. Serve hot garnished with parsley.

Chicken–Chile Relleno Casserole

MAKES 4 SERVINGS

All of the wonderful flavors of classic Mexican chiles rellenos are included in this casserole, but with far less work. This is a very simple one-dish meal: all you need are a salad and your favorite gluten-free bread or tortillas. If you like your Mexican food very mild, reduce the green chiles to one-half can. This dish works best using dairy cheese.

1 cup mozzarella cheese, shredded (reserve ¼ cup)

1 cup mild Cheddar or Colby cheese, shredded (reserve ¼ cup)

1 cup cooked chicken, cut in ½-inch cubes

1 can (4 ounces) diced green chiles

4 large eggs, at room temperature

1 cup sour cream or sour cream alternative, such as Tofutti, at room temperature

1 teaspoon baking powder

½ teaspoon chopped fresh oregano or ¼ teaspoon dried

¼ teaspoon ground cumin

⅛ teaspoon chili powder

Paprika, for garnish

¼ cup chopped fresh cilantro, for garnish

1 Place a rack in the middle of the oven. Preheat the oven to 350°F. Generously grease an 8-inch square baking dish.

2 Layer the ingredients in the dish, starting with the cheeses, then the chicken, and then the chiles, ending with the reserved ¼ cup of each of the cheeses.

3 In a medium bowl, whisk together the eggs, sour cream, baking powder, oregano, cumin, and chili powder and pour over the cheese mixture. Sprinkle generously with paprika.

4 Bake 30 to 45 minutes, or until the top is puffy and golden. Serve immediately, garnished with chopped cilantro.

Turkey Rice Casserole

MAKES 4 SERVINGS

Leftover turkey (or chicken) is resurrected in this simple, down-home casserole. Instant brown rice is a marvelous invention for harried cooks, so keep it on hand at all times. If you keep cooked turkey on hand in the freezer (as I often do) then you'll always have the makings for this dish.

2 cups cooked turkey, cut in 1-inch pieces

1 cup instant brown rice

1 can (7 ounces) sliced water chestnuts, drained

1 can (7 ounces) sliced mushrooms, drained

1 small red bell pepper, in vertical thin slices

4 tablespoons finely diced onion or 1 tablespoon dried minced onion

1½ teaspoons curry powder

1 teaspoon chopped fresh thyme or ½ teaspoon dried

¼ teaspoon garlic powder

3 tablespoons sweet rice flour

1¼ cups 1% milk (cow's, rice, soy, potato, or nut)

1 cup gluten-free low-sodium chicken broth, such as Swanson's Natural Goodness, or homemade Chicken Broth (page 676)

1 tablespoon canola oil

2 tablespoons wheat-free tamari soy sauce, such as Crystal or San-J

2 teaspoons chopped fresh parsley or 1 teaspoon dried

2 tablespoons sliced almonds

1 Place a rack in the middle of the oven. Preheat the oven to 350°F. Generously grease an 11 × 7-inch glass baking dish. Arrange turkey in dish and pour brown rice around it. Put water chestnuts, mushroom, and bell peppers on top.

2 In a medium saucepan, whisk together onion, curry powder, thyme, garlic powder, and sweet rice flour until thoroughly blended. Add milk and broth and cook over medium heat, whisking constantly, until mixture comes to a boil and slightly thickens, about 2 to 3 minutes. Remove from heat and whisk in canola oil and soy sauce. Gently pour over mixture in prepared dish. Tilt dish to make sure liquid gets to corners. Sprinkle with parsley and almonds. Cover loosely with foil.

3 Bake 20 to 25 minutes or until juices are bubbly and rice is tender. Remove foil during last 5 minutes of baking. Remove from oven and serve immediately.

Arroz con Pollo

MAKES 4 SERVINGS

The name of this dish means "rice with chicken" in Spanish and has many versions, but any way you prepare it is a meal in itself. You can transfer the ingredients to a decorative casserole dish before baking, but I often just bake it right in the oven-proof skillet in which I browned the chicken. Then I serve it, family-style, right in the skillet—saving another dish from the dishwasher.

2 pounds chicken legs and thighs (about 8 pieces)

2 teaspoons gluten-free seasoned salt, such as Lawry's

½ teaspoon freshly ground black pepper

¼ cup cornstarch

¼ cup canola oil

½ cup finely diced onion or 2 tablespoons dried minced onions

1 can (14 to 15 ounces) petite diced tomatoes, including juice

1½ cups long-grain white rice

1 can (14 to 15 ounces) or 1¾ cups gluten-free, low-sodium chicken broth, such as Swanson's Natural Goodness, or homemade Chicken Broth (page 676)

1 can (4 ounces) sliced mushrooms, including juice

¼ cup dry sherry

1 garlic clove, minced

1 bay leaf

⅛ teaspoon crushed red pepper

⅛ teaspoon crushed saffron threads

1 cup frozen green peas, thawed

2 tablespoons chopped fresh parsley, for garnish

1 Place a rack in the middle of the oven. Preheat the oven to 375°F. Generously grease 11 × 7-inch or 12 × 8-inch casserole dish. Sprinkle chicken pieces with seasoned salt and pepper. Roll each piece in cornstarch to coat thoroughly.

2 In a large, heavy skillet, heat the oil over medium-high heat. Cook chicken pieces until browned on all sides, about 5 minutes per side. Place chicken in prepared casserole. Combine onion, tomatoes, rice, chicken broth, mushrooms, sherry, garlic, bay leaf, red pepper, and saffron and mix thoroughly. Pour over chicken. Cover tightly with lid or aluminum foil.

3 Bake 40 to 45 minutes. Add green peas and continue baking, covered, 10 to 15 minutes more or until liquid is absorbed. Remove bay leaf. Serve hot, garnished with chopped parsley.

Baked Aloha Pineapple Chicken

MAKES 4 SERVINGS

This is a perfect dish for your dinner guests. I serve it routinely because it is fail-safe and always receives rave reviews due to the unexpected, yet tantalizing combination of savory-sweet tarragon and thyme with the sweet-tart pineapple. It can be assembled ahead of time—perhaps that morning— and then baked just prior to serving. Add a side of basmati rice and sautéed red and green peppers for a colorful plate.

4 boneless skinless chicken breasts (about 1¼ pounds)
½ teaspoon salt
¼ teaspoon freshly ground black pepper
2 tablespoons olive oil
1 can (8 ounces) crushed pineapple, including juice
½ cup dry white wine
1 tablespoon gluten-free Worcestershire sauce, such as French's
1 tablespoon Dijon mustard
1 garlic clove, minced
1 teaspoon chopped fresh thyme or ½ teaspoon dried
½ teaspoon chopped fresh tarragon or ¼ teaspoon dried
1 teaspoon cornstarch mixed with 1 tablespoon water (optional)
2 tablespoons chopped fresh parsley or cilantro, for garnish
¼ cup chopped macadamia nuts or slivered almonds, for garnish

1 Place a rack in the middle of the oven. Preheat the oven to 375°F. Sprinkle the chicken with salt and pepper. In a 10-inch ovenproof skillet, heat the oil over medium-high heat. Cook chicken until dark golden brown on both sides, about 10 minutes.

2 In a small bowl, whisk the pineapple, wine, Worcestershire sauce, mustard, garlic, thyme, and tarragon and pour over chicken. Cover and bake 45 to 50 minutes. Uncover, turn chicken over and bake 10 minutes more.

3 Remove skillet from oven and transfer chicken to a plate. Cover with foil to keep warm. Place skillet over medium heat and boil juices. If they are thick enough, return chicken to pan and serve. If not, mix cornstarch with water to form paste. Stir cornstarch mixture into boiling juices and cook over medium heat until mixture thickens.

4 To serve, pour pineapple mixture over chicken breasts. Garnish with parsley and nuts.

Paella

MAKES 6 SERVINGS

Paella is a Spanish rice dish that typically includes shellfish and chicken, but it can take many different forms. I serve this dish often to guests but always ask if any of them have allergies to its ingredients. If anybody is allergic to fish, I simply omit it and add a bit more chicken. Sometimes I use gluten-free pepperoni slices by Hormel, which complement the flavors in the chorizo.

2 tablespoons extra-virgin olive oil
6 mixed chicken pieces (drumsticks, thighs, or chicken breast halves)
¼ pound gluten-free chorizo, such as Publix, cut in ¼-inch slices
½ cup chopped onion
1 can (28 ounces) diced tomatoes, including juice
3 garlic cloves, minced
1 tablespoon paprika
4 teaspoons chopped fresh oregano or 2 teaspoons dried
½ teaspoon crushed saffron threads
1 teaspoon salt
¼ teaspoon freshly ground black pepper
4½ cups gluten-free, low-sodium chicken broth, such as Swanson's Natural Goodness, or homemade Chicken Broth (page 676)
1½ cups uncooked, short-grain white rice
1 package (9 ounces) frozen artichoke or 1 can (14 to 15 ounces) artichoke hearts, drained
½ small jar (3 ounces) pimientos (optional)
½ pound shrimp, peeled and deveined
1 cup green peas
2 tablespoons chopped fresh parsley, for garnish
2 fresh lemons, cut into half, for drizzling over chicken

1 In a large ovenproof skillet or paella pan, heat the olive oil over medium heat. Cook chicken until browned on all sides, about 5 minutes per side. Remove chicken from skillet. Add chorizo and onion and cook over medium heat until lightly browned, about 5 minutes. Add tomatoes, garlic, paprika, oregano, saffron, salt, pepper, chicken broth, rice, and artichokes. Bring mixture to a boil, reduce heat and simmer, covered, 15 minutes.

2 Return chicken to pan. Cover and simmer 30 minutes. (If using an ovenproof skillet, you may bake in oven at 350°F for 30 minutes.) Uncover, add pimentos, shrimp, and green peas and cook 5 minutes more or until shrimp is cooked through. Serve immediately, garnished with fresh parsley and a drizzle of fresh lemon juice.

Chicken Divan

MAKES 4 SERVINGS

My version of this old favorite has the broccoli on top for a more colorful dish, but if you prefer the traditional way of having it under the chicken, you may do that too. There is no additional salt in this recipe because reducing the chicken broth intensifies the salt level, but you can always add salt and pepper if you wish.

2 tablespoons unsalted butter, or buttery spread, such as Earth Balance, or canola oil, divided

1 pound broccoli, cut into 1-inch florets (3 cups)

1 pound boneless skinless chicken breasts, sliced thin

2 tablespoons finely chopped onion

1½ cups gluten-free, low-sodium chicken broth, such as Swanson's Natural Goodness, or homemade Chicken Broth (page 676)

½ cup heavy cream or soy milk

¼ cup dry sherry

2 teaspoons gluten-free Worcestershire sauce, such as French's

⅛ teaspoon freshly grated nutmeg

1 cup grated Parmesan cheese or soy alternative, such as Soyco, divided

3 large egg yolks

1 tablespoon lemon juice

½ cup slivered almonds

1 Heat 1 tablespoon of the butter in a large, heavy ovenproof skillet over medium heat. Add broccoli, cover with lid, and cook 1 to 2 minutes. Transfer broccoli to plate.

2 Heat the remaining tablespoon of butter in same skillet over medium-high heat. Add chicken and onion and cook until cooked through and golden brown on both sides, about 3 to 5 minutes per side. Transfer chicken to plate with broccoli.

3 Place a broiler rack about 6 inches away from the heat source. Preheat the broiler. Add broth and cream to skillet. Cook, scraping bottom of skillet, until sauce is reduced to 1 cup, about 7 to 10 minutes. Add sherry, Worcestershire sauce, and nutmeg. Simmer again until reduced to 1 cup.

4 Stir in ¾ cup of the Parmesan cheese. In a small bowl, whisk egg yolks and lemon juice. Whisk ¼ cup sauce into egg mixture and then whisk mixture back into skillet. Return chicken to skillet. Arrange broccoli in single layer on chicken and spoon some of the sauce over the broccoli. Sprinkle remaining ¼ cup Parmesan cheese over broccoli. Sprinkle almonds on broccoli.

5 Broil until bubbly and golden brown. Watch carefully to avoid burning. Serve immediately.

ROTISSERIE CHICKENS

Many cooks use store-bought rotisserie chicken from the deli as a time-saving convenience. While you too may be tempted to simply buy a rotisserie chicken instead of roasting one at home, don't—unless it is guaranteed to be gluten-free by the store or the manufacturer (for example, Perdue). Otherwise, if you purchase it in the typical deli environment, you don't know if it has come into contact with gluten—from ingredients in its preparation, from touching other gluten-containing foods in the store, or from being handled by someone who has touched gluten.

Chicken Pot Pie

MAKES 4 SERVINGS

A pot pie is a perfect way to use up leftover cooked chicken. If you prefer a creamy filling, replace half of the chicken broth with whole cream. This delicious home-style dish is comfort food at its best.

FILLING

2 cups cooked chicken, cut in ½-inch pieces

½ cup chopped onion

¼ pound broccoli, cut in 1-inch florets (½ cup)

1 small carrot, peeled and thinly sliced

¼ cup frozen corn kernels

¼ cup frozen green peas

1 small cooked russet potato, peeled and cubed

1 ripe plum or Roma tomato, cut in ½-inch cubes

1 tablespoon Dijon mustard

1 teaspoon salt

2 teaspoons chopped fresh thyme or 1 teaspoon dried

1 teaspoon chopped fresh rosemary or ½ teaspoon dried, crushed

¼ teaspoon summer savory, crushed (optional)

¼ teaspoon freshly ground black pepper

Dash of freshly grated nutmeg

1 cup gluten-free, low-sodium chicken broth, such as Swanson's Natural Goodness, or homemade Chicken Broth (page 676)

1 tablespoon cornstarch stirred into 2 tablespoons cold water

TOPPING

1 cup Carol's Sorghum Blend (page x)

1 teaspoon sugar

1 teaspoon baking powder

¼ teaspoon baking soda

1 teaspoon xanthan gum

2 teaspoons chopped fresh parsley or 1 teaspoon dried

¼ teaspoon celery salt

2 tablespoons butter or buttery spread, such as Earth Balance, melted

½ cup 1% milk (cow's, rice, soy, potato, or nut)

1 large egg white

1 Place a rack in the middle of the oven. Preheat the oven to 375°F. Generously grease 8- or 9-inch round deep baking dish.

2 Place all filling ingredients (except cornstarch) in dish and mix together. (At this point, you may refrigerate the filling until you want to bake it—either the next day or that night.)

3 Bake mixture, covered, 30 minutes or until mixture is bubbling. Remove from oven.

4 While filling bakes, combine biscuit ingredients in a small bowl and whisk together. Drop by tablespoons onto hot filling. Return chicken pot pie to oven and bake 20 to 25 minutes or until biscuit topping is golden brown and crisp. Serve hot.

Chicken-Artichoke-Mushroom Casserole

MAKES 4 SERVINGS

A family friend frequently served her own version of this dish to guests and I always loved visiting her home knowing it would be on the menu. I adapted that dish to the current version you see here, using sorghum flour and gluten-free bread crumbs for the crispy coating. All you need is some crusty gluten-free French bread and a crispy salad to round it out.

4 boneless skinless chicken breast halves (about 1¼ pounds)

1 cup gluten-free bread crumbs, such as Ener-G, or homemade Plain Bread Crumbs (page 117)

¼ cup sorghum flour

1 large egg, lightly beaten with 1 tablespoon water

1 tablespoon olive oil

1 tablespoon unsalted butter, or buttery spread, such as Earth Balance, or canola oil

½ teaspoon salt

¼ teaspoon freshly ground black pepper

1 can (6.5 ounces) sliced mushrooms, drained

1 jar (6.5 ounces) marinated artichokes, drained

¼ cup dry sherry or dry white wine

½ cup shredded Provolone cheese or 4 large slices of Provolone, or cheese alternative such as Vegan Gourmet

Juice of 1 lemon, for drizzling over chicken

Additional salt and pepper, to taste

1 Place a rack in the middle of the oven. Preheat the oven to 375°F. Generously grease an 8-inch baking dish.

2 Cut each breast into thin slices. Combine bread crumbs and sorghum flour in pie plate. Dip chicken pieces into beaten egg, then into the bread crumbs.

3 In a heavy skillet, heat olive oil and butter over medium-high heat. Cook chicken slices until golden brown, about 5 minutes per side. Season each side with salt and pepper.

4 Layer chicken slices on bottom; top with mushrooms and artichokes. Pour sherry over chicken.

5 Bake 25 to 30 minutes or until liquid is bubbly. Place cheese on top of chicken and return to oven for 5 minutes more. Just before serving, squeeze fresh lemon juice over casserole. Add salt and pepper to taste. Serve immediately.

Coq au Vin

MAKES 4 SERVINGS

This classic French dish means "chicken in wine." The secret to achieving its wonderful flavor is to deeply brown the chicken, onions, and carrots before adding the broth and wine. This is the perfect dish for a cold winter's day when you want something hearty in the oven, filling the kitchen with a heavenly aroma.

1 slice bacon, uncooked

1 teaspoon olive oil

8 chicken legs and thighs

1 package (10 ounces) frozen pearl onions, thawed

1 can (8 ounces) sliced mushrooms, drained

1 cup gluten-free, low-sodium chicken broth, such as Swanson's Natural Goodness, or homemade Chicken Broth (page 676)

1 cup dry red wine

1 tablespoon gluten-free Worcestershire sauce, such as French's

2 garlic cloves, peeled and crushed

2 teaspoons chopped fresh thyme or 1 teaspoon dried

1 teaspoon sugar

½ teaspoon freshly ground black pepper

1 bay leaf

1 pound baby carrots

½ teaspoon salt

½ cup chopped fresh parsley, for garnish

1 In a Dutch oven or other deep, heavy pot with a tight-fitting lid, brown the bacon slice until crisp. Remove bacon from pan and remove pan from heat, leaving the bacon drippings in the Dutch oven. Reserve the bacon.

2 Pat chicken dry with paper towels. Return Dutch oven to medium heat. Add 1 teaspoon olive oil to bacon drippings. Cook chicken pieces until browned on all sides, about 3 to 5 minutes per side. Remove chicken from pan and set aside.

3 Place a rack in the middle of the oven. Preheat the oven to 400°F. In the same Dutch oven, brown the onions for about 5 minutes. Add the mushrooms and sauté 5 minutes more. Slowly pour in the chicken broth, wine, and Worcestershire sauce. Add the garlic, thyme, sugar, black pepper, and bay leaf. Return chicken to the pan and add the reserved bacon slice.

4 Bake, covered, 30 minutes. Reduce heat to 350°F, add carrots and salt and continue cooking 30 minutes more. Remove bay leaf and serve hot, garnished with parsley.

Chicken Cacciatore

MAKES 4 SERVINGS

Though there are many variations to this hearty dish, this version absolutely delights my family or dinner guests on cold, snowy nights. Often called Hunter's Stew, legend has it that Italian wives prepared it for their husbands to fortify them during hunting season. I like to think that my guests leave well-fortified for their journey home.

4 boneless skinless chicken breast halves (about 1¼ pounds)

2 tablespoons olive oil

1 can (8 ounces) chopped mushroom pieces

½ cup finely chopped red bell pepper

1 small onion, finely diced

1 garlic clove, minced

1 can (14 to 15 ounces) whole peeled tomatoes with juice (chop whole tomatoes with kitchen shears)

½ cup dry red wine

2 tablespoons drained and rinsed capers (optional)

2 tablespoons fresh lemon juice

1 tablespoon tomato paste

4 teaspoons chopped fresh oregano or 2 teaspoons dried

2 teaspoons chopped fresh thyme or 1 teaspoon dried

1 teaspoon sugar

½ teaspoon salt

¼ teaspoon crushed red pepper

¼ teaspoon freshly ground black pepper

2 teaspoons cornstarch mixed in 2 tablespoons cold water until smooth

4 cups hot cooked gluten-free pasta, such as Tinkyada

1 In a Dutch oven or other deep, heavy pot with a tight-fitting lid, heat the oil over medium-high heat. Add chicken breasts and cook until golden brown on all sides, about 5 minutes per side. Transfer chicken to plate. Add mushrooms, red bell peppers, onion, and garlic to skillet. Cook vegetables, stirring often, until they begin to soften.

2 Add tomatoes, wine, capers, lemon juice, tomato paste, oregano, thyme, sugar, salt, crushed red pepper, and black pepper and bring to boil. Return chicken to skillet, reduce heat to low and simmer, covered, 30 minutes.

3 To thicken sauce before serving, stir cornstarch mixture into sauce over medium heat, stirring until sauce thickens. Serve sauce over chicken and pasta.

Chicken Fricassee

MAKES 4 SERVINGS

Fricassee is a mixture of stewed chicken and vegetables that can be served over dumplings, biscuits, or rice, as in this easy version here. Amazingly versatile, it can be made ahead and reheated the next day for even better flavor.

8 chicken thighs (about 1 pound)

½ teaspoon salt

½ teaspoon freshly ground black pepper

2 tablespoons olive oil, divided

1 can (8 ounces) sliced mushrooms, drained

2 garlic cloves, minced

2 teaspoons chopped fresh rosemary or 1 teaspoon dried, crushed

2 teaspoons chopped fresh thyme or 1 teaspoon dried

¼ teaspoon crushed red pepper

1 cup dry white wine

1 cup gluten-free, low-sodium chicken broth, such as Swanson's Natural Goodness, or homemade Chicken Broth (page 676)

1 tablespoon cornstarch whisked with 2 tablespoon cold water until smooth

12 cherry tomatoes, halved

12 Nicoise olives, pitted

4 cups hot cooked white rice

¼ cup chopped fre sh parsley, for garnish

1 Sprinkle the chicken thighs with salt and pepper.

2 Heat the olive oil in a heavy medium saucepan or skillet over medium heat. Cook the chicken thighs, turning frequently, until well-browned, about 5 minutes per side. Add the mushrooms, garlic, rosemary, thyme, red pepper, wine, and broth and cook about 3 minutes, scraping the bottom of the skillet with a wooden spoon. Reduce the heat to low; cover, and simmer gently 1 hour. Stir the cornstarch mixture into the pan and cook over medium heat, stirring constantly, until thickened.

3 Sprinkle the tomatoes and olives over the chicken, cover, remove from the heat, and let stand 5 minutes. Serve over hot cooked rice, garnished with parsley.

Chicken Curry

MAKES 4 SERVINGS

This is an especially quick, simple curry. For more timid palates, use ¼ teaspoon ground cayenne. For the more adventurous, increase that to ½ teaspoon. Beyond that, you're on your own! This may seem like a lot of measuring, but curry is—by definition—a flavorful dish and requires lots of spices.

4 cups hot Coconut Rice (page 218) or hot cooked white basmati rice
2 tablespoons canola oil
1 pound (about 1¾ cups) cubed chicken breast
1 cup petite diced tomatoes, including juice
½ teaspoon ground mustard
¼ teaspoon ground cayenne, or to taste
¼ teaspoon ground cumin
¼ teaspoon ground turmeric
¼ teaspoon curry powder
¼ teaspoon salt
⅛ teaspoon ground cloves
¾ cup coconut milk
2 tablespoons chopped fresh cilantro, for garnish

1 Prepare coconut rice. Then, in a large skillet, heat the oil over medium-high heat. Add chicken and cook until darkly browned on all sides, about 5 to 7 minutes.

2 Stir in tomatoes, mustard, cayenne, cumin, turmeric, curry powder, salt, cloves and coconut milk until blended. Reduce heat to low and simmer 10 minutes or until chicken is completely cooked through and juices reduce down slightly. Serve over hot coconut rice, garnished with cilantro.

Chicken Mole

MAKES 4 SERVINGS

Mole is a Mexican sauce traditionally made with many ingredients, including chocolate, which adds rich flavor, but not sweetness. I add cocoa, which is easier to have on hand and contributes less fat to the dish. A mole is usually thickened with bread or tortillas, but I've revised it so it just naturally thickens on its own.

8 chicken legs and thighs
Juice of 2 limes
½ teaspoon salt
¼ teaspoon freshly ground black pepper
1 can (14 to 15 ounces) petite diced tomatoes, including juice
½ small onion, chopped
1 garlic clove, minced
2 tablespoons blanched almonds, toasted
2 tablespoons chopped fresh cilantro
½ teaspoon ground cinnamon
½ teaspoon chipotle chile powder, such as McCormick's
¼ teaspoon ground cumin
⅛ teaspoon ground allspice
⅛ teaspoon ground cloves
Dash of gluten-free liquid smoke seasoning, such as Durkee or Spice Islands
2 tablespoons unsweetened cocoa powder (Dutch-process or alkali)
¼ cup water (or more)
2 tablespoons olive oil

1 Sprinkle chicken with lime juice, then sprinkle with salt and pepper. Let stand while preparing other ingredients.

2 In a blender, combine tomatoes, onion, garlic, almonds, cilantro, cinnamon, chipotle chile powder, cumin, allspice, cloves, liquid smoke, cocoa, and water. Puree until very, very smooth. Add more water if mixture is too thick. Set aside.

3 In a large, heavy skillet, heat oil over medium-high heat and cook chicken until golden brown on all sides, about 5 minutes per side. Remove skillet from heat.

4 Pour mole sauce over chicken and slowly bring to boil. Immediately reduce heat to low, cover, and simmer 15 minutes. Serve immediately.

Chicken Provençal

MAKES 4 SERVINGS

The term Provençal *refers to the style of Provence cooking, and I didn't understand the American romance with southern France until I visited that lovely region for myself. Now I too have developed a fondness for Mediterranean fare like this one, which incorporates all the typical flavors—tomatoes, olives, olive oil, and herbs—of that delightful corner of the world.*

4 boneless skinless chicken breast halves (about 1¼ pounds)
1 teaspoon salt
½ teaspoon freshly ground black pepper
2 tablespoons olive oil
1 garlic clove, minced
½ cup dry white wine
2 teaspoons snipped fresh rosemary or 1 teaspoon dried, crushed
1 tablespoon Dijon mustard
2 green onions, sliced
¼ cup pitted kalamata olives
1 teaspoon capers, drained and rinsed
2 ripe plum or Roma tomatoes or 6 grape tomatoes, seeded and diced
2 tablespoons chopped fresh parsley, for garnish

1 Sprinkle chicken breasts with salt and pepper.

2 In a large, heavy skillet, heat the oil over medium heat. Add chicken and cook until golden brown on all sides, about 5 minutes per side depending on size or until juice is no longer pink when cut in the thickest part. Transfer chicken to plate and cover with foil to keep warm.

3 In the same skillet, add garlic and wine and cook about 1 minute, scraping up browned bits from bottom of skillet. Add rosemary, mustard, onions, olives, and capers and cook 1 minute more. Add tomatoes and heat to serving temperature. Pour over chicken and serve, garnished with chopped parsley.

Chicken Saltimbocca

MAKES 4 SERVINGS

Saltimbocca literally means "jumps in the mouth" in Italian. This dish's full flavor makes it a fitting name. Often made with veal, my version is simply thin slices of chicken breasts, prosciutto, and Provolone cheese braised in white wine. It is very easy to assemble. It is easier if you use thin-sliced chicken breasts, but regular chicken breasts halves will work, too. You just have to pound them more to get the ⅛-inch thickness. If they are particularly large, slice them horizontally in half.

4 thin-sliced boneless skinless chicken breast halves (about 1¼ pounds)
4 thin slices prosciutto (about 4 ounces total)
2 large garlic cloves, minced
1 tablespoon rubbed sage
½ teaspoon freshly ground black pepper
1 tablespoon butter or buttery spread, such as Earth Balance
1 tablespoon olive oil
4 thin slices provolone cheese or cheese alternative, such as Vegan Gourmet
Juice and zest of 1 lemon
2 tablespoons chopped fresh parsley or 1 tablespoon dried, for garnish

1 Place a rack in the middle of the oven. Preheat the oven to 325°F. With a meat mallet, pound each piece of chicken breast to a ⅛-inch thickness between two sheets of plastic wrap. Remove the plastic wrap and lay each breast on a slice of prosciutto. Rub the minced garlic, sage, and pepper on top side of chicken. Fold chicken and prosciutto in half and secure with a toothpick at open end, if necessary.

3 In a nonstick ovenproof skillet, heat the butter and olive oil over medium heat. Place each prosciutto-wrapped chicken breast in the skillet and cook until brown on the bottom, about 3 to 5 minutes. Turn and brown on the other side, about 3 to 5 minutes more. Cover and place skillet in preheated oven, about 12 to 15 minutes, depending on the size and thickness of chicken breasts, until juice is no longer pink when centers of thickest pieces are cut.

4 Five minutes before serving, place a slice of cheese on each breast and return it to the oven until cheese melts. Remove from oven, squeeze fresh lemon juice over chicken breasts, and garnish with parsley. Serve immediately.

Chicken Stroganoff

MAKES 4 SERVINGS

Stroganoff originated in Russia and is typically made with beef, but I know that many people prefer chicken, instead, which tastes just as good. I use dark meat from chicken thighs for full flavor. The juices are thickened to a silky smoothness with sweet rice flour, rather than the traditional wheat flour.

2 tablespoons olive oil
1 can (8 ounces) sliced mushrooms, drained
1 pound boneless chicken thighs, cut in 1-inch pieces
1 teaspoon salt
½ teaspoon freshly ground black pepper
2 large garlic cloves, minced
2 green onions, finely chopped
1 teaspoon chopped fresh thyme or ½ teaspoon dried
¼ cup dry sherry
2 tablespoons gluten-free Worcestershire sauce, such as French's
½ cup dry white wine
½ cup sour cream or sour cream alternative, such as Tofutti
1 teaspoon sweet rice flour stirred into 1 tablespoon cold water
2 tablespoons chopped fresh parsley, for garnish

1 In a heavy skillet, heat the oil over medium heat. Add mushrooms and cook undisturbed until lightly browned. Turn and cook mushrooms until browned on other side. Transfer mushrooms to a plate.

2 Sprinkle chicken with salt and pepper. Add chicken to same skillet and cook over medium heat until chicken is golden brown on all sides, about 5 to 7 minutes. Add garlic, onions, thyme, sherry, and Worcestershire sauce and cook 1 more minute. Add white wine and simmer, covered, 15 minutes. Remove from heat.

3 Slowly stir in sour cream, return to low heat, and gently bring to serving temperature, but do not boil. If mixture is not thick enough, stir sweet rice flour mixture into pan until thickened slightly. Serve immediately, garnished with a sprinkle of chopped parsley.

Chicken Tagine in a Slow Cooker

MAKES 4 SERVINGS

Tagine refers to both a Moroccan dish and the clay pot in which it is cooked. But I think a slow cooker is a perfect way for busy cooks to prepare it. You can prepare, then chill, the ingredients (chicken through carrots) in a heavy duty food-storage bag overnight, so all you have to do is put them in the slow cooker the next morning to have a delicious dish awaiting you that evening.

4 boneless skinless chicken breast halves (about 1¼ pounds)

1¼ teaspoons salt

1 teaspoon ground cinnamon

1 teaspoon ground ginger

½ teaspoon ground coriander

½ teaspoon ground turmeric

½ teaspoon ground cumin

½ teaspoon freshly ground black pepper

1 medium red onion, halved and thinly sliced

2 large carrots, peeled and sliced diagonally in ¼-inch pieces

1 large garlic clove, minced

1 cup gluten-free, low-sodium chicken broth, such as Swanson's Natural Goodness, or homemade Chicken Broth (page 676)

2 tablespoons honey

1 tablespoon fresh lemon juice

1 tablespoon tomato paste

¼ cup dark raisins

¼ cup finely chopped dried apricots

2 cups cooked hot white basmati rice (with pinch of saffron added during cooking), for serving

1 tablespoon cornstarch whisked into 2 tablespoons cold water

¼ cup chopped fresh cilantro, for garnish

¼ cup sliced almonds, for garnish

2 tablespoons sliced, pitted green olives, for garnish (optional)

1 In a 6-quart slow cooker, add the chicken, salt, cinnamon, ginger, coriander, turmeric, cumin, pepper, onion, carrots, and garlic. In a small bowl or measuring cup, whisk together the broth, honey, lemon juice, and tomato paste and pour into the slow cooker. Sprinkle with raisins and apricots. Cover.

2 Cook 5 hours on High heat. Or, cook 8 hours on Low heat and just before serving, turn slow cooker to High. Whisk cornstarch mixture into liquid in slow cooker and replace lid. The juices should thicken slightly. Serve over hot basmati rice, garnished with cilantro, almonds, and green olives.

Chicken Enchiladas
MAKES 4 SERVINGS

For people who live in the Southwest, enchiladas are a weekly item on dinner menus. They are highly versatile, lending themselves to innovation and creativity. You can either follow this recipe with its thick, chunky homemade red enchilada sauce, or use a store-bought gluten-free red enchilada sauce such as Las Palmas or La Victoria.

SAUCE

3 tablespoons olive oil, divided

1 small onion, finely chopped

1 small garlic clove, minced

1 can (14 to 15 ounces) petite diced tomatoes, including juice

1 small can (6 ounces) tomato paste

1 teaspoon chili powder

1 teaspoon chopped fresh oregano or ½ teaspoon dried

¼ teaspoon ground cumin

2 tablespoons chopped fresh cilantro

¾ teaspoon salt, or to taste

1 teaspoon sugar

½ cup gluten-free, low-sodium chicken broth, such as Swanson's Natural Goodness, or homemade Chicken Broth (page 676)

FILLING

2 cups grated Cheddar cheese or cheese alternative, such as Vegan Gourmet

2 cups cooked, shredded chicken

8 gluten-free corn tortillas, such as Tamxico

½ cup sour cream or sour cream alternative, such as Tofutti, for garnish

½ cup chopped green onions, for garnish

1 Place a rack in the middle of the oven. Preheat the oven to 350°F. Coat an 11 × 7-inch baking dish with cooking spray.

2 Make the sauce: In a heavy, medium saucepan, cook the onion and garlic in 1 tablespoon of the oil until transparent, about 3 to 5 minutes. Add tomatoes, tomato paste, chili powder, oregano, cumin, cilantro, salt, and sugar. Bring to boil. Reduce heat, cover, and simmer 5 minutes. If sauce is too thick, add ¼ to ½ cup chicken broth to reach desired consistency. This sauce makes about 2½ cups and can be refrigerated for 3 days.

3 While sauce is simmering, combine cheese and chicken for filling. Heat remaining 2 tablespoons of the oil in a small skillet over medium heat. Using tongs, dip tortillas into hot oil, one at a time, to soften and then drain on paper towels.

4 Dip each tortilla in the sauce. Lay tortilla on a plate. Fill with ¼ cup of chicken filling and 3 tablespoons enchilada sauce and roll up. Place enchilada seam-side down in baking dish. Repeat with remaining tortillas. Top with remaining sauce. Bake 30 minutes. To serve, top with sour cream and onions.

Creole Chicken Gumbo

MAKES 4 SERVINGS

Creole cooking is probably the ultimate fusion cooking, that is, it is a blend of many different cultures. And, we're the lucky recipients because there is no need for any gluten-containing ingredients. I use Cajun-style andouille chicken sausage in this recipe but you can use any type you wish.

2 tablespoons canola oil

4 chicken legs

¼ cup chopped onion

¼ pound gluten-free andouille sausage, such as Applegate Farms, cut in ¼-inch slices

1 rib celery, finely sliced

1 small green pepper, finely chopped

½ cup petite diced tomatoes, including juice

2 garlic cloves, smashed

3 cups gluten-free, low-sodium chicken broth, Swanson's Natural Goodness, or homemade Chicken Broth (page 676)

1 teaspoon tomato paste

2 bay leaves

2 teaspoons paprika

1 teaspoon chopped fresh thyme or ½ teaspoon dried

1 teaspoon chopped fresh basil or ½ teaspoon dried

½ teaspoon salt

½ teaspoon freshly ground black pepper

1 can (12 ounces) okra, okra pieces halved, drained

1 teaspoon file powder

2 tablespoons cold water

1 cup cooked, diced dark meat chicken

4 ounces fresh or canned crab meat

2 cups hot cooked white rice

2 tablespoons chopped flat-leaf parsley

1 In a Dutch oven or other deep, heavy pot with a tight-fitting lid, heat the oil over medium heat. Add chicken in one part of skillet and put onion, sausage, celery and green pepper in separate area of skillet. Cook until chicken is browned on all sides. Stir vegetables and sausage occasionally so they brown on all sides, transferring to plate if they finish browning before chicken. Stir in tomatoes, garlic, broth, tomato paste, bay leaves, paprika, thyme, basil, salt, and black pepper (and return browned vegetables to skillet, if removed). Gradually bring to boil and reduce heat. Simmer gently, uncovered, 15 minutes.

2 Add okra to pot and continue to simmer 5 minutes more. In a small bowl, blend file powder and cold water. Add to soup and stir briskly. Add chicken and crab meat and heat to serving temperature over medium heat, but do not boil. Serve piping hot over hot cooked rice, garnished with parsley.

Turkey Bacon–Onion Pie

MAKES 6 SERVINGS

This pie is similar to a quiche and makes a lovely brunch dish. Although I use turkey bacon, you can use any type you like.

CRUST
Basic Pastry Crust dough for 9-inch pie, single crust (page 587)

FILLING
4 strips turkey bacon, finely diced
4 large eggs, beaten
½ teaspoon salt
¼ teaspoon freshly ground black pepper
2 teaspoons chopped fresh chives
⅛ teaspoon freshly grated nutmeg
2 large onions, finely diced
2 tablespoons grated Parmesan cheese or soy alternative, such as Soyco

1 Place a rack in both the bottom and middle positions of the oven. Preheat the oven to 350°F. Roll out pie crust following directions on page 118. Fit into 9-inch nonstick (gray, not black) pie pan and flute edges. Refrigerate.

2 In a large, heavy skillet cook bacon over medium heat until crispy. Transfer bacon to a large mixing bowl, leaving bacon fat in skillet. Add eggs, salt, pepper, chives, and nutmeg to bowl and whisk until smooth.

3 Cook onions in bacon fat, over medium-low heat, covered, 10 to 12 minutes, or until translucent and lightly browned. Remove piecrust from refrigerator and arrange cooked onions evenly on bottom of crust. Pour egg mixture over onions. Sprinkle with Parmesan cheese.

4 Bake on bottom rack of oven 10 minutes. Move pie pan to middle rack and bake 15 to 20 more minutes, or until filling is firm and lightly browned. Remove from oven and cool on wire rack 10 minutes. Cut into 6 slices and serve immediately.

Turkey Tetrazzini

MAKES 4 SERVINGS

This is an excellent way to use up leftover turkey or chicken. It's hearty and comforting and can be conveniently assembled the night before so all you have to do is bake it the next day. Whole milk (or even cream) works best in this recipe, but for those trying to reduce calorie intake, 1% or 2% milk will work just fine.

PASTA AND TURKEY
8 ounces (1 box) uncooked gluten-free fettuccine or spaghetti, such as Pastariso or Tinkyada
2 cups chopped cooked light and dark meat turkey or chicken

SAUCE AND VEGETABLES

1 cup gluten-free, low-sodium chicken broth, such as Swanson's Natural Goodness, or homemade Chicken Broth (page 676)

½ cup whole milk (cow, rice*, soy, potato*, or nut)

½ cup dry white wine

¼ cup (½ stick) unsalted butter or buttery spread, such as Earth Balance, or canola oil

¼ cup grated Parmesan cheese or soy alternative, such as Soyco

1 teaspoon celery salt

1 teaspoon chopped fresh thyme or ½ teaspoon dried

¼ teaspoon freshly ground black pepper

Dash of freshly grated nutmeg

1 garlic clove, minced

2 tablespoons sweet rice flour stirred into 3 tablespoons water

1 small onion, finely chopped

1 can (7 ounces) sliced mushrooms, drained

½ cup frozen pearl onions, thawed and drained or ½ cup finely chopped fresh onion

½ cup frozen green peas, thawed

½ cup finely chopped red bell pepper

2 tablespoons chopped fresh parsley or 1 tablespoon dried

TOPPING

¼ cup grated Parmesan cheese or soy alternative, such as Soyco

½ cup gluten-free bread crumbs, such as Ener-G, or homemade Plain Bread Crumbs (page 117)

¼ cup sliced almonds

Cooking spray

2 teaspoons chopped fresh parsley or 1 teaspoon dried

1 Place a rack in the middle of the oven. Preheat the oven to 375°F. Generously grease a 2-quart casserole dish. Prepare the pasta and turkey: Break the uncooked fettuccine or spaghetti in half and scatter it over the bottom of the casserole dish. Top it with the cooked turkey pieces.

2 Prepare the sauce and vegetables: In a medium saucepan, combine chicken broth, milk, wine, butter, Parmesan cheese, celery salt, thyme, black pepper, nutmeg, and garlic. Cook over medium heat until mixture has bubbles around the edge of the pan. Stir sweet rice flour into water until it is smooth and whisk it into the hot milk mixture. Continue to cook it, stirring constantly, until it thickens slightly.

3 Pour half of the sauce over the turkey and pasta in pan. Stir onion, mushrooms, pearl onions, green peas, bell pepper, and parsley into remaining sauce and pour into pan.

4 Make the topping: In a bowl, combine Parmesan cheese and bread crumbs and sprinkle on top. Sprinkle almonds on top, then spray lightly with cooking spray.

5 Bake 30 to 35 minutes or until the sauce is bubbly and the crust is lightly browned. Remove casserole from oven and garnish with parsley. Serve immediately.

If you use rice milk or potato milk, increase sweet rice flour to 3 tablespoons.

WHOLE BIRDS

Simple Roasted Chicken

MAKES 4 SERVINGS

I roast a whole chicken frequently; not only do I love the chicken prepared this way, but I then have leftover meat for soups and sandwiches. I also make a chicken broth using the bones and freeze it for later use. The cornstarch makes the chicken skin a little crisper. The mild seasoning means kids will love it.

1 whole chicken (about 3 pounds)
Juice of 1 lemon
¼ cup cornstarch
1 bay leaf
2 teaspoons celery salt
½ teaspoon freshly ground black pepper
¼ cup hot water

1 Place a rack in the middle of the oven. Preheat the oven to 400°F. Grease a heavy-duty roasting pan (preferably one with a lid).

2 Check the chicken for pin feathers, trim off any extra fat, and pat it dry with paper towels. Squeeze lemon juice all over the chicken and inside the cavity. Dust it with cornstarch either by sprinkling it on or tossing chicken with cornstarch in paper bag. Place lemon and bay leaf in cavity of chicken.

3 Place chicken breast-side up on rack in greased baking pan. Pierce skin on breast and legs with fork. Sprinkle celery salt and black pepper on chicken. Add ½ cup hot water to pan, cover with lid, and roast 1 ½ to 2 hours or until skin is browned. The chicken is done when the juices run clear when the thigh is pierced and the temperature in the thickest part of the thigh and the thickest part of the breast is 170°F on an instant-read thermometer. Remove pan from oven and let chicken sit, covered, on a wire rack for 15 minutes. Carve chicken, remove bay leaf, and serve. Refrigerate any leftovers for up to 3 days.

Roast Chicken with Cranberry Chutney

MAKES 4 SERVINGS

You're familiar with cranberry sauce but cranberry chutney is far more flavorful. Try this fresh take on cranberries and you'll love how it complements poultry or fish dishes.

CHICKEN
1 fryer chicken (4 pounds)
½ teaspoon poultry seasoning
½ teaspoon salt
¼ teaspoon freshly ground black pepper

CHUTNEY
1 bag (12 ounces) fresh cranberries, rinsed and picked over
1 cup sugar
1 cup chopped onions
¼ cup dry white wine or water
¼ cup cider vinegar
1 garlic clove, minced
1-inch piece of fresh ginger, minced
¼ teaspoon freshly grated nutmeg
¼ teaspoon ground allspice
⅛ teaspoon ground cloves
¼ teaspoon salt
⅛ teaspoon crushed red pepper

1 Place a rack in the middle of the oven. Preheat the oven to 400°F. Spray chicken with cooking spray. Sprinkle with poultry seasoning, salt, and pepper. Place chicken on rack in greased roasting pan. Roast chicken 1 ½ to 2 hours, basting occasionally with pan juices, or until skin is browned. The chicken is done when the juices run clear when the thigh is pierced and the temperature in the thickest part of the thigh and the thickest part of the breast is 170°F on an instant-read thermometer. Remove pan from oven and let chicken sit, covered, on a wire rack for 15 minutes

2 While the chicken roasts, combine all chutney ingredients in a heavy medium pan over medium-high heat. Cook until cranberries are popped, about 10 to 12 minutes. Remove from heat and let stand until chicken is ready. You will have about 2 cups of chutney.

3 Carve chicken into serving pieces and serve immediately with cranberry chutney. Refrigerate any chicken leftovers for up to 3 days. Refrigerate leftover chutney in a glass or ceramic container for up to a week.

Southwestern Roast Chicken with Avocado Salsa

MAKES 4 SERVINGS

When you want something a little different from traditional roasted chicken, use this recipe. The rub makes it very flavorful.

CHICKEN
2 teaspoons Southwestern Chicken Rub (page 668)
1 fryer chicken (4 pounds)
Cooking spray
½ teaspoon salt
¼ teaspoon freshly ground black pepper

SALSA
2 ripe plum or Roma tomatoes, seeded and chopped
2 tablespoons diced red onion
2 tablespoons chopped fresh cilantro
1 tablespoon fresh lime juice
1 tablespoon rice vinegar
1 garlic clove, minced
¼ teaspoon hot pepper sauce, such as Frank's
¼ teaspoon salt
⅛ teaspoon white pepper
1 small avocado, halved, seeded, peeled and chopped into ½-inch cubes

1 Prepare the southwestern chicken rub. Place a rack in the middle of the oven. Preheat the oven to 400°F. Spray chicken with cooking spray. Sprinkle with salt and pepper and then evenly sprinkle rub all over chicken. Place chicken, breast-side down, on rack in greased roasting pan. Roast 30 minutes or until back is gently browned.

2 Turn chicken breast-side up and continue to roast 1½ hours. The chicken is done when the juices run clear when the thigh is pierced and the temperature in the thickest part of the thigh and the thickest part of the breast is 170°F on an instant-read thermometer. Remove pan from oven and let chicken stand, covered, on a wire rack for 15 minutes.

3 While the chicken is roasting, make the salsa: In a serving bowl, combine tomatoes, onion, cilantro, lime juice, vinegar, garlic, hot pepper sauce, salt, and white pepper and toss gently. Just before serving, add chopped avocado and toss gently. Carve chicken into serving pieces and serve immediately with avocado salsa. Refrigerate any leftovers for up to 3 days.

CAST-IRON CAUTION

While you may be tempted to haul out that antique cast-iron skillet from the back of the closet, check it first. If it has been used for foods containing gluten, the pan could be contaminated. Examine the pan carefully before using, or even better, start over with a brand new cast-iron skillet and reserve it for gluten-free foods. You can buy seasoned, ready-to-use skillets at Lodge (www.lodgemfg.com).

Chicken Under a Brick

MAKES 4 SERVINGS

I have always been curious about this dish, but didn't taste it until a couple of years ago at the famed Chez Panisse restaurant in Berkeley, California. The concept is simple: cook chicken in a skillet, weighted down so a crispy crust forms. Surprisingly easy to make at home, it works best in a cast-iron skillet. If you don't have a brick, use another (smaller) skillet to weight the chicken down and add food cans in the top skillet to increase the weight. Make sure you don't get a chicken larger than 3 pounds or it won't fit in the skillet.

1 whole chicken (3 pounds)
2 teaspoons kosher salt
2 garlic cloves, minced
¼ cup olive oil
1 cup chopped fresh herbs, preferably basil, oregano, parsley, rosemary, sage, and thyme
1 teaspoon grated lemon zest
½ teaspoon crushed red pepper
Juice from 1 whole lemon for drizzling over cooked chicken

1 Remove and discard giblets from chicken and cut away fat around tail. With kitchen shears, remove backbone by cutting along both sides. Pat chicken dry. Place chicken skin side up on flat surface, pressing breastbone with hand to flatten or cut breastbone with shears so it will lie flat.

2 In a small bowl, combine salt and garlic, and rub all over chicken. Place flattened chicken in 13 × 9-inch baking dish. Combine 2 tablespoons of olive oil with herbs, zest, and crushed red pepper. Pat herb mixture onto chicken. Return chicken to dish and refrigerate overnight.

3 Place remaining 2 tablespoons of olive oil in bottom of a 10-inch cast-iron skillet or heavy ovenproof skillet. Place flattened chicken, skin-side down, in skillet. Wrap brick in aluminum foil and place on top of chicken. Or use another skillet as described above.

4 Place a rack in the middle of the oven. Preheat the oven to 400°F. Cook chicken in skillet 15 minutes over medium heat, then place skillet in oven to roast 30 to 45 minutes. The chicken is done when the juices run clear when the thigh is pierced and the temperature in the thickest part of the thigh and the thickest part of the breast is 170°F on an instant-read thermometer.

5 Remove skillet from oven and let stand 15 minutes, covered, before lifting chicken from skillet with a thin metal spatula, taking care not to tear the skin. Cut into serving pieces. Drizzle with fresh lemon juice and serve. Refrigerate any leftovers for up to 3 days.

Herbes de Provence Roasted Chicken on Garlic Croutons

MAKES 4 SERVINGS

Herbes de Provence is a mixture of flavorful herbs typically used in Provence. Crispy, crunchy garlic croutons form a bed for this succulent roasted chicken. Brown the croutons just before serving and, for the crunchiest results, don't reheat leftovers in a microwave oven.

2 cups (½-inch) homemade Croutons (see Caesar Salad, page 151)
1 whole chicken (3 to 4 pounds)
2 large yellow onions, thinly sliced
¼ cup extra-virgin olive oil, divided
1½ teaspoons salt, divided
½ teaspoon freshly ground black pepper
1 to 2 teaspoons herbes de Provence, depending on taste
1 fresh lemon, quartered
2 tablespoons unsalted butter or buttery spread, such as Earth Balance, melted, or canola oil
2 tablespoons hot water
1 garlic clove, minced

1 Prepare the croutons; set aside. Place a rack in the middle of the oven. Preheat the oven to 400°F. Generously grease a roasting pan. Remove giblets and pin feathers and wash chicken inside and out. Cut off all excess fat with kitchen scissors or a sharp knife. Tuck wing tips behind bird. Toss onions with 1 tablespoon olive oil in roasting pan. Place chicken on onions and sprinkle cavity with half of salt and pepper. Place lemons inside chicken. Pat chicken dry with paper towels, brush with melted butter, and sprinkle with 1 teaspoon salt, ¼ teaspoon pepper, and the herbes de Provence. Add hot water to bottom of pan.

2 Roast 1 hour 15 minutes to 1½ hours, basting occasionally with pan juices, or until skin is browned. The chicken is done when the juices run clear when the thigh is pierced and the temperature in the thickest part of the thigh and the thickest part of the breast is 170°F on an instant-read thermometer. Remove pan from oven and let chicken stand, covered, on a wire rack for 15 minutes.

3 While chicken roasts, in a large nonstick skillet, heat remaining 3 tablespoons of oil and minced garlic over medium heat. Toss bread cubes in skillet in oil to coat thoroughly. Cook bread cubes, turning frequently, until nicely browned and crunchy, about 10 to 12 minutes.* Watch carefully and add more olive oil, if needed. Sprinkle with remaining ½ teaspoon salt and remaining ¼ teaspoon pepper.

4 Place croutons on serving platter and put roasted sliced onions on top. Slice chicken and place it on onions. Pour pan juices over chicken and croutons. Sprinkle with additional salt and pepper, if desired, and serve hot. Refrigerate any leftovers for up to 3 days.

Note: As an alternative to pan-roasted croutons, toss them in olive oil and garlic and bake on a parchment-lined 13 × 9-inch baking sheet at 350°F. Turn croutons once to promote even browning. Sprinkle with remaining ½ teaspoon salt and ¼ teaspoon freshly ground black pepper. Serve immediately.

Middle Eastern–Spiced Chicken with Homemade Harissa Sauce

MAKES 4 SERVINGS

This nicely spiced chicken is served with my version of harissa, an essential and very potent ingredient that is quite common in many Middle Eastern cultures. Ground coriander can be found in the baking aisle of your grocery store and is made from the dried seeds of the coriander plant, whose bright, green leaves are called cilantro.

2 teaspoons homemade Harissa Sauce (page 673)
¼ cup extra-virgin olive oil
2 teaspoons ground coriander
1 teaspoon salt
½ teaspoon ground cumin
¼ teaspoon ground cinnamon
1 whole chicken (about 4 pounds)

1 Prepare the harissa. Place a rack in the middle of the oven. Preheat the oven to 400°F. Make the rub: In a food processor, combine oil, 2 teaspoons of the harissa, coriander, salt, cumin, and cinnamon and process until smooth. Taste and adjust seasonings, if desired.*

2 Generously grease a heavy-duty roasting pan with rack and lid. Place chicken on rack. Rub cavity and skin of the chicken with the harissa mixture. Cover roasting pan.

3 Roast the chicken until tender, about 1½ to 2 hours or until skin is browned The chicken is done when the juices run clear when the thigh is pierced and the temperature in the thickest part of the thigh and the thickest part of the breast is 170°F on an instant-read thermometer. Remove pan from oven and let chicken stand, covered, on a wire rack for 15 minutes.

4 Carve the chicken and serve with extra harissa sauce. Refrigerate leftovers for up to 3 days.

* Serve harissa sparingly as a sauce for meats or as an ingredient in sauces. Store in the refrigerator, tightly covered, for up to a month.

Cornish Game Hens with Orange-Apricot Glaze

MAKES 4 SERVINGS

Cornish game hens nestled on a bed of rice make a lovely dinner for guests. Don't split the hens if you prefer to serve them whole, but it does take longer to roast whole hens.

4 Cornish game hens (about 1 pound each), split in half lengthwise (backs discarded)
Canola oil or cooking spray
2 teaspoons salt
1 teaspoon freshly ground black pepper
1 cup apricot preserves
½ cup orange juice
1 tablespoon olive oil
1 teaspoon white wine vinegar (or cider vinegar)

1 Place a rack in the middle of the oven. Preheat the oven to 350°F. Lightly coat a roasting pan and rack with cooking spray. Arrange hens skin-side up on rack and coat with cooking spray. Sprinkle inside and skins of hens with salt and pepper.

2 Roast 30 minutes. Meanwhile, in a small bowl, whisk apricot preserves, orange juice, olive oil, and vinegar to make smooth glaze.

3 Remove roasting pan from oven. Spoon ⅓ glaze over each hen to coat well. Return pan to oven and continue to roast, basting again after 10 minutes of roasting. Check for doneness and continue roasting and basting for another 20 minutes or until hens are browned Hens are done when the juices run clear when the thigh is pierced and the temperature in the thickest part of the thigh and the thickest part of the breast is 170°F on an instant-read thermometer. Remove pan from oven and let hens stand, covered, on a wire rack 15 minutes. Remove from oven and serve immediately. Refrigerate leftovers for up to 3 days.

Cornish Game Hens with Gremolata Pesto

MAKES 4 SERVINGS

Gremolata is a blend of fresh herbs. Rather than leave it "chunky" I prefer to put it in a blender to get a pesto-like texture. It is especially good during the summer months, when fresh herbs are bounteous; I grow my own, but you can purchase fresh herbs in the produce section of any grocery store. There are many variations of gremolata—and no one absolute way to make it—so use the herbs available to you. You can also stir any leftover gremolata into cooked white rice for a flavor variation.

CORNISH GAME HENS

4 Cornish game hens (about 1 pound each), split in half lengthwise (backs discarded)
Juice of 1 lemon
1 teaspoon salt
½ teaspoon freshly ground black pepper

PESTO

Grated zest of 1 lemon
¼ cup finely chopped fresh chives
¼ cup finely chopped fresh parsley (preferably flat-leaf)
¼ cup finely chopped fresh thyme
¼ cup finely chopped fresh savory or chervil or basil
2 garlic cloves, minced
2 tablespoons olive oil

1 Place a rack in the middle of the oven. Preheat the oven to 350°F. Lightly coat a roasting pan and rack with cooking spray. Arrange hens, skin-side up, on rack and squeeze lemon juice inside cavity and on skin of hens. Coat hen with cooking spray. Sprinkle salt and pepper in cavity and on skin of hens.

2 Roast hens 45 minutes to 1 hour or until skin is browned. The hens are done when the juices run clear when the thigh is pierced and the temperature in the thickest part of the thigh and the thickest part of the breast is 170°F on an instant-read thermometer. Remove pan from oven and let hens stand, covered, on a wire rack for 15 minutes.

3 While hens are roasting, make the pesto: In a small blender or chopper, combine lemon zest, chives, parsley, thyme, savory (or other herb), garlic, and olive oil and pulse until it resembles pesto. Cover and hold at room temperature.

4 Carve roasted hens and serve with ¼ cup gremolata spooned over each hen. Refrigerate leftovers for up to 3 days.

Roasted Cornish Game Hens with Root Vegetable Puree

MAKES 4 SERVINGS.

As the hens roast, their spiced juices drip on the root vegetables nestled on the bottom of the roasting pan. When pureed, those wonderful flavored juices become a key part of the dish. Serve this dish with cranberry sauce for a flavorful and colorful addition.

CORNISH GAME HENS AND MARINADE

2 whole Cornish game hens
1 cup chopped yellow onion
½ cup apple cider vinegar
4 garlic cloves, peeled
¼ cup honey
1 small jalapeno, seeded
1½ teaspoons ground ginger
1 tablespoon chopped fresh thyme or 1½ teaspoons dried thyme
1½ teaspoons salt
½ teaspoon chili powder
½ teaspoon ground allspice
½ teaspoon ground cinnamon
¼ teaspoon ground nutmeg

ROOT VEGETABLE PUREE

2 medium russet potatoes, peeled and chopped
2 ripe, but firm pears, peeled, cored, and chopped
2 Granny Smith apples, peeled, cored, and chopped
1 large parsnip, peeled and chopped
1 celery root, peeled and chopped
¼ cup (½ stick) unsalted butter or buttery spread, Earth Balance, melted, or canola oil
¼ teaspoon salt
¼ teaspoon freshly ground black pepper

1 Place hens in a large, heavy-duty food storage plastic bag. Combine the marinade ingredients in a blender and process until smooth. Pour the marinade into the bag, seal, and refrigerate overnight, making sure hens are immersed as much as possible in the marinade.

2 Preheat the oven to 400°F. Generously grease a heavy-duty roasting pan. Arrange root vegetables on the bottom of the roasting pan. Remove hens from the marinade. With marinade still on the hens, place hens directly on vegetables. Cover roasting pan with lid.

3 Roast hens for 45 to 60 minutes or until browned. The hens are done when the juices run clear when the thigh is pierced and the temperature in the thickest part of the thigh and the thickest part of the breast is 170°F on an instant-read thermometer. Remove pan from oven and let hens stand, covered, on a wire rack for 15 minutes. Transfer hens to a serving platter and cover with foil to keep warm.

4 Transfer roasted vegetables to a food processor and puree them or mash them with an electric mixer. Add melted butter, salt, and pepper and enough of the pan juices to reach the consistency of soft mashed potatoes. Cover and keep warm while slicing each game hen in half. Serve hens with puree on the side. Refrigerate any leftovers for up to 3 days.

Brined Turkey

MAKES 24 SERVINGS

My method of preparing roast turkey involves brining a fresh turkey, which really means soaking the whole turkey in salted water overnight. I prefer a smaller turkey (around 12 pounds) because it fits more easily into the refrigerator during brining and is easier to handle. You can use a pot, but there are now giant, heavy-duty resealable food-storage bags that are suitable for this technique. If brining isn't practical for your situation, you can skip this procedure and still have a delicious turkey.

½ cup salt

⅓ cup sugar

2 large bay leaves

2 tablespoons chopped fresh thyme or 1 tablespoon dried

¼ teaspoon ground cloves

½ teaspoon freshly ground black pepper

2 gallons water, divided

1 (12- to 14-pound) fresh turkey

Butter or oil for coating turkey

Additional salt and freshly ground pepper

1 In a stockpot or canning pot, combine the salt, sugar, bay leaves, thyme, cloves, pepper, and 2 cups of the water. Bring the mixture to a boil, stirring until the salt dissolves. Remove from the heat and add the remaining water, using ice cubes as part of the remaining water to cool it down quickly. If the pot is too small to hold the turkey, transfer the cooled brine to a larger container such as a cooler, a large clean pail, or heavy-duty food-storage bag.

2 Rinse the fresh turkey and remove the pin feathers with fingers. Remove the giblets and wash the cavities thoroughly. Place the turkey, breast-side down, in the brine. If the turkey isn't covered by the water, add more water. Cover and refrigerate the turkey 24 hours.

3 Rinse the turkey and discard the brine. Pat the turkey dry with paper towels. I use a heavy, lidded, dark, porcelain-coated, cast-iron roasting pan which can hold a turkey as large as 22 pounds. These roasting pans are probably antiques, but you can buy contemporary, lighter-weight versions called "granite ware" at kitchen stores. These roasting pans brown the turkey beautifully but don't dry it out because the lid locks in moisture.

4 Coat the turkey with butter or oil and then lightly season it inside and out with salt and pepper (you won't need as much salt if you brine the turkey because the turkey has been soaking in salted water). If I'm stuffing it, I do that next. I set it on a rack in the roasting pan, which has been coated with cooking spray, and pour about 1 to 2 cups of boiling water in the bottom of the pan. This liquid prevents scorching but is also the basis for delicious pan juices (drippings) that flavor the gravy.

5 Roast the turkey at 350°F for 15 to 20 minutes per pound, basting it often with the pan juices. The turkey is done when the juices run clear when the thigh is pierced and the temperature in the thickest part of the thigh and the thickest part of the breast is 170°F on an instant-read thermometer. Remove pan from oven and let turkey stand, covered, on a wire rack for 30 minutes. It will continue to cook and the turkey should reach 180°F as it rests. Carve the turkey and serve. Refrigerate any leftovers for up to 3 days.

STUFFINGS

Bread Pudding Stuffing

MAKES 12 SERVINGS

Unlike many stuffing recipes, this one is more like a bread pudding with a custard-like texture. I make this at holiday time and my guests like it because it is so moist. Made with chicken broth rather than milk, it will turn out less like custard.

BREAD STUFFING

1 pound gluten-free bread, such as homemade White Sandwich Yeast Bread (page 85), crusts removed and cut into ½-inch cubes

1 teaspoon celery salt

2 tablespoons chopped fresh thyme

¼ cup extra-virgin olive oil

1 large garlic clove, minced

CUSTARD

1 stick (½ cup) unsalted butter or buttery spread, such as Earth Balance, melted

1 cup finely chopped celery

1 cup finely chopped onions

1 can (7 ounces) sliced mushrooms

½ cup chopped fresh parsley

7 large eggs, at room temperature

3½ cups whole milk or gluten-free, low-sodium chicken broth, such as Swanson's Natural Goodness, or homemade Chicken Broth (page 676)

2 teaspoons salt or to taste

½ teaspoon freshly ground black pepper or to taste

1 Place a rack in the middle of the oven. Preheat the oven to 325°F. Generously grease a 13 × 9 × 2-inch nonstick (gray, not black) baking dish. Make the stuffing: Toss the bread cubes with the celery salt, thyme, olive oil and garlic in a large bowl until well coated. Place cubes on a large, foil-lined baking sheet in a single layer.

2 Toast the bread cubes for 20 to 25 minutes, or until they are dry and lightly browned. Turn or shake cubes halfway through to assure even toasting. The time required to brown the cubes will vary depending on type of bread and its moisture content. Remove the bread cubes from the oven and place in a large bowl.

3 While the bread is toasting, make the custard: In a large, heavy skillet, heat the butter over medium-high heat. Add the celery, onions, and mushrooms and cook until the vegetables are soft. Add vegetables and parsley to bread cubes. In a separate bowl, whisk the eggs, milk, salt, and pepper. Pour over the bread cubes and toss until the bread is well soaked. Transfer bread pudding to prepared dish.

4 Bake uncovered until the top is firm and golden, about 1 hour. Remove from oven and let stand 10 minutes before serving. Cut into pieces with a sharp knife and serve hot as a side dish.

Cornbread Stuffing with Sausage and Fruit

MAKES 6 SERVINGS

The addition of chopped apple in this stuffing lends a sweet note and complements the savory sage. This is intended to be cooked with the turkey or other whole bird.

2 cups gluten-free bread cubes, from White Sandwich Yeast Bread (page 85)

2 cups gluten-free cornbread cubes, from Cornbread (page 68)

5 tablespoons unsalted butter or buttery spread, such as Earth Balance

1 small onion, finely chopped

2 stalks celery, finely chopped

1 small unpeeled apple (such as Granny Smith or Gala), finely chopped

½ teaspoon salt

½ cup gluten-free sausage, such as Jimmy Dean, Johnsonville, or Publix, browned and drained

½ cup dried cranberries

¼ cup chopped Italian-flat leaf parsley

2 teaspoons chopped fresh sage (or ½ teaspoon dried sage)

½ to 1 cup gluten-free low-sodium chicken broth, such as Swanson's Natural Goodness, or homemade Chicken Broth (page 676)

1 Place a rack in the middle of the oven. Preheat the oven to 325°F and line a 13 × 9-inch rimmed baking sheet with foil. Arrange bread and corn-bread cubes on sheet.

2 Bake 20 to 25 minutes or until dry and lightly browned. Remove from oven and cool slightly.

3 While bread is toasting, in a medium skillet, heat the butter over medium heat until melted. Sauté onion, celery, and apple until soft. Toss toasted bread with salt in a large bowl and add sausage, cranberries, parsley, and sage. Mix with spatula or your hands until thoroughly blended. Add enough chicken broth to moisten the mixture thoroughly. Use stuffing as directed in your recipe.

Cornbread Stuffing with Dried Fruit and Pomegranate Seeds

MAKES 6 SERVINGS

This makes a perfect stuffing for a small turkey (under 14 pounds) or for 6 pork chops. The dried fruit and pomegranate seeds lend a slightly sweet flavor and good, chewy texture.

4 cups gluten-free corn bread cubes from Cornbread (page 68) or half recipe Corn Muffins (page 46)
1 teaspoon salt
Cooking spray
2 tablespoons unsalted butter or buttery spread, such as Earth Balance
1 small onion, finely chopped
2 stalks celery, finely chopped
1 cup pomegranate seeds
½ cup chopped dried apricots
½ cup dried cranberries
¼ cup chopped Italian-leaf parsley
2 teaspoons chopped fresh sage or 1 teaspoon dried
½ to 1 cup gluten-free low-sodium chicken broth, such as Swanson's Natural Goodness, or home-made Chicken Broth (page 676), or apple juice

1 Place a rack in the middle of the oven. Preheat the oven to 350°F. Toss the corn bread cubes with salt and coat evenly with olive oil cooking spray. Place on parchment-lined 13 × 9-inch baking sheet.

2 Bake 20 to 25 minutes or until the corn bread is lightly browned. Remove from oven and cool.

3 In a medium skillet, heat the butter over medium heat until melted. Cook onion and celery until translucent. Add to bread cubes, along with pomegranate seeds, apricots, cranberries, parsley, and sage and mix with spatula or your hands until thoroughly blended. Add broth and stir until corn bread is thoroughly moistened. Use stuffing as directed in your recipe.

MEATS

Beef Steaks and Chops

Grilled Filet Mignon with Southwestern Mango-Corn Salsa

Grilled Ancho-Coffee–Rubbed Filot Mignon

Chipotle Grilled Steaks

Grilled Steak Florentine

Grilled Flank Steak with Fresh Herbs

Grilled Flank Steak with Chimichurri Sauce

Grilled Mustard-Marinated Flank Steak

Grilled Kiwi-Marinated Flank Steak

Grilled Beef Kabobs

Pan-Seared Filet Mignon with Caramelized Onions

Steak Diane

Chicken-Fried Steak with Simple White Gravy

Cube Steak with Marinara Sauce

Swiss Steak

Veal Piccata

Beef Roasts

Braised Pot Roast with Vegetables

Italian Pot Roast

Red Wine–Braised Pot Roast with Mushrooms

Marinated Tri-Tip Roast with Spice Rub and Chipotle Sour Cream Sauce

Herbed Roast Beef with Yorkshire Pudding

Sauerbraten

Corned Beef and Cabbage

Mini Beef Wellingtons

Beef Casseroles and Stir-Fries

Beef Burgundy

Beef Stroganoff

Pepper Steak

Beef Short Ribs

Carne Asada

Osso Buco

Reuben Casserole

Shepherd's Beef Pie

Smoked Paprika Beef in Savory Crepes

Asian Stir-Fry Beef Over Brown Rice

Ground Beef

Meat Loaf

Barbecued Meat Loaf

Italian Meat Loaf

Southwestern Meat Loaf

Swedish Meatballs

Piccadillo

Hungarian Beef Goulash

Mexican Skillet Beef and Rice

Stuffed Trio of Sweet Peppers

Stuffed Cabbage Rolls

Pork Chops and Cutlets

Braised Pork Chops with Red-Wine Plums

Sage-Dusted Pork Chops with Autumn Spiced Apples

Grilled Pork Chops with Minted Pineapple Salsa

Q = Quick **V** = Vegetarian

Cumin-Dusted Pork Chops with
Orange-Onion Salsa

Pork Chops with Spicy Orange-
Cilantro Sauce

Rosemary Pork Chops with
Pomegranate Molasses

Smothered Pork Chops

Pork Chops with Cornbread
Stuffing with Dried Fruits and
Pomegranate Seeds

Pork Cutlets with Marsala Wine
and Mushrooms

Pork Cutlets Milanese

Chicken-Fried Pork Cutlets with
Vinegar Gravy

Roasted Pork Medallions with
Orange-Ginger Sauce

Pork Schnitzel

Pork Tenderloins and
Roasts

Chipotle-Lime Pork Tenderloin
with Black Bean–Orange Salsa

Cumin-Rubbed Pork Tenderloin
with Citrus Marmalade

Mustard-Sage Crusted Pork
Tenderloin with Pear-Cranberry
Compote

Roasted Pork Tenderloin with
Apricot Chutney

Grilled Pork Tenderloin with
Herb Salsa

Oven-Roasted Pork Tenderloin
with Sage-Apple-Cranberry Relish

Roasted Pork Tenderloin with
Morels

Jamaican Jerk Pork Roast

Thyme-Rubbed Roast Pork
with Dried Apricot Stuffing

Baked Ham with Clementine
Marmalade Glaze

Pork Ribs, Stir-Fries,
and Casseroles

Barbecued Baby Back Ribs

Green Chile with Pork

Pork Stew in a Slow Cooker

Pork Adobado in a Slow Cooker

Pork Carnitas in a Slow Cooker

Sweet-and-Sour Pork

Family-Style Cassoulet with
Kielbasa

Pork Sausage

Beer Brats with Onions, Pepper,
and Sauerkraut

Corn Dogs

Creole Red Beans and Rice

Sausage with Warm Lentils
and Polenta

Lamb

Pan-Grilled Rosemary
Lamb Chops

Lamb Daube

Crown Roast of Lamb

Moussaka

Greek Lamb and Vegetable
Kabobs with Pita Pockets

Whether you're fixing a special meal for your family, hosting a small, informal dinner party, or entertaining in grand style, you'll find plenty of flavorful options in this chapter of beef, veal, pork, ham, and lamb dishes. Main meals aren't the first things that come to mind when contemplating the gluten-free diet, but they can contain gluten, just like everything else. Rest assured, my recipes use other ingredients to substitute for wheat—or leave it out altogether—without any loss of flavor or appearance.

But just where does gluten lurk in main meat dishes? It is in the flour used to thicken sauces, to dredge meats so they brown better, as the base in commercial seasoning mixes, or as an extender or filler in seasoning blends. Most people don't think about this source of wheat because, unlike breads and pasta—where it is visible—the wheat in main dishes is usually hidden. But it is just as damaging.

Despite growing up in the heartland, my life experiences—including traveling the globe—have exposed me to a wide variety of cuisines that broadened my culinary horizons. So, there are dishes from around the world, including Steak Florentine and Paella from the Mediterranean; Grilled Chimichurri Flank Steak or Grilled Ancho-Coffee–Rubbed Filet Mignon for a Latin American touch; and dishes with Asian influences such as Asian Stir-Fry Beef and Sweet-and-Sour Pork. Many ethnic entrees are perfect for gluten-free diets because they don't rely on wheat or the wheat is easily omitted or replaced. The herbs and spices in ethnic foods awaken our palates and make eating such a pleasure.

I have also included a wide variety of family favorites, ranging from all-American comfort food dishes like Meat Loaf, Breaded Pork Chops, Barbecued Baby Back Ribs, and Pot Roast, to more upscale dishes like Beef Wellington and Osso Buco.

You may even get some ideas for transforming your own favorite main dishes into gluten-free winners.

For those who count calories, use lean cuts of beef or pork (e.g., pork tenderloin is just as lean as skinless chicken breasts).

Short on time? There are a number of suggested quick tips and shortcuts, including some slow-cooker recipes. The new slow cookers are easier to monitor and have removable liners that make cleanup a breeze, but you can also line your old—but perfectly functional—slow cooker with the new disposable liners.

BEEF STEAKS AND CHOPS

Grilled Filet Mignon with Southwestern Mango-Corn Salsa

MAKES 4 SERVINGS

Serving sizzling steaks from the grill is one of my favorite ways to entertain in the summer. This full-bodied spice rub pairs nicely with the salsa's sweet, mellow mango and crunchy vegetables. If you want less heat, coat the steaks with only half of the rub.

FILET MIGNON AND RUB

2 teaspoons ground cumin

2 teaspoons chili powder

1 teaspoon dried oregano

2 garlic cloves, minced

½ teaspoon salt

¼ teaspoon freshly ground black pepper

2 tablespoons fresh lime juice

4 filet mignon (about 4 ounces each), 1½ inches thick

SALSA

¼ teaspoon homemade Southwestern Seasoning (page 668) or to taste

1 cup fresh corn kernels (about 2 small ears)

½ cup chopped fresh cilantro

½ cup red onion, finely chopped

¼ cup pitted black olives, halved

¼ cup red bell pepper, chopped

1 ripe but firm mango, peeled, seeded, and diced

1 small avocado, diced

2 tablespoon olive oil

2 tablespoon red wine vinegar

¼ teaspoon salt

⅛ teaspoon freshly ground black pepper

1 Prepare the rub and the filet mignon: In a small bowl, combine the cumin, chili powder, oregano, garlic, salt, and pepper with lime juice to form a paste. Spread the paste on both sides of each steak and refrigerate at least 2 hours.

2 Place a barbecue grill about 6 inches away from the heat source. Preheat the grill to medium heat. Grill the steaks 3 to 4 minutes. Turn the meat over with tongs and cook on the other side, about 4 minutes more for rare, or 5 to 6 minutes more for medium-rare. To check for doneness, make a small cut in the thickest part. For longer cooking, move the steaks to a cooler part of the grill. Transfer the steak from the grill to a plate and cover with foil to keep warm; let stand 10 minutes.

3 While the steaks cook, make the salsa: Combine all of the salsa ingredients in a medium bowl. Toss to mix thoroughly. Serve the salsa with the steaks.

Grilled Ancho-Coffee–Rubbed Filet Mignon

MAKES 4 SERVINGS

Ancho chiles are dried poblanos, and they bring great flavor and a little kick to this dish without being overly hot. Coffee might seem unusual as a rub for meat, but it is often used in Mexican cuisine such as moles, and it lends an irresistible complexity to this special cut of meat.

RUB

4 tablespoons ground coriander

1 tablespoon espresso or coffee powder

1 tablespoon salt

1 tablespoon black pepper

2 teaspoons ancho chile powder

1 teaspoon dry mustard

1 teaspoon ground cumin

½ teaspoon garlic powder

¼ teaspoon ground cayenne

FILET MIGNON

2 teaspoons gluten-free Worcestershire sauce, such as French's

1 teaspoon Dijon mustard

4 filet mignon (about 4 ounces each)

Additional salt and freshly ground pepper to taste

1 Make the rub: Combine all ingredients in a glass container. Transfer 2 tablespoons to a small bowl. Store the rest in the container with a tight-fitting lid.

2 Prepare the steaks: To the small bowl with the rub, add the Worcestershire sauce and mustard to make a paste. Rub a thin layer on both sides of the steaks; let stand 15 minutes at room temperature.

3 Place a barbecue grill about 6 inches away from the heat source. Preheat the grill. Grill the steaks 3 to 4 minutes. Turn the meat over with tongs and cook on the other side, about 3 minutes more for rare, or 4 minutes more for medium-rare. To check for doneness, make a small cut in the thickest part. For longer cooking, move the steaks to a cooler part of the grill. Serve immediately.

Chipotle Grilled Steaks

MAKES 4 SERVINGS

If you like flavorful steaks—especially those with extraordinarily bold ingredients such as chipotle chile powder—try this very easy idea.

4 filet mignon or New York strips (about 4 ounces each)

1 tablespoon Montreal steak seasoning, such as McCormick's or seasoning of choice

¼ teaspoon chipotle chile powder, such as McCormick's

Additional salt and freshly ground pepper to taste

1 Pat the beef dry with paper towels. Combine the seasoning and chili powder and rub it on both sides of the steaks. Let the steaks stand at room temperature for 15 minutes.

2 Place a barbecue grill about 6 inches away from the heat source. Preheat the grill to medium-high heat. Grill the steaks 4 to 5 minutes. Turn the

meat over with tongs and cook on the other side, about 4 minutes more for rare, or 5 to 6 minutes more for medium-rare. To check for doneness, make a small cut in the thickest part. For longer cooking, move the steaks to a cooler part of the grill. Transfer steaks to a plate, cover, and let stand 5 to 10 minutes. Sprinkle with additional salt and pepper to taste and serve immediately.

Grilled Steak Florentine

MAKES 4 SERVINGS

It was a Friday night in Florence, Italy. My friend and I forgot to make dinner reservations (a mistake in a popular tourist city like Florence) and also forgot that the restaurants don't open until 7 p.m. So, here we were, two starving tourists patiently sitting on the doorstep of an unknown restaurant that, based on the menu posted on its door, served the famed Steak Florentine. We absolutely had to taste it before leaving Florence the next morning, and it was definitely worth the wait. We ate it with a simple tossed salad and grilled vegetables. For a dish that tasted so good, its preparation at home is surprisingly simple. I prefer to cook the steaks on a grill, but you can achieve similar results indoors with a grill pan.

2 large garlic cloves, minced

4 small T-bone steaks (about 4 ounces each)

1 teaspoon salt

½ teaspoon freshly ground black pepper

2 lemons, halved

2 teaspoons olive oil

Additional salt and freshly ground pepper to taste

1 Rub the minced garlic over the steaks and sprinkle with salt and pepper. Place in a heavy duty food-storage bag, and refrigerate 1 hour to allow seasoning to permeate meat. Let steaks stand at least 20 minutes at room temperature before grilling.

2 Place a barbecue grill about 6 inches away from the heat source. Preheat the grill to medium-high heat. Grill the steaks 3 to 4 minutes. Turn the meat over with tongs and cook on the other side, about 3 minutes more for rare, or 4 minutes more for medium-rare. To check for doneness, make a small cut in the thickest part. For longer cooking, move the steaks to a cooler part of the grill. Remove steaks from grill and allow to rest, covered with foil, 10 minutes.

3 Transfer the steaks to a serving platter. Squeeze half a lemon over each steak, then drizzle with olive oil and serve immediately, adding additional salt and pepper if desired. (You may also remove the bones and cut the steaks into thin slices for serving, instead.)

Grilled Flank Steak with Fresh Herbs

MAKES 8 SERVINGS

Once you make this dish and taste the balance of flavors, feel free to change the herbs based on your preferences and what's available in your garden or at the store. The steak yields a very flavorful sauce even if you omit the smoked paprika, but it's worth using. If you can't find it at your local gourmet store, order it at www.spanishtable.com or www.tienda.com.

HERB SAUCE
1 cup extra-virgin olive oil
1 cup chopped flat-leaf parsley
½ cup red wine vinegar or champagne vinegar
¼ cup chopped fresh basil leaves
¼ cup chopped yellow onion
2 tablespoons fresh lemon juice
1 tablespoon chopped fresh oregano leaves
2 garlic cloves, halved
1 teaspoon smoked paprika
1 teaspoon salt
½ teaspoon freshly ground black pepper
¼ teaspoon crushed red pepper

STEAK
2 pounds flank steak
Additional salt and freshly ground pepper to taste

1 Make the herb sauce: In a food processor, process the oil, parsley, vinegar, basil, onion, lemon juice, oregano, garlic, paprika, salt, pepper, and crushed red pepper until smooth. Refrigerate half of the sauce; place the remaining sauce in a glass dish or heavy duty food storage bag. Add flank steak and refrigerate overnight to marinate.

2 Make the steak: Place a barbecue grill about 6 inches away from the heat source. Preheat the grill to medium heat. Remove the steak from the sauce, pat dry (or it will cause the fire in the barbecue grill to flame up), and bring to room temperature. Sprinkle with salt and pepper. Discard sauce. Grill the steaks 3 to 4 minutes. Turn the meat over with tongs and cook on the other side, about 3 minutes more for rare, or 4 minutes more for medium-rare. To check for doneness, make a small cut in the thickest part. For longer cooking, move the steaks to a cooler part of the grill.

3 Transfer the steak from the grill to a plate and cover with foil to keep warm; let stand 5 to 10 minutes. Slice against the grain in very thin strips with a serrated knife or an electric knife. Serve with reserved, chilled herb sauce that has been brought to room temperature.

Grilled Flank Steak with Chimichurri Sauce

MAKES 8 SERVINGS

Chimichurri sauce is commonly served with meat in Argentina, but you can serve it with just about anything. It is made of herbs that pack a lot of flavor; but I recommend fresh herbs for best results.

1 cup minced flat-leaf parsley
½ cup extra-virgin olive oil
½ cup red wine vinegar
1 tablespoon chopped onion
2 garlic cloves, whole
2 teaspoons ground cumin
½ teaspoon salt
½ teaspoon freshly ground black pepper
¼ teaspoon crushed red pepper
1 pound flank steak
Additional salt and freshly ground pepper to taste

1 Make the sauce: In a food processor, place the parsley, oil, vinegar, onion, garlic, cumin, salt, black pepper, and crushed red pepper and pulse until combined. Refrigerate half of sauce; place remaining sauce in glass dish or heavy-duty food storage bag. Add the flank steak and refrigerate overnight.

2 Place a barbecue grill about 6 inches away from the heat source. Preheat the grill to medium heat. Remove steak from chimichurri sauce (discard sauce), pat dry (or it will cause the fire in the barbecue grill to flame up dangerously), and bring to room temperature. Sprinkle with additional salt and pepper to taste. Grill the steaks 3 to 4 minutes. Turn the meat over with tongs and cook on the other side, about 3 minutes more for rare, or 4 minutes more for medium-rare. To check for doneness, make a small cut in the thickest part. For longer cooking, move the steaks to a cooler part of the grill.

3 Transfer the steak from the grill to a plate and cover with foil to keep warm; let stand 5 to 10 minutes. Remove foil and slice against the grain in very thin strips with serrated knife or electric knife. Serve with reserved, chilled, chimichurri sauce that has been brought to room temperature.

Grilled Mustard-Marinated Flank Steak

MAKES 4 SERVINGS

Robust marinades like this one not only boost the flavor, but also tenderize this economical cut of meat. It is very important to slice flank steak on the diagonal (across the grain) to assure that every bite is as tender as possible.

¼ cup red wine vinegar
¼ cup lemon juice
2 tablespoons olive oil
2 tablespoons packed light brown sugar
2 tablespoons Dijon mustard
1 large garlic clove, minced
1 teaspoon salt
2 teaspoons fresh oregano or 1 teaspoon dried
Dash of hot pepper sauce, such as Frank's
1 pound flank steak

1 In a medium bowl, whisk together vinegar, lemon juice, oil, brown sugar, mustard, garlic, salt, oregano, and hot pepper sauce until thoroughly combined. Pour into a heavy-duty food storage bag. Add the flank steak and marinate up to 24 hours or at least overnight.

2 Place a barbecue grill about 6 inches away from the heat source. Preheat the grill. Remove steaks from marinade; pat dry. Grill the steaks 3 to 4 minutes. Turn the meat over with tongs and cook on the other side, about 3 minutes more for rare, or 4 minutes more for medium-rare. To check for doneness, make a small cut in the thickest part. For longer cooking, move the steaks to a cooler part of the grill. Transfer the steak from the grill to a plate and cover with foil to keep warm; let stand 10 minutes. Slice diagonally with a sharp knife or an electric knife. Serve warm.

Grilled Kiwi-Marinated Flank Steak

MAKES 4 SERVINGS

Kiwi fruit—yes, the same lovely green kiwi we use in fruit salads—has a natural enzyme that softens meat fairly quickly while adding its own wonderfully unique flavor. You'll be amazed at how delicious these steaks are, and kiwi may become a staple in your future marinades.

1 pound flank steak

2 kiwi fruit, peeled and coarsely chopped

¼ cup canola oil

¼ cup wheat-free tamari soy sauce, such as Crystal or San-J

2 tablespoons gluten-free Worcestershire sauce, such as French's

2 tablespoons balsamic vinegar

2 tablespoons dry white wine or lemon juice

2 garlic cloves, minced

1 Place the flank steak in a heavy-duty food storage bag.

2 In a blender, puree the kiwi fruit, oil, soy sauce, Worcestershire sauce, balsamic vinegar, wine, and garlic until very smooth. Pour over the tenderloin, seal the bag tightly, and refrigerate up to 2 hours.

3 Place a barbecue grill about 6 inches away from the heat source. Preheat the grill. Remove steak from the marinade; pat dry. Discard marinade. Grill the steaks 3 to 4 minutes. Turn the meat over with tongs and cook on the other side, about 3 minutes more for rare, or 4 minutes more for medium-rare. To check for doneness, make a small cut in the thickest part. For longer cooking, move the steaks to a cooler part of the grill. Transfer the steak from the grill to a plate and cover with foil to keep warm; let stand 10 minutes. Slice against the grain, diagonally, and serve warm.

Grilled Beef Kabobs

MAKES 4 SERVINGS

Kabobs are easy to prepare; in fact, they can be assembled ahead and marinated overnight. The next day, you simply heat the grill and cook them. Depending on your choice of vegetables, they can be extremely colorful, as well.

4 wood skewers

1 pound beef sirloin steak, cut in 1-inch cubes

1 medium onion, peeled and cut in quarters

1 large red bell pepper, cut in 1-inch pieces

1 large green bell pepper, cut in 1-inch pieces

½ pound button mushrooms, cleaned

½ cup gluten-free teriyaki sauce, such as Crystal or Premier Japan

¼ cup wheat-free tamari soy sauce, such as Crystal or San-J

2 tablespoons gluten-free hoisin sauce, such as Premier Japan

2 tablespoons spicy brown mustard

1 tablespoon olive oil

2 garlic cloves, minced

1 Thread 4 wood skewers with cubes of beef, onions, bell peppers, and mushrooms, alternating meat and vegetables as desired. Place the skewers in a 13 × 9-inch baking dish.

2 In a small bowl, whisk together the teriyaki sauce, soy sauce, hoisin sauce, mustard, oil, and garlic. Pour over the kabobs in the baking dish, pressing the kabobs into the marinade. Refrigerate overnight or at least 4 hours.

3 Place a barbecue grill about 6 inches away from the heat source. Preheat the grill to the desired temperature and oil the grill grate. Remove the kabobs from the marinade and arrange on the grill while not exposing the skewers to direct heat if they are wooden; discard the marinade.

4 Grill the skewers 10 minutes, turning them occasionally, until done to taste. Serve immediately.

Pan-Seared Filet Mignon with Caramelized Onions

MAKES 4 SERVINGS

Caramelized onions provide a sweet complement to the full body of the filet mignon rub. The steaks are seared in a pan on the stovetop, so this dish is especially good for a cold winter's night when you don't want to clear a path through the snow to reach the barbecue grill—or if you don't have a barbecue grill at all.

FILET MIGNON

½ teaspoon garlic powder

½ teaspoon onion powder

1 teaspoon chopped fresh oregano or ½ teaspoon dried

¼ teaspoon salt

¼ teaspoon ground black pepper

¼ teaspoon ground cayenne (optional)

4 filet mignon (about 4 ounces each)

ONIONS

2 tablespoons canola oil, divided

2 cups onions, sliced in thin vertical strips (about 2 large onions)

⅛ teaspoon salt

⅛ teaspoon ground black pepper

1 Prepare the steaks: In a bowl, combine the garlic powder, onion powder, oregano, salt, pepper, and cayenne and dredge the steaks in the mixture. Let the steaks stand at room temperature while cooking the onions.

2 Prepare the onions: Heat 1 tablespoon of the canola oil in large, heavy-duty skillet over medium-high heat. Add the sliced onions, sprinkle with salt and pepper, and cook until nicely browned, about 10 to 15 minutes. Transfer the onions to a plate and cover with foil while the steak cooks.

3 Heat the remaining tablespoon of olive oil in the skillet over medium-high and cook the steaks until nicely browned, 4 to 5 minutes. Turn the meat over with tongs and cook on the other side,

about 4 minutes for rare, or 5 to 6 minutes for medium-rare. To check for doneness, make a small cut in the thickest part. For longer cooking time, reduce the heat to medium. Serve with onions on top of each steak.

Steak Diane

MAKES 4 SERVINGS

This classic restaurant dish is often flumed tableside in a dramatic performance. My easy version omits the flaming and is so simple you probably won't need a recipe the next time you make it. Feel free to vary the ingredients, such as using more mushrooms or more lemon juice, depending on your tastes.

4 filet mignon (about 4 ounces each)

½ teaspoon + ⅛ teaspoon salt

½ teaspoon freshly ground black pepper

2 tablespoon unsalted butter or buttery spread, such as Earth Balance, divided

1 can (8 ounces) sliced mushrooms, drained

2 tablespoons finely chopped green onion

1 tablespoon brandy, or 1 teaspoon brandy extract (optional)

2 teaspoons gluten-free Worcestershire sauce, such as French's

1 teaspoon Dijon mustard

1 garlic clove, crushed

1 tablespoon fresh lemon juice

2 tablespoons snipped fresh parsley leaves

1 Sprinkle the steaks with ½ teaspoon of the salt and the pepper. Let stand while preparing the sauce.

2 In a large skillet, melt 1 tablespoon butter over medium heat. Add the mushrooms, onion, brandy (if using), Worcestershire sauce, mustard, garlic, lemon juice, and the remaining ⅛ teaspoon salt, and cook, stirring, until the onions are tender. Stir in the parsley. Pour the sauce into a small metal bowl or saucepan, cover, and keep warm on a burner.

3 To cook the steaks, melt the remaining tablespoon of butter in the skillet. Cook the steaks over medium-high heat until nicely browned, 4 to 5 minutes. Turn the meat over with tongs and cook on the other side, about 4 minutes for rare, or 5 to 6 minutes for medium-rare. To check for doneness, make a small cut in the thickest part. For longer cooking, move the steaks to a cooler part of the grill. Serve the steaks with the mushroom sauce.

Chicken-Fried Steak with Simple White Gravy

MAKES 4 SERVINGS

Served with mashed potatoes and green peas, this is a classic comfort food meal. Even if you're not a big fan of fried foods, this is one you'll want to try. The gravy will be creamier if you use whole milk rather than 2% milk.

1 cup Carol's Sorghum Blend (page x)

1 cup finely crushed gluten-free savory crackers (about 25 crackers the size of saltines), such as Edward & Sons

4 teaspoons gluten-free seasoned salt, such as Lawry's

¼ teaspoon freshly ground black pepper

½ cup 1% milk (cow's, rice, soy, potato, or nut)

2 large eggs

4 cube steaks (about 1 pound)

¼ cup canola oil for frying

1 recipe Simple White Gravy (see page 675)

1 In a shallow bowl, combine the sorghum blend, crackers, seasoned salt, and pepper. In another shallow bowl, whisk the milk and eggs together until all of the egg membrane is broken up and the mixture is very smooth.

2 With a meat mallet, pound the cube steak until it is ¼ to ⅓ inch thick. Dip the steaks first in the sorghum mixture, then in the egg mixture, and then in sorghum mixture again.

3 In a large, heavy skillet, heat the oil over medium-high heat. Fry the steaks until golden brown, about 4 to 5 minutes per side, turning only once. If you turn them more than once, the coating will fall off. Transfer the steaks to a platter; cover with foil to keep warm. Serve with the white gravy.

Cube Steak with Marinara Sauce Ⓠ

MAKES 4 SERVINGS

This is one of my "fix-it-quick" recipes that I learned from a fellow graduate student long ago when we were seriously time-challenged. While it's certainly easy to purchase ready-made marinara sauce in a jar, my homemade version is so simple and so flavorful—it beats the store-bought versions hands down. I keep small batches of it in my freezer so I can heat in the microwave and quickly make easy dishes like this one. You can keep serving-size pieces of cube steak in the freezer, too. Just heat them in the microwave oven, along with the sauce, sear them quickly in a skillet, and dinner will be ready in no time at all. This is a great dish for kids.

1 tablespoon canola oil

4 cube steaks (about 1 pound)

1 teaspoon salt

½ teaspoon freshly ground black pepper

1 cup gluten-free marinara sauce, such as Classico, or homemade Marinara Sauce (page 672)

½ cup shredded mozzarella cheese or cheese alternative, such as Vegan Gourmet

1 In a heavy-duty skillet, heat the oil over medium heat. Sprinkle the steaks with salt and pepper, add to the pan, and brown on both sides, about 1 to 2 minutes per side. To check for doneness, make a small cut in the thickest part.

2 Top each steak with ¼ cup marinara sauce and 2 tablespoons of the mozzarella cheese. Cover the skillet with a lid for 1 minute and cook over low heat or until the cheese melts. Serve immediately.

Swiss Steak

MAKES 4 SERVINGS

Most Swiss steak recipes don't use smoked paprika, but I discovered this marvelous spice while traveling in Portugal and Spain, and I just love the robust flavor it lends to dishes. If you can't find it at your local gourmet store, order it at www.spanishtable.com or www.tienda.com. You can use plain paprika, if you wish, but once you try the smoked version you'll be hooked.

4 beef cutlets (about 4 ounces each)
1 teaspoon salt
½ teaspoon freshly ground black pepper
½ cup cornstarch, divided
2 tablespoons canola oil
1 large onion, thinly sliced
1 large garlic clove, minced
2 stalks celery, chopped
1 can (14 to 15 ounces) petite diced tomatoes, including juice
1 tablespoon tomato paste
2 teaspoons gluten-free Worcestershire sauce, such as French's
1 teaspoon smoked paprika or regular paprika
2 teaspoons chopped fresh oregano or 1 teaspoon dried
1 can (14 to 15 ounces) or 1¾ cups gluten-free, low-sodium beef broth, such as Swanson's, or homemade Beef Broth (page 675)
2 tablespoons fresh chopped parsley, for garnish

1 Sprinkle both sides of the cutlets with salt and pepper. Place all but 1 tablespoon of cornstarch in a shallow bowl or paper bag. Dredge cutlets on both sides in the cornstarch.

2 In a Dutch oven or other deep, heavy pot with a tight-fitting lid, heat the oil over medium-high heat. Add the cutlets, being careful not to overcrowd them or they will steam rather than sear. Cook until golden brown on both sides, about 2 minutes per side. Transfer the steaks to a plate.

3 In the same skillet, add the onion, garlic, and celery. Cook 2 minutes or until the onion is softened. Add the tomatoes, tomato paste, Worcestershire sauce, paprika, oregano, and beef broth and stir to combine. Return cutlets to the skillet. Cover and simmer on low heat 30 to 35 minutes.

4 Transfer the cutlets to a serving platter and cover with foil to keep warm. If juices need thickening, stir remaining tablespoon of cornstarch into 2 tablespoons cold water until smooth. Stir enough cornstarch mixture into juices over medium-high heat until juices thicken. Pour over cutlets and serve immediately, garnished with parsley.

Veal Piccata

MAKES 4 SERVINGS

This Milanese dish comes together very quickly; it actually requires your close attention because veal cutlets cook so fast. Be sure to have all the other dishes in the meal ready to serve before you start to cook.

4 veal cutlets (about 1 pound), pounded ⅛-inch thick
2 teaspoons salt
½ teaspoon freshly ground black pepper
½ cup cornstarch
1½ tablespoons olive oil
4 tablespoons unsalted butter or buttery spread, Earth Balance, divided
1 cup dry white wine
¼ cup fresh lemon juice
1 garlic clove, chopped
2 tablespoon capers, drained
1 tablespoon chopped parsley leaves + parsley sprigs for garnish

1 Sprinkle both sides of the veal with the salt and pepper. Place the cornstarch in a shallow bowl and dredge the veal in it, shaking to remove any excess.

2 In a large skillet, heat the oil over medium-high heat. Add 1½ tablespoons of the butter and, working quickly, cook the veal in batches until golden brown on both sides, about 1 minute per side. Transfer the veal to a plate.

3 Add the wine to the pan and bring to a boil, scraping to remove any browned bits from the bottom of the pan. When the wine has reduced to half, add the lemon juice, garlic, and capers and cook 5 minutes, or until the sauce has thickened slightly. Whisk in the remaining 2½ tablespoons of butter and the chopped parsley. When the butter has melted, return the veal to the pan and cook until heated through and the sauce has thickened, about 1 minute. Garnish with parsley sprigs and serve immediately.

BEEF ROASTS

Braised Pot Roast with Vegetables

MAKES 4 SERVINGS

When I was growing up, we always had a beef roast for Sunday's midday meal, and the Sunday night meal was roast beef sandwiches. If that didn't finish off the roast beef, it reappeared in vegetable soup later that week. I didn't know it then, but I was already an expert at making the most of every meal. Today, whenever I make a roast, I plan our next few meals around it. Then I take the bones or a good chunk of the meat and make beef broth, which I freeze in 2-cup containers for future use.

1 boneless chuck roast (about 2 pounds), trimmed of excess fat

½ teaspoon salt

½ teaspoon freshly ground black pepper

1 tablespoon canola oil

1 medium onion, diced

1 garlic clove, minced

1 can (14 to 15 ounces) petite diced tomatoes, including juice

¼ cup red wine vinegar

1 tablespoon firmly packed light brown sugar

1 bay leaf

1 (3-inch) strip of orange rind (no white part)

1 teaspoon chopped fresh thyme or ½ teaspoon dried thyme

1 cup gluten-free, low-sodium beef broth, such as Swanson's, or homemade Beef Broth (page 675)

2 cups baby carrots

1 pound very small red potatoes, washed (or 4 medium red potatoes, quartered)

1½ tablespoons cornstarch dissolved in 2 tablespoons cold water

1 tablespoon chopped fresh parsley, for garnish

1 Place a rack in the middle of the oven. Preheat the oven to 350°F. Pat the beef dry with paper towels and sprinkle with salt and pepper on all sides.

2 In a large, heavy Dutch oven, heat the oil over medium-high heat. Cook the beef until browned on all sides. Transfer the beef to a plate, add onions and garlic to the Dutch oven, and cook over moderate heat, stirring, until the onion is golden. Stir in the tomatoes, vinegar, brown sugar, bay leaf, orange rind, thyme, and broth. Carefully place the roast in the liquid and bring the mixture to a boil.

3 Roast the beef in the oven, covered, 1 hour. Add carrots and potatoes and continue cooking, covered, 45 minutes more.

4 Transfer the beef and vegetables to a plate and let stand, covered with foil, 10 minutes. If you wish to serve beef with gravy, skim the fat from top of the cooking liquid and discard bay leaf and orange rind. Bring the liquid to a boil. Stir the cornstarch into water until smooth and add enough to the boiling liquid, whisking constantly, to thicken into gravy of desired consistency. Simmer gravy, stirring occasionally, for 1 minute more. Add additional salt and pepper, if desired. Slice beef, arrange on serving platter, and transfer vegetables to platter. Spoon some gravy over beef and serve remaining gravy on the side. Garnish beef with parsley. Serve hot.

Italian Pot Roast

MAKES 6 SERVINGS

Italian pot roast is much like American pot roast—slowly cooked beef in a covered pot—except for the wonderfully aromatic Italian herbs that make this dish so special. The narrower and deeper the pot—for example, a stock pot—the better for this roast so that most of it is submerged in the sauce as it cooks.

1 tablespoon canola oil

1 boneless beef chuck roast (about 2 pounds)

¾ teaspoon salt

½ teaspoon freshly ground black pepper

1 medium onion, finely chopped

2 garlic cloves, minced

1 cup dry red wine

1 can (14 to 15 ounces) petite diced tomatoes, including juice

1 tablespoon balsamic vinegar

1 teaspoon sugar

2 teaspoons Italian seasoning

¼ teaspoon crushed red pepper

1 bay leaf

1 tablespoon cornstarch dissolved in 2 tablespoons cold water

1 Place a rack in the middle of the oven. Preheat the oven to 350°F. Season the roast with the salt and pepper. In a tall, deep pot, heat the oil over medium heat. Place the roast in the pot and cook until browned evenly on all sides.

2 Add the onion, wine, tomatoes, vinegar, sugar, seasoning, crushed red pepper, and bay leaf to the pot and cook over medium heat until the sauce bubbles. Transfer the pot to the oven and roast, covered, 2 hours. Remove pot from the oven and let stand 10 minutes.

3 Transfer the beef roast to a plate and cover with foil to keep warm. Remove the bay leaf. Discard all but 2 cups of the sauce, using a fat separator to discard any unwanted fat. Place pot on medium heat and add cornstarch mixture. Cook, stirring constantly, until mixture thickens.

4 Cut roast diagonally into slices and serve with the sauce.

Red Wine–Braised Pot Roast with Mushrooms

MAKES 12 SERVINGS

Perfect for a Sunday dinner or Sunday night supper, marinate this pot roast overnight and then cook it low and slow in a Dutch oven or other deep, heavy pot with a tight-fitting lid until it's mouthwateringly tender.

MARINADE

1 cup dry red wine

¼ cup wheat-free tamari soy sauce, Crystal or San-J

2 tablespoons gluten-free Worcestershire sauce, such as French's

2 tablespoons olive oil

1 tablespoon tomato paste

1 teaspoon packed light brown sugar

1 teaspoon onion powder

2 teaspoons chopped fresh thyme or 1 teaspoon dried

¼ teaspoon garlic powder

1 garlic clove, minced

1 teaspoon salt

1 teaspoon freshly ground black pepper

POT ROAST

1 bottom round beef roast (about 4 pounds)

1 tablespoon olive oil

2 tablespoons cornstarch mixed in 3 tablespoons cold water

1 can (8 ounces) sliced mushrooms, drained

1 Make the marinade: Combine all the marinade ingredients in a large, heavy-duty food storage bag. Add the roast and seal tightly. Refrigerate overnight.

2 Make the pot roast: Remove the roast from marinade and pat dry. Reserve the marinade. In a Dutch oven or other deep, heavy pot with a tight-fitting lid, heat the oil over medium-high heat.

Cook the beef on both sides until nicely browned, about 10 minutes per side. Add the reserved marinade to the Dutch oven, cover, and simmer on low heat for 3 hours or until the meat is tender. Turn meat once during cooking so both sides cook in the marinade.

3 Transfer the beef to a platter and cover with foil to keep warm. Add the cornstarch mixture to pot and stir to combine with the marinade. Increase the heat to medium and cook, stirring constantly, until the juices thicken. Slice beef and serve with the thickened juices.

Marinated Tri-Tip Roast with Spice Rub and Chipotle-Sour Cream Sauce

MAKES 4 SERVINGS

A tri-tip roast—a boneless cut of meat from the bottom sirloin, also called a "triangular" roast because of its shape—is versatile and so easy to prepare, plus there's almost no waste. This cut of meat is very popular in some parts of the country, but you may also use boneless top sirloin or London broil instead. Try slicing this dish for sandwiches or serve it on its own with sauces such as the Chimichurri Sauce (page 330) or the Chipotle–Sour Cream Sauce (shown here).

MARINADE

1 cup dry red wine

⅓ cup wheat-free tamari soy sauce, such as Crystal or San-J

2 tablespoons packed light brown sugar

4 teaspoons chopped fresh thyme or 2 teaspoons dried

4 teaspoons chopped fresh rosemary or 2 teaspoons dried, crushed

1 teaspoon Dijon mustard

1 tri-tip roast (about 1½ pounds)

RUB

1 tablespoon chili powder

1½ teaspoons lemon pepper

1½ teaspoons onion powder

½ teaspoon ground cumin

½ teaspoon ground coriander

½ teaspoon garlic powder

SAUCE

1 container (8 ounces) sour cream or sour cream alternative, such as Tofutti

1 to 2 teaspoons homemade Chipotle Adobo Sauce (page 673) or to taste

1 In a large shallow bowl, combine all the marinade ingredients. Immerse the roast in the marinade and refrigerate 2 to 3 hours, covered. Remove the roast from the marinade; reserve the marinade. Pat the roast completely dry with paper towels.

2 In a medium bowl, combine the spice rub ingredients and pat evenly all over the roast. Let the roast stand at room temperature while barbecue grill heats to medium-high heat.

3 Sear the roast, with the fat side up, over medium-high heat. Then, flip the roast over, reduce the heat to medium and roast 20 minutes for medium-rare (145°F) with an instant-read thermometer inserted into the center of the roast), or longer depending on the desired degree of doneness. Transfer the roast to a plate and cover with a foil tent for 10 minutes.

4 While the roast stands, make the sauce: Blend sauce into sour cream until smooth.

5 Place the reserved marinade in a small saucepan and boil 3 to 5 minutes. Remove the foil and slice the roast diagonally across the grain in thin slices. Pour the heated marinade over slices and serve immediately with the sour cream sauce.

Herbed Roast Beef with Yorkshire Pudding

MAKES 6 SERVINGS

Yorkshire pudding is an English dish made from a savory batter (much like popovers), but the batter is baked in the drippings from the roast beef. This is a perfect entree for the holidays or a special dinner party. Prepare the batter ahead and keep it at room temperature so all you have to do is fill the molds and bake them while the roast is standing.

1 recipe Yorkshire Pudding batter (page 57)

1 top round roast (about 4½ to 5 pounds), rinsed and patted dry

Fresh rosemary sprigs

10 garlic cloves, peeled

1 tablespoon finely chopped fresh rosemary

2 teaspoons salt

1 teaspoon freshly ground black pepper

2 tablespoons olive oil

1 Prepare the Yorkshire pudding batter. Then, place a rack in the middle of the oven. Preheat the oven to 400°F. Place a rack in a small roasting pan and place the fresh rosemary sprigs on the rack. Place the roast on the rosemary, bone side down. Make ten ½-inch-deep slits in the meaty side of the roast and press a garlic clove deeply into each slit. Combine the chopped rosemary, salt, and pepper in a small bowl, stir in the oil to make a paste. Rub the paste on all sides of the roast.

2 Roast 1 hour. Remove the pan from the oven and turn the roast for even browning. Reduce the oven temperature to 350°F and continue roasting until an instant-read thermometer inserted in the thickest part of the roast reads 125 to 130°F for medium-rare, about 45 minutes, or 140°F for medium, about 1 hour. Remove ¼ cup of drippings from the bottom of the pan, adding canola oil to make ¼ cup if necessary.

3 Let the roast stand, covered, 20 to 30 minutes before carving. Bake the Yorkshire Pudding. Carve the roast and serve with the Yorkshire pudding.

Sauerbraten

MAKES 6 SERVINGS

Sauerbraten is beef pot roast marinated in wine and spices, then served with sweet, spicy gravy. It is German or Austrian in origin and there are many versions, most requiring crushed ginger- snaps to flavor and thicken the gravy. While it takes several ingredients and 3 days to marinate in your refrigerator, it's well worth the effort. Juniper berries come from an evergreen native to Europe and are responsible for the unique flavor of gin. They are available at specialty markets, but you can omit them here if you wish.

1 chuck roast (about 4 pounds), trimmed of excess fat
2 teaspoons salt, divided
1 cup dry red wine
1 cup red wine vinegar
1 can (14 to 15 ounces) or 1¾ cups gluten-free, low-
    sodium beef broth, such as Swanson's,
    or homemade Beef Broth (page 675)
1 tablespoon tomato paste
1 medium onion, sliced
1 teaspoon whole black peppercorns
1 teaspoon whole mustard seed
1 teaspoon juniper berries, crushed (optional)
5 allspice berries, or 1 teaspoon ground allspice
2 bay leaves
3 whole cloves, or ½ teaspoon ground cloves
¼ cup cornstarch
3 tablespoons canola oil
6 gluten-free gingersnaps, such as Pamela's, or
    homemade Gingersnaps (page 417) crushed

1 Rub the beef with 1 teaspoon of the salt and place it in a large glass or ceramic bowl. Add the wine, vinegar, beef broth, tomato paste, onion, peppercorns, mustard seeds, juniper berries (if using), allspice, bay leaves, and cloves. Cover and marinate in the refrigerator 3 days, turning often.

2 Remove the beef from the marinade; reserve the marinade. Pat the beef dry and dust with cornstarch. In a Dutch oven or other deep, heavy pot with a tight-fitting lid, heat the oil on medium heat and brown the beef on all sides. Add the reserved marinade and remaining 1 teaspoon of salt. Cover and simmer slowly over low heat 3 hours or until tender. You can also roast the beef in a 325°F oven for 3 hours.

3 Transfer the beef to a plate, remove the bay leaves and cloves, and cover with foil to keep warm. Pour the marinade through a sieve to remove the whole spices. Return the marinade to the Dutch oven and add the crushed gingersnaps. Stir until mixture thickens. If it isn't thick enough, mix 1 tea- spoon cornstarch with 1 tablespoon cold water until smooth and stir into the marinade over medium heat until mixture thickens further into gravy-like consistency. Cut the beef into serving slices, drizzle with some of the gravy, and serve with the remaining gravy in a pitcher.

Corned Beef and Cabbage

MAKES 6 SERVINGS

When I visited Ireland a few years ago, I was eager to try this traditional Irish dish. However, I was disappointed to learn that it was not on the menu anywhere and is served only at special occasions—somewhat like our Thanksgiving turkey dinner in America. That said, it is still luscious whenever you do get to enjoy it. If you use an uncured brisket, typically found at natural food stores, you may want to add more salt to the simmering water.

SAUCE

½ cup each mayonnaise or dairy-free mayonaise, such as Nasoya Nayonnaise, and sour cream or sour cream alternative, such as Tofutti

2 tablespoons bottled horseradish

½ teaspoon grated orange rind

1 teaspoon salt (or to taste)

⅛ teaspoon freshly ground black pepper

CORNED BEEF AND CABBAGE

1 corned beef brisket (about 3 pounds)

4 quarts cold water

1 garlic clove

2 bay leaves

2 tablespoons packed light brown sugar

1 tablespoon whole black peppercorns, cracked

2 teaspoons chopped fresh thyme or 1 teaspoon dried

¾ teaspoon ground allspice

½ teaspoon paprika

3 whole cloves

½ small head green cabbage (¾ to 1 pound)

8 small new potatoes, washed

3 small carrots, peeled and halved

1 small onion, halved

1 Make the sauce: In a small bowl, combine all the sauce ingredients and refrigerate. Let stand at room temperature 20 minutes before serving with the corned beef.

2 Prepare the corned beef and cabbage: Place a rack in the middle of the oven. Preheat the oven to 300°F. Rinse the corned beef with cold water. Fill a large Dutch oven or other deep, heavy pot with a tight-fitting lid with water and bring to a gentle simmer. Place the corned beef in the pot and add garlic, bay leaves, brown sugar, peppercorns, thyme, allspice, paprika, and cloves. Return water to a simmer, cover, and roast 3 to 3½ hours in oven.

3 One hour before serving, place the cabbage, potatoes, carrots, and onion in pot of salted water and simmer, covered, 30 to 45 minutes. Remove the corned beef from the Dutch oven and let stand 15 minutes, covered. Remove the bay leaves. Slice the corned beef and arrange on a serving platter, surrounded by the vegetables. Serve hot with sauce.

Mini Beef Wellingtons

MAKES 4 SERVINGS

Beef Wellington is an English dish of beef tenderloin, topped with pâté, and then wrapped in pie crust and baked. Mini versions of this famous dish using small filets mignons—rather than the full-size tenderloins—are easier to assemble with our gluten-free pastry, and are much easier to serve. If pâté isn't to your liking, use your favorite pesto instead.

4 ounces gluten-free goose or duck liver pâté

4 center-cut filets mignons (about 3 ounces each), 1½ inches thick)

1 teaspoon salt

½ teaspoon freshly ground black pepper

½ recipe Basic Pastry Crust (page 587), rolled into four 7-inch squares

1 tablespoon cornstarch

1 large egg, beaten + 2 teaspoons water for egg wash

Cooking spray

1 Place a rack in the middle of the oven. Preheat the oven to 375°F. Line 13 × 9-inch nonstick (gray, not black) baking sheet with parchment paper and set aside.

2 Season each filet with ¼ teaspoon salt and ⅛ teaspoon pepper. Heat the oil in a large heavy skillet over medium-high heat. Add the filets and sear

1 minute on each side for medium-rare. Transfer to plate to cool so you can handle them.

3 Top each filet with 1 ounce of pâté, pressing to flatten the pâté into the meat. Place a pastry square on a flat surface that is dusted with cornstarch. Place filet, pâté side down, in the center of the pastry square. Fold pastry over the filet as though wrapping a package and press edges to seal. Repeat with remaining filets and pastry squares.

4 Place Beef Wellingtons seam-side down on the baking sheet. Brush egg wash over tops and sides and bake until the pastry is golden brown and an instant-read thermometer inserted into center of filet registers 140°F for medium-rare, about 20 minutes. Remove from oven; cover loosely with foil, and let stand 10 minutes before serving. The meat will continue to cook during this period. Serve immediately.

BEEF CASSEROLES AND STIR-FRIES

Beef Burgundy

MAKES 6 SERVINGS

When my son went away to college, this rich and saucy dish was one he frequently requested when he returned home on vacations. It's a great dish for dinner guests as you can prepare it ahead of time, then reheat it in the oven while you're preparing everything else. In fact, it tastes better when made a day ahead and reheated—the flavors are deeper and more pronounced.

1 bacon slice
1 pound beef sirloin steak, cut in 1-inch cubes
1 teaspoon salt
½ teaspoon freshly ground black pepper
1 cup pearl onions
1 cup baby carrots
1½ cups Burgundy wine
1 can (14 to 15 ounces) or 1¾ cups gluten-free low-sodium beef broth, such as Swanson's, or homemade Beef Broth (page 675)
2 tablespoons tomato paste
1 bay leaf
2 tablespoons fresh thyme or 1 tablespoon dried
1 can (8 ounces) sliced mushrooms
2 garlic cloves, minced
1½ tablespoons cornstarch stirred into 2 tablespoons water until smooth
½ cup chopped fresh parsley
1 pound hot cooked gluten-free pasta, such as Tinkyada

1 In a Dutch oven or other deep, heavy pot with a tight-fitting lid, cook the bacon over medium heat until brown. Remove with tongs, leaving the drippings in pan; reserve cooked bacon. Sprinkle the beef with salt and pepper and brown in bacon oil over medium heat, about 5 minutes. Add the cooked bacon, onions, carrots, wine, broth, tomato paste, bay leaf, thyme, mushrooms, and garlic to the pan. Stir thoroughly and bring to a boil.

2 Cover and bake in 325°F oven 1 hour or until the meat is very tender. If the mixture needs thickening, stir the cornstarch mixture into the dish and heat over medium heat until the juices thicken. Remove the bay leaf and serve over hot cooked pasta.

Beef Stroganoff

MAKES 4 SERVINGS

My first taste of this dish was as a student teacher in a rural Nebraska town; my supervisor prepared it for a colleague and me. I married soon after and began preparing it myself. It's been a family favorite ever since. Using less expensive cuts of meat, such as a chuck roast, yields a more flavorful stroganoff due to the higher fat content, but I have also used sirloin steak and round steak successfully.

1½ pounds chuck roast, cut in ½-inch cubes
1 teaspoon salt
½ teaspoon freshly ground black pepper
2 tablespoons canola oil
1 can (8 ounces) sliced mushrooms, drained
1 medium onion, chopped
1 garlic clove, minced
3 cups gluten-free, low-sodium beef broth, such as Swanson's, or homemade Beef Broth (page 675)
2 tablespoons tomato paste
1 tablespoon brandy
1 tablespoon Dijon mustard
2 teaspoons chopped fresh dill or 1 teaspoon dried
¼ cup sweet rice flour
½ cup sour cream or sour cream alternative, such as Tofutti
Additional salt and freshly ground pepper to taste
1 pound hot cooked gluten-free pasta, such as Tinkyada, or Orgran, or pasta of choice
2 tablespoons chopped fresh parsley, for garnish
Dash of paprika, for garnish

1 Sprinkle the beef with salt and pepper. In a large, heavy skillet, heat the oil over medium-high heat and cook the beef until it is dark brown on all sides. Add the mushrooms, onion, and garlic. Cook 5 minutes over low-medium heat, stirring constantly.

2 Add 2¾ cups beef broth, increase the heat to medium and cook, scraping the drippings from the bottom of skillet. Stir in tomato paste, brandy, mustard, and dill. Cover and simmer on low heat 30 minutes.

3 Combine the sweet rice flour with the remaining ¼ cup of beef broth until smooth. Add to the skillet, increase the heat to medium and cook, stirring constantly, until the mixture thickens. Reduce the heat to low and stir in the sour cream. Heat to serving temperature, but do not boil or the sour cream will curdle. Add additional salt and pepper, to taste, if necessary. Serve over pasta. Garnish with chopped parsley and dash of paprika.

Pepper Steak

MAKES 4 SERVINGS

Ordinarily, this dish relies on the flavors of beef and bell peppers, but my version is jazzed up with Beau Monde, a seasoning mix available in the spice section of your grocery section, and sherry for even fuller flavor.

2 tablespoons wheat-free tamari soy sauce, such as Crystal or San-J

1 pound sirloin steak tips, sliced very thin against the grain

2 tablespoons canola oil, divided

1 medium green bell pepper, sliced thin

1 medium red bell pepper, sliced thin

1 medium onion, sliced thin

1 garlic clove, minced

½ cup gluten-free, low-sodium beef broth, such as Swanson's, or homemade Beef Broth (page 675)

1 teaspoon Beau Monde seasoning by Spice Islands

1 can (14 to 15 ounces) petite diced tomatoes, including juice

2 tablespoons dry sherry

1 tablespoon gluten-free Worcestershire sauce, such as French's

1 tablespoon cornstarch

4 cups hot cooked white rice

1 In a large heavy-duty food storage bag, combine the soy sauce and sliced steak; set aside to marinate while assembling the remaining ingredients.

2 In a large, heavy 10-inch skillet, heat 1 tablespoon of the oil over medium-high heat. Cook steak until lightly browned, about 3 to 5 minutes. You may have to cook the steak in two batches if your skillet isn't big enough. Transfer the steak to a clean plate.

3 In the same skillet, add the remaining tablespoon of canola oil and peppers, onion, and garlic. Cook until the vegetables begin to soften, about 3 minutes. Add the beef broth and Beau Monde seasoning, cover, and simmer 5 minutes.

4 Return the beef to the skillet, add tomatoes, and simmer 5 minutes. In a small bowl or cup, combine sherry and Worcestershire sauce and stir in cornstarch until mixture is smooth. Stir into skillet and cook until sauce is thickened, about

2 minutes. Serve immediately over cooked white rice.

Beef Short Ribs

MAKES 4 SERVINGS

Today's slow cookers are a marvelous improvement over the original versions, since you can remove and wash the pot in the dishwasher, or, use disposable plastic liners that make clean-up a breeze. This easy dish is perfect for a winter's day when you want dinner waiting for you when you walk in the door.

2 tablespoons canola oil

4 pounds beef shortribs, trimmed, and cut into 4-rib sections

1 cup ketchup

⅓ cup gluten-free Worcestershire sauce, such as French's

¼ cup fresh lemon juice

2 tablespoons packed light brown sugar

1 medium onion, sliced

1 teaspoon dry mustard

1 teaspoon chili powder

1 teaspoon salt

1 teaspoon hot pepper sauce, such as Frank's

2 cups gluten-free, low-sodium chicken broth, such as Swanson's Natural Goodness, or homemade Chicken Broth (page 676)

1 In a large skillet, heat the oil over medium-high heat. Cook ribs, meat side down, until nicely browned, working in batches until all ribs are browned.

2 Lightly coat the slow cooker with cooking spray. Combine the remaining ingredients until thoroughly blended and add to the slow cooker. Place the ribs in the slow cooker and cook 6 to 8 hours on low heat.

Carne Asada

MAKES 4 SERVINGS

Carne asada—*meaning "grilled meat"—is one of the easiest dishes to make and can be eaten plain, in sandwiches, or in tacos or fajitas. It is a good dish for busy nights because you put the flank steak in the marinade, refrigerate overnight, and grill it the next day. Chipotle Adobo Sauce (page 673)—a common Southwestern ingredient made of chipotle peppers and a tomato sauce that usually contains wheat—can be made ahead of time and frozen so you have it on hand for dishes like this.*

2 teaspoons homemade Chipotle Adobo Sauce
    (page 673)
¼ cup red wine or cider vinegar
¼ cup canola oil
1 small onion, sliced
¼ teaspoon garlic powder
½ bunch cilantro with stems, washed
2 teaspoons salt
1 pound flank steak

1 In a large heavy-duty food storage bag, combine the chipotle adobo sauce, wine, oil, onion, garlic powder, cilantro, and salt. Add the flank steak, seal, and refrigerate overnight. Let the steak stand at room temperature while the grill heats up. Remove beef from marinade and pat dry; discard the marinade.

2 Place a barbecue grill about 6 inches away from the heat source. Preheat the grill to medium-high heat. Grill the steak 3 to 4 minutes. Turn the meat over with tongs and cook on the other side, about 3 minutes more for rare, or 4 minutes more for medium-rare. To check for doneness, make a small cut in the thickest part. For longer cooking, move the steak to a cooler part of the grill. Slice in thin pieces, diagonally, across the grain. Serve immediately.

Osso Buco

MAKES 4 SERVINGS

Osso buco *literally means "bone with a hole" and the hole contains the rich marrow, a delicacy for some who eat it with special small spoons. The traditional Milanese version is often served on Saffron Risotto (page 222), but my version is served on soft polenta—which works best in a wide shallow bowl, rather than a plate, so all the juices are captured. Look for shanks cut from the hind legs, which will be meatier.*

4 veal or beef shanks (about 3 inches long each)
¼ cup cornstarch
1 tablespoon Beau Monde seasoning by Spice
    Islands
½ teaspoon freshly ground black pepper
1 tablespoon unsalted butter or buttery spread, such
    as Earth Balance
1 tablespoon olive oil
1 cup gluten-free, low-sodium beef broth,
    such as Swanson's, or homemade Beef Broth
    (page 675)
½ cup dry red wine
¼ cup tomato paste
1 teaspoon Italian seasoning
2 garlic cloves, minced
1 small carrot, sliced diagonally in ½-inch slices
2 tablespoons chopped fresh flat-leaf parsley,
    divided
1 tablespoon dried celery flakes
1 teaspoon grated lemon or orange zest
4 cups hot cooked polenta

1 Dip the veal shanks into cornstarch and sprinkle with the seasoning and pepper. In a Dutch oven or other deep, heavy pot with a tight-fitting lid, heat the butter and oil over medium heat. Add the shanks and cook until browned, about 10 minutes on each side.

2 Add the broth, wine, tomato paste, Italian seasoning, garlic, carrot, 1 tablespoon of the parsley, celery flakes, and lemon zest and bring to a boil. Reduce the heat and simmer, covered, 1 to 1½ hours. If there is too much liquid, remove the lid so the liquid can evaporate as it cooks. (If you prefer a thicker sauce, mix 2 teaspoons sweet rice flour with 2 tablespoons cold water until smooth and whisk into the sauce until thickened.)

3 Serve each shank on top of hot polenta, topped with the remaining tablespoon of parsley for garnish.

Reuben Casserole

MAKES 4 SERVINGS

If you like Reuben sandwiches, then you'll love this easy casserole. Assemble it the night before and bake the next day. It blends all those wonderful flavors from the Reuben sandwich, in an easy-to-prepare dish that goes great with a gluten-free beer.

1 can (8 ounces) sauerkraut, drained

½ teaspoon caraway seed

6 slices homemade Pumpernickel French Yeast Bread (page 103) or Quinoa Pumpernickel Yeast Bread (page 97)

1 teaspoon salt, divided

¼ cup Thousand Island dressing, such as Litehouse Foods

¼ pound thin sliced corned beef, finely chopped with scissors

1 teaspoon fresh dill or ½ teaspoon dried

8 ounces grated Swiss cheese or cheese alternative, such as Vegan Gourmet, divided

2 plum tomatoes, sliced very thin

1½ cups 1% milk (cow's, rice, soy, potato, or nut)

3 large eggs

½ cup chopped onion or 2 tablespoons dried minced onions

¼ cup grainy mustard

½ teaspoon freshly ground black pepper

2 tablespoons fresh parsley or 1 tablespoon dried

1 Generously grease an 8-inch nonstick (gray, not black) pan; set aside.

2 Arrange the sauerkraut in a thin layer on the bottom of the pan. Sprinkle with caraway seed. Arrange the 6 bread slices in a single layer on top, cutting some pieces, if necessary, to fit in. Sprinkle with ½ teaspoon of salt.

3 Spread the Thousand Island dressing over the bread. Arrange the chopped corned beef on the dressing. Top with ¾ of the Swiss cheese (about 6 ounces), reserving the final two ounces for sprinkling on top. Arrange the tomato slices on top.

4 In a bowl, whisk together the milk, eggs, onions, mustard, remaining ½ teaspoon salt and pepper until completely blended. Pour over mixture in pan. Wrap tightly with foil and refrigerate overnight.

5 Bring the casserole to room temperature. Place a rack in the middle of the oven. Preheat the oven to 350°F.

6 Bake 30 minutes, uncovered. Loosely cover with foil and continue baking 20 to 25 minutes more or until a knife inserted in the center comes out almost clean. Sprinkle the reserved Swiss cheese on top and return to oven for 5 to 10 minutes more or until the cheese is melted. Remove from oven and sprinkle with parsley. Serve immediately.

Shepherd's Beef Pie

MAKES 4 SERVINGS

Although shepherd's pie typically features ground lamb, this pot pie uses flavorful beef topped with mashed potatoes. It is an especially good way to use up leftovers. The beer adds a robust taste, but you may use wine instead. Heating tomato paste enhances the tomato flavor and adds depth to this dish.

FILLING

1 tablespoon unsalted butter or buttery spread, such as Earth Balance

½ pound lean beef cubes, about ½-inch size

1 small onion, diced

2 medium carrots, peeled and cut in ⅛-inch slices

1 tablespoon tomato paste

2 cups gluten-free, low-sodium chicken broth, such as Swanson's Natural Goodness, or homemade Chicken Broth (page 676)

½ cup gluten-free beer, such as Bard's Tale or Redbridge, or red wine

2 tablespoons wheat-free tamari soy sauce, such as Crystal or San-J

1 teaspoon chopped fresh thyme or 1½ teaspoons dried

1 cup frozen peas

2 tablespoons sweet rice flour

¼ cup 1% milk (cow's, rice, soy, potato, or nut)

TOPPING

2 tablespoons unsalted butter or buttery spread, such as Earth Balance, at room temperature

2 tablespoons grated Parmesan cheese or soy alternative, such as Soyco

1 large egg, beaten

2 cups leftover mashed potatoes, at room temperature

1 Place a rack in the middle of the oven. Preheat the oven to 375°F. Generously grease an 8-inch or 1-quart ovenproof baking dish.

2 Make the filling: In a heavy, large skillet, heat the butter over medium heat. Add the beef, onion, and carrots and cook until the beef is browned, about 8 to 10 minutes. Add the tomato paste and cook 1 minute, stirring constantly. Add the broth, beer, soy sauce, thyme, and peas and continue to cook, covered, 10 minutes more.

3 Stir the sweet rice flour into the milk until smooth. Stir it into the beef mixture and cook on medium until it thickens slightly, about 1 to 2 minutes. Transfer to the casserole dish.

4 Make the topping: In a bowl, stir the butter, cheese, egg, and mashed potatoes. Drop by spoonfuls around the perimeter of the dish, mashing potatoes up against side of dish so that they form a

continuous circle around the entire dish—leaving the center uncovered.

5 Bake 20 to 25 minutes or until the filling is bubbly and the potatoes start to brown. If the leftover mashed potatoes have not been brought to room temperature, the baking time will be longer. Let stand 10 minutes before serving.

Smoked Paprika Beef in Savory Crepes

MAKES 4 SERVINGS

I often make this dish after a dinner party at which we've had steak and red wine because it is a perfect way to use any leftovers. If the steak is grilled and has some "char" on it, that only adds to the flavor. Smoked paprika gives this dish a marvelous smoky depth. The crepe batter makes 9 crepes (2 for each serving and 1 to be a test or a snack.)

CREPES

⅔ cup sifted Carol's Sorghum Blend (page x)

¼ teaspoon xanthan gum

⅛ teaspoon salt

1 cup 1% milk (cow's, rice, soy, potato, or nut)

2 large eggs

1 tablespoon canola oil

Additional canola oil or cooking spray for frying

STEAK

1 pound leftover cooked steak, cut in ½-inch cubes

1 medium red bell pepper, seeded and cut in very thin slices

2 teaspoons smoked paprika

1 large tomato (or 2 plum or Roma tomatoes), seeded and chopped

½ cup dry red wine

1 teaspoon sugar

½ teaspoon salt

¼ teaspoon freshly ground black pepper

½ cup sour cream or sour cream alternative, such as Tofutti, divided, plus more for serving (optional)

Dash of paprika, for garnish

2 tablespoons chopped fresh parsley, for garnish

1 Make the crepes: In a blender, combine sorghum blend, xanthan gum, salt, milk, eggs, and oil and process until smooth.

2 Heat an 8-inch skillet or seasoned crepe pan over medium-high heat until a drop of water dances on the surface. Lightly coat the pan with oil or cooking spray. Pour a scant ¼ cup batter into pan and immediately tilt pan to coat bottom evenly. Cook until underside of crepe is brown and cook other side for about 20 to 30 seconds. (Often the first crepe will not turn out as well as succeeding ones, because the pan hasn't yet reached the ideal temperature.) Remove the crepe from pan and lay on a sheet of wax paper. Repeat with remaining batter, replenishing the oil or cooking spray as needed to prevent the crepes from sticking. Cover the crepes to keep them warm.

3 Prepare the steak: In a medium saucepan, combine the steak, bell pepper, paprika, tomato, wine, sugar, salt, and pepper. Bring to a boil over medium heat, reduce the heat to low, and simmer, covered, 15 to 20 minutes. Remove from the heat and stir in ⅓ cup of the sour cream. Cool the mixture 5 minutes. Mixture can be prepared ahead to this point and then refrigerated.

4 Place a rack in the middle of the oven. Preheat the oven to 375°F. Generously grease a glass or ceramic 11 × 7-inch baking dish. Lay each crepe, golden-brown side down, on a flat surface. Using a slotted spoon, put ⅛ of the steak mixture in a line down the center of the crepe. Roll the crepe into a cylinder and place, seam down, in a prepared dish. Repeat with the remaining 7 crepes filling. There will be liquid remaining in saucepan. Stir remaining sour cream into liquid and pour over crepes.

5 Bake 30 to 35 minutes or until the crepes are heated through. Serve with a scant tablespoon of sour cream, if using, a dash of paprika, and a sprinkle of parsley.

Asian Stir-Fry Beef over Brown Rice

MAKES 4 SERVINGS

The flavors in this dish are phenomenal, due to the Chinese 5-spice powder which is a mixture of cinnamon, fennel, star anise, cloves, and Szechwan pepper. Freeze the beef for 15 minutes to make it easier to slice thin.

2 tablespoons wheat-free tamari soy sauce, such as Crystal or San-J , divided

1 teaspoon sesame oil

2 garlic cloves, minced

2 teaspoons packed light brown sugar

1 teaspoon Chinese 5-spice powder

½ teaspoon crushed red pepper

1 pound lean beef sirloin, cut in very thin strips

2 tablespoons peanut oil, divided

3 tablespoons fresh ginger, grated

1 small onion, chopped

1 pound broccoli, cut into 1-inch florets (about 3 cups)

1 large red bell pepper, cut in thin strips

1¼ cups gluten-free, low-sodium beef broth, such as Swanson's, or homemade Beef Broth (page 675)

1 tablespoon cornstarch

2 cups hot cooked brown rice

1 In a medium bowl, combine 1 tablespoon of the soy sauce with the sesame oil, garlic, sugar, 5-spice powder, and crushed red pepper. Add the beef and toss to coat thoroughly. Marinate at room temperature 15 minutes.

2 In a large, heavy skillet or wok, heat 1 tablespoon of the peanut oil over medium heat. Add the beef with the marinade, ginger, and onion and stir-fry over medium heat until just browned, about 2 minutes. Transfer the beef, ginger, and onion to a plate.

3 Increase the heat to medium-high and add the remaining tablespoon of peanut oil and the remaining tablespoon of soy sauce to the skillet. Add the broccoli and bell pepper and cook 1 minute.

4 Stir the cornstarch into ¼ cup of broth until smooth. Add to the skillet, along with the remaining broth and stir until blended. Cover and cook 2 minutes more.

5 Return the beef to the skillet and heat to serving temperature. Serve over hot rice.

GROUND BEEF

Meat Loaf

MAKES 6 SERVINGS

You don't have to be gluten-free to enjoy this meat loaf—even my non-gluten-free friends—and their kids—love this version. You may be surprised to learn that this savory dish contains allspice, but the proof is in the taste—it gives this all-American dish a certain something, or je ne sais quoi, *as the French would say.*

1 pound lean ground beef (or use half ground beef and half ground turkey)

1 cup (8 ounces) tomato sauce

1 tablespoon packed light brown sugar

1 tablespoon gluten-free Worcestershire sauce, such as French's

½ teaspoon celery salt

¼ teaspoon ground allspice

1 cup chopped onions or ¼ cup dried minced onion

1 large egg, beaten

2 tablespoons chopped fresh parsley or 1 tablespoon dried

1 tablespoon Dijon mustard

½ teaspoon salt

½ teaspoon freshly ground black pepper

½ cup gluten-free bread crumbs, such as Ener-G, or homemade Plain Bread Crumbs (page 117)

1 Place a rack in the middle of the oven. Preheat the oven to 350°F. Generously grease an 8 × 4-inch nonstick (gray, not black) loaf pan or line a 13 × 9-inch nonstick (gray, not black) baking sheet with foil and coat it with cooking spray.

2 Place the ground beef in a large mixing bowl. Put the tomato sauce in a small bowl and stir in the brown sugar, Worcestershire sauce, celery salt, and allspice. Add half of the tomato mixture to the ground beef; reserve the other half for topping.

3 Add the onions, egg, parsley, mustard, salt, pepper, and bread crumbs to the ground beef and mix with your hands to blend thoroughly. Spread the mixture in the loaf pan or into an 8-inch circle on the baking sheet. Brush the remaining tomato sauce mixture on top.

4 Bake the loaf 1 hour or until the internal temperature reaches 160°F on an instant-read thermometer. Let stand 10 minutes before slicing. Serve hot.

Barbecued Meat Loaf

MAKES 6 SERVINGS

Barbecue sauce, fragrant with molasses, vinegar, and spices, makes this meat loaf extra-flavorful. The sauce that goes on top is key to the success of this dish. You don't have to use the smoked paprika, but it adds a wonderful depth.

1 pound lean ground beef (or use half ground beef and half ground turkey)

½ cup chopped onion or 2 tablespoons dried minced onions

1 teaspoon salt

1 teaspoon chopped fresh thyme of ½ teaspoon dried

½ teaspoon freshly ground black pepper

1 can (8 ounces) tomato sauce

2 tablespoons packed light brown sugar

2 tablespoons molasses (not blackstrap)

1 tablespoon red wine vinegar

1 teaspoon Dijon mustard

½ teaspoon ground cumin

½ teaspoon smoked paprika, if available

¼ teaspoon garlic powder

½ cup gluten-free bread crumbs, such as Ener-G, or homemade Plain Bread Crumbs (page 117) soaked in ¼ cup 1% milk (cow's, rice, soy, potato, or nut)

1 large egg

1 Place a rack in the middle of the oven. Preheat the oven to 375°F. Generously grease an 8 × 4-inch nonstick (gray, not black) loaf pan or line a 13 × 9-inch nonstick (gray, not black) baking sheet with foil and coat with cooking spray.

2 In a large mixing bowl, place the ground beef and stir in the onion, salt, thyme, and pepper.

3 Put the tomato sauce in a small bowl and whisk in the sugar, molasses, vinegar, mustard, cumin, paprika, and garlic powder. Stir half of the tomato sauce mixture into the ground beef; reserve the other half for topping. Stir the bread crumbs and egg into the ground beef and mix thoroughly.

4 Shape the ground beef into an 8 × 4-inch loaf on baking sheet or transfer to the loaf pan. Spread the remaining tomato mixture on top of the meat loaf.

5 Bake the loaf 1 hour or until the internal temperature reaches 160°F on an instant-read thermometer. Let stand 10 minutes and slice. Serve hot.

Italian Meat Loaf

MAKES 6 SERVINGS

Italian seasoning, fennel, and Parmesan cheese transform ordinary meat loaf into something extraordinary. This version makes especially good meat loaf sandwiches.

1½ pounds lean ground beef (or use half ground beef and half ground turkey)

1 can (8 ounces) tomato sauce

1 tablespoon gluten-free Worcestershire, such as French's

1 tablespoon sugar

3 teaspoons Italian seasoning, divided

½ cup gluten-free bread crumbs, such as Ener-G, or homemade Plain Bread Crumbs (page 117)

½ cup grated Parmesan cheese or soy alternative, such as Soyco

1 cup chopped onion or ¼ cup dried minced onion

4 tablespoons chopped fresh parsley or 2 tablespoons dried

1 teaspoon salt

½ teaspoon garlic powder or 1 large garlic clove, minced

¼ teaspoon freshly ground black pepper

1 large egg

½ teaspoon fennel seeds

1 Place a rack in the middle of the oven. Preheat the oven to 350°F. Generously grease an 8 × 4-inch nonstick (gray, not black) loaf pan or line a 13 × 9-inch nonstick (gray, not black) baking sheet with foil and coat with cooking spray.

2 Place the ground beef in a large mixing bowl. Put the tomato sauce in a small bowl and stir in the Worcestershire sauce, sugar, and 1 teaspoon of the Italian seasoning and add half to the ground beef; reserve the other half for topping.

3 Add the bread crumbs, Parmesan cheese, onion, parsley, salt, garlic, pepper, egg, and the remaining 2 teaspoons Italian seasoning to the beef mixture, and mix with your hands to blend thoroughly. Shape the ground beef into an 8 × 4-inch loaf on the baking sheet or transfer to the loaf pan. Stir fennel seeds into the remaining tomato sauce and brush on top.

4 Bake the loaf 1 hour or until the internal temperature reaches 160°F on an instant-read thermometer. Let stand for 10 minutes before slicing. Serve hot.

Southwestern Meat Loaf

MAKES 6 SERVINGS

Depending on the Mexican salsa you choose, this meat loaf will take on different personalities. I once made it with a peach-based tomato salsa and it was fabulous, so let your creativity fly. If you plan to use the leftover meat loaf in sandwiches, be sure to save some of the salsa as a sauce.

1 pound lean ground beef (or use half ground beef and half ground turkey)

1½ cups gluten-free Mexican tomato salsa, such as Publix or Tostitos

½ cup gluten-free bread crumbs, such as Ener-G, or homemade Plain Bread Crumbs (page 117) or ¼ cup quick-cooking white rice

1 can (4 ounces) diced green chiles, undrained

2 teaspoons homemade Southwestern Seasoning (page 668)

1 cup chopped onions or ¼ cup dried minced onion

4 teaspoons chopped fresh oregano or 2 teaspoons dried

1 teaspoon salt

½ teaspoon garlic powder or 1 large garlic clove, minced

¼ teaspoon freshly ground black pepper

1 large egg

1 Place a rack in the middle of the oven. Preheat the oven to 350°F. Generously grease an 8 × 4-inch nonstick (gray, not black) loaf pan or line a 13 × 9-inch nonstick (gray, not black) baking sheet with foil and coat with cooking spray.

2 Place the ground beef in a large mixing bowl. Add 1 cup of the salsa to the ground beef; reserve the other half for topping.

3 Add the remaining ingredients to the ground beef and mix with your hands to thoroughly blend. Shape the ground beef into an 8 × 4-inch loaf on the baking sheet or transfer to the loaf pan. Spread the remaining salsa on top.

4 Bake the loaf 1 hour or until the internal temperature reaches 160°F on an instant-read thermometer. Let stand 10 minutes before slicing. Serve hot.

Swedish Meatballs

MAKES 4 SERVINGS (24 MEATBALLS)

There are some classics that people never get tired of. This is one of them. You can use any combination of ground meat you wish; in fact, I sometimes use combinations of ground beef, pork, or chicken for variety and richer flavor. This dish is easily assembled ahead of time up to the step when you add the sour cream, making it a great dish for company. Fresh dill sprinkled as a garnish is absolutely fabulous.

1 pound ground beef

½ cup gluten-free bread crumbs, such as Ener-G, or homemade Plain Bread Crumbs (page 117)

1 tablespoon chopped onion or 1 teaspoon dried minced onion

1 large egg, slightly beaten

2 garlic cloves, minced

3 teaspoons chopped fresh dill or 1 teaspoon dried + pinch for sour cream sauce

½ teaspoon ground allspice + pinch for sour cream sauce

¼ teaspoon freshly grated nutmeg + pinch for sour cream sauce

½ teaspoon salt

¼ teaspoon freshly ground black pepper

1 tablespoon cornstarch

1 cup gluten-free, low-sodium beef broth, such as Swanson's, or homemade Beef Broth (page 675)

1 tablespoon brandy (optional) or 1 teaspoon brandy extract

1 cup sour cream or sour cream alternative, such as Tofutti

1 pound hot cooked gluten-free pasta, such as Heartland's finest or Tinkyada

2 tablespoons chopped fresh parsley or fresh dill, for garnish

1 Place a rack in the middle of the oven. Preheat the oven to 350°F. Line a 13 × 9-inch nonstick (gray, not black) baking sheet with foil. In a large bowl, combine the beef, bread crumbs, onion, egg, garlic, dill, allspice, nutmeg, salt, and pepper. Shape into 24 meatballs, each 1 inch in diameter.

2 Place the meatballs on the baking sheet. Bake 20 minutes or until browned.

3 Whisk the cornstarch into ¼ cup of the beef broth. Heat the remaining beef broth in a large saucepan. Add the cornstarch mixture and stir over medium heat until thickened. Add the meatballs and brandy to the pan and simmer gently 10 minutes. Stir in the sour cream and remaining pinches of dill, allspice, and nutmeg, but do not boil or the sour cream will curdle. Serve immediately over hot cooked pasta, garnished with parsley or dill.

Piccadillo

MAKES 4 SERVINGS

This Cuban ground-beef dish has several variations, with many fascinating flavor components—savory, sweet (from the raisins), and a bit salty (from the capers and olives). And, it can be eaten in many different ways. This versatile concoction can be used to stuff peppers, eaten over cooked white rice, made into a stew with the addition of beef or chicken broth, or used as a filling for tacos or fajitas.

1 tablespoon olive oil

1 pound lean ground beef

½ teaspoon salt

¼ teaspoon freshly ground black pepper

½ cup chopped white onion

½ cup diced red bell pepper

½ cup diced yellow bell pepper

1 can (14 to 15 ounces) petite diced tomatoes, including juice

1 garlic clove, minced

1 teaspoon ground cumin

1 teaspoon chopped fresh thyme or ½ teaspoon dried

¼ teaspoon freshly grated nutmeg

¼ cup sliced green olives

¼ cup almond slices

¼ cup golden raisins

1 bay leaf

1 tablespoon cider vinegar

¼ cup fresh parsley, chopped, for garnish

1 In a heavy-duty skillet, heat the oil over medium heat. Season ground beef with salt and pepper and place in skillet, along with onion and peppers. Cook, stirring frequently, until the meat is fully browned and the vegetables are softened, about 5 minutes.

2 Stir in the tomatoes, garlic, cumin, thyme, nutmeg, olives, almonds, raisins, and bay leaf. Mix thoroughly until well incorporated. Simmer, covered, 10 to 15 minutes to blend the flavors. Add the vinegar and bring to serving temperature. Adjust seasonings, if necessary. Serve hot, garnished with parsley.

Hungarian Beef Goulash

MAKES 4 SERVINGS

Goulash is a stew made with beef and vegetables and flavored with Hungarian sweet paprika, which can be found in the spice section of your grocery store or in specialty shops. I grew up eating this dish, not fully understanding "why" until, as an adult I realized that my mother came from a Czech community where Eastern European dishes such as this one were quite common.

1 slice uncooked bacon

1 tablespoon olive oil

1 pound boneless beef, trimmed and cut in 2-inch cubes

2 tablespoons cornstarch

1 teaspoon salt

½ teaspoon freshly ground black pepper

1 can (14 to 15 ounces) petite diced tomatoes

1 tablespoon red wine vinegar

1 can (14 to 15 ounces) or 1¾ cups gluten-free, low-sodium beef broth, such as Swanson's, or homemade Beef Broth (page 675)

1 small onions, chopped

1 garlic clove, minced

1 tablespoon Hungarian sweet paprika

1 teaspoon sugar

1 teaspoon caraway seed

2 teaspoons chopped fresh oregano or 1 teaspoon dried

¼ cup sour cream or sour cream alternative, such as Tofutti

2 tablespoons chopped flat-leaf parsley, for garnish

1 pound hot cooked gluten-free pasta, such as Tinkyada

1 Heat a heavy-duty skillet over medium heat. Add the bacon and fry until crisp, about 5 minutes. Remove bacon with tongs, leaving bacon drippings in the skillet, and reserve. Add olive oil to the pan.

2 In the skillet, heat the oil over medium heat. Dust the beef with cornstarch, sprinkle it with salt and pepper, and add it to the hot skillet. Cook until evenly browned on all sides, about 5 to 8 minutes.

3 Stir in the tomatoes, vinegar, beef broth, onion, garlic, paprika, sugar, caraway, and oregano. Return the bacon to skillet and bring to a boil. Lower the heat to a simmer and cook 1 hour, covered, stirring occasionally.

4 Just before serving, remove the goulash from the heat and stir in sour cream. Do not boil or the sour cream will curdle. Garnish with chopped parsley. Serve over hot cooked pasta.

Mexican Skillet Beef and Rice ⓠ

MAKES 4 SERVINGS

Save this dish for really busy nights, when you and the kids are starving and want dinner on the table right away. Serve it with a tossed salad and some corn tortillas, wrapped in damp paper towels and heated gently in the microwave.

½ pound lean ground beef

¼ cup chopped onion or 1 tablespoon dried minced onion

1½ tablespoons chili powder

1 teaspoon fresh oregano or ½ teaspoon dried

½ teaspoon ground cumin

¼ teaspoon salt

1 cup cooked brown rice (instant brown rice is fine)

1 can (14 to 15 ounces) pinto beans or black beans, drained and rinsed

1 can (4 ounces) diced green chiles

2 medium Roma or plum tomatoes, seeded and chopped

2 tablespoons chopped fresh cilantro, for garnish

1 In a large skillet, cook the ground beef over medium-high heat until browned, about 5 minutes, stirring to crumble the beef. The beef will be more flavorful is it is fully browned and all the liquid has evaporated.

2 Add the onion, chili powder, oregano, cumin, and salt. Stir in the rice, beans, and chiles and bring to serving temperature. Top with the chopped tomato; garnish with chopped cilantro. Serve immediately.

Stuffed Trio of Sweet Peppers

MAKES 6 SERVINGS

Although this is a home-style dish, the colorful peppers look very elegant nestled on a bed of white basmati rice. It can be used for everyday dining but also makes a lovely dish for guests who like home-style cooking.

6 medium-size bell peppers (2 red, 2 yellow, 2 green)

½ pound lean ground beef

2 cups gluten-free marinara sauce, such as Classico, or homemade Marinara Sauce (page 672)

3 cups cooked white rice

1 small onion, finely chopped

1 teaspoon chopped fresh oregano or ½ teaspoon dried

1 teaspoon chopped fresh thyme or ½ teaspoon dried

½ teaspoon salt

½ teaspoon freshly ground black pepper

1 garlic clove, minced

4 cups hot cooked white basmati rice

1 Halve each pepper lengthwise, from stem to base. Remove seeds and cut off stem. Place on plate and cook in microwave oven on high, covered with waxed paper, 5 minutes. Remove and let cool. Coat a 13 × 9-inch glass baking dish with cooking spray; set aside.

2 In a heavy skillet, cook the ground beef over medium-high heat until nicely browned and the liquid has evaporated, about 5 minutes. Stir in 1 cup of the marinara sauce, cooked rice, onion, oregano, thyme, salt, pepper, and garlic. Spoon the mixture into the peppers. Spoon any leftover mixture around peppers. Or, freeze to spoon over white rice later for a quick meal. (You may prepare this dish the night before; cover, and refrigerate to bake the next day.)

3 Place a rack in the middle of the oven. Preheat the oven to 375°F. Bake 20 minutes, covered, or until the sauce is bubbling. Remove from the oven. Heat the remaining 1 cup of marinara sauce to serving temperature and drizzle it over the stuffed peppers. Serve on a bed of hot cooked rice.

Stuffed Cabbage Rolls

MAKES 6 SERVINGS

Although there are many versions of this homey dish, I prefer the Russian and Czech influences of dill here—possibly because I grew up near a Czech community and because I've been eating stuffed cabbage at a Russian café near my home for many years.

CABBAGE ROLLS

1½ cups cooked white short-grain rice

½ pound raw lean ground beef

½ cup gluten-free bread crumbs, such as Ener-G, or homemade Plain Bread Crumbs (page 117)

2 tablespoons fresh parsley or 1 tablespoon dried

1 tablespoon sugar

2 teaspoons chopped fresh dill or 1 teaspoon dried

1 garlic clove, minced

2 teaspoons salt, or to taste

1 teaspoon freshly ground black pepper

12 large cabbage leaves, preferably Savoy cabbage

SAUCE

2 tablespoons extra-virgin olive oil

1 cup finely diced yellow onion

1 garlic clove, minced

1 tablespoon tomato paste

4 teaspoons sweet paprika

2 cups gluten-free, low-sodium chicken broth, such as Swanson's Natural Goodness, or homemade Chicken Broth (page 676)

1 cup tomato sauce

2 tablespoons red wine vinegar

1 tablespoon sugar

2 teaspoons chopped fresh dill or 1 teaspoon dried

2 teaspoons chopped fresh thyme or 1 teaspoon dried

½ teaspoon salt

½ teaspoon freshly ground black pepper

1 Make the cabbage rolls: In a bowl, combine rice, beef, bread crumbs, parsley, sugar, dill, garlic, salt, and pepper and mix thoroughly with your hands. Cover and refrigerate.

2 Bring a large pot of salted water to a boil. Fill a large bowl with ice water. Add the cabbage leaves to boiling water and cook just until slightly wilted, about 1 minute. Remove the leaves from the boiling water with tongs and immediately plunge into the ice water. When cool, remove and pat dry with paper towels. Or, line a lettuce spinner with paper towels and spin cabbage leaves until dry.

3 Cut the thick part of the stem from each cabbage leaf with a sharp knife or kitchen shears. Place a scant 3 tablespoons filling in the center of each cabbage leaf. Fold sides of leaf over filling, overlapping them slightly. Then, starting at stem end, roll up leaf into bundle, securing with toothpicks. Place rolls, overlapped side down, in 13 × 9-inch glass greased baking dish; set aside.

4 Place a rack in the middle of the oven. Preheat the oven to 375°F.

5 Make the sauce: In a heavy skillet, heat the oil over medium-high heat. Add the onion and cook until they are translucent. Add the remaining ingredients and simmer 10 minutes. Pour the sauce over the cabbage rolls and bake 30 to 45 minutes or until the cabbage is tender. To serve, spoon the sauce over the rolls.

PORK CHOPS AND CUTLETS

Braised Pork Chops with Red-Wine Plums

MAKES 4 SERVINGS

Braising means cooking meat slowly on the stovetop in a little bit of liquid—with the spices adding marvelous flavor to these pork chops. Or, cut pork tenderloin into 1-inch-thick boneless chops called medallions for this recipe. You can feel virtuous after eating this dish because the red wine and dried plums contain high levels of antioxidants (and also because you prepared such a delicious dish).

1 tablespoon olive oil

4 lean pork chops (about 6 ounces each)

½ teaspoon salt

½ teaspoon freshly ground black pepper

1 large onion, peeled and cut in ¼-inch slices

½ cup pitted dried plums, halved

1 cup dry red wine

1 strip orange peel

¼ teaspoon ground cinnamon

⅛ teaspoon ground cloves

⅛ teaspoon ground allspice

1 tablespoon packed light brown sugar

1 In a medium, heavy skillet, heat the oil over medium-high heat. Sprinkle the pork with salt and pepper and cook until the pork is browned on both sides, about 3 to 4 minutes per side. Add the onion around the pork and then put the dried plums on top of the onion.

2 In a bowl, whisk together the wine, orange peel, cinnamon, cloves, allspice, and brown sugar and pour over the onion and plums. Cover and cook over low heat about 30 minutes, or until the pork is tender. Transfer the pork, plums, and onion to a serving platter and cover with foil to keep warm.

3 Increase the heat to medium-high and boil the juices until they reduce somewhat and become syrupy; pour this mixture over the pork and serve immediately.

Sage-Dusted Pork Chops with Autumn Spiced Apples

MAKES 4 SERVINGS

To me, the smell of apples and spices is one of autumn's signature aromas. The addition of sage is like the proverbial frosting on the cake. I prefer to leave apples unpeeled for added texture and nutrients, but peel them if you wish.

PORK CHOPS

4 boneless pork chops (about 4 ounces each), ½ inch thick

1 teaspoon salt

1 teaspoon rubbed sage

½ teaspoon freshly ground black pepper

1 tablespoon olive oil

SPICED APPLES

2 tablespoons unsalted butter or buttery spread, such as Earth Balance

3 apples (such as Granny Smith or Honey Crisp), cored, and sliced in ½-inch-thick wedges

2 teaspoons fresh thyme leaves

¼ cup dried cranberries

1 can (6 ounces) apple juice

Juice of 1 lemon

1 teaspoon Dijon mustard

1 tablespoon packed light brown sugar (double the sugar if apples are tart)

¼ teaspoon ground cinnamon

¼ teaspoon ground cloves

¼ teaspoon salt

¼ teaspoon freshly ground black pepper

1 Place a rack in the middle of the oven. Preheat the oven to 350°F. Prepare the pork chops: Sprinkle both sides of pork with salt, sage, and pepper.

2 In a heavy skillet, heat the oil over medium-high heat. Cook the pork chops until nicely browned, about 4 to 5 minutes per side. Transfer the pork to an ovenproof serving dish and roast 15 to 20 minutes in the oven or until the internal temperature reads 140°F to 145°F when tested with an instant-read thermometer.

3 Prepare the apples: Without wiping the skillet, melt the butter over medium-low heat. Add the apples and thyme and cook until apples are lightly browned. Add the cranberries and apple juice, stirring to scrape up brown bits on the bottom of skillet. Cook until the juice reduces somewhat. Add lemon juice, mustard, brown sugar, cinnamon, cloves, salt, and pepper. Simmer 10 to 15 minutes, covered, or until apples soften.

4 Remove the pork from the oven and place on a serving platter. Spoon the cooked apples over and around the pork chops. Serve immediately.

Grilled Pork Chops with Minted Pineapple Salsa

MAKES 4 SERVINGS

The sweet tanginess of the salsa elevates an ordinary pork chop to new and attractive culinary heights, while the fruit and vegetables supply important nutrients and fiber.

½ cup Minted Pineapple Salsa (page 671)
4 pork chops (about 4 ounces each)
½ teaspoon salt
¼ teaspoon freshly ground black pepper
1 teaspoon chopped fresh thyme or ½ teaspoon dried

Make the salsa. Sprinkle the pork chops with salt and pepper; sprinkle with thyme. Grill or fry pork chops until browned, about 3 to 4 minutes per side, or to desired degree of doneness. Serve with 2 tablespoons of the salsa on each pork chop.

Cumin-Dusted Pork Chops with Orange-Onion Salsa

MAKES 4 SERVINGS

Sweet mandarin oranges contrast nicely with the tartness of the red onions and the unique smoky flavor of cumin. Ground from cumin seeds, cumin is a key ingredient in Southwestern and Indian dishes and brings distinction to anything you use it in. Start out using it sparingly and increase the amount as you wish.

SALSA

2 cans (11 ounces each) mandarin oranges, drained
½ cup chopped red onion
2 tablespoons fresh chopped cilantro
1 tablespoon white wine vinegar
1 tablespoon honey
1 tablespoon grated orange zest
1 teaspoon olive oil
½ teaspoon chili powder
¼ teaspoon ground cumin
⅛ teaspoon salt
⅛ teaspoon freshly ground black pepper

PORK CHOPS

4 pork chops (about 4 ounces each), ½ inch thick
1 teaspoon salt
½ teaspoon ground cumin
¼ teaspoon freshly ground black pepper
1 tablespoon olive oil

1 Make the salsa: Gently toss all the salsa ingredients in a small bowl. Cover and hold at room temperature until serving time.

2 Prepare the pork chops: Sprinkle both sides of chops with salt, cumin, and pepper. In a heavy skillet, heat the oil over medium heat. Cook the pork chops to the desired degree of doneness. Or, cook pork chops on barbecue grill to desired degree of doneness. Serve with salsa.

Pork Chops with Spicy Orange-Cilantro Sauce

MAKES 4 SERVINGS

The fresh citrus flavors of orange and cilantro are the perfect complements to the distinctive smokiness of cumin in this lovely pork dish.

4 boneless pork chops (about 4 ounces each),
    ½ inch thick
1 teaspoon ground cumin
1 teaspoon salt
¼ teaspoon freshly ground black pepper
1 tablespoon canola oil
1 cup fresh orange juice
1 tablespoon rice vinegar
1 teaspoon grated orange zest
¼ teaspoon garlic powder
⅛ teaspoon ground cayenne
½ cup chopped fresh cilantro

1 Rub both sides of the pork chops with the cumin, salt, and pepper.

2 In a large heavy-duty skillet, heat the oil over medium-high heat. Add the pork chops and cook on both sides until nicely browned, about 3 to 4 minutes on each side.

3 Add the orange juice, vinegar, orange zest, garlic, and cayenne to the skillet. Reduce the heat to low, and simmer, covered, 10 minutes or until the chops are done. Transfer the chops to a plate and cover with foil to keep warm. Add all but 2 tablespoons of the cilantro and continue simmering the sauce until reduced by half and slightly syrupy.

4 Pour the sauce over chops, garnish with remaining 2 tablespoons of cilantro, and serve immediately.

Rosemary Pork Chops with Pomegranate Molasses

MAKES 4 SERVINGS

With all the interest in the health benefits of pomegranates, you're likely to find pomegranate molasses at your local natural food store or the gourmet section of your grocery store, but if you can't, see below for an easy way to make pomegranate syrup. In this very simple recipe, the pomegranate complements the rosemary and adds a delightfully different flavor to the pan juices.

4 thin-cut boneless pork chops (about 1 pound)
½ teaspoon salt
½ teaspoon freshly ground black pepper
2 tablespoons fresh rosemary or 1 tablespoon dried,
    very finely crushed
2 tablespoons canola oil
¼ cup pomegranate molasses or pomegranate syrup*
2 tablespoons chopped fresh parsley or 1 tablespoon
    dried, for garnish

1 Sprinkle both sides of the pork chops with salt, pepper, and rosemary and let stand at room temperature for 30 minutes while you prepare the rest of the meal.

2 In a heavy skillet, heat the oil over medium heat. Add the pork chops and cook them until they are browned on both sides, about 3 to 5 minutes per side.

3 Transfer the pork chops to a plate and cover with foil to keep them warm. Add the pomegranate molasses to the pan and cook with the juices over medium heat about 1 minute or until it is heated to serving temperature. If the mixture is too thin, cook it a little longer to reduce the juices. Pour over the pork chops and serve, garnished with parsley.

*To make pomegranate syrup: Simmer 1 cup of pure pomegranate juice until it is reduced to ¼ cup.

Smothered Pork Chops

MAKES 4 SERVINGS

The flexibility of this dish allows you to choose what to smother on the pork chops—a tomato-based sauce or a mushroom-based sauce, for example. In this case, it's an onion and garlic-based gravy, thickened and creamed with buttermilk.

4 boneless pork chops (about 4 ounces each),
    ½ inch thick
½ cup cornstarch + 2 tablespoons
1 teaspoon onion powder
¼ teaspoon ground cayenne
¼ teaspoon garlic powder
1 teaspoon salt
¼ teaspoon freshly ground black pepper
¼ cup canola oil
1 cup gluten-free, low-sodium chicken broth, such
    as Swanson's Natural Goodness, or homemade
    Chicken Broth (page 676)
½ cup buttermilk or homemade Buttermilk
    (page 677)
Additional salt and freshly ground pepper to taste
    (optional)
Chopped fresh flat-leaf parsley, for garnish

1 Pat the pork chops dry with paper towels. Put ½ cup cornstarch in a shallow bowl and add onion powder, cayenne, garlic powder, salt, and pepper. Whisk with fork to distribute ingredients thoroughly. Dip the pork chops in the cornstarch mixture.

2 In a large, heavy skillet, heat the oil over medium heat. Lay the pork chops in the skillet in a single layer, taking care not to crowd them. If they are too close together, they will steam rather than brown. Fry 7 to 10 minutes on each side or until golden brown.

3 Remove the pork chops from the skillet. Add all but ¼ cup of chicken broth and cook over medium heat until the liquid is reduced slightly. Stir 2 tablespoons of the remaining cornstarch mixture in remaining ¼ cup of the chicken broth and add to the skillet. Cook over medium heat until slightly thickened. Reduce the heat to low and stir in the buttermilk.

4 Return the pork chops to the skillet, spooning the sauce over them. Cover and simmer 5 minutes or until the pork is cooked through. Season with additional salt and pepper, if desired, and serve immediately, garnished with parsley.

Pork Chops and Cornbread Stuffing with Dried Fruits and Pomegranate Seeds

MAKES 4 SERVINGS

Serve this elegant version of a down-home dish to your guests and they'll marvel at the combination of flavorful ingredients. The pomegranate seeds will trigger the most curiosity.

4 boneless pork chops (4 ounces each),
    ¾ inch thick
1 teaspoon salt
½ teaspoon freshly ground black pepper
2 tablespoons canola oil
1 recipe Cornbread Stuffing with Dried Fruit and
    Pomegranate Seeds (page 324)
Fresh sage leaves, for garnish

1 Place a rack in the middle of the oven. Preheat oven to 400° F. Cut a pocket horizontally in each pork chop to hold the stuffing. Sprinkle both sides of pork chops with salt and pepper. Fill the pocket of each pork chop with the stuffing, squeezing it with your fingers so it fits in pocket. There will be leftover stuffing which you will put under the pork chops as they bake.

2 In a large, heavy skillet, heat the oil over medium heat. Gently place the stuffed pork chops in the skillet, taking care not to dislodge the stuffing. Cook the pork chops until browned on both sides, about 5 to 7 minutes for each side.

3 Spoon the remaining stuffing into a generously greased quart casserole or ovenproof serving dish. (To shorten baking time, heat stuffing in microwave oven until warm.) Lay the browned pork chops on top of the stuffing, taking care not to dislodge stuffing from the pork chops. Cover tightly with foil.

4 Bake 25 to 30 minutes or until the stuffing is heated through and the pork chops are done. Remove from oven and let stand 10 minutes, with the foil resting loosely on top. Serve immediately, garnished with sage leaves.

Pork Cutlets with Marsala Wine and Mushrooms

MAKES 4 SERVINGS

This classic Italian dish is delicious served over soft polenta, with the pan juices drizzled on top. It's great when you're pressed for time, but it's also a wonderful dish to prepare while guests watch you in the kitchen—which is what usually happens at my house. Marsala is a wine from the Sicilian city of the same name and is often used in Italian cooking (either sweet or dry Marsala will work).

4 pork cutlets (about 4 ounces each), about ½ inch thick
½ teaspoon salt
½ teaspoon black pepper
1 tablespoon olive oil
¼ cup Marsala wine
1 teaspoon balsamic vinegar
1 can (8 ounces) sliced mushrooms, with juice
1 garlic clove, minced
1 tablespoon fresh chopped rosemary
4 cups hot cooked polenta

1 Pat the cutlets dry and sprinkle with salt and pepper; set aside.

2 In a large, heavy skillet, heat the oil over medium heat. Add the cutlets and cook until lightly browned, about 3 to 4 minutes. Turn and

cook until other side is browned and crispy, about 2 to 3 minutes more.

3 Add the Marsala, vinegar, mushrooms and their juices, garlic, and rosemary. Simmer gently 3 to 5 minutes or until the cutlets are cooked through and the juices have reduced slightly. Transfer the cutlets to a serving platter and pour the reduced juices and mushrooms on top. Serve immediately on hot cooked polenta.

Pork Cutlets Milanese

MAKES 4 SERVINGS

Milanese is a descriptive name typically given to dishes that are pounded thin, breaded, and fried. It originated in Milan, Italy, hence the name. While there a few years ago, my non-gluten-free dinner companions loved the huge cutlets, which nearly covered the whole plate. My version is smaller, less cumbersome, and highly worthy of praise.

4 pork cutlets (about 4 ounces each), pounded to ¼ inch thick
1 teaspoon salt
½ teaspoon freshly ground black pepper
1 large egg, beaten to foam
1 cup gluten-free bread crumbs, such as Ener-G, or homemade Plain Bread Crumbs (page 117)
½ cup grated Parmesan cheese or soy alternative, such as Soyco
2 tablespoons olive oil, or more as needed
2 lemons, cut in half
2 tablespoons chopped fresh parsley, for garnish

1 Place a rack in the middle of the oven. Preheat the oven to 300°F. Line a 13 × 9-inch baking sheet (not nonstick) with foil and coat it with cooking spray.

2 Sprinkle the pork cutlets with salt and pepper. Put an egg in a shallow bowl and the bread crumbs and cheese in another shallow bowl. Dip each cutlet into the egg and then into the bread crumbs. Lay on a large plate until ready to fry.

3 In a heavy, large skillet, heat the oil over medium-high heat. Cook the pork cutlets until golden brown; turn and cook until golden brown on the other side. Transfer the cutlets to a baking sheet and put in the heated oven to finish cooking 10 to 15 minutes more. Serve hot with a wedge of lemon and a sprinkle of parsley.

Chicken-Fried Pork Cutlets with Vinegar Gravy

MAKES 4 SERVINGS

This dish is like traditional Chicken-Fried Steak, only using pork cutlets instead. Vinegar gravy may seem unusual, but it is a wonderful complement to the rich flavor and crispy texture of the pork cutlet. If you prefer things more traditional, try the Simple White Gravy (page 675).

PORK CUTLET

4 pork cutlets (about 4 ounces each), about ½ inch thick

2 teaspoons salt

1 teaspoon freshly ground black pepper

½ cup cornstarch

1 cup 1% milk (cow's, rice, soy, potato, or nut)

2 large eggs

¼ cup canola oil or peanut oil for frying

GRAVY

¾ cup mayonnaise

½ cup cider vinegar

¼ teaspoon salt

⅛ teaspoon white pepper

⅛ teaspoon hot pepper sauce, such as Frank's

1 Prepare the cutlets: Sprinkle both sides of the cutlets with salt and pepper on both sides and let stand at room temperature while assembling the remaining ingredients. In a shallow bowl, place the cornstarch. In another shallow bowl, whisk the milk and eggs together until all of the egg membrane is broken up and the mixture is very smooth.

2 Dip the steak first in cornstarch, then in egg mixture, then in cornstarch again. Repeat with each cutlet.

3 In a large, heavy skillet (preferably cast-iron), heat the oil over medium-high heat. Fry the cutlets until golden brown, about 4 to 5 minutes per side, turning only once. If you turn them again, the coating falls off. If your skillet isn't big enough, fry two at a time and keep fried cutlets warm in a 200°F oven on a foil-lined baking sheet.

4 Make the gravy: In a small saucepan, whisk the gravy ingredients together and cook over medium heat until slightly thickened. If mixture is too thick, thin with milk to reach desired consistency. Transfer cutlets to serving platter, pour the gravy over the cutlets, and serve immediately.

Roasted Pork Medallions with Orange-Ginger Sauce

MAKES 4 SERVINGS

Medallions are simply circles of pork tenderloin. The orange-ginger sauce is a marvelous complement to pork and is a perfect dinner dish for company.

½ cup orange juice concentrate, thawed

¼ cup gluten-free, low-sodium chicken broth, such as Swanson's Natural Goodness, or homemade Chicken Broth (page 676)

2 teaspoons cornstarch

1 tablespoon minced fresh ginger

1 teaspoon onion powder

¼ teaspoon garlic powder

1 tablespoon wheat-free tamari soy sauce, such as Crystal or San-J

¼ teaspoon crushed red pepper

¼ teaspoon white pepper

1 tablespoon canola oil

1 pound pork tenderloin, trimmed of fat

Chopped fresh chives, for garnish

1 In a bowl, combine the orange juice and chicken broth with the cornstarch, stirring until smooth. Add the ginger, onion powder, garlic powder, soy sauce, crushed red pepper, and white pepper. Set aside.

2 Place a rack in the middle of the oven. Preheat the oven to 400°F. Heat the oil in a heavy, oven-proof skillet over medium heat. Add the pork and cook until browned on all sides, about 5 minutes. Cover with an ovenproof lid or foil and transfer to the oven.

3 Roast 15 to 20 minutes or until the center of the pork registers 140°F when inserted with an instant-read thermometer. Transfer to a serving platter and let stand, covered, 15 minutes.

4 Place the same skillet over medium heat and add the orange juice mixture. Cook, stirring constantly to loosen the bits of browned meat on the bottom of the skillet, until the mixture thickens, about 3 to 5 minutes. Remove from heat. Slice pork tenderloin into 1-inch circles or medallions and pour the orange sauce over. Garnish with fresh chives and serve immediately.

Pork Schnitzel

MAKES 4 SERVINGS

My daughter-in-law's parents are Austrian and German and she grew up eating schnitzel. It's one of her favorite dishes and she serves this version often. I love it, too; it satisfies my love of crispy and crunchy foods—too often missing when eating gluten-free.

1 pound pork tenderloin, cut in ¼-inch slices
½ cup cornstarch
1 teaspoon seasoned salt, such as Lawry's
¼ teaspoon freshly ground black pepper
2 large eggs, thoroughly beaten
1 cup gluten-free bread crumbs, such as Ener-G, or homemade Plain Bread Crumbs (page 117)
¼ cup canola oil, plus more as needed
Additional salt and freshly ground pepper (optional)
1 lemon, quartered

1 Place a rack in the middle of the oven. Preheat the oven to 180°F. Line a 15 × 10-inch baking sheet with foil and lightly coat with cooking spray.

2 Place the pork slices in a single layer in a heavy-duty food storage bag. With the smooth side of a meat mallet, pound the pork to a ¼-inch thickness. Cut the bag open with kitchen scissors, leaving the pounded pork intact.

3 In a shallow bowl, combine the cornstarch, seasoned salt, and pepper. Place the eggs in a second shallow bowl and the bread crumbs in a third shallow bowl

4 Dip each pork slice into the cornstarch mixture, then into the eggs, and finally in the bread crumbs.

5 In a large, nonstick (gray, not black) skillet, heat the oil over medium-high heat. Cook the pork, a few pieces at a time, until golden brown, about 5 to 7 minutes per side. Remove the browned pork from the skillet and keep warm in the oven until all the cutlets are cooked. Add salt and pepper to taste, if desired. Serve immediately with a squeeze of fresh lemon.

PORK TENDERLOINS AND ROASTS

Chipotle-Lime Pork Tenderloin with Black Bean–Orange Salsa

MAKES 4 SERVINGS

Chipotle Adobo Sauce (page 673) is a very popular ingredient in Southwestern dishes. However, it is often made with wheat flour to thicken the sauce. To be safe, I recommend making your own, which is really quite simple.

PORK

1 pork tenderloin (about 1 pound), trimmed of excess fat

1 teaspoon homemade Chipotle Adobo Sauce (page 673)

1 tablespoon red wine vinegar

1 teaspoon onion powder

2 teaspoons chopped fresh oregano or 1 teaspoon dried

½ teaspoon ground cumin

½ teaspoon salt

¼ teaspoon garlic powder

¼ teaspoon freshly ground black pepper

Juice of 1 lime

SALSA

1 teaspoon homemade Chipotle Adobo Sauce (page 673)

1 cup red and yellow grape tomatoes, halved

1 can (14 to 15 ounces) black beans, rinsed and drained

½ cup chopped fresh cilantro

¼ cup chopped red onion

Juice and grated zest of 1 lime

¼ teaspoon ground cumin

1 small can (11 ounces) mandarin oranges, drained

1 Prepare the pork: Place the pork in a heavy-duty food storage bag. Add the remaining ingredients and massage the bag to blend the ingredients, making sure the pork is submerged in the marinade. Refrigerate overnight.

2 Place a barbecue grill about 6 inches away from the heat source. Preheat the grill to medium-high heat. Remove the pork from the marinade (discard marinade) and grill about 7 minutes on one side to form grill marks. Turn and grill another 7 minutes to form grill marks on other side. Continue cooking another 5 to 7 minutes or until the internal temperature reaches 145°F to 150°F on an instant-read thermometer when inserted into the center. Transfer the tenderloin to a serving plate. Wrap in foil and let stand 10 minutes before slicing.

3 Make the salsa: In a bowl, combine all of the salsa ingredients, except oranges, and mix well. Just before serving, gently stir the oranges into the salsa. Slice the pork and serve immediately with the salsa.

Cumin-Rubbed Pork Tenderloin with Citrus Marmalade

MAKES 4 SERVINGS

The tangy flavors of citrus marmalade provide a nice contrast to the savory pork. Use any citrus flavor you like, such as clementine, orange, or kumquat.

1 pork tenderloin (about 1 pound)

1 teaspoon ground cumin

1 teaspoon salt

½ teaspoon freshly ground black pepper

1 tablespoon canola oil

1 teaspoon homemade Clementine Marmalade (page 678), or citrus-flavored marmalade of choice

1 Place a rack in the middle of the oven. Preheat the oven to 400°F. Rub the pork tenderloin with cumin, then sprinkle with salt and pepper.

2 In a large, ovenproof skillet, heat the oil over medium heat. Cook the pork tenderloin until browned on all sides, about 5 to 7 minutes.

3 Cover skillet with an ovenproof lid or foil and place in the oven. Roast 20 to 25 minutes or until the internal temperature reaches 145°F to 150°F on an instant-read thermometer when inserted into the center. Transfer the pork to a serving platter and let stand, covered, 10 minutes. Slice the pork and serve with the marmalade.

Mustard-Sage Crusted Pork Tenderloin with Pear-Cranberry Compote

MAKES 4 SERVINGS

The beauty of this dish is that you can prepare most of it ahead of time and chill it. Gently reheat the Pear-Cranberry Compote in the microwave before serving. Brown the pork tenderloin the day before (or the morning of the dinner) and finish roasting just in time for dinner.

COMPOTE

2 ripe pears (peeled, cored, and diced)
2 tablespoons honey
¼ cup dried cranberries
⅛ teaspoon ground cinnamon
⅛ teaspoon freshly grated nutmeg
⅛ teaspoon salt
⅛ teaspoon freshly grounded black pepper
2 tablespoons apple cider vinegar

PORK TENDERLOIN

1 boneless pork tenderloin (about 1 pound)
2 tablespoons dry mustard
2 tablespoons ground sage
1 teaspoon salt
¼ teaspoon freshly ground black pepper
1 tablespoon canola oil

1 Place a rack in the middle of the oven. Preheat the oven to 400°F. Make the compote: In a small, heavy saucepan, combine the pears, honey, dried cranberries, cinnamon, nutmeg, salt, pepper, and vinegar. Bring to a simmer and cook 20 minutes, covered, over low-medium heat. Remove from heat and cool slightly.

2 Prepare the tenderloin: Sprinkle the tenderloin with dry mustard, sage, salt, and pepper and press the mixture onto the meat with your fingers.

3 In a medium, heavy skillet, heat the oil over medium heat. Add the pork and brown all sides, about 5 minutes per side. Add 2 tablespoons water to skillet, cover with an ovenproof lid or foil, and transfer to oven.

4 Roast 20 to 25 minutes or until an instant-read thermometer registers 145°F to 150°F when inserted into the center of the roast. Transfer to a serving platter and let stand, covered, 10 minutes. Slice diagonally into 1-inch pieces and serve immediately with the compote.

Roasted Pork Tenderloin with Apricot Chutney

MAKES 4 SERVINGS

Chutney is a spicy side dish and can take many different forms. Some versions can be sharp and sour, while others, like this apricot version, are sweet and spicy. Chutneys are usually served with meat to enhance its flavor. I also look at chutneys as a way to incorporate more fruits (or vegetables) into my diet. And, that's a good thing.

1½ cup dried apricots, chopped
¼ cup finely chopped onion
2 tablespoons packed light brown sugar
2 tablespoons dried sweetened cranberries
2 tablespoons cider vinegar
½ teaspoon pumpkin pie spice
½ teaspoon dry mustard
⅛ teaspoon crushed red pepper
1⅛ teaspoons salt, divided
1 pork tenderloin (about 1 pound)
½ teaspoon freshly ground black pepper
1 tablespoon canola oil

1 In a small, heavy saucepan, place the apricots, onion, sugar, cranberries, vinegar, pumpkin pie spice, mustard, crushed red pepper, and ⅛ teaspoon of the salt. Bring to a boil, reduce the heat to low, and cook, covered, about 20 to 25 minutes. Transfer the chutney to a small serving bowl, cover, and let stand at room temperature until serving time. (The chutney can be made the day before, covered and chilled. Bring to room temperature before serving.)

2 Place a rack in the middle of the oven. Preheat the oven to 400°F. Sprinkle the pork tenderloin with the remaining 1 teaspoon salt and the pepper.

3 Heat the oil in a large, ovenproof skillet. Cook the pork tenderloin until browned on all sides, about 5 minutes per side. Cover the skillet with an ovenproof lid or foil and place in the oven.

4 Roast 20 to 25 minutes or until an instant-read thermometer registers 145°F to 150°F when inserted into the center of the roast. Transfer to a serving platter and let stand, covered, 10 minutes.

5 Slice the pork and serve immediately with the chutney.

Grilled Pork Tenderloin with Herb Salsa

MAKES 4 SERVINGS

I love the fresh herbs in this salsa, especially when their flavors are heightened with vinegar and fresh lemon juice. You can vary the proportions of herbs, depending on what's in your garden or available at the grocery store.

1 pork tenderloin (about 1 pound)
1 teaspoon salt
½ teaspoon freshly ground black pepper
2 teaspoons chopped fresh thyme or 1 teaspoon dried
Herb Salsa (see page 671)

1 Sprinkle the pork with salt and pepper. Sprinkle it all over with the thyme. Let stand 30 minutes.

2 Heat the grill to medium heat and cook the pork tenderloin until an instant-read thermometer registers 145°F to 150°F when inserted into the center of tenderloin. Remove from the grill and cover with foil; let stand 10 minutes.

3 While the pork is grilling, prepare the Herb Salsa (page 671). Slice the pork and serve immediately with the salsa.

Oven-Roasted Pork Tenderloin with Sage-Apple-Cranberry Relish

MAKES 4 SERVINGS

Sage is a natural flavor partner for pork; this dish takes advantage of that relationship and heightens the flavor with Granny Smith apples—another ingredient that complements pork.

PORK TENDERLOIN

1 tablespoon dry mustard
1 teaspoon rubbed sage
1 teaspoon salt + pinch for relish
½ teaspoon freshly ground black pepper + pinch for relish
¼ teaspoon ground cayenne
1 pork tenderloin (about 1 pound)
1 tablespoon canola oil

RELISH

1 large Granny Smith apple, cored and diced
¼ cup dried cranberries
¼ cup diced red onion
2 large fresh sage leaves, finely chopped
1 tablespoons chopped fresh chives
1 tablespoon cider vinegar
1 tablespoon honey

1 Place a rack in the middle of the oven. Preheat the oven to 375°F. Prepare the tenderloin: In a small bowl, stir together the mustard, sage, salt, pepper, and cayenne. Pat the pork tenderloin dry with paper towel and press the mixture on all sides of pork.

2 In a medium, heavy ovenproof skillet, heat the oil over medium heat. Add the pork tenderloin and cook until browned on all sides, about 5 minutes. Cover the skillet with an oven-proof lid and transfer to the oven.

3 Roast the pork until the internal temperature reaches 145°F to 150°F when an instant-read thermometer is inserted in the center. Remove from oven and let stand, covered, 10 minutes.

4 While pork is roasting, make the relish: In a bowl, combine the apple, cranberries, red onion, sage, chives, vinegar, honey, and remaining pinches of salt and pepper and toss thoroughly. Slice pork into 1½-inch slices and serve with relish.

Roasted Pork Tenderloin with Morels

MAKES 4 SERVINGS

Growing up in Eastern Nebraska, we knew the best time to hunt for fresh morel mushrooms was right after a spring rain. We would coat them in cornmeal, fry them, and eat our fill—until the next spring rain enticed us to the timbered area near our home once again. Unless you're lucky enough to have access to fresh morels, dried morels will suffice in this dish.

2 ounces dried morels

1 pork tenderloin (about 1 pound)

1 teaspoon salt

½ teaspoon freshly ground black pepper

2 tablespoons chopped fresh thyme or 3 teaspoons dried, divided

2 tablespoons canola oil, divided

½ cup gluten-free yellow cornmeal, such as Albers, Lamb's, Kinnikinnick, or Shiloh Farms

2 shallots, minced

1 teaspoon rubbed sage

½ cup dry white wine

1 tablespoon unsalted butter or buttery spread, such as Earth Balance

1 Soak the dried morels in 1 cup boiling water 30 minutes. Drain, check for sand or grit, soak again and rinse again; set aside.

2 Place a rack in the middle of the oven. Preheat the oven to 400°F. Sprinkle the pork with salt, pepper, and 2 teaspoons of the thyme.

3 Heat 1 tablespoon of the canola oil in a heavy, ovenproof skillet over medium heat. Brown the pork on all sides, about 5 minutes per side. Cover the skillet with an ovenproof lid or foil and transfer to the oven.

4 Roast 40 to 45 minutes or until an instant read thermometer registers 145°F to 150°F when inserted in the center of the roast. Transfer the pork to a serving platter, cover with foil, and let stand 10 minutes.

5 While the pork is roasting, dip half of the cleaned and drained morels in cornmeal. Heat the remaining tablespoon of oil in a small skillet and fry the morels until golden brown. Drain on paper towels; set aside.

6 Without wiping the skillet used to roast the pork, add shallots, sage, wine, and remaining morels to the skillet. Cook, scraping up browned bits from the bottom of skillet, 5 to 10 minutes to reduce juices. Add butter and stir while mixture thickens slightly. Slice the pork thinly, and drizzle reduced juices on top. Garnish with fried morels. Serve immediately.

Jamaican Jerk Pork Roast

MAKES 10 SERVINGS

Store-bought Jamaican jerk seasoning is packed with flavor and is one of only three ingredients you have to add to make this fabulous pork roast. The leftovers make wonderful sandwiches, too.

1 boneless pork loin or tenderloin (about 3 pounds)

⅓ cup gluten-free Jamaican Jerk seasoning, such as Durkee, Tone, or Spice Islands, or homemade Jamaican Jerk Seasoning (page 669)

2 tablespoons dry mustard

2 teaspoons salt

1 Place a rack in the middle of the oven. Preheat the oven to 375°F. Coat a roasting pan with cooking spray. Pat the pork loin dry with paper towels. In a bowl, combine the jerk seasoning, ground mustard, and salt. Sprinkle the mixture on all sides of pork loin.

2 Roast 50 minutes to 1 hour, or until an instant-read thermometer registers 145°F to 150°F when inserted into the center of the pork.

3 When the pork is done, remove the pan from the oven and let stand, covered, 10 minutes. (The temperature will rise 10 degrees more, to 160°F). Slice the pork and serve warm.

Thyme-Rubbed Roast Pork with Dried Apricot Stuffing

MAKES 4 SERVINGS

Ask your butcher to butterfly the pork tenderloin and pound it to a ½-inch thickness so that you can stuff it. Otherwise, it will be too thick to roll and you won't achieve the desired results.

½ cup chopped dried apricots

¼ cup chopped onion or 1 tablespoon dried minced onion

½ cup dry red wine

1 teaspoon chopped fresh thyme or ½ teaspoon dried

1½ teaspoons salt, divided

¼ teaspoon freshly ground black pepper

1 pork tenderloin (about 1 pound), prepared for stuffing

2 teaspoons dried thyme leaves

½ teaspoon freshly ground black pepper

1 tablespoon canola oil

½ cup gluten-free, low-sodium chicken broth, such as Swanson's Natural Goodness, or homemade Chicken Broth (page 676)

½ cup dry white wine

1 Combine the apricots, onion, wine, thyme, ½ teaspoon of the salt and the pepper. Let sit at room temperature 30 minutes or until wine is absorbed.

2 Place a rack in the middle of the oven. Preheat the oven to 350°F. Lay the pork flat on cutting board. Spread the fruit mixture over meat in even layer. Roll pork, starting from short side, and tie with cotton kitchen twine or string. Spray the roast with cooking spray. Sprinkle thyme, the remaining 1 teaspoon of salt, and pepper over pork, pressing mixture onto meat with fingers if necessary. Tie with kitchen string, if necessary.

3 In a large, ovenproof skillet, heat the oil over medium heat. Gently transfer rolled pork to skillet and cook until brown on all sides, about 2 to 3 minutes per side.

4 Cover skillet with an ovenproof lid or foil and place in preheated oven.

5 Roast 30 to 35 minutes or until the meat registers 145°F to 150°F when an instant-read thermometer is inserted in the center. Transfer the roast to a serving platter and let stand, covered, with foil to keep it warm, 10 minutes.

6 Place the skillet over medium heat, add the chicken broth and wine and bring to a boil, scraping up any brown bits from the bottom of the skillet. Simmer until the pan juices reduce slightly or mix 1 teaspoon cornstarch into 1 tablespoon cold water and stir into the juices, until slightly thickened. Slice the pork diagonally into 1-inch slices and serve hot with the pan juices in a small pitcher.

Baked Ham with Clementine Marmalade Glaze

MAKES ABOUT 20 SERVINGS

I'm a huge fan of Clementine Marmalade (page 678) and always have a supply in my freezer, but you can also use orange marmalade on this ham if you wish. Be sure to wait until the end of the baking time to brush on the glaze. Its high sugar content will cause the ham to burn if it is added at the beginning.

The amount of servable meat in a ham varies by type: generally, for boneless ham, expect about 4 to 5 servings per pound; for semi-boneless ham, about 3 to 4 servings per pound; for bone-in ham, about 2 to 3 servings per pound.

1 lean bone-in ham (7 to 9 pounds)
¼ cup homemade Clementine Marmalade (page 678) or orange marmalade
¼ cup packed light brown sugar
¼ teaspoon ground mustard
⅛ teaspoon ground cloves

1 Place an oven rack in the lower third of the oven. Preheat the oven to 325°F.

2 Prepare the ham by scoring the fat ¼-inch deep every two inches in a cross-hatch fashion. Place the ham on a rack in a pan that has been coated with cooking spray. Add water as needed to maintain ¼-inch depth.

3 Bake 1 to 2 hours or until an instant-read thermometer registers 110°F when inserted into the center of the ham.

4 Combine the marmalade, brown sugar, mustard, and cloves in a saucepan over medium-low heat and cook, stirring well, until melted.

5 Increase the oven heat to 375°F. Brush the glaze on the ham, replenish the water to a depth of ¼-inch, and return the ham to the oven to bake 10 to 15 minutes more or until the glaze begins to darken. The internal temperature of the ham should read 140°F. Let the ham stand, covered, 10 minutes, before carving.

PORK RIBS, STIR-FRIES, AND CASSEROLES

Barbecued Baby Back Ribs

MAKES 12 SERVINGS

You can adjust the heat intensity in this light but flavorful sauce by how much chili powder and crushed red pepper you put in. I prefer pork baby back ribs because I think they're more flavorful, but you can use any ribs you wish.

RIBS AND RUB
1 recipe Southwestern Seasoning (page 668)
8 pounds baby back pork ribs (about 6 or 7 slabs)
Salt and freshly ground pepper to taste

SAUCE
1 small can (8 ounces) tomato sauce
¼ cup red wine vinegar
¼ cup molasses (not blackstrap)
2 tablespoons packed light brown sugar
2 tablespoons grated fresh onion
1 tablespoon gluten-free Worcestershire sauce, such as French's
½ to 1 teaspoon crushed red pepper
2 teaspoons chopped fresh oregano or 1 teaspoon dried
½ teaspoon freshly ground black pepper
¼ to ½ teaspoon chili powder
½ teaspoon salt
1 garlic clove, minced

1 Make the ribs and rub: Prepare the seasoning. Then, sprinkle the meaty side of the ribs with salt and pepper and dust with seasoning. Wrap ribs in foil and bake in 250°F oven for 6 to 7 hours. (This step can be done the day before. Refrigerate, covered.)

2 Make the sauce: In a small saucepan, combine all the sauce ingredients. Bring to a boil, reduce the heat to low, and simmer 10 to 15 minutes or until the sauce is reduced by one-third. This will be a fairly thin sauce, meant for brushing on the meat in a thin glaze and served as a light sauce at mealtime.

3 Heat the ribs to serving temperature, bone side down, on barbecue over low heat about 6 inches from the heat source. During last 10 minutes of heating, brush sauce on ribs. Serve immediately. Transfer remaining sauce to small pitcher and serve with meal.

Green Chile with Pork

MAKES 6 SERVINGS

For many of us (particularly those living in the Southwest), we must have our "green chile fix" at least once a week. Usually the term "green chile" refers to a sauce that is eaten over burritos or enchiladas. The leftover chile can be refrigerated, tightly covered, for another meal yet that week.

1 teaspoon canola oil or light olive oil

½ pound pork chops or pork shoulder, cut in ¼-inch cubes

½ cup onion, finely diced

2 garlic cloves, minced

4 cups gluten-free. low-sodium chicken broth, such as Swanson's Natural Goodness, or homemade Chicken Broth (page 676)

1 small can (4 ounces) diced green chiles

3 large plum tomatoes, diced and seeded

1 teaspoon ground coriander

1 teaspoon ground oregano

½ teaspoon ground cumin

½ teaspoon salt

¼ teaspoon sugar

¼ cup chopped fresh cilantro

1 tablespoon cornstarch

2 tablespoons water

1 tablespoon fresh lime juice

1 In a heavy skillet, heat the oil over medium heat and cook the pork until lightly browned, about 5 minutes. Add the onions and cook until just tender, about 3 to 5 minutes, stirring constantly. Add all remaining ingredients except cornstarch,

water, and lime juice and simmer, covered, 20 to 25 minutes.

2 Stir the cornstarch into water until smooth. Add to green chile sauce and bring to a boil, stirring constantly, until the mixture thickens slightly. Remove from heat. Add the fresh lime juice and serve immediately.

Pork Stew in a Slow Cooker

MAKES 4 SERVINGS

This is a perfect dish when you're away from the house all day, yet want to be greeted with dinner when you walk in the door. For fuller flavor, brown the pork, kielbasa, onions, and carrots before putting them in the slow cooker. You can use your favorite herbs in place of the thyme and marjoram, but use the allspice for a mysteriously wonderful note.

2 tablespoons olive oil

½ pound boneless pork shoulder or tenderloin, cut in ½-inch cubes

½ teaspoon salt

½ teaspoon freshly ground black pepper

½ pound kielbasa or Polish sausage, such as Boar's Head or Jennie-O, cut in ½-inch slices

1 cup chopped onion

4 carrots, peeled and cut diagonally in ½-inch slices

1 tablespoon tomato paste

2 teaspoons chopped fresh thyme or 1 teaspoon dried

2 teaspoons chopped fresh marjoram or 1 teaspoon dried

⅛ teaspoon ground allspice

1 can (14 to 15 ounces) white kidney or cannellini beans, drained and rinsed

1 can (14 to 15 ounces) or 1¾ cups gluten-free, low-sodium chicken broth, such as Swanson's Natural Goodness, or homemade Chicken Broth (page 676)

1 can (14 to 15 ounces) petite diced tomatoes, including juice

1 In a heavy skillet, heat 1 tablespoon of the oil over medium heat. Sprinkle pork with salt and pepper. Add pork and kielbasa to skillet and cook to deep brown color on both sides, about 10 minutes. Transfer to slow cooker.

2 Add the remaining tablespoon of olive oil to the skillet and cook onions and carrots over medium heat until slightly tender. Add the tomato paste, thyme, marjoram, and allspice and cook until tomato paste is incorporated into the ingredients. Add the mixture to the slow cooker, along with beans, chicken broth, and tomatoes. Stir to blend all ingredients.

3 Cook 4 to 5 hours on High heat or 8 to 10 hours on low heat. Serve hot.

Pork Adobado in a Slow Cooker

MAKES 4 SERVINGS

When food is cooked in adobo or marinade it is said to be adobado. In fact, adobo means marinade, so this dish is really pork marinated in a red chile sauce. Cooking it in a slow cooker results in a low-effort but very tender, flavorful dish.

1 pork tenderloin (about 1 pound), trimmed of excess fat

1 can (8 ounces) tomato sauce

½ teaspoon medium-strength red chile powder*

½ teaspoon homemade Chipotle Adobo Sauce (page 673)

½ teaspoon sugar

¼ teaspoon ground cumin

½ teaspoon chopped fresh oregano or ¼ teaspoon dried

¼ teaspoon ground coriander

¼ teaspoon garlic powder

¼ teaspoon salt

1 Coat the liner of a slow cooker with cooking spray. Cut the pork tenderloin coarsely into 1 to ½-inch chunks and add to slow cooker.

2 Stir together remaining ingredients and pour over pork. Cook 4 hours on high heat. Or, cook all day on low heat.

3 Remove pork from slow cooker. Serve as main dish, spooning remaining sauce in slow cooker over

pork. Or, shred pork and serve as filling for tacos, mixed with remaining sauce in slow cooker.

*Note: Red chile powder is available in the international food aisle at grocery stores. It is made from dried peppers and is not the same as chili powder, which is actually a blend of herbs and spices. I buy mine in Santa Fe, New Mexico, and it is labeled by the region or city of New Mexico in which the chiles are grown. For example, Dixon medium or Hatch mild refers to the towns of Dixon or Hatch.

Pork Carnitas in a Slow Cooker

MAKES 4 SERVINGS

The word carnitas in Spanish literally means "little meats". In this case the meat is shredded into little pieces. This is one of my favorite Southwestern dishes because it is simple to prepare, yet so flavorful and versatile. Pork tenderloin works great because there are no bones and virtually no waste, but, pork shoulder works very well, too. I eat this dish on top of polenta and in fajitas and tacos. If you don't want to use a slow cooker, try making this dish in a Dutch oven.

1 pork tenderloin or pork shoulder (about 1 pound), trimmed of excess fat

½ cup gluten-free, low-sodium chicken broth, such as Swanson's Natural Goodness, or homemade Chicken Broth (page 676)

½ cup gluten-free Mexican salsa, such as Newman's Own or Pace

1 tablespoon tomato paste

½ teaspoon ground coriander

½ teaspoon salt

¼ teaspoon garlic powder

¼ teaspoon chipotle chile powder, such as McCormick's

¼ teaspoon freshly ground black pepper

1 Place a rack in the middle of the oven. Preheat the oven to 325°F. Cut the pork tenderloin into ½ inch chunks and add to a Dutch oven or other deep, heavy pot with a tight-fitting lid. Or, put it in a slow cooker that has been coated with cooking spray.

2 Combine the remaining ingredients in a bowl, pour over the pork, and cover. Cook 6 hours in slow cooker on low heat or roast the pork in the oven for 4 hours.

3 Serve the pork as a main dish, spooning the sauce over it. Or, shred the pork and serve it as a filling for tacos, using the remaining liquid in the Dutch oven as sauce.

Sweet-and-Sour Pork

MAKES 4 SERVINGS

I love the flavors in this dish, probably because I think that sweet ingredients (such as pineapple) are a welcome addition to savory dishes. It is easy to make using the "pinch" method: adding whatever amount looks and feels about right. Once you make it and get a sense of your preferences, you'll see that it works just fine in this dish.

2 tablespoons canola oil, divided

1 small onion, cut vertically in ¼-inch slices

1 carrot, cut diagonally in ¼-inch slices

1 small red bell pepper, seeded and chopped

1 small green bell pepper, seeded and chopped

¾ pound pork (cooked or raw), cut in 1-inch cubes

2 cans (8 ounces each) pineapple chunks, including juice

⅓ cup cider vinegar

¼ cup packed light brown sugar

3 tablespoons wheat-free tamari soy sauce, such as Crystal or San-J

1 tablespoon grated fresh ginger

2 garlic cloves, minced

⅛ teaspoon freshly ground white pepper

1 tablespoon cornstarch mixed in 2 tablespoons cold water until smooth

4 cups hot cooked white rice or brown rice

1 In a heavy, medium wok, heat 1 tablespoon of the oil over medium-high heat. Cook the onion, carrot, and red and green bell peppers, stirring frequently, until they are softened and the onion starts to brown, about 5 minutes. Transfer the vegetables

to a plate. Add the remaining tablespoon of oil and cook the pork, stirring occasionally, until cooked through and darkly browned.

2 Add the pineapple chunks (including juice), vinegar, brown sugar, soy sauce, ginger, garlic, and white pepper and simmer 2 to 3 minutes. Stir the cornstarch mixture into the skillet, continuing to stir until the mixture thickens slightly. Return the vegetables to the wok, bring to serving temperature, and serve over hot cooked rice.

Family-Style Cassoulet with Kielbasa

MAKES 4 SERVINGS

Fix this on a cold winter day when you want a hearty, hot meal—but don't want to spend a lot of time in the kitchen. Let the beans simmer in your slow-cooker while you're at work, then assemble the cassoulet when you get home and bake it while you prepare the remainder of the meal. For extra flair, bake in 4 individual cassoulet pots. Serve with a crispy, tossed salad, gluten-free French Yeast Bread (page 100) and a glass of red wine.

2 cups dried white (navy) beans

4 cups water

1 teaspoon salt

1 bay leaf

½ pound gluten-free kielbasa, such as Boar's Head or Jennie-O, cut in ¼-inch slices

1 large onion, chopped

2 garlic cloves, minced

1 can (14 to 15 ounces) petite diced tomatoes, including juice

½ cup dry white wine

1 cup chopped fresh kale or spinach leaves, chopped

½ cup sun-dried tomatoes, chopped

2 teaspoons chopped fresh rosemary or 1 teaspoon dried

2 teaspoons chopped fresh thyme or 1 teaspoon dried

½ teaspoon freshly ground black pepper

½ teaspoon celery salt

1 Rinse and pick over the white beans. Add beans, water, salt, and bay leaf to a slow cooker and cook 6 to 8 hours, all day, or overnight on low heat.

2 Place a rack in the middle of the oven. Preheat the oven to 400°F. In a large, heavy ovenproof skillet, cook kielbasa and onion over medium heat until lightly browned. Transfer the kielbasa and onion to drain on a plate lined with paper towels.

3 Add cooked beans (drained and bay leaf removed) to pan. Return kielbasa and onion to pan and add remaining ingredients. Bring to a boil over medium-high heat. Cover with an oven-proof lid or foil.

4 Bake 15 minutes. Uncover and bake 15 minutes more. Serve hot.

PORK SAUSAGE

Beer Brats with Onions, Pepper, and Sauerkraut

MAKES 4 SERVINGS

If you're serving this for a backyard picnic, place the cooked bratwurst (or brats, as I call them) in a disposable aluminum foil pan, pour on the reserved beer, and cover with aluminum foil. Keep it in the grill, on low heat. The brats stay warm and moist until your guests are ready for them and you can dispose of the foil container later.

4 gluten-free bratwurst sausages, such as Boar's Head or Johnsonville
1 medium large onion, peeled and thinly sliced
1 medium green bell pepper, seeded and thinly sliced
2 bottles gluten-free beer, such as Bard's Tale or Redbridge
1 package (16 ounces) sauerkraut, such as Boar's Head
1 tablespoon sugar
1 tablespoon caraway seed
4 homemade Hot Dog Buns (page 107)
Dijon mustard or yellow mustard

1 Place the brats in a saucepan that's just big enough to hold them so that they are close together. Add the onion and bell pepper. Add enough beer to cover the brats, onion, and green pepper.

2 Cook over medium heat approximately 15 to 20 minutes, or until the brats are done. Transfer the brats to the barbecue grill, reserving the beer. Grill the brats over very low heat until golden brown, turning occasionally to put grill marks on all sides of brats. Return the brats to the beer mixture to keep them hot until ready to serve.

3 While the brats are grilling, place the sauerkraut, sugar, and caraway seed in a medium saucepan. Add the cooked onions and peppers. Cook over medium heat to reach serving temperature.

4 To serve, place a brat in a bun and top with onion bell pepper mixture and sauerkraut. Serve with mustard.

Corn Dogs

MAKES 6 SERVINGS

Kids love corn dogs, which are simply skewered hot dogs that are deep-fried in a cornmeal batter. Your choice of utensils affects the ease of preparing this old-time favorite. Prepare the batter in a tall, narrow jar or measuring cup to make it easier to roll the skewered hot dog; use wood skewers that won't burn your fingers; and fry the corn dogs in a wide, shallow skillet (rather than a tall, narrow pot) to make it easier to quickly immerse the whole corn dog.

1 cup gluten-free cornmeal, such as Albers, Lamb's, Kinnikinnick, or Shiloh Farms

½ cup Carol's Sorghum Blend (page x)

1 tablespoon sugar

½ teaspoon baking soda

¼ teaspoon salt

¾ cup 1% milk (cow's, rice, soy, potato, or nut)

1 tablespoon cider vinegar

1 large egg

6 gluten-free hot dogs, such as Boars Head, Buffalo Guys, Ballpark, or Applegate Farms

6 wood skewers

¼ cup white rice flour, for dusting

Peanut oil for frying

1 In a tall, narrow jar or measuring cup, whisk together the cornmeal, sorghum blend, sugar, baking soda, and salt. In a small bowl or measuring cup, whisk together the milk, vinegar, and egg until all of the egg membrane is broken up. Whisk the egg-buttermilk mixture into the dry ingredients until the batter is very smooth. Let the batter stand 5 minutes. It should be the consistency of pancake batter, thick enough to coat a spoon. If the batter is too stiff, add water, a tablespoon at a time.

2 Insert a wood skewer into the end of each hotdog. Pat the hot dogs dry with paper towels and dust them with white rice flour.

3 Heat the oil to a depth of 3 inches in a wide shallow skillet. Holding the end of the skewer, dip the hotdog in the batter to coat it thoroughly. Immerse the hotdog in the oil and fry until lightly browned, turning if necessary to make sure all of the batter is browned.

4 Remove the corn dog from the oil and drain on paper towels. Serve immediately.

Creole Red Beans and Rice

MAKES 4 SERVINGS

This is a perfect recipe for the slow cooker and it will fill your house with mouth-watering aromas. The "heat" in this dish is introduced by the andouille sausage, of course, but is also determined by the amount of ground cayenne you use, so try it with ¼ teaspoon and then increase it if you wish. If you can't find andouille sausage, try kielbasa as a good substitute.

1 bacon slice, uncooked

1 stalk celery, chopped

1 small yellow onion, chopped

1 pound dried red beans (not kidney beans)

2 garlic cloves, crushed

2 teaspoons fresh basil or 1 teaspoon dried

1 teaspoon crushed dried rosemary

1 teaspoon fresh oregano or ½ teaspoon dried

1 teaspoon fresh thyme or ½ teaspoon dried

2 teaspoons salt

1 teaspoon freshly ground black pepper

2 tablespoons packed light brown sugar

⅛ teaspoon ground cayenne

1 bay leaf

¼ pound gluten-free andouille sausage, such as Applegate Farms, halved lengthwise and cut in ¼-inch pieces

Water to cover beans

4 cups hot cooked white rice

1 tablespoon chopped fresh parsley (optional)

1 In a medium, heavy skillet, cook the bacon over medium heat or until the fat is rendered. Remove the bacon; add the celery and onion to the remaining bacon fat and cook over medium heat until translucent, about 8 minutes. Remove from heat.

2 Rinse and pick over the beans to remove stones or debris. Place in a slow cooker, along with garlic, basil, rosemary, oregano, thyme, salt, black pepper, sugar, cayenne, bay leaf, and andouille sausage. Add the bacon, celery, and onion.

3 Add enough water to cover the beans and cook 6 to 8 hours on low heat, or until the beans are done. Serve over cooked rice, garnished with parsley.

Sausage with Warm Lentils and Polenta

MAKES 4 SERVINGS

Beans and lentils play a particularly important role in gluten-free diets because they are a safe, tasty, and relatively inexpensive form of protein and are very versatile. They provide lots of nutrients and fiber, too. This comfort-food dish is perfect on a cold winter day, accompanied by homemade gluten-free French Yeast Bread (page 100), a tossed salad, and perhaps a glass of your favorite wine to soothe the soul.

SAUSAGE AND LENTILS

1 tablespoon olive oil

½ pound (8 ounces) smoked kielbasa or other smoked sausage, such as Boar's Head or Jennie-O, diagonally sliced in ¼-inch pieces

1 large carrot, peeled and diced

2 ribs celery, diced

¼ teaspoon garlic powder

1½ cups French green lentils or brown lentils (not split peas)

4 cups gluten-free, low-sodium chicken broth, such as Swanson's Natural Goodness, or homemade Chicken Broth (page 676)

1 tablespoon chopped onion or 1 teaspoon dried minced onion

1 tablespoon chopped fresh thyme or ½ teaspoon dried

1 teaspoon salt

¼ teaspoon freshly ground black pepper

DRESSING

¼ cup extra-virgin olive oil

¼ cup fresh orange juice

2 tablespoons red wine vinegar

1 tablespoon Dijon mustard

POLENTA

3 cups gluten-free, low-sodium chicken broth, such as Swanson's Natural Goodness, or homemade Chicken Broth (page 676)

1 cup gluten-free yellow cornmeal, such as Albers, Lamb's, Kinnikinnick, or Shiloh Farms

1 tablespoon olive oil

1 teaspoon salt

1 Prepare the sausage and lentils: In a medium, heavy saucepan, heat the oil over medium heat. Add the kielbasa and cook until browned, about 2 to 3 minutes per side. Transfer the kielbasa to a plate; set aside.

2 In the same pan, add the carrot, celery, and garlic powder and cook over medium heat, stirring occasionally, until the vegetables are tender, about 5 to 7 minutes. Add the lentils, chicken broth, onion, thyme, salt, and black pepper to pan. Increase the heat to high and bring to a boil. Reduce heat to low and simmer, covered, 15 minutes or until the lentils are done. Remove from heat.

3 Make the dressing: Place all the dressing ingredients in a jar with a screw-top lid and shake well. Drain the lentils and return to the pan. Add the dressing and kielbasa and toss to coat thoroughly. Place over low heat to keep warm

4 Prepare the polenta: In a separate medium pan, bring the chicken broth to a boil over high heat. Whisk in the cornmeal, oil, and salt. Reduce the heat to medium and cook, whisking constantly, until done. It may take 15 to 20 minutes to cook and may require more liquid before it is done. Cover the polenta, remove from heat, and let stand 5 minutes. To serve, divide polenta among 4 serving bowls. Top with sausage and lentils and serve immediately.

LAMB

Pan-Grilled Rosemary Lamb Chops ⓠ

MAKES 4 SERVINGS

Rosemary works well with lamb in this simple main dish. It can be ready in less than 15 minutes, so have all the remaining dishes ready before you prepare the lamb. This dish is great for evenings when you're in a hurry, yet want a nice, filling main dish.

2 tablespoons extra-virgin olive oil
2 tablespoons minced fresh rosemary leaves, divided
8 loin lamb chops (about 6 ounces each), trimmed of excess fat
½ teaspoon salt, or to taste
¼ teaspoon freshly ground black pepper, or to taste
2 garlic cloves, minced
½ cup gluten-free, low-sodium chicken broth, such as Swanson's Natural Goodness, or homemade Chicken Broth (page 676)
Additional salt and freshly ground pepper to taste

1 In a large skillet, heat the oil and 1 tablespoon of the rosemary over medium-high heat. Pat the lamb chops dry with paper towels and sprinkle with salt and pepper. Lay chops in the pan and cook about 4 minutes per side, turning once, until the internal temperature reads 125°F on an instant-read thermometer inserted into the side of the lamb. When the lamb is cooked on each side, stand the chops on their edges and brown, about 2 minutes more. Reduce the heat if needed so the browned bits remaining in the pan don't burn. Transfer the chops to a plate and cover with foil.

2 Pour off all but 1 tablespoon fat from the skillet. Add the garlic, tilting the skillet to keep the garlic submerged in the fat, and cook over low heat until golden, about 1 minute. Add the broth, stirring up browned bits from the bottom of the pan, and simmer over high heat until mixture reduces slightly. Pour sauce over the lamb chops, sprinkle with remaining rosemary and season with additional salt and pepper, to taste. Serve immediately.

Lamb Daube

MAKES 4 SERVINGS

A daube (pronounced dohb) is a French-style lamb stew simmered in wine, tomatoes, and herbs—with a hint of citrus. For the heartiest flavor, it should be marinated overnight or all day so plan ahead when deciding to serve it. My version has a slight Provencal slant and is equally good, if not better, when reheated the second day. Serve it with a crusty homemade gluten-free French Yeast Bread (page 100) and you have a wonderful meal for a cool night.

1 lamb shoulder (about 2 pounds), cut in 1½-inch cubes
2 large whole yellow onions, peeled and cut into ½-inch slices
24 baby carrots
2 garlic cloves, minced
2 strips orange zest
1 bay leaf
1 tablespoon dried herbes de Provence
2 teaspoons salt
1 teaspoon freshly ground black pepper
½ bottle dry red wine (1½ cups)
¼ cup cornstarch
2 tablespoons olive oil
1 can (14 to 15 ounces) petite diced tomatoes, including juice
1 tablespoon anchovy paste (optional)

1 In a heavy-duty food storage bag, combine the lamb, onions, carrots, garlic, orange zest, bay leaf, herbes de Provence, salt, pepper, and wine. Marinate all day or overnight, stirring occasionally. Remove the lamb and the onions with a slotted spoon or ladle and transfer to a plate covered with paper towels to drain; reseal and set aside the bag of marinade.

2 Place a rack in the middle of the oven. Preheat the oven to 325°F. Pat the lamb cubes dry and dust the lamb and onions with cornstarch.

3 In a Dutch oven or other deep, heavy pot with a tight-fitting lid, heat the oil over medium heat and cook the lamb and onions, a few pieces at a time, until well-browned on all sides. Add the reserved marinade, tomatoes and anchovy paste (if using) to the Dutch oven, increase the heat to high, and bring the daube to a boil. Cover the Dutch oven and transfer it to the preheated oven.

4 Cook the daube 1½ to 2 hours or until the lamb is very tender. Stir occasionally, adding water (or wine) if the stew looks dry. Serve hot.

Crown Roast of Lamb

MAKES 6 SERVINGS

If you would prefer to make this dish without any bread crumbs, omit them and use one rather than two lemons. Save this dish for company when presentation is part of the menu because it is a gorgeous dish. Enhance the presentation by filling the center of the crown roast with a side dish, such as Herbed Brown Rice (page 218).

1 crown roast of lamb (about 3 pounds)
1 teaspoon salt
½ teaspoon freshly ground black pepper
2 tablespoons olive oil
Juice and grated zest of 2 lemons
½ cup gluten-free bread crumbs, such as Ener-G, or homemade gluten-free Plain Bread Crumbs (page 117), or more, to taste
3 large garlic cloves, peeled and minced
2 tablespoons chopped fresh parsley, divided
1 tablespoon chopped fresh sage
2 teaspoons chopped fresh rosemary
1 teaspoon chopped fresh thyme

1 Place a rack in the middle of the oven. Preheat the oven to 425°F. Season the lamb with salt and pepper. Place a rack inside a roasting pan and lightly coat the rack and the pan with cooking spray. Set the lamb on the wire rack.

2 In a small bowl, combine the oil, lemon juice and zest, bread crumbs, garlic, 1 tablespoon of the parsley, sage, rosemary, and thyme. Stir until well blended. Brush the herb mixture on meat.

3 Roast 20 to 30 minutes or until an instant-read thermometer registers 145°F for medium-rare. Remove the lamb from the oven and cover with foil 10 minutes while the lamb continues to cook. Slice into 6 servings and garnish with the remaining tablespoon of fresh parsley.

Moussaka

MAKES 4 SERVINGS

Moussaka (pronounced moo-sah-KAH) can refer to any dish of vegetables and ground meat created in layers but we most often think of moussaka as this Greek dish with eggplant and lamb.

2 small eggplants
1 teaspoon salt, divided
½ teaspoon freshly ground black pepper, divided
1 tablespoon extra-virgin olive oil
½ cup chopped onion
1 garlic cloves, minced
1 bunch fresh oregano leaves, chopped
1 bunch fresh flat-leaf parsley, chopped
1 pound ground lean lamb
¼ teaspoon ground cinnamon
Pinch of freshly grated nutmeg
1 tablespoon tomato paste
½ can (half of 14 to 15 ounces) whole tomatoes, drained and coarsely chopped
½ cup dry red wine
4 ounces feta cheese crumbles, divided
½ cup grated Parmesan cheese or soy alternative, such as Soyco, divided
½ cup gluten-free bread crumbs, such as Ener-G, or homemade Plain Bread Crumbs (page 117)
Cooking spray

1 Cut off the stems of the eggplants and remove the skin with a vegetable peeler. Cut each eggplant in half lengthwise; cut each half into ½-inch thick slices. Season the eggplant slices on both sides with ½ teaspoon of the salt and ¼ teaspoon of the pepper.

2 In a large skillet, heat the oil over medium heat. Working in batches, fry the eggplant slices in a single layer, 1 to 2 minutes per side turning once, until brown on both sides adding more oil, if necessary. Drain the eggplant slices on paper towels.

3 Add the onion, garlic, oregano, and parsley to skillet. Cook over medium heat, stirring, until soft and fragrant, about 3 minutes. Add the ground lamb, stirring to break up the meat; add the remaining ½ teaspoon salt and remaining ¼ teaspoon pepper. Cook until lamb is lightly browned, about 5 minutes. Add cinnamon, nutmeg, tomato paste, tomatoes, and wine and simmer until the liquid has evaporated, stirring occasionally. Remove from the heat.

4 Place a rack in the middle of the oven. Preheat the oven to 350°F. Generously grease an 8-inch square baking dish. Layer the bottom of the dish with ⅓ of the eggplant, leaving no gaps between slices. Spread ½ of the meat sauce over the eggplant, leveling it with a spatula. Sprinkle with ½ of the feta cheese and Parmesan cheese. Repeat the layers again, ending with a final layer of eggplant. Sprinkle bread crumbs evenly over moussaka. Coat bread crumbs with cooking spray. Cover baking dish with foil.

5 Bake 20 minutes, then remove the foil and bake 15 more minutes or until the juices are bubbly and the bread crumbs are browned. Let cool 5 minutes before serving.

Greek Lamb and Vegetable Kabobs with Pita Pockets

MAKES 4 SERVINGS

Kabob is a Middle-Eastern term for cubes of meat or vegetables threaded on a skewer and roasted or grilled. Serve them with your own homemade pita pockets.

8 wood skewers, or more as needed

LAMB AND MARINADE
2 pounds lamb loin, cut in 1½-inch cubes
¼ cup extra-virgin olive oil
¼ cup fresh lemon juice
2 tablespoons honey
2 garlic cloves, minced
1 large white onion, finely chopped
2 tablespoons chopped fresh mint leaves
1 tablespoon chopped fresh oregano leaves
1 teaspoon chopped fresh rosemary leaves
1 teaspoon salt
¼ teaspoon freshly ground black pepper

VEGETABLES
12 porcini mushrooms, cleaned
1 large white onion, cut in 2-inch squares
1 green bell pepper, cut in 2-inch squares
1 orange bell pepper, cut in 2-inch squares
1 red bell pepper, cut in 2-inch squares
1 yellow bell pepper, cut in 2-inch squares
4 homemade Pita Breads (page 113)

1 Soak wood skewers in water for 30 minutes.

2 Prepare the lamb and marinade: Combine the lamb and marinade ingredients in a heavy-duty food storage bag and mix well. Seal the bag tightly and marinate in the refrigerator at least 2 hours, preferably overnight, rotating the bag occasionally to thoroughly coat the lamb.

3 Heat a barbecue grill to medium heat. Remove lamb with from the marinade about 30 minutes before grilling and bring the meat to room temperature.

4 Assemble the kabobs: Fill skewers, alternating lamb with mushrooms, onion, and peppers until all ingredients are used.

5 Grill skewers, rotating to brown the lamb on all sides, until cooked to desired doneness, about 7 to 8 minutes for medium-rare. Serve with warmed pita pockets.

VEGETABLES

Stuffed Artichokes

Asparagus with
Hollandaise Sauce

Simple Roasted Beets

Ginger-Garlic Baby Bok Choy

Broccoli with
Creamy Lemon Sauce

Broccoli with Cheese Sauce

Red Cabbage with Apples

Sweet and Sour Red Cabbage

Baby Carrots with
Dill-Maple Syrup

Collard Greens

Roasted Fresh Corn with
Fresh Chive Butter

Creamed Corn

Sweet Corn Casserole

Sweet Corn Cakes

Green Bean Casserole with
Onion Topping

Crispy Baked Smashed Potatoes

Roasted Potatoes with
Rosemary and Capers

Spicy Roasted
Fingerling Potatoes

Crispy Potato Wedges

Garlic Mashed Potatoes

Mashed Garlic Potatoes and
Celery Root

Parmesan Potato Puffs

Potato Gratin

Savory Potato Kugel

Scalloped Potatoes

Sweet Potato Casserole with
Pineapple-Pecan Topping

Home-Style Potato Salad

Italian-Style Spinach

Baked Acorn Squash with
Candied Nut Stuffing

Broiled Tomatoes

Spiced Roasted Vegetables

Marinated Vegetable Stir-Fry

Vegetable Tempura with
Dipping Sauce

 = Quick    = Vegetarian

Vegetables bring lively color, satisfying textures, and a wide variety of enticing flavors to meals. I can't imagine living without juicy red tomatoes, crunchy carrots, leafy greens such as romaine lettuce or spinach, and, as you can tell by the recipes in this chapter, a personal favorite—potatoes.

Vegetables are a critical component of any diet, and many of them taste just great eaten raw or simply steamed with a little butter or oil, salt, and pepper. The USDA recommends that you get 5 to 9 servings per day of fruits and vegetables. Oldways Preservation Trust, in cooperation with the World Health Organization, developed the Mediterranean Diet Pyramid that emphasizes food from plant sources, including fruits and vegetables, and seasonally fresh and locally grown foods, which often maximizes their health-promoting micronutrient and antioxidant content. Although all vegetables contain important nutrients, many experts advocate eating those that represent the colors of the rainbow: red, yellow, blue, and green.

This chapter includes recipes that represent a cross-section of healthy vegetables prepared in a wide variety of ways—ranging from raw, dressed with sauces, steamed, roasted, and grilled. There are lots of potato recipes since many of the classics you know and love, such as Scalloped Potatoes, actually contain wheat. I also include vegetables from the rainbow of colors mentioned above, such as Grilled Vegetables, Polenta, and Green Been Casserole. Let these recipes be a starting point for your own creativity.

Stuffed Artichokes

MAKES 4 SERVINGS

Use the biggest artichokes you can find for this satisfying recipe, which combines one of my favorite vegetables with a rich, flavorful Italian bread crumb stuffing that is sure to please. You'll be licking your fingers when you're done.

1 teaspoon salt

4 large artichokes

2 lemons, each cut in 4 wedges, divided

1 bay leaf

1 tablespoon unsalted butter or buttery spread, such as Earth Balance, or olive oil

¼ cup finely diced onion

1 garlic clove, minced

2 teaspoons chopped fresh basil or 1 teaspoon dried

1 cup gluten-free bread crumbs, such as Ener-G, or homemade Plain Bread Crumbs (page 117)

1 teaspoon grated lemon zest

3 tablespoons grated Parmesan cheese or soy alternative, such as Soyco, + additional for garnish

¼ cup olive oil, divided + additional for drizzling

Salt and freshly ground pepper to taste

1 Fill a Dutch oven or other deep, heavy pot with a tight-fitting lid with water and bring to a boil over high heat. Add the salt and reduce the temperature to low to keep the water simmering and ready for the artichokes.

2 Cut the stem from each artichoke so the base is flat. Lay each artichoke on its side and, with a sharp knife, cut off the upper third. With kitchen shears, clip the prickly leaf tips from each remaining leaf. Rub the cut sides and bottom with the wedges from 1 lemon, squeezing lemon juice onto the cut areas and set aside.

3 Place the prepared artichokes, squeezed lemon wedges, and bay leaves in the boiling water and simmer, partially covered, until the bottom is tender and can be pierced with a sharp knife and an outer leaf pulls out easily, about 25 to 30 minutes.

4 Place a rack in the middle of the oven. Preheat the oven to 400°F. While the artichokes are cooking, heat the butter in a small skillet over medium heat. Add the onion and cook until soft and translucent, about 4 to 5 minutes.

5 To the onion, add the garlic and basil and cook another 30 seconds, stirring constantly.

6 Remove from the heat and stir in the bread crumbs, lemon zest, Parmesan, and 2 tablespoons of the olive oil. Mix well and adjust seasonings with salt and freshly ground black pepper.

7 Remove the artichokes from the boiling water and drain upside down in a colander or on a dish towel. Cool.

8 With your fingers, press the leaves away from the center to reveal the inner choke and prickly leaves. Pull out the cone of undeveloped white leaves and gently scrape out the choke with a spoon, trying not to damage the heart. Gently pull all of the leaves away from the center until they open slightly, leaving room for the stuffing.

9 Fill the artichoke cavities with bread stuffing, and pack a little bit into the space between the leaves.

10 Place the artichokes in a glass or ceramic baking dish and drizzle the tops with the remaining 2 tablespoons of olive oil.

11 Pour ½ cup of water into the bottom of the dish and place in the oven. Bake until the artichokes are golden brown and the bread crumbs become crusty, about 10 to 15 minutes.

12 Transfer the artichokes to a serving plate, lightly drizzle with olive oil, and sprinkle with grated Parmesan. Sprinkle with salt and pepper, to taste. Serve with the 4 remaining lemon wedges.

Asparagus with Hollandaise Sauce Ⓠ Ⓥ

MAKES 4 SERVINGS

Tender spears of green asparagus nestled under a creamy hollandaise sauce make a lovely accompaniment to any meal. I use tofu instead of heavy cream so my hollandaise contains less butter than traditional versions; you'll never miss it.

SAUCE

2 large egg yolks
1 cup soft silken tofu, such as Mori-Nu
3 tablespoons fresh lemon juice
¼ teaspoon xanthan gum
2 tablespoons unsalted butter or buttery spread, such as Earth Balance, or canola oil

ASPARAGUS

¼ teaspoon salt
¼ teaspoon dry mustard
⅛ teaspoon ground cayenne
⅛ teaspoon white pepper
1 pound medium asparagus, ends trimmed

1 Make the sauce: Blend the egg yolks, tofu, lemon juice, and xanthan gum in a blender until light and fluffy. Place the mixture in the top of a double boiler that sits over, but does not touch, simmering, not boiling, water. Add the butter, whisking constantly until the mixture thickens, adding 1 tablespoon or more hot water until it easily pours from a spoon.

2 Prepare the asparagus: Remove the sauce from the heat and stir in the salt, mustard, cayenne, and pepper. Keep warm over simmering water while cooking the asparagus, up to about 30 minutes. If it starts to separate or thicken too much, add a teaspoon of boiling water and whisk briskly until it easily pours from a spoon.

3 Cook the asparagus in boiling salted water until just tender, about 4 to 6 minutes, depending on their size. Remove from the water, drain, and pat dry with paper towels. Serve immediately, drizzled with the sauce.

Simple Roasted Beets

MAKES 4 SERVINGS

Roasted beets are extremely simple to prepare, and beets are also quite high in antioxidants, which gives them their deep red color. This simple recipe uses fresh herbs and a drizzle of vinaigrette to bring out the deep roasted-beet flavor.

6 medium beets (about ¾ pound)
Kosher salt and freshly ground black pepper, to taste
3 sprigs fresh thyme or savory
2 tablespoons + ¼ cup extra-virgin olive oil
2 tablespoons balsamic vinegar
1 teaspoon Dijon mustard
Salt and freshly ground black pepper to taste

1 Place a rack in the middle of the oven. Preheat the oven to 400°F. Scrub the beets well and place them on a large piece of aluminum foil. Sprinkle with salt and pepper, add thyme sprigs, and drizzle with 2 tablespoons of the olive oil. Wrap the foil around the beets tightly and bake until the beets are tender, about 1 hour. Set aside to cool.

2 When the beets are just slightly warm, slip off their skins (wearing plastic gloves to protect your hands from stains) and slice them in ¼-inch slices into the serving bowl; set aside.

3 In a small bowl, whisk together the balsamic vinegar and mustard until smooth. Slowly pour in the remaining ¼ cup of olive oil, whisking constantly, until it thickens slightly. Add salt and pepper to taste. Serve the beets at room temperature, drizzled with the vinaigrette.

Ginger-Garlic Baby Bok Choy

MAKES 4 SERVINGS

Bok choy is an Asian member of the cabbage family and has a milder flavor than most cabbage. I prefer baby bok choy because it is smaller and more tender than the larger variety. Cooking it in white wine infuses wonderful flavor, which is enhanced by the ginger and garlic.

1 cup dry white wine
8 baby bok choy, trimmed, and cut lengthwise in half through core
2 garlic cloves, minced
1 tablespoon minced fresh ginger
1 teaspoon sesame oil
½ teaspoon salt
¼ teaspoon freshly ground black pepper

1 Bring the wine to a boil in a large pot over high heat. Add the bok choy, reduce the heat to medium-high, and cook, covered, until crisp-tender, turning occasionally, about 5 minutes. Drain the bok choy and return it to the pot.

2 Toss the bok choy with garlic, ginger, and oil and cook 1 to 2 minutes more over medium heat, stirring constantly. Sprinkle with salt and pepper. Serve immediately.

Broccoli with Creamy Lemon Sauce

MAKES 4 SERVINGS

Vibrantly green broccoli and a beautiful yellow lemon sauce were meant for each other, as you'll see in this colorful side dish. I especially like to serve bright dishes like this with less colorful entrées such as grilled or roasted meats. The sauce is best made with half-and-half, but you may use your favorite nondairy milk, if necessary.

2 tablespoons fresh lemon juice

2 tablespoons white wine

½ teaspoon grated lemon zest

⅛ teaspoon garlic powder

¾ cup gluten-free, low-sodium chicken broth, such as Swanson's Natural Goodness, or homemade Chicken Broth, divided

1½ teaspoons cornstarch

½ cup half-and-half

Salt and freshly ground pepper to taste

1 pound broccoli, cut into 1-inch florets (3 cups)

1 In a medium saucepan, combine the lemon juice, white wine, lemon zest, garlic powder, and ½ cup of the chicken broth over medium heat.

2 Bring the mixture a boil. Whisk the cornstarch into the remaining ¼ cup of chicken broth until smooth, then whisk into the boiling mixture. Cook, whisking constantly, until the mixture thickens. Remove from the heat and stir in the half-and-half. Taste and add salt and pepper, if necessary. Cover and keep warm while cooking the broccoli.

3 Cook the broccoli in boiling salted water until just tender, about 4 to 6 minutes, depending on the size of the florets. Remove from the water, drain, and pat dry with paper towels. Serve immediately, drizzled with the lemon sauce.

Broccoli with Cheese Sauce Q V

MAKES 4 SERVINGS

Cheddar cheese and broccoli just taste good together and make a very colorful side dish as well. Since kids love cheese, this might be a good way to encourage them to eat broccoli—one of the healthiest vegetables on earth due to its calcium, vitamin C, folic acid, and iron content.

1¼ cups half-and-half or milk (cow's, soy, rice, potato, or nut)

1 tablespoon cornstarch

1 small garlic clove, minced

1 cup shredded Cheddar cheese, Colby cheese, longhorn cheese, or cheese alternative, such as Vegan Gourmet

¼ teaspoon salt

⅛ teaspoon ground cayenne

1 tablespoon fresh lemon juice

1 pound broccoli, cut into 1-inch florets (3 cups)

1 In a medium saucepan, whisk together ¼ cup of the half-and-half and the cornstarch over medium heat until smooth. Add the remaining half-and-half and garlic and cook, whisking constantly, until the mixture thickens slightly.

2 Remove saucepan from the heat and add the cheese, stirring until it melts. Add salt and cayenne and taste, possibly adding more if needed. Stir in the lemon juice and keep warm while the broccoli cooks.

3 Cook the broccoli in boiling salted water until just tender, about 4 to 6 minutes, depending on the size of the florets. Remove from the water, drain, and pat dry with paper towels. Serve immediately, drizzled with the cheese sauce.

Red Cabbage with Apples

MAKES 4 SERVINGS

Red cabbage is similar to green cabbage in flavor, but gets added nutrition from anthocyanins, which are powerful antioxidants that lend it that distinctive red color. The acid in the wine and vinegar in this recipe help maintain the marvelous red color during cooking. The apples lend a nice touch of sweetness.

½ large head red cabbage (about 1½ pounds)
1 tablespoon canola oil
1 small onion, finely chopped
1 medium apple, peeled, cored, and finely chopped
¼ cup dry red wine
¼ cup apple cider vinegar
2 teaspoons sugar
½ teaspoon salt
¼ teaspoon ground cloves
1 small bay leaf

1 Wash cabbage. Shred either by hand with a knife or using a food processor.

2 In a medium, heavy pot, heat the oil over medium heat. Add the onion and cook until softened. Add remaining ingredients and bring to boil. Reduce heat and simmer, covered, 1 hour. Remove bay leaf. Serve immediately.

Sweet and Sour Red Cabbage Ⓥ

MAKES 4 SERVINGS

This is a very common dish in Austria, so I ate it quite often during my recent visit there. Red cabbage is chock-full of nutrients and it makes a colorful contrast to other foods on your plate. I like to serve it with Pork Schnitzel (page 362), but it's also great with smoked pork chops and any other hearty main dishes.

1 small head red cabbage, shredded (about 1 pound)
¼ cup water
¼ cup apple cider vinegar
¼ cup packed light brown sugar
1 tablespoon canola oil
¼ cup chopped onion or 1 tablespoon dried minced onion
½ teaspoon ground allspice
¼ teaspoon ground cloves
½ teaspoon salt
¼ teaspoon freshly ground black pepper

Combine all ingredients in a heavy-duty saucepan with lid. Bring to boil, reduce heat to low, and simmer, covered, 45 to 60 minutes or until the cabbage is very tender. Serve immediately

Baby Carrots with Dill-Maple Syrup Ⓠ Ⓥ

MAKES 4 SERVINGS

I often serve these carrots when I have dinner guests because they add color to the plate and their slightly sweet flavor complements savory entrees. I find that most people like carrots if they are not overcooked, so I only cook them until they are barely tender.

1 pound baby carrots, washed and trimmed
½ teaspoon salt
2 tablespoons maple syrup
1 tablespoon chopped fresh dill weed or
    2 teaspoons dried
Dash of freshly ground white pepper

1 In a medium saucepan, combine baby carrots and salt with enough water to cover over high heat. Bring to a boil and simmer, covered, for 6 to 8 minutes or until the carrots are barely tender. Drain thoroughly.

2 Toss carrots with maple syrup, dill weed, and white pepper. Serve immediately.

Collard Greens

MAKES 4 SERVINGS

Collards, or collard greens, are a member of the cabbage family but grow as green leaves rather than a head. They are very nutritious, but must be cooked thoroughly before eating. The amount of salt you need to add will depend on the saltiness of the ham hock. If you choose to omit the ham hock, use more garlic to increase the flavor and add more salt to taste.

1 ham hock

1 small onion, peeled and diced

1 tablespoon unsalted butter or buttery spread, such as Earth Balance, or canola or olive oil

1 garlic clove, minced

3 cups water

3 bunches collard greens or a 1-pound bag, cleaned, rinsed, and cut into 1-inch pieces

Salt and freshly ground pepper to taste

1 In a large deep pot, combine the ham hock, onion, butter, and minced garlic. Add the water and bring to a simmer over medium heat for 30 minutes.

2 Gradually add the collard greens to the pot in batches, letting each batch wilt down before adding more. Reduce the heat to low and allow the greens to simmer, covered, for 1 to 1½ hours. Taste and add salt and pepper, if necessary. Serve immediately.

Roasted Fresh Corn with Fresh Chive Butter ⓥ

MAKES 4 SERVINGS

Once you try this simple idea you'll be hooked. Don't husk the corn before you cook it; the husks provide the perfect container to hold in moisture and flavor while the corn cooks inside, still on the cob. While you should always use unsalted butter in baking, you can use salted butter on these ears of corn. I also cook the unhusked ears in the microwave oven when time is short.

4 ears fresh corn, unhusked

¼ cup butter or buttery spread, such as Earth Balance

2 tablespoons chopped fresh chives

1 Place a rack in the middle of the oven. Preheat the oven to 350°F. Place unhusked ears of corn on the baking sheet that is lined with foil.

2 Bake 30 to 45 minutes (depending on size of corn ear). Remove pan from oven and let cool until you can comfortably handle the corn. Remove corn husks and silks and discard.

3 Melt the butter in the microwave oven and stir in the chives. Serve with the corn.

Grilled Fresh Corn with Fresh Chive Butter: Heat the outdoor grill to high. Peel the husks back from the corn; discard silks, and brush with the butter and chives. Close the husks. Wrap each ear separately in foil and lay the ears on the grill. Cook about 30 minutes, or until ears are tender, turning frequently. Cooking time will vary with the size of the ears and the temperature of the grill.

Creamed Corn

MAKES 4 SERVINGS

The wonderful fresh taste of the sweet corn really shines through in this comfort-food dish that is quite simple to make. If possible, use fresh corn from your garden or your local farmer's market, although frozen ears of corn will work nicely as well. Kids just love the smooth texture.

4 ears of sweet corn

1⅓ cups 1% milk (cow's, rice, soy, potato, or nut)

1 tablespoon unsalted butter or buttery spread, such as Earth Balance

1 tablespoon cornstarch

1 teaspoon sugar or to taste

½ teaspoon salt or to taste

¼ teaspoon freshly ground black pepper

1 With a sharp knife, cut the kernels from the ear of corn. You should have about 2 cups. Using the dull side of the knife, scrape the milk and remaining pulp from the cobs and add it to the kernels.

2 In a food processor, place 1 cup of the kernels along with the milk, butter, cornstarch, sugar, salt, and pepper and process until smooth.

3 Place the mixture and the remaining corn kernels in a medium saucepan over medium heat and bring to a boil. Reduce the heat and simmer for 2 to 3 minutes or until the mixture thickens slightly. Serve immediately.

Sweet Corn Casserole

MAKES 4 SERVINGS

Make this dish when fresh sweet corn is plentiful, rather than using frozen or canned corn. You'll agree that it's worth the wait because the casserole will be creamier.

1½ cups Savory Biscotti sticks (page 73), crushed

3 slices pancetta, diced

1 small onion, finely diced

2 ears sweet yellow corn, shucked, kernels cut off the cob

¾ cup whole milk (cow's, rice, soy, potato, or nut)

½ teaspoon salt

¼ teaspoon freshly ground black pepper

1½ tablespoons honey

2 large eggs

1 tablespoon chopped fresh parsley or 1 teaspoon dried, for garnish

Dash of paprika, for garnish

1 Prepare the biscotti. Then, place a rack in the middle of the oven. Preheat the oven to 400°F. Generously grease a 1- to 1½-quart baking dish.

2 In a heavy, large skillet, cook the diced pancetta over medium heat until browned and crisp. Remove from heat and stir in onion, corn, milk, salt, pepper, and honey until thoroughly blended. Stir in eggs and 1¼ cups of the crushed biscotti until blended. Transfer the mixture to the baking dish. Sprinkle remaining crumbs on top.

3 Bake 20 minutes or until the top is golden brown. Top with parsley and a dash of paprika. Serve immediately.

Sweet Corn Cakes

MAKES 8 CAKES

If sweet corn is in season, cut the kernels from one ear and use them for this recipe; otherwise, use the frozen variety. These savory little cakes make a great side dish in a Southwestern meal and are especially good topped with your favorite salsa or guacamole. Kids love them, too.

½ cup (1 stick) unsalted butter or buttery spread, such as Earth Balance, at room temperature, or canola oil

1 cup frozen corn kernels, thawed

½ cup instant masa harina*

¼ cup gluten-free yellow cornmeal, such as Albers, Lamb's, Kinnikinnick, or Shiloh Farms

¼ cup sugar

¾ teaspoon baking powder

½ teaspoon onion powder

½ teaspoon xanthan gum

½ teaspoon salt

¼ cup hot water

1 In a medium bowl, beat the butter with an electric mixer on medium speed until smooth. Add the remaining ingredients and mix until smooth. Form into 8 balls and press each into a 3-inch patty, ½-inch thick.

2 Coat a 10-inch cast-iron skillet or heavy-duty pan with cooking spray. Fry the cakes over medium heat until lightly browned on the bottom, approximately 3 to 5 minutes. Turn cakes and brown on other side. Serve hot.

*Available at specialty stores and the Hispanic section of some supermarkets. Masa harina is finely ground corn. Some masas contain lime, which improves the nutritional qualities of the corn; they will work in this recipe as well.

Green Bean Casserole with Onion Topping Ⓥ

MAKES 4 SERVINGS

Another classic you can still enjoy! This is traditional green bean casserole that most of you grew up with—minus the canned cream of mushroom soup with its wheat flour and wheat-coated fried onions. My adaptation uses sweet rice flour as a thickener for the green beans and cornstarch for dredging the fried onions.

TOPPING

2 medium yellow onions, peeled and sliced
    in ⅛-inch rings
½ cup cornstarch
Canola for frying
Salt and freshly ground pepper to taste

CASSEROLE

¼ cup sweet rice flour
1¼ cups 1% milk (cow's, rice, soy, potato, or nut)
1 tablespoon wheat-free tamari soy sauce, such as
    Crystal or San-J
1 tablespoon gluten-free Worcestershire sauce, such
    as French's
½ teaspoon onion powder
½ teaspoon celery salt
½ teaspoon salt
¼ teaspoon garlic powder (optional)
¼ teaspoon freshly ground black pepper
1 can (14 to 15 ounces) cut green beans
1 can (7 ounces) sliced mushrooms, drained

1 Make the onion topping: Dust the onions with cornstarch or place both in paper bag and shake thoroughly.

2 Heat 1-inch of canola oil in a heavy skillet over medium heat. Fry a few onion rings at a time until golden brown and drain on paper towels. Sprinkle with salt and pepper immediately.

3 Place a rack in the middle of the oven. Preheat the oven to 350°F. Generously grease a 1 quart ovenproof casserole dish.

4 Stir sweet rice flour into ¼ cup of the milk until smooth. Place this mixture and remaining milk in heavy, medium saucepan. Add soy sauce, Worcestershire sauce, onion powder, celery salt, salt, garlic, and pepper. Cook over medium heat, stirring constantly, until mixture thickens.

5 Add green beans, mushrooms, and half of the onion topping and stir to combine. Pour mixture into prepared dish.

6 Bake 25 to 30 minutes or until casserole is bubbling. Top with remaining onion topping. Return to the oven for another 10 minutes or until onions are hot. Serve immediately.

Crispy Baked Smashed Potatoes Ⓥ

MAKES 4 SERVINGS

Although this recipe shows you how to prepare this dish from scratch, I often make it when I have leftover mashed potatoes. It is a great way to reinvent them for a future meal.

1 pound small red potatoes, washed and halved
1 garlic clove, smashed
1 cup warm (110°F) buttermilk or homemade
    Buttermilk (page 677)
4 teaspoons chopped fresh rosemary or 2 teaspoons
    dried, finely crushed
Kosher salt and freshly ground black pepper to taste
¼ cup olive oil
2 tablespoons grated Parmesan cheese or soy alter-
    native, such as Soyco

1 Place a rack in the middle of the oven. Preheat the oven to 400°F. Scrub the potatoes and boil them in salted water to cover until they are fork tender. Drain the potatoes (reserving ¼ cup of the potato water) and mash to a coarse texture (a few lumps are fine, that's what "smashed" means) along with buttermilk and rosemary. Season with salt and pepper, adding some reserved potato water, if necessary.

2 Heat the olive in a 10-inch cast-iron skillet over medium heat. Add the smashed potatoes when the oil is very hot, but not smoking. Cook until the bottom starts to brown. Transfer to the oven.

3 Bake, uncovered, 25 to 30 minutes, or until the potatoes are golden and crispy on the bottom.

4 Using oven mitts, carefully invert the skillet onto a plate and cut the potatoes into wedges. Dust with Parmesan cheese. Serve immediately.

Roasted Potatoes with Rosemary and Capers

MAKES 4 SERVINGS

Small potatoes are best for this recipe because they cook quickly and you get lots of crispy crust on the outside to contrast to the smooth potato inside.

2 pounds baby red potatoes or fingerlings
2 tablespoons olive oil
1 tablespoon finely chopped fresh rosemary or
    1 teaspoon dried, crushed
1 teaspoon salt
¼ teaspoon freshly ground black pepper
3 tablespoons capers, rinsed

1 Place a rack in the middle of the oven. Preheat the oven to 400°F. Wash the potatoes, pat dry, and cut in half. Add the oil to a cast-iron skillet. Arrange the potatoes, cut side down, on the skillet. Sprinkle with rosemary, salt, and pepper.

2 Roast potatoes 30 to 45 minutes or until fork tender. During the last 5 minutes of roasting, sprinkle with capers. Serve immediately.

Spicy Roasted Fingerling Potatoes

MAKES 4 SERVINGS

Fingerlings are small, elongated potatoes and are usually available in the produce section of natural food stores or some supermarkets. If you can't find them, use baby red potatoes instead.

10 fingerling potatoes, washed and cut in half
    lengthwise
2 tablespoons olive oil
½ teaspoon salt
½ teaspoon chopped fresh basil or ¼ teaspoon dried
½ teaspoon chopped fresh thyme or ¼ teaspoon dried
¼ teaspoon garlic powder
¼ teaspoon ground paprika
¼ teaspoon freshly ground black pepper

1 Place a rack in the middle of the oven. Preheat the oven to 375°F. In a medium bowl, toss together the potatoes and olive oil.

2 In a small bowl, combine the salt, basil, thyme, garlic powder, paprika, and pepper until well blended. Add to potatoes and toss to coat well. Place the potatoes, cut side down, on 13 × 9-inch nonstick (gray, not black) pan.

3 Bake 30 to 35 minutes or until the potatoes are done. Roasted time may vary with thickness of potatoes. Serve hot.

Crispy Potato Wedges

MAKES 4 SERVINGS

While there are several steps to making these delightfully crunchy potatoes, the crispy coating is very satisfying and worth every minute of their preparation. White rice flour is the secret to the marvelous texture.

2 large russet potatoes cut in ¼-inch wedges

1 teaspoon salt

1½ teaspoons onion powder

1 teaspoon chopped fresh oregano or ½ teaspoon dried

¼ teaspoon garlic powder

¼ teaspoon ground cayenne

¼ teaspoon freshly ground black pepper

½ cup cornstarch

¼ teaspoon baking soda

1 large egg

2 tablespoons fresh lemon juice

1 cup white rice flour

Canola oil or peanut oil, for frying

Additional salt to taste

1 Place the potato wedges in a large microwave-safe bowl. In a small bowl, whisk together the salt, onion powder, oregano, garlic powder, cayenne, and pepper in a small bowl. Sprinkle the spices over the potatoes and toss until the potatoes are thoroughly coated.

2 Lay a sheet of crumpled wax paper over the bowl, and cook on high 5 minutes, or until potatoes are not quite done. Let the potatoes cool slightly.

3 In a shallow bowl, whisk together the cornstarch, baking soda, egg, and lemon juice, adding water if necessary to reach a thin consistency. In a second shallow bowl, place the white rice flour.

4 Heat 2 inches of oil in a deep heavy pot to 360°F. Dip the potatoes in the rice flour, then the egg mixture, and again in the rice flour. Immediately fry the potatoes in batches until browned and crispy. Drain on paper towels. Add more salt to taste, if desired. Serve hot.

Garlic Mashed Potatoes

MAKES 4 SERVINGS

This really flavorful dish is easy to make. Boiling raw garlic along with the potatoes makes it slightly sweet and soft enough to mash right into the cooked potatoes. Chicken broth, rather than milk, lends flavor and keeps it dairy-free. Yukon Gold potatoes mash up creamier than other varieties, but you can use russets, too.

1 pound Yukon Gold potatoes, peeled and cut into uniform chunks

2 garlic cloves, peeled

2 tablespoons extra-virgin olive oil or herb-flavored oil, if desired

¾ teaspoon salt

¼ teaspoon freshly ground black pepper

1 cup hot (120°F) gluten-free, low-sodium chicken broth, such as Swanson's Natural Goodness, or homemade Chicken Broth (page 676)

1 tablespoon chopped fresh parsley or 1 teaspoon dried, for garnish

1 In a large pot, combine the potatoes and garlic with enough water to cover by 1 inch. Cover and bring to boil over high heat. Reduce the heat to medium-low and boil until the potatoes are done, about 15 to 20 minutes. Remove from heat and drain thoroughly. Mash thoroughly.

2 Add the olive oil, salt, and pepper. Continue to mash the potatoes and garlic, adding enough chicken broth as needed to reach desired consistency. Serve immediately, garnished with parsley.

Garlic-Parmesan Mashed Potatoes: For extra flavor, add ½ cup grated Parmesan cheese or soy alternative, such as Soyco, when you add the oil and seasonings in Step 2.

Mashed Potatoes and Celery Root

MAKES 4 SERVINGS

Whole celery root looks like a gnarled woody ball, but once it is peeled, cooked, and mashed it looks like regular mashed potatoes. In fact, you won't be able to differentiate the celery root from the potatoes in this dish, though you will notice the wonderful light herbaceous celery flavor.

2 large Idaho potatoes (about 2 pounds), peeled and cut into 2-inch pieces

1 celery root (about ½ pound), peeled and cut into 2-inch pieces

2 large garlic cloves, peeled and minced

2 cups gluten-free, low-sodium chicken broth such as Swanson's Natural Goodness, or homemade Chicken Broth (page 676) + enough water to cover potatoes and celery root, if necessary

½ cup warm (110°F) 1% milk (cow's, rice, soy, potato, or nut) or as needed

2 tablespoons unsalted butter or buttery spread, such as Earth Balance, or canola oil

½ cup chopped fresh chives

Salt and freshly ground black pepper to taste

1 In a large saucepan, combine the potatoes, celery root, and garlic cloves. Add the chicken broth and enough water, if necessary, to cover. Bring to a boil, reduce the heat to medium and simmer, covered, 10 to 15 minutes, or until the potatoes and celery root are tender.

2 Drain the potatoes, celery root, and garlic and return to the saucepan. Add the milk and butter and mash by hand or with an electric mixer until smooth, using as much milk as necessary. Stir in chives. Add salt and pepper to taste.

Parmesan Potato Puffs

MAKES 4 SERVINGS (3 PUFFS EACH)

This dish is a marvelous way to use up left-over mashed potatoes; the Parmesan cheese and crunchy bread crumb coating add depth of flavor and mouth-pleasing texture.

¼ cup Carol's Sorghum Blend (page x)

½ cup grated Parmesan cheese or soy alternative, such as Soyco

2 cups leftover mashed potatoes

1 cup gluten-free bread crumbs, such as Ener-G, or homemade Plain Bread Crumbs (page 117)

Cooking spray

1 Line a 13 × 9-inch nonstick (gray, not black) rimmed baking sheet with parchment paper.

2 Stir the sorghum blend and Parmesan cheese into the mashed potatoes. Shape into 12 balls using a tablespoon or a #50 metal spring-action ice cream scoop to make equal portions. Coat hands with cooking spray. Shape each portion into a round ball with hands. Dip into bread crumbs and place on prepared pan. Refrigerate 30 minutes. Coat each ball with cooking spray.

3 Place a rack in the middle of the oven. Preheat the oven to 350°F. Bake potato puffs 25 to 30 minutes or until golden brown. Remove from oven and serve immediately.

Potato Gratin

MAKES 4 SERVINGS

A mandoline makes slicing the potatoes really easy, but isn't necessary to make this dish. For added richness, use whole milk or half-and-half in place of the 1% milk. Although I use a 1-quart casserole, a really deep dish helps prevent spillovers that are so characteristic of dishes like this.

3 medium russet potatoes, peeled and thinly sliced

2 teaspoon chopped fresh thyme or 1 teaspoon dried

¼ teaspoon white pepper

¼ teaspoon garlic salt

3 tablespoons grated Parmesan cheese or soy alternative, such as Soyco

1 tablespoon sweet rice flour

1 cup gluten-free bread crumbs, such as Ener-G, or homemade Plain Bread Crumbs (page 117)

2 tablespoons unsalted butter or buttery spread, such as Earth Balance, chopped into pieces, or canola oil

¾ cup 1% milk (cow's, rice, soy, potato, or nut)

1 Place a rack in the middle of the oven. Preheat the oven to 375°F. Generously grease a 1-quart baking dish.

2 Layer half of the potatoes in the baking dish. Sprinkle the potatoes with half of the Parmesan cheese, half of the sweet rice flour, and half of the bread crumbs. Layer the remaining half of the potatoes on top and sprinkle with the remaining cheese, flour, and crumbs. Dot with pieces of butter. Pour the milk over the top. Cover with an ovenproof lid or foil.

3 Bake 40 minutes. Remove the cover and bake another 15 minutes or until the potatoes are tender and the top is golden brown. Serve immediately.

Savory Potato Kugel

MAKES 6 SERVINGS

A kugel is a crusty, baked pudding often served for Jewish holidays and can be sweet or savory; potatoes are paired with cheese and eggs in this typical savory version of a comfort-food side dish.

1 large package (8 ounces) cream cheese or cream cheese alternative, such as Tofutti, at room temperature

3 large eggs, beaten

2 tablespoons unsalted butter or buttery spread, such as Earth Balance, or canola oil

¼ cup sweet rice flour or 2 tablespoons cornstarch

1 teaspoon salt

½ teaspoon baking powder

1 small onion, chopped

4 cups frozen shredded hash browns, thawed and drained

1 large leek, white part only, cleaned, rinsed, and cut in ¼-inch slices

1 Place a rack in the middle of the oven. Preheat the oven to 350°F. Generously grease an 8-inch nonstick (gray, not black) pan; aside.

2 In a food processor, process the cream cheese, eggs, and butter until very smooth. Add the sweet rice flour, salt, and baking powder and process until very smooth. Add the onion, hash browns, and leek and process until the batter is thick and chunky. Spoon into the prepared pan.

3 Bake 45 minutes or until the top is golden brown and crusty. Serve immediately.

Scalloped Potatoes

MAKES 6 SERVINGS

This is comfort food, American-style! The creamy white sauce is thickened with potato starch rather than wheat flour. You may be surprised to see nutmeg in this dish; the amount is so small that you won't detect it, yet it definitely perks up the flavor. To speed up the baking time, heat the milk in the microwave oven until steaming. This dish reheats very well.

4 medium russet potatoes (peeled, sliced)
1 small onion, peeled and thinly sliced
¼ cup potato starch
2 tablespoons grated Parmesan cheese or soy alternative, such as Soyco
1 teaspoon salt
1 teaspoon onion powder
1 teaspoon dry mustard
¼ teaspoon white pepper
⅛ teaspoon freshly grated nutmeg
2 cups hot (120°F) 1% milk (cow's, rice, soy, potato, or nut)
1 tablespoon canola oil
1 tablespoon butter or buttery spread, such as Earth Balance, cut in ¼-inch cubes, or canola oil
Paprika, for garnish

1 Place a rack in the middle of the oven. Preheat the oven to 375°F. In a large bowl, toss the potatoes and onion with the potato starch, Parmesan cheese, salt, onion powder, mustard, pepper, and nutmeg. Spread evenly in a 1½-quart baking dish.

2 Combine the hot milk and oil and pour over potatoes; dot with butter cubes. Lightly dust with paprika. Cover with an ovenproof lid or foil.

3 Bake 45 minutes. Remove the lid and continue baking another 15 minutes, or until the sauce is bubbly and the potatoes are lightly browned.

Scalloped Potatoes with Ham: Add 1 cup of ¼-inch cubes of ham and reduce onion salt to ½ teaspoon.

Sweet Potato Casserole with Pineapple-Pecan Topping

MAKES 6 SERVINGS

This is a creative way of serving traditional sweet potatoes at a holiday meal. Pineapple lends additional sweetness, complemented by the crunchy texture of the pecans.

1 large can (14 to 15 ounces) sweet potatoes, drained, or 3 large cooked and peeled sweet potatoes
2 large eggs
2 tablespoons unsalted butter or buttery spread, such as Earth Balance, melted, or canola oil
2 tablespoons packed light brown sugar, divided
¾ teaspoon salt
½ teaspoon ground cinnamon
½ teaspoon freshly grated nutmeg
1 small can (8 ounces) pineapple tidbits, drained
¼ cup chopped pecans

1 Place a rack in the middle of the oven. Preheat the oven to 375°F. Generously grease an 8-inch baking dish.

2 In a medium bowl, mash sweet potatoes. Stir in the eggs, butter, half of the sugar, salt, cinnamon, and nutmeg until thoroughly blended. Spread the sweet potato mixture in the baking dish.

3 In a small bowl, combine the pineapple, pecans, and remaining sugar and sprinkle mixture over the sweet potatoes. Coat with cooking spray and cover with foil.

4 Bake 25 to 30 minutes. Remove the foil and spray with cooking spray again. Bake another 10 to 15 minutes or until the top is browned and bubbly. Serve immediately.

Home-Style Potato Salad

MAKES 6 SERVINGS

This is the potato salad I grew up with. We never measured any of the ingredients, but simply dumped them in and then made adjustments based on taste. When I make it for my family, I never peel the potatoes—keeping the nutrients and fiber found in the well-scrubbed skins—and I think the red skins lend a pleasing color and texture to the potato salad. But you may peel the potatoes if you wish.

4 cups new red potatoes, boiled, peeled, diced
4 large eggs, hard-boiled, peeled, chopped
½ cup celery, finely chopped
¼ cup green onion, finely chopped
½ cup mayonnaise or dairy-free mayonnaise, such as Nasoya Nayonnaise
3 tablespoons sweet pickle relish
2 tablespoons Dijon mustard
2 tablespoons apple cider vinegar
1 teaspoon sugar
1 teaspoon celery salt
½ teaspoon celery seed
½ teaspoon yellow mustard
¼ teaspoon white pepper
1 tablespoon chopped fresh parsley or 1 teaspoon dried, for garnish
1 teaspoon paprika, for garnish
Additional salt and freshly ground pepper to taste

1 Combine the potatoes, eggs, celery, and green onion in a large bowl.

2 In a small bowl, whisk together the mayonnaise, relish, mustard, vinegar, sugar, celery salt, celery seed, mustard, and white pepper until thoroughly blended. Pour over potatoes and toss with spatula until the potatoes and eggs are thoroughly coated. Sprinkle with parsley and paprika for garnish. Chill until serving time. Let stand at room temperature 15 minutes before serving.

Italian-Style Spinach

MAKES 4 SERVINGS

This is a perfect choice for those nights when you want a super-healthy side dish, but don't have much time. Spinach is chock-full of nutrients and the onion, garlic, red pepper flakes, and Parmesan cheese—traditional Italian ingredients—add marvelous flavor and a distinctly Italian flair.

2 tablespoons extra virgin olive oil
1 medium onion, peeled and diced
2 garlic cloves, minced
1 bag (10 ounces each) fresh baby spinach, washed
½ cup gluten-free vegetable broth, such as Imagine, or homemade Vegetable Broth (page 677), or dry white wine
¼ teaspoon salt, or to taste
¼ teaspoon freshly ground black pepper, or to taste
¼ teaspoon crushed red pepper
2 tablespoons grated Parmesan cheese or soy alternative, such as Soyco, for garnish, optional

1 In a Dutch oven or other deep, heavy pot with a tight-fitting lid, heat the oil over medium heat. Add the onion and cook, stirring occasionally, until the onion is soft and translucent, about 5 minutes.

2 Add the garlic, spinach, broth, salt, pepper, and red pepper and cook, covered, until the spinach is wilted. Sprinkle with the Parmesan cheese, if using, and serve immediately.

Italian-Style Spinach with Sausage: Just before serving, add ½ pound hot cooked, crumbled gluten-free Italian sausage, such as Applegate Farm. Toss to mix and serve.

Baked Acorn Squash with Candied Nut Stuffing

MAKES 4 SERVINGS

Acorn squash, a member of the squash family, is known for its lovely yellow-orange flesh. The sweet, nutty topping contrasts nicely with the squash's smooth, creamy texture.

2 small acorn squash, about 1 pound each
Kosher salt and freshly ground black pepper
Cooking spray
¼ cup (½ stick) unsalted butter or buttery spread, such as Earth Balance, softened
1 cup finely chopped almonds, walnuts, or pecans
½ cup packed light brown sugar
1 teaspoon ground cinnamon
⅛ teaspoon freshly grated nutmeg
3 tablespoons orange juice concentrate

1 Place a rack in the middle of the oven. Preheat the oven to 350°F. With a very sharp knife, cut the squash in half through the equator and scrape out the seeds with a spoon. Set the squash halves, cut sides up, on a baking sheet and sprinkle with salt and pepper. Coat with cooking spray and cover tightly with foil.

2 Bake 25 to 30 minutes.

3 Meanwhile, in a medium bowl, combine the butter, nuts, brown sugar, cinnamon, nutmeg, and orange juice concentrate. Remove the foil from the squash and fill the centers of each acorn with the stuffing.

4 Return the squash to the oven and bake another 15 to 20 minutes, uncovered, or until the stuffing is lightly browned. Serve hot.

Broiled Stuffed Tomatoes

MAKES 4 SERVINGS

This colorful side dish is great any time of year, but it's especially delicious at summer's end when tomatoes are plentiful and at their best.

¾ cup gluten-free bread crumbs, such as Ener-G, or homemade Plain Bread Crumbs (page 117)
1 cup chopped flat-leaf parsley
½ cup grated Parmesan cheese or soy alternative, such as Soyco
1 small garlic clove, minced
Pinch of crushed red pepper
4 vine-ripened medium tomatoes, ½ inch of tops removed, seeded
¼ cup extra-virgin olive oil
Kosher salt and freshly ground black pepper to taste

1 Prepare the bread crumbs. Then, place a rack in the middle of the oven. Preheat the oven to 400°F. Lightly oil an 8-inch glass baking dish.

2 In the bowl of a food processor, pulse the bread crumbs, parsley, Parmesan cheese, garlic, and red pepper until well combined.

3 With a spoon, fill the tomatoes lightly with the bread crumb mixture. Place the stuffed tomatoes in the baking dish. Drizzle with oil and sprinkle with salt and pepper. Add ½ cup water to bottom of baking dish. Cover dish lightly with foil.

4 Bake tomatoes until tender and the stuffing has cooked through, about 15 to 20 minutes.

5 Preheat the broiler. Remove baking dish from oven and remove the foil. Place the dish 8 to 10 inches from the heat and broil until the stuffing is crisp and slightly browned, 2 to 3 minutes. Serve immediately.

Spicy Roasted Vegetables Ⓥ

MAKES 4 SERVINGS

This is a favorite side dish during the winter months. Roasting accentuates the vegetables' flavor and brings out their natural sweetness. You can vary the vegetables based on what's available in your grocery store or farmer's market. This is a very versatile dish: you can use a few of the vegetables in larger quantities or substitute other vegetables such as eggplant and tomatoes. You can also try different seasonings.

¼ cup extra-virgin olive oil

¼ cup balsamic vinegar

1 small bag (10 ounces) pearl onions

1 tablespoon chopped fresh oregano or 1 teaspoon dried

2 garlic cloves, minced

½ teaspoon ground coriander

½ teaspoon ground cumin

½ teaspoon salt

¼ teaspoon freshly ground black pepper

2 teaspoons molasses (not blackstrap)

2 medium carrots, halved lengthwise

1 large red bell pepper, cut in ¼-inch strips

1 large yellow bell pepper, cut in ¼-inch strips

1 medium zucchini, sliced ¼-inch thick

1 medium sweet potato, peeled and cut in ½-inch cubes

1 small fennel bulb, sliced thinly

1 Combine all the ingredients in a large bowl and toss thoroughly. Let stand 30 minutes. Toss again.

2 Place a rack in the middle of the oven. Preheat the oven to 400°F. Drain the vegetables and reserve the marinade. Arrange the vegetables on a 15 × 10-inch rimmed baking sheet that has been lined with foil.

3 Roast the vegetables, uncovered, 30 to 45 minutes, stirring occasionally. Transfer the vegetables to a serving platter. Heat the reserved marinade to serving temperature and pour over the vegetables. Toss lightly and serve hot.

Marinated Vegetable Stir-Fry Ⓥ

MAKES 4 SERVINGS

Marinating the vegetables produces deep flavor in this stir-fry. Serve it alone, as a side, or over brown rice for a heartier dish.

3 tablespoons olive oil, divided

¼ cup balsamic vinegar

1 teaspoon chopped fresh oregano or ½ teaspoon dried

1 garlic clove, minced

½ teaspoon ground coriander

¼ teaspoon ground cumin

¼ teaspoon salt

¼ teaspoon freshly ground black pepper

2 teaspoons molasses (not black strap)

1 large onion, peeled and cut in ¼-inch vertical slices

4 medium carrots, peeled and cut in ¼-inch slices

2 medium zucchini squash, cut in ¼-inch slices

2 small yellow summer squash, cut in ¼-inch slices

1 large red bell pepper, cut in ¼-inch slices

1 large yellow bell pepper, cut in ¼-inch slices

1 Combine 1 tablespoon of the oil, balsamic vinegar, oregano, garlic, coriander, cumin, salt, black pepper, and molasses in a large bowl. Add the vegetables and let stand 30 minutes. Drain vegetables and reserve marinade.

2 Heat the remaining oil in a wok or large, deep skillet. Cook the onions and carrots, stirring constantly, until they are crisp-tender, about 5 to 7 minutes. Add the zucchini, yellow squash and cook, stirring constantly, another 2 minutes. Add the bell peppers and cook another minute, stirring constantly.

3 Add 2 to 3 tablespoons of the reserved marinade to the vegetables and cook, stirring constantly, another minute or until the vegetables and marinade are hot. Serve immediately.

Vegetable Tempura with Dipping Sauce ⓥ

MAKES 4 SERVINGS

This dish is great to serve at a casual get-together where everybody gathers in the kitchen and eats the fried vegetables as soon as they're done. White rice flour gives this batter a nice crunchiness.

SAUCE

½ cup wheat-free low-sodium tamari soy sauce, such as Crystal or San-J

2 tablespoons rice wine vinegar

2 teaspoons honey

Juice of 1 lemon

BATTER

1½ cups white rice flour, divided

¼ cup cornstarch

1 cup cold sparking mineral water

1 egg yolk, cold from the refrigerator

Peanut oil, for frying

Salt for sprinkling

VEGETABLES

1 zucchini, cut lengthwise in thin slices

6 thin asparagus stalks, tough ends trimmed off

⅓ pound broccoli, cut into florets (1 cup)

2 medium carrots, peeled and sliced diagonally in very thin strips

1 small Japanese eggplant, halved and cut in ¼-inch slices

1 medium sweet potato, peeled and cut in ¼-inch slices

2 large Portobello mushrooms, thinly sliced

1 red bell pepper, seeded and cut in ½-inch strips

1 Make the dipping sauce by whisking together the soy sauce, vinegar, honey, and lemon juice. Set aside.

2 Make the batter: Whisk together 1 cup of the rice flour and the cornstarch in a bowl. Whisk in the sparkling water until the batter is smooth. Add the egg yolk and whisk until the batter is the consistency of heavy cream.

3 Heat 2 to 3 inches of oil to 375°F in a wok or deep fryer.

4 Pat the vegetables dry with paper towels and dust with the remaining ½ cup rice flour; shake off excess. Dip the vegetables into the batter and gently place 4 or 5 pieces of the same type of vegetable at a time in the hot oil. Do not overcrowd the wok or fryer. Fry the vegetables until golden brown, turning once, about 3 minutes. Between batches, skim off the small bits of batter that float in the oil. Drain the vegetables on paper towels; season them with salt. Serve immediately with the dipping sauce.

COOKIES AND BARS

Drop Cookies

Chocolate Chip Cookies

Double Chocolate Chip Cookies

Decadent Chocolate Cookies

Chocolate Peanut Butter Cookies

Chocolate Cherry
Coconut Cookies

Chocolate-Cranberry Cookies

White Chocolate–Cherry Cookies

Cranberry-Orange White
Chocolate Cookies

Trail Mix Cookies

Coconut Nests

Coconut Macaroons with a
Chocolate Drizzle

Coconut Raisin Cookies

Cornflake Cookies

Peanut Butter Cookies

Crunchy Almond Cookies

Chai Almond Cookies

Pecan Sandies or Sables

Mesquite Pecan Cookies

Chestnut Cookies

Sesame Cookies

Flax Cookies

Hemp Seed Cookies

Italian Pignoli Cookies

Date-Nut Cookies

Dried Cherry and Nut Cookies

Millet and Dried Fruit Cookies

Oatmeal Raisin Cookies

Montina Raisin Cookies

Old-Fashioned Molasses
Sorghum Cookies

Gingersnaps

Frosted Spice Cookies

Sugar Cookies

Lemon Cookies with Lemon Glaze

Amaretti

Meringue Cookies

Oven-Baked Caramel Corn

Popcorn Balls

No-Bake Cookies

Bourbon Balls

Chocolate Mocha Balls

Dark Chocolate Truffles

White Chocolate–Apricot-Almond
Balls

Canadian Cookies

Peanut Butter Balls

Shaped, Cut-Out, and Rolled Cookies

Holiday Cut-Out Cookies

Snickerdoodles

Springerle Cookies

Spritz Cookies

Lemon-Anise Biscotti

Apricot-Almond Biscotti

Chocolate-Cherry-Walnut Biscotti

White Chocolate–Dipped Pistachio-Cranberry Biscotti

Gingerbread People

Pfeffernusse

Graham Crackers

Chocolate Sandwich Cookies with Orange Filling

Hamantaschen

Rugelach

Ladyfingers

Madeleines

Mexican Wedding Cakes

Swedish Tea Cakes

Pizzelles

Ice Cream Cones

Tuilles

Florentines

Rosettes

Bars

Chocolate Brownies

Chocolate Peanut Butter Brownies

Fudgy Vegan Chocolate Brownies

Black Bean Brownies with Espresso Ganache

Brownie Fruit Pizza

Mocha Brownie Sandwiches

Chocolate-Coconut Bars

Black and White Blondies

Pineapple-Coconut Blondies

Toffee Bars

Lemon Bars

Key Lime Bars

Coconut-Date Bars

Apple Pie Bars

Banana Bars with Orange Frosting

Cranberry Oatmeal Bars

Raspberry Bars

Fig Bars

Pumpkin Bars

Shortbread

Cranberry Shortbread Bars

Lebkuchen Bars

Marshmallow Rice Treats

Peanut Butter Ice Cream Bars with Fudge Sauce

The first cookies were created by people who used a small amount of cake batter to test the oven temperature before baking a large cake. These test cakes were called *koekje,* meaning "little cake" in Dutch. In fact, old cookbooks, such as an 1896 cookbook in my library, don't have a separate category for cookies but list them under cakes instead.

Cornflake Cookies were the first cookies I baked as a child and I have recreated that recipe here. There are other favorites that kids love, such as Chocolate Chip Cookies, Peanut Butter Cookies, Gingersnaps, and good old-fashioned Oatmeal Raisin Cookies—made with gluten-free oats.

Holiday favorites like Spritz Cookies and Snickerdoodles are included, plus Graham Crackers, biscotti, Madeleines, Ladyfingers, Rosettes, and Rugelach. There are even some No-Bake cookies and truffles. And, you'll find many of your favorite bars including brownies, blondies, marshmallow rice bars, and lemon bars.

I make it all easy by starting with Carol's Sorghum Blend (page x). Prepare a batch of this blend and keep it in your pantry, so you're always ready to bake.

If you avoid dairy, I offer substitutions for cow's milk, butter, and cream cheese. I call for 1% milk in most of these recipes because it is lower in fat and calories, but you can use your favorite milk instead. Be sure to shake store-bought buttermilk thoroughly before measuring it because the solids tend to settle on the bottom of the carton, making the first few cups much thinner than the final cup. If your buttermilk is extremely thick, add a little water.

Although I mention specific brands by name, you should always read labels because manufacturers can change ingredients.

Whether you bake your cookies from scratch with the recipes in this chapter or use a store-bought mix, here are helpful hints to avoid common mistakes in gluten-free baking, and achieve cookie-baking success. Don't forget: have fun and get the family and/or friends involved.

- Beat the butter and sugar just until blended, and no more. Make sure the butter or buttery spread is the temperature specified in the recipe. If your butter is melted when the recipe calls for room temperature, you will end up with cookie dough that is too soft and far more likely to spread during baking—yielding thin, crispy cookies that spread into each other on the baking sheet. Some buttery spreads, such as Spectrum Naturals, tend to spread less. If you want the dough to spread, simply press the dough ball down to the desired height with the bottom of an oiled drinking glass.

- The type of fat used can also affect how cookies spread. For example, shortening inhibits spread while butter increases it; more sugar increases the spread while less sugar decreases it. Baking at a higher temperature reduces spread because the cookie exterior sets up faster. Some bakers chill the cookie dough before shaping it so that the outside of the cookies "set up" from the oven heat.

- Use nonstick pans only if the recipe suggests them. Cookies brown quickly, especially on the bottom, because they have a high sugar content and are usually small and thin. Some are better baked on dull gray aluminum baking sheets rather than the nonstick variety recommended for breads and cakes. Light-color baking sheets reflect radiant heat—rather than absorbing it, as do the gray nonstick sheets—so they are a better choice for most cookies. Each recipe in this chapter has instructions for what type of baking sheet to use.

- Regardless of what type of cookie you are baking, it is best to bake them on parchment paper. It reduces their tendency to spread, the pan doesn't have to be greased (which promotes spreading), and parchment paper can be used again and again, which makes it an economical investment in your baking success.

- Most cookies are best when removed from the oven while they are still slightly underbaked. Remove them from the baking sheet after 2 or 3 minutes—or just long enough to slightly firm up. The baking sheet retains heat and still continues to bake the cookies after they leave the oven, so quickly getting them off the baking sheet and onto a wire rack to cool completely is important to avoid extra-brown bottoms.

- The amount of time required to bake cookies can vary across different ovens. Stay close to your oven when baking cookies and watch them closely—especially the first time you make any recipe—so that you'll know what's right for you.

- Real butter browns cookies best, but non-hydrogenated buttery spreads, such as Earth Balance, can also work. To enhance browning, brush the dough with cream, milk, or beaten egg just before baking.

- Start with a cool baking sheet each time you bake a batch of cookies so that the cookie dough won't spread. This means either having extra baking sheets on hand or you can rest a slightly warm baking sheet on a pile of towel-covered frozen vegetable bags for a few minutes to cool it down before baking the next batch.

DROP COOKIES

Chocolate Chip Cookies
MAKES 24 SERVINGS

America's favorite cookie is easy to make and sure to delight everyone. If you wish, you can buy chocolate chunks or chop the chocolate yourself rather than use chocolate chips—as long as you verify the chocolate's gluten-free status. Try replacing the nuts with raisins, dried cranberries, or caramel chips. Serve these cookies by themselves or with ice cream.

¼ cup (½ stick) unsalted butter or buttery spread, such as Earth Balance, at room temperature, but not melted

¾ cup granulated sugar

½ cup packed light brown sugar

1 large egg, at room temperature

2 teaspoons pure vanilla extract

2 cups Carol's Sorghum Blend (page x)

1 teaspoon xanthan gum

½ teaspoon salt

¼ teaspoon baking soda

¾ cup gluten-free chocolate chips, such as Tropical Source

¼ cup finely chopped pecans or walnuts (optional)

1 Place a rack in the lower-middle position and another in the upper-middle position of the oven. Preheat the oven to 375°F. Line two 15 × 10-inch baking sheets (not nonstick) with parchment paper.

2 In a large mixing bowl, beat the butter, granulated sugar, and brown sugar with an electric mixer on low speed until very smooth, about 1 minute. Beat in the egg and vanilla extract until thoroughly blended.

3 In a small bowl, whisk together the sorghum blend, xanthan gum, salt and baking soda, and then gradually beat into the egg mixture on low speed just until blended. Stir in the chocolate chips and nuts, if using. Knead the dough with your hands a few times to make sure the chips and nuts are thoroughly incorporated.

4 Using a wet tablespoon or a #50 metal spring-action ice cream scoop, drop 1½-inch balls of dough at least 2 inches apart on the baking sheets, 12 per sheet. Place one sheet on the lower–middle rack and another on the upper-middle rack of the oven.

5 Bake 12 to 15 minutes, rotating the baking sheets between racks halfway through baking, or until the cookies start to brown around the edges. Cool the cookies 2 to 3 minutes on the baking sheet, then transfer them to a wire rack to cool completely. Store, tightly covered, for up to 2 days or in the freezer for up to 1 month.

Double Chocolate Chip Cookies Ⓥ

MAKES 24 SERVINGS

If you love chocolate, then this double chocolate cookie (with cocoa powder and chocolate chips) is for you. Use gluten-free chocolate chunks instead of chips, if you like.

¼ cup (½ stick) unsalted butter or buttery spread, such as Earth Balance, at room temperature, but not melted

½ cup granulated sugar

½ cup packed light brown sugar

1 large egg

2 teaspoons pure vanilla extract

1½ cups Carol's Sorghum Blend (page x)

½ cup unsweetened cocoa powder (not Dutch-process or alkali)

1 teaspoon xanthan gum

¼ teaspoon baking soda

½ teaspoon salt

1 cup gluten-free chocolate chips, such as Tropical Source

1 Place a rack in the lower-middle position and another in the upper-middle position of the oven. Preheat the oven to 375°F. Line two 15 × 10-inch baking sheets (not nonstick) with parchment paper.

2 In a large mixing bowl, beat the butter, granulated sugar, and brown sugar with an electric mixer on low speed until very smooth, about 1 minute. Beat in the egg and vanilla. Gradually add the sorghum blend, cocoa, xanthan gum, baking soda, and salt and beat on low speed just until blended. Stir in the chocolate chips.

3 Using a wet tablespoon or a #50 metal spring-action ice cream scoop, drop 1½-inch balls of dough at least 2 inches apart on the baking sheets, 12 per sheet. Place one sheet on the lower-middle rack and another on the upper-middle rack of the oven.

4 Bake 12 to 15 minutes, rotating the baking sheets between racks halfway through baking. Cool the cookies 2 to 3 minutes on the baking sheet, then transfer them to a wire rack to cool completely. Store, tightly covered, for up to 2 days or in the freezer for up to 1 month.

Decadent Chocolate Cookies Ⓥ

MAKES 48 SERVINGS

Chocoholics will adore this cookie! Mostly chocolate, sugar, eggs, and nuts—with only a little flour for stability—the deep, rich chocolate flavor really shines through.

9 ounces gluten-free bittersweet (at least 60%) chocolate, such as Scharffen Berger or Tropical Source

5 tablespoons (about ⅓ cup) unsalted butter or buttery spread, such as Earth Balance

3 large eggs

1 cup sugar

½ teaspoon pure vanilla extract

½ cup sorghum flour

¼ teaspoon baking soda

¼ teaspoon xanthan gum

¼ teaspoon salt

1 cup finely chopped walnuts

1 bag (12 ounces) gluten-free chocolate chips, such as Tropical Source

1 In a medium microwave-safe bowl, heat the chocolate and butter on low in a microwave oven for 1 to 2 minutes, or until melted. Stir until well blended; set aside.

2 In a large bowl, beat the eggs, sugar, and vanilla with an electric mixer on low speed until thick, about 1 minute. In a small bowl, whisk together the flour, baking soda, xanthan gum, and salt and beat into the eggs on low speed until no flour streaks remain. Beat in the chocolate mixture. Stir in the walnuts and chocolate chips. The dough will be very soft. Cover the bowl tightly and refrigerate 2 hours.

3 Place an oven rack in the middle position of the oven. Preheat the oven to 375°F. Line a 15 × 10-inch baking sheet (not nonstick) with parchment paper.

4 Shape the dough into 48 walnut-size balls with your hands and place 12 balls, at least 1½ inches apart, on the sheet. Keep remaining balls of dough chilled.

5 Bake 10 to 12 minutes or just until the cookies look shiny and the crust starts to crack. Cool the cookies 2 minutes on the pan; then transfer to a wire rack to cool completely. Repeat with remaining balls of chilled dough, 12 per sheet. Store, tightly covered, for up to 2 days or in the freezer for up to 1 month.

Chocolate Peanut Butter Cookies Ⓥ

MAKES 20 SERVINGS

Chocolate and peanut butter are a winning combination, especially in these pretty cookies with their crackled appearance. If you prefer a nutty texture, use crunchy peanut butter; if not, use the creamy style. Either way, these cookies are delightful.

1½ cups Carol's Sorghum Blend (page x)

½ cup unsweetened cocoa powder (not Dutch-process or alkali)

½ teaspoon baking soda

½ teaspoon xanthan gum

¼ teaspoon salt

¼ cup unsalted butter or buttery spread, such as Earth Balance, at room temperature, but not melted

½ cup granulated sugar + 2 tablespoons, for rolling

½ cup packed light brown sugar

¼ cup creamy or crunchy peanut butter

1 large egg

1 teaspoon pure vanilla extract

1 Place a rack in the middle of the oven. Preheat the oven to 375°F. Line a 15 × 10-inch baking sheet (not nonstick) with parchment paper.

2 In a small bowl, whisk together the sorghum blend, cocoa, baking soda, xanthan gum, and salt; set aside. In a medium bowl, beat the butter, ½ cup of the granulated sugar, brown sugar, and peanut butter with an electric mixer on medium speed until blended. Add the egg and vanilla and beat on medium speed just until blended. Reduce the speed to low and gradually beat in the dry ingredients until smooth.

3 With wet hands, roll the dough into 20 balls, each 1-inch in diameter. Dip each cookie in the remaining 2 tablespoons of sugar, and place 2 inches apart on the baking sheet. Lightly coat the bottom of a drinking glass with cooking spray and flatten each cookie to about ½ inch thick.

4 Bake 7 to 10 minutes or until the cookies are firm around the edges and look crackly. Cool the cookies 2 to 3 minutes on the baking sheet, then transfer them to a wire rack to cool completely. Store, tightly covered, for up to 2 days or in the freezer for up to 1 month.

Chocolate Cherry Coconut Cookies Ⓥ

MAKES 24 SERVINGS

This is one of my favorite cookies because it combines some of the flavors I love best. Shredded coconut gives them a nice chewy quality and dried cherries provide a dose of tartness.

¼ cup (½ stick) unsalted butter or buttery spread, such as Earth Balance, at room temperature, but not melted

½ cup granulated sugar

¾ cup packed light brown sugar

1 large egg

2 teaspoons pure vanilla extract

1½ cups Carol's Sorghum Blend (page x)

½ cup unsweetened cocoa powder (not Dutch-process or alkali)

1 teaspoon xanthan gum

½ teaspoon salt

¼ teaspoon baking soda

¾ cup gluten-free chocolate chips, such as Tropical Source

½ cup dried sweetened cherries

¼ cup sweetened shredded coconut

1 Place a rack in the lower-middle position and another in the upper-middle position of the oven. Preheat the oven to 375°F. Line two 15 × 10-inch baking sheets (not nonstick) with parchment paper.

2 In a large mixing bowl, beat the butter, granulated sugar, and brown sugar with an electric mixer on low speed until very smooth, about 1 minute. Beat in the egg and vanilla.

3 In a small bowl, whisk together the sorghum blend, cocoa, xanthan gum, salt, and baking soda

and gradually beat into the egg mixture on low speed just until blended. Stir in the chocolate chips, cherries, and coconut. Knead the dough with your hands a few times to make sure the chips, cherries, and coconut are thoroughly incorporated.

4 Using a wet tablespoon or a #50 metal spring-action ice cream scoop, drop 1½-inch balls of dough at least 2 inches apart on the baking sheets, 12 per sheet. Use the bottom of a drinking glass to flatten the cookies slightly. Place one sheet on the lower-middle rack and another on the upper-middle rack of the oven.

5 Bake 12 to 15 minutes, rotating the baking sheets between racks halfway through baking, or until the cookies are firm. Cool the cookies 2 to 3 minutes on the baking sheet, then transfer them to a wire rack to cool completely. Store, tightly covered, for up to 2 days or in the freezer for up to 1 month.

Chocolate-Cranberry Cookies

MAKES 24 SERVINGS

This is one of my personal favorites because I love the combination of cranberry and chocolate. I often freeze a few cookies in a resealable plastic bag; then they're ready to take with me when I'm traveling.

¼ cup unsalted butter or buttery spread, such as Earth Balance, at room temperature, but not melted

½ cup granulated sugar

¾ cup packed light brown sugar

1 large egg

2 teaspoons pure vanilla extract

1½ cups Carol's Sorghum Blend (page x)

½ cup unsweetened cocoa powder (not Dutch-process or alkali)

1 teaspoon xanthan gum

½ teaspoon salt

¼ teaspoon baking soda

¾ cup gluten-free chocolate chips, such as Tropical Sources

½ cup dried sweetened cranberries

¼ cup finely chopped walnuts

1 Place a rack in the lower-middle position and another in the upper-middle position of the oven. Preheat the oven to 375°F. Line two 15 × 10-inch baking sheets (not nonstick) with parchment paper.

2 In a large mixing bowl, beat the butter, granulated sugar, and brown sugar with an electric mixer on low speed until very smooth, about 1 minute. Beat in the egg and vanilla.

3 In a small bowl, whisk together the sorghum blend, cocoa, xanthan gum, salt, and baking soda and gradually beat into the egg mixture on low speed just until blended. Stir in the chocolate chips, cranberries, and walnuts. Knead the dough with your hands a few times to make sure the chips, cranberries, and nuts are thoroughly incorporated.

4 Using a wet tablespoon or a #50 metal spring-action ice cream scoop, drop 1½-inch balls of dough at least 2 inches apart on the baking sheets, 12 per sheet. Use the bottom of a drinking glass to flatten the cookies slightly. Place one sheet on the lower-middle rack and another on the upper-middle rack of the oven.

5 Bake 12 to 15 minutes, rotating the baking sheets between racks halfway through baking, or until the cookies are firm. Cool the cookies 2 to 3 minutes on the baking sheet, then transfer them to a wire rack to cool completely. Store, tightly covered, for up to 2 days or in the freezer for up to 1 month.

White Chocolate–Cherry Cookies Ⓥ

MAKES 24 SERVINGS

White chocolate is not really chocolate—it contains only cocoa butter, not cocoa solids. (Make sure you buy the kind that doesn't have other additives.) Nonetheless, it's delicious and you'll love these cookies. Don't use nonstick baking sheets; the cookies will brown too quickly and might burn.

½ cup (1 stick) unsalted butter or buttery spread, such as Earth Balance, at room temperature, but not melted

1 cup granulated sugar

1 tablespoon packed light brown sugar

1 large egg

2 teaspoons pure vanilla extract

2 cups Carol's Sorghum Blend (page x)

1 teaspoon xanthan gum

½ teaspoon baking powder

½ teaspoon salt

3.5 ounces gluten-free white chocolate bar, such as Organica, chopped in ¼-inch chunks

¼ cup dried cherries

1 Place a rack in the lower-middle position and another in the upper-middle position of the oven. Preheat the oven to 375°F. Line two 15 × 10-inch baking sheets (not nonstick) with parchment paper.

2 In a large mixing bowl, beat the butter, granulated sugar, and brown sugar with an electric mixer on low speed until very smooth, about 1 minute. Beat in the egg and vanilla. Gradually add the sorghum blend, xanthan gum, baking powder, and salt and beat on low speed just until blended. Stir in the white chocolate chunks and cherries.

3 Using a wet tablespoon or a #50 metal spring-action ice cream scoop, drop 1½-inch balls of dough at least 2 inches apart on the baking sheets, 12 per sheet. Spray the bottom of a drinking glass with cooking spray and flatten the cookies slightly. Place one sheet on the lower-middle rack and another on the upper-middle rack of the oven.

4 Bake 12 to 15 minutes, rotating the baking sheets between racks halfway through baking. Cool the cookies 2 to 3 minutes on the baking sheet, then transfer them to a wire rack to cool completely. Store, tightly covered, for up to 2 days or in the freezer for up to 1 month.

Cranberry-Orange–White Chocolate Cookies

MAKES 24 SERVINGS

Cranberry and orange are wonderful in this cookie, and the white chocolate chunks complement both flavors with its creaminess.

½ cup (1 stick) unsalted butter or buttery spread, such as Earth Balance, at room temperature, but not melted

1 cup granulated sugar

1 tablespoon packed light brown sugar

1 large egg

1 tablespoon grated orange zest

2 teaspoons pure vanilla extract

2 cups Carol's Sorghum Blend (page x)

1 teaspoon xanthan gum

½ teaspoon baking powder

½ teaspoon salt

½ cup dried sweetened cranberries

½ cup gluten-free white chocolate chunks, chopped from white chocolate bar such as Organica

1 Place a rack in the lower-middle position and another in the upper-middle position of the oven. Preheat the oven to 375°F. Line two 15 × 10-inch baking sheets (not nonstick) with parchment paper.

2 In a large mixing bowl, beat the butter, granulated sugar, and brown sugar with an electric mixer on low speed until smooth, about 1 minute. Beat in the egg, orange zest, and vanilla until smooth. In a small bowl, whisk together the sorghum blend, xanthan gum, baking powder, and salt and gradually beat into the egg mixture on low speed just until blended. Stir in the cranberries and white chocolate chunks.

3 Using a wet tablespoon or a #50 metal spring-action ice cream scoop, drop 1½-inch balls of dough at least 2 inches apart on the baking sheets,

12 per sheet. Spray the bottom of a drinking glass with cooking spray and flatten the cookies slightly. Place one sheet on the lower-middle rack and another on the upper-middle rack of the oven.

4 Bake 12 to 15 minutes, rotating the baking sheets between racks halfway through baking, or until the cookies are lightly browned around the edges. Cool the cookies 2 to 3 minutes on the baking sheet, then transfer them to the wire rack to cool completely. Store, tightly covered, for up to 2 days or in the freezer for up to 1 month.

White-Chocolate-Cherry Cookies: Omit the orange zest, and replace the dried sweetened cranberries with dried cherries.

Trail Mix Cookies

MAKES 24 SERVINGS

Everyone knows what trail mix is, yet not everyone can eat it because of nut allergies. Enjoy Life Foods makes a gluten-free and nut-free trail mix that works beautifully in these yummy cookies.

½ cup (1 stick) unsalted butter or buttery spread, such as Earth Balance, at room temperature, but not melted

1 cup granulated sugar

1 tablespoon packed light brown sugar

1 large egg

1 teaspoon pure vanilla extract

1 teaspoon almond extract

2 cups Carol's Sorghum Blend (page x)

1 teaspoon xanthan gum

½ teaspoon baking powder

½ teaspoon salt

1 cup gluten-free trail mix, such as Enjoy Life Foods

1 Place a rack in the lower-middle position and another in the upper-middle position of the oven. Preheat the oven to 350°F. Line two 15 × 10-inch baking sheets (not nonstick) with parchment paper.

2 In a large mixing bowl, beat the butter, granulated sugar, and brown sugar with an electric mixer on low speed until very smooth, about 1 minute. Beat in the egg, vanilla, and almond extract. Gradually add the sorghum blend, xanthan gum, baking powder, and salt and beat on low speed just until blended. Stir in the trail mix.

3 With wet hands, shape the dough into 1½-inch balls and place 2 inches apart on the baking sheet, 12 per sheet. Press the balls lightly with your fingers to flatten slightly.

4 Bake 15 to 18 minutes, rotating the baking sheets between racks halfway through baking. Cool the cookies 2 to 3 minutes on the baking sheet, then transfer them to a wire rack to cool. Store, tightly covered, for up to 2 days or in the freezer for up to 1 month.

Coconut Nests

MAKES 18 SERVINGS

Use these delightful little nests to hold jelly beans at Easter time, truffles on Valentine's Day, or holiday candies at Christmas. Or, just bake them as plain cookies without the indentation.

2 cups sweetened shredded coconut, divided
½ cup sweetened condensed milk
¼ cup cornstarch
⅛ teaspoon salt
½ teaspoon pure vanilla extract
¼ teaspoon almond extract
1 to 2 drops green food coloring (optional)

1 Place a rack in the middle of the oven. Preheat the oven to 350°F. Line a 15 × 10-inch baking sheet (not nonstick) with parchment paper.

2 In a medium bowl, beat 1½ cups of the coconut plus all the remaining ingredients together with an electric mixer on low speed until well blended. Shape into balls of 1 teaspoon each, dip in the

remaining ½ cup of coconut and place, 1 inch apart, on the baking sheet. Press down the center of each nest with the back of a teaspoon or your finger to create an indentation.

3 Bake 10 to 15 minutes, or until the nests are golden brown and the coconut is lightly toasted. Cool the nests 5 minutes on the baking sheet and press the indentation again with your finger. Transfer to a wire rack to cool completely. Store, tightly covered, for up to 2 days or in the freezer for up to 1 month.

Coconut Macaroons with Chocolate Drizzle Ⓥ

MAKES 16 SERVINGS

I used to buy macaroons at a local coffee shop to eat with my coffee before I became gluten-free, and now I'm delighted to have my own delicious version. These moist and chewy cookies are especially wonderful when drizzled with chocolate.

1 package (14 ounces) sweetened shredded coconut
1 cup powdered sugar, divided
½ cup cornstarch
1 teaspoon xanthan gum
3 large egg whites, at room temperature
⅛ teaspoon salt
1 teaspoon pure vanilla extract
½ cup gluten-free chocolate chips, such as Tropical Source

1 Place a rack in the middle of the oven. Preheat the oven to 350°F. Line a 13 × 9-inch baking sheet (not nonstick) with parchment paper; set aside.

2 In a small bowl, whisk together the coconut, ¾ cup of the powdered sugar, cornstarch, and xanthan gum; set aside.

3 In a separate bowl, beat the egg whites and salt with an electric mixer on medium speed until the whites are foamy. Add the remaining ¼ cup of the powdered sugar, a tablespoon at a time, and continue to beat just to the stiff peak stage. Stir in the vanilla. Fold the coconut flake mixture into the egg whites. The dough will be somewhat stiff.

4 With wet hands, form 16 balls, each 1½ inches in diameter, on a baking sheet, leaving at least 1 inch between the cookies.

5 Bake 15 to 20 minutes or until the cookies start to brown around edges and the coconut looks toasted. Cool the macaroons 10 minutes on the baking sheet, then transfer them to a wire rack to cool completely. When cool, transfer to a serving platter.

6 Melt the chocolate chips in the microwave on low. With a spoon, drizzle the melted chocolate back and forth across the cookies. Cool completely until chocolate is set. Store, tightly covered, for up to 2 days or in the freezer for up to 1 month.

Coconut Raisin Cookies

MAKES 10 SERVINGS

As they say, necessity is often the mother of invention. This recipe came about when I arrived at a cooking school a few years ago to do a demonstration using rolled rice flakes. As it turned out, we couldn't find the rolled rice flakes, so we quickly improvised with large natural coconut flakes (sometimes called coconut chips) and sliced almonds; together, their texture somewhat resembles rolled rice flakes. The students loved them, and a new cookie was born!

1 cup Carol's Sorghum Blend (page x)
¼ cup potato flour (not potato starch)
2 tablespoons tapioca flour
½ cup packed light brown sugar
1 teaspoon xanthan gum
1 teaspoon ground cinnamon
½ teaspoon baking soda
½ teaspoon baking powder
½ teaspoon salt
1 large egg
¼ cup unsalted butter or buttery spread, such as Earth Balance, at room temperature, but not melted
½ cup applesauce, drained
2 tablespoons molasses (not blackstrap)
½ teaspoon pure vanilla extract
½ cup natural raw coconut flakes
⅓ cup sliced almonds
¾ cup dark raisins

1 Place a rack in the middle of the oven. Preheat the oven to 325°F. Line a 13 × 9-inch baking sheet (not nonstick) with parchment paper.

2 In a food processor, blend all the ingredients except the coconut, almonds, and raisins until smooth.

3 Add the coconut and almonds and pulse just until mixed. Add the raisins and pulse a couple of times just to blend the dough. Drop 10 tablespoons of dough at least 2 inches apart on the prepared baking sheet.

4 Bake 20 to 25 minutes or until the cookies are lightly browned. Cool the cookies 5 minutes on the pan on a wire rack. Store, tightly covered, for up to 2 days or in the freezer for up to 1 month.

Cornflake Cookies

MAKES 12 SERVINGS

This is the first recipe I recall making as a child. In fact, back when I was an active child and calories didn't matter as much, I could devour the whole batch in one day. I added dried cranberries for additional color and chewiness in this updated version. Now that you can buy gluten-free corn-flakes, you can enjoy cookies like these too, but in moderation. For best results, don't use a nonstick baking sheet because the dark surface absorbs heat readily and the cookies might burn.

½ cup (1 stick) unsalted butter or buttery spread, such as Earth Balance, at room temperature, but not melted

½ cup sugar

1 large egg

½ teaspoon xanthan gum

½ teaspoon baking powder

¼ teaspoon salt

1¼ cups Carol's Sorghum Blend (page x)

1 cup gluten-free cornflakes, such as Erewhon or Nature's Path, divided

½ cup sweetened coconut flakes

½ cup dried cranberries

1 Place a rack in the middle of the oven. Preheat oven to 375°F. Line a 15 × 10-inch baking sheet (not nonstick) with parchment paper.

2 In a medium mixing bowl, beat butter, sugar, and egg with electric mixer on high speed until smooth, about 1 minute. Reduce speed to low and beat in xantham gum, baking powder, salt, sorghum blend, and ½ cup cornflakes until well blended. Stir in remaining ½ cup cornflakes plus coconut and cranberries. Dough will be stiff. Drop 12 heaping tablespoons about 2 inches apart on prepared baking sheet.

3 Bake 12 to 15 minutes or until the edges are lightly browned. Remove baking sheet from oven and let cookies cool on baking sheet 5 minutes, then transfer to a wire rack to cool completely. Store, tightly covered, for up to 2 days or in the freezer for up to 1 month.

Peanut Butter Cookies

MAKES 20 SERVINGS

As delicious as the classic cookie we grew up with was, you can't go wrong with this one. If you like, bake half of the dough and freeze the remainder in 1½-inch logs. Then simply cut ½-inch circles to bake on another day.

¾ cup creamy peanut butter

1 cup packed light brown sugar

1 teaspoon pure vanilla extract

1 large egg

1⅓ cups Carol's Sorghum Blend (page x)

1 teaspoon xanthan gum

½ teaspoon salt

½ teaspoon baking soda

¼ cup chopped peanuts

1 Place a rack in the middle of the oven. Preheat the oven to 350°F. Line a 15 × 10-inch nonstick (gray, not black) baking sheet with parchment paper.

2 In a mixing bowl, beat the peanut butter, sugar, vanilla, and egg with an electric mixer on low speed until well blended, about 1 minute.

3 Whisk together the sorghum blend, xanthan gum, salt, and baking soda and beat into the peanut butter mixture on low speed just until blended. Stir in the peanuts.

4 Shape the dough into 20 balls, each 1½ inches in diameter, and refrigerate on a plate, covered, 1 hour. Place the balls 2 inches apart on the baking sheet. Flatten each cookie slightly with the tines of a fork in a crisscross pattern.

5 Bake 10 to 12 minutes or until the edges of the cookies start to set and begin to brown. Cool the cookies 5 minutes on the pan; then transfer to a wire rack to cool completely. Store, tightly covered, for up to 2 days or in the freezer for up to 1 month.

Peanut Butter Chocolate Chip Cookies: Stir ½ cup gluten-free chocolate chips, such as Tropical Source, into the dough. Bake as directed. Store, tightly covered, for up to 2 days or in the freezer for up to 1 month.

Crunchy Almond Cookies

MAKES 12 SERVINGS

This is one of those recipes that is greatly simplified by a food processor. If you don't have almond meal, place 1½ cups whole almonds in a food processor and pulse with the sugar until it resembles coarse meal. Add the remaining ingredients to the food processor and proceed with the directions. These cookies work great in Tiramisu (page 651).

1 cup almond meal, such as Bob's Red Mill
⅓ cup sugar
½ cup Carol's Sorghum Blend (page x)
1 tablespoon canola oil
1 teaspoon xanthan gum
½ teaspoon baking powder
¼ teaspoon salt
1 large egg
1 teaspoon almond extract

1 Place a rack in the middle of the oven. Preheat the oven to 350°F. Line a 13 × 9-inch baking sheet (not nonstick) with parchment paper or aluminum foil. Blend all ingredients in food processor until thoroughly mixed. Shape the dough into 12 balls, about 1 inch in diameter, and place at least 2 inches apart on the baking sheet.

2 Bake 10 to 12 minutes or until the cookies are firm. The cookies will appear dry and won't brown very much. Cool the cookies 2 to 3 minutes on the baking sheet then transfer them to a wire rack to cool completely. Store, tightly covered, for up to 2 days or in the freezer for up to 1 month.

Chai Almond Cookies

MAKES 24 SERVINGS

The unmistakable flavor of chai—traditionally in tea—is very popular right now. That unique flavor is actually based on spices commonly found in baked goods.

½ cup (1 stick) unsalted butter or buttery spread, such as Earth Balance, at room temperature, but not melted
1 cup granulated sugar
1 tablespoon packed light brown sugar
1 large egg
2 teaspoons pure vanilla extract
1 teaspoon almond extract
2 cups Carol's Sorghum Blend (page x)
1 teaspoon xanthan gum
¾ teaspoon ground allspice
¾ teaspoon ground cardamom
½ teaspoon ground cinnamon
½ teaspoon baking powder
½ teaspoon salt
½ cup finely chopped toasted almonds
½ cup powdered sugar, for rolling

1 Place a rack in the lower-middle position and another in the upper-middle position of the oven. Preheat the oven to 375°F. Line two 15 × 10-inch baking sheets (not nonstick) with parchment paper.

2 In a large mixing bowl, beat the butter, sugar, and brown sugar with an electric mixer on low speed until very smooth, about 1 minute. Beat in the egg, vanilla, and almond extract. Gradually add the sorghum blend, xanthan gum, allspice, cardamom, cinnamon, baking powder, and salt and beat on low speed just until blended. Stir in the almonds.

3 With wet hands, shape a tablespoon of dough into a ball and place 2 inches apart on the baking sheets, 12 per sheet. Place one sheet on the lower-middle rack and another on the upper-middle rack of the oven.

4 Bake 12 to 15 minutes, rotating the baking sheets between racks halfway through baking. Cool the cookies 2 to 3 minutes on the baking sheet. Roll the hot cookies in powdered sugar. Cool completely on a wire rack, then roll the cookies in powdered sugar again. Serve immediately. Store, tightly covered, for up to 2 days or in the freezer for up to 1 month. You may roll the cookies in powdered sugar again, just before serving.

Pecan Sandies or Sables
MAKES 24 SERVINGS

Some people refer to these cookies as "sandies" because the ground pecans lend a sandy feel while others call them "sables." Either way, this cookie is sure to delight pecan lovers. It is common to shape these cookies by forming the dough into a log and then slicing the log into cookies, but that may lead to irregularly-shaped cookies, since the log tends to flatten as you put pressure on it during cutting. If you wish, shape the cookies into balls with your hands and flatten them slightly with the bottom of a drinking glass.

1 cup pecans, toasted and cooled, plus 24 pecans, halved
½ cup powdered sugar
½ cup packed light brown sugar
2 cups Carol's Sorghum Blend (page x)
1 teaspoon xanthan gum
½ teaspoon salt
¼ cup (½ stick) unsalted butter or buttery spread, such as Earth Balance, at room temperature, cut into 2-tablespoon chunks
1 large egg yolk
2 teaspoons pure vanilla extract

1 In a food processor, process the cup of pecans with the powdered sugar and brown sugar until the pecans are finely ground. Add the sorghum blend,

xanthan gum, and salt and process until blended, scraping down the side of the bowl with a spatula. Scatter the butter chunks on top and process until well blended. Add the egg yolk and vanilla and process until the dough comes together in a ball or in several clumps. Remove the dough from the food processor and knead it with your hands for a few seconds or until it is smooth.

2 Divide the dough in half and shape each half into a 6-inch log. Wrap each log tightly with plastic wrap and refrigerate for at least 2 hours.

3 Place a rack in the lower-middle position and another in the upper-middle position of the oven. Preheat the oven to 325°F. Line two 15 × 10-inch baking sheets (not nonstick) with parchment paper.

4 Cut each log into ¼-inch slices, rotating the log slightly each time to keep its cylindrical shape. Place the slices 1 inch apart on the baking sheets, 12 per sheet. Press a pecan half in the center of each slice. Place one sheet on the lower-middle rack and another on the upper-middle rack of the oven.

5 Bake 15 to 20 minutes, or until the cookies start to brown around the edges, rotating the baking sheets between racks halfway through baking. Cool the cookies 2 to 3 minutes on the baking sheet, then transfer them to a wire rack to cool completely. Store, tightly covered, for up to 2 days or in the freezer for up to 1 month.

Mesquite Pecan Cookies
MAKES 24 SERVINGS

Mesquite, ground from the pods of the mesquite tree that grows abundantly in the Southwest, adds a unique, cinnamonlike flavor to these cookies. Mesquite also enhances the browning process so watch these cookies carefully to make sure they don't burn.

½ cup (1 stick) unsalted butter or buttery spread, such as Earth Balance, at room temperature, but not melted

1 cup granulated sugar

1 tablespoon packed light brown sugar

1 large egg

2 teaspoons pure vanilla extract

1¾ cups Carol's Sorghum Blend (page x)

¼ cup mesquite flour, such as Casadefruta

1 teaspoon xanthan gum

½ teaspoon ground cinnamon

½ teaspoon baking powder

½ teaspoon salt

½ cup finely chopped pecans

1 Place a rack in the lower-middle position and another in the upper-middle position of the oven. Preheat the oven to 375°F. Line two 15 × 10-inch baking sheets (not nonstick) with parchment paper.

2 In a large mixing bowl, beat the butter, granulated sugar, and brown sugar on low speed until smooth, about 1 minute. Beat in the egg and vanilla. In a small bowl, whisk together the sorghum blend, mesquite, xanthan gum, cinnamon, baking powder, and salt and gradually beat into the egg mixture on low speed just until blended. Stir in the pecans.

3 With wet hands, shape the dough into 1½-inch balls and place them 2 inches apart on the baking sheets, 12 per sheet. Coat the bottom of a drinking glass with cooking spray and gently flatten each cookie to 1-inch thickness. Place one sheet on the lower-middle rack and another on the upper-middle rack of the oven.

4 Bake 15 to 18 minutes, rotating the baking sheets between racks halfway through baking. Cool the cookies 2 to 3 minutes on the baking sheet, then transfer them to a wire rack to cool completely. Store, tightly covered, for up to 2 days or in the freezer for up to 1 month.

Chestnut Cookies

MAKES 18 SERVINGS

Chestnut flour, ground from chestnuts, is light, delicate, and slightly sweet and it makes wonderful cookies. You can find it at natural food stores or by mail order from www.dowdandrogers.com, a company that specializes in gluten-free products made from chestnuts.

½ cup (1 stick) unsalted butter or buttery spread, such as Earth Balance, at room temperature, but not melted

1 cup sugar + 2 tablespoons for rolling

1 tablespoon packed light brown sugar

1 large egg

1 teaspoon pure vanilla extract

1 teaspoon almond extract

1 cup Carol's Sorghum Blend (page x)

1 cup chestnut flour

1 teaspoon xanthan gum

½ teaspoon baking powder

½ teaspoon salt

½ cup pine nuts or chopped pecans

1 Place a rack in the lower-middle position and another in the upper-middle position of the oven. Preheat the oven to 375°F. Line two 15 × 10-inch baking sheets (not nonstick) with parchment paper.

2 In a large mixing bowl, beat the butter, sugar, and brown sugar with an electric mixer on low speed until very smooth, about 1 minute. Beat in the egg, vanilla, and almond extract. Gradually add the sorghum blend, xanthan gum, baking powder, and salt and beat on low speed just until blended. Stir in the nuts.

3 With wet hands, shape the dough into 1½-inch balls and place them 2 inches apart on the baking sheets, 9 per sheet. Place one sheet on the lower-middle rack and another on the upper-middle rack of the oven.

4 Bake 12 to 15 minutes, rotating the baking sheets between racks halfway through baking. Cool the cookies 2 to 3 minutes on the baking sheet, then transfer them to a wire rack to cool completely. Store, tightly covered, for up to 2 days or in the freezer for up to 1 month.

Sesame Cookies

MAKES 18 SERVINGS

Sesame seeds come from the sesame plant and the term "open sesame" from the seed pod's tendency to burst open when ripe. These cookies are sometimes called "benne wafers" because benne is African for sesame. We often think of sesame seeds as an ingredient in savory dishes, but they are delightful in this cookie, which is commonly served in the South.

½ cup (1 stick) unsalted butter or buttery spread, such as Earth Balance, at room temperature, but not melted

1 cup granulated sugar

1 tablespoon packed light brown sugar

1 large egg, at room temperature

1 tablespoon grated lemon zest

2 teaspoons pure vanilla extract

2 cups Carol's Sorghum Blend (page x)

1 teaspoon xanthan gum

½ teaspoon baking powder

½ teaspoon salt

1 cup sesame seeds

1 Place a rack in the lower-middle position and another in the upper-middle position of the oven. Preheat the oven to 375°F. Line two 15 × 10-inch baking sheets (not nonstick) with parchment paper.

2 In a large mixing bowl, beat the butter, granulated sugar, and brown sugar with an electric mixer on low speed until smooth, about 1 minute. Beat in the egg, lemon zest, and vanilla until smooth. In a small bowl, whisk together the sorghum blend, xanthan gum, baking powder, and salt and gradually beat into the egg mixture on low

speed just until blended. Shape the dough into a flat disk, tightly wrap it, and chill 1 hour.

3 Place the sesame seeds in a wide shallow bowl. With wet hands, divide the dough into 18 pieces about the size of a golf-ball. Shape each piece into a log, 2½ inches long and ¾ inch in diameter, and roll the logs in the sesame seeds. Place the logs at least 1½ inches apart on the baking sheets, 9 logs per sheet. Place one sheet on the lower–middle rack and another on the upper-middle rack of the oven.

4 Bake 15 to 20 minutes, rotating the baking sheets between racks halfway through baking, until the sesame seeds are fragrant and the cookies are well-browned. Cool the cookies 2 to 3 minutes on the baking sheet and then transfer them to a wire rack to cool completely. Store, tightly covered, for up to 2 days or in the freezer for up to 1 month.

Flax Cookies

MAKES 12 SERVINGS

Flax seed supplies a nut-like flavor and wonderful nutrients such as fiber, omega-3 fatty acids, and protein to any diet. These cookies travel well; I take a stash with me when I'm on the road. They are great for school lunches and picnics, too.

1 cup flaxseed meal

½ cup Carol's Sorghum Blend (page x)

½ cup pecan meal

2 teaspoons baking powder

½ teaspoon salt

2 teaspoons ground cinnamon

1 teaspoon xanthan gum

1 teaspoon ground ginger

½ teaspoon allspice

1 large egg

2 tablespoons unsalted butter or buttery spread, such as Earth Balance, at room temperature, but not melted

½ cup pure maple syrup

1 teaspoon pure vanilla extract

1 Place a rack in the middle of the oven. Preheat the oven to 325°F. Generously grease a 13 × 9-inch nonstick (gray, not black) baking sheet or line it with parchment paper.

2 Blend all of the ingredients thoroughly in a food processor. Or mix together in a medium bowl with an electric mixer on low speed until smooth, about 1 minute. Gather the dough into a large ball. Using a wet tablespoon or a #50 metal spring-action ice cream scoop, drop 1½-inch balls of dough at least 2 inches apart on the baking sheet. Use a fork to flatten each ball in a criss-cross design.

3 Bake 20 minutes or until the cookies are firm. Cool cookies 5 minutes on the baking sheet, then transfer to a wire rack to cool completely. Store, tightly covered, for up to 2 days or in the freezer for up to 1 month.

Hemp Seed Cookies

MAKES 24 SERVINGS

Hemp ingredients or foods can be found in health food stores and are especially nutritious. This recipe uses shelled hemp seeds, which have a proper ratio of omega-3 and six essential fatty acids, and are also high in protein and fiber. Hemp seeds resemble sunflower seeds in flavor and lend a hearty, earthy taste to these cookies. The manufacturers recommend that baking temperatures not exceed 350°F to avoid damaging these precious nutrients.

½ cup (1 stick) unsalted butter or buttery spread, such as Earth Balance, at room temperature but not melted
1 cup granulated sugar + ¼ cup for rolling
1 tablespoon packed light brown sugar
1 large egg
1 teaspoon pure vanilla extract
1 teaspoon almond extract
2 cups Carol's Sorghum Blend (page x)
1 teaspoon xanthan gum
½ teaspoon baking powder
½ teaspoon salt
½ cup shelled hemp seed, such as Manitoba Harvest

1 Place a rack in the lower-middle position and another in the upper-middle position of the oven. Preheat the oven to 350°F. Line two 15 × 10-inch baking sheets (not nonstick) with parchment paper.

2 In a large mixing bowl, beat the butter, granulated sugar, and brown sugar with an electric mixer on low speed until very smooth, about 1 minute. Beat in the egg, vanilla, and almond extract. Gradually add the sorghum blend, xanthan gum, baking powder, and salt and beat on low speed just until blended. Stir in the hemp seeds.

3 With wet hands, shape the dough into 1½-inch balls, roll them in the remaining ¼ cup sugar, and place 2 inches apart on the baking sheets, 12 per sheet. Coat the bottom of a drinking glass with cooking spray and gently flatten each cookie to 1-inch thickness. Sprinkle the cookies with any sugar that remains after rolling. Place one sheet on the lower-middle rack and another on the upper-middle rack of the oven.

4 Bake 15 to 18 minutes, rotating the baking sheets between racks halfway through baking. Cool the cookies 2 to 3 minutes on the baking sheet, then transfer them to a wire rack to cool completely. Store, tightly covered, for up to 2 days or in the freezer for up to 1 month.

Italian Pignoli Cookies

MAKES 24 SERVINGS

Pignoli (commonly called pine nuts) are delicious edible seeds from the cones of pine trees. They are quite popular in Italy, but are also very plentiful in the United States, especially in the Southwest where they are called piñon. They are very aromatic when heated, and add a distinctive taste to these cookies.

1 can (8-ounces) gluten-free almond paste, such as Love'n Bake, or homemade Almond Paste (page 678)

2 large egg whites

1 teaspoon almond extract

1½ cups Carol's Sorghum Blend (page x)

½ cup sugar

¼ teaspoon xanthan gum

⅛ teaspoon salt

½ cup pignoli (pine nuts)

2 tablespoons powdered sugar, for dusting

1 Place a rack in the middle of the oven. Preheat the oven to 300°F. Line two 15 × 10-inch baking sheets (not nonstick) with parchment paper. Lightly grease the parchment paper with shortening.

2 In a large mixing bowl, crumble the almond paste into very small pieces. Add the egg whites and almond extract and beat with an electric mixer on low speed until blended. Beat in the sorghum blend, sugar, xanthan gum, and salt in a medium bowl and lightly toss with a fork. Place the pine nuts in a shallow bowl.

3 With wet hands, shape a teaspoon of the dough into a ball with your hands and dip it into the pine nuts, pressing the nuts into the cookies with your hands. Repeat with the remaining dough and place the balls on the cookie sheets, 2 inches apart. Stick any remaining pine nuts on the balls of dough.

4 Bake 20 to 25 minutes. Cool the cookies on the baking sheet 1 minute, then transfer them to a wire rack to cool completely. Dust with powdered sugar.

Date-Nut Cookies

MAKES 24 SERVINGS

Recipes for sweet, old-fashioned date cookies are often found in church cookbooks, which is where my mother's recipe came from. As a child, I didn't appreciate dates, but today I love eating them plain as a snack or in cookies such as this one.

½ cup (1 stick) unsalted butter or buttery spread, such as Earth Balance, at room temperature, but not melted

1 cup granulated sugar + ¼ cup for rolling

1 tablespoon packed light brown sugar

1 large egg

2 teaspoons grated lemon zest

1 teaspoon pure vanilla extract

2 cups Carol's Sorghum Blend (page x)

1 teaspoon xanthan gum

½ teaspoon baking powder

½ teaspoon ground cinnamon

½ teaspoon ground nutmeg

½ teaspoon salt

1 cup chopped pitted dates

¼ cup chopped pecans

1 Place a rack in the middle of the oven. Preheat the oven to 375°F. Line two 15 × 10-inch baking sheets (not nonstick) with parchment paper.

2 In a large mixing bowl, beat the butter, granulated sugar, and brown sugar with an electric mixer on low speed until very smooth, about 1 minute. Beat in the egg, lemon zest, and vanilla. Gradually add the sorghum blend, xanthan gum, baking powder, cinnamon, nutmeg, and salt and beat on low speed just until blended. Stir in the dates and pecans.

3 With wet hands, shape the dough into 1½-inch balls and place them 2 inches apart on the baking sheets, 12 per sheet. Place one sheet on the lower-middle rack and another on the upper-middle rack of the oven.

4 Bake 12 to 15 minutes, or until the cookies spring back when touched with a finger. Cool the cookies 2 to 3 minutes on the baking sheet, then transfer them to a wire rack to cool completely. Store, tightly covered, for up to 2 days or in the freezer for up to 1 month.

Dried Cherry and Nut Cookies ⓥ

MAKES 24 SERVINGS

Dried cherries are not only flavorful, but they are nutritious and provide a delicious "chew" to these cookies. You can use any nuts you wish.

½ cup (1 stick) unsalted butter or buttery spread, such as Earth Balance, at room temperature, but not melted

1 cup granulated sugar + ¼ cup for rolling

1 tablespoon packed light brown sugar

1 large egg

1 teaspoon pure vanilla extract

1 teaspoon almond extract

2 cups Carol's Sorghum Blend (page x)

1 teaspoon xanthan gum

½ teaspoon baking powder

½ teaspoon salt

1 cup dried cherries

¼ cup finely chopped walnuts

1 Place a rack in the lower-middle position and another in the upper-middle position of the oven. Preheat the oven to 375°F. Line two 15 × 10-inch baking sheets (not nonstick) with parchment paper.

2 In a large mixing bowl, beat the butter, 1 cup of the granulated sugar, and brown sugar with an electric mixer on low speed until very smooth, about 1 minute. Beat in the egg, vanilla, and almond extract. Gradually add the sorghum blend, xanthan gum, baking powder, and salt and beat on low speed just until blended. Stir in the cherries and nuts.

3 With wet hands, shape the dough into 1½-inch balls, roll them in the remaining ¼ cup sugar, and place them 2 inches apart on the baking sheets, 12 per sheet. Coat the bottom of a drinking glass with cooking spray and gently flatten each cookie to 1 inch thickness. Sprinkle the cookies with any sugar that remains after rolling. Place one sheet on the lower-middle rack and another on the upper-middle rack of the oven.

4 Bake 12 to 15 minutes, rotating the baking sheets between racks halfway through baking. Cool the cookies 2 to 3 minutes on the baking sheet, then transfer them to a wire rack to cool completely. Store, tightly covered, for up to 2 days or in the freezer for up to 1 month.

Millet and Dried Fruit Cookies ⓥ

MAKES 24 SERVINGS

Millet's mild flavor and light color make it versatile for use in many foods. If you can't find millet flour, grind enough whole grain millet for this recipe with a clean coffee grinder until it reaches the consistency of flour. Refrigerate millet grains for up to a year or freeze them for up to 2 years. I don't recommend storing millet flour in the pantry because it can quickly turn rancid.

½ cup (1 stick) unsalted butter or buttery spread, such as Earth Balance, at room temperature, but not melted

1 cup granulated sugar

1 tablespoon packed light brown sugar

1 large egg

2 teaspoons pure vanilla extract

1 tablespoon grated lemon zest

1½ cups Carol's Sorghum Blend (page x)

½ cup millet flour

1 teaspoon xanthan gum

½ teaspoon baking powder

½ teaspoon salt

¾ cup chopped dried fruit of choice (apricots, cherries, cranberries, or blueberries)

½ cup finely chopped pecans

1 Place a rack in the lower-middle position and another in the upper-middle position of the oven. Preheat the oven to 375°F. Line two 15 × 10-inch baking sheets (not nonstick) with parchment paper.

2 In a large mixing bowl, beat the butter, granulated sugar, and brown sugar with an electric mixer on low speed until very smooth, about 1 minute. Beat in the egg, vanilla, and lemon zest. Gradually add the sorghum blend, millet flour, xanthan gum, baking powder, and salt and beat on low speed just until blended. Stir in the dried fruit and pecans.

3 With wet hands, shape the dough into 1½-inch balls and place them 2 inches apart on the baking sheets, 12 per sheet. Coat the bottom of a drinking glass with cooking spray and gently flatten each cookie to 1-inch thickness. Place one sheet on the lower-middle rack and another on the upper-middle rack of the oven.

4 Bake 15 to 18 minutes, rotating the baking sheets between racks halfway through baking. Cool the cookies 2 to 3 minutes on the baking sheet, then transfer them to a wire rack to cool completely. Store, tightly covered, for up to 2 days or in the freezer for up to 1 month.

Oatmeal Raisin Cookies

MAKES 18 SERVINGS

You'll enjoy this classic treat that you likely grew up eating and loving. These are large cookies, like grandma used to make. If oats are not for you, try the Coconut Raisin Cookies (page 406).

¼ cup (½ stick) unsalted butter or buttery spread, such as Earth Balance, at room temperature, but not melted

½ cup granulated sugar

½ cup packed light brown sugar

1 large egg

1 tablespoon molasses (not blackstrap)

2 teaspoons pure vanilla extract

2 cups Carol's Sorghum Blend (page x)

1½ teaspoons xanthan gum

½ teaspoon ground cinnamon

¼ teaspoon ground nutmeg

½ teaspoon baking powder

½ teaspoon salt

1½ cups gluten-free rolled oats* or rolled soy flakes**†

½ cup golden or dark raisins

¼ cup chopped walnuts

1 Place a rack in the lower-middle position and another in the upper-middle position of the oven. Preheat the oven to 375°F. Line two 15 × 10-inch nonstick (gray, not black) baking sheets with parchment paper.

2 In a large mixing bowl, beat the butter, granulated sugar, and brown sugar with an electric mixer on low speed until smooth, about 1 minute. Beat in the egg, molasses, and vanilla just until blended. Gradually add the sorghum blend, xanthan gum, cinnamon, nutmeg, baking powder, and salt and beat on low speed just until blended. Do not overbeat. Stir in the oatmeal, raisins, and walnuts. The dough will be fairly stiff.

3 Shape 18 balls of dough, each 1½ inches in diameter, and place the balls at least 2 inches apart on the prepared baking sheet, 9 cookies per sheet. Roll the balls in hands for uniform shapes.

Place one sheet on the lower-middle rack and another on the upper-middle rack of the oven.

4 Bake 15 to 18 minutes, or until the cookies start to brown around the edges, rotating the baking sheets between racks halfway through baking. Cool the cookies 2 to 3 minutes on the baking sheet, then transfer them to a wire rack to cool completely. Store, tightly covered, for up to 2 days or in the freezer for up to 1 month.

*Available at www.bobsredmill.com, www. creamhillestates.com, www.giftsofnature.net, www. glutenfreeoats.com, and www.onlyoats.com.

**Available at natural food stores.

†Check with your physician before using gluten-free oats.

Montina Raisin Cookies

MAKES 24 SERVINGS

Montina is the trade name given to a flour ground from the seeds of Indian ricegrass. This relative newcomer to the gluten-free scene is grown primarily in the Northwestern corner of the United States, with the company headquarters located in Montana—hence the name Montina. It is widely available under the name of Montina Pure Supplement in health food stores or at www.amazing grains.com. It is very nutritious and full of fiber, but is best used in smaller amounts in baking.

¼ cup (½ stick) unsalted butter or buttery spread, such as Earth Balance, at room temperature, but not melted

1 cup granulated sugar

1 tablespoon packed light brown sugar

1 large egg

2 teaspoons pure vanilla extract

1¾ cups Carol's Sorghum Blend (page x)

¼ cup Montina Pure Supplement

1½ teaspoons xanthan gum

½ teaspoon ground cinnamon

½ teaspoon baking powder

½ teaspoon salt

½ cup dark raisins

½ cup finely chopped pecans

1 Place a rack in the lower-middle position and another in the upper-middle position of the oven. Preheat the oven to 375°F. Line two 15 × 10-inch baking sheets (not nonstick) with parchment paper.

2 In a large mixing bowl, beat the butter, granulated sugar, and brown sugar with an electric mixer on low speed until smooth, about 1 minute. Beat in the egg and vanilla. Gradually add the sorghum blend, Montina, xanthan gum, cinnamon, baking powder, and salt and beat on low speed just until blended. Do not overbeat. Stir in the raisins and pecans. The dough will be fairly stiff.

3 With wet hands, shape the dough into 1¼-inch balls and place them 2 inches apart on the baking sheets, 12 per sheet. Coat the bottom of a drinking glass with cooking spray and gently flatten each cookie to 1 inch thickness. Place one sheet on the lower-middle rack and another on the upper-middle rack of the oven.

4 Bake 15 to 18 minutes, rotating the baking sheets between racks halfway through baking. Cool the cookies 2 to 3 minutes on the baking sheet, then transfer them to a wire rack to cool completely. Store, tightly covered, for up to 2 days or in the freezer for up to 1 month.

Old-Fashioned Molasses Sorghum Cookies

MAKES 24 SERVINGS

There is actually a type of molasses made from sorghum but it is not widely available in all parts of the country, so I just use regular molasses. If you don't need all of these cookies at one time, freeze half of the dough in a 1½-inch log so you can make refrigerator or icebox cookies later. When the need for cookies arises, cut the log into ½-inch slices and bake as directed below.

¼ cup (½ stick) unsalted butter or buttery spread, such as Earth Balance, at room temperature

¾ cup packed light brown sugar

1 large egg

¼ cup molasses (not blackstrap)

¼ teaspoon pure vanilla extract

2 cups sorghum flour

2 teaspoons ground cinnamon

1 teaspoon ground ginger

½ teaspoon xanthan gum

½ teaspoon baking soda

¼ teaspoon salt

2 tablespoons sanding (or granulated) sugar, for rolling

1 Place a rack in the middle of the oven. Preheat the oven to 350°F. Line a 15 × 10-inch baking sheet (not nonstick) with parchment paper.

2 In a large mixing bowl, beat the butter and brown sugar with an electric mixer on low speed until well blended, about 1 minute. Add the egg, molasses, and vanilla and beat until smooth.

3 In a separate bowl, sift together the sorghum, cinnamon, ginger, xanthan gum, baking soda, and salt. Gradually beat the flour mixture into the butter mixture on low speed until well blended, scraping down the side of the bowl if necessary. The dough will be stiff.

4 Shape the dough into 24 balls, each 1 inch in diameter with your hands. Flatten each ball slightly between your palms and dredge both sides of it in the sanding (or granulated) sugar. Place the balls on the prepared baking sheet about 1 to 2 inches apart.

5 Bake 7 to 10 minutes or until cookies are just set. Cool the cookies 2 to 3 minutes on the baking sheet, then transfer them to a wire rack to cool completely. Store, tightly covered, for up to 2 days or in the freezer for up to 1 month.

Gingersnaps Ⓥ

MAKES 24 SERVINGS

Gingersnaps are wonderful for traveling, for dipping in coffee, and as cookie-crumb crusts for pies. Their delicious flavor and intoxicating aroma are perfect at any holiday festivity.

½ cup (1 stick) unsalted butter or buttery spread, such as Earth Balance, at room temperature, but not melted

1 cup packed light brown sugar

1 large egg

3 tablespoons molasses (not blackstrap)

1 teaspoon pure vanilla extract

1 teaspoon almond extract

2½ cups Carol's Sorghum Blend (page x)

1 teaspoon xanthan gum

1½ teaspoons ground ginger

1½ teaspoons ground cinnamon

½ teaspoon baking powder

½ teaspoon salt

¼ teaspoon ground nutmeg

¼ teaspoon ground cloves

2 tablespoons granulated sugar, for rolling

1 Place a rack in the lower-middle position and another in the upper-middle position of the oven. Preheat the oven to 375°F. Line two 15 × 10-inch baking sheets (not nonstick) with parchment paper.

2 In a large mixing bowl, beat the butter and brown sugar with an electric mixer on low speed until smooth, about 30 seconds. Beat in the egg, molasses, vanilla, and almond extract. Gradually add the sorghum blend, xanthan gum, ginger, cinnamon, baking powder, salt, nutmeg, and cloves and beat on low speed just until blended.

3 With wet hands or a #50 metal ice cream scoop, shape the dough into 1½-inch balls, roll them in the sugar, and place them 2 inches apart on the baking sheets, 12 per sheet. Sprinkle the cookies with any sugar that remains after rolling. Place one sheet on the lower–middle rack and another on the upper-middle rack of the oven.

4 Bake 15 to 20 minutes, rotating the baking sheets between racks halfway through baking. Cool the cookies 2 to 3 minutes on the baking sheet, then transfer them to a wire rack to cool completely. Store, tightly covered, for up to 2 days or in the freezer for up to 1 month.

Frosted Spice Cookies

MAKES 24 SERVINGS

These cookies are especially appropriate at the holidays with their warm, spicy flavors (but you can enjoy them any time).

COOKIES

½ cup (1 stick) unsalted butter or buttery spread, such as Earth Balance, at room temperature, but not melted

½ cup granulated sugar + 2 tablespoons sugar, for rolling

½ cup packed light brown sugar

1 large egg

2 teaspoons pure vanilla extract

2 cups Carol's Sorghum Blend (page x)

1 teaspoon xanthan gum

1½ teaspoons ground cinnamon

1 teaspoon ground ginger

½ teaspoon ground nutmeg

½ teaspoon baking powder

½ teaspoon salt

¼ teaspoon ground allspice

¼ teaspoon ground cloves

FROSTING

1 cup powdered sugar

1 tablespoon water, or as needed

1 teaspoon unsalted butter or buttery spread, such as Earth Balance, at room temperature

½ teaspoon pure vanilla extract

1 Place a rack in the lower-middle position and another in the upper-middle position of the oven. Preheat the oven to 375°F. Line two 15 × 10-inch baking sheets (not nonstick) with parchment paper.

2 Make the cookies: In a large mixing bowl, beat the butter, ½ cup granulated sugar, and brown sugar with an electric mixer on low speed until very smooth, about 1 minute. Beat in the egg and vanilla. Gradually add the sorghum blend, xanthan gum, cinnamon, ginger, xanthan gum, nutmeg, baking powder, salt, allspice, and cloves and beat on low speed just until blended. Gather the dough into a ball, knead it with your hands until it is smooth, flatten into a disk, wrap tightly, and chill 2 hours.

3 With wet hands or a #50 metal ice cream scoop, shape the dough into 1½-inch balls and place 2 inches apart on the baking sheets, 12 per sheet. Place one sheet on the lower-middle rack and another on the upper-middle rack of the oven.

4 Bake 12 to 15 minutes, rotating the baking sheets between racks halfway through baking. Cool the cookies 2 to 3 minutes on the baking sheet, then transfer them to a wire rack to cool completely. Store, tightly covered, for up to 2 days or in the freezer for up to 1 month.

5 Make the frosting: Whisk together the powdered sugar, water, butter, and vanilla until very smooth. Add more sugar or water, as needed, to reach the desired consistency. Spread each cookie with a scant teaspoon of frosting and place it on a wire rack to dry. Serve immediately; frosted cookies will not freeze very well.

Sugar Cookies

MAKES 24 SERVINGS

This is a basic dough for making vanilla cookies, but it is quite versatile and can also be the basis for many of your family favorites. Don't use nonstick baking sheets; the cookies will brown too quickly and might burn.

½ cup (1 stick) unsalted butter or buttery spread, such as Earth Balance, at room temperature, but not melted

1 cup granulated sugar + ¼ cup for rolling

1 tablespoon packed light brown sugar

1 large egg

1 teaspoon pure vanilla extract

1 teaspoon almond extract

2 cups Carol's Sorghum Blend (page x)

1 teaspoon xanthan gum

½ teaspoon baking powder

½ teaspoon salt

1 Place a rack in the lower-middle position and another in the upper-middle position of the oven. Preheat the oven to 375°F. Line two 15 × 10-inch baking sheets (not nonstick) with parchment paper.

2 In a large mixing bowl, beat the butter, 1 cup granulated sugar, and brown sugar with an electric mixer on low speed until very smooth, about 1 minute. Beat in the egg, vanilla, and almond extract. Gradually add the sorghum blend, xanthan gum, baking powder, and salt and beat on low speed just until blended.

3 With wet hands, shape the dough into 1½-inch balls, roll them in the remaining ¼ cup sugar, and place 2 inches apart on the baking sheet, 12 per sheet. Coat the bottom of a drinking glass with cooking spray and gently flatten each cookie to 1 inch thickness. Sprinkle the cookies with any sugar that remains after rolling. Place one sheet on the lower-middle rack and another on the upper-middle rack of the oven.

4 Bake 12 to 15 minutes, rotating the baking sheets between racks halfway through baking.

Cool the cookies 2 to 3 minutes on the baking sheet, then transfer them to a wire rack to cool completely. Store, tightly covered, for 2 days or in the freezer for up to 1 month.

Lemon Cookies with Lemon Glaze

MAKES 24 SERVINGS

Tart, yet delicate, this is the perfect cookie for tea or a ladies luncheon. If you prefer a milder lemon flavor, start with 1 tablespoon lemon zest and adapt the recipe according to your taste.

COOKIES

½ cup (1 stick) unsalted butter or buttery spread, such as Earth Balance, at room temperature, but not melted

1 cup granulated sugar + 1 tablespoon for sprinkling

1 tablespoon packed light brown sugar

1 large egg

2 teaspoons pure vanilla extract

1 to 2 tablespoons grated lemon zest, or to taste

2 cups Carol's Sorghum Blend (page x)

1 teaspoon xanthan gum

½ teaspoon baking powder

½ teaspoon salt

GLAZE

1 cup powdered sugar

1 tablespoon fresh lemon juice

1 Place a rack in the lower-middle position and another in the upper-middle position of the oven. Preheat the oven to 375°F. Line two 15 × 10-inch baking sheets (not nonstick) with parchment paper.

2 Make the cookies: In a large mixing bowl, beat the butter, 1 cup granulated sugar, and brown sugar with an electric mixer on low speed until smooth, about 30 seconds. Beat in the egg, vanilla, and lemon zest. In a small bowl, whisk together the sorghum blend, xanthan gum, baking powder, and salt and gradually beat on low speed just until blended.

3 With wet hands, shape the dough into 1½-inch balls and place 2 inches apart on the baking sheet, 12 per sheet. Coat the bottom of a drinking glass with cooking spray and gently flatten each cookie to 1 inch thickness. Place one sheet on the lower-middle rack and another on the upper-middle rack of the oven.

4 Bake 15 to 18 minutes, rotating the baking sheets between racks halfway through baking. Cool the cookies 2 to 3 minutes on the baking sheet, then transfer to a wire rack to cool completely

5 Make the glaze: Combine the powdered sugar and lemon juice until smooth. Brush the cookies with the glaze, and sprinkle with the remaining tablespoon of granulated sugar. Store, tightly covered, for up to 2 days or in the freezer for up to 1 month.

Amaretti

MAKES 16 SERVINGS

I devour these marvelous almond macaroonlike cookies by the bag whenever I visit Italy. I bring home as many bags as I can fit in my suitcase then freeze them to use when making Tiramisu (page 651), instead of the traditional Ladyfingers (page 436). But you don't have to go all the way to Italy— they are really quite simple to make at home.

1 cup whole blanched almonds
⅔ cup sugar
1 large egg white
½ teaspoon almond extract
⅛ teaspoon salt

1 Place a rack in the middle of the oven. Preheat the oven to 350°F. Line a 13 × 9-inch baking sheet (not nonstick) with parchment paper.

2 In a food processor, process the almonds and sugar until the almonds are finely ground. Add the egg white, almond extract, and salt and pulse until combined. Roll the dough into 16 balls, about 1 inch in diameter and place about 2 inches apart on the baking sheet. Slightly flatten the balls slightly with a drinking glass that has been coated with cooking spray.

3 Bake 10 minutes, or until the cookies are pale golden in color. Cool the cookies on the pan on a wire rack. The amaretti keep 4 days in an airtight container at room temperature or can be frozen for up to 1 month.

Meringue Cookies

MAKES 24 SERVINGS

Meringues are usually white (though they can be altered with food coloring) and look like airy clouds; they melt as soon as you pop them in your mouth. You will often see these cookies— sometimes called kisses—in bakeries, but they are simple to make at home.

3 large egg whites, at room temperature
⅔ cup sugar
⅛ teaspoon cream of tartar
½ teaspoon pure vanilla extract
¼ cup powdered sugar

1 Place a rack in the middle of the oven. Preheat the oven to 225°F. Line a 13 × 9-inch baking sheet (not nonstick) with parchment paper; set aside.

2 In a medium bowl, beat the egg whites with an electric mixer on medium-high speed until frothy, about 30 seconds. Gradually add 1 tablespoon of the sugar and beat 1 minute. Increase the mixer speed to high and beat in the cream of tartar, vanilla, and the remaining sugar; continue to beat about 2 minutes, or until the whites are glossy and the peaks stand straight up rather than curling over at the top. Gradually sift the powdered sugar into the beaten egg whites, 2 tablespoons at a time, in two batches and gently fold it in.

3 Spoon the mixture into a heavy-duty plastic freezer bag with ¼-inch of the corner cut off. Pipe 24 cookies, about a tablespoon each, 1 inch apart on the baking sheet.

4 Bake 1¼ hours in the middle of the oven, or until the cookies are dry. Turn off the heat and leave the meringues in the oven 30 more minutes.

Remove the meringues from the oven and cool on the baking sheet. Store, tightly covered, for up to 2 days or in the freezer for up to 1 month.

Peppermint Meringue Cookies: Add ½ teaspoon peppermint extract along with the vanilla extract.

Oven-Baked Caramel Corn

MAKES 5 CUPS

A treat more than a cookie, it is so simple that I'm amazed I waited so many years to make it, always assuming that it was difficult and tedious. Unlike the store-bought variety, my version has no trans fats, is not overly sweet, and you can even use noncaloric sucralose (Splenda) in place of up to half of the sugar. Kids will gobble it up.

1 quart (5 cups) popped corn (start with ⅓ cup popcorn kernels)
6 tablespoons unsalted butter or buttery spread, such as Earth Balance
½ cup packed light brown sugar
¼ cup light corn syrup
¼ teaspoon salt
¼ teaspoon pure vanilla extract
¼ teaspoon baking soda

1 Place a rack in the middle position of the oven. Preheat the oven to 200°F. Place the popped corn in a 13 × 9 × 3-inch or larger glass baking dish.

2 In a small, heavy saucepan, combine the butter, brown sugar, corn syrup, and salt over medium heat. Bring to a boil, reduce the heat to low, and simmer about 3 minutes, stirring occasionally. Remove the caramel from the heat and stir in the vanilla and baking soda until foamy. Pour the caramel evenly over the popcorn.

3 Bake 45 minutes, stirring every 15 minutes. Remove the dish from the oven and transfer the popcorn to a sheet of waxed paper to cool thoroughly. Store, tightly covered, for up to 2 days.

Popcorn Balls

MAKES 6 SERVINGS

Popcorn balls are a relatively healthy snack for kids if you don't load them up with too much caramel. Be sure to wait until the caramel is cool enough to handle or you could suffer severe burns. Handling them with clean protective gloves (the kind you wear to do dishes) is a good idea.

1 quart (5 cups) popped corn (start with ⅓ cup popcorn kernels)
½ cup (1 stick) unsalted butter or buttery spread, such as Earth Balance
⅔ cup packed light brown sugar
⅓ cup light corn syrup
¼ teaspoon salt
¼ teaspoon pure vanilla extract
¼ teaspoon baking soda

1 Place an oven rack in the middle position of the oven. Preheat the oven to 200°F. Place the popped corn in a glass baking dish that is at least 13 × 9 × 3 inches or larger.

2 In a small, heavy saucepan, combine the butter, brown sugar, corn syrup, and salt over medium heat. Bring to a boil, reduce the heat to low, and simmer about 3 minutes, stirring occasionally. Remove the caramel from the heat and stir in the vanilla and baking soda until the caramel is foamy. Pour the mixture evenly over the popcorn, tossing gently to coat.

3 Bake 45 minutes, stirring every 15 minutes. This thoroughly coats all of the popcorn and sets the caramel. Remove the dish from the oven and transfer the popcorn to a sheet of waxed paper to cool. When the mixture is still warm, but cool enough to handle safely, firmly press the popcorn into 3-inch balls (or balls of preferred size), wearing plastic gloves that are coated with cooking spray. Cool the balls completely on the waxed paper. Store, tightly covered, for up to 2 days.

NO-BAKE COOKIES

Bourbon Balls

MAKES 30 SERVINGS

This is my mother's recipe, adapted to be gluten-free, and she always made these powerful little balls during the holidays. If you prefer a non-alcoholic cookie, use orange juice instead.

4 or 5 gluten-free mild-flavored cookies (or enough to equal 1 cup) crushed, such as Pamela's Butter Shortbread or Pecan Shortbread, or homemade mild-flavored cookies of choice
¾ cup powdered sugar + ¼ cup for rolling
1 cup finely chopped pecans, toasted and cooled
2 tablespoons unsweetened cocoa powder (Dutch-process or natural)
1 tablespoon light corn syrup
2 tablespoons bourbon or orange juice

1 In a food processor, process the cookies, ¾ cup of the powdered sugar, pecans, and cocoa until the cookies and nuts are finely ground.

2 Add the corn syrup and bourbon and pulse until the mixture is crumbly. Remove the mixture from the food processor, press it into a flat disk, wrap tightly, and chill 1 hour.

3 With lightly oiled hands, compress a tablespoon of dough into a little ball, roll it in the remaining ¼ cup of powdered sugar, and place on a sheet of wax paper. Store, tightly covered, for up to 2 days or in the freezer for up to 1 month. At serving time, roll in powdered sugar again and serve in mini-muffin paper liners.

Chocolate Mocha Balls

MAKES 16 SERVINGS

Keep these on hand in your freezer during the holidays and you'll always have a quick dessert for unexpected guests. They're especially cute when served in foil or paper candy liners. If you prefer a nonalcoholic version you may use cold brewed coffee instead of the liqueur.

1 package (9 cookies) Pamela's Dark Chocolate, Chocolate Chunk Cookies
1 teaspoon instant espresso powder
1 tablespoon coffee-flavored liqueur, such as Kahlua, or strong, cold brewed coffee
¼ cup (1 stick) unsalted butter or buttery spread, such as Earth Balance, at room temperature
2 tablespoons unsweetened cocoa powder (Dutch-process or natural)

1 In a food processor, process the cookies and espresso powder until the cookies are very finely ground. You will have almost 2 cups of cookie crumbs. Add the liqueur and butter and process until the mixture forms a ball or clumps. Shape the mixture into a flat disk, wrap tightly, and chill 2 hours.

2 Compress a tablespoon of dough into a ball, roll in the cocoa, and place on a foil-lined baking sheet. Chill 1 hour. Serve in foil or paper candy liners. Store, tightly covered, for up to 2 days or in the freezer for up to 1 month.

Dark Chocolate Truffles

MAKES 18 SERVINGS

These chocolate bites are luxuriously rich and delicious. Because truffles are prone to melting, keep these little gems cool.

4 ounces gluten-free semisweet chocolate, such as Scharffen Berger or Tropical Source

3 ounces gluten-free bittersweet chocolate, such as Scharffen Berger or Tropical Source

⅓ cup powdered sugar

⅓ cup heavy cream or soy or almond milk

1 tablespoon almond liqueur, such as Amaretto, or hazelnut liqueur, such as Frangelico (optional)

2 tablespoons unsweetened cocoa powder (Dutch-process or alkali preferred)

1 Line a 13 × 9-inch baking sheet with wax paper and set aside.

2 In a food processor, combine chocolates and powdered sugar and process until chocolate is finely chopped.

3 In a medium saucepan, heat the cream over medium heat just until it starts to simmer. With the food processor on, pour the hot cream mixture through lid and process until the mixture is smooth. Add liqueur (if using). Scrape mixture onto pan and press down with spatula to an equal thickness. Chill 2 hours.

4 Working quickly, cut the chocolate into 18 equal-sized pieces. With your hands, quickly roll each piece into a ball and put it on a plate. Chill 15 minutes.

5 Remove the truffles from the refrigerator and quickly dredge 3 balls at a time in the cocoa powder. Place each ball in a mini-foil or paper candy liner and refrigerate in an airtight container. Bring to room temperature just before serving.

White Chocolate–Apricot-Almond Balls

MAKES 24 SERVINGS

Serve these dainty little cookie balls during the holidays or at dinner parties in little foil or paper candy liners. Their small size makes them ideal for those who just want a little something sweet, not an entire dessert.

1 cup whole almonds

⅔ cup powdered sugar

2 cups (about 12 ounces) dried apricots

2 tablespoons light or dark rum or orange juice

2 teaspoons grated orange zest

1 teaspoon pure vanilla extract

1 bar (3.5 ounces) gluten-free white chocolate bar, such as Organica, chopped or broken in ¼-inch chunks

1 In a food processor, process the almonds and powdered sugar until the almonds are very finely ground. Add the apricots and pulse until the apricots are very finely chopped.

2 Add the rum, orange zest, vanilla, and white chocolate and pulse until the mixture is just blended. With lightly oiled hands, compress the dough into 24 balls, each 1 inch in diameter. Refrigerate. Serve in mini-muffin paper liners. Store, tightly covered, for up to 2 days or in the freezer for up to 1 month.

Canadian Cookies

MAKES 12 COOKIES

For reasons I never fully understood, my grandmother referred to these cookies as "Canadian Cookies." They were always piled high in a green glass dish in the little hutch in her dining room, waiting for us. This recipe is from a dog-eared recipe card, written in my mother's handwriting, which I've cherished all these years. I made only one change: To make the soy flakes resemble quick-cooking oats ordinarily used in this recipe, and to add stickiness, I give the soy flakes a whirl in a food processor along with ¼ teaspoon of xanthan gum. You can also use gluten-free oats if your physician approves.

1½ cups rolled soy flakes* or gluten-free rolled oats,**†
¼ teaspoon xanthan gum
1 cup sugar
¼ cup (½ stick) unsalted butter or buttery spread, such as Earth Balance
¼ cup 1% milk (cow's, rice, soy, potato, or nut)
½ cup sweetened coconut flakes
3 tablespoons unsweetened cocoa powder (not Dutch-process)
⅛ teaspoon salt
½ teaspoon pure vanilla extract

1 Line a 13 × 9-inch baking sheet with wax paper; set aside. In a food processor, whirl the soy flakes and xanthan gum a few times to slightly crush them so they more closely resemble quick-cooking oats; set aside.

2 In a medium heavy saucepan, combine the sugar, butter, and milk over medium-high heat. Bring to a boil, reduce the heat to medium, and boil 1 minute.

3 Remove the pan from the heat. Working quickly, stir in the soy flake mixture, coconut, cocoa, salt, and vanilla until thoroughly combined.

4 Drop by tablespoons on the wax paper. Cool at room temperature. Store in an airtight container for up 2 days.

Available at natural food stores.

**Available at www.bobsredmill.com, www. creamhillestates.com, www.giftsofnature.net, www. glutenfreeoats.com, and www.onlyoats.com.*

†Check with your physician before using gluten-free oats.

Peanut Butter Balls
MAKES 36 SERVINGS

The beauty of this cookie is that it doesn't require baking, which is probably one of the reasons I found it in my mother's recipe box. Like me, she appreciated a quick dessert that didn't require turning on the oven. I have modified her recipe somewhat to include more contemporary ingredients, but it is very similar to her version.

¼ cup crunchy peanut butter
⅓ cup honey
1 teaspoon pure vanilla extract
1 cup gluten-free rolled oats*† or natural raw coconut
½ cup cornstarch
2 tablespoons finely chopped peanuts
2 tablespoons ground flax meal
¼ teaspoon xanthan gum
¼ teaspoon salt
2 tablespoons powdered sugar (or enough to roll 36 balls)

1 Place the peanut butter, honey, and vanilla in a food processor and pulse a few times to blend. Add the oats, cornstarch, peanuts, flax, xanthan gum, and salt and process until the ingredients are well blended. Scrape down the sides of the bowl and process again.

2 With wet or lightly oiled hands, shape the dough into 24 balls, each 1 inch in diameter, and place on a sheet of wax paper to firm up. Roll in powdered sugar. Store, tightly covered, up to 2 days.

Available at www.bobsredmill.com, www.creamhillestates. com, www.giftsofnature.net, www.glutenfreeoats.com, and www.onlyoats.com.

†Check with your physician before using gluten-free oats.

SHAPED, CUT-OUT, AND ROLLED COOKIES

Holiday Cut-Out Cookies

MAKES ABOUT 24 SERVINGS (DEPENDING ON CUT-OUT SHAPES AND SIZES)

This recipe makes a thin, crisp cookie, suitable for cut-out shapes that kids can decorate or frost. You can also vary the extracts, using more or less—or use a combination of flavors such as almond, anise, lemon, peppermint, or vanilla—to suit your tastes. Read labels of decorations carefully to identify any gluten. If you don't plan to decorate the cookies and prefer a plumper cookie, bake them at 375°F just until the edges start to brown.

2¼ cups Carol's Sorghum Blend (page x)

1 teaspoon xanthan gum

½ teaspoon baking powder

½ teaspoon salt

½ cup (1 stick) unsalted butter or buttery spread, such as Earth Balance, at room temperature and cut into tablespoons

1 cup granulated sugar

1 tablespoon packed light brown sugar

1 large egg

1 teaspoon pure vanilla extract

1 teaspoon almond extract

White rice flour for dusting

1 In a large mixing bowl, whisk together the sorghum blend, xanthan gum, baking powder, and salt. With the mixer on low speed, beat in the butter pieces until smooth. Beat in the granulated sugar, brown sugar, egg, vanilla, and almond

TIPS FOR MAKING CUT-OUT COOKIES

1 To avoid having the batter stick to cookie sheets, use silicone baking liners (such as Silpat) or parchment paper.

2 Cookies will brown much faster on a nonstick (gray, not black) cookie sheet than they will on a light-colored shiny cookie sheet. For cookies that brown too quickly, try using the light-colored shiny cookie sheets rather than the gray nonstick type. Lining the sheet with parchment paper will also help reduce excessive browning. Or, try insulated baking sheets to assure even baking.

3 Use metal cookie cutters instead of plastic ones to make sharper cuts.

4 If the chilled dough is too stiff, leave it at room temperature 15 to 20 minutes, or knead dough with hands to make it more pliable. If the dough is too soft after rolling, chill or freeze it until firm, then cut into desired shapes. Do not roll dough thinner than ¼ inch.

5 If you're having trouble transferring cut-out cookies to the baking sheet, roll the dough onto parchment paper or nonstick liners, cut out desired shapes, remove scraps of dough (leaving cut-out cookies on paper) and transfer paper or liner, cookies and all, to baking sheet.

6 Chill shaped cookies 30 minutes before baking.

extract until well-blended. Remove the dough from the mixing bowl and knead it with your hands until it is very smooth. Divide the dough in half and pat each half into a flat 1-inch disk. Wrap each disk tightly and refrigerate 1 hour.

2 Place a rack in the middle of the oven. Preheat the oven to 375°F. Line a 15 × 10-inch baking sheet (not nonstick) ready and line with parchment paper and have it ready.

3 Put half of the chilled dough on a 15-inch square piece of parchment paper that is dusted with white rice flour. Cut a piece of plastic wrap the same size as the parchment paper, lay it on top of the dough, sprinkle it with white rice flour, and roll the dough to ¼-inch thickness. Remove the plastic wrap and cut out the desired shapes, reserving the scraps. Arrange the cookies 1 inch apart on the baking sheet. Cut the second half of the dough into shapes. Reroll the scraps from both halves, cut more cookies, and arrange on the baking sheet. If your sheet won't hold all of the shapes, bake two batches.

4 Bake 10 to 15 minutes, rotating the sheet halfway through baking. Cool the cookies on the baking sheet on a wire rack 2 minutes. Remove the cookies from the baking sheet and cool completely on the wire rack. Bake the second half of the cookies and cool in the same manner. Store undecorated cookies, tightly covered, for up to 2 days or in the freezer for up to 1 month.

5 Decorate as desired with frosting, sprinkles, coconut, raisins, chocolate chips, and so on.

Snickerdoodles

MAKES 24 SERVINGS

Snickerdoodles are sugar cookies rolled in sugar and cinnamon. The origin of this cookie's name is unclear, but one theory claims they are a Dutch creation named after St. Nicholas. This is adapted from my mother-in-law's recipe, which was always served during the holidays.

2 cups Carol's Sorghum Blend (page x)
1 teaspoon xanthan gum
½ teaspoon baking powder
½ teaspoon salt
½ cup (1 stick) unsalted butter or buttery spread, such as Earth Balance, at room temperature and cut into tablespoons
1 cup granulated sugar + 3 tablespoons for rolling
1 tablespoon packed light brown sugar
1 large egg
1 teaspoon pure vanilla extract
1 teaspoon almond extract
¼ teaspoon ground cinnamon

1 In a large mixing bowl, whisk together the sorghum blend, xanthan gum, baking powder, and salt. With the mixer on low speed, beat in the butter, a tablespoon at a time, until smooth. Beat in 1 cup of the granulated sugar, brown sugar, egg, vanilla, and almond extract until well-blended. Remove the dough from the mixing bowl and knead it with your hands until it is very smooth. Divide the dough in half and pat each half into a flat disk. Wrap each disk tightly and refrigerate 1 hour.

2 Place a rack in the lower-middle position and another in the upper-middle position of the oven. Preheat the oven to 375°F. Line two 15 × 10-inch baking sheets (not nonstick) with parchment paper to fit the baking sheet.

3 Combine the remaining 3 tablespoons sugar with the cinnamon in a shallow bowl. Working with 1 disk at a time, shape the dough into 12 walnut-sized balls and roll each ball in the cinnamon-sugar mixture. Place the balls 2-inches apart on the baking sheet. Repeat with the remaining disk on the remaining sheet. Place one sheet on the lower-middle rack and another on the upper-middle rack of the oven.

4 Bake 12 to 15 minutes, rotating the baking sheets between racks halfway through baking, or until the cookies are golden brown around the edges. Cool the cookies 2 to 3 minutes on the baking sheet, then transfer them to a wire rack to cool completely. Store, tightly covered, for up to 2 days or in the freezer for up to 1 month.

Springerle Cookies

MAKES 18 SERVINGS

These are white, anise-flavored cookies tradition-ally served at Christmas in Austria and Bavaria. They are crisp and great for dunking in coffee—or tea or hot chocolate, too. They are rolled with a special wooden rolling pin with etched designs that transfer to the dough. The dough has to chill before it's rolled and then it dries overnight, so plan ahead to leave enough time. Springerle rolling pins are available at specialty shops and kitchen catalogs.

2¼ cups Carol's Sorghum Blend (page x)
½ pound powdered sugar
½ teaspoon baking powder
¼ teaspoon xanthan gum
¼ teaspoon salt
2 large eggs
1 tablespoon unsalted butter or buttery spread, such as Earth Balance, at room temperature
2 teaspoons grated lemon zest
1 teaspoon anise extract
½ teaspoon pure vanilla extract

1 In a small bowl, whisk together the sorghum blend, powdered sugar, baking powder, xanthan gum, and salt; set aside.

2 In a medium bowl, beat the eggs and butter with an electric mixer on medium speed until smooth, about 30 seconds. Beat in the lemon zest, anise extract, and vanilla. With the mixer on low speed, gradually beat in the flour mixture until blended. Knead the dough with your hands until it is soft and smooth. Divide the dough into two balls, flatten to two 1-inch disks, wrap tightly, and chill two hours.

3 Place one of the disks on a sheet of parchment paper. Top with a sheet of heavy-duty plastic wrap. With a regular rolling pin, roll the dough to ½-inch thick. Remove the plastic and then roll again with a springerle rolling pin to make designs on the dough, flattening it to ⅜-inch. Cut the frames apart at the borders. Repeat the process with the remaining disk of dough, rolled out on a second sheet of parchment paper. Cover the cookies with a tea towel (not a terry towel) and allow the cookies to stand overnight, resting on the parchment paper, so that they dry out and the design firms up.

4 Place a rack in the middle of the oven. Preheat the oven to 325°F. Transfer the parchment paper (with the dried cookie shapes on them) to two 15 × 10-inch baking sheets (not nonstick), 9 cookies per sheet. Place one sheet on the lower-middle rack and another on the upper-middle rack of the oven.

5 Bake 7 to 10 minutes, rotating the baking sheets between racks halfway through baking, or until the cookies look dry. Cool the cookies 10 minutes on the pan on a wire rack, then transfer them to the wire rack to cool completely. The cookies will be very crisp. To soften them, place in a tightly-covered container with a slice of fresh apple. The longer the cookies are stored, the more prominent the anise flavor. Store, tightly covered, for up to 2 days or in the freezer for up to 1 month.

Spritz Cookies

MAKES 24 SERVINGS

My mother-in-law always makes these delicate butter cookies during the holidays; they are a popular Swedish tradition. You will need a cookie press since these are traditionally piped onto the baking sheet in decorative shapes. This recipe tastes best when made with real butter, but the buttery spread listed below will also work. Just be sure that you do not use a diet or whipped buttery spread because they contain too much water for baking.

2½ cups Carol's Sorghum Blend (page x)

½ teaspoon xanthan gum

¼ teaspoon salt

½ cup (1 stick) unsalted butter or buttery spread, such as Earth Balance, at room temperature

¾ cup sugar

3 egg yolks

1 tablespoon 1% milk (cow's, rice, soy, potato, or nut)

1 teaspoon pure vanilla extract

½ teaspoon almond extract

1 Place a rack in the middle of the oven. Preheat the oven to 375°F. Have a 15 × 10-inch ungreased baking sheet (not nonstick) ready. Have your cookie press and plates ready. In a small bowl, whisk together the sorghum blend, xanthan gum, and salt until well blended; set aside.

2 In a medium bowl, beat the butter and sugar with an electric mixer on medium speed until well blended. Beat in the egg yolks, milk, vanilla, and almond extract. Reduce the speed to low and gradually beat in the flour mixture until the dough is smooth. Gather the dough into a ball and knead with it with your hands until it is smooth. It should be soft and pliable, not stiff and hard. Divide the dough into four balls; tightly wrap 3 of them so they don't dry out and place on the countertop. Do not refrigerate the dough.

3 Following the directions accompanying the cookie press, roll the ball of dough into a log and fill the cookie press. Press the cookies onto the baking sheet about 1 inch apart. If the dough is the right consistency, you will not need to exert force to get the dough onto the baking sheet. If the dough is too stiff, return all the dough to the mixing bowl and beat in another tablespoon of milk. If it too wet, add more sorghum blend, a tablespoon at a time.

4 Bake 10 to 12 minutes or just until the edges of the cookies turn golden. Do not overbake. With a very thin metal spatula, immediately transfer the cookies to a wire rack to cool completely. If you leave them on the cookie sheet too long, they will

be hard to remove. Store, tightly covered, for up to 2 days or in the freezer for up to 1 month.

Lemon-Anise Biscotti

MAKES 16 SERVINGS

The flavors of anise and lemon complement each other nicely, and the crisp cookies are perfect when dipped in a steaming cup of coffee or espresso, or in a glass of afternoon sherry. Biscotti are naturally crisp, but for added crisp, turn off the oven and leave the baking sheet inside, with the door closed, for an additional 10 to 15 minutes.

2 cups Carol's Sorghum Blend (page x)

1 cup sugar

¼ cup Expandex modified tapioca starch

1 tablespoon anise seed

1½ teaspoons xanthan gum

1 teaspoon baking powder

½ teaspoon salt

2 large eggs, at room temperature

¼ cup unsalted butter or buttery spread, such as Earth Balance, at room temperature

2 tablespoons grated lemon zest

2 teaspoons pure vanilla extract

1 Place a rack in the middle of the oven. Preheat the oven to 350°F. Line a 13 × 9-inch nonstick (gray, not black) baking sheet with parchment paper.

2 In a food processor, combine the sorghum blend, sugar, modified tapioca starch, anise seed, xanthan gum, baking powder, and salt. Pulse a few times until the ingredients are thoroughly blended.

3 Add the eggs, butter, lemon zest, and vanilla and pulse on and off about 20 times to moisten the dough, then process until the dough forms a ball. Break the dough into big clumps, and process until the dough forms a ball again.

4 Remove the dough from the food processor and knead it with your hands until smooth. On the baking sheet, shape the dough into a ball, divide the ball in half, and shape each half into a log, 12 inches long, 2 inches wide, and ½ inch thick. Wet your hands with water if the dough is sticky or shape the log with a wet spatula.

5 Bake 20 minutes, or until the dough cracks on top and begins to brown at the edges. Remove the baking sheet from the oven and cool the logs 10 minutes. Reduce the oven temperature to 325°F but leave the oven on.

6 With a sharp knife (an electric knife works especially well), cut each log diagonally into ¾-inch thick slices. Arrange the slices, cut side down, ½-inch apart on the baking sheet and return the sheet to the oven.

7 Bake 20 minutes, turning the cookies over, cut-side up, halfway during baking. Transfer the cookies to a wire rack for cooling. Store, tightly covered, for up to 2 days or in the freezer for up to 1 month.

Apricot-Almond Biscotti

MAKES 16 SERVINGS

Biscotti keep and travel well because they're crisp and don't get stale quickly. I often take them on trips to Europe or other places where there may not be gluten-free desserts on the menu, so I can have dessert with my coffee.

¼ cup whole or slivered almonds

2 cups Carol's Sorghum Blend (page x)

1 cup sugar

¼ cup Expandex modified tapioca starch

1½ teaspoons xanthan gum

1 teaspoon baking powder

½ teaspoon salt

2 large eggs, at room temperature

¼ cup unsalted butter or buttery spread, such as Earth Balance, at room temperature

2 tablespoons grated orange zest

2 teaspoons pure vanilla extract

½ teaspoon almond extract

½ cup chopped dried apricots

1 Place a rack in the middle of the oven. Preheat the oven to 350°F. Line a 13 × 9-inch nonstick (gray, not black) baking sheet with parchment paper.

2 In a food processor, process the almonds for 15 seconds to partially chop them, then add the sorghum blend, sugar, modified tapioca starch, xanthan gum, baking powder, and salt. Pulse a few times until the ingredients are thoroughly blended.

3 Add the eggs, butter, orange zest, vanilla, and almond extract, and pulse on and off about 20 times to moisten the dough, then process until the dough forms a ball. Break the dough into big clumps, add the dried apricots, and process until the dough forms a ball again.

4 Remove the dough from the food processor and knead it with your hands to make sure the almonds and apricots are evenly distributed throughout the dough. On the baking sheet, shape the dough into a ball, divide the ball in half, and shape each half into a log, 12 inches long, 2 inches wide, and ½ inch thick, and place on the baking sheet at least 3 inches apart. If the dough is sticky, wet your hands with water or use a wet spatula to shape the dough.

5 Bake 20 minutes, or until the dough cracks on top and begins to brown at the edges. Remove the baking sheet from the oven and cool the logs 10 minutes. Reduce the oven temperature to 300°F but leave the oven on.

6 With a sharp knife (an electric knife works especially well), cut each log diagonally into ¾-inch-thick slices. Arrange the slices, cut side down, ½ inch apart on the baking sheet and return the sheet to the oven.

7 Bake 20 minutes, turning the cookies over, cut-side up, halfway during baking. Transfer the cookies to a wire rack for cooling. Store, tightly covered, for up to 2 days or in the freezer for up to 1 month.

Chocolate-Cherry-Walnut Biscotti ⓥ

MAKES 24 SERVINGS

Serve these biscotti plain or drizzle White Chocolate Dip (page 431) across them for a decorative touch and added decadence. You can also make this a dark chocolate drizzle by substituting dark chocolate for the white chocolate.

1¾ or 2 cups Carol's Sorghum Blend (page x)
¾ cup packed light brown sugar
½ cup unsweetened Dutch-process cocoa powder
¼ cup Expandex modified tapioca starch
1½ teaspoons xanthan gum
1 teaspoon instant espresso powder (optional)
1 teaspoon baking powder
½ teaspoon salt
¼ cup unsalted butter or buttery spread, such as Earth Balance, at room temperature
¼ cup corn syrup
2 large eggs, at room temperature
¾ cup dried tart cherries
¼ cup finely chopped walnuts

1 Place a rack in the middle of the oven. Preheat the oven to 350°F. Line a 13 × 9-inch nonstick (gray, not black) baking sheet with parchment paper.

2 In a food processor, combine the sorghum blend, brown sugar, cocoa, modified tapioca starch, xanthan gum, espresso powder (if using), baking powder, and salt. Pulse a few times until the ingredients are thoroughly blended.

3 Add the butter, corn syrup, and eggs and pulse on and off about 20 times to moisten the dough, then process until the dough forms a ball. Break the dough into big clumps, add the cherries and walnuts and process until the dough forms a ball again.

4 Remove the dough from the food processor and knead it with your hands to make sure the cherries and walnuts are evenly distributed. On the baking sheet, shape the dough into a ball, divide it in half, and shape each half into a log, 12 inches long, 2 inches wide, and ½ inch thick. If the dough is sticky, wet your hands with water or use a wet spatula to shape the dough.

5 Bake 20 minutes, or until the dough cracks on top and is firm at the edges. Remove the baking sheet from the oven and cool the logs 10 minutes. Reduce the oven temperature to 300°F but leave the oven on.

6 With a sharp knife (an electric knife works especially well), cut each log diagonally into ¾-inch-thick slices. Arrange the slices, cut side down, ½ inch apart on the baking sheet and return the sheet to the oven.

7 Bake another 20 minutes. Transfer the biscotti to a wire rack for cooling. Store, tightly covered, for up to 2 days or in the freezer for up to 1 month.

White Chocolate–Dipped Pistachio-Cranberry Biscotti ⓥ

MAKES 16 SERVINGS

The green and red colors from the pistachios and dried cranberries, make this cookie a perfect dessert during the holidays. For a brighter look, substitute chopped candied red cherries. The decadent white chocolate dip is fabulous.

BISCOTTI
2 cups Carol's Sorghum Blend (page x)
1½ teaspoons xanthan gum
2 teaspoons baking powder
½ teaspoon salt
¾ cup packed light brown sugar
2 large eggs
¼ cup (½ stick) unsalted butter or buttery spread, such as Earth Balance, at room temperature
1 teaspoon pure vanilla extract
¾ cup shelled pistachios, chopped
¾ cup dried cranberries or chopped candied red cherries

DIP

½ cup gluten-free white chocolate, chopped, from a white chocolate bar, such as Organica

1 teaspoon unsalted butter or buttery spread, such as Earth Balance

1 Place a rack in the middle of the oven. Preheat the oven to 350°F. Line a 13 × 9-inch nonstick (gray, not black) baking sheet with parchment paper.

2 In a food processor, combine sorghum blend, xanthan gum, baking powder, salt, and brown sugar. Pulse until thoroughly mixed.

3 Add eggs, butter, and vanilla. Process until the dough forms a ball. Break the ball into several clumps and process until dough forms ball again.

4 Remove the dough from the food processor and massage the pistachios and cranberries into the dough by hand. Wet your hands with water if the dough is sticky. Divide the dough in half. On the baking sheet, shape each half into a log measuring 2 inches wide by 12 inches long by ½ inch thick.

5 Bake 20 minutes. Remove the baking sheet from the oven and cool the logs 10 minutes. Reduce the oven temperature to 300°F.

6 Place the logs on a cutting board. With an electric knife or sharp, serrated knife cut each log diagonally into ¾-inch slices. Place each slice on baking sheet, cut side down and return the sheet to the oven.

7 Bake another 20 minutes, turning the slices over, cut-side up, halfway through baking. Transfer the biscotti to a wire rack for cooling.

8 Make the dip: In a 1-quart saucepan, heat the chocolate and butter over low heat, stirring constantly, until melted. Dip each cookie halfway into the melted chocolate and place it on waxed paper to cool or refrigerate until chocolate is set. Bring to room temperature before serving. Store, tightly covered, for up to 2 days or in the freezer for up to 1 month.

Gingerbread People

MAKES ABOUT 16 SERVINGS (DEPEND-ING ON SIZE OF COOKIE CUTTER)

Kids and adults will enjoy decorating these delightful little gingerbread people. Using modified tapioca starch yields a crisp cookie. Be sure to press cookie cutters straight down on the dough, for best results.

½ cup (1 stick) unsalted butter or buttery spread, such as Earth Balance, at room temperature, but not melted

¾ cup packed light brown sugar

1 large egg

3 tablespoons molasses (not blackstrap)

1 teaspoon pure vanilla extract

2½ cups Carol's Sorghum Blend (page x)

2 tablespoons Expandex modified tapioca starch, or additional Carol's Sorghum Blend (page x)

1 teaspoon xanthan gum

1½ teaspoons ground ginger

1½ teaspoons ground cinnamon

½ teaspoon baking powder

½ teaspoon salt

¼ teaspoon ground nutmeg

¼ teaspoon ground cloves

1 Place a rack in the lower-middle position and another in the upper-middle position of the oven. Preheat the oven to 375°F. Line two 15 × 10-inch baking sheets (not nonstick) with parchment paper.

2 In a large mixing bowl, beat the butter and brown sugar with an electric mixer on low speed until smooth, about 30 seconds. Beat in the egg, molasses, vanilla, and almond extract. Gradually add the sorghum blend, modified tapioca starch, xanthan gum, ginger, cinnamon, baking powder, salt, nutmeg, and cloves and beat on low speed just until blended. Gather the dough into a ball and knead it with your hands until it is soft and pliable. Flatten it into a disk, wrap tightly, and chill 2 hours.

3 Divide the dough in half and place half in a food storage bag to prevent drying out. Position a 12 × 12-inch sheet of parchment paper on the countertop, dust it with white rice flour, and place half of the dough in the middle. Cover with a sheet of heavy-duty plastic wrap. With a rolling pin, roll the dough to a ¼-inch thick rectangle. Cut out 8 gingerbread people with a cookie cutter. (The number of cookies you can cut from this dough will vary with the size of your cookie cutter.) Transfer the cookies to the baking sheet. Repeat the process with the remaining half of the dough. You can re-roll the leftover scraps and cut more cookies. Place one sheet on the lower-middle rack and another on the upper-middle rack of the oven.

4 Bake 15 to 20 minutes, rotating the baking sheets between racks halfway through baking. Cool the cookies 2 to 3 minutes on the baking sheet, then transfer them to a wire rack to cool completely. Decorate as desired. Store, tightly covered, for up to 2 days or in the freezer for up to 1 month.

Pfeffernusse

MAKES 24 SERVINGS

This traditional German "peppernut" cookie is popular during the holidays. Don't be swayed by the long list of spices—including the black pepper; they give these cookies their unique flavor. Serve them with robust coffee.

½ cup (1 stick) unsalted butter or buttery spread, such as Earth Balance, at room temperature, but not melted
1 cup packed light brown sugar
1 large egg
1 teaspoon pure vanilla extract
2 cups Carol's Sorghum Blend (page x)
1½ teaspoons ground cinnamon
1 teaspoon xanthan gum
½ teaspoon instant coffee powder
½ teaspoon freshly ground black pepper
½ teaspoon anise seed
½ teaspoon baking powder
½ teaspoon salt
¼ teaspoon ground nutmeg
¼ teaspoon ground cloves
¼ teaspoon ground allspice
¼ cup powdered sugar, for rolling

1 Place a rack in the lower-middle position and another in the upper-middle position of the oven. Preheat the oven to 375°F. Line two 15 × 10-inch baking sheets (not nonstick) with parchment paper.

2 In a large mixing bowl, beat the butter and brown sugar with an electric mixer on low speed until smooth, about 30 seconds. Beat in the egg and vanilla. Gradually add the sorghum blend, cinnamon, xanthan gum, coffee, pepper, anise seed, baking powder, salt, nutmeg, cloves, and allspice and beat on low speed just until blended. Gather the dough into a ball and massage it with your hands until it is soft and supple. Flatten it into a dish, wrap tightly, and chill 1 hour.

3 With wet hands, shape the dough into 24 walnut-sized balls and place them 2 inches apart on the baking sheets, 12 per sheet. Place one sheet on the lower-middle rack and another on the upper-middle rack of the oven.

4 Bake 15 to 20 minutes, rotating the baking sheets between racks halfway through baking. Cool the cookies 2 to 3 minutes on the baking sheet. Roll in powdered sugar and then transfer them to a wire rack to cool. Roll again in more powdered sugar, if necessary, before serving. Store, tightly covered, for up to 2 days or in the freezer for up to 1 month.

Graham Crackers

MAKES 24 SERVINGS

Graham crackers are universally loved by children and adults and they are such a versatile cookie. They also make great crumb crusts for pies. Mesquite flour has a unique, cinnamonlike taste and gives these crackers a lovely golden color. You can also use all sorghum blend instead. Modified tapioca starch gives the crackers their characteristic snap. Instead of using a fork to make holes in the dough, make the traditional evenly-spaced perforations in the graham crackers with a docker, a rolling pin–like tool with protruding prongs.

1¼ cups Carol's Sorghum Blend (page x)
¼ cup mesquite flour, such as Casadefruta
2 tablespoons Expandex modified tapioca starch
½ teaspoon ground cinnamon
½ teaspoon xanthan gum
½ teaspoon salt
¼ teaspoon baking powder
⅛ teaspoon ground mace
⅛ teaspoon ground ginger
⅓ cup packed light brown sugar
1 tablespoon honey
1 tablespoon pure vanilla extract
¼ cup unsalted butter or buttery spread, such as Earth Balance, at room temperature
1 to 2 tablespoons water, if needed

1 Place all the ingredients in a food processor and process until the mixture forms a ball or large clumps. (Or mix the ingredients with an electric mixer on low speed for 2 minutes, or until well blended.) Add a tablespoon of water to the mixture if necessary. Gather the dough into your hands and knead it into a soft ball. Divide the dough into two 1-inch-thick disks, wrap tightly, and refrigerate 1 hour.

2 Place a rack in the middle of the oven. Preheat the oven to 325°F. Have two 15 × 10-inch rimmed baking sheets ready. Lay a 10 × 10-inch sheet of parchment paper on a flat surface. Place one of the disks of dough on the parchment paper and top with a sheet of heavy-duty plastic wrap. Using a rolling pin, roll the dough to an 8-inch square, about ⅛-inch thick. Transfer the dough, still between the parchment paper and plastic wrap, to one of the baking sheets, with the parchment side down. Remove the plastic wrap. Using a sharp knife, cut the dough into 2¼-inch squares and prick them lightly with a fork. (Or use the docker.) Repeat with the remaining disk of dough, placing it on the second baking sheet.

3 Bake the first sheet 15 to 20 minutes or until the crackers are browned; watch carefully since the crackers can burn easily. Remove the crackers from the oven, cut the lines again with a sharp knife and cool 2 minutes on the baking sheet. Transfer the parchment paper (with the crackers still on it) to a wire rack and cool completely. Repeat with the second sheet. The crackers become crisp as they cool. Since it is hard to roll the dough to perfectly shaped 8-inch squares, freeze the cut-away portions of the crackers for use in pie crusts. Store, tightly covered, for up to 2 days or in the freezer for up to 1 month.

Chocolate Sandwich Cookies with Orange Filling ⓥ

MAKES 18 SERVINGS

Chocolate and orange complement one another and are one of my favorite flavor combinations, so this unique little sandwich cookie is very popular at my house. You can use this chocolate cookie recipe for cookie-crumb pie crusts as well.

COOKIES

¼ cup (½ stick) unsalted butter or buttery spread, such as Earth Balance, at room temperature, but not melted

½ cup packed light brown sugar

1 large egg

1 tablespoon grated orange zest

1 teaspoon pure vanilla extract

1½ cups Carol's Sorghum Blend (page x)

½ cup unsweetened cocoa powder (not Dutch-process or alkali)

1 teaspoon xanthan gum

½ teaspoon salt

¼ teaspoon baking powder

Pinch ground cloves

FILLING

¼ cup (½ stick) unsalted butter or buttery spread, such as Earth Balance, at room temperature

1 cup powdered sugar

Grated zest of half an orange

Pinch salt

1 Make the cookies: In a large mixing bowl, beat the butter, brown sugar, egg, orange zest, and vanilla with an electric mixer on low speed until smooth, about 30 seconds.

2 In a small bowl, whisk together the sorghum blend, cocoa, xanthan gum, salt, baking powder, and cloves. With the mixer on low speed, gradually beat in the flour mixture just until the sorghum blend is no longer visible. The dough will look like little clumps. Gather the dough with your hands into a rough ball and knead it for a few minutes until it is soft and pliable. Shape it into two 1-inch thick disks, wrap tightly, and chill 1 hour.

3 Place a rack in the lower-middle position and another in the upper-middle position of the oven. Preheat the oven to 325°F. Line two 15 × 10-inch baking sheets (not nonstick) with parchment paper.

4 Roll out one of the disks between two sheets of plastic wrap to a thickness of ⅛ to ¼ inch. Use a 1¾-inch round cookie cutter to cut 12 cookies and place them on one of the baking sheets at least 1½ inches apart. Repeat the process with the other disk of dough and place the 12 cookies on the second baking sheet. Roll the scraps of cookie dough and cut another 6 cookies from each disk for a total of 12 additional cookies; set aside until the first batch of cookies is baked. Place one sheet on the lower-middle rack and another on the upper-middle rack of the oven.

5 Bake 15 to 20 minutes or until the cookies look dry on top, rotating the baking sheets between racks halfway through baking. Cool the cookies 2 to 3 minutes on the baking sheet and then transfer them to a wire rack to cool. Cool the baking sheet another 10 minutes and then bake the remaining 12 cookies. Cool as directed. At this point, you can store the cookies, tightly covered, for up to 2 days or in the freezer for up to 1 month.

6 Make the filling: In a medium bowl, beat the butter, powdered sugar, orange zest, and salt until smooth and place about 1 teaspoon on a cookie. Top with another cookie and press the cookies together to form 18 sandwiches. Refrigerate to firm up the filling; let stand at room temperature 15 minutes before serving. Filled cookies do not freeze well.

Hamantaschen

MAKES 18 SERVINGS

Hamantaschen are triangular-shaped pastry cookies with poppy seed, prune, raspberry, or apricot filling. They are a traditional Eastern European treat and often served for the Jewish holiday Purim.

½ cup (1 stick) unsalted butter or buttery spread, such as Earth Balance, at room temperature, but not melted
1 cup granulated sugar
1 tablespoon packed light brown sugar
1 large egg
1 tablespoon fresh orange juice
2 teaspoons grated orange zest
1 teaspoon pure vanilla extract
2 cups Carol's Sorghum Blend (page x)
1 teaspoon xanthan gum
¼ teaspoon baking soda
¼ teaspoon salt
½ cup raspberry or apricot preserves
White rice flour for dusting

1 In a large mixing bowl, beat the butter, granulated sugar, and brown sugar with an electric mixer on low speed until very smooth, about 1 minute. Beat in the egg, orange juice, orange zest, and vanilla until smooth.

2 In a small bowl, whisk together the sorghum blend, xanthan gum, baking soda, and salt until blended and then gradually beat into the butter mixture on low speed until well blended. Gather the dough into a ball and knead it with your hands until soft and smooth. Flatten the dough into two disks, wrap each tightly in plastic wrap, and chill at least 3 hours or up to two days.

3 Place a rack in the middle of the oven. Preheat the oven to 375°F. Line a 15 × 10-inch baking sheet (not nonstick) with parchment paper. Unwrap one of the disks of dough (keep remaining disk chilled) and knead with your hands until it pliable. Roll the disk of dough to a ¼-inch thickness between two sheets of plastic wrap that are dusted with white rice flour. A wet paper towel beneath the plastic wrap helps prevent slippage. With a 3-inch cutter, cut out as many rounds as possible. Transfer rounds with a metal spatula to the baking sheet, arranging about ½ inch apart. Reroll the scraps and cut out more rounds.

4 With a pastry brush, brush a light coating of water around the edge of each round before putting a teaspoon of raspberry preserves in the center. This makes the dough stick together better. Pinch the edges very tightly together in 3 places to form a triangle, yet leave the preserves exposed. Make sure the sides of the triangle are taut enough to prevent the preserves from leaking as the cookies bake.

5 Bake 12 to 15 minutes, or until the cookies are lightly browned. Cool the cookies on the baking sheet 5 minutes and transfer to wire racks to cool completely. Repeat the process with the remaining disk of dough. Store, tightly covered, for up to 2 days or in the freezer for up to 1 month.

Rugelach V

MAKES 32 SERVINGS

Rugelach are little rolled pastries filled with any number of fillings such as cinnamon-sugar or various types of jam or preserves.

PASTRY

2¼ cups Carol's Sorghum Blend (page x)
1 cup granulated sugar
1 tablespoon packed light brown sugar
1 teaspoon xanthan gum
½ teaspoon baking powder
½ teaspoon salt
⅛ teaspoon baking soda
½ cup (1 stick) unsalted butter or buttery spread, such as Earth Balance, at room temperature, and cut into tablespoons
1 large egg
1 teaspoon pure vanilla extract
1 teaspoon almond extract
White rice flour for rolling

FILLING

½ cup apricot or raspberry preserves

½ cup granulated sugar mixed with 1 teaspoon ground cinnamon

1 large egg, beaten, for egg wash

1 tablespoon granulated sugar, for sprinkling on cookies

1 Make the pastry: In a food processor, combine sorghum blend, granulated sugar, brown sugar, xanthan gum, baking powder, salt, and baking soda. Add the butter, egg, vanilla extract, and almond extract, and process until the mixture forms a ball or several clumps. Remove dough from food processor and knead with your hands until it is soft and pliable. Flatten the dough into fourths, wrap each fourth tightly in plastic, and refrigerate 1 hour.

2 Place a rack in the middle of the oven. Preheat oven to 350°F. Line a 15 × 10-inch baking sheet (not nonstick) with parchment paper. Lay a moistened paper towel on flat surface, such as a countertop. Cut a 10 × 10-inch piece of heavy-duty plastic wrap. Place one sheet directly on the dampened paper towel.

3 Unwrap one quarter of dough (leaving remaining three quarters tightly covered on countertop) and work with hands until dough is no longer cool. Flatten into disk and place on plastic wrap that is dusted with white rice flour. Cut another 10 × 10-inch piece of plastic wrap and place on disk. With rolling pin, roll into a 9-inch circle, taking care to roll from the inside of the circle out to the edge and working in a clockwise fashion to keep the dough at an even thickness. Remove top sheet of plastic wrap.

4 Make the filling: Spread dough evenly with 2 tablespoons of the preserves and 2 tablespoons of the cinnamon sugar. Cut the circle into 8 equal wedges. Use a flat metal spatula or knife to gently lift the first wedge away from the circle to make it easier to roll. Starting from the wide end, roll each wedge up. Place the cookies, points tucked under, on prepared baking sheet. Repeat with remaining

3 quarters of dough. Brush cookies with beaten egg. Sprinkle with granulated sugar.

5 Bake 15 to 20 minutes or until lightly browned. Remove from oven, cool cookies on pan 5 minutes, then transfer them to a wire rack to cool completely. Store, tightly covered, for up to 2 days or in the freezer for up to 1 month.

Ladyfingers

MAKES 18 SERVINGS

In Italy, these delicacies are called savioardi. *They are the basis for the wonderful Italian dessert Tiramisu (page 651) and can also be used in trifles. They freeze nicely so they can be made ahead.*

2 large eggs, at room temperature

⅓ cup sugar

1 teaspoon pure vanilla extract

⅛ teaspoon salt

1 cup potato starch

¼ cup Carol's Sorghum Blend (page x)

1 teaspoon Expandex modified tapioca starch, or Carol's Sorghum Blend (page x)

⅛ teaspoon baking soda

⅛ teaspoon xanthan gum

1 Place a rack in the middle of the oven. Preheat the oven to 400°F. Generously grease two 15 × 10-inch baking sheets (not nonstick) or line with parchment paper.

2 Separate the eggs; set aside the whites. Beat the egg yolks with half of the sugar and the vanilla until the mixture is pale yellow, about 5 minutes.

3 Beat the egg whites with the salt until stiff peaks form. Gently fold the egg whites into the egg yolks. In a small bowl, whisk together the potato starch, sorghum blend, modified tapioca starch, baking soda, and xanthan gum; gently fold it into the egg mixture, one-fourth at a time. Put the dough into a pastry bag fitted with a ½-inch tip, or a quart-size heavy-duty food storage bag with a ½-inch corner cut off.

4 Squeeze the dough out of the bag onto the sheet in 3 × 1-inch logs, at least 2 inches apart, 9 per sheet. For best results, hold the bag of dough upright as you squeeze, rather than at an angle. Also, hold the bag with the corners perpendicular to the baking sheet, rather than horizontal, for a better-shaped cookie. Use a wet fingertip to shape the cookies, if necessary.

5 Bake 10 to 12 minutes or until the cookies are golden brown around the edges and firm. Cool the cookies 2 minutes on the sheet on a wire rack. Transfer the cookies to finish cooling on the wire rack. Dust with powdered sugar. Store, tightly covered, for up to 2 days or in the freezer for up to 1 month. After freezing, roll again in powdered sugar just before serving.

*Dr. Schär makes savioardi and may be ordered from www.schaer.com.

Madeleines

MAKES 12 SERVINGS

Madeleines are shell-shaped and have a texture similar to delicate little cakes. I use a nonstick madeleine pan for this recipe, and the oven temperature is geared to this type of pan. If you wish to make more cookies, cool the pan, wipe it clean, and grease it again before you whip up the second batch.

¾ cup Carol's Sorghum Blend (page x)
1 tablespoon Expandex modified tapioca starch
½ teaspoon baking powder
¼ teaspoon xanthan gum
⅛ teaspoon salt
1 large egg, at room temperature
6 tablespoons granulated sugar
1 tablespoon packed light brown sugar
1 tablespoon grated lemon zest
¼ cup (½ stick) unsalted butter or buttery spread, such as Earth Balance, at room temperature, melted
2 tablespoons powdered sugar, for dusting

1 Place a rack in the middle of the oven. Preheat the oven to 375°F. Generously grease or butter a madeleine pan.

2 In a small bowl, sift together the sorghum blend, modified tapioca starch, baking powder, xanthan gum, and salt; set aside.

3 In a medium mixing bowl, beat the egg, granulated sugar, brown sugar, and lemon zest with an electric mixer on low speed until the eggs are a pale yellow and the mixture has doubled in volume, 3 to 5 minutes.

4 Gently fold the flour mixture into the eggs and then fold in the lemon zest and butter. Spoon a scant tablespoon of batter into each mold, filling it about two-thirds full.

5 Bake 5 minutes, then reduce the heat to 350°F and bake 2 to 3 minutes more or until the madeleines are golden brown around the edges and a toothpick inserted into the centers comes out clean. Invert the madeleines onto a wire rack and cool 10 minutes. Dust with powdered sugar. Store, tightly covered, for up to 2 days or in the freezer for up to 1 month.

Mexican Wedding Cakes V

MAKES 30 SERVINGS

You'll find these little round cookies in any Mexican or Southwestern cookbook. They're very easy to make; in fact, you can get the kids to help you roll the dough into little balls.

¾ cup unsalted butter or buttery spread, such as Earth Balance, at room temperature
½ cup powdered sugar + ¼ cup for rolling
1 teaspoon pure vanilla extract
2 cups Carol's Sorghum Blend (page x)
1½ teaspoons xanthan gum
½ teaspoon salt
½ cup very finely chopped toasted almonds

1 In a food processor, place the butter, ½ cup powdered sugar, and vanilla and process until well blended. Add the sorghum blend, xanthan gum, salt, and almonds and process just until the mixture forms a ball or several clumps on one side. Remove the dough from the food processor and knead it with your hands until it is smooth. Shape the dough into a 1-inch disk, wrap tightly, and refrigerate at least 3 hours.

2 Place a rack in the middle of the oven. Preheat the oven to 375°F. Line a 15 × 10-inch baking sheet (not nonstick) with parchment paper. (An insulated cookie sheet works very well for this cookie.) Shape the dough into 1-inch balls and place on the baking sheet at least 1½ inches apart.

3 Bake 15 to 20 minutes or until the cookies are set. Cool the cookies 5 minutes on the pan on a wire rack. While the cookies are still warm, roll them in powdered sugar. Once cookies have completely cooled, roll again in powdered sugar. Store, tightly covered, for up to 2 days or in the freezer for up to 1 month. After freezing, roll again in powdered sugar just before serving.

Swedish Tea Cakes

MAKES 30 SERVINGS

These classic little holiday gems are so simple and are best made with fresh, quality ingredients. Use butter, if possible, for its wonderful flavor, but a buttery spread will work for those who are dairy-sensitive. Be sure to avoid using whipped or diet spreads because they contain too much water for baking.

¾ cup unsalted butter or buttery spread, such as Earth Balance, at room temperature
¼ cup granulated sugar
½ cup powdered sugar + ¼ cup for rolling
2 teaspoons pure vanilla extract
2 cups Carol's Sorghum Blend (page x)
1½ teaspoons xanthan gum
½ teaspoon salt
½ cup finely chopped toasted pecans

1 In a food processor, place the butter, granulated sugar, ½ cup powdered sugar, and vanilla and process until just blended. Add the sorghum blend, xanthan gum, salt, and pecans and process just until the dough forms a ball or several clumps on one side of the bowl. Remove the dough from the food processor and knead it with your hands until it is smooth.

2 Shape the dough into a 1-inch disk, wrap tightly, and refrigerate at least 3 hours.

3 Place a rack in the middle of the oven. Preheat the oven to 375°F. Line a 15 × 10-inch baking sheet (not nonstick) with parchment paper. (An insulated cookie sheet will work very well.) Shape the dough into 1-inch balls and place on the baking sheet at least 1½ inches apart.

4 Bake 15 to 20 minutes or until the cookies are set. Cool the cookies 5 minutes on the pan. While cookies are still warm, roll in powdered sugar. Once cookies have completely cooled, roll again in powdered sugar. Store, tightly covered, for up to 2 days, or in the freezer for up to 1 month. After freezing, roll again in powdered sugar just before serving.

Pizzelles

MAKES ABOUT 36 SERVINGS

Pizzelles are thin, crisp wafer cookies that are baked on a special pizzelle iron and then dusted with powdered sugar. Italian versions use anise flavor, but you can use vanilla if you prefer. Pizzelle irons differ, so follow the baking directions provided by the manufacturer. You may need to experiment with the amount of batter and baking time, depending on the iron.

1¾ cups Carol's Sorghum Blend (page x)

2 teaspoons baking powder

¼ teaspoon xanthan gum

⅛ teaspoon salt

3 large eggs

¾ cup granulated sugar

¼ cup (½ stick) unsalted butter or buttery spread, such as Earth Balance, melted

1 teaspoon pure vanilla extract or anise extract, or to taste

Canola oil for the pizzelle iron

¼ cup powdered sugar, for dusting

1 In a small bowl, sift together the sorghum blend, baking powder, xanthan gum, and salt; set aside.

2 In a medium bowl, beat the eggs and granulated sugar with an electric mixer on medium speed until thick and pale yellow, about 30 seconds. On low speed, beat in the melted butter and vanilla and then gradually beat in the flour mixture just until the batter is smooth.

3 Heat the pizzelle iron and brush with oil. Drop 1 tablespoon of batter onto each circle on the iron. (You may need to experiment with the amount of batter and baking time for your iron.)

4 Bake 5 to 20 seconds, or until steam no longer comes out of the iron. Carefully remove cookies from the iron and cool completely on a wire rack before storing in an airtight container. Just before serving, dust the cookies lightly with powdered sugar.

Ice Cream Cones

MAKES 36 SERVINGS

Until I developed this recipe, I hadn't eaten ice cream cones for about 20 years—especially waffle cones. I was amazed at how easy it is to make them; the kids will love them.

I use a pizzelle iron to make these cones, since it imprints a beautiful pattern on the cookie. Then while still warm from the oven, the cookie is quickly wrapped around a wooden cone and allowed to harden. They are better when made with real butter, but you may use the buttery spread listed below.

1¾ cups Carol's Sorghum Blend (page x)

2 teaspoons baking powder

¼ teaspoon xanthan gum

⅛ teaspoon salt

3 large eggs

¾ cup sugar

¼ cup (½ stick) unsalted butter or buttery spread, such as Earth Balance, melted

1 teaspoon pure vanilla extract or to taste

Canola oil for the pizzelle iron

Gluten-free ice cream, sherbet, frozen yogurt, or sorbet of choice

1 Prepare cookies following Steps 1 and 2 of Pizelles recipe (page 438).

2 Heat the pizzelle iron and brush with oil. Drop 1 tablespoon of batter onto each circle on the iron, slightly off-center toward the back of the iron.

3 Bake 5 to 20 seconds, or until steam no longer comes out of the iron. Baking times will vary by machine; mine took only 5 seconds to fully cook the cookies.

4 Use the tines of a fork to carefully remove cookies from the iron and wrap around the wooden cone or shape by hand into a cone, sealing the bottom shut with your fingers. Stand the cone upright in a drinking glass or wire stand to cool completely. The cones will harden further as they cool. Store, tightly covered, for up to 2 days or in the freezer for up to 1 month. Fill with your choice of frozen treat and serve.

Tuiles

MAKES 16 SERVINGS

These thin, crisp cookies are traditionally draped over a glass or a rolling pin right after they come out of the oven and are still warm and pliable. The word tuile *is pronounced "tweel" and is French for "tile," which is what these cookies look like when they're shaped.*

¼ cup Carol's Sorghum Blend (page x)

⅛ teaspoon xanthan gum

⅛ teaspoon salt

¼ cup unsalted butter or buttery spread, such as Earth Balance, at room temperature

⅔ cup sugar

2 large egg whites

½ teaspoon pure vanilla extract

1 cup very finely ground almonds or store-bought almond meal, such as Bob's Red Mill

1 Place a rack in the middle of the oven. Preheat the oven to 375°F. Line a 15 × 10-inch baking sheet (not nonstick) with parchment paper and grease lightly with butter or shortening or use a silicon baking mat.

2 In a small bowl, whisk together the sorghum blend, xanthan gum, and salt; set aside.

3 In a medium bowl, beat the butter and sugar with an electric mixer on low speed until smooth, about 30 seconds. Beat in the egg whites until fully incorporated and then the vanilla.

4 With the mixer on low speed, gradually beat in the flour mixture and almonds until just combined.

5 Plan to bake 3 cookies at a time, or 2 cookies at a time if your baking sheet is smaller than 15 × 10-inches. Starting at the top of baking sheet, drop three tablespoons of batter each at least 2 inches apart. Use a wet spatula to spread the batter to a diameter of 3 inches.

6 Bake 5 to 8 minutes or until the cookies are lightly browned around the edges. Remove the baking sheet from the oven and let the cookies cool for a few seconds. While the cookies are still hot, remove them with a thin spatula and drape them over a glass or a rolling pin that is covered with wax paper. Allow the cookie to sit a few minutes to harden and then transfer to a wire rack to cool completely. For a tightly-wrapped tuille, wrap the cookie around the handle of a wooden spoon. Allow the cookie to cool slightly, then carefully slip it off the wooden handle and cool on a wire rack. Repeat the process with the remaining batter.

Florentines

MAKES 12 SERVINGS

Florentines are delicious thin, flat Italian cookies made of ground nuts. They will stick to the parchment paper if you don't grease it. Stack three of them with your favorite ice cream in between the cookies and drizzle a complementary sauce over the top. If you prefer your florentines plain, omit the chocolate drizzle.

½ cup pecans

⅓ cup sugar

¼ cup Carol's Sorghum Blend (page x)

⅛ teaspoon xanthan gum

⅛ teaspoon salt

5 tablespoons unsalted butter or buttery spread, such as Earth Balance, at room temperature

2 large egg whites, beaten to a foam

1 teaspoon grated orange zest (optional)

½ cup gluten-free chocolate chips, such as Tropical Source

1 Place a rack in the middle of the oven. Preheat the oven to 350°F. Line a 15 × 10-inch baking sheet (not nonstick) with parchment paper; lightly grease it with butter or shortening.

2 In a food processor, pulse the pecans until they resemble very fine crumbs. Add the sugar, sorghum blend, xanthan gum, and salt and pulse until blended. Add the butter, egg whites, and orange zest and process until well blended.

3 Using a wet 1-teaspoon measuring spoon or a 25mm metal spring-action ice cream scoop, drop 1-inch balls of dough at least 3 inches apart on the baking sheets, 6 per sheet.

4 Bake 10 to 15 minutes, rotating the baking sheet halfway through baking, or until the cookies are brown around the edges. Remove the pan from the oven and cool 5 minutes. Transfer the parchment paper with the cookies still on it to a wire rack. Cool the baking sheet for 5 to 10 minutes, line it with fresh parchment paper and repeat with the remaining cookie dough.

5 When the cookies are firm, transfer them to a platter. Place the chocolate chips in a small food storage bag. Immerse the bag into barely simmering water until the chips are melted. Snip a small corner off the bag. Pipe a chocolate squiggle onto each cookie. Allow the chocolate to harden before storing the cookies.

Rosettes

MAKES 40 LARGER SERVINGS OR
60 SMALLER SERVINGS

Rosettes are deep-fried batter formed into delicately beautiful shapes with a special rosette iron that are then dusted with powdered sugar. They taste like funnel cake from a county fair. I ate my share of this Scandinavian treat during the holidays while living in Fargo, North Dakota. Look for rosette irons, preferably cast iron (not cast aluminum) in kitchen stores, specialty catalogs, or online. Follow the directions that come with the iron.

1 cup Carol's Sorghum Blend (page x)
1 tablespoon sugar
¼ teaspoon xanthan gum
¼ teaspoon salt
2 large eggs
1 cup 1% milk (cow's, rice, soy, potato, or nut)
½ teaspoon pure vanilla extract
Canola oil, for deep frying

1 In a small bowl, whisk together the sorghum blend, sugar, xanthan gum, and salt; set aside.

2 In a medium bowl, beat the eggs with an electric mixer on low speed. Beat in the flour mixture and milk alternately, blending until smooth. Stir in the vanilla. Chill the batter overnight. Line a baking sheet with paper towels to drain the rosettes; set aside.

3 In a deep fryer or heavy deep pot, heat 3 inches of oil to 350°F to 365°F. Place a rosette iron in the hot oil for 30 to 60 seconds to heat it. Dip the hot iron ¾ of the way into the batter, making sure NOT to let the batter run over the top of the iron or the cookie will be impossible to remove. Immerse the coated iron in the hot oil and fry 25 to 30 seconds or until light brown. Remove the rosette from the oil and slip the cookie off onto a paper towel. Sprinkle with powdered sugar when cool. Repeat with the remaining batter, making that the oil remains between 350°F and 365°F. Serve immediately.

BARS

Chocolate Brownies

MAKES 16 SERVINGS

Two kinds of chocolate assure that this fudgy brownie is packed with chocolate flavor. For extra fun, try the Rocky Road Brownies and Chocolate Chai Brownies variations.

3 ounces gluten-free semisweet baking chocolate, such as Tropical Source, melted

⅓ cup unsalted butter or buttery spread, such as Earth Balance, melted, or canola oil

¾ cup packed light brown sugar

2 large eggs, at room temperature

1 teaspoon pure vanilla extract

1 cup Carol's Sorghum Blend (page x)

½ cup unsweetened cocoa powder (not Dutch-process or alkali)

1 teaspoon xanthan gum

½ baking powder

½ teaspoon salt

¼ cup hot (120°F) water or freshly brewed coffee

¼ cup chopped walnuts

1 Place a rack in the middle of the oven. Preheat the oven to 350°F. Generously grease an 8-inch square glass dish.

2 In a medium mixing bowl, combine the melted chocolate with butter and brown sugar and beat with an electric mixer on low speed until smooth, about 30 seconds Beat in eggs and vanilla until thoroughly blended. Add sorghum blend, cocoa, xanthan gum, baking powder, and salt and beat until thoroughly blended. Blend in hot water. Stir in walnuts. Transfer batter to prepared pan and smooth top with a wet spatula.

3 Bake 20 minutes. Don't overbake. Remove from oven and cool on a wire rack for 20 minutes. Brownies will firm up as they cool. Cut into 16 squares and serve at room temperature.

Chocolate Chai Brownies: Add ¼ teaspoon each ground cinnamon, ground allspice, ground cloves, and ground cardamom to the dry ingredients. Bake as directed.

Rocky Road Brownies: Bake brownies 15 minutes. Sprinkle 1 cup miniature marshmallows, ½ cup chopped pecans, and ½ cup gluten-free chocolate chips, such as Tropical Source, on top. Bake 5 minutes more or until marshmallows and chips melt slightly. Remove from oven and cool completely before cutting into squares.

Chocolate Peanut Butter Brownies ⓥ

MAKES 16 SERVINGS

Chocolate and peanut butter just naturally go together. For a nice fudgy texture that is particularly pleasing with this combination, remove brownies from the oven before the center is done. They will continue to cook a bit, but won't be overdone. If you use chunky peanut butter, you may want to omit any additional chopped peanuts.

1 cup Carol's Sorghum Blend (page x)

½ cup unsweetened cocoa powder (not Dutch-process or alkali)

½ teaspoon baking powder

½ teaspoon salt

1 teaspoon xanthan gum

1 cup light brown sugar

⅓ cup peanut butter, at room temperature

1 large egg, at room temperature

2 teaspoons pure vanilla extract

½ cup warm (110°F) water

¼ cup each gluten-free chocolate chips, such as Tropical Source; peanut butter chips, such as Hy-Vee; and chopped peanuts

Powdered sugar, for dusting

1 Place a rack in the middle of the oven. Preheat the oven to 350°F. Generously grease an 8-inch square nonstick (gray, not black) pan.

2 In a large mixing bowl, beat sorghum blend, cocoa, baking powder, salt, xanthan gum, and brown sugar with an electric mixer on low speed until blended, about 30 seconds. Beat in peanut butter, egg, vanilla, and water until well combined. Stir in chocolate chips, peanut butter chips, and peanuts. Spread batter in prepared pan.

3 Bake 15 to 20 minutes or until the top is firm. Remove from oven and cool on a wire rack for 20 minutes. Brownies will firm up as they cool. Cut into 16 squares and serve at room temperature, dusted with powdered sugar.

Fudgy Vegan Chocolate Brownies Ⓥ

MAKES 16 SERVINGS

For those who can't eat wheat, dairy, or eggs, this is your special treat—you'll never miss what's not in it. And what is in it is good for you; the cocoa, coffee, and dried plums are very high in antioxidants. You've probably never made bars quite this way before, but you'll love the results.

⅓ cup unsweetened cocoa powder (not Dutch-
     process or alkali)
1 cup pitted dried plums
¾ cup hot (120°F) brewed coffee
⅔ cup Carol's Sorghum Blend (page x)
½ cup packed light brown sugar
1 teaspoon baking powder
½ teaspoon xanthan gum
½ teaspoon salt
¼ teaspoon baking soda
2 teaspoons pure vanilla extract
1½ cups gluten-free chocolate chips, such as Tropical
     Source, divided
¼ cup finely chopped toasted walnuts

1 Place a rack in the middle of the oven. Preheat the oven to 350°F. Generously grease an 8-inch square nonstick (gray, not black) pan; set aside.

2 In the bowl of a food processor, combine the cocoa, dried plums, and hot coffee and let stand 5 minutes. Pulse a few times, holding a towel over the lid to avoid splatters, until the prunes are pureed.

3 Add the sorghum blend, brown sugar, baking powder, xanthan gum, salt, baking soda, and vanilla and process until smooth. Add ½ cup of the chocolate chips and nuts to the batter, and pulse just a few times. Spread the batter in the prepared pan.

4 Bake 20 to 25 minutes, or until a toothpick inserted into the center comes out with a little batter still on it. Remove the pan from the oven and immediately sprinkle the remaining cup of chocolate chips on top. As the chocolate melts, spread it with a knife. Cool the brownies on a wire rack for 20 minutes. Brownies will firm up as they cool. Cut into 16 squares and serve at room temperature.

Black Bean Brownies with Espresso Ganache Ⓥ

MAKES 16 SERVINGS

Yes, beans in brownies! But no one will know by the taste. This brownie recipe is a great way to pump up the nutritional value of snacks, especially of fiber and other nutrients that might be missing in a gluten-free diet. If you don't have any bean flour, you can use the same amount of Carol's Sorghum Blend (page x).

1 can (14 to 15 ounces) black beans, drained and rinsed

3 large eggs, at room temperature

¾ cup packed light brown sugar

½ cup unsweetened cocoa powder (not Dutch-process or alkali)

¼ cup bean flour (chickpea, navy*, pinto*, or white bean), or Carol's Sorghum Blend (page x)

¼ cup maple syrup

3 tablespoons finely ground dark roast coffee beans

1 tablespoon pure vanilla extract

1 teaspoon baking powder

1 teaspoon xanthan gum

½ teaspoon salt

¼ cup chopped walnuts or pecans

3 ounces gluten-free chocolate chips, such as Tropical Source

⅓ cup freshly brewed espresso

1 Place a rack in the middle of the oven. Preheat the oven to 350°F. Generously grease an 8-inch square nonstick (gray, not black) pan.

2 Place the beans, eggs, and brown sugar in a food processor and process until the beans are smooth. Add the remaining ingredients, except walnuts, chocolate chips, and espresso and process until smooth. Stir in walnuts.

3 Spread the batter in the pan and bake 20 to 25 minutes or until a toothpick inserted in center comes out not quite clean. Place the pan on a wire rack to cool for 20 minutes.

4 Meanwhile, place the chocolate chips in a heat-proof bowl. In a small saucepan, bring espresso to a boil, pour it over the chocolate, and stir until melted. Cool to room temperature and then use a wet spatula to spread the ganache over the cooled brownies. Cool the brownies another 20 minutes. Cut into 16 squares and serve at room temperature.

Available at www.heartlandsfinest.com.

Brownie Fruit Pizza

MAKES 8 SERVINGS

Kids love this delicious treat. Keep a well-sealed bag of the decadent brownie mix on hand so you can make this dessert at a moment's notice. You can also make it with two batches of homemade Chocolate Brownies (page 442). Use fresh fruit, but if you drain canned fruit and pat it very dry, that will work, too.

BROWNIES

1 package (21 ounces) Bob's Red Mill Gluten-Free Brownie Mix or 2 recipes homemade Chocolate Brownies (page 442)

¾ cup or 1½ sticks unsalted butter or buttery spread, such as Earth Balance, melted

1 large egg, at room temperature

2 teaspoons pure vanilla extract

¾ cup warm (110°F) water

TOPPINGS

1 tablespoon powdered sugar

1 teaspoon pure vanilla extract

1 package (8 ounces) cream cheese or cream cheese alternative, such as Tofutti, at room temperature

½ pint (1 cup) fresh strawberries, washed, stemmed, and halved

1 cup fresh blueberries

1 cup fresh raspberries

1 can (11 ounces) mandarin oranges, drained and patted dry

½ cup store-bought orange marmalade

½ cup gluten-free chocolate syrup, such as Hershey's

1 Place a rack in the middle of the oven. Preheat the oven to 350°F. Generously grease 12-inch nonstick (gray, not black) pizza pan.

2 Make the brownies: In a medium mixing bowl, blend brownie mix with butter, egg, vanilla, and water with an electric mixer on medium speed until well mixed, following package directions. (Or prepare 2 recipes of the homemade Chocolate

Brownie batter as directed on page 442.) Spread evenly on prepared pizza pan, making sure outer edges are slightly higher to hold topping.

3 Bake brownie 20 minutes or until center is firm. Remove from oven and cool pan completely on wire rack. Do not remove brownie from pan.

4 Make the toppings: In a medium bowl, mix the powdered sugar and vanilla into the softened cream cheese and spread evenly on cooled brownie pizza to within 1 inch of outer edges. Arrange fruit in decorative circular pattern on cream cheese. In small pan, heat marmalade slightly and brush on fruit with pastry brush to give sheen. Let brownie pizza stand 15 minutes on a wire rack to allow marmalade and cream cheese to set up. Cut into 8 wedges, just as you would cut pizza. Drizzle with chocolate syrup. Serve immediately.

Mocha Brownie Sandwiches Ⓥ

MAKES 8 SERVINGS

This easy recipe uses very thin bars of brownies, stacked with espresso-flavored whipped cream. Drizzle it with your favorite store-bought chocolate sauce or use the homemade Chocolate Sauce (page 622). They make especially pretty individual desserts for dinner guests.

1 package (21 ounces) Bob's Red Mill Gluten-Free Brownie Mix or 2 recipes homemade Chocolate Brownies (page 442)

2 cups heavy cream, or 1 tub (ounces) whipped topping, such as Lucerne or Soyatoo

2 tablespoons sugar

1 package (3 ounces) cream cheese or cream cheese alternative, such as Tofutti, softened

1 tablespoon espresso powder

1 tablespoon pure vanilla extract

1 cup homemade Chocolate Sauce (page 622)

Fresh raspberries or strawberries and fresh mint, for garnish

1 Place a rack in the middle of the oven. Preheat the oven to 350°F. Generously grease a 15 × 10-inch rimmed nonstick (gray, not black) baking sheet and line it with parchment paper. Prepare the store-bought brownie batter as directed on the package (or 2 recipes of the homemade Chocolate Brownie batter as directed on page 442), spreading the batter as evenly as possible in the pan; the batter will barely cover the pan.

2 Bake 12 to 15 minutes or just until the center of the brownies firms up—overbaking will result in a dry brownie. Immediately remove the pan from oven and let the brownies cool completely in the baking sheet on a wire rack. They must be cool to cut well.

3 With a 2½-inch metal biscuit cutter, cut 16 rounds from the brownie layer.

4 Just before serving, in a medium bowl, beat the heavy cream with an electric mixer on medium speed until soft peaks form. Beat in the sugar until stiff peaks form and then beat in the cream cheese, espresso, and vanilla until smooth.

5 Place 8 of the brownie layers on dessert plates or a serving platter. Top with 2 tablespoons of whipped cream. Place a second brownie layer on top and then place a dollop of whipped cream on top and drizzle with chocolate sauce. Serve immediately, garnished with fresh berries and mint.

Chocolate-Coconut Bars

MAKES 16 SERVINGS

If you love the flavors of chocolate and coconut together, you'll love these bars. For more interesting texture, use coconut flakes, which are larger, instead of shredded coconut. I use Health Valley Rice Bran Crackers (a staple in my kitchen) but any gluten-free cookie will do. Of course, each cookie type will lend its own flavor and character to this simple bar.

¼ cup (½ stick) unsalted butter or buttery spread, such as Earth Balance, at room temperature

1½ cups finely crushed gluten-free cookies, such as Pamela's, Healthy Valley Rice Bran Crackers, or Mi-Del Arrowroot Cookies

½ teaspoon xanthan gum

1 cup sweetened coconut flakes, divided

½ cup chopped pecans

½ cup gluten-free chocolate chips, such as Tropical Source

½ cup evaporated milk, whole milk, or 1% milk (cow's, rice, soy, potato, or nut)

2 tablespoons sugar

1 teaspoon pure vanilla extract

1 Place a rack in the middle of the oven. Preheat the oven to 350°F. Use a microwave to melt the butter in an 8-inch glass baking pan. Add the crushed cookies and xanthan gum and mix well, or use a food processor to blend the butter with the cookies and xanthan gum instantly. Press the mixture firmly onto the bottom of the pan to form a crust.

2 Sprinkle half of the coconut, pecans, and chocolate chips over crust.

3 In a small bowl, stir together milk, sugar, and vanilla. Pour over mixture in pan. Sprinkle remaining ½ cup of coconut on top.

4 Bake 20 to 25 minutes or until the coconut is lightly browned. Remove from oven and cool bars in the pan for 20 minutes on wire rack. Cut into 16 squares and serve at room temperature.

Black and White Blondies

MAKES 16 SERVINGS

Think of this as a "blonde" brownie, dense and chewy, with both dark chocolate chips and white chocolate chunks. You may use white chocolate chips, but be mindful that they contain dairy.

¼ cup (½ stick) unsalted butter or buttery spread, such as Earth Balance, at room temperature

2 large eggs

½ cup packed light brown sugar

1 teaspoon pure vanilla extract

1 cup Carol's Sorghum Blend (page x)

1 teaspoon xanthan gum

¼ teaspoon salt

¼ cup gluten-free chocolate chips, such as Tropical Source

¼ cup gluten-free white chocolate chunks chopped from white chocolate bar, such as Organica

2 tablespoons chopped pecans

1 Place a rack in the middle of the oven. Preheat the oven to 350°F. Generously grease an 8-inch square nonstick (gray, not black) pan.

2 In a medium bowl, beat the butter, eggs, brown sugar, and vanilla with an electric mixer on low speed until thoroughly combined, about 2 minutes. Add sorghum blend, xanthan gum, and salt and beat on medium speed until smooth. Stir in chocolate and pecans. Transfer dough to prepared pan.

3 Bake 20 minutes or until the bars are golden brown. Cool the brownies in the pan 20 minutes on a wire rack before cutting. Cut into 16 squares and serve at room temperature.

Pineapple-Coconut Blondies

MAKES 16 SERVINGS

These bars are dense and satisfying, largely due to the pineapple and coconut, and the macadamia nuts add a nice crunch.

¼ cup (½ stick) unsalted butter or buttery spread, such as Earth Balance, at room temperature
2 large eggs, at room temperature
1 can (8 ounces) crushed pineapple, drained well
½ cup packed light brown sugar
1 teaspoon rum extract
1 cup Carol's Sorghum Blend (page x)
1 teaspoon xanthan gum
½ teaspoon baking powder
½ teaspoon salt
½ cup sweetened shredded coconut
¼ cup chopped macadamia nuts or pecans

1 Place a rack in the middle of the oven. Preheat the oven to 350°F. Generously grease an 8-inch square nonstick (gray, not black) pan.

2 In a medium mixing bowl, beat the butter, eggs, pineapple, brown sugar, and rum extract with an electric mixer on low speed until thoroughly combined, about 1 minute. Add sorghum blend, xanthan gum, baking powder, and salt and beat on medium speed until smooth. Stir in coconut and macadamia nuts. The batter will be somewhat stiff. Spread the batter evenly in the prepared pan.

3 Bake 25 to 30 minutes or until the bars are golden brown and a toothpick inserted into the center comes out clean. Cool the bars in the pan 20 minutes on a wire rack. Cut into 16 squares and serve at room temperature.

Toffee Bars

MAKES 16 SERVINGS

This cookie is somewhat like toffee candy, which I absolutely love. My mother made these bars, which is probably what got me started on my love for toffee. If you prefer dark chocolate or can't have dairy, use dark chocolate instead of milk chocolate.

5 tablespoons unsalted butter or buttery spread, such as Earth Balance, at room temperature
½ cup packed light brown sugar
1 large egg yolk
1 cup Carol's Sorghum Blend (page x)
1½ teaspoons xanthan gum
¼ teaspoon salt
6 ounces gluten-free milk chocolate, such as Scharffen Berger
⅓ cup finely chopped toasted almonds

1 Place a rack in the middle of the oven. Preheat the oven to 350°F. Generously grease an 8-inch square nonstick (gray, not black) baking pan; set aside.

2 In a medium mixing bowl, beat the butter, brown sugar, and egg yolk with an electric mixer on low speed until thoroughly blended, about 2 minutes. Gradually beat in the sorghum blend, xanthan gum, and salt until well blended. Spread or press the dough into the prepared pan.

3 Bake 15 to 20 minutes or until the bar is lightly browned. Remove the pan from the oven and immediately lay the chocolate bars on top. As the bar melts, spread the chocolate evenly with a knife. Let the brownies cool in the pan for 20 minutes on a wire rack. Cut into 16 squares and serve at room temperature.

Lemon Bars ⓥ

MAKES 16 SERVINGS

By their very nature, lemon bars involve a multi-step process because they have at least two layers, each of which must be baked and cooled. But I've streamlined this recipe so that it's a breeze and virtually fail-safe. It's one of my favorites.

CRUST

1 cup Carol's Sorghum Blend (page x)

2 tablespoons sugar

¼ cup (½ stick) cold unsalted butter or buttery spread, such as Earth Balance

¼ teaspoon xanthan gum

¼ teaspoon salt

FILLING

1 cup sugar

2 large eggs, at room temperature

2 tablespoons fresh lemon juice

2 teaspoons grated lemon zest

⅛ teaspoon salt

1 Place one rack in the bottom position and another at the middle position of the oven. Preheat the oven to 325°F. Generously grease an 8-inch square pan and line with parchment paper. Grease parchment paper.

2 Make the crust: In a food processor, blend the sorghum blend, sugar, butter, xanthan gum, and salt just until crumbly. Press evenly into prepared pan.

3 Bake crust 15 minutes on bottom rack, then move pan to middle shelf and bake another 10 minutes or until lightly browned at edges. Cool crust in the pan 15 minutes on wire rack.

4 Make the filling: In a food processor, combine sugar, eggs, lemon juice, lemon zest, and salt until thoroughly blended. Spread over baked crust.

5 Bake bars 20 to 25 minutes on middle shelf or until edges and top start to brown. Cool the bars in the pan for 20 minutes on a wire rack. Cut into 16 squares and serve at room temperature.

Key Lime Bars ⓥ

MAKES 16 SERVINGS

These subtly flavored key lime squares are part cheesecake and part bar cookie. If you like key lime, you'll love these bars. Pamela's Biscotti works especially well in this dessert since the six cookies in each package make exactly 1 cup of crushed crumbs. The bars are baked in a water bath for a smoother, less grainy texture.

1 cup crushed gluten-free cookies, such as Pamela's Biscotti or homemade Sugar Cookies (page 419)

¼ cup finely ground macadamia nuts or pecans

¼ cup sweetened shredded coconut

2 tablespoons unsalted butter or buttery spread, such as Earth Balance

⅔ cup sugar

1 tablespoon cornstarch

½ teaspoon baking powder

⅛ teaspoon salt

2 large eggs, lightly beaten

2 tablespoons fresh key lime juice

2 teaspoons grated key lime zest

1 Place a rack in the middle of the oven. Preheat the oven to 350°F. Generously grease an 8-inch square nonstick (gray, not black) baking dish; set aside. Have a 13 × 9-inch pan and a kettle of boiling water ready for the water bath.

2 In a medium bowl, combine the crushed cookies, nuts, coconut, and butter until the crumbs are well coated with butter. Press firmly onto the bottom of the pan.

3 Bake 5 minutes, or until the crust is lightly browned around the edges and fragrant. Watch carefully; the crust can burn quickly. Cool the crust in the pan on a wire rack while making the filling, but leave the oven on.

4 In a small bowl, whisk together the sugar, cornstarch, baking powder, and salt until blended. In a separate bowl, beat the eggs, lime juice, and lime zest with an electric mixer on low speed just until blended. Pour over the crust. Place a tea towel in the bottom of the 13 × 9-inch pan. Place the cheesecake pan in the water and pour boiling water in the larger pan until it comes up 1 inch on the sides of the cheesecake pan.

5 Bake 35 to 40 minutes or until the center is firm. Remove the cheesecake pan from the water-bath and cool bars in the pan for 20 minutes on a wire rack and then refrigerate for 2 to 3 hours before cutting into 16 squares.

Coconut-Date Bars

MAKES 16 SERVINGS

Coconut lovers will appreciate this yummy bar; the dates add sweetness as well as their own rich flavor.

½ cup buttermilk, well-shaken, or homemade Buttermilk (page 677)

½ cup finely chopped dates

¼ cup unsalted butter or buttery spread, such as Earth Balance, at room temperature, or canola oil

½ cup sugar

1 large egg, at room temperature

1 teaspoon pure vanilla extract

1 cup Carol's Sorghum Blend (page x)

1 teaspoon xanthan gum

½ teaspoon salt

¼ teaspoon baking powder

¼ teaspoon baking soda

½ cup sweetened shredded coconut

Powdered sugar, for dusting

1 Place a rack in the middle of the oven. Preheat the oven to 325°F. Generously grease an 8-inch nonstick (gray, not black) pan; set aside.

2 In a small saucepan, heat the buttermilk over medium heat until bubbles form around the edge of the pan. Remove the pan from the heat and add the dates. Let stand 10 minutes or until the dates are soft.

3 In a medium mixing bowl, beat the butter with an electric mixer on medium speed until light and

fluffy, about 30 seconds. Beat in the sugar, egg, and vanilla until smooth.

4 In a small bowl, whisk together the sorghum blend, xanthan gum, salt, and baking powder. Beat the flour mixture into the butter mixture on low speed, alternating with the cooled buttermilk, beginning and ending with the dry ingredients. Stir in the coconut. Spread the batter evenly in the pan.

5 Bake 25 to 30 minutes or until a toothpick inserted into the center comes out clean. Cool the bars in the pan on a wire rack. Cut the bars into 16 squares and dust with powdered sugar.

Apple Pie Bars

MAKES 8 SERVINGS

When you crave apple pie—but don't have the time to make it—these bars are the perfect solution. Granny Smith apples provide a nice tart contrast to the sweet, rich cream cheese frosting.

BARS

1 small apple (such as Granny Smith or Jonathan), peeled, cored, and very finely diced

Juice and grated zest of 1 lemon

¼ cup unsalted butter or buttery spread, such as Earth Balance, at room temperature

½ cup packed light brown sugar

¼ cup granulated sugar

1 large egg, at room temperature

1 teaspoon pure vanilla extract

1 cup Carol's Sorghum Blend (page x)

1½ teaspoons apple pie spice

1 teaspoon xanthan gum

½ teaspoon baking powder

½ teaspoon salt

½ cup chopped pecans, divided

FROSTING

½ cup powdered sugar

1 small package (3 ounces) cream cheese or cream cheese alternative, such as Tofutti, softened

1 Make the bars: Place a rack in the middle of the oven. Preheat the oven to 350°F. Generously grease an 8-inch square nonstick (gray, not black) pan. In a medium bowl, toss the apples with the lemon juice and zest; set aside.

2 In a medium bowl, beat the butter, brown sugar, granulated sugar, egg, and vanilla with an electric mixer on medium speed 1 minute. Gradually add the sorghum blend, apple pie spice, xanthan gum, baking powder, and salt and beat on low speed until well combined. Stir in the apples and half of the pecans. The batter will be stiff. Spread the batter evenly in the pan.

3 Bake 25 to 30 minutes, or until a toothpick inserted in the center comes out clean. Cool the bars in the pan 20 minutes on a wire rack, With a thin metal spatula, cut between the bars and edge of pan to loosen. Cut into 8 squares with a sharp knife.

4 Make the frosting: Combine the powdered sugar and cream cheese and spread on top of the bars. Sprinkle with the remaining pecans. Refrigerate, tightly covered, for up to 2 days.

Banana Bars with Orange Frosting Ⓥ

MAKES 16 SERVINGS

Save those over-ripe bananas for tasty tropical bars like these. Just peel and store them in freezer bags until the baking urge strikes; then thaw them gently in the microwave before incorporating them into the batter.

BARS

¼ cup (½ stick) unsalted butter or buttery spread, such as Earth Balance, at room temperature

½ cup sugar

1 large egg, at room temperature

1 large very ripe banana, mashed

1 teaspoon pure vanilla extract

1 teaspoon lemon juice

1 cup Carol's Sorghum Blend (page x)

1 teaspoon xanthan gum

½ teaspoon baking soda

½ teaspoon salt

¼ cup finely chopped walnuts

FROSTING

2 tablespoons fresh orange juice

1 teaspoon canola oil

1 teaspoon pure vanilla extract

½ teaspoon grated orange zest

1½ cups powdered sugar

⅛ teaspoon salt

1 Place a rack in the middle of the oven. Preheat the oven to 350°F. Generously grease an 8-inch square nonstick (gray, not black) pan; set aside.

2 Make the bars: In a large bowl, beat the butter and sugar with an electric mixer on low speed until smooth. Beat in the egg, banana, vanilla, and lemon juice until smooth; gradually beat in the sorghum blend, xanthan gum, baking soda, and salt on low speed until blended. Stir in the walnuts. Spread the batter evenly in the pan.

3 Bake 20 to 30 minutes or until a toothpick inserted into the center comes out clean. Cool the bars in the pan 30 to 35 minutes on a wire rack.

4 Make the frosting: In a medium bowl, mix together the orange juice, oil, vanilla, and orange zest until smooth. Beat in the powdered sugar, and salt until smooth, adding water, if necessary, a teaspoon at a time to reach the proper consistency. Spread the frosting over the cooled bars. Let stand 20 to 30 minutes for frosting to firm up. Cut into 16 squares and serve at room temperature.

Cranberry Oatmeal Bars

MAKES 16 SERVINGS

This festive bar is often seen in bakeries around the holidays, but I could eat them any day of the year. The hearty oatmeal topping is very filling and the flavors are addictive, so be prepared.

SHORTBREAD LAYER

½ cup (1 stick) unsalted butter or buttery spread, such as Earth Balance at room temperature (but not melted)

¾ cup packed light brown sugar

2 cups Carol's Sorghum Blend (page x)

¼ cup Expandex modified tapioca starch

2 tablespoons chopped walnuts

2 tablespoons rolled soy flakes* or gluten-free rolled oats**†

½ teaspoon xanthan gum

½ teaspoon salt

¼ cup 1% milk (cow's, rice, soy, potato, or nut)

1 tablespoon molasses (not blackstrap)

2 teaspoons pure vanilla extract

TOPPING

¼ cup (½ stick) unsalted butter or buttery spread, such as Earth Balance, melted

1 teaspoon pure vanilla extract, divided

½ cup Carol's Sorghum Blend (page x)

½ cup rolled soy flakes or gluten-free rolled oats**†

½ cup packed light brown sugar

¼ cup sliced almonds

½ teaspoon ground cinnamon

¼ teaspoon xanthan gum

¼ teaspoon salt

1 can (14 to 15 ounces) or 1½ cups whole (not jellied) cranberry sauce

1 Place a rack in the middle of the oven. Preheat the oven to 350°F. Generously grease an 11 × 7-inch nonstick (gray, not black) pan.

2 Make the shortbread layer: In a food processor, pulse the butter and brown sugar a few times until fluffy. Add sorghum blend, modified tapioca starch, walnuts, soy flakes, xanthan gum, and salt, and pulse a few times until blended. Add milk, molasses, and vanilla, and pulse a few times, then process until mixture forms ball. Dough will be somewhat stiff. Pat dough evenly into prepared pan.

3 Make the topping: In a food processor, pulse the butter, vanilla, sorghum blend, soy flakes, sugar, almonds, cinnamon, xanthan gum, and salt a few times, then process until mixture is crumbly and well blended. Spread cranberry sauce evenly on batter. Sprinkle topping evenly on cranberry sauce, pressing mixture lightly with hands.

4 Bake 35 to 40 minutes or until topping is golden brown. Cool the bars 20 minutes in the pan on a wire rack. Cut into 16 squares and serve at room temperature.

*Available at natural food stores.

**Available at www.bobsredmill.com, www.creamhillestates. com, www.giftsofnature.net, www.glutenfreeoats.com, and www.onlyoats.com.

†Check with your physician before using gluten-free oats.

Raspberry Bars

MAKES 16 SERVINGS

I freeze these bars in little plastic bags and put them in my handbag when I travel. They're a perfect little pick-me-up or a great treat when none of the desserts on the menu are appropriate. If you're a fan of coconut, as I am, stir ¼ cup sweetened shredded coconut into the topping.

½ cup (1 stick) unsalted butter or buttery spread, such as Earth Balance, melted

2 teaspoons pure vanilla extract, divided

1 cup Carol's Sorghum Blend (page x)

1 cup rolled soy flakes* or gluten-free oats**†

½ cup sugar

1½ teaspoons xanthan gum

1 teaspoon grated lemon zest

½ teaspoon salt

⅔ cup raspberry preserves or jam

1 Place a rack in the middle of the oven. Preheat the oven to 375°F. Generously grease an 8-inch nonstick (gray, not black) pan or line it with foil that extends over the edges to make handles for easy removal. Grease the foil.

2 In a medium mixing bowl, combine the melted butter and 1 teaspoon of the vanilla. Stir in the sorghum blend, soy flakes, sugar, xanthan gum, lemon zest, and salt until thoroughly blended. Press 1 cup of this mixture firmly on bottom of prepared pan.

3 Mix remaining teaspoon of vanilla with raspberry preserves and spread evenly over bottom crust in pan. Sprinkle remaining soy flake mixture over preserves and pat firmly to make the top layer smooth and even.

4 Bake 20 to 25 minutes or until top is nicely browned. Cool the bars in the pan 30 minutes on a wire rack. Cut into 16 squares and serve at room temperature.

*Available at natural food stores.

**Available at www.bobsredmill.com, www.glutenfreeoats. com. www.giftsofnature.net, and www.creamhillestates.com.

†Check with your physician before using gluten-free oats.

Fig Bars

MAKES 16 SERVINGS

If you can't find rolled soy flakes, you may use the same amount of natural coconut flakes found in natural food stores. These flakes are larger than shredded coconut and have a texture somewhat similar to rolled soy flakes. If you wish, you may also use the same amount of gluten-free oats.*†

½ cup (1 stick) unsalted butter or buttery spread, such as Earth Balance, melted
2 teaspoons pure vanilla extract, divided
1 cup Carol's Sorghum Blend (page x)
1 cup rolled soy flakes, or raw natural coconut flakes
½ cup packed light brown sugar
1½ teaspoons xanthan gum
½ teaspoon ground cinnamon
¼ teaspoon salt
1 tablespoon Port wine (optional)
1 jar (8 ounces) fig preserves

1 Place a rack in the middle of the oven. Preheat the oven to 375°F. Generously grease an 8-inch square nonstick (gray, not black) baking pan.

2 In a medium mixing bowl, combine the melted butter and 1 teaspoon of the vanilla. Stir in the sorghum blend, soy flakes, brown sugar, xanthan gum, cinnamon, and salt until thoroughly blended. Press 1 cup of the mixture firmly to form a crust on the bottom of the pan.

3 Whisk the Port wine, if using, and the remaining teaspoon of vanilla into the preserves until smooth. Spread the preserves evenly over the crust. Sprinkle the remaining soy flake mixture over the preserves and pat firmly to make the top layer smooth and even.

4 Bake 20 to 25 minutes or until the top is nicely browned. Cool the bars in the pan 20 minutes on a wire rack. Cut into 16 squares and serve at room temperature.

*Available from www.bobsredmill.com, www. creamhillestates.com, www.glutenfreeoats.com, www.giftsofnature.net, and www.onlyoats.com.

†Check with your physician before using gluten-free oats.

Pumpkin Bars

MAKES 16 SERVINGS

Pumpkin is what I call a "double-hitter." It is not only a very healthful food, but the rich taste blends beautifully with very flavorful spices.

BARS

2 large eggs, at room temperature

¾ cup sugar

½ cup canola oil

¾ cup (about half of 14 to 15 ounce can) canned pumpkin puree (not pie filling)

1 cup Carol's Sorghum Blend (page x)

1 teaspoon xanthan gum

1 teaspoon baking powder

½ teaspoon baking soda

½ teaspoon salt

½ teaspoon ground cinnamon

¼ teaspoon ground ginger

¼ teaspoon ground cloves

¼ teaspoon grated nutmeg

FROSTING

1 small package (3 ounces) cream cheese or cream cheese alternative, such as Tofutti, softened

1 cup sifted powdered sugar

1 teaspoon pure vanilla extract

¼ cup finely chopped pecans or walnuts (optional)

1 Place a rack in the middle of the oven. Preheat the oven to 350°F. Generously grease a 13 × 9-inch nonstick (gray, not black) pan.

2 Make the bars: In a medium bowl, beat the eggs, sugar, oil and pumpkin with an electric mixer on medium speed until light and fluffy. Add sorghum blend, xanthan gum, baking powder, baking soda, salt, cinnamon, ginger, cloves, and nutmeg to the pumpkin mixture and mix at low speed until thoroughly combined and batter is smooth. Spread batter evenly in prepared pan. Bake 15 to 20 minutes or until done. Let cool completely in the pan for 20 minutes on a wire rack.

3 Make the frosting: In a medium bowl, beat the cream cheese with an electric mixer on low speed until smooth. Add sugar and vanilla and mix at low speed until combined. Spread on cooled pumpkin bars. Sprinkle evenly with nuts, if using. Cut into 16 squares and serve at room temperature.

Shortbread

MAKES 8 SERVINGS

Shortbread is a rich, crumbly cookie usually made without eggs or leavening, so it doesn't rise— hence the name shortbread. It is actually quite versatile, and you can vary the flavors with different extracts, such as orange or anise extract, in the same amounts.

½ cup (1 stick) unsalted butter or buttery spread, such as Earth Balance, at room temperature, but not melted

½ cup powdered sugar

2 cups Carol's Sorghum Blend (page x)

¼ cup Expandex modified tapioca starch

½ teaspoon xanthan gum

½ teaspoon salt

2 teaspoons grated lemon zest

2 teaspoons pure vanilla extract

1 teaspoon almond extract

¼ cup 1% milk (cow's, rice, soy, potato, or nut)

1 tablespoon granulated sugar

1 Place a rack in the middle of the oven. Preheat the oven to 350°F. Line a 13 × 9-inch baking sheet (not nonstick) with parchment paper.

2 In a food processor, pulse the butter and powdered sugar a few times until fluffy. Add sorghum blend, modified tapioca starch, xanthan gum, salt, lemon zest, and vanilla and almond extracts and pulse a few times until blended. Add the milk and pulse a few times, then process until mixture forms a ball. The dough will be somewhat stiff.

3 Pat the dough into an 8-inch circle on the prepared sheet. Sprinkle with granulated sugar.

4 Bake 30 to 35 minutes or until the edges are golden brown. Cool the shortbread on the pan 10 minutes on a wire rack. Cut into wedges.

Chocolate Chip Shortbread: Omit lemon zest. Add ¼ cup gluten-free chocolate chips, such as Tropical Source, to the dough with a few pulses of the food processor. Press into an 8-inch square nonstick (gray, not black) pan, lined with foil and sprayed with cooking spray. Bake 30 minutes. Remove from oven and sprinkle with ¾ cup chocolate chips. Let chips melt 5 minutes; spread with knife. Cool completely on a wire rack before slicing into 8 pieces.

Chocolate-Orange Shortbread Bars: Spread 1 cup store-bought orange marmalade evenly over 1 baked shortbread baked in an 8-inch square pan or 8-inch circle. Sprinkle with ½ cup finely chopped, toasted walnuts. Melt 1 cup gluten-free chocolate chips, such as Tropical Source on low in microwave oven, stirring occasionally until smooth. Add milk, a teaspoon at a time, to reach the desired consistency. Drizzle on top of the shortbread. Let cool on a wire rack. Cut the shortbread into 8 bars or wedges. Serve immediately.

Cranberry Shortbread Bars Ⓥ

MAKES 16 SERVINGS

A crispy shortbread crust is topped by a cream cheese filling in this bar. For added punch, add ¼ cup chopped crystallized ginger (also called candied ginger) to the dough. It will enhance the ginger in the crust and complement the cranberry flavor. You'll find it in natural food stores and specialty shops.

CRUST

¼ cup (½ stick) unsalted butter or buttery spread, such as Earth Balance, at room temperature

¼ cup packed light brown sugar

1 teaspoon grated orange zest

1 teaspoon pure vanilla extract

1 cup Carol's Sorghum Blend (page x)

1 teaspoon xanthan gum

½ teaspoon ground ginger

½ teaspoon salt

1 large egg yolk

¼ cup dried sweetened cranberries

¼ cup gluten-free white chocolate chunks, chopped from white chocolate bar, such as Organica

CREAM CHEESE LAYER

1 small package (3 ounces) cream cheese or cream cheese alternative, such as Tofutti, at room temperature

½ cup powdered sugar

1 teaspoon orange extract

1 teaspoon pure vanilla extract or ¼ teaspoon vanilla powder

1 teaspoon fresh lemon juice

2 tablespoons chopped dried sweetened cranberries

DRIZZLE

½ cup powdered sugar

1 teaspoon fresh lemon juice

1 teaspoon canola oil

Enough water to form thin frosting

1 Place a rack in the middle of the oven. Preheat the oven to 325°F. Lightly grease 9 × 9-inch nonstick (gray, not black) pan.

2 Make the crust: In a food processor, combine butter, brown sugar, orange zest, and vanilla and process until smooth. Add sorghum blend, xanthan gum, ginger, and salt and process until well blended. Scrape down sides with spatula. Add cranberries and white chocolate and process until blended again. With a wet spatula, press dough evenly into pan.

3 Bake 15 to 20 minutes, or just until edges start to brown. Cool the bars 10 minutes in the pan on a wire rack.

4 Make the cream cheese layer: Blend the cream cheese, powdered sugar, orange and vanilla extracts, and lemon juice until smooth. With a spatula, spread the cream cheese layer evenly over the crust and immediately sprinkle with chopped cranberries. Chill the bars for at least 2 hours.

5 Make the drizzle: In a bowl, whisk together powdered sugar, lemon juice, oil, and water until smooth. Drizzle the frosting in a thin line back and forth across the pan. Chill again for 2 hours before serving. Cut into 16 squares and serve at room temperature.

Lebkuchen Bars

MAKES 24 SERVINGS

Lebkuchen is a chewy German cookie similar to gingerbread in flavor and often served at Christmas. The term lebkuchen *is thought to be derived from the term "honey cake" since the cookie usually includes honey. Traditionally, these are baked as individual cookies, but my bar version is much simpler. My sister-in-law lived in Europe for many years and often sent these treats to us during the holidays. We became hooked on their distinctive flavor, so I began making this version in a pan and have continued with that tradition.*

2 cups Carol's Sorghum Blend (page x)
1 teaspoon xanthan gum
1½ teaspoons ground cinnamon
¼ teaspoon ground cardamom
¼ teaspoon ground allspice
¼ teaspoon ground nutmeg
¼ teaspoon ground ginger
⅛ teaspoon ground cloves
½ teaspoon baking soda
½ cup packed light brown sugar
1 large egg
¼ cup molasses (not blackstrap)
2 tablespoons honey
2 tablespoons canola oil
½ cup finely chopped almonds
2 cups powdered sugar
2 tablespoons water (or enough to form a stiff frosting)
1 tablespoon unsalted butter or buttery spread, such as Earth Balance, at room temperature, or canola oil
¼ teaspoon pure vanilla extract

1 Place a rack in the middle of the oven. Preheat the oven to 325°F. Generously grease a 13 × 9-inch pan (not nonstick); set aside.

2 In a small bowl, sift together the sorghum blend, xanthan gum, cinnamon, cardamom, allspice, nutmeg, ginger, cloves, and baking soda; set aside.

3 In a medium bowl, beat the brown sugar, egg, molasses, honey, and oil with an electric mixer on medium speed until blended, about 1 minute. With the mixer on low, gradually beat in the flour mixture until the dough is smooth. Beat in the almonds. The dough will be very sticky, so use a wet spatula to spread it evenly in the pan.

4 Bake 15 to 20 minutes or until the dough appears dry and firm around the edges. Cool the bars in the pan on a wire rack 30 minutes.

5 In a medium bowl, sift the powdered sugar. Beat in the water, butter, and vanilla until smooth. Spread evenly on the cooled lebkuchen. Cool the cookies in the pan 20 minutes on wire rack until the frosting is set. Cut into 24 bars with a sharp knife.

Marshmallow Rice Treats

MAKES 24 SERVINGS

The traditional version of this treat requires crispy brown rice cereal, which was once off limits. Today, kids can enjoy this treat made with safe versions of the cereal.

½ cup unsalted butter or buttery spread, such as Earth Balance
2 teaspoons vanilla extract
1 package (5½ cups) miniature marshmallows or 55 large marshmallows
6 cups gluten-free crispy brown rice cereal, such as Erewhon, crushed

1 In a large saucepan, melt the butter, vanilla, and salt over low heat. Add the marshmallows and stir until melted and the mixture is smooth. Remove from the heat.

2 Immediately add the cereal and stir with a spatula until all the ingredients are thoroughly mixed together.

3 Lightly oil your hands and immediately press the mixture into a greased 13 × 9-inch pan. You can also lay a sheet of plastic wrap over the bars to make pressing them easier. Cool completely before cutting into 24 bars.

Peanut Butter Ice Cream Bars with Fudge Sauce Ⓥ

MAKES 10 SERVINGS

This dessert must be kept frozen, but that means it can be made ahead. It blends two of the greatest flavors on earth—chocolate and peanut butter—and it delights the senses with several different textures from the frozen ice cream, the crunchy, nutty crust, and the warm, creamy chocolate sauce.

CRUST

¼ cup (½ stick) unsalted butter or buttery spread, such as Earth Balance, at room temperature

¼ cup chunky peanut butter

¼ cup packed light brown sugar

1 large egg, at room temperature

1 cup Carol's Sorghum Blend (page x)

1 teaspoon xanthan gum

½ teaspoon salt

¼ teaspoon baking powder

⅛ teaspoon baking soda

ICE CREAM LAYER

1 pint (2 cups) gluten-free vanilla ice cream, such as Ben & Jerry's, Dreyer's Grand, or Häagen-Dazs, softened

SAUCE

¼ cup (½ stick) unsalted butter or buttery spread, such as Earth Balance

⅓ cup packed light brown sugar

¼ cup unsweetened cocoa powder (natural or Dutch-process)

½ cup heavy cream or soy milk

⅛ teaspoon salt

2 tablespoons peanut butter (smooth or creamy)

½ teaspoon pure vanilla extract

1 Place a rack in the middle of the oven. Preheat the oven to 325°F. Generously grease a 9-inch springform pan and line the bottom with wax paper or parchment paper.

2 Make the crust: In a food processor, process the butter, peanut butter, brown sugar, and egg, until thoroughly blended. Add the sorghum blend, xanthan gum, salt, baking powder, and baking soda and process until blended. It will look crumbly. Press the batter evenly on the bottom and 2-inches up the sides of the prepared pan.

3 Bake 10 to 12 minutes, or until the edges of the crust start to brown and the peanut butter smells fragrant. Cool the crust completely on a wire rack, leaving it in the pan.

4 Make the ice cream layer: Spread the ice cream gently but evenly on top of the cooled crust with a spatula. Cover the pan tightly with plastic wrap and freeze 4 hours or until the ice cream is very firm.

5 Make the sauce: In a small saucepan, combine all the ingredients except the peanut butter and vanilla over medium-low heat. Bring to a simmer and cook, whisking constantly, until the sauce thickens slightly, about 2 to 3 minutes. Stir in the peanut butter and vanilla. Cool the sauce to room temperature.

6 To serve, wrap a hot wet dish towel around the perimeter of the pan to release the ice cream from the pan. Remove the side of the springform pan. Slice the cake into 10 bars or wedges with a long thin knife dipped in hot water and wiped dry between cuts. Transfer bars to small plates. Garnish each with a drizzle of the sauce. Serve immediately. Freeze leftovers.

CAKES AND CUPCAKES

Coffee Cakes

Buttermilk Coffee Crumb Cake

Blueberry-Lemon Coffee Cake

Lemon Coffee Cake with Lemon Glaze

Sour Cream Apple Coffee Cake

Hazelnut Coffee Cake with Maple Sugar Crust

White and Yellow Cakes

Yellow Cake

White Cake

Bundt Pound Cake

Lemon-Thyme Pound Cake with Lemon Frosting

Harvey Wallbanger Cake with Galliano Glaze

Angel Food Cake

Strawberry Jello Cake

Cakes with Fruit, Nuts, and Fillings

Italian Cream Layer Cake

Italian Rosemary-Lemon Layer Cake

Lady Baltimore Cake with Soaked Fruit Frosting

Banana Layer Cake with Maple Cream Cheese Frosting

Banana–Coconut Custard Layer Cake

Banana–Hemp Seed Layer Cake with Cinnamon Frosting

Coconut Layer Cake with Whipped Cream Frosting

Orange-Coconut Cake with Fluffy Orange Frosting

Orange-Date Cake with Brandy Sauce

Poppy Seed–Orange Pound Cake with Orange Glaze

Pineapple-Filled Layer Cake

Polynesian Layer Cake with Coconut–Cream Cheese Frosting

Boston Cream Pie with Chocolate Ganache

Polenta Cake

Pear-Almond Cake

Rhubarb-Almond Cake

Old-Fashioned Strawberry Shortcake

Strawberry Swirl Cake with Fluffy Pink Frosting

Strawberries and Cream Layer Cake

Chestnut Cake with Marrons Glacés Whipped Cream

Black Walnut Bundt Cake with Caramel Frosting

Cream-Filled Cakes

Chocolate Cakes

Chocolate Bundt Cake

Chocolate-Raspberry Bundt Cake

Vegan Chocolate Spice Cake

Vegan Chocolate Layer Cake with Chocolate Mocha Frosting

Chocolate Mayonnaise Cake

Mini Chocolate Peanut Butter Cakes

Chocolate Molten Lava Cakes with Crème Anglaise

Devil's Food Layer Cake with Fudge Frosting

Mexican Chocolate Layer Cake with Cinnamon Frosting

Mocha Latte Layer Cake

German Chocolate Cake with Coconut-Pecan Frosting

Black Forest Layer Cake

Chocolate Cookie Cake

Sacher Torte

Carob Torte with Caramel Topping

Carob-Cinnamon Cake with Cinnamon Frosting

Spice Cakes

Apple Spice Cake

Carrot Layer Cake with Coconut-Cream Cheese Frosting

Chai Spice Cake with Vanilla

Cream-Cheese Frosting

Old-Fashioned Molasses Cake

Gingerbread Cake with Spiced Cream Cheese Frosting

Tomato Soup Spice Cake with Cream Cheese Frosting

Holiday and Special Occasion Cakes

Babka

Bûche de Noël

Fruitcake

Panforte

Pear Kuchen

Christmas Beer Cake

Petit Fours

Pumpkin Roll Cake

Red Velvet Bundt Cake

Cheesecakes

One-Dish Rustic Cheesecake

Simple Pumpkin Cheesecake

New York–Style Cheesecake

Cheesecake Bars

Lime Cheesecake

Green Tea Cheesecake

Black and White Cheesecake

Simple Chocolate Cheesecake Cups

Mini-Chocolate Cheesecakes

Chocolate Espresso Cheesecake with Espresso-Caramel Sauce

Peanut Butter Cheesecake with Cookie Crust

Pineapple-Coconut Cheesecake with Nut Crust

Nectarine Cheesecake Tart

Raspberry White Chocolate Cheesecake

White Chocolate Cheesecake with Caramel-Pecan Topping

Cupcakes

Yellow Cupcakes

White Cupcakes

Pound Cake Cupcakes

Old-Fashioned Molasses Cupcakes

Coconut Cupcakes with
Coconut Frosting

Orange-Coconut Cupcakes with
Orange-Coconut Frosting

Mini Coconut-Pecan Cupcakes

Banana Cupcakes with
Maple–Cream-Cheese Frosting

Black Walnut Cupcakes with
Caramel Frosting

Polynesian Cupcakes with
Coconut Cream-Cheese Frosting

Tiramisu Cupcakes

Harvey Wallbanger Cupcakes

Vegan Chocolate Cupcakes with
Mocha Frosting

Chocolate Peanut Butter
Cupcakes

Mini Mexican Chocolate
Cupcakes with
Cinnamon Frosting

Black Forest Cupcakes

German Chocolate Cupcakes with
Coconut-Pecan Frosting

Mini Sacher Torte Cupcakes

Mini Chocolate Peppermint
Ice Cream Cupcakes

Mini Carob Cupcakes with
Caramel Topping

Carob-Cinnamon Cupcakes

Autumn-Spice Apple Cupcakes

Mini Carrot Cake Cupcakes

Mini Pumpkin-Spice Cupcakes

Mini Chai-Spice Cupcakes

Flourless Cakes

Flourless Honey Almond Cake

Flourless Hazelnut Cake

Flourless Walnut-Orange Torte

Flourless Almond-Apricot Torte

Flourless Pumpkin Seed Cake

Flourless Clementine Cake

Flourless Limoncello Almond
Cake with Limoncello Glaze

Flourless Dark Chocolate Cake

Flourless Chocolate
Espresso Cake

Haroset (Fruit and Nut Cake)

Pudding Cakes and Upside-Down Cakes

Citrus Pudding Cake

Coconut Pudding Cake

Hot Fudge Pudding Cake

Praline Pudding Cake

Apple-Butterscotch Upside-Down
Cake

Pineapple Upside-Down Cake

Apricot Upside-Down Cake

Caramelized Pear–Gingerbread
Upside-Down Cake

Cranberry-Walnut
Upside-Down Cake

Ice Cream Cakes

Angel Food Ice Cream Cake

Fresh Peach Ice Cream Cake

Chocolate Peppermint
Ice Cream Cake

We celebrate special times in life with cakes, and there are plenty in this chapter—from flourless cakes to cheesecakes to coffee cakes to fabulous favorites such as Devil's Food Chocolate, Angel Food, Old-Fashioned Strawberry Shortcake, Carrot Cake, and Apple Spice Cake. You can always use one of the many store-bought gluten-free cake mixes, but I offer unique cakes such as German Chocolate Cake, Sacher Torte, Boston Cream Pie, Lady Baltimore Cake, and a Chocolate Molten Lava Cake with Creme Anglaise that you won't find in any store-bought mix.

Flourless cakes are super-simple to whip up and creamy, rich cheesecakes—such as the classic New York Style or decadent Chocolate Espresso Cheesecake with Espresso-Caramel Sauce—are sure to please your most discerning guests. Luscious toppings and frostings, including homemade Basic Whipped Cream (page 624), and a special fondant recipe for special-occasion cakes, help make even the simplest cake a work of art.

All these cakes come in myriad shapes and styles including Bundt cakes, layer cakes, sheet cakes, roll cakes, upside-down cakes, ice cream cakes, pound cakes, and coffee cakes.

Cupcakes, once reserved for children because they are easier to eat, have grown up. Now they appear at weddings, showers, holiday parties, and black-tie events—in exotic flavors and decorated to the hilt. In this chapter you'll find cupcakes from the simplest—Yellow Cupcakes or White Cupcakes with frosting that every child loves—to the sophisticated, such as Tiramisu Cupcakes, Black Forest Cupcakes, and Polynesian Cupcakes with Coconut-Cream Cheese Frosting. With these easy recipes, you'll be able to pack snacks in lunch boxes, serve treats at dinner, and celebrate fun kid's parties and other special occasions with cupcakes that rise to any occasion.

Prepare a batch of Carol's Sorghum Blend (page x) and keep it in your pantry, so you're always ready to bake. Beating the ingredients together in a mixing bowl creates an emulsion by blending liquid and dry ingredients to form a cohesive batter. Any ingredient added later—such as more water or milk or eggs or vanilla or flour—should be thoroughly blended in to maintain that emulsion; otherwise, the cake won't bake properly.

Be sure to use the type and size of pan stated in the recipe. Gray (not black) nonstick pans work best. All of these recipes are calibrated to fit in the pan specified in the directions. If your pan is too small, the batter may overflow while baking. If your pan is too large—perhaps an 11 × 7-inch pan rather than a 9 × 5-inch pan—the batter will bake much more quickly, resulting in a much thinner cake.

If you avoid dairy, I offer substitutions for cow's milk, butter, buttermilk, sour cream, and cream cheese. 1% milk is called for in most of these recipes because it is lower in fat and calories, but you can substitute any milk. Be sure to shake store-bought buttermilk thoroughly before measuring it because the solids tend to settle on the bottom of the carton, making the first few cups much thinner than the final cup. If your buttermilk is extremely thick, thin it with a little water. Although everything tastes wonderful with real butter, try replacing it with non-dairy buttery spreads such as Earth Balance; Spectrum Naturals also works well in baking but it will not melt if you use it in frostings or sauces. Try the homemade Nondairy Whipped Topping (page 624) in place of Basic Whipped Cream (page 624), or use store-bought soy-based whipped topping, such as Lucerne or Soyatoo.

COFFEE CAKES

Buttermilk Coffee Crumb Cake Ⓥ

MAKES 10 SERVINGS

This delicious coffee cake makes a great brunch dish. A version of this recipe has been in my family for nearly thirty-five years. It's rich and satisfying, and is sure to become a favorite in your family, too.

CRUMB CAKE

5 tablespoons unsalted butter or buttery spread, such as Earth Balance, at room temperature

1 cup firmly packed light brown sugar

1 large egg, at room temperature

1 cup buttermilk, well-shaken, or homemade Buttermilk (page 677)

2 teaspoons pure vanilla extract

1½ cups Carol's Sorghum Blend (page x)

1½ teaspoons xanthan gum

1 teaspoon ground cinnamon

¾ teaspoon baking soda

¾ teaspoon salt

TOPPING

¼ cup Carol's Sorghum Blend (page x)

¼ cup firmly packed light brown sugar

2 tablespoons unsalted butter or buttery spread, such as Earth Balance, at room temperature

1 Place a rack in the middle of the oven. Preheat the oven to 350°F. Generously grease an 11 × 7-inch nonstick (gray, not black) rectangular pan.

2 Make the cake: In a large mixing bowl, beat the butter and brown sugar with an electric mixer until light and fluffy. Beat in egg on medium speed until smooth. Combine buttermilk and vanilla extract in a separate bowl.

3 In a small bowl, whisk together the 1½ cups sorghum blend, xanthan gum, cinnamon, baking soda, and salt. With the mixer on low speed, beat the sorghum mixture into the egg mixture, alternating with the buttermilk mixture, beginning and ending with the dry ingredients. Beat just until the batter is smooth and thickens slightly. Spread the batter evenly in the pan.

4 Make the topping: Combine the sorghum blend and brown sugar in a small bowl. Cut in the butter with a fork until the mixture resembles coarse crumbs. Sprinkle on top of coffee cake.

5 Bake 35 minutes or until the top of the cake is golden brown and a toothpick inserted into center comes out clean. Cool the cake in the pan 10 minutes on a wire rack. Serve warm.

Blueberry-Lemon Coffee Cake Ⓥ

MAKES 10 SERVINGS

This cake is equally good whether you use dried or fresh blueberries, but it will be decidedly sweeter with dried blueberries because their sugar is more concentrated.

LIQUID INGREDIENTS

2 large eggs, at room temperature

¾ cup buttermilk, well-shaken, or homemade Buttermilk (page 677)

⅓ cup unsalted butter or buttery spread, such as Earth Balance, at room temperature, or ¼ cup canola oil

1 tablespoon grated lemon zest

1 teaspoon pure vanilla extract

DRY INGREDIENTS

1½ cups Carol's Sorghum Blend (page x)

¾ cup sugar

1 teaspoon xanthan gum

½ teaspoon baking powder

½ teaspoon baking soda

⅓ teaspoon salt

1 cup dried blueberries (or fresh)

1 cup Streusel Topping (page 566)

1 Place a rack in the middle of the oven. Preheat the oven to 350°F. Generously grease an 11 × 7-inch nonstick (gray, not black) rectangular pan.

2 In a large mixing bowl, beat the eggs, buttermilk, butter, lemon zest, and vanilla extract with an electric mixer on medium speed until smooth.

3 In a small bowl, whisk together the sorghum blend, sugar, xanthan gum, baking powder, baking soda, and salt. With the mixer on low speed, gradually beat the dry ingredients into the liquid ingredients just until the batter is smooth. Stir in the blueberries. Spread the batter into the pan. Sprinkle the streusel topping on top.

4 Bake 35 minutes or until the top is golden brown and a toothpick inserted into the center of the cake comes out clean. Cool the cake in the pan 10 minutes on a wire rack. Serve warm.

Lemon Coffee Cake with Lemon Glaze Ⓥ

MAKES 10 SERVINGS

Lemon glaze makes this popular coffee cake more contemporary. The flavor is quite strong, so omit the lemon zest if you want it milder.

COFFEE CAKE
5 tablespoons unsalted butter or buttery spread, such as Earth Balance, or ¼ cup canola oil

1 cup sugar

3 tablespoons grated lemon zest

2 large eggs, at room temperature

⅔ cup 1% milk (cow's, rice, soy, potato, or nut)

2 tablespoons fresh lemon juice

1 teaspoon pure vanilla extract

1½ cups Carol's Sorghum Blend (page x)

1 teaspoon xanthan gum

½ teaspoon baking powder

½ teaspoon baking soda

½ teaspoon salt

GLAZE
1 cup powdered sugar

¼ cup fresh lemon juice

2 teaspoons grated lemon zest

1 Place a rack in the middle of the oven. Preheat the oven to 350°F. Generously grease an 11 × 7-inch nonstick (gray, not black) rectangular pan.

2 Make the cake: In a large mixing bowl, beat the butter, sugar, and lemon zest with an electric mixer on medium speed until very smooth. Beat in eggs until smooth.

3 In a small bowl, combine the milk, lemon juice, and vanilla extract. In a medium bowl, whisk together the sorghum blend, xanthan gum, baking powder, baking soda, and salt.

4 With the mixer on low speed, beat the dry ingredients into egg mixture, alternating with milk mixture, beginning and ending with dry ingredients. Spread the batter in the pan.

5 Bake 30 to 35 minutes or until a toothpick inserted into the center of the cake comes out clean. Cool the cake in the pan 10 minutes on a wire rack.

6 Make the glaze: Combine the ingredients in a small bowl until smooth. Gently spread glaze over warm cake. Serve warm.

Sour Cream Apple Coffee Cake Ⓥ

MAKES 10 SERVINGS

The rich flavors of the butter and sour cream complement the apples' tart sweetness. This coffee cake makes a great brunch dish, but you could also serve it as dessert after dinner, with or without a dollop of homemade Basic Whipped Cream (page 624).

½ cup unsalted butter or buttery spread, such as Earth Balance, at room temperature, or ⅓ cup canola oil

1 cup sugar

2 large eggs, at room temperature

1 cup (8 ounces) sour cream or sour cream alternative, such as Tofutti

1 teaspoon pure vanilla extract

½ teaspoon almond extract

2 cups Carol's Sorghum Blend (page x)

1 teaspoon ground cinnamon

1 teaspoon baking powder

½ teaspoon baking soda

1 teaspoon salt

2 cups finely chopped and peeled apples (2 medium apples, preferably Jonathan or Granny Smith)

½ cup dark raisins

1 tablespoon sugar

1 Place a rack in the middle of the oven. Preheat the oven to 350°F. Generously grease a 13 × 9-inch non-stick (gray, not black) pan.

2 In a large mixing bowl, beat the butter and sugar with an electric mixer on medium speed until smooth. Add the eggs and beat until smooth, then beat in sour cream, vanilla extract and almond extract.

3 In a bowl, whisk together the sorghum blend, cinnamon, baking powder, baking soda, and salt. Beat dry ingredients into egg mixture on low speed until blended. Stir in the apples and raisins. Spread the batter in the pan and sprinkle with the sugar.

4 Bake 30 to 35 minutes or until the top is lightly browned and a toothpick inserted into the center comes out clean. Cool the cake in the pan 15 minutes on a wire rack. Serve warm.

Hazelnut Coffee Cake with Maple-Sugar Crust **V**

MAKES 10 SERVINGS

Hazelnuts bring a wonderful flavor to this coffee cake, but you can use almond meal (finely ground nuts) in place of the hazelnut meal, if you wish. This cake is not overly sweet, so to dress it up try serving it with a dollop of homemade Basic Whipped Cream (page 624) dusted with maple sugar.

2 large eggs, at room temperature

¼ cup pure maple syrup

¼ cup canola oil

1 teaspoon pure vanilla extract

1 teaspoon maple extract (optional)

1½ cups Carol's Sorghum Blend (page x)

½ cup hazelnut meal*

¾ cup sugar

1¼ teaspoons baking powder

1 teaspoon xanthan gum

½ teaspoon baking soda

½ teaspoon salt

½ cup buttermilk, well shaken, or homemade Buttermilk (page 677)

3 tablespoons maple sugar, or 3 tablespoons sugar blended with 1 teaspoon pure maple syrup

1 Place a rack in the middle of the oven. Preheat the oven to 350°F. Generously grease an 11 × 7-inch nonstick (gray, not black) rectangular pan.

2 In a large mixing bowl, beat together the eggs, syrup, oil, vanilla extract, and maple extract with an electric mixer on medium speed until very smooth.

3 In a medium bowl, whisk together the sorghum blend, hazelnut meal, sugar, baking powder, xanthan gum, baking soda, and salt. With the mixer on low speed, beat the sorghum mixture into the egg mixture, alternating with buttermilk, beginning and ending with dry ingredients. Spread the batter in the pan and sprinkle with maple sugar.

4 Bake 25 to 30 minutes or until a toothpick inserted into center of cake comes out clean. Cool the cake in the pan 10 minutes on a wire rack. Serve warm.

*Available at www.bobsredmill.com.

WHITE AND YELLOW CAKES

Yellow Cake

MAKES 12 SERVINGS

I think of yellow cake as the dessert equivalent of the little black dress. It can be served simply or dressed up or down, to suit any occasion such as a birthday or even a wedding. Every gluten-free cook needs an excellent basic yellow cake recipe like this one that can be adapted as needed.

½ cup (1 stick) unsalted butter or buttery spread, such as Earth Balance, at room temperature, or ⅓ cup canola oil

¾ cup sugar

2 large eggs, at room temperature

1½ cups Carol's Sorghum Blend (page x)

1 teaspoon xanthan gum

½ teaspoon salt

¼ teaspoon baking powder

¼ teaspoon baking soda

¾ cup buttermilk, well-shaken, or homemade Buttermilk (page 677)

1 teaspoon pure vanilla extract

½ teaspoon almond extract

1 Place a rack in the middle of the oven. Preheat the oven to 325°F. Generously grease two 8-inch round nonstick (gray, not black) cake pans and line the bottoms with parchment paper or wax paper. Generously grease the pans again; set aside.

2 In a large mixing bowl, beat the butter with an electric mixer on medium speed until smooth. Gradually beat in the sugar until smooth. Add the eggs, one at a time, beating well after each addition.

3 In another bowl, sift together the sorghum blend, xanthan gum, salt, baking powder, and baking soda. In a measuring cup, whisk together the buttermilk, vanilla extract, and almond extract.

4 With the mixer on low speed, beat the sorghum mixture into the egg mixture, alternating with the buttermilk, beginning and ending with the sorghum mixture. Spread the batter evenly in the pans.

5 Bake 20 to 25 minutes or until the tops of the cakes are golden brown and a toothpick inserted into the center of the cake comes out clean. Cool the cakes in the pan 10 minutes on a wire rack. Invert the cakes onto the wire rack, remove and discard the paper, and invert the cakes to rest on their bottoms while they cool completely on the wire rack.

White Cake

MAKES 12 SERVINGS

Another wonderful basic cake recipe, this deliciously moist cake can be adapted in so many ways using your favorite extracts (such as lemon or orange), different fillings, glazes, and frostings, such as Fudge Frosting (page 494). The possibilities are limitless.

½ cup (1 stick) unsalted butter or buttery spread, such as Earth Balance, at room temperature, or ⅓ cup canola oil

¾ cup sugar

3 large egg whites, at room temperature

1½ cups Carol's Sorghum Blend (page x)

1 teaspoon xanthan gum

½ teaspoon salt

¼ teaspoon baking powder

¼ teaspoon baking soda

¾ cup buttermilk, well-shaken, or homemade Buttermilk (page 677)

1 teaspoon pure vanilla extract

½ teaspoon almond extract (optional)

1 Place a rack in the middle of the oven. Preheat the oven to 325°F. Generously grease two 8-inch round nonstick (gray, not black) cake pans and line the bottoms with parchment paper or wax paper. Generously grease the pans again; set aside.

2 In a large mixing bowl, beat the butter with an electric mixer on medium speed until smooth. Gradually beat in the sugar until smooth. Add the egg whites, one at a time, beating well after each addition.

3 In another bowl, sift together the sorghum blend, xanthan gum, salt, baking powder, and baking soda. In a measuring cup, whisk together the buttermilk, vanilla extract, and almond extract, if using.

4 With the mixer on low speed, beat the sorghum mixture into the egg mixture, alternating with the buttermilk, beginning and ending with the sorghum mixture. Spread the batter evenly in the pans.

5 Bake 20 to 25 minutes or until the tops of the cakes are golden brown and a toothpick inserted into the center of the cake comes out clean. Cool the cakes in the pans 10 minutes on a wire rack. Remove the cakes from the pans with a thin metal spatula, discard the paper, and invert the cakes to rest on their bottoms while they cool completely on the wire rack.

Bundt Pound Cake

MAKES 12 SERVINGS

This cake is more dense than a classic white or yellow cake, but like those, you can easily enhance the taste with flavored extracts. For example, instead of vanilla, try almond, lemon, or rum extracts. I like to bake it in a large Bundt pan because the pretty slices showcase the pound cake's lovely, traditionally rich texture and crumb. This cake is best served while still slightly warm from the oven.

½ cup unsalted butter or buttery spread, such as Earth Balance, at room temperature, or ⅓ cup canola oil

2 cups sugar

4 large eggs, at room temperature

3 cups Carol's Sorghum Blend (page x)

1½ teaspoons xanthan gum

¾ teaspoon salt

½ teaspoon baking powder

½ teaspoon baking soda

1½ cups buttermilk, well-shaken, or homemade Buttermilk (page 677)

1 tablespoon grated lemon zest

2 teaspoons pure vanilla extract

1 Place a rack in the middle of the oven. Preheat the oven to 325°F. Generously grease a 10-inch non-stick Bundt pan; set aside.

2 In a large mixing bowl, beat the butter with an electric mixer on medium speed until smooth. Add sugar and continue beating on medium speed until well blended. Mix in eggs, one at a time, beating well after each addition.

3 In a medium bowl, sift together the sorghum blend, xanthan gum, salt, baking powder, and baking soda. In a measuring cup, combine buttermilk, lemon zest, and vanilla extract. On low speed, beat the dry ingredients into the egg mixture, alternating with the buttermilk and ending with the sorghum mixture. Spread the batter in the prepared pan.

4 Bake 1 hour, or until the top is golden brown and a toothpick inserted into the center of the cake comes out clean. Cool the cake in the pan 10 minutes on a wire rack. Remove cake from the pan and cool completely on the wire rack.

Lemon-Thyme Pound Cake with Lemon Frosting

MAKES 12 SERVINGS

Lemon and thyme complement one another; the thyme provides an unexpected, yet delicious twist to the otherwise traditionally sweet lemon flavor. Blueberries provide a lovely garnish and further complement the lemony flavor.

POUNDCAKE

½ cup unsalted butter or buttery spread, such as Earth Balance, at room temperature, or ⅓ cup canola oil

2 cups sugar

4 large eggs, at room temperature

3 cups Carol's Sorghum Blend (page x)

1½ teaspoons xanthan gum

¾ teaspoon salt

½ teaspoon baking powder

½ teaspoon baking soda

1½ cups buttermilk, well-shaken, or homemade Buttermilk (page 677)

2 tablespoon grated lemon zest

2 teaspoons pure vanilla extract

1 tablespoon chopped fresh thyme leaves

FROSTING

1½ cups powdered sugar

2 tablespoons fresh lemon juice

1 teaspoon grated lemon zest

2 cups fresh blueberries

1 Place a rack in the middle of the oven. Preheat oven to 325°F. Generously grease a 10-inch non-stick (gray, not black) Bundt pan; set aside.

2 Make the cake: In a large mixing bowl, beat the butter with an electric mixer on medium speed until smooth. Add sugar and continue beating on medium speed until well blended. Mix in eggs, one at a time, beating well after each addition.

3 In a medium bowl, sift together the sorghum blend, xanthan gum, salt, baking powder, and baking soda. On low speed, beat the dry ingredients into the egg mixture, alternating with the buttermilk and ending with the sorghum mixture. Stir in the lemon zest, vanilla extract, and thyme. Spread the batter evenly in the pan.

4 Bake 1 hour or until the top is golden brown and a toothpick inserted into the center of the cake comes out clean. Cool the cake in the pan 10 minutes on a wire rack. Remove the cake from the pan with a thin metal spatula and cool completely on the wire rack.

5 Make the frosting: In a medium bowl, whisk together the powdered sugar, lemon juice, and lemon zest until smooth. Pour over the top of the cake, letting the frosting fall down the sides in puddles. Let the frosting set up 10 minutes. Place the blueberries in the hole of the Bundt pan and a few around the edges of the plate for garnish. Serve immediately.

Harvey Wallbanger Cake with Galliano Glaze Ⓥ

MAKES 12 SERVINGS

For sophisticated or retro celebratory gatherings, walk down memory lane with this cake based on the popular Harvey Wallbanger cocktail, which features Galliano, a vanilla-flavored liqueur. The glaze will be very thin and should soak into the cake rather than look like a frosting.

CAKE

⅓ cup (5 tablespoons) unsalted butter or buttery spread, such as Earth Balance, at room temperature, or ¼ cup canola oil

1 cup sugar

2 large eggs, at room temperature

1½ cups Carol's Sorghum Blend (page x)

1 teaspoon xanthan gum

¼ teaspoon baking powder

¼ teaspoon baking soda

¼ teaspoon salt

½ cup buttermilk, well-shaken, or homemade Buttermilk (page 677)

¼ cup Galliano liqueur

1 tablespoon grated orange zest

2 teaspoons pure vanilla extract

GLAZE

1 cup powdered sugar

½ cup fresh orange juice

1 tablespoon Galliano liqueur

1 tablespoon vodka

Pinch of salt

1 Place a rack in the middle of the oven. Preheat the oven to 325°F. Generously grease a 10-cup nonstick (gray, not black) Bundt cake pan; set aside.

2 Make the cake: In a large mixing bowl, beat the butter with an electric mixer on medium speed until smooth. Gradually beat in the sugar until smooth. Add the eggs, one at a time, beating well after each addition.

3 In another bowl, sift together the sorghum blend, xanthan gum, baking powder, baking soda, and salt. In a measuring cup, whisk together the buttermilk, liqueur, orange zest, and vanilla extract.

4 With the mixer on low speed, beat the sorghum mixture into the egg mixture, alternating with the buttermilk, beginning and ending with the sorghum mixture. Pour the batter into the pan, spreading evenly.

5 Bake 55 minutes to 1 hour or until the top of the cake is golden brown and a toothpick inserted into the center of the cake comes out clean. Cool the cake in the pan 10 minutes on a wire rack. Remove the cake from the pan with a thin metal spatula and cool completely on the wire rack. Transfer the cake to serving plate

6 Make the glaze: In a medium bowl, beat the powdered sugar with the orange juice, liqueur, vodka, and salt with electric mixer until smooth. Drizzle the glaze over the cake. Serve immediately.

Angel Food Cake

MAKES 12 SERVINGS

Dessert can be a light finish with this airy cake. It is very important to sift the powdered sugar, potato starch, and cornstarch before measuring to aerate these ingredients and remove any lumps. After measuring, sift them together 3 times before adding to the egg whites to assure the lightest texture possible.

1 cup powdered sugar
½ cup cornstarch
½ cup potato starch
½ teaspoon xanthan gum
1 cup egg whites (about 14 egg whites), at room temperature
1 teaspoon cream of tartar
½ teaspoon salt
1 teaspoon almond extract
1 teaspoon pure vanilla extract
¾ cup granulated sugar

1 Place a rack in the lower-middle position of the oven. Preheat the oven to 375°F. Set an ungreased 10-inch (16-cup) tube pan with a removable bottom nearby. If the pan bottom is not removable, line it with parchment or wax paper.

2 In a small bowl, sift together the powdered sugar, cornstarch, potato starch and xanthan gum 3 times; set aside.

3 In a large, clean mixing bowl, place the egg whites, cream of tartar, salt, almond extract, and vanilla extract. With the mixer on medium-high speed, beat with clean beaters until the whites become frothy. Increase the speed to high, add the granulated sugar, 2 tablespoons at a time, and continue beating until the sugar dissolves and the whites just start to form stiff white peaks.

4 With a wide spatula, gently fold in ¼ of the dry ingredients at a time, until they disappear into the egg whites. Transfer the batter to the tube pan. Run a butter knife or chopstick through the batter a few times to break up any air bubbles.

5 Bake 30 minutes, then reduce the heat to 325°F and continue baking until the cake is golden brown and the top springs back when pressed firmly, about 50 minutes to 1 hour.

6 Quickly invert the pan onto its prongs or invert the pan over the neck of a wine bottle so that air can circulate all around it.

can circulate all around it. Let the cake cool completely, about 2 to 3 hours.

7 To unmold the cake, run a sharp knife around edge between the cake and the pan, being careful not to separate the golden crust from the cake. Slide the cake out of the pan and insert a knife between the cake and the removable bottom to release, or peel off parchment or wax paper, if used.

8 Place the cake, bottom-side up, on a platter. Cut slices by sawing gently with an electric or serrated knife. Serve immediately.

Strawberry Jello Cake

MAKES 12 SERVINGS

This yummy, old-fashioned cake will take you back to your childhood. You can vary the fruit, for example, using fresh peaches and peach gelatin or fresh raspberries and raspberry gelatin. Commercial whipped topping in a tub works better if you plan to eat the cake a few hours later; if you make your own whipped cream topping, eat the cake right away because the topping won't hold its shape very long.

½ cup (1 stick) unsalted butter or buttery spread, such as Earth Balance, at room temperature, or ⅓ cup canola oil

¾ cup sugar

3 large egg whites, at room temperature

1½ cups Carol's Sorghum Blend (page x)

1 teaspoon xanthan gum

½ teaspoon salt

¼ teaspoon baking powder

¼ teaspoon baking soda

¾ cup buttermilk, well-shaken, or homemade Buttermilk (page 677)

1 teaspoon pure vanilla extract

½ teaspoon almond extract

1 package (3 ounces) strawberry-flavored gelatin

2 cups homemade Basic Whipped Cream (page 624) or whipped topping, such as Lucerne or Soyatoo

1 Place a rack in the middle of the oven. Preheat the oven to 350°F. Generously grease an 11 × 7-inch or 10-inch round nonstick (gray, not black) cake pan; set aside.

2 In a large mixing bowl, beat the butter with an electric mixer on medium speed until smooth. Gradually beat in the sugar until smooth. Add the egg whites, one at a time, beating well after each addition.

3 In another bowl, sift together the sorghum blend, xanthan gum, salt, baking powder, and baking soda. In a measuring cup, whisk together the buttermilk, vanilla extract, and almond extract.

4 With the mixer on low speed, beat the sorghum mixture into the egg mixture, alternating with the buttermilk, beginning and ending with the sorghum mixture. Pour the batter into the pan and spread it evenly with a wet spatula.

5 Bake 30 to 35 minutes or until the top of the cake is golden brown and a toothpick inserted into the center of the cake comes out clean. Cool the cake in the pan 20 minutes on a wire rack.

6 In a bowl, dissolve the gelatin powder in ¾ cup warm (120°F) water and let stand 10 minutes. Make several holes in the top of the cake about 1 inch deep (the pointed end of a chopstick works great) and then pour the gelatin mixture over the cake, making sure it penetrates all of the holes. Refrigerate the cake overnight. Just before serving, frost the cake with the whipped cream. Serve immediately. Refrigerate any leftovers.

CAKES WITH FRUITS, NUTS, AND FILLINGS

Italian Cream Layer Cake

MAKES 12 SERVINGS

Delicate and creamy with flavors of coconut and pecan, this lovely layer cake is perfect for special occasions that require a show-stopping dessert. Although there is an Italian cream cake called cassata, *the sweet, rich flavors of this cake make it clear why this is a true Southern favorite.*

CAKE

⅓ cup unsalted butter or buttery spread, such as Earth Balance, at room temperature, or ¼ cup canola oil

1 cup sugar

2 large eggs, at room temperature, separated

1½ cups Carol's Sorghum Blend (page x)

1 teaspoon xanthan gum

½ teaspoon baking powder

½ teaspoon baking soda

½ teaspoon salt

¾ cup buttermilk or homemade Buttermilk (page 677)

1 teaspoon pure vanilla extract

1 teaspoon coconut extract

5 tablespoons finely chopped toasted pecans, divided

FROSTING

1 small package (3 ounces) cream cheese or cream cheese alternative, such as Tofutti, at room temperature

1 tablespoon unsalted butter or buttery spread, such as Earth Balance, at room temperature, or canola oil

3 cups powdered sugar

1 teaspoon coconut extract

1 Place a rack in the middle of the oven. Preheat the oven to 325°F. Generously grease two 8-inch round nonstick (gray, not black) cake pans and line the bottoms with parchment paper or wax paper. Grease again; set aside.

2 Make the cake: In a large mixing bowl, beat the butter with an electric mixer on medium speed until creamy and smooth. Gradually beat in the sugar until smooth. Add the egg yolks, one at a time, beating well after each addition.

3 In another bowl, sift together the sorghum blend, xanthan gum, baking powder, baking soda, and salt. In a measuring cup, whisk together the buttermilk, vanilla extract, and coconut extract.

4 With the mixer on low speed, beat the sorghum mixture into the egg mixture, alternating with the buttermilk, beginning and ending with the sorghum mixture. Add 4 tablespoons of the pecans, scrape down the side of the bowl, and beat just until smooth.

5 In a clean large bowl with clean beaters, beat the egg whites on high speed until stiff peaks form. Fold the egg whites into the batter; and spread the batter evenly in the pans.

6 Bake 30 to 35 minutes or until the tops of the cakes are golden brown and a toothpick inserted into the center of the cake comes out clean. Cool the cakes in the pans 10 minutes on a wire rack. Remove the cakes from the pan with a thin metal spatula, discard the paper, and cool completely on the wire rack.

7 Make the frosting: Beat the cream cheese and butter in a medium bowl with an electric mixer on medium speed until smooth and creamy. Gradually beat in the powdered sugar on low speed. Add coconut extract and beat well.

8 Place 1 cake layer, topside down, on a serving plate; spread with one-third of the frosting. Top with the other cake layer, topside up. Spread remaining frosting evenly over the top and sides of the cake. Sprinkle with remaining tablespoon of chopped pecans. Cut with a serrated knife. Serve immediately.

Italian Rosemary-Lemon Layer Cake Ⓥ

MAKES 12 SERVINGS

Marmalade makes a quick, easy filling for this layer cake. Rosemary is usually thought of as an herb for savory dishes, and is used a great deal in Italian dishes, but it is a delightful surprise in this citrus-flavored cake.

1½ cups Carol's Sorghum Blend (page x)

1 teaspoon xanthan gum

½ teaspoon baking soda

½ teaspoon baking powder

½ teaspoon salt

2 large eggs, at room temperature

1 cup sugar

⅓ cup light olive oil

½ cup buttermilk, well-shaken, or homemade Buttermilk (page 677)

¼ cup orange liqueur, such as Triple Sec, or orange juice

1 tablespoon grated lemon zest

2 teaspoons finely chopped fresh rosemary, divided

6 tablespoons orange marmalade

2 tablespoons powdered sugar, for garnish

2 fresh rosemary sprigs, for garnish

1 Place a rack in the middle of the oven. Preheat the oven to 350°F. Generously grease two 8-inch round nonstick (gray, not black) pans. Line the bottoms with parchment paper and grease again; set aside.

2 In a small bowl, whisk together the sorghum blend, xanthan gum, baking soda, baking powder, and salt; set aside.

3 In a medium mixing bowl, beat the eggs with an electric mixer on medium speed until light yellow. Beat in the sugar and olive oil until well blended. In a measuring cup, combine the buttermilk, and liqueur. Gradually beat in the sorghum mixture on low speed, alternating with the buttermilk mixture, beginning and ending with the sorghum mixture. Stir in the lemon zest and 1½ teaspoons of the chopped rosemary. Spread the batter evenly in the pans.

4 Bake 30 to 35 minutes or until the cakes pull away from the edge of the pan and a toothpick inserted into the center comes out clean. Cool the cakes in the pans 10 minutes on a wire rack. Run a sharp knife around the edge of the pan to loosen the cake.

5 To assemble, place one layer on a plate, topside down. Spread the marmalade on the top. Add the second cake layer, topside up, dust with powdered sugar, and sprinkle the remaining 1 teaspoon rosemary evenly over the cake. Garnish with rosemary sprigs. Serve immediately.

Lady Baltimore Cake with Soaked Fruit Frosting Ⓥ

MAKES 16 SERVINGS

The origins of this elegant Southern classic with its fruit-filled layers are unclear: it was either named after royalty, or a tea room that served it, or it was introduced in a novel: it's a mystery! Plan ahead to make the frosting for this cake by soaking the dried fruit in sherry overnight. If you would rather not use sherry, use almond extract instead. With three layers, this is a fairly large cake, so have plenty of family and friends available so you're not tempted to eat it all yourself!

DRIED FRUIT FOR FROSTING

½ cup finely chopped dried figs, + sliced dried figs for garnish

½ cup chopped raisins

¼ cup chopped candied cherries

¼ cup chopped candied pineapple

¼ cup dry sherry (or 1 tablespoon almond extract plus 1 tablespoon water)

CAKE

½ cup unsalted butter or buttery spread, such as Earth Balance, at room temperature, or ⅓ cup canola oil

1½ cups sugar

4 large eggs, separated

3 cups Carol's Sorghum Blend (page x)

1½ teaspoons xanthan gum

½ teaspoon baking powder

½ teaspoon baking soda

¾ teaspoon salt

1¾ cups buttermilk, well-shaken, or homemade Buttermilk (page 677)

2 teaspoons pure vanilla extract

1 teaspoon almond extract

FROSTING

4 large egg whites, at room temperature

1¼ cups sugar

¼ teaspoon cream of tartar

3 tablespoons cold water

1 cup pecans, toasted lightly and chopped fine, divided

1 Prepare the dried fruit: The night before, soak the chopped figs, raisins, cherries and pineapple in the sherry in a covered bowl.

2 Make the cake: Place a rack in the middle of the oven. Preheat the oven to 325°F. Generously grease three 8-inch round nonstick (gray, not black) cake pans and line the bottoms with parchment paper or wax paper. Grease again and set aside.

3 In a large mixing bowl, beat the butter with an electric mixer on medium speed until smooth. Gradually beat in the sugar until smooth. Add the egg yolks, one at a time, beating well after each addition.

4 In another bowl, sift together the sorghum blend, xanthan gum, baking powder, baking soda, and salt. In a measuring cup, whisk together the buttermilk, vanilla extract, and almond extract.

5 With the mixer on low speed, beat the sorghum mixture into the egg mixture, alternating with the buttermilk, beginning and ending with the sorghum mixture.

6 In a clean bowl with clean beaters, beat the egg whites on high speed until stiff peaks form. Fold the egg whites into the batter; spread the batter into the prepared pans, dividing evenly.

7 Bake 30 to 35 minutes or until the tops of the cakes are golden brown and a toothpick inserted into the center of the cake comes out clean. Cool the cakes in the pans 10 minutes on a wire rack. Remove the cakes from the pans with a thin metal spatula, discard the paper, and cool the cakes completely on the wire rack. Trim ¼ inch from the rounded tops of the cakes to make them more uniformly thick and more stable when stacked.

8 Make the frosting: In a double boiler over simmering water, combine the egg whites, sugar, cream of tartar, and cold water. Beat 7 minutes with a portable electric mixer, or until the mixture reaches the consistency of frosting. Remove frosting from the heat. Remove ⅓ of the frosting and stir soaked dried fruit and ½ cup of the pecans into it.

9 Place 1 cake layer on a serving plate and spread with half of the dried-fruit frosting. Top with the second cake layer. Spread with the remaining half of the dried-fruit frosting. Top with the third cake layer. Spread the reserved ⅔ of the frosting evenly over the top and sides of the cake. Sprinkle with the remaining ½ cup of chopped pecans. Serve immediately.

Banana Layer Cake with Maple–Cream Cheese Frosting Ⓥ

MAKES 12 SERVINGS

The flavors of banana and maple complement one another in this home-style dessert. It's lovely baked in a Bundt pan, but you can also use a 10-inch round cake pan. Be sure to reduce the frosting recipe by half, if you use the round pan, since there will be less cake surface to frost.

POUND CAKE

5 tablespoons unsalted butter or buttery spread, such as Earth Balance, at room temperature, or ¼ cup canola oil

1 cup sugar

2 large eggs, at room temperature

1 large very ripe banana, mashed

1½ cups Carol's Sorghum Blend (page x)

1 teaspoon xanthan gum

½ teaspoon baking powder

½ teaspoon baking soda

¼ teaspoon salt

¾ cup buttermilk, well-shaken, or homemade Buttermilk (page 677)

1 teaspoon pure vanilla extract

1 teaspoon banana-flavored extract (optional)

1 teaspoon maple-flavored extract (optional)

1 cup finely chopped pecans, divided

FROSTING

1 small package (3 ounces) cream cheese or cream cheese alternative, such as Tofutti, at room temperature

¼ cup (½ stick) unsalted butter or buttery spread, such as Earth Balance, at room temperature

4 teaspoons pure maple syrup

⅛ teaspoon maple-flavored extract (optional)

3 cups powdered sugar

Pinch of salt

1 Place a rack in the middle of the oven. Preheat the oven to 325°F. Generously grease a 10-inch nonstick (gray, not black) Bundt cake pan; set aside.

2 Make the cake: In a large mixing bowl, beat the butter with an electric mixer on medium speed until creamy and smooth. Gradually beat in the sugar until smooth. Add the eggs, one at a time, beating well after each addition. Beat in the mashed banana until the batter is smooth.

3 In another bowl, sift together the sorghum blend, xanthan gum, baking powder, baking soda, and salt. In a measuring cup, whisk together the buttermilk, vanilla extract, and the banana-flavored and maple-flavored extracts, if using.

4 With the mixer on low speed, beat the sorghum mixture into the egg mixture, alternating with the buttermilk, beginning and ending with the sorghum mixture. Add ¾ cup of the pecans, scrape down the side of the bowl, and beat just until smooth. Spread the batter in the pan.

5 Bake 55 minutes to 1 hour or until a toothpick inserted into the center of the cake comes out clean. Cool the cake in the pan 5 minutes on a wire rack. Remove the cake from the pan with a thin metal spatula and cool completely on the wire rack.

6 Make the frosting: In a medium bowl, beat the cream cheese, butter, maple syrup, and maple extract with an electric mixer on medium speed until smooth and creamy. Gradually beat in the powdered sugar and salt until the frosting is smooth.

7 Place the cake on a serving plate. Spread the frosting evenly over the top and part way down the sides of the cake. Sprinkle the top of the cake with the remaining pecans. Serve immediately or refrigerate until serving time.

Banana–Coconut Custard Layer Cake Ⓥ

MAKES 12 SERVINGS

Coconut lovers will certainly want to try this cake, which is especially moist thanks to the bananas. The luscious coconut filling makes this cake a winner.

CAKE

5 tablespoons unsalted butter or buttery spread, such as Earth Balance, at room temperature, or ¼ cup canola oil

1 cup sugar

4 egg whites, at room temperature

1 large very ripe banana, mashed

1½ cups Carol's Sorghum Blend (page x)

1 teaspoon xanthan gum

½ teaspoon baking powder

½ teaspoon baking soda

½ teaspoon salt

¾ cup buttermilk, well-shaken, or homemade Buttermilk (page 677)

2 teaspoons pure vanilla extract

½ cup sweetened coconut flakes

FILLING

¾ cup sugar

¼ cup cornstarch

1 cup 1% milk (cow's, rice, soy, potato, or nut)

1 can (14 to 15 ounces) light coconut milk

4 egg yolks, at room temperature

1 teaspoon coconut extract

¼ cup toasted coconut, for sprinkling on top of cake

1 Place a rack in the middle of the oven. Preheat oven to 325°F. Generously grease two 8-inch round nonstick (gray, not black) cake pans and line the bottoms with parchment paper or wax paper. Grease again and set aside.

2 Make the cake: In a large mixing bowl, beat the butter with an electric mixer on medium speed until creamy and smooth. Gradually beat in the sugar until smooth. Add the egg whites, one at a time, beating well after each addition. Beat in the mashed banana.

3 In another bowl, sift together the sorghum blend, xanthan gum, baking powder, baking soda, and salt. In a measuring cup, whisk together the buttermilk and vanilla extract.

4 With the mixer on low speed, beat the sorghum mixture into the egg mixture, alternating with the buttermilk, beginning and ending with the sorghum mixture. Add the coconut flakes, scrape down the side of the bowl, and beat just until smooth. Spread the batter in the pans.

5 Bake 30 to 35 minutes or until the cakes are golden brown and a cake tester inserted into the center of the cake comes out clean. Cool the cakes in the pans 10 minutes on a wire rack. Remove the cakes from the pan with a thin metal spatula, discard the paper, and cool completely on the wire rack.

6 Make the filling: In a small, heavy saucepan, whisk together the sugar and cornstarch. Add the milk, coconut milk, and egg yolks and cook over medium heat, whisking constantly, for 1 minute, or until the mixture thickens. Immediately transfer the pan to a bowl of ice water to cool it quickly.

7 To assemble the cake, place one layer on a serving plate, topside down. Spread it with 1 cup of the filling. Place the second layer on top and spread the top with the remaining filling. Sprinkle with the toasted coconut. Serve immediately or refrigerate.

Banana–Hemp Seed Layer Cake with Cinnamon Frosting Ⓥ

MAKES 12 SERVINGS

Hemp has been grown for thousands of years for fiber and food. Shelled hemp seed, the type used in this recipe, is gaining popularity as a healthful snack and baking ingredient because it is one of the most balanced sources of omega-3 and -6 essential fatty acids (EFAs). Sprinkle it on yogurt, salads, and cereal. Here, I add it to a banana-flavored layer cake, keeping the baking temperature below 350°F to preserve the integrity of the fatty acids.

CAKE

½ cup unsalted butter or buttery spread, such as Earth Balance, at room temperature, or ⅓ cup canola oil

1 cup sugar

1 large very ripe banana, mashed

2 large eggs, at room temperature

1½ cups Carol's Sorghum Blend (page x)

1 teaspoon xanthan gum

½ teaspoon salt

½ teaspoon baking powder

½ teaspoon baking soda

¾ cup buttermilk, well-shaken, or homemade Buttermilk (page 677)

1 teaspoon pure vanilla extract

½ teaspoon almond extract

¼ cup shelled hemp seed, such as Manitoba Harvest

FROSTING

2 cups powdered sugar

¼ teaspoon ground cinnamon

Pinch of salt

2 tablespoons unsalted butter or buttery spread, such as Earth Balance, at room temperature

¼ cup 1% milk (cow's, rice, soy, potato, or nut)

1 teaspoon pure vanilla extract

2 tablespoons shelled hemp seed, such as Manitoba Harvest, for garnish

1 Place a rack in the middle of the oven. Preheat the oven to 325°F. Generously grease two 8-inch round nonstick (gray, not black) cake pans and line the bottoms with parchment paper or wax paper. Generously grease the pans again; set aside.

2 Make the cake: In a large mixing bowl, beat the butter with an electric mixer on medium speed until smooth. Gradually beat in the sugar and the mashed banana until smooth. Add the eggs, one at a time, beating well after each addition.

3 In another bowl, sift together the sorghum blend, xanthan gum, salt, baking powder, and baking soda. In a measuring cup, whisk together the buttermilk, vanilla extract, and almond extract.

4 With the mixer on low speed, beat the sorghum mixture into the egg mixture, alternating with the buttermilk, beginning and ending with the sorghum mixture. Stir in the hemp seed. Spread the batter evenly in the pans.

5 Bake 30 to 35 minutes or until the tops of the cakes are golden brown and a toothpick inserted into the center of the cakes comes out clean. Cool the cakes 10 minutes in the pans on a wire rack. Remove the cakes from the pans with a thin metal spatula, discard the paper, and cool completely on the wire rack.

6 Make the frosting: In a medium bowl, whisk together the powdered sugar, cinnamon, and salt. With an electric mixer on low speed, or by hand with a spatula, beat in the butter, milk, and vanilla until the frosting is smooth, adding more powdered sugar or milk to reach the right consistency, if necessary.

7 To assemble the cake, place one layer on a serving plate, topside down. Spread the cake with 1 cup of the frosting. Place the second layer on top and spread the top with the remaining frosting. Sprinkle with the shelled hemp seed. Serve immediately.

Coconut Layer Cake with Whipped Cream Frosting
MAKES 12 SERVINGS

I knew my husband for only a few months before we married, which wasn't long enough to learn that he detested coconut. You can imagine his surprise (and mine!) when I popped the ritualistic piece of coconut-flavored wedding cake into his mouth at our wedding reception. I, on the other hand, adore coconut and love this coconut-intensive cake.

CAKE

⅓ cup (5 tablespoons) unsalted butter or buttery spread, such as Earth Balance, at room temperature, or ¼ cup canola oil

1 cup sugar

2 large eggs, at room temperature

1½ cups Carol's Sorghum Blend (page x)

1 teaspoon xanthan gum

¼ teaspoon baking powder

¼ teaspoon baking soda

¼ teaspoon salt

¾ cup buttermilk, well-shaken, or homemade Buttermilk (page 677)

2 teaspoons pure vanilla extract

1 teaspoon coconut extract

½ cup sweetened shredded coconut

FROSTING

2 cups cold heavy cream

¼ cup sugar

1 teaspoon coconut extract

2 cups sweetened coconut flakes, divided

1 Place a rack in the middle of the oven. Preheat the oven to 325°F. Generously grease two 8-inch round nonstick (gray, not black) cake pans and line the bottoms with parchment paper or wax paper. Generously grease the pans again; set aside.

2 Make the cake: In a large mixing bowl, beat the butter with an electric mixer on medium speed until smooth. Gradually beat in the sugar until smooth. Add the eggs, one at a time, beating well after each addition.

3 In another bowl, sift together the sorghum blend, xanthan gum, baking powder, baking soda, and salt. In a measuring cup, whisk together the buttermilk, vanilla extract, and coconut extract.

4 With the mixer on low speed, beat the sorghum mixture into the egg mixture, alternating with the

> ## HOW TO TOAST COCONUT
>
> Place a rack in the middle of the oven. Preheat the oven to 325°F. Spread the coconut on a rimmed baking sheet (not nonstick). Toast in the oven until some of the shreds are golden brown, about 10 to 15 minutes, stirring 2 or 3 times. Watch carefully since oven temperatures and baking times may vary. Cool to room temperature before using.

buttermilk, beginning and ending with the sorghum mixture. Stir in the coconut flakes. Spread the batter evenly in the pans.

6 Bake 20 to 25 minutes or until the tops of the cakes are golden brown and a toothpick inserted into the center of the cake comes out clean. Cool the cakes in the pans 10 minutes on a wire rack. Remove the cakes from the pans with a thin metal spatula, discard the paper, and cool completely on the wire rack.

7 Make the frosting: Beat the whipping cream and sugar until stiff peaks form. Stir in the sugar and coconut extract.

8 Place one cake layer on a serving plate, topside down, and spread with 1 cup of the frosting. Sprinkle with 1 cup of the coconut. Top with the other cake layer, topside up. Frost the sides and then the top of the cake with the whipped cream. Sprinkle the remaining 1 cup of coconut on top of the cake. Refrigerate 1 hour before serving. Refrigerate leftovers.

Orange Coconut Cake with Fluffy Orange Frosting Ⓥ

MAKES 12 SERVINGS

This makes a lovely dessert for a casual luncheon, bridge club, or a special event such as a bridal shower. Rather than frost the sides, just put the frosting between the layers and on top, lending a "lighter" look to this otherwise rich, elegant cake.

CAKE

⅓ cup (5 tablespoons) unsalted butter or buttery spread, such as Earth Balance, at room temperature, or ¼ cup canola oil

1 cup sugar

2 large eggs, at room temperature

1½ cups Carol's Sorghum Blend (page x)

1 teaspoon xanthan gum

¼ teaspoon baking powder

¼ teaspoon baking soda

¼ teaspoon salt

¾ cup buttermilk, well-shaken, or homemade Buttermilk (page 677)

1 tablespoon grated orange zest

2 teaspoons pure vanilla extract

1 teaspoon orange extract (optional)

½ cup sweetened shredded coconut

FROSTING

3 large egg whites

1 cup sugar

¼ teaspoon cream of tartar

3 tablespoons fresh orange juice

1 teaspoon grated orange zest

1 teaspoon pure vanilla extract

1 teaspoon coconut extract (optional)

1 cup sweetened shredded coconut, toasted

1 Place a rack in the middle of the oven. Preheat oven to 325°F. Generously grease two 8-inch round nonstick (gray, not black) cake pans and line the bottoms with parchment paper or wax paper. Generously grease the pans again and set aside.

2 Make the cake: In a large mixing bowl, beat the butter with an electric mixer on medium speed until smooth. Gradually beat in the sugar until smooth. Add the eggs, one at a time, beating well after each addition.

3 In another bowl, sift together the sorghum blend, xanthan gum, baking powder, baking soda, and salt. In a measuring cup, whisk together the buttermilk, orange zest, vanilla extract, and orange extract, if using.

4 With the mixer on low speed, beat the sorghum mixture into the egg mixture, alternating with the buttermilk, beginning and ending with the sorghum mixture. Stir in the coconut. Pour the batter into the prepared pans, dividing evenly.

5 Bake 20 to 25 minutes or until the tops of the cakes are golden brown and a toothpick inserted into the center of the cake comes out clean. Cool the cakes in the pans 10 minutes on a wire rack. Remove the cakes from the pans with a thin metal spatula, discard the paper, and cool completely on the wire rack.

6 Make the frosting: In a double boiler over simmering water, combine the egg whites, sugar, cream of tartar, and orange juice. Beat 7 minutes with a portable electric mixer, or until the mixture reaches the consistency of frosting. Remove frosting from the heat and stir in the orange zest, vanilla extract, and coconut flavoring, if using.

7 Place one cake layer on a serving plate, topside down; spread with half of the frosting. Top with the second cake layer, topside up. Spread the top with the remaining half of the frosting. Sprinkle with the toasted coconut. Serve immediately.

Orange-Date Cake with Brandy Sauce Ⓥ

MAKES 12 SERVINGS

My grandmother often made a date cake for me when I was home from college, so I think of her every time I make it. I have updated it here with orange flavor, and I serve it drizzled with a hearty warm brandy sauce, making it perfect for a winter evening.

CAKE

¾ cup buttermilk, well-shaken, or homemade Buttermilk (page 677)

¾ cup finely chopped dates

Grated zest from 1 orange

6 tablespoons unsalted butter or buttery spread, such as Earth Balance, at room temperature, or ⅓ cup canola oil

1 cup sugar

2 large eggs, at room temperature

2 teaspoons pure vanilla extract

1½ cups Carol's Sorghum Blend (page x)

1 teaspoon xanthan gum

½ teaspoon salt

¼ teaspoon baking powder

¼ teaspoon baking soda

Pinch of freshly grated nutmeg

½ cup finely chopped walnuts

SAUCE

½ cup sugar

¼ cup cold water

1 teaspoon unsalted butter or buttery spread, such as Earth Balance, at room temperature, or canola oil

1 teaspoon pure vanilla extract

2 tablespoons brandy

1 Place a rack in the middle of the oven. Preheat the oven to 325°F. Generously grease an 11 × 7-inch nonstick (gray, not black) pan.

2 Make the cake: In a small saucepan, heat the buttermilk over medium heat until bubbles form around the edge of the pan. Remove the pan from the heat and add the dates and orange zest. Let cool 10 minutes or until the dates are soft.

3 In a medium mixing bowl, beat the butter on medium speed with an electric mixer until light and fluffy. Beat in the sugar, eggs, and vanilla extract until smooth.

4 In a small bowl, whisk together the sorghum blend, xanthan gum, salt, baking powder, baking soda, and nutmeg. Beat the sorghum mixture into the egg mixture on low speed, alternating with the cooled buttermilk, beginning and ending with the

sorghum mixture. Stir in the walnuts. Spread the batter evenly in the pan.

5 Bake 30 to 35 minutes or until a toothpick inserted into the center of the cake comes out clean. Cool the cake in the pan 10 minutes on a wire rack.

6 Make the sauce: In a heavy saucepan, heat the sugar and water over medium-high heat. Bring to a boil and then cook, swirling the pan occasionally, until the sugar is golden brown. Remove the pan from the heat and stir in the butter until smooth. Stir in the vanilla and then the brandy. Serve immediately, over slices of cake.

Poppy Seed–Orange Pound Cake with Orange Glaze Ⓥ

MAKES 12 SERVINGS

Pound cakes are extraordinarily versatile, as illustrated in this version that pairs poppy seed with orange flavoring. A yummy orange glaze further accentuates the fresh citrus flavor. You can also use lemon zest and lemon juice if you prefer.

POUND CAKE

½ cup (1 stick) unsalted butter or buttery spread, such as Earth Balance, at room temperature, or ⅓ cup canola oil

2 cups sugar

4 large eggs, at room temperature

3 cups Carol's Sorghum Blend (page x)

1½ teaspoons xanthan gum

¾ teaspoon salt

½ teaspoon baking powder

½ teaspoon baking soda

1½ cups buttermilk, well-shaken, or homemade Buttermilk (page 677)

2 tablespoons grated orange zest

2 teaspoons pure vanilla extract

⅓ cup poppy seed

GLAZE

¼ cup orange juice

¼ cup sugar

1 teaspoon grated orange zest

1 Place a rack in the middle of the oven. Preheat the oven to 325°F. Generously grease a 10-inch nonstick (gray, not black) Bundt pan; set aside.

2 Make the cake: In a large mixing bowl, beat the butter with an electric mixer on medium speed until smooth. Add sugar and continue beating on medium speed until well blended. Mix in eggs one at a time, beating well after each addition.

3 In a medium bowl, sift together the sorghum blend, xanthan gum, salt, baking powder, and baking soda. In a measuring cup, combine buttermilk, orange zest, and vanilla extract. With the mixer on low speed, beat the sorghum mixture into the egg mixture, alternating with the buttermilk and ending with the sorghum mixture. Mix in the poppy seed. Spread the batter in the prepared pan.

4 Bake 1 hour or until the top is golden brown and a toothpick inserted into the center of the cake comes out clean. Cool the cake in the pan 10 minutes on a wire rack. Remove cake from the pan and cool completely on the wire rack. Transfer cake to a serving plate.

5 Make the glaze: In a small saucepan, combine the orange juice, sugar, and orange zest and cook over medium heat until syrupy, about 5 minutes. Brush the cake with the warm glaze and serve immediately.

Pineapple-Filled Layer Cake ⓥ

MAKES 12 SERVINGS

If you like pineapple, you'll love this cake. For best results, serve the cake immediately after icing it; the frosting is prettiest when freshly made.

CAKE

⅓ cup (5 tablespoons) unsalted butter or buttery spread, such as Earth Balance, at room temperature, or ¼ cup canola oil

1 cup sugar

2 large eggs, at room temperature

1½ cups Carol's Sorghum Blend (page x)

1 teaspoon xanthan gum

¼ teaspoon baking powder

¼ teaspoon baking soda

½ teaspoon salt

¾ cup buttermilk, well-shaken, or homemade Buttermilk (page 677) or half buttermilk and half pineapple juice

2 teaspoons pure vanilla extract

FILLING

1 can (8 ounces) crushed pineapple, including juice

¼ cup sugar

1 tablespoon cornstarch

FROSTING

3 large egg whites

1 cup sugar

¼ teaspoon cream of tartar

3 tablespoons pineapple juice

1 teaspoon pure vanilla extract

¼ cup dried pineapple pieces for garnish (optional)

1 Place a rack in the middle of the oven. Preheat the oven to 325°F. Generously grease two 8-inch round nonstick (gray, not black) cake pans and line the bottoms with parchment paper or wax paper. Generously grease the pans again; set aside.

2 Make the cake: In a large mixing bowl, beat the butter with an electric mixer on medium speed until smooth. Gradually beat in the sugar until smooth. Add the eggs, one at a time, beating well after each addition.

3 In another bowl, sift together the sorghum blend, xanthan gum, baking powder, baking soda, and salt. In a measuring cup, whisk together the buttermilk (or buttermilk and pineapple juice) and vanilla extract.

4 With the mixer on low speed, beat the sorghum mixture into the egg mixture, alternating with the buttermilk, beginning and ending with the sorghum mixture. Spread the batter in the pans, dividing evenly.

5 Bake 20 to 25 minutes or until the tops of the cakes are golden brown and a toothpick inserted into the center of the cake comes out clean. Cool the cakes in the pans 10 minutes on a wire rack.

Remove the cakes from the pans with a thin metal spatula, discard the paper, and cool completely on the wire rack before filling and frosting.

6 While the cakes are cooling, make the filling: Stir together the crushed pineapple, sugar, and cornstarch in a small pan until very smooth. Cook over

FONDANT FOR SPECIAL-OCCASION CAKES

Fancy cakes are not off limits to a gluten-free diet. Mary Schaefer, of the Notter School of Pastry Arts in Florida, offers this fondant to transform any cake into an elaborate treat. Fondant is an icing that is rolled out and draped over a cake for a smooth look. Use this recipe on any basic 9-inch cake in this chapter or a smaller or larger cake.

COVERS UP TO A 10-INCH ROUND CAKE

1 tablespoon unflavored gelatin powder, such as Knox
¼ cup cold water
½ cup glucose
4 teaspoons glycerine
2 tablespoons solid white shortening, such as Crisco or Spectrum Vegetable
2 pounds powdered sugar (about 7½ cups)
Vanilla, almond, orange or flavoring of choice to taste (optional)
Food coloring as desired (optional)

1 Sprinkle the gelatin over the cold water in a 2-cup heatproof glass measuring cup or a stainless steel bowl. Bloom the gelatin, allowing to stand for 5 minutes. Set the bowl in a small pan of simmering water and heat, swirling the gelatin until dissolved.

2 Add the glucose and glycerin and mix well with a spoon. Add the shortening and stir until melted. Remove from heat. Cool to lukewarm, about 10 to 15 minutes.

3 Sift the powdered sugar and put in a large bowl. Make a well in the center of the sugar. Pour the lukewarm gelatin mixture into the well and stir first with a spoon and then with your hands until you have a smooth consistency. If the gelatin mixture is too hot when added to the powdered sugar you will have to add too much powdered sugar to get the proper consistency.

4 If using flavoring and/or food coloring, add and mix again. If the dough is too soft, add more sugar; if too stiff, add water, a drop at a time. Wrap tightly with plastic wrap and allow to rest for several hours in an airtight container before using.

Using Fondant: First, prepare your cake and frost it according to the recipe directions. Next, on a flat surface dusted lightly with cornstarch, use a rolling pin to roll fondant to a 17-inch circle, ⅛-inch thick. Wrap fondant around rolling pin, then unroll it over cake, starting at one side and continuing over top to other side. Use sides of a drinking glass to smooth out the top and sides, then cut off excess fondant around bottom of cake with a sharp paring knife or pizza cutter. Consult a cake decorating book for more details on using fondant.

medium-low heat, whisking constantly, until the mixture thickens. Chill the filling until it is firm.

7 Make the frosting: Combine the egg whites, sugar, cream of tartar, and pineapple juice in a double boiler over simmering water being careful not to let the pan touch the water. Beat on medium speed with a portable electric mixer 7 minutes or until the mixture reaches the consistency of frosting and is very glossy. Remove frosting from the heat and stir in the vanilla extract. Proceed directly to icing the cake.

8 Place one cake layer on a serving plate, topside down; spread evenly with the pineapple filling. Top with the second cake layer, topside up. Spread the top and sides with the frosting, using the spatula to make decorative dips and swirls. Serve immediately, garnished with dried pineapple.

Polynesian Layer Cake with Coconut–Cream Cheese Frosting **Ⓥ**

MAKES 12 SERVINGS

This cake is filled with the luscious Polynesian flavors of pineapple, banana, and coconut and is wonderful for a casual brunch or for those who prefer lightly-flavored cakes. It is a very moist, dense cake, so it takes longer to bake than other cakes of similar size.

CAKE
1½ cups Carol's Sorghum Blend (page x)
1 cup sugar
1 teaspoon xanthan gum
1 teaspoon baking soda
½ teaspoon salt
¼ teaspoon ground cinnamon
2 large eggs, at room temperature
⅓ cup canola oil
2 teaspoons pure vanilla extract
1 large ripe banana, mashed
1 can (8 ounces) crushed pineapple, undrained
½ cup sweetened coconut flakes
½ cup chopped pecans

FROSTING
1 package (8 ounces) cream cheese or cream
    cheese alternative, such as Tofutti, at room
    temperature
¼ cup (½ stick) unsalted butter or buttery
    spread, such as Earth Balance, at room
    temperature
3 cups powdered sugar
1 teaspoon coconut extract
¼ cup toasted coconut flakes, for sprinkling on top
    of cake

1 Place a rack in the middle of the oven. Preheat the oven to 325°F. Generously grease two 8-inch nonstick (gray, not black) round pans. Line the bottoms with parchment paper or wax paper and grease again; set aside.

2 Make the cake: In a large mixing bowl, whisk together the sorghum blend, sugar, xanthan gum, baking soda, salt, and cinnamon. Add the eggs, oil, and vanilla extract and beat with an electric mixer on low speed until blended, scraping down the side of the bowl with a spatula. Beat in the banana on medium speed until well blended. Stir in the pineapple, coconut, and pecans. Spread the batter evenly in the pans.

3 Bake 40 to 45 minutes or until the cakes pull away from the edges of the pan and a toothpick inserted into the center of the cakes comes out clean. Cool the cakes in the pans 15 minutes on a wire rack. Remove the cakes from the pans with a thin metal spatula, discard the paper, and cool completely on the wire rack.

4 Make the frosting: In a medium bowl, beat the cream cheese and butter with an electric mixer until smooth. Gradually sift in the powdered sugar and beat until smooth. Beat in the coconut extract. Place one cake layer, topside down, on a serving plate. Spread with 1 cup of the frosting. Place the second layer, topside up, on top and frost the top and sides. Sprinkle the top with toasted coconut. Refrigerate 1 hour before serving; refrigerate any leftovers.

Boston Cream Pie with Chocolate Ganache ⓥ

MAKES 12 SERVINGS

This dessert is actually not a pie but a layered cake. I'm not sure if it is from Boston, but the combination of yellow cake, vanilla pudding, and a delicious chocolate ganache make a lovely dessert. For best results, make the vanilla pudding ahead of time and refrigerate it so it holds its shape when serving.

PUDDING

2 tablespoons sugar

1½ tablespoons cornstarch

⅛ teaspoon salt

1 cup 1% milk (cow's, rice, soy, potato, or nut)

1 teaspoon pure vanilla extract

CAKE LAYERS

½ cup unsalted butter or buttery spread, such as Earth Balance, at room temperature, or ⅓ cup canola oil

¾ cup sugar

2 large eggs, at room temperature

1½ cups Carol's Sorghum Blend (page x)

1 teaspoon xanthan gum

½ teaspoon salt

¼ teaspoon baking powder

¼ teaspoon baking soda

¾ cup buttermilk, well-shaken, or homemade Buttermilk (page 677)

1 teaspoon pure vanilla extract

½ teaspoon almond extract

GANACHE

⅓ cup heavy cream or ¼ cup whole milk (cow's, rice, soy, potato, or nut)

9 ounces gluten-free bittersweet chocolate, such as Scharffen Berger, finely chopped

1 Make the pudding: In a medium saucepan, stir together the sugar, cornstarch, and salt until thoroughly blended. Add the milk and cook over medium heat, stirring constantly, until mixture thickens. Remove from the heat and stir in the vanilla. Lay a piece of plastic wrap directly on the pudding and refrigerate for at least 3 hours.

2 Place a rack in the middle of the oven. Preheat the oven to 325°F. Generously grease two 8 inch round nonstick (gray, not black) cake pans and line the bottoms with parchment paper or wax paper. Generously grease the pans again; set aside.

3 Make the layers: In a large mixing bowl, beat the butter with an electric mixer on medium speed until smooth. Gradually beat in the sugar until smooth. Add the eggs, one at a time, beating well after each addition.

4 In another bowl, sift together the sorghum blend, xanthan gum, salt, baking powder, and baking soda. In a measuring cup, whisk together the buttermilk, vanilla extract, and almond extract.

5 With the mixer on low speed, beat the sorghum mixture into the egg mixture, alternating with the buttermilk, beginning and ending with the sorghum mixture. Spread the batter evenly in the pans.

6 Bake 20 to 25 minutes or until the tops of the cakes are golden brown and a toothpick inserted into the center of the cake comes out clean. Cool the cakes in the pans 10 minutes on a wire rack. Remove cakes from the pans with a thin metal spatula, discard the paper, and cool completely on the wire rack.

7 Make the ganache: Place the chopped chocolate in a heatproof bowl. Heat the cream to boiling and then pour over the chocolate. Let stand about 3 minutes and then stir until smooth. Immediately proceed to assembling the cake before the chocolate hardens.

8 To assemble the cake, place one cake layer, topside down, on a serving plate. Spread the vanilla pudding on top. Place the second layer on top, topside up. Drizzle the chocolate ganache over the top of the cake and spread it to the edges, letting a little run over the sides, if desired. Serve immediately before the chocolate hardens. Refrigerate leftovers.

Polenta Cake

MAKES 8 SERVINGS

This easy cake is amazingly versatile and you can vary its taste with the type of liqueur you use. I like Frangelico (hazelnut), Triple Sec (orange), or limoncello (lemon), but you can also use milk if you wish. The cornmeal, dried fruit, nuts, and fennel lend an interesting texture and flavor to this cake, which is best served slightly warm with a dollop of whipped cream. You may also bake the cake in a heart-shaped cake pan for a special Valentine's Day treat.

1 cup cornstarch

1 cup gluten-free yellow cornmeal, such as Albers, Lamb's, Kinnikinnick, or Shiloh Farms

1 teaspoon baking powder

1 teaspoon salt

1 teaspoon xanthan gum

½ cup (1 stick) unsalted butter or buttery spread, such as Earth Balance, at room temperature

1 cup sugar

3 large eggs, at room temperature

¼ cup liqueur of choice (see headnote) or 1% milk (cow's, rice, soy, potato, or nut)

1 teaspoon pure vanilla extract

¼ cup pine nuts

¼ cup dark raisins

1 tablespoon fennel seeds

½ cup homemade Basic Whipped Cream (page 624), for serving

1 Place a rack in the middle of the oven. Preheat the oven to 325°F. Generously grease a 9-inch round cake pan. Line the bottom with parchment paper or wax paper and grease again; set aside.

2 In a small bowl, whisk together the cornstarch, cornmeal, baking powder, salt, and xanthan gum; set aside.

3 In a large mixing bowl, beat the butter and sugar with an electric mixer on medium speed until light and fluffy. Add the eggs one at a time, beating well after each addition. Beat in liqueur and vanilla

extract. Gradually add the pine nuts, raisins, and fennel seeds, beating just until smooth. Spread the batter in the prepared pan, smoothing the top with a wet spatula.

4 Bake 45 minutes, or until a toothpick inserted into the center of the cake comes out clean. Cool the pan 15 minutes on a wire rack. Remove the cake from pan with a thin metal spatula, discard the paper, and cool completely on the wire rack. Serve each slice with a tablespoon of whipped cream.

Pear-Almond Cake

MAKES 12 SERVINGS

This is an elegant—but not too sweet—dessert and it looks like something you would see in a pastry shop in Europe. I like it simply dusted with powdered sugar, but it is also wonderful with whipped cream. Enhance the flavor by adding a tablespoon of pear liqueur to the homemade Basic Whipped Cream (page 624).

⅓ cup (5 tablespoons) unsalted butter or buttery spread, such as Earth Balance, at room temperature, or ¼ cup canola oil

¾ cup sugar + 1 tablespoon for sprinkling

2 large eggs, at room temperature

1½ cups Carol's Sorghum Blend (page x)

1 teaspoon xanthan gum

½ teaspoon salt

¼ teaspoon baking powder

¼ teaspoon baking soda

½ cup buttermilk, well-shaken, or homemade Buttermilk (page 677)

¼ cup pear liqueur or almond liqueur or ¼ cup buttermilk, well-shaken (optional)

1 teaspoon pure vanilla extract

½ teaspoon almond extract (optional)

1 can (14 to 15 ounces) pear halves drained and cut in ¼-inch slices

2 tablespoons sliced almonds

2 tablespoons powdered sugar, for dusting

1 Place a rack in the middle of the oven. Preheat the oven to 325°F. Generously grease a 10-inch round nonstick (gray, not black) springform pan with a removable bottom. Line the bottom with parchment paper or wax paper. Grease again. You may also use a regular 10-inch nonstick cake pan, but it will be harder to cut the cake.

2 In a large mixing bowl, beat the butter with an electric mixer on medium speed until smooth. Gradually beat in ¾ cup sugar until smooth. Add the eggs, one at a time, beating well after each addition.

3 In another bowl, sift together the sorghum blend, xanthan gum, salt, baking powder, and baking soda. In a measuring cup, whisk together the buttermilk, liqueur, if using, vanilla extract, and almond extract, if using.

4 With the mixer on low speed, beat the sorghum mixture into the egg mixture, alternating with the buttermilk, beginning and ending with the sorghum mixture. Spread the batter in the pan. Arrange the sliced pears in a pinwheel design on top of the cake. Sprinkle with the sliced almonds and the remaining tablespoon of sugar.

5 Bake 25 to 30 minutes or until the top of the cake is golden brown and a toothpick inserted into the center of the cake comes out clean. Cool the cake 10 minutes in the pan on a wire rack. Remove the cake from the pan with a thin metal spatula, discard the paper, and cool 20 minutes on the wire rack. Serve warm with a dusting of powdered sugar.

Rhubarb-Almond Cake

MAKES 8 SERVINGS

Make this home-style cake in the spring when rhubarb is in season. You can also find fresh rhubarb in the produce section of grocery stores in spring and early summer. We transplanted a rhubarb plant from our old house to our current house seventeen years ago and it faithfully produces every year.

RHUBARB

4 cups (1 pound) rhubarb, sliced in ½-inch pieces
⅔ cup sugar
¼ teaspoon ground cinnamon
¼ teaspoon freshly grated nutmeg
2 tablespoons sliced almonds, toasted

CAKE

1 cup Carol's Sorghum Blend (page x)
⅔ cup sugar
1 teaspoon baking powder
½ teaspoon salt
½ cup 1% milk (cow's, rice, soy, potato, or nut)
¼ cup canola oil
1 large egg, at room temperature
2 teaspoons almond extract
1 teaspoon pure vanilla extract
2 tablespoons powdered sugar, for dusting

1 Place a rack in the middle of the oven. Preheat the oven to 350°F. Generously grease an 8-inch square nonstick (gray, not black) baking pan.

2 Prepare the rhubarb: In a medium bowl, toss the rhubarb with the sugar, cinnamon, and nutmeg and place in the baking pan. Sprinkle with almonds.

3 Make the cake: Place all of the cake ingredients in a medium mixing bowl and beat with electric mixer on medium speed until thoroughly blended and slightly thickened. Spread batter evenly over the rhubarb.

4 Bake 40 to 50 minutes or until a toothpick inserted into the center of the cake comes out clean. Cool the cake in the pan 20 minutes on a wire rack. Serve warm with a dusting of powdered sugar.

Old-Fashioned Strawberry Shortcake Ⓥ

MAKES 10 SERVINGS

This is the classic dessert that we all remember from our childhood. The bright red strawberries are gorgeous, and the mix of textures teases with velvety whipped cream and slightly crunchy shortcake. The dessert is best eaten when the cake is warm, soon after it is baked.

STRAWBERRIES

2 pints (4 cups) fresh strawberries, washed, stemmed, and halved

¼ cup sugar, or to taste

1 teaspoon pure vanilla extract

SHORTCAKE

¾ cup Carol's Sorghum Blend (page x)

¾ cup potato starch

½ cup sugar + 1 tablespoon for sprinkling

1 tablespoon baking powder

½ teaspoon baking soda

1 teaspoon xanthan gum

1 teaspoon guar gum

½ teaspoon salt

¼ cup unsalted butter or buttery spread, such as Earth Balance, at room temperature, or ¼ cup canola oil

1 cup buttermilk, well-shaken, or homemade Buttermilk (page 677), at room temperature

1 teaspoon pure vanilla extract

White rice flour for dusting and rolling

2 tablespoons 2% milk (or cream) for brushing biscuit tops

2 cups homemade Basic Whipped Cream (page 624) or whipped topping, such as Lucerne or Soyatoo

1 Prepare the strawberries: In a medium bowl, toss the strawberries with the sugar and vanilla extract; set aside.

2 Place a rack in the middle of the oven. Preheat the oven to 375°F. Generously grease a 13 × 9-inch nonstick (gray, not black) baking sheet or line with parchment paper. Dust the surface lightly with white rice flour.

3 Make the shortcake: In a food processor, pulse the sorghum blend, potato starch, ½ cup of the sugar, baking powder, baking soda, xanthan gum, guar gum, and salt to mix thoroughly. Add the butter, buttermilk, and vanilla extract. Blend until the dough forms ball, scraping down the side of the bowl with a spatula, if necessary. The dough will be very, very soft, but dusting it with rice flour makes it more manageable.

4 Place the dough on the prepared baking sheet. Lightly dust the dough with white rice flour to facilitate easier handling. Gently pat the dough to a 1-inch thick circle and cut it into 10 circles, 2 inches in diameter, with a floured, metal biscuit cutter. For better rising, push the biscuit cutter straight down on the dough rather than twisting it while cutting. Shape the remaining dough to 1-inch thick and cut again, lightly dusting the dough again with white rice flour to prevent sticking, if necessary. Arrange the shortcakes evenly on the baking sheet and brush the tops with milk. Sprinkle with the remaining tablespoon of sugar. (As an alternative, you may divide the dough evenly in a generously-greased, 12-cup nonstick (gray, not black) muffin pan and bake for 10 to 15 minutes, or until the shortcakes are nicely browned.)

5 Bake 15 to 20 minutes or until the shortcakes are browned and crisp to your liking. Remove them from the oven and cool slightly.

6 To assemble the shortcakes, cut them in half horizontally. Arrange strawberries on the bottom half and replace the top. Drizzle more strawberries on top and top with 2 generous tablespoons of whipped cream.

Strawberry Swirl Cake with Fluffy Pink Frosting Ⓥ

MAKES 12 SERVINGS

This cake nearly shouts "springtime" with its pretty pink swirl—which is actually very easy to make—and fluffy pink frosting. It's perfect for a little girl's birthday party.

CAKE

½ cup (1 stick) unsalted butter or buttery spread, such as Earth Balance, at room temperature, or ⅓ cup canola oil

¾ cup sugar

3 large egg whites, at room temperature

1½ cups Carol's Sorghum Blend (page x)

1 teaspoon xanthan gum

½ teaspoon salt

¼ teaspoon baking powder

¼ teaspoon baking soda

¾ cup buttermilk, well-shaken, or homemade Buttermilk (page 677)

1 teaspoon pure vanilla extract

½ teaspoon almond extract

1 package (4 ounces) strawberry-flavored gelatin

1½ cups (about 1 pint container) hulled and sliced fresh strawberries (reserve a few whole, unhulled strawberries for garnishing the top of the cake)

FROSTING

3 large egg whites, at room temperature

1 cup sugar

¼ teaspoon cream of tartar

3 tablespoons cold water

1 to 2 drops red food coloring (enough to make the frosting pink, but not red)

1 teaspoon pure vanilla extract

1 Place a rack in the middle of the oven. Preheat the oven to 350°F. Generously grease two 9-inch nonstick (gray, not black) round pans. Line the bottoms with parchment paper and grease again; set aside.

2 Make the cake: In a large mixing bowl, beat the butter with an electric mixer on medium speed until smooth. Gradually beat in the sugar until smooth. Add the egg whites, one at a time, beating well after each addition.

3 In another bowl, sift together the sorghum blend, xanthan gum, salt, baking powder, and baking soda. In a measuring cup, whisk together the buttermilk, vanilla extract, and almond extract.

4 With the mixer on low speed, beat the sorghum mixture into the egg mixture, alternating with the buttermilk, beginning and ending with the sorghum mixture. Pour half of the batter into a separate bowl and add the gelatin powder, stirring until well blended. From opposite sides of the pan, simultaneously pour half of the white batter and half of the strawberry batter—side by side— into each pan.

5 Draw the blade of a butter knife back and forth through the batter in two S shapes, going from the strawberry side to the white side and back to the strawberry side. Don't swirl the batter too much or it will be all pink, rather than swirls of pink and white.

6 Bake 30 to 35 minutes or until the tops of the cakes are golden brown and a cake tester inserted into the center of the cakes comes out clean. Cool the cakes in the pans 10 minutes on a wire rack. Remove the cakes from the pans with a thin metal spatula, discard the paper, and cool completely on the wire rack before frosting.

7 Make the frosting: In a double boiler over simmering water, combine the egg whites, sugar, cream of tartar, and cold water. Beat on medium speed 7 minutes with an electric mixer, or until the mixture reaches the consistency of frosting and is very glossy. Quickly beat in enough drops of red food coloring to reach the desired pink color and vanilla extract, and proceed directly to icing the cake.

8 Place one cake layer, topside down, on a serving plate. Spread with 1 cup of the frosting. Arrange the strawberries slices in a single layer on top of the frosting. Place the second layer on top, topside up, and frost the top and sides, using a spatula to make decorative dips and swirls. Just before serving, garnish the top of the cake with the reserved whole strawberries. Refrigerate any leftovers.

Strawberries and Cream Layer Cake Ⓥ

MAKES 10 SERVINGS

This is a casually arranged, yet stunningly beautiful dessert that will impress your guests. In the cream filling, I use mascarpone cheese, a very rich Italian cow's milk cheese similar to cream cheese, but if you are dairy-sensitive, you can use nondairy cream cheese instead. Or, try another filling such as Pineapple Filling (page 478). This cake is prettiest when served fairly soon after it is assembled before the strawberry filling sets up completely. You want the filling oozing out of the layers, not firm and hard.

CAKE

½ cup unsalted butter or buttery spread, such as Earth Balance, at room temperature but not melted, or ⅓ cup canola oil

2 cups sugar

4 large eggs, at room temperature

3 cups Carol's Sorghum Blend (page x)

1½ teaspoons xanthan gum

¾ teaspoon salt

½ teaspoon baking powder

½ teaspoon baking soda

1½ cups buttermilk, well-shaken, or homemade Buttermilk (page 677)

1 tablespoon grated lemon zest

1 teaspoon pure vanilla extract

½ teaspoon almond extract

FILLING

½ cup sugar

1 tablespoon cornstarch

Pinch salt

½ cup cold water

1 tablespoon light corn syrup

2 tablespoons strawberry gelatin powder

½ teaspoon pure vanilla extract

1 drop red food coloring (optional)

3 cups fresh strawberries (about 1 pound whole strawberries), divided

FILLING

1 tub (8 ounces) mascarpone cheese or cream cheese alternative, such as Tofutti + ½ teaspoon almond extract

2 cups homemade Basic Whipped Cream (page 624) or whipped topping, such as Lucerne or Soyatoo

1 Place a rack in the middle of the oven. Preheat the oven to 325°F. Generously grease a 9 × 5-inch nonstick (gray, not black) loaf pan; set aside.

2 Make the cake: In a large mixing bowl, cream the butter with an electric mixer on medium speed until smooth. Add sugar and continue beating on medium speed until well blended. Mix in eggs, one at a time, beating well after each addition.

3 In a medium bowl, sift together the sorghum blend, xanthan gum, salt, baking powder, and baking soda. In a measuring cup, combine buttermilk, lemon zest, vanilla extract, and almond extract. On low speed, beat the sorghum mixture into the egg mixture, alternating with the buttermilk and ending with the sorghum mixture. Spoon the batter into the prepared pan and smooth the top with a spatula.

4 Bake 1 hour, or until the top is golden brown and a toothpick inserted into the center of the cake comes out clean. Cool the cake in the pan 10 minutes on a wire rack. Remove the cake from the pan and cool completely on the wire rack.

Slice the cake horizontally into three equal layers; set aside.

5 Make the strawberry filling: In a medium saucepan, whisk together the sugar, cornstarch, and salt until blended. Then whisk in the water. Cook over medium-high heat, whisking constantly, until the mixture is thick and clear. Remove from the heat and stir in the corn syrup, gelatin, vanilla extract, and food coloring; cool 15 minutes.

6 Slice 2 cups of the strawberries and gently stir them into the cooled gelatin. Set aside while making the cream filling.

7 Make the cream filling: In a medium bowl, beat the mascarpone cheese and almond extract with an electric mixer on medium speed until smooth. Fold in the whipped cream.

8 To assemble the cake, place the bottom layer on a serving platter and spread it with 1 cup of the cream filling. Top it with half of the strawberry filling. Place the second cake layer on top and spread with 1 cup of the cream filling and the remaining strawberry filling. Place the third cake layer on top and spread with the remaining cream filling. Halve the remaining 1 cup of strawberries and arrange them on top in an informal but decorative fashion letting some of them fall on the serving plate. Serve immediately. Refrigerate leftovers.

Chestnut Cake with Marrons Glacés Whipped Cream Ⓥ

MAKES 10 SERVINGS

Chestnut flour is commonly used in Italian baking, but is gaining popularity in the United States because it is gluten-free. If you can't find candied chestnuts, which are usually available at specialty shops, use your favorite chopped nuts instead.

CAKE

½ cup (1 stick) unsalted butter or buttery spread, such as Earth Balance, at room temperature, or ⅓ cup canola oil

¾ cup sugar

2 large eggs, at room temperature

¾ cup Carol's Sorghum Blend (page x)

¾ cup chestnut flour

1 teaspoon xanthan gum

½ teaspoon salt

½ teaspoon baking powder

½ teaspoon baking soda

¾ cup buttermilk, well-shaken, or homemade Buttermilk (page 677)

1 teaspoon pure vanilla extract

1 teaspoon rum extract

WHIPPED CREAM

2 cups homemade Basic Whipped Cream (page 624) or whipped topping, such as Lucerne or Soyatoo

1 tablespoon dark rum or 1 teaspoon rum extract

½ cup finely chopped marrons glacés (candied chestnuts)

1 Place a rack in the middle of the oven. Preheat the oven to 325°F. Generously grease a 9-inch round nonstick (gray, not black) springform pan with a removable bottom. Line the bottom with parchment paper or wax paper. Grease again.

2 Make the cake: In a large mixing bowl, beat the butter with an electric mixer on medium speed until smooth. Gradually beat in the sugar until smooth. Add the eggs, one at a time, beating well after each addition.

3 In another bowl, sift together the sorghum blend, chestnut flour, xanthan gum, salt, baking powder, and baking soda. In a measuring cup, whisk together the buttermilk, vanilla extract, and rum extract.

4 With the mixer on low speed, beat the sorghum mixture into the egg mixture, alternating with the buttermilk, beginning and ending with the sorghum mixture. Spread the batter in the prepared pan.

5 Bake 25 to 30 minutes or until the top of the cake is golden brown and a cake tester inserted into the center of the cake comes out clean. Cool the cake in the pan 10 minutes and then remove the springform pan sides. Cool the cake completely on the wire rack. Discard the paper liner.

6 Make the whipped cream: In medium bowl, place the whipped cream and stir in the rum and candied chestnuts. Serve each piece of cake with a dollop of whipped cream.

Black Walnut Bundt Cake with Caramel Frosting Ⓥ

MAKES 12 SERVINGS

When I was growing up, there was a huge black walnut tree just outside our back door. As a small child, I learned how to separate the tough outside husk from the hard black shell and I grew to love this earthy fruit. This cake has a deep, rich, nutty flavor people will find irresistible.

CAKE

5 tablespoons unsalted butter or buttery spread, such as Earth Balance, at room temperature, or ¼ cup canola oil

1 cup sugar

2 large eggs, divided

1½ cups Carol's Sorghum Blend (page x)

1 teaspoon xanthan gum

½ teaspoon baking powder

½ teaspoon baking soda

½ teaspoon salt

¾ cup buttermilk, well-shaken, or homemade Buttermilk (page 677)

1 teaspoon pure vanilla extract

1 teaspoon black walnut extract (optional)

¼ cup finely chopped black walnuts

FROSTING

¼ cup (½ stick) unsalted butter or buttery spread, such as Earth Balance, at room temperature

1 cup packed dark brown sugar

2 tablespoons 1% milk (cow's, rice, soy, potato, or nut), or more if necessary

1 tablespoon pure vanilla extract

1 box (16 ounces) powdered sugar

¼ cup finely chopped black walnuts, for garnish

1 Place a rack in the middle of the oven. Preheat the oven to 325°F. Generously grease a 10-inch nonstick (gray, not black) Bundt cake pan; set aside.

2 Make the cake: In a large mixing bowl, beat the butter with an electric mixer on medium speed until creamy and smooth. Gradually beat in the sugar until smooth. Add the eggs, one at a time, beating well after each addition.

3 In another bowl, sift together the sorghum blend, xanthan gum, baking powder, baking soda, and salt. In a measuring cup, whisk together the buttermilk, vanilla extract, and black walnut extract, if using.

4 With the mixer on low speed, beat the sorghum mixture into the egg mixture, alternating with the buttermilk, beginning and ending with the sorghum mixture. Add the black walnuts, scrape down the side of the bowl, and beat just until smooth. Spread the batter in the pan.

5 Bake 55 minutes to 1 hour or until the cake is golden brown and a toothpick inserted into the center of the cake comes out clean. Cool the cake in the pan 10 minutes on a wire rack. Remove the cake from the pan with a thin metal spatula and cool completely on the wire rack.

6 Make the frosting: Beat the butter in a medium bowl with an electric mixer on medium speed until smooth and creamy. Beat in the brown sugar, milk, and vanilla extract. Gradually beat in the powdered sugar until smooth.

7 Place the cake on a serving plate. Spread frosting evenly over the top and sides of the cake. Sprinkle the top evenly with the black walnuts. Serve immediately.

Cream-Filled Cakes

MAKES 8 SERVINGS

Similar to "Twinkies," these are yellow cakes filled with marshmallow cream—a treat well known by young and old alike. You need a special pan with eight indentations—variously known as an éclair pan, a canoe cake pan, or a cream twinkle pan—readily available at kitchen stores or online.

CAKES

½ cup (1 stick) unsalted butter or buttery spread, such as Earth Balance, at room temperature, or ⅓ cup canola oil

1 cup sugar

2 large eggs, at room temperature

1¼ cups Carol's Sorghum Blend (page x)

1 teaspoon xanthan gum

½ teaspoon salt

¼ teaspoon baking powder

¼ teaspoon baking soda

¾ cup buttermilk, well-shaken, or homemade Buttermilk (page 677)

1 teaspoon pure vanilla extract

½ teaspoon lemon extract or grated lemon zest

Drop of yellow food coloring (optional)

FILLING

1 jar (7 ounces) marshmallow creme, such as Marshmallow Fluff by Norbest

¼ cup white shortening, such as Spectrum Vegetable, at room temperature

3 tablespoons powdered sugar

¼ teaspoon pure vanilla extract

1 Place a rack in the middle of the oven. Preheat the oven to 325°F. Generously grease a nonstick (gray, not black) pan (see headnote) and set aside.

2 Make the cakes: In a large mixing bowl, beat the butter with an electric mixer on medium speed until smooth. Gradually beat in the sugar until smooth. Add the eggs, one at a time, beating well after each addition.

3 In another bowl, sift together the sorghum blend, xanthan gum, salt, baking powder, and baking soda. In a measuring cup, whisk together the buttermilk, vanilla extract, lemon extract. and food coloring, if using.

4 With the mixer on low speed, beat the sorghum mixture into the egg mixture, alternating with the buttermilk, beginning and ending with the sorghum mixture. Divide the batter evenly in the pan, filling each indentation half full.

5 Bake 20 to 25 minutes or until the tops of the cakes are golden brown and a cake tester inserted into the center comes out clean. Cool the cakes in the pan 5 minutes on a wire rack. Remove the cakes from the pans with a thin metal spatula and cool completely on the wire rack.

6 Make the filling: In a medium bowl, beat the marshmallow fluff and shortening together with an electric mixer on medium speed until well blended. Beat in the powdered sugar and vanilla extract until smooth. Transfer the filling to a gallon-size, heavy-duty food storage bag or a pastry bag fitted with a plastic tip.

7 Poke holes in 3 to 4 places down the center of the cake's flat side (the top as it bakes). Place the tip into the flat side of the cake and squirt a little of the filling into the holes. Be careful not to squirt too much or too hard or it will break the cake. Serve at room temperature.

CHOCOLATE CAKES

Chocolate Bundt Cake

MAKES 12 SERVINGS

A Bundt pan makes a pretty-shaped cake and a nice presentation for guests. It is especially festive if you sprinkle powdered sugar on top and fill the center with bright red cherry pie filling. It also freezes well, so bake it ahead for later use.

½ cup (1 stick) unsalted butter or buttery spread, such as Earth Balance, at room temperature, or ⅓ cup canola oil

1¼ cups sugar

3 large eggs, at room temperature

⅔ cup 1% milk, (cow, rice, soy, potato, or nut) at room temperature

1 tablespoon pure vanilla extract

2 cups Carol's Sorghum Blend (page x)

⅔ cup unsweetened cocoa powder (not Dutch-process or alkali)

1 teaspoon baking soda

1 teaspoon xanthan gum

¾ teaspoon salt

⅔ cup hot (120°F) brewed coffee

½ cup powdered sugar, for dusting

1 can (14 to 15 ounces) cherry pie filling, such as Wilderness or Comstock for serving

1 Place a rack in the middle of the oven. Preheat the oven to 325°F. Generously grease a 10-cup nonstick (gray, not black) Bundt pan.

2 In a large mixer bowl, beat the butter and sugar with an electric mixer on medium speed until light and fluffy. Beat in eggs, one at a time, until thoroughly blended. Beat in milk and vanilla extract.

3 In a separate bowl, whisk together sorghum blend, cocoa, baking soda, xanthan gum, and salt. Beat sorghum mixture into the egg mixture on low speed, alternating with hot coffee, beginning and ending with sorghum mixture. Spread the batter in the pan, smoothing the top of the batter with a spatula.

4 Bake 45 to 50 minutes or until a toothpick inserted into center of cake comes out clean. Cool the cake in the pan 15 minutes on a wire rack. Remove the cake from the pan with a thin metal spatula, and cool completely on the wire rack.

5 Place the cake on a serving plate, dust the top with powdered sugar, and then fill the center of the cake with cherry pie filling. Serve immediately.

Chocolate-Raspberry Bundt Cake

MAKES 12 SERVINGS

I once ordered a chocolate birthday cake for my husband and was pleasantly surprised to find the unmistakable taste of raspberries. It was absolutely delicious and the raspberries made the cake very moist. So, now I often add crushed raspberries to my chocolate cakes.

⅔ cup unsalted butter or buttery spread, such as Earth Balance, at room temperature, or ½ cup canola oil

1½ cups packed light brown sugar

2 large eggs, at room temperature

2 teaspoons pure vanilla extract

2⅔ cups Carol's Sorghum Blend (page x)

⅔ cup unsweetened cocoa powder (not Dutch-process or alkali)

1½ teaspoons xanthan gum

1 teaspoon baking soda

½ teaspoon salt

¾ cup 1% milk (cow's, rice, soy, potato, or nut)

1 cup crushed fresh raspberries (or frozen raspberries, thoroughly drained)

1 Place a rack in the middle of the oven. Preheat the oven to 325°F. Generously grease a 10-cup nonstick (gray, not black) Bundt pan.

2 In the bowl of an electric mixer, beat the butter and sugar on low speed until light and fluffy. Beat in the eggs and vanilla extract.

3 In a separate bowl, whisk together the sorghum blend, cocoa powder, xanthan gum, baking soda, and salt. Beat into the egg mixture alternately with the milk, beginning and ending with the sorghum mixture. Stir in the crushed raspberries. Spread the batter in the pan.

4 Bake 45 to 50 minutes or until a toothpick inserted into the center of the cake comes out clean. Cool the cake in the pan 15 minutes on a wire rack. Remove the cake from the pan with a thin metal spatula, and cool completely on the wire rack. Serve immediately.

Vegan Chocolate Spice Cake Ⓥ

MAKES 8 SERVINGS

This easy one-bowl cake is for those who love chocolate and spice together, and vegans will appreciate that it is free of dairy and eggs. If you prefer not to use all the spices, you can leave out one such as the cloves, and add a ¼ teaspoon more of another such as the cinnamon.

1¾ cups Carol's Sorghum Blend (page x)

1 cup sugar

⅓ cup unsweetened cocoa powder (not Dutch-process or alkali)

1 teaspoon baking soda

1 teaspoon ground cinnamon

¾ teaspoon xanthan gum

¾ teaspoon salt

½ teaspoon freshly grated nutmeg

¼ teaspoon ground cloves

⅓ cup canola oil

1 tablespoon cider vinegar

2 teaspoons pure vanilla extract

1 cup hot (120°F) water

1 Place a rack in the middle of the oven. Preheat the oven to 350°F. Generously grease an 8-inch square nonstick (gray, not black) baking pan; set aside.

2 Place all of the ingredients in a medium mixing bowl. Beat with an electric mixer on low speed until thoroughly blended. Transfer the batter to the prepared pan, spreading evenly with a wet spatula. Let stand 10 minutes.

3 Bake 25 to 30 minutes or until a toothpick inserted into the center of the cake comes out clean. Cool the cake in the pan 20 minutes on a wire rack. Serve warm or at room temperature.

Vegan Chocolate Layer Cake with Mocha Frosting Ⓥ

MAKES 12 SERVINGS

This incredibly easy cake is for chocolate lovers who also avoid dairy and eggs. Coffee in the frosting enhances the chocolate flavor.

CAKE

1¾ cups Carol's Sorghum Blend (page x)

1 cup sugar

⅓ cup unsweetened cocoa powder (not Dutch-process or alkali)

1 teaspoon baking soda

¾ teaspoon xanthan gum

¾ teaspoon salt

1 cup hot (120°F) water

⅓ cup canola oil

1 tablespoon cider vinegar

1 tablespoon pure vanilla extract

FROSTING

2 cups powdered sugar

2 tablespoons unsweetened cocoa powder (Dutch-process or alkali)

2 tablespoons unsalted butter or buttery spread, such as Earth Balance, at room temperature

¼ cup hot, (120°F) strongly-brewed espresso or coffee

Pinch salt

1 Place a rack in the middle of the oven. Preheat the oven to 350°F. Generously grease two 8-inch round nonstick (gray, not black) pans. Line each with parchment paper or wax paper and grease again.

2 Make the cake: In a medium mixing bowl, sift together the sorghum blend, sugar, cocoa, baking soda, xanthan gum, and salt. Add the water, oil, vinegar, and vanilla extract. Beat with an electric mixer on low speed until thoroughly blended. Spread the batter evenly in the pans with a wet spatula. Let stand 10 minutes before baking.

3 Bake 20 to 25 minutes or until a toothpick inserted into the center of the cakes comes out clean. Cool the cakes in the pans 10 minutes on a wire rack. Remove cakes from pans with a thin metal spatula, discard parchment paper, and cool completely on the wire rack.

4 Make the frosting: In a medium bowl, beat all ingredients except coffee until blended. Add coffee gradually, one tablespoon at a time, until frosting reaches desired consistency.

5 Place a cake layer on a serving plate, topside down, and spread with 1 cup frosting. Top with the second layer, topside side up, and spread the remaining frosting on top. Serve immediately.

Chocolate Mayonnaise Cake Ⓥ

MAKES 12 SERVINGS

This cake is moist and flavorful, belying its unconventional mayonnaise base. (The flavor blends in easily; no one will know it's there.) Use real mayonnaise; reduced-fat mayonnaise may be used, but the cake won't be quite as moist. The technique of soaking cocoa in boiling water deepens its chocolate flavor, so don't skip this important step. It can be done quickly while you're assembling the other ingredients.

¾ cup boiling water
⅓ cup unsweetened cocoa powder (not Dutch-process or alkali)
¾ cup real mayonnaise (not reduced fat or salad dressing)
1 cup sugar
1 teaspoon pure vanilla extract
2 cups Carol's Sorghum Blend (page x)
1 teaspoon baking soda

1 Place a rack in the middle of the oven. Preheat oven to 350°F. Generously grease a 9-inch square nonstick (gray, not black) cake pan or two 8-inch round nonstick (gray, not black) cake pans. If planning to frost as layer cakes, line 8-inch pans with parchment paper or wax paper. Grease again.

2 In small bowl, pour boiling water over cocoa and stir until smooth. Set aside while you measure remaining ingredients.

3 In a large mixing bowl, beat mayonnaise, sugar, and vanilla extract with an electric mixer at medium speed 1 minute. Reduce speed to low and beat in cocoa mixture just until incorporated. Gradually add flour and soda, beating just until batter thickens slightly. Spread batter in the pan(s).

4 Bake 25 to 30 minutes or until a cake tester inserted in the center comes out clean. Remove pan(s) from oven and cool 10 minutes on wire rack. Remove the cake(s) from pan(s) with a thin metal spatula, discard paper, if using, and cool completely on the wire rack. Serve immediately.

Mini Chocolate Peanut Butter Cakes Ⓥ

MAKES 4 SERVINGS

These scrumptious little chocolate cakes are filled with a perfect combination of peanut butter and chocolate. If you can't find gluten-free peanut butter chips, use gluten-free chocolate chips and stir one tablespoon of peanut butter into the filling.

CAKES

1¼ cups Carol's Sorghum Blend (page x)

½ cup unsweetened cocoa powder (not Dutch-process or alkali)

1 teaspoon xanthan gum

¾ teaspoon baking soda

¾ teaspoon salt

½ cup unsalted butter or buttery spread, such as Earth Balance, or ⅓ cup canola oil

1 cup packed light brown sugar

½ cup 1% milk (cow's, rice, soy, potato, or nut)

1 large egg, at room temperature

2 teaspoons pure vanilla extract

¾ cup hot (120°F) brewed coffee

½ cup heavy cream

FILLING

½ teaspoon unflavored gelatin powder, such as Knox

1½ tablespoons cold water

2 ounces gluten-free peanut butter chips, such as Hy-Vee

GLAZE

¼ cup (½ stick) unsalted butter or buttery spread, such as Earth Balance, at room temperature

¼ cup gluten-free chocolate chips, such as Tropical Source

1 tablespoon light corn syrup

1 Place a rack in the middle of the oven. Preheat the oven to 325°F. Generously grease 4 mini 4-inch springform pans and line the bottoms with parchment paper or wax paper. Grease again; set aside.

2 Make the cake: In a small bowl, whisk together the sorghum blend, cocoa, xanthan gum, baking soda, and salt; set aside.

3 In a large mixing bowl, beat the butter and brown sugar with an electric mixer on medium speed about 30 seconds. Beat in the milk, egg, and vanilla extract until thoroughly blended.

4 On low speed, beat the sorghum mixture into the egg mixture, alternating with the hot coffee, beginning and ending with the sorghum mixture. Spread the batter evenly with a wet spatula in the pans.

5 Bake 20 to 25 minutes or until a toothpick inserted into the center of the cakes comes out clean. Cool the cakes in the pans 10 minutes on a wire rack. Remove cakes from pans with a thin metal spatula, discard the paper, and cool completely on the wire rack. Slice the cakes, crosswise, about ¾ quarters of the way to create a pocket; set aside.

6 Make the filling: Sprinkle the gelatin on the cold water in a small heavy saucepan and stir; let stand 1 minute. Heat the mixture over low heat until the gelatin dissolves. Add the peanut butter chips and stir until the mixture is smooth and the chips are melted, then stir into the cream. Chill 15 minutes. Whip the mixture until stiff peaks form. Transfer the filling to a heavy-duty food storage bag and cut off ½ inch from one corner. Pipe ¼ of the filling into the middle of each cake through the pocket. Place the cakes on a wire rack.

7 Make the glaze: In a glass bowl set over a saucepan of simmering water, combine the butter, chocolate, and corn syrup. Stir until the chocolate is melted and the mixture is smooth. Remove from the heat and let stand 5 minutes. Pour the glaze over the cakes and refrigerate them to set the glaze. Let the cakes stand at room temperature 10 minutes before serving.

Chocolate Molten Lava Cakes with Crème Anglaise Ⓥ

MAKES 6 SERVINGS

These cakes are just like those you see on restaurant menus, yet they are amazingly simple. They can be assembled ahead of time and refrigerated, then baked during dinner to tantalize your guests with their heavenly aroma. The crème anglaise triples in volume as you beat it, so be sure to use a bowl that is big enough to accommodate this expansion.

CAKES

9 ounces bittersweet dark chocolate, such as Scharffen Berger, chopped

¼ cup (½ stick) unsalted butter or buttery spread, such as Earth Balance, or 3 tablespoons canola oil

1 teaspoon pure vanilla extract

¼ teaspoon salt

4 large eggs, at room temperature

1½ tablespoons granulated sugar

2 tablespoons powdered sugar, for dusting

Fresh raspberries and a sprig of fresh mint, for garnish

CRÈME ANGLAISE

½ cup heavy cream or whole milk (cow's, soy, or nut)

2 large egg yolks

¼ cup sugar

1 teaspoon pure vanilla extract

1 Generously grease 6 small (4 ounce), ovenproof ramekins with butter or buttery spread and set aside. Have a 13 × 9-inch baking sheet (not nonstick) ready.

2 Make the cakes: In a medium glass bowl, combine chocolate, butter, vanilla extract, and salt. Heat on high for 1 ½ to 2 minutes in microwave oven or until mixture is melted. Stir to thoroughly combine. Set aside to cool to room temperature.

3 In another medium bowl, whip the eggs and sugar with an electric mixer until very light and tripled in volume, about 5 minutes. Fold the egg mixture into the chocolate with a spatula. Divide mixture among the 6 ramekins. Place the ramekins on the baking sheet. (Or chill the ramekins, covered, until baking time.)

4 Bake 8 to 10 minutes (or 12 to 15 minutes if chilled) at 400°F or until the tops are just set and look firm. Don't overbake or the insides will not be like "molten lava."

5 While the cakes bake, make the crème anglaise: Whisk the cream, egg yolks, and sugar in a medium glass bowl until creamy. Place the bowl over a pan of simmering water, being careful not to let the bowl touch the water.

6 Using an electric hand mixer, beat the crème anglaise on high until it triples in volume and is very thick and creamy, about 3 to 4 minutes. Remove from the heat and stir in the vanilla extract.

7 To serve: Wearing oven mitts, loosen edges of the cakes with a sharp knife and invert on a serving plate. Pour ¼ cup of the crème anglaise around each cake. Dust with powdered sugar and garnish with fresh raspberries and mint leaves. Serve immediately,

Devil's Food Layer Cake with Fudge Frosting Ⓥ

MAKES 8 SERVINGS

I have to say that this chocolate cake is "devilishly" good. The recipe makes a small cake that's perfect for small families or dinner parties.

CAKE LAYERS

1½ cups Carol's Sorghum Blend (page x)

1 cup sugar

½ cup unsweetened cocoa powder (not Dutch-process or alkali)

¾ teaspoon baking soda

1 teaspoon xanthan gum

¾ teaspoon salt

1 cup buttermilk, well-shaken, (thinned with ¼ cup water if thick) or homemade Buttermilk (page 677)

1 tablespoon pure vanilla extract

½ cup unsalted butter or buttery spread, such as Earth Balance, at room temperature, or ⅓ cup canola oil

1 cup sugar

2 large eggs, at room temperature

FROSTING

½ cup (1 stick) unsalted butter or buttery spread, such as Earth Balance, or ⅓ canola oil

⅓ cup 1% milk (cow's, rice, soy, potato, or nut)

3½ cups powdered sugar

¼ cup unsweetened cocoa powder (natural or Dutch-process)

⅛ teaspoon salt

1 tablespoon pure vanilla extract

¼ cup chopped walnuts

1 Place a rack in the middle of the oven. Preheat the oven to 350°F. Generously grease two 8-inch round nonstick (gray, not black) cake pans. Line with parchment paper or wax paper and grease again; set aside.

2 Make the layers: In a medium bowl, sift together the sorghum blend, sugar, cocoa, baking soda, xanthan gum, and salt; set aside. In a measuring cup, combine the buttermilk and vanilla extract; set aside.

3 In a large mixing bowl, beat the butter and sugar with an electric mixer on low speed 1 minute, scraping down the side of the bowl with a spatula. Add the eggs, one at a time, beating thoroughly after each addition.

4 With the mixer on low speed, add the sorghum mixture alternately with the buttermilk, beginning and ending with the sorghum mixture. Spread the batter evenly in the pans.

5 Bake 25 to 30 minutes; or until the cakes start to pull away from the edges of the pan and a toothpick inserted into the center of the cakes comes out clean. Cool the pans 10 minutes on a wire rack. Remove the cakes from the pans with a thin metal spatula, discard the paper, and cool completely on the wire rack.

6 Make the frosting: In a medium saucepan, combine the butter and milk and cook over medium heat until the butter is melted. Add the powdered sugar, cocoa, and salt and bring to a boil. Beat with an electric mixer on medium speed until the frosting reaches the consistency of thin fudge. Stir in the vanilla extract; use immediately.

7 To frost the cake, place one cake layer, topside down, on a serving platter. Spread ¼ of the frosting on top and out to the edges. Place the remaining layer on top of frosting, topside up. Spread ¼ of the frosting on top. Spread remaining frosting on sides of cake. Sprinkle with nuts. Serve immediately.

Mexican Chocolate Layer Cake with Cinnamon Frosting Ⓥ

MAKES 12 SERVINGS

Cinnamon is commonly used with chocolate in Mexico, but the addition of cloves adds a mysterious and lovely note to this cake. You can bake the cake ahead of time, freeze it for up to two weeks, and defrost it on your countertop, but the frosting should be used immediately after it is made.

CAKE LAYERS

2 cups Carol's Sorghum Blend (page x)

1½ teaspoons baking soda

1 teaspoon baking powder

½ cup unsweetened cocoa powder (not Dutch-process or alkali)

1 teaspoon xanthan gum

½ teaspoon ground cinnamon

½ teaspoon salt

Pinch ground cloves (optional)

1 cup buttermilk, well shaken, (thinned with ¼ cup water if thick) or homemade Buttermilk (page 677)

1 tablespoon pure vanilla extract

½ cup unsalted butter or buttery spread, such as Earth Balance, at room temperature, or ⅓ cup canola oil

1½ cups sugar

2 large eggs, at room temperature

FROSTING

3 large egg whites
1¼ cups sugar
¼ teaspoon ground cinnamon
¼ teaspoon cream of tartar
3 tablespoons cold water
1 teaspoon pure vanilla extract

1 Place a rack in the middle of the oven. Preheat the oven to 325°F. Generously grease two 8-inch round nonstick (gray, not black) cake pans. Line the bottoms with parchment paper or wax paper, then grease them again; set aside.

2 Make the layers: In a medium bowl, whisk together the sorghum blend, baking soda, baking powder, cocoa, xanthan gum, cinnamon, salt, and cloves; set aside. In a measuring cup, combine the buttermilk and vanilla extract; set aside.

3 In a large mixing bowl, beat the butter with an electric mixer on medium speed until it is smooth and creamy. Add the sugar and beat 1 minute, scraping down the side of the bowl with a spatula. Add the eggs, one at a time, beating thoroughly after each addition.

4 With the mixer on low speed, add the sorghum mixture alternately with the buttermilk, beginning and ending with the sorghum mixture. Be sure to beat the dry ingredients thoroughly each time before adding the buttermilk. Spread the batter in the pans.

5 Bake 30 to 35 minutes or until a toothpick inserted into the center of the cakes comes out clean. Cool cakes in the pans 10 minutes on a wire rack. Remove the cakes from the pans with a thin metal spatula, discard the paper, and cool completely on the wire rack.

6 Make the frosting: Combine the egg whites, sugar, cinnamon, cream of tartar, and cold water in a double boiler over boiling water, being careful not to let the top bowl touch the water. Beat with

an electric mixer on medium speed 5 to 7 minutes until glossy and the mixture reaches the desired spreading consistency. Stir in vanilla extract. Use immediately.

7 To frost the cake, place one cake layer on a serving platter, topside down. Spread ½ cup of the frosting evenly on top. Place the second cake on top, topside up. Frost the top and sides with the remaining frosting, using a spatula to make attractive dips and swirls in the frosting. Serve immediately.

Mocha Latte Layer Cake
MAKES 12 SERVINGS

Fans of café lattés will appreciate the flavors in this cake. For the "latté" touch, sprinkle the top of the cake with a little ground cinnamon, nutmeg, or Dutch-process cocoa.

CAKE LAYERS

½ cup (1 stick) unsalted butter or buttery spread, such as Earth Balance, at room temperature, or ⅓ cup canola oil
1 cup sugar
2 large eggs, at room temperature
1½ cups Carol's Sorghum Blend (page x)
4 teaspoons instant espresso powder
1 teaspoon xanthan gum
¾ teaspoon baking soda
¾ teaspoon salt
1 cup buttermilk, well-shaken, (thinned with ¼ cup water if thick) or homemade Buttermilk (page 677)
1 teaspoon pure vanilla extract

FROSTING

3 cups homemade Basic Whipped Cream (page 624) or whipped topping, such as Lucerne or Soyatoo
1 tablespoon instant espresso powder
1 teaspoon pure vanilla extract
Ground cinnamon, for garnish
Freshly grated nutmeg, for garnish
Dutch-process cocoa, for garnish

1 Place a rack in the middle of the oven. Preheat the oven to 325°F. Generously grease two 8-inch round nonstick (gray, not black) pans. Line the bottom with parchment paper or wax paper and grease again; set aside.

2 Make the layers: In a large mixing bowl, beat the butter and sugar with an electric mixer on medium speed about 30 seconds. Beat in the eggs, one at a time, until thoroughly blended.

3 Whisk together the sorghum blend, espresso powder, xanthan gum, baking soda, and salt in a small bowl. On low speed, beat the sorghum mixture into the egg mixture, alternating with the buttermilk, beginning and ending with the sorghum mixture. Stir in the vanilla extract. Spread the batter evenly in the pans with a wet spatula.

4 Bake 25 to 30 minutes or until a tester inserted into the center of the cakes comes out clean. Cool the cakes in the pans 10 minutes on a wire rack. Remove cakes from pans with a thin metal spatula, discard the paper, and cool completely on the wire rack.

5 Make the frosting: Place whipped cream in a medium bowl. Stir in the espresso powder until well-blended. Reserve ½ cup of the whipped cream for garnish.

6 Place a cake layer on a serving plate, topside down, and spread with half of the frosting. Top with the second layer, bottom side down, and swirl the remaining frosting over the top of the cake. Serve immediately, garnished with a sprinkle of cinnamon, nutmeg, and cocoa. Refrigerate leftovers.

German Chocolate Cake with Coconut-Pecan Frosting Ⓥ

MAKES 12 SERVINGS

This rich cake is not from Germany, but rather named after a Mr. German who developed a particular kind of chocolate bar. Since German chocolate is sometimes hard to find, I use regular cocoa instead. Dissolving the cocoa in water to help intensify the overall chocolate flavor. This big, showy cake, with its luscious frosting, makes a lovely presentation for guests.

CAKE

⅓ cup unsweetened cocoa powder (not Dutch-process or alkali)

½ cup boiling water

2 cups Carol's Sorghum Blend (page x)

1 teaspoon salt

1 teaspoon baking soda

½ cup (1 stick) unsalted butter or buttery spread, such as Earth Balance, at room temperature, or ⅓ cup canola oil

1 cup granulated sugar

¾ cup packed light brown sugar

3 large eggs, at room temperature

1 tablespoon pure vanilla extract

FROSTING

3 egg yolks

¾ cup 1% milk (cow's, rice, soy, potato, or nut)

1 cup sugar

1 tablespoon unsalted butter or buttery spread, such as Earth Balance

1 package (7 ounces) sweetened shredded coconut (about 1⅔ cups)

1 teaspoon pure vanilla extract

1 cup chopped pecans

1 Place a rack in the middle of the oven. Preheat oven to 325°F. Generously grease two 8-inch non-stick (gray, not black) round cake pans. Line the bottoms with parchment paper or wax paper nd grease again; set aside.

2 Make the cake: In a measuring cup, combine the cocoa and boiling water and let stand 5 minutes while the cocoa dissolves. Sift together the sorghum blend, salt, and baking soda; set aside.

3 In a large mixing bowl, beat the butter and sugars with an electric mixer on medium-low speed for about 30 seconds. Increase the speed to medium-high and beat 2 minutes, scraping down the bowl with a spatula halfway through mixing. Add the eggs one at a time on medium speed, beating well after each addition. Add the sorghum mixture alternately with the dissolved chocolate, beginning and ending with sorghum mixture. Beat in the vanilla extract until smooth. Spread the batter equally among the three pans.

4 Bake 25 to 30 minutes or until a toothpick inserted into the center of the cakes comes out clean. Cool the cakes in the pans 10 minutes on a wire rack. Invert the cakes onto a greased wire rack, discard the paper, and cool to room temperature before frosting, about 2 hours.

5 Make the frosting: In a medium saucepan, beat the egg yolks, milk, sugar, and butter until smooth. Cook over medium heat about 10 or 12 minutes, stirring until the mixture thickens. Remove the pan from the heat and stir in the coconut and vanilla extract. Cool the frosting completely and refrigerate. Stir in the pecans just before using so they retain their crispness.

6 Place a cake layer, topside down, on a serving plate. Spread the cake with half of the frosting. Add the second layer, topside up, and spread with the remaining half of the frosting. Serve immediately.

Black Forest Layer Cake

MAKES 12 SERVINGS

Black Forest Cake is a chocolate layer cake filled with layers of whipped cream and cherries. I saw many cakes like this in Germany and Austria and I vowed to make a gluten-free version when I returned home from my vacation.

CAKE

½ cup unsalted butter or buttery spread, such as Earth Balance, at room temperature, or ⅓ cup canola oil

1 cup packed light brown sugar

1 large egg, at room temperature

½ cup 1% milk (cow's, rice, soy, potato, or nut), at room temperature

2 teaspoons pure vanilla extract

1½ cups Carol's Sorghum Blend (page x)

½ cup unsweetened cocoa powder (not Dutch-process or alkali)

¾ teaspoon baking soda

¾ teaspoon salt

1 teaspoon xanthan gum

¾ cup hot (120°F) brewed coffee

FILLING

4 cups homemade Basic Whipped Cream (page 624) or whipped topping, such as Lucerne or Soyatoo, divided

1 teaspoon kirschwasser (cherry brandy) or vanilla extract

1 can (14 to 15 ounces) cherry pie filling, such as Wilderness or Comstock

2 ounces gluten-free dark chocolate, such as Scharffen Berger or Tropical Source, shaved, for garnish

1 Place a rack in the middle of the oven. Preheat the oven to 325°F. Generously grease two 8-inch round nonstick (gray, not black) pans. Line the bottoms with parchment paper or wax paper. Grease again; set aside.

2 Make the cakes: In a large mixing bowl, beat the butter with an electric mixer on low speed 30 seconds. Add the sugar and beat on low speed until well blended. Beat in the egg, milk, and vanilla extract until they are well blended. In a small bowl, whisk together the sorghum blend, cocoa, baking soda, salt, and xanthan gum.

3 On low speed, beat the sorghum mixture into the egg mixture, alternating with the hot coffee, beginning and ending with the sorghum mixture. Spread the batter in the pans, dividing evenly.

4 Bake 25 to 30 minutes or until a toothpick inserted in the center of the cakes comes out clean. Cool the cakes in the pans 10 minutes. Remove cakes from the pan with a thin metal spatula, discard the paper liners, and cool the cakes on the wire rack.

5 Make the filling: In a medium bowl, place the whipped cream. Stir in kirschwasser or vanilla extract.

6 To assemble the cake, place one cake layer on a serving plate and spread the top with 1½ cups of the whipped cream. Top with ½ cup of the cherry pie filling. Place the second cake layer on top. Spread the top with 2 cups of whipped cream, reserving the final 1 cup for garnish. Spoon the remaining cherry pie filling on the whipped cream and spread to within 1 inch of cake edges. Garnish with chocolate shavings. Serve immediately with a dollop of the reserved ½ cup whipped cream on each side.

Chocolate Cookie Cake

MAKES 16 SERVINGS

Once assembled, this whimsical cake resembles a huge version of the cream-filled chocolate cookies that children and children-at-heart love. It would be perfect for a child's birthday party.

CAKE

1½ cups Carol's Sorghum Blend (page x)

1 cup sugar

½ cup unsweetened cocoa powder (not Dutch-process or alkali)

1 teaspoon xanthan gum

¾ teaspoon baking soda

¾ teaspoon salt

Pinch ground cloves (optional)

1 cup buttermilk, well-shaken, (thinned with ¼ cup water if thick) or homemade Buttermilk (page 677)

1 tablespoon pure vanilla extract

½ cup unsalted butter or buttery spread, such as Earth Balance, at room temperature, or ⅓ cup canola oil

1 cup sugar

2 large eggs, at room temperature

FILLING

1 package (8 ounces) cream cheese or cream cheese alternative, such as Tofutti, at room temperature

2 cups homemade Basic Whipped Cream (page 624) or whipped topping, such as Lucerne or Soyatoo

FROSTING

1 cup powdered sugar

¼ cup unsweetened cocoa powder (natural or Dutch-process)

1 tablespoon unsalted butter or buttery spread, such as Earth Balance, at room temperature

1 tablespoon water (or more if needed)

1 Place a rack in the middle of the oven. Preheat the oven to 325°F. Generously grease two 8-inch round nonstick (gray, not black) cake pans. Line the bottoms with parchment paper or wax paper, then grease again; set aside.

2 Make the cake: In a medium bowl, whisk together the sorghum blend, sugar, cocoa, xanthan gum, baking soda, salt, and cloves; set aside. In a measuring cup, combine the buttermilk and vanilla extract; set aside.

3 In a large mixing bowl, beat the butter with an electric mixer on medium speed until it is smooth and creamy. Add the sugar and beat 1 minute, scraping down the side of the bowl with a spatula. Add the eggs, one at a time, beating thoroughly after each addition.

4 With the mixer on low speed, add the sorghum mixture alternately with the buttermilk, beginning and ending with the sorghum mixture. Be sure to beat the dry ingredients thoroughly each time before adding the buttermilk. Spread the batter evenly in the pans.

5 Bake 25 to 30 minutes; or until a toothpick inserted into the center of the cakes comes out clean. Cool the cakes in the pans 10 minutes on a wire rack. Remove the cakes from the pans with a thin metal spatula, discard the paper, and cool completely on the wire rack.

6 Make the filling: In a medium bowl, beat the cream cheese on low speed until smooth. Gently fold the whipped cream into the cream cheese; set aside.

7 Make the frosting: In a small bowl, whisk together the powdered sugar and cocoa. Stir in the butter and water until the glaze is smooth, adding more water if necessary—1 teaspoon at a time—to reach spreading consistency.

8 To assemble the cake, place one layer on a serving plate, topside down. Spread evenly with all of the filling. Place remaining cake layer on top, topside up, and spread with the glaze. Serve immediately and refrigerate the leftovers.

Sacher Torte

MAKES 8 SERVINGS

This cake with a storied history is named after the famous Sacher Hotel in Vienna, Austria. The hotel's version of the cake is served with a traditional "S" carved on top. Despite its celebrated origin, it is really quite simple to make at home— it's just a basic chocolate layer cake with a filling of apricot preserves topped by a simple chocolate glaze. If you want more chocolate frosting, use the Fudge Frosting recipe on page 494.

If you don't have a double boiler, use a heatproof glass bowl set over a pan of simmering water, being careful not to let the bowl touch the water. Or, heat the chocolate and corn syrup on low in the microwave in 30-second increments, stirring after each increment.

1 cup packed light brown sugar
½ cup (1 stick) unsalted butter or buttery spread, such as Earth Balance, or ⅓ cup canola oil
2 large eggs, at room temperature
¾ cup buttermilk, well-shaken, or homemade Buttermilk (page 677)
1 tablespoon pure vanilla extract
1½ cups Carol's Sorghum Blend (page x)
½ cup unsweetened cocoa powder (not Dutch-process or alkali)
1 teaspoon xanthan gum
¾ teaspoon baking soda
¼ teaspoon salt
¾ cup apricot preserves
2 tablespoons apricot brandy or plain brandy
9 ounces gluten-free bittersweet chocolate, such as Scharffen Berger, chopped
2 tablespoons light corn syrup

1 Place a rack in the middle of the oven. Preheat the oven to 350°F. Generously grease two 8-inch round nonstick (gray, not black) cake pans. Line the bottoms of the pans with parchment paper or wax paper and grease again; set aside.

2 In a large bowl, beat the sugar and butter with an electric mixer on medium speed until smooth. Add the eggs, buttermilk, and vanilla extract and mix until well blended. It may look curdled, but will become smooth after the dry ingredients are added.

3 In a small bowl, whisk together the sorghum blend, cocoa, xanthan gum, baking soda, and salt and beat in ½ cup at a time on low speed until completely blended. Scrape down the side of the bowl with a spatula. Spread the batter evenly in the pans with a wet spatula.

4 Bake 25 to 30 minutes or until the cakes start to pull away from sides of the pans and a tooth-pick inserted into the center of the cakes comes out clean. Cool the cakes in the pans 10 minutes on a wire rack. Remove the cake from the pan with a thin metal spatula, discard the paper, and cool completely on the wire rack.

5 To assemble the cake, place one cake layer, topside down, on a serving platter. Combine the apricot preserves and brandy and spread on the top of the cake. Place the second cake layer, top-side up, on top.

6 In the top of a double boiler over simmering water, stir the chocolate and corn syrup until the chocolate is melted. With a spatula, slowly spread the frosting over the top of the cake then spread some of the frosting on the sides. Let chocolate harden slightly before serving.

Carob Torte with Caramel Topping Ⓥ

MAKES 6 SERVINGS

I am frequently asked for desserts that are free of gluten, dairy, and eggs, so I developed this lus-cious torte. You won't miss those ingredients, and your family and friends are sure to enjoy it.

TORTE

½ cup carob powder

1 cup Carol's Sorghum Blend (page x)

1 cup packed light brown sugar

1 teaspoon ground cinnamon

¾ teaspoon baking soda

¾ teaspoon salt

½ teaspoon xanthan gum

½ teaspoon baking powder

¼ teaspoon instant espresso powder

Pinch of ground cloves (optional)

⅓ cup canola oil

2 teaspoons pure vanilla extract

3 jars (4 ounces each) prune baby food

⅓ cup hot (120°F) water + 2 teaspoons

½ cup finely chopped walnuts (optional)

TOPPING

½ cup packed light brown sugar

2 tablespoons light corn syrup

¼ cup (½ stick) unsalted butter or buttery spread, such as Earth Balance

¼ cup 1% milk (cow's, rice, soy, potato, or nut)

1 teaspoon pure vanilla extract

1 Place a rack in the middle of the oven. Preheat the oven to 325°F. Grease an 8-inch nonstick (gray, not black) springform pan. Set aside. Toast the carob powder in a dry saucepan 2 minutes, stirring constantly, or until it is aromatic and turns one shade darker.

2 Make the torte: In a large bowl, mix the carob powder, sorghum blend, brown sugar, cinnamon, baking soda, salt, xanthan gum, baking powder, espresso powder, cloves, oil, and vanilla extract with an electric mixer on low speed to make a dry, crumbly mixture. Set aside ½ cup of this mixture.

3 Beat the prune baby food and ⅓ cup hot water into the mixture until the batter is smooth. Spread the batter in the pan. Stir the nuts and the remaining 2 teaspoons water into the reserved ½ cup dry cake mixture and sprinkle it over the cake.

4 Bake 50 to 55 minutes or until the top is firm and the edges of the cake pull away from the pan. Cool the cake 10 minutes on a wire rack. Remove the cake from the pan with a thin metal spatula and cool completely on the wire rack. The cake may fall slightly in the center after cooling.

5 Make the topping: In a small saucepan, cook the brown sugar, corn syrup, and butter over medium heat until it boils. Reduce the heat to low and simmer it gently 5 minutes, stirring to make sure it doesn't burn. Remove from the heat and stir in the milk and vanilla extract until smooth. Serve warm, spooned over each slice of the carob torte.

Carob-Cinnamon Cake with Cinnamon Frosting Ⓥ

MAKES 10 SERVINGS

Cinnamon is a marvelous complement to carob in this cake, and the cinnamon-flavored frosting certainly accentuates this effect. Carob is actually a legume and toasting intensifies its flavor, so don't omit this important step.

CAKE

⅓ cup carob powder

½ cup (1 stick) unsalted butter or buttery spread, such as Earth Balance, at room temperature, or ⅓ cup canola oil

1 cup sugar

2 large eggs, at room temperature

1½ cups Carol's Sorghum Blend (page x)

1 teaspoon xanthan gum

¾ teaspoon salt

½ teaspoon ground cinnamon

¼ teaspoon baking powder

¼ teaspoon baking soda

1 cup 1% milk (cow's, rice, soy, potato, or nut)

1 teaspoon pure vanilla extract

FROSTING

3 cups powdered sugar

1 teaspoon ground cinnamon

1 teaspoon pure vanilla extract

1 to 3 tablespoons milk (cow's, rice, soy, potato, or nut)

1 Place a rack in the middle of the oven. Preheat the oven to 350°F. Generously grease a 10-inch round nonstick (gray, not black) cake pan. Line the bottom with parchment paper or wax paper and grease again; set aside.

2 Make the cake: Toast the carob powder for 2 minutes in a heavy, medium saucepan over medium heat, stirring constantly, or until it is aromatic and one shade darker.

3 In a large mixing bowl, beat the butter with an electric mixer on medium speed until smooth. Gradually beat in the sugar until well blended. Add the eggs, one at a time, beating well after each addition.

4 In another bowl, whisk together the sorghum blend, toasted carob powder, xanthan gum, salt, cinnamon, baking powder, and baking soda. In a measuring cup, whisk together the milk and vanilla extract.

5 With the mixer on low speed, beat the sorghum mixture into the butter, alternating with the milk, beginning and ending with the sorghum mixture. Spread the batter evenly in the pan with a wet spatula.

6 Bake 40 to 45 minutes or until the cake starts to pull away from the edge of the pan and a toothpick inserted into the center of the cake comes out clean. Cool the cake in the pan 30 minutes on a wire rack.

7 Make the frosting: In a medium bowl, beat the powdered sugar, cinnamon, vanilla extract, and enough of the milk with an electric mixer on low speed to reach the proper consistency. Frost the top and sides of the cake and serve immediately.

SPICE CAKES

Apple Spice Cake

MAKES 12 SERVINGS

This cake is perfect for a crisp fall day, with the scent of apples and spices to fill your kitchen. Jonathan or Braeburn apples work well in this cake because of their sweet yet slightly tart taste, but you can use any type of apple available.

2 small cooking apples, peeled, cored, and very finely diced

Juice and grated zest of 1 lemon

½ cup unsalted butter or buttery spread, such as Earth Balance, at room temperature, or ⅓ cup canola oil

1 cup packed light brown sugar

3 large eggs, at room temperature

1½ cups Carol's Sorghum Blend (page x)

1 teaspoon xanthan gum

1 teaspoon baking powder

1½ teaspoons ground cinnamon

¾ teaspoon ground cloves

½ teaspoon ground allspice

½ teaspoon freshly grated nutmeg

½ teaspoon baking soda

½ teaspoon salt

1 teaspoon pure vanilla extract

½ cup raisins or currants

¼ cup chopped pecans

½ cup powdered sugar, for dusting

1 Place a rack in the middle of the oven. Preheat the oven to 350°F. Generously grease a 9-inch springform nonstick (gray, not black) pan and line the bottom with parchment paper. Grease it again. In a medium bowl, toss the apples with the lemon juice and zest; set aside.

2 In a large mixing bowl, beat the butter and sugar with an electric mixer on medium speed 2 minutes. Add the eggs, one at a time, beating thoroughly after each addition. Gradually add the sorghum blend, xanthan gum, baking powder, cinnamon, cloves, allspice, nutmeg, baking soda, and salt and beat on low speed until well combined. Stir in the apples, vanilla extract, raisins, and pecans. Spread the batter in the pan.

3 Bake 35 to 45 minutes, or until a toothpick inserted in the center of the cake comes out clean. Cool the cake in the pan 15 minutes on a wire rack. Remove the cake from the pan and cool completely on the wire rack. Dust with powdered sugar before serving.

Carrot Layer Cake with Coconut Cream-Cheese Frosting

MAKES 12 SERVINGS

Carrot cake is one of my most-requested cakes. When topped with cream cheese frosting, I have to agree that it is certainly one of the best desserts on earth. This makes a large cake, so you will need 3 cake pans, each 9 inches in diameter.

CAKE

3 cups Carol's Sorghum Blend (page x)

1½ teaspoons xanthan gum

1 teaspoon baking soda

2 teaspoons pumpkin pie spice

1 teaspoon ground ginger

¾ teaspoon salt

4 large eggs, at room temperature

1 cup sugar

¾ cup packed light brown sugar

½ cup (1 stick) unsalted butter or buttery spread, such as Earth Balance, at room temperature, or ⅓ cup canola oil

¾ cup buttermilk, well-shaken, or homemade Buttermilk (page 677)

1 teaspoon pure vanilla extract

2 cups finely shredded carrots

1 can (8 ounces) crushed pineapple, drained very well (discard the juice)

1 cup sweetened shredded coconut

½ cup finely chopped walnuts, divided

FROSTING

1 small package (3 ounces) cream cheese or cream cheese alternative, such as Tofutti, at room temperature

2 tablespoons 1% milk (cow's, rice, soy, potato, or nut) or pineapple juice

1 teaspoon pure vanilla extract

3 cups powdered sugar

1 cup sweetened shredded coconut, toasted

Pinch of salt

1 Place a rack in the middle of the oven. Preheat the oven to 325°F. Generously grease three round 9-inch nonstick (gray, not black) cake pans. Line the bottom of the pans with parchment paper or wax paper and grease again; set aside.

2 Make the cakes: In a medium bowl, sift the sorghum blend, xanthan gum, baking soda, pumpkin pie spice, ginger, and salt; set aside.

3 In a large mixing bowl, beat the eggs, sugars, oil, yogurt, buttermilk, and vanilla extract with an electric mixer on medium speed until smooth. Add sorghum mixture slowly on low speed, then increase speed to medium and beat until smooth. With a large spatula, fold in the carrots, pineapple, coconut, and ⅓ cup of the walnuts. Spread the batter evenly in the pans.

4 Bake 40 to 45 minutes or until the cakes pull way from the sides of the pans and a toothpick inserted in the center of the cakes comes out clean. Cool the cakes in the pans 15 minutes on a wire rack. Remove the cakes from the pans with a thin metal spatula, discard the paper, and cool completely on the wire rack.

5 Make the frosting: In a medium bowl, beat the cream cheese, milk, and vanilla extract with an electric mixer on medium speed until very smooth. With the mixer on low speed, gradually beat in the powdered sugar until smooth. Stir in the coconut and salt.

6 Place one cake layer, topside down, on a serving plate. Spread ⅓ of the frosting on top. Place the sec-

ond layer on top, and spread ⅓ of the frosting over the top. Add the third layer and top with the remaining frosting. Sprinkle with the remaining chopped walnuts. Serve immediately. Refrigerate leftovers.

Chai Spice Cake with Vanilla Cream-Cheese Frosting Ⓥ

MAKES 12 SERVINGS

Many people drink chai tea and chai lattes these days, so why not chai cakes? This delicious cake captures those exotic spice flavors and the vanilla-accented frosting enhances them even more.

CAKE

½ cup (1 stick) unsalted butter or buttery spread, such as Earth Balance, at room temperature, or ⅓ cup canola oil

1 cup sugar

2 large eggs, at room temperature

1½ cups Carol's Sorghum Blend (page x)

1½ teaspoons ground cinnamon

1 teaspoon ground cardamom

1 teaspoon xanthan gum

½ teaspoon baking soda

½ teaspoon baking powder

½ teaspoon ground cloves

½ teaspoon freshly ground black pepper

¼ teaspoon freshly grated nutmeg

½ teaspoon salt

¾ cup buttermilk, well-shaken, or homemade Buttermilk (page 677)

1 tablespoon pure vanilla extract

1 cup finely chopped pecans, divided

FROSTING

1 small package (3 ounces) cream cheese or cream cheese alternative, such as Tofutti, at room temperature

2 tablespoons unsalted butter or buttery spread, such as Earth Balance, melted

1 tablespoon pure vanilla extract

2 cups powdered sugar

1 Place a rack in the middle of the oven. Preheat the oven to 350°F. Generously grease a 10-inch round nonstick (gray, not black) cake pan; set aside.

2 Make the cake: In a large mixing bowl, beat the butter with an electric mixer on medium speed until smooth. Gradually beat in the sugar until smooth. Add the eggs, one at a time, beating well after each addition.

3 In another bowl, whisk together the sorghum blend, cinnamon, cardamom, xanthan gum, baking soda, baking powder, cloves, black pepper, nutmeg, and salt. In a measuring cup, whisk together the buttermilk and vanilla extract.

4 With the mixer on low speed, beat the sorghum mixture into the butter, alternating with the buttermilk, beginning and ending with the sorghum mixture. Stir in ½ cup of the pecans. Spread the batter evenly in the pan with a wet spatula.

5 Bake 35 to 40 minutes or until the cake starts to pull away from the edge of the pan and a toothpick inserted into the center of the cake comes out clean. Cool the cake in the pan 30 minutes on a wire rack.

6 Make the frosting: In a medium mixing bowl, beat the cream cheese, butter, and vanilla extract with an electric mixer on low speed until it is smooth. Beat in the powdered sugar gradually until it is smooth.

7 Spread the frosting on the top of the cake, sprinkle it with the remaining pecans, and serve immediately. Refrigerate leftovers.

Old-Fashioned Molasses Cake Ⓥ

MAKES 12 SERVINGS

Molasses is a traditionally popular flavoring in spice cakes because it lends such depth. This simple cake captures those rich flavors.

½ cup (1 stick) unsalted butter or buttery spread, such as Earth Balance, at room temperature, or ⅓ cup canola oil
¾ cup packed light brown sugar
2 large eggs, at room temperature
¼ cup molasses (not blackstrap)
1 teaspoon pure vanilla extract
2 cups Carol's Sorghum Blend (page x)
2 teaspoons ground cinnamon
1 teaspoon ground ginger
1 teaspoon xanthan gum
1 teaspoon baking soda
½ teaspoon salt

1 Place a rack in the middle of the oven. Preheat the oven to 350°F. Generously grease an 8-inch square nonstick (gray, not black) baking pan.

2 In a large mixing bowl, beat the butter with an electric mixer on low speed until smooth. Add the brown sugar and continue beating on low speed until well blended. Add the eggs, molasses, and vanilla extract and beat until the batter is smooth.

3 In a separate bowl, whisk together the sorghum blend, cinnamon, ginger, xanthan gum, baking soda, and salt. Gradually beat the sorghum mixture into the egg mixture on low speed, scraping down sides of bowl if necessary, until well blended and slightly thickened. Spread the batter in the prepared pan.

4 Bake 25 to 30 minutes or until a toothpick inserted into the center of the cake comes out clean. Cool the cake in the pan 10 minutes on a wire rack. Serve slightly warm.

Gingerbread Cake with Spiced Cream-Cheese Frosting Ⓥ

MAKES 10 SERVINGS

This gingerbread cake is complemented by a spicy cream cheese frosting.

CAKE

1½ cups Carol's Sorghum Blend (page x)

1 teaspoon baking soda

1½ teaspoons ground ginger

1 teaspoon ground cinnamon

½ teaspoon ground cloves

½ teaspoon salt

¼ cup (½ stick) unsalted butter or buttery spread, such as Earth Balance, at room temperature, or canola oil

½ cup packed light brown sugar

1 large egg, at room temperature

½ cup molasses (not blackstrap)

1 teaspoon pure vanilla extract

½ cup buttermilk, well-shaken, or homemade Buttermilk (page 677)

FROSTING

1 package (8 ounces) cream cheese or cream cheese alternative, such as Tofutti, softened

1 teaspoon pure vanilla extract

2 cups powdered sugar

1½ teaspoons pumpkin pie spice

1 Place a rack in the middle of the oven. Preheat the oven to 350°F. Generously grease a round 9-inch nonstick (gray, not black) cake pan and line the bottom with parchment paper; set aside.

2 Make the cake: Sift together the sorghum blend, baking soda, ginger, cinnamon, cloves, and salt in a medium bowl; set aside.

3 In a large bowl, beat the butter with an electric mixer on medium speed until smooth. Add the brown sugar, egg, and molasses, and beat well. In a measuring cup, whisk together the buttermilk, and vanilla extract and add alternately with the sorghum mixture to the egg mixture, beginning and ending with the sorghum mixture. Spread the batter into the pan.

4 Bake 25 to 30 minutes or until a toothpick inserted into the center comes out clean. Cool the cake in the pan 10 minutes on a wire rack. Remove the cake from the pan with a thin metal spatula, discard paper, and cool completely on the wire rack.

5 Make the frosting: In a small bowl, beat the cream cheese with an electric mixer on low speed until smooth. Add the vanilla extract and beat until thoroughly blended. On low speed gradually beat in the powdered sugar and pumpkin pie spice until the frosting is smooth.

6 Place the cake on a serving platter. Spread the frosting evenly on the top and sides of the cake. Serve immediately, or refrigerate until serving time.

Tomato Soup Spice Cake with Cream Cheese Frosting Ⓥ

MAKES 12 SERVINGS

This looks like an ordinary spice cake so no one will recognize its tomato soup base.

CAKE

½ cup unsalted butter or buttery spread, such as Earth Balance, at room temperature, or ⅓ cup canola oil

1 cup sugar

2 large eggs, at room temperature

1½ cups Carol's Sorghum Blend (page x)

2 tablespoons unsweetened cocoa powder (not Dutch-process or alkali)

1 teaspoon xanthan gum

1 teaspoon baking soda

1 teaspoon ground cinnamon

½ teaspoon ground cloves

¼ teaspoon freshly grated nutmeg

¼ teaspoon salt

¾ cup gluten-free tomato soup, such as Amy's Kitchen, Imagine, or Pacific Foods

1 tablespoon pure vanilla extract

½ cup dark raisins

½ cup toasted walnut pieces

FROSTING

1 small package (3 ounces) cream cheese, or cream cheese alternative, such as Tofutti, at room temperature

2 tablespoons unsalted butter or buttery spread, such as Earth Balance, melted

2 cups powdered sugar

1 teaspoon pure vanilla extract

1 Place a rack in the middle of the oven. Preheat the oven to 350°F. Generously grease a 10-inch round nonstick (gray, not black) cake pan; set aside.

2 Make the cake: In a large mixing bowl, beat the butter with an electric mixer on medium speed until smooth. Gradually beat in the sugar until smooth. Add the eggs, one at a time, beating well after each addition.

3 In another bowl, whisk together the sorghum blend, cocoa, xanthan gum, baking powder, baking soda, cinnamon, cloves, nutmeg, and salt. In a measuring cup, whisk together the tomato soup and vanilla extract.

4 With the mixer on low speed, beat the sorghum mixture into the butter, alternating with the tomato soup, beginning and ending with the sorghum mixture. Stir in the raisins. Spread the batter evenly in the pan with a wet spatula.

5 Bake 30 to 35 minutes or until the cake starts to pull away from the edge of the pan and a toothpick inserted into the center of the cake comes out clean. Cool the cake in the pan 20 minutes on a wire rack.

6 While the cake bakes, make the frosting: In a medium mixing bowl, beat the cream cheese and butter with an electric mixer on low speed until it is smooth. Add the powdered sugar gradually until it is smooth. Beat in the vanilla extract until smooth.

7 Place the cake on a serving platter. Spread the frosting evenly on the top and sides of the cake, sprinkle it with walnuts, and serve immediately. Refrigerate leftovers.

HOLIDAY AND SPECIAL OCCASION CAKES

Babka

MAKES 10 SERVINGS

Babka is an eastern European dessert—part bread, part coffeecake—traditionally served at Easter. It's best served warm, soon after it is baked.

TOPPING

2 tablespoons Carol's Sorghum Blend (page x)

2 tablespoons packed light brown sugar

1 tablespoon unsalted butter or buttery spread, such as Earth Balance, at room temperature

¼ teaspoon ground cinnamon

CAKE

2¼ teaspoons (1 packet) active dry yeast

1½ cups warm (110°F) orange juice

3 cups Carol's Sorghum Blend (page x)

2 teaspoons xanthan gum

1 teaspoon salt

½ cup (1 stick) unsalted butter or buttery spread, such as Earth Balance, at room temperature, or ⅓ cup canola oil

½ cup sugar

3 large eggs, at room temperature

1 tablespoon pure vanilla extract

¼ cup dried currants

¼ cup dried cranberries

¼ cup pine nuts

Grated zest of 1 lemon

Grated zest of 1 orange

¼ cup powdered sugar, for dusting

1 Make the topping: Generously grease a 10-inch nonstick (gray, not black) Bundt pan. Combine the sorghum blend, brown sugar, butter, and cinnamon until crumbly. Sprinkle on the bottom of the pan; set aside.

2 Make the cake: In a small bowl, combine the yeast and orange juice; set aside to foam.

3 In a small bowl, whisk together the sorghum blend, xanthan gum, and salt until blended. In the bowl of a heavy-duty mixer, beat the butter and sugar on low speed until blended. Add the eggs, one at a time, beating well after each addition. Stir the vanilla extract into the yeast-orange juice mixture. Still on low speed, gradually beat in the sorghum mixture alternately with the yeast-orange juice mixture, beginning and ending with the sorghum mixture. Increase the speed to medium and beat until the mixture thickens slightly, about 30 seconds. Stir in the dried fruits, nuts, lemon zest, and orange zest.

4 Transfer the batter to the pan and smooth the top with a wet spatula. Place the pan in a warm place (75°F to 80°F), cover, and let rise until doubled in volume, about 45 minutes.

5 Place a rack in the middle of the oven. Preheat the oven to 350°F. Bake 45 to 50 minutes or until a toothpick inserted into the center of the cake comes out clean. Cool the cake in the pan 15 minutes on a wire rack. Invert the cake onto the wire rack and cool completely. Dust with powdered sugar just before serving.

Bûche de Noël

MAKES 12 SERVINGS

I transformed my mother-in-law's recipe into the traditional Bûche de Noël, *which is French for yule log. This log-shaped cake symbolizes the tree branches that the ancient Celts burned while celebrating the winter solstice. Despite the fancy name, my version of this dessert is simply a chocolate cake roll filled with an orange mousse and covered with chocolate frosting. Orange is not traditional, but citrus is in season in the winter and brightens up the taste of the cake.*

CAKE

¾ cup Carol's Sorghum Blend (page x)

¼ cup unsweetened cocoa powder (not Dutch process or alkali)

¾ teaspoon xanthan gum

¼ teaspoon baking soda

¼ teaspoon salt

4 large eggs, at room temperature

¾ cup sugar

1 teaspoon pure vanilla extract

½ cup powdered sugar, divided, for dusting

FILLING

2 tablespoons boiling water

1 teaspoon unflavored gelatin powder, such as Knox

3 cups homemade Basic Whipped Cream (page 624) or whipped topping, such as Lucerne or Soyatoo

1 teaspoon grated orange zest

½ teaspoon vanilla extract

FROSTING

2 cups powdered sugar

2 tablespoons unsweetened cocoa powder (Dutch-process or alkali)

2 tablespoons unsalted butter or buttery spread, such as Earth Balance, melted, or canola oil

¼ cup hot (120°F) water or brewed coffee

⅛ teaspoon salt

1 Preheat the oven to 350°F. Generously grease a 15 × 10-inch rimmed baking sheet (not nonstick) and line it with parchment paper. Grease again and set aside.

2 Make the cake: In a small bowl, sift together the sorghum blend, cocoa, xanthan gum, baking soda, and salt. For the best results, sift again to assure that all ingredients are thoroughly blended; set aside.

3 In a large mixing bowl, beat the eggs with an electric mixer on medium speed until pale yellow, about 5 minutes. Beat in the sugar until smooth. Gradually beat in the sorghum mixture on low speed until thoroughly combined. Spread the batter on the baking sheet and smooth the top with a wet spatula.

4 Bake 15 to 18 minutes, or until the cake springs back when lightly touched. Immediately, loosen the edges and flip the cake onto a clean tea towel (not terry) that is sprinkled with ¼ cup of the powdered sugar. Discard the parchment paper and dust the cake with the remaining ¼ cup of the powdered sugar. Fold the towel over the short edge of the cake and roll it up in the towel, jelly-roll fashion. Refrigerate, seam side down, covered, for at least 2 hours.

5 Make the filling: In a small bowl, sprinkle the gelatin over the boiling water, stirring until smooth; set aside. Place the whipped cream in a large bowl and beat the softened gelatin, orange zest, and vanilla extract into the whipped cream. Refrigerate while making the frosting.

6 Make the frosting: Sift together the powdered sugar and cocoa over a medium bowl. Stir in the melted butter, hot water, and salt and continue stirring until smooth. If frosting is too thin, add more powdered sugar, ¼ cup at a time; if too thick, add more water, 1 tablespoon at a time until the frosting reaches proper spreading consistency.

7 To fill the cake, gently remove it from the tea towel. Spread the filling to within 1 inch of the cake's edge. Reroll the cake and place it on a serving platter, seam side down. Frost the cake with the Chocolate Frosting. Refrigerate the cake, tightly wrapped. To serve, slice with a serrated or electric knife. Refrigerate leftovers.

Fruitcake

MAKES 16 SERVINGS

Joke all you want about fruitcakes, but if not too dense and eaten fresh, they can be good. I have received many compliments on this recipe. If you use the mini pans, be sure not to overbake the fruitcakes or they will end up dry.

CAKE

2 large eggs, at room temperature

⅓ cup canola oil

¼ cup orange liqueur, such as Triple Sec, or orange juice

1 tablespoon grated orange zest

1 teaspoon almond extract

1½ cups Carol's Sorghum Blend (page x)

½ cup sugar

1 teaspoon xanthan gum

½ teaspoon baking powder

¼ teaspoon salt

¼ teaspoon ground cinnamon

⅛ teaspoon freshly grated nutmeg

1 cup finely chopped walnuts, pecans, or almond slivers, or a mixture of all three nuts

2 cups (about ½ pound) chopped dried fruits (blueberries, cranberries, cherries, apricots, or pineapple)

GLAZE

¼ cup water

¼ cup sugar

2 tablespoons orange liqueur, such as Triple Sec, or orange juice

1 Place a rack in the middle of the oven. Preheat the oven to 325°F. Generously grease three 5 × 3-inch nonstick (gray, not black) loaf pans or a 9 × 5-inch nonstick (gray, not black) loaf pan.

2 Make the cake: In a medium mixing bowl, combine the eggs, oil, liqueur, orange zest, and almond extract. Beat with an electric mixer on medium speed until thoroughly blended. Add the sorghum blend, sugar, xanthan gum, baking powder, salt, cinnamon, and nutmeg. Reduce speed to low and beat until well blended.

3 Add the nuts and dried fruits, increase the speed to medium, and beat until thoroughly blended. The batter will be stiff and sticky. Transfer the dough to the pan(s), smoothing the top(s) with a wet spatula.

4 Bake small loaves 1 hour to 1 hour 15 minutes; large loaf 1 hour 15 minutes to 1 hour 30 minutes or until a toothpick inserted into the center of the loaf comes out clean. Cool the fruitcakes in the pans 15 minutes on a wire rack. Remove fruitcakes from pans with a thin metal spatula and let cool on the wire rack 30 minutes.

5 Make the glaze: In a small saucepan, combine the water and sugar and heat over medium heat until the sugar is dissolved. Remove from heat and stir in the liqueur. Cool 30 minutes. Brush all sides of fruitcakes with glaze. Place fruitcakes in sealed container and refrigerate.

Panforte

MAKES 16 SERVINGS

Panforte is a Christmas sweet from Tuscany. The word itself means "strong bread," possibly because it is a fairly hearty treat. I saw this sold in decorative boxes and tins in gift shops all over northern Italy just before the holidays; it makes a lovely gift. And, no two were alike, which means yours will be perfect no matter how it turns out.

1¾ cups chopped toasted nuts,* (pecans, walnuts, pine nuts, almonds, or hazelnuts, or a mixture of your favorites)

½ cup dried sweetened cranberries, such as Craisins, or mixed candied fruit, or a combination of both

⅓ cup dried currants

2 teaspoons grated orange zest

⅔ cup Carol's Sorghum Blend (page x)

3 tablespoons unsweetened cocoa powder (natural or Dutch-process)

2 ounces gluten-free bittersweet or semisweet chocolate, such as Scharffen Berger or Tropical Source, grated

1½ teaspoons ground cinnamon

¼ teaspoon freshly ground black pepper

¼ teaspoon ground cloves

¼ teaspoon freshly grated nutmeg

¼ teaspoon ground coriander

⅛ teaspoon ground cardamom

⅛ teaspoon salt

⅔ cup honey

½ cup sugar

2 tablespoons water

1 teaspoon unsalted butter or buttery spread, such as Earth Balance, at room temperature

2 tablespoons powdered sugar, for dusting

1 Place a rack in the middle of the oven. Preheat the oven to 325°F. Generously grease a 10-inch nonstick (gray, not black) springform pan. Line it with parchment paper and grease again.

2 In a large mixing bowl, combine the nuts, cranberries, currants, orange zest, sorghum blend, cocoa, chocolate, cinnamon, black pepper, cloves, nutmeg, coriander, cardamom, and salt. Toss to coat evenly.

3 In a medium, heavy saucepan, bring the honey and sugar to a boil, stirring to dissolve the sugar, and boil 3 minutes. Remove from the heat and stir in the water and butter. Pour the hot syrup over the fruit and nut mixture, stirring to coat evenly. The batter will be thick and sticky.

4 Press the mixture evenly in the prepared pan by placing a sheet of plastic wrap on top and pressing with fingers or a spatula. Remove the plastic wrap.

5 Bake 30 minutes at 325°F or until just firm in center. Cool the cake in the pan 15 minutes on a wire rack, then loosen from sides of pan by running a knife around the edge the pan. Cool completely in pan. Turn out onto large cutting board and remove parchment paper. Cut the panforte into wedges with a sharp knife. Serve at once, dusted with powdered sugar.

*To toast nuts: Place a rack in the middle of the oven. Preheat the oven to 325°F. Place the nuts in a thin layer on a 15x10-inch baking sheet (not nonstick). Bake 5 minutes, then start watching for browning as you bake another 5 to 8 minutes. Some nuts will brown more quickly than others, so if you use a blend of nuts you may have to bake them separately. Cool and then chop.

Pear Kuchen

MAKES 8 SERVINGS

Kuchen is a German yeast cake, usually filled with fruit and nuts, plus lots of wonderful spices. I served this cake at an Easter brunch and it disappeared quickly.

CAKE

2 firm-ripe Bosc pears, peeled, cored, and very finely diced

Juice and grated zest of 1 lemon

1½ teaspoons active dry yeast

¼ cup warm (110°F) 1% milk (cow's, rice, soy, potato, or nut)

½ cup unsalted butter or buttery spread, such as Earth Balance, at room temperature, or ⅓ cup canola oil

1 cup packed light brown sugar

2 large eggs, at room temperature

1 teaspoon pure vanilla extract

1½ cups Carol's Sorghum Blend (page x)

1 teaspoon xanthan gum

1 teaspoon ground cinnamon

½ teaspoon ground allspice

¼ teaspoon freshly grated nutmeg

½ teaspoon salt

¼ teaspoon ground cloves

TOPPING

3 tablespoons sliced almonds or chopped pecans

3 tablespoons Carol's Sorghum Blend (page x)

2 tablespoons packed light brown sugar

1 tablespoon unsalted butter or buttery spread, such as Earth Balance, at room temperature

2 tablespoons powdered sugar, for dusting

1 Generously grease a 9-inch springform pan and line the bottom with parchment paper or wax paper. Grease it again; set aside. In a medium bowl, toss the pears with the lemon juice and zest; set aside. Combine the yeast and warm milk and let stand 5 minutes.

2 Make the cake: In a medium mixing bowl, beat the butter and sugar with an electric mixer on medium speed 2 minutes. Add the eggs, one at a time, beating thoroughly after each addition. Beat in the yeast mixture and vanilla extract. Gradually add the sorghum blend, xanthan gum, cinnamon, allspice, nutmeg, salt, and cloves and beat on low speed until well combined. Stir in the pears. Spread the batter evenly in the pan.

3 Make the topping: Combine the almonds, sorghum blend, brown sugar, and butter until crumbly. Sprinkle on the batter, leaving a 1-inch border around the edge of the pan. Cover the pan loosely and put it in a warm place (75° to 80°) to rise 45 to 50 minutes.

4 Place a rack in the middle of the oven. Preheat the oven to 350°F. Bake the cake 35 to 45 minutes, or until a toothpick inserted in the center of the cake comes out clean. Cool the cake in the pan 15 minutes and then remove the sides and bottom; discard the paper. Serve the cake slightly warm, dusted with powdered sugar.

Christmas Beer Cake

MAKES 12 SERVINGS

Renee Zonka is the Associate Dean of Culinary at Kendall College near Chicago. Her passion for gluten-free cooking was honed during stints at the Culinary Institute of America and other training. Gluten-free beer lends a distinctive note to this rich cake she created, but you could use hard cider, such as Woodchuck, instead.

CAKE

1½ cups sorghum flour

½ cup tapioca flour

½ cup potato starch

2 teaspoons baking powder

1 teaspoon baking soda

½ teaspoon salt

2 teaspoons xanthan gum

¾ cup unsalted butter or buttery spread, such as Earth Balance, softened, or ⅔ cup canola oil

1½ cups sugar

3 large eggs, at room temperature

1½ cups sour cream or sour cream alternative, such as Tofutti

½ cup gluten-free beer, such as Bard's Tale or Redbridge

1½ teaspoons pure vanilla extract

FILLING/TOPPING

½ cup sugar

2 teaspoons ground cinnamon

⅔ cup finely chopped walnuts

1 Place a rack in the middle of the oven. Preheat oven to 350°F. Generously grease a 10-inch non-stick (gray, not black) tube pan or Bundt pan; set aside.

2 Make the cake: In a large mixing bowl, whisk together the flours, potato starch, baking powder, baking soda, salt, and xanthan gum.

3 In a small mixing bowl, beat the butter and sugar with an electric mixer on low speed. Add the eggs, sour cream, beer, and vanilla extract and beat for 2 minutes. Add to the sorghum mixture and mix on low speed until all ingredients are well blended.

4 Make the filling/topping: In a small bowl, whisk together the sugar, cinnamon, and walnuts.

5 Spoon ⅓ of the cake batter into the pan. Sprinkle with ⅓ of the filling/topping. Spoon on another third of the cake batter and again sprinkle on a ⅓ of the filling/topping. Spoon the remaining ⅓ of the cake batter into the pan and sprinkle with the remainder of the filling/topping.

6 Bake 55 minutes to 1 hour 5 minutes or until the cake is brown and a toothpick inserted into the center of the cake comes out clean. Cool the cake in the pan 10 minutes on a wire rack. Remove the cake from the pan with a thin metal spatula and cool completely on the wire rack.

Petit Fours

MAKES ABOUT 18 CAKES

Despite their cute French name, these are simply tiny squares of cake with a light icing or glaze. The term petit fours *means "small ovens" and were created as a way for patisseries to use up leftovers while the ovens cooled down at the end of the day's bake. Traditionally made of almond sponge cake, my version uses yellow cake layers*

sandwiched with jam and then glazed with icing. Sometimes petit fours are decorated with candy flowers, which you can find at cooking specialty shops. My version is simple and one of the easiest ways to make this dessert, but you can dress it up as you please.

CAKE

½ cup unsalted butter or buttery spread, such as Earth Balance, at room temperature, or ⅓ cup canola oil

¾ cup sugar

2 large eggs, at room temperature

1½ cups Carol's Sorghum Blend (page x)

1 teaspoon xanthan gum

½ teaspoon salt

¼ teaspoon baking powder

¼ teaspoon baking soda

¾ cup buttermilk, well-shaken, or homemade Buttermilk (page 677)

1 teaspoon pure vanilla extract

½ teaspoon almond extract

1 small jar (10 ounces) seedless jam of choice

ICING

¼ cup 1% milk (cow's, rice, soy, potato, or nut)

Food coloring, if desired

1 cup powdered sugar

1 Place a rack in the middle of the oven. Preheat the oven to 325°F. Generously grease a 15 × 10-inch jellyroll pan. Line with parchment paper or wax paper and grease again; set aside.

2 Make the cake: In a large mixing bowl, beat the butter with an electric mixer on medium speed until smooth. Gradually beat in the sugar until smooth. Add the eggs, one at a time, beating well after each addition.

3 In another bowl, whisk together the sorghum blend, xanthan gum, salt, baking powder, and baking soda. In a measuring cup, whisk together the buttermilk, vanilla extract, and almond extract.

4 With the mixer on low speed, beat the sorghum mixture into the egg mixture, alternating with the buttermilk, beginning and ending with the sorghum mixture. Spread the batter evenly in the pan.

5 Bake 12 to 15 minutes or until the top of the cake is golden brown and a toothpick inserted into the center of the cake comes out clean. Cool the cake in the pan 10 minutes on a wire rack. Invert the cake onto a sheet of wax paper, discard the paper on the bottom of the cake, and cool the cake completely. It will be fairly thin.

6 Cut the cooled cake into two of each shape—small squares, rectangles, or triangles—with metal cookie cutters. Spread the top of half of the cakes with jam. Place a second cake of the same shape on top and arrange the cakes in rows on a wire rack or glazing screen with plenty of space between the rows. Set the rack over a shallow pan or wax paper to catch the drips.

7 Make the icing: In a bowl, stir the milk and food coloring, if using, into the powdered sugar until smooth. It should be thinner than regular frosting. Spoon or pour the icing over the small cakes, allowing the drippings to fall onto the pan below. The drippings may be scraped off of the pan or paper, and reheated for use again. Allow the cakes to set until completely dry. Lift the cakes from the rack with a metal spatula, and trim the bottom edges with a sharp knife. Set into small muffin papers for easy handling or on a dessert plate lined with a paper doily. Decorate as desired. Serve as soon as the icing is set.

Pumpkin Roll Cake

MAKES 12 SERVINGS

Pumpkin always makes cakes moist and delicious, and pumpkin roll cakes are one of my frequently requested recipes. Despite their lovely, but intricate look, rolled cakes are really easy to make, since they are basically just a thin cake rolled around a sweet, creamy filling. My easy directions make it fail proof.

CAKE

¾ cup Carol's Sorghum Blend (page x)

1½ teaspoons ground cinnamon

1 teaspoon baking powder

1 teaspoons ground ginger

¾ teaspoon ground allspice

¾ teaspoon xanthan gum

¼ teaspoon freshly grated nutmeg

¼ teaspoon salt

4 large eggs, at room temperature

½ cup granulated sugar

½ cup packed light brown sugar

⅔ cup canned pumpkin (not pumpkin pie filling)

1 teaspoon fresh lemon juice

½ cup powdered sugar, for dusting, divided

FILLING

1 large package (8 ounces) cream cheese or cream cheese alternative, such as Tofutti, at room temperature

1 cup powdered sugar + 2 tablespoons for dusting

2 tablespoons unsalted butter or buttery spread, such as Earth Balance at room temperature, or canola oil

1 teaspoon pure vanilla extract

1 Place a rack in the middle of the oven. Preheat the oven to 350°F. Generously grease a 15 × 10-inch baking sheet (not nonstick) and line it with parchment paper; spray the paper with cooking spray.

2 In a small bowl, whisk together the sorghum blend, cinnamon, baking powder, ginger, allspice, xanthan gum, nutmeg and salt; set aside. In a large mixing bowl, beat the eggs on medium speed until pale yellow, about 5 minutes. Beat in the granulated sugar, brown sugar, pumpkin, and lemon juice until smooth. Gradually beat in the sorghum mixture on low speed until thoroughly combined. Spread the batter on the baking sheet and smooth the top with a wet spatula.

3 Bake 15 to 18 minutes, or until the cake springs back when lightly touched. Immediately dust the cake with ¼ cup of the powdered sugar. Immediately, loosen the edges and flip the cake onto a clean tea towel (not terry). Discard the parchment paper and dust the cake with the remaining ¼ cup of the powdered sugar. Fold the towel over the short edge of the cake and roll it up in the towel, jelly-roll fashion. Cool completely, with the seam edge down, for 1 hour in the refrigerator.

4 Carefully unroll the cake and gently remove it from the towel. Beat the cream cheese with an electric mixer on low speed until smooth. Gradually beat in 1 cup of the powdered sugar, butter, lemon juice, and vanilla extract until smooth. Gently spread the filling on the cake to within 1 inch of the edges. Roll up the cake, starting with a short end, into a jelly roll and place it on a serving plate, seam side down. Dust the cake with the remaining 2 tablespoons powdered sugar. Refrigerate until serving time.

Red Velvet Bundt Cake

MAKES 10 SERVINGS

Legend says that this cake originated in the 1950s at a restaurant in New York's Waldorf-Astoria Hotel. Others think it originated during the Civil War. Regardless of the source, this cake's deep red color makes it perfect for the holidays, topped with white fluffy frosting and garnished with fresh holly. Be careful with the red food coloring—it will stain anything it touches, including your hands.

½ cup (1 stick) unsalted butter or buttery spread, such as Earth Balance, or ⅓ cup canola oil

1½ cups sugar

2 large eggs, at room temperature

3 cups Carol's Sorghum Blend (page x)

2 tablespoons unsweetened cocoa powder (not Dutch-process or alkali)

1½ teaspoons xanthan gum

1 teaspoon salt

1 cup buttermilk, well-shaken, or homemade Buttermilk (page 677)

1 bottle (1 ounce) or 3 tablespoons red food coloring

2 teaspoons pure vanilla extract

1 tablespoon cider vinegar

1 teaspoon baking soda

1 Place a rack in the middle of the oven. Preheat the oven to 350°F. Generously grease a 10-cup nonstick (gray, not black) Bundt pan.

2 Beat the butter and sugar in a large bowl with electric mixer for 2 minutes. Thoroughly beat in the eggs on low speed.

3 Whisk together the sorghum blend, cocoa, xanthan gum, and salt in a small bowl. In a small measuring cup, combine the buttermilk, food coloring, and vanilla extract. With the mixer on low speed, beat in the sorghum mixture alternately with the buttermilk mixture, beginning and ending with the sorghum mixture. Whisk together the vinegar and soda and stir it into the batter. Spread the batter in the pan.

4 Bake 55 to 60 minutes or until a toothpick inserted in the center of the cake comes out clean. Cool the cake in the pan 10 minutes on a wire rack. Remove the cake from the pan and cool completely on the wire rack.

CHEESECAKES

One-Dish Rustic Cheesecake Ⓥ

MAKES 4 SERVINGS

Handed down to my mother-in-law from her Swedish aunt, this rustic, no-crust cheesecake recipe, called Ost Kaka, *now resides on a tattered index card in my little wooden box of family favorites. A Scandinavian comfort food, it's amazingly easy to assemble because it can be mixed and baked in the same dish.*

1 cup cottage cheese, at room temperature

2 large eggs, at room temperature

½ cup 1% milk (cow's, rice, soy, potato, or nut—or whole cow's milk for fuller body)

1 teaspoon pure vanilla extract

2 teaspoons cornstarch

¼ cup sugar

¼ cup homemade Basic Whipped Cream (page 624) or whipped topping, such as Lucerne or Soyatoo, for garnish

1 Place a rack in the middle of the oven. Preheat oven to 325°F. Coat a 1-quart baking dish with cooking spray. In the same dish, whisk together the cottage cheese, eggs, milk, and vanilla extract until smooth. Stir the cornstarch into the sugar before adding it to the mixture so it doesn't clump.

2 Place the dish in a 13 × 9-inch baking pan. Pour boiling water into the baking pan to depth of 1 inch.

3 Bake 40 to 45 minutes or until the top is set. Cool the baking dish on a wire rack. Serve warm or at room temperature with a dollop of whipped cream.

Simple Pumpkin Cheesecake Ⓥ

MAKES 12 SERVINGS

This cheesecake is particularly good nestled atop a Cookie Crust (page 585) made from Gingersnaps (page 417), but it is so flavorful that you can also serve it without a crust, as I do in this recipe. Serve it with a dollop of homemade Basic Whipped Cream (page 624) and a dusting of cinnamon or chopped crystallized ginger. At holiday time, I drizzle a little sweet cranberry sauce on it for color and lovely flavor and texture contrast.

3 packages (8 ounces each) cream cheese or cream cheese alternative, such as Tofutti, at room temperature

¾ cup packed light brown sugar

3 large eggs, at room temperature

1 can (14 to 15 ounces) pumpkin puree (not pumpkin pie filling)

2 tablespoons Carol's Sorghum Blend (page x)

2½ teaspoons pumpkin pie spice

¼ teaspoon salt

1 tablespoon brandy or brandy extract

1 teaspoon pure vanilla extract

1 Place a rack in the middle of the oven. Preheat oven to 325°F. Generously grease a 9-inch non-stick (gray, not black) springform pan.

2 Process cream cheese and sugar in food processor until smooth. Add eggs, pumpkin puree, sorghum blend, pumpkin pie spice, salt, brandy, and vanilla extract, and process just until smooth. Pour into pan and smooth top with spatula.

3 Bake 1 hour to 1 hour 15 minutes or until top is firm. Remove from oven and cool in pan 30 minutes on a wire rack. Refrigerate at least 2 hours before serving.

New York–Style Cheesecake

MAKES 12 SERVINGS

This is the quintessential cheesecake. Serve it plain or topped with fruit, such as strawberries or blueberries.

CRUST

1 package (9 cookies) gluten-free vanilla or lemon-flavored cookies, such as Pamela's Lemon Shortbread, or homemade Lemon Cookies (page 419)

1 tablespoon sugar

2 tablespoons unsalted butter or buttery spread, such as Earth Balance, melted, or canola oil

FILLING

3 packages (8 ounces each) cream cheese or cream cheese alternative, such as Tofutti, cut into 1-inch cubes and softened

1 cup sugar

¼ cup sour cream or sour cream alternative, such as Tofutti, at room temperature

Juice and grated zest of 1 lemon

1½ teaspoons pure vanilla extract

⅛ teaspoon salt

3 large eggs, at room temperature

1 Place a rack in the middle of the oven. Preheat the oven to 325°F. Generously grease the bottom and sides of a 9-inch nonstick (gray, not black) springform pan; set aside.

2 Place the cookies and sugar in a food processor and process until they are fine crumbs. Add the butter and process until the mixture is crumbly. Pat the crust onto the bottom of the pan. Bake 10 to 12 minutes or just until the crust is fragrant. Cool the crust while preparing the filling, but leave the oven on.

3 In a large mixing bowl, beat the cream cheese with an electric mixer on medium speed until light and fluffy. Add the sugar and sour cream and beat 1 minute, scraping the side of the bowl. Add the lemon juice and zest, vanilla extract, and salt and beat until smooth. Beat in the eggs, one a time, just until blended. Pour the filling over the crust and smooth with a spatula.

4 Bake 1 hour or until the top is firm. Cool the cheesecake 15 minutes on a wire rack. Run a sharp knife around the outer edge of the cake to loosen the edges and remove the sides of the pan. Wrap the cheesecake in plastic and refrigerate overnight. Slide a thin metal knife between the cheesecake and the pan and slide the cheesecake to a serving plate. Let stand at room temperature. Cut with a knife dipped in hot water, then dried. Refrigerate leftovers.

Cheesecake Bars **V**

MAKES 12 SERVINGS

Think of these as thin cheesecakes, served in tinier portions, rather than a typical cheesecake.

CRUST

½ cup (1 stick) unsalted butter or buttery spread, such as Earth Balance, at room temperature, but not melted, or ⅓ cup canola oil

½ cup powdered sugar

2 cups Carol's Sorghum Blend (page x)

¼ cup Expandex modified tapioca starch

½ teaspoon xanthan gum

½ teaspoon salt

2 teaspoons grated lemon zest

2 teaspoons pure vanilla extract

1 teaspoon almond extract

¼ cup 1% milk (cow, rice, soy, potato, or nut)

FILLING

2 tablespoons unsalted butter or buttery spread, such as Earth Balance, melted, or canola oil

2 packages (8 ounces each) cream cheese or cream cheese alternative, such as Tofutti, at room temperature

½ cup sugar

1 teaspoon pure vanilla extract

2 large eggs, at room temperature

TOPPING

1 cup sour cream or sour cream alternative, such as Tofutti

2 tablespoons sugar

½ teaspoon pure vanilla extract

1 Have all ingredients at room temperature.

2 Beat the eggs only long enough to incorporate them into the cream cheese. Overbeating may cause the cheesecake to rise and then fall during cooling, which causes cracks.

3 Bake the cheesecake just until the center is just set, but still looks slightly underdone. It will firm up as it cools.

1 Place a rack in the middle of the oven. Preheat oven to 325°F. Line a 13 × 9-inch nonstick (gray, not black) baking pan with foil, letting the foil hang over at least 2 inches on each end.

2 Make the crust: Beat the butter in a medium mixing bowl with an electric mixer on low speed until smooth. Add the sugar and beat 1 minute. Add the sorghum blend, tapioca starch, xanthan gum, salt, lemon zest, vanilla extract, almond extract, and milk. Beat until thoroughly blended. With fingers, press the dough evenly onto the bottom of the pan; set aside.

3 Make the filling: Wipe out the mixing bowl, and place the butter, cream cheese, sugar, and vanilla extract in the bowl. Beat with an electric mixer on low speed until the mixture is smooth. Add the eggs, one at a time, and beat just until the eggs are incorporated. Spread the mixture over the crust. Bake 25 minutes or until a knife inserted into the filling 1-inch from the edge comes out clean.

4 Make the topping: In a small bowl, whisk together the sour cream, sugar, and vanilla until smooth. Carefully spread it in a very thin layer on top of the cheesecake. Bake 10 minutes more. Cool the cheesecake in the pan 10 minutes on a wire rack. Refrigerate 3 hours. When ready to serve, remove the cheesecake from the pan by lift-ing the foil handles and place on a cutting board for easier slicing. Refrigerate leftovers.

Lime Cheesecake

MAKES 12 SERVINGS

This is very much like a lemon cheesecake, but with a delightful lime flavor instead.

CRUST

1 package (9 cookies) gluten-free vanilla or lemon-flavored cookies, such as Pamela's Lemon Shortbread, or homemade Lemon Cookies (page 419)

1 tablespoon sugar

2 tablespoons unsalted butter or buttery spread, such as Earth Balance, melted, or canola oil

2 teaspoons grated lime zest

FILLING

3 packages (8 ounces each) cream cheese or cream cheese alternative, such as Tofutti, cut into 1-inch cubes and softened

1 cup sugar

¼ cup sour cream or sour cream alternative, such as Tofutti, at room temperature

Juice and grated zest of 2 limes

1½ teaspoons pure vanilla extract

⅛ teaspoon salt

3 large eggs, at room temperature

1 cup homemade Basic Whipped Cream (page 624) or whipped topping, such as Lucerne, or Soyatoo

1 lime, thinly sliced, for garnish

1 Place a rack in the middle of the oven. Preheat the oven to 325°F. Generously grease the bottom and sides of a 9-inch nonstick (gray, not black) springform pan; set aside.

2 Place the cookies and sugar in a food processor and process until they are fine crumbs. Add the butter and lime zest and process until the mixture is crumbly. Pat the crust onto the bottom of the pan. Bake 10 to 12 minutes or just until the crust is fragrant. Cool the crust while preparing the fill-ing, but leave the oven on.

3 In the bowl of a stand mixer, beat the cream cheese on medium speed until light and fluffy. Add the sugar and beat 1 minute, scraping the side of the bowl. Add the lime juice and zest, vanilla extract, and salt and beat until smooth. Beat in the eggs, one a time, just until blended. Pour the filling over the crust and smooth with a spatula.

4 Bake 1 hour or until the top is firm. Cool the cheesecake 15 minutes on a wire rack. Run a sharp knife around the outer edge of the cake to loosen the edges and remove the sides of the pan. Wrap the cheesecake in plastic and refrigerate overnight. Slide a thin metal knife between the cheesecake and the pan and slide the cheesecake to a serving plate.

5 Bring the cheesecake to room temperature; slice with a knife dipped in hot water, then dried. Serve with a dollop of whipped cream, garnish with a lime slice. Refrigerate leftovers.

Green Tea Cheesecake

MAKES 12 SERVINGS

Green tea and ginger are two of the most popular new flavors for sweets and make this an unusual and special dessert. For a more intense green tea flavor, add the green tea powder to the refrigerated sour cream the night before. I used the China Zen flavor by Tazo, which has a hint of mint. A drop of green food coloring will heighten the cake's visual appeal. I served this cheesecake as one of four cheesecake flavors to a large family gathering and it was everyone's favorite (over chocolate, mocha, and pineapple-flavored cheesecakes).

CRUST

1 package (9 cookies) gluten-free vanilla or lemon-flavored cookies, such as Pamela's Lemon Shortbread, or homemade Lemon Cookies (page 419)

1 tablespoon sugar

2 tablespoons unsalted butter or buttery spread, such as Earth Balance, melted, or canola oil

FILLING

3 packages (8 ounces each) cream cheese or cream cheese alternative, such as Tofutti, cut into 1-inch cubes and softened

1 cup sugar

¼ cup sour cream or sour cream alternative, such as Tofutti, at room temperature

1 tablespoon pure vanilla extract

⅛ teaspoon salt

3 large eggs, at room temperature

2 teaspoons grated fresh ginger

2 teaspoons Japanese green tea powder (matcha), or use a spice grinder to grind the tea from 4 green tea bags into a very fine powder

Drop of green food coloring (optional)

1 Place a rack in the middle of the oven. Preheat the oven to 325°F. Generously grease the bottom and sides of a 9-inch nonstick (gray, not black) springform pan; set aside.

2 Make the crust: Place the cookies and sugar in a food processor and process until they are fine crumbs. Add the butter and process until the mixture is crumbly. Pat the crust onto the bottom of the pan. Bake 10 to 12 minutes or just until the crust is fragrant. Cool the crust while preparing the filling, but leave the oven on.

3 Make the filling: In the bowl of a stand mixer, whip the cream cheese on medium speed until light and fluffy. Add the sugar, sour cream, vanilla extract, and salt and beat 1 minute, scraping the side of the bowl with a spatula. Beat in the eggs, one a time, just until blended. Stir in the ginger, green tea powder, and food coloring, if using. Pour the filling over the crust and smooth with a spatula.

4 Bake 1 hour or until the top is firm. Cool the cheesecake 15 minutes on a wire rack. Run a sharp knife around the outer edge of the cake to loosen the edges and remove the sides of the pan. Wrap the cheesecake in plastic and refrigerate overnight. Slide a thin metal knife between the cheesecake and the pan and slide the cheesecake to a serving plate. Let stand at room temperature; slice with a knife dipped in hot water, then dried. Refrigerate leftovers.

Black and White Cheesecake

MAKES 12 SERVINGS

With its black bottom and top layers, and creamy cheesecake in between, this cake is eye-catching—and irresistibly delicious.

1 package (9 cookies) gluten-free chocolate cookies, such as Pamela's Dark Chocolate, Chocolate Chunk Cookies

2 tablespoons unsalted butter or buttery spread, such as Earth Balance, melted, or canola oil

2 packages (8 ounces each) cream cheese or cream cheese alternative, such as Tofutti, at room temperature

½ cup sugar

1 teaspoon pure vanilla extract

2 large eggs, at room temperature

1 tablespoon sweet rice flour

1 Place a rack in the middle of the oven. Preheat oven to 325°F. Generously grease a 9-inch non-stick (gray, not black) spring-form pan with removable sides.

2 Place cookies in food processor and process 30 to 45 seconds or until finely ground (a few small clumps are fine).

3 Remove half of crumbs to use for topping. To remaining crumbs in food processor, add butter and process until thoroughly blended. Press crumbs firmly on bottom of springform pan.

4 Wipe out food processor with paper towel. Add cream cheese, sugar, vanilla extract, eggs, and sweet rice flour and process until thoroughly blended. Pour batter over crumbs in pan.

5 Bake 40 to 45 minutes or until center is almost firm. Sprinkle reserved cookie crumbs evenly on top. Cool cake in the pan 10 minutes on a wire rack. Refrigerate 4 hours or overnight. Remove sides of pan. Bring to room temperature; slice with a knife dipped in hot water, then dried. Refrigerate leftovers.

Simple Chocolate Cheesecake Cups

MAKES 4 SERVINGS

Sometimes it's more fun to serve cheesecakes in little wine goblets than as a wedge cut from a large cake. This approach can also be quite elegant if you decorate each serving with something special, such as a chocolate-covered espresso bean, a long-stemmed strawberry or maraschino cherry, or even a shaving of bitter-sweet chocolate.

¾ cup gluten-free chocolate syrup, such as Hershey's, divided

2 tablespoons honey or agave nectar

1 teaspoon pure vanilla extract

⅛ teaspoon salt

2 cups homemade Basic Whipped Cream (page 624) or whipped topping, such as Lucerne or Soyatoo

1 small package (3 ounces) cream cheese or cream cheese alternative, such as Tofutti, softened and cut into 8 pieces

4 teaspoons apricot preserves or orange marmalade, for garnish

1 Stir together ½ cup of the chocolate syrup with 2 tablespoons of the honey, vanilla extract, and salt. Set aside.

2 In a large mixing bowl, place 1½ cups of whipped cream; refrigerate remaining ½ cup of whipped cream for garnish.

3 Add cream cheese pieces to bowl and beat into the whipped cream. Gently fold chocolate mixture into the whipped cream mixture until there are no streaks. Divide mixture among 4 goblets or stemmed wine glasses. Chill at least 1 hour.

4 To serve, top each cheesecake with 1 table-spoon of the reserved chocolate syrup, then 2 tablespoons of the reserved whipped cream. Garnish each with 1 teaspoon orange marmalade or raspberry preserves.

Mini-Chocolate Cheesecakes Ⓥ

MAKES 12 SERVINGS

This recipe is designed for the mini 12-cheese-cake pans. It's a fun way to serve cheesecake and requires no cutting. Freeze any of the leftover cheesecakes for another day.

CRUST

1 package (9 cookies) gluten-free chocolate cookies, such as Pamela's Dark Chocolate, Chocolate Chunk, or homemade Chocolate Sandwich Cookies (page 434)

FILLING

2 tablespoons boiling water

6 ounces gluten-free dark chocolate, such as Tropical Source, finely chopped

2 packages (8 ounces each) cream cheese or cream cheese alternative, such as Tofutti, cut into 1-inch cubes and softened

¾ cup sugar

2 teaspoons pure vanilla extract

⅛ teaspoon salt

2 large eggs, at room temperature

1 Place a rack in the middle of the oven. Preheat the oven to 325°F. Generously grease a nonstick (gray, not black) mini 12-cheesecake pan; set aside.

2 Place the cookies in a food processor and process until they are fine crumbs. Sprinkle the crumbs evenly onto the bottoms of the 12 cheesecake molds.

3 Melt the chocolate in the boiling water; set aside.

4 In a large mixing bowl, beat the cream cheese with an electric stand mixer on medium speed until light and fluffy. Add the sugar, vanilla extract, and salt and beat 1 minute, scraping the side of the bowl. Beat in the chocolate mixture and then beat in the eggs, one a time, just until blended. Pour the filling into the molds, dividing evenly.

5 Bake 20 to 25 minutes or until the tops are firm. Cool the cheesecakes in the pan 15 minutes on a wire rack. Then release the cheesecakes by pushing up from the bottom. Refrigerate overnight. Let stand at room temperature 10 minutes before serving.

Chocolate-Espresso Cheesecake with Espresso-Caramel Sauce Ⓥ

MAKES 12 SERVINGS

If you love the flavors of chocolate and coffee as much as I do, then you'll love this cheesecake. To keep things simple, you can serve it without the sauce, but it does add a certain lusciousness that's nice for special occasions. Serve it with a robust, dark roast coffee for added impact.

CRUST

1 package (9 cookies) gluten-free chocolate cookies, such as Pamela's Dark Chocolate, Chocolate Chunk or homemade Chocolate Sandwich Cookies (page 434)

2 tablespoons sugar

2 tablespoons unsalted butter or buttery spread, such as Earth Balance, melted, or canola oil

FILLING

2 tablespoons instant espresso powder

2 tablespoons water

5 ounces semi-sweet chocolate, such as Scharffen Berger or Tropical Source, cut in ½-inch pieces

3 packages (8 ounces each) cream cheese or cream cheese alternative such as Tofutti, cut in 1-inch cubes and softened

1 cup sugar

¼ cup sour cream or sour cream alternative, such as Tofutti, at room temperature

1 tablespoon coffee liqueur, such as Kahlúa (optional)

1 tablespoon pure vanilla extract

⅛ teaspoon salt

4 large eggs, at room temperature

SAUCE

½ cup packed light brown sugar

2 tablespoons light corn syrup

¼ cup (½ stick) unsalted butter or buttery spread, such as Earth Balance

¼ cup 1% milk (cow's, rice, soy, potato, or nut)

1 teaspoon pure vanilla extract

2 tablespoons brewed espresso

1 tablespoon coffee liqueur, such as Kahlúa (optional)

1 Place a rack in the middle of the oven. Preheat the oven to 350°F. Generously grease a 9-inch nonstick (gray, not black) springform pan set aside.

2 Make the crust: Place the cookies and sugar in a food processor and process until they are fine crumbs. Add the butter and process until the mixture is crumbly. Pat the crust onto the bottom of the pan. Bake 10 to 12 minutes or just until the crust is fragrant. Refrigerate the crust while preparing the filling, but leave the oven on.

3 Make the filling: In a microwave-safe measuring cup, heat the espresso powder in water in the microwave on high until the water boils. Remove from the microwave and stir until the espresso is dissolved. Stir in the chocolate until it is melted; set aside.

4 In a large mixing bowl, whip the cream cheese with an electric mixer on medium speed until light and fluffy. Add the sugar, sour cream, coffee liqueur (if using), vanilla extract, and salt and beat 1 minute, scraping the side of the bowl. Beat in the eggs, one a time, just until blended. Add the espresso-chocolate mixture and beat in just until blended. Pour the filling over the crust and smooth with a spatula.

5 Bake 1 hour or until the top is just set. Cool the cheesecake 15 minutes on a wire rack. Run a sharp knife around the outer edge of the cake to loosen the edges and remove the sides of the pan. Wrap the cheesecake in plastic and refrigerate overnight.

Slide a thin metal knife between the cheesecake and the pan and slide the cheesecake to a serving plate. Let stand at room temperature and then slice with a knife dipped in hot water, then dried.

6 Make the sauce: In a small saucepan, cook the brown sugar, corn syrup, and butter over medium heat until it boils. Reduce the heat to low and simmer gently 5 minutes, stirring to make sure it doesn't burn. Remove from the heat and stir in the milk, vanilla, espresso, and liqueur, if using, until smooth. Serve warm. If the sauce hardens, reheat it gently in a saucepan over low heat.

Peanut Butter Cheesecake with Cookie Crust Ⓥ

MAKES 12 SERVINGS

The peanut butter in this cheesecake provides a subtle background note, not a dominant element, but the peanut butter cookie crust adds a burst of peanut butter flavor. Garnish with salted peanuts and a drizzle of warmed peanut butter if you really want to pack a peanut butter punch.

CRUST

1 package (9 cookies) gluten-free peanut butter cookies, such as Pamela's Peanut Butter or homemade Peanut Butter Cookies (page 407)

2 tablespoons unsalted butter or buttery spread, such as Earth Balance, at room temperature, or canola oil

FILLING

2 packages (8 ounces each) cream cheese or cream cheese alternative, such as Tofutti, softened

½ cup sugar

2 tablespoons creamy peanut butter

2 large eggs, at room temperature

1 tablespoon cornstarch

1 teaspoon pure vanilla extract

1 Place a rack in the middle of the oven. Preheat oven to 325°F. Generously grease the bottom and sides of an 8-inch nonstick (gray, not black) springform pan; set aside.

2 Make the crust: Process cookies in food processor until crushed into fine crumbs. Add butter and process until thoroughly combined. Press mixture on bottom of springform pan.

3 Bake 10 minutes or just until fragrant and remove from oven. Leave oven on.

4 Make the filling: Wipe out the food processor with damp paper towel. Process the cream cheese and sugar in the food processor until smooth. Add peanut butter, eggs, cornstarch, and vanilla extract and process until very smooth. Pour into prepared crust and smooth top with spatula.

5 Bake 40 to 45 minutes or until the top is firm. Remove from oven and cool cake in the pan 30 minutes on a wire rack. Refrigerate overnight. Slide a thin metal knife between the cheesecake and the pan and slide cheesecake to a serving plate. Let stand at room temperature, then slice with a knife dipped in hot water, then dried.

Pineapple-Coconut Cheesecake with Nut Crust ⓥ

MAKES 12 SERVINGS

The flavors of the tropics are melded in this luscious cheesecake that combines pineapple, coconut, and macadamia nuts.

CRUST

1½ cups crushed gluten-free vanilla or lemon-flavored cookies, such as Pamela's Lemon Shortbread, or homemade Lemon Cookies (page 419)

2 tablespoons sugar

⅓ cup (5 tablespoons) unsalted butter or buttery spread, such as Earth Balance

½ cup chopped macadamia nuts

FILLING

3 packages (8 ounces each) cream cheese or cream cheese alternative, such as Tofutti, cut into 1-inch cubes and softened

1 cup sugar

¼ cup sour cream or sour cream alternative, such as Tofutti, at room temperature

1 tablespoon pure vanilla extract

1 teaspoon coconut extract

⅛ teaspoon salt

3 large eggs, at room temperature

1 small can (8 ounces) crushed pineapple, thoroughly drained

½ cup sweetened shredded coconut

1 Place a rack in the middle of the oven. Preheat the oven to 325°F. Generously grease the bottom and sides of a 9-inch nonstick (gray, not black) springform pan; set aside.

2 Place the cookies and sugar in a food processor and process until they are fine crumbs. Add the butter and process until the mixture is crumbly; add the nuts and process again until they are coarsely ground. Pat the crust onto the bottom of the pan. Bake 10 to 12 minutes or just until the crust is fragrant. Cool the crust on a wire rack while preparing the filling, but leave the oven on.

3 In a large mixing bowl, beat the cream cheese with an electric mixer on medium speed until light and fluffy. Add the sugar, sour cream, vanilla extract, coconut extract, and salt and beat 1 minute, scraping the side of the bowl with a spatula. Beat in the eggs, one a time, just until blended. Stir in the pineapple and coconut flakes. Pour the filling over the crust and smooth with a spatula.

4 Bake 1 hour or until the top is firm. Cool the cheesecake 15 minutes on a wire rack. Run a sharp knife around the outer edge of the cake to loosen the edges and remove the sides of the pan. Wrap the cheesecake in plastic and refrigerate overnight. Slide a thin metal knife between the cheesecake and the pan and slide the cheesecake to a serving plate. Let stand at room temperature and then slice with a knife dipped in hot water, then dried.

Nectarine-Cheesecake Tart Ⓥ

MAKES 12 SERVINGS

Make this cheesecake in the summer when fresh nectarines are available. If you can't find a tart pan with a removable bottom, then use a spring-form pan of the same size.

CRUST

1 package (9 cookies) gluten-free vanilla or lemon-flavored cookies, such as Pamela's Lemon Shortbread, or homemade Lemon Cookies (page 419)

1 tablespoon sugar

2 tablespoons unsalted butter or buttery spread, such as Earth Balance, melted, or canola oil

FILLING

3 packages (8 ounces each) cream cheese or cream cheese alternative, such as Tofutti, cut into 1-inch cubes and softened

½ cup sugar

¼ cup sour cream or sour cream alternative, such as Tofutti, at room temperature

2 teaspoons pure vanilla extract

⅛ teaspoon salt

3 large eggs, at room temperature

2 large fresh nectarines, pitted and thinly sliced

3 tablespoons apple jelly, melted

1 Place a rack in the middle of the oven. Preheat the oven to 325°F. Generously grease the bottom and sides of a 9-inch nonstick (gray, not black) tart pan with a removable bottom; set aside.

2 Place the cookies and sugar in a food processor and process until they are fine crumbs. Add the butter and process until the mixture is crumbly. Pat the crust into the pan.

3 Bake 10 to 12 minutes or just until the crust is fragrant. Cool the crust while preparing the filling, but leave the oven on.

4 In a large mixing bowl, beat the cream cheese with an electric mixer on medium speed until light and fluffy. Add the sugar, sour cream, vanilla extract, and salt and beat 2 minutes, scraping the side of the bowl. Beat in the eggs, one a time, just until blended. Pour the filling over the crust and smooth with a spatula.

5 Bake 1 hour or until the top is firm. Cool the cheesecake on a wire rack while preparing the nectarines and apple jelly. Arrange the nectarine slices in a concentric circle on the tart; brush with the apple jelly. Bake 10 minutes. Cool the cheesecake 15 minutes on the wire rack and refrigerate overnight.

Raspberry-White Chocolate Cheesecake Ⓥ

MAKES 12 SERVINGS

Raspberries and white chocolate make a lovely combination in this cheesecake.

CRUST

1 package (9 cookies) gluten-free vanilla or lemon-flavored cookies, such as Pamela's Lemon Shortbread, or homemade Lemon Cookies (page 419)

½ cup macadamia nuts (or nuts of choice)

1 tablespoon sugar

2 tablespoons unsalted butter or buttery spread, such as Earth Balance, melted, or canola oil

FILLING

3 packages (8 ounces each) cream cheese or cream cheese alternative, such as Tofutti, cut into 1-inch cubes and softened

1 cup sugar

¼ cup sour cream or sour cream alternative, such as Tofutti, at room temperature

3.5 ounces gluten-free white chocolate, such as Organica, melted

1½ teaspoons pure vanilla extract

⅛ teaspoon salt

4 large eggs, at room temperature

½ cup raspberry preserves

2 packages (6 ounces each) fresh raspberries, washed

1 Place a rack in the middle of the oven. Preheat the oven to 325°F. Generously grease the bottom and sides of a 9-inch nonstick (gray, not black) springform pan; set aside.

2 Make the crust: Place the cookies, nuts, and sugar in a food processor and process until they are fine crumbs. Add the butter and process until the mixture is crumbly. Pat the crust onto the bottom of the pan and 1-inch up the sides. Bake 8 to 10 minutes or just until the crust is fragrant. Cool the crust while preparing the filling, but leave the oven on.

3 Make the filling: In a large mixing bowl, beat the cream cheese with an electric mixer on medium speed until light and fluffy. Add the sugar, sour cream, white chocolate, vanilla extract, and salt and beat 1 minute until smooth, scraping the side of the bowl. Beat in the eggs, one at a time, just until blended. Pour the filling over the crust and smooth with a spatula.

4 Bake 1 hour or until the top is firm. Cool the cheesecake 15 minutes on a wire rack. Run a sharp knife around the outer edge of the cake to loosen the edges and remove the sides of the pan. Wrap the cheesecake in plastic and refrigerate overnight. Slide a thin, metal knife between the cheesecake and the pan and slide the cheesecake to a serving plate.

5 In a small saucepan, melt the raspberry preserves over low heat. Remove from the heat and stir in fresh raspberries. Let the cheesecake stand at room temperature and then slice with a knife dipped in hot water, then dried. Spoon raspberry sauce on each slice. Refrigerate leftovers.

White Chocolate Cheesecake with Caramel-Pecan Topping Ⓥ

MAKES 12 SERVINGS

White chocolate lovers will adore this cheesecake. It sits in a dark chocolate crust and is topped with a crunchy, mouth-watering pecan sauce that will win your heart.

CRUST

1 package (9 cookies) gluten-free chocolate cookies, such as Pamela's Dark Chocolate, Chocolate Chunk, or homemade Chocolate Cookies (page 434)

2 tablespoons sugar

2 tablespoons unsalted butter or buttery spread, such as Earth Balance, melted, or canola oil

FILLING

3 packages (8 ounces each) cream cheese or cream cheese alternative, such as Tofutti, cut into 1-inch cubes and softened

1 cup sugar

½ cup sour cream or sour cream alternative, such as Tofutti, at room temperature

1 tablespoon almond extract

⅛ teaspoon salt

4 large eggs, at room temperature

1 gluten-free white chocolate baking bar (3.5 ounces) such as Ghirardelli, melted

SAUCE

½ cup packed light brown sugar

2 tablespoons light corn syrup

¼ cup (½ stick) unsalted butter or buttery spread, such as Earth Balance, or 3 tablespoons canola oil

¼ cup 1% milk (cow's, rice, soy, potato, or nut)

1 teaspoon pure vanilla extract

½ cup chopped pecans, toasted

1 Place a rack in the middle of the oven. Preheat the oven to 325°F. Generously grease the bottom and sides of a 9-inch nonstick (gray, not black) springform pan; set aside.

2 Make the crust: Place the cookies and sugar in a food processor and process until they are fine crumbs. Add the butter and process until the mixture is crumbly. Pat the crust onto the bottom of the pan. Bake 10 to 12 minutes or just until the crust is fragrant. Cool the crust while preparing the filling, but leave the oven on.

3 Make the filling: In a large mixing bowl, beat the cream cheese with an electric mixer on medium speed until light and fluffy. Add the sugar and sour cream and beat 1 minute, scraping the side of the bowl. Add the almond extract and salt and beat until smooth. Beat in the eggs, one a time, just until blended. Stir in the melted white chocolate. Pour the filling over the crust and smooth with a spatula.

4 Bake 1 hour or until the top is firm. Cool the cheesecake 15 minutes on a wire rack. Run a sharp knife around the outer edge of the cake to loosen the edges and remove the sides of the pan. Wrap the cheesecake in plastic and refrigerate overnight. Slide a thin metal knife between the cheesecake and the pan and slide the cheesecake to a serving plate. Let stand at room temperature and then slice with a knife dipped in hot water, then dried.

5 Make the topping: In a small saucepan, cook the brown sugar, corn syrup, and butter over medium heat until it boils. Reduce the heat to low and simmer gently 5 minutes, stirring to make sure it doesn't burn. Remove from the heat and stir in the milk and vanilla until smooth. Stir in the pecans. Serve cheesecake with the warm sauce poured over each piece. If the sauce hardens, reheat it gently in a saucepan over low heat.

CUPCAKES

Yellow Cupcakes
MAKES 12 SERVINGS

Kids love cupcakes because they are easy to eat, and adults love them because they're just the right size. These simple, yellow cupcakes are versatile and an important recipe for every gluten-free cook's repertoire.

½ cup (1 stick) unsalted butter or buttery spread, such as Earth Balance, at room temperature, or ⅓ cup canola oil
¾ cup sugar
2 large eggs, at room temperature
1½ cups Carol's Sorghum Blend (page x)
1 teaspoon xanthan gum
½ teaspoon salt
¼ teaspoon baking powder
¼ teaspoon baking soda
¾ cup buttermilk, well-shaken, or homemade Buttermilk (page 677)
1 teaspoon pure vanilla extract
½ teaspoon almond extract

1 Place a rack in the middle of the oven. Preheat the oven to 325°F. Generously grease the cups of a standard 12-cup nonstick (gray, not black) muffin pan or line with paper liners. Spray the insides of the liners with cooking spray.

2 In a large mixing bowl, beat the butter with an electric mixer on medium speed until smooth. Gradually beat in the sugar until smooth. Add the eggs, one at a time, beating well after each addition.

3 In another bowl, sift together the sorghum blend, xanthan gum, salt, baking powder, and baking soda. In a measuring cup, whisk together the buttermilk, vanilla extract, and almond extract.

4 With the mixer on low speed, beat the sorghum mixture into the egg mixture, alternating with the buttermilk, beginning and ending with the sorghum mixture. Divide the batter evenly in the pan.

5 Bake 20 to 25 minutes or until a toothpick inserted into the center of a cupcake comes out clean. Cool the cupcakes in the pan 5 minutes and then place them on a wire rack to finish cooling completely. Serve plain or with your favorite frosting.

White Cupcakes

MAKES 12 SERVINGS

Simple white cupcakes are wonderfully versatile and they are often much more appropriate for a party than a cake because everyone gets their own little treat to savor.

½ cup (1 stick) unsalted butter or buttery spread, such as Earth Balance, at room temperature, or ⅓ cup canola oil

¾ cup sugar

3 large egg whites, at room temperature

1½ cups Carol's Sorghum Blend (page x)

1 teaspoon xanthan gum

½ teaspoon salt

¼ teaspoon baking powder

¼ teaspoon baking soda

¾ cup buttermilk, well-shaken, or homemade Buttermilk (page 677)

1 teaspoon pure vanilla extract

½ teaspoon almond extract (optional)

1 Place a rack in the middle of the oven. Preheat the oven to 325°F. Generously grease the cups of a standard 12-cup nonstick (gray, not black) muffin pan or line with paper liners. Spray the insides of the liners with cooking spray.

2 In a large mixing bowl, beat the butter with an electric mixer on medium speed until smooth. Gradually beat in the sugar until smooth. Add the egg whites, one at a time, beating well after each addition.

3 In another bowl, sift together the sorghum blend, xanthan gum, salt, baking powder, and baking soda. In a measuring cup, whisk together the buttermilk, vanilla, and almond extract.

4 With the mixer on low speed, beat the sorghum mixture into the egg mixture, alternating with the buttermilk, beginning and ending with the sorghum mixture. Divide the batter evenly in the pan.

5 Bake 25 to 30 minutes or until a toothpick inserted into the center of a cupcake comes out clean. Cool the cupcakes in the pan 5 minutes on a wire rack. Remove cupcakes from pan and place on a wire rack to finish cooling completely.

YELLOW AND WHITE CUPCAKES

Yellow cupcakes and white cupcakes are very versatile, so always keep a batch in your freezer. Vary the taste with different extracts, such as lemon or coconut, or by adding grated citrus zest. Vary the look with a vanilla or chocolate frosting—or just a simple dusting of powdered sugar. Sliced in half, horizontally, and layered with sliced strawberries and whipped cream, cupcakes make perfect strawberry shortcakes. Regardless of the frosting you choose, there are lots of ways you can add decorative touches to your cupcakes. Bake the cupcakes in paper liners, either colored ones or gold or silver. After they have thoroughly cooled, place each cupcake in yet another paper liner of the same color and tie a pretty ribbon around the liner. Decorate the cupcake with fresh fruit, chocolate shavings, candied fruuit, cocoa nibs, chocolate-covered espresso beans, nuts—the options are limitless.

Pound Cake Cupcakes

MAKES 12 SERVINGS

We traditionally think of pound cakes as large cakes, but the dense batter also makes terrific cupcakes. These cupcakes are best served while still slightly warm from the oven—plain, with a light dusting of powdered sugar, or topped with strawberries and a dollop of whipped cream.

½ cup unsalted butter or buttery spread, such as Earth Balance, at room temperature, or ⅓ cup canola oil

2 cups sugar

4 large eggs, at room temperature

3 cups Carol's Sorghum Blend (page x)

1½ teaspoons xanthan gum

¾ teaspoon salt

½ teaspoon baking powder

½ teaspoon baking soda

1½ cups buttermilk, well-shaken, or homemade Buttermilk (page 677)

1 tablespoon grated lemon zest

2 teaspoons pure vanilla extract

1 Place a rack in the middle of the oven. Preheat oven to 325°F. Generously grease the cups of a standard 12-cup nonstick (gray, not black) muffin pan or line with paper liners. Spray the insides of the liners with cooking spray.

2 In a large mixer bowl, beat the butter with an electric mixer on medium speed until smooth. Add sugar and continue beating on medium speed until well blended. Mix in eggs, one at a time and beating well after each addition.

3 In a medium bowl, whisk together the sorghum blend, xanthan gum, salt, baking powder, and baking soda. In a measuring cup, combine buttermilk, lemon zest, and vanilla extract. On low speed, beat the sorghum mixture into the egg mixture, alternating with the buttermilk and ending with

the sorghum mixture. Divide the batter evenly in the pan.

4 Bake 25 to 30 minutes or until a toothpick inserted into the center of a cupcake comes out clean. Cool the cupcakes in the pan 5 minutes on a wire rack. Remove cupcakes from pan and place on a wire rack to finish cooling completely.

Old-Fashioned Molasses Cupcakes

MAKES 12 SERVINGS

These spice cupcakes use molasses, which was a very popular flavoring in old-time cookbooks.

½ cup (1 stick) unsalted butter or buttery spread, such as Earth Balance, at room temperature, or ⅓ cup canola oil

¾ cup packed light brown sugar

2 large eggs, at room temperature

¼ cup molasses (not blackstrap)

1 teaspoon pure vanilla extract

2 cups Carol's Sorghum Blend (page x)

2 teaspoons ground cinnamon

1 teaspoon ground ginger

1 teaspoon xanthan gum

1 teaspoon baking soda

½ teaspoon salt

1 Place a rack in the middle of the oven. Preheat the oven to 350°F. Generously grease the cups of a 12-cup nonstick (gray, not black) muffin pan or line with paper liners. Spray the insides of the liners with cooking spray.

2 In a large mixing bowl, beat the butter with an electric mixer on low speed until smooth. Add the brown sugar and continue beating on low speed until well blended. Add the eggs, molasses, and vanilla extract and beat until the batter is smooth.

3 In a separate bowl, sift together the sorghum blend, cinnamon, ginger, xanthan gum, baking soda, and salt. Gradually beat the sorghum mixture into the egg mixture on low speed, scraping down side of bowl if necessary, until well blended and slightly thickened. Divide the batter evenly in the pan.

4 Bake 20 to 25 minutes or until a toothpick inserted into the center of a cupcake comes out clean. Cool the cupcakes in the pan 5 minutes on a wire rack. Remove cupcakes from pan and place them on a serving platter or dessert plates.

Coconut Cupcakes with Coconut Frosting Ⓥ

MAKES 12 SERVINGS

Coconut is one of my favorite flavors, so I love these coconut-intensive cupcakes.

CUPCAKES

⅓ cup (5 tablespoons) unsalted butter or buttery spread, such as Earth Balance, at room temperature, or ¼ cup canola oil

1 cup sugar

2 large eggs, at room temperature

1½ cups Carol's Sorghum Blend (page x)

1 teaspoon xanthan gum

¼ teaspoon baking powder

¼ teaspoon baking soda

¼ teaspoon salt

¾ cup buttermilk, well-shaken, or homemade Buttermilk (page 677)

2 teaspoons pure vanilla extract

1 teaspoon coconut extract

½ cup sweetened coconut

FROSTING

2 cups homemade Basic Whipped Cream (page 624) or whipped topping, such as Lucerne or Soyatoo

1 teaspoon coconut extract

2 cups sweetened shredded coconut

1 Place a rack in the middle of the oven. Preheat the oven to 325°F. Generously grease the cups of a standard 12-cup nonstick (gray, not black) muffin pan or line with paper liners. Spray the insides of the liners with cooking spray.

2 Make the cupcakes: In a large mixing bowl, beat the butter with an electric mixer on medium speed until smooth. Gradually beat in the sugar until smooth. Add the eggs, one at a time, beating well after each addition.

3 In another bowl, whisk together the sorghum blend, xanthan gum, baking powder, baking soda, and salt. In a measuring cup, whisk together the buttermilk, vanilla extract, and coconut extract.

4 With the mixer on low speed, beat the sorghum mixture into the egg mixture, alternating with the buttermilk, beginning and ending with the sorghum mixture. Stir in the coconut flakes. Divide the batter evenly in the pan.

5 Bake 20 to 25 minutes or until a toothpick inserted into the center of a cupcake comes out clean. Cool the cupcakes in the pan 5 minutes and then place them on a wire rack to finish cooling completely.

6 Make the frosting: In a medium bowl, place the whipping cream. Stir in the coconut extract. Spread each cupcake with frosting and sprinkle with coconut flakes. Serve immediately.

Orange-Coconut Cupcakes with Orange-Coconut Frosting Ⓥ

MAKES 12 SERVINGS

The combination of coconut and orange is irresistible in these cupcakes. They make a lovely dessert for a casual luncheon or bridal shower when displayed on a three-tier cake stand.

CUPCAKES

⅓ cup (5 tablespoons) unsalted butter or buttery spread, such as Earth Balance, at room temperature, or ¼ cup canola oil

1 cup sugar

2 large eggs, at room temperature

1½ cups Carol's Sorghum Blend (page x)

1 teaspoon xanthan gum

¼ teaspoon baking powder

¼ teaspoon baking soda

¼ teaspoon salt

¾ cup buttermilk, well-shaken, or homemade Buttermilk (page 677)

1 tablespoon grated orange zest

2 teaspoons pure vanilla extract

1 teaspoon orange extract (optional)

½ cup sweetened shredded coconut

FROSTING

3 large egg whites

1 cup sugar

¼ teaspoon cream of tartar

3 tablespoons fresh orange juice

1 teaspoon grated orange zest

1 teaspoon pure vanilla extract

1 teaspoon coconut extract (optional)

¾ cup sweetened shredded coconut, toasted

1 Place a rack in the middle of the oven. Preheat oven to 325°F. Generously grease the cups of a standard 12-cup nonstick (gray, not black) muffin pan or line with paper liners. Spray the insides of the liners with cooking spray.

2 Make the cupcakes: In a large mixing bowl, cream the butter with an electric mixer on medium speed until smooth. Gradually beat in the sugar until smooth. Add the eggs, one at a time, beating well after each addition.

3 In another bowl, sift together the sorghum blend, xanthan gum, baking powder, baking soda, and salt. In a measuring cup, whisk together the buttermilk, orange zest, vanilla extract, and orange extract, if using.

4 With the mixer on low speed, beat the sorghum mixture into the egg mixture, alternating with the buttermilk, beginning and ending with the sorghum mixture. Stir in the shredded coconut. Divide the batter evenly in the pan.

5 Bake 25 to 30 minutes or until a toothpick inserted into the center of a cupcake comes out clean. Cool the cupcakes in the pan 5 minutes on a wire rack. Remove cupcakes from pan and cool completely on the wire rack.

6 Make the frosting: In a double boiler over simmering water, combine the egg whites, sugar, cream of tartar, and orange juice. Beat 7 minutes with a portable electric mixer, or until the mixture reaches the consistency of frosting. Remove frosting from the heat and stir in the orange zest, vanilla extract, and coconut extract, if using. Spread each cupcake generously with frosting, sprinkle with coconut, and serve immediately.

Mini Coconut-Pecan Cupcakes Ⓥ

MAKES 24 SERVINGS

The creamy coconut flavor in these tiny cupcakes, accented by crunchy pecans, can't be beat.

CUPCAKES

⅓ cup unsalted butter or buttery spread, such as Earth Balance, at room temperature, or ¼ cup canola oil

1 cup sugar

2 large eggs, at room temperature, divided

1½ cups Carol's Sorghum Blend (page x)

1 teaspoon xanthan gum

½ teaspoon baking powder

½ teaspoon baking soda

½ teaspoon salt

¾ cup buttermilk or homemade Buttermilk (page 677)

1 teaspoon pure vanilla extract

1 teaspoon coconut extract

4 tablespoons finely chopped toasted pecans

FROSTING

1 tablespoon unsalted butter or buttery spread, such as Earth Balance, at room temperature, or canola oil

1 small package (3 ounces) cream cheese or cream cheese alternative, such as Tofutti, at room temperature

1 teaspoon coconut extract

3 cups powdered sugar

½ cup shredded coconut, for garnish

1 Place a rack in the middle of the oven. Preheat the oven to 325°F. Generously grease the cups of a mini 12-cup nonstick (gray, not black) muffin pan or line with paper liners. Spray the insides of the liners with cooking spray.

2 Make the cupcakes: In a large mixing bowl, beat the butter with an electric mixer on medium speed until creamy and smooth. Gradually beat in the sugar until smooth. Add the egg yolks, one at a time, beating well after each addition.

3 In another bowl, whisk together the sorghum blend, xanthan gum, baking powder, baking soda, and salt. In a measuring cup, whisk together the buttermilk, vanilla extract, and coconut extract.

4 With the mixer on low speed, beat the sorghum mixture into the egg mixture, alternating with the buttermilk, beginning and ending with the sorghum mixture. Add the pecans, scrape down the side of the bowl, and beat just until smooth.

5 In a large clean bowl with clean beaters, beat the egg whites on high speed until stiff peaks form. Fold the egg whites into the batter. Divide the batter evenly in the pan.

6 Bake 15 to 17 minutes or until the tops of the cupcakes feel firm to the touch. Cool the cupcakes in the pan 5 minutes on a wire rack. Remove cupcakes from pan and place on a serving platter or dessert plates. Repeat with the remaining batter.

7 Make the frosting: In a medium bowl, beat the butter, cream cheese, and coconut extract with an electric mixer on medium speed until smooth and creamy. Gradually beat in the powdered sugar on low speed. Spread each mini cupcake with 2

teaspoons of frosting and sprinkle with a teaspoon of shredded coconut.

Banana Cupcakes with Maple–Cream-Cheese Frosting Ⓥ

MAKES 12 SERVINGS

Banana and maple are natural partners in these flavorful cupcakes.

CUPCAKES

5 tablespoons unsalted butter or buttery spread, such as Earth Balance, at room temperature, or ¼ cup canola oil

1 cup sugar

2 large eggs, at room temperature

1 large very ripe banana, mashed

1½ cups Carol's Sorghum Blend (page x)

1 teaspoon xanthan gum

½ teaspoon baking powder

½ teaspoon baking soda

¼ teaspoon salt

¾ cup buttermilk, well-shaken, or homemade Buttermilk (page 677)

1 teaspoon pure vanilla extract

1 teaspoon banana-flavored extract (optional)

1 teaspoon maple-flavored extract (optional)

1 cup finely chopped pecans, divided

FROSTING

1 small package (3 ounces) cream cheese or cream cheese alternative, such as Tofutti, at room temperature

¼ cup (½ stick) unsalted butter or buttery spread, such as Earth Balance, at room temperature, or canola oil

4 teaspoons pure maple syrup

⅛ teaspoon maple-flavored extract (optional)

3 cups powdered sugar

Pinch salt

1 Place a rack in the middle of the oven. Preheat the oven to 325°F. Generously grease the cups of a standard 12-cup nonstick (gray, not black) muffin pan or line with paper liners. Spray the insides of the liners with cooking spray.

2 Make the cupcakes: In a large mixing bowl, beat the butter with an electric mixer on medium speed until creamy and smooth. Gradually beat in the sugar until smooth. Add the eggs, one at a time, beating well after each addition. Beat in the mashed banana until the batter is smooth.

3 In another bowl, whisk together the sorghum blend, xanthan gum, baking powder, baking soda, and salt. In a measuring cup, whisk together the buttermilk, vanilla extract, and banana-flavored and maple-flavored extracts, if using.

4 With the mixer on low speed, beat the sorghum mixture into the egg mixture, alternating with the buttermilk, beginning and ending with the sorghum mixture. Add ¾ cup of the pecans, scrape down the side of the bowl, and beat just until smooth. Divide the batter evenly in the pan.

5 Bake 20 to 25 minutes or until a toothpick inserted into the center of a cupcake comes out clean. Cool the cupcakes in the pan 5 minutes . Remove cupcakes from pan and place on a wire rack to finish cooling.

6 Make the frosting: In a medium bowl, beat the cream cheese, butter, maple syrup, and maple extract with an electric mixer on medium speed until smooth and creamy. Gradually beat in the powdered sugar until the frosting is smooth.

7 Spread the frosting evenly on the top of each cupcake and then sprinkle each with the remaining pecans. Serve immediately or refrigerate.

Black Walnut Cupcakes with Caramel Frosting Ⓥ

MAKES 12 SERVINGS

The fabulous flavor of black walnuts is unique— not at all like English walnuts—and especially delicious when combined with caramel frosting.

CUPCAKES

5 tablespoons unsalted butter or buttery spread, such as Earth Balance, at room temperature, or ¼ cup canola oil

1 cup sugar

2 large eggs, divided

1½ cups Carol's Sorghum Blend (page x)

1 teaspoon xanthan gum

½ teaspoon baking powder

½ teaspoon baking soda

½ teaspoon salt

¾ cup buttermilk, well-shaken, or homemade Buttermilk (page 677)

1 teaspoon pure vanilla extract

1 teaspoon black walnut extract (optional)

¼ cup finely chopped black walnuts

FROSTING

¼ cup (½ stick) unsalted butter or buttery spread, such as Earth Balance, at room temperature, or 3 tablespoons canola oil

1 cup packed dark brown sugar

2 tablespoons 1% milk (cow's, rice, soy, potato, or nut), or more if necessary

1 tablespoon pure vanilla extract

1 box (16 ounces) powdered sugar

¼ cup finely chopped black walnuts, for garnish

1 Place a rack in the middle of the oven. Preheat the oven to 350°F. Generously grease the cups of a standard 12-cup nonstick (gray, not black) muffin pan or line with paper liners. Spray the insides of the liners with cooking spray.

2 Make the cupcakes: In a large mixing bowl, beat the butter with an electric mixer on medium speed until creamy and smooth. Gradually beat in the sugar until smooth. Add the eggs, one at a time, beating well after each addition.

3 In another bowl, whisk together the sorghum blend, xanthan gum, baking powder, baking soda, and salt. In a measuring cup, whisk together the buttermilk, vanilla extract, and black walnut extract, if using.

4 With the mixer on low speed, beat the sorghum mixture into the egg mixture, alternating with the buttermilk, beginning and ending with the sorghum mixture. Add the black walnuts, scrape down the side of the bowl, and beat just until smooth. Divide the batter evenly in the pan.

5 Bake 20 to 25 minutes or until a toothpick inserted into the center of a cupcake comes out clean. Cool the cupcakes in the pan 5 minutes and then place them on a wire rack to finish cooling.

6 Make the frosting: In a medium bowl, beat the butter with an electric mixer on medium speed until smooth and creamy. Beat in the brown sugar, milk, and vanilla extract. Gradually beat in the powdered sugar until smooth.

7 Spread the frosting evenly on the top of each cupcake and then sprinkle each with the black walnuts. Serve immediately.

Polynesian Cupcakes with Coconut Cream-Cheese Frosting Ⓥ

MAKES 12 SERVINGS

If you love the Polynesian flavors of bananas, pineapple, and coconut in one bite, then these cupcakes are perfect for you. They are somewhat dense because of all these wonderful flavors, but that just makes them all the more satisfying.

CUPCAKES

1½ cups Carol's Sorghum Blend (page x)
1 cup sugar
1 teaspoon xanthan gum
1 teaspoon baking soda
½ teaspoon salt
¼ teaspoon ground cinnamon
2 large eggs, at room temperature
⅓ cup canola oil
2 teaspoons pure vanilla extract
1 large ripe banana, mashed
1 can (8 ounces) crushed pineapple, undrained
½ cup sweetened coconut flakes
½ cup chopped pecans

FROSTING

1 package (8 ounces) cream cheese or cream cheese alternative, such as Tofutti, at room temperature
¼ cup (½ stick) unsalted butter or buttery spread, such as Earth Balance, at room temperature, or 3 tablespoons canola oil
1 teaspoon coconut extract
2 cups powdered sugar
¼ cup sweetened shredded coconut, toasted, for garnish

1 Place a rack in the middle of the oven. Preheat the oven to 325°F. Generously grease the cups of a standard 12-cup nonstick (gray, not black) muffin pan or line with paper liners. Spray the insides of the liners with cooking spray.

2 Make the cupcakes: In a large mixing bowl, whisk together the sorghum blend, sugar, xanthan gum, baking soda, salt, and cinnamon. Add the eggs, oil, and vanilla extract and beat with an electric mixer on low speed until blended, scraping down the side of the bowl with a spatula. Beat in the banana on medium speed until well blended. Stir in the pineapple, coconut, and pecans. Divide the batter evenly in the pan.

3 Bake 25 to 30 minutes or until a toothpick inserted into the center of a cupcake comes out clean. Cool the cupcakes in the pan 5 minutes on a wire rack. Remove cupcakes from pan and cool completely on the wire rack.

4 Make the frosting: In a medium bowl, beat the cream cheese, butter, and coconut extract with an electric mixer on medium speed until smooth. Gradually sift in the powdered sugar and beat until smooth. Spread each cupcake with frosting and sprinkle with toasted coconut.

Tiramisu Cupcakes

MAKES 12 SERVINGS

Tiramisu means "pick me up" in Italian, and these cute little cakes will certainly give you a lift. They are yet another way of transforming a simple yellow cupcake into a delicious dessert with very little effort.

½ cup (1 stick) unsalted butter or buttery spread, such as Earth Balance, at room temperature, or ⅓ cup canola oil

¾ cup sugar

2 large eggs, at room temperature

1½ cups Carol's Sorghum Blend (page x)

1 teaspoon xanthan gum

½ teaspoon salt

¼ teaspoon baking powder

¼ teaspoon baking soda

¾ cup buttermilk, well-shaken, or homemade Buttermilk (page 677)

1 teaspoon pure vanilla extract

½ teaspoon almond extract

½ cup freshly brewed espresso

⅓ cup gluten-free dark chocolate, such as Scharffen Berger or Tropical Source, shaved

1 recipe Cream Cheese Frosting (page 449)

2 tablespoons Dutch-process cocoa powder, for dusting

1 Place a rack in the middle of the oven. Preheat the oven to 325°F. Generously grease the cups of a standard 12-cup nonstick (gray, not black) muffin pan or line with paper liners. Spray the insides of the liners with cooking spray.

2 In a large mixing bowl, beat the butter with an electric mixer on medium speed until smooth. Gradually beat in the sugar until smooth. Add the eggs, one at a time, beating well after each addition.

3 In another bowl, whisk together the sorghum blend, xanthan gum, salt, baking powder, and baking soda. In a measuring cup, whisk together the buttermilk, vanilla extract, and almond extract.

4 With the mixer on low speed, beat the sorghum mixture into the egg mixture, alternating with the buttermilk, beginning and ending with the sorghum mixture. Divide the batter evenly in the pan.

5 Bake 20 to 25 minutes or until a toothpick inserted into the center of a cupcake comes out clean. Cool the cupcakes in the pan 5 minutes on a wire rack. Remove cupcakes from pan and cool completely place on the wire rack.

6 With a toothpick, poke several holes in each cupcake. Brush the tops with espresso and let stand 15 minutes. Spread the cream cheese frosting on each cupcake, and garnish with shaved dark chocolate and a dusting of cocoa.

Harvey Wallbanger Cupcakes

MAKES 12 SERVINGS

Galliano is a vanilla-flavored liqueur that brings a lovely flavor to these treats for adults, but you may also use Cointreau or Frangelico. The glaze will soak into the cupcakes rather than look like a frosting.

CUPCAKES

⅓ cup (5 tablespoons) unsalted butter or buttery spread, such as Earth Balance, at room temperature, or ⅓ cup canola oil

1 cup sugar

2 large eggs, at room temperature

1½ cups Carol's Sorghum Blend (page x)

1 teaspoon xanthan gum

¼ teaspoon baking powder

¼ teaspoon baking soda

¼ teaspoon salt

½ cup buttermilk, well-shaken, or homemade Buttermilk (page 677)

¼ cup Galliano liqueur

1 tablespoon grated orange zest

2 teaspoons pure vanilla extract

GLAZE

1 cup powdered sugar
½ cup fresh orange juice
1 tablespoon Galliano liqueur
1 tablespoon vodka
Pinch salt

1 Place a rack in the middle of the oven. Preheat the oven to 325°F. Generously grease the cups of a standard 12-cup nonstick (gray, not black) muffin pan or line with paper liners. Spray the insides of the liners with cooking spray.

2 In a large mixing bowl, beat the butter with an electric mixer on medium speed until smooth. Gradually beat in the sugar until smooth. Add the eggs, one at a time, beating well after each addition.

3 In another bowl, whisk together the sorghum blend, xanthan gum, baking powder, baking soda, and salt. In a measuring cup, whisk together the buttermilk, liqueur, orange zest, and vanilla extract.

4 With the mixer on low speed, beat the sorghum mixture into the egg mixture, alternating with the buttermilk, beginning and ending with the sorghum mixture. Divide the batter equally in the pan.

5 Bake 20 to 25 minutes or until a toothpick inserted into the center of a cupcake comes out clean. Cool the cupcakes in the pan 5 minutes and then place them on a wire rack to finish cooling completely.

6 Make the glaze: In a medium bowl, beat the powdered sugar with the orange juice, liqueur, vodka, and salt until smooth. Holding a cupcake by the bottom, twirl the cupcake top in the glaze and place upright on a plate to set up. Serve immediately.

Vegan Chocolate Cupcakes with Mocha Frosting (V)

MAKES 24 SERVINGS

These simple chocolate cupcakes are perfect for those who avoid dairy and eggs. Coffee enhances the chocolate flavor in the frosting.

CUPCAKES

1¾ cups Carol's Sorghum Blend (page x)
1 cup sugar
⅓ cup unsweetened cocoa powder (not Dutch-process or alkali)
1 teaspoon baking soda
¾ teaspoon xanthan gum
¾ teaspoon salt
1 cup hot (120°F) water
⅓ cup canola oil
1 tablespoon cider vinegar
1 tablespoon pure vanilla extract

FROSTING

2 cups powdered sugar
2 tablespoons unsweetened cocoa powder (Dutch-process or alkali)
2 tablespoons unsalted butter or buttery spread, such as Earth Balance, at room temperature, or canola oil
¼ cup hot (120°F), strongly brewed espresso or coffee
Pinch salt

1 Place a rack in the middle of the oven. Preheat the oven to 325°F. Generously grease the cups of a mini 12-cup nonstick (gray, not black) muffin pan or line with paper liners. Spray the insides of the liners with cooking spray.

2 Make the cupcakes: Whisk together the sorghum blend, sugar, cocoa, baking soda, xanthan gum, and salt in a medium mixing bowl. Add the water, oil, vinegar, and vanilla extract. Beat with an electric mixer on low speed until thoroughly blended. Divide the batter evenly in the pan. Let batter stand 10 minutes.

3 Bake 15 to 17 minutes or until a toothpick inserted into the center of a cupcake comes out clean. Cool the cupcakes in the pan 5 minutes and then place them on a serving platter or dessert plates. Repeat with remaining batter.

4 Make the frosting: In a medium bowl, beat all ingredients except coffee with an electric mixer on low speed until blended. Add coffee gradually until frosting reaches desired consistency. Spread each cupcake with frosting. Serve immediately.

Chocolate Peanut Butter Cupcakes Ⓥ

MAKES 12 SERVINGS

The flavors of chocolate and peanut butter complement each other beautifully in these yummy cupcakes. If you can't find gluten-free peanut butter chips, use gluten-free chocolate chips and stir a tablespoon of peanut butter into the cupcake batter.

CUPCAKES

1¼ cups Carol's Sorghum Blend (page x)

½ cup unsweetened cocoa powder (not Dutch-process or alkali)

1 teaspoon xanthan gum

¾ teaspoon baking soda

¾ teaspoon salt

½ cup unsalted butter or buttery spread, such as Earth Balance, or ⅓ cup canola oil

1 cup packed light brown sugar

½ cup 1% milk (cow's, rice, soy, potato, or nut)

1 large egg, at room temperature

2 teaspoons pure vanilla extract

¾ cup hot (120°F) brewed coffee or hot water

2 ounces gluten-free peanut butter chips, such as Hy-Vee

GLAZE

¼ cup (½ stick) unsalted butter or buttery spread, such as Earth Balance, at room temperature, or 3 tablespoons canola oil

¼ cup gluten-free chocolate chips, such as Tropical Source

1 tablespoon light corn syrup

1 Place a rack in the middle of the oven. Preheat the oven to 325°F. Generously grease the cups of a standard 12-cup nonstick (gray, not black) muffin pan or line with paper liners. Spray the insides of the liners with cooking spray.

2 Make the cupcakes: In a small bowl, sift together the sorghum blend, cocoa, xanthan gum, baking soda, and salt; set aside.

3 In a large mixer bowl, beat the butter and brown sugar with an electric mixer on medium speed about 30 seconds. Beat in the milk, egg, and vanilla extract until thoroughly blended.

4 Beat the sorghum mixture into the egg mixture on low speed, alternating with the hot coffee, beginning and ending with the sorghum mixture. Divide the batter evenly in the pan.

5 Bake 20 to 25 minutes or until a toothpick inserted into the center of a cupcake comes out clean. Cool the cupcakes in the pan 5 minutes on a wire rack. Remove cupcakes from pan and cool completely on the wire rack. Remove the paper liners from cupcakes, if using.

6 Make the glaze: Combine the butter, chocolate, and corn syrup in a glass bowl set over a saucepan of simmering water. Stir until the chocolate is melted and the mixture is smooth. Remove from the heat and let stand 5 minutes. Pour the glaze over the cupcakes and refrigerate them to set the glaze. Let the cupcakes stand at room temperature 10 minutes before serving.

Mini Mexican Chocolate Cupcakes with Cinnamon Frosting Ⓥ

MAKES 24 SERVINGS

Cinnamon is commonly used with chocolate in Mexico. You can bake the cupcakes ahead of time, freeze for up to two weeks, and defrost them on your countertop before frosting but the frosting itself should be used immediately after it is made.

CUPCAKES

2 cups Carol's Sorghum Blend (page x)

1½ teaspoons baking soda

1 teaspoon baking powder

½ cup unsweetened cocoa powder (not Dutch-
process or alkali)

1 teaspoon xanthan gum

½ teaspoon ground cinnamon

½ teaspoon salt

1 cup thin buttermilk, well-shaken, (or ¾ cup buttermilk
mixed with ¼ cup water) or 1 cup homemade
Buttermilk (page 677)

1 tablespoon pure vanilla extract

½ cup unsalted butter or buttery spread, such as Earth
Balance, at room temperature, or ⅓ cup canola oil

1½ cups sugar

2 large eggs, at room temperature

FROSTING

3 large egg whites

1¼ cups sugar

¼ teaspoon ground cinnamon

¼ teaspoon cream of tartar

3 tablespoons cold water

1 teaspoon pure vanilla extract

1 Place a rack in the middle of the oven. Preheat the oven to 325°F. Generously grease the cups of a mini 12-cup nonstick (gray, not black) muffin pan or line with paper liners. Spray the insides of the liners with cooking spray.

2 Make the cupcakes: In a medium bowl, whisk together the sorghum blend, baking soda, baking powder, cocoa, xanthan gum, cinnamon, and salt; set aside. In a measuring cup, combine the buttermilk and vanilla extract; set aside.

3 In the large mixing bowl of a stand mixer, beat the butter until it is smooth and creamy. Add the sugar and beat 1 minute, scraping down the side of the bowl with a spatula. Add the eggs, one at a time, beating thoroughly after each addition.

4 With the mixer on low speed, add the sorghum mixture alternately with the buttermilk, beginning and ending with the sorghum mixture. Be sure to beat the sorghum mixture thoroughly each time before adding the buttermilk. Divide the batter evenly in the pan.

5 Bake the cupcakes 15 to 17 minutes or until the tops of the cupcakes are firm to the touch. Cool the cupcakes in the pan 5 minutes on a wire rack and then place them on a serving platter or dessert plates. Repeat with remaining batter.

6 Make the frosting: Combine the egg whites, sugar, cinnamon, cream of tartar, and cold water in a double boiler over simmering water, being careful not to let the top of the pan touch the water. Beat with a portable electric mixer 5 to 7 minutes until glossy and the mixture reaches the desired spreading consistency. Stir in the vanilla extract. Immediately, spread each cupcake with 1 tablespoon of frosting. Serve immediately.

Black Forest Cupcakes

MAKES 12 CUPCAKES

The flavors of these cupcakes—chocolate and cherry—originated in the Black Forest region of Germany, which is also known for producing sour cherries. Cherry brandy or kirschwasser *is distilled, so it is safe for gluten-free diets, but you may also use pure vanilla extract.*

CUPCAKES

½ cup unsalted butter or buttery spread, such as Earth
Balance, at room temperature, or ⅓ cup canola oil

1 cup packed light brown sugar

1 large egg, at room temperature

½ cup 1% milk (cow's, rice, soy, potato, or nut), at
room temperature

2 teaspoons pure vanilla extract

1½ cups Carol's Sorghum Blend (page x)

½ cup unsweetened cocoa powder (not Dutch-
process or alkali)

¾ teaspoon baking soda

¾ teaspoon salt

1 teaspoon xanthan gum

¾ cup hot (120°F) brewed coffee

FROSTING

2 cups homemade Basic Whipped Cream (page 624) or whipped topping, such as Lucerne or Soyatoo

1 teaspoon kirschwasser (cherry brandy), optional

½ can (14 to 15 ounces) cherry pie filling, such as Wilderness or Camstock

2 squares gluten-free dark chocolate, such as Scharffen Berger or Tropical Source, shaved

1 Place a rack in the middle of the oven. Preheat the oven to 325°F. Generously grease the cups of a standard 12-cup nonstick (gray, not black) muffin pan or line with paper liners. Spray the insides of the liners with cooking spray.

2 Make the cupcakes: In a large mixing bowl, beat the butter with an electric mixer on low speed 30 seconds. Add the sugar and beat on low speed until well blended. Beat in the egg, milk, and vanilla extract until they are well blended. In a small bowl, whisk together the sorghum blend, cocoa, soda, salt, and xanthan gum.

3 On low speed, beat the dry ingredients into the egg mixture, alternating with the hot coffee, beginning and ending with the sorghum mixture. Divide the batter evenly in the pan.

4 Bake 20 to 25 minutes or until a toothpick inserted in the center of a cupcake comes out clean. Cool the cupcakes in the pan 5 minutes and then place them on a wire rack to finish cooling.

5 Make the frosting: Place the whipped cream in a medium bowl. Stir in kirschwasser.

6 Spread the whipped cream on top of each cupcake and garnish with a tablespoon of cherry pie filling and a dusting of shaved chocolate. Serve immediately. Refrigerate leftovers.

German Chocolate Cupcakes with Coconut-Pecan Frosting Ⓥ

MAKES 12 SERVINGS

This was a very popular cake when I was growing up, but I like making it into cupcakes for entertaining. These showy sweets are especially pretty when arranged on a three-tier cake stand and used as a centerpiece or placed on a buffet table.

CUPCAKES

⅓ cup unsweetened cocoa powder (not Dutch-process or alkali)

½ cup boiling water

2 cups Carol's Sorghum Blend (page x)

1 teaspoon salt

1 teaspoon baking soda

½ cup (1 stick) unsalted butter or buttery spread, such as Earth Balance, at room temperature, or ⅓ cup canola oil

1 cup granulated sugar

¾ cup packed light brown sugar

3 large eggs, at room temperature

1 tablespoon pure vanilla extract

FROSTING

3 egg yolks

¾ cup 1% milk (cow's, rice, soy, potato, or nut)

1 cup sugar

1 tablespoon unsalted butter or buttery spread, such as Earth Balance, or canola oil

1 package (7 ounces) sweetened shredded coconut (about 1⅔ cups)

1 teaspoon pure vanilla extract

1 cup chopped pecans

1 Place a rack in the middle of the oven. Preheat oven to 325°F. Generously grease the cups of a standard 12-cup nonstick (gray, not black) muffin pan or line with paper liners. Spray the insides of the liners with cooking spray.

2 Make the cupcakes: Combine the cocoa and boiling water in a measuring cup and let stand 5 minutes while the cocoa dissolves. Sift together the sorghum blend, salt, and baking soda; set aside.

3 In the bowl of a stand mixer, beat the butter and sugars at medium-low speed, about 30 seconds. Increase the speed to medium-high and beat 2 minutes, scraping down the bowl with a spatula halfway through mixing. Add the eggs one at a time on medium speed, beating well after each addition. Add the sorghum mixture alternately with the dissolved chocolate, beginning and ending with sorghum mixture. Beat in the vanilla extract until smooth. Divide the batter evenly in the pan.

4 Bake 20 to 25 minutes or until a toothpick inserted into the center of a cupcake comes out clean. Cool the cupcakes in the pan 5 minutes on a wire rack and then place them on a wire rack to finish cooling completely.

5 Make the frosting: Beat the egg yolks, milk, sugar, and butter in a medium saucepan until smooth. Cook over medium heat about 10 or 12 minutes, stirring until the mixture thickens. Remove the pan from the heat and stir in the coconut and vanilla extract. Cool the frosting completely and refrigerate. Stir in the pecans just before using. Spread each cupcake with the frosting and serve immediately.

Mini Sacher Torte Cupcakes

MAKES 24 SERVINGS

These adorable little treats will delight your guests and are especially fun to serve at a dinner party. Garnish each with a dried apricot, dipped in some of the chocolate ganache.

CUPCAKES

½ cup (1 stick) unsalted butter or buttery spread, such as Earth Balance, at room temperature, or canola oil

1 cup packed light brown sugar

2 large eggs, at room temperature

¾ cup thin buttermilk, well-shaken, (or ½ cup buttermilk mixed with ¼ cup water) or homemade Buttermilk (page 677)

1 teaspoon pure vanilla extract

1½ cups Carol's Sorghum Blend (page x)

½ cup unsweetened cocoa powder (not Dutch-process or alkali)

1 teaspoon xanthan gum

¾ teaspoon baking soda

¼ teaspoon salt

1 tablespoon pure vanilla extract

¾ cup apricot preserves

2 tablespoons apricot brandy or plain brandy

GLAZE

9 ounces gluten-free bittersweet chocolate, such as Scharffen Berger, chopped

2 tablespoons light corn syrup

1 Place a rack in the middle of the oven. Preheat the oven to 325°F. Generously grease the cups of a mini 12-cup nonstick (gray, not black) muffin pan or line with paper liners. Spray the insides of the liners with cooking spray.

2 Make the cupcakes: In a large mixing bowl, beat the butter and sugar on medium speed with an electric mixer 2 minutes. until smooth. Add the eggs, buttermilk, and vanilla extract and mix until well blended. The mixture may look curdled, but will become smooth after the dry ingredients are added.

3 In a small bowl, whisk together the sorghum blend, cocoa, xanthan gum, soda, and salt, and beat in ½ cup at a time on low speed until completely blended. Divide the batter evenly in the pans.

4 Bake 15 to 17 minutes or until a toothpick inserted into the center of a cupcake comes out clean. Cool the cupcakes in the pan for 5 minutes and then place them on a wire rack to finish cooling completely. Repeat with remaining batter.

5 To assemble the cupcakes, divide them in half horizontally. Combine the apricot preserves and brandy and spread a generous teaspoon of this mixture on the bottom half of each cupcake. Replace the top half of each cupcake and place them on a wire rack.

6 Make the glaze: In the top of a double boiler over simmering water, stir the chocolate and corn syrup until the chocolate is melted. Or, heat the chocolate and corn syrup in a glass bowl in a microwave oven on high until the chocolate is melted. Slowly spread the glaze over the cupcakes. Let chocolate set up for about 10 to 15 minutes before serving. Refrigerate any leftover glaze for 1 week.

Mini Chocolate Peppermint Ice Cream Cupcakes Ⓥ

MAKES 24 SERVINGS

This is a perfect dessert for a large party because it makes 24 cupcakes. They are especially pretty if you serve them on chilled serving plates, garnished with fresh mint, and perhaps a dusting of crushed peppermint candies.

½ cup (1 stick) unsalted butter or buttery spread, such as Earth Balance, at room temperature, or ⅓ cup canola oil

1¼ cups sugar

3 large eggs, at room temperature

⅔ cup 1% milk, (cow, rice, soy, potato, or nut), at room temperature

1 tablespoon pure vanilla extract

1 teaspoon peppermint extract

2 cups Carol's Sorghum Blend (page x)

⅔ cup unsweetened cocoa powder (not Dutch-process or alkali)

1 teaspoon baking soda

½ teaspoon salt

1 teaspoon xanthan gum

⅔ cup hot (120°F) brewed coffee

1 pint gluten-free peppermint ice cream, such as Hood Regular or Skondra's (or 1 pint gluten-free vanilla ice cream, such as Ben & Jerry's, with ½ cup crushed peppermint candies)

2 cups homemade Basic Whipped Cream (page 624) or whipped topping, such as Lucerne or Soyatoo

1 cup gluten-free chocolate syrup, such as Hershey's, or homemade Chocolate Sauce (page 622)

1 Place a rack in the middle of the oven. Preheat the oven to 325°F. Generously grease the cups of a mini 24-cup nonstick (gray, not black) muffin pan or line with paper liners. Spray the insides of the liners with cooking spray.

2 In a large mixer bowl, beat butter and sugar with an electric mixer on medium speed until light and fluffy. Beat in eggs, one at a time, until thoroughly blended. Beat in milk, vanilla extract, and peppermint extract.

3 In a separate bowl, whisk together sorghum blend, cocoa, baking soda, salt, and xanthan gum. On low speed, beat sorghum mixture into the egg mixture, alternating with hot coffee, beginning and ending with sorghum mixture. Divide the batter evenly in the pan.

4 Bake 15 to 17 minutes or until a toothpick inserted into the center of a cupcake comes out clean. Cool the cupcakes in the pan 5 minutes on a wire rack.

Remove cupcakes from the pan and cool completely on the wire rack. Repeat with remaining batter.

5 Cut each cupcake in half, horizontally. Remove the top half. Working quickly, spread a generous tablespoon of ice cream on the bottom layer. Replace the top half, wrap tightly, and freeze at least 2 hours. When ready to serve, quickly frost the cupcakes with the whipped cream, drizzle with chocolate sauce, and serve immediately. Freeze leftovers, tightly wrapped.

Mini Carob Cupcakes with Caramel Topping Ⓥ

MAKES 24 SERVINGS

I get many requests from people who want a chocolate-like cupcake, but without the chocolate. Others have asked for an egg-free, dairy-free cupcake. So I created these cupcakes using carob, a member of the legume family, instead of cocoa, and other ingredients (such as prune baby food) instead of eggs. These dainty little morsels are complemented by the caramel topping and are especially pretty when you remove them from the paper liners, place two or three on a small dessert plate while they are still warm, and drizzle the warm caramel topping over them.

CUPCAKES

½ cup carob powder
1 cup Carol's Sorghum Blend (page x)
1 cup packed light brown sugar
1 teaspoon ground cinnamon
¾ teaspoon baking soda
¾ teaspoon salt
½ teaspoon xanthan gum
½ teaspoon baking powder
¼ teaspoon instant espresso powder
Pinch cloves
⅓ cup canola oil
2 teaspoons pure vanilla extract
3 jars (4 ounces each) prune baby food
⅓ cup hot (120°F) water + 2 teaspoons
½ cup finely chopped walnuts (optional)

TOPPING

½ cup packed light brown sugar
2 tablespoons light corn syrup
¼ cup (½ stick) unsalted butter or buttery spread, such as Earth Balance
¼ cup 1% milk (cow's, rice, soy, potato, or nut)
1 teaspoon pure vanilla extract

1 Place a rack in the middle of the oven. Preheat the oven to 325°F. Generously grease the cups of a mini 12-cup nonstick (gray, not black) muffin pan or line with paper liners. Spray the insides of the liners with cooking spray. Set aside. Toast the carob powder in a dry saucepan 2 minutes, stirring constantly, or until it is aromatic and turns one shade darker.

2 Make the cupcakes: In a large mixing bowl, combine the carob powder, sorghum blend, brown sugar, cinnamon, baking soda, salt, xanthan gum, baking powder, espresso powder, and cloves together with the oil and vanilla extract with an electric mixer on low speed to make a dry, crumbly mixture. Set aside ½ cup of this mixture.

3 Beat the prune baby food and ⅓ cup hot water into the large bowl until the batter is smooth. Spread the batter in the cupcake pans, dividing evenly. Stir the nuts and the remaining 2 teaspoons water into the remaining ½ cup dry cake mixture and sprinkle ¼ cup of it evenly over the cupcakes.

4 Bake 15 to 17 minutes or until the tops are firm to the touch. Cool the cupcakes in the pan 5 minutes and then place them on a serving platter or dessert plates. Repeat with the remaining batter.

5 Make the topping: In a small saucepan, cook the brown sugar, corn syrup, and butter over medium heat until it boils. Reduce the heat to low and simmer it gently 5 minutes, stirring to make sure it doesn't burn. Remove from the heat and stir in the milk and vanilla extract until smooth. Serve warm, spooned over the carob cupcakes.

Carob-Cinnamon Cupcakes Ⓥ

MAKES 12 SERVINGS

Cinnamon is a natural complement to carob in these delicious cupcakes that replicate the chocolate look—without the actual chocolate. Toasting intensifies the carob flavor, so it is an important step.

CUPCAKES

⅓ cup carob powder

½ cup (1 stick) unsalted butter or buttery spread, such as Earth Balance, at room temperature, or ⅓ cup canola oil

1 cup sugar

2 large eggs, at room temperature

1½ cups Carol's Sorghum Blend (page x)

1 teaspoon xanthan gum

¾ teaspoon salt

½ teaspoon ground cinnamon

¼ teaspoon baking powder

¼ teaspoon baking soda

1 cup 1% milk (cow's, rice, soy, potato, or nut)

1 teaspoon pure vanilla extract

FROSTING

3 cups powdered sugar

1 teaspoon ground cinnamon

1 teaspoon pure vanilla extract

1 to 3 tablespoons 1% milk (cow's, rice, soy, potato, or nut)

1 Place a rack in the middle of the oven. Preheat the oven to 350°F. Generously grease the cups of a standard 12-cup nonstick (gray, not black) muffin pan or line with paper liners. Spray the insides of the liners with cooking spray.

2 Make the cupcakes: Toast the carob powder for 2 minutes in a heavy, medium saucepan over medium heat, stirring constantly, or until it is aromatic and one shade darker.

3 In a large mixing bowl, beat the butter with an electric mixer on medium speed until smooth. Gradually beat in the sugar until well blended. Add the eggs, one at a time, beating well after each addition.

4 In another bowl, whisk together the sorghum blend, carob powder, xanthan gum, salt, cinnamon, baking powder, and baking soda. In a measuring cup, whisk together the milk and vanilla extract.

5 With the mixer on low speed, beat the sorghum mixture into the butter, alternating with the milk, beginning and ending with the sorghum mixture. Divide the batter evenly in the pan.

6 Bake 20 to 25 minutes or until a toothpick inserted into the center of a cupcake comes out clean. Cool the cupcakes in the pan 5 minutes on a wire rack and then place them on a wire rack to finish cooling.

7 Make the frosting: In a medium bowl, beat the powdered sugar, cinnamon, vanilla extract, and enough of the milk with an electric mixer on low speed to reach the proper consistency. Spread the frosting on the tops of the cupcakes and serve.

Autumn-Spice Apple Cupcakes Ⓥ

MAKES 12 SERVINGS

The wonderful aromatic spices in these cupcakes complement apples very nicely, making them one of my favorite recipes for autumn when apples are at their best. Jonathan or Braeburn apples work well because of their sweet, yet slightly tart taste, but you can use any variety.

2 small cooking apples, peeled, cored, and very finely diced

Juice and grated zest of 1 lemon

½ cup unsalted butter or buttery spread, such as Earth Balance, at room temperature, or ⅓ cup canola oil

1 cup packed light brown sugar

3 large eggs, at room temperature

1½ cups Carol's Sorghum Blend (page x)

1 teaspoon xanthan gum

1 teaspoon baking powder

1½ teaspoons ground cinnamon

¾ teaspoon ground cloves

½ teaspoon ground allspice

½ teaspoon freshly grated nutmeg

½ teaspoon baking soda

½ teaspoon salt

1 teaspoon pure vanilla extract

½ cup raisins or currants

¼ cup chopped pecans

½ cup powdered sugar, for dusting

1 Place a rack in the middle of the oven. Preheat the oven to 350°F. Generously grease the cups of a standard 12-cup nonstick (gray, not black) muffin pan or line with paper liners. Spray the insides of the liners with cooking spray. In a medium bowl, toss the apples with the lemon juice and zest; set aside.

2 In a mixing bowl, beat the butter and sugar on medium speed 2 minutes. Add the eggs, one at a time, beating thoroughly after each addition. Gradually add the sorghum blend, xanthan gum, baking powder, cinnamon, cloves, allspice, nutmeg, baking soda, and salt and beat on low speed until well combined. Stir in the apples, vanilla extract, raisins, and pecans. Divide the batter evenly in the pan.

3 Bake 25 to 30 minutes, or until a tester inserted in the center of a cupcake comes out clean. Cool the cupcakes in the pan 5 minutes on a wire rack. Remove cupcakes from the pan and cool completely on the wire rack to finish cooling. Dust with powdered sugar before serving.

Mini Carrot Cake Cupcakes Ⓥ

MAKES 48

These mini carrot cupcakes are perfect treat if you want a taste of this moist, delicious cake, but not a whole slice of cake. This recipe makes 48 cupcakes which freeze well and thaw quickly because they're small, so keep a stash in your freezer for unexpected company.

CUPCAKES

3 cups Carol's Sorghum Blend (page x)

1½ teaspoons xanthan gum

1 teaspoon baking soda

2 teaspoons pumpkin pie spice

1 teaspoon ground ginger

¾ teaspoon salt

4 large eggs, at room temperature

1 cup sugar

¾ cup packed light brown sugar

½ cup (1 stick) unsalted butter or buttery spread, such as Earth Balance, at room temperature, or ⅓ cup canola oil

¾ cup buttermilk, well-shaken, or homemade Buttermilk (page 677)

1 teaspoon pure vanilla extract

2 cups finely shredded carrots

1 can (8 ounces) crushed pineapple, drained very well (discard the juice)

1 cup sweetened shredded coconut

½ cup finely chopped walnuts, divided

FROSTING

1 small package (3 ounces) cream cheese or cream cheese alternative, such as Tofutti, at room temperature

2 tablespoons 1% milk (cow's, rice, soy, potato, or nut) or pineapple juice

1 teaspoon pure vanilla extract

Pinch salt

3 cups powdered sugar

1 cup sweetened shredded coconut, toasted

1 Place a rack in the middle of the oven. Preheat the oven to 325°F. Generously grease the cups of a mini 24-cup nonstick (gray, not black) muffin pan or line with paper liners. Spray the insides of the liners with cooking spray.

2 Make the cupcakes: In a medium bowl, sift the sorghum blend, xanthan gum, baking soda, pumpkin pie spice, ginger, and salt; set aside.

3 In large mixer bowl, beat the eggs, sugars, oil, buttermilk, and vanilla extract with electric mixer until smooth. Add sorghum mixture slowly on low speed, then increase speed to medium and beat until smooth. With a large spatula, stir in the carrots, pineapple, coconut, and ⅓ cup of the walnuts. Divide the batter evenly in the pan.

4 Bake 17 to 20 minutes or until the top of the cake feels firm to the touch. Cool the cupcakes in the pan 5 minutes on a wire rack and then place them on a serving platter or dessert plates. Repeat with the remaining batter.

5 Make the frosting: In a medium bowl, beat the cream cheese, milk, vanilla extract, and salt with an electric mixer on medium speed until very smooth. With the mixer on low speed, gradually beat in the powdered sugar until the frosting is smooth. Spread a tablespoon of frosting on top of each cupcake, sprinkle with toasted coconut, and serve immediately. Refrigerate leftovers.

Mini Pumpkin-Spice Cupcakes (V)

MAKES 24 SERVINGS

Serve these delicious cupcakes anytime but they are especially nice to serve during the holidays instead of the traditional pumpkin pie. All of the lovely flavors are there, just in an easy-to-serve cupcake rather than a slice of pie.

CUPCAKES

¾ cup Carol's Sorghum Blend (page x)

1½ teaspoons ground cinnamon

1 teaspoon baking powder

1 teaspoon ground ginger

¾ teaspoon ground allspice

¾ teaspoon xanthan gum

¼ teaspoon freshly grated nutmeg

¼ teaspoon salt

4 large eggs, at room temperature

½ cup granulated sugar

½ cup packed light brown sugar

⅔ cup canned pumpkin puree (not pumpkin pie filling)

1 teaspoon fresh lemon juice

½ cup powdered sugar, for dusting

FROSTING

1 package (8 ounces) cream cheese or cream cheese alternative, such as Tofutti, at room temperature

1 cup powdered sugar

2 tablespoons unsalted butter or buttery spread, such as Earth Balance, at room temperature, or canola oil

1 teaspoon pure vanilla extract

1 Place a rack in the middle of the oven. Preheat the oven to 325°F. Generously grease the cups of a mini 24-cup nonstick (gray, not black) muffin pan or line with paper liners. Spray the insides of the liners with cooking spray.

2 Make the cupcakes: In a small bowl, whisk together the sorghum blend, cinnamon, baking powder, ginger, allspice, xanthan gum, nutmeg and salt; set aside. In a large mixing bowl, beat the eggs on medium speed until pale yellow, about 5 minutes. Beat in the granulated sugar, brown sugar, and pumpkin until smooth. Gradually beat in the sorghum mixture on low speed until thoroughly combined. Divide the batter evenly in the pan.

3 Bake 15 to 17 minutes, or until the tops of the cupcakes feel firm to the touch. Cool the cupcakes in the pan 5 minutes and then place them on a serving platter or dessert plates. Repeat with remaining batter.

4 Make the frosting: In a medium bowl, beat the cream cheese with an electric mixer on low speed until smooth. Gradually beat in powdered sugar, butter, and vanilla extract until smooth. Spread each mini-cupcake with 1 tablespoon frosting and serve immediately. Refrigerate leftovers.

Mini Chai-Spice Cupcakes

MAKES 24 SERVINGS

Mini-cupcakes are such fun to eat, especially when they are packed with this delightful chai flavor.

CUPCAKES

½ cup (1 stick) unsalted butter or buttery spread, such as Earth Balance, at room temperature or ⅓ cup canola oil

1 cup sugar

2 large eggs, at room temperature

1½ cups Carol's Sorghum Blend (page x)

1½ teaspoons ground cinnamon

1 teaspoon xanthan gum

½ teaspoon baking soda

½ teaspoon baking powder

1 teaspoon ground cardamom

½ teaspoon ground cloves

½ teaspoon freshly ground black pepper

¼ teaspoon freshly grated nutmeg

½ teaspoon salt

¾ cup buttermilk, well-shaken, or homemade Buttermilk (page 677)

1 tablespoon pure vanilla extract

1 cup finely chopped pecans, divided

FROSTING

1 small package (3 ounces) cream cheese or cream cheese alternative, such as Tofutti, at room temperature

2 tablespoons unsalted butter or buttery spread, such as Earth Balance, melted, or canola oil

1 tablespoon pure vanilla extract

2 cups powdered sugar

1 Place a rack in the middle of the oven. Preheat the oven to 350°F. Generously grease the cups of a mini 12-cup nonstick (gray, not black) muffin pan or line with paper liners. Spray the insides of the liners with cooking spray.

2 Make the cupcakes: In a large mixing bowl, beat the butter with an electric mixer on medium speed until smooth. Gradually beat in the sugar until smooth. Add the eggs, one at a time, beating well after each addition.

3 In another bowl, whisk together the sorghum blend, cinnamon, xanthan gum, baking soda, baking powder, cardamom, cloves, black pepper, nutmeg, and salt. In a measuring cup, whisk together the buttermilk and vanilla extract.

4 With the mixer on low speed, beat the sorghum mixture into the butter, alternating with the buttermilk, beginning and ending with the sorghum mixture. Stir in ½ cup of the pecans. Divide the batter evenly in the pan.

5 Bake 15 to 17 minutes or until the top of the cupcakes are firm to the touch. Cool the cupcakes in the pan 5 minutes and then place them on a serving platter or dessert plates. Repeat with the remaining batter.

6 Make the frosting: In a medium mixing bowl, beat the cream cheese, butter, and vanilla extract with an electric mixer on low speed until smooth. Beat in the powdered sugar gradually until the frosting is smooth. Spread the frosting on the tops of the cupcakes and serve immediately.

FLOURLESS CAKES

Flourless Honey Almond Cake

MAKES 10 SERVINGS

Lavender honey is a very popular and delicate flavor combination. So you can serve this cake knowing you're at the pinnacle of food trends. If you can't find lavender honey, use regular honey. The cake will taste great anyway.

2 cups almonds (measure before grinding)
3 large eggs, at room temperature
⅔ cup lavender honey or regular honey
¼ cup (½ stick) unsalted butter or buttery spread,
    such as Earth Balance, melted, or canola oil
1 tablespoon pure vanilla extract
½ teaspoon salt
¼ teaspoon baking soda

1 Place a rack in the middle of the oven. Preheat the oven to 350°F. Generously grease an 8-inch nonstick (gray, not black) springform pan with removable sides. Line the bottom with wax paper or parchment paper and grease again.

2 Grind the nuts in a food processor to a fine meal.

3 Add the eggs, honey, butter, vanilla extract, salt, and baking soda and process 30 to 40 seconds. Scrape down the side of the bowl and process another 30 seconds or until the mixture is thoroughly blended. Spread the batter evenly in the pan.

4 Bake 35 to 40 minutes or until a toothpick inserted into center comes out clean. The cake rises as it bakes, then may fall slightly as it cools. Cool the cake 15 minutes in the pan on a wire rack. Cut gently around edge of pan with a sharp knife to loosen the cake. Release the pan sides; discard paper liner. Serve at room temperature.

Flourless Hazelnut Cake

MAKES 10 SERVINGS

Frangelico is a liqueur made from hazelnuts that lends a wonderful note to this cake. For a lighter texture, separate the eggs and beat the egg whites to soft peaks with your electric mixer. Blend remaining ingredients together; then fold into egg whites by hand.

2 cups skinless hazelnuts (measure before grinding)
¾ cup packed light brown sugar
4 large eggs, at room temperature
½ teaspoon baking powder
½ cup (1 stick) unsalted butter or buttery spread,
    such as Earth Balance, melted, or light olive oil
Grated zest of 1 lemon
¼ cup hazelnut liqueur, such as Frangelico
½ teaspoon salt
2 tablespoons powdered sugar for dusting

1 Place a rack in the middle of the oven. Preheat the oven to 350°F. Generously grease; then line the bottom of an 8-inch springform pan with wax paper or parchment paper. Grease again; set aside.

2 Grind the nuts in a food processor to a fine meal.

3 Add the brown sugar, eggs, baking powder, butter, lemon zest, liqueur, and salt to the food processor and process 30 to 40 seconds. Scrape down the side of bowl and process another 30 seconds. Spread the batter evenly in the prepared pan.

4 Bake 40 to 45 minutes or until a toothpick inserted into the center comes out clean. The cake rises as it bakes, then falls slightly as it cools. Cool the cake in the pan 15 minutes on a wire rack. Cut around edge of the cake with a sharp knife to loosen the cake. Release the pan sides; discard paper liner. Serve at room temperature dusted with powdered sugar.

Flourless Walnut-Orange Torte Ⓥ

MAKES 10 SERVINGS

Ground walnuts make this cake creamy and smooth, almost like walnut-orange fudge. For a lighter texture, separate the eggs and beat the egg whites to soft peaks with your electric mixer. Blend remaining ingredients together; then fold into egg whites by hand.

2 cups walnut pieces (measure before grinding)

¾ cup sugar

4 large eggs, at room temperature

½ teaspoon baking powder

½ cup (1 stick) unsalted butter or buttery spread, such as Earth Balance, melted, or canola oil

Grated zest of 1 large orange

¼ cup orange juice concentrate

½ teaspoon salt

2 tablespoons powdered sugar, for dusting

1 Place a rack in the middle of the oven. Preheat the oven to 350°F. Generously grease, then line the bottom of an 8-inch round nonstick (gray, not black) springform pan with wax paper or parchment paper. Grease it again; set aside.

2 Grind the nuts in a food processor to a fine meal.

3 Add the sugar, eggs, baking powder, butter, orange zest, orange juice concentrate, and salt to the food processor and process 30 to 40 seconds. Scrape down sides of the bowl with a spatula and process 30 seconds more. Spread the batter evenly in the pan.

4 Bake 40 to 45 minutes or until a toothpick inserted into the center comes out clean. The cake rises as it bakes, then falls slightly as it cools. Cool the cake in the pan 15 minutes on a wire rack. Cut around edge of the pan with a sharp knife to loosen the cake. Release pan sides; discard paper liner. Dust with powdered sugar and serve.

Flourless Almond-Apricot Torte Ⓥ

MAKES 10 SERVINGS

Almonds and dried apricots are both packed with nutrients, and their strong flavors make a delicious combination in this flourless, not-too-sweet cake.

2 cups almonds (measure before grinding)

½ cup sugar

¾ cup finely chopped dried apricots

½ cup apricot preserves, divided, + 3 tablespoons for garnish

⅓ cup unsalted butter or buttery spread, such as Earth Balance, melted, or canola oil

½ teaspoon baking powder

Grated zest of 1 orange

4 large eggs, at room temperature

1 teaspoon almond extract

½ teaspoon salt

2 tablespoons powdered sugar for dusting

1 Place a rack in the middle of the oven. Preheat the oven to 350°F. Generously grease an 8-inch round nonstick (gray, not black) springform pan and line it with parchment paper. Grease again; set aside.

2 Grind the nuts in a food processor to a fine meal.

3 Add the sugar, dried apricots, ¼ cup of the apricot preserves, butter, baking powder, orange zest, eggs, almond extract, and salt and blend 30 to 40 seconds. Scrape down the side of the bowl with a spatula, and blend again 30 to 40 seconds or until all the ingredients are thoroughly blended. Spread the batter evenly in the pan.

4 Bake 35 to 40 minutes or until a toothpick inserted in the center comes out clean. Cool the cake in the pan 15 minutes on a wire rack. Gently run a sharp knife around the edge of the pan to loosen the cake. Remove the outer rim; discard the paper, and invert the cake onto a serving plate.

5 Spread remaining ¼ cup of the apricot preserves over top of the cake while it is still warm. Serve with a dusting of powdered sugar and a scant teaspoon of apricot preserves as a garnish.

Flourless Pumpkin Seed Cake

MAKES 10 SERVINGS

This delightful cake uses roasted pumpkin seeds (which are from the squash family) rather than nuts, so it's safe for those with nut allergies. Serve this instead of pumpkin pie at your next holiday gathering.

2 cups toasted pumpkin seeds* (measure before grinding)

1 cup packed light brown sugar

4 large eggs, at room temperature

¼ teaspoon baking soda

½ cup (1 stick) unsalted butter or buttery spread, such as Earth Balance, melted, or canola oil

½ cup canned pumpkin puree (not pumpkin pie filling)

1 tablespoon pure vanilla extract

2 teaspoons pumpkin pie spice

½ teaspoon salt

2 tablespoons powdered sugar, for dusting

1 Place a rack in the middle of the oven. Preheat the oven to 350°F. Generously grease an 8-inch round non-stick (gray, not black) springform pan and line the bottom with parchment paper. Grease again; set aside.

2 Grind the pumpkin seeds in a food processor to a fine meal.

3 Add remaining ingredients to the food processor and process 30 to 40 seconds. Scrape down sides of bowl and process another 30 to 45 seconds or until batter is thoroughly smooth and blended. Spread the batter evenly in the prepared pan.

4 Bake 35 to 40 minutes or until a toothpick inserted into the center of the cake comes out clean. The cake rises as it bakes, then may fall slightly as it cools. Cool the cake in the pan 15 minutes on a wire rack. Cut around the edge of the pan with a sharp knife to loosen the cake. Release the pan sides; discard the paper liner. Dust with powdered sugar before serving.

*To toast pumpkin seeds: stir 1 cup seeds in large dry skillet over medium heat three to five minutes or just until they start to turn light brown. Remove from skillet. Repeat with remaining one cup of pumpkin seeds. Cool. (This step can be completed ahead of time; store roasted pumpkin seeds in the refrigerator.)

Flourless Clementine Cake V

MAKES 10 SERVINGS

This is a great recipe to serve your guests during the winter months, when clementines are available by the carton. They'll surely ask, "What's in this fabulous cake?" There is no oil in the cake because the peels of the clementines provide plenty. For a lighter-textured cake, separate the eggs and beat the egg whites with an electric mixer to stiff peaks. Blend remaining ingredients together, then fold into egg whites by hand. If you happen to have homemade Clementine Marmalade (page 678) on hand, use 1¼ cups plus another 3 tablespoons for garnish.

5 clementines, washed, quartered and seeded, divided

1 cup sugar

2 cups whole almonds (measure before grinding)

¼ cup packed light brown sugar

¼ teaspoon baking soda

1 teaspoon xanthan gum

5 large eggs, at room temperature

1 teaspoon pure vanilla extract

½ teaspoon salt

2 tablespoons powdered sugar, for dusting

1 Place a rack in the middle of the oven. Preheat the oven to 350°F. Generously grease an 8-inch nonstick (gray, not black) springform pan and line the bottom with parchment paper. Grease again; set aside.

2 Process the clementines in food processor until finely pureed. Put pureed clementines and sugar in a large microwave-safe bowl and cook, covered with waxed paper, on medium-high 10 minutes, stirring occasionally. Set aside to cool. Refrigerate 3 tablespoons of marmalade for garnish.

3 In the same food processor (no need to wash or wipe out), grind the almonds to a fine meal. Add the brown sugar, baking soda, xanthan gum, eggs, vanilla extract, salt, and clementine puree (or marmalade), and blend 30 to 40 seconds. Scrape down the sides with a spatula, and blend another 30 to 40 seconds or until all the ingredients are thoroughly blended. Spread the batter evenly in the pan.

4 Bake 35 to 45 minutes or until a toothpick inserted into the center of the cake comes out clean. Cover with foil during the last 20 minutes of baking to avoid overbrowning. Cool the cake in the pan 10 minutes on a wire rack. Gently run a sharp knife around the edge of the pan to loosen the cake. Remove outer rim; discard the paper. Cool the cake completely on the wire rack. Invert onto a serving plate. Serve with a dusting of powdered sugar and a scant teaspoon of the clementine marmalade per serving.

Flourless Limoncello Almond Cake with Limoncello Glaze ⓥ

MAKES 10 SERVINGS

Limoncello is very popular in Italy. In fact, I not only found it in gourmet stores but in the truck stops along the Autostrada *(Italy's equivalent of our interstate system). For a lighter texture, separate the eggs and beat the egg whites to soft peaks with your electric mixer. Blend the remaining*

ingredients together; then fold into the egg whites by hand.

CAKE
2 cups whole almonds (measure before grinding)
¾ cup packed light brown sugar
½ cup unsalted butter or buttery spread, such as Earth Balance, melted, or canola oil
¼ teaspoon baking soda
Grated zest of 1 lemon
¼ cup Limoncello liqueur or fresh lemon juice
4 large eggs, at room temperature
½ teaspoon almond extract
½ teaspoon salt

GLAZE
1 cup powdered sugar
2 tablespoons unsalted butter or buttery spread, such as Earth Balance, at room temperature, or canola oil
2 tablespoons Limoncello liqueur or fresh lemon juice

1 Place a rack in the middle of the oven. Preheat oven to 350°F. Generously grease an 8-inch springform pan and line the bottom with parchment paper; grease again and set aside.

2 Make the cake: Grind the nuts in a food processor to a fine meal.

3 Add the brown sugar, butter, baking soda, lemon zest, liqueur, eggs, almond extract, and salt to the food processor and blend 30 to 40 seconds. Stop the machine, scrape down sides with a spatula, and blend another 30 to 40 seconds or until all the ingredients are blended. Spread the batter evenly in the springform pan.

4 Bake 40 to 45 minutes or until a toothpick inserted in the center comes out clean. Cool the cake in the pan 10 minutes on a wire rack. Gently run a sharp knife around the edge of the pan to loosen the cake and remove outer rim; discard paper. Cool the cake completely on the wire rack. Invert the cake onto a serving plate.

5 Make the glaze: In a small bowl, sift the powdered sugar. Add the butter and liqueur and whisk until smooth. Spread over cooled cake.

Flourless Dark Chocolate Cake V

MAKES 10 SERVINGS

Hershey's Special Dark cocoa, available in grocery stores, works especially well in this recipe. Dissolving cocoa in hot water before baking enhances its flavor. This is a very dark cake—perfect for special occasions because it looks so rich and decadent.

½ cup unsweetened cocoa powder

½ cup boiling water

2 cups whole almonds (measure before grinding)

¾ cup packed light brown sugar

3 large eggs, at room temperature

⅓ cup unsalted butter or buttery spread, such as Earth Balance, melted, or canola oil

1 tablespoon pure vanilla extract

½ teaspoon salt

2 tablespoons powdered sugar, for dusting

1 Place a rack in the middle of the oven. Preheat the oven to 350°F. Generously grease; then line the bottom of an 8-inch springform pan with parchment paper or wax paper. Grease again; set aside.

2 Dissolve the cocoa in the boiling water; set aside. Meanwhile, grind the nuts in a food processor to a fine meal.

3 Add the brown sugar, eggs, butter, vanilla extract, and salt to the food processor and process 30 to 40 seconds. Scrape down sides of bowl and process another 30 seconds or until mixture is thoroughly blended. Spread the batter evenly in the pan.

4 Bake 40 to 45 minutes or until a toothpick inserted into the center of the cake comes out clean. The cake rises as it bakes, then may fall slightly as it cools. Cool the cake in the pan 10 minutes on a wire rack. Gently run a sharp knife around edge of pan to loosen the cake. Release pan sides; discard paper liner. Dust with powdered sugar before serving.

Flourless Chocolate-Orange Cake: In Step 3, add the grated zest of one orange along with the sugar.

Flourless Chocolate Espresso Cake V

MAKES 10 SERVINGS

This cake is for those, like me, who believe that coffee and chocolate were meant for each other.

½ cup unsweetened cocoa powder (Dutch-process)

½ cup hot (120°F), strong brewed espresso

2 cups whole almonds (measure before grinding)

¾ cup packed light brown sugar

¼ teaspoon baking soda

2 large eggs, at room temperature

⅓ cup unsalted butter or buttery spread, such as Earth Balance, melted, or canola oil

1 teaspoon pure vanilla extract

½ teaspoon salt

2 tablespoons powdered sugar, for dusting

10 gluten-free chocolate-covered espresso beans, such as Trader Joes (optional)

1 Place a rack in the middle of the oven. Preheat the oven to 350°F. Grease; then line the bottom of an 8-inch nonstick (gray, not black) springform pan with wax paper or parchment paper. Grease again; set aside.

2 Dissolve the cocoa in the hot espresso; set aside. Grind the nuts in a food processor to a fine meal.

3 Add the brown sugar, baking soda, eggs, butter, vanilla extract, and salt to the food processor and process 30 to 40 seconds. Scrape down the side of the bowl with a spatula and process another 30 seconds or until the mixture is thoroughly blended. Spread the batter evenly in the pan.

4 Bake 35 to 40 minutes or until a toothpick inserted into the center of the cake comes out clean. The cake rises as it bakes, then may fall slightly as it cools. Cool the cake in the pan 15 minutes on a wire rack. Cut gently around edge of the pan with a sharp knife to loosen the cake. Release the pan sides; discard paper liner. Dust with powdered sugar before serving and garnish with chocolate covered espresso beans, if desired.

Haroset (Fruit and Nut Cake)

MAKES 12 SERVINGS

This luscious almond and apple cake is very dense and heavy because it is a Passover sweet that represents the mortar used by Jewish slaves in Egypt. It can be made in a number of different ways, using various forms of dried fruit.

2 cups whole almonds (measure before grinding)

¾ cup packed light brown sugar

1 teaspoon ground cinnamon

½ teaspoon salt

1 tart apple (such as Granny Smith), peeled, cored, and diced

1 teaspoon grated fresh ginger

2 tablespoons white dessert wine, such as Muscat or Vin Santo, or orange juice

Grated zest of 1 lemon

4 large eggs, at room temperature

2 tablespoons powdered sugar, for dusting

1 Place a rack in the middle of the oven. Preheat the oven to 350°F. Generously grease a 9-inch nonstick (gray, not black) springform pan and line the bottom with wax paper or parchment paper. Grease again.

2 Place the almonds, brown sugar, cinnamon, and salt in a food processor and grind them to a fine meal. Add the apples, ginger, wine, and lemon zest and process until smooth.

3 Add the eggs and process 30 to 40 seconds. Scrape down the side of the bowl with a spatula and process another 30 to 45 seconds or until the batter is thoroughly smooth and blended.

4 Bake 35 to 40 minutes or until a toothpick inserted into the center comes out clean. The cake will rise as it bakes, then may fall slightly as it cools. Cool the cake in the pan 15 minutes on a wire rack. Cut around the edge with a sharp knife to loosen the cake from the pan. Release the pan side, discard the paper, and cool the cake completely on the wire rack. Dust with powdered sugar before serving.

PUDDING CAKES AND UPSIDE-DOWN CAKES

Citrus Pudding Cake

MAKES 8 SERVINGS

If you like the citrus flavors of orange, lemon, and lime, then you'll love this cake. Plus, it contains no eggs, making it perfect for those with egg sensitivities.

CAKE

1 cup Carol's Sorghum Blend (page x)

⅓ cup sugar

2 teaspoons baking powder

½ teaspoon xanthan gum

¼ teaspoon salt

¼ cup 1% milk (cow's, rice, soy, potato, or nut)

¼ cup orange juice concentrate

2 tablespoons unsalted butter or buttery spread, such as Earth Balance, melted, or canola oil

2 tablespoons grated orange zest

1 teaspoon grated lemon zest

1 teaspoon pure vanilla extract

TOPPING

⅔ cup sugar

1 tablespoon Carol's Sorghum Blend (page x)

¼ teaspoon salt

1 cup hot (120°F) water

½ cup hot (120°F) fresh lemon juice

1 Place a rack in the middle of the oven. Preheat the oven to 350°F. Generously grease a 9-inch square nonstick (gray, not black) pan.

2 Make the cake: In a medium mixing bowl, whisk the sorghum blend, sugar, baking powder, xanthan gum, and salt. Beat in the milk, orange juice concentrate, butter, orange zest, lemon zest, and vanilla extract with an electric mixer on low speed (or by hand with a whisk) until smooth. Spread the batter evenly in the pan.

3 Make the topping: In a small bowl, whisk together the sugar, sorghum blend, and salt until thoroughly blended. Sprinkle the mixture evenly over the entire surface of the batter. Combine the hot water and hot lemon juice and pour slowly and gently over the sugar mixture.

4 Bake 40 to 45 minutes or until the cake starts to pull away from the edge of the pan. Do not overbake; the sauce under the cake will look very thin. Remove the cake from the oven and cool 20 to 25 minutes on a wire rack before serving. Spoon the cake out of the pan and drizzle the sauce from the bottom of the pan over the cake.

Coconut Pudding Cake

MAKES 8 SERVINGS

Pudding cakes create their own pudding, hence the name. Even though you put the liquid on top, the creamy pudding forms on the bottom of the cake and should be poured over the cake when it is served. Coconut flour is ground from fresh coconut meat and is high in fiber. It absorbs a lot of water during baking. It can be found in many natural food stores and online. This cake is perfect for those who avoid eggs.

CAKE

½ Carol's Sorghum Blend (page x)

¼ cup coconut flour, such as Bob's Red Mill

⅓ cup sugar

2 teaspoons baking powder

½ teaspoon xanthan gum

¼ teaspoon salt

½ cup 1% milk (cow's, rice, soy, potato, or nut)

½ cup sweetened shredded coconut

2 tablespoons unsalted butter or buttery spread, such as Earth Balance, melted, or canola oil

1 teaspoon coconut extract

1 teaspoon pure vanilla extract

TOPPING

⅔ cup sugar

1 tablespoon Carol's Sorghum Blend (page x)

¼ teaspoon salt

1 can (14 to 15 ounces or 1½ cups) hot (120°F) coconut milk, stirred

¼ cup sweetened shredded coconut, toasted

1 Place a rack in the middle of the oven. Preheat the oven to 350°F. Generously grease a 9-inch square nonstick (gray, not black) pan or 2-quart baking dish.

2 Make the cake: Whisk the sorghum blend, coconut flour, sugar, baking powder, xanthan gum, and salt into a medium mixing bowl. With electric mixer on low (or by hand with a whisk) beat in the milk, coconut, butter, coconut extract, and vanilla extract. Spread the batter evenly in the pan.

3 Make the topping: In a small bowl, whisk together the sugar, sorghum blend, and salt until thoroughly blended. Sprinkle the mixture evenly over the entire surface of the batter. Pour the hot coconut milk slowly and gently over the sugar mixture.

4 Bake 40 to 45 minutes or until the cake starts to pull away from edges of the pan. Do not overbake. Remove the cake from the oven and cool 20 to 25 minutes on a wire rack before serving. Spoon the cake out of the pan and drizzle the sauce from the bottom of the pan over the cake. Top with toasted coconut flakes.

Hot Fudge Pudding Cake

MAKES 8 SERVINGS

As the name indicates, the recipe creates its own hot fudge sauce as it bakes. You can then drizzle this sauce over the cake when you serve it. This cake is perfect for those who avoid eggs.

CAKE

1 cup Carol's Sorghum Blend (page x)

½ cup sugar

⅓ cup unsweetened cocoa powder (Dutch-process)

2 teaspoons baking powder

1 teaspoon xanthan gum

¼ teaspoon salt

¼ teaspoon instant espresso powder (optional)

½ cup 1% milk (cow's, rice, soy, potato, or nut)

2 tablespoons unsalted butter or buttery spread, such as Earth Balance, melted, or canola oil

1 tablespoon pure vanilla extract

TOPPING

⅓ cup packed light brown sugar

⅓ cup granulated sugar

¼ cup unsweetened cocoa powder (Dutch-process)

¼ teaspoon salt

1½ cups hot (120°F) water

1 Place a rack in the middle of the oven. Preheat the oven to 350°F. Generously grease a 9-inch square nonstick (gray, not black) pan.

2 Make the cake: In a medium mixing bowl, whisk the sorghum blend, sugar, cocoa, baking powder, xanthan gum, salt, and espresso powder (if using.) With an electric mixer on low (or by hand with a whisk) beat in the milk, butter, and vanilla extract until smooth. Spread the batter evenly into prepared pan.

3 Make the topping: In a medium bowl, whisk together the brown sugar, granulated sugar, cocoa, and salt until thoroughly blended. Sprinkle the mixture evenly over the entire surface of the batter. Pour the hot water slowly and gently over the cocoa mixture.

4 Bake 40 to 45 minutes or until the cake starts to pull away from the edge of the pan. Do not overbake; the sauce under the cake will look very thin. Remove the cake and cool 20 to 25 minutes on a wire rack before serving. Spoon the cake out of the pan and drizzle the sauce from the bottom of the pan over the cake.

Praline Pudding Cake

MAKES 8 SERVINGS

Praline is the term used to describe a confection of nuts, sugar, and cream that is typically browned to produce a caramel flavor. This cake, with its caramel flavor and pecans, is a perfect example. It is also an egg-free cake, making it ideal for those who avoid eggs.

CAKE

1 cup Carol's Sorghum Blend (page x)

½ cup packed dark brown sugar

¼ cup finely chopped pecans

2 teaspoons baking powder

½ teaspoon xanthan gum

¼ teaspoon salt

½ cup 1% milk (cow's, rice, soy, potato, or nut)

2 tablespoons unsalted butter or buttery spread, such as Earth Balance, melted, or canola oil

1 tablespoon pure vanilla extract

1 tablespoon rum extract

TOPPING

⅔ cup packed light brown sugar

1 tablespoon Carol's Sorghum Blend (page x)

¼ teaspoon salt

1½ cups hot (120°F) water

1 Place a rack in the middle of the oven. Preheat the oven to 350°F. Generously grease a 9-inch nonstick (gray, not black) square pan or a 2-quart baking dish.

2 Make the cake: Whisk the sorghum blend, brown sugar, pecans, baking powder, xanthan gum, and salt in a medium mixing bowl. With an electric mixer on low beat in the milk, butter, and vanilla extract and rum extracts until the batter is smooth. Spread the batter evenly in the pan.

3 Make the topping: Whisk together the brown sugar, sorghum blend, and salt until thoroughly blended. Sprinkle the mixture evenly over the entire surface of the batter. Pour the hot water slowly and gently over the brown sugar mixture.

4 Bake 40 to 45 minutes or until the cake starts to pull away from the edge of the pan. Do not overbake; the sauce under the cake will look very thin. Cool the cake in the pan 20 to 25 minutes on a wire rack before serving. Spoon the cake out of the pan and drizzle the sauce from the bottom of the pan over the cake.

Apple-Butterscotch Upside-Down Cake Ⓥ

MAKES 10 SERVINGS

Upside-down cakes represent old-fashioned good-ness and they're great for beginners because they are virtually fail-proof. This one is especially deli-cious in the fall when apples are at their best and the aromatic spices make your kitchen smell so good.

TOPPING

¼ cup unsalted butter or buttery spread, such as Earth Balance, at room temperature, or canola oil

2 small Jonathan or Granny Smith apples, peeled, cored, and cut in ⅛-inch slices

2 tablespoons fresh lemon juice

¼ cup packed light brown sugar

½ cup gluten-free butterscotch morsels, such as Safeway, Hy-Vee, or Publix

CAKE

½ cup unsalted butter or buttery spread, such as Earth Balance, at room temperature, or ⅓ cup canola oil

1 cup packed light brown sugar

3 large eggs, at room temperature

1½ cups Carol's Sorghum Blend (page x)

1 teaspoon xanthan gum

1 teaspoon baking powder

1½ teaspoons ground cinnamon

¾ teaspoon ground cloves

½ teaspoon ground allspice

½ teaspoon freshly grated nutmeg

½ teaspoon baking soda

½ teaspoon salt

1 teaspoon pure vanilla extract

2 small cooking apples, peeled, cored, and very finely diced

Juice and grated zest of 1 lemon

½ cup raisins or currants

¼ cup chopped pecans

½ cup powdered sugar, for dusting

1 Make the topping: Place a rack in the middle of the oven. Preheat the oven to 350°F. Generously grease a 10-inch cast-iron or ovenproof skillet. Melt the butter in the skillet over medium heat. Add the apples and lemon juice and cook until slightly tender, about 3 to 5 minutes, turning halfway through cooking. Remove the skillet from the heat and use tongs to arrange the apple slices attractively in a pinwheel fashion in the skillet. Sprinkle evenly with brown sugar and butter-scotch morsels; set aside.

2 Make the cake: In a mixing bowl, beat the butter and sugar on medium speed 2 minutes. Add the eggs, one at a time, beating thoroughly after each addition. Gradually add the sorghum blend, xanthan gum, baking powder, cinnamon, cloves, allspice, nutmeg, baking soda, salt, and vanilla extract and beat on low speed until well combined. Toss the apples with the lemon juice and zest and stir them into the batter, along with the raisins and pecans. Carefully spoon the batter evenly onto the filling in the skillet. Gently spread it with a wet spatula so you don't dislodge the apple slices.

3 Bake 30 to 35 minutes, or until a tester inserted in the center of the cake comes out clean. Cool the cake in the skillet 15 minutes. Place a serving plate on top of the skillet, topside down, and then use oven mitts on both hands to hold the skillet and plate tightly together and invert. The cake will drop on to the plate. Serve the cake warm, dusted with powdered sugar.

Pineapple Upside-Down Cake Ⓥ

MAKES 10 SERVINGS

Who doesn't like this old-time favorite? It's a sure bet no one will turn down this all-American des-sert, which is so simple to make.

TOPPING

½ cup packed light brown sugar

1 can (16 ounces) pineapple rings in juice (about 7 rings), drained, and juice reserved for cake

7 maraschino cherries, drained

CAKE

½ cup unsalted butter or buttery spread, such as Earth Balance, at room temperature, or ⅓ cup canola oil

¾ cup sugar

2 large eggs, beaten

1½ cups Carol's Sorghum Blend (page x)

1½ teaspoons xanthan gum

¼ teaspoon baking powder

¼ teaspoon baking soda

¼ teaspoon salt

1 teaspoon pure vanilla extract

½ cup homemade Basic Whipped Cream (page 624), or whipped topping, such as Lucerne or Soyatoo, for garnish (optional)

1 Place a rack in the middle of the oven. Preheat oven to 325°F. Generously grease a 10-inch nonstick (gray, not black) cake pan or a cast-iron skillet.

2 Make the topping: Sprinkle the brown sugar evenly over the bottom of the pan. Arrange pineapple rings on the brown sugar and place a cherry in the center of each ring. Set aside.

3 Make the cake: In a large mixing bowl, beat the butter and sugar with an electric mixer on medium speed until light and fluffy. Beat in the eggs on low speed just until blended.

4 In a medium bowl, whisk together the sorghum blend, xanthan gum, baking powder, baking soda, and salt. In another medium bowl, combine the reserved pineapple juice (with enough water added to equal ¾ cup), and vanilla extract. On low speed, beat the sorghum mixture into the egg mixture, alternating with the pineapple juice, beginning and ending with sorghum mixture. Mix just until combined. Carefully spread the batter over the pineapple and smooth the top with a wet spatula.

5 Bake 35 to 40 minutes or until the top springs back when touched. Cool the cake in the pan 15 minutes. Place a serving plate on top of the pan, topside down, and then use oven mitts on both hands to hold the pan and plate tightly together and invert. The cake will drop onto the plate. Serve the cake warm with a dollop of whipped cream.

Apricot Upside-Down Cake

MAKES 10 SERVINGS

This apricot cake is an interesting twist on an old favorite, the pineapple upside-down cake. It is best when made with fresh apricots so wait until summer when fresh apricots are plentiful.

CAKE

⅓ cup (5 tablespoons) unsalted butter or buttery spread, such as Earth Balance, or ¼ cup canola oil, at room temperature

1 cup sugar

2 large eggs, at room temperature

1½ cups Carol's Sorghum Blend (page x)

1 teaspoon xanthan gum

¼ teaspoon baking powder

¼ teaspoon baking soda

¼ teaspoon salt

¾ cup buttermilk, well-shaken, or homemade Buttermilk (page 677)

1 teaspoon pure vanilla extract

1 teaspoon almond extract

TOPPING

½ cup packed light brown sugar

2 tablespoons light corn syrup

12 fresh apricots, halved and pitted

¾ cup homemade Basic Whipped Cream (page 624), or whipped topping, such as Lucerne or Soyatoo, for garnish

1 Place a rack in the middle of the oven. Preheat the oven to 325°F. Generously grease a 10-inch round nonstick (gray, not black) pie pan or an 11 × 7-inch nonstick (gray, not black) pan.

2 Make the cake: In a large mixer bowl, beat the butter and sugar with an electric mixer on medium speed until light and fluffy. With the mixer on low speed, mix in eggs, one at a time, beating well after each addition.

3 In a medium bowl, whisk together the sorghum blend, xanthan gum, baking powder, baking soda, and salt. In another medium bowl, combine buttermilk, vanilla extract, and almond extract. On low speed, beat the sorghum mixture into the egg mixture, alternating with buttermilk—beginning and ending with the sorghum mixture. Mix just until combined. Set aside.

4 Make the topping: Sprinkle the brown sugar evenly over the bottom of the pan and drizzle the corn syrup on top. Arrange the apricot halves in a single layer, cut side up, on the sugar. Spread the cake batter evenly over the apricots and smooth the batter with a wet spatula.

5 Bake 35 to 40 minutes or until the top of the cake springs back when touched. Cool the cake in the skillet 15 minutes. Place a serving plate on top of the skillet, topside down, and then use oven mitts on both hands to hold the skillet and plate tightly together and invert. The cake will drop on to the plate. Serve the cake warm with a dollop of whipped cream.

Caramelized Pear–Gingerbread Upside-Down Cake Ⓥ

MAKES 12 SERVINGS

While most of us are familiar with the popular pineapple upside-down cake made with yellow cake, this version combines caramelized pears and spicy gingerbread for a very flavorful twist on this all-American dish. Baking it in a cast-iron skillet heightens the caramel flavor.

TOPPING
¾ cup packed light brown sugar
2 tablespoons water
3 firm ripe pears

CAKE
1½ cups Carol's Sorghum Blend (page x)
1 teaspoon baking soda
1½ teaspoons ground ginger
1 teaspoon ground cinnamon
½ teaspoon ground cloves
½ teaspoon salt
¼ cup (½ stick) unsalted butter or buttery spread, such as Earth Balance, at room temperature, or canola oil
½ cup packed light brown sugar
1 large egg, at room temperature
½ cup molasses (not blackstrap)
½ cup buttermilk, well-shaken, or homemade Buttermilk (page 677)
1 teaspoon pure vanilla extract

1 Place a rack in the middle of the oven. Preheat the oven to 350°F. Generously grease a 10-inch cast-iron skillet.

2 Make the topping: In the cast-iron skillet, combine the sugar and water. Bring to a simmer over low heat, swirling the pan occasionally, until the sugar dissolves. Cook 1 minute, gently swirling the pan so the sugar dissolves evenly. Remove the pan from the heat. Cool 10 minutes.

3 Wash and peel the pears. Cut in half, lengthwise; then in quarters. Remove the core from each quarter and cut into 3 uniformly-sized wedges. Arrange pears in pin-wheel design in skillet.

4 Make the cake: In a medium bowl, whisk together the sorghum blend, baking soda, ginger, cinnamon, cloves, and salt; set aside.

5 In a large bowl, beat the butter, brown sugar, and egg with an electric mixer on medium speed until smooth. In a measuring cup, whisk together the molasses, buttermilk, and vanilla extract and add alternately with the sorghum mixture, beginning and ending with the sorghum mixture. Carefully spread the batter on top of the pears.

6 Bake 30 minutes or until a toothpick inserted into the center comes out clean. Cool the cake in the pan 10 minutes on a wire rack. Loosen the edges of the cake with a knife. Lay a serving platter, top side down, on the skillet. Using oven mitts, invert. The cake will drop onto the serving plate. Remove the skillet. Serve slightly warm.

Cranberry-Walnut Upside-Down Cake

MAKES 12 SERVINGS

The addition of cranberries makes this a nice holiday dessert, but with dried cranberries available year-round it can be enjoyed any time of the year. For extra holiday flair, add a couple tablespoons of chopped crystallized ginger to the topping.

CAKE

6 tablespoons unsalted butter or buttery spread, such as Earth Balance, at room temperature, or canola oil

1 cup sugar

2 large eggs, at room temperature

1½ cups Carol's Sorghum Blend (page x)

1½ teaspoons xanthan gum

½ teaspoon salt

¼ teaspoon baking powder

¼ teaspoon baking soda

¾ cup buttermilk, well-shaken, or homemade Buttermilk (page 677)

1 teaspoon pure vanilla extract

1 teaspoon almond extract

TOPPING

½ cup packed light brown sugar

2 tablespoons light corn syrup

1 cup dried sweetened cranberries

½ cup chopped walnuts

½ cup homemade Basic Whipped Cream (page 624), or whipped topping, such as Lucerne or Soyatoo, for garnish

1 Place a rack in the middle of the oven. Preheat the oven to 325°F. Generously grease a 10-inch round nonstick (gray, not black) pie pan or an 11 × 7-inch nonstick (gray, not black) pan.

2 Make the cake: In a large mixer bowl, beat the butter and sugar with an electric mixer on medium speed until light and fluffy. Beat in eggs one at a time, on low speed, beating well after each addition.

3 In a medium bowl, whisk together the sorghum blend, xanthan gum, salt, baking powder, and baking soda. In a measuring cup, combine the buttermilk, vanilla extract, and almond extract. On low speed, beat the sorghum mixture into the egg mixture, alternating with the buttermilk, beginning and ending with the sorghum mixture. Beat just until combined, about 30 seconds; set aside.

4 Make the topping: Sprinkle the brown sugar evenly over the bottom of the pan and drizzle the corn syrup on top. Arrange the cranberries and walnuts on the sugar. Spread the cake batter evenly on top and smooth the batter with a wet spatula, if necessary.

5 Bake 35 to 40 minutes or until the top of the cake springs back when touched. Cool the cake in the pan 10 minutes on a wire rack. Loosen the edges of the cake with a thin metal spatula. Lay a serving platter, topside down, on the pan. Using oven mitts, invert the cake onto the serving plate. Remove the pan. Serve slightly warm, garnished with whipped cream.

ICE CREAM CAKES

Angel Food Ice Cream Cake Ⓥ

MAKES 12 SERVINGS

My mother always made this cake for our birthday parties when we were growing up. I don't know anyone else who makes this cake, so it remains special in my childhood memories.

1 homemade Angel Food Cake (page 467)
1 pint gluten-free Neapolitan ice cream
4 cups homemade Basic Whipped Cream (page 624), or whipped topping, such as Lucerne or Soyatoo

1 Cut the angel food cake in half cross-wise with a serrated knife. Remove the top half and set it on a plate.

2 Soften the ice cream so that it can be cut or scooped. Put a layer of ice cream about 1½ inches thick on the bottom layer of angel food cake. Replace the top layer.

3 With a spatula, frost the cake with the whipped cream and make attractive dips and swirls on the top and sides.

4 Freeze the cake for at least 2 hours before serving. To serve, slice with an electric or serrated knife. Freeze leftovers, tightly wrapped.

Fresh Peach Ice Cream Cake Ⓥ

MAKES 12 SERVINGS

Fresh peaches taste far better than canned ones in this summertime dessert, so save this cake for a time when you have access to the sweetest peaches you can find.

½ cup unsalted butter or buttery spread, such as Earth Balance, at room temperature, or ⅓ cup canola oil
¾ cup sugar
3 large egg whites, at room temperature
1½ cups Carol's Sorghum Blend (page x)
1 teaspoon xanthan gum
¼ teaspoon baking powder
¼ teaspoon baking soda
½ teaspoon salt
¾ cup buttermilk, well-shaken, or homemade Buttermilk (page 677)
1 teaspoon pure vanilla extract
½ teaspoon almond extract
1 pint gluten-free peach ice cream, sorbet, or frozen yogurt, such as Häagen-Dazs or Publix, softened
2 fresh peaches, washed, seeded, and finely chopped (about 2 diced cups)
3 cups homemade Basic Whipped Cream (page 624) or whipped topping, such as Lucerne or Soyatoo

1 Place a rack in the middle of the oven. Preheat the oven to 325°F. Generously grease a 10-inch nonstick (gray, not black) Bundt cake pan; set aside.

2 In a large mixing bowl, beat the butter with an electric mixer on medium speed until creamy and smooth. Gradually beat in the sugar until smooth. Add the egg whites, one at a time, beating well after each addition.

3 In another bowl, whisk together the sorghum blend, xanthan gum, baking powder, baking soda, and salt. In a measuring cup, whisk together the buttermilk, vanilla extract, and almond extract.

4 With the mixer on low speed, beat the sorghum mixture into the egg mixture, alternating with the buttermilk, beginning and ending with the sorghum mixture. Pour the batter into the pan.

5 Bake 55 minutes to 1 hour or until the cake is golden brown and a cake tester inserted into the center of the cake comes out clean. Cool the cake in the pan 10 minutes on a wire rack. Remove the cake from the pan with a thin metal spatula and cool completely on the wire rack.

6 Cut the cake in half, horizontally. Remove the top half. Stir the chopped fresh peaches into the softened peach ice cream. Working quickly, spread the ice cream mixture on the bottom cake layer. Replace the top half, wrap tightly, and freeze the cake until the ice cream is solid. When ready to serve, frost the cake with whipped cream and serve immediately. Freeze leftovers, tightly wrapped.

Chocolate Peppermint Ice Cream Cake Ⓥ

MAKES 12 SERVINGS

Cool peppermint complements the chocolate in this frozen concoction.

½ cup (1 stick) unsalted butter or buttery spread, such as Earth Balance, at room temperature or ⅓ cup canola oil

1¼ cups sugar

3 large eggs, at room temperature

⅔ cup 1% milk, (cow, rice, soy, potato, or nut), at room temperature

1 tablespoon pure vanilla extract

1 teaspoon peppermint extract

2 cups Carol's Sorghum Blend (page x)

⅔ cup unsweetened cocoa powder (not Dutch-process or alkali)

1 teaspoon baking soda

1 teaspoon xanthan gum

⅔ cup hot (120°F) brewed coffee

1 pint gluten-free peppermint ice cream, such as Hood Regular or Skondra's (or 1 pint gluten-free vanilla ice cream, such as Ben & Jerry's, with ½ cup crushed peppermint candies), softened

3 cups homemade Basic Whipped Cream (page 624) or whipped topping, such as Lucerne or Soyatoo

1 Place a rack in the middle of the oven. Preheat the oven to 325°F. Generously grease a 10-cup nonstick (gray, not black) Bundt pan.

2 In a large mixer bowl, beat butter and sugar with an electric mixer on medium speed until light and fluffy. Beat in eggs, one at a time, until thoroughly blended. Beat in milk, vanilla extract, and peppermint extract

3 Whisk together sorghum blend, cocoa, baking soda, and xanthan gum in a separate bowl. On low speed, beat sorghum mixture into the egg mixture, alternating with hot coffee, beginning and ending with the sorghum mixture. Transfer the batter to the prepared pan, smoothing the top of the batter with a spatula.

4 Bake 55 minutes to 1 hour or until a toothpick inserted into the center of the cake comes out clean. Cool the cake in the pan 15 minutes on a wire rack. Remove the cake from the pan with a thin metal spatula and transfer the cake to a serving platter and cool completely.

5 Cut the cake in half, horizontally. Remove the top half. Working quickly, spread the ice cream evenly on the bottom cake layer. Replace the top half, wrap tightly, and freeze the cake. When ready to serve, frost the cake with the whipped cream and serve immediately. Freeze leftovers, tightly wrapped.

Mini Chocolate Peppermint Ice Cream Cupcakes: Generously grease the cups of a mini 12-cup muffin pan or line with paper liners. Spray the insides of the liners with cooking spray. Divide the batter evenly into each cupcake. Place a rack in the middle of the oven. Preheat the oven to 325°F and bake 15 to 17 minutes. Repeat with the remaining batter. Cut the cupcakes in half, crosswise, and spread the bottom half of each cupcake with 1 tablespoon of ice cream. Replace the top half of the cupcake and freeze just until the ice cream is hard. To serve, drizzle gluten-free chocolate syrup, such as Hershey's, or homemade Chocolate Sauce (page 622) on top.

PIES AND PASTRIES

Fruit Pies and Tarts

Cherry Pie

Apricot Pie

Raspberry Pie

Strawberry Pie with
Whipped Cream

Mixed Berry Pie

Top-Crust Peach Pie

Top-Crust Apple Pie

Dutch Apple Pie with
Streusel Topping

Rhubarb Custard Pie

Easy Summer Fruit Tart

Apricot-Almond Tart

Limoncello Tart

Linzertorte

Individual Fresh Peach Tarts
in Coconut Crust

Pear-Almond Tart

Rhubarb Meringue Tart

Rustic Plum Almond Tart

Plum-Cream Cheese Tart

Rustic Nectarine Frangipane Tart

Summer Raspberry Cream Tart

Apple-Cranberry Galette

Peach Tarte Tatin

Plum Tatin

Ice Cream Pies

Frozen Margarita Pie

Cappuccino Ice Cream Pie with
Chocolate Sauce

Individual Chocolate
Baked Alaskas

Orange Butter Ice Cream Pie

Pineapple Icebox Dessert

Nut Pies

Pecan Pie

Chocolate Pecan Tart

Bourbon-Laced Mocha Walnut Pie

Pine Nut Pie with
Chocolate Sauce

Macadamia-Walnut Pie

Granola Pie

Pie Crusts

Cookie Crust

Nutty Cookie Crumb Crust

Cream Cheese Pie Crust

Basic Pastry Crust for Single-
or Double-Crust Pies

Cream and Chiffon Pies

Banana Cream Pie with
Mile-High Meringue

Banana Cream Pie Brownie

Chocolate Cream Pie

Chocolate Cream Pie with White
Chocolate Cream

Chocolate Fudge Pie

Chocolate Fudge Espresso Pie

Chocolate Meringue Pie

Black Bottom Pie

French Silk Pie

Coconut Chess Pie

Coconut Cream Pie

Q = Quick   V = Vegetarian

Butterscotch Pie

Praline Pumpkin Pie

Sweet Potato Pie

Sour Cream–Raisin Pie

Raspberry Chiffon Pie in Almond Crust

Strawberry Chiffon Pie in a Coconut Crust

Pineapple Meringue Pie

Eggnog Custard Pie with Whipped Cream Topping

Peanut Butter Pie

Key Lime Pie in Coconut Crumb Crust

Lemon Meringue Tart

Lime Curd Tart

Mango Blueberry Tart

Torta della Nonna (Grandmother's Cake)

Pastries and Doughnuts

Crullers

Yeast-Free Crullers

Doughnuts

Baked Apple Doughnuts with Powdered Sugar Glaze

Beignets

Sopaipillas

Yeast-Free Sopaipillas

Danish Puffed Pancakes

Funnel Cakes

Corn Fritters

Cream Puffs

Éclairs

Baklava

Apple Strudel

Crepes

Dessert Crepes

Austrian Crepes in Custard

Crepes with Ricotta Filling and Chocolate Sauce

Crepes Suzette

Jam-Filled Crepes

Fondue, Sauces, and Toppings

Caramel Fondue

Dark Chocolate Fondue

Milk Chocolate Fondue

Chocolate Sauce

Caramel Sauce

Praline Sauce

Rum Sauce

Basic Whipped Cream

Nondairy Whipped Topping

Next to yeast breads, pies, tarts, and pastries are the foods that inspire the most trepidation in gluten-free bakers—mostly because of the crusts. It is possible to make delicious pies at home, but to make a successful gluten-free pie crust, you'll have to learn from scratch or relearn a few important aspects of handling the ingredients.

The shortening or butter must be at room temperature—rather than cold—for the most thorough and effective blending. It is much faster and more thorough to blend the ingredients in a food processor than using a pastry cutter or an electric mixer. You can't overwork this pie dough because there is no gluten to toughen the crust, so a food processor works best here. The liquid is added slowly and the mixture is processed until it forms a ball or several large clumps on one side of the bowl. The resulting dough will be a bit wetter than traditional pie dough, but this is normal.

You can also roll and reroll the dough, freezing leftover bits and pieces for use again and again—as long as they're stored in a heavy-duty food storage bag or air-tight container to prevent drying out.

Innovative techniques—such as baking the crust on the bottom rack of the oven for a portion of the baking time—prevent sogginess by browning the crust, making it less likely to absorb moisture from the pie filling. The remaining baking time is done on the middle rack of the oven to assure even browning all around, including the top pie crust.

Nonstick pans (gray, not black) are critical for promoting this important browning process. Pies, especially those with pastry crusts, won't brown at all in glass or ceramic pie pans. It is important to note that most nonstick pans (gray, not black) are deep-dish, requiring a bit more filling than traditional glass or ceramic pie pans.

The pastry pie crust in this book works best for pies that do not bake for extended periods of time, but instead bake just long enough to brown the crust, not necessarily to fully cook the filling. So, if you are using the pie crust for some of your own fruit pie recipes you might want to cook the fruit fillings beforehand. If the crust starts to brown too quickly, lay a sheet of foil on top of the pie.

It's easy to produce a beautiful, golden crust by brushing it with beaten egg, apple juice, milk, cream, or corn syrup. Meringues should use superfine sugar or powdered sugar rather than granulated sugar and spread over a slightly warm—rather than cold—filling for best results. Most pies in this chapter are best served on the same day they're made and will taste better at room temperature. If you refrigerate any leftovers, cover them with plastic wrap or foil to prevent absorption of fridge odors—although this will make the crust soft. To warm up pies before serving, gently heat them in a 250°F oven rather than reheating them in a microwave, which will make the crust soggy.

The Basic Pastry Crust recipe (page 587) makes enough for a double-crust pie. If you're making a single-crust pie, freeze the remaining dough and thaw it on the countertop at room temperature or overnight in the refrigerator—never in a microwave oven. Better yet, roll a few pie crusts to a 10-inch circle and freeze them between layers of parchment paper, tightly sealed in a food storage bag or a box. These crusts will thaw quickly when removed from the freezer while you're making the filling. For many types of pie—and for those cooks who remain challenged by pie crust—there are several no-bake crusts in this book that are quite simple to construct and complement the fillings nicely.

You may use your favorite shortening in the pie crusts, but I also suggest non-hydrogenated versions, such as Earth Balance and Spectrum Vegetable that work beautifully. If you avoid dairy, I offer substitutions for cow's milk, butter, and cream cheese. Try making homemade Nondairy Whipped Topping (page 624) or store-bought, soy-based whipped topping in place of homemade Basic Whipped Cream (page 624).

FRUIT PIES AND TARTS

Cherry Pie

MAKES 6 SERVINGS

Nothing says summer like cherry pie, especially if you find fresh cherries in season, preferably at a farmer's market. Since most nonstick pie pans (gray, not black) are "deep-dish size," this pie holds lots of filling. This cherry filling firms up nicely because you first cook it with cornstarch to thicken it before filling the pie crust.

1 cup sugar + 1 tablespoon for sprinkling on crust
¼ cup cornstarch
Dash of salt
4 cups fresh tart red cherries or 3 cans (14 to 15 ounces each), thoroughly drained
1 teaspoon almond extract
White rice flour for dusting
2 tablespoons unsalted butter or buttery spread, such as Earth Balance, at room temperature and cut in 6 pieces
Basic Pastry Crust dough for a 9-inch pie, double crust (page 587)
1 tablespoon heavy cream, or apple juice, or beaten egg white for brushing on the crust

1 In a medium, heavy saucepan, whisk together 1 cup of the sugar, cornstarch, and salt until well blended. Add the cherries and cook over medium heat, stirring constantly, until the mixture thickens and becomes clear. Remove from the heat, stir in almond extract, and set aside to cool.

2 Place a rack in the bottom position and another in the middle position of the oven. Preheat the oven to 375°F. Prepare the double-crust pastry dough as directed in Step 1 on page 587. Then, roll the bottom pie crust and fit it into the pie pan following directions in Step 4 on page 587. Spread the cooled cherry filling evenly in the pie crust. Dot with pieces of butter. Continue with the top crust, as directed in Step 4 on page 587.

3 Freeze the pie 10 minutes. Brush with the cream and sprinkle with the remaining tablespoon of sugar. Place the pie on a nonstick (gray, not black) baking sheet.

4 Bake 15 to 20 minutes on the bottom rack of the oven. Move the pie to the middle rack and bake 25 to 35 minutes more, or until the crust is golden brown. Cover the crust with foil if it browns too quickly. Remove from oven and cool completely on a wire rack before cutting.

Apricot Pie

MAKES 8 SERVINGS

Fresh apricot pie is one of life's utmost pleasures. Interestingly, fresh apricots are far more flavorful when cooked, and you can use apricots in this pie even if they're not totally ripe. Canned apricots do not taste nearly as good as fresh apricots, so don't make any substitutions.

1 cup sugar + 1 tablespoon for sprinkling on crust
¼ cup quick-cooking tapioca
Pinch of salt
Pinch of freshly grated nutmeg
4 cups pitted and halved fresh apricots, thoroughly drained
1 tablespoon fresh lemon juice
½ teaspoon almond extract
Basic Pastry Crust dough for a 9-inch pie, double crust (page 587)
White rice flour for dusting
2 tablespoons unsalted butter or buttery spread, such as Earth Balance, at room temperature and cut in 6 pieces
1 tablespoon apple juice or milk or beaten egg white for brushing on the pie crust
¼ teaspoon ground cinnamon

1 In a large bowl, whisk 1 cup of the sugar with the tapioca, salt, and nutmeg. Add the apricots, lemon juice, and almond extract and toss until completely blended. Set aside.

2 Place a rack in the bottom position and another in the middle position of the oven. Preheat the oven to 375°F. Prepare the double-crust pastry dough as directed in Step 1 on page 587. Then, roll the bottom pie crust and fit it into the pie pan following directions in Step 4 on page 587. Continue with the top crust, as directed in Step 4 on page 587. Freeze the pie 10 minutes. Brush the crust with apple juice and sprinkle with the remaining tablespoon of sugar and the cinnamon. Place the pie on a nonstick (gray, not black) baking sheet.

3 Bake 15 to 20 minutes on the bottom rack of the oven. Move the pie to the middle rack and bake 30 to 40 minutes more, or until the crust is golden brown. Cover the crust with foil if it browns too quickly. Remove from oven and cool completely on a wire rack before cutting.

Raspberry Pie

MAKES 6 SERVINGS

This pie is best in summer, when fresh raspberries are especially flavorful and plentiful. The lovely deep red filling looks wonderful with the creamy white topping.

Nutty Cookie Crumb Crust (page 585)
2 containers (6 ounces each) fresh raspberries, picked over, washed, and patted dry
3 tablespoons cornstarch
¼ cup sugar
1 cup raspberry-cranberry concentrate, thawed but not diluted
¾ cup cold water

1 Prepare the crust as directed on page 585 in a 9-inch pie pan. Arrange the raspberries evenly in the crust. In a small saucepan, whisk the cornstarch and sugar until well blended. Whisk in the raspberry-cranberry concentrate and water, place the saucepan over medium heat, and continue whisking until the mixture boils. Boil 1 minute, whisking constantly. Set the pan aside to cool the filling completely.

2 Pour cooked filling into the crust and refrigerate 2 to 3 hours or until set. Serve chilled or at room temperature.

Strawberry Pie with Whipped Cream

MAKES 8 SERVINGS

Nothing reminds me of spring more than this luscious dessert with its bright red, shiny strawberries. The whipped cream is truly the "frosting on the cake."

Nutty Cookie Crumb Crust (page 585)
1 cup sugar
2 tablespoons cornstarch
⅛ teaspoon salt
1 cup cold water
2 tablespoons light corn syrup
4 tablespoons strawberry gelatin powder
½ teaspoon pure vanilla extract
1 drop red food coloring (optional)
1 quart (4 cups) fresh strawberries, washed and hulled
¾ cup homemade Basic Whipped Cream (page 624) or whipped topping, such as Lucerne or Soyatoo

1 Prepare the crust as directed on page 585 in a 9-inch pie pan.

2 In a medium saucepan, whisk together the sugar, cornstarch, and salt until blended. Then whisk in the water. Cook over medium-high heat, whisking constantly, until the mixture is thick and clear. Remove from the heat and stir in the corn syrup, gelatin, vanilla extract, and food coloring if using; cool completely.

3 Pat the strawberries dry with paper towels, then slice. Gently stir the strawberries into the cooled gelatin. Pour the filling into the pie crust. Refrigerate until firm, about 3 to 4 hours.

4 Serve each slice of pie chilled or at room temperature, topped with 2 tablespoons of whipped cream. Refrigerate leftovers.

Mixed Berry Pie

MAKES 6 SERVINGS

Berry pies say "summer" in the most delicious way. I use two kinds of thickeners to make sure the filling firms up nicely, since berries have lots of juice. This pie is especially good if you make the pie crust with butter, rather than shortening.

CRUST

Basic Pastry Crust dough for a 9-inch pie, double crust (page 587)

White rice flour for dusting

1 egg yolk whisked with 1 tablespoon water for egg wash

1 tablespoon sugar

FILLING

⅔ cup sugar, or to taste + 1 tablespoon for sprinkling on crust

2 tablespoons cornstarch

2 tablespoons quick-cooking tapioca

8 cups (2 pounds) fresh raspberries, blueberries, and blackberries

1 tablespoon fresh lemon juice

1 tablespoon orange liqueur, such as Triple Sec or Cointreau (optional)

1 tablespoon unsalted butter or buttery spread, such as Earth Balance, cut in 3 pieces

1 Make the crust: Prepare the double-crust pastry dough as directed in Step 1 on page 587.

2 While the dough chills, make the filling: In a large bowl, mix together ⅔ cup of sugar, cornstarch, and tapioca. Add the berries and toss well. Once you have the berries mixed with the sugar, taste to see if more sugar is needed. Add the lemon juice and liqueur, if using, and toss well; set aside.

3 Place a rack in the bottom position and another in the middle position of the oven. Preheat the oven to 375°F. Roll the bottom pie crust and fit it into the pie pan following directions in Step 4 on page 587. Fill with the fruit mixture, but limit the extra juice to 2 tablespoons. Dot the filling with the butter pieces. Continue with the top crust as directed

in Step 4 on page 587. Freeze the pie 10 minutes. Brush the crust with the egg wash and sprinkle with the remaining tablespoon of sugar. Place it on a nonstick (gray, not black) baking sheet.

4 Bake 15 minutes on the bottom oven rack. Move the pie to the middle rack and bake 25 to 35 minutes more, or until the top crust is nicely browned. Cover loosely with foil if the crust browns too much. Remove from oven and cool completely on a wire rack before cutting. Serve at room temperature.

Top-Crust Peach Pie

MAKES 6 SERVINGS

A peach pie can be assembled fairly quickly if you don't peel the peaches and only use a top crust, which can be as rustic as you like. The result? A fabulous pie—without all the work.

CRUST

Basic Pastry Crust dough for a 9-inch pie, single crust (page 587)

1 egg white and 1 teaspoon water beaten to foam for egg wash

FILLING

6 medium peaches, pitted, and cut in ½-inch slices

2 tablespoons potato starch

2 tablespoons fresh lemon juice

½ cup sugar + 1 tablespoon for sprinkling on crust

1 teaspoon almond extract

1 teaspoon pure vanilla extract

¼ teaspoon ground cinnamon

⅛ teaspoon freshly grated nutmeg

¼ teaspoon salt

1 Make the crust: Prepare the single-crust pastry dough as directed in Step 1 on page 587. Roll pie crust to 8 × 8-inch square, trimming edges so crust is same size as dish. Reserve, covered in plastic wrap.

2 Place a rack in the middle of the oven. Preheat the oven to 375°F. Generously grease an 8 × 8-inch glass baking dish.

3 Make the filling: Combine peaches, potato starch, lemon juice, ½ cup sugar, almond extract, vanilla extract, cinnamon, nutmeg, and salt in medium bowl. Mix well and transfer to prepared baking dish.

4 Remove top piece of plastic wrap and invert pie crust over dish, centering it exactly over dish before removing remaining piece of plastic wrap. Brush crust with egg wash. Sprinkle with remaining tablespoon of sugar.

5 Bake 30 to 35 minutes or until pie crust is golden brown and peaches are bubbling. Remove from oven and cool 30 minutes on a wire rack before cutting. Serve at room temperature.

Top-Crust Apple Pie

MAKES 6 SERVINGS

This easy pie just uses a top crust rather than both a top and bottom crust, making it quick to assemble and very forgiving if you're not adept at handling pie crust. The thinner you can roll the pie crust, the better it will be.

FILLING

4 cups unpeeled, sliced apples (Gala, Granny Smith, or your choice)

½ cup sugar

2 tablespoons cornstarch

1 teaspoon cinnamon or apple pie spice

¼ teaspoon salt

2 tablespoons unsalted butter or buttery spread, such as Earth Balance, melted

1 tablespoon fresh lemon juice

CRUST

Basic Pastry Crust dough for a 9-inch pie, single crust (page 587)

1 egg white beaten with 1 tablespoon water for egg wash

1 teaspoon sugar for sprinkling on crust

1 Place a rack in the middle of the oven. Preheat the oven to 375°F. Generously grease a 9-inch round microwave-safe pie pan.

2 Make the filling: In a large bowl, toss the apples with the sugar, cornstarch, cinnamon, and salt. Add the melted butter and lemon juice and toss to coat the apples thoroughly. Add to prepared pie pan. Place pan in microwave oven and cook on high 5 minutes to partially cook apples. (If you can't microwave the apples, cook this mixture in a saucepan on the stove 5 minutes to soften the apples.) Set aside to cool.

3 Make the crust: Prepare the single-crust pastry crust dough as directed in Step 1 on page 587. Then, roll pie crust to a 9-inch circle, trimming edges so crust is same size as pan. Remove top piece of plastic wrap and invert pie crust over apples, centering it exactly over pan before removing remaining top sheet of plastic wrap. Tuck edges of pastry down around inside edge of pan. If the pie crust tears or breaks, simply pinch it together if possible. If not, that break simply becomes a vent to let steam escape. Brush the pie crust with egg wash and sprinkle with sugar.

4 Bake 20 to 25 minutes or until the pie crust is golden brown and apples are tender. Remove from oven and cool completely on wire rack before cutting. Serve at room temperature.

Dutch Apple Pie with Streusel Topping

MAKES 6 SERVINGS

The crunchy topping on this pie is a nice alternative to traditional pastry crusts and is quite simple to make. The streusel topping adds luscious flavor (plus, you get extra nutrients from the flax cereal).

CRUST

Basic Pastry Crust dough for a 9-inch pie, single crust (page 587)

FILLING

5 cups apples, peeled, cored, and cut in ⅛-inch slices

Juice and grated zest of 1 lemon

¾ cup sugar

2 tablespoons sweet rice flour or 1 tablespoon cornstarch

½ teaspoon ground cinnamon

¼ teaspoon freshly grated nutmeg

¼ teaspoon ground allspice

¼ teaspoon salt

2 tablespoons unsalted butter or buttery spread, such as Earth Balance, at room temperature and cut in 6 pieces

TOPPING

½ cup Carol's Sorghum Blend (page x)

½ cup gluten-free flax cereal, such as Perky's Nutty Flax, or rice cereal, such as Perky's Nutty Rice

½ cup packed light brown sugar

½ teaspoon ground cinnamon

¼ teaspoon salt

¼ cup (½ stick) unsalted butter or buttery spread, such as Earth Balance, cut in ¼-inch cubes

1 Place a rack in the bottom position and another in the middle position of the oven. Preheat the oven to 375°F.

2 Make the crust: Prepare the single-crust pastry dough as directed in Step 1 on page 587. Then, fit it into a 9-inch nonstick (gray, not black) pie pan, as directed in Steps 2 and 3. Flute the edges

decoratively as instructed for a single-crust pie. Put the crust in the freezer while preparing the filling. (You may prepare the crust ahead and freeze, tightly covered, for up to a week.)

3 Make the filling: In a large bowl, toss together the apples, and lemon juice and zest. In a small bowl, whisk together the sugar, sweet rice flour, cinnamon, nutmeg, allspice, and salt until thoroughly blended and toss with the apple mixture until well blended.

4 Remove the pie crust from the freezer. Place the apple mixture in the pie crust and dot with the butter pieces. Lay a sheet of aluminum foil lightly on top of filling, but do not seal.

5 Bake 15 minutes on the bottom rack of the oven. Move the pie to the middle rack and bake 15 minutes more, still covered with foil.

6 While the pie bakes, make the topping: in a medium bowl, toss together the sorghum blend, cereal, brown sugar, cinnamon, and salt until well blended. With your fingers, blend in the butter until moist clumps form. Remove pie from oven. Discard the foil and sprinkle the streusel topping evenly over the apples. Return pie to the oven on the middle rack.

7 Bake 10 to 15 minutes more, or until the streusel is browned and the apples are tender. Remove from oven and cool completely on wire rack before cutting. Serve at room temperature.

Rhubarb Custard Pie

MAKES 6 SERVINGS

Rhubarb makes its appearance in my garden every spring, heralding the warmer weather to come. I usually make simple rhubarb pie with it, but I'm always eager to try something new, such as this one, which has a custard-like texture surrounding the rhubarb.

CRUST

Basic Pastry Crust dough for a 9-inch pie, double crust (page 587)

2 pounds fresh rhubarb, cut in ½-inch pieces

1 egg white beaten with 1 tablespoon water for egg wash

1 teaspoon sugar for sprinkling on crust

FILLING

1¼ cups sugar

1 tablespoon cornstarch

½ teaspoon freshly grated nutmeg

Pinch of ground cinnamon

2 large eggs, at room temperature

1 tablespoon 1% milk (cow's, rice, soy, potato, or nut)

3 drops red food coloring (optional)

2 tablespoons unsalted butter or buttery spread, such as Earth Balance at room temperature and cut in 6 pieces

1 Make the crust: Prepare the double-crust pastry dough as directed in Step 1 on page 587.

2 Place a rack in the bottom position and another in the middle position of the oven. Preheat the oven to 375°F. Fit the pastry into a 9-inch non-stick (gray, not black) pie pan, as directed in Steps 2 and 3 on page 587. Spread the rhubarb evenly in the crust.

3 Make the filling: In a medium bowl, whisk together the sugar, cornstarch, nutmeg, and cinnamon. Beat in the eggs, milk, and red food coloring, if using, with an electric mixer on low speed until smooth. Pour the mixture over the rhubarb. Dot the filling with the butter pieces.

4 Continue with the top crust, as directed in Step 4 on page 587. Prick the crust several times with a fork to allow the steam to escape. Freeze the pie 10 minutes. Brush the crust with the egg wash and sprinkle with the sugar. Place the pie on a nonstick baking sheet.

5 Bake 15 to 20 minutes on the bottom rack of the oven. Move the pie to the middle rack and bake 25 to 35 minutes more, or until the crust is golden brown. Cover the crust with foil if it browns too quickly. Remove from oven and cool completely on a wire rack before cutting.

Easy Summer Fruit Tart

MAKES 6 SERVINGS

If you feel challenged by rolling and shaping traditional pie crusts, this easy tart is the answer. Just press the dough into a tart pan that has a pretty fluted edge, rather than rolling and shaping it. Remove the side, and you have a pretty fluted edge, thanks to the tart pan. The fruit filling is as simple to prepare as the crust. Simply arrange the fresh fruit in a decorative way on a bed of jam or marmalade.

Basic Pastry Crust dough for a 9-inch pie, single crust (page 587)

1 tablespoon sugar

½ teaspoon almond extract

1 cup fresh blackberries, washed and dried

1 cup sliced fresh peaches, pitted and cut in ¼-inch slices

1 cup fresh raspberries, washed and dried

1 jar (8 ounces) orange marmalade or 1 cup homemade Clementine Marmalade (page 678)

1 Place a rack in the bottom position of the oven. Preheat the oven to 375°F. Lightly butter a 9-inch nonstick (gray, not black) tart pan with a removable bottom; set aside.

2 Prepare the pastry dough as directed in Step 1 on page 587. Freeze two-thirds of the dough for another use. Return the remaining one-third of dough to the food processor, add the sugar and almond extract and process until well blended. Press the dough into the tart pan evenly and into the edges of the pan, leveling it off so it is even with the top edge of the pan, forming a pretty edge for the finished tart. Prick the bottom of the tart with a fork several times. Put in the freezer 15 minutes.

3 Bake crust 15 minutes. Cool in the pan 15 minutes on a wire rack.

4 Arrange the fruit decoratively on the tart crust, with a row of blackberries around the outer edge of the tart, then a circle of overlapping sliced peaches, and the raspberries placed in the center.

5 Place the marmalade in a heat-proof bowl and heat in the microwave on medium until it starts to boil. Pour it over the fruit. Cool completely before serving at room temperature.

Apricot-Almond Tart

MAKES 6 SERVINGS

Some cooks like to peel apricots before using, but I prefer to reap the benefits of the nutrients and fiber in the skins. Plus, the skins on apricots aren't that tough. This is a very easy dessert to assemble, especially if you keep a stash of pie crust dough in your freezer. Or, better yet, keep a stash of pie crusts that are already rolled out to a 10-inch circle.

CRUST

Basic Pastry Crust dough for a 9-inch pie, single crust (page 587)

FILLING

¼ cup apricot preserves + 1 tablespoon for brushing on the crust

1 teaspoon almond extract

⅔ cup very finely ground slivered almonds

⅓ cup sugar

10 fresh apricots, pitted and halved

1 tablespoon unsalted butter or buttery spread, such as Earth Balance, cut in 4 pieces

2 tablespoons powdered sugar, for dusting

1 Place a rack in the bottom position and another in the middle position of the oven. Preheat the oven to 375°F. Generously grease a 9-inch nonstick (gray, not black) tart pan with removable sides.

2 Make the crust: Prepare the single-crust pastry dough as directed in Step 1 on page 587. Then, roll it to a 9-inch diameter between 2 sheets of plastic wrap with a wet paper towel on the countertop to anchor the plastic wrap. Remove the top sheet of plastic wrap and trim the pie crust to same size as bottom tart pan. Invert pie crust on bottom of tart pan, centering it exactly before removing remaining top sheet of plastic wrap. Pierce the bottom of the crust with a fork. Bake 10 to 12 minutes on the bottom rack of the oven, or until the crust is firm and dry. Remove and cool 10 minutes on a wire rack.

3 Make the filling: In a small saucepan, heat the preserves and almond extract, and then spread on the bottom of the cooled crust. In a small bowl, combine the ground almonds and sugar and sprinkle on the preserves. Arrange the apricots, cut side down, on top of the almonds and dot with the butter pieces.

4 Bake 30 to 35 minutes on middle rack of the oven, or until the apricots are tender and the filling is syrupy. Remove from oven and cool completely on a wire rack before removing the sides of the tart pan. Dust the tart with powdered sugar just before serving. Serve at room temperature.

Limoncello Tart

MAKES 8 SERVINGS

Limoncello is a lemon-flavored liqueur that is very popular in Italy, but is also easily found in most liquor stores in the United States. You'll love the contrast of the sweet and crunchy pine nut crust against the creamy tartness of the lemon filling.

CRUST

1 cup Carol's Sorghum Blend (page x)

¼ cup (½ stick) unsalted butter or buttery spread, such as Earth Balance, at room temperature

¼ cup pine nuts, toasted

2 tablespoons sugar

¼ teaspoon xanthan gum

¼ teaspoon salt

1 egg yolk whisked with 1 tablespoon water for egg wash

FILLING

1 cup sugar

3 tablespoons cornstarch

½ cup 1% milk (cow's, rice*, soy, potato*, or nut)

¼ cup fresh lemon juice

¼ cup Limoncello, or fresh lemon juice

1 teaspoon lemon zest

2 large eggs, slightly beaten

1 large egg yolk

1 tablespoon unsalted butter or buttery spread, such as Earth Balance, at room temperature

Fresh raspberries or strawberries, for garnish

1 Place a rack in the bottom position of the oven. Preheat the oven to 375°F. Generously grease a 9-inch round nonstick (gray, not black) tart pan with removable sides or a 6 × 10-inch rectangular nonstick (gray, not black) tart pan with removable sides.

2 Make the crust: In a food processor, blend sorghum blend, butter, pine nuts, sugar, xanthan gum, and salt until crumbly. Press evenly into the prepared pan with your fingers. Brush the entire crust with the egg wash.

3 Bake 10 to 12 minutes on the bottom rack or until the crust is lightly browned and becomes fragrant. Remove from oven and cool completely on a wire rack.

4 Make the filling: In a heavy medium saucepan, whisk together the sugar and cornstarch. Whisk in the milk, lemon juice, liqueur, and lemon zest until well blended. Whisk in the eggs and egg yolk until smooth. Cook 7 to 9 minutes over medium heat, whisking constantly, or until the mixture thickens. Do not let it boil. Remove the pan from the heat and stir in the butter.

5 Spread the filling evenly into the pie crust with a spatula. Chill the tart until the filling is set, about 6 to 8 hours, before removing the side of the pan. Serve at room temperature, garnished with fresh berries. Refrigerate leftovers.

Note: If using rice milk or potato milk, increase the cornstarch to 4 tablespoons.

Linzertorte

MAKES 6 SERVINGS

The Linzertorte comes from Linz, Austria, and has a jam filling and lattice-top crust. A gluten-free pie crust is too delicate to weave the typical lattice design, so I use a lattice cutter, often found at kitchen stores and discount outlets. If you can't find one, simply cut little squares from the frozen crust to assemble on top of the filling in a lattice pattern.

1 cup very finely ground hazelnuts or walnuts

¾ cup Carol's Sorghum Blend (page x)

¼ cup sweet rice flour

¼ cup granulated sugar

¼ cup packed light brown sugar

½ teaspoon ground cinnamon

¼ teaspoon xanthan gum

Pinch salt

Pinch ground cloves

¼ cup (½ stick) unsalted butter or buttery spread, such as Earth Balance, chilled and cut in 8 pieces

1 large egg, lightly beaten

½ teaspoon lemon zest

⅔ cup raspberry jam

2 tablespoons powdered sugar, for dusting

1 In a food processor, combine the ground nuts, sorghum blend, sweet rice flour, granulated sugar, brown sugar, cinnamon, xanthan gum, salt, and cloves. Pulse a couple of times. Place the butter pieces evenly around the edge of the bowl and process until the mixture resembles coarse crumbs. Add the egg and lemon zest and pulse until the dough forms a ball. Flatten the dough into 2 flat disks, each ½-inch thick, wrap tightly in plastic wrap, and refrigerate 2 hours.

2 Place a rack in the bottom position and another in the middle position of the oven. Preheat the oven to 350°F. Unwrap one of the disks, keeping the other one tightly wrapped. Massage the disk in your hands until it no longer feels cold. Place it between two sheets of heavy-duty plastic wrap and roll it to a 10-inch circle. Place the circle of dough, still between the plastic wrap, on a 10-inch plate and freeze it while preparing the bottom crust and filling.

3 Unwrap the other disk of dough and massage it in your hands until it no longer feels cold. Press it evenly into an ungreased 9-inch round nonstick (gray, not black) tart pan with a fluted edge and a removable bottom. Spread the jam evenly over the bottom of the crust.

4 Remove the chilled pie crust from the freezer and lay it on a flat surface. Remove the top layer of plastic wrap. Press a lattice pie top cutter into the pie crust, creating a lattice design. Leaving the plastic wrap intact, invert and center the crust over the pie, plastic wrap up, and drape it over the filling. Remove the remaining plastic wrap and let the dough come to room temperature before trimming the edge and then rolling the outside edge of the torte to form a neat edge.

5 Bake 15 minutes on the bottom rack of the oven. Move the torte to the middle rack and bake 20 to 25 minutes more, or until the torte is bubbly and the crust is browned. Remove from oven and cool completely on a wire rack. Serve at room temperature dusted with powdered sugar.

Individual Peach Tarts in Coconut Crusts Ⓥ

MAKES 4 SERVINGS

This is especially nice to make when fresh peaches are in season. The coconut crusts provide a crunchy contrast to the fruit and are a wonderful alternative to the flour crusts traditionally used in these tarts. If you are dairy-sensitive and use a cream cheese alternative, the texture of the filling may be a little less creamy, but delicious nonetheless.

CRUST

1½ cups sweetened shredded coconut

1 tablespoon sweet rice flour

¼ teaspoon salt

1 teaspoon pure vanilla extract

2 tablespoons unsalted butter or buttery spread, such as Earth Balance, at room temperature

¾ cup homemade Basic Whipped Cream (page 624) or whipped topping, such as Lucerne or Soyatoo

FILLING

1 teaspoon almond extract

¾ cup mascarpone cheese or cream cheese alternative, such as Tofutti, softened

2 whole fresh peaches, peeled, halved, and seeded or 4 canned peach halves, drained

½ cup peach preserves

1 Place a rack in the middle of the oven. Preheat the oven to 325°F. Generously grease 4 nonstick (gray, not black) mini-springform pans and put them on a baking sheet; set aside.

2 Make the crust: In a large bowl, toss the coconut with the sweet rice flour and salt until blended. Add the vanilla and melted butter and toss until the coconut is coated. Press the mixture evenly into the 4 pans.

3 Bake 15 minutes, or until the coconut crust is lightly browned, rotating the baking sheet halfway through baking. Remove from oven and cool completely on a wire rack.

4 While crusts cool, make the filling: Stir the almond extract into the whipped cream. Fold the mixture into the cheese. Fill the 4 tarts evenly with the cheese mixture. Place a peach half, cut side down, on the cheese mixture.

5 In a small saucepan, heat the preserves until they are thinned and pour evenly over the peaches. Let the tarts stand at room temperature until the preserves firm up, about 30 minutes, before removing the sides of the pans. Serve at room temperature.

Pear-Almond Tart

MAKES 6 SERVINGS

This is a photo-worthy fancy dessert. The arrangement of the thinly sliced pears is what lends this dessert that professional touch. Contrary to its sophisticated look, this tart is quite easy to prepare.

CRUST

1 cup Carol's Sorghum Blend (page x)

¼ cup (½ stick) unsalted butter or buttery spread, such as Earth Balance, at room temperature

2 tablespoons sugar

¼ teaspoon xanthan gum

¼ teaspoon salt

FILLING

1 cup blanched almonds or almond slivers

½ cup sugar

¼ cup (½ stick) unsalted butter or buttery spread, such as Earth Balance, at room temperature

¼ teaspoon salt

1 large egg, at room temperature

1 teaspoon pure vanilla extract

1 teaspoon almond extract

2 large ripe but firm Bosc pears

¼ cup apple or red currant jelly, melted

1 Place a rack in the bottom position and another in the middle position of the oven. Preheat the oven to 375°F. Generously grease a 9-inch round nonstick (gray, not black) tart pan with removable sides or a 10 × 6-inch rectangular nonstick (gray, not black) tart pan with removable sides.

2 Make the crust: In a food processor, blend all crust ingredients until crumbly. Press the crust evenly with your fingers into the prepared pan; set aside.

3 Make the filling: In the same food processor, process the almonds to a fine meal. Add the sugar, butter, salt, egg, vanilla, and almond extract and process until thoroughly blended. With a wet spatula, spread the filling evenly in the crust.

4 Peel the pears; cut each pear in half lengthwise and remove core and stem. Place each half on the cutting board, cut side down, and slice crosswise into ¼-inch slices. Arrange the pear slices close together on the filling, either in concentric circles in the round tart pan or in two long rows in the rectangular pan. Gently brush the pears with the melted jelly.

5 Bake 15 minutes on the bottom rack of the oven. Move the pan to the middle rack and bake 30 minutes more, covering the top with foil if it browns too quickly. Remove from oven and cool completely on a wire rack.

Rhubarb Meringue Tart

MAKES 6 SERVINGS

Some might call this a bar since it's quite thin, but I think of it as a very thin pie. It's a nice alternative to rhubarb pie. This dessert was served at my baby shower many years ago and I will always associate it with a very happy time in my life.

CRUST

1 cup Carol's Sorghum Blend (page x)

2 tablespoons sugar

¼ cup (½ stick) unsalted butter or buttery spread, such as Earth Balance, at room temperature

½ teaspoon xanthan gum

¼ teaspoon salt

FILLING

2 large eggs (reserve whites for meringue, see below)

1 tablespoon cornstarch

⅓ cup sugar

1 cup rhubarb, finely diced

½ teaspoon pure vanilla extract

1 drop red food coloring (optional)

MERINGUE

2 large egg whites, at room temperature (separated from egg yolks, above)

⅛ teaspoon cream of tartar

2 tablespoons superfine sugar

½ teaspoon pure vanilla extract

1 Place a rack in the bottom position and another in the middle position of the oven. Preheat the oven to 350°F. Generously grease a 9-inch round nonstick (gray, not black) springform pan.

2 Make the crust: In a food processor, blend all crust ingredients until crumbly. Press evenly into the pan.

3 Bake 10 to 15 minutes on the bottom rack of the oven or until the crust is lightly browned at the edges. Remove from oven and cool 15 minutes on a wire rack. Leave the oven on.

4 Make the filling: In a heavy, nonreactive saucepan, combine the egg yolks, cornstarch, sugar, and rhubarb. Cook over medium heat until the mixture thickens, about 5 minutes. Add the vanilla extract and red food coloring, if using. Spread the filling over the cooled crust.

5 Make the meringue: Increase the oven to 425°F. In a medium bowl, beat egg whites and cream of tartar with an electric mixer on medium speed until foamy. Continue beating, adding sugar a tablespoon at a time, just until stiff peaks form. Gently stir in vanilla.

6 Spread the meringue over the rhubarb, making attractive dips and swirls and making sure the meringue touches the crust all around its edge. Place pan on the middle rack of the oven. Bake

5 to 8 minutes, or until the meringue is light golden brown. Browning time varies with different ovens—watch carefully so it doesn't burn. Remove and cool for 1 hour on a wire rack. Refrigerate 2 to 3 hours. Let stand at room temperature for 20 minutes before serving.

Rustic Plum Almond Tart

MAKES 6 SERVINGS

You can have all the wonderful components of pie in this tart, but without as much work. This is a rustic treat—beautiful in its simplicity. The glaze is important because it provides a lovely sheen to the fruit.

Basic Pastry Crust dough for a 9-inch pie, single crust (page 587)

1 teaspoon almond-flavored extract

1 can (8 ounces) almond paste, such as Love'n Bake or homemade Almond Paste (page 678)

10 fresh Italian or prune plums, pitted and halved

¼ teaspoon ground cinnamon

⅛ teaspoon salt

1 egg white, for egg wash

3 tablespoons sugar

1 Place a rack in the middle of the oven. Preheat the oven to 375°F. Line a 13 × 9-inch nonstick (gray, not black) baking sheet with parchment paper.

2 Prepare the single-crust pastry dough as directed in Step 1 on page 587, adding the almond extract before blending the ingredients in the food processor. Lay a wet paper towel on flat surface. Place sheet of heavy-duty, premium plastic wrap on top and then roll pastry dough between two sheets of plastic wrap to 10-inch diameter. Remove top plastic wrap sheet and then invert pie crust onto baking sheet. Remove plastic wrap.

3 Place almond paste between same two sheets of plastic wrap and roll to 8-inch diameter. Place almond paste in center of pie crust. Arrange plums, cut side down, on almond paste. Roll edges of pie crust toward center of pie and crimp or flute edges. Pie crust may break or tear, but simply press broken pieces together. Sprinkle cinnamon and salt over plums. Brush crust with beaten egg white. Sprinkle 2 tablespoons of sugar over plums and the remaining tablespoon on the pie crust.

4 Bake 30 minutes or until the crust is browned and the plums are tender. Remove from oven and cool 20 minutes on a wire rack.

Plum-Cream Cheese Tart

MAKES 6 SERVINGS

Make this delightful tart in summer when plums are plentiful and at their best. The crust bakes up like a crisp cookie, which complements the creamy cheese filling and delectable plums. Be sure the plums are ripe, but not soft or their juices will overwhelm the filling.

CRUST

1 cup Carol's Sorghum Blend (page x)

¾ cup tapioca flour

½ cup sweet rice flour

2 tablespoons sugar

2 teaspoons lemon zest

2 teaspoons xanthan gum

½ teaspoon salt

¼ teaspoon baking soda

½ cup shortening, such as Crisco, Earth Balance, or Spectrum Vegetable

½ cup 1% milk (cow's, rice, soy, potato, or nut)

1 large egg, at room temperature

FILLING

1 package (8 ounces) cream cheese or cream cheese alternative, such as Tofutti, at room temperature

¼ cup sugar, divided

2 teaspoons lemon zest

1 teaspoon pure vanilla extract

1 teaspoon almond extract

5 small, ripe but firm plums, pitted and thinly sliced (10 slices per plum)

¼ cup apple jelly

1 Place a rack in the bottom position and another in the middle position of the oven. Preheat the oven to 325°F.

2 Make the crust: In a food processor, combine sorghum blend, flours, sugar, lemon zest, xanthan gum, salt, baking soda, and shortening. Pulse a few times to blend ingredients. Add milk and pulse a few times to blend, then process on high until mixture forms a ball. Remove dough and knead a few times with hands to form soft ball. Place half of dough in heavy-duty food storage bag and refrigerate or freeze for another use.

3 Shape remaining half of dough into flat disk and place on center of parchment paper. Cover with sheet of heavy-duty plastic wrap. Roll dough to 10-inch circle. Remove top plastic wrap and invert crust, centering it over a 9-inch nonstick (gray, not black) pie pan. Remove remaining plastic wrap and press into place. If dough is hard to handle press entire bottom crust in place with your fingers. Flute rim decoratively, pushing dough down the edges of pan a bit to make more shallow crust.

4 Place egg in a mixing bowl. Dip pastry brush into egg white and brush crust. Prick bottom of crust with fork a few times. Leave egg in bowl.

5 Bake 10 minutes on bottom rack of oven or until just lightly browned. Remove from oven and cool crust slightly in the pan on a wire rack.

6 While crust is baking, make the filling: In the mixing bowl with the egg, add cream cheese, 3 tablespoons sugar, lemon zest, vanilla extract, and almond extract and beat with electric mixer on medium-low to thoroughly combine. Spread evenly over baked crust, making edges a bit higher to contain any plum juices. Arrange plum slices in concentric circles over cheese. Sprinkle with remaining tablespoon of sugar.

7 Bake 15 minutes on the middle rack or until the crust is completely browned. Remove from oven and cool 10 minutes on a wire rack. In a small bowl, melt the jelly in the microwave on high until melted and gently brush it over the plums to give them a nice sheen. Cool and then serve at room temperature.

Rustic Nectarine Frangipane Tart Ⓥ

MAKES 6 SERVINGS

A frangipane (frahn-gee-PAH-ne) consists of an almond filling or batter, usually baked in a sweet pastry crust with fruit on top. The flavor of almonds and nectarines just naturally go together. An added bonus to using nectarines is that you don't have to peel them, and their lovely red skin is especially pretty in this tart.

Basic Pastry Crust dough for a 9-inch pie, single crust (page 587)

1 can (8 ounces) almond paste, such as Love'n Bake, or homemade Almond Paste, page 678

4 firm, ripe nectarines, pitted and cut in ¼-inch wedges

1 teaspoon almond extract

¼ teaspoon salt

3 tablespoons sugar, divided

⅓ cup apple jelly, melted

1 tablespoon water

1 Place a rack in the bottom position and another in the middle position of the oven. Preheat the oven to 375°F. Have a 13 × 9-inch nonstick (gray, not black) baking sheet ready.

2 Prepare the single-crust pastry dough as directed in Step 1 on page 587. Then, lay a wet paper towel on a flat surface such as the countertop. Place a sheet of parchment paper on the countertop and then roll the pie crust dough between the parchment paper and a sheet of heavy duty plastic wrap to a 10-inch diameter. Remove the top sheet of plastic wrap and slide the parchment paper (with the pie crust on it) onto the baking sheet.

3 Place the almond paste between two sheets of plastic wrap and roll it to an 8-inch diameter. Remove one of the sheets of plastic wrap, invert the almond paste over the crust, and put in the center of the pie crust. Remove the plastic wrap.

4 Toss the nectarines with the almond extract and the salt. Arrange the slices in a concentric circle (or pattern of your choice) on the almond paste. Roll or push the edges of the pie crust toward center of pie and crimp or flute edges. The pie crust may break or tear; simply press the tears together. Sprinkle 2 tablespoons of sugar over the nectarines and the remaining tablespoon on the pie crust.

5 Bake 15 minutes on the bottom rack of the oven. Move to the middle rack of the oven and bake 15 minutes more, or until the pie crust is browned and the nectarines are tender. Remove from oven. Combine the melted apple jelly with water and brush on the nectarines and the pie crust. Cool completely on a wire rack.

Summer Raspberry Cream Tart Ⓥ

MAKES 6 SERVINGS

Make this gorgeous tart in the summer when fresh raspberries are in season. Choose the best raspberries—all of a similar size—and showcase them on the delectable almond cream. If your raspberries are different sizes, you can just scatter them randomly over the almond cream.

CRUST

1 cup Carol's Sorghum Blend (page x)

¼ cup (½ stick) unsalted butter or buttery spread, such as Earth Balance, at room temperature

2 tablespoons sugar

¼ teaspoon xanthan gum

¼ teaspoon salt

1 egg yolk + 1 tablespoon water for egg wash

FILLING

½ cup sugar

2 tablespoons cornstarch

⅛ teaspoon salt

1 cup 1% milk (cow's, rice, soy, potato, or nut)

2 large egg yolks

½ teaspoon almond extract

3 containers (6 ounces each) fresh raspberries, washed and patted dry with paper towels

3 tablespoons apple jelly or red currant jelly

1 Place a rack in the bottom position of the oven. Preheat the oven to 375°F. Generously grease a 9-inch, nonstick (gray, not black) tart pan with removable sides or 9-inch nonstick (gray, not black) pie pan.

2 Make the crust: In a food processor, blend the crust ingredients except for the egg wash, just until crumbly. Press it evenly on the bottom and up the sides of the pan. Brush the entire crust with the egg wash.

3 Bake 5 to 10 minutes on the bottom rack, or until the crust is firm, slightly fragrant, and the edges just start to brown. Remove from oven and cool the crust on a wire rack.

4 Make the filling: In a medium-heavy saucepan, whisk together the sugar, cornstarch, and salt. In a small bowl, whisk together the milk and egg yolks until smooth and whisk into the saucepan.

5 Cook the filling over medium heat, whisking constantly, until the mixture boils, then thickens and becomes much harder to whisk. Stir in the almond extract. Transfer the filling to a shallow bowl, press plastic wrap directly on the surface, and chill 2 hours.

6 Remove the plastic wrap from the chilled filling and spread it evenly in the crust with a spatula. Top with the raspberries, starting from the center and working out to the edge of the tart in neat, concentric circles. Melt the jelly in a small bowl in the microwave on medium until melted and gently brush it over the raspberries. Chill the tart 15 minutes or until the jelly firms up. Serve at room temperature. Refrigerate leftovers.

Apple-Cranberry Galette

MAKES 6 SERVINGS

A galette is a free-form pie, rather than one that is fitted into a pie pan. If the crust breaks or doesn't look perfect don't worry—it is supposed to look rustic and casually formed, rather than perfectly shaped.

Basic Pastry Crust dough for a 9-inch pie, single crust (page 587)

2 large apples, peeled, cored, and cut in ¼-inch slices

½ cup dried cranberries

2 tablespoons sugar, divided

¼ cup chopped walnuts

¼ teaspoon ground cinnamon

2 tablespoons fresh lemon juice

2 tablespoons corn syrup

1 teaspoon boiling water

1 Place a rack in the middle of the oven. Preheat the oven to 375°F. Have a 13×9-inch nonstick (gray, not black) rimmed baking sheet ready.

2 Prepare the single-crust pastry dough as directed in Step 1 on page 587. Freeze one of the disks for another use. Then, massage the remaining disk of dough until it is smooth and pliable. Place a 13 × 9-inch sheet of parchment paper on a flat surface such as the countertop and lightly dust it with white rice flour. Place the dough on the paper and cover it with a sheet of heavy-duty plastic wrap anchored on a wet paper towel to prevent slippage.

3 With a rolling pin, roll the dough to a 10-inch circle, ⅛-inch thick. Transfer the parchment paper, with the crust and plastic wrap on it, to the baking sheet. Remove the plastic wrap.

4 In a large bowl, toss the apple slices, cranberries, 1 tablespoon of the sugar, nuts, cinnamon, and lemon juice and arrange the mixture in the center of the pie crust but no closer than 2 inches from the edge. With a thin metal spatula, lift up the sides of the crust slightly and gently flip it toward the center, covering the filling by about 1 inch. Overlap the crust slightly as you work around the circle of the crust, gently lifting it up and toward the center of the pie. If the crust breaks, simply press it together with your fingers.

5 Bake 20 minutes. Whisk the corn syrup and water together and brush it on the crust. Sprinkle the remaining tablespoon of sugar on the crust and over the apple filling. Bake 15 to 20 minutes more, or until the crust is golden brown and the apples are tender. Cool the galette 20 minutes on a wire rack. Serve warm or at room temperature.

Peach Tarte Tatin

MAKES 6 SERVINGS

Make this dessert in late summer when fresh peaches are at their best. I prefer to leave the skins on fruit desserts because I like the texture, the nutrients, and the color that the skins lend to the final dish. But you may peel the peaches if you wish.

½ cup + 1 tablespoon sugar

2 tablespoons water

2 teaspoons fresh lemon juice

⅛ teaspoon salt

1 tablespoon unsalted butter or buttery spread, such as Earth Garden

1 teaspoon almond extract

7 fresh medium peaches

Basic Pastry Crust dough for a 9-inch pie, single crust (page 587)

1 egg yolk whisked with 1 tablespoon water, for egg wash

1 Place a rack in the middle of the oven. Preheat the oven to 375°F. In a heavy 10-inch ovenproof skillet, whisk together ½ cup of the sugar, water, lemon juice, and salt. Cook 2 minutes over medium heat, or until the mixture turns a light gold. Swirl the pan occasionally, but do not stir. Remove the skillet from the heat and stir in the butter and almond extract. Cool slightly.

2 Pit and quarter 6 of the peaches and half of the seventh peach. Place remaining ½ peach in the center of the skillet, cut side down, and arrange the peach quarters decoratively around it. Return the skillet to medium heat and cook about 10 minutes or until the mixture is bubbly, but do not stir. Remove from heat.

3 Make the single-crust pastry dough as directed in Step 1 on page 587. Freeze one of the disks for another use. Then, massage the remaining disk between your hands until it is warm and pliable.

Roll the dough between two sheets of heavy-duty plastic wrap, anchored on a wet paper towel to prevent slippage. Remove the top layer of plastic wrap and trim the crust to a 10-inch circle. Center the rolled crust over the skillet before removing the top layer of plastic wrap. Press the dough down on the peaches and around the edges of the skillet. Brush it with the egg wash and sprinkle with the remaining tablespoon of sugar.

4 Bake 20 to 25 minutes, or until the crust is lightly browned and firm. Cool the skillet 10 minutes on a wire rack. Place a serving platter, top down, on the skillet. Using both hands and oven mitts, carefully invert the tart onto the serving plate. Cool 10 minutes more or until the peaches have firmed up. Serve warm.

Plum Tatin

MAKES 6 SERVINGS

This is more like an upside-down plum cake. The yummy caramel sauce surrounding the plums will simply melt in your mouth. For added decadence, serve with a dollop of sweetened crème fraîche or homemade Basic Whipped Cream (page 624), but the powdered sugar dusting works very well, too.

12 fresh Italian or prune plums, pitted and halved

1½ cups sugar, divided

⅓ cup water

½ cup unsalted butter or buttery spread, such as Earth Balance, at room temperature

2 large eggs, at room temperature

1½ cups Carol's Sorghum Blend (page x)

1 teaspoon xanthan gum

½ teaspoon salt

¼ teaspoon baking powder

¼ teaspoon baking soda

¾ cup well-shaken buttermilk or homemade Buttermilk (page 677)

1 teaspoon pure vanilla extract

½ teaspoon almond extract

2 tablespoons powdered sugar, for dusting

1 Place a rack in the middle of the oven. Preheat the oven to 350°F. Generously grease a 9-inch round nonstick (gray, not black) pie pan and arrange the plums in the dish, cut side up.

2 In a small saucepan, make the caramel sauce. Combine ¾ cup of the sugar and water and cook over high heat until it turns a warm amber color. Swirl the pan, but do not stir the caramel sauce. Pour it evenly over the plums. If any of the plums become dislodged, rearrange them with a fork (not your fingers, since the caramel will be very hot).

3 In a large mixing bowl, beat the butter with an electric mixer on medium speed until smooth. Gradually beat in the remaining ¾ cup of sugar until smooth. Add the eggs, one at a time, beating well after each addition.

4 In another bowl, sift together the sorghum blend, xanthan gum, salt, baking powder, and baking soda. In a measuring cup, whisk together the buttermilk, vanilla, and almond extract. With the mixer on low speed, beat the sorghum mixture into the egg mixture, alternating with the buttermilk mixture, beginning and ending with the sorghum mixture.

5 Pour the batter evenly over the plums and bake 30 to 40 minutes until a cake tester comes out clean. Cool the cake in the pan 15 minutes; invert the cake onto a flat serving plate. If a plum becomes dislodged, replace it. Dust with powdered sugar. Serve warm or at room temperature.

ICE CREAM PIES

Frozen Margarita Pie

MAKES 10 SERVINGS

The crunchy saltiness of the pretzel crust is a perfect complement to the sweet, smooth, creamy margarita filling. I take this dessert to neighborhood parties during the summer and it disappears in a flash.

CRUST

2 cups (4 ounces) gluten-free pretzels, such as Ener-G or Glutano

⅓ cup sugar

¼ cup (½ stick) unsalted butter or buttery spread, such as Earth Balance, melted

¼ teaspoon salt (taste first before adding)

FILLING

1 can (14 to 15 ounces) sweetened condensed milk (not evaporated milk)

2 tablespoons fresh lime juice

2 tablespoons fresh orange juice or orange liquer, such as Triple Sec

1 tablespoon grated lime zest

1 tablespoon tequila (optional)

3 cups homemade Basic Whipped Cream (page 624) or whipped topping, such as Lucerne or Soyatoo

GARNISH

1 tablespoon grated lime zest

1 whole lime, cut in 10 thin slices

10 pretzels, gently crushed

1 Coat a 9-inch glass pie plate with cooking spray. Make pretzel crust: In food processor, process pretzels and sugar until pretzels resemble medium-size crumbs. Add melted butter and salt, if using, and process until crumbs are coated with butter. Press crumbs onto bottom of pie plate and up the sides, then freeze.

2 Wipe out food processor with paper towels. Make margarita filling: Add sweetened condensed milk, lime juice, orange juice, lime zest, and tequila and process until smooth. Set aside.

3 In a medium bowl, place 2 cups of the whipped cream. Gently fold in the margarita filling and spread in the frozen pretzel crust. Return the pie to the freezer, uncovered, for 5 or 6 hours. Then wrap tightly in plastic wrap until serving time.

4 When ready to serve, let pie sit at room temperature 10 minutes. Cut the pie into 10 slices. Garnish each with a tablespoon of the reserved whipped cream, a dusting of grated lime zest, a slice of lime, and a sprinkle of crushed pretzels.

Frozen Strawberry Margarita Pie: Fold 1½ cups diced fresh strawberries into the margarita filling just before spreading it in the crust in Step 3 above.

Cappuccino Ice Cream Pie with Chocolate Sauce Ⓥ

MAKES 6 SERVINGS

The simplicity of this pie belies its stunning presentation. Assembling the pie is quite easy, but the layers have to freeze as they're created, so be sure to plan ahead and allow enough time.

CRUST

½ cup pine nuts or slivered almonds

¾ cup Carol's Sorghum Blend (page x)

½ cup powdered sugar

¼ cup unsweetened cocoa powder (Dutch-process or natural cocoa)

¼ teaspoon salt

6 tablespoons unsalted butter or buttery spread, such as Earth Balance, chilled and cut into 12 pieces

2 large egg yolks, slightly beaten

Water, if needed

FILLING

1 pint gluten-free chocolate ice cream, such as Ben & Jerry's, Dreyer's Grand, Edy's, or Häagen-Dazs, slightly softened

1 pint gluten-free coffee ice cream, such as Ben & Jerry's, Edy's, or Starbucks, slightly softened

Homemade Chocolate Sauce (page 622), divided

1 Make the crust: In a food processor, process the nuts until finely ground. Add the sorghum blend, powdered sugar, cocoa, and salt and pulse a few times. Add the butter and pulse until the texture resembles coarse cornmeal, about 10 to 15 seconds. With the motor running, add the egg yolks and process until mixture forms a ball or several clumps. If the dough seems dry, add water 1 tablespoon at a time and pulse to mix. Remove the dough from the food processor and knead with your hands until smooth.

2 Press the dough evenly with your fingers into a 9-inch round nonstick (gray, not black) pie pan and refrigerate 1 hour. Place a rack in the middle of the oven. Preheat the oven to 375°F. Bake the chilled crust 10 to 12 minutes or until just set. Watch the crust carefully so it doesn't burn. Cool the crust 15 minutes on a wire rack.

3 Make the filling: Spread the chocolate ice cream evenly in the pie crust. Freeze 30 minutes. Spoon ½ cup of the chocolate sauce evenly over the ice cream. Freeze 15 minutes. Spread the coffee ice cream over the chocolate sauce. Freeze 30 minutes. Serve frozen with the remaining chocolate sauce drizzled over each slice.

Individual Chocolate Baked Alaskas Ⓥ

MAKES 6 SERVINGS

Although you can make a single large Baked Alaska and cut it into serving pieces, I like each guest to have his or her own personal one. You can vary the basic idea of Baked Alaska by choosing your own flavors of cake and ice cream. In addition to the chocolate combinations here, try other flavor combinations like vanilla pound cake with strawberry ice cream, or gingerbread with lemon sorbet. Refrigerate leftover egg yolks for 2 to 4 days and use in puddings, custards, or zabaglione. If you don't want to use fresh egg whites, use Just Desserts egg white powder and follow the manufacturer's directions.

Homemade Chocolate Brownies (page 442)

1 pint gluten-free chocolate ice cream, such as Ben & Jerry's, Dreyer's Grand, Edy's, or Häagen-Daaz, slightly softened

8 large egg whites or powdered egg whites to equal 8 egg whites, such as Just Whites

Pinch salt

¾ cup sugar

1 Prepare the brownies. Then, line a 13 × 9-inch baking sheet with foil or parchment paper. Using a 2½-inch round cookie cutter, cut the brownies into 6 rounds and place the rounds at least 2 inches apart on the sheet. Cover the sheet tightly with plastic wrap and freeze 30 minutes.

2 Top each brownie round with a scoop of ice cream (about ⅓ cup), then freeze, covered, just until the ice cream is hard, about 30 minutes. Or, slice the ice cream into rounds that fit the brownie tops.

3 Place a rack in the middle of the oven. Preheat the oven to 450°F. In a large mixing bowl, beat the egg whites and salt with an electric mixer on high speed until they reach the soft peak stage. Add the sugar a little at a time, beating at high speed, and continue beating until the whites reach the stiff peak stage, about 5 minutes in a standing mixer or about 12 minutes with a hand-held mixer.

4 Remove the baking sheet from the freezer. Working quickly, spread the meringue on the ice cream and cake, mounding it on top and covering the ice cream and cake completely. Make attractive dips and swirls with a spatula.

5 Immediately bake 6 minutes or until the meringues are golden brown. With a thin spatula, quickly transfer each Baked Alaska to a serving plate and serve immediately.

Orange Butter Ice Cream Pie

MAKES 6 SERVINGS

I've been making this ice cream pie for many summers and it remains a family favorite. You make this in stages, freezing each layer before adding the next one. Start making it a day or two ahead to give you enough time to complete all of the different stages.

1 quart gluten-free vanilla ice cream, such as Ben & Jerry's, Dryers Grand, or Häagen-Dasz or homemade Vanilla Ice Cream (page 657), softened

Basic Pastry Crust for a 9-inch pie, single crust (page 587), baked

ORANGE BUTTER

⅓ cup unsalted butter or buttery spread, such as Earth Balance

½ cup sugar

⅓ cup orange juice concentrate

3 large eggs, separated (reserve whites for meringue, below)

Grated zest of 2 oranges

Grated zest of 2 lemons

¼ teaspoon salt

MERINGUE

3 large egg whites, at room temperature (separated from egg yolks, above)

¼ teaspoon cream of tartar

¼ teaspoon salt

⅓ cup sugar

1 Prepare the single-crust pastry dough as directed in Step 1 on page 587. Use an ice cream scoop to layer half of the ice cream on bottom of the baked pie shell. With a spatula, press the ice cream scoops together to cover the bottom evenly. Freeze until hard.

2 Make the orange butter: In the top of a double boiler, combine the butter, sugar, orange juice concentrate, egg yolks, orange zest, lemon zest, and salt. Cook over simmering water, beating constantly with wire whisk, until mixture thickens. Remove from heat. Cool, covered, in refrigerator until firm.

3 Spread half of the orange butter over frozen ice cream. Freeze until hard.

4 Spread remaining half of ice cream over the orange butter. Freeze until hard.

5 Top with the remaining orange butter. Freeze until hard.

6 Place a rack in the middle of the oven. Preheat the oven to 475°F.

7 Make the meringue: Beat the reserved egg whites with an electric mixer on low speed until foamy. Add the cream of tartar and salt, increase the speed to high, and beat until soft peaks form. Beat in the sugar, 1 tablespoon at a time, until the meringue is smooth and glossy.

8 Spread the meringue over top of frozen pie, using a spatula to make attractive dips and swirls. Make sure the edges of the meringue touch the pie crust. Place pie on a baking sheet.

9 Bake 3 to 5 minutes or until the meringue is browned. Freeze immediately. Remove the pie from the freezer 5 minutes before serving.

Pineapple Icebox Dessert

MAKES 8 SERVINGS

Desserts like as this one were classics when I was growing up. You can use any type of cookies you like, including your own homemade versions.

CRUST

1 package (9 cookies) gluten-free cookies, such as Pamela's Lemon Shortbread, or homemade Graham Crackers (page 433), divided

2 tablespoons unsalted butter or buttery spread, such as Earth Balance, at room temperature

FILLING

½ cup sugar

2 tablespoons cornstarch

1 large can (14 to 15 ounces) crushed pineapple, including juice

TOPPING

2 cups homemade Basic Whipped Cream (page 624) or whipped topping, such as Lucerne or Soyatoo

1½ cups miniature marshmallows

1 Generously butter an 11 × 7-inch baking dish. Make the crust: In a food processor, process the cookies until finely ground. Add the butter and blend until crumbly. Press all but ½ cup of the mixture evenly on the bottom and ½ inch up the sides of the baking dish; set aside.

2 Make the filling: In a medium-heavy saucepan, whisk together the sugar and cornstarch until blended. Add the crushed pineapple and its juice and cook over medium-low heat, whisking constantly, until the mixture thickens. Pour the hot filling evenly on the crumb crust. Refrigerate 30 minutes or until the filling is firm.

3 Make the topping: In a medium bowl, place the whipped cream and stir in the marshmallows. Spread it evenly on top of the pineapple filling. Sprinkle with the remaining cookie crumbs. Refrigerate 2 hours or until firm. Refrigerate leftovers.

NUT PIES

Pecan Pie

MAKES 6 SERVINGS

This is perhaps my favorite pie because I love pecans and caramel flavors. I've streamlined the recipe to make it super-easy for you. A food processor makes short work of the filling.

Basic Pastry Crust dough for a 9-inch pie, single crust (page 587)

1 egg, beaten to a foam, for egg wash

2 cups pecan halves

½ cup homemade Basic Whipped Cream (page 624) or whipped topping, such as Lucerne or Soyatoo, for garnish

FILLING

1 cup packed dark brown sugar

4 large eggs, at room temperature

2 cups dark (or light) corn syrup

2 tablespoons unsalted butter or buttery spread, such as Earth Balance, at room temperature

2 tablespoons cornstarch

1 tablespoon pure vanilla extract

¼ teaspoon salt

1 Place a rack in the bottom position and another in the middle position of oven. Preheat the oven to 375°F. Prepare the single-crust pastry dough as directed in Step 1 on page 587. Freeze half of the dough for another use. Then fit the remaining half into a 9-inch nonstick (gray, not black) pie pan, as directed in Steps 2 and 3 on page 587. Flute the edges decoratively as instructed for a single-crust pie. Brush outer edges of crust with beaten egg to encourage browning. Arrange pecan halves on bottom of pie crust.

2 Make the filling: In a food processor, combine filling ingredients and blend until thoroughly combined. Pour mixture over pecans in pie shell. Place pie pan on nonstick (gray, not black) baking sheet and place baking sheet on bottom rack of oven.

3 Bake 20 minutes on bottom rack of oven. Move pie to middle rack and continue baking for 30 to 35

minutes more or until filling is set. If crust starts to brown too quickly, cover with aluminum foil.

4 Remove pie and cool completely on wire rack before cutting. Refrigerate for at least 1 hour before serving to make sure pie is firm enough to cut. Cut into 8 slices. Serve with a generous tablespoon of whipped cream.

Chocolate Pecan Tart

MAKES 8 SERVINGS

A tart is generally shorter in height than a pie, so consider this tart like a thin pecan pie. There is a hint of chocolate here, for added decadence. Serve this with a dollop of whipped cream.

Basic Pastry Crust dough for a 9-inch pie, single crust (page 587)

1 egg, beaten to a foam, for egg wash

1 cup chopped pecans

⅔ cup gluten-free chocolate chips, such as Tropical Source

½ cup homemade Basic Whipped Cream (page 624) or whipped topping, such as Lucerne or Soyatoo, for garnish

FILLING

½ cup light corn syrup

¼ cup packed dark brown sugar

2 large eggs, at room temperature

2 tablespoons unsalted butter or buttery spread, such as Earth Balance, melted

1 tablespoon pure vanilla extract

¼ teaspoon salt

1 Place a rack in the bottom position and another in the middle position of the oven. Preheat the oven to 375°F. Prepare the single-crust pastry dough as directed in Step 1 on page 587. Freeze half of the dough for another use, then fit the remaining half into a 9-inch nonstick (gray, not black) pie pan, as directed in Steps 2 and 3 on page 587. Flute the edges decoratively, as instructed, for a single-crust pie. Brush the outer edges of the crust with beaten egg. Arrange the pecans and chocolate chips on the bottom of the crust.

2 Make the filling: In a medium bowl, beat the filling ingredients with an electric mixer on low speed until thoroughly blended and very smooth.

3 Pour the mixture into the crust. Place the tart pan on a baking sheet.

4 Bake 10 minutes on bottom rack of the oven. Lay a sheet of foil over the pie and move to the middle rack and continue baking 15 to 20 minutes more or until the filling is set.

5 Remove from oven and cool completely on a wire rack. Refrigerate at least 1 hour before serving to make sure the pie is firm enough to cut. Serve each slice garnished with a tablespoon of whipped cream.

Bourbon-Laced Mocha Walnut Pie Ⓥ

MAKES 8 SERVINGS

Nut pies are always decadent, but I dressed this one up a bit to include bourbon and chocolate, so it will hit the spot when you are going all out. If you prefer not to use bourbon, you may use white wine or hot coffee instead.

Basic Pastry Crust dough for a 9-inch pie, single crust (page 587)
1 egg, beaten to a foam for egg wash
2 cups chopped walnuts
½ cup gluten-free chocolate chips, such Tropical Source

FILLING
¼ cup packed dark brown sugar
1 tablespoon instant espresso powder
2 large eggs, at room temperature
½ cup corn syrup (dark or light)
2 tablespoons unsalted butter or buttery spread, such as Earth Balance, softened
1 tablespoon cornstarch
2 tablespoons bourbon, white wine, or hot coffee
1 teaspoon pure vanilla extract
¼ teaspoon salt

1 Place a rack in the bottom position and another in the middle position of the oven. Preheat the oven to 375°F. Prepare the single-crust pastry dough as directed in Step 1 on page 587. Freeze half of the dough for another use, then fit the remaining half into a 9-inch nonstick (gray, not black) pie pan, as directed in Steps 2 and 3 on page 587. Flute the edges decoratively, as instructed, for a single crust pie. Brush outer edges of crust with egg wash and arrange the walnuts and chocolate chips on the bottom of the pie crust.

2 Make the filling: In a medium bowl, beat filling ingredients with an electric mixer on low speed until thoroughly combined and very smooth. Pour mixture into pie shell. Place pie pan on nonstick (gray, not black) baking sheet and place baking sheet on bottom rack of oven.

3 Bake 10 minutes on the bottom rack of the oven. Lay a sheet of foil over the pie and move it to the middle rack and continue baking 15 to 20 minutes more or until the filling is set.

4 Remove from oven and cool completely on a wire rack. Refrigerate for at least 1 hour before serving to make sure pie is firm enough to cut.

Pine Nut Pie with Chocolate Sauce Ⓥ

MAKES 8 SERVINGS

Pine nuts come from the piñon, *or pine tree, and are very popular in Mediterranean and Southwestern cuisines. In Italy, they come from the pignoli tree, but are quite similar and used in the same way in baking.*

1 cup homemade Chocolate Sauce (page 622)
Basic Pastry Crust dough for a 9-inch pie, single crust (page 587)
1 egg, beaten to a foam, for egg wash
2 cups pine nuts

FILLING

½ cup light corn syrup

¼ cup packed dark brown sugar

2 large eggs, at room temperature

2 tablespoons unsalted butter or buttery spread, such as Earth Balance, melted

1 tablespoon pure vanilla extract

¼ teaspoon salt

1 Prepare the chocolate sauce; set aside. Place an oven rack in the bottom position of the oven and another one in the middle position. Preheat the oven to 375°F. Prepare the single-crust pastry dough as directed in Step 1 on page 587. Freeze half of the dough for another use and then fit the remaining half into a 9-inch nonstick (gray, not black) pie pan, as directed in Steps 2 and 3 on page 587. Flute the edges decoratively as instructed, for a single-crust pie. Brush outer edges of crust with egg wash to encourage browning. Arrange the pine nuts on the bottom of the crust.

2 In a medium bowl, beat filling ingredients with an electric mixer on low speed until thoroughly combined and very smooth. Pour mixture over pine nuts. Place pie pan on nonstick (gray, not black) baking sheet and place baking sheet on bottom rack of oven.

3 Bake 10 minutes on the bottom rack of the oven. Lay a sheet of foil over the pie and move it to the middle rack and continue baking for 15 to 20 minutes more or until the filling is set.

4 Cool the pie completely on a wire rack. Refrigerate for at least 1 hour before serving to make sure pie is firm enough to cut. Serve each slice garnished with 2 tablespoons of chocolate sauce.

Macadamia-Walnut Pie

MAKES 8 SERVINGS

Macadamia nuts are native to Australia, but most of us associate them with Hawaii, where they are also grown. They have a rich, buttery flavor and, combined with walnuts, make this pie wonderfully decadent. Make sure the nuts are fresh.

Basic Pastry Crust dough for a 9-inch pie, single crust (page 587)

1 egg, beaten to a foam, for egg wash

1½ cups toasted macadamia nuts (see Toasting Nuts footnote, page 510)

1 cup walnuts

½ cup (1 stick) unsalted butter or buttery spread, such as Earth Balance, at room temperature

½ cup packed light brown sugar

¼ cup corn syrup

1 large egg, at room temperature

1 teaspoon pure vanilla extract

½ teaspoon grated orange zest

¼ teaspoon salt

1 cup homemade Chocolate Sauce (page 622)

1 Place a rack in the bottom position and another in the middle position of the oven. Preheat the oven to 375°F. Prepare the single-crust pastry dough as directed in Step 1 on page 587. Freeze half of the dough for another use and then fit the remaining dough into 9-inch nonstick (gray, not black) pie pan. Flute the edges decoratively, as instructed, for a single crust pie. Brush outer edges of crust with egg wash to encourage browning. Chop the roasted macadamia nuts and walnuts coarsely and arrange them on the bottom of the crust.

2 In a medium bowl, beat the butter, brown sugar, corn syrup, egg, vanilla, orange zest, and salt with an electric mixer on medium speed 1 minute, or until light and fluffy. Pour the mixture into the pan and place on a nonstick (gray, not black) baking sheet.

3 Bake 10 minutes on the bottom rack of the oven. Lay a sheet of foil on top of the pie and move to the middle rack and continue baking 15 to 20 minutes more. The filling will be somewhat soft but firms up when cooled.

4 Cool the pie completely on a wire rack. Refrigerate at least 1 hour before serving to make sure the pie is firm enough to cut. Serve each slice garnished with 2 tablespoons of Chocolate Sauce.

Granola Pie

MAKES 6 SERVINGS

This isn't a pie that uses a granola crust, but the filling is made of granola. You'll love the crunchy texture. I use the Naked Gluten-Free Granola (page 11) recipe from this book. You can add dried fruits to the granola for a fruitier flavor and chewier texture. Rest assured, it's good no matter what type of granola you use.

Basic Pastry Crust for a 9-inch pie, single crust (page 587)

1 cup Naked Gluten-Free Granola† (page 11), divided

½ cup (1 stick) unsalted butter or buttery spread, such as Earth Balance, at room temperature

½ cup packed light brown sugar

½ cup corn syrup (dark or light)

⅛ teaspoon salt

1 teaspoon pure vanilla extract

3 eggs, at room temperature and lightly beaten

¼ cup gluten-free chocolate chips, such as Tropical Source

½ cup homemade Basic Whipped Cream (page 624) or whipped topping, such as Lucerne or Soyatoo, for garnish

1 Place a rack in the bottom position and another in the middle position of the oven. Preheat the oven to 350°F. Prepare the single-crust pastry dough as directed in Step 1 on page 587. Freeze half of the dough for another use. Then, fit the remaining dough into a 9-inch nonstick (gray, not black) pie pan and flute the edges decoratively as directed for a single-crust pie. Place pan in freezer.

2 Place ⅓ cup of granola in food processor and process until finely ground. Add butter, brown sugar, corn syrup, salt, vanilla and eggs until thoroughly blended. Add remaining granola and chocolate chips and pulse just until blended. Remove pie crust from freezer and spread filling in crust. Place pie pan on nonstick (gray, not black) baking sheet.

3 Bake 20 minutes on the bottom rack of oven. Move pie to the middle rack, cover edges with foil to prevent excessive browning, and bake 15 to 20 minutes or until filling is set and crust is golden brown. Remove from oven and cool 30 minutes on wire rack. Serve at room temperature, each slice garnished with a tablespoon of whipped cream. Refrigerate leftovers.

†Check with your physician before using gluten-free oats.

PIE CRUSTS

Cookie Crust

MAKES A 9-INCH PIE CRUST

This incredibly versatile crust is designed for no-bake fillings such as puddings and custards. It works with almost any light-colored basic cookie. If the cookies are especially sweet, use less sugar; if they're not very sweet, such as the Health Valley Rice Bran crackers, use more sugar.

The type of cookies used in cookie crumb crusts affect the browning of the crust and its sweetness. Crusts made with light-colored cookies will visibly brown around the edges of the pan. Darker-colored cookies, such as gingersnaps, may not exhibit visible browning so you need to rely on their fragrance as your cue to remove the crust from the oven. Cookies that are sweeter will brown more quickly because they contain more sugar; those that are less sweet may take longer to brown. Once the crusts starts to brown, it will finish very quickly. The bottom line? Monitor these crusts carefully to prevent burning.

1½ cups plain gluten-free cookie crumbs (about 8 or 9 cookies), such as Ener-G, or homemade Sugar Cookies (page 419) or cookies of choice

1 teaspoon sugar

2 tablespoons unsalted butter or buttery spread, such as Earth Balance, at room temperature but not melted

1 teaspoon pure vanilla extract

1 Place a rack in the middle of the oven. Preheat the oven to 350°F. In a food processor, process the cookies and sugar until the cookies are fine crumbs. Add the butter and vanilla and process until the cookie crumbs are thoroughly coated with butter.

2 Press the crumbs evenly on the bottom and up the sides of a 9-inch nonstick (gray, not black) pan. The edge of the crust should be level with the top of the pie pan. Use the bottom edge of a ¼-cup metal measuring cup to firmly press the crumbs where the bottom of the pan meets the side.

3 Bake 5 to 8 minutes or just until the crust smells fragrant and there is visible browning around the edge of the pan. It can burn easily so remove it from the oven at the first signs and smells of browning. Cool the crust on a wire rack completely before adding the filling.

Nutty Cookie Crumb Crust

MAKES A 9-INCH PIE CRUST

This basic crust pairs perfectly with no-bake fillings, such as chiffon pies or pudding pies. Since pie crusts made from cookies are more likely to burn during long baking times, like some fruit pies or pumpkin pies, I don't recommend using those fillings in cookie crusts. You can vary the nuts and the cookies, making a wonderful array of flavors and textures to complement your choice of filling.

1 cup pecans or walnuts (whole nuts or pieces)

2 tablespoons sugar

¾ cup gluten-free cookies, such as Pamela's Lemon Shortbread or Pecan Shortbread

2 tablespoons unsalted butter or buttery spread, such as Earth Balance, at room temperature, but not melted

1 teaspoon pure vanilla extract

1 Place a rack in the middle of the oven. Preheat the oven to 350°F. In a food processor, process the nuts and sugar until the nuts are finely ground. Add the cookies and process until they are finely ground. Add the butter and vanilla and process until the mixture is crumbly.

2 Press the crumbs evenly on the bottom and up the sides of a 9-inch nonstick (gray, not black) pan. The edge of the crust should be level with the top of the pie pan. Use the bottom edge of a ¼-cup metal measuring cup to firmly press the crumbs where the bottom of the pan meets the side.

3 Bake 5 to 8 minutes or until the crust is fragrant and the edges of the crust just start to brown. Cool the crust on a wire rack completely before adding the filling.

Cream Cheese Pie Crust

MAKES ONE 9-INCH DOUBLE-CRUST PIE CRUST OR TWO 9-INCH SINGLE-CRUST PIE CRUSTS

Use this pie crust for any pie where dairy flavor is desired, such as a cream pies or custard pies. The cream cheese makes the pie crust dough a bit stiffer to roll out, but it tastes great.

1 cup Carol's Sorghum Blend (page x)
¾ cup tapioca flour
½ cup sweet rice flour
3 tablespoons sugar
1 teaspoon xanthan gum
1 teaspoon guar gum
⅛ teaspoon baking soda
½ teaspoon salt
1 package (8 ounces) cream cheese or cream cheese alternative, such as Tofutti, at room temperature
2 tablespoons 1% milk (cow's, rice, soy, potato, or nut)
1 teaspoon cider vinegar or lemon juice
1 egg yolk whisked in 1 tablespoon cold water for egg wash

1 In a food processor, place the sorghum blend, tapioca, sweet rice flour, 2 tablespoons of the sugar, xanthan gum, guar gum, baking soda, and salt and process to blend thoroughly. Add the cream cheese and butter and process until the mixture is crumbly. With the motor running, add the milk gradually and blend until the dough forms a ball. If it doesn't form a ball, use a spatula to break up the dough into pieces and process again, scraping down sides if necessary. Remove dough from food processor and knead with hands until smooth. Shape the dough into two 1-inch-thick disks, wrap tightly with plastic wrap, and refrigerate 1 hour.

For a Single-Crust Pie:

2 Massage a disk of dough between your hands until it is warm and pliable, making the crust easier to handle. Roll to a 10-inch circle between two pieces of heavy-duty plastic wrap dusted with rice flour. (Use a damp paper towel between countertop and plastic wrap to anchor plastic.) Move the rolling pin from the center of the dough to the outer edge, moving around the circle in clockwise fashion to assure uniform thickness.

3 Remove the top plastic wrap and invert the crust, centering it over a 9-inch nonstick (gray, not black) pie pan. Remove the remaining plastic wrap and press into place. Trim the edges to an even over-hang all around the pan.

For a Double-Crust Filled Pie

4 Follow Steps 1, 2, and 3. Add filling as directed in your recipe. Roll remaining disk of dough to 10-inch circle, invert, and center on the filled crust. Don't remove the top plastic wrap until the dough is centered. Trim the top crust to the same over-hang as bottom crust. Press the two crusts together and shape a decorative edge around rim of pie plate. Freeze 15 minutes. Brush with beaten egg for glossier crust. Sprinkle with remaining tablespoon of sugar. Prick the top crust several times with a fork to allow the steam to escape. Place the pan on a nonstick baking sheet.

5 Place a rack in the bottom position and another in the middle position of the oven. Preheat the oven to 375°F. Bake 15 minutes on the bottom position to brown bottom crust. Move to middle position and bake 25 to 35 minutes more or until the top crust is nicely browned. Cover loosely with foil if the edges brown too much. Cool completely on a wire rack before cutting.

Basic Pastry Crust for Single- or Double-Crust Pies (V)

MAKES ONE 9-INCH DOUBLE-CRUST PIE
CRUST OR TWO 9-INCH SINGLE-CRUST
PIE CRUSTS

This will be your go-to crust for any pie that calls for a pastry crust. Keep a supply of Carol's Sorghum Blend (page x) on hand so you're always ready to bake a pie crust. It is very simple to work with and is very soft, supple, and pliable, so it drapes over the pie pan easily. If it does break, simply press the tear with your fingers to mend it. If you only need enough pie dough for a single-crust pie, freeze the remaining half for another pie.

1 cup Carol's Sorghum Blend (page x)

¾ cup tapioca flour

½ cup sweet rice flour

3 tablespoons sugar, divided

1 teaspoon xanthan gum

1 teaspoon guar gum

½ teaspoon salt

⅛ teaspoon baking soda

½ cup shortening, such as Crisco or Spectrum Vegetable, or buttery sticks, such as Earth Balance*

½ cup 1% milk (cow's, rice, soy, potato, or nut)

1 teaspoon vinegar or lemon juice

1 egg white beaten with 1 tablespoon water for egg wash (optional)

1 Place the sorghum blend, tapioca flour, sweet rice flour, 2 tablespoons of the sugar, xanthan gum, guar gum, salt, baking soda, and shortening in a food processor and process until crumbly. Add the milk and vinegar and process until the dough forms a ball. If it doesn't form a ball, use a spatula to break up the dough into pieces and process again, scraping down sides if necessary. Remove the dough from the food processor and knead with your hands until smooth. Shape the dough into two 1-inch-thick disks, wrap tightly with plastic wrap, and refrigerate 1 hour.

For a Single-Crust Pie:

2 Massage a disk of dough between your hands until it is warm and pliable, making the crust easier to handle. With a rolling pin, roll to a 10-inch circle between two pieces of heavy-duty plastic wrap dusted with rice flour. (Use a damp paper towel between countertop and plastic wrap to anchor plastic.) Move the rolling pin from the center of the dough to the outer edge, moving around the circle in clockwise fashion to assure uniform thickness.

3 Remove the top plastic wrap and invert the crust, centering it over a 9-inch nonstick (gray, not black) pie pan. Remove the remaining plastic wrap and press into place. Trim the edges to an even overhang all around the pan. Shape a decorative edge around rim of pan if you are making a single-crust pie. If not, leave the over-hang in place.

For a Double-Crust Filled Pie

4 Follow Steps 1, 2, and 3. Add filling as directed in your recipe. Roll remaining disk of dough to a 10-inch circle, invert, and center on the filled crust. Do not remove the top plastic wrap until the dough is centered. Trim the top crust to the same over-hang as bottom crust. Press the two crusts together and shape a decorative edge around rim of pan. Freeze 15 minutes. Brush with beaten egg. Sprinkle with remaining tablespoon of sugar. Prick the top crust several times with a fork to allow the steam to escape. Place the pan on a nonstick baking sheet.

5 Place a rack in the bottom position and another in the middle position of the oven. Preheat the oven to 375°F oven. Bake 15 minutes to brown bottom crust. Move to middle position and bake 25 to 35 minutes more or until the top crust is nicely browned. Cover loosely with foil if the edges brown too much. Cool completely on a wire rack before cutting.

Nonhydrogenated shortenings, by Spectrum Vegetable or Earth Balance, are available at natural food stores.

CREAM AND CHIFFON PIES

Banana Cream Pie with Mile-High Meringue Ⓥ

MAKES 8 SERVINGS

I always marvel at pies with very tall meringue topping. Well, now you can do the same thing at home. The secret to those high meringues is simply to use many egg whites. The gelatin in the banana cream filling ensures that it holds its shape after the pie is cut into wedges.

Basic Pastry Crust dough for a 9-inch pie, single crust (page 587)

1 teaspoon unflavored gelatin powder, such as Knox

2 tablespoons boiling water

½ cup sugar

3 tablespoons cornstarch

¼ teaspoon salt

1½ cups 1% milk (cow's, rice, soy, potato, or nut)

6 large eggs, separated (reserve whites for meringue, below)

1 tablespoon unsalted butter or buttery spread, such as Earth Balance

1 teaspoon pure vanilla extract

2 large bananas, peeled and cut in ¼-inch slices

MERINGUE

6 large egg whites, at room temperature (separated from egg yolks, above)

¼ teaspoon cream of tartar

⅛ teaspoon salt

¼ cup superfine sugar

½ teaspoon pure vanilla extract

1 Place a rack in the bottom position of the oven. Preheat the oven to 375°F. Prepare the single-crust pastry dough as directed in Step 1 on page 587. Fit the pie crust into a 9-inch nonstick (gray, not black) pie pan and flute the edges, decoratively, as directed, for a single-crust pie. Bake 15 minutes or until crust is lightly browned. Cool the crust in the pan on a wire rack. Leave the oven on.

2 In a small bowl, stir the gelatin into the boiling water until dissolved; set aside.

3 In a heavy saucepan, whisk together the sugar, cornstarch, and salt until they are thoroughly combined. In a medium bowl, whisk milk and egg yolks together until they are completely blended. Add to saucepan. Cook over medium heat, whisking constantly, until the mixture thickens, about 5 minutes. Remove from heat and whisk in the butter, vanilla, and gelatin mixture until it is very smooth. Set aside to cool slightly in the pan.

4 Layer the sliced bananas evenly in the crust. Using a spatula, spread the custard evenly over the bananas.

5 Make the meringue: In a medium bowl, beat the egg whites, cream of tartar, and salt with an electric mixer on medium speed until they are frothy. Gradually beat in the sugar, 1 tablespoon at a time, just until stiff peaks form. Stir in the vanilla.

6 Use a spatula to spread the meringue on top of the pie in decorative dips and swirls. The meringue will be very high. Make sure the meringue touches the edges of the pie crust to prevent shrinkage while baking.

7 Bake 10 to 15 minutes or until the meringue is nicely browned. Remove the pie from the oven and cool 15 minutes on a wire rack. Refrigerate 4 hours and serve the same day; refrigerate the leftovers.

Banana Cream Pie Brownie

MAKES 8 SERVINGS

There are many ways to pair chocolate and bananas. This easy, yet innovative dessert makes it possible to have your pie and eat it too. If you wish, you may use store-bought whipped topping in place of the whipped cream and buy ready-made gluten-free chocolate brownies.

Homemade Chocolate Brownies (page 442)

2 cups homemade Basic Custard (page 643) or 2 cups gluten-free vanilla pudding, such as Giant, Hy-Vee, or Royal

1 teaspoon banana-flavored extract (optional)

1 medium banana, peeled and sliced in ¼-inch slices

2 cups homemade Basic Whipped Cream (page 624) or whipped topping, such as Lucerne or Soyatoo

Shaved gluten-free chocolate, such as Tropical Source, for garnish

1 Place a rack in the middle of the oven. Preheat the oven to 350°F. Generously grease a 10-inch deep-dish pie pan (nonstick, gray not black); set aside.

2 Prepare the brownies as directed on page 442, but with the following changes:

  a. reduce the butter or canola oil to ¼ cup

  b. reduce the baking powder to ¼ teaspoon

Use a wet spatula to press and spread the batter evenly in the bottom and up the sides of the pie pan to form the brownie crust. The batter will be fairly stiff and will stay in place when pressed up the sides of the pan.

3 Bake 15 to 20 minutes or until the crust is nearly done and a toothpick inserted into the edge has some batter on it; it will continue to cook when removed from the oven. The crust may look rough and uneven, but the custard will cover it up. Cool the crust in the pan on a wire rack while preparing the filling.

4 Prepare the custard as directed on page 643. Stir in the banana extract, if using. Press a layer of plastic wrap directly on top of the custard and refrigerate until firm.

5 Layer the sliced bananas evenly in the brownie crust. Spread the custard on top. Chill about 4 hours.

6 Use a spatula to spread the whipped cream evenly over the custard and make decorative dips and swirls. Garnish with shaved chocolate. Serve immediately. Refrigerate leftovers.

Chocolate Cream Pie

MAKES 8 SERVINGS

Old-fashioned favorites like this are always a sure hit with family and friends. Refrigerate the leftovers, if there are any.

Basic Pastry Crust for a 9-inch pie, single crust (page 587)

1¼ cups sugar

¼ cup cornstarch

¼ teaspoon salt

3 cups 1% milk (cow's, rice*, soy, potato*, or nut)

3 large egg yolks, at room temperature

1 large egg, at room temperature

6 ounces gluten-free bittersweet chocolate, such as Scharffen Berger, finely chopped

2½ tablespoons unsalted butter or buttery spread, such as Earth Balance

1 tablespoon pure vanilla extract

2 cups homemade Basic Whipped Cream (page 624) or whipped topping, such as Lucerne or Soyatoo

1 Prepare the single-crust pastry dough, as instructed in Steps 1, 2, and 3 on page 587. Bake 15 minutes or until crust is lightly browned. Cool the crust in the pan on a wire rack.

2 In a heavy saucepan, whisk together the sugar, cornstarch, and salt until thoroughly blended. Add the milk, egg yolks, and egg and cook, stirring constantly, over medium heat until the mixture comes to a boil. Continue to cook, stirring constantly, 7 to 8 minutes more, or until the mixture thickens. Remove from the heat.

3 Stir in the chocolate, whisking until it is melted. Whisk in the butter and 1 tablespoon of the vanilla. Pour the filling into the pie crust. Press a piece of plastic wrap on the top of the pie. Refrigerate the pie 3 hours.

4 Remove the plastic wrap from the pie and use a spatula to spoon the whipped cream on top of the filling. Refrigerate leftovers.

Chocolate Banana Cream Pie: Cut 2 ripe but firm peeled bananas into ¼-inch slices and layer them on the bottom of the crust before proceeding to Step 2 above.

*Note: Increase the cornstarch to 5 tablespoons if using rice milk or potato milk.

Chocolate Cream Pie with White Chocolate Cream Ⓥ

MAKES 8 SERVINGS

For best results, make this luscious creamy pie a day ahead. Big shavings of bittersweet chocolate on top add a really decadent touch that will rival any gourmet pie you can buy. If you have a pretty ceramic pie plate you've been saving, use it for this special pie. I took this pie to a dinner party when I tested it, and everyone loved it—the pie plate was empty within seconds.

CRUST

1 package (9 cookies) gluten-free chocolate cookies, such as Pamela's Dark Chocolate, Chocolate Chunk Cookies or homemade Chocolate Cookies (page 434)

¼ teaspoon salt

2 tablespoons unsalted butter or buttery spread, such as Earth Balance, melted

FILLING

1 cup sugar

6 tablespoons cornstarch

½ teaspoon salt

3 cups whole milk, preferred but may use 1% milk (cow's, rice, soy, potato, or nut)

5 large whole egg yolks

2 tablespoons unsalted butter or buttery spread, such as Earth Balance, cut into small pieces

6 ounces gluten-free bittersweet or dark chocolate, such as Scharffen Berger, chopped

1 tablespoon pure vanilla extract

CREAM

3.5 ounces gluten-free white chocolate bar, such as Organica, broken into pieces

¼ cup 1% milk (cow's, rice, soy, potato, or nut)

½ teaspoon unflavored gelatin powder, such as Knox

2 cups homemade Basic Whipped Cream (page 624) or whipped topping, such as Lucerne or Soyatoo

Shaved gluten-free bittersweet chocolate, for garnish

Optional garnishes: fresh raspberries, blueberries, or strawberries; fresh mint leaves; dusting of cocoa powder

1 Place a rack in the middle of the oven. Preheat the oven to 350°F. Make the crust: Place the cookies and salt in a food processor and process until the cookies resemble fine crumbs. You will have between 1½ and 2 cups of crumbs. Pour the melted butter evenly over the crumbs and pulse a few times to blend it into the crumbs.

2 Firmly press the crumbs onto the bottom and up the sides of a 9-inch pie pan. Bake the crust 10 minutes. Remove from the oven and cool on a wire rack while preparing the filling.

3 Make the filling: In a medium, heavy saucepan, whisk together the sugar, cornstarch, and salt until well blended. Add the milk and egg yolks and cook over medium heat, whisking constantly and scraping the bottom and sides of the pan, until the mixture thickens. Continue to stir it for another minute, whisking constantly.

4 Remove the pan from the heat and stir in the butter and chocolate until they are completely melted and smooth. Add the vanilla extract and stir well. Pour the filling into the crust and chill thoroughly.

5 Make the cream: Melt the white chocolate and milk in microwave oven on low until the chocolate melts. Stir until it is smooth and then cool it for 5 minutes. Whisk in the gelatin powder until it is completely dissolved.

6 In a medium bowl, place the whipped cream. Fold in the white chocolate-gelatin mixture. Spread it over the chilled pie, making dips and swirls with a spatula. Sprinkle chocolate shavings on top. Add additional garnishes, if using. Refrigerate the pie for at least 3 hours before serving. Refrigerate leftovers.

Chocolate Fudge Pie

MAKES 8 SERVINGS

This is my favorite pie to serve at dinner parties because it's always a sure hit with guests—and they have no idea how easy it is to make. There is no crust to fuss with and I quickly mix it up in a bowl and pour into a pie pan.

9 ounces gluten-free bittersweet chocolate, such as Scharffen Berger, chopped

½ cup (1 stick) unsalted butter or buttery spread, such as Earth Balance, cut in cubes

1 tablespoon pure vanilla extract

1 cup sugar

2 large eggs, at room temperature

½ cup Carol's Sorghum Blend (page x)

¼ cup sweet rice flour

½ teaspoon salt

¼ teaspoon xanthan gum

1 Place a rack in the middle of the oven. Preheat the oven to 350°F. Generously grease a 9-inch nonstick (gray, not black) pie pan.

2 In a microwave-safe mixing bowl, combine the chocolate and butter. Microwave on medium in 2- or 3-minute increments until the chocolate melts. Cool 5 minutes. Stir in the vanilla extract.

3 Beat the sugar into the chocolate mixture with an electric mixer on low speed until smooth. Beat

in the eggs, one at a time, until smooth. Add the sorghum blend, sweet rice flour, salt, and xanthan gum, and beat on low speed until well blended. Pour the batter into the prepared pan and smooth the top with a wet spatula.

4 Bake 20 to 25 minutes or until a toothpick inserted into the center comes out wet but the outer edges of the pie are firm to the touch. The idea is to bake it just enough to set it but not dry it out by baking it too long. Cool the pan 30 minutes on a wire rack before serving. The pie may be served at room temperature or slightly warm.

Chocolate Fudge Espresso Pie

MAKES 12 SERVINGS

Eating this delectable pie is like eating pure fudge nestled on top of a chocolate-coffee crust. I use a particular form of cocoa that is very dark, giving the pie a "serious chocolate" appearance. As I often tell my daughter-in-law, "There's no such thing as too much chocolate." This pie demonstrates that conviction. When you want to dress it up for company, add a few chocolate-covered espresso beans as an additional garnish. If coffee isn't your cup of tea (pardon the pun), just omit the espresso. I suggest cutting this pie into very tiny wedges because it is so rich.

CRUST

1 package (9 cookies) gluten-free chocoalte cookies, such as Pamela's Espresso Chocolate Chunk cookies, or homemade Chocolate Cookies (page 434)

1 large egg, at room temperature

FILLING

¾ cup Hershey's Special Dark cocoa

½ cup (1 stick) unsalted butter or buttery spread, such as Earth Balance, at room temperature

2 large eggs, at room temperature

½ cup sugar

1 teaspoon instant espresso powder

1 teaspoon pure vanilla extract

¾ cup homemade Basic Whipped Cream (page 624) or whipped topping, such as Lucerne or Soyatoo

3 tablespoons cocoa nibs, such as Scharffen Berger, for sprinkling on top (optional)

1 Place a rack in the middle of the oven. Preheat the oven to 350°F. Generously grease a 9-inch springform pan with removable sides.

2 Make the crust: Place cookies in food processor. Process until thoroughly crushed. Add egg and pulse until mixture is thoroughly blended.

3 Press mixture into bottom of pan with hands, covering it with plastic wrap to avoid sticking to your hands if necessary.

4 Make the filling: Wipe bowl of food processor with damp paper towel to remove remnants of crust and add cocoa, butter, eggs, sugar, espresso powder, and vanilla extract. Process until thoroughly blended. Spread filling in baked crust, smoothing with a wet spatula.

5 Bake 15 to 20 minutes or until filling starts to set around edges and crust browns. Remove from oven; filling will continue to cook for awhile. Cool 30 minutes on wire rack. Refrigerate 2 hours before serving. Garnish each slice with a tablespoon of whipped cream and a teaspoon of cocoa nibs, if using.

Chocolate Meringue Pie

MAKES 8 SERVINGS

My mother only made pies for very special occasions, but this is the one I remember best from my childhood. Since chocolate was my family's favorite flavor, this pie was always greeted with jubilation.

CRUST AND FILLING

Basic Pastry Crust for a 9-inch pie, single crust (page 587)

1¼ cups sugar

¼ cup cornstarch

¼ teaspoon salt

3 cups 1% milk (cow's, rice*, soy, potato*, or nut)

4 large eggs, separated (reserve whites for meringue, below)

6 ounces gluten-free bittersweet chocolate, such as Scharffen Berger, finely chopped

2½ tablespoons unsalted butter or buttery spread, such as Earth Balance

1 tablespoon pure vanilla extract

MERINGUE

4 large egg whites, at room temperature (separated from egg yolks, above)

¼ cup sugar

¼ teaspoon cream of tartar

⅛ teaspoon salt

½ teaspoon pure vanilla extract

1 Prepare the single-crust pastry crust, as instructed in Steps 1, 2, and 3 on page 587, freezing the remaining half of the dough for another use. Bake on a rack in the bottom position of a preheated 375°F oven 15 minutes or until the crust is lightly browned. Cool the crust in the pan on a wire rack.

2 In a heavy saucepan, whisk together the sugar, cornstarch, and salt until thoroughly blended. Add the milk and egg yolks and cook, stirring constantly, over medium heat until the mixture comes to a boil. Continue to cook, stirring constantly, 7 to 8 minutes more, or until the mixture thickens. Remove from the heat.

3 Stir in the chocolate, whisking until it is melted. Whisk in the butter and vanilla extract. Pour the filling into the pie crust. Press a piece of plastic wrap directly on the top of the pie but do not chill.

4 Place a rack in the middle of the oven. Preheat the oven to 425°F. In a medium bowl, beat the egg whites, sugar, cream of tartar, and salt with an electric mixer on medium speed until soft peaks form. Stir in the vanilla extract. Remove the plastic wrap from the filling and use a spatula to spread the meringue in decorative dips and swirls. Make sure the meringue touches the edges of the pie crust to avoid shrinkage during baking.

5 Bake 10 to 12 minutes or until the meringue is nicely browned. Cool the pie 15 minutes on a wire rack, then refrigerate 3 hours or until the filling is firm. Refrigerate leftovers.

*Note: Increase the cornstarch to 5 tablespoons if using rice milk or potato milk.

Black Bottom Pie

MAKES 8 SERVINGS

Black Bottom Pie is a rich chocolate cream pie with a rum-flavored custard on top, smothered with a creamy topping. The recipe typically requires many steps, but I've simplified it for you. Most recipes include an uncooked egg white topping, but I use a whipped cream topping for safety. If you prefer the egg-white topping but don't want the risk of raw eggs, use Just Whites egg white powder and follow the package directions.

CRUST

1 package (9 cookies) gluten-free chocolate cookies, such as Pamela's Dark Chocolate, Chocolate Chunk Cookies or homemade Chocolate Cookies (page 434) (1½ cups of crumbs)

1 tablespoon sugar

2 tablespoons unsalted butter or buttery spread, such as Earth Balance, at room temperature

FILLING AND TOPPING

1 envelope (2½ teaspoons) unflavored gelatin powder, such as Knox

2 tablespoons rum or 1 teaspoon rum extract, divided

1 tablespoon water

1 cup sugar

6 tablespoons cornstarch

½ teaspoon salt

3 cups whole milk (cow's, rice, soy, potato, or nut)

4 large egg yolks

6 ounces gluten-free bittersweet or dark chocolate, such as Scharffen Berger, finely chopped

1 tablespoon pure vanilla extract

4 cups homemade Basic Whipped Cream (page 624) or whipped topping, such as Lucerne or Soyatoo

Chocolate shavings, for garnish

1 Place a rack in the middle of the oven. Preheat the oven to 350°F. Generously grease a 9-inch nonstick (gray, not black) pie pan. Place the chocolate cookies and sugar in a food processor and process until the cookies resemble fine crumbs. Add the butter and process until thoroughly combined. Press the crumb mixture firmly onto the bottom and up the sides of the pie pan to form a thin crust.

2 Bake 8 to 10 minutes, or just until the crust is fragrant. Do not overbake it. Cool the pie crust in the pan completely on a wire rack.

3 In a small bowl, stir together the gelatin, 1 tablespoon of the rum, and the water; set aside until the gelatin softens, about 5 minutes.

4 Meanwhile, in a medium saucepan, whisk together the sugar, cornstarch, and salt. Whisk in the milk and egg yolks until thoroughly combined. Heat over medium heat until the mixture comes to a boil and thickens, whisking constantly. Remove from the heat and whisk in the vanilla and gelatin mixture until smooth. (If the gelatin has hardened, add a tiny bit of water to soften it before adding to the hot custard.) Remove the pan from the heat and reserve ½ cup of the custard in a medium bowl, covered. Stir the chocolate into the remaining custard mixture in the saucepan until completely melted and smooth. Pour the filling into the crust and chill, lightly covered, 30 minutes.

5 In a medium bowl, fold 1 cup of the whipped cream into to the reserved ½ cup custard mixture and add the remaining tablespoon of rum. Spread this layer over the chocolate filling. Spread the remaining whipped cream on top and refrigerate the pie overnight or until completely set. Serve each slice with a sprinkle of chocolate shavings. Refrigerate leftovers.

French Silk Pie

MAKES 8 SERVINGS

I used to serve this decadent chocolate pie in a plain pastry crust, but now I prefer it in a crunchy cookie crust, which contrasts nicely with the silky smooth filling.

Homemade Cookie Crust for a 9-inch pie (page 585)
1 teaspoon unflavored gelatin powder, such as Knox
2 tablespoons boiling water
¾ cup sugar
¼ cup cornstarch
¼ teaspoon salt
4 large egg yolks, beaten
1½ cups 1% milk (cow's, rice*, soy, potato*, or nut)
1 tablespoon unsalted butter or buttery spread, such as Earth Balance, at room temperature
6 ounces gluten-free bittersweet chocolate, such as Scharffen Berger, cut in 1-inch pieces
3 cups homemade Basic Whipped Cream (page 624) or whipped topping, such as Lucerne or Soyatoo

1 Prepare the pie crust. Then, make the filling: In a small bowl, stir the gelatin into the boiling water until dissolved and set aside. In a heavy saucepan, whisk together the sugar, cornstarch, and salt. With an electric mixer, beat in the eggs on high speed until pale yellow, about 4 minutes. Add the milk, place the pan over medium heat, and cook,

whisking constantly, until the mixture boils and then thickens slightly. Immediately remove the pan from heat and stir in the butter and chocolate. Continue to stir until the chocolate and butter are melted and the mixture is very smooth.

2 Pour the mixture into the prepared pie crust and refrigerate at least 4 hours.

3 Spread the whipped cream over the filling and to the outside edges of the crust. Refrigerate 2 hours. Serve chilled and refrigerate leftovers.

Note: If using rice milk or potato milk, increase the cornstarch to 5 tablespoons.

Coconut Chess Pie

MAKES 6 SERVINGS

This is the dessert you can turn to when you want something creamy, comforting, and easy to assemble. Chess pies are crustless custard pies, which save time and are lower in calories than pies in crusts.

2 large eggs, at room temperature
½ cup sugar
¼ cup 1% milk (cow's, rice, soy, potato, or nut)
¼ cup (½ stick) unsalted butter or buttery spread, such as Earth Balance at room temperature
1 tablespoon sweet rice flour
1 teaspoon pure vanilla extract
1 teaspoon coconut extract (optional)
¼ teaspoon salt
1 cup sweetened shredded coconut

1 Place a rack in the middle of the oven. Preheat the oven to 350°F. Lightly grease a 9-inch glass or ceramic pie pan.

2 Place all ingredients in mixing bowl. With electric mixer, beat ingredients on medium until thoroughly blended. Pour into pie pan.

3 Bake 25 to 30 minutes or until the top is golden brown. If it browns too much, cover with foil during the final minutes of baking. Remove pie from oven and cool completely on wire rack. Serve at room temperature. Refrigerate leftovers.

Chocolate Chess Pie: Omit the shredded coconut and coconut extract. Beat in ¼ cup Dutch-process cocoa with the other ingredients in Step 2. Bake as directed.

Coconut Cream Pie

MAKES 8 SERVINGS

I particularly love the smell of coconut when it toasts in the oven and when combined with the creamy, mellow custard filling this pie is heavenly.

CRUST

1¼ cups (about 60) gluten-free crackers, such as Health Valley Rice Bran

¼ cup unsalted butter or buttery spread, such as Earth Balance, at room temperature

2 tablespoons sugar

⅛ teaspoon salt

FILLING

¾ cup sugar

⅓ cup cornstarch

¼ heaping teaspoon salt

3¼ cups 1% milk (cow's rice, soy, potato, or nut)

6 large egg yolks, at room temperature

2 tablespoons unsalted butter or buttery spread, such as Earth Balance, at room temperature

1 teaspoon pure vanilla extract

1 teaspoon coconut extract (optional)

¾ cup sweetened shredded coconut

TOPPING

1 cup homemade Basic Whipped Cream (page 624) or whipped topping, such as Lucerne or Soyatoo

¼ cup sweetened shredded coconut, toasted (see How to Toast Coconut, page 475)

1 Place a rack in the middle of the oven. Preheat the oven to 350°F. Make the crust: Process the crackers in a food processor until very fine. Add butter, sugar and salt and process again until thoroughly blended. Press into 9-inch pie pan. Bake

10 minutes or just until crust begins to firm up. Remove from oven and cool.

2 Make the filling: In a medium-size, heavy saucepan, whisk together sugar, cornstarch, and salt over medium heat. Add all but ½ cup of the milk. To remaining ½ cup milk, whisk in egg yolks until thoroughly blended and all egg membrane is broken up.

3 Add egg-milk mixture to pan and cook over medium heat, stirring constantly with a wire whisk, until mixture thickens, about 5 minutes, depending on the temperature of the ingredients. It is very important to keep whisking throughout the cooking time or the mixture may become lumpy. Remove from the heat and stir in butter, vanilla, and coconut extract, if using, until smooth. Then stir in coconut.

4 Using a spatula, spread filling evenly in crust. Refrigerate at least 4 hours.

5 To serve, top each slice with 2 tablespoons whipped cream and a sprinkle of toasted coconut.

Butterscotch Pie

MAKES 6 SERVINGS

Butterscotch is a wonderful flavor. If you like butterscotch pudding, you will love this pie.

CRUST

Basic Pastry Crust for a 9-inch pie, single crust (page 587)

FILLING

1 cup packed light brown sugar

4 tablespoons cornstarch

¼ teaspoon salt

2 cups evaporated skim milk or 1¾ cups whole milk (cow's, rice*, soy)

3 large egg yolks

3 tablespoons unsalted butter or buttery spread, such as Earth Balance

1 teaspoon pure vanilla extract

1 teaspoon bourbon or whiskey (optional)

½ teaspoon butter-flavored extract (optional)

TOPPING

2 cups homemade Basic Whipped Cream (page 624) or whipped topping, such as Lucerne or Soyatoo

1 Make the crust: Prepare the single-crust pastry crust, as instructed in Steps 1, 2, and 3 on page 587. Bake 15 minutes or until crust is lightly browned. Cool the crust in the pan on a wire rack. Then, make the filling: In a large, heavy saucepan, whisk together the sugar, cornstarch, and salt over medium heat. Whisk in the milk gradually. Then whisk in the egg yolks and bring the mixture to a boil, continuing to whisk constantly. Immediately reduce the heat to low and continue to boil 1 to 2 minutes, or until the mixture turns slightly darker. (This boiling time is critical because it develops the butterscotch flavor—but be careful, the mixture may splatter as it boils.)

2 Remove the pan from the heat and stir in the butter, vanilla, bourbon, if using, and butter extract, if using. Pour into a nonreactive bowl and press a sheet of plastic wrap directly onto the pudding. Chill 2 hours.

3 Remove the plastic wrap and spread the cooled pudding in the pie crust and chill another 2 hours. Before serving, spread the whipped cream over the filling, making sure it touches the edges of the crust all around. Serve immediately. Refrigerate leftovers.

*Note: If using rice milk, increase the cornstarch to 3 tablespoons.

Praline Pumpkin Pie

MAKES 6 SERVINGS

If you want a basic recipe for pumpkin pie, make this recipe without the topping (see variation). But for some marvelous crunch to the smooth, creamy filling, add the praline topping during the final minutes of baking.

CRUST

Basic Pastry Pie Crust dough for a 9-inch pie, single crust (page 587)

FILLING

1 can (14 to 15 ounces) canned pumpkin puree (not pie filling)
¾ cup sugar
2 teaspoons pumpkin pie spice
1 teaspoon ground cinnamon
¾ teaspoon salt
2 large eggs, at room temperature
¾ cup 1% milk (cow's, rice, soy, potato, or nut)

PRALINE TOPPING

½ cup pecans, chopped fine in food processor
¼ cup packed dark brown sugar
1 tablespoon dark corn syrup
1 teaspoon pure vanilla extract
⅛ teaspoon salt

1 Place a rack in the bottom position and another in the middle position of the oven. Preheat the oven to 425°F. Make the crust: Prepare the single-crust pastry dough as directed in Step 1 on page 587. Freeze half of the dough for another use. Then, fit the remaining dough into a 9-inch nonstick (gray, not black) pie pan and flute the edges decoratively as directed, for a single-crust pie. Place pan in freezer.

2 Make the filling: In a medium bowl, combine all filling ingredients and beat with electric mixer until smooth.

3 Remove pie crust from freezer and pour filling into crust. Place pie pan on nonstick (gray, not black) baking sheet. Bake 15 minutes on bottom rack. Move pie to middle rack; reduce heat to 350°F and bake 35 to 40 minutes or until center barely jiggles when shaken.

4 While the pie is baking, toss the pecans and sugar together. Add the corn syrup, vanilla extract, and salt and stir until the mixture is thoroughly blended. Sprinkle evenly on the pie. Continue baking 10 minutes more or until the praline topping is bubbling and lightly browned. Cool 2 hours on a wire rack. Refrigerate until serving time. Serve chilled or at room temperature. Refrigerate leftovers.

Pumpkin Pie: Eliminate the pecan topping in Step 4.

Sweet Potato Pie

MAKES 6 SERVINGS

Sweet potatoes are tasty, versatile, very healthy, and one of the least allergenic foods on earth. I prefer red garnet sweet potatoes for this pie because of their magnificent color, but you can use your favorite sweet potato.

Basic Pastry Crust dough for a 9-inch pie, single crust (page 587)

2 cups mashed cooked red garnet sweet potatoes

¾ cup sugar

1 teaspoon ground cinnamon

¾ teaspoon salt

½ teaspoon ground allspice

½ teaspoon freshly grated nutmeg

½ teaspoon ground ginger

¼ teaspoon ground cloves

2 teaspoons lemon juice

2 teaspoons grated orange zest

2 large eggs, at room temperature

½ cup 1% milk (cow's, rice, soy, potato, or nut)

¼ cup unsalted butter or buttery spread, such as Earth Balance, melted

1 Place a rack in the middle of the oven. Preheat the oven to 425°F. Make the crust: Prepare the pastry dough as directed in Step 1 on page 587. Freeze half of the dough for another use. Then, fit the remaining dough into a 9-inch nonstick (gray, not black) pie pan and flute the edges decoratively as directed, for a single-crust pie. Place pan in freezer while preparing the sweet potato filling.

2 In a medium bowl, combine the mashed sweet potatoes, sugar, cinnamon, salt, allspice, nutmeg, ginger, cloves, lemon juice, orange zest, eggs, milk and butter and beat with electric mixer on medium speed until smooth.

3 Remove pie crust from freezer and pour filling into crust. Place pie pan on nonstick (gray, not black) baking sheet. Bake 15 minutes in preheated oven on lower rack. Move pie to center rack; reduce heat to 350°F and bake 35 to 40 minutes or center barely jiggles when shaken. Cover the edges of the pie crust with foil to prevent burning the crust. Cool 2 hours on a wire rack. Refrigerate until serving time. Refrigerate leftovers.

Sour Cream–Raisin Pie

MAKES 6 SERVINGS

This is a creamy concoction of vanilla custard and raisins accented with nutmeg and cloves. Often found in older cookbooks, my version blends memories of old-time favorites with modern simplicity.

Basic Pastry Crust dough for a 9-inch pie, single crust (page 587)

1 cup dark raisins

2 large eggs, at room temperature

1 cup sour cream or sour cream alternative, such as Tofutti

¾ cup sugar

1 teaspoon pure vanilla extract

¼ teaspoon salt

¼ teaspoon freshly grated nutmeg

Pinch ground cloves

½ cup chopped pecans (optional)

1 Prepare the pastry dough as directed in Step 1 on page 587. Freeze half of the dough for another use. Then, fit the remaining dough in to a 9-inch nonstick (gray, not black) pie pan and flute the edges decoratively as directed, for a single-crust pie in Steps 2 and 3 on page 587. Place pan in freezer while preparing the filling.

2 Place a rack in the bottom position and another in the middle position of the oven. Preheat the oven to 375°F. Place the raisins in a small heavy saucepan and add just enough water to cover.

Bring to a boil, remove the pan from the heat, and let stand 15 minutes to plump.

3 Meanwhile, in a large bowl, beat the eggs, sour cream, sugar, vanilla, salt, nutmeg, and cloves with an electric mixer on medium until smooth. Drain the raisins well and stir them in. Stir in the nuts, if using. Pour the filling into the pie crust, making sure the raisins are evenly distributed. Place pie pan on nonstick (gray, not black) baking sheet.

4 Bake 15 minutes on the bottom rack of the oven. Move the pie to the middle rack and bake 25 minutes more or until the filling is set. Cool completely on a wire rack before serving. Serve at room temperature. Refrigerate leftovers.

Raspberry Chiffon Pie in Almond Crust Ⓥ

MAKES 6 SERVINGS

Smooth and airy, this pie literally melts in your mouth. Its creamy texture is the result of blending the gelatin and cream, and this contrasts nicely with the slightly crunchy crust.

CRUST

1 cup whole almonds

¾ cup crushed gluten-free vanilla cookies, such as Midel Arrowroot, or homemade Sugar Cookies (page 419)

2 tablespoons sugar

2 tablespoons unsalted butter or buttery spread, such as Earth Balance, at room temperature, but not melted

FILLING

¼ cup water

1 envelope (2½ teaspoons) unflavored gelatin powder, such as Knox

¾ cup sugar

½ teaspoon almond extract

1 package (12 ounces) frozen raspberries, not thawed or drained

1½ cups homemade Basic Whipped Cream (page 624) or whipped topping, such as Lucerne or Soyatoo

1 Place a rack in the middle of the oven. Preheat the oven to 350°F. Make the crust: In a food processor, process the almonds until they are coarsely ground. Add the cookies and sugar and process until the cookies resemble fine bread crumbs. Add the butter and process until the mixture is crumbly and the crumbs are shiny. Press the crumbs evenly on the bottom and up the sides of a 9-inch nonstick (gray, not black) pie pan. The edge of the crust should be level with the top of the pie pan.

2 Bake 5 to 8 minutes, or until the crust is fragrant and the edges of the crust just start to brown. Cool the crust on a wire rack while assembling the filling.

3 Make the filling: Place the water in a medium saucepan and sprinkle the gelatin on top, stirring until it is incorporated. Let stand 5 minutes. Add sugar and bring the mixture to a simmer over medium heat, stirring until the sugar is dissolved.

4 Remove from the heat and stir in the almond extract and raspberries until thoroughly blended. Let the mixture stand 5 minutes; it will cool quickly and thicken slightly.

5 In a large bowl, place the whipped cream. Gently fold the raspberry mixture into the whipped cream and spread the mixture evenly in the crust. Refrigerate until the filling is set, at least 4 hours or preferably overnight. Serve chilled. Refrigerate leftovers.

Strawberry Chiffon Pie in a Coconut Crust

MAKES 6 SERVINGS

The smooth fluffy texture of the strawberry chiffon filling contrasts nicely with the crunchy coconut crust. Serve this lovely pink dessert, flecked with chunks of red strawberries, for a casual luncheon or a summertime dinner party.

CRUST

1½ cups sweetened shredded coconut

1 tablespoon sweet rice flour

¼ teaspoon salt

1 teaspoon pure vanilla extract

2 tablespoons unsalted butter or buttery spread, such as Earth Balance, at room temperature

FILLING

1 quart (4 cups) fresh strawberries, chopped

¾ cup sugar

1 envelope (2½ teaspoons) unflavored gelatin powder, such as Knox

½ cup cold water

2 teaspoons fresh lemon juice

½ teaspoon almond extract

4 cups homemade Basic Whipped Cream (page 624) or whipped topping, such as Lucerne or Soyatoo

1 Place a rack in the middle of the oven. Preheat the oven to 325°F. Lightly butter a 9-inch round nonstick (gray, not black) pie pan; set aside.

2 Make the crust: In a small bowl, toss together the coconut, sweet rice flour, and salt until blended. Add the vanilla extract and butter and toss until the coconut is well coated. Press the mixture onto the bottom and up the sides of the pie pan.

3 Bake 20 to 25 minutes or until the crust is lightly browned, covering the edges loosely with foil to prevent overbrowning, if necessary. Cool the crust on a wire rack.

4 Make the filling: In a large bowl, combine the strawberries and sugar; let stand 15 minutes to let the sugar dissolve. In a small saucepan, sprinkle the gelatin over the cold water. Let stand 1 minute and then cook over medium heat, stirring constantly, until the gelatin is dissolved. Remove from the heat and stir in the lemon juice and almond extract. Stir the cooled gelatin into the strawberries. Cool to room temperature, about 15 to 20 minutes.

5 In a medium bowl, place the whipped cream and fold in the strawberries. Pour the filling into the crust and smooth the top with a spatula. Refrigerate at least 4 hours before serving.

Pineapple Meringue Pie

MAKES 6 SERVINGS

Cream pies are actually quite easy to make, but there are several steps that have to happen in sequence, so they do take some planning ahead. Nonetheless, they are delicious and well worth the effort. Fruit-based pies like this one are perfect for summer days.

Basic Pastry Crust dough for 9-inch pie, single crust, (page 587)

1 teaspoon unflavored gelatin powder, such as Knox

2 tablespoons boiling water

1 cup sugar, divided

¼ cup cornstarch

¼ teaspoon salt

1½ cups 1% milk (cow's, rice, soy, potato, or nut)

3 large eggs, separated

2 tablespoons unsalted butter or buttery spread, such as Earth Balance

½ teaspoon rum extract

1 can (8 ounces) crushed pineapple, very thoroughly drained

¼ teaspoon cream of tartar

1 Prepare the single-crust pastry dough as directed in Step 1 on page 587. Freeze half of the dough for another use. Then, fit the remaining dough into a 9-inch nonstick (gray, not black) pie pan and flute the edges decoratively as directed, for a single-crust pie in Steps 2 and 3 on page 587. Place pan in freezer while preparing filling and topping. In a small bowl, stir the gelatin into the boiling water until dissolved and set aside.

2 In a heavy medium saucepan, whisk together ⅔ cup of the sugar, cornstarch, and salt until well blended. Gradually whisk in the milk and egg yolks until thoroughly blended and smooth.

3 Place the saucepan over medium heat and cook the mixture, whisking constantly, until it thickens or about 7 to 8 minutes. Do not let it boil. Remove from the heat and stir in the butter, rum extract, gelatin mixture, and very thoroughly drained crushed pineapple. Pour the filling into the pie crust.

4 Place a rack in the middle of the oven. Preheat the oven to 375°F. In a medium bowl, beat the egg whites, the remaining ⅓ cup of sugar, and the cream of tartar with an electric mixer on medium speed until stiff peaks form. Spread the meringue on the filling and out to the edges of the pie, touching the crust to avoid shrinkage during baking. Make attractive dips and swirls with a spatula.

5 Bake 6 to 10 minutes or until the meringue is golden brown. Cool the pie 25 minutes on a wire rack, refrigerate 2 hours, and serve on the same day. Refrigerate leftovers.

Eggnog Custard Pie with Whipped Cream Topping

MAKES 8 SERVINGS

The delicious flavors of eggnog—nutmeg, vanilla, and rum—are captured in this luscious pie. If you prefer, use brandy in place of the rum. Since eggnog is only available during the holidays, put this pie on your list of holiday desserts.

CRUST
Basic Pastry Crust dough for a 9-inch pie, single crust (page 587)

FILLING
2⅔ cups eggnog

4 large eggs, at room temperature

2 tablespoons rum or 2 teaspoons rum extract (optional)

1 teaspoon pure vanilla extract

⅓ cup sugar

⅛ teaspoon salt

¼ teaspoon freshly grated nutmeg plus additional for garnish

WHIPPED CREAM TOPPING
2 cups homemade Basic Whipped Cream (page 624) or whipped topping, such as Lucerne or Soyatoo

2 teaspoons rum or 2 drops of rum flavoring

1 Place a rack in the bottom position and another in the middle position of the oven. Preheat the oven to 375°F. Make the crust: Prepare the single-crust pastry dough as directed in Step 1 on page 587. Freeze half of the dough for another use. Then, fit the remaining dough into a 9-inch nonstick (gray, not black) pie pan and flute the edges decoratively as directed, for a single-crust pie in Steps 2 and 3 on page 587. Do not prick the bottom of the crust. Place the pie pan on a nonstick (gray, not black) baking sheet. Bake 5 to 10 minutes on the bottom rack of the oven or until the crust starts to brown. Cool the crust on a wire rack. Reduce the oven heat to 350°F, but leave the oven on.

2 Make the filling: In a large bowl, beat the eggnog, eggs, rum, and vanilla with an electric mixer on medium until smooth. Add the sugar, salt, and nutmeg and mix well. Pour into the pie crust. Cover with foil.

3 Bake 25 minutes on the middle rack of the oven; remove the foil, and continue baking 30 to 40 minutes or until a knife inserted into the center of the pie comes out clean. Cool the pie on a wire rack 15 minutes.

4 Make the topping: In a medium bowl, place the whipped cream. Stir in the rum flavoring. Spread evenly over the eggnog custard, using a spatula to make attractive dips and swirls. Refrigerate 3 hours before serving. Refrigerate leftovers.

Peanut Butter Pie

MAKES 6 SERVINGS

If you're a peanut butter purist, this luscious pie can stand alone. For chocolate–peanut butter lovers out there, the chocolate sauce drizzled over this peanut butter pie is the perfect topping.

CRUST

6 gluten-free chocolate cookies, such as Pamela's Dark Chocolate, Chocolate Chunk Cookies or homemade Chocolate Cookies (page 434)

1 tablespoon sugar

2 tablespoons unsalted butter or buttery spread, such as Earth Balance, at room temperature

FILLING

1 package (8 ounces) cream cheese or cream cheese alternative, such as Tofutti, softened (not lite)

½ cup packed light brown sugar

¼ cup creamy peanut butter

2 teaspoons pure vanilla extract

1½ cups homemade Basic Whipped Cream (page 624) or whipped topping, such as Lucerne or Soyatoo

⅓ cup crushed salted peanuts

½ cup gluten-free chocolate syrup, such as Hershey's, or homemade Chocolate Sauce (page 622)

1 Place a rack in the middle of the oven. Preheat the oven to 350°F. Make the crust: In a food processor, process the cookies until they are finely ground. Add the sugar and butter and process until thoroughly blended. Press the mixture on the bottom and up the sides of a 9-inch round nonstick (gray, not black) pie pan.

2 Bake 5 to 10 minutes or just until the crust is fragrant. Watch carefully because the crust may burn easily depending on the cookies used. Refrigerate to cool.

3 Make the filling: Wipe out the food processor with a damp paper towel. Add the cream cheese, brown sugar, peanut butter, and vanilla and process until thoroughly combined. Transfer to a large bowl.

4 In a separate bowl, place the whipped cream. Fold the peanut butter–cream cheese mixture into the whipped cream with a spatula until no white streaks remain.

5 Pour into the prepared crust and chill at least 2 hours before serving. To serve, cut into slices, sprinkle with peanuts, and drizzle with chocolate syrup. Refrigerate leftovers.

Key Lime Pie in Coconut Crumb Crust Ⓥ

MAKES 8 SERVINGS

This is my version of a wonderful key lime pie that my husband enjoyed recently at a Denver restaurant while I looked on, taking notes, so I could recreate it at home. The coconut in the crust provides an interesting textural contrast to the smooth, creamy, slightly tart filling. Key limes are quite small, which can make it a challenge to squeeze by hand, but an electric juicer makes quick work of them. You can also purchase key lime juice. If you prefer less lime flavor, use half lime juice and half lemon juice.

FILLING

1 can (14 to 15 ounces) sweetened condensed milk

½ cup fresh key lime juice

1 teaspoon grated key lime zest

3 drops green food coloring (optional)

2 cups homemade Basic Whipped Cream (page 624) or whipped topping, such as Lucerne or Soyatoo

CRUMB CRUST

1 cup crushed gluten-free cookies, such as Midel Arrowroot, or homemade Graham Crackers (page 433)

2 tablespoons sugar

½ cup sweetened shredded coconut

3 tablespoons unsalted butter or buttery spread, such as Earth Balance, melted

1 Whisk together the sweetened condensed milk, lime juice, lime zest, and food coloring (if using); set aside to let the mixture thicken.

2 Place a rack in the middle of the oven. Preheat the oven to 325°F. In a food processor, process the cookies and sugar until they are fine crumbs. Sprinkle the coconut evenly over the crumbs. Pour the melted butter evenly over the coconut and pulse a few times just until the ingredients are blended. Firmly press the crumb mixture onto the bottom and all the way up the sides of a 9-inch nonstick (gray, not black) pie pan.

3 Bake 5 to 10 minutes or until it is fragrant and the coconut starts to brown. Watch carefully because different crackers or cookies may burn more easily than others. Cool the crust 10 minutes on a wire rack.

4 Fold the whipped cream into the lime mixture until there are no more white streaks. Pour it into the crust, smoothing the top with a spatula. Chill 3 to 4 hours or until the filling firms up. Serve chilled or at room temperature. Refrigerate leftovers.

Lemon Meringue Tart

MAKES 8 SERVINGS

You'll love my version of old-fashioned lemon meringue pie, but in a crunchy crust of almond meal rather than a plain pastry crust and a thinner filling. For a more fancy presentation, use a pastry bag or heavy-duty food storage bag to pipe the meringue onto the filling in decorative swirls or patterns.

CRUST

¾ cup Carol's Sorghum Blend (page x)

2 tablespoons almond meal, chestnut flour, or Carol's Sorghum Blend (page x)

¼ cup powdered sugar

⅛ teaspoon salt

2 tablespoons unsalted butter or buttery spread, such as Earth Balance, at room temperature

FILLING

1 cup sugar

3 tablespoons cornstarch

1 teaspoon grated lemon zest

½ cup 1% milk (cow's, rice*, soy, potato*, or nut)

½ cup fresh lemon juice

2 large eggs, slightly beaten

1 large egg yolk, slightly beaten

1 tablespoon unsalted butter or buttery spread, such as Earth Balance

MERINGUE

3 large egg whites, at room temperature

¼ teaspoon cream of tartar

¼ cup superfine sugar

¼ teaspoon pure vanilla extract

1 Generously grease an 8-inch nonstick (gray, not black) fluted tart pan with a removable bottom. Make the crust: In a food processor, combine the sorghum blend, almond meal, sugar, salt, and butter and process until the dough forms a smooth ball Remove the dough and knead with your hands until smooth. Roll the dough to a 10-inch circle between two pieces of plastic wrap. Remove the top piece of plastic wrap and invert the dough onto the tart pan, centering it before removing the plastic wrap. With your fingers, press the dough into the pan and up the sides. Refrigerate 30 minutes.

2 Place a rack in the bottom position and another in the middle position of the oven. Preheat the oven to 325°F. Bake the crust 15 to 20 minutes on the bottom rack or until the edges are slightly browned. Cool the pan 15 minutes on a wire rack. Leave the oven on.

3 Make the filling: In a heavy saucepan, whisk together the sugar, cornstarch, and lemon zest. Whisk in the milk and lemon juice until blended. Bring to a boil over medium heat and cook 1 minute, stirring constantly. Remove the pan from the heat.

4 In a small bowl, whisk the eggs and egg yolk until smooth. Whisk 3 tablespoons of the hot lemon mixture into the egg mixture and then add the egg mixture to the lemon mixture, stirring constantly. Cook the mixture over medium heat 1 minute, stirring constantly, until thickened. Remove from the heat and stir in the butter. Press a sheet of plastic wrap directly onto the filling and set aside while preparing the meringue.

5 Make the meringue: Beat the egg whites and cream of tartar with an electric mixer on medium speed just until soft peaks form. Continue beating, gradually adding the sugar, a tablespoon at a time, just until stiff peaks form. Stir in the vanilla.

6 Remove the plastic wrap from the filling and use a spatula to spread it into the crust. Spread the meringue over the lemon filling, making sure the meringue touches the pie crust to avoid shrinking during baking. Bake the pie on the middle rack 20 minutes or until the meringue is light golden brown. Watch carefully so it doesn't burn. Cool the pie on a wire rack 30 minutes and serve. Refrigerate any leftovers.

Note: If using rice milk or potato milk, increase the cornstarch to 6 tablespoons.

Lime Curd Tart

MAKES 6 SERVINGS

Lime curd is just like lemon curd—a thick, creamy spread. You can use this versatile lime curd in any way you would use a lemon curd. This tart has a tremendous amount of flavor, so very small slices are appropriate.

CRUST

1 cup gluten-free cookie crumbs, such as Midel Arrowroot or homemade Graham Crackers (page 433)

2 teaspoons sugar

1 tablespoon unsalted butter or buttery spread, such as Earth Balance, at room temperature

FILLING

3 large eggs, at room temperature

2 large egg yolks, at room temperature

1 cup sugar

1 tablespoon cornstarch

½ cup fresh lime juice

⅛ teaspoon salt

¼ cup unsalted butter or buttery spread, such as Earth Balance

¼ teaspoon grated lime zest

2 cups homemade Basic Whipped Cream (page 624) or whipped topping, such as Lucerne or Soyatoo

1 Place a rack in the middle of the oven. Preheat the oven to 350°F. Generously grease an 8-inch round nonstick (gray, not black) springform pan; set aside.

2 Make the crust: In a food processor, process the cookies and sugar to a fine meal-like texture. Add the butter and process until crumbly. Press the mixture into the bottom and 1-inch up the sides of the pan.

3 Bake 5 to 10 minutes on the middle rack or until the crust is fragrant. Watch carefully since the crust can burn quickly depending on the type of cookies used. Cool the crust 15 minutes on a wire rack.

4 Make the filling: Place the eggs and egg yolks in a medium bowl and whisk together until smooth; set aside. In a medium saucepan, whisk together the sugar and cornstarch until blended. Add the lime juice and salt and bring to a boil, whisking constantly. Whisk ¼ cup of the mixture into the eggs and then whisk the entire mixture into the eggs. Using a spatula, scrape all of the mixture from the bowl back into the saucepan and cook over medium heat about 5 minutes, whisking constantly, or until the mixture thickens and coats the back of a spoon. Be careful not to bring the mixture to a boil. Remove the pan from the heat and stir in the butter and lime zest.

5 If the filling is lumpy, strain it through a wire-mesh strainer or sieve into the cooled pie crust. Place a piece of plastic wrap directly on the filling and refrigerate at least 2 hours or preferably overnight. Remove the plastic wrap before spreading the lime curd in the crust.

6 Spread the whipped cream evenly over the lime curd, using a spatula to make attractive dips and swirls. Serve immediately. Refrigerate any leftovers.

Mango Blueberry Tart

MAKES 4 SERVINGS

Mango and blueberry, with their lovely orange and dark blue colors, are especially pretty in this tart. Arrange them artfully on the filling and this tart will take its place proudly on a dinner table.

CRUST

1½ cups Carol's Sorghum Blend (page x)

½ cup sugar

½ teaspoon xanthan gum

⅛ teaspoon salt

½ cup (1 stick) unsalted butter or buttery spread, such as Earth Balance, at room temperature and cut into 8 pieces

1 teaspoon pure vanilla extract

FILLING

½ cup sour cream or sour cream alternative, such as Tofutti

1 small package (3 ounces) cream cheese or cream cheese alternative, such as Tofutti, softened

¼ cup sugar

2 tablespoons fresh lemon juice

1 large mango, peeled, seeded and diced

1 cup fresh blueberries

Grated zest of 1 lime for garnish

1 Lightly butter a 9-inch round nonstick (gray, not black) tart pan or springform pan with removable sides.

2 Make the crust: In a food processor, pulse the sorghum blend, sugar, xanthan gum, and salt to blend. Add the butter pieces and vanilla and process until the mixture resembles coarse crumbs. Remove the dough from the food processor and knead it with your hands until it is smooth. Press the dough into the pan as thinly as possible, pressing it about 1-inch up the sides. Freeze 30 minutes.

3 While the crust is chilling, place a rack in the bottom position of the oven. Preheat the oven to 350°F. Bake the crust about 20 minutes, or until the pastry is lightly browned around the edges. Cool completely on a wire rack.

4 Make the filling: In a large bowl, beat the sour cream, cream cheese, sugar, and lemon juice until smooth. Spread it in the baked pastry shell. Arrange the diced mango and blueberries evenly over the filling. Refrigerate 2 to 3 hours or until firm. Dust the pie lightly with lime zest before serving. Refrigerate leftovers.

Torta della Nonna

MAKES 8 SERVINGS

Even though the Italians call this a Grandmother's Cake, it qualifies as a pie because it has a crust and a cream cheese filling. I've wanted to make it since a recent trip to Italy when I saw how much my tour guide, Anria Novelli Del Pizzo, enjoyed this dessert at an open-air café in Milan, just steps away from the Duomo and La Scala opera house. Later, Anria graciously shared her recipe that was handed down from her mother-in-law, Antonietta Santarelli Del Pizzo, and I've adapted it to be gluten-free. Grazie (thank you), ladies.

CRUST

1 cup Carol's Sorghum Blend (page x)

¾ cup tapioca flour

¼ cup sweet rice flour

½ cup sugar

Grated zest and juice of 1 lemon

2 teaspoons xanthan gum

½ teaspoon salt

¼ teaspoon baking soda

½ cup shortening, such as Crisco or Spectrum Vegetable, or buttery sticks, such as Earth Balance

⅓ cup 1% milk (cow's, rice, soy, potato, or nut)

1 teaspoon pure vanilla extract

FILLING

2 cups ricotta cheese (drained overnight with liquid discarded)

3 large eggs, at room temperature

½ cup sugar

2 tablespoons cornstarch

¼ teaspoon salt

Grated zest of 1 lemon

1 tablespoon pure vanilla extract

GARNISH

1 tablespoon powdered sugar (or more to taste)

1 Place a rack in the bottom position and another in the middle position of the oven. Preheat the oven to 375°F. Have a 9-inch nonstick (gray, not black) pie pan ready.

2 Make the crust: In a food processor, combine the sorghum blend, tapioca flour, rice flour, sugar, lemon zest, lemon juice, sugar, xanthan gum, salt, baking soda, and shortening. Pulse a few times to blend ingredients. Add milk and vanilla extract, pulse a few times to blend, then process until mixture forms a ball. Remove the dough from the food processor and massage it a few times with hands to form a soft ball. Place half of dough in a heavy duty food storage bag to keep it from drying out.

3 Shape the remaining half of dough into a flat disk and place it on the center of a sheet of heavy-duty plastic wrap that is anchored on a wet paper towel. Place a sheet of plastic wrap on top and roll dough to a 10-inch circle. Remove the top plastic wrap and invert crust, centering it over pie pan. Remove the remaining plastic wrap and press the dough into place. Roll the crust edges slightly toward the center of pan in preparation for top crust, which will be rolled around it and sealed.

4 Make the filling: In a medium bowl, beat all of the filling ingredients with an electric mixer on medium speed until thoroughly blended. Spread the filling evenly in the crust.

5 Roll the remaining half of the dough to a 10-inch circle between sheets of plastic wrap. Remove the top plastic sheet and invert the dough and center it on the filled crust. Remove the second plastic wrap once the dough is centered. Roll outer edges of top crust around bottom crust edges, press together, and flute or shape decorative edge around rim of pie pan. Place the pie on a nonstick (gray, not black) baking sheet.

6 Bake on the bottom rack 15 minutes. Move the pie to the middle rack and bake 20 to 25 minutes more, or until the crust is nicely browned. The top crust will rise up during baking and then fall while cooling. Cover the crust loosely with foil if edges brown too much during baking. Cool completely on a wire rack before cutting. Place powdered sugar in a small sieve and dust the entire top crust. This is best served at room temperature.

PASTRIES AND DONUTS

Crullers

MAKES 12 SERVINGS

A cruller is a cakelike doughnut shaped into a long twist, deep fried, and sprinkled with powdered sugar.

2 packets (2¼ teaspoons each) instant dry yeast
⅓ cup warm (110°F) water
½ cup sugar, divided
2 tablespoons unsalted butter or buttery spread, such as Earth Balance, melted
1 large egg, at room temperature
1 teaspoon pure vanilla extract
1 cup Carol's Sorghum Blend (page x)
1 cup cornstarch
¼ cup Expandex modified tapioca starch
2 teaspoons baking powder
1½ teaspoons xanthan gum
½ teaspoon salt
¼ teaspoon freshly grated nutmeg
⅛ teaspoon baking soda
Canola oil for oiling hands and deep frying
Powdered sugar for dusting

1 In a small bowl, dissolve yeast in warm water, along with 1 teaspoon of the sugar. Set aside 5 minutes to foam.

2 In the mixing bowl of a stand mixer, combine butter, egg, vanilla, and remaining sugar. Beat on low speed to blend ingredients. Add sorghum blend, cornstarch, modified tapioca starch, xanthan gum, salt, nutmeg, and baking soda and the yeast mixture, and beat on low until dough is thoroughly blended. Dough will be somewhat stiff and sticky.

3 With very lightly oiled hands, shape about 2 tablespoons of dough into 12 strips, each about 1 inch in diameter and 5 inches long. Gently twist strips and place on parchment paper.

4 Heat oil to 375°F at a depth of 4 inches in a heavy-duty saucepan on the stove or an electric fryer (following manufacturer's directions). When fat has reached 375°F, use a slotted spoon to carefully ease crullers into fat, 1 at a time. Fry about 2 minutes until golden brown all over, using tongs to turn. Drain on paper towels. Dust with powdered sugar and serve warm.

Yeast-Free Crullers

MAKES 12 SERVINGS

The traditional French cruller is made from pâte a choux *(pat-ah-shoo), the basic dough used for cream puffs. Here, I use a modified cream puff dough and shape the crullers on a baking sheet before frying them in hot oil. Then they are brushed or dipped into a powder sugar frosting to produce the characteristic glaze. These are best eaten within 30 minutes of frying, so plan accordingly. The white vanilla powder I refer to here is the kind commonly served with coffee at coffeehouses, but you can also buy it in the spice section of some grocery stores, or from Authentic Foods or Gifts of Nature.*

½ cup white rice flour
¼ cup potato starch
2 tablespoons Expandex modified tapioca starch
2 large eggs plus 1 egg white, at room temperature
¾ cup water
¼ cup unsalted butter or buttery spread, such as Earth Balance
2 teaspoons sugar
1 teaspoon pure vanilla extract or ½ teaspoon white vanilla powder
¾ teaspoon salt
¼ teaspoon freshly grated nutmeg
Canola oil for frying

GLAZE

1 cup powdered sugar
1 teaspoon unsalted butter or buttery spread, such as Earth Balance
½ teaspoon pure vanilla extract or ¼ teaspoon white vanilla powder

1 Line a 15 × 10-inch baking sheet (not nonstick) with parchment paper and coat with cooking spray. Have a quart-size, heavy-duty food storage bag and scissors ready

2 Whisk together the flour, potato starch, and modified tapioca starch together and have ready by the stove. Have eggs in a small bowl ready as well.

3 Bring the water, butter, sugar, vanilla extract, salt, and nutmeg to a boil over medium-high heat. When the mixture starts to boil, add the flour mixture all at once and stir with wooden spoon until mixture pulls away from sides of pan and film forms on pan bottom.

4 Remove the pan from the heat and cool dough at least 5 minutes, but no longer than 10 minutes. Using a hand mixer, add eggs one at a time, beating until smooth after each addition. The dough should be thick but fall slowly and steadily if the beaters are raised up. If it doesn't, add more water a tablespoon at a time until it does. The dough must be somewhat soft so it can be piped into shapes.

5 Fill a food storage bag with dough. Cut a ¼-inch opening in one of the bottom corners. Twist the top of the bag to force dough out through the hole. Pipe the dough into 12 rings onto prepared baking sheet, beginning in the center and making continuous concentric circles to a diameter of 3 inches. Place baking sheet in the freezer 15 to 20 minutes.

6 Heat the oil to 375°F at a depth of 4 inches in a heavy-duty saucepan on the stove or an electric fryer (following manufacturer's directions). Use a slotted spoon to lower a cruller in hot oil. Fry until golden brown on underside, then turn with a slotted spoon. The crullers will take longer to brown than other fried foods because they are frozen. Fry to a deep golden brown, then drain on paper towels.

7 Make the glaze: In a medium bowl, mix the powdered sugar, butter, vanilla, and enough water to form a smooth thin frosting. When crullers are cool enough to handle, dip each in glaze or use a brush to brush the glaze on them. Serve immediately.

Doughnuts Ⓥ

MAKES 12 SERVINGS

The techniques used to create these doughnuts — for example, creating a little hothouse for rising— may seem a little unusual, but your reward will be heavenly doughnuts that rise high and light. Make plenty—the kids will love 'em.

2 packets (2¼ teaspoons each) instant dry yeast

½ cup warm (110°F) water

½ cup sugar, divided

2 tablespoons unsalted butter or buttery spread, such as Earth Balance, melted

1 large egg, at room temperature

1 teaspoon pure vanilla extract

1 cup Carol's Sorghum Blend (page x)

1 cup cornstarch

¼ cup Expandex modified tapioca starch

1½ teaspoons xanthan gum

½ teaspoon salt

½ teaspoon ground cardamom

¼ teaspoon ground cinnamon

¼ teaspoon ground mace

Canola oil for oiling hands

Vegetable shortening or canola oil, for deep fat frying

1½ cups superfine sugar mixed with 1 teaspoon cinnamon

1 In a small bowl, dissolve yeast in warm water, along with 1 teaspoon of the sugar. Set aside 5 minutes to foam.

2 In the mixing bowl of a stand mixer, combine butter, egg, and remaining sugar. Beat on low speed to blend ingredients. Add remaining ingredients, including yeast mixture, and beat on low until dough is thoroughly blended. Dough will be somewhat stiff and sticky.

3 With lightly oiled hands, shape 2 generous tablespoons dough into 12 balls. With your hands, flatten each ball to 3-inch circle and punch hole in center. Pull gently to make 3-inch diameter doughnut shape, ½-inch thick with a 1-inch diameter hole. Place on large baking sheet lined with parchment paper. Repeat with remaining balls of dough, continuing to lightly oil hands as needed to prevent sticking. Place this baking sheet on a heating pad turned to "high." Cover with upside-down baking sheet to form a little moist hothouse for the doughnuts to rise. For added warmth, place two heated Hot Socks* on the top, upside-down baking sheet to assure heat from both top and bottom. Or use a second heating pad. Let doughnuts rise to desired height. Rising time will vary by your altitude and weather conditions.

4 Preheat oil. Remove cover from doughnuts. When fat has reached 375°F, use a slotted spoon to carefully ease doughnuts into fat, 1 at a time. Fry about 2 minutes until golden brown all over, using tongs to turn. Drain on paper towels. Dust with cinnamon-sugar.

Whipped-Cream Filled Doughnuts: Follow Steps 1 and 2. Follow Step 3, except do not punch hole in flattened 3-inch ball of dough. Proceed with Step 4. When doughnuts are fried, drain on paper towel until cool enough to touch. Cut ½-inch slit horizontally in side of doughnut. Insert nozzle of aerosol whipped cream into slit and press nozzle to fill with approximately 1 tablespoon whipped cream per doughnut. Dust each doughnut with 1 teaspoon powdered sugar or granulated sugar. Serve immediately.

Jam-Filled Doughnuts: Follow instructions for Whipped Cream–Filled Doughnuts. Fill heavy-duty, quart-size food storage bag with ¾ cup raspberry jam (or jam of your choice) that has been warmed slightly. Twist top of bag to force jam into one corner. Cut ¼ inch off same corner of bag and insert corner into slit in doughnut. Exert gentle pressure to press 1 tablespoon jam into each doughnut. Dust each doughnut with 1 teaspoon powdered sugar or granulated sugar. Serve immediately or wrap securely until serving time.

DOUGHNUT TIPS

- Never fry more than 4 doughnuts at a time to allow for even cooking.

- Keep fat as near to 375°F as possible. If oil is too hot, doughnuts will brown before they cook inside. If it too cold, they won't brown and may dry out before they are cooked through.

- Always remember that hot oil is very dangerous so keep your fryer on a safe, level surface.

- Frying with hot oil requires your complete attention so avoid distractions and don't have pets or children in the area while you're frying.

Hot Socks: Fill a clean, white tube sock with uncooked white rice. Tie the sock at open end in a firm knot. To heat, place in microwave oven on high for 2 to 3 minutes, depending on sock size.

Baked Apple Doughnuts with Powdered Sugar Glaze ⓥ

MAKES 12 SERVINGS

Yes, can you can bake doughnuts instead of frying them. This yeast-free donut is very flavorful and will have your family gathering in the kitchen to find out what smells so good. Because they aren't fried, they contain far less fat than donuts you can buy or even others you can make, so you can indulge with less guilt. Nonstick mini-Bundt molds are usually black (rather than the gray version I recommend) so I have lowered the oven temperature from the usual 350°F to 325°F. If your pans are gray, bake the doughnuts at 350°F. Watch the doughnuts carefully to avoid burning because they are quite small.

DRY INGREDIENTS

1¾ cups Carol's Sorghum Blend (page x)

¼ cup Expandex modified tapioca starch, or ¼ cup Carol's Sorghum Blend (page x)

¼ cup packed light brown sugar

2 teaspoons baking powder

1 teaspoon ground cinnamon

1 teaspoon xanthan gum

½ teaspoon salt

¼ teaspoon ground cloves

¼ teaspoon freshly grated nutmeg

¼ teaspoon ground allspice

LIQUID INGREDIENTS

1 cup unsweetened apple juice concentrate, thawed but not diluted

1 large egg, at room temperature

¼ cup canola oil

2 tablespoons molasses (not blackstrap)

1 teaspoon pure vanilla extract

GLAZE

1 cup powdered sugar

1 tablespoon molasses (not blackstrap)

2 tablespoons water

1 Place a rack in the middle of the oven. Preheat the oven to 325°F. Very generously grease the 6 molds of a mini-Bundt or mini-angel food cake pan; set aside. You will need to bake the doughnut batter in two batches.

2 In large mixing bowl, whisk together the dry ingredients. Add the liquid ingredients and beat with an electric mixer on low speed just until well blended. Fill each mold with 2 tablespoons batter and use a wet spatula to evenly distribute the batter. (Note: This may appear to be an insufficient amount of batter—don't worry, the batter rises to fill the mold. If you happen to overfill the molds for the first batch of doughnuts and don't have enough batter to fill all molds for the second batch, fill as many as you can and put ¼ cup water in each of the empty molds to avoid damaging the pan.)

3 Bake 20 to 25 minutes or until the tops of the doughnuts are firm and lightly browned. Cool the doughnuts 5 minutes in the pan and then gently loosen the edges with a sharp knife and transfer the doughnuts to a wire rack to cool completely. Bake the remaining half of batter.

4 When the doughnuts are cool, whisk together the powdered sugar, molasses, and water until smooth. Dip the patterned side of each doughnut into frosting. Place on plate to dry. Serve immediately.

Beignets

MAKES 24 SERVINGS

Beignets are like doughnuts—fried and dusted with powdered sugar—but without the holes,. Serve them with the darkest, richest coffee you can find. I especially like a coffee-chicory blend for New Orleans authenticity. For added sophistication, use powdered sugar in which you've stored a whole vanilla bean for at least a month. Or, stir vanilla powder into the powdered sugar for the same effect.

1 tablespoon active dry yeast

½ cup warm (110°F) water + 2 tablespoons

1 tablespoon sugar, divided

1 cup Carol's Sorghum Blend (page x)

¾ cup potato starch

¼ cup sweet rice flour

½ teaspoon xanthan gum

1 teaspoon salt

1 tablespoon canola oil or unsalted butter or buttery spread, such Earth Balance, melted

1 teaspoon pure vanilla extract

White rice flour for dusting

Canola oil for frying

Powdered sugar for dusting

1 In a small bowl, dissolve 1 teaspoon of the sugar in ½ cup warm water and stir in yeast until thoroughly mixed. Set aside 5 minutes to foam.

2 In a large mixing bowl, combine sorghum blend, potato starch, sweet rice flour, remaining sugar, xanthan gum, and salt. Add yeast mixture, oil, and vanilla. Blend with electric mixer on low, adding remaining 2 tablespoons of warm water to form thick but soft dough. Or, place all ingredients in food processor and process until thoroughly blended and dough forms a soft ball.

3 Wrap half of dough in plastic wrap. Roll out half of dough to an 8-inch square, and ⅛-inch thickness between sheets of heavy-duty plastic wrap dusted with white rice flour. To prevent slipping, place a wet paper towel under plastic wrap to anchor it. Cut into 2 × 2-inch squares, trimming away any ragged edges. Repeat with remaining dough.

4 Heat 4 inches oil to 375°F in a heavy-duty saucepan on the stove, or an electric fryer (following manufacturer's directions).

5 Use a slotted spoon to carefully place squares of dough into hot oil. When dough rises to the top, turn over to help beignet puff evenly. Cook until pale gold on both sides, turning several times to encourage even browning (1 to 2 minutes total cooking time). Remove with slotted spoon and drain on paper towels. Repeat with remaining half of dough. Serve immediately with a generous dusting of powdered sugar.

Sopaipillas Ⓥ

MAKES 24 SERVINGS

Sopaipillas are puffy, fried breads. A well-known restaurant called Rancho de Chimayo in New Mexico serves the best sopaipillas I've ever tasted. They come to your table in a basket, fresh from the fryer, looking like fluffy little pillows and it's always a major decision: "Should I eat one with my meal, or save one for dessert, or simply cave in and eat the whole basket now?" For dessert, the standard procedure is to bite off a corner and drizzle honey into the pocket (New Mexico honey is also great, but that's another story). I haven't eaten a wheat-flour sopaipilla for nearly 20 years,
but I create my own version at home and you can, too. They're surprisingly easy.

1 tablespoon active dry yeast
½ cup + 2 tablespoons warm (110°F) water
1 tablespoon sugar, divided
1 cup Carol's Sorghum Blend (page x)
¾ cup potato starch
¼ cup sweet rice flour
½ teaspoon xanthan gum
1 teaspoon salt
1 tablespoon canola oil
Canola oil, for frying
Honey or powdered sugar, for garnish

1 Dissolve 1 teaspoon of the sugar in ½ cup of the warm water and stir in yeast until thoroughly mixed. Set aside 5 minutes to foam.

2 In the large bowl of a stand mixer, combine sorghum blend, potato starch, sweet rice flour, remaining sugar, xanthan gum, and salt. Add yeast mixture and oil. Blend with electric mixer on low, adding the 2 tablespoons of warm water to form thick but soft dough. Or place all ingredients in food processor and process until thoroughly blended and dough forms a soft ball.

3 Wrap half of dough in plastic wrap. Roll out other half to 8 × 8-inch square, and ⅛-inch thickness between sheets of heavy-duty plastic wrap. For easier rolling, place wet paper towel under plastic wrap to anchor it. Cut into 2 × 2-inch squares, trimming away any ragged edges. Repeat with remaining dough.

4 Heat the oil to 375°F at a depth of 2 to 3 inches in a deep, 3 to 4-quart pan on the stove, or an electric fryer (following manufacturer's directions).

5 Use a slotted spoon to carefully place squares of dough into hot oil, flat side down. When dough rises to the top, turn over to help sopaipillas puff evenly. Cook until pale gold on both sides, turning several times to encourage even browning (1 to 2 minutes total cooking time). Remove with slotted spoon and drain on paper towels. Repeat with remaining half of dough. Serve immediately with honey or powdered sugar.

Yeast-Free Sopaipillas

MAKES 24 SERVINGS

To facilitate the puffing of the dough for these light and sweet Mexican donuts, gently press the "puffed" portion of the dough into the hot oil as it fries. Turn them frequently during frying to facilitate even browning on both sides. If one side browns too much it won't puff up. These little pillows are best served immediately with honey or powdered sugar.

¾ cup + 2 tablespoons warm (110°F) 1% milk (cow's, rice, soy, potato, or nut) or water
1 tablespoon canola oil
1 cup Carol's Sorghum Blend (page x)
¾ cup potato starch
¼ cup sweet rice flour
1 tablespoon sugar
2 teaspoons baking powder
1 teaspoon salt
½ teaspoon xanthan gum
White rice flour for dusting
Canola oil for frying
Honey or powdered sugar, for garnish

1 In a food processor, place the milk and oil and then all the remaining ingredients and process until thoroughly blended and mixture forms a ball or several small balls. Remove the dough from the food processor and knead it with your hands a few times until it is a smooth ball. Divide the dough in half.

2 Prepare the sopaipillas as directed in Steps 3, 4, and 5 on page 610. Serve immediately with honey or powdered sugar.

Danish Puffed Pancakes

MAKES 30 SERVINGS (DEPENDING ON PAN SIZE)

These Danish desserts are also called Aebleskiver *or* Poffertj *and are cooked in a special cast-iron pan called an* aebleskiver (ebelskiver) *or "monk's pan," which is available at kitchen stores or online. They are perfect for kids because they are small. I use a small 7-hole gray cast-iron pan and use 1 tablespoon batter per hole. Other types of pans may be larger and require more batter so follow the manufacturer's directions for batter amounts and baking times.*

3 large eggs, at room temperature
1½ cups Carol's Sorghum Blend (page x)
½ cup potato starch
1 teaspoon xanthan gum
1 teaspoon baking powder
1 teaspoon baking soda
1 teaspoon ground cardamom or grated lemon zest
½ teaspoon salt
⅔ cup sugar
1 teaspoon pure vanilla extract
4 tablespoons unsalted butter or buttery spread, such as Earth Balance, melted
1 cup buttermilk, well-shaken, or homemade Buttermilk (page 677)
Canola oil for frying
Powdered sugar for dusting
½ cup raspberry jam, for garnish

1 Separate the eggs; set the egg yolks aside. In a medium bowl, beat the egg whites with an electric mixer on medium speed just until stiff peaks form; set aside.

2 Whisk the sorghum blend, potato starch, xanthan gum, baking powder, baking soda, cardamom (or lemon zest) and salt into a medium bowl. With an electric mixer at medium speed, beat the sugar, vanilla, egg yolks, and butter in a large bowl until thoroughly blended. Whisk in the sorghum mixture alternately with the buttermilk, beginning and ending with the dry ingredients. Fold the egg whites into the batter, which will be similar to thick cake batter.

3 Preheat the aebleskiver pan over medium-low heat. Put 1 teaspoon oil in each indentation and then fill each indentation with 1 tablespoon of batter.

4 Cook until sides of each aebleskiver are set and golden brown, about 3 to 5 minutes. Insert a clean knitting needle or skewer into the pancake and carefully turn aebleskivers over. Bake until the bottom is golden brown, about 2 to 3 minutes more. Repeat with remaining oil and batter.

5 Transfer aebleskivers to a platter. Sprinkle generously with powdered sugar and drizzle raspberry jam over them. Serve immediately.

Funnel Cakes

MAKES 6 SERVINGS

This delicate-looking treat reminds me of summertime and county fairs. Although the name suggests that you use a funnel to drop the batter into the hot oil, I found that it's easier to just carefully pour the batter into the hot oil from a spouted measuring cup. If you still want to use a funnel, choose one with at least a ⅜-inch opening and fill it with ¼ cup batter each time you make a funnel cake.

1 cup Carol's Sorghum Blend (page x)

¼ cup cornstarch

2 tablespoons sugar

½ teaspoon baking powder

½ teaspoon baking soda

¼ teaspoon salt

¼ teaspoon xanthan gum

1 large egg, at room temperature

¾ cup 1% milk (cow's, rice, soy, potato, or nut), at room temperature

Canola oil for frying

1 tablespoon powdered sugar, for dusting

Syrup or honey, for serving (optional)

1 In a 4-cup glass measuring bowl or other bowl or container with a pour spout, whisk together the sorghum blend, cornstarch, sugar, baking powder, baking soda, salt, and xanthan gum. Whisk in the egg and milk until smooth.

2 Heat the oil to 375°F at a depth of 2 inches in a heavy-duty deep skillet on the stove or to the depth specified for your electric fryer (follow manufacturer's directions). Transfer ¼ cup batter to a small glass measuring cup with a spout or to a funnel, preferably with a ⅜-inch opening. If you use the funnel, hold your finger over the funnel opening while you fill it and release your finger when you're ready to drizzle the batter into the hot oil.

3 Pour ¼ cup batter into the hot oil in a slow circular motion. If you've never eaten (or even seen) a funnel cake before, imagine a circular mound of fried bread. Fry until golden brown, turning once. Funnel cakes fry quickly, so have a slotted spoon ready to remove them from the oil. Drain on a paper towel-lined plate and sprinkle with powdered sugar. Serve hot with syrup or honey, if desired.

Corn Fritters

MAKES 24 SERVINGS

Serve these crispy morsels as a side dish or instead of bread. To assure they cook thoroughly, I suggest making the fritters no larger than about 2 inches in diameter. For savory fritters, replace the powdered sugar with 1 teaspoon dried parsley.

1½ cups Carol's Sorghum Blend (see page x)
½ cup potato starch
2 teaspoons baking powder
½ teaspoon sugar
1 teaspoon xanthan gum
1 teaspoon onion powder
1 teaspoon salt
2 large eggs, separated, at room temperature
1 tablespoon canola oil
½ to ⅔ cup 1% milk (cow's, rice, soy, potato, or nut)
½ cup fresh corn kernels (or frozen and thawed)
1 tablespoon powdered sugar, for garnish
Canola, for frying

1 Sift the dry ingredients into a mixing bowl. Whip the egg whites to stiff peaks and set aside.

2 Whisk the egg yolks, canola oil, and enough milk into the dry ingredients to form a smooth batter. Gently fold in the egg whites and corn kernels. The batter should be fairly stiff.

3 Heat 4 inches of oil to 375°F in a heavy-duty saucepan on the stove or an electric fryer (following manufacturer's directions). Use a spoon or a metal, spring-action ice cream scoop to carefully place about 2 tablespoons batter into the hot oil and fry until golden brown on the underside. Turn and cook until the other side turns golden. Watch carefully so fritters do not burn. Cooking time will vary depending on your saucepan, the type and size of fryer you are using, and how many fritters you fry at one time. Avoid overcrowding with too many fritters because this causes the temperature of the oil to drop.

4 Remove the fritters with a slotted spoon and drain on paper towels. Garnish with chopped parsley, for savory fritters, or for a sweeter finish, with powdered sugar. Serve immediately.

Cream Puffs

MAKES 12 FULL-SIZE CREAM PUFFS OR 24 MINI-CREAM PUFFS

These decadent little puffs are really very easy to make, so give them a try. I once froze over a hundred of them, successfully transported them on an airplane, and served them during a speaking engagement. I purchased the whipped cream in aerosol cans at my destination and we had great fun poking the whipped cream into the cream puffs. Cream puffs may also be filled with savory fillings such as chicken, tuna, ham, or egg salad for a luncheon entrée.

½ cup white rice flour
¼ cup potato starch
2 tablespoons Expandex modified tapioca starch
2 large eggs plus 1 egg white, at room temperature
⅔ cup water
¼ cup unsalted butter or buttery spread, such as Earth Balance
1 teaspoon sugar
¼ teaspoon salt
1 cup homemade Basic Whipped Cream (page 624) or whipping topping, such as Lucerne or Soyatoo
Powdered sugar, for garnish

1 Place a rack in the middle of the oven. Preheat the oven to 400°F. Line a 15 × 10-inch baking sheet (not nonstick) with parchment paper.

2 Whisk the flour, potato starch, and modified tapioca starch together in a small bowl, and have ready by the stove. Have eggs ready in a small bowl as well.

3 In a medium heavy saucepan, bring the water, butter, sugar, and salt to a boil over medium-high heat. When mixture starts to boil, add the flour mixture all at once and stir with a wooden spoon until the mixture pulls away from the sides of pan and a film forms on the bottom of the pan.

4 Immediately remove the pan from heat and cool at least 5 minutes, but no longer than 10 minutes. Using a handheld electric mixer, add the eggs, one at a time—beating until smooth after each addition.

5 Use a #14 spring-action metal ice cream scoop, and drop 12 mounds, each 2 inches in diameter, onto the baking sheet. Or, for mini cream puffs, drop 24 mounds, each 1 inch in diameter. With wet fingers, smooth any points that protrude and gently shape all mounds into circles so they bake and brown evenly.

6 Bake 35 to 45 minutes for full-size cream puffs (30 minutes for mini-cream puffs), or until cream puffs turn a deep golden brown. Transfer cream puffs to a wire rack and immediately cut a 1-inch horizontal slit in the side of each cream puff, right where you'll eventually cut them completely in half. Cool completely on the wire rack.

7 When the cream puffs are cool, use a serrated knife to cut each completely in half horizontally along the slit and discard the soft dough inside. Fill with whipped cream and replace the top. Dust with powdered sugar and serve immediately.

Éclairs Ⓥ

MAKES 20 SERVINGS

Éclairs are cream puffs formed into a slightly elongated shape. I give you suggested dimensions for the éclairs, but you can make them any shape or size you like. Drizzle them with melted chocolate after dusting with powdered sugar. Like the Cream Puffs (page 613), they can also be treated as a delicate sandwich with savory fillings such as chicken, tuna, ham, or egg salad.

½ cup white rice flour
¼ cup potato starch
2 tablespoons Expandex modified tapioca starch
2 large eggs plus 1 egg white, at room temperature
⅔ cup water
¼ cup unsalted butter or buttery spread, such as Earth Balance
1 teaspoon sugar
¼ teaspoon salt
1 cup homemade Basic Whipped Cream (page 624) or whipped topping, such as Lucerne or Soyatoo
Powdered sugar for garnish

1 Place a rack in the middle of the oven. Preheat the oven to 400°F. Line a 15 × 10-inch baking sheet (not nonstick) with parchment paper.

2 Whisk the flour, potato starch, and modified tapioca starch together in a small bowl and have ready by the stove. Have eggs ready in a small bowl as well.

3 In a medium heavy saucepan, bring the water, butter, sugar, and salt to a boil over medium-high heat. When mixture starts to boil, add the flour mixture all at once and stir with a wooden spoon until the mixture pulls away from the sides of pan and a film forms on the bottom of the pan.

4 Immediately remove the pan from heat and cool at least 5 minutes, but no longer than 10 minutes. Using a handheld electric mixer, add the eggs, one at a time, beating until smooth after each addition.

5 Spoon the dough into a heavy-duty food storage bag. Cut a bottom corner diagonally to make a ½-inch opening. Pipe 20 strips of dough, each 4 inches long and 3 inches apart, onto a parchment-lined baking sheet (not nonstick).

6 Bake 30 minutes or until deep golden brown and firm. Cool the éclairs on a wire rack and split in half, lengthwise, to form a top and bottom.

7 When the eclairs are cool, use a serrated knife to cut each one completely in half horizontally along the slit and discard the soft dough inside. Fill with whipped cream and replace the top. Dust with powdered sugar and serve immediately.

Baklava ⓥ

MAKES 24 SERVINGS

Once upon a time, this Greek-inspired dessert was my favorite, and I often rated restaurants and coffee shops by whether they offered Baklava and how well they made it. Today, I make my own. There are several steps, but the results are well worth the effort. The key is to roll the dough as thin as possible without breaking it.

DOUGH

1 cup Carol's Sorghum Blend (page x)

¾ cup tapioca flour

¼ cup sweet rice flour

¼ cup Expandex modified tapioca starch

1 tablespoon sugar

1 teaspoon xanthan gum

1 teaspoon guar gum

½ teaspoon salt

¼ teaspoon active dry yeast

½ cup shortening, such as Crisco, Earth Balance, or Spectrum Vegetable, at room temperature

2 tablespoons unsalted butter or buttery spread, such as Earth Balance, at room temperature

½ cup 1% milk (cow's, rice, soy, potato, or nut)

FILLING

2 cups finely ground walnuts

2 cups finely ground almonds

⅔ cup packed light brown sugar

1 tablespoon ground cinnamon

Cooking spray

SYRUP

2 cups sugar

1 cup water

1 tablespoon fresh lemon juice

1 teaspoon pure vanilla extract

1 large strip orange peel

1 (3-inch) piece cinnamon stick

3 whole cloves

¼ cup honey

1 Make the dough: In a food processor, combine sorghum blend, tapioca flour, sweet rice flour, modified tapioca starch, sugar, xanthan gum, guar gum, salt, yeast, shortening and butter and process 30 seconds. Add the milk and process until the dough forms a ball or large clump on one side of the bowl. If it doesn't form a ball, use a spatula to break up the dough into pieces and process it again, scraping down the side of the bowl if necessary. Remove the dough from the food processor and knead it with your hands until it is smooth. Flatten the dough to a 1-inch-thick disk, wrap tightly in plastic wrap, and chill 1 hour to let the ingredients meld together.

2 Generously butter two 8-inch square pans; set aside. Divide the dough into six equal pieces; return five of the pieces to the plastic wrap so they don't dry out. Massage the dough in your hands until it is warm and pliable. Cut two 14-inch strips of heavy-duty plastic wrap and place one on the countertop. Place a damp paper towel between the countertop and the plastic wrap to reduce slipping. Place the dough on top of the plastic wrap and cover with the second piece of plastic wrap. Roll the dough to a very thin 14-inch strip between the two sheets of plastic wrap.

3 Remove the top plastic wrap and invert the dough over one of the prepared pans, centering the crust so that the dough fits up the sides and overhangs a little bit. Press the dough into place before removing the remaining plastic wrap. Repeat the same step with another ball of dough for the second prepared pan. Lightly spray the dough with cooking spray.

4 Make the filling: Whisk together the nuts, brown sugar, and cinnamon until blended. Sprinkle 1 cup of the nuts over the dough in each pan.

5 Roll another two balls of the dough to 14-inch strips, fitting them into each of the pans as described above. Coat the dough with cooking spray. Sprinkle another cup of nut filling on top of dough in each pan.

6 Roll the final two balls of dough to 14-inch strips and fit into the two pans. Evenly trim the edge of the dough, leaving enough to roll under decoratively around the edge of the pan. With a very sharp knife, cut each pan of baklava into twelve 2 inch squares.

7 Place a rack in the bottom position and another in the middle position of the oven. Preheat the oven to 350°F. Lightly coat the bars with cooking spray and refrigerate 30 minutes.

8 Bake 15 minutes on the bottom rack of the oven. Move the pans to the middle rack and bake another 10 to 15 minutes, or until the baklava is light golden.

9 While the baklava bakes, make the syrup: In a heavy, medium pan, bring the sugar, water, lemon juice, vanilla, orange peel, cinnamon stick, and cloves to a boil and simmer 10 minutes, or until it is slightly thickened and syrupy. Whisk in the honey. Remove from the heat, discard the orange peel and cinnamon stick.

10 When the baklava is done, cut completely through the scores, all the way to the bottom of the pan. Use a tablespoon or a coffee measure to drizzle small amounts of the warm syrup over the bars and into the cuts. Cool completely and let stand several hours before serving.

Apple Strudel
MAKES 12 SERVINGS

Strudel is a traditional Austrian pastry, but it is actually a pie crust wrapped around an apple filling. It is best eaten as soon as it has cooled to room temperature.

DOUGH
1 cup Carol's Sorghum Blend (page x)
¾ cup tapioca flour
½ cup sweet rice flour
¼ cup sugar, divided
1 teaspoon xanthan gum
1 teaspoon guar gum
½ teaspoon salt
½ teaspoon active dry yeast
½ cup shortening, such as Crisco, Earth Balance, or Spectrum Vegetable, or buttery sticks, such as Earth Balance, at room temperature
⅓ cup 1% milk (cow's, rice, soy, potato, or nut)
1 teaspoon vinegar or lemon juice
1 egg, beaten to a foam, for brushing
White rice flour or cornstarch, for dusting

FILLING
4 large apples, peeled and diced
2 teaspoons fresh lemon juice
1 tablespoon unsalted butter or buttery spread, such as Earth Balance, at room temperature
½ cup sugar
½ cup raisins
¼ cup finely chopped walnuts
½ teaspoon ground cinnamon
¼ teaspoon salt

1 Make the dough: Place the sorghum blend, tapioca, sweet rice flour, 3 tablespoons of the sugar, xanthan gum, guar gum, salt, yeast, and shortening in a food processor. Process until blended. Add the milk and vinegar and process until the dough forms a ball. If it doesn't form a ball, use a spatula to break up the dough into pieces and process again, scraping down sides if necessary. Remove the dough from the food processor and knead it with your hands until smooth. Flatten the dough to two 1-inch-thick disks, wrap tightly in plastic wrap, and chill 1 hour.

2 Massage one of the disks between your hands until it is warm and pliable. (Keep remaining disk wrapped tightly to avoid drying out.) Place the disk on a 15-inch sheet of parchment paper that has been dusted with white rice flour. Cover the dough with plastic wrap, and roll it to a ⅛-inch thin rectangle about 10 × 12 inches. Remove the top plastic wrap.

3 Place a rack in the middle of the oven. Preheat the oven to 350°F.

4 While the oven preheats, make the filling: In a medium bowl, toss the apples with the lemon juice and then with the melted butter, sugar, raisins, walnuts, cinnamon, and salt until well blended. Place half of the apple mixture down the middle of the dough. Turn in the ends, and, beginning at the long side, use the parchment paper to help roll and nudge the dough up and over the apples. Press the dough together on top to seal in the apples. Carefully lift the parchment paper and transfer the strudel to one side of the 15 × 10-inch baking sheet.

5 Repeat steps 2 and 3 with the remaining disk of dough and remaining apple mixture and transfer the strudel to the other side of the baking sheet. Trim away any excess parchment paper.

6 Bake 30 minutes on the middle rack or until the crust starts to brown and the apples are tender. Brush the strudel with the egg mixture, sprinkle with the remaining 1 tablespoon of sugar, and return to the oven to bake 10 minutes more or until the strudel is completely browned. Cool the strudels on the pan on a wire rack 15 minutes. Cut each strudel into 6 slices. Serve warm or at room temperature.

CREPES

Dessert Crepes

MAKES 8 SERVINGS

Crepes are thin pancakes and are very popular in certain parts of Europe, especially Austria. They are surprisingly easy to make once the pan reaches the right temperature. And, they form the basis for several other desserts such as Austrian Crepes in Custard (page 618), Crepes Suzette (page 619), Crepes with Ricotta Filling and Chocolate Sauce (page 618), and Jam-Filled Crepes (page 620).

⅔ cup sifted Carol's Sorghum Blend (page x)
1 tablespoon sugar
¼ teaspoon xanthan gum
⅛ teaspoon salt
1 cup 1% milk (cow's, rice, soy, potato, or nut)
2 large eggs
1 tablespoon canola oil
1 teaspoon pure vanilla extract

1 Combine all the ingredients in a blender and process until very smooth. Heat an 8-inch skillet or seasoned crepe pan over medium-high heat until a drop of water dances on the surface. Lightly oil the pan with canola oil.

2 Pour a scant ¼ cup (or more, if using a larger pan) batter into the pan and immediately tilt the pan to coat the bottom evenly. Cook until the underside of the crepe is brown; turn the crepe over and cook other side for about 20 to 30 seconds. Remove crepe from pan and lay on a sheet of wax paper. Repeat with remaining batter, layering the crepes between wax paper or parchment paper.

Austrian Crepes in Custard

MAKES 4 SERVINGS

Despite their elegant appearance, crepes are actually quite easy to make. Frying crepes is just like making pancakes, except they don't have leavening so they don't rise. Once they're cooked, you can assemble this European dish—which is jam-filled crepes baked in a creamy custard—in no time.

8 homemade Dessert Crepes (page 617)
½ cup boiling water
¼ cup dried currants
1 package (8 ounces) cream cheese, or cream cheese alternative, such as Tofutti, softened
¼ cup apricot preserves
2 large eggs, at room temperature, separated
½ teaspoon grated lemon zest
2 tablespoons sugar, divided
1 teaspoon pure vanilla extract
Pinch salt
¾ cup whole milk (cow's, rice, soy, potato, or nut)
¼ cup powdered sugar for dusting

1 Prepare the dessert crepes; set aside. Then, put the boiling water and currants in a heatproof bowl and let stand 15 minutes. Drain the currants well and pat them dry between paper towels; set aside.

2 In a medium bowl, beat the cream cheese, preserves, 1 egg yolk, lemon zest, 1 tablespoon of the sugar, and vanilla extract with an electric mixer on medium speed until well blended; set aside.

3 In a separate clean bowl with clean beaters, beat 1 of the egg whites with a pinch of salt to the soft peak stage. Add the remaining 1 tablespoon of the sugar and beat until it forms stiff peaks. Gently fold the cheese mixture into beaten egg white and then fold in the currants.

4 Preheat the oven to 400°F and lightly butter a 13 × 9-inch glass baking dish. Place an oven rack in the middle position of the oven. Spread 2 generous tablespoons of the filling on each crepe, leaving a ½-inch border all around, and roll up the crepes jelly-roll fashion. Place the crepes in the prepared baking dish, seam-side down.

5 In a small bowl, whisk together the remaining egg yolk, egg white, and 1 tablespoon of sugar, and milk and pour over crepes.

6 Bake 30 to 35 minutes or until crepes are puffed and the custard is set. Cool the crepes 15 minutes on a wire rack until they are just warm. Dust with powdered sugar and serve immediately.

Crepes with Ricotta Filling and Chocolate Sauce Ⓥ

MAKES 8 SERVINGS

Make the crepes a few hours before dinner and let them stand between sheets of parchment paper or wax paper at room temperature. Assemble them just before serving or, for extra fun, let your guests help. This dessert is really simple to assemble once you have the crepes made. It's a great dessert for guests because it really is quite elegant.

CREPES

⅔ cup sifted Carol's Sorghum Blend (page x)
¼ teaspoon xanthan gum
⅛ teaspoon salt
1 cup 1% milk (cow's, rice, soy, potato, or nut)
2 large eggs, at room temperature
6 teaspoons unsalted butter or buttery spread, such as Earth Balance, melted, or canola oil, divided
1 teaspoon almond extract

FILLING

1 cup ricotta cheese, at room temperature
1 tablespoon powdered sugar
1 teaspoon pure vanilla extract
½ teaspoon almond extract
Homemade Chocolate Sauce (page 622), for garnish

1 Make the crepes: Combine the sorghum blend, xanthan gum, salt, milk, eggs, 2 teaspoons of the butter, and almond extract in a blender and process until very smooth.

2 Heat an 8-inch nonstick skillet or seasoned crepe pan over medium-high heat until a drop of water dances on the surface. Add enough of the remaining 4 teaspoons butter (about ½ teaspoon per crepe) to lightly coat the skillet, adding more as necessary to fry all 8 crepes.

3 Pour a scant 2 tablespoons batter into the crepe pan and immediately tilt pan to coat the bottom evenly. Cook until the underside of the crepe is brown; cook other side for about 20 to 30 seconds until it is also lightly browned. Fry another 7 crepes with the remaining batter and butter. Stack the crepes with layers of parchment paper or aluminum foil between them.

4 Make the filling: In a food processor, place the cheese, powdered sugar, vanilla extract, and almond extract and blend until smooth.

5 To serve, place each of the 8 crepes on a dessert plate and spread 2 tablespoons of filling in the center of each and then fold it in half. Drizzle each crepe with 2 tablespoons of the chocolate sauce. Serve immediately.

Crepes Suzette
MAKES 4 SERVINGS

Crepes Suzette are simply crepes filled with orange jam. Its fancy French name implies "difficult," yet this is actually quite simple. Navel oranges work best because they are seedless. Traditional versions of this dish include flaming a liqueur, but I omitted that step for safety and simplicity. As a tasty shortcut, thin your favorite orange marmalade with a little orange juice and pour the mixture over the crepes.

⅔ cup sifted Carol's Sorghum Blend (page x)
¼ teaspoon xanthan gum
⅛ teaspoon salt
1 cup 1% milk (cow's, rice, soy, potato, or nut)
2 large eggs, at room temperature
6 teaspoons unsalted butter or buttery spread, such as Earth Balance, melted, or canola oil
1 teaspoon pure vanilla extract or orange extract
1½ cups fresh orange juice
2 tablespoons powdered sugar
2 teaspoons grated orange zest
2 tablespoons orange liqueur, such as Triple Sec (optional)
3 naval oranges, peeled and sectioned
Powdered sugar, as garnish

1 In a blender, combine the sorghum blend, xanthan gum, salt, milk, eggs, 2 teaspoons of the butter, and vanilla and process until very smooth.

2 Heat an 8-inch nonstick skillet or seasoned crepe pan over medium-high heat until a drop of water dances on the surface. Add enough of the remaining 4 teaspoons butter (about ½ teaspoon per crepe) to lightly coat the skillet, adding more as necessary to fry all 8 crepes.

3 Pour a scant 2 tablespoons batter into the crepe pan and immediately tilt pan to coat the bottom evenly. Cook until the underside of the crepe is brown; cook other side for about 20 to 30 seconds until it is also lightly browned. Fry another 7 crepes using the remaining batter and butter. Stack the crepes with layers of parchment paper or aluminum foil between them.

4 In a small, heavy saucepan, bring the orange juice, sugar, and orange zest to a boil over medium-high heat. Reduce the heat to low and simmer about 5 minutes, stirring occasionally, until it reduces down and becomes syrupy. Remove from the heat and stir in the liqueur and oranges; gently bring to serving temperature again.

5 Gently fold the crepes into quarters and lay, overlapping slightly, in an 11 × 7-inch baking dish. Pour the sauce over the crepes and serve immediately, sprinkled with powdered sugar.

Jam-Filled Crepes

MAKES 6 SERVINGS

Palacsinta is the Hungarian name for jam-filled crepes. Berry jams are especially tasty, but I also like to use apricot preserves. Dusted with powdered sugar, these little gems are sure to please the kids.

⅔ cup Carol's Sorghum Blend (page x)
¼ teaspoon xanthan gum
⅛ teaspoon salt
1 cup 1% milk (cow's, rice, soy, potato, or nut)
2 large eggs, at room temperature
6 teaspoons unsalted butter or buttery spread, such as Earth Balance, melted, or canola oil
1 teaspoon almond extract
¾ cup raspberry or strawberry or blackberry jam
¼ cup powdered sugar for dusting

1 Combine the sorghum blend, xanthan gum, salt, milk, eggs, 2 teaspoons of the butter, and almond extract in a blender and process until very smooth. Transfer to a large glass jar or container and refrigerate at least 30 minutes.

2 Heat an 8-inch nonstick skillet or seasoned crepe pan over medium-high heat until a drop of water dances on the surface. Add enough of the remaining 4 teaspoons butter (about ½ teaspoon per crepe) to lightly coat the skillet, adding more as necessary to fry all 12 crepes.

3 Pour a scant 2 tablespoons batter into the crepe pan and immediately tilt pan to coat the bottom evenly. Cook until the underside of the crepe is brown; cook other side for about 20 to 30 seconds until it is also lightly browned. Fry another 7 crepes using the remaining batter and butter. Stack the crepes with layers of parchment paper or aluminum foil between them.

4 Spread a tablespoon of jam over each crepe and roll up, jelly-roll style. Or, fill the crepe with jam and then fold in half, then in half again. Serve immediately, dusted with powdered sugar.

FONDUE, SAUCES, AND TOPPINGS

Caramel Fondue

MAKES 4 SERVINGS (1½ CUPS)

Rich, creamy caramel tastes good on just about anything, and caramel fondue is a nice way to serve and share dessert with friends and family. It is fun, tasty, and promotes lots of conversation because you're all focused on the fondue pot in the center of the table. I've attended large parties where there was a small fondue pot for every 2 to 3 people, and it worked very nicely.

1 cup sugar

¼ cup water

¼ cup heavy cream or 3 tablespoons 1% milk (cow's, rice, soy, potato, or nut)

¼ cup (½ stick) unsalted butter or buttery spread, such as Earth Balance, at room temperature

½ teaspoon pure vanilla extract

¼ teaspoon salt

Dippers: apple slices, banana slices, peeled clementine sections, 1-inch cubes of gluten-free pound cake, large marshmallows, whole strawberries, chunks of fresh pineapple, Mary's Gone Crackers original flavor, or Ener-G pretzels

1 In a heavy, medium saucepan, combine the sugar and water over medium-low heat. Stir until the sugar is dissolved. Increase the heat to medium-high and boil, swirling the pan occasionally without stirring, until the caramel sauce turns a deep amber color, about 7 minutes. As the mixture boils, wipe down sides of pan frequently with wet pastry brush to prevent the crystallization of the sugar.

2 Remove the sauce from the heat and stir in the cream with a long-handled spoon, carefully avoiding the splatters as it bubbles up. Add the butter, reduce the heat to low and return the pan to the heat, stirring until the butter melts and the caramel is smooth. Stir in the vanilla and the salt.

3 Place the mixture in a fondue pot. Arrange the dippers on a platter and provide forks or bamboo skewers for guests to dunk food into the warm caramel. If the caramel starts to firm up, add a tablespoon more corn syrup and transfer it from the fondue pot to a microwave-safe dish and reheat it in the microwave. Return it to the fondue pot.

Dark Chocolate Fondue

MAKES 4 SERVINGS (1½ CUPS)

For those who think dark chocolate is the "only" chocolate, this fondue is for you. At a big trade show a few years ago, I noticed one of my favorite cracker companies—Mary's Gone Crackers—was exhibiting right next to a company that produced delicious chocolate. We joked that we should combine the two products into one, that is, the crackers dipped in chocolate. That was the inspiration for using savory crackers as a dipper and, although it's a little unusual, it's incredibly delicious—sort of like chocolate-covered pretzels.

12 ounces gluten-free dark chocolate, such as Scharffen Berger, coarsely chopped

2 tablespoons light corn syrup

Dippers: apple slices, banana slices, peeled clementine sections, 1-inch cubes of gluten-free pound cake, large marshmallows, whole strawberries, chunks of fresh pineapple, Mary's Gone Crackers original flavor, or Ener-G pretzels

1 In a small, microwave-safe bowl, melt the chocolate and syrup on low in a microwave, stirring every 30 seconds until the chocolate is melted and smooth. Different chocolate bars have differing levels of stabilizers, which affect this sauce. If it is too thick, add water, a tablespoon at a time, until it is just thick enough to coat the dippers.

2 Place the mixture in a fondue pot. Arrange the dippables on a platter and provide forks or bamboo skewers for guests to dunk food into the warm chocolate. If the chocolate starts to firm up, add a tablespoon more corn syrup and transfer it from the fondue pot to a microwave-safe dish and reheat it in the microwave. Return it to the fondue pot.

Milk Chocolate Fondue

MAKES 4 SERVINGS (1½ CUPS)

This fondue is for milk chocolate lovers. Some chocolate bars will have more gums and stabilizers than others, so the amount of cream or milk required to reach the right dipping consistency may vary.

½ cup heavy cream or ⅓ cup 1% milk (cow's, rice, soy, potato, or nut)

12 ounces gluten-free milk chocolate, such as Scharffen Berger, coarsely chopped

Dippers: apple slices, banana slices, peeled clementine sections, 1-inch cubes of gluten-free pound cake, large marshmallows, whole strawberries, fresh chunks of pineapple, Mary's Gone Crackers original flavor, or Ener-G pretzels

1 Heat the cream in a heavy glass or stainless steel pan over moderate heat until bubbles form around edges of pan.

2 Remove the pan from the heat, add the chocolate and let stand in the hot cream 3 to 5 minutes to soften. Whisk chocolate and cream together until smooth.

3 Transfer chocolate sauce to a fondue pot or set the mixing bowl on a rack above a small lit candle. If the chocolate becomes too thick, stir in more cream, 1 tablespoon at a time, to reach the desired consistency. Arrange dippables on a platter and provide forks or bamboo skewers for guests to dunk food into chocolate mixture.

Chocolate Sauce

MAKES 10 SERVINGS (1¼ CUPS)

Many purchased varieties of chocolate sauce have undesirable ingredients. My version is so simple and if you choose your gluten-free chocolate chips carefully, you'll have little else but chocolate in this tempting sauce.

1 cup gluten-free, chocolate chips, such as Tropical Source

¼ cup unsalted butter or buttery spread, such as Earth Balance

½ teaspoon pure vanilla extract

Dash salt

Place all the ingredients in a small saucepan and melt over low heat just until the chocolate chips start to soften. Remove the pan from heat and stir the sauce thoroughly. Use immediately.

Caramel Sauce

MAKES 4 SERVINGS (½ CUP)

Making caramel sauce often includes lots of splattering since it involves boiling sugar. Not so with this simple version. It makes a small batch because each tablespoon packs a punch in flavor and calories. If you don't have any cream on hand, just use whole milk. No whole milk? Use whatever type of milk you have on hand, but only use 1½ tablespoons because it is much thinner than heavy cream.

½ cup packed dark brown sugar

¼ cup (½ stick) unsalted butter or buttery spread, such as Earth Balance

⅛ teaspoon salt

2 tablespoons heavy cream or 1% milk (cow's, rice, soy, potato, or nut)

½ teaspoon pure vanilla extract

1 Combine the brown sugar, butter, and salt in a small, heavy saucepan. Whisk over medium heat until the sugar and butter are melted. Whisk in the cream and continue cooking, whisking constantly, for 2 minutes more as the mixture simmers and thickens slightly. Remove from the heat and stir in the vanilla extract.

2 Store the sauce in a glass, airtight container in the refrigerator. Heat it gently in the microwave oven to restore pouring consistency.

Praline Sauce

MAKES 8 SERVINGS (1 CUP)

Similar to a caramel sauce but lighter in color and more delicate in taste, this sauce has less butter and cream than traditional caramel sauce, making it less rich.

2 tablespoons packed light brown sugar
1 tablespoon cornstarch
1 cup light corn syrup
¼ cup chopped pecans
1 teaspoon pure vanilla extract
⅛ teaspoon butter-flavored extract
⅛ teaspoon salt

1 Whisk the sugar and cornstarch together in a small, heavy saucepan until thoroughly blended. Stir in the corn syrup.

2 Cook over medium heat, stirring constantly, until the mixture boils. Remove from heat and stir in pecans, vanilla extract, butter extract, and salt. Cool slightly. Spoon over ice cream or other desserts. Refrigerate leftover sauce and heat gently in microwave to soften before serving again.

Rum Sauce

MAKES 8 SERVINGS (1 CUP)

You can use any liquor you wish for this easy sauce, depending on how you're going to serve it. For example, rum complements a rum cake; bourbon would be great as a sauce for fruitcake; whisky would be ideal for a chocolate cake. If you want the flavor without the alcohol, just use a teaspoon of rum extract and 3 tablespoons water. This recipe is also a good one for using up leftover egg yolks.

HOMEMADE WHIPPED CREAM FOR EVERY RECIPE

Use the chart below when making your own homemade whipped cream.

BEAT TO SOFT PEAKS: HEAVY CREAM	STIR IN: SUPERFINE SUGAR	PURE VANILLA EXTRACT	YIELD: WHIPPED CREAM
¼ cup	2 teaspoons	½ teaspoon	½ cup
⅓ cup	2½ teaspoons	¾ teaspoon	⅔ cup
6 tablespoons	2¾ teaspoons	1 teaspoon	¾ cup
½ cup	1 tablespoon	1¼ teaspoons	1 cup
¾ cup	1½ tablespoons	1½ teaspoons	1½ cups
1 cup	2 tablespoons	1¾ teaspoons	2 cups (1 pint)
1½ cups	3 tablespoons	2 teaspoons	3 cups
2 cups	¼ cup	2¼ teaspoons	4 cups (1 quart)

½ cup sugar

¼ cup unsalted butter or buttery spread, such as Earth Balance

¼ cup rum (dark or light)

4 egg yolks

1 teaspoon pure vanilla extract

In a small, heavy saucepan, whisk together sugar, butter, rum and egg yolks over medium heat. Whisk constantly until mixture thickens slightly. Remove from heat and stir in vanilla extract. Serve warm or store in refrigerator 3 days. Reheat on low in microwave to bring to serving consistency.

Basic Whipped Cream

MAKES 6 SERVINGS (2 CUPS)

Nothing tastes quite like homemade whipped cream. Its creamy texture makes it the perfect pair to just about any dessert, including pies, cakes, and even fresh fruit. Homemade whipped cream lacks the stabilizers found in commercial whipped toppings and will not hold its shape very long, so for best results, serve immediately.

1 cup heavy cream

2 tablespoons superfine sugar

1¾ teaspoons pure vanilla extract

In a medium bowl, beat the heavy cream with an electric mixer on medium-high speed until soft peaks form. Add the sugar and vanilla extract and beat until stiff peaks form.

Nondairy Whipped Topping Q V

MAKES 12 SERVINGS (ABOUT 3 CUPS)

The beauty of this topping is that it can be made very quickly and is best served immediately. There is no waiting for it to set up; in fact, if you refrigerate it too long it gets too stiff. This alternative to dairy-based whipped cream is appropriate for lactose-intolerant people but some brands contain sodium caseinate, which is not suitable for those allergic to dairy.

Nondairy creamers are meant to flavor coffee but they can add flavor to dessert toppings, too. Look in the dairy section of your grocery store. I prefer coffee creamers that contain no hydrogenated oils. If you can't find flavored coffee creamers—or a flavor you like—buy a plain variety such as Silk Creamer, and add a teaspoon of your favorite extract such as almond, chocolate, or lemon and additional sugar to taste.

⅓ cup powdered sugar

¼ cup instant ClearJel, such as King Arthur Flour*

2 cups cold nondairy creamer, such as Silk, in your preferred flavor

Dash salt

Blend together the sugar and ClearJel in a blender. Add the nondairy creamer and blend on high speed just until the mixture is smooth and thickens slightly. Serve immediately as a soft whipped topping; refrigerate for 30 minutes for a stiffer topping. If you refrigerate it any longer, it becomes too stiff.

*Available at www.kingarthurflour.com.

FRUIT AND CUSTARD DESSERTS

Fruit Desserts

Balsamic Strawberries with Whipped Cream

Berries in Gelatin

Candied Clementines

Fresh Figs with Goat Cheese and Honey

Bananas Foster on a Crispy Tortilla Shell

Roasted Pears with Macaroon Crumbles

Baked Apples with Granola Filling

Crisps, Cobblers, and Clafoutis

Apple Crisp with Streusel Topping

Apple Crisp with Oat Crumble Topping

Cherry Crisp

Peach Crisp

Fresh Peach-Raspberry Crisp

Cardamom-Ginger Pear Crisp

Strawberry-Rhubarb Crisp

Rhubarb-Banana Crisp

Apple Betty

Apple Pandowdy

Nectarine-Macaroon Crunch

Apricot-Almond Cobbler

Cherry Cobbler

Fresh Peach-Blueberry Cobbler

Cherry Clafouti

Dried Plum Clafouti

Pear Clafouti

Peach Clafouti

Custards, Puddings, and Flans

Basic Custard for Pies

Instant Vanilla Pudding

Butterscotch Pudding

Black and White Chocolate Pudding

Chocolate Pots de Crème

Southern Banana Pudding

Almond-Millet Pudding

Baked Rice Pudding

Coconut Rice Custard

Crème Brûlée

Simplest Flan

Classic Flan

Polenta Pudding

Indian Pudding with
Pomegranate Syrup

Panna Cotta

Espresso Dairy-Free Panna Cotta

Tiramisu

Next Thing to Robert Redford
Dessert

Sweet Pineapple-Raisin Kugel

Pavlova

Fudge Sundaes on Crisp Tortillas

Clementine Zabaglione

Mousses, Sorbets, and Soufflés

Chocolate Mousse

White Chocolate Mousse

Peanut Butter Mousse

Viennese Cinnamon-Mocha
Mousse

Vanilla Ice Cream

Chocolate Espresso Sorbet

Lemon Sorbet with Limoncello

Individual Chocolate
Espresso Soufflés

Piña Colada Soufflé with
Coconut Whipped Cream

Bread Puddings and Trifles

Raisin Bread Pudding with
Cinnamon Sauce

Chocolate-Cappuccino Bread
Pudding with Brandy Sauce

Eggnog Bread Pudding with
Rum Sauce

Pumpkin Bread Pudding with
Clementine Crème Anglaise

Black Forest Trifle

Chocolate Orange Trifle with
Orange Custard

Strawberry, Lemon Curd,
and Kiwi Trifle

Even in a healthy diet, desserts satisfy an innate need for sweets, and they provide balance to a savory or spicy meal. A simple piece of fruit can make for a satisfying ending to a great meal. Fruit-based desserts are particularly important because they bring a multitude of delectable flavors and textures while supplying important fiber and nutrients. Some all-American classics, like fruit crisps and cobblers, are listed in this chapter, plus more exotic dishes like a Cherry Clafouti, Figs with Goat Cheese and Honey, or Bananas Foster on a Crispy Tortilla Shell.

Custard-based desserts offer a mouth-watering creamy richness. Airy soufflés, delectable mousses, and luscious-layered trifles, zabaglione, and panna cotta can adorn your dessert table. Or, for the kids, try all-American puddings in vanilla and chocolate with versatile instant versions that are great by themselves or as fillings for pies. Many of these creamy desserts are dairy-based but if you avoid dairy, I offer substitutions for cow's milk, butter, sour cream, and cream cheese. Make your own Nondairy Whipped Topping (page 624) or use store-bought, soy-based whipped topping in place of whipped cream.

Many of your favorites are naturally gluten-free, but even for those that require some adaptation, your desserts can be lovely and enticing. The wide variety of dessert choices in this chapter ensures you'll find something to satisfy everyone's cravings.

FRUIT DESSERTS

Balsamic Strawberries with Whipped Cream Ⓥ

MAKES 4 SERVINGS

The sweetness of fresh strawberries marries with the sweet, yet tart, nature of balsamic vinegar to produce a truly extraordinary taste. Sweetened whipped cream provides a soft, velvety contrast.

2 pints strawberries, washed, hulled, and halved
¼ cup balsamic vinegar (raspberry-flavored balsamic vinegar works well, too)
1 tablespoon sugar
1 teaspoon pure vanilla extract
1 cup homemade Basic Whipped Cream (page 624) or whipped topping, such as Lucerne or Soyatoo

1 In a shallow bowl or plastic freezer bag, combine strawberries, vinegar, sugar, and vanilla to marinate at room temperature 30 minutes.

2 Divide strawberries and their juices among 4 wine glasses or goblets. Top with a large dollop of whipped cream. Serve immediately.

Berries in Gelatin

MAKES 6 SERVINGS

Serve this simple dessert in your prettiest goblets and your guests will be impressed—both at this dessert's beauty and at its wonderful, light flavor. You can vary the fruit depending on what's in season, but try to get at least three different colors for the prettiest effect. Glass serving dishes work well because they showcase the fruit's lovely colors. A dollop of fat-free yogurt and fresh mint leaves make an attractive topping.

2 tablespoons unflavored gelatin powder, such as Knox
1 cup white grape juice, cold
3 cups white grape juice, very hot
1 cup mandarin oranges
½ cup fresh blueberries
½ cup fresh raspberries

1 In a large bowl, stir the gelatin powder and the cold white grape juice. Add the hot white grape juice, stirring thoroughly until the gelatin is dissolved.

2 Chill the gelatin in the refrigerator until it just begins to set (it will begin to resist when you try to stir it with a spoon). Stir in the fruit until it is thoroughly distributed. Transfer the mixture to 6 goblets or dessert serving bowls. Chill all day or overnight. Serve chilled.

Candied Clementines

MAKES 4 SERVINGS

While anything made with chocolate is the top choice at my house, some people prefer fruit-based desserts. Here is one that is so simple, yet so elegant, that you'll want to try it for your next party. Serve the clementines in goblets, garnished with a sprig of fresh mint, for a special touch.

8 whole clementines, peeled
½ cup sugar
2 tablespoons water
1 tablespoon fresh lemon juice
2 tablespoons orange liqueur, such as Triple Sec, or
    fresh orange juice
Fresh mint, for garnish

1 Arrange clementines in a wide shallow bowl or 13 × 9-inch glass baking dish, pulling the tops of each clementine's segments slightly apart without detaching the bottoms—sort of like opening up the petals of a flower.

2 In a medium saucepan, combine sugar, water, and lemon juice over medium heat. Bring to a boil, reduce heat to low, and simmer, stirring constantly, until the mixture is clear. Remove from heat and stir in orange liqueur. Cool 15 minutes or until syrup is lukewarm.

3 Pour syrup over clementines, making sure each they are well coated. Refrigerate for 2 hours. Bring to room temperature before serving. Place 2 clementines in serving goblet or glass, drizzle syrup over it, and top with a mint sprig.

Fresh Figs with Goat Cheese and Honey Q V

MAKES 4 SERVINGS

I tasted this unique combination a few years ago and never forgot it. Working from my memory and the suggestions of others, I've combined fresh Black Mission figs, a salty cheese such as Parmigiano-Reggiano or Asiago, and good-quality honey. This is a dessert, despite a dusting of freshly ground black pepper. The black pepper offers surprisingly pleasurable contrast to the sweetness, further enhancing this already special dish.

4 slices or shavings of Parmigiano-Reggiano or
  Asiago cheese
8 fresh Black Mission figs, washed and halved
  lengthwise
¼ cup honey or agave nectar
1 tablespoon freshly ground black pepper

1 Place a slice of cheese on each of 4 serving
plates or in each of 4 goblets.

2 Place 2 fresh figs, cut side up, on cheese.

3 Drizzle the figs with honey and sprinkle with
pepper. Serve at room temperature.

Bananas Foster on a Crispy Tortilla Shell Ⓥ

MAKES 4 SERVINGS

*Reminiscent of New Orleans, this classic dish is
typically served on vanilla (or rum raisin or pecan)
ice cream, and it's fabulous. And by placing the
bananas and ice cream on a crispy, salty piece of
baked tortilla, you've added another level of delight.*

TORTILLA SHELL
1 gluten-free tortilla, such as Food for Life or
  La Tortilla Factory
1 tablespoon unsalted butter or buttery spread,
  such as Earth Balance, melted
Dash salt

SAUCE
⅓ cup unsalted butter or buttery spread, such as
  Earth Balance
½ cup packed light brown sugar
¼ cup light corn syrup
¼ teaspoon salt
1 tablespoon dark rum (or rum extract)
1 teaspoon pure vanilla extract
2 ripe, but firm medium bananas
1 pint gluten-free vanilla ice cream, such as Ben &
  Jerry's, Dreyer's Grand, or Häagen-Dazs, or
  homemade Vanilla Ice Cream (page 657)

1 Make the tortilla shells: Place a rack in the
middle of the oven. Preheat the oven to 425°F.
Brush the top of the whole tortilla with melted
butter. Cut the tortilla into quarters with kitchen
scissors and place the quarters on a foil-lined baking sheet or pizza pan (not nonstick). Lay an ovenproof wire rack (the kind used under roasts) over
the tortillas to prevent them from curling.

2 Bake the tortilla quarters 3 to 5 minutes or just
until they look golden brown. Watch carefully
because they can burn quickly. Remove them
from the oven, sprinkle lightly with salt, and let
cool while making the caramel-rum sauce.

3 Make the sauce: In a medium skillet, combine
the butter, brown sugar, corn syrup, and salt over
medium heat. Bring to a boil, reduce heat to low,
and simmer about 4 minutes, stirring occasionally. Remove skillet from heat and stir in rum and
vanilla.

4 Peel bananas, cut into ½-inch slices, and add to
caramel mixture in skillet. Return skillet to low
heat and cook gently just until bananas are heated
through.

5 Place the 4 tortilla quarters on 4 dessert plates.
Spoon ½ cup ice cream on each tortilla quarter.
Drizzle banana-caramel mixture on each and serve
immediately.

Roasted Pears with Macaroon Crumbles Ⓥ

MAKES 4 SERVINGS

*This is an easy last-minute dessert that is perfect
during the fall and winter when pears are at their
best (I prefer the Bosc variety because they hold
their shape). It's also a good way to use up leftover
macaroons.*

2 firm Bosc pears, halved and cored

1 tablespoon unsalted butter or buttery spread, such as Earth Balance

3 tablespoons sugar, divided

2 tablespoons almond liqueur, such as Amaretto, or orange juice

⅓ cup boiling water

2 gluten-free coconut macaroons, such as Manischewitz, or homemade Coconut Macaroons (without Chocolate Drizzle) (page 405), finely crumbled

¼ cup homemade Basic Whipped Cream (page 624) or whipped topping such as Lucerne or Soyatoo, crème fraîche or plain yogurt for garnish

1 Place a rack in the middle of the oven. Preheat the oven to 425°F. Spread the butter on the bottom of an 8-inch baking dish. Sprinkle 2 tablespoons of the sugar on the bottom of the dish and arrange the pears, cut side up, on the sugar. Coat the cut side of the pears with cooking spray and sprinkle them with the remaining tablespoon of sugar.

2 Roast the pears, uncovered, 20 minutes. Add the boiling water and the liqueur to the dish and stir until the sugar from the bottom of the pan is dissolved. Baste the pears with the pan juices. Sprinkle the top of each pear with crumbled macaroons.

3 Roast the pears for 15 minutes more, or until they are tender and the macaroons are toasted and crunchy. Serve warm, with a dollop of whipped cream, crème fraîche, or yogurt.

Baked Apples with Granola Filling Ⓥ

MAKES 4 SERVINGS

The heavenly aroma of apples baking is one of the great joys of autumn. This easy recipe uses home-made Naked Gluten-Free Granola (page 11) and bakes while you're eating dinner. It is a good way to get the kids to eat their apples.

½ cup homemade Naked Gluten-Free Granola† (page 11)

4 McIntosh apples, washed and dried

1 tablespoon packed light brown sugar

½ teaspoon ground cinnamon

¼ teaspoon freshly grated nutmeg

1 tablespoon unsalted butter or buttery spread, such as Earth Balance, melted

1 tablespoon honey

1 Prepare the granola. Then, place a rack in the middle of the oven. Preheat the oven to 400°F. Generously grease an 8-inch glass baking dish. Remove stems and use apple corer to core apples. Use knife or potato peeler to remove ½ inch of skin from around top of apple. Place apples in baking dish.

2 Mix granola, brown sugar, cinnamon, nutmeg, butter, and honey until well blended. Press 2 tablespoons of mixture into core of each apple. Cover tightly with foil.

3 Bake 40 to 45 minutes or until apples are done. Remove from oven and cool the apples in the pan 30 minutes on a wire rack. Serve warm.

†Check with your physician before using gluten-free oats.

CRISPS, COBBLERS, AND CLAFOUTIS

Apple Crisp with Streusel Topping

MAKES 6 SERVINGS

This version of the classic apple dessert is for those who prefer not to use any grains, such as oats, in the topping. To speed up baking time, cook the sliced apples in the microwave oven on high while you prepare the topping. Granny Smith apples hold their shape but take longer to cook; McIntosh or Jonathan apples are wonderful in the fall.

FILLING

4 cups thinly sliced apples, unpeeled (4 large Gala, Granny Smith, or your choice)

½ cup apple juice

2 tablespoons fresh lemon juice

1 teaspoon pure vanilla extract

1 teaspoon ground cinnamon or apple pie spice

TOPPING

½ cup Carol's Sorghum Blend (page x)

½ cup granulated sugar

¼ cup packed light brown sugar

½ cup (1 stick) unsalted butter or buttery spread, such as Earth Balance, at room temperature

½ cup chopped walnuts

⅛ teaspoon salt

1 Place a rack in the middle of the oven. Preheat the oven to 350°F. Generously grease an 8-inch baking dish.

2 Make the filling: In a glass baking dish, place the apples and toss with the apple juice, lemon juice, vanilla extract, and cinnamon.

3 Make the topping: Prepare the sorghum blend. In a medium bowl, beat the sugar and butter with an electric mixer on low speed until smooth. Blend in the sorghum blend, walnuts, and salt on low speed until the mixture is crumbly. Sprinkle evenly over the apples.

4 Bake 30 to 40 minutes or until the apples are tender and the streusel is browned. Lay a sheet of aluminum foil over dish if the topping browns too much before the apples are done. Cool the apple crisp in the pan on a wire rack 20 minutes. Serve slightly warm.

Note: For added crispness in the topping, make it before you prepare the apples. Crumble the dough onto a foil-lined baking sheet. Bake at 350°F for 10 to 15 minutes. Sprinkle the pre-baked nuggets on top of the apples and bake as directed in recipe.

Apple Crisp with Oat Crumble Topping

MAKES 6 SERVINGS

The scent of cinnamon and apples in this dish always reminds me of autumn. I prefer to leave the fruit unpeeled for the added nutrients and fiber, but you can peel the apples if you wish. Try substituting pears in this dessert, for variety.

FILLING

4 cups thinly sliced apples, unpeeled (4 large Gala, Granny Smith, or your choice)

2 tablespoons raisins

2 tablespoons packed light brown sugar

2 tablespoons cornstarch

½ teaspoon ground cinnamon

¼ teaspoon salt

2 tablespoons unsalted butter or buttery spread, such as Earth Balance, at room temperature

2 tablespoon fresh lemon juice

2 tablespoons hot water

1 tablespoon apple cider or apple juice (optional)

1 teaspoon pure vanilla extract

TOPPING

1 cup gluten-free rolled oats*†

½ cup Carol's Sorghum Blend (page x)

¼ cup finely chopped walnuts

2 tablespoons maple syrup (or more to taste)

2 tablespoons unsalted butter or buttery spread, such as Earth Balance, at room temperature

1 teaspoon pure vanilla extract

¼ teaspoon ground cinnamon

¼ teaspoon salt

1 Place a rack in the middle of the oven. Preheat the oven to 375°F. Generously grease an 8-inch microwave-safe baking pan.

2 Make the filling: In a medium bowl, toss apples with raisins, sugar, cornstarch, cinnamon, and salt until well blended. Add butter, lemon juice, hot water, apple cider, if using, and vanilla extract and mix thoroughly. Add to pan.

3 Cover filling with wax paper. Microwave on high 5 minutes to soften the apples. (You may also cook this apple mixture 5 minutes in a saucepan over medium heat.)

4 Make the topping: In a small bowl, blend the oats, sorghum blend, walnuts, maple syrup, butter, vanilla extract, cinnamon, and salt with your fingers until crumbly and sprinkle on the apples. Coat streusel with cooking spray.

5 Bake 25 minutes or until the oat crumble topping is crisp and the apples are tender. Cool the apple crisp in the pan 20 minutes on a wire rack. Serve slightly warm.

*Available at www.bobsredmill.com, www. creamhillestates.com, www.giftsofnature.net, www. glutenfreeoats.com, and www.onlyoats.com.

†Check with your physician before using gluten-free oats.

Cherry Crisp Ⓥ

MAKES 6 SERVINGS

If you're lucky enough to have fresh cherries, this dessert will be sublime. But it is also very good when made with canned cherries, so go ahead and enjoy one of America's traditional desserts any time of year.

FILLING

2 cans (about 14 to 15 ounces each) tart red cherries, drained (or 2 cups fresh tart cherries)

½ cup sugar

1 tablespoon cornstarch

1 teaspoon almond-flavored extract

¼ teaspoon salt

TOPPING

¼ cup (½ stick) unsalted butter or buttery spread, such as Earth Balance, at room temperature

¼ cup packed light brown sugar

¼ cup granulated sugar

½ cup Carol's Sorghum Blend (page x)

1 teaspoon ground cinnamon

½ teaspoon salt

½ cup rolled soy flakes or gluten-free rolled oats*†

1 Place a rack in the middle of the oven. Preheat the oven to 375°F. Grease a 1-quart ovenproof baking dish.

2 Make the filling: In the baking dish, stir together cherries, sugar, cornstarch, almond extract, and salt until thoroughly combined. Let stand while preparing topping.

3 Make the topping: In a food processor, combine butter, brown sugar, granulated sugar, sorghum blend, cinnamon, and salt and process until mixture is crumbly. Add soy flakes and process until combined. Sprinkle the topping evenly over the fruit filling.

4 Bake 25 to 30 minutes or until the topping is browned. Cool the cherry crisp in the pan 20 minutes on a wire rack. Serve slightly warm.

Available from www.bobsredmill.com, www. creamhillestates.com, www.giftsofnature.net, www. glutenfreeoats.com, and www.onlyoats.com.

†*Check with your physician before using gluten-free oats.*

Peach Crisp

MAKES 8 SERVINGS

As a member of Slow Food Utah, Jane Bauer— an avid cook since her teens — is an advocate for locally grown food that supports local farmers and decreases cost and impact on the environment. For this crisp, she favors local, late-summer peaches grown in Utah or Colorado, rather than those which may have traveled over 1,500 miles to her table. To preserve the bounty of locally- grown summer peaches for year-round use, Jane suggests freezing them: Wash, pat dry, and freeze in heavy-duty food storage bags. Once the peaches are thawed, the skins will easily peel.

FILLING

6 cups fresh peaches, peeled and sliced (¼-inch slices)
¾ cup sugar
¼ cup cornstarch

TOPPING

1 cup Carol's Sorghum Blend (page x)
⅔ cup gluten-free yellow cornmeal, such as Alber's, Lamb's, Kinnikinnick, or Shiloh Farms
½ cup packed light brown sugar
1 teaspoon salt
⅔ cup very cold unsalted butter or buttery spread, such as Earth Balance, cut in small pieces
¾ cup toasted pine nuts

1 Place a rack in the middle of the oven. Preheat the oven to 375°F. Generously grease a 10 × 7-inch nonstick (gray, not black) baking dish; set aside.

2 Make the filling: In a medium bowl, combine the peaches, sugar, and cornstarch and mix with a spoon until well combined. Spread the mixture evenly in the baking dish.

3 Make the topping: In a medium bowl, mix together the sorghum blend, cornmeal, brown sugar, and salt. Using an electric mixer on low speed or your hands, mix in the cold butter until the mixture looks like coarse crumbs, working quickly so the butter does not melt. Stir the pine nuts into the mixture.

4 Cover the fruit evenly with the topping. Set the pan on a nonstick (gray, not black) baking sheet so it doesn't spill into the oven when the peaches bubble up.

5 Bake 45 minutes or until the fruit is bubbling and tender and the topping is golden brown. Cool the peach crisp in the pan 20 minutes on a wire rack. Serve slightly warm.

Fresh Peach-Raspberry Crisp 🅥

MAKES 4 SERVINGS

This dessert will taste far better when made with fresh peaches and raspberries so use them when they're in season and at their best.

FILLING

4 large fresh peaches
1 cup fresh raspberries, washed
Grated zest of 1 orange
½ cup orange juice
1 teaspoon pure vanilla extract
2 teaspoons cornstarch
½ teaspoon ground cinnamon

TOPPING

½ cup granulated sugar

¼ cup packed light brown sugar

½ cup (1 stick) unsalted butter or buttery spread, such as Earth Balance, at room temperature

½ cup Carol's Sorghum Blend (page x)

½ cup chopped walnuts

⅛ teaspoon salt

Cooking spray

1 Place a rack in the middle of the oven. Preheat the oven to 350°F. Generously grease an 8-inch baking dish.

2 Make the filling: Peel the peaches by dipping them into boiling water for 30 seconds and then into ice water. The skins will slip off easily. Remove the pit and slice the peaches in ½-inch wedges. In a large bowl, toss the peaches and raspberries with the orange zest, orange juice, and vanilla. Sprinkle with the cornstarch and cinnamon and toss until well blended. Spread the mixture evenly in the baking dish.

3 Make the topping: In the same large bowl, beat the granulated sugar, brown sugar, and butter with an electric mixer on low speed until smooth. Beat in the sorghum blend, walnuts, and salt on low speed until the mixture is crumbly; sprinkle evenly over the peaches. Lightly spray with cooking spray.

4 Bake 30 to 40 minutes or until the peaches are tender and the streusel is browned. Lay a sheet of aluminum foil over dish if the topping browns too much before the filling is done. Cool the crisp in the pan 20 minutes on a wire rack. Serve slightly warm.

Cardamom-Ginger Pear Crisp Ⓥ

MAKES 6 SERVINGS

Cardamom is commonly used in Scandinavian baking and is one of the more expensive spices on earth. This is a wonderful winter dessert, when pears are in season.

FILLING

6 ripe but firm Bosc pears (6 cups), peeled, thinly sliced, and cut into 1-inch pieces

2 tablespoons fresh lemon juice

1 tablespoon unsalted butter or buttery spread, such as Earth Balance, melted

1 teaspoon pure vanilla extract

¼ cup packed light brown sugar

2 tablespoons granulated sugar

2 teaspoons cornstarch

2 tablespoons finely diced crystallized ginger

TOPPING

¼ cup granulated sugar

¼ cup packed light brown sugar

¼ cup (½ stick) unsalted butter or buttery spread, such as Earth Balance, melted

1 cup Carol's Sorghum Blend (page x)

½ cup finely chopped walnuts

½ teaspoon ground cinnamon

⅛ teaspoon salt

Cooking spray

1 Place a rack in the middle of the oven. Preheat the oven to 400°F. Generously grease an 8-inch baking dish.

2 Make the filling: In a large bowl, toss the pears with the lemon juice, butter, and vanilla. In a small bowl, whisk together the brown sugar, granulated sugar, cornstarch, and ginger until well blended. Toss with the pears until they are thoroughly coated. Spread evenly in the prepared pan.

3 Make the topping: In the same large bowl, use a pastry blender, a fork, or your fingers to mix the granulated sugar, brown sugar, butter, sorghum blend, walnuts, cinnamon, and salt together until crumbly. Sprinkle evenly over the pears. Coat the topping lightly with cooking spray.

4 Bake 25 to 30 minutes until the pears are tender and the topping is browned. Cover dish loosely with foil if the topping browns too much before the pears are done. Cool the crisp in the pan 20 minutes on a wire rack. Serve slightly warm.

Strawberry-Rhubarb Crisp

MAKES 8 SERVINGS

This is a summertime treat, just like Grandma used to make. Rhubarb can be found in grocery stores during the spring and in mid-to-late summer, and also at farmer's markets throughout the summer. You can use a teaspoon of orange extract in place of the orange juice and orange zest, if you wish.

FILLING

1 cup sugar

2 tablespoons cornstarch

Pinch salt

4 cups diced rhubarb

4 cups fresh strawberries, washed, hulled, and quartered

2 teaspoons fresh orange juice

2 teaspoons grated orange zest

1 teaspoon pure vanilla extract

TOPPING

¼ cup (½ stick) unsalted butter or buttery spread, such as Earth Balance, at room temperature

¼ cup granulated sugar

¼ cup packed light brown sugar

1 cup Carol's Sorghum Blend (page x)

¼ teaspoon salt

1 Place a rack in the middle of the oven. Preheat the oven to 375°F. Generously grease a 2-quart baking dish; set aside.

2 Make the filling: In a large bowl, whisk together the sugar, cornstarch, and salt. Add the rhubarb, strawberries, orange juice, orange zest, and vanilla extract and toss together until thoroughly combined. Using a slotted spoon, transfer the mixture to the prepared pan; discard any juices remaining in the bowl.

3 Make the topping: In the same large bowl, use a pastry blender, a fork, or your fingers to mix the butter, granulated sugar, brown sugar, sorghum blend, and salt together until crumbly. Sprinkle evenly over the rhubarb.

4 Bake 30 minutes; reduce the heat to 325°F and bake 20 to 25 minutes longer, or until the fruit filling is bubbling and the topping is browned. Cover dish with foil if topping browns before rhubarb is done. Cool the crisp in the pan 20 minutes on a wire rack. Serve slightly warm.

Rhubarb-Banana Crisp

MAKES 4 SERVINGS

Yes, that's rhubarb and banana in the same dessert—an unusual combination, but one that I found in my mother's old recipe collection—and delicious. I've streamlined it by baking it in an ovenproof saucepan—the same one you cook the rhubarb in—to save time.

FILLING

1 tablespoon unsalted butter or buttery spread, such as Earth Balance

2 cups chopped fresh rhubarb

1 tablespoon water

¼ cup packed light brown sugar

½ teaspoon grated orange zest

¼ teaspoon salt

¼ teaspoon ground cinnamon

⅛ teaspoon freshly grated nutmeg

1 large or 2 small ripe (but not mushy) bananas, peeled and sliced in ½-inch rounds

TOPPING

½ cup (about 16) crushed gluten-free cookies such as Health Valley Rice Bran Crackers or cookies of choice

¼ cup Carol's Sorghum Blend (page x)

¼ cup rolled soy flakes or gluten-free rolled oats*†

2 tablespoons unsalted butter or buttery spread, such as Earth Balance

2 tablespoons packed light brown sugar

¼ teaspoon ground cinnamon

¼ teaspoon salt

⅛ teaspoon baking soda

¼ cup sliced almonds

1 Place a rack in the middle of the oven. Preheat the oven to 400°F. Spray a 2-quart, ovenproof saucepan with cooking spray. (A glass pan works well, but a stainless steel pan can also work.)

2 Make the filling: In the saucepan, melt butter over low heat. Add rhubarb, water, brown sugar, orange zest, salt, cinnamon, and nutmeg. Cover and cook over low heat 10 minutes. Remove from heat and stir in sliced bananas.

3 Make the topping: In a food processor, process crackers until they resemble cracker crumbs. Add remaining ingredients and pulse until blended. Sprinkle topping over rhubarb mixture. Cover saucepan tightly with foil.

4 Bake 20 minutes. Remove foil and bake 5 minutes more or until topping looks crisp. Cool the crisp in the pan 20 minutes on a wire rack.

Available from www.bobsredmill.com, www.creamhillestates.com, www.giftsofnature.net, www.glutenfreeoats.com, and www.onlyoats.com.

†*Check with your physician before using gluten-free oats.*

Apple Betty

MAKES 4 SERVINGS

Apple Betty is a classic, old-fashioned dish, which is often served with vanilla ice cream. I never peel fruit in dishes such as this, preferring to reap the benefits of the fiber and nutrients residing in the skin, but you may peel the apples if you wish. I especially like Jonathans in the fall when they're great; otherwise, use a blend of Delicious and Granny Smith apples.

FILLING

4 cups apples (such as Jonathan), cored and chopped

½ cup apple juice or cider

2 tablespoons sugar

2 tablespoons fresh lemon juice

1 teaspoon pure vanilla extract

1 teaspoon cornstarch

½ teaspoon ground cinnamon

¼ teaspoon freshly grated nutmeg

¼ teaspoon salt

TOPPING

½ cup rolled soy flakes or gluten-free rolled oats*†

¼ cup Carol's Sorghum Blend (page x)

¼ cup finely chopped walnuts

2 tablespoons packed dark brown sugar

2 tablespoons unsalted butter or buttery spread, such as Earth Balance, melted

1 teaspoon pure vanilla extract

½ teaspoon ground cinnamon

½ teaspoon xanthan gum

¼ teaspoon salt

1 Place a rack in the middle of the oven. Preheat the oven to 350°F. Generously grease a 1-quart baking dish.

2 Make the filling: In a large bowl, toss the filling ingredients together and spread the filling evenly in the dish.

3 Make the topping: In the same large bowl, toss the topping ingredients together until thoroughly combined and crumbly. Sprinkle evenly over apples. Cover dish with aluminum foil.

4 Bake 30 minutes. Remove aluminum foil and bake 10 minutes more. Cool the crisp in the pan 20 minutes on a wire rack. Serve slightly warm.

*Available from www.bobsredmill.com, www. creamhillestates.com, www.giftsofnature.net, www. glutenfreeoats.com, or www.onlyoats.com.

†Check with your physician before using gluten-free oats.

Apple Pandowdy

MAKES 8 SERVINGS

A pandowdy is a rustic American dessert of cooked fruit covered with pie crust. The unique feature of this dessert is the pie crust, which is pushed down into the fruit halfway during the baking process, causing it to caramelize slightly. I like using Granny Smith apples because they are somewhat tart and hold their shape.

Basic Pastry Crust dough for 9-inch pie, single crust (page 587)

1 tablespoon cornstarch

⅛ teaspoon salt

⅓ cup + 1 tablespoon sugar

⅛ teaspoon fresh grated nutmeg

¼ teaspoon ground cinnamon

4 apples (such as Granny Smith), peeled, cored and sliced in ⅛-inch slices

2 tablespoons unsalted butter or buttery spread, such as Earth Balance

Juice and zest of 1 lemon

¼ cup orange liqueur, such as Triple Sec, or orange juice

1 Prepare the pastry crust dough as directed in Step 1 on page 587. Freeze half of the dough for another use. Roll the remaining half to ⅛-inch thickness between sheets of heavy-duty plastic wrap. Set aside. Then, place a rack in the middle of the oven. Preheat the oven to 400°F. Whisk the cornstarch with the salt, ⅓ cup of sugar, nutmeg, and cinnamon in a large mixing bowl until well blended. Add the apples and toss to coat thoroughly. Stir in the butter, lemon, juice, lemon zest, and liqueur and toss until thoroughly blended. Transfer the mixture to a 9-inch ovenproof skillet.

2 Remove the top sheet of plastic wrap from the crust and invert it, centering it over the apple mixture. Remove the remaining plastic wrap and trim the edges of the crust flush with the edges of the skillet. With the tines of a fork, poke several steam vents in the pie crust. Sprinkle with the remaining tablespoon of sugar. Heat the skillet over medium heat so it is hot to the touch.

3 Bake 30 minutes. Remove skillet from the oven and reduce the oven temperature to 350°F. Using a sharp knife, cut the crust into 1-inch squares and then press the squares down into the filling. Return the pandowdy to the oven and bake until golden brown, about 15 minutes longer. Cool the pandowdy in the pan 15 to 20 minutes on a wire rack. Serve slightly warm.

Nectarine-Macaroon Crunch

MAKES 4 SERVINGS

In summer, ripe nectarines are absolutely gorgeous with their bright red skins, and I especially like their flavor in baked desserts like this one. The blueberries add sweetness and beautiful color to the dish. The heavy cream is an optional topping, but certainly adds a mellow richness that can't be beat.

TOPPING

½ cup Carol's Sorghum Blend (page x)

2 tablespoons packed light brown sugar

2 tablespoons granulated sugar

¾ cup sliced almonds

½ cup (1 stick) unsalted butter or buttery spread, such as Earth Balance, at room temperature

1 cup (about 6 to 8) gluten-free coconut macaroons, such as Manischewitz, coarsely chopped

FILLING

3 tablespoons sugar

1 tablespoon potato starch

4 nectarines, pitted and sliced into thick wedges

½ cup fresh blueberries, washed and patted dry with paper towels

1 tablespoon pure vanilla extract

½ heavy cream, for garnish (optional)

1 Place a rack in the middle of the oven. Preheat the oven to 350°F. Generously grease an 8-inch square glass baking dish; set aside.

2 Make the topping: In a medium bowl, whisk together the sorghum blend, brown sugar, and granulated sugar. Add the almonds and mix well. Add the butter and rub it in with your fingers until moist clumps form. Stir in the crushed macaroons; set aside.

3 Make the filling: In a large bowl, whisk together the sugar and potato starch. Add the nectarines and blueberries, and toss to combine. Stir in the vanilla extract. Spread the fruit in the prepared dish. Sprinkle the topping over the fruit.

4 Bake 30 to 40 minutes, or until the nectarines are tender and the topping is golden and crisp. Cool the crunch in the dish 10 minutes on a wire rack. Serve slightly warm, drizzled with 2 tablespoons heavy cream per serving, if you wish.

Apricot-Almond Cobbler

MAKES 6 SERVINGS

Fresh apricots are one of nature's most delicious gifts. This dessert won't be as tasty if you use canned apricots, so wait until fresh ones are in season, during summer, for the best results.

FRUIT

4 cups fresh apricot halves

1 tablespoon unsalted butter or buttery spread, such as Earth Balance, at room temperature

1 teaspoon almond extract

½ cup sugar

1 tablespoon cornstarch

⅛ teaspoon salt

TOPPING

1¼ cups Carol's Sorghum Blend (page x)

½ cup sugar + 1 tablespoon for sprinkling on top

1 teaspoon baking powder

½ teaspoon xanthan gum

¼ teaspoon salt

¼ cup (½ stick) unsalted butter or buttery spread, such as Earth Balance, melted, + 1 tablespoon for brushing

1 large egg, at room temperature

1 teaspoon grated lemon zest

1 teaspoon almond extract

¼ cup buttermilk, well-shaken, or homemade Buttermilk (page 677)

2 tablespoons sliced almonds

1 Place a rack in the middle of the oven. Preheat the oven to 375°F. Generously grease an 11 × 7-inch nonstick (gray, not black) pan.

2 Prepare the fruit: In a medium bowl, toss the apricots with the butter and almond extract. Add the sugar, cornstarch, and salt until and toss until well combined. Spread in the pan.

3 Make the topping: In the same medium bowl, whisk together the sorghum blend, ½ cup sugar, baking powder, xanthan gum, and salt. Beat in ¼ cup of the butter, egg, lemon zest, almond extract, and buttermilk with an electric mixer on low speed, just until blended. Drop by table-spoonfuls on the apricots; the topping will spread as it bakes. Sprinkle with the remaining table-spoon of sugar and the sliced almonds.

4 Bake 35 to 40 minutes or until the topping is lightly browned and crispy. Cool the cobber in the pan 5 minutes on a wire rack and then brush with the remaining tablespoon of melted butter. Serve slightly warm.

Cherry Cobbler

MAKES 6 SERVINGS

Cobblers are American deep-dish fruit desserts, a variation on pies that are easy and quick to make.

FRUIT

6 cups pitted tart red cherries, drained thoroughly; reserve ¼ cup juice

1 teaspoon almond extract

1 cup sugar

4 teaspoons potato starch

⅛ teaspoon salt

1 tablespoon unsalted butter or buttery spread, such as Earth Balance, melted

TOPPING

1 cup Carol's Sorghum Blend (page x)

½ cup sugar + 1 tablespoon for sprinkling

1 teaspoon baking powder

½ teaspoon ground cinnamon

½ teaspoon xanthan gum

¼ teaspoon salt

¼ cup (½ stick) unsalted butter or buttery spread, such as Earth Balance, melted, + 1 tablespoon for brushing

1 large egg, at room temperature

1 teaspoon grated lemon zest

1 teaspoon almond extract

⅓ cup buttermilk, well-shaken, or homemade Buttermilk (page 677)

2 tablespoons sliced almonds

1 Place a rack in the middle of the oven. Preheat the oven to 375°F. Generously grease an 8-inch square nonstick (gray, not black) pan.

2 Prepare the fruit: In a medium bowl, toss the cherries with the reserved cherry juice and almond extract. Add the sugar, potato starch, and salt and toss until well combined; spread in the prepared pan. Drizzle the melted butter over the fruit.

3 Make the topping: In the same medium bowl, whisk together the sorghum blend, ½ cup sugar, baking powder, cinnamon, xanthan gum, and salt. Beat in the butter, egg, lemon zest, almond extract, and buttermilk with an electric mixer on low speed, just until blended. Drop by tablespoonfuls on the cherries; the topping will spread as it bakes. Sprinkle with the remaining tablespoon of sugar and the sliced almonds.

4 Bake 35 to 40 minutes or until the topping is lightly browned and crispy. Cool the cobbler in the pan 5 minutes on a wire rack and then brush with the remaining tablespoon of melted butter. Cool another 15 minutes. Serve slightly warm.

Fresh Peach-Blueberry Cobbler Ⓥ

MAKES 6 SERVINGS

Fresh peaches and blueberries go together very nicely in this home-style dessert. Canned peaches will not taste nearly as good, so save this dessert for summer when good-quality peaches are available. Bourbon lends a classy flavor, but orange juice works well, too (or use a blend of both).

FRUIT

5 cups fresh peaches

1 cup fresh blueberries

2 tablespoons orange juice or bourbon

1 tablespoon unsalted butter or buttery spread, such as Earth Balance, at room temperature

1 teaspoon almond extract

½ cup sugar

1 tablespoon potato starch

⅛ teaspoon salt

TOPPING

1 cup Carol's Sorghum Blend (page x)

½ cup sugar + 1 tablespoon for sprinkling

1 teaspoon baking powder

½ teaspoon ground cinnamon

½ teaspoon xanthan gum

¼ teaspoon salt

¼ cup (½ stick) unsalted butter or buttery spread, such as Earth Balance, melted, + 1 tablespoon for brushing

1 large egg, at room temperature

1 teaspoon almond extract

⅓ cup buttermilk, well-shaken, or homemade Buttermilk (page 677)

2 tablespoons sliced almonds

1 Place a rack in the middle of the oven. Preheat the oven to 375°F. Generously grease an 11x7-inch square nonstick (gray, not black) pan. Dip the peaches in boiling water 30 seconds and then in ice water. The skins will slip right off. Remove the pits and cut each peach into 6 wedges.

2 Prepare the fruit: In a large bowl, toss the peaches and blueberries with the orange juice, butter, and almond extract. Add the sugar, potato starch, and salt and toss until well combined; spread in the prepared pan.

3 Make the topping: In the same large bowl, whisk together the sorghum blend, ½ cup sugar, baking powder, cinnamon, xanthan gum, and salt. Beat in the butter, egg, almond extract, and buttermilk with an electric mixer on low speed, just until blended. Drop by tablespoonfuls on the peaches and blueberries; the topping will spread as it bakes. Sprinkle with the remaining tablespoon of sugar and the sliced almonds.

4 Bake 35 to 40 minutes or until the topping is lightly browned and crispy. Cool the cobbler in the pan 5 minutes on a wire rack and then brush with the remaining tablespoon of melted butter. Cool another 15 minutes. Serve slightly warm.

Cherry Clafouti

MAKES 6 SERVINGS

Cherries are probably the most common fruit used in a clafouti *(clah-FOO-tee), a French dessert that is a combination of a custard and pancake. It is an excellent dessert for beginning cooks because it is so simple to make, it always works, and it never fails to please anyone who eats it.*

FRUIT

2 cups pitted canned Bing cherries, drained

1 tablespoon sugar

1 tablespoon cherry brandy, such as kirschwasser, optional

1 teaspoon almond-flavored extract

BATTER

3 large eggs, at room temperature

¼ cup sugar, divided

½ cup Carol's Sorghum Blend (page x)

½ cup 1% milk (cow's, rice, soy, potato, or nut)

1 teaspoon pure vanilla extract

1 teaspoon almond extract

¼ teaspoon salt

1 tablespoon sliced almonds

2 tablespoons powdered sugar, for garnish

1 Place a rack in the middle of the oven. Preheat the oven to 350°F. Generously grease a 9-inch round ovenproof cake pan or pie pan.

2 Prepare the fruit: In the pan, add the cherries, sugar, brandy, and almond extract and toss well.

3 Make the batter: In a blender, combine the eggs, 3 tablespoons of the sugar, sorghum blend, milk, vanilla, almond extract, and salt until smooth and pour over the cherries. Sprinkle with almonds and the remaining 1 tablespoon of the sugar.

4 Bake 40 to 45 minutes or until the clafouti is firm to the touch. Cool the clafouti in the pan 15 minutes on a wire rack. Serve slightly warm, garnished with powdered sugar.

Dried Plum Clafouti

MAKES 6 SERVINGS

Clafouti is a French dessert that is simple to make when you whip up the batter in a blender. This version uses dried plums—really, prunes—which are a healthy, antioxidant-rich fruit. Have the fruit rest in the port for 30 minutes to enhance the fruit's natural flavor. Serve with a dollop of whipped cream that has ½ teaspoon grated orange zest in it or a teaspoon of port, or even both.

FRUIT

2 cups pitted dried plums, cut in half

¼ cup port wine

1 tablespoon sugar

1 teaspoon grated orange zest

¼ teaspoon ground cinnamon

¼ teaspoon salt

BATTER

3 large eggs, at room temperature

½ cup Carol's Sorghum Blend (page x)

½ cup 1% milk (cow's, rice, soy, potato, or nut)

2 tablespoons sugar, divided

1 teaspoon pure vanilla extract or brandy-flavored extract

1 tablespoon sliced almonds, for garnish

2 tablespoons powdered sugar, for garnish

1 Prepare the fruit: In a shallow bowl, combine the plums and port. Let stand 30 minutes, then drain port (better yet, drink it). Generously grease an 8-inch ovenproof cake pan or pie pan.

2 Place a rack in the middle of the oven. Preheat the oven to 350°F. Prepare the fruit: In a medium bowl, combine the dried plums, wine, sugar, orange zest, cinnamon, and salt and arrange evenly in the prepared pan.

3 Make the batter: In a blender, combine the eggs, flour blend, milk, 1 tablespoon of the sugar, and the vanilla until smooth.

4 Pour the batter over dried plums and sprinkle with the almonds and the remaining 1 tablespoon of sugar.

5 Bake 40 to 45 minutes or until the clafouti is firm to the touch. Cool the clafouti in the pan 15 minutes on a wire rack. Serve slightly warm, garnished with powdered sugar.

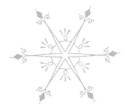

Pear Clafouti

MAKES 8 SERVINGS

Bosc pears work especially well in this dessert because they hold their shape nicely during the baking process. If they aren't available, use Anjou instead.

FRUIT

3 large ripe, firm Bosc pears, unpeeled, cored, and cut in ⅛-inch slices

2 tablespoons packed light brown sugar

1 tablespoon pear liqueur, such as Aqua Perfect, or fresh lemon juice

BATTER

3 large eggs, at room temperature

⅓ cup sugar, divided

½ cup Carol's Sorghum Blend (page x)

½ cup 1% milk (cow's, rice, soy, potato, or nut)

2 teaspoons pure vanilla extract

1 teaspoon almond extract

1 teaspoon grated lemon zest

⅛ teaspoon salt

2 tablespoons pear liqueur, such as Aqua Perfect, or fresh lemon juice

1 tablespoon sliced almonds

2 tablespoons powdered sugar, for garnish

1 Place a rack in the middle of the oven. Preheat the oven to 350°F. Generously grease a 9-inch ovenproof cake pan or pie pan.

2 Prepare the fruit: In the pan, place the pears and toss with the brown sugar and liqueur.

3 Make the batter: In a blender, combine the eggs, 4 tablespoons of the sugar, sorghum blend, milk, vanilla extract, almond extract, lemon zest, salt, and liqueur until smooth; pour over the pears. Sprinkle with almonds and the remaining sugar.

4 Bake 40 to 45 minutes or until the clafouti is firm to the touch. Cool 5 minutes on a wire rack. Serve warm, garnished with powdered sugar.

Peach Clafouti

MAKES 8 SERVINGS

Fresh peaches taste much better than canned peaches in this dessert, so make it in the summer when fresh peaches are plentiful. You can also use the same amount of fresh apricots instead.

FRUIT

3 cups fresh peaches, washed, peeled and sliced (or 2 peaches)

1 tablespoon fresh lemon juice

1 teaspoon pure vanilla extract

3 tablespoons sugar

BATTER

3 large eggs, at room temperature

⅓ cup sugar, divided

½ cup Carol's Sorghum Blend (page x)

½ cup 1% milk (cow's, rice, soy, potato, or nut)

1 teaspoon pure vanilla extract

1 teaspoon almond extract

1 teaspoon grated lemon zest

⅛ teaspoon salt

1 tablespoon sliced almonds

2 tablespoons powdered sugar, for garnish

1 Place a rack in the middle of the oven. Preheat the oven to 350°F. Generously grease a 9-inch ovenproof cake pan or pie pan.

2 Prepare the fruit: Place peaches in the pan and toss with the lemon juice and vanilla extract. Sprinkle the sugar on top.

3 Make the batter: In a blender, combine the eggs, 4 tablespoons of the sugar, sorghum blend, milk, vanilla, almond extract, lemon zest, and salt until smooth; pour over the peaches. Sprinkle with almonds and the remaining sugar.

4 Bake 40 to 45 minutes or until the clafouti is spongelike. Cool the clafouti in the pan 15 minutes on a wire rack. Serve slightly warm, garnished with powdered sugar.

CUSTARDS, PUDDINGS, AND FLANS

Basic Custard for Pies

MAKES 2 CUPS FOR A 9-INCH PIE OR
FOUR ½-CUP INDIVIDUAL SERVINGS

*Smooth, creamy, and rich, this custard has
enough body for pies. For a really wonderful flavor, use homemade Vanilla Sugar, which is very
easy to make.*

1 teaspoon unflavored gelatin powder, such as Knox
2 tablespoons boiling water
½ cup sugar or homemade Vanilla Sugar*
3 tablespoons cornstarch
¼ teaspoon salt
1½ cups 1% milk (cow's, rice, soy, potato, or nut)
5 large egg yolks, beaten
1 tablespoon unsalted butter or buttery spread, such
    as Earth Balance, at room temperature
1 teaspoon pure vanilla extract

1 In a small bowl, stir the gelatin into the boiling
water until dissolved and set aside.

2 In a heavy saucepan, whisk together sugar,
cornstarch, and salt until they are thoroughly
combined. In a medium bowl, whisk together milk
and egg yolks until completely blended. Add to
saucepan.

3 Cook over medium heat, whisking constantly,
until mixture thickens, about 5 minutes. Remove
from heat and whisk in butter, vanilla extract, and
gelatin mixture until very smooth.

4 Pour the custard into the prepared crust. Press
plastic wrap directly onto the surface. Chill until
set, at least 4 hours. Remove plastic wrap and
serve.

**To make Vanilla Sugar, place 1 cup of sugar in a glass
jar with a screw-top lid. Slit 1 vanilla bean lengthwise
from top to bottom. Spread it open slightly to expose the
seeds and put it in the jar. (If you don't want the little
black vanilla flecks in your sugar, leave the bean whole
rather than slitting it.) Seal the jar tightly and store in a
dark, dry place. As you use the sugar, replenish it with
more so you always have vanilla sugar on hand.*

Instant Vanilla Pudding

MAKES 4 SERVINGS

*Keep a batch of this pudding's dry ingredients
mixed up in your pantry and you can use it in
other recipes that call for instant pudding. Using
richer milk will yield richer pudding. Dairy-
sensitive folks can use soy or nut milks instead
and still have a tasty, though somewhat thinner,
pudding.*

¼ cup dry milk powder, such as Better Than Milk
    Soy Powder
¼ cup powdered sugar, or to taste
¼ cup instant ClearJel, by King Arthur Flour
¼ teaspoon salt
1 cup cold 2% milk (cow's, soy, nut)*
1 cup cold half-and-half or whole milk or 1% milk
    (cow's, soy, nut)
1 teaspoon pure vanilla extract

In a blender or the bowl of a standing mixer, mix
the soy powder, sugar, ClearJel, and salt together
until they are thoroughly blended. Add the milk,
half-and-half, and vanilla extract and blend until
smooth. If the mixture is too thick, add 1 tablespoon of milk at a time to reach desired consistency. It will thicken further as it chills in the
refrigerator. Divide the mixture into 4 serving
bowls. Refrigerate 1 to 2 hours.

Instant Lemon Pudding: Add 1 tablespoon freshly grated lemon zest and 2 tablespoons fresh lemon juice to the milk.

Instant Chocolate Pudding: Add ⅓ cup gluten-free chocolate syrup, such as Hershey's, with the milk and blend as directed.

*Note: Rice milk and potato milk will not thicken in this pudding.

Butterscotch Pudding ⓥ

MAKES 4 SERVINGS

I recently ate at a restaurant that specializes in all-American dishes and I had the most wonderful butterscotch pudding—something I hadn't eaten for a very long time. It reminded me of home-cooked meals and I just knew the recipe had to be in this book. If you want this pudding to be really decadent and rich, use half-and-half or whole milk.

⅔ cup firmly packed dark brown sugar

2 tablespoons cornstarch

¼ teaspoon salt

2 cups 1% milk (cow's, rice*, soy, potato*, or nut)

1 large egg yolk

1 tablespoon unsalted butter or buttery spread, such as Earth Balance

1 tablespoon pure vanilla extract

1 teaspoon butter-flavored extract (optional)

¼ cup homemade Basic Whipped Cream (page 624) or whipped topping, such as Lucerne or Soyatoo

1 In a large heavy saucepan, whisk together the brown sugar, cornstarch, and salt until thoroughly blended. Add the milk gradually, whisking constantly, and then whisk in the egg yolk.

2 Bring the mixture to a boil over medium heat, whisking constantly. Immediately reduce the heat to low and continue to boil, stirring constantly, 1 minute more. (This boiling time is critical because it develops the caramel, butterscotch flavor, but be careful, the mixture may splatter as it boils.)

3 Remove the pudding from the heat and stir in the butter, vanilla extract, and butter extract, if using. Divide among 4 dessert cups and chill for at least 2 hours. Serve with a dollop of whipped cream.

*Note: If using rice milk or potato milk, increase the cornstarch to 3 tablespoons.

Black and White Chocolate Pudding ⓥ

MAKES 4 SERVINGS

Topped with a big, bright red strawberry this multi-layered classy-looking dessert is amazingly easy to make and can be prepared ahead of time. Be warned . . . it's really rich.

¼ cup sugar

3 tablespoon cornstarch

¼ teaspoon salt

2 cups 1% milk (cow's, rice, soy, potato, or nut)

½ cup gluten-free white chocolate, chopped from a white chocolate bar, such as Organica

½ cup chopped gluten-free chocolate, such as Tropical Source

1 teaspoon pure vanilla extract

2 tablespoons shaved gluten-free dark chocolate, such as Tropical Source, for garnish

1 In a medium saucepan, stir together the sugar, cornstarch, and salt until thoroughly blended. Add the milk and cook over medium heat, stirring constantly, until mixture thickens, about 5 minutes.

2 Remove pan from heat and stir in vanilla. Place half of pudding (about 1 cup) in another saucepan. Stir the white chocolate into the first pan until they melt. Stir chocolate chips into the second pan until they melt.

3 Have 4 small wine glasses or stemmed goblets ready. Start with the white chocolate pudding and assemble the puddings in 4 layers, beginning and ending with the white chocolate pudding. Top with 1½ teaspoons shaved chocolate. Chill at least 2 hours before serving.

Chocolate Pots de Crème

MAKES 6 SERVINGS

This elegant, yet simple dessert in martini glasses or espresso cups is a perfect ending to a dinner party. Top with a dollop of whipped cream, a dusting of cinnamon, fresh strawberries, chocolate-covered espresso beans, or cocoa nibs.

3 tablespoons unsweetened cocoa powder (Dutch-process or alkali)

¾ cup packed light brown sugar

3 tablespoons cornstarch

1½ teaspoons instant espresso powder

3 cups whole milk (cow's, rice*, soy, potato*, or nut)

2 ounces gluten-free chocolate, such as Tropical Source

¼ teaspoon salt

1½ teaspoons pure vanilla extract

1 teaspoon orange-flavored liqueur (optional)

1 In a medium saucepan, whisk together the cocoa, brown sugar, cornstarch, and espresso powder. Over medium heat, whisk in the milk, chocolate, and salt until the chocolate melts and the mixture thickens, about 5 to 8 minutes.

2 Remove the mixture from the heat and stir in the vanilla extract and liqueur, if using. Pour evenly into individual dessert bowls. Chill until firm.

*Note: If using rice milk or potato milk, increase cornstarch to 4 tablespoons.

Southern Banana Pudding

MAKES 8 SERVINGS

This pudding and cookie-layered dessert is a Southern classic, with many variations. Some versions are topped with a meringue, but I use whipped cream instead because it's easier to make and provides a creamier effect.

½ cup sugar

3 tablespoons cornstarch

¼ teaspoon salt

1½ cups 1% milk (cow's, rice*, soy, potato*, or nut)

6 large egg yolks, beaten

1 tablespoon unsalted butter or buttery spread, such as Earth Balance

1 teaspoon pure vanilla extract

30 gluten-free cookies (about 3 packages), such as Glutino's Vanilla, Pamela's Lemon Shortbread or Pecan Shortbread, Midel's Arrowroot Crackers, or Health Valley Rice Bran Crackers

3 medium ripe, but firm bananas, sliced

1 cup homemade Basic Whipped Cream (page 624) or whipped topping, such as Lucerne or Soyatoo

1 In a heavy saucepan, whisk together the sugar, cornstarch, and salt until they are thoroughly combined. In a medium bowl, whisk the milk and eggs together until they are completely blended and add to the saucepan.

2 Cook over medium heat, whisking constantly, until the mixture thickens, about 5 minutes. Remove from heat and whisk in butter and vanilla. Let cool 10 minutes.

3 Layer ⅓ of the cookies on the bottom of a glass, straight-sided serving bowl, breaking cookies into small pieces to fill in the gaps. Spread ½ of the pudding on top. Place 1 of the sliced bananas evenly over the pudding. Layer another ⅓ of the cookies on top of the bananas. Spread the remaining half of the pudding evenly on top. Layer another sliced banana on top and top with the remaining ⅓ of the cookies. Cover tightly with plastic wrap and refrigerate 3 hours or more. To serve, top with whipped cream.

*Note: If using rice milk or potato milk, increase the cornstarch to 4 tablespoons.

Almond-Millet Pudding

MAKES 4 SERVINGS

This comfort-food dessert featuring millet satisfies your sweet tooth while adding whole grains into your diet. Millet is an especially nutritious gluten-free grain that is easy to digest because of its high lysine (an amino acid) content.

¼ cup sugar
2 tablespoons cornstarch
2 cups 1% milk (cow's, rice, soy, potato, or nut)
2 large eggs
¼ teaspoon salt
1 teaspoon pure vanilla extract
1 teaspoon almond extract
1 cup cooked whole grain millet
2 tablespoons sliced almonds, for garnish

1 In a medium, heavy saucepan, stir together sugar and cornstarch until well blended. Stir in the milk, eggs, and salt and whisk until the eggs are thoroughly blended.

2 Place the saucepan over medium heat and cook, stirring constantly, until the mixture thickens, about 3 to 5 minutes. Remove from the heat and stir in the vanilla extract, almond extract, and cooked millet.

3 Divide the mixture evenly among 4 dessert goblets or stemmed wine glasses. Sprinkle almonds on the pudding. You can serve this immediately as a creamy, warm dessert or chill it for at least an hour for a cool treat.

Baked Rice Pudding

MAKES 4 SERVINGS

This lush dessert makes excellent use of leftover cooked white rice. Use either basmati or regular long-grain white rice. Your choice of milk will affect the color of the pudding: cow's milk yields white pudding; rice milk yields gray pudding; soy milk yields tan pudding. Regardless of color, this dessert is delicious.

2 cups cooked white rice
1 cup 1% milk (cow's, rice, soy, potato, or nut)
1 large egg, whisked or beaten
1 tablespoon unsalted butter or buttery spread, such as Earth Balance
¼ teaspoon salt
½ cup dark or golden raisins
¼ cup sugar
¼ teaspoon ground cinnamon, plus a little extra for dusting
1 teaspoon pure vanilla extract
1 cup homemade Basic Whipped Cream (page 624) or whipped topping, such as Lucerne or Soyatoo (optional)
Ground cinnamon, for dusting

1 In a medium, heavy saucepan, heat rice and milk over medium-high heat. Whisk in egg, butter, salt, and raisins. Heat until mixture forms bubbles around the edge, then turn down heat to low, cover, and simmer 20 to 30 minutes or until milk is absorbed. Stir occasionally so mixture doesn't scorch.

2 Stir in sugar, cinnamon, and vanilla. For extra creaminess, stir in 1 cup of whipped cream. Transfer to a bowl, cover, and chill. Serve in 4 dessert bowls or goblets, dusted lightly with ground cinnamon.

Coconut Rice Custard

MAKES 4 SERVINGS

It seems I always have leftover cooked rice, and—not wanting to waste anything—I developed this delicious dessert to use it up. This recipe uses white rice, but brown rice will produce a lovely, though somewhat heartier and chewier, texture. And, it will be far more nutritious, as well.

¼ cup sugar

2 tablespoons cornstarch

2 cups 1% milk (cow's, rice*, soy, potato*, or nut)

2 large eggs

¼ teaspoon salt

2 teaspoon coconut-flavored extract (optional)

2 cups cooked white rice

Optional garnishes: toasted coconut, homemade Basic Whipped Cream (page 624), maraschino cherry

1 In a medium, heavy saucepan, whisk together the sugar and cornstarch until thoroughly blended. Add the milk, eggs, and salt and whisk until the eggs are thoroughly blended.

2 Place the saucepan over medium heat and cook, stirring constantly, until the mixture thickens, about 3 to 5 minutes. Remove the pan from the heat and stir in the coconut extract and cooked white rice.

3 Divide the mixture among 4 goblets or wine glasses. You can eat the custard immediately as a creamy, warm dessert or chill it for at least an hour for a cool treat.

*Note: If using rice milk or potato milk, increase the cornstarch to 3 tablespoons.

Crème Brûlée

MAKES 4 SERVINGS

You don't have to be a restaurant chef to make this classic French dessert; it's actually simple enough to create at home. There is something exotic and mysterious about using a whole vanilla bean, the only edible fruit of the lily family. Although it comes from such a simple-looking little pod, the most delicious flavor emerges. If you don't have a vanilla bean, use a tablespoon of good-quality, pure vanilla extract instead.

2 cups heavy cream

1 whole vanilla bean, split lengthwise and scraped (see Vanilla Sugar footnote, page 643)

5 large egg yolks

⅓ cup sugar + 2 teaspoons for broiling

1 Generously grease four 6-ounce custard cups or ramekins; set aside.

2 In a medium, heavy saucepan, heat the cream, vanilla bean pod, and the scraped seeds over medium heat until bubbles begin to form around the edge of the pan. Remove the pan from the heat and let stand 30 minutes to cool.

3 In a medium bowl, beat the egg yolks and ⅓ cup of the sugar with the electric mixer on medium speed until the eggs are lemon-colored and thick, about 2 minutes. Remove the vanilla bean from the cooled cream and pour the egg yolks into the cream.

4 Cook without boiling over low heat until the mixture thickens and coats the back of a metal spoon. Remove the pan from the heat and pour the mixture into the prepared cups. Cover and refrigerate 3 hours or until set.

5 About 2 hours before serving, sprinkle the remaining 2 teaspoons sugar evenly over custards and brown with a kitchen torch. Or, put the cups in an 8-inch square ovenproof baking dish and broil 6 inches from the heat until the sugar turns brown and hardens. The broiling time will vary depending on your oven and how far the custards are from the heat, so watch carefully and remove them from the oven as soon as the sugar is browned to your liking. Refrigerate until serving time.

Simplest Flan

MAKES 4 SERVINGS

Flan is a luscious, soothing dessert from Spain that works well to balance hot, spicy meals. My super-simple version here uses a microwave to cook the flan. This dessert tastes best made with dairy products, so I don't offer alternatives here.

½ cup sugar
2 tablespoons water
3 large eggs, at room temperature
¾ sweetened condensed milk
1 cup evaporated skim milk
⅓ cup half-and-half
2 teaspoons pure vanilla extract

1 Grease four 4-ounce custard cups or ramekins; set aside.

2 In a 2-cup glass (not plastic) measuring cup, microwave the sugar and water on high heat 5 to 7 minutes or until the mixture boils and turns a walnut-brown color. (Watch carefully after 5 minutes of cooking, since the mixture can easily burn.) Quickly, pour the mixture into the bottom of the ramekins, dividing evenly.

3 In a large bowl, whisk the eggs until they are well blended, then whisk in the milks, half-and-half, and vanilla extract. Divide the egg mixture evenly among the ramekins. Arrange the ramekins in a circle in the microwave oven.

MAKING CARAMEL FOR THE FLAN

Melting sugar to make caramel may seem daunting, but all it takes is patience. At first, the sugar will appear to do nothing. Then it starts to melt, very slowly, and may appear to harden and look like crusty snow. You can swirl the skillet or pan, but do not stir the sugar. It will continue to melt slowly and will gradually become liquid. Let it continue to melt and turn a deep golden brown before removing it from the heat. Watch it carefully because it can burn quickly if left untended.

4 Microwave on medium heat 12 to 15 minutes, rotating the ramekins a quarter turn every 4 minutes. (If your microwave has a turntable, you don't have to rotate the ramekins.) The flan is done when a knife inserted into edges comes out clean, but when inserted into center of custard comes out thickly coated with custard. (The center will firm up after chilling.)

5 Cool the flans in the custard cups 30 minutes on a wire rack. Refrigerate at least 4 to 6 hours.

6 To serve, run a thin knife around the edge of each custard cup and invert onto a serving plate or bowl. Serve immediately.

Classic Flan

MAKES 4 TO 6 SERVINGS

Known as flan in Spain, this rich and creamy dessert is called crème caramel in France. For the creamiest texture, this dessert is best when made with whole milk and half-and-half, but you may use soy milk or almond milk. Nonfat or rice milk will not produce a creamy texture.

1½ cups sugar, divided
¼ cup water
5 large eggs, at room temperature
¼ teaspoon salt
1½ cups half-and-half
1 cup heavy cream
1 teaspoon pure vanilla extract
Fresh mint sprigs, for garnish

1 Place a rack in the middle of the oven. Preheat the oven to 350°F. Generously butter six 4-ounce custard cups or ramekins and place them in an 11 × 7-inch baking dish that is lined with a folded tea towel.

2 In a small, heavy saucepan, cook ¾ cup of the sugar with the water over medium heat, swirling the pan occasionally until the mixture is golden brown and syrupy, about 7 minutes. Do not stir it. Immediately pour it into the buttered cups.

3 In a large bowl, beat the eggs, salt, and the remaining ¾ cup of sugar with an electric mixer on low speed until the eggs are lemon-colored, about 2 minutes. Gradually beat in the half-and-half, cream, and vanilla extract. Let the mixture stand 5 minutes, then divide it evenly among the prepared ramekins. Pour boiling water into the baking pan up to within 1 inch of the top of the custard cups.

4 Bake 1 hour or until a knife inserted in the center of the custard comes out clean. Remove the custards from the water and cool 15 minutes on a wire rack. To serve, run a sharp knife around the inside edge of the custard cup and invert onto a serving plate or bowl.

Polenta Pudding

MAKES 6 SERVINGS

Apple butter—a highly flavorful spread—makes this dessert easy to prepare because it takes the place of the several ingredients needed if making the dish from scratch. Make this pudding the night before and have it for a quick and easy breakfast.

2 tablespoons slivered almonds
3 cups 1% milk (cow, rice, soy, potato, or nut)
1 cup gluten-free yellow cornmeal, such as Albers, Lamb's, Kinnikinnick, or Shiloh Farms
⅛ teaspoon salt
¾ cup apple butter
¼ cup dried cranberries
1 teaspoon pure vanilla extract

1 Toast the almonds in a heavy 2-quart saucepan over medium heat, shaking the pan occasionally until they are fragrant. Add the milk, cornmeal, and salt and cook, whisking constantly, until the mixture thickens, about 2 to 3 minutes. (Some versions of cornmeal may take longer to cook.)

2 Remove the cornmeal from the heat and stir in the apple butter, cranberries, and vanilla extract. Divide evenly among 6 small dessert bowls or goblets. Serve warm or chilled.

Indian Pudding with Pomegranate Syrup

MAKES 6 SERVINGS

This New England classic makes a wonderful autumn dessert. Serve it with a drizzle of pomegranate syrup (perhaps even a few fresh pomegranate seeds) and a dollop of whipped cream or crème fraîche. Although the pudding is typically served for dessert, you will sometimes see it on breakfast menus in restaurants. For a breakfast treat, simply reheat it in the microwave and sprinkle a few raisins and yogurt on top.

PUDDING

2 cups 1% milk (cow's, rice, soy, potato, or nut)

2 tablespoons unsalted butter or buttery spread, such as Earth Balance

2 tablespoons sugar

¼ teaspoon salt

⅓ cup gluten-free yellow cornmeal, such as Albers, Lamb's, Kinnikinnick, or Shiloh Farms

½ teaspoon ground ginger

¼ teaspoon ground cinnamon

¼ teaspoon grated orange zest

2 tablespoons molasses

2 large egg yolks

SYRUP

2 cups pomegranate juice

2 teaspoons sugar

⅛ teaspoon salt

1 Place a rack in the middle of the oven. Preheat the oven to 275°F. Generously grease a 1-quart shallow baking dish.

2 Make the pudding: In a medium, heavy saucepan, bring the milk, butter, sugar, and salt to a boil over medium-high heat. Whisk in the cornmeal and cook, whisking constantly, until the mixture thickens, about 4 to 5 minutes. Remove the pan from the heat and stir in the ginger, cinnamon, and orange zest.

3 In a small bowl, stir molasses and egg yolks together until smooth. Add ¼ cup of hot cornmeal mixture to molasses and stir together. Stir it back into hot cornmeal mixture and whisk thoroughly until combined. Pour into the prepared dish.

4 Bake 1 hour 15 minutes or until the pudding barely moves when the pan is touched. Cool the pudding to room temperature on a wire rack. Cover and chill 2 hours.

5 Make the syrup: In a heavy, medium saucepan, bring the pomegranate juice, sugar, and salt to a boil over medium-high heat. Reduce the heat just enough to let the juice simmer, but not boil. Cook until the mixture is reduced to ¾ cup. Remove the

pan from the heat and cool slightly. The syrup will firm up as it cools. Serve the pudding in dessert bowls or goblets with 2 tablespoons warm syrup drizzled over each serving.

Panna Cotta

MAKES 4 SERVINGS

Panna cotta is actually just creamy gelatin with a lovely Italian name, which means "cooked cream." If heavy cream isn't right for you, use the heaviest, thickest nondairy milk you can find, such as almond milk or soy milk. Add a strip of lemon peel for a little extra flavor.

2 teaspoons unflavored gelatin powder, such as Knox

2 cups heavy cream (or half cream and half milk) or milk (cow's, soy, or almond)

⅓ cup sugar

1 whole vanilla bean, halved and scraped (see Vanilla Sugar footnote, page 643), or 1 tablespoon pure vanilla extract

1 teaspoon almond extract

⅛ teaspoon salt

1 (3-inch) strip lemon zest

1 cup fresh strawberries or raspberries

Fresh mint, for garnish

1 Lightly grease a decorative ring mold or four 4-inch custard cups or ramekins. In a small bowl, sprinkle the gelatin powder over ¼ cup of the cream. Let stand 3 to 5 minutes to soften.

2 In another saucepan, heat the remaining cream with the sugar, salt, and vanilla bean, if using, until tiny bubbles form around the edge of the pan (do not boil.) Remove the cream from the heat and remove the vanilla bean, if using. Whisk in the gelatin mixture until smooth and the vanilla extract if you're not using the vanilla bean. Add the almond extract.

3 Pour the panna cotta into the prepared mold and refrigerate 6 hours or overnight, until firm.

4 To serve, quickly dip the bottom of the mold in lukewarm water and then dry the bottom of the mold with a paper towel. Loosen the edge of the panna cotta with a sharp knife and unmold onto a dessert plate. Garnish each with ¼ cup berries and a spring of fresh mint. Serve immediately.

Coconut Panna Cotta: Use the same amount of light coconut milk in place of the cream. Omit the vanilla bean or extract and replace the almond extract with coconut extract. Prepare as directed. Divide ½ cup toasted coconut evenly among servings as a garnish.

Espresso Dairy-Free Panna Cotta Ⓥ

MAKES 4 SERVINGS

You can use regular yogurt in this dessert, but I designed it for those who can't have dairy. Use a store-bought soy-based yogurt instead or your own homemade yogurt.

2 cups low-fat vanilla yogurt (cow's) or soy yogurt, such as Whole Soy, + ¼ cup for garnish

2 tablespoons coffee liqueur, such as Kahlúa

1 tablespoon sugar + 2 teaspoons for the topping

⅓ cup fresh brewed espresso, cooled to room temperature

1½ teaspoons unflavored gelatin powder, such as Knox

1 can (11 ounces) mandarin oranges, drained (reserve 12 orange sections for garnish)

2 tablespoons cocoa nibs, such as Scharffen Berger, for garnish (optional)

12 chocolate-covered espresso beans, for garnish (optional)

1 In a small bowl, whisk together 2 cups of the yogurt, 1 tablespoon of the liqueur, and sugar until smooth; set aside. Lightly grease 4 ramekins, sauce dishes, or mini-Bundt pans, each about 4½ inches in diameter.

2 In a small saucepan, combine the espresso and 1 tablespoon of the liqueur. Stir the gelatin in until it is well blended; let stand 1 minute.

3 Place the saucepan over low heat and cook, stirring constantly, until the gelatin is dissolved, about 25 to 30 seconds. Remove the pan from the heat and whisk the warm gelatin into the yogurt mixture until smooth.

4 Pour the mixture into the prepared ramekins. Refrigerate at least 4 hours or until set.

5 Unmold a panna cotta onto each of 4 dessert plates and arrange 3 orange segments around each serving. Serve each with 1 tablespoon of yogurt and a sprinkling of cocoa nibs and espresso beans, if using.

Tiramisu Ⓥ

MAKES 8 SERVINGS

Tiramisu means "pick me up" in Italian and its sweet, creamy texture is sure to give you a boost. About 30 minutes before you make this heavenly Italian dessert, put the 2-quart bowl and beaters from your electric mixer in the refrigerator to chill. This will make the cream whip higher and lighter.

2 cups homemade Basic Whipped Cream (page 624) or whipped topping, such as Lucerne or Soyatoo

1 package (8 ounces) cream cheese or cream cheese alternative, such as Tofutti, softened

1 tub (8 ounces) mascarpone, or cream cheese alternative, such as Tofutti, softened

¾ cup powdered sugar

½ cup very strong brewed coffee or espresso

2 tablespoons coffee liqueur, such as Kahlúa

2 teaspoons pure vanilla extract

18 homemade Ladyfingers (page 436), or gluten-free cookies, such as Pamela's Pecan Shortbread

2 tablespoons unsweetened cocoa powder (Dutch-process or alkali)

¼ cup gluten-free grated chocolate, such as Tropical Source, for garnish

1 Coat an 8-inch square pan with cooking spray. Set aside.

2 Using the chilled 2-quart bowl and beaters (see headnote), make the whipped cream.

3 In another 2-quart bowl using the same beaters, beat together the cream cheese, mascarpone, and sugar until thoroughly combined. With a spatula, fold in ¼ of the whipped cream into the cream cheese-mascarpone mixture. Carefully fold in remaining whipped cream.

4 Combine coffee, coffee liqueur, and vanilla in shallow bowl. Quickly and lightly dip each cookie in the mixture only halfway. (Do not saturate the cookies or they will fall apart.) Place 9 of the cookies in a single layer on the bottom of the prepared pan. Spoon on half of the mascarpone and smooth it with a spatula.

5 Dip the remaining cookies in the coffee mixture and arrange in a single layer on top of the mascarpone. Top with the remaining mascarpone and smooth it with a spatula. Place the cocoa in a fine-mesh sieve and gently dust over the mascarpone.

6 Cover with plastic wrap and refrigerate at least 4 hours. (The flavor will be more fully developed if the tiramisu is chilled overnight.) Garnish each slice with a scant tablespoon of grated chocolate.

Next Thing to Robert Redford Dessert Ⓥ

MAKES 16 SERVINGS

Handwritten in the corner of the tattered recipe card I have, and written in our neighbor's unmistakably familiar handwriting, was the word "great." She lived next door to my parents for two decades and I still remember the day she brought this dessert to our house. At the time, it was very popular because Robert Redford was a hit at the box office, as Brad Pitt is today. This dessert will be a "hit" at your house, too.

BOTTOM LAYER

1 cup Carol's Sorghum Blend (page x)

½ cup (1 stick) unsalted butter or buttery spread, such as Earth Balance, at room temperature

1 cup finely chopped pecans

1 teaspoon xanthan gum

MIDDLE LAYER

1 package (8 ounces) cream cheese or cream cheese alternative, such as Tofutti, softened

1 cup powdered sugar

3 cups Basic Whipped Cream (page 624) or whipped topping, such as Lucerne or Soyatoo, thawed and divided

TOP LAYER

2 cups homemade Basic Custard for Pies (page 643) or 2 cups gluten-free vanilla pudding, such as Giant, Hy-Vee, or Royal

2 cups Chocolate Pots de Crème (page 645) or 2 cups gluten-free chocolate pudding, such as Giant, Hy-Vee, or Royal

¼ cup chopped pecans

3 ounces gluten-free dark chocolate, such as Tropical Source, shaved, for garnish

1 Place a rack in the middle of the oven. Preheat the oven to 350°F. Make the bottom layer: in a medium bowl, beat the sorghum blend, butter, pecans, and xanthan gum with an electric mixer on low speed until crumbly and press the mixture on the bottom of a 13 × 9-inch nonstick (gray, not black) pan that has been lightly coated with cooking spray.

2 Bake 15 to 20 minutes or until lightly browned. Cool the pan completely on a wire rack.

3 Make the middle layer: In a medium bowl, beat the cream cheese and sugar with an electric mixer on medium speed until smooth. Fold in half of the whipped cream and spread on the cooled crust. Chill 2 hours or until this layer firms up.

4 Make the top layer: Prepare the puddings.

over the vanilla pudding. Spread the remaining whipped topping over the chocolate pudding. Refrigerate at least 2 hours or overnight to firm up. Sprinkle with pecans and chocolate shavings before cutting in serving pieces.

Sweet Pineapple-Raisin Kugel

MAKES 8 SERVINGS

Kugel are casseroles served at traditional eastern European meals. They can be sweet or savory and are made with a variety of ingredients. You can use any fruit you choose in place of the pineapple and raisins, but be sure to drain canned fruits if you use them.

1 package (8 ounces) gluten-free fettuccine, such as Heartland's Finest or Thai Kitchen
2 tablespoons unsalted butter or buttery spread, such as Earth Balance, at room temperature
2 small packages (3 ounces each) cream cheese or cream cheese alternative, such as Tofutti, softened
3 large eggs, at room temperature
⅓ cup sour cream or sour cream alternative, such as Tofutti, at room temperature
½ cup sugar
½ teaspoon ground cinnamon
1 teaspoon pure vanilla extract
1 cup 1% milk (cow's, rice, soy, potato, or nut)
½ cup crushed pineapple, drained
¼ cup golden raisins

TOPPING

¼ cup finely chopped walnuts
¼ cup sugar
¼ cup (½ stick) unsalted butter or buttery spread, such as Earth Balance, at room temperature
1 teaspoon pure vanilla extract
½ teaspoon ground cinnamon

1 Place a rack in the middle of the oven. Preheat the oven to 350°F. Generously grease an 8-inch baking pan.

2 Cook the fettucine in salted, boiling water for 5 to 7 minutes until al dente, stirring frequently; drain and set aside in a large bowl.

3 In a medium bowl, beat the butter, cream cheese, eggs, sour cream, sugar, cinnamon, vanilla extract, and milk with an electric mixer on low speed until very smooth. Stir in the pineapple and raisins and fold this mixture into the noodles. Transfer to the prepared baking pan.

4 Bake 35 minutes. Meanwhile, make topping: In a separate medium bowl, mix together the walnuts, sugar, butter, and cinnamon. Sprinkle over the egg noodle mixture and bake 15 minutes more or until bubbly and lightly browned. Serve warm.

Pavlova

MAKES 4 SERVINGS

Pavlova is simply a baked meringue filled with whipped cream that makes a lovely presentation for guests. The meringue can be made ahead and kept in an airtight container for two days prior to serving. Serve one large pavlova, or individual ones, to each guest. Instead of whipped cream, you can fill the meringue with lemon curd or your favorite nondairy pudding. Top the pavlova with any type of fresh fruit you want—the more colorful the better.

3 large egg whites, at room temperature
1 teaspoon fresh lemon juice
⅛ teaspoon salt
¾ cup sugar, divided
1 teaspoon pure vanilla extract, divided
1 teaspoon cornstarch
⅛ teaspoon cream of tartar
2 cups homemade Basic Whipped Cream (page 624) or whipped topping, such as Lucerne or Soyatoo, divided
1 kiwi, peeled and sliced thinly, crosswise
1 cup fresh strawberries, stemmed and sliced
½ cup fresh blueberries, washed, hulled, and dried
½ cup mandarin oranges, drained
Fresh mint leaves, for garnish

1 Place a rack in the middle of the oven. Preheat the oven to 250°F. Line a 13 × 9-inch baking sheet (not nonstick) with parchment paper. Outline an 8-inch circle in the center of the parchment paper; set aside.

2 In a large bowl, combine the egg whites, lemon juice, and salt. Set the bowl over a pan of simmering water, being careful not to let the bowl touch the water. Beat the egg whites with an electric mixer on medium speed until they double in volume. Gradually add ½ cup of the sugar, 1 tablespoon at a time, until the meringue stands in soft peaks. Total beating time should be about 10 minutes. Fold in the cornstarch and vanilla.

3 Spread the meringue onto the baking sheet within the marked circle. Using a spoon or spatula, make a large indentation in the center of meringue to hold the whipped cream and fruit.

4 Bake 1 hour or until center if rim and edges are set. Turn off the oven, open the door slightly, and allow the meringue to cool 2 hours in the oven. Transfer the meringue to a wire rack to cool completely.

5 To assemble the pavlova, remove the meringue from the baking sheet with a long, wide spatula and place it on a serving plate. Fill the hollow of the meringue with whipped cream, reserving ½ cup for garnish.

6 Top the whipped cream with strawberries, kiwi, blueberries, and mandarin oranges. To serve, cut the crisp pavola carefully but firmly with an electric knife or a long, serrated knife dipped in hot water, then wiped dry. Garnish each serving with 2 tablespoons of the reserved whipped cream and a fresh mint leaf.

Fudge Sundaes on Crisp Tortillas Ⓠ Ⓥ

MAKES 4 SERVINGS

You know that craving: You want something sweet and creamy, with a little texture, for contrast— and you want it fast. These sundaes fill the bill. Add chopped toasted nuts and other toppings, if you like.

2 gluten-free flour tortillas, such as Food for Life or La Tortilla Factory

¼ teaspoon salt

Canola oil for frying

1 pint gluten-free vanilla ice cream, such as Ben & Jerry's, Dreyer's Grand, or Häagen-Dazs, or homemade Vanilla Ice Cream (page 657)

½ cup gluten-free chocolate syrup, such as Hershey's, or homemade Chocolate Sauce (page 622)

1 Cut each tortilla into 4 quarters with kitchen scissors or a sharp knife. Put enough canola oil in a heavy saucepan to cover the tortilla.

2 Cook the tortillas, one at a time, over medium heat until they turn light golden brown. Push tortilla down with tongs to submerge fully in oil and turn once to brown both sides. Watch carefully because the tortilla can crisp quickly, especially if it is at room temperature.

3 Remove the tortilla from the oil with tongs and drain it on paper towels. Immediately sprinkle salt lightly on tortilla. Repeat with remaining wedges.

4 Serve two wedges per person, each wedge topped with a scoop of vanilla ice cream and a drizzle of 2 tablespoons chocolate syrup.

Clementine Zabaglione

MAKES 4 SERVINGS

Zabaglione (tsah-bahl-YO-neh) is an Italian dessert sauce, usually made with Vin Santo, a sweet Italian wine, or sweet Marsala. You can always make it the traditional way, but I know you'll fall in love with my flavorful, nonalcoholic version that uses sweet, juicy clementines now available almost year-round in supermarkets (although I think their flavor is better during the winter months). Serve this creamy sauce over fresh berries or in place of crème anglaise.

3 large egg yolks
¼ cup sugar
3 tablespoons fresh clementine juice, or Vin Santo, or sweet Marsala wine
Grated zest of 1 clementine

1 In a large glass bowl, beat the egg yolks, sugar, and juice until the color is pale orange. Place the bowl over a pan of simmering water, being careful not to let the bowl touch the water.

2 Beat the sauce with an electric mixer on high speed until it is tripled in volume and is very thick and creamy, about 3 to 4 minutes. Stir in the grated clementine zest. Serve the sauce immediately.

MOUSSES, SORBETS, AND SOUFFLÉS

Chocolate Mousse

MAKES 4 SERVINGS

This is probably one of the simplest mousses you can make. You can serve it as is and let it speak for itself or add some colorful preserves. Whipped cream is a classic topping.

¾ cup gluten-free chocolate syrup, such as Hershey's, or homemade Chocolate Sauce (page 622)
2 tablespoons honey or agave nectar
½ teaspoon pure vanilla extract
⅛ teaspoon salt
2½ cups homemade Basic Whipped Cream (page 624) or whipped topping, such as Lucerne or Soyatoo
4 teaspoons apricot preserves or orange marmalade, for garnish (optional)

1 Stir together ¼ cup of the chocolate syrup, the honey, vanilla extract, and salt.

2 In a large mixing bowl, place 2 cups of the whipped cream; refrigerate ½ cup for garnish. Gently fold the chocolate mixture into the 2 cups whipped cream until there are no streaks. Divide the mousse evenly among 4 dessert goblets or stemmed wine glasses. Chill at least 1 hour.

3 To serve, top each serving with 2 tablespoons of the reserved chocolate syrup, then 2 tablespoons of the reserved whipped cream. To garnish, if using, top each with 1 teaspoon fruit jam of your choice such as orange marmalade, or raspberry or apricot preserves.

Chocolate Mint Mousse: Add ½ teaspoon peppermint extract to chocolate syrup mixture.

White Chocolate Mousse

MAKES 4 SERVINGS

I'm normally a fan of dark chocolate, but this white chocolate mousse is fantastic. For added decadence on special occasions, drizzle it with a gluten-free liqueur, such as Kahlúa. The gelatin powder gives the mousse extra body, but if you prefer a softer mousse, omit it.

3.5 ounces gluten-free white chocolate, such as Organica, broken into pieces

¾ cup homemade Basic Whipped Cream (page 624) or whipped topping, such as Lucerne or Soyatoo

⅛ teaspoon salt

¼ teaspoon unflavored gelatin powder, such as Knox

1 teaspoon pure vanilla extract

Optional garnishes: fresh raspberries, blueberries, or strawberries; fresh mint leaves or a dusting of cocoa powder

1 Melt the white chocolate, ¼ cup of whipped cream, and salt in microwave oven on low until the chocolate melts. Stir until smooth and then let cool 5 minutes. Whisk in the gelatin powder until completely dissolved.

2 In a small mixer bowl, beat the remaining ¼ cup of whipped cream with the vanilla extract on medium-high speed until stiff peaks form (do not overbeat).

3 Fold the melted white chocolate mixture into the whipped cream (or remaining ½ cup of whipped topping). Divide evenly among 4 small martini goblets or espresso cups and refrigerate it at least 1 hour before serving. Garnish as desired.

Peanut Butter Mousse

MAKES 4 SERVINGS

Smooth and creamy, this dessert can be made ahead, and it looks especially pretty served in little martini glasses or dessert goblets.

1 package (8 ounces) cream cheese or cream cheese alternative, such as Tofutti, softened

½ cup packed light brown sugar

¼ cup creamy peanut butter

1 tablespoon pure vanilla extract

1 cup homemade Basic Whipped Cream (page 624) or whipped topping, such as Lucerne or Soyatoo

2 tablespoons chopped peanuts, for garnish

1 In a medium mixing bowl, beat the cream cheese, sugar, peanut butter, and vanilla extract and blend until thoroughly combined. In a separate bowl, beat the heavy cream with an electric mixer on medium-high speed to the soft peak stage. Reserve ¼ cup whipped cream for garnish.

2 Using a spatula, fold the whipped cream into the cream cheese mixture until there are no white streaks. Divide evenly among 4 dessert bowls. Refrigerate at least 2 hours. To serve, garnish each serving with a tablespoon of whipped cream and a sprinkling of peanuts.

Viennese Cinnamon-Mocha Mousse

MAKES 4 SERVINGS

Jazz up this dessert with a tablespoon of your favorite gluten-free liqueur. Soaking the cocoa in the hot coffee further enhances the deep chocolate flavor. If you want this mousse to be creamier, melt 1 tablespoon gluten-free white chocolate, such as Organica, in the hot coffee. The servings are small and perfect for a dainty tea cup.

⅓ cup unsweetened cocoa powder (Dutch-process or alkali)

¼ teaspoon ground cinnamon

4 teaspoons unflavored gelatin powder, such as Knox

1 cup 1% milk (cow, rice, soy, potato, or nut), divided

¾ cup freshly brewed coffee (or, see headnote)

1 teaspoon pure vanilla extract

¼ cup sugar

½ cup homemade Basic Whipped Cream (page 624) or whipped topping, such as Lucerne or Soyatoo, for garnish

2 tablespoons cocoa nibs, such as Scharffen Berger, or chocolate-covered espresso beans, for garnish

1 In a measuring cup, dissolve the cocoa and cinnamon in the hot coffee and let stand 5 minutes.

2 In a blender, sprinkle the gelatin in ¼ cup of the milk and let stand 5 minutes or until the gelatin softens. Add the hot coffee mixture and blend 30 seconds. Add the remaining ¾ cup of the milk, vanilla extract, and sugar and blend until very smooth.

3 Divide the mixture evenly among 4 espresso cups or martini goblets. Chill at least 4 hours. Serve, garnished with a dollop of whipped cream and a sprinkling of cocoa nibs or chocolate-covered espresso beans.

Vanilla Ice Cream

MAKES 1 QUART

Rich, creamy, homemade vanilla ice cream relies on a few simple ingredients—cream, eggs, sugar, and vanilla—without the stabilizers found in store-bought versions. Electric ice cream makers simplify the process. You can vary this vanilla version by adding fresh strawberries or chocolate chips—whatever you like.

¾ to 1 cup sugar

2 tablespoons arrowroot

¼ teaspoon salt

2 cups heavy cream

2 cups half-and-half

4 large egg yolks

1 tablespoon pure vanilla extract

1 In a medium, heavy saucepan, whisk together sugar, arrowroot, and salt. Whisk in heavy cream and half-and-half. Place saucepan over medium-low heat and bring to a simmer, whisking constantly. Remove from heat.

2 In a medium bowl, whisk egg yolks until very smooth. Whisk ½ cup of the hot cream mixture into eggs, and then slowly pour egg mixture into saucepan in a slow steady stream, continuing to whisk constantly until well-blended.

3 Return saucepan to medium-low heat and cook, stirring constantly, until mixtures registers 175°F and coats the back of a spoon. Remove from heat, stir in vanilla extract, and pour custard into a medium bowl. Let stand at room temperature 15 minutes, stirring occasionally. Cover and refrigerate overnight or until temperature reaches 40°F.

4 Freeze in ice cream maker, according to manufacturer's directions. Serve immediately or transfer to freezer-safe container and freeze, tightly covered, up to 1 week.

Fresh Strawberry Ice Cream: Stir 1 cup fresh, hulled, sliced strawberries and 2 drops of red food coloring into chilled custard before churning.

Chocolate Chip Ice Cream: Stir 1 cup semi-sweet chocolate chips, such as Tropical Source or Ghirardelli, into chilled custard before churning.

Chocolate Espresso Sorbet

MAKES 1 QUART

Sorbet can be light but this one has a rich, rewarding flavor. Sorbet doesn't usually contain dairy so it's safe for dairy-sensitive folks who can't eat ice cream, sherbet, or gelato.

2 cups sugar
1½ cups unsweetened cocoa powder (not Dutch-process or alkali)
½ teaspoon xanthan gum
½ teaspoon salt
4 cups water
1 cup freshly brewed espresso or coffee
1 tablespoon pure vanilla extract
1 tablespoon brandy or 1 teaspoon brandy extract

1 In a medium, heavy saucepan, whisk together the sugar, cocoa, xanthan gum, and salt. Add the water and brewed coffee and whisk to blend. Bring mixture to a boil, then reduce the heat to low, and simmer 20 minutes, stirring occasionally, or until the mixture is slightly reduced. Add the vanilla extract and brandy. Refrigerate the mixture to 40°F.

2 Pour the sorbet into the freezer container of an electric ice cream freezer. Freeze according to manufacturer's directions.

Lemon Sorbet with Limoncello

MAKES 1 QUART

You can find Limoncello everywhere in Italy—at least I certainly did. It was so ubiquitous that I even found it at truck stops. But you don't have to travel to Italy; you can find it here, in most liquor stores. The sorbet may not freeze as stiffly because of the Limoncello, but it's still delicious.

1 packet (2½ teaspoons) unflavored gelatin powder, such as Knox
2¼ cups cold water, divided
1 cup sugar
¾ cup fresh lemon juice
2 tablespoons grated lemon zest
2 tablespoons Limoncello liqueur (optional)
Fresh mint, for garnish

1 In a medium, heavy, saucepan, whisk gelatin into ¼ cup of the water. Let stand 5 minutes to dissolve. Add the remaining 2 cups of water and the sugar. Cook over medium heat until sugar and gelatin completely dissolve. Remove from heat; stir in the lemon juice and lemon zest. Refrigerate the mixture to 40°F.

2 Pour the mixture into an electric ice cream freezer and follow the manufacturer's directions. Remove sorbet by using melon baller or a spring-action ice cream scoop. Serve immediately in 6 dessert goblets with a drizzle of Limoncello liqueur, if using. Garnish with fresh mint.

Individual Chocolate Espresso Soufflés

MAKES 4 SERVINGS

Chocolate and coffee just naturally go together. In fact, I think of chocolate and coffee as two of my favorite food groups, so I just love this soufflé. It's great for company, who can't help but be impressed when they first catch the chocolate aroma wafting from the kitchen and then when you bring out the soufflés, hot from the oven.

1 tablespoon butter or buttery spread, such as Earth Balance, for buttering ramekins

½ cup sugar

⅓ cup cornstarch

3 tablespoons unsweetened cocoa powder (Dutch-process)

1 teaspoon instant espresso powder

¼ cup 1% milk (cow's, rice, soy, potato, or nut)

1 teaspoon coffee liqueur, such as Kahlúa, or brewed coffee

2 large egg whites, at room temperature

¼ teaspoon cream of tartar

1 tablespoon powdered sugar for dusting

4 chocolate-covered espresso beans, for garnish

1 Place a rack in the middle of the oven. Preheat the oven to 375°F. Generously butter four 3 inch ceramic ramekins and dust each with some of the sugar. Shake any excess sugar out into a small saucepan.

2 Whisk together the sugar, cornstarch, cocoa, and espresso powder in the small saucepan. Whisk in the milk and cook about 2 to 3 minutes on medium heat, or until the mixture is smooth. Remove the heat, stir in the liqueur, and let cool 5 minutes.

3 In a medium bowl, beat the egg whites and cream of tartar to the stiff peak stage. Gently whisk the chocolate mixture into the egg whites until there are almost no white streaks. Spoon a generous ¼ cup of the mixture into the prepared ramekins and place them on a baking sheet (not nonstick).

4 Bake 20 to 25 minutes, or until the soufflés rise but the centers remain slightly soft. Serve immediately, dusted with powdered sugar. Garnish with a chocolate-covered espresso bean.

Piña Colada Soufflé with Coconut Whipped Cream

MAKES 4 SERVINGS

This soufflé is deceptively rich, so I recommend small portions, perhaps served in stemmed wine glasses, small goblets, or tea cups. When making soufflés, you can gently whisk the beaten egg whites into the other ingredients, rather than the usual folding. Just be careful not to deflate the air beaten into the egg whites, which makes the soufflé airy and delicate.

⅓ cup sugar + 1 tablespoon for ramekins

1 can (8 ounces) crushed pineapple, thoroughly drained (discard juice)

2 tablespoons cornstarch

¼ cup 1% milk (cow's, rice, soy, potato, or nut)

1 tablespoon unsalted butter or buttery spread, such as Earth Balance

2 large egg whites, at room temperature

¼ teaspoon cream of tartar

1 teaspoon coconut extract (or vanilla extract)

½ cup homemade Basic Whipped Cream (page 624) or whipped topping, such as Lucerne or Soyatoo

¼ cup sweetened shredded coconut, toasted, for garnish (see How to Toast Coconut, page 475)

1 Place a rack in the middle of the oven. Preheat the oven to 375°F. Generously grease four 3-inch ceramic ramekins with butter and then dust with 1 tablespoon of the sugar; tap out the excess into the food processor.

2 In the food processor, process ⅓ cup of the sugar, pineapple, cornstarch, and milk until very smooth.

3 In a medium, heavy saucepan, combine pine-apple mixture and butter and cook 2 minutes over medium-low heat, whisking constantly, or until it thickens. Remove the pan from the heat. Whisk in the coconut extract; set aside.

4 In a medium bowl, beat the egg whites and cream of tartar with an electric mixer on medium speed until the egg whites reach the stiff peak stage. Fold ¼ of the whites into the pineapple mixture. Gently fold this mixture back into the egg whites just until the white streaks disappear. Divide the mixture evenly among the 4 prepared ramekins.

5 Bake 20 to 25 minutes or until the soufflés are puffed and golden. They should jiggle slightly in the center. Serve immediately with 2 tablespoons of the whipped topping and a sprinkling of toasted coconut.

BREAD PUDDINGS AND TRIFLES

Raisin Bread Pudding with Cinnamon Sauce Ⓥ

MAKES 8 SERVINGS

Save those last few slices of Cinnamon Raisin Yeast Bread (page 84) and use it in this home-style dessert. Topped with the Cinnamon Sauce—which can also be used on apple and pear dishes—this dessert is delightfully comforting.

BREAD PUDDING

6 slices gluten-free bread such as Ener-G Cinnamon Loaf or leftover homemade Cinnamon Raisin Yeast Bread (page 84)

½ cup dark raisins

2 cups 1% milk (cow's, rice, soy, potato, or nut)

1 cup sugar

4 large eggs, at room temperature

1 teaspoon pure vanilla extract

¼ teaspoon ground cinnamon

⅛ teaspoon freshly grated nutmeg

¼ teaspoon salt

SAUCE

⅓ cup packed light brown sugar

2 teaspoons cornstarch

½ teaspoon ground cinnamon

⅛ teaspoon salt

⅔ cup water

1 tablespoon unsalted butter or buttery spread, such as Earth Balance

½ teaspoon grated lemon zest

1 teaspoon fresh lemon juice

1 Place a rack in the middle of the oven. Preheat the oven to 325°F. Generously grease an 8-inch nonstick (gray, not black) baking dish.

2 Make the bread pudding: Slice the crusts off the bread and cut into 1-inch cubes. Place the cubed bread in the prepared dish. Sprinkle raisins over the bread.

3 In a medium shallow bowl, whisk together the milk, sugar, eggs, vanilla extract, cinnamon, salt, and nutmeg until smooth and pour evenly over the bread cubes. Press down on bread and let stand 15 minutes. Cover with aluminum foil.

4 Bake 35 to 40 minutes. Remove the foil and bake 10 to 15 minutes more or until the top is golden brown. Cool the bread pudding 10 minutes on a wire rack.

5 While the bread pudding bakes, make the sauce: In a small saucepan, stir together sugar, cornstarch, cinnamon, and salt over medium-high heat. Stir in water and bring to boil, stirring constantly. Reduce heat to medium and boil until thick.

6 Remove from heat and add butter, lemon zest, and lemon juice, stirring until butter is melted and sauce is smooth. Serve the bread pudding warm with 2 tablespoons of the sauce per portion.

Chocolate-Cappuccino Bread Pudding with Brandy Sauce Ⓥ

MAKES 8 SERVINGS

If you want the crust of the bread pudding to be browned and crisp, use a nonstick (gray, not black) pan. If you prefer the crust to be soft, use a glass baking dish instead.

BREAD PUDDING

6 slices gluten-free bread, such as Whole Foods, or White Sandwich Yeast Bread (page 85)

½ cup sugar

3 tablespoons unsweetened cocoa powder (Dutch-process)

1 teaspoon ground cinnamon

¼ teaspoon salt

2 cups 1% milk (cow's, rice, soy, potato, or nut)

4 large eggs, at room temperature

1 tablespoon coffee liqueur, such as Kahlúa (optional)

1 teaspoon pure vanilla extract

1 cup gluten-free chocolate chips, such as Tropical Source

SAUCE

¼ cup (½ stick) unsalted butter or buttery spread, such as Earth Balance, at room temperature

½ cup packed light brown sugar

¼ cup heavy cream or 2 tablespoons whole milk (cow's, rice, soy, potato, or nut)

2 tablespoons brandy or 2 teaspoons brandy extract

1 teaspoon pure vanilla extract

1 Place a rack in the middle of the oven. Preheat the oven to 325°F. Generously grease an 8-inch nonstick (gray, not black) baking dish.

2 Make the bread pudding: Slice crusts off the bread and cut it into 1-inch cubes. Place the cubed bread in the prepared dish.

3 In a small bowl, whisk together the sugar, cocoa, cinnamon, and salt until blended. Whisk in the eggs, liqueur, if using, and vanilla extract until very smooth. Pour evenly over the bread cubes. Sprinkle with the chocolate chips. Press down on the bread and let stand 15 minutes so the bread can absorb the mixture. Cover with aluminum foil.

4 Bake 35 to 40 minutes. Remove the foil and bake 10 to 15 minutes more or until the top is golden brown and crisp. Cool the bread pudding in the pan 10 minutes on a wire rack.

5 Make the sauce: In a heavy saucepan, heat the butter over medium heat. Add the brown sugar and simmer 2 minutes. Remove from the heat and stir in the cream. The mixture will spatter and harden, but return it to the heat and continue to stir until smooth. Remove from the heat and stir in the brandy and vanilla. Serve immediately drizzled over the warm bread pudding.

Eggnog Bread Pudding with Rum Sauce Ⓥ

MAKES 8 SERVINGS

This dish is fun to serve at the holidays when eggnog is available. If you want the crust of the bread pudding to be browned and crisp, use a nonstick (gray, not black) pan. If you prefer the crust to be soft, use a glass baking dish instead.

BREAD PUDDING

6 slices gluten-free bread, such as Whole Foods, or White Sandwich Yeast Bread (page 85)

¾ cup sugar

¼ teaspoon salt

¼ teaspoon freshly grated nutmeg

2 cups eggnog (cow's milk or soy, such as Silk)

4 large eggs, at room temperature

¼ cup dark rum or orange juice

1 teaspoon pure vanilla extract

½ cup golden raisins

SAUCE

¼ cup (½ stick) unsalted butter or buttery spread, such as Earth Balance, at room temperature

½ cup packed light brown sugar

¼ cup heavy cream or 2 tablespoons whole milk (cow's, rice, soy, potato, or nut)

2 tablespoons dark rum or 2 teaspoons rum-flavored extract

1 teaspoon pure vanilla extract

1 Place a rack in the middle of the oven. Preheat the oven to 325°F. Generously grease an 8-inch nonstick (gray, not black) dish.

2 Make the bread pudding: Slice crusts off the bread and cut it into 1-inch cubes. Place the cubed bread in the prepared dish.

3 Whisk together the sugar, salt, and nutmeg until blended. Whisk in the eggnog, eggs, rum, and vanilla extract until very smooth. Pour evenly over the bread cubes. Sprinkle with the raisins. Press down on the bread and let stand 15 minutes so the bread can absorb the mixture. Cover with aluminum foil.

4 Continue preparing bread pudding and sauce as directed in Steps 4 and 5 of the Chocolate-Cappuccino Bread Pudding (page 661).

Pumpkin Bread Pudding with Clementine Crème Anglaise Ⓥ

MAKES 8 SERVINGS

Clementines are similar to tangerines and are sold by the carton in the produce section year-round, but are better and more plentiful during the winter months. Be sure to use a glass bowl big enough to hold the crème anglaise, which will triple in volume as you beat it.

BREAD PUDDING

6 slices gluten-free bread, such as Whole Foods, or White Sandwich Yeast Bread (page 85)

½ cup chopped pecans

¾ cup golden raisins

2 cups 1% milk (cow's, rice, soy, potato, or nut)

1 cup sugar

3 large eggs, at room temperature

½ cup canned pumpkin puree (not pie filling)

1½ teaspoons ground cinnamon

1 teaspoon pure vanilla extract

1 teaspoon ground ginger

½ teaspoon ground cloves

¼ teaspoon freshly grated nutmeg

¼ teaspoon salt

CRÈME ANGLAISE

3 large egg yolks
¼ cup sugar
3 tablespoons clementine juice
Grated zest of 1 clementine

1 Place a rack in the middle of the oven. Preheat the oven to 350°F. Generously grease an 8-inch nonstick (gray, not black) baking dish.

2 Make the bread pudding: Slice the crusts off bread and cut into 1-inch cubes. Place cubed bread in prepared dish. Top with pecans and raisins.

3 In a medium bowl, whisk together the milk, sugar, eggs, pumpkin, cinnamon, vanilla extract, ginger, cloves, nutmeg, and salt. Pour evenly over the bread cubes. Press down on the bread and let stand 15 minutes so it can absorb the liquid. Cover the dish with aluminum foil.

4 Bake 35 to 40 minutes. Remove the foil and bake 10 to 15 minutes more or until the top is golden brown. Cool the bread pudding in the dish 10 minutes on a wire rack.

5 While the bread pudding bakes, make the crème anglaise: In a large glass bowl, beat the egg yolks, sugar, and juice until the color is pale orange. Place the bowl over a pan of simmering water, being careful not to let the bowl touch the water.

6 Beat the sauce with an electric mixer on high speed until it is tripled in volume and is very thick and creamy, about 3 to 4 minutes. Stir in the grated clementine zest. Serve the bread pudding warm, with 2 tablespoons of the crème anglaise per serving.

Black Forest Trifle

MAKES 12 SERVINGS

Although this elegant dessert may seem complicated, it is one of the easiest—yet one of the showiest—in this book. You can find trifle bowls at kitchen stores or discount stores, but you can also use any large, straight-sided glass bowl. If you don't have the exact amounts of ingredients for this dish, just use what you have, as long as all the amounts are in proportion. Be aware, however, that if you whip your own cream or use the aerosol can variety, it will not hold its shape for very long, so it's best to serve right away.

1 recipe homemade Chocolate Brownies (page 442)
1 recipe homemade Instant Vanilla Pudding (page 643) or pudding of your choice
1 tablespoon cherry brandy, such as kirschwasser (optional)
1 can (14 to 15 ounces) cherry pie filling
4 cups homemade Basic Whipped Cream (page 624) or whipped topping, such as Lucerne or Soyatoo
1 can (11 ounces) mandarin oranges, drained and patted dry
2 tablespoons unsweetened cocoa powder (Dutch-process), for garnish
Fresh mint leaves, for garnish (optional)

1 Prepare the brownies. Prepare the pudding. Then, cut the brownies into 1-inch pieces and place half in a layer on the bottom and along sides of trifle bowl.

2 Stir the cherry brandy into the cherry pie filling and spoon all but 1 tablespoon over the brownies. Smooth the cherry filling with a spatula and press filling firmly against sides of bowl.

3 Fold whipped topping into pudding. Spoon mixture over cherries. Smooth with spatula and press it firmly against sides of bowl.

4 Place the remaining brownies around the edge of the bowl, creating a ring of brownies around the top. Arrange a circle of mandarin oranges next to the brownies.

5 To serve, garnish the top with the remaining 1 tablespoon of cherry pie filling. Dust with cocoa and garnish with mint leaves, if using. Serve immediately.

Chocolate Orange Trifle with Orange Custard ⓥ

MAKES 12 SERVINGS

This is a wonderful finale for a dinner party and also makes a stunning addition to a buffet table, if you have time to assemble it just before serving. The rich texture of the orange cream and little bits of orange peel in the marmalade complement the chocolate cake. It takes some time and effort to get all the ingredients ready but the dish can be assembled fairly quickly. Everyone's pleasure (including your own) at seeing and enjoying this dessert, will be your reward.

CAKE

½ cup (1 stick) unsalted butter or buttery spread, such as Earth Balance

1 cup packed light brown sugar

1¼ cups Carol's Sorghum Blend (page x)

1 large egg, at room temperature

½ cup unsweetened cocoa powder (not Dutch-process or alkali)

1 teaspoon xanthan gum

¾ teaspoon salt

½ teaspoon baking soda

2 teaspoons pure vanilla extract

½ cup 1% milk (cow's, rice, soy, potato, or nut)

½ cup hot (120°F) water or coffee

1½ cups orange marmalade or homemade Clementine Marmalade (page 678)

2 small cans (11 ounces each) mandarin oranges, drained (12 sections reserved for garnish)

Fresh mint leaves, for garnish (optional)

CUSTARD

½ cup sugar

¼ cup cornstarch

¼ teaspoon salt

2 cups 1% milk (cow's, rice, soy, potato, or nut)

1 small container (3 ounces) orange juice concentrate, thawed but not reconstituted

1 teaspoon grated orange zest

1 teaspoon pure vanilla extract

1 tablespoon unsalted butter or buttery spread, such as Earth Balance

4 cups homemade Basic Whipped Cream (page 624) or whipped topping, such as Lucerne or Soyatoo

1 Place a rack in the middle of the oven. Preheat the oven to 350°F. Generously grease an 11 × 7-inch nonstick (gray, not black) pan.

2 Make the cake: In a large bowl, beat butter with an electric mixer on low-medium speed until smooth. Beat in sugar, then egg. Add sorghum blend, cocoa, xanthan gum, salt, baking soda, vanilla, and milk and blend thoroughly. Blend in hot water. Pour batter into pan, smooth top with spatula, and bake 25 to 30 minutes or until tooth-pick inserted in center of cake comes out clean. Remove from oven and cool in the pan 30 minutes on wire rack. Cut cake into 1-inch cubes.

3 Make the custard: In a small saucepan, whisk together the sugar, cornstarch, and salt. Whisk in the milk, orange juice concentrate, and orange zest.

4 Cook the mixture over medium heat, whisking constantly, about 5 to 8 minutes or until it thickens. Remove it from heat; stir in the vanilla extract and butter, and transfer to a shallow bowl or 11 × 7-inch pan. Press plastic wrap directly onto the orange custard and chill 30 minutes. Stir half the whipped cream into the chilled orange custard.

5 Assemble the trifle: In the bottom of a trifle bowl or a straight-sided glass bowl layer half of the cake cubes, ½ cup of marmalade, 1 can of mandarin oranges (minus 12 for garnish), and 2 cups of orange custard. Continue with a second layer of cake, ½ cup marmalade, and the second can of mandarin oranges, ending with the remaining orange custard. Cover the top with remaining whipped cream and spread the remaining half-cup of marmalade in the center of the whipped cream. Arrange the reserved mandarin oranges around the edge of bowl and mint leaves for garnish. Serve immediately.

Strawberry, Lemon Curd, and Kiwi Trifle Ⓥ

MAKES 12 SERVINGS

A trifle is best served to a large group and makes an impressive presentation. Bring it to the table after dinner and serve each guest a portion in a glass goblet or dessert bowl. It is fun to try different approaches as you assemble the layers of a trifle, so feel free to experiment a bit.

LEMON CURD

3 large eggs
2 large egg yolks
¾ cup sugar
⅓ cup fresh lemon juice
¼ cup (½ stick) unsalted butter or buttery spread, such as Earth Balance,
1 tablespoon grated lemon zest

TRIFLE

1 (9-inch) layer from homemade Yellow Cake (page 464)
2 cups hulled and sliced fresh strawberries
¼ cup sugar
2 tablespoons lemon liqueur, such as Limoncello, or orange liqueur, such as Triple Sec, or fresh orange juice
1½ cups lemon curd or homemade Lemon Curd
4 cups homemade Basic Whipped Cream (page 624) or whipped topping, such as Lucerne or Soyatoo
2 cups peeled and sliced fresh kiwi
¼ cup sliced almonds
Fresh mint leaves, for garnish (optional)

1 Make the lemon curd: Fill the bottom of a double boiler with 2 inches of water. In the top of the double boiler, whisk all the ingredients together over medium heat until smooth. Cook the sauce until thick, about 10 to 12 minutes, stirring constantly. Remove from the heat and cool. Chill 30 minutes before using in the trifle.

2 Make the trifle: Cut the yellow cake into 1-inch pieces and place half of the pieces in a layer on the bottom and along the sides of a trifle bowl or a straight sided glass bowl.

3 In a medium bowl, combine the strawberries, sugar, and liqueur and spoon all but ¼ cup over the cake and arrange some of the slices, cut side in, firmly against the sides of the bowl so they are visible from the outside.

4 Spread half of the lemon curd over the strawberries and top with ½ cup of the whipped cream. Arrange all but ¼ cup of the sliced kiwi fruit over the whipped topping.

5 Arrange the remaining pieces of cake on top and around the edge of the bowl, creating a layer of cake. Spread the remaining half of the lemon curd and ½ cup of the whipped cream on top. Arrange the remaining strawberries and kiwi fruit on the top decoratively.

6 To serve, sprinkle with the sliced almonds and garnish with mint leaves, if using. Serve immediately.

HOMEMADE GLUTEN-FREE INGREDIENTS

Seasonings

Lemon Pepper Seasoning

Mediterranean Herb Seasoning

Southwestern Seasoning

Southwestern Chicken Rub

Adobo Seasoning

Blackening Seasoning

Jamaican Jerk Seasoning

Onion Soup Mix

Seafood Seasoning

Sauces and Salsas

Basic Vinaigrette

Raspberry Vinaigrette

Pico de Gallo

Tomato, Corn, or Bean Salsa

Herb Salsa

Garlic-Thyme Herbed Butter

Basil Pesto

Marinara Sauce

Harissa Sauce

Chipotle Adobo Sauce

Chipotle Mayonnaise

Blue Cheese Dipping Sauce

Bechamel Sauce

Simple Cream Sauce

Simple White Gravy

Miscellaneous

Beef Broth

Chicken Broth

Shrimp Stock

Vegetable Broth

Buttermilk

Almond Milk

Almond Paste

Honey Butter

Cinnamon Applesauce

Clementine Marmalade

Q = Quick   V = Vegetarian

There are several commercially prepared ingredients used throughout this book that you might not be able to find in stores or that contain something you can't eat. I recommend making your own for the best and freshest flavor and control over what goes into your food. Many of the recipes here, such as the seasonings, rely on a small spice grinder or coffee grinder to grind and blend them. These inexpensive grinders are typically found in kitchen stores or stores that sell whole-bean coffee. It is best to reserve separate grinders for spice-grinding and coffee-grinding because the aroma of the spices can linger in the machine and will certainly flavor any coffee that is ground in it (and vice versa).

Although many experts suggest grinding pieces of bread in a grinder to clean it, I prefer using white rice kernels instead. The kernels dislodge any remnants of spice clinging to the blades or those lodged in the crevices of the machine. Once the rice is ground to a fine powder, throw it away and then wipe out the spice grinder with a damp paper towel to capture any remaining debris. For spices that are particularly oily or strongly flavored, such as cumin or cinnamon, brush the blades and crevices of the grinder with a new or sterilized toothbrush to make sure all parts are clean.

SEASONINGS

Lemon Pepper Seasoning Q V

MAKES 3 TABLESPOONS

This homemade lemon pepper seasoning packs a lot more flavor than the store-bought version and is wonderful sprinkled on meats, fish, or poultry.

2 tablespoons grated lemon zest
1 teaspoon freshly ground black pepper
¼ teaspoon salt
¼ teaspoon celery seed
¼ teaspoon onion powder
⅛ teaspoon garlic powder
⅛ teaspoon sugar

Place ingredients in a small spice or coffee grinder and process until finely ground. Refrigerate, tightly covered, for up to 2 weeks.

Mediterranean Herb Seasoning Q V

MAKES ABOUT 2½ TABLESPOONS

This diverse mix of herbs and spices combines to bring the sunny flavors of the Mediterranean to your table. Savory is sometimes hard to find, so you may omit it.

1 teaspoon dried parsley
1 teaspoon dried thyme
1 teaspoon dried oregano
½ teaspoon dried savory (optional)
½ teaspoon dried orange zest
¼ teaspoon dried rosemary
¼ teaspoon dried marjoram
⅛ teaspoon fennel seeds
⅛ teaspoon celery seed
⅛ teaspoon garlic powder
⅛ teaspoon sugar

Combine all of the ingredients in a coffee grinder and process until the fennel seeds are ground. Transfer to a jar with a screw-top lid. Store in a dark, dry place for up to 3 months.

Southwestern Seasoning

MAKES ½ CUP

This flavorful blend of spices evokes the smoky ambience of the Southwest with its chili, oregano, and cumin spices. For fuller flavor, use a tablespoon of coriander seeds rather than the ground variety. Like many seasonings of the Southwest, this one is spicy and full-bodied, so start out with a little less than the recipe calls for and add more to taste.

2 tablespoons chili powder
2 tablespoons dried oregano
1 tablespoon ground coriander
1 tablespoon salt
1 teaspoon paprika
1 teaspoon ground cumin
1 teaspoon cayenne pepper
1 teaspoon crushed red pepper
1 teaspoon freshly ground black pepper
1 teaspoon garlic powder
½ teaspoon sugar

Combine all of the ingredients in a coffee grinder and process until the crushed red pepper flakes (and whole coriander seeds, if using) are ground. Transfer to a jar with a screw-top lid. Store in a dark, dry place for up to 3 months.

Southwestern Chicken Rub

MAKES ⅔ CUP

This rub is a little milder than Southwestern Seasoning (page 668) and not nearly as smoky because it has no cumin in it. It is perfect for using on roasted whole chickens, Cornish game hens, or turkey, but you an also use it when frying chicken parts.

2 teaspoons salt
2 teaspoons ground cumin
2 teaspoons ground chili powder
2 teaspoons ground coriander
2 teaspoons onion powder
1 teaspoon dried oregano
½ teaspoon sugar
½ teaspoon freshly ground black pepper

Combine all of the ingredients in a coffee grinder and process until the oregano leaves are ground. Transfer to a jar with a screw-top lid. Store in a dark, dry place for up to 3 months.

Adobo Seasoning

MAKES ABOUT 3 TABLESPOONS

Adobo is the Spanish word for "seasoning," and it is sometimes used to indicate when meat is stewed in spices like this. This blend is easy to make and can be used wherever adobo seasoning is required, as in Chipotle Adobo Sauce (page 673).

1 tablespoon onion powder
1 tablespoon garlic powder
2 teaspoons salt
1 teaspoon dried oregano
½ teaspoon chili powder
½ teaspoon ground cumin
½ teaspoon freshly ground black pepper
½ teaspoon paprika

Combine all of the ingredients in a coffee grinder and process until the oregano leaves are ground. Transfer to a jar with a screw-top lid. Store in a dark, dry place for up to 3 months.

Blackening Seasoning

MAKES ABOUT 5 TEASPOONS

Some restaurants use wheat flour or bread crumbs to make blackening seasonings. You can easily make your own blend at home and be sure it is safe.

1 teaspoon salt
½ teaspoon dried thyme
½ teaspoon dried oregano
½ teaspoon sweet paprika
½ teaspoon freshly ground black pepper
½ teaspoon onion powder
½ teaspoon fennel seeds
¼ teaspoon cayenne pepper
¼ teaspoon garlic powder

Combine all of the ingredients in a small coffee grinder and process until the fennel seeds are ground. Transfer to a jar with a screw-top lid. Store in a dark, dry place for up to 3 months.

Jamaican Jerk Seasoning

MAKES ABOUT 5 TEASPOONS

Use this flavorful blend any time a recipe calls for it instead of buying it ready-made. It works well on chicken and pork, and I often use it on fish fillets before grilling them.

2 teaspoons sugar
1 teaspoon ground allspice
½ teaspoon ground ginger
½ teaspoon onion powder
½ teaspoon garlic powder
½ teaspoon salt
¼ teaspoon ground nutmeg
¼ teaspoon cayenne pepper
⅛ teaspoon ground cloves

Combine all of the ingredients in a coffee grinder and process until the fennel seeds are ground. Transfer to a jar with a screw-top lid. Store in a dark, dry place for up to 3 months.

Onion Soup Mix

MAKES A GENEROUS ½ CUP

One of the realities of a gluten-free diet is that the little bag of commercial onion soup mix useful for so many recipes is now off-limits. But the good news is you can make your own.

½ cup dried minced onion
1 teaspoon onion salt
¼ teaspoon garlic powder
¼ teaspoon sugar
¼ teaspoon celery salt
1 tablespoon sweet rice flour
½ teaspoon gluten-free beef-flavored base (bouillon granules), such as Ener-G or Vogue Cuisine
¼ teaspoon apple pectin powder or unflavored gelatin powder

Combine all the ingredients in a jar with a screw-top lid. Use in the same proportions as commercial onion soup mix. Double or triple the recipe, if needed. Store in the refrigerator for up to 3 months.

Seafood Seasoning

MAKES ABOUT 5 TEASPOONS

Use this seasoning in seafood dishes, such as crab cakes, grilled fish, or in fish casseroles.

1 teaspoon salt
1 teaspoon paprika
½ teaspoon dry mustard, such as McCormick's
½ teaspoon celery salt
½ teaspoon dried thyme
½ teaspoon dried marjoram
½ teaspoon garlic powder
¼ teaspoon onion powder
⅛ teaspoon freshly grated nutmeg
⅛ teaspoon ground allspice
⅛ teaspoon dried dill weed

Combine all of the ingredients in a coffee grinder and process until the thyme leaves are ground. Transfer to a jar with a screw-top lid. Store in a dark, dry place for up to 3 months.

SAUCES AND SALSAS

Basic Vinaigrette

MAKES 1 CUP

Keep this basic vinaigrette on hand to dress your mixed green salads or cooked vegetables. Add a teaspoon of finely chopped shallots or your favorite fresh herbs, such as basil, for variation.

2 teaspoons Dijon mustard
¼ cup vinegar (red wine, white wine, Champagne, or Sherry)
½ teaspoon honey
½ teaspoon salt, or to taste
Freshly ground black pepper
¾ to 1 cup extra virgin olive oil

In a small mixing bowl, whisk together the mustard, vinegar, honey, salt, and pepper. Gradually whisk in half of the oil. Taste the dressing and continue whisking in more oil, then tasting, until the dressing is smooth and tastes balanced. Use immediately or refrigerate, covered, for up to 1 week.

Raspberry Vinaigrette

MAKES 1¼ CUPS

The flavor of raspberries adds a fruity note to mixed green salads, but it can be used on whole grain salads or tossed with fresh fruit. This fruity note is also lovely when the vinaigrette is used to marinate poultry.

½ cup fresh raspberries
¼ cup sherry vinegar or champagne vinegar
1 teaspoon Dijon mustard
1 teaspoon honey
½ teaspoon onion powder
¼ teaspoon salt
⅛ teaspoon xanthan gum
½ cup olive oil

In a blender, puree all of the ingredients except the olive oil until the vinaigrette is smooth. With the blender running, add the oil in a thin stream until the vinaigrette thickens slightly. Refrigerate, tightly covered, for up to 1 week.

Pico de Gallo

MAKES ABOUT 1 CUP

Pico de gallo is a Spanish term used for fresh Mexican salsa. It is not cooked or mashed, so it has less liquid than other salsas, and is typically served with Mexican, or Southwestern foods such as tacos and fajitas.

2 vine-ripened tomatoes, seeded and finely diced
½ jalapeño pepper, seeded and finely diced
¼ cup red onion, finely diced
2 tablespoons chopped fresh cilantro
2 tablespoons fresh lime juice
1 small garlic clove, minced
Dash hot pepper sauce, such as Frank's (or additional jalapeño; optional)
¼ teaspoon salt
⅛ teaspoon white pepper

In a small bowl, combine all ingredients and toss to mix thoroughly. Store in glass bowl, tightly covered, at room temperature for up 1 hour before serving or refrigerate until serving time. Bring to room temperature before serving.

Tomato, Corn, or Bean Salsa

MAKES 1½ CUPS

Use this basic recipe as a starting point for a wide variety of delicious salsas. You can focus on just the tomatoes or combine the main ingredients to make tomato-corn salsa, corn and bean salsa or your preference. I like to add a little sweetness to the salsa for balance but you can leave out the honey or agave.

1 cup of one of the following: chopped plum tomatoes, cooked corn kernels, or canned black beans (rinsed and drained) or a combination
¼ cup diced red onion
2 tablespoons diced red bell pepper
1 tablespoon rice vinegar
1 tablespoon honey or agave nectar
1 teaspoon olive oil
¼ teaspoon salt
¼ teaspoon freshly ground black pepper
⅛ teaspoon crushed red pepper flakes (optional)

In a small bowl, toss together the corn, beans or tomatoes, red onion, bell pepper, vinegar, honey, oil, salt, pepper, and crushed red pepper flakes, if using. Serve immediately.

Minted Pineapple Salsa: Replace the corn, beans, or tomatoes with 1 can (8 ounces) drained pineapple tidbits. Stir in 3 tablespoons chopped fresh mint and serve immediately.

Herb Salsa

MAKES 1 CUP

This is a cross between a salsa and a sauce. Use it to perk up any simply flavored chicken, meat, fish, or vegetable dish or toss it with some cooked pasta or rice.

1 tablespoon Dijon mustard
1 tablespoon champagne vinegar or sherry vinegar
1 garlic clove, minced
½ cup fresh flat-leaf parsley
½ cup fresh basil
½ cup fresh mint
¼ cup fresh thyme
2 teaspoons grated lemon zest
¼ teaspoon salt
2 tablespoons olive oil

Place all ingredients (except olive oil) in a small food processor and pulse to chop them coarsely, but not pulverize them. Add oil and pulse a few times to combine it with the herbs.

Garlic-Thyme Herbed Butter Ⓠ Ⓥ

MAKES ½ CUP

Herbed butter, sometimes called compound butter, is simply butter to which herbs and spices have been added. Place on top of grilled steaks or vegetables just before serving, so the marvelous flavor seeps into the food as it melts. Keep a log in the freezer at all times so you can pop a slice onto food at a moment's notice.

½ cup (1 stick) unsalted butter or buttery spread, such as Earth Balance at room temperature
1 garlic clove, minced
2 teaspoons chopped fresh thyme
⅛ teaspoon salt, or to taste

1 In a small bowl, blend the butter, garlic, thyme, and salt with a spatula. Transfer the butter to a large strip of plastic wrap.

2 With a spatula, shape the butter into a 1-inch log and roll up the plastic around the log, twisting the ends to seal. Gently roll the log to evenly round out the shape. Place the log in the freezer to make the butter cold enough to slice again.

3 When ready to serve, remove the log from the plastic wrap, slice it in ½-inch pieces with a sharp knife that has been dipped in hot water, and place the butter on top of your food.

Basil Pesto Ⓠ Ⓥ

MAKES ½ CUP

Of course, you can buy ready-made basil pesto but if you have your own basil plants it is quite simple and economical to make your own. You will need a food processor to puree the leaves, since a blender cannot handle the stiff nature of the pesto.

¼ cup toasted pine nuts
2 cups lightly packed fresh basil, washed and patted dry
1 garlic clove, minced
⅓ cup extra-virgin olive oil plus more to top stored pesto
3 tablespoons grated Parmesan cheese or soy alternative, such as Soyco
Dash salt and pepper to taste

1 In a food processor, process the pine nuts until they are finely ground. Add the basil and garlic and process just until a little bit of texture remains. With the food processor running, add the oil through the feed tube.

2 Remove the pesto from the food processor and stir in the Parmesan cheese, salt, and pepper. Serve immediately or refrigerate any leftover pesto for 2 days with a thin layer of olive oil on top to prevent discoloration.

Marinara Sauce Ⓥ

MAKES 4½ CUPS

This easy, yet flavorful marinara sauce is perfect with spaghetti or lasagna. Freeze leftover sauce in meal-size quantities and thaw in the microwave for a quick meal.

1 large can (24 ounces) tomato juice
1 can (6 ounces) tomato paste
⅛ cup chopped fresh basil or 1 tablespoon dried
2 tablespoons chopped fresh parsley or 1 tablespoon dried
2 teaspoons sugar
2 teaspoons chopped fresh oregano or 1 teaspoon dried
2 teaspoons finely snipped fresh rosemary or 1 teaspoon dried, crushed
½ teaspoon salt, or to taste
¼ teaspoon crushed red pepper
¼ teaspoon freshly ground black pepper
1 garlic clove, minced
1 bay leaf
2 tablespoons grated Romano cheese or soy alternative, such as Soyco (optional)

In a slow cooker, whisk together all of ingredients. Mix well. Cook 6 to 8 hours on low heat, stirring occasionally. Or combine all ingredients in a medium-size, heavy saucepan. Bring to boil, reduce heat to low, and simmer, covered, 30 to 45 minutes. Remove bay leaf before serving.

Harissa Sauce
MAKES ABOUT ½ CUP

Harissa is a garlicky North African chile sauce used in meat dishes, couscous, or as an ingredient in sauces. Ground coriander can be found in the baking aisle of your grocery store and is made from the dried seeds of the coriander plant, whose bright, green leaves are called cilantro.

¼ cup extra-virgin olive oil
¼ cup chopped yellow onion
2 tablespoons fresh lime juice
2 purchased, jarred roasted red peppers
¼ small seeded jalapeño pepper
2 garlic cloves, peeled
Palm-size bunch of fresh cilantro
2 teaspoons ground coriander
½ teaspoon ground cumin
1 whole cardamom seed
¼ teaspoon salt
⅛ teaspoon freshly ground black pepper
Pinch ground cloves

In a food processor, combine all of the ingredients and process until smooth. Taste and adjust seasonings, if desired. Store in the refrigerator, tightly covered, for up to a month.

Chipotle Adobo Sauce
MAKES ½ CUP

This may seem like an unusual ingredient but you'll find that it's actually quite common in Southwestern dishes. Since most of the chipotles in adobo sauce are manufactured outside the United States, and wheat flour is known to be used in certain brands, it is much safer to make your own at home.

¼ cup ketchup
2 tablespoons cider vinegar
2 tablespoons chipotle chile powder, such as McCormick's
½ teaspoon homemade Adobo Seasoning (page 668)
¼ teaspoon salt

In a small bowl, stir the ingredients together until well blended. Refrigerate, tightly covered, for up to 1 week. Or freeze for up to 1 month.

Chipotle Mayonnaise
MAKES ½ CUP

This is a great spread for grilled hamburgers or fish. Start with 1 teaspoon Chipotle Adobo Sauce (page 673) then add more, ½ teaspoon at a time, to taste.

½ cup mayonnaise
2 teaspoons homemade Chipotle Adobo Sauce (page 673)
1 teaspoon fresh lime juice
⅛ teaspoon garlic powder
Pinch ground cumin
Salt to taste

In a small bowl, whisk the ingredients together with a spoon until well blended. Refrigerate, tightly covered, for 2 days.

Blue Cheese Dipping Sauce

MAKES 1 CUP

Blue cheese adds tons of flavor and is safe, as long as you use the gluten-free brands here. Use this sauce for Buffalo Wings or dipping vegetables.

½ cup crumbled gluten-free blue cheese, such as Boar's Head or Sargento

¼ cup buttermilk or homemade Buttermilk (page 677), well-shaken

2 tablespoons fresh lemon juice

¼ cup finely snipped fresh chives

¼ teaspoon seasoning blend, such as Morton's Nature's Seasons or dash each of parsley, garlic powder, celery salt, and freshly ground black pepper

In a small bowl, mash blue cheese into buttermilk and lemon juice with a fork to form a paste with just a few chunks remaining. Stir in fresh chives and seasoning blend. Serve sauce at room temperature with wings.

Bechamel Sauce

MAKES 1 CUP

Sometimes called a white sauce and traditionally made with flour, bechamel *(BESH-a-mel) is useful for drizzling on a number of dishes ranging from meat, fish, vegetables, or pasta.*

1 tablespoon sweet rice flour

1 teaspoon gluten-free instant chicken soup and seasoning base, such as Vogue Cuisine

¼ teaspoon dry mustard

⅛ teaspoon freshly ground white pepper

Dash freshly grated nutmeg (optional)

1 cup whole milk (cow's, rice, soy, potato, or nut)

1 tablespoon unsalted butter or buttery spread, such as Earth Balance

Salt to taste

1 In a small saucepan, whisk together flour, soup base, mustard, white pepper, and nutmeg (if using) until well blended.

2 Whisk in milk, place pan over medium-low heat, and cook, whisking constantly, until mixture thickens. Remove from heat and whisk in butter until melted. For a thicker sauce, increase sweet rice flour to 1½ tablespoons.

Simple Cream Sauce

MAKES 2¼ CUPS

Use this creamy sauce whenever you recipe calls for white sauce or Bechamel sauce.

1 tablespoon unsalted butter or buttery spread, such as Earth Balance

2 cups 2% milk (cow's, rice, soy, potato, or nut)

¼ cup sweet rice flour

1 cup grated Parmesan cheese or soy alternative, such as Soyco

1 large egg, beaten until smooth

In a medium heavy saucepan, melt the butter over medium heat. Add 1½ cups of the milk. Stir sweet rice flour into remaining ½ cup milk until smooth, add it to the pan, and cook, whisking constantly, until slightly thickened and bubbling. Add 1 cup Parmesan cheese and stir until melted. Stir 2 tablespoons of milk-cheese mixture into the beaten egg, then add egg to the pan. Cook another 3 to 4 minutes, whisking constantly. The mixture will thicken slightly. Serve immediately.

Simple White Gravy

MAKES 2 ½ CUPS

This simple gravy, richer than the simple cream sauce, is perfect with Chicken-Fried Steak, mashed potatoes, or baking powder biscuits.

1 teaspoon canola oil
1 strip uncooked bacon
2½ cups whole milk (cow's, rice, soy, potato, or nut)
4 teaspoons sweet rice flour
½ teaspoon salt
½ teaspoon freshly ground black pepper

1 In a large heavy skillet, heat the oil over medium-high heat. Fry the bacon until crisp. Remove the bacon and pour off all but 1 tablespoon of the oil, leaving any browned bits in the skillet.

2 Add 2 cups of the milk to the skillet. Stir the sweet rice flour, salt, and pepper into remaining ½ cup milk until the mixture is very smooth. Stir it into skillet and cook over medium-high heat, whisking constantly, until the mixture thickens, about 7 to 10 minutes. Crumble the bacon and add it to the gravy. Serve immediately.

MISCELLANEOUS

Beef Broth

MAKES ABOUT 4 QUARTS (16 CUPS)

The nice thing about making your own beef broth is that you can control the salt. Make a batch of this easy beef broth and store it in 2-cup containers in your freezer. Then, defrost it overnight in the refrigerator or quickly in the microwave and it is ready to use in many of the recipes in this book.

½ pound beef stew meat, cut in 1-inch cubes
1 large onion, peeled and quartered
1 large carrot, sliced lengthwise
2 ribs celery, halved horizontally
1 large tomato, quartered
1 tablespoon tomato paste
2 large garlic cloves, peeled
4 quarts cold water
2 tablespoons chopped fresh parsley
2 teaspoons chopped fresh thyme or 1 teaspoon dried
1 teaspoon salt
6 whole black peppercorns
1 large bay leaf
1 tablespoon tomato paste

1 Place the beef, onion, and carrot in large baking pan and roast in a 400°F oven for 20 to 30 minutes, or until the beef is darkly browned. Transfer to a 6-quart stockpot and add the remaining ingredients. Discard fat from the roasting pan and add just enough water to cover the bottom of the pan. Deglaze the pan over medium-high heat, scraping up browned bits. Add this mixture to the stockpot.

2 Bring the mixture in the stockpot slowly to a simmer, cover, and continue to simmer, covered, 2 hours. (Avoid bringing to boil rapidly since this produces foam that you'll have to skim off.)

3 Strain the mixture through a sieve and ladle into freezer-safe containers. Refrigerate until cool, then remove fat. Freeze, labeled and tightly covered, for up to 3 months.

Chicken Broth

MAKES ABOUT 4 QUARTS (16 CUPS)

Chicken broth is one of those versatile items that serves as the basis for many dishes. I prefer to make my own so I can control the salt and keep it pure and flavorful with fresh herbs. With this easy recipe, you'll see how convenient it is to make your own.

16 cups water

Bones of 1 chicken with some meat left on, fatty parts cut off

1 small onion, halved

3 medium tomatoes

2 ribs celery

1 whole carrot

1½ tablespoons salt, or to taste

1 tablespoon tomato paste (optional)

6 whole black peppercorns

1 tablespoon chopped fresh parsley or 2 teaspoons dried

1 tablespoon chopped fresh thyme or 2 teaspoons dried

½ teaspoon poultry seasoning

6 dill seeds

1 Fill a 6-quart stockpot with water and add all the ingredients.

2 Bring the water to a boil slowly over medium heat (coming to a boil too quickly produces foam and cloudy broth). Quickly turn heat down to low when it starts to boil and simmer, covered, 2 hours.

3 Strain the mixture through a sieve and ladle into freezer-safe containers. Refrigerate until cool, then remove fat. Freeze, labeled and tightly covered, for up to 3 months.

Shrimp Stock

MAKES 2 QUARTS (8 CUPS)

Shrimp stock is made like chicken broth but uses shrimp shells in place of chicken bones. It is commonly added to Southern dishes such as gumbo. You can often replace shrimp stock with clam broth, but homemade shrimp stock lends an extra special flavor and is worth the effort.

2 tablespoons canola oil

1 rib celery, roughly chopped

1 small onion, chopped

1 small carrot, roughly chopped

Shells from 1½ pounds medium shrimp

½ cup white wine

7 cups water

3 whole black peppercorns

1 bay leaf

1 teaspoon chopped fresh thyme or ½ teaspoon dried

1 In a 3-quart saucepan or stockpot, heat the oil over medium-high heat. Add the celery, onion, and carrot and cook about 5 minutes, or until the vegetables are slightly softened. Then, add the shrimp shells and cook, stirring constantly, until shells are pink and fragrant.

2 Add the wine and cook until reduced by half. Add water, peppercorns, bay leaf, and thyme. Bring to a boil and immediately reduce heat to low. Simmer 30 to 45 minutes, uncovered, or until reduced by one-third or to about 5 cups.

3 Strain the mixture through a sieve and ladle into freezer-safe containers. Refrigerate until cool. Freeze, labeled and tightly covered, for up to 3 months.

Vegetable Broth

MAKES 4 QUARTS (16 CUPS)

Homemade vegetable broth is extraordinarily flavorful and fresh-tasting. It is also quite easy to make, using mild, yet pleasantly flavored vegetables that complement each other. Fresh herbs enhance the blast of flavor from the tomato paste, but dried herbs will also work here. This broth is especially useful in vegetarian soups, stews, and any dish that requires a mild-flavored broth.

16 cups water
1 large onion, halved
4 medium tomatoes, halved
2 ribs celery, trimmed
2 whole carrots, peeled and coarsely chopped
1½ tablespoons salt, or to taste
1 tablespoon tomato paste (optional)
6 whole black peppercorns
1 bunch fresh parsley or 1 tablespoon dried
1 small bunch fresh thyme sprigs or 1 teaspoon dried thyme
6 dill seeds

1 Fill a 6-quart stockpot with water and add all the ingredients.

2 Bring the water to a boil slowly over medium heat. Quickly turn heat down to low when it starts to boil and simmer, covered, 2 hours.

3 Strain the mixture through a sieve and ladle into freezer-safe containers. Refrigerate until cool. Freeze, labeled and tightly covered, for up to 3 months.

Buttermilk

MAKES 1 CUP

Note that rice milk will not thicken, so reduce the amount of rice-based buttermilk in recipes by 25 percent. If you need more than 1 cup, simply double or triple the ingredients as needed. Be sure to shake or whisk the buttermilk well before measuring.

1 tablespoon cider vinegar or fresh lemon juice
2% milk (cow's, rice, soy, potato, or nut) to equal 1 cup

Put the vinegar in a measuring cup. Whisk in enough milk to equal 1 cup. Let stand 10 minutes to thicken slightly. Refrigerate unused portions, tightly covered, for up to 1 week.

Almond Milk

MAKES 2 CUPS

Nut milk is a wonderful substitute for cow's milk in baking and makes great smoothies. For a lighter-colored milk, use almonds without skins.

½ cup blanched almonds
2 cups warm water
1 teaspoon honey
¼ teaspoon pure vanilla extract
⅛ teaspoon xanthan gum
⅛ teaspoon salt, or to taste

In a blender, process all of the ingredients until very, very smooth. Strain through colander lined with cheesecloth and refrigerate in an airtight container for up to 3 days.

Almond Paste

MAKES 1½ CUPS

This very simple almond paste can be used in place of commercially prepared almond paste on a 1:1 ratio. Many recipes call for a whole can of almond paste; this one makes the equivalent of two cans, 8 ounces or ¾ cup each. You can use one can (¾ cup) and freeze the remainder in a heavy-duty food storage bag. You will need a food processor, not a blender, to grind the almonds.

1½ cups slivered blanched almonds
½ cup sugar
⅛ teaspoon salt
½ cup corn syrup
1 teaspoon almond extract

Place almonds, sugar, and salt in food processor and pulse until very finely ground. Add corn syrup and almond extract and process until mixture comes together and forms a ball or clump on one side of the bowl. Break up into smaller clumps with spatula and process until it forms ball again. Makes equivalent of 2 cans (¾ cup in each can) of almond paste. Freeze remaining ¾ cup for up to a month.

Honey Butter

MAKES ½ CUP

Honey butter is simply butter blended with honey. It makes a delicious spread for fresh baked muffins, waffles, and pancakes but you can use it in any way you wish.

1 tablespoon honey, or to taste
½ cup (1 stick) unsalted butter or buttery spread
   such as Earth Balance, at room temperature

In a small bowl, mix the honey into the softened butter until smooth. Serve at room temperature. Refrigerate leftovers.

Cinnamon Applesauce

MAKES 1 CUP

Serve this applesauce with potato latkes or use as it a topping for waffles or pancakes—or as a tasty snack. For thicker applesauce, drain in a coffee filter for 1 hour; discard the liquid.

1 cup plain applesauce
¼ to ⅓ teaspoon ground cinnamon, or to taste
⅛ teaspoon grated nutmeg (optional)
Dash salt (optional)

In a small bowl, stir ingredients together until well blended. Refrigerate, tightly covered, for up to a week. Serve at room temperature.

Clementine Marmalade

MAKES ABOUT 1½ CUPS

I fell in love with clementines (also known as tangerines) a couple of years ago and found that they make a marvelous marmalade—a bit sweeter than oranges and with less bitterness from the pulp. My easy version uses the microwave and doesn't need pectin or other additives to make it gel.

3 clementines, washed but unpeeled
¾ cup sugar

1 Cut the clementines into quarters, removing any seeds or white pithy centers. Place the quartered clementines in a blender or food processor and pulse until the peel reaches the desired size (⅛-inch to ¼-inch pieces are best). Place the mixture in a microwave-safe glass dish or bowl and add the sugar.

2 Microwave on high 1 minute. Stir, then heat again for 30 seconds. Repeat in 30-second increments on high until the mixture thickens slightly. Store, tightly covered, in the refrigerator for up to 1 week.

INDEX

692   Index